THE
ALMANAC
OF
AMERICAN
HISTORY

THE
ALMANAC
OF
AMERICAN
HISTORY

General Editor:

ARTHUR M. SCHLESINGER, JR.

Executive Editor: JOHN S. BOWMAN

Consultants: Marcus Cunliffe Robert H. Ferrell S.L. Mayer
Richard C. Wade Gordon S. Wood

🐂 **A Bison Book**

A PERIGEE BOOK

Perigee Books
are published by
The Putnam Publishing Group
200 Madison Avenue
New York, NY 10016

Produced by Bison Books Corp.
17 Sherwood Place
Greenwich, CT 06830
U.S.A.

Library of Congress Cataloging in Publication Data
Main entry under title:

The Almanac of American history.

  "A Bison book."
  Includes index.
  1. United States—History—Chronology.
I. Schlesinger, Arthur Meier, date. II. Bowman,
John Stewart, date.
E174.5.A45 1984   973'.02'02   84-7736
ISBN 0-399-51082-6

Printed in the United States of America

  2 3 4 5 6 7 8 9 10

Grenade throwers in France—October 26, 1918.

CONTENTS

INTRODUCTION

ARTHUR M. SCHLESINGER JR.
Albert Schweitzer Chair in the Humanities, City University of New York

INTRODUCTION

"In the beginning," wrote John Locke in the *Second Treatise on Civil Government*, "all the world was America." Locke intended only a metaphor for the state of nature that preceded the establishment of civil society. But his metaphor evokes much more. It implies a way America was first seen from Europe—as a new beginning, a break in the long, sad continuities of history, a fresh chance for fallen humanity.

The red men, the Native Americans, lived in something close to Locke's state of nature. Even whites in America were liberated, in part at least, from the deadweights of the past. They brought certain ideas and institutions from the older civilization, but transformed these in the hard experience of subduing a wilderness and pushing on to ever-receding frontiers. Other ideas and institutions, like feudalism, they simply left behind; and the absence of feudalism assured a separate political evolution in the new land. "The great advantage of the Americans," as Alexis de Tocqueville said in *Democracy in America*, "is that they have arrived at a state of democracy without having to endure a democratic revolution, and that they are born equal without becoming so."

As early as 1782, while American commissioners in Paris were negotiating for British recognition of American independence, a French immigrant to Orange County, New York, propounded a question that still echoes today: "What then is the American, this new man?" They were a motley group, these white Americans, a "promiscuous breed," Hector de St. John de Crèvecoeur, the American essayist, called them in his *Letters from an American Farmer*, composed of English, Scotch, Irish, French, Dutch, Germans, Swedes, yet "melted into a new race of men, whose labours and posterity will one day cause great changes in the world." Crèvecoeur went on to answer his own question: "*He* is an American, who, leaving behind him all his ancient prejudices and manners, receives new ones from the new mode of life he has embraced, the new government he obeys, and the new rank he holds . . . . The American is a new man, who acts upon new principles."

Many nationalities joined in making the new society. But the British influence predominated, supplying the language, the law, the religion, the culture, the training in self-government, even the very political theory that led to the overthrow of British rule. Yet everything subtly altered after the transatlantic passage. Nor was the frontier the only agency of Americanization. The new land moved through a series of historic stages; or, to put it differently, history imposed a succession of overlapping tasks on the men and women who settled the new continent. Each task created its own agenda, its own set of priorities for the evolving nation. Each new agenda determined how the American people allocated their attention, their resources and their hopes during each historic stage. And each agenda further modified old ideas and institutions and, on occasion, invented new ones, thereby developing a distinctive American order of life.

The first of these historic tasks was invasion and conquest. For North America was not an unpopulated wilderness. No one knows how many Indians there were when the white men first arrived. Estimates range from one to four million. They were widely scattered across the vast continent, mostly nomadic, fragmented by tribe, language and ritual. But they were there, with cultures and identities of their own. The establishment of the white man in the new land meant the expulsion of the red man, as it also meant the unceasing adaptation of European ideas and institutions to American circumstance.

This process of adaptation widened the American deviation from Europe, fostered impulses of separatism and thereby led on to the second historic task: the achievement of nationhood. In the last quarter of the 18th century, when travel and communication were slow and laborious, Americans faced the challenge of converting 13 colonies with local concerns and local loyalties into a democratic republic with national identity, national loyalty and a national government. Two great documents—the Declaration of Independence and the Constitution—crystallized the American creed, affirming that all men were created equal with unalienable rights to life, liberty and the pursuit of happiness and defining the polity within which those rights were to be exercised. Years after, in the late 20th century, Americans watched Third World countries in an equivalent travail of nationhood. But the pursuit of national identity had been a good deal easier for Americans, blessed as they were by abundant natural resources, by a literate population, by a Calvinist work ethic, by antecedent traditions of self-government, by relative isolation from foreign aggression. Yet even with these advantages it required a bloody civil war before the travail was over.

From the task of establishing nationhood Americans moved to the task of settling the continent. They relentlessly pressed their invasion of the wilderness until white America at last stretched from sea to sea over the smashed cultures and crushed bodies of the Native Americans. As white men moved farther, forever westward, they also began to confront the most glaring contradiction between the American creed and the American reality. This contradiction committed Americans to their next national task: the abolition of slavery, the destruction of the system by which one person owned another as private property. It took four years of savage fraternal war before that task was completed in a legal sense. A century and a quarter later it had not yet been completed in the fundamental sense. The plight of racial minorities, though Americans have become infinitely more sensitive to that plight in the last generation, remains a realm of inequality in a society allegedly dedicated to equal rights.

After the Civil War the nation faced the task of industrializing an agricultural economy, transforming a predominantly rural society of farmers and planters into an increasingly urban (and in time suburban) society of capitalists and workers. This process brought with it marked improvement in standards of living. It brought also marked increase in the social tensions bred by inequality.

The pressure of these social tensions forced the nation into the next historic agenda: the humanization of the new industrial order. The first 40 years of the 20th century witnessed the conversion of a laissez-faire, devil-take-the-hindmost economy into a society that acknowledged a responsibility to act against mass unemployment, to assure civilized standards of life and labor, to protect the poor and the helpless, even to open doors to those heretofore barred from opportunity by virtue of race or sex.

Industrialization, resources, entrepreneurial ingenuity, the work ethic—all had made the United States a world power by the end of the 19th century. Years before, the Founding Fathers had had a clear perception of the relationship between national security and the international balance of power. "It cannot be to our interest," Jefferson wrote in a letter to Thomas Leiper in 1814, "that all Europe should be reduced to a single monarchy," and he warned of the threat to America should "the whole force of Europe [be] wielded by a single hand." But this realistic insight was obscured as America turned to its continental tasks. American security in the later 19th century seemed more a consequence of isolation and virtue than of an international equilibrium secured by the British fleet. With the 20th century, however, the United States itself became one of the mighty, inextricably absorbed into world power politics. Americans now waged two great hot wars and thereafter a long, grueling cold war in the interest of maintaining the international balance of power.

This renewed involvement in the world posed the seventh historic task: the development of a responsible foreign policy that would defend vital national interests without succumbing to the temptations of ideological or commercial crusades. Americans saw a general interest in the promotion of free institutions abroad. But wise leaders concluded that this could be done more effectively by setting an example of a working democracy in the United States than by crusading intervention in foreign lands. "Wherever the standard of freedom and independence has been or shall be unfurled," John Quincy Adams said of America in an address, July 4, 1821, "there will her heart, her benedictions and her prayers be. But she goes not abroad in search of monsters to destroy."

"We have plenty of sins of our own to war against," said Theodore Roosevelt in his Annual Message, December 6, 1904, "and under ordinary circumstances we can do more for the general uplifting of humanity by striving with heart and soul to put a stop to civic corruption, to brutal lawlessness and violent race prejudices here at home than by passing resolutions about wrong-doing elsewhere."

Certainly America enjoyed its greatest influence in the world when, as in the days of Wilson, of Franklin Roosevelt and of Kennedy, its democratic professions were validated by progressive policies at home and therefore commanded the confidence of plain people in other lands. America has succeeded internationally less through the force of its arms than through the splendor of its ideals.

In the 20th century, change plowed inexorably along, propelled by the self-generating momentum of scientific discovery and technological innovation. Henry Adams was the first American to proclaim the transcendent significance of the ever accelerating velocity of history. "The world," he wrote in *The Degradation of the Democratic Dogma* in 1909, "did not double or treble its movement between 1800 and 1900, but, measured by any standard known to science—by horse-power, calories, volts, mass in any shape—the tension and vibration and volume and so-called progression of society were fully a thousand times greater in 1900 than in 1800"—and, as he well understood, would be exponentially greater in the century ahead.

As the 20th century draws to a close, Americans are confronting a new crisis produced by the onward rush of science and technology. The old basic, mass-production "smokestack" industries—steel, automobiles, rubber, glass, textiles—are losing their competitive advantages to the third world. From the industrial age, it seems, America must pass into a new age of high-technology, based on the computer, the semiconductor and the microchip. The electronic age looming ahead once more prescribes new tasks and demands new priorities.

So a succession of tasks created a succession of agendas. Agreement on a new agenda was never smoothly nor painlessly attained. Just as the nation grew accustomed to one set of priorities, a new crisis imposed itself, bringing its own challenges, its own agonizing problems, its own capacity to threaten and frighten and divide. The passage from one national agenda to another is always a time of confusion, strain and foreboding. People have vested interests, emotional as well as material, in cherished ideas and institutions. Abandoning the familiar and embracing the novel causes stress. In every case, whether Manifest Destiny or abolition or the New Deal, the emerging agenda, the incipient priorities, roused resistance which was always vocal, often powerful. Alarmed debate and angry division have always characterized the transition from one agenda to another.

So the law of acceleration leaves turmoil in its wake. But America never was a homogeneous nation. Crevecoeur's "promiscuous breed" became more promiscuous still in the 19th century, as new waves of immigration enriched and diversified the American population. "Here," said Walt Whitman in "By Blue Ontario's Shore", "is not merely a nation but a teeming nation of nations." The process of Americanizing the immigrant did not cease. But Americanization involved its share of paradox, and paradoxes compounded confusion. "It's a complex fate, being an American," observed Henry James.

Let us consider some of the paradoxes. First one

INTRODUCTION

must note the contradiction between the American addiction to experiment and the American susceptibility to ideology. On the one hand, Americans are famous for their faith in the experimental approach to life and society; for finding the meaning of propositions in practical results; for regarding trial and error as the means to truth. Experiment has always been a key word. George Washington in his First Inaugural Address saw the destiny of republican government as finally "staked on the experiment intrusted to the hands of the American people." The country needs "bold, persistent experimentation," said Franklin D Roosevelt a century and a half later. In an address at Oglethorpe University, May 22, 1932, he said, "It is common sense to take a method and try it: If it fails, admit it frankly and try another. But above all, try something."

The greatest of American philosophers. William James, summed up this strain in the national temperament in the doctrines he variously called "pragmatism" or "radical empiricism." He stood for what he called an "unfinished universe" and affirmed the intractable reality of growth, pluralism, ambiguity, mystery and contingency. he perceived a world where free men could gain partial and limited truths—truths that worked for them—but where no one could get an absolute grip on ultimate truth. He stood against monism—the idea that the world could be understood from a single point of view; against faith in a central body of unified dogma; against the notion of a closed universe framed in unalterable and reconcilable principles; in short, against the tyranny of ideology.

Yet at the same time that Americans live by experiment they also show a recurrent weakness for ideology. This is not altogether surprising. The intellectual origins of the nation, after all, were saturated in one of the profoundest ideologies ever devised—the theology of Calvinism. No 18th century thinker anywhere had a sharper analytical mind than Jonathan Edwards of Massachusetts, whose vigorous advocacy of Calvinism founded a distinct school of American theology. Any people so conditioned is bound to have a vulnerability to spacious abstractions ever after. "The ideas of the Americans," Tocqueville said in *Democracy in America,* "are all either extremely minute and clear or extremely general and vague." So in the 19th century a man in the Calvinist tradition, John C. Calhoun, applied his considerable powers of abstract thought to the construction of an ideology designed to justify the institution of human slavery. So in the 20th century another man in the Calvinist tradition, John Foster Dulles, sought to construct a sacred ideology of private enterprise against godless communism. The propensity to dogma explains why the theory of American society as expounded by some Americans—the theory of unfettered laissez-faire—differs from the reality of pragmatic government intervention in the economic order. The tension between experiment and ideology remains perennial in American democracy.

A second paradox, already touched upon, lies in the antagonism between the American affirmation of equality and the American tolerance of inequality. "A land of freedom, boastfully so-called, with human slavery at the heart of it," wrote William James in *Memories and Studies,* " . . .what was it but a thing of falsehood and horrible self-contradiction?" It is hard to overstate the effects of this paradox on the American character. Americans could not devote so much of their early energy to killing red men, enslaving black men, rejecting yellow men, without injecting a deep conviction of racial superiority into themselves and their society. To preserve their illusions of innocence, Americans resorted to the process Freud called "repression"—keeping disagreeable things out of consciousness. American historians no doubt provided meticulous accounts of Indian wars, slavery and oriental exclusion policies; but they held the phenomena at a distance, treating them as isolated events of an extinct time, rarely perceiving them in organic relation to the American community. The intensities buried by the mechanisms of repression burst out in another way—in American literature. The national literature has involuntarily seen race as near the heart of American life. From the start American novels—from Cooper and Melville through Mark Twain to Faulkner—were pervaded by images of racial unrest, aggression and guilt. What white America declined to confront in its conscious thoughts, it could not escape in fantasy. Leatherstocking and Uncas, Ishmael and Queequeg, Huck and Jim—in such characters and relationships the national unconscious sought to come to terms with the tragic paradox denied in the national consciousness.

A third paradox is the continuing tension between order and violence in American life. On the one hand, Americans have always prided themselves on devotion to the rule of law. On the other, American history has been marked by war, insurrection, riot, mobs, duels, murders, lynchings, muggings. In his first notable speech to the Young Men's Lyceum of Springfield, Illinois, January 27, 1838, the young Abraham Lincoln identified the propensity toward violence as the supreme threat to American institutions. "Whenever the vicious portion of population shall be permitted to . . . burn churches, ravage and rob provision-stores, throw printing-presses into rivers, shoot editors, and hang and burn obnoxious persons at pleasure, and with impunity; depend on it, this Government cannot last."

No one saw more poignantly than Lincoln the desperate need to control and transcend this national propensity. No one understood more keenly that the ultimate answer to violence was not law-as-order but law-as-justice. It was fortunate as well as ironic that this man who perceived so profoundly the curse of violence should have been President during the greatest explosion of violence in American history. Throughout the Civil War, Lincoln strove to hold the destructive impulse in check. He said it all in his Second Inaugural Address, "With malice toward none; with charity for all; with firmness in the right, as God gives us to see the right, let us strive on to finish the work we are in; to bind up the nation's wounds." In the end, at Ford's Theater, the greatest American foe of violence and hate became the greatest American victim of violence and hate.

The 20th century saw violence unabated. The decision to drop the atomic bomb on Japan may well have been inescapable, but the deed was one of the great acts of destruction in all human history. From crime in the streets through riots in the cities to the assassination of admired national leaders, the resort to violence remained part of the American character, even as Americans righteously denounced proclivities to violence on the part of other peoples.

A fourth national paradox lies in the question of conformity versus diversity. Observers of the United States have long claimed to detect powerful social pressures toward conformity. The most perceptive of them all, Tocqueville, saw a "tyranny of the majority" as endemic in American society and added: "I know of no country in which there is so little independence of mind and freedom of discussion as in the United States." The impression spread in later years of the United States as a nation where the tyrannous majority and the ever-boiling melting pot wiped out all ethnic, regional and philosophical differences, leaving a bland and undifferentiated mass.

Yet, at the same time, any traveler can find a large, sprawling, diverse nation, with ethnic enclaves in the great cities and emphatic regional variations in accent, food, dress and folkways. If the world saw America half a century ago as a land of Babbitts, it was after all an American novelist who created Babbitt—which should have reminded the world that America is a nation given to abundant and mordant self-exposure. In the 1960s, dissent in the land of Babbitts took so many forms and had such urgency behind it that it almost threatened to rend the social fabric itself. America has always been simultaneously a society of complacency and a society of criticism. Few nations have shown a greater knack for self-adulation and for sanctimonious preachments to lesser breeds without the law. No nation has more precisely and vividly documented its own errors, injustices and shames.

Still another contradiction manifest through American history is between materialism and idealism in the national life. Tocqueville professed to know of "no country . . . where the love of money has taken stronger hold on the affections of men"—strong words indeed from a Frenchman. Three quarters of a century later, in 1906, William James deplored in a letter to H. G. Wells the "moral flabbiness" among his fellow countrymen "born of the exclusive worship of the bitch-goddess *Success*. That—with the squalid cash interpretation put on the word success—is our national disease." Americans and foreigners alike have seen the United States as the triumph of the gross bourgeoisie, acquisitive, materialistic and vulgar.

Yet Americans are plainly capable of being greatly stirred by idealism. No nation in history has given so much of its treasure to the aid of other nations. No society in history has devoted so much of its resources and zeal to philanthropy and to non-profit enterprises of humanitarian and social benefit. The Peace Corps is at least as faithful an expression of the American spirit as the Standard Oil Company—and even the Standard Oil Company spawned the Rockefeller Foundation.

A final paradox has to do with the nature of the American experiment itself. Many Americans have seen themselves as a chosen people, their country as a "redeemer nation," commissioned by a wonder-working Providence to regenerate suffering mankind and thereby qualitatively different in motive and destiny from all other nations. This was the view of the Puritans who had been providentially despatched to New England, they believed, because (as Edward Johnson wrote in 1653) "this is the place where the Lord will create a new Heaven and a new Earth." "We Americans," wrote Herman Melville in *White-Jacket* in 1850, "are the peculiar chosen people—the Israel of our time; we bear the ark of the liberties of the world." "America is the only idealistic nation in the world," said Woodrow Wilson in a speech at Sioux Falls, South Dakota, in 1919. "I have always believed," said Ronald Reagan in his 1982 Thanksgiving Day Proclamation, "that this anointed land was set apart in an uncommon way, that a divine plan placed this great continent here between the oceans to be found by people from every corner of the earth who had a special love of faith and freedom."

Yet others, equally redoubtable, wonder whether America has enjoyed this divine immunity to temptation and corruption and ask whether the United States is, after all, qualitatively different from other states. "We, as well as the other inhabitants of the globe," was the realistic view of Alexander Hamilton in *The Federalist*, "are yet remote from the happy empire of perfect wisdom and perfect virtue." "Angelic impulses and predatory lusts," said William James, "divide our heart exactly as they divide the heart of other countries." No one more searchingly questioned the idea of a "redeemer nation" than the greatest American theologian of the 20th century, Reinhold Niebuhr. "Nations, as individuals, who are completely innocent in their own esteem, are insufferable in their human contacts." Let the self-righteous nation understand, Niebuhr warned in *The Irony of American History,* that divine judgment punishes human pretension—and never forget "the depth of evil to which individuals and communities may sink, particularly when they try to play the role of God in history."

The point about paradox is that both sides may be true. Walt Whitman asked in "Song of Myself:"

Do I contradict myself?
Very well then I contradict myself.
(I am large, I contain multitudes.)

The American contradictions reflect accurately what William James in his *Pragmatism* called "the common-sense world, in which we find things partly

INTRODUCTION

joined and partly disjoined" and where no "great single-word answers to the world's riddle." From the paradoxes two images of America emerge—the America of ideology, racism, violence, conformity, materialism, a nation anointed by God; and the America of experiment, equality, justice, diversity, idealism, one nation among many. Walt Whitman in his *Democratic Vistas*, saw the contest between the two Americas as a grand theme of history, "the battle advancing, retreating, between democracy's convictions, aspirations, and the people's crudeness, vice, caprices."

Yet, through all the unresolved paradoxes of the American character, through all the turmoil produced by unrelenting scientific and technological change, there winds a thread of historic and moral continuity. For America does have a single advantage over most nations. For the Declaration of Independence and the Constitution explicitly set forth the values and purposes of the republic in documents that defined goals, implied commitments and measured achievement. The men who signed the Declaration, said Lincoln, in Springfield, June 26, 1857, "meant to set up a standard maxim for a free society, which could be familiar to all, and revered by all; constantly looked to, constantly labored for, and even though never perfectly attained, constantly approximated, and thereby constantly spreading and deepening its influence, and augmenting the happiness and value of life to all people of all colors everywhere." Together the two national charters established the standards by which to set the American course and to judge the American performance.

The great engine of social change in America has been the determination to close the gap between performance and promise, between the reality and the ideal. The impulse toward reform is inherent in the American experiment. "America," said the Swedish author of *An American Dilemma*, Gunnar Myrdal, "is continuously struggling for its soul." The struggle in its nature must favor the America of experiment, justice and diversity; for these are the values affirmed by the American creed. In spite of periodic frustration, defeat and tragedy, the national experience has seen a steady narrowing of the gap between the promises embodied in the great charters and the realities of everyday life.

The struggle, as Whitman noted, sways back and forth and has done so throughout the history of the republic, and longer. "The two parties which divide the State," wrote Emerson in "The Conservative", "the party of Conservatism and that of innovation, are very old, and have disputed the possession of the world ever since it was made." As a people, Americans regularly go through seasons of action, passion, idealism and reform until energies languish. Then they long for respite and enter into seasons of withdrawal, neglect, hedonism and cynicism.

So in the first two decades of the 20th century two demanding Presidents, Theodore Roosevelt and Woodrow Wilson, exhorted the American people first to democratize political and economic institutions at home

and then to make the world safe for democracy. After 20 years of activism, the American people were emotionally exhausted. They yearned for "normalcy" and in 1920 got Warren G. Harding. The politics of purpose gave way to the politics of drift.

After the do-nothing 20s came a new burst of innovation, of action, passion and reform—Franklin Roosevelt and the New Deal, the Second World War, Harry Truman and the Fair Deal. Once again two activist decades left the people tired and drained. The Eisenhower lull provided a needed interlude of repose amidst the recurrent storms of the 20th century. Yet once more, as time passed, Americans felt the need to get their country moving again. As the 1920s made the 1930s necessary, so the 1950s led into the 1960s and a new rush of commitment: Kennedy and the New Frontier, Johnson and the Great Society, the racial revolution, the war against poverty.

This time desperate events—the assassination at Dallas, the Vietnam War—gave activism a sinister turn, an edge of hysteria. There followed riots in the cities, turmoil on the campuses, two more terrible assassinations, drugs and violence, Watergate and the fall of a President, until people feared that the social fabric itself might be unravelling. So much trauma compressed in so short a time produced national exhaustion in less than the customary two decades. By the 1970s America became once again, as it had been in the 1920s and the 1950s, a spent nation, fearful of responsibility, self-absorbed and cynical—the "me" decade, the "culture of narcissism."

Two things happen during the conservative swings of the cycle. On the one hand, rest recharges the national batteries and replenishes the national energies. On the other, the problems neglected in the years of drift become acute, threaten to become unmanageable and demand remedy. Each activist epoch has a detonating issue—a problem growing in magnitude and menace and beyond the capacity of the marketplace to control. At the turn of the century, the detonating issue was the concentration of private economic power in the trusts; in the 1930s it was depression and mass unemployment; in the 1960s it was racial injustice. As the republic rallies its forces to meet such problems, it develops new agendas and discharges impulses of innovation and reform against social anomalies across the board.

America in the 1980s faced a new set of issues— not only the transition from smokestacks to high technology, but the restoration of an infrastructure— roads, dams, bridges, harbors, water supply and sewage systems—in dangerous disrepair, and the control of a propensity toward inflation as deeply rooted in the structure of the economy as the propensity toward depression had been before the New Deal. If the unregulated marketplace could not meet these problems, then the nation might expect a new swing of the cycle with a new agenda and new priorities. Sometime in the 1980s, the dam would again break, as it had broken at the turn of the century, again in the 1930s, again in the 1960s, with a comparable release of innovation and reform in national affairs. So the long labor to fulfill the promises of American life would continue into the inscrutable future.

The law of acceleration dooms modern society to inexorable change. But, as Emerson wrote a century and a half ago in "The American Scholar", "If there is any period one would desire to be born in, is it not the age of Revolution; when the old and the new stand side by side and admit of being compared; when the energies of all men are searched by fear and by hope; when the historic glories of the old can be compensated by the rich possibilities of the new era? This time, like all times, is a very good one, if we but know what to do with it."

Steelmills and homes of workers, Pittsburgh, 1909.

FOUNDING A NATION

986–1787

GORDON S. WOOD
Professor of History, Brown University

FOUNDING A NATION 986-1787

Although the United States began with the Declaration of Independence in 1776, the actual origins of the American people go much further back in time—to at least the 16th century when the Spanish set up posts in Florida and in the western parts of the North American continent. America thus began as an outpost of Europe. Columbus's discovery of the New World on behalf of the Spanish crown in 1492 and the subsequent exploration and settlement of the Western Hemisphere by Spain and other European states were all aspects of the great explosion of Western energies that took place at the beginning of modern times. Over a period of 500 years, from the age of Columbus to the sudden collapse of the European empires in our own time, the states of Europe extended their influence—their languages, their economies and their peoples—over all parts of the globe. The United States was only the most important and most dramatic product of this outward thrust during the past half-millennium of world history.

During the 16th century Spain and Portugal dominated Europe's expansion into the Western Hemisphere. For more than a half century after Columbus's discovery England remained tied commercially to the European continent and made no effort to follow up its own claim to the New World established by the explorations of John Cabot in 1497. Then under Elizabeth I England suddenly turned away from Europe ·and began to earn its modern reputation as a great maritime power. During the course of the next cen-

A Timacua chief dispensing justice, 1590

tury, England, a tiny island in the northwest corner of Europe, spread its entrepreneurial energy over the world. The origins of the North American colonies that later became the United States lay in this outburst of English exploration and settlement.

England's settlement of the New World differed from that of the other European powers in a variety of ways. First of all, England transplanted more of its people abroad. While Spain during the first century of its colonization sent about 240,000 people to America, Britain in a like period sent 400,000 with over 100,000 more going to Ireland. And unlike the Spanish migrants, many of the English colonists went as families. The natures of the native American societies that received these Spanish and English settlers also differed. Whereas the Spanish colonists confronted large and flourishing Indian populations, the English found only scattered and sparsely populated tribes of natives. Instead, therefore, of ruling from above and racially mixing with the Indians, as the Spanish colonists did, the English displaced the natives, either by destroying them through war and disease or by driving them back into the hinterland.

Spanish South America and English North America contrasted in other ways, too. In the Spanish colonies the direction and government of the settlements came from above, from the crown and the Roman Catholic Church, and this central control resulted almost immediately in elaborate bureaucratic hierarchies that reached from Spain to the remotest parts of the Spanish empire. In English North America, however, the impetus for settlement came largely from below, from private entrepreneurs in search of profits or from religious dissidents in search of the freedom to worship. For nearly a century after England began its probes into the Western Hemisphere, the English Crown's role was confined to granting legal authority to exploit the New World, either to individuals or to groups of its subjects organized as commercial companies. Until the mid and late 17th century neither the English monarchy nor the established English Church paid much attention to what their own people were doing in the New World. Consequently, at the very outset the English settlement developed an extreme localist and de-

Mariners observing the North Star, 1575.

centralized nature that in subsequent centuries came to characterize much of American life.

The first permanent English settlement in America began with Jamestown in 1607, organized by the Virginia Company. The Virginia Company was a profit-seeking joint stock organization; it was modelled on such companies as the Levant and East India Companies that had been commercially successful in other parts of the world. But the barren, sparsely populated North American wilderness was not what the English investors in the Virginia Company expected. There were few mineral resources to exploit and no large numbers of natives to trade with or harness for labor. Consequently the Virginia Company, like the dozen or so other English companies created to exploit the New World, lost money immediately and struggled on until its collapse in 1624. Tobacco came too late to save the company but it did save the colony of Virginia. The European demand for tobacco, the first mass luxury product, soon was making fortunes for those Virginia settlers able to command labor and stay alive. Until the middle of the 17th century the Virginia settlers died like flies, mostly, it seems, from malaria. Only the immigration of an average of 1500 white bonded servants a year kept the colony and tobacco production growing. Tobacco production demanded large numbers of laborers as well as huge amounts of land. The result was that tobacco planters of the Chesapeake brought in thousands of servants from England and scattered themselves along the many rivers of the region. Much to the horror of some, this tobacco producing area, which had begun with a town in 1607, developed few other towns in the course of the next century or more.

Perhaps the most important characteristic of the English migrants to the New World, compared to those that came from other European countries, was their religious diversity. While Spain and France ensured that only orthodox Catholics went to their colonies, England was willing to send any of its people regardless of their religious beliefs. Out of the turmoil of the Reformation, England, by the late 16th century, had become the principal Protestant power in Europe. But many Englishmen were not happy with the way Queen Elizabeth had halted the momentum of the Reformation; they wanted to carry it further and to purify the English Church of all remnants of Catholicism. These Puritans, as they were called, differed among themselves over how they would reorganize the national church. Many Puritans wanted to cleanse the Church of England from within, abolishing bishops and numerous rituals. Still others wanted to do away altogether with the very structure of a national church and form only separate congregations of believers. Some extreme Protestants like the Quakers went even further and made every person his or her own church. Then, too, there were still many English Roman Catholics who never accepted England's break with Rome.

The English crown and church leaders were not happy with all this religious disorder and dissidence, and they attempted to compel greater orthodoxy and uniformity of belief. In reaction to such compulsion by the early 17th century many Englishmen looked to America as a place where they might settle and worship as they pleased. The most numerous and important of these religious dissidents were the Puritans, who settled largely in New England.

Puritan migrations to New England had begun with a small group of extreme Separatists who came to Plymouth via Holland in 1620. But these Pilgrims, as they came to be called, were a poor and humble group, and their few numbers were overwhelmed by the thousands of Puritan migrants who founded Boston and the Massachusetts Bay Colony ten years later. These Massachusetts Puritans were not Separatists; they had no desire to break from the established English Church. Instead they hoped to reform it from afar. They came with money and with a fierce determination to build a new model society of saints in the wilderness. Within a few years this Puritan society had towns scattered all over eastern Massachusetts Bay and south and west along the Connecticut River. In 1639 these Connecticut towns banded together and formed their own separate Puritan colony.

The Puritan leaders were not modern believers in religious freedom. They believed as firmly as did the Anglicans from whom they had fled that the church's beliefs must be orthodox and uniform and that the state had the obligation to support the church and its beliefs. Hence they punished Quakers and other dissenters in their midst as harshly as the Anglicans in England had punished them. Those such as Ann Hutchinson and Roger Williams, who would not conform to Massachusetts's orthodoxy, found refuge in settlements around Narragansett Bay to the south of Boston. Eventually these dissidents and refugees came together to form the colony of Rhode Island.

Although no English colony had quite the religious power of those of New England, other English colonies were settled for religious purposes. In 1632 Charles I granted the Roman Catholic Lord Baltimore a proprietary charter to a large wedge of territory north of Virginia. Both Baltimore and later his son sought to make the colony of Maryland into a feudal system of manors and an asylum for their fellow Catholics. But the manorial system never materialized and Protestants in the colony soon outnumbered Catholics. Later in the century another proprietor, William Penn, also sought to establish a religious haven for his

Puritans going to a Sunday service.

co-religionists, in his case, Quakers. In 1681 Charles II gave Penn proprietary rights to what became the huge colony of Pennsylvania, where Penn hoped to create a peaceful community filled with brotherly love and religious toleration. The Quakers and religious freedom thrived in this prosperous colony but brotherly love did not. Pennsylvania soon became one of the most ethnically diverse and faction-ridden of the English colonies.

The English, however, were not the only colonists in North America. North and west of the English colonies, in what became Canada, were limited numbers of French settlers; by 1700 they totalled only about 15,000. Although France had begun settling North America at about the same time as England, its bureaucratic government, its restrictive land-owning policies and its fear of allowing any but French Catholics to colonize retarded the development of French Canada. The Dutch also set up a post in North America. In the mid–1620s the Dutch West India company organized New Netherlands with its center on Manhattan Island, called New Amsterdam. The colony was thinly populated, and its many tiny settlements were not well-equipped to defend themselves against Indian raids. In 1664, when an English fleet captured New Amsterdam, this Dutch colony was ripe for the taking by the English Crown. It became New York.

By 1700, with the creation of other proprietary colonies in the Carolinas and the Jerseys in the last quarter of the century, the English had consolidated their control of a strip along the eastern edge of the North American continent. None of these settlements extended more than a couple of hundred miles inland, and their total population was only about 250,000. They were repeatedly disrupted by border clashes and warfare with the French, Spanish and Indians, and they were often racked by disorder and even rebellions, like that of Nathaniel Bacon in Virginia in 1676. Yet despite all these difficulties and turmoil these primitive English colonies were prospering and growing rapidly, more rapidly indeed than any people in the western world.

During the last part of the 17th century, the English government became increasingly interested in these fast-growing and prosperous outposts. The Crown began to take back what it had so freely given away to private individuals and groups at the beginning of the century and to assert greater control over the government of the colonies. From the 1660s on, the Crown began confiscating many of the company and proprietary charters and placing these private governments under royal jurisdiction. In 1685 James II brought these imperial efforts to a head with his short-lived Dominion of New England, the most radical attempt the English government ever made in America to create a centralized viceroyalty, like that of imperial Spain operating directly on the colonists. Although this extreme royal venture collapsed with the overthrow of James II in England in the Glorious Revolution of 1688-69, the crown did not stop its piecemeal efforts to extend its rule over the colonies. By the

middle of the 18th century only four North American colonies remained outside the Crown's direct management—the proprietary colonies of Pennsylvania and Maryland and the small chartered colonies of Connecticut and Rhode Island; even these were circumscribed by the English government's jurisdiction in new ways. All the rest were royal colonies whose governors were appointed by the crown 3000 miles away.

This royal control, however, never went deep into colonial affairs. In each colony locally-elected assemblies inhibited the governors' power over the societies they ruled. The empire that emerged by the beginning of the 18th century was thus a superficial mercantile one—confined largely to the regulation of colonial trade. As early as the mid-17th century the English Parliament began passing a number of navigation acts designed to control the movement of goods in and out of the colonies. Certain valuable "enumerated" goods such as tobacco and sugar had to be sent to England before shipment elsewhere in the world, and nearly all European goods imported into the colonies had to go through England. The mother country sent to the colonies an increasing number of officials—customs collectors, revenue officers, and vice-admiralty judges—to enforce the new navigation system. Yet the colonists repeatedly bribed these imperial officials and evaded many of the trade regulations. The English government's control over its colonies remained therefore slight and shallow; it scarcely interfered with the colonists' pursuit of their own local interests. And because both the colonies and England were prospering, few politicians in the mother country worried much about the superficial and decentralized character of their empire.

By the early decades of the 18th century, colonial society was becoming more stable. Local elites or aristocracies emerged in each of the colonies, and social distinctions became more durable and inheritable than they ever had been during the early chaotic decades of settlement of the 17th century. The rich became richer and if the poor did not become poorer they at least were becoming more and more separated from those large landowners and wealthy merchants at the top of the social pyramid. Yet America's social hierarchy, by English and European standards, remained remarkably stunted and flat. These provincial colonies located on the very edges of the civilized world had no titled nobility to speak of, no court life, no great cities and none of the fabulous wealth and artworks displayed by the 18th century English and European aristocracies. As rich and distinguished as aristocrats like William Byrd or Robert Livingston may have been in Virginia or New York, they remained only minor gentry in comparison with 18th century English aristocrats; their estates were miniature set against the magnificent palaces the English nobility built for themselves.

Moreover, at the same time as American society was missing the topmost tiers of a traditional European society, it was also without the bottommost levels, at least among the white colonists. There were some poor in America, particularly in what passed as cities, but their numbers were miniscule compared to the destitute of England and France. The American colonists suffered no food crises; they probably enjoyed the highest standard of living in the world. Yet in France and other parts of Europe famine continued to be a recurrent problem; even in more prosperous England half the population was periodically dependent for subsistence on some form of charity. Unlike England where land was scarce and the mass of farmers were tenants paying rent to gentry and aristocratic landlords, most American white farmers owned their own land. No doubt Americans had distinctions of gentility and differences of wealth, but compared to what people had known of societies through history, their social world seemed remarkably middling and equal. Indeed, so remote, so flat and so unelegant did American society seem that many Europeans regarded the colonists as little better than savages.

In the 18th century this prosperous, largely yeoman population continued to grow by leaps and bounds, doubling every 25 years or so. In 1680 Pennsylvania had a population of only about 4000; by 1740 it was over 80,000 and rising rapidly. People were living longer and marrying earlier and having more surviving children. But this extraordinary growth of population was also fed by immigration, immigration that was very different from that of the 17th century. The earlier exclusively English migration declined; the only Englishmen now encouraged to go to the colonies were convicts and paupers. Georgia, the last British colony in what would become the United States, was in fact founded in 1732 as a philanthropic refuge for the English poor. But as the numbers of English immigrants slackened, their places were taken by tens of thousands of others—mainly Scots, Scotch-Irish and Irish from the British Isles and Germans from the upper Rhine valley. These people poured into the middle colonies, especially into Pennsylvania; many made their way westward or south down the Appalachian valley into the Carolinas. From 1700 to 1775 perhaps as many as 300,000 white immigrants journeyed to America. By the time of the Revolution, colonial society was much less English and more heterogeneous than it had been.

Most conspicuously adding to the diversity of 18th century colonial society were the hundreds of thousands of black African slaves. Black servants had appeared in Virginia as early as 1619, but it was not until the end of the 17th century—when the colonists' incessant demand for labor, particularly in the tobacco plantations of the Chesapeake and the newly opened rice fields of South Carolina, could no longer be met by white indentured servants—that black slaves were brought into the colonies in large numbers. Already by 1680 the number of blacks in the Chesapeake area was well over 4000; by 1720 it was 37,000 and increasing rapidly. Altogether between 1700 and 1775 perhaps 250,000 blacks were imported into the North American colonies. By the time of the Revolution

blacks made up nearly a half million out of a total American population of two million.

Blacks were everywhere in America—perhaps constituting as much as 14% of the population of New York—but nine out of ten of them were in the Southern Colonies; in 1740 two-thirds of the population of South Carolina was black. Some of these Afro-Americans were free, though their status as free men declined steadily in the 18th century. But most were slaves, bought and sold as property in an oppressive system of hereditary lifetime servitude unlike anything Englishmen had ever known. The debasement of the blacks was distinctive and brutal, even for that callous age, but it differed in different regions of the colonies—milder among the household servants of the northern cities, severe but stable in the long-existing Afro-American slave communites of the Chesapeake tobacco colonies, but becoming incredibly savage and lethal in the disease-ridden rice and indigo swamps of South Carolina.

The increasing diversity of colonial society expressed itself in a thousand different ways—in German newspapers, increased whisky drinking and new dances and dialects. But most impressive was the greater variety of religions. At the same time as the English crown was extending its control over the governments of the colonies, the established Church of England sought to bring the colonists' religious life more into line with that of the mother country. But by the early 18th century the English Church confronted an American religious world that was almost totally contrary to what the age expected. Instead of having a government-supported nationally integrated orthodox church that at best tolerated nonconformists and dissenters, America had unintentionally created a crazy mosaic made up of dozens, if not hundreds, of different and often competing religious groups; many people in fact had no religion at all. To be sure, some of the colonies, especially in the South, did have formal Anglican establishments, but nowhere did these establishments duplicate the hierarchical Church of the Mother Country. There were no bishops in America, indeed no hierarchy at all, and everywhere Anglican clergymen remained weak and dependent on their local congregations. Even in Virginia, where the Church of England was strongest, Anglican clergymen were in a running battle with planter-dominated vestries. In the other colonies the Anglican establishment existed virtually in name only, overwhelmed in numbers by dissenting groups of Presbyterians, Congregationalists, Baptists, Quakers or whatever. Both Pennsylvania and Rhode Island even formally rejected the very idea of an established church. Only in New England—in Connecticut and Massachusetts—were there tax-supported religious establishments that resembled that of England. Yet these establishments, to the unending chagrin of the Anglicans, were Puritan; and the Church of England was humiliatingly forced to compete in New England as a tolerated dissenting sect.

Most colonial clergymen were not very happy with this unexpected religious chaos, and everywhere they sought to organize and centralize religious affairs and to bring more people into the embrace of the churches. Even the Puritans in New England tried to counter the extreme localism of their separate congregations and to blur the once vital distinction between saved and damned in order to increase church membership. In all the colonies, clergymen of different religious persuasions competed with one another for communicants. They lowered their distinctive beliefs to the commonest denominator and stressed formal rituals and external behavior at the expense of inner piety. And in so doing they often failed to meet the emotional and spiritual needs of their communities.

The inevitable reaction came, first with the hell-fire preaching of the learned Jonathan Edwards during the 1730s in the Connecticut River Valley, and later with enthusiastic revivals inspired by the great itinerant English preacher, George Whitefield. Between 1739 and 1741 Whitefield traveled up and down the continent and released a flood of pent-up evangelical fervor. Itinerant preachers of various persuasions sprung up and tore into established parishes with their dire warnings of sin and hopeful promises of rebirth. They preached everywhere and anywhere, sometimes in church buildings, but often in barns and open fields. They drew huge crowds of crying, sobbing people, thousands upon thousands of desperate souls asking what they must do to be saved.

This was the Great Awakening. Nothing like it on such a scale had ever happened before in America. Within a few years the height of the fever had passed, but the effects of the Awakening were lasting. Religious life in America would never again be the same.

Not only did such revivals become the dominant mode of American religious expression, but the Great Awakening had the effect of clarifying religious developments in America that hitherto had been only dimly understood. Instead of reversing the religious diversity and chaos of the early 18th century, it added to it. Beliefs and doctrines became more blurred, religious groups were further splintered, and the authority of the clergy slipped more and more into the hands of their congregations. Religion lost much of its traditional concern for the whole community and became more a matter of individual choice—of personal acts of conversion. Finally, the idea that government had an obligation to support one religious truth or group over another was considerably weakened. American religious life now seemed to be little more than a marketplace of disparate Christian organizations or denominations, none more orthodox or privileged than another, all in competition for souls.

By the middle of the 18th century the English government was becoming both more interested in these burgeoning prosperous colonies and more alarmed by the confusion and chaos of their behavior. Royal officials complained incessantly of the colonists' increased defiance of authority and their continued evasions of the navigation acts. The colonial population was growing faster than anyone could have believed possible and was becoming an ever larger and more important part of the whole British world. In 1700 the American colonists had been only one-twentieth of the British and Irish combined; by 1770 they were nearly one-fifth. In the 20 years after 1745 the value of their exports to Britain doubled, and their imports from Britain rose even faster. British officials realized with heightened apprehension that these remote and half-savage North American provinces were becoming the most important and expanding segment of the British Empire; already one-half of all British shipping was engaged in American commerce. The colonists, too, were aware of their surprising growth and prided themselves on it. It seemed a sign of some great future destiny; already writers on both sides of the Atlantic were talking about the inevitable movement of civilization westward. Some far-sighted colonists such as Benjamin Franklin were even predicting that sooner or later the metropolitan center of the British Empire would have to shift to America.

It was in the context of heightened concern for the North American colonies that British officials and imperial-minded colonists prepared for a renewal of war with France. Since the 17th century, England had engaged in repeated struggles with France and Spain for the mastery of Europe, struggles into which the colonists were inevitably drawn. Now by 1750 it became clear to all antagonists that the central theater of the next phase of this periodic European warfare would take place in North America. France, alarmed by the growth of the British colonies, tried to secure its hold on the Ohio Valley by building a string of forts. The colonists resisted and unofficial fighting began. In 1754 at a meeting at Albany, imperial officials tried to organize the separate colonies against the French and Indian threat, but the plan of union was rejected by the colonies. That such a colonial union should even have been drawn up, however, suggested the unprecedented nature of the developing crisis. In 1755 Major General Edward Braddock, Commander-in-Chief of the British forces in America, suffered a disastrous defeat at the hands of the French and Indians, and the war in America became a titanic struggle for empire. After a series of setbacks, the British government reorganized itself under the leadership of William Pitt and the superiority of British wealth and colonial numbers slowly began to tell. With Brigadier General James Wolfe's capture of Quebec in 1759, a British victory inevitably followed. By the Peace of Paris of 1763, Britain acquired from the defeated powers, France and Spain, all of Canada, Nova Scotia, East and West Florida and millions of fertile acres between the Appalachians and the Mississippi. Since France was forced to cede to Spain the huge territory of Louisiana in compensation for Spain's entering the war, France—Britain's most fearsome enemy—was removed once and for all from the North American continent. Great Britain stood astride an empire that was as large and prosperous as any since the fall of Rome.

The consequences of this Seven Years' War (or the French and Indian War, as it was called in America)

GORDON S. WOOD

ultimately proved to be the undoing of the British empire. The newly acquired territory in North America had to be policed, and the Indians in the trans-Appalachian area had to be protected from land-hungry settlers. Thus the British Army in North America could not be not be sent home, but had to be retained in western posts at great expense. When this expense was added to the £137 million of British war debt, the overall cost of the war and the peace became staggering to a hardpressed British government. It was natural, therefore, for the British government to look to its colonies to help provide revenue to support this newly enlarged empire. Following a royal proclamation in 1763 that prohibited white settlement in the trans-Appalachian West and reserved it for the Indians, the British Parliament enacted a momentous series of measures. In just a few short years Great Britain attempted to centralize its decentralized empire and to reverse a half-century of what Edmund Burke called the "salutary neglect" of its colonies. Under that neglect the colonists had developed too keen a sense of their local rights and privileges to accept any intrusion on them lying down. They were driven first into resistance and finally into revolution.

In 1764 came the Sugar Act, a wide-ranging successor to the great navigation acts of the 17th century. It not only added duties to a number of products imported into the colonies, but it tightened up the navigation system in a variety of ways with the aim of curbing colonial evasion and smuggling. In 1765 came the Stamp Act, the first direct tax that Parliament had ever laid on America. It aroused a storm of colonial protest and was repealed in 1766. Next, in 1767, the British government, under the leadership of Chancellor of the Exchequer Charles Townshend, tried to raise revenue by levying still more customs duties; at the same time the bureaucracy of the empire was further strengthened and many of the British troops were moved from the West into the coastal ports. These measures in turn provoked angry agreements among the colonists not to import British goods until the duties were withdrawn. Conflict with the British army in Boston in 1770 erupted in a riot in which the troops killed five civilians—the "Boston Massacre." Although Britain eventually repealed all the Townshend duties except that on tea, by the early 1770s the nerves of both the British and the colonists were on edge and their patience exhausted. When the colonists on December 16, 1773 dumped £10,000 worth of tea into Boston Harbor, the final crisis was at hand. Britain retaliated in 1774 with a series of coercive acts, including the closing of the port of Boston. A clash of arms followed on April 19, 1775 at Lexington and Concord, and Britain and its colonies were at war.

The war went on for eight years—the longest war in United States history until that of Vietnam nearly two centuries later. The Americans lost many of the battles, but under General George Washington's leadership they kept their faith in the cause and their army in the field. They defeated the British when it counted, at Saratoga in the fall of 1777, which brought France into the struggle against Britain, and finally at Yorktown in 1781. This victory led inevitably to the peace treaty of 1783, in which Britain finally recognized the independence of the United States and agreed to generous boundaries for the new country: on the west, the Mississippi River; on the south, the Spanish-held Floridas; on the north, roughly the present boundary with Canada. Even the French were stunned by what America's peace negotiators—Benjamin Franklin, John Adams and John Jay—achieved.

But the peace of 1783 was not the whole of the American Revolution. What had begun in the 1760s as a struggle within the British Empire for colonial autonomy became in the end a world-shattering event that went well beyond a simple colonial war for independence. During the imperial debate in the 1760s and 1770s the colonists were compelled to explain to themselves why they differed so much from Great Britain and other European nations. In the process the Americans came to see that all the discrepancies between themselves and Europeans were not really as bad and shameful as they often had been made to think. All of America's social characteristics that earlier had been seen as deficiencies—the incomplete development of an established church, the chaos of religious groups, the lack of a titled nobility, the unfinished social hierarchy, the insufficiency of elegance and luxury, and the general immaturity and mediocrity of colonial life—all these characteristics could now be viewed as good and desirable. For decades enlightened reformers in Europe and Britain had suggested that the colonists of the New World—in their simplicity, equality, prosperity and freedom—represented an ideal young republican society that stood in glaring contrast to the corruption and decadence of monarchical and aristocratic Europe. Now in the crises of revolution, Americans came to believe all this with a new intensity and to see that they were not after all in the backwaters of history and on the remote edges of civilization, but were in fact in the vanguard of history—a special people with a special destiny to show the world the republican way toward equality and liberty.

Even before the independence of the colonies from Great Britain was declared on July 4, 1776, Americans began creating new republican state constitutions. The formation of these separate state constitutions in place of the former royal colonial governments was, said Thomas Jefferson in 1776, "the whole object of the present controversy." For the Revolution aimed not just to free Americans from British tyranny but to prevent all future tyrannies. They incorporated their constitutions in written documents that prescribed both the powers of government and the rights of citizens and thus permanently changed the thinking of the world about what a constitution ought to be. These new state governments quickly moved to embody the liberal values of the 18th century Enlightenment: by expanding the suffrage and popular representation in government; by equalizing the laws of inheritance; by prohibiting monopolies and other forms of legal privilege; by reforming the law and softening the harshness of the traditional penal codes; by drawing up plans for popular education; by providing for new roles for republican women; and, most important, by beginning an attack on the existence of black slavery. For over a century slavery had existed in America without substantial criticism; now in the libertarian atmosphere of the Revolution, slavery was suddenly seen to be an aberration, a "peculiar institution" that could no longer be automatically accepted as part of the nature of things. if slavery were to continue, as it did in the Southern States, it would now have to be anxiously defended; and for the first time the South began to be self-conscious of its distinctiveness as a region.

At the same time as the new republican states were creating their separate governments, Americans were busy forming a confederation of these governments, the "United States of America." As the failure of the Albany Plan of Union in 1754 showed, Americans were very reluctant to surrender the independence of their separate governments to any superintending body. The Articles of Confederation, sent to the states for ratification in 1777, provided for a "firm league of friendship" among these states. Although the confederation gained some substantial powers, the crucial powers to tax and regulate commerce remained with the individual states. Weak as it was, this union was not ratified by all the states until March 1781. By the time of the peace treaty with Britain in 1783, the central government of the United States had already shown itself to be too impotent to govern. The location and decentralized nature of American life that had baffled the British for over a century now threatened to undo this new experiment in republican liberty even as it began. It was becoming obvious to many Americans that their Revolution and their efforts at national union were not over in 1783, but in some senses had just begun.

CHRONOLOGY

986
Discovery Norse navigator Bjarni Herjulfson is blown off course while searching for Eric the Red's coastal Greenland settlement, founded in 986. Herjulfon's ship is driven to the south and he reports there the sighting of an unidentified land mass, probably the shores of mainland North America.

1000
Exploration Lief Ericson, a son of Eric the Red, explores the east coast of North America. As he sails southward, he names the areas he encounters in his voyage: Helluland (the land of flat rocks), Markland (forest land) and Vinland (wine land). Recent archeological discoveries (1961-1968) have found a Norse settlement at L'Anse-aux-Meadows in the northern peninsula of Newfoundland, and the general topographic features strongly suggest this was the site of Vinland. Traces of at least eight buildings have been found—one some 25 feet by 17 feet, with a hearth in the center and sleeping platforms on the walls—and these, along with finds of artifacts (iron nails and rivets, a stone lamp, a spindle whorl and more) all can be traced to Norse practices and sources of this period. It is believed that this settlement was abandoned after only 25 to 50 years of residence at most, and in any case it did not become known to the world at large until our own time.

1004-1008
Exploration Lief Ericson's brothers, Thorvald and Thorstein, further explore the North American coast.

A Norse boat used as shelter in the Americas.

EARLY MAN, INDIANS AND THE MOUND BUILDERS

When the first European explorers arrived, they did not find a continent empty of human beings. Awaiting them were some two million indigenous Indians, the members of some 600 tribes and the speakers of about 500 distinct languages. These Indians were the descendants of a far earlier group of immigrants. According to all present evidence, the species *Homo sapiens* did not evolve in the new world. Instead, between the years 40,000 to 8,000 B.C., early Asiatic peoples crossed over the Bering Strait land bridge at a time when the ocean level was low because so much water was in great ice sheets.

Over millennia, these newcomers penetrated southward, eventually spreading widely over the North and South American continents. Basically hunting, fishing and gathering cultures, these early people left fossil remains and evidences of settlement in North America. The Minnesota Woman from the glacial Lake Agassiz and the Midland man from Texas are two of the most ancient; and radiocarbon dating indicates settlements occurring from 35,000 to 8000 B.C. The Bat Cave site in central New Mexico offers an early example of a primitive form of corn, from 3000 to 2000 B.C.

Unlike the complex civilizations of the Maya, Aztecs and Incas that later developed from Mexico to Peru, the peoples north of the Rio Grande River essentially remained strongly individualistic and unregimented, as far as can be determined. The North American Indian cultures ranged from nomadic groups to the inhabitants of century-old towns.

The most fascinating and monumental architectural remains in North America are those of the Mound Builders. The ancestors of present-day Indians, the Mound Builders occupied a wide area in the Mississippi River valley. They left a series of elaborate earthworks, some over 2000 years old and some as recent as the mid-16th century. As sedentary farmers, the Mound Builders created impressive weavings, pottery, stone carvings, and other artifacts. Their mounds, which served as foundations for temples and dwellings, as fortifications, as burial chambers and as religious sites and totems, varied in size from 1 to 100 acres. Eclecticism also characterized the shapes of the mounds—which included cones, pyramids and representations of animal forms. The largest still-existing structure is the Cahokia mound near East St. Louis, Illinois. This 100-foot tall truncated pyramid sits on a 17-acre base. The most complex mound is the Ohio Great Serpent Mound—the elaborate coiled earthwork representing a snake is 5 feet high and 1350 feet long.

The European advance into the American interior eventually eradicated all remnants of this mound-building culture, although the earliest French arrivals in the late 1600s still found the Natchez Indians using mounds for temples and habitations.

1010-1013
Exploration An Icelandic trader, Thorfinn Karlsevni, sails in a voyage of discovery to the North

FOUNDING A NATION 986-1787

American coast, probably exploring areas other than those already seen by Leif Ericson and his brothers. Possibly Karlsevni also sails into Hudson Bay.

1014-1015
Exploration The last Norse voyage to the new world takes place. According to the Greenland Saga, Eric's daughter Freydis sails with Karlsevni on the final trip to the mainland.

1542
Discovery Portuguese explorers Diogo de Tieve and Pedro Vasquez discover the Atlantic islands Corvo and Flores of the Azores, and their ships are subsequently blown northward by a storm until they reach what may have been the Grand Bank of Newfoundland before they sail back to Portugal.

1480-1481
Exploration Voyages from Bristol, England are made by Thomas Lloyd and others toward America.

12 OCTOBER 1492
Discovery After over two months at sea, Christopher Columbus first sights the Bahamas, one of which he names San Salvador. This voyage, the first of four, is funded by the Spanish Crown and private sponsors who wish to find a western sea route to Asia. Sailing on the *Santa Maria,* Columbus commands a fleet of two other ships, the *Niña* and the *Pinta.*

25 DECEMBER 1492
Exploration The *Santa Maria* is wrecked off Hispaniola (Santo Domingo) during an exploratory voyage to the coasts of Cuba and Hispaniola. After founding the settlement of La Navidad there, Columbus returns to Spain.

3-4 MAY 1493
Exploration In two papal bulls, Pope Alexander VI grants to Spain all lands not under Christian rule that fall west of a demarcation line 100 leagues west of the Azores.

11 JUNE 1493
Exploration On his second voyage to the new

The landing of Columbus at San Salvador.

CHRISTOPHER COLUMBUS, c. 1451-1506

Although it is now known that the arrival of Christopher Columbus in the Americas was preceded by the voyages and even brief settlement in Newfoundland of Norse seamen some five centuries earlier, this does not diminish Columbus' achievement. The voyages of Columbus took a much longer southerly route and, most importantly, were followed by widespread, rapid and permanent European settlement in the New World.

Aside from his discovery of America, Columbus himself was a remarkable man for his era. Born in humble circumstances to a Genoese weaver father, and largely self-educated both in the basic skills of literacy and in navigation, he made an excellent marriage into a distinguished and propertied Genoese family. He was rewarded for his daring first voyage to the Americas by the Spanish titles of admiral and viceroy, and by a coat of arms. Thus Columbus was a self-made man who rose to the highest levels of society.

Before his historic voyages, Columbus had some 37 years of practical experience in seamanship, beginning on trading voyages at the age of 14, first along the Italian coast, and then to Marseilles and Tunis. Shipwrecked while on a voyage to Flanders and England, he landed penniless in Lisbon, Portugal, then the main European center of overseas exploration. Possibly he became involved here in selling navigation charts with his brother. He also continued his passage on mercantile trips to Iceland, Ireland, Madeira and West Africa.

Columbus' original agreement with the Spanish Crown for his 1492 voyage enabled him to "discover islands and mainland in the Ocean Sea," the "islands" and "mainland" referring to Cipangu and Cathay—Marco Polo's names for Japan and China. As the world already was accepted as round and there was no knowledge of an intervening continent, Columbus' proposal was deemed quite reasonable and based on respectable authority. But Columbus' calculations were based on Marco Polo's overestimate of the east-west area of Asia and on Ptolemy's underestimate of the circumference of the globe—hence setting the distance to the orient at 3000 nautical miles rather than at the actual distance of 10,000 nautical miles. Thus when Columbus landed on the Bahamian cay of San Salvador in October 1492, he erroneously regarded the island as an outlying Japanese island. To the end of his days Columbus persisted in this misapprehension. On his fourth and last voyage he explored the western reaches of the Caribbean Sea in search of the Malayan peninsula and India. His characteristic stubbornness and sense of divine guidance led him to reject all contradictory evidence.

Regardless of these errors, Columbus was an able sea commander, a courageous explorer and a creative geographical theorist. But his greatest skill was as an unerringly accurate navigator. In spite of his very conservative navigation techniques, using only the simplest type of celestial navigation, he possessed an uncanny sense of dead reckoning which always led him directly to any place he had once visited. For example, on his third voyage, he sailed directly from the Venezuela coast to the new Spanish settlement on Hispaniola.

Like most of the other early European explorers, Columbus was an adventurer in obsessive search of gold. This led to a only half-hearted participation in the Hispaniola colonization efforts and to an at-times brutal treatment of the native Caribbean peoples. In his last years in Spain, Columbus enjoyed a substantial income from his West Indian discoveries, along with a tarnished reputation. He died in Valladolid in relative obscurity, and it remained to his illegitimate younger son Fernando to rescue his reputation and to raise Columbus to legendary status.

King Ferdinand pointing across the Atlantic.

world, Columbus sets out with more than 1200 men on 17 ships from Cadiz. In this trip of nearly three years Columbus explores the Leeward Islands, Puerto Rico, the Cuban coast, Jamaica and Hispaniola.

28 NOVEMBER 1493
Settling Coming back to Hispaniola, Columbus finds his colonial outpost of La Navidad destroyed.

2 JANUARY 1494
Settling Columbus establishes a second port of Isabela on Santo Domingo. The settlement also experiences problems caused by a poor choice of site, inadequate gold and the rebelliousness of the local native peoples. These difficulties lead to its abandonment, to be followed by the 1496 establishment of the city of Santo Domingo.

7 JUNE 1494
Discovery Portugal and Spain sign the Treaty of Tordesillas which moves the demarcation line created by the papal bulls of 1493 to 370 leagues west of the Cape Verde Islands. In this treaty, Portugal is given control of any territories east of the line. Possibly, unknown to Spain, Portugal has already discovered Brazil to which it now has a legal right.

10 MARCH 1496
Exploration At the conclusion of his second voyage of discovery, Columbus sets sail for the return trip to Spain. He leaves his brother Bartolomeo in command in Santo Domingo.

24 JUNE 1497
Discovery John Cabot, in possession of a trade monopoly issued by Henry VII of England, first sights the land mass of the North American continent, probably Newfoundland. He claims this area for the English monarch and then sails southward along the coast, probably reaching Maine, before he returns to Bristol, England in early August.

MAY 1498
Exploration In early May, John Cabot leaves on his second voyage to America and this time he explores the east coast of the continent, possibly as far south as Delaware or even Chesapeake Bay.

30 MAY 1498
Exploration With a fleet of seven ships, Columbus sets sail on his third voyage of discovery to the Americas. This time taking a more southerly route, he comes upon Trinidad and views the coast of South America.

31 AUGUST 1498
Settling Columbus arrives at Santo Domingo to find the port in the midst of an uprising caused by poor administration of the colony. The Brothers Columbus are sent home as prisoners, and the Spanish Crown replaces them with a new governor.

27 JUNE 1499
Discovery Amerigo Vespucci, sailing on a Spanish voyage of discovery led by Alonso de Hajeda, first sights the South American coast, explores southward along this coast and then sails around the Bahamas on his return trip to Spain.

19 MARCH 1501
Exploration King Henry VII of England grants a

patent to three English merchants and three from the Azores, who then supposedly complete two expeditions to the new world.

13 MAY 1501
Exploration Amerigo Vespucci, now sailing under the Portuguese flag, voyages again to the South American coast. The Portuguese have already sent representatives to the new world in the persons of João Fernandes (1499) and Gaspar Corte-Real (1500), to be followed by Miguel Corte-Real (1502), who explore northern waters in the area of Labrador and Newfoundland. Upon his return to Portugal, Vespucci writes several letters to his former patron, Lorenzo de'Medici, stating his belief that his voyages have been to a new continent.

11 MAY 1502
Exploration With a fleet of four ships, Columbus sets sail on his fourth and last voyage to the Americas.

15 JUNE 1502
Exploration Columbus lands at Martinique. Then, after a stop at Santo Domingo, he explores central America from the area of the Honduras to Panama.

9 DECEMBER 1502
Exploration A second patent is granted by Henry VII of England to the "Company of Adventures to the New World," an Anglo-Portuguese group. This patent results in a series of transatlantic voyages through 1505, probably reaching the mid–Atlantic coast of North America.

25 JUNE 1503
Exploration Returning from his Central American expedition, Columbus is shipwrecked and marooned in Jamaica before his return to Spain.

20 MAY 1506
Exploration Columbus dies in Valladolid, Spain still believing that his voyages have been to Asia, rather than to an entirely new continent.

25 APRIL 1507
Discovery Geographer Martin Waldseemuller first uses the name "America" to indicate the new world in his book *Cosmographiae Introductio*, apparently erroneously crediting the Italian navigator Amerigo Vespucci with the discovery of the continent.

2-8 APRIL 1513
Discovery During an era of Spanish exploration and exploitation of the Caribbean islands, the conqueror of Puerto Rico, Juan Ponce de Leon, sights Florida in the area of St. Augustine. Ponce de Leon subsequently explores both the eastern and western coasts of Florida. Later Spanish voyages around the Florida and Atlantic coast include those by Alvarez Pineda in 1519; Francisco de Gordillo who in 1521 covered the coastal area from Florida to South Carolina; Esteban

Gomez in 1524 who sailed from Nova Scotia to Florida; and Pedro de Quexos (1524-25) who traveled as far north as the mid–Atlantic states.

20 FEBRUARY 1521
Settling Ponce de Leon, having received a patent from the Spanish crown to colonize Florida, sets sail from Puerto Rico with a company of 200 men. Landing in Florida probably at Charlotte Harbor, Ponce de Leon is wounded in an attack by the natives and his group returns to Cuba, where he dies. But this abortive attempt to establish a settlement on the mainland is not to discourage the Spaniards for long.

19 MARCH 1524
Exploration Sent by Francis I of France to find a route to the east Indies, Giovanni de Verrazano sights land around the area of the Carolinas.

17 APRIL 1524
Discovery Verrazano reaches New York harbor and discovers the Hudson River. Then he sails on northward to Narragansett Bay and continues on to Nova Scotia before his return to France. It is some ten years before the French crown sponsors another voyage to the new world.

JULY 1526
Settling The Spanish Crown grants Lucas Vasquez de Ayllon a patent to colonize Florida and he sails from Hispaniola with 500 prospective colonists for the Cape Fear area of North Carolina. He tries to establish a settlement there near the Pedee River. During the fall and severe winter Ayllon and 350 others die. The survivors give up and return to Hispaniola.

10 JUNE 1527
Exploration Two English ships, the *Samson* and the *Mary Guilford* sail from Plymouth for North America. The *Samson* is lost at sea but the *Mary Guilford* voyages southward down the coast from Labrador, reaching the West Indies in November.

14 APRIL 1528
Settling A group of 400 Spanish colonists led by Panfilo de Narvaez lands in Florida at Tampa Bay. They trek north to the village of Apalachee near Tallahassee in a fruitless search for gold. Disappointed, they set sail for Mexico on September 22. Of the two men who survive the subsequent shipwreck, Cabeza de Vaca reaches Mexico City in 1536 and his version of the trip reinforces the legend of the immensely wealthy Seven Cities of Cibola, located somewhere in New Mexico.

10 JUNE 1534
Exploration Sponsored by Francis I of France, Jacques Cartier (who may also have sailed with Verrazano in 1524) arrives at the Strait of Belle Isle, voyages southward along the coasts of Newfoundland, Prince Edward Island and Gaspe Bay before his return to France.

9 AUGUST 1535
Exploration On his second voyage to North America, Jacques Cartier travels up the St. Lawrence River to Quebec and then with smaller boats goes on to Montreal. He spends the winter in Quebec and returns to France the following year.

28 MAY 1539
Exploration The governor of Cuba, Hernando de Soto, lands on the Florida coast at either Tampa Bay or Charlotte Harbor with 600 Spanish soldiers. They explore the western half of Florida and spend the winter of 1539-40 in Apalachee, visited some 11 years earlier by Narvaez's expedition. The following spring they march northward to the Savannah River area, then westward to the Blue Ridge Mountains and finally back to the Gulf of Mexico near Mobile. After spending the winter of 1540-41 in the delta country, de Soto and his men again march north, crossing the Mississippi River near Memphis. They then pass west through the Ozark Mountains and spend a third winter (1541-42) in eastern Oklahoma. After their return to the Mississippi River, de Soto falls ill and dies. The rest of the company, led by Luis Moscoso de Alvarado, travels west to the upper Brazos River and spends its fourth and last winter (1542-43) by the Mississippi River near the mouth of the Arkansas River. The following summer they end their expedition by sailing down the Mississippi. This epic journey into the American wilderness by the Spaniards marks their serious and concerted effort to claim America as their own.

8 JULY 1539
Exploration Spaniard Francisco de Ulloa embarks from Acapulco, Mexico to sail northward in the Gulf of California, around the tip of Baja California and northward up the coast of the peninsula.

7 JULY 1540
Exploration Spaniard Francisco Vasquez de Coronado captures a Zuñi Indian pueblo at Hawikuh in western New Mexico, believing it to be one of the legendary wealthy Seven Cities of Cibola. This pueblo was originally discovered by Franciscan Fray Marcos de Niza in 1539. From this base camp of Hawikuh, renamed Granada-Cibola by its conquerors, Don Garcia Lopez de Cardenas leads a westward expedition of discovery to the Grand Canyon. Hernando de Alvarado travels eastward from Granada-Cibola to Albuquerque and the Texas Panhandle looking for the wealthy legendary kingdom of Quivéra.

25 AUGUST 1540
Exploration In support of Coronado, Hernando de Alarcon sets out from Acapulco to explore the Gulf of California and journeys up the Colorado River to a point near its junction with the Gila River.

26 MAY 1541
Exploration After spending the winter near Albuquerque, Francisco de Coronado leads an expeditionary force northwest, finally reaching Kansas, before he returns to Mexico City.

AUGUST 1541
Exploration On his third and last voyage, Jacques Cartier returns to Quebec to conquer, with the aid of Roberval, the kingdom of the Saguenay, which he believed to be fabulously wealthy. Cartier returns to France with a shipload of fool's gold and quartz, which he thought to be diamonds. After an unsuccessful trip up the Saguenay River, Roberval soon follows.

27 JUNE 1542
Exploration Juan Rodriguez Cabrillo voyages up the California coast and claims the territory for Spain.

1 MARCH 1543
Exploration Bartolome Ferrelo, Cabrillo's successor, sails north along the California coast and reaches what is probably Oregon.

26 JUNE 1549
Indians In one of the first missionary efforts by the Spanish, Dominican Fray Luis Cancer de Babastro is killed by the Indians when he arrives in Florida from Vera Cruz for the purpose of converting the Indians to Christianity.

11 JUNE 1559
Settling Spaniard Don Tristan de Luna y Arellano sails from Vera Cruz with 1500 settlers. This party is unable to found a settlement on Pensacola Bay in Florida but they explore inland in the region of Alabama before their departure.

29 MAY 1561
Settling Angel de Villafane, having taken command of the Arellano colonists, sets sail northward and possibly reaches Cape Hatteras. Again, this attempt by the Spanish to colonize the Atlantic coast of North America proves unsuccessful.

23 SEPTEMBER 1561
Settling Issuing a royal order, King Philip II of Spain forbids any more attempts to establish settlements in the Florida region. The Spanish have been discouraged by their past failures at colonization in this region. But when the French step into the vacuum left by the Spanish, the Spanish then rethink their policy toward the Atlantic coastal area.

30 APRIL 1562
Settling With the approval of King Charles IX of France, Jean Ribault arrives on the northeast Florida coast with two ships carrying some 150 prospective settlers in an attempt to found a Huguenot colony. The group establishes a settlement at Parris Island, North Carolina, named Port Royal. In early 1564 the colony disbands when essential supplies do not arrive. In the same year, a second French Huguenot group led by René de Laudonniere settles at Ft. Caroline

near the St. John's River in Florida. Reinforcements in the form of more settlers and supplies arrive in the spring of 1565. Startled into action by the bold movements of the French into this region, the Spanish determine to remove them and renew their own efforts at colonization.

28 AUGUST 1565
Settling Spaniard Pedro Menendez de Aviles arrives at St. Augustine with a party of 1500 prospective colonists as part of the Spanish plan to regain complete control of the Florida (including Georgia and South Carolina) coast and to oust the French.

8 SEPTEMBER 1565
Settling Menendez founds the first permanent European colony in North America at St. Augustine.

10 SEPTEMBER 1565
Settling Jean Ribault sets sail with an attack force from Ft. Caroline (some 40 miles to the north) in order to destroy the Spanish settlement at St. Augustine, but his fleet is wrecked in a storm.

20 SEPTEMBER 1565
Settling Menendez leads a land force to Ft. Caroline, which he captures, in the process killing most the French defenders. He renames the fort San Mateo. He establishes a military force there and builds a number of forts to maintain the new Spanish gains.

12 APRIL 1568
Settling Dominique de Gourgues arrives from France with a fleet of three ships and 100 soldiers. With the help of the Indians, he captures two Spanish ports at the mouth of the St. John's River, as well as San Mateo. He follows this victory by a massacre of Spanish prisoners.

5 AUGUST 1570
Indians Fray Batista Segura leads a group of Spanish Jesuits to the Chesapeake Bay area to convert the Indians.

14-18 FEBRUARY 1571
Indians The missionary Jesuits in the Segura group are murdered by the Indians they came to convert on Chesapeake Bay. This leads to the withdrawal of all Jesuits from Florida.

JUNE 1576
Exploration To find the Northwest Passage, a supposed northern sea route to Asia, Martin Frobisher leaves England on the first of three voyages. On this trip he reaches Baffin Land, Frobisher Bay and Hudson Strait, where he investigates indigenous mineral resources. Subsequent English explorers also search for the Northwest Passage—John Davis in 1585-87, George Weymouth in 1602 and John Knight in 1606.

JULY 1577
Settling Acting Spanish governor Pedro Menendez

THE NORTHWEST PASSAGE

Although the European search for the Northwest Passage—a water route through the North American continent to Asia—was to prove futile during the colonial era, the possibility of the seaway's existence was a beacon that drew explorers and adventurers in an intermittent stream for the nearly three centuries before the American Revolution. Navigators from all nations sought the elusive Northwest Passage, beginning with John Cabot in 1497. After a voyage along Cape Breton Island and the Nova Scotia coastline, Cabot came upon Newfoundland which he mistakenly thought to be China. In 1524 Giovanni da Verrazano, sailing under the French flag, determined the passage to be north of Newfoundland; and ten years later Jacques Cartier sailed up the St. Lawrence River to the site of Montreal in pursuit of the passage. Forty years later Martin Frobisher reached Hudson Bay which he took to be the elusive strait. John Davis continued Frobisher's investigations, and in 1610 Henry Hudson explored Hudson Bay. He was followed by William Baffin who erroneously thought Baffin Bay landlocked, thus discouraging further navigation along this route for two centuries. The voyages of Luke Foxe and Thomas James ended the first great era of the search. The "sea of the west" was also sought in overland treks by Samuel Champlain and La Vérendrye. In 1778, James Cook tried to explore the Pacific end of the passage, but success was not to come until the 19th century. In 1818 John Ross again mistakenly thought Baffin Bay landlocked. The following year William Edward Parry nearly navigated the route from east to west; and in 1845 John Franklin and his crew disappeared while searching for the Northwest Passage. In the end, it was an Englishman who found the passage in 1854. Robert McClure crossed the route north of the continent by sailing eastward from Bering Strait, and then by abandoning his ship and completing the journey over ice. Not until 1906 did Roald Amundsen make the transit entirely by sea. In the 19th century the Northwest Passage was to prove of little use as a short trade route to China because of the prevalent icy conditions. In spite of the apparent uselessness of the search for the Northwest Passage, the numerous exploratory expeditions that sought the route brought other benefits. They resulted in the establishment of North Atlantic cod fisheries and in the initiation of trade with Russia. But most importantly, these expeditions exponentially increased European knowledge of the geography of the North American continent and added immense land areas to the colonial empires, particularly that of Great Britain.

Marques (nephew of the earlier Menendez) rebuilds the fort at Santa Elena on Parris Island in South Carolina after Indian hostility had forced an earlier abandonment of the Florida garrisons.

APRIL 1578
Indians Marques burns the large Indian village at Copocay in Florida and also takes many prisoners. This method of dealing with the Indians is a prototype of the methods pursued in the centuries that follow.

11 JUNE 1578
Settling Sir Humphrey Gilbert receives a patent from the English crown to explore and colonize America. He completes two exploratory voyages but

lacks the financial support to found a settlement to oppose the ever increasing influence of the Spanish in the new world. Returning to England in 1583, his ship is lost at sea while four others reach port.

17 JUNE 1579
Discovery Francis Drake sails into San Francisco Bay and claims the region for Queen Elizabeth. This is during his voyage of circumnavigation of the globe, during which he attacks and captures Spanish ships carrying gold from Peru across the Pacific Ocean.

17 JULY 1580
War In Florida, Marques defeats a French naval force led by Gilberto Gil, who is killed in the battle. This signals the end of French influence in the coastal Florida area.

25 MARCH 1584
Settling Sir Walter Raleigh, who accompanied Sir Humphrey Gilbert on his last voyage, renews Gilbert's patent to explore and settle in North America. After a survey of Spanish defenses in the Caribbean, the expedition lands on Roanoke Island in July. Raleigh names this newly discovered land Virginia in honor of Queen Elizabeth.

27 JULY 1585
Settling Sir Walter Raleigh sends a colonizing expedition, led by Richard Grenville and Ralph Lane, which lands at Roanoke. Beleaguered by Indians and the Spanish, this first settlement lasts for a year and then is abandoned when Francis Drake, after

Sir Francis Drake.

a privateering voyage to the Caribbean, offers the settlers passage home. Several weeks later, Grenville, who has in the meantime returned to England, arrives at the abandoned colony with supplies. He leaves 15 men at Roanoke.

JUNE-JULY 1586
Settling Francis Drake attacks and levels the Spanish fort and other buildings at St. Augustine. He also attacks the Spanish Santa Elena colony.

22 JULY 1587
Settling John White leads an expedition to the English Roanoke colony. He finds no trace of the Grenville settlers. White leaves off another group of settlers there and returns to England for supplies.

18 AUGUST 1587
Settling Virginia Dare, John White's grandchild, is born in Roanoke. She is the first English child to be born in America.

1588
Arts/Culture Thomas Harriot, a member of Sir Walter Raleigh's Roanoke settlement group, publishes his eyewitness account of the new world, *A Briefe and True Account of the New Found Land of Virginia*. The failure of this first attempt by the English to settle America had discouraged further investment in such ventures. Harriot's book functions as propaganda to encourage further investment, as it emphasizes the positive aspects of America while it downplays the elements of risk. Such is also the nature of many other "true accounts" that are to follow throughout the 17th century.

17 AUGUST 1590
Settling Delayed by the Spanish Armada's attack on England, John White returns to Roanoke to find that all the settlers have disappeared without a trace.

OTHER EVENTS OF 1590
Arts/Culture Richard Hakluyt, who accompanied Sir Walter Raleigh on his Roanoke expedition, publishes his comprehensive anthology of reports of notable voyages of discovery entitled *The Principall Navigations, Voiages and Discoveries of the English Nation, Made by Sea or Overland to the Most Remote and Farthest Distant Quarters of the Earth at Any Time within the Compasse of these 1500 Years*. A second enlarged edition of this work, enriched with accounts by the most recent Elizabethan world travelers, including Francis Drake, Martin Frobisher, Humphrey Gilbert, Richard Hawkins and Walter Raleigh, appears in three folio sized volumes during the years between 1598 and 1600. The publication of the *Principall Navigations* is a milestone marking the prevailing 16th century European interest and activity in the discovery and exploration of the new world.

1591
Arts/Culture Engravings of the drawings of Jacques

le Moyne de Morgues appear in the second book of voyages published by De Bry. Le Moyne is a professional artist who joined the French Huguenot expedition led by Rene de Laudonniere to settle Florida. These drawings of North America depict Indians employed in fishing and hunting activities. In published form, these works are the first eyewitness visual representations of the North American scene to reach the European public.

23 SEPTEMBER 1595

Indians After the Spanish Crown launches a successful missionary effort in Florida, it follows up with an intensive campaign led by Fray Juan de Silva. The Spanish divide the American southeast into mission provinces comprising Florida, Georgia and South Carolina. They build chapels in many locations. In the years 1595 and 1596, some 1500 native Americans are converted to Christianity, according to Spanish accounts. But increasing hostility and attacks by the Guale Indians leads to the abandonment of most missions north of St. Augustine. These missionary efforts reflect the growing belief of the Spanish and other Europeans that perhaps conversion to Christianity rather than the use of arms is a more effective method of pacifying the Indians.

10 OCTOBER 1599

Indians The Spanish send a military force out of St. Augustine to punish the Indians for their attacks on the missionaries. The Spanish destroy Indian villages and crops. Faced by the ferocity of this attack, the Indians seek peace.

15 MAY 1602

Exploration Captain Bartholomew Gosnold anchors his ship the *Concord* at New Bedford, Massachusetts. He thus becomes the first Englishman to land on the New England coast and he is credited with naming Cape Cod, Martha's Vineyard and other sites.

JUNE 1604

Settling The French establish their first settlement on the north Atlantic coast. Holding a patent from the French monarch, Pierre du Guast Sieur de Monts founds the Maine colony on Neutral Island in the St. Croix River. This colony is later moved to Nova Scotia.

5 MARCH 1605

Settling Sponsored by English Catholic aristocracy, George Weymouth voyages to the Maine coast and Nantucket with the purpose of founding a Catholic English colony. The published account of this expedition encourages two groups of merchants to seek and receive in 1606 patents for colonization. This results in the creation of two Virginia companies—the London Company for the colonization of South Virginia (or the present Washington, D.C. area) and the Plymouth Company for the colonization of North Virginia (or the present New York City area).

20 JULY 1605

Exploration French explorer Samuel Champlain sails as far south as Cape Cod during one of his eleven trips to Canada. He later establishes a garrison at Quebec and focuses his efforts on achieving friendly relations with the Indians and on developing the fur trade.

AUGUST 1606

Exploration The Plymouth Company sends out its first expedition to reconnoiter the territory of North Virginia to which they have received colonization rights. The voyage ends in disaster when the Spanish capture them in the Caribbean.

OCTOBER 1606

Exploration Sponsored by Sir John Popham, the Plymouth Company sends out a second expedition to North America. A detailed investigation of the Atlantic coast is completed by Thomas Hanham and Martin Pring, who return to England fired with enthusiasm for all they have seen of America.

20 DECEMBER 1606

Settling A colonizing expedition of 144 men sponsored by the London Company sets sail for Virginia in three ships, the *Discovery,* the *Goodspeed* and the *Sarah Constant.* The captain of the fleet is Christopher Newport.

24 MAY 1607

Settling Colonists land at Jamestown, Virginia under the patent of the London Company. Starvation and disease reduce the original 105 settlers to 32 during the first seven months. The dismal situation is improved the following year with the election of Captain John Smith as council president, the arrival of new provisions and the institution of self-supporting agricultural crops such as corn.

15 JUNE 1607

Settling After an intensive building program, the Jamestown colonists erect their forts as a defense against Spanish and Indian attacks.

22 JUNE 1607

Settling Leaving Jamestown, Captain Newport sets sail on the return trip to England. He takes with him a cargo of what proves to be fool's gold. This early export reflects the strong economic motivations of investors in the Virginia colony. Meanwhile the settlers back in Jamestown face a period of dissension, disease and malnutrition.

7 AUGUST 1607

Exploration Sponsored by Sir Ferdinando Gorges, the third expedition of the Plymouth Company anchors off coastal Maine near Monhegan.

14 AUGUST 1607

Settling The Plymouth Company expedition reaches Popham Beach on the Sagadahoc River in Maine and

The first day at Jamestown.

raises a fort there encompassing other structures. This first colony of the Plymouth Company fails because of dissension within the ranks and an unwillingness to work. A number of early colonies failed because the colonists were in actuality adventurers who sought quick wealth rather than a long-term commitment to settlement in the American wilderness.

10 SEPTEMBER 1607
Colonial Affairs In Jamestown, the first president of the Virginia colony Edward M. Wingfield is ousted from his position. His successor is John Ratcliffe.

10 DECEMBER 1607
Indians Captain John Smith leaves Jamestown in an attempt to obtain food from the Indians for the starving colonists. He is captured by Chief Powhatan and the two men who accompany him are killed. According to Smith's own account, he is saved by Pocahontas, Powhatan's daughter.

OTHER EVENTS OF 1607
Colonial Affairs In one of the first rebellious incidents in the English American colonies, a plot is revealed against the governing council of Jamestown; the leader of the cabal, George Kendall, is executed.
Science/Technology The Jamestown settlers have brought knowledge of the art of glassmaking to Virginia and they produce glass artifacts, including beads which are to be used as articles of trade with the Indians.

2 JANUARY 1608
Settling Captain Newport returns from England bringing reinforcements of supplies and 110 additional colonists to find the Jamestown population decimated by disease and starvation.
Colonial Affairs Captain John Smith returns to Jamestown following his imprisonment by the Indians. His adversaries in the Jamestown council throw him into prison with the intent of executing him. Captain Newport arrives just in time to save him from death at the hands of the colonists.

7 JANUARY 1608
Colonial Affairs Further disaster strikes Jamestown

when the fort burns, leaving the colonists defenseless against attack by Indians and the Spanish.

9 APRIL 1608
British Policy Leaving Jamestown on the return voyage to England, Captain Newport transports a second cargo of gold back to eager English investors. The "gold" is in reality mica, which has no value.

24 JULY-7 SEPTEMBER 1608
Exploration Once again free, John Smith leaves Jamestown to explore Chesapeake Bay, as well as the Potomac and Rappahannock Rivers. While he is away, the Jamestown colonists undergo another bout of disease and starvation. This suffering points up the dependence of the colonists on English food supplies and their need to achieve self-sufficiency in producing adequate crops to feed themselves.

13 AUGUST 1608
Arts/Culture In London, John Smith's account of the early days of the Jamestown colony, *A True Relation of Such Occurrences and Accidents of Noate as Hath Hapned in Virginia Since the First Planting of That Collony,* is submitted for publication.

10 SEPTEMBER 1608
Colonial Affairs On his return from the exploratory expedition to the north, John Smith is chosen as the new president of the Jamestown council. He is granted wise powers of governance, as the colonists realize the need for extraordinary means to ensure the success of the Jamestown colony which is now threatened with failure.

29 SEPTEMBER 1608
British Policy Captain Newport arrives from England on his second supply run of the year. The colonists are still almost totally dependent on English food provisions for their survival.

DECEMBER 1608
British Policy Leaving the Jamestown colonists to face their second winter in America, Captain Newport sets sail for the return trip to England. He carries with him the first shipment of commodities intended for the export trade. Included among the goods are ashes, glass items, pitch, soap, tar, lumber and iron ore. Captain Newport also takes with him John Smith's second account of progress in the Jamestown settlement, as well as Smith's reports and maps of his explorations of Chesapeake Bay.

OTHER EVENTS OF 1608
Industry The London Company dispatches glass workers to the Jamestown colony for the purpose of further developing the glass industry. They are to erect glass furnaces.
Agriculture Captain John Smith is taught by the Indians how to cultivate Indian corn. The following spring he plants 40 acres of corn. This new indigenous grain will serve to ward off starvation for the

colonists but eventually the monotony of this diet will excite opposition. This leads to some revision, at least in the colonies, of the idea of America as a land of plenty.

Settling English religious separatist John Robinson leads his English congregation into exile in The Netherlands. Robinson's is only one group of many that leaves England for the continent in order to escape religious persecution under the rule of King James I. Robinson's group finds religious tolerance in first Amsterdam and later Leyden. Twelve years later many members of this group will sail to America on the *Mayflower*. Robinson, who dies in 1625, is unable to follow his parishioners to the Plymouth colony.

25 MARCH 1609
Exploration Henry Hudson sets out in a seven-month voyage of exploration for the Dutch East India Company that takes him to the new world. His original assignment is to find a shorter route from The Netherlands to Asia to facilitate trade with the Orient. Hudson's voyage is followed by a number of other exploratory trips by Dutch mariners, including Adriaen Block.

1 MAY 1609
Settling The Pilgrim separatists led by John Robinson and William Brewster move to Leyden from Amsterdam. In spite of the welcome religious tolerance they encounter in The Netherlands, they feel uneasy about the political future of the region after the truce between Holland and Spain expires in 1621. Also they see their offspring losing contact with their native English culture and they themselves are prevented from participating in the Dutch guild system. In 1616 they are to initiate contact with the Virginia Company with an eye toward emigrating to the new world.

5 MAY 1609
Exploration Samuel Argall sets sail from England under the auspices of the London Company to find a more direct sea route to the Virginia territory.

23 MAY 1609
British Policy The English Crown grants a new charter to the London Company, which will be now titled the Virginia Company. The charter provides for its incorporation as a joint stock company, thus providing the company with an infusion of much needed capital. The Virginia company is also granted land and greatly increased powers of government in the American colony. Sir Thomas Smith is named treasurer of the Virginia Company.

8 JUNE 1609
Settling As a result of the conditions of its new charter, the Virginia Company is able to dispatch nine ships carrying some 800 prospective settlers to Jamestown. Only seven of the ships reach Jamestown two months later. The remaining two ships, carrying Captain Newport, Sir George Somers and deputy gover-

Henry Hudson on the Hudson River.

nor–elect Sir Thomas Gates, are wrecked in the Bermudas. Sir Thomas Gates and the settlers accompanying him will arrive in Jamestown a year later.

JULY 1609
Exploration In the course of his explorations for the French in Canadian territory, Samuel Champlain, guided by Algonquin and Huron Indians, travels up the Richelieu River into Lake Champlain. A few weeks later, Champlain's party attacks a group of Iroquois Indians in the Ticonderoga area. This sets the precedent for the emnity between the French and Iroquois in the years to follow.

AUGUST 1609
Settling Seven Virginia Company ships carrying reinforcements of supplies and new settlers arrive at Jamestown, unaccompanied by deputy governor–elect Sir Thomas Gates who was shipwrecked in Bermuda.

28 AUGUST 1609
Exploration Diverted from his original search for trade routes to the Orient, Henry Hudson arrives in Delaware Bay.

13 SEPTEMBER 1609
Exploration Henry Hudson reaches the Hudson River. He sails upstream as far as Albany before continuing his explorations of the North American coast.

5 OCTOBER 1609
Colonial Affairs In Jamestown John Smith is severely injured in a powder explosion and is ousted from his leadership of the Virginia colony. He returns to England in one of the ships in the Sir Thomas Gates fleet. Meanwhile Jamestown is undergoing another period of internal disorder in the absence of Gates, who is still delayed in Bermuda.

DECEMBER 1609
Settling The Jamestown colonists, reinforced by

nearly 500 new settlers, face another dismal winter, their third in America. Before the next spring, a great many colonists die from starvation.

OTHER EVENTS OF 1609
Arts/Culture In England Richard Hakluyt publishes the last work in his epic series on the literature of discovery. *Virginia Richly Valued* is based on an originally Portuguese eyewitness account of the travels of de Soto through the hinterlands of the American South in the years 1539 to 1543. Some scholars suggest that de Soto himself was the author of the original narration.
Life/Customs In the first European marriage performed in the American settlements, Anne Barrows and John Laydon are wed in Virginia.
Settling The city of Santa Fe is founded by the Spanish in New Mexico.

28 FEBRUARY 1610
British Policy The Virginia Company takes further steps toward instituting absolutist rule when it appoints Thomas West, Lord Delaware, as the first lord-governor and captain–general of the Virginia colony. The broad political and military powers granted to Lord Delaware reflect the growing English concern with placing the colony on a sound footing in terms of both political and economic organization.

23 MAY 1610
Colonial Affairs Long delayed by a shipwreck in Bermuda, deputy–governor Sir Thomas Gates, accompanied by Sir George Somers and Captain Newport, finally reaches Jamestown to find the settlement demoralized by the wide-scale suffering and deaths of the previous winter.

6 JUNE 1610
Colonial Affairs Newly appointed lord-governor of the Virginia colony, Lord Delaware, sails into Chesapeake Bay with three ships carrying new colonists and additional supplies. He receives word that deputy governor Sir Thomas Gates has finally reached Jamestown. He also hears that Gates, discouraged by the conditions that met him in the colony, plans to leave Jamestown with the surviving settlers in order to rescue them from starvation.

8 JUNE 1610
Colonial Affairs Enroute to Newfoundland with a group of demoralized settlers, Jamestown deputy governor Sir Thomas Gates encounters the newly arriving governor of the Virginia colony, Lord Delaware, in the James River. Lord Delaware commands Gates to return to Jamestown.

10 JUNE 1610
Colonial Affairs Lord Delaware finally reaches Jamestown. Taking stock of the poor conditions there, he dispatches Sir George Somers and Samuel Argall to Bermuda to procure food for the malnourished colonists. He also orders the construction of a garri-

son at Point Comfort to increase the defensive capabilities of the settlers.

10 SEPTEMBER 1610
Colonial Affairs Deputy governor of Jamestown Sir Thomas Gates leaves for England. He has been ordered to do so by the Virginia Company and Lord Delaware, his mission being to report to investors whether there is any hope of the colony ever becoming a commercially viable enterprise. While Gates presents a relatively optimistic report in England, Lord Delaware spurs the colonists on to greater efforts in agriculture by threatening them with punishment if they do not work hard enough.

DECEMBER 1610
Colonial Affairs The fourth winter of the Jamestown colony proves to be somewhat less severe than the previous winters, thanks to the increased agricultural activity and additional food bartered from the Indians. Still, times are hard.

OTHER EVENTS OF 1610
Arts/Culture In London, William Strachey publishes his experiences as a colonist in Virginia in *A True Repertory of the Wrack and Redemption of Sir Thomas Gates, Knight, upon and from the Islands of the Bermudas, His Coming to Virginia and the Estate of that Colony Then and after the Government of Lord La Ware*. (Some scholars believe that this is one of the books that may have inspired Shakespeare's *Tempest*.) Strachey, who was secretary of the colony under Gates, presented a somewhat romanticized view of the colony that downplayed its serious shortcomings and served to rekindle enthusiasm for the venture by English investors. Strachey's book reflects the essential importance of such promotional literature, however misleading, in persuading English investors to pursue ventures in America.
Science/Technology The first doctor to come to the English colonies, Lawrence Bohune, arrives in Virginia. Ten years later he will be designated as Surgeon General of the London Company in Virginia. Though the arrival of a professional physician is undoubtedly important to the colony, there is little he can do against rampant disease as long as malnutrition persists.

28 MARCH 1611
Colonial Affairs Beset by ill health, Lord Delaware leaves Jamestown for England. Since his arrival in the colony, Delaware has suffered from ague, dysentery and scurvy—a tribute to the abysmal diet of even the leaders of the colony.

10 MAY 1611
Settling Sir Thomas Dale arrives in Virginia with 300 men, as well as provisions and livestock, on three ships.

23 MAY 1611
Colonial Affairs Sir Thomas Dale replaces Lord

FOUNDING A NATION 986-1787

Delaware as leader of the Jamestown colony. Dale seeks to control the ongoing dissension by means of the "Dale Code" which threatens lawbreakers with harsh punishments. This judicial code is essentially one of martial law, probably a necessary evil for the survival of the colony. In any case it constitutes a desperate measure and a last ditch effort to turn the colony into a successful commercial venture. Dale also starts to build a fort and a series of stockades up the James River. These projects will later be finished under Sir Thomas Gates.

21 JUNE 1611
Exploration In Hudson Bay, Henry Hudson is sent out in an open boat to his death by his ship's crew. This occurs after a series of misfortunes in which his ship *Discovery* is marooned by ice, supplies run low, and the crew eventually mutinies. On this, his fourth voyage of exploration, Hudson has discovered Hudson Bay while seeking a northern sea route to the Orient for the English.

SEPTEMBER 1611
Settling Sir Thomas Dale is sent by Sir Thomas Gates to establish a new town named Henrico some 40 miles north of Jamestown. Within a stockaded wall the settlement includes storehouses, a church and dwelling houses. This project constitutes the first expansion of the Jamestown colony and marks the renewed resolve of British investors to establish a viable permanent colony in America.

OTHER EVENTS OF 1611
Ideas/Beliefs Puritan minister Alexander Whitaker arrives in Jamestown from Cambridge, England to found the first Presbyterian church in the Virginia colony. Two years later he is to instruct and convert Pocahontas to Christianity.
Colonial Affairs Spanish King Philip III has the English colonizers in Virginia kept under constant surveillance. When three of his men sail into the James River for this purpose, they are captured and imprisoned in Jamestown for the next five years. Yet the Spanish spies are able to maintain contact with the Spanish Crown. They press for the destruction of the Jamestown settlement.

22 MARCH 1612
British Policy The Virginia Company receives a third charter for its Virginia colony. This document spells out the wider political powers of the governing members and also gives the Virginia Company power over Bermuda which has been an important source of provisions for the floundering colony.

OTHER EVENTS OF 1612
Settling Based on the original claim of Henry Hudson, the Dutch establish a foothold in the new world on the island of Manhattan. The ships *Tiger* and *Fortune* sail to America to found a preliminary post on Manhattan to expedite trade with the Indians of the Hudson River valley.

Arts/Culture In England Captain John Smith publishes *A Map of Virginia*. This book describes and extolls the virtues of the Virginia colony. In the same year the Dale Code is also published in London. Titled *Laws Divine Morall and Martial,* this harsh judicial code has been compiled by Sir Thomas Dale, Sir Thomas Gates and William Strachey. Its publication informs prospective colonists to the Virginia colony of what they may expect when they arrive. Instituted in 1611, the code will remain in effect until 1619 when the Virginia House of Burgesses sits for the initial session of the first legislative assembly in America. As economic and social conditions gradually improve in the Virginia colony, a severe code becomes less necessary.
Agriculture John Rolfe, who arrived in Virginia in 1609, successfully plants and harvests a native tobacco crop. From this time onward tobacco becomes a primary export crop for the Virginia settlements.

TOBACCO

When architect Benjamin Latrobe inventively designed a tobacco leaf capital to top the classical-style columns in the new United States Capitol, he created a tribute to what had become colonial America's most important cash crop. Tobacco was already an important agricultural product of the indigenous North American Indian cultures when Columbus arrived in the Caribbean. One of his seamen reported in Cuba, "many people, with a firebrand in the hand, and herbs to drink the smoke thereof." The archeological relics of the Mound Builders indicate that pipe smoking was an ancient custom, for both ritual and pleasurable ends, in the new world. And the early explorers of the interior found the smoking of tobacco to be a widespread habit among the Indians from the Great Lakes to the Gulf of Mexico. To produce sufficient quantities, the Indians had developed specialized agricultural techniques and, reportedly, a tribe near Lake Huron was already producing tobacco on a commercial scale in order to sell to other tribes during the early 16th century.

By the early 17th century, tobacco use had become familiar to all of the European countries. At first employed for what were supposed to be its miraculously curative powers, tobacco indulgence later came to be regarded as a pernicious antisocial and morally evil habit—a judgment that had little effect on its users. Indeed, the world market for tobacco became virtually insatiable.

Therefore, when planter John Rolfe successfully introduced the European commercial culture of tobacco in Virginia, the survival of the colony was assured. Although tobacco soon became the main source of revenue for Virginia, Maryland and North Carolina, the crop had a number of agricultural, social and economic disadvantages. Its great potential for profit led to the organization of enormous single-crop plantations, requiring a large body of slave labor. The inevitable depletion of the soil required ever larger acreages devoted to tobacco, leading to a geographic shift westward into Tennessee and Kentucky, also introducing the institution of slavery into these regions. The dangers of the single cropping method were apparent in the effects of the climate—one bad year could lead to bankruptcy, while an extremely good year could result in an overall drop in market prices. Also, widespread tobacco culture tended to discourage the development of other crops leading to colonial self-sufficiency; instead the tobacco-based settlements remained overly dependent on import goods. The real winners in the tobacco market were the British tobacco merchants who sold the product for three times its cost to them. The widespread southern culture of tobacco as a cash crop also led to its frequent use as commodity currency during the colonial era. After the Revolutionary War, Virginia and North Carolina growers established factories for the production of pipe and chewing tobacco and snuff, which served as the basis of the great tobacco empires that developed during the course of the 19th century.

APRIL 1613
Indians Pocahontas is seized by Sir Samuel Argall and held as a hostage by the Jamestown colonists to force the release of settlers imprisoned by the Indians. She is converted by the Puritan clergyman Alexander Whitaker to Christianity. Though she is often cited as the first Indian to convert under the English, Manteo was baptized in the Church of England by members of Sir Walter Raleigh's Roanoke expedition in 1587. Also in the previous century, the Spanish conducted an ambitious missionary effort in Florida. Pocahontas is given the Christian name of Rebecca.

JULY 1613
Colonial Affairs Sir Thomas Dale dispatches a group of Englishmen led by Sir Samuel Argall from Virginia to successfully attack the French colonial outposts in Maine. Argall's force burns the French settlement at Port Royal and expels the Jesuit post on Mount Desert Island. Argall brings 15 French prisoners back to Virginia.

NOVEMBER 1613
Colonial Affairs Enroute back from his attacks on the French settlements in Maine, Sir Samuel Argall anchors at the newly established Dutch fort on Manhattan. He forces the Dutch to raise the English flag. These raids of the English against other European colonists in America mark the widening imperial interests of England in the new world.

OTHER EVENTS OF 1613
Settling In the Virginia colony, Sir Thomas Dale establishes the settlement of Bermuda Hundred. This further expansion of the Jamestown colony reflects the growing success of the English colonial effort in Virginia. In the same year, the Dutch build a permanent trading post on lower Manhattan Island along with a fort on the tip of the island. Intended primarily to protect the lucrative Dutch fur trading activities with the Indians of the lower Hudson River valley, this initial settlement effort is led by Adriaen Block and Hendrick Christianson. Christianson remains to govern the settlement while Block returns to Amsterdam from his third voyage to the new world. After leaving Manhattan, Block discovers and explores the Connecticut and Housatonic Rivers, Long Island Sound and the New England coast as far north as Salem, Massachusetts. Block Island is named after him. He also completes several maps of these newly explored geo-graphical areas. His map of Manhattan is the first to show it as separate from Long Island.

Arts/Culture In yet another book published in England about the new world, Samuel Purchas in *Purchas His Pilgrims* expresses an unconventionally disparaging attitude about the virtues of life in the American colonies. He condemns the paucity of culture in America and praises the institutions of European civilization. This book is a contrast to the usually propagandistic accounts of the new world, possibly because it is not primarily inspired by motives of commercial gain.

27 MARCH 1614
Discovery The Estates-General of The Netherlands passes the Ordinance of 1614. To encourage exploration and colonization efforts by the Dutch, this legislation offers the lure of trade monopolies in the newly claimed areas. Meanwhile Dutch navigator Cornelius May explores the Atlantic coastal area from Long Island to Delaware Bay. Cape May, New Jersey, is named in his honor.

14 APRIL 1614
Life/Customs Virginia planter John Rolfe marries Pocahontas, daughter of Indian Chief Powhatan who continues his hostility toward the colonists. Pocahontas was converted to Christianity the preceding year.

1 OCTOBER 1614
Exploration Dutch trader and navigator Adriaen Block returns to Amsterdam from his exploratory voyage of the New England rivers and coast. He brings with him his detailed maps of these regions. The favorable information brought by Block encourages Dutch to organize large–scale colonial ventures in the new world.

11 OCTOBER 1614
Settling Organized by a group of Dutch merchants and shipowners engaged in trade with the Hudson River Valley Indians, the New Netherland Company is granted a charter by the Dutch government. This charter grants the company a three–year trade monopoly in America between 40°N and 45°N.

OTHER EVENTS OF 1614
Settling Dutch fur traders establish the first important settlement in America when they erect a stockaded fort on the upper Hudson River near Albany.

Colonial Affairs In Virginia, Sir Thomas Dale institutes a system of private land ownership for colonists. Settlers are granted three-acre plots of land.

Agriculture After two years of successful tobacco harvests in the Virginia settlements, John Rolfe sends the first export cargo of tobacco back to England on the ship *Elizabeth*.

Exploration In a return trip to the new world, Captain John Smith leads a large fishing fleet up the Atlantic coast. In the bounteous waters off Maine, fishermen catch over 60,000 fish in one month. During this voyage Smith maps the New England coast, investigates min-

FOUNDING A NATION 986-1787

Dutch traders in the New Netherlands.

eral resources and the whale population.

SEPTEMBER-OCTOBER 1615
Exploration On his seventh exploratory trip for the French, Samuel Champlain discovers Lake Huron and facilitates routes for fur traders into the interior of the North American continent. Meanwhile Etienne Brule, a fellow explorer, leaves the Champlain party to follow the Susquehanna River to its mouth in Chesapeake Bay.

1616
British Policy Accompanied by Virginia planter John Rolfe and his Indian wife Pocahontas, deputy governor of Jamestown Sir Thomas Dale returns to England to report on the progress of the English colonial effort in Virginia. Pocahontas is presented at court to English monarch King James I.
Arts/Culture Adding to his literature on the new world, Captain John Smith publishes *A Description of New England*.
Indians A large-scale smallpox epidemic decimates the New England Indian population from Maine to Rhode Island. In the years that follow, Indians are infected often by diseases introduced by European settlers and against which the Indians lack immunity.

23 DECEMBER 1617
British Policy The English Crown institutes a penal colony in Virginia which is to receive habitual criminals who are exiled from their native country.

OTHER EVENTS OF 1617
Settling The immigration of women of a higher social status begins in the Virginia colony. The arrival of these women sets the foundation for the sustained growth of the colony and for the establishment of stable institutions and communities. Meanwhile, in a continuation of their settlement activity along the Hudson River, the Dutch move Fort Nassau at Castle Island across to the west bank of the Hudson, locating the fort at the site of present–day Albany.
Colonial Affairs Samuel Argall becomes the new deputy governor of Virginia. His stewardship of the colony is a period of exploitation and poor government.

18 NOVEMBER 1618
Colonial Affairs Sir Samuel Argall is removed from the governorship of the Virginia colony, concluding a two–year period of misrule. During his tenure, Argall has proclaimed strict laws supporting religious practices. The failure to attend church services is punishable by imprisonment and forced labor. The Sabbath is strictly enforced with all forms of amusement banned on this day. Such regulation serves only to excite the opposition of the colonists.
British Policy In London, the Virginia Company enacts a new charter of privileges, orders and laws. This charter grants the Virginia colonists some voice in the legislative process.

OTHER EVENTS OF 1618
Colonial Affairs The governor of Virginia, Lord Delaware, sets sail for the colony with reinforcements of settlers and provisions. He dies during the Atlantic crossing.

Matoaks als Rebecka daughter to the mighty Prince Powhatan Emperour of Attanoughkomouck als Virginia converted and baptized in the Christian faith, and Wife to the wor.ᵗᵗ Mʳ Tho: Rolff.

Pocahontas painted in Elizabethan costume.

British Policy In London, Sir Edwin Sandys and the Earl of Southampton obtain control of the Virginia Company. They institute much–needed reforms, repeal the harsh legal code and replace deputy governor Argall with George Yeardley. Yeardley will not arrive in the colony until the following year.

19 APRIL 1619
Colonial Affairs Sir George Yeardley arrives in Virginia to assume the post of governor. His appointment heralds an era of reform and renewed development. He brings with him the 1618 charter of privileges granted by the Virginia Company and he is empowered to organize a council and establish a general assembly.

28 APRIL 1619
British Policy In London, Sir Edwin Sandys officially assumes control of the Virginia Company when he is elected treasurer. Replacing Thomas Smith in this post, Sandys is of a more liberal philosophy.

19 JUNE 1619
Settling The Leyden Pilgrim separatists are granted a patent in the name of English clergyman John Wyncop, enabling them to establish a colony in Virginia. Subject to royal approval, this petition is granted with the aid and intercession of Sir Edwin Sandys, treasurer of the Virginia Company.

30 JULY 1619
Colonial Affairs The first legislative assembly in the American colonies is elected by Virginia planters. Twenty-two burgesses are chosen, two from each of 11 plantations. This political body will meet with the governor and his council and it will function in a judicial role.

9-14 AUGUST 1619
Colonial Affairs The Virginia House of Burgesses, the first representative assembly in America, sits for its initial session in Jamestown. The independence of this body is limited in that any laws enacted are subject to the acquiescence of the Virginia Company in London.

AUGUST 1619
Slavery Twenty African blacks are brought to Jamestown on a Dutch ship for sale as indentured servants. In reality, this is the beginning of slavery in the Virginia colony.

OTHER EVENTS OF 1619
Industry Virginia colonists establish the first iron works in the English settlements at Falling Creek.
Settling The Virginia Company sends to the colonies a shipload of young women of marriageable age. Virginia planters are to pay 120 pounds of tobacco for the passage of each woman. In addition, 100 London slum children are dispatched to Virginia where they will become apprentices.
Colonial Affairs The Virginia legislature passes ex-

The first Africans arriving, Jamestown, 1619.

plicit blue laws to regulate ostentation in dress. This sumptuary code requires colonists to select clothing that befits their social rank and any excesses in clothing are subject to taxation. Also a new land policy is instituted in the Virginia colony. Provisions of the 1609 charter are finally carried out to grant 100 acres to settlers who arrived before 1616. A further innovation is the head right, which grants 50 acres to investors to pay for the sea passage of each new colonist. This new availability of land considerably motivates immigration from England.

FEBRUARY 1620
Settling The government of Holland extends a formal invitation to the Leyden separatists to settle permanently in The Netherlands. The Leyden group turns this offer down as they are expecting English royal approval of their American colonization patent.

20 FEBRUARY 1620
Settling Two English merchants, London ironmonger Thomas Weston and London clothmaker John Peirce, are granted a patent by the Virginia Company and they suggest that the Leyden separatists join in their venture.

3 MARCH 1620
Settling Sir Ferdinando Gorges represents the Plymouth Company in its petition to King James I for a charter granting it settlement rights in the New England region. The agents of the Plymouth Company have been encouraged to seek this northern location by the reported presence of rich cod fishing waters off the coast of Maine.

FOUNDING A NATION 986-1787

18 JUNE 1620
British Policy The Earl of Southampton, Henry Wriothesley, is chosen as treasurer of the Virginia Company to replace his friend and business partner Sir Edwin Sandys. Southampton is also of a liberal philosophy. He remains in this post until the dissolution of the Virginia Company in 1624.

29 JUNE 1620
British Policy In an agreement between the English Crown and the Virginia Company, the growing of tobacco in England is prohibited, hence granting a virtual monopoly in the production of this commodity to the Virginia colony. In return for this privilege, the Virginia Company is to pay the Crown a duty of one shilling per pound of tobacco.

JULY 1620
Settling The Leyden separatists agree to join with Thomas Weston and John Peirce who hold a patent for settlement in America from the Virginia Company. A joint stock company is organized to raise capital for the Atlantic crossing.

22 JULY 1620
Settling Boarding the *Speedwell*, 35 Pilgrims from the Leyden separatists led by William Brewster leave Holland for England. The *Speedwell* is later abandoned in Plymouth, England as it turns out to be unseaworthy.

16 SEPTEMBER 1620
Settling The *Mayflower* sets sail for America with 101 colonists in addition to the ship's crew. Most of the colonists are not Pilgrims. The group includes Miles Standish, hired as military leader, 14 indentured servants and several hired craftsmen.

9 NOVEMBER 1620
Settling The *Mayflower* reaches Cape Cod and the Pilgrims decide to disembark in this territory even though they are outside the area of the Virginia Company. Possibly this course is taken because there are serious doubts about the legality of their patent.

11 NOVEMBER 1620
Colonial Affairs Aboard the *Mayflower* the prospective settlers sign the Mayflower Compact while their ship is anchored in Provincetown harbor. Signed by the 41 men aboard, this document is drafted by the Pilgrim leaders who wish to exert control over rebellious members of the group. The Mayflower Compact outlines a form of government based on a social compact—essentially an agreement to obey laws they might pass.

13 NOVEMBER 1620
British Policy King James I of England grants in a charter to the Council for New England rights to the land area in America from sea to sea between 40°N and 48°N. The Council for New England is a new entity resulting from the reorganization of the

Plymouth Company. This body now represents aristocracy rather than merchants and its goal is that of a land company instead of a trading organization. It does nevertheless receive a trading and fishing monopoly for the area under its control. In its charter it receives land title to all of New England and makes the land grants that form the basis of five colonies—Plymouth, Massachusetts, New Hampshire, Maine and Connecticut—in the years that follow.

21 DECEMBER 1620
Settling After an initial exploratory expedition, the *Mayflower* anchors off Plymouth, concluding its 63–day voyage. The colonists begin to disembark.

DECEMBER 1620
Ideas/Beliefs The Plymouth Puritans, led by William Brewster, William Bradford and Edward Winslow, establish a separatist church. These three Puritan leaders were originally members of the Leyden congregation. Ralph Smith, the first pastor of this church, arrives later.

OTHER EVENTS OF 1620
Arts/Culture Virginia settlers organize the first public library in the American colonies at the proposed college in Henrico. The volumes for the library are donated by English landowners.
Population An epidemic rages in Virginia and more than 1000 settlers die.

21 MARCH 1621
Settling The final group of colonists disembarks from the *Mayflower* which has remained anchored off the Plymouth colony all winter in support of the new settlers.

22 MARCH 1621
Indians The Plymouth Pilgrims and the Wampanoag Indians led by chief Massassoit reach a treaty agreement. The Pilgrims and Indians form a defensive alliance and enact a peace pact. Squanto, an Indian who can speak English (because he had spent two years in England after being captured in 1615), facilitates the treaty. This is one of the first documented treaties between Europeans and American Indians.

5 APRIL 1621
Settling The *Mayflower* sets sail on the return trip to England, leaving the Plymouth colonists on their own.

21 APRIL 1621
Colonial Affairs When Deacon John Carver, the first governor of the Plymouth colony dies, William Bradford is chosen as the second governor. He will hold this position until 1656.

1 JUNE 1621
British Policy In London, John Peirce receives a second patent from the Council for New England. This patent grants land title jointly to the Plymouth colony investors and settlers, with 100 acres going to

MASSASSOIT AND KING PHILIP

The two New England Wampanoag Indian chiefs Massassoit (c. 1580-1661) and Metacomet (c. 1640-1676), more familiarly known as King Philip, were father and son. But this family unity did not extend to their relations with the early English settlers. While the leadership of Massassoit was characterized by amity and unbroken peace, the rule of King Philip erupted into the most devastating Indian war in New England's history.

When the Pilgrims arrived at Plymouth, Massassoit, or "Yellow Feather," already was familiar with Europeans. Probably he was the "king of the country" encountered by Captain John Smith during his New England coastal expedition. The territory under Massassoit's control apparently extended from Massachusetts Bay to Narragansett Bay, including Cape Cod and encompassing much of eastern Massachusetts and Rhode Island. Massassoit's willingness to seek friendship with the Pilgrims possibly was motivated by the weak condition of his tribe because of a recent epidemic and from continuing hostilities with the Narragansett Indians. With all the pomp he could muster, Plymouth leader John Carver received Massassoit and his escort to transact a peace treaty after the suitable rituals had been observed and the Indians had been offered a drink of whiskey. In the following years, Massassoit and the Massachusetts settlers visited back and forth frequently—Massassoit was invited to share the Pilgrims' first Thanksgiving dinner; Massassoit returned a lost settler; the colonists cured Massassoit of a serious illness; Massassoit warned the settlers of a planned Indian attack against the Weston plantation; Massassoit sought refuge in Plymouth from the Narragansett Indians; Roger Williams made peace with Massassoit in Rhode Island; and Massassoit visited Boston twice to be entertained by Massachusetts Bay Colony Governor John Winthrop.

After Massassoit's death, his son Metacomet succeeded to the leadership of the Wampanoag Indians. Sardonically called King Philip by the colonists because of his haughty and aristocratic manner, as well as for his claim of equality with his "brother" King Charles II of England, Metacomet feared that the unchecked territorial expansion of the British settlers in New England was making the Indian a stranger in his own land. Although his attempted alliance of the New England Indian tribes to oppose and eject the colonists was never entirely successful, the relatively brief conflict known as King Philip's War was relentlessly bloody. When the war ended with the killing of Metacomet, nearly half of the English settlements had been destroyed. The colonists had Metacomet's body beheaded, drawn and quartered; and as befitting a traitor, Metacomet's head was displayed in Plymouth for a number of years.

each colonist. Fifteen hundred acres are set aside as public land. The boundaries of the colony are not spelled out.

3 JUNE 1621
Settling In order to organize trade and colonial efforts in the American areas frequented by Dutch traders and ships, a leading Dutch merchant Willem Usselinx and other merchants some together to establish the Dutch West India Company. The charter granted to this group by the Dutch government provides them with a trading monopoly and the right to establish settlements in North America. Furthermore, the Amsterdam merchants receive authority over New Netherland, or present–day New York.

JUNE 1621
Settling A group of 50 Englishmen led by Andrew Weston arrives at the Plymouth colony. They decide to settle at Wessagusset to found a fishing and trading post. This Wessagusset colony fails two years later because of ineffective administration and Indian raids.

OCTOBER 1621
Colonial Affairs Following his appointment by the Virginia Company in London, Sir Francis Wyatt arrives in Jamestown to assume the position of governor. He carries with him the Ordinance and Constitution granted the colony by the Virginia Company.

10 NOVEMBER 1621
Settling Thirty additional settlers arrive in Plymouth on the *Fortune*.

13 DECEMBER 1621
Settling The *Fortune* leaves Plymouth for England carrying a cargo of lumber and furs bartered from the Indians. The vessel is seized by the French before it reaches its destination.

8 MARCH 1622
British Policy The lottery which was a fund–raising device for the Virginia Company is banned by the Privy Council. This undermines the financial basis of the Virginia Company and sends the organization into receivership.

22 MARCH 1622
Indians In Virginia, the Opechancanough Indians attack and massacre some 350 colonists. This disaster frustrates the attempt of Virginians to establish an ironworks at Falling Creek. The colonists retaliate with a series of raids on the Indians.

10 AUGUST 1622
British Policy Sir Ferdinando Gorges and John Mason receive a grant from the Council for New Eng-

Pilgrims landing at Plymouth, 1620.

FOUNDING A NATION 986-1787

PURITANISM

The beliefs and practices of the New England Puritans have had a profound effect on American life in the social and political area, as well as in the moral and intellectual sphere. Yet the nature of Puritanism is so complex that there is considerable disagreement as to its character. While some historians have cited Puritanism as the source of the American ideals of liberty, tolerance and human rights, the prevailing popular view is that Puritanism epitomizes intolerance, authoritarianism and a rejection of the cultural and aesthetic. There is some basis to both opinions. The Pilgrims who arrived on the *Mayflower* as a vanguard of the great Puritan migrations to Massachusetts were unwelcome religious nonconformists in their native England. The movement, which began during the reign of Elizabeth I, originally sought to "purify" the Anglican Church of irreligious vestments and images, and later came to oppose the authority of the bishops and of the monarchy.

The Massachusetts Bay Colony Puritans were moderate nonconformists who acknowledged the Church of England, but instituted autonomous or Congregationalist churches. The Puritans upheld the Calvinist doctrines of original sin, predestination, and salvation through grace. Good works were regarded as an obligation of all men. Their strict enforcement of the Sabbath was accompanied by a ban on theater, sports, religious music and the celebration of Christmas, which they saw as pagan. Another basic tenet of Puritanism was the idea of a convenant between God and man, both in the matter of grace and salvation, and in the matter of instituting a civil government to maintain social order and obedience to religious rules. This government was led by learned laymen, and the right to vote was restricted to male church members. Puritans had little tolerance for dissent in their ranks and hence banished such nonconformists as Anne Hutchinson, Roger Williams, and Quakers, of whom they even executed several.

A growing secularism beginning in the 1660s gradually weakened Puritan society, as did the unfortunate role of the clergy in the 1692 Salem witchcraft trials. Though the Puritans were restrictive of excesses and of diversionary pursuits, they were remarkably advanced in other realms—their divorce laws were more liberal than English ones, and their governmental legislation pioneered in promoting certain individual rights. In colonial America the Puritans were notable for their intellectual activity, as seen in the works of John Winthrop and of Cotton Mather. And through their strong support of education, they transmitted to future generations their rationalism and other humanist traditions.

land deeding them all land between the Merrimac and Kennebec Rivers, in the Maine-New Hampshire area.

6 NOVEMBER 1622
British Policy The Council for New England is granted further protection of its trading and fishing monopoly and its authority to grant licenses for such activity. This monopoly is confirmed by a royal proclamation.

30 DECEMBER 1622
British Policy The Council for New England ap-

points Robert Gorges, son of Sir Ferdinando Gorges, as the first lieutenant general of the New England territory. In addition he receives a 300–square–mile land grant along Boston Bay.

MARCH 1623
Settling Plymouth colonist Miles Standish saves the group of Wessagusset settlers from the Indians. The Wessagusset settlement is located at the site of present-day Weymouth on Massachusetts Bay. The settlers, who have survived a severe winter of starvation, decide to return to England.

29 JUNE 1623
Settling The Atlantic coast from Maine to Rhode Island is divided and granted to 20 patentees by the Council for New England.

JULY 1623
British Policy In danger of bankruptcy, the Virginia Company in London comes under the management of the Privy Council. This leads to eventual royal rule of the Virginia colony.

AUGUST 1623
Settling A steady stream of colonists begins to arrive to reinforce the ranks of the Plymouth colonists.

SEPTEMBER 1623
Settling Lieutenant general of New England Robert Gorges dispatches a group of English settlers to occupy the now abandoned Weston colony at Wessagusset. After a severe winter most of the colonists return to England, and Gorges loses interest in pursuing his plans for a fishing and trading post at this site.

3 NOVEMBER 1623
Settling The officials of the Dutch West India Company pass a provision allowing for Dutch colonization in the new world. Amsterdam investors are authorized to send five or six Dutch families to New Netherland to initiate a permanent colony.

OTHER EVENTS OF 1623
Settling Land grants from the Council for New England permit the establishment of settlements at Portsmouth and Dover, New Hampshire and Casco Bay and Saco Bay, Maine under the sponsorship of Sir Ferdinando Gorges and John Mason. With another grant from the Council, merchants from Dorchester, England, found a fishing colony at Gloucester on Cape Ann.
Colonial Affairs Laws which discriminate on the basis of social status are applied in the Virginia colony. The upper classes are exempted from the punishment of whipping.
Agriculture Governor Bradford orders the Plymouth colonists to plant corn to supplement their scarce food rations. Friendly Indians advise them on successful cultivation techniques. The abundant fish and lobster also comprise an important part of the Plymouth colo-

nists' diet. Farther south, the Virginia legislature orders settlers to plant mulberry trees. The leaves of the mulberry will be used to feed silkworms. The colony is still trying to develop more commodities for the export market.

Industry New England settlers begin a salt works at Piscataqua, New Hampshire, and construct a sawmill near York, Maine.

MARCH 1624
Agriculture Edward Winslow, a leader of the Plymouth colony, imports from England what prove to be the first cattle in New England.

28 MARCH 1624
Colonial Affairs In passing the Provisional order, the Dutch West India Company provides its North American colonists with a detailed plan of governmental organization. This document also regulates the social behavior as well as agricultural and economic activity of the colonists.

30 MARCH 1624
Settling In the first group of Dutch colonists sponsored by the Dutch West India Company are some 30 families who leave Amsterdam on the ship of Captain Cornelis May. The Dutch West India Company also names May as the colony's first director. When the settlers arrive at New York, they are split up. Most of them are taken up the Hudson River to Fort Nassau. While others are sent to the Delaware River area in New Jersey, some are left on Governor's Island in New York Bay. Possibly some settlers may have remained on Manhattan Island while others proceeded to Long Island. This dispersal of the settlers marks the attempt of the Dutch to secure as many sites as possible.

24 MAY 1624
British Policy In London, the charter of the Virginia Company is revoked and the colony of Virginia is now designated a royal colony.

15 JULY 1624
British Policy The Privy Council designates a committee of 40 men to manage Virginia colonial affairs in the place of the dissolved Virginia Company.

24 AUGUST 1624
British Policy Sir Francis Wyatt is officially appointed governor of the now royal Virginia colony by King James I. Wyatt was also Virginia governor under the former administration of the Virginia Company. This decision to maintain a continuity of power in the colony marks a desire to ensure the continued stability of Virginia.

OTHER EVENTS OF 1624
Arts/Culture John Smith publishes in London a narration of his travels in North America, the *General History of Virginia, the Summer Isles and New England*. This book includes the story of his rescue by

Pocahontas. Edward Winslow also publishes his *Good News from New England* in London.

Ideas/Beliefs The legal code of the Virginia colony mandates church attendance on Sunday. Those who do not attend are required to pay a fine of one pound of tobacco. In addition, each plantation must set aside at least a room for the purpose of religious worship. This religious regulation reflects the religious tendencies of King James I. Meanwhile the English sponsors of the Plymouth colony send an unordained Puritan minister, John Lyford, to America. The colonists are angered by his unprofessional status. They accuse him of Anglican bias and of planning to found a rival settlement. He is tried and punished by banishment from the colony.

JANUARY 1625
Colonial Affairs The Dutch West India Company sends out a second colonial director in the person of Willem Verhulst to its North American settlements. Verhulst replaces sea captain Cornelis May. Verhulst is supported by a council of Dutch mariners and two assistants.

OTHER EVENTS OF 1625
External Affairs King James I of England dies. He is succeeded by King Charles I.

14 MARCH 1626
Colonial Affairs George Yeardley is appointed by the English Crown as governor of the Virginia colony, replacing Sir Francis Wyatt.

4 MAY 1626
Settling Peter Minuit arrives in New Netherland on the ship *Sea-Mew*. He settles on Manhattan Island with other Dutch colonists. Later this year he buys Manhattan from the Indians for 60 guilders, or about $24. This price is paid in goods. Minuit names the island New Amsterdam. Dutch colonists from New Jersey move to New Amsterdam.

SEPTEMBER 1626
Colonial Affairs Willem Verhulst, the second director of New Netherland, is relieved of his duties because of incompetence. He is replaced in this position by Peter Minuit. Minuit is later removed as director in 1631 when his policies in dealing with the patroons are judged too liberal.

15 NOVEMBER 1626
Colonial Affairs The Plymouth Pilgrims, bolstered by growing prosperity and their increasing numbers, reach a decision to buy out their London stockholders for £1900 and to take over the repayment of the company debt of £600. Eight colonists guarantee the agreement in exchange for a trade monopoly and a tax on shareholders until the debt is repaid.

OTHER EVENTS OF 1626
Settling Led by Roger Conant, colonists from Cape Ann establish the settlement of Naumkeag, or Salem.

FOUNDING A NATION 986-1787

Industry Dutch settlers in New Amsterdam build the first flour mill in the colonies.

14 JUNE 1627
Settling The Dutch settlement on the Delaware River is completely deserted as the last of the colonists leave to join the group of Dutch now settled at New Amsterdam on Manhattan Island, where Peter Minuit governs as director.

NOVEMBER 1627
Colonial Affairs Francis West is appointed governor of the royal colony of Virginia by the English Crown, replacing George Yeardley.

OTHER EVENTS OF 1627
Settling In an urgent attempt to provide adequate numbers of settlers for the Virginia colony, the London managers send over a shipload of some 1500 kidnapped children, some of whom are quite young.
Colonial Affairs The New Amsterdam colony and the Plymouth colony establish a trading relationship. The Plymouth colony also erects a trading post on the Kennebec River in Maine under a patent from the Council for New England. French Cardinal Richelieu founds the Company of New France, granting the company a monopoly in fur trading on the North American continent and title to all of the land area from Florida to the Arctic.
Ideas/Beliefs The leader of the Merrymount Colony at Quincy, Massachusetts, Thomas Morton, erects a maypole to mock the ascetic religious practices of the neighboring Puritans.

19 MARCH 1628
Colonial Affairs The newly formed New England Company in Massachusetts, led by nonconformist clergyman John White, is awarded a patent to the land between the Merrimac and Charles Rivers. Most of this group's 90 participants are Puritans, and some of them were members of the Dorchester Company of 1624 that had unsuccessfully sought to settle Cape Ann.

26 MARCH 1628
Colonial Affairs Following a period of four years, the Virginia House of Burgesses again convenes, called together by Francis West, governor of Virginia.

1 MAY 1628
Life/Customs The Massachusetts colonists at Merrymount led by Thomas Morton celebrate May Day with a may pole, dancing and drinking. The revival of this pagan festival in the new world horrifies the Plymouth Pilgrims.

JUNE 1628
Colonial Affairs The Plymouth Pilgrims send Miles Standish to eradicate the Merrymount settlement at Quincy. Established in 1623 by Captain Wollaston and governed by Thomas Morton, the colony enjoyed considerable success at Indian trading. Morton is reviled by the Pilgrims for his dissolute life style and after his capture by Miles Standish he is sent back to England.

6 SEPTEMBER 1628
Settling A group of some 40 English settlers led by John Endecott arrives by ship at present–day Salem. Roger Conant and his colonists are already in residence there. After governing the settlement for two years, Endecott is succeeded by John Winthrop. This marks the beginning of the Massachusetts Bay Colony.

OTHER EVENTS OF 1628
Ideas/Beliefs The Dutch settlers in New Amsterdam found the Dutch Reformed Church there.

10 MARCH 1629
British Policy King Charles I of England dissolves Parliament and reigns without it until 1640. This spurs immigration to the American colonies.

19 MARCH 1629
Colonial Affairs The newly organized Massachusetts Bay Company—arising out of the former New England Company—is granted a charter by the English Crown. As no site for the company's annual meeting is included in the charter, the company later takes advantage of this omission to remove the organization to New England and there to make the company into a virtually independent Puritan commonwealth.

7 JUNE 1629
Colonial Affairs The government of The Netherlands grants to the Dutch West India Company the Charter of Freedoms and Exemptions. This document is intended to encourage agriculturally based colonization that will render the colony self–supporting with a surplus that will supply the company's vast merchant fleet. The Dutch West India Company is given authority to issue large land grants to patroons in exchange for their sponsorship and transport of 50 or more settlers to the colonies. The patroons are to be granted freedom from taxation for eight years and feudal rights.

29 JUNE 1629
Settling Four hundred settlers arrive on five ships at Salem to supplement the colonists ruled by John Endecott.

10 JULY 1629
Ideas/Beliefs The two clergymen, Francis Higginson and Samuel Skelton, establish the first nonseparatist Congregational church in Salem.

5 SEPTEMBER 1629
Colonial Affairs In England, 12 Puritan members of the Massachusetts Bay Company sign the Cambridge Agreement which formally provides for the transfer of the Massachusetts Bay Company charter and govern-

ment to New England. This action is instigated by the growing political insecurity in England after the dissolution of Parliament in March and the commercial disruptions of the Thirty Year's War in Europe.

20 OCTOBER 1629
Colonial Affairs In England, John Winthrop is elected as the governor of the Massachusetts Bay Company. This action is made possible by the provisions of the Cambridge Agreement.

7 NOVEMBER 1629
Colonial Affairs The Council for New England grants the territory of New Hampshire between the Merrimac and Piscataqua Rivers to John Mason.

17 NOVEMBER 1629
Colonial Affairs John Mason and Sir Ferdinando Gorges receive from the Council for New England an extensive trading grant. They are to have exclusive trading rights in an undefined area extending from Maine and New Hampshire north to the St. Lawrence River and west to Lake Champlain.

OTHER EVENTS OF 1629
Industry New England colonists establish a brick kiln in Salem and a leather tannery at the site of Lynn, Massacusetts.
Settling In England, King Charles I grants to Sir Robert Heath the territory between 31°N and 36°N. This area is named Carolina, after Charles. As yet, no colonization plans are developed for this region.

13 JANUARY 1630
Colonial Affairs The Council for New England grants the Plymouth Patent to William Bradford and other members of the Plymouth colony. This grant clarifies the limits of the 1621 grant.

JANUARY 1630
Colonial Affairs Under the authority of the June 1629 Charter of Freedoms and Exemptions, the Dutch West India Company has by now granted five patroonships in North America to directors of the company. Of the five patroonships, only three are colonized—Pavonia, which includes Staten Island; Swaanendael on Delaware Bay; and Rensselaerswyck on the upper Hudson River. Of these three patroonships, only Rensselaerswyck proves to be a success. Amsterdam merchant Kiliaen Van Rensselaer rules as an absentee patroon of a territory that spreads 24 miles on both sides of the Hudson River and that is home to several thousand Dutch tenants. In 1638 the tenants of Rensselaerswyck will be afforded the opportunity to own land.

29 MARCH 1630
Settling Beginning a wave of immigration into the Massachusetts Bay colony, newly elected governor John Winthrop leaves in the first group of ships sailing from Southampton, England. These five ships carry some 900 colonists and the company's charter.

JOHN WINTHROP, 1588-1649

John Winthrop, the first governor of the Massachusetts Bay Colony, labored long and hard in the service of an independent Puritan theocracy that was founded on essentially anti-democratic principles. Winthrop's own sometimes liberal tendencies were held in check by the criticisms of the all-powerful Puritan clergy. Yet his deeply-felt Puritanism was based on a religious fundamentalism that demanded literal Biblical prototypes for all the institutions and activities of the new colony—a colony that was meant to be a dynamic earthly expression of the will of God. Born in England the son of a socially-elite Suffolk land-holding family, Winthrop studied at Cambridge University before he entered Gray's Inn to practice law in London. The troubled British political scene and the uneasy future of nonconformist religious sects encouraged him to take an interest in the recently-formed Massachusetts Bay Company, with an eye toward emigration.

As one of the London organizers of the proposed settlement, he supported the decision to transfer the company and its charter physically to America. This foresighted move was eventually to result in the creation of a self-governing commonwealth. Winthrop was chosen governor before the 1630 departure of the *Arabella*, carrying some 700 colonists. Although the term of the Massachusetts Bay Colony governorship was for only one year, Winthrop was chosen to that post in the years 1629-1634, 1637-1640, 1642-1644 and 1646-1649. He also served as deputy governor for a total of ten years. After choosing Boston as the site of the seat of government, Winthrop met and dealt with a number of crises—including the opposition of the freemen to the concentration of power in the hands of the magistrates, the religious controversy over the teachings of Anne Hutchinson, and the banishment of Roger Williams. An early supporter of the defensive New England Confederation, Winthrop was chosen its first president in 1643. His personal journal, later known as *The History of New England*, started just before his departure for America and continuing intermittently until his death, became an invaluable source for the historical events, as well as the religious and social organization, of the Puritan commonwealth.

---

29 MAY 1630
Arts/Culture John Winthrop begins to write an extensive historical narrative covering the years 1630 to 1649. This journal, later known as *The History of New England* is not published in full until 1825. It is important not only as a primary historical source and as a social and intellectual record, but also as a touchstone of literary inspiration for 19th century American writers, including Longfellow.

12 JUNE 1630
Settling After a two-and-a-half-month voyage, the Southampton ships carrying John Winthrop and his colonists anchor in Salem Harbor. John Endecott hands over the Salem government to Winthrop and leaves for Charlestown.

23 AUGUST 1630
Colonial Affairs The new governor of the Massachusetts Bay colony, John Winthrop, convenes the first session of the court of assistants at Charlestown.

FOUNDING A NATION 986-1787

Labor The first session of the Massachusetts Bay colony of assistants led by John Winthrop mandates a wage ceiling of two shillings a day for workers in the building trades. This action represents the first regulation of labor in the colonies.

17 SEPTEMBER 1630
Settling The settlement of Boston is officially established by Massachusetts Bay colonists led by John Winthrop. The original Indian name of the site is Shawmut, or "living fountain." Boston is named after an English county town and it is the offshoot of the Salem colony led by John Endecott.

30 SEPTEMBER 1630
Life/Customs The first public execution in the American colonies takes place when Pilgrim John Billington is hanged for the murder of a compatriot during a quarrel.

19 OCTOBER 1630
Colonial Affairs The first meeting of the general court takes place in the Massachusetts Bay colony. During this session, more than 100 colonists plead for admission as freemen of the Massachusetts Bay Company.

9 NOVEMMBER 1630
Transportation The first ferry route is established across the river between Boston and Charlestown. Licensed ferry operators are limited to a passenger fare of one penny, with the same amount to be charged for 100 pounds of cargo.

OTHER EVENTS OF 1630
Ideas/Beliefs The first Boston church is established by Puritan clergyman John Wilson with the support of John Winthrop, Thomas Dudley and Isaac Johnston. This Congregational church had been located earlier in Charlestown across the river from Boston.
Arts/Culture In a task that will take 20 years, the second governor of the Plymouth colony, William Bradford, begins to set down his *History of Plymouth Plantation*. Bradford's account of the *Mayflower* voyage and the early years of the Plymouth colony will not be published until 1856.
Population At the beginning of this year, there are some 3000 colonists in Virginia and 300 in the Plymouth colony. In the years 1630-1640, the great migration will bring some additional 16,000 colonists to the Massachusetts Bay colony.

5 FEBRUARY 1631
Ideas/Beliefs Clergyman Roger Williams arrives in New England, where he will serve in the Salem and Plymouth churches. He questions the legality of the Massachusetts Bay colony charter and advocates separation of church and state.

18 MAY 1631
Colonial Affairs In the Massachusetts Bay Colony, 118 additional male settlers are permitted to assume the status of the original 12 freemen. But in violation of the company charter, only church members are allowed to become freemen who may vote for officials.

2 DECEMBER 1631
Settling Sir Ferdinando Gorges receives a third land grant of 24,000 acres on the York River in the Maine-New Hampshire area. He begins to settle this region.

3 FEBRUARY 1632
Colonial Affairs In the Massachusetts Bay Colony, Watertown settlers state their opposition to a tax ordered by the court of assistants in which they have no voice. This later leads to a general court decision to admit two delegates from each town to advise the tax committee.

19 MARCH 1632
Settling The Council for New England grants a large tract of land near the mouth of the Connecticut River to a group of Puritans led by Lord Saye and Sele and Lord Brooke.

19 MAY 1632
Colonial Affairs In the Massachusetts Bay Colony, the general court is granted the right to choose the governor and deputy governor. The assistants are to be elected by the freemen, who are also permitted to send deputies to the general court. This marks a first step toward representative government, but only church members may become freemen.

30 JUNE 1632
Settling Charles I grants the Maryland Charter to Roman Catholic Lord Baltimore. It grants the proprietor the right to make "laws with the consent of the freemen and that are "agreeable" to the laws of England. Religious freedom is also provided for in the charter. Initially Lord Baltimore rules as an absentee proprietor through the first governor Leonard Calvert, his brother. Calvert is able to institute the system of manorial government proposed in the charter and to develop a friendly relationship with the Maryland Indians.

OCTOBER 1632
Exploration Edward Winslow of the Plymouth colony explores the Connecticut River valley, indicating Puritan interest in westward expansion.

6 DECEMBER 1632
Settling The Dutch-settled patroonship of Swaanendael located on the west bank of Delaware Bay has been eradicated by hostile Indians by this date.

19 JANAURY 1633
British Policy An attempt to revoke the Massachusetts Bay Company charter comes before the English Privy Council. This move is promoted by Thomas Morton, who has been deported twice from the colony by Puritans, and by Sir Ferdinando Gorges.

8 JUNE 1633
Settling A Dutch ship from New Amsterdam sails up the Connecticut River as far as Hartford to build Fort Good Hope, a trading post.

3 JULY 1633
British Policy The Privy Council rejects Virginia's claim to its territory that was included in the Maryland charter granted to Lord Baltimore. This sets the stage for later border disputes.

JULY 1633
Settling Plymouth governor William Bradford and Edward Winslow fail to arrange a combined Plymouth-Massachusetts Bay colony expedition inland to the Connecticut River to open the area up to colonization.

4 SEPTEMBER 1633
Ideas/Beliefs Prompted by political disorder in England, the notable church leader John Cotton arrives in New England. He is followed by Thomas Hooker, another influential Puritan clergyman.

SEPTEMBER 1633
Settling Massachusetts Bay Colony settler John Oldham leads a group inland to the Connecticut Valley. They spend the winter at Wethersfield, Connecticut. Meanwhile Edward Winslow of Plymouth commissions William Holmes to erect a trading post on the Connecticut River above Hartford.

8 OCTOBER 1633
Colonial Affairs The Massachusetts Bay Colony settlement of Dorchester organizes the first town government.

22 NOVEMBER 1633
Settling The first group of 200 settlers, many of them Catholic, led by governor Leonard Calvert, sets sail for Maryland.

OTHER EVENTS OF 1633
Education Dutch schoolmaster Adam Roelantsen arrives in New Amsterdam to establish the first school in America. This school, which has endured as the present-day Collegiate Church of New York City, is created as an offshoot of the Dutch Reformed Chuch. Soon after, the Boston Latin school is established as the first public school. Its classical curriculum is based on English models.

27 FEBRUARY 1634
Settling The group of Maryland-bound colonists arrives in Virginia and travels north up Chesapeake Bay to Blakiston's Island.

28 APRIL 1634
British Policy The English Privy Council creates the Commission for Foreign Plantations, better known as the Laud Commission. In spite of its wide mandate for governance, this body is to have little real influence in the colonies.

14 MAY 1634
Colonial Affairs A representative form of government is organized by the Massachusetts Bay Company when town deputies insist on seeing the company charter.

26 FEBRUARY 1635
Colonial Affairs The freemen of the Maryland colony meet in an assembly and formulate a legislative code. They act without the approval of Lord Baltimore, who subsequently repudiates their document.

23 APRIL 1635
Colonial Affairs A naval skirmish occurs in the waters off Virginia between the ships of Virginia trader William Claiborne and Lord Baltimore. This incident results from the boundary dispute between Maryland and Virginia. The Virginia settlement on Kent Island had been included in the royal grant to Lord Baltimore. Another such confrontation occurs in May.

MAY 1635
British Policy After two years of consideration, the Laud Commission orders the revocation of the Massachusetts Bay Company charter, asserting that it had been illegally procured and its mandate had been overstepped. The colony refuses to submit to this.

7 JULY 1635
Colonial Affairs John Winthrop the Younger is appointed to govern the area around the mouth of the Connecticut River.

AUGUST 1635
Colonial Affairs New Amsterdam colonists forcibly remove a group of Virginians from the abandoned Dutch Fort Nassau on the Delaware River. The Dutch then set up a military garrison, thus ensuring their trading rights in the New Jersey area.

13 SEPTEMBER 1635
Ideas/Beliefs The Massachusetts general court orders Roger Williams into exile. This action is provoked by his criticism of the Massachusetts Bay Company charter and his promotion of the separation of church and state. Relenting somewhat, the court permits Williams to spend the winter in Salem before his banishment.

OCTOBER 1635
Settling Massachusetts Bay colonists arrive at the Connecticut River to settle in the Hartford area. An earlier Massachusetts group from Dorchester has already been at Windsor since spring. Plymouth has original claim to the Windsor area where they have a trading post.

JANUARY 1636
Ideas/Beliefs Roger Williams escapes from Salem as he fears imprisonment and deportation. He spends the rest of the winter with the Indians. Other dissenters join him in the spring. This group tries to settle at

FOUNDING A NATION 986-1787

Plymouth but they are not permitted to do so.

13 MARCH 1636

Settling The Massachusetts Bay general court creates an administrative plan for the settlement at the mouth of the Connecticut River governed by John Winthrop the Younger. The plan contains the explicit provision that the settlers have ultimate control over their own destiny.

Colonial Affairs In the same session, the general court enacts the Township Act which allows Massachusetts towns a degree of self government by freemen.

25 MAY 1636

Colonial Affairs A Puritan of aristocratic birth, Sir Henry Vane, is elected governor of the Massachusetts Bay colony. Vane, John Cotton and other Boston church members are influenced by the religious views of Anne Hutchinson. She advocates a personal and mystical religion, one that lessens the importance of the clergy as interpreters of the scriptures.

31 MAY 1636

Settling Clergyman Thomas Hooker and his followers arrive in Hartford, Connecticut, from Newton, Massachusetts, in a further wave of inland migration. He founds the first church in the territory and he and his followers declare their freedom from all but divine authority.

JUNE 1636

Ideas/Beliefs After purchasing land from the Indians, Roger Williams founds the present day city of Providence, Rhode Island. The new colony becomes a haven of religious tolerance.

20 JULY 1636

Indians New England trader John Oldham is killed by the Pequot Indians. His murder leads to a series of punitive expeditions against the Pequots who live in the Rhode Island-Long Island-Connecticut area.

24 AUGUST 1636

Indians To pursue the Pequot Indian warfare, Massachusetts governor John Endecott organizes a military force.

28 OCTOBER 1636

Education The Massachusetts general court appropriates money to found Harvard College. The first president of the college is clergyman Henry Dunster, and the entrance requirements for incoming students specify a sound classical education.

20 JANUARY 1637

Ideas/Beliefs In a Boston sermon, John Wheelwright supports the considerable religious influence of Anne Hutchinson—with her advocacy of grace over works and of personal revelation that downplays the role of the clergy. As a result of this attack, Wheelwright is convicted of contempt and sedition.

3 MAY 1637

British Policy In the matter of the revocation of the Massachusetts Bay Company charter, the English Privy Council instructs Sir Ferdinando Gorges to serve a writ on the Massachusetts administrators and to bring back the charter. Gorges is unable to accomplish his mission as his ship breaks down.

27 MAY 1637
Colonial Affairs In the Massachusetts Bay Colony election, John Winthrop defeats Governor Henry Vane, who has the support of pro-Hutchinson Boston, by relocating the voting to Newtown.

5 JUNE 1637
Indians In another episode in the Pequot Indian war, Captain John Mason leads a force against the main Pequot camp near Stonington, Connecticut, and destroys it.

28 JULY 1637
Indians Near New Haven, the Pequot Indians who escaped the slaughter at Stonington are massacred by a united force of Connecticut, Massachusetts Bay Colony and Plymouth colonists near Fairfield, Connecticut. The Pequot tribe is virtually eradicated and 40 years of peace on the frontier follow.

30 AUGUST 1637
Ideas/Beliefs To deal with the religious dissension instigated by the doctrines of Anne Hutchinson, a synod of 25 Puritan clergymen meets in Newtown to clarify the nature of Puritan doctrine.

2 SEPTEMBER 1637
Colonial Affairs Director Van Twillen of the New Amsterdam colony is removed from office for various offenses, including mismanagement, religious intolerance and illegal trading. His successor is Amsterdam merchant Willem Kieft.

12 NOVEMBER 1637
Ideas/Beliefs John Wheelwright is sentenced to banishment by the Massachusetts general court. At the same session, Anne Hutchinson is ordered to be tried for sedition and contempt. She is found guilty and sentenced to banishment.

31 DECEMBER 1637
Settling Peter Minuit, now in the service of the Swedish, leads a group of Swedish settlers to the Delaware River area under a grant from the New Sweden Company. The New Sweden Company is a combined group of Dutch and Swedish investors.

7 MARCH 1638
Ideas/Beliefs After Anne Hutchinson is tried and excommunicated by an ecclesiastical court, she leaves with her family for the Rhode Island colony of Roger Williams.

4 APRIL 1638
British Policy The English Crown rules against Virginia and William Claiborne in the Maryland-Virginia boundary dispute. Claiborne is denied his claim to Kent Island. He later recaptures the island when political conditions disintegrate in England.

APRIL 1638
Settling William Coddington leads a group of Boston exiles to Roger Williams' Providence colony. Coddington purchases Aquidneck Island from the Indians and together with Anne Hutchinson establishes Pocasset, or Portsmouth.

31 MAY 1638
Ideas/Beliefs In a Hartford sermon, Thomas Hooker expresses the view that political power should rest on the consent of the governed.

JUNE 1638
Settling Sailing back to Sweden after delivering colonists to the Delaware River area, Peter Minuit dies when his ship sinks.

OTHER EVENTS OF 1638
Arts/Culture Stephen Daye establishes the first colonial printing press in Cambridge, Massachusetts. The next year he issues the broadside "Oath of a Free Man," which promotes freedom of conscience.

24 JANUARY 1639
Colonial Affairs The Connecticut settlements of Hartford, Wethersfield and Windsor enact the Fundamental orders, a confederate governmental plan that allows for popular consent but places constraints on religious membership and limits voting to freemen. Written by Roger Ludlow, this document remains in effect with amendments until 1818.

3 APRIL 1639
Colonial Affairs A royal charter names Sir Ferdinando Gorges proprietor and governor of Maine, confirming the grant from the Council for New England.

8 MAY 1639
Settling William Coddington founds Newport, Rhode Island, after he separates from Anne Hutchinson's neighboring Pocasset colony.

14 JULY 1639
Colonial Affairs Settlers in New Hampshire led by John Wheelwright sign the Exeter Compact, patterned after the Mayflower Compact.

12 MARCH 1640
Settling The two Rhode Island settlements of Newport and Pocasset, founded by William Coddington and Anne Hutchinson, are combined.

APRIL 1640
Settling Swedish reinforcements arrive at the Delaware River settlement. The new arrivals include governor Peter Hollender Ridder, Lutheran clergyman Reorus Torkillus, and farm animals.

25 JUNE 1640
Colonial Affairs A provincial court is set up in York, Maine, in an attempt to establish the Maine territory as an independent entity.

19 JULY 1640
Settling Revising its 1629 document, the Dutch gov-

ernment issues a new Charter of Freedoms and Exemptions. Its intent is to facilitate Dutch colonization of New Netherland. The land area of the patroonships is limited to 200 acres for those who undertake to bring over five settlers. The charter also establishes a plan of local self-government.

NOVEMBER 1640
Settling Dutch colonists originally from Utrecht arrive to settle in the Delaware River area, close to the Fort Christina Swedish colony.

2 MARCH 1641
Colonial Affairs The Plymouth land patent is deeded to the freemen of the colony by trustee William Bradford who received it from the Council for New England.

14 JUNE 1641
Colonial Affairs The Massachusetts Bay Colony assumes jurisdiction of the Dover-Portsmouth, New Hampshire, area, with the proprietors keeping their land rights.

10 DECEMBER 1641
Colonial Affairs The Massachusetts general court formally adopts the Body of Liberties, a legal code compiled by Nathaniel Ward. The court rejects the more Mosaic code proposed by John Cotton in *Moses His Judicialls* (1636). Issued to counter criticism that the magistrates exercise too much discretion, the Body of Liberties also bases its criminal code on the Old Testament.

21 JANUARY 1642
Indians Director of the New Netherland colony Willem Kieft calls a meeting of the Twelve (family representatives) to organize a military response to the increasing raids of Hudson River Valley Indians. The Indians are finding themselves hemmed in more and more by the Iroquois tribes of the north and the growing European colonization to their south.

18 FEBRUARY 1642
Colonial Affairs The heads of influential Dutch colonial families petition for representation in the New Netherland government.

MARCH 1642
Indians The Dutch campaign against the Hudson River Valley Indians proves unsuccessful. Instead a settler on the Bronx River, Jonas Bronck, makes a truce that is to last for one year.

11 DECEMBER 1642
Colonial Affairs In response to English colonial incursions into the New York and Long Island area, New Netherland director Willem Kieft creates the office of English Secretary.

OTHER EVENTS OF 1642
External Affairs Civil war breaks out in England

between the royalist supporters of King Charles I and the Parliamentarians and Puritans. Oliver Cromwell emerges as the Puritan leader.

25-26 DECEMBER 1643
Indians Hudson River valley Indians fleeing from the attacks of the Mohawk Indians are massacred by the Dutch when they seek safety in the Dutch settlements. The Indians then retaliate with a series of raids against Dutch colonists.

MARCH 1643
Colonial Affairs Roger Williams leaves for England in order to obtain a charter for his Rhode Island colony.

19 MAY 1643
Colonial Affairs. In Boston, representatives from the four New England colonies of Connecticut, Massachusetts, Plymouth and New Hampshire meet to confederate as the United Colonies of New England. This is in response to the military shortcomings pointed up by the Pequot Indian wars and to deal with Dutch territorial incursions. Under the articles of confederation, the territorial integrity of the member colonies is respected. The governing board of eight commissioners, two from each colony, has authority to declare war for both defensive and offensive purposes. The costs of any military action are to be shared proportionally by the colonies. The commissioners also have authority over Indian affairs, fugitives and disagreements between colonies.

AUGUST 1643
Indians Anne Hutchinson and most of her family are murdered by Indians near Eastchester, Long Island, where she has moved after her husband's death.

SEPTEMBER 1643
Indians Leader of the New Netherland colony Willem Kieft convenes a meeting of the Eight to seek assistance in dealing with the increasingly destructive Indians raids on settlements in the New York and Long Island area.

29 SEPTEMBER 1643
Indians Connecticut colonist John Underhill leads a force to the aid of beleaguered Dutch colonists in the campaign against the Indians.

23 OCTOBER 1643
Colonial Affairs Following the lead of Guilford and Stamford, the independent Connecticut town of Milford unites with the New Haven colony under a single government.

6 NOVEMBER 1643
Colonial Affairs The New Haven Colony general court draws up a plan for representative government. This Frame of Government proposes a legal system based on the Ten Commandments, restricts the vote to church members and does not allow for jury trial.

7 MARCH 1644
Colonial Affairs The Massachusetts Bay Colony legislature becomes bicameral as a result of the legal case, *Shearman* v. *Keayne.*

18 MARCH 1644
Indians In Virginia the Opechancanough Indians rise up against the settlers but after two years they will be defeated decisively. The Indians are forced to give up all the land between the James and York Rivers. The peace between the Indians and settlers lasts until 1675.

24 MARCH 1644
British Policy In England Roger Williams is formally granted a charter for his Rhode Island Colony, allowing the towns of Providence, Portsmouth, Newport and Warwick to establish a general assembly.

18 JUNE 1644
Colonial Affairs Increasingly dissatisfied with the inept Indian policy of New Netherland director Willem Kieft, representatives of the Dutch colonists refuse to agree to new excise taxes.

29 NOVEMBER 1644
Indians The Massachusetts general court passes legislation promoting the conversion of New England Indians. This motivates clergyman John Eliot to learn Indian languages in preparation for the widespread conversion of New England Indians to Christianity.

9 AUGUST 1645
Indians Peace is finally declared between the Dutch and the Hudson River valley Indians. Facilitated by the Mohawk Indians, this pact concludes four years of hostilities in which numerous Dutch and English settlements were destroyed.

30 AUGUST 1645
Indians The New England Confederation commissioners arrange a peace treaty in Boston with the Narragansett Indians.

28 JULY 1646
Colonial Affairs Willem Kieft is removed from his position as director of the New Netherland colony, largely because of his ill-judged Indian policy that resulted in four years of war.

4 NOVEMBER 1646
Ideas/Beliefs The Massachusetts general court passes a law that makes heresy punishable by death.

14 NOVEMBER 1646
Ideas/Beliefs In a continuing controversy, Robert Child and others protest the intolerance of Massachusetts Puritans toward those of other faiths—an intolerance expressed in religious and civil discrimination. Child also criticizes the Puritan fathers for not adhering to the more liberal principles of English common law. In response to these charges, Governor John

THE IROQUOIS CONFEDERACY

In 1779, when American Revolutionary forces on a punitive mission arrived in western New York's Mohawk River valley, they were astounded at the evidences of the remarkable Iroquois culture that greeted them. Before them lay broad cultivated fields of corn, squash, potatoes, beans and peas; expertly pruned apple, peach and pear orchards; and well–equipped farms with domesticated animals and livestock. In the eyes of the common soldiers, the Iroquois lived better in their wood frame and stone houses with brick chimneys and glazed windows than most of the European settlers in the region.

Around 1650, the Iroquois achieved the most advanced native American civilization north of the Rio Grande. When European colonists began to settle on the eastern seaboard, the most powerful Iroquois tribes—the Cayuga, Mohawk, Oneida, Onondaga, and Seneca—had already formed the political association known as the Iroquois Confederacy, or the Five Nations, in order to end intertribal warfare. In 1722, the Five Nations became the Six Nations when they were joined by the Tuscarora Indians, driven out of the South by settlers.

According to tradition, this loose confederacy had been organized in the 16th century by the Mohawk visionary Dekanawida and his disciple Hiawatha, who made a life's work of persuading village after village to sign the "great peace." By the 17th century the territory controlled by the Iroquois extended from New England to the Mississippi River in the West and to the Tennessee River in the South. The unique political structure of the confederacy, of independence and interdependence among the tribes, delegated a special place to women. Not only was the lineage based on the maternal line, but women also nominated the 50 *sachems* who sat on the governing council of the Five Nations, as well as the male representatives to the tribal councils. Although the league did not interfere in tribal affairs, it did mediate successfully in many intertribal conflicts.

Due mainly to the influence of Indian superintendent Sir William Johnson, the Iroquois sided with the British against the French in the European struggle for territory and for the fur trade. Except for the Tuscaroras and half of the Oneidas, the Iroquois also sided with the British in the Revolutionary War—a choice that turned out to be disastrous for the Indians. After the participation of Iroquois in the 1778 Cherry Valley and Wyoming Valley massacres, General George Washington ordered the devastating punitive expedition led by General John Sullivan. By the end of the 18th century, war and disease had reduced the Iroquois by one-quarter, and they eventually lost most of their territory, often through treaty violation and land fraud by real estate speculators.

In their heyday, the Iroquois exercised an influence far beyond their numbers—some 16,000 at their height. Not only were they able to hold two great European empires, Great Britain and France, at bay, but they also organized a sophisticated political structure that reportedly served as a model for some of Benjamin Franklin's proposals for the new United States Federal Government.

Winthrop and the magistrates justify their policies and banish Child.

JANUARY 1647
Colonial Affairs In Maryland, the first woman barrister in the colonies, Margaret Brent, seeks and is

denied the right to vote in the assembly.

11 MAY 1647
Colonial Affairs Peter Stuyvesant arrives in New Amsterdam to assume the position of leader of the New Netherland colony, replacing Willem Kieft.

29 MAY 1647
Colonial Affairs A general assembly of Rhode Island freemen from the towns of Newport, Portsmouth, Providence and Warwick meets in Portsmouth to draft a constitution that allows for separation of church and state, permits public referenda on legislation and gives towns the right to initiate legislation.

11 NOVEMBER 1647
Education The Massachusetts general court passes legislation requiring each sizeable town to institute some form of public education. The smaller towns must hire a teacher, while larger towns must organize a grammar school.

27 APRIL 1648
Colonial Affairs New Netherland governor Peter Stuyvesant orders the construction of Fort Beversrede on the Schuylkill River at the site of present-day Philadelphia. The erection of this fort marks the growing competition of the Dutch and Swedes for the lands south of New York. Governor Johan Bjornsson Prinz of the New Sweden colony constructs a series of forts, concluding with Fort New Krisholm near the mouth of the Schuylkill River. Stuyvesant therefore meets the challenge of the Swedish by erecting Fort Beversrede across the river from the Swedish fort.

MAY 1648
Colonial Affairs The Swedish forces from Fort New Krisholm burn the Dutch Fort Beversrede.

JUNE 1648
Ideas/Beliefs The Massachusetts general court finds Margaret Jones guilty of witchcraft and orders her hanged in Boston. The previous year a witch had been executed in Hartford. Fourteen witches will be executed in Connecticut and Massachusetts during the years 1647 to 1662.

18 OCTOBER 1648
Labor The Massachusetts general court grants a charter to the shoemakers of Boston and the first labor organization in America is born.

NOVEMBER 1648
Colonial Affairs The Dutch Fort Beversrede is burned a second time by Swedish forces. Nevertheless the Dutch hang on stubbornly to the site until their 1651 erection of Fort Casimir to control the routes into the New Sweden colony.

30 JANUARY 1649
British Policy In England King Charles I is executed and the Commonwealth is established. Responding to these events, Virginia declares its loyalty to the English royal house of Stuart and offers itself as a haven for fleeing cavaliers.

24 APRIL 1649
Ideas/Beliefs The Toleration Act is passed in Maryland during the administration of Protestant deputy governor William Stone. The act provides for religious freedom for all Christians, including Catholics.

19 JULY 1649
Ideas/Beliefs Through the efforts of Edward Winslow, the Society for Propagating the Gospel in New England is established in London. This society promotes the conversion of Indians to Christianity.

13 OCTOBER 1649
Colonial Affairs The New Netherland advisory council of The Nine, dissatisfied with the government provided by the Dutch West India Company under Peter Stuyvesant, petitions the government of Holland for assistance in instituting reforms. The dissidents particularly seek a provision for self government by each settlement.

OCTOBER 1649
Colonial Affairs William Coddington, who opposes the union of the four Rhode Island towns of Newport, Portsmouth, Providence and Warwick under the charter granted to Roger Williams, leaves for England in order to obtain his own charter for the island of Aquidneck.

16 OCTOBER 1649
Ideas/Beliefs The independent Maine government passes legislation that grants religious freedom to its citizens, with the stipulation that those of other religious persuasions behave decorously.

6 APRIL 1650
Colonial Affairs Lord Baltimore grants Maryland a bicameral assembly, with a lower house of delegates and an upper house of councillors.

23-29 SEPTEMBER 1650
Colonial Affairs In the Treaty of Hartford, New Netherland governor Peter Stuyvesant and the commissioners of the New England Confederacy delineate the boundaries between the Dutch and English settlements in the southern New England and Long Island area. The Dutch are permitted to keep their lands in Hartford. This treaty is respected by both parties until the conquest of New Netherland by the English.

30 OCTOBER 1650
British Policy To reduce Dutch supremacy in trade and shipping, the English Parliament bans foreign ships without a special license from trading in the American colonies.

OCTOBER 1650
British Policy In response to the Virginia colony's

declaration of allegiance to the Crown, the English Parliament declares a naval blockade on Virginia.

MARCH 1651
Colonial Affairs In England, William Coddington is granted a separate Rhode Island charter for the island of Aquidneck that reinforces his opposition to the Providence Plantations of Roger Williams.

19 JULY 1651
Ideas/Beliefs In a series of continuing acts of religious intolerance in Massachusetts, three Baptists are tried and banished.

Colonial Affairs Dutch colonists from New Netherland erect and occupy Fort Casimir on the Delaware River. This garrison controls the routes into the territory of the New Sweden colony. The Swedish and Dutch are in competition for the same land area in the Philadelphia-New Jersey region.

9 OCTOBER 1651
British Policy In the second of a series of trade acts, the English Interregnum Parliament rules that no goods may be imported from the colonies into England in non-English ships or from locations other than the point of production. Enforcement of these trade acts is to be carried out by colonial governors. Since the English lack the necessary shipping stock to assume all the required import functions, supply shortages arise. This leads to dissent in the colonies where there is a demand for freedom of trade, protection of all merchants—including foreign shippers—and a declared intention of continuing to use Dutch shippers. This act, known is the first Navigation Act, serves to instigate the Anglo-Dutch War (1652-1654).

5 NOVEMBER 1651
Colonial Affairs In the continuing hostilities between Swedish and Dutch colonists, the new governor of the New Sweden colony, Johan Classen Rising, is able to defeat the Dutch and capture Fort Casimir.

15 NOVEMBER 1651
British Polity Catholic royalist Thomas Green, named deputy governor of the Maryland colony by departing governor William Stone, states his allegiance to Charles II as rightful successor to the English throne. This provokes the English government to send parliamentary commissioners to the colony to investigate. Among the commissioners is William Claiborne who had opposed Maryland in the earlier boundary dispute over Kent Island.

5 DECEMBER 1651
Colonial Affairs The government of Maine appeals to the English Parliament for support against the territorial expansionism of the Mssachusetts colonies. This attempt to place Maine's independence on a legal footing fails.

12 MARCH 1652
British Policy Virginia Governor Sir William Berkeley and his council submit to the representatives dispatched by the English Parliament on two armed vessels. An election follows and Richard Bennett, one of the parliamentary commissioners, is chosen as new governor by the burgesses. William Claiborne is elected secretary of state. For the next eight years, Virginia enjoys a period of virtual self–rule.

29 MARCH 1652
British Policy The English parliamentary commissioners sent out to investigate Maryland deputy governor Thomas Green, who invited attention by professing loyalty to Charles II, relieve him of his authority and name William Fuller governor in his place. Lord Baltimore is relieved of his proprietory powers for the interim.

APRIL 1652
Colonial Affairs In response to the pleas of Dutch colonists for self–government, the government of The Netherlands issues an order to permit the settlement at New Amsterdam to organize a city government.

18 MAY 1652
Slavery The Rhode Island colony enacts the first American law declaring slavery illegal. In the same year, The Netherlands agrees to permit the export of black slaves to the New Netherland colony. In the Dutch colony legislation is passed to regulate treatment of slaves by their masters. Slaves may be punished by whipping only with the express permission of the colonial authorites.

31 MAY 1652
Colonial Affairs The Massachusetts general court passes legislation including the territory of Maine within the boundaries of the Bay Colony, thus dashing Maine's hopes for continued independence. Massachusetts sets her northern border at a point three miles north of the Merrimac River source. This brings all of the settlements of Sir Ferdinando Gorges as far north as Saco Bay under the authority of the Massachusetts Bay colony.

7 JUNE 1652
Finance In defiance of English law, the Massachusetts general court establishes a mint and coins the pine tree shilling.

JULY 1652
External Affairs War breaks out between the English and the Dutch. This European war affects colonial relations, since the New England Confederation and the New Netherland colony intensify hostilities.

29 OCTOBER 1652
Colonial Affairs In a further act of defiance toward England, the Massachusetts Bay colony proclaims itself an independent commonwealth.

OCTOBER 1652
Colonial Affairs In the Rhode Island Colony, Roger

Williams is able to get the English government to revoke William Coddington's separate charter for the island of Aquidneck.

20 NOVEMBER 1652
Colonial Affairs The May annexation of Maine territory by the Massachusetts Bay Colony becomes reality when the settlement of Kittery submits to the authority of Massachusetts. It is the first Maine community to come under the rule of Massachusetts.

2 FEBRUARY 1653
Colonial Affairs As ordered by the Dutch government, Peter Stuyvesant takes offical steps to grant a degree of self government to the New Amsterdam settlement. Stuyvesant formally declares New Amsterdam a municipality. Although he makes municipal office appointments, he reserves the power to enact laws and pass ordinances for the governor and his council.

2 JUNE 1653
Colonial Affairs The Massachusetts Bay Colony refuses to support the New England Confederation vote for war against the Dutch colonists in New Netherland. The New Englanders fear that the Dutch are conspiring with the Nyantic Indians against English settlers in the Connecticut colony.

5 JULY 1653
Colonial Affairs The Dutch garrison of Fort Good Hope at Hartford, Connecticut, is annexed by the Connecticut colony. Although this action occurs during the course of the Anglo-Dutch War (1652-1654), the colonial outposts of these European nations do not formally enter into a state of war against each other.

10 DECEMBER 1653
Colonial Affairs Peter Stuyvesant calls the first session of the representative assembly of New Netherland. Attending are both Dutch and English representatives from incorporated towns close to New Amsterdam. The delegates continue to oppose the arbitrary government of New Netherland under the direction of the Dutch West India Company.

OTHER EVENTS OF 1653
Indians Missionary John Eliot publishes the first book printed in an Indian language, *Catechism in the Indian Language*. Eliot will later translate the Bible into the Algonquian language.

7 MARCH 1654
Colonial Affairs Massachusetts colonists seek to widen their power over the recently annexed Maine territory. Supported by a grant from Parliament, Plymouth colonist Thomas Prince travels to the Kennebec River to organize the settlement.

MAY 1654
Colonial Affairs New Netherland governor Peter Stuyvesant calls a second session of the assembly to consider the escalation of hostilities with the colonies of the New England Confederation.

20 JUNE 1654
Colonial Affairs New England colonists hear of the peace treaty between the English and Dutch just as a military force is about to leave Boston to march against the Dutch settlement at New Amsterdam.

SEPTEMBER 1654
Settling Jewish immigration to America begins with the arrival of 23 Sephardic Jews in New Amsterdam. These new settlers come from Brazil, driven out by the Spanish Inquisition in effect there. Jacob Barsimon was the first Jew to arrive in July. The Dutch West India Company supports their right to remain over the objections of New Netherland governor Peter Stuyvesant.

30 OCTOBER 1654
Colonial Affairs Maryland Governor William Fuller, who has been appointed to his post by English parliamentarians, follows his inauguration by revoking the Toleration Act, withdrawing the protection of the law from Catholics and by denying the proprietor Lord Baltimore authority over the colony.

25 MARCH 1655
Colonial Affairs The civil war in Maryland between royalist Catholics and Puritan parliamentarians concludes with the victory of the Puritan faction led by Maryland Governor William Fuller. Former royalist governor William Stone, who is wounded during the fighting, is imprisoned and the victorious Puritans execute four of his followers.

26 SEPTEMBER 1655
Colonial Affairs Peter Stuyvesant is able to recapture the Dutch Fort Casimir from the Swedish in the Delaware territory. This defeat effectively ends all royal Swedish influence on the American continent. The city of New Amsterdam, which has carried on the 15–year military campaign against the New Sweden colony, receives in payment a large land grant from the Dutch West India Company of territory in the Delaware River area.

OTHER EVENTS OF 1655
Life/Customs In one of the few cases of women's suffrage in the colonial era, Lady Deborah Moody is permitted to vote in a Long Island town meeting. The status of women is also reflected in their illiteracy rates. The strong educational bias of the Massachusetts colony is reflected in a 50 percent illiteracy rate for women, while the figure is 60 percent in New Netherland and 75 percent in Virginia. (These determinations are made on the basis of women's ability to sign their names to documents with either an "X" or a written signature.)

JANUARY 1656
British Policy Lord Baltimore regains his authority

over the Maryland colony thanks to the intercession of the English Committee of Trade. The restoration of his privileges is dependent on the choice of Josias Fendall as the new governor of the colony.

MARCH 1656
Colonial Affairs In Rhode Island, William Coddington finally drops his opposition to the authority of the Providence Plantations—a union of the towns of Newport, Portsmouth, Providence and Warwick created in the charter obtained by Roger Williams.

10 JULY 1656
Colonial Affairs Josias Fendall is elected Maryland governor to replace Governor William Fuller. This permits the reinstatement of Lord Baltimore as proprietor.

JULY-AUGUST 1656
Ideas/Beliefs Massachusetts Bay Colony Puritans greet the first Quakers to arrive in Boston with imprisonment, physical beatings and banishment without benefit of trial. Similar incidents occur in 1657 and 1659.

17 SEPTEMBER 1656
Ideas/Beliefs The commissioners of the United Colonies of New England federation support the actions of Massachusetts Puritans toward Quakers.

22 SEPTEMBER 1656
Life/Customs In a provincial court session in Patuxent, Maryland, the first colonial all-woman jury sits to hear the case of Judith Catchpole who is accused of murdering her unborn child. The jury acquits her of the charges.

2 OCTOBER 1656
Ideas/Beliefs In a further act of hostility against Quakers, Connecticut enacts legislation to fine and banish Quakers. Later on in October, the Massachusetts general court passes similar legislation in support of earler Massachusetts actions against Quakers.

21 APRIL 1657
Colonial Affairs A group of 167 Dutch settlers from New Amsterdam arrives at Fort Casimir in the Delaware territory. Led by Jacob Alrichs, the settlers rename the community New Amstel. Two years later, Alrichs is replaced by Alexander d'Hinoyossa as leader.

AUGUST 1657
Ideas/Beliefs Governor Peter Stuyvesant greets with harsh treatment five Quakers who come to New Amsterdam. After rigorous punishment, they are banished to Rhode Island.

29 MAY 1658
Ideas/Beliefs The Massachusetts general court passes further legislation opposing religious freedom for Quakers. This law specifically bars the holding of Quaker meetings.

13 JULY 1658
Colonial Affairs The Massachusetts Bay colony completes its annexation of Maine territory when the settlement of Casco Bay, or present-day Falmouth, comes under its jurisdiction.

27 OCTOBER 1659
Ideas/Beliefs William Robinson and Marmaduke Stevenson, two Quakers who defy the Massachusetts Bay colony expulsion order and return to the colony, are hanged.

DECEMBER 1659
British Policy The death of Virginia governor Samuel Matthews marks the end of British parliamentary power in the Virginia colony during Oliver Cromwell's Protectorate. With the demise of the Protectorate in England, the Virginia burgesses place themselves under 'supreme power' until lawful authority issues from England.

OTHER EVENTS OF 1659
Ideas/Beliefs Clergyman John Eliot publishes *The Christian Commonwealth,* a book that treats the Puritan concept of the inextricable interrelationship of church and state.

10 MARCH 1660
Colonial Affairs The Maryland assembly declares itself independent of the proprietory control of Lord Baltimore and of the control of his deputies. Governor Josias Fendall is removed from power.

12 MARCH 1660
Colonial Affairs Royalist Sir William Berkeley is elected governor by the Virginia general assembly in anticipation of the return of royal rule in England. Governor Berkeley is officially commissioned by King Charles II of England in July.

29 MAY 1660
External Affairs The royal house of Stuart is restored to power in England as Charles II returns to claim the throne.

1 JUNE 1660
Ideas/Beliefs Mary Dyer, a former supporter of Anne Hutchinson, defies an expulsion order and returns to the Massachusetts Bay colony. She is hanged.

JUNE 1660
Indians Dutch authorities enact legislation to discourage the illegal activities of those who interfere with Iroquois Indian fur traders in the area of Fort Orange.

10 OCTOBER 1660
British Policy The English Crown approves an expanded Navigation Act of 1660. This act requires that only English-built and owned vessels, with a crew of whom three-quarters are English, may be used for trade in the English colonies; and that certain com-

TOWN MEETINGS

The earliest and most enduring example of grass–roots democracy in America is the New England town meeting. In the early colonial era, the town meeting developed as an open forum to consider matters of local interest, including taxation, charity for the needy, the organization and operation of schools, the legislation and implementation of public law and the initiation and construction of public works projects, such as roads. The town meeting chose selectmen as executive officers to carry out the proposals and policies decided upon by the meeting. In most communities, all free male citizens were allowed to vote in the town meeting, regardless of whether they possessed the privilege of suffrage in the colony as a whole. The town meeting as an institution probably evolved from the Congregationalist parish meeting, which was organized to deal with secular matters affecting the church. In the era leading up to the Revolutionary War, New England town meetings became hotbeds of anti-British protest and activity.

The town meeting was the most popular, literally and figuratively, form of local government in New England, but eventually the increasing size of some communities forced restrictions on participation in the meetings. For instance, in 1822 a Boston town meeting was unable to accommodate its total of 7000 eligible inhabitants, so the full town meeting was replaced with a session of the elected representatives of the people. But in the more rural areas of the Northeast, the institution of the town meeting persists as an effective instrument of self government into the present day. Although the town meeting concept was generally confined to the New England area, these "elementary republics," as Thomas Jefferson called them, did provide a model for the organization of townships in other areas of the country, as well as provide the national government with a practical example for some of its democratic procedures.

modities—including indigo, sugar and tobacco—of colonial origin can be shipped only to England or her colonies.

18 OCTOBER 1660
Colonial Affairs Rhode Island is the first of the New England colonies to support the restoration of Charles II to the English throne.

NOVEMBER 1660
Colonial Affairs Philip Calvert is appointed governor by the Maryland assembly.

14 MARCH 1661
Colonial Affairs The Connecticut colony proclaims the restoration of Charles II to the English throne, followed by New Haven in June and Massachusetts in August.

24 MARCH 1661
Ideas/Beliefs Massachusetts continues to enforce harsh penalties against Quakers when William Leddra is hanged for defying an expulsion order.

SEPTEMBER 1661
Ideas/Beliefs Severe penalties against Quakers are opposed by a royal order that requires the release of all imprisoned Quakers to representatives of the English Crown who will transport them to England for trial. Massachusetts does release its Quaker prisoners, but instead of sending them to England, lets them leave the Bay colony.

7 DECEMBER 1661
Ideas/Beliefs Under duress from Parliament, Massachusetts suspends the corporal punishment act that imposes harsh penalties on Quakers and other religious nonconformists.

DECEMBER 1661
Colonial Affairs By this time a number of Dutch and English settlements on Long Island and in New Jersey have been incorporated as towns with some degree of self government.

OTHER EVENTS OF 1661
Ideas/Beliefs John Eliot publishes his translation of the Bible into the Algonquian Indian language. This is also the first Bible ever to be printed in the American colonies and the remarkable event is hailed by Increase Mather, among others.

3 MAY 1662
Colonial Affairs The Connecticut Colony under John Winthrop, Jr. finally obtains a royal charter through the agency of Lord Saye and Sele. This charter defines the boundaries of Connecticut to include the independent colonies of Guilford, Milford, New Haven and Stamford.

18 OCTOBER 1662
Ideas/Beliefs The Massachusetts general court reinstates the corporal punishment act that imposes severe penalties on Quakers and other religious nonconformists, thus returning to its stance of defying British policy.

4 NOVEMBER 1662
Colonial Affairs The freemen of New Haven vote to maintain the independent status of the colony and to oppose its annexation by the Connecticut colony, as provided for in the charter of May 1662.

Penn making a treaty with the Indians.

OTHER EVENTS OF 1662

Arts/Culture Michael Wigglesworth publishes his book of Puritan poetry, *Day of Doom; or, A poetical description of the great and last Judgement*. This 17th century best seller vividly evokes the torments of hellfire awaiting sinners.

British Policy The English Crown confirms the Massachusetts Bay Colony charter provided that the colony permits Anglicans the freedom to worship and that all landowners receive the vote, regardless of their religious affiliation.

24 MARCH 1663

British Policy King Charles II creates the colony of Carolina by granting the territory to eight loyal supporters. The proprietors of Carolina include Sir William Berkeley, former governor of Virginia, and the proprietors of Jersey—John Lord Berkeley and Sir George Carteret. In contrast to the more democratic makeup of the northern colonies, the proprietors of Carolina plan to establish a feudal society patterned on the English estate system.

7 JUNE 1663

Indians Relations between the Hudson River Valley Indians and Dutch colonists disintegrate to the point that the Indians attack the village of Wiltwyck, near present-day Kingston, New York. This leads the Dutch to conduct three retaliatory raids against the Indian strongholds which they destroy.

10 JUNE 1663

Colonial Affairs The Duke of Norfolk and Samuel Vassal contest the legality of the Carolina charter issued by Charles II. This is to be followed by a challenge from the Cape Fear Company. They all have prior claims to the Carolina territory.

8 JULY 1663

Colonial Affairs Rhode Island, whose earlier charters were found to have no sound legal basis, is granted a royal charter that guarantees religious freedom for the colonists.

27 JULY 1663

British Policy The second Navigation Act is passed by Parliament. Designed to benefit English and Colonial merchants, this act states that all imports (with certain exceptions such as salt, wine, servants and horses) to the American colonies from other European countries or colonies must be transported from England on English vessels. Again the responsibility for enforcement rests with the colonial governors.

3 MARCH 1664

Colonial Affairs New Netherland governor Peter Stuyvesant is forced to submit in the matter of the English towns on Long Island. Although these towns lie within the mutually recognized boundary of Dutch territory, they now come under English control. This turn of events occurs when the Connecticut Colony sends James Christie to Long Island to obtain an oath of allegiance from the English settlers and to oust the Dutch magistrates.

12 MARCH 1664

British Policy The Duke of York obtains a grant that gives him authority over all lands between the Connecticut and Delaware Rivers. This land grant includes all Dutch holdings in North America.

2 APRIL 1664

British Policy The Duke of York names Colonel Richard Nicolls as the head of a commission to conquer New Netherland.

16 MAY 1664

Indians The Hudson River valley Indians surrender the Esopus valley to the Dutch.

24 JUNE 1664

British Policy The Duke of York makes a proprietory grant of the land between the Hudson and Delaware Rivers to his loyal supporters, Sir George Carteret and John, Lord Berkeley. This area is named New Jersey in honor of Carteret who served as governor of the Isle of Jersey. Berkeley and Carteret expect to realize large profits from sales of real estate.

23 JULY 1664

Colonial Affairs The Massachusetts Bay colony makes a pretense of allowing nonchurch members the vote based on the size of their estate. But Massachusetts refuses to comply with the other provisions required by the king's commissioners.

29 AUGUST 1664

British Policy An English fleet of four vessels, led by Colonel Richard Nicolls, arrives in New York harbor. Nicolls is empowered by the Duke of York to capture New Netherland.

7 SEPTEMBER 1664

British Policy Following a naval blockade and without a shot fired, Governor Peter Stuyvesant surrenders New Netherland to the English force led by Richard Nicolls. Stuyvesant is forced to submit as he lacks the support of the colonists in opposing the English. The English generously grant the Dutch colonists religious freedom and property inheritance rights, as well as trade privileges. Nicolls changes the name of New Amsterdam to New York, in honor of the Duke of York.

20 SEPTEMBER 1664

British Policy Colonel George Cartwright, a commissioner sent by the Duke of York, accepts the surrender of the Dutch at Fort Orange (Albany) on the Hudson River.

24 SEPTEMBER 1664

British Policy After the annexation of the Dutch Fort Orange, the English become allies of the Five Nations of the Iroquois in place of the Dutch.

FOUNDING A NATION 986-1787

10 OCTOBER 1664
British Policy The English obtain control of the Dutch Fort Casimir in Delaware.

OCTOBER 1664
Colonial Affairs William Drummond is appointed governor of Albemarle, or present-day North Carolina. The Carolina proprietors subsequently compile a Concessions and Agreements, which provides for a representative assembly, freedom of conscience and liberal land grants.

14 DECEMBER 1664
Colonial Affairs The charter granted to the Duke of York in March 1664 has the effect of persuading the independent colonies of Guilford, Milford and Stamford to join Connecticut. New Haven still holds out against annexation.

OTHER EVENTS OF 1664
Slavery The Maryland Colony passes a law that mandates the lifelong servitude of black slaves. This law is deemed necessary because legal precedents in England allow for the freeing of those slaves who convert to Christianity and establish legal residence in the country. The colonial assemblies of New York, New Jersey, North Carolina, South Carolina and Virginia will also pass such laws.

5 JANUARY 1665
Colonial Affairs The New Haven colony finally allows itself to be annexed by Connecticut.

10 FEBRUARY 1665
Colonial Affairs Philip Carteret, a relative of Sir George Carteret, is named governor of New Jersey. The Dutch settlers accept his authority but the English settlers oppose him. He leads a group of colonists in establishing a settlement at Elizabethtown.

17 FEBRUARY 1665
British Policy The Plymouth Colony agrees to comply with the orders of the king's commissioners who come to New England to examine the colonial administration, settle border disputes and to enforce the Navigation Act. In order to be in compliance with the king's commissioners, the colonists must swear allegiance to the Crown and permit freedom of religion.

20 FEBRUARY 1665
Colonial Affairs Sir George Carteret and John, Lord Berkeley, the proprietors of New Jersey, present their Concessions and Agreements. This document calls for a representative assembly, freedom of conscience and liberal leasing of land.

23 FEBRUARY 1665
British Policy While the Second Anglo-Dutch War rages in Europe, the deputy of the Duke of York, Richard Nicolls, orders the annexation of all property belonging to the Dutch West India Company in what was formerly New Netherland.

11 MARCH 1665
Colonial Affairs Thirty-four deputies from English and Dutch towns in Westchester and Long Island meet at Hempstead to approve a judicial code known as the Duke's Laws. This code also provides for municipal reorganization and for freedom of conscience.

20 APRIL 1665
Colonial Affairs Connecticut joins the Plymouth Colony in agreeing to comply with the conditions of the king's commissioners.

3 MAY 1665
Colonial Affairs The Rhode Island Colony also agrees to comply with the king's commissioners, following the lead of Plymouth and Connecticut.

19-24 MAY 1665
Colonial Affairs When the Massachusetts Bay Colony refuses to conform to the requirements of the king's commissioners, the commissioners recommend that the Massachusetts charter be revoked. On receiving this advice, the English Crown orders Massachusetts representatives to come to London to answer the charges of the commissioners. Once again the Massachusetts general court defies these royal orders.

JUNE 1665
Colonial Affairs The Dutch municipal officials of New Amsterdam, now New York under the English, are replaced by the traditional English offices of alderman, mayor and sheriff. The new charter granted to New York limits trading activities to freemen and disallows self government.

10 JULY 1665
Colonial Affairs A second charter for the Carolina territory extends its southern borders to include Florida.

22 AUGUST 1665
British Policy The English Privy Council voids all previous claims to the Carolina territory, making the 1663 patent of Charles II the only valid one.

OCTOBER 1665
British Policy The king's commissioners found an independent government in Maine that will last until 1668.

10 OCTOBER 1665
British Policy In the New York Colony, formerly New Netherland, the Duke of York's deputy Richard Nicolls orders the confiscation of property belonging to Dutch colonists who refuse to declare loyalty to the English king.

3 MAY 1666
Agriculture When the overproduction of tobacco results in a glutted market, the Maryland assembly passes legislation to forbid the cultivation of tobacco as a commercial crop for the period of one year.

OTHER EVENTS OF 1671

OTHER EVENTS OF 1666
Settling Connecticut colonists from New Haven arrive to settle the area of Newark, New Jersey, after receiving land grants from New Jersey governor Carteret. The colonists pattern their new settlement after a New England town.

5 JUNE 1667
Colonial Affairs In Virginia, five Dutch warships enter the James River to attack the merchant shipping on this waterway. The Dutch are able to capture and take away 18 ships owned by English merchants.

21 JULY 1667
External Affairs The Peace of Breda which formally ends the Second Anglo-Dutch War, officially establishes English sovereignty over the former Dutch territory of New Netherland.

23 SEPTEMBER 1667
Slavery The Virginia House of Burgesses passes legislation stating that the conversion of blacks to Christianity does not bring about their release from servitude. The law encourages slave owners in conversion efforts.

30 NOVEMBER 1667
British Policy The English Crown formally recognizes the claims of the Connecticut colony to territory west of the Connecticut River.

21 APRIL 1668
British Policy The Duke's Laws, a judicial code issued by the Duke of York, already in effect in the Westchester and Long Island area since March 1665, is now put into force in Delaware. The Duke's Laws include a plan for municipal organization and provide for freedom of conscience.

4 JUNE 1668
Colonial Affairs The first meeting of the New Jersey general assembly takes place. This governmental body has been provided for in the fairly liberal Concessions and Agreement issued by proprietors Sir George Carteret and John, Lord Berkeley in 1665.

6 JULY 1668
Colonial Affairs Massachusetts is able to annex Maine when Maine colonists send representatives to a special convention at York that submits to the authority of Massachusetts.

11 MARCH 1669
British Policy The English proprietors of Carolina issue the Fundamental Constitutions to replace the Concessions and Agreements of 1665. It is thought that John Locke and proprietor Sir Anthony Ashley authored this document. This detailed governmental blueprint combines an aristocratic social plan with liberal principles and religious tolerance. Although the original and complete Fundamental Constitutions is not enacted by the colonial legislatures, the document

is an important influence on colonial religious practices in the Carolinas.

MAY 1669
Colonial Affairs Following the annexation of Maine by Massachusetts, three Maine deputies arrive to represent the Maine territory in the Massachusetts court.

1 MARCH 1670
Colonial Affairs A second amended version of the Fundamental Constitutions of 1669 is enacted in the Carolinas.

MARCH 1670
Settling A group of English colonists led by Joseph West settles in the Carolina territory at Port Royal Sound.

APRIL 1670
Settling In the Carolina territory, the settlers led by Joseph West move north and establish Charles Town, near present Charleston.

20 APRIL 1670
British Policy The Virginia assembly votes to end the English practice of deporting habitual criminals as indentured servants to the Virginia colony. The English Parliament supports this legislation for a while but then revokes it in 1717.

8 JULY 1670
External Affairs The Treaty of Madrid is signed by England and Spain. Each nation agrees to respect the other's rights in the American territories they occupy.

3 OCTOBER 1670
Colonial Affairs In Virginia, the assembly reserves the privilege of voting for landowners. A similar measure is enforced in Maryland by Lord Baltimore in December.

OTHER EVENTS OF 1670
Slavery The Virginia assembly passes another slavery law. This legislation disallows lifelong servitude for those blacks who became Christians before their arrival in the colony. This law is a reaction to the moral issues raised by the enslavement of Christians.

10 APRIL 1671
Indians Following a series of Indian hostilities against Massachusetts colonists, the Plymouth leaders require King Philip, chief of the Wampanoag Indians, to surrender his arms and he complies by giving up only part of his arsenal. King Philip is the colonists' name for Metacomet, a son of Massassoit.

OTHER EVENTS OF 1671
Westward Movement French explorers reach Sault Saint Marie and claim the interior of the North American continent for their monarch, King Louis XIV. In the same year, Virginia explorers Thomas Batts and Robert Fallam trek into the interior and discover the Falls of the Great Kanawha.

FOUNDING A NATION 986-1787

Indians Carolina colonists vanquish the Coosa Indians. A number of Indian captives are enslaved, thus initiating an experiment with Indian slavery.

Slavery Maryland broadens its 1664 slavery law by declaring the conversion of blacks either before or after their importation irrelevant to their fate of lifelong servitude. This enactment eases the economic apprehensions of slave importers and encourages the conversion of slaves to Christianity.

MARCH 1672

External Affairs The Third Anglo-Dutch War beings in Europe. It will last for two years. the Dutch plan a campaign to win back their New Netherland colonies from the English.

15 MAY 1672

Arts/Culture The first copyright law is passed in the colonies by the Massachusetts general court. This legislation provides for a seven-year copyright and a sizeable fine for infringement. Bookseller John Usher receives the first copyright for his edition of *The General Laws and Liberties of the Massachusetts Colony.*

OTHER EVENTS OF 1672

Slavery The Royal Africa Company is granted a monopoly of the English slave trade.

Ideas/Beliefs English Quaker leader George Fox tours the American colonies. This expedition is to pave the way for a Quaker effort to settle in America.

Colonial Affairs The Duke of York invalidates the 1664 land grants made to New Jersey settlers by his deputy Richard Nicolls.

1 JANUARY 1673

Life/Customs The first regular mail service between Boston and New York is established. The mail is carried by a horseback rider through wilderness areas by way of Hartford.

25 FEBRUARY 1673

British Policy All of Virginia is granted to proprietors Lord Arlington and Lord Culpepper for a period of 31 years by King Charles II. Later this grant is amended and the territory finally reverts to the king, who agrees to pay Lord Culpepper £600 a year until 1684.

17 MAY 1673

Westward Movement Two French explorers, Jesuit missionary Father Jacques Marquette and fur trader Louis Joliet, set out on a journey of discovery into the interior of North America. They travel from Lake Michigan southward and down the Mississippi River as far as the Arkansas River before they return north again.

7 AUGUST 1673

War A Dutch naval task force enters New York harbor in an attempt to win back from the English the territory of New Netherland. The Dutch ships bombard the English garrison on Manhattan.

JACQUES MARQUETTE, 1637-1675

One of the greatest French explorers of the American interior, Jesuit missionary Jacques Marquette together with Louis Joliet discovered the upper Mississippi River and traced its course downstream as far as the mouth of the Arkansas River before returning to the Great Lakes. This epic 2500-mile four-month journey of exploration in 1673 was completed in two birch–bark canoes paddled by Marquette and Joliet's five companions. Marquette wrote in his journal, "Indian corn, with some smoked meat constituted all our provisions." This expedition, carried out under such primitive conditions, led to the territorial expansion of the French colonial empire from the St. Lawrence River to the Gulf of Mexico.

Father Marquette was born in Laon, France, to a prominent military and political family. Becoming a Jesuit novice at 17, he went on to study philosophy and then to teach in Rheims and other towns. After his 1666 arrival in New France, he mastered the Ottawa Indian language and served among the Ottawa and Huron Indians in the upper Great Lakes region. Among the Indians who came to visit his mission were the Illinois, who reported crossing a great river on their way.

Four years after his first meeting with explorer Louis Joliet, Marquette was designated by the governor of New France to join Joliet on an expedition to find the great river spoken of by the Illinois Indians. Marquette and Joliet did not proceed southward on the Mississippi beyond the Arkansas River, as they then learned from Indians that the Spanish were on the lower Mississippi, which flowed into the Gulf of Mexico. The arduous journey broke Marquette's health, and he never really recovered. Two years later he died, after completing the journal that was to be the only record of the expedition (as Joliet's journal and maps were later lost near the Montreal rapids in a river mishap). But in dying in the new world wilderness, Marquette fulfilled his pious dream of following in the footsteps of St. Francis Xavier, who had also died as a missionary in a far-off land.

---

12 AUGUST 1673

War Captain Anthony Clove, leader of the Dutch military force, accepts the surrender of the English garrison on Manhattan. Captain Clove is subsequently appointed governor general of New Netherland.

15 AUGUST 1673

War Dutch military forces proceed up the Hudson River and recapture Esopus (New Kingston) and Albany.

17 AUGUST 1673

War Dutch authorities are named to head New Orange (New York). Most English towns in New Jersey and on eastern Long Island submit peacefully to restored Dutch rule, although five settlements in Suffolk object.

OTHER EVENTS OF 1673

British Policy The Navigation Act of 1673, passed by the English Parliament, sets duties on certain goods passing from one plantation to another and establishes the office of customs commissioner to collect these duties. This act is drafted to prevent the evasion of English duties by traders who stop their ship at a colonial port on the way to Europe.

19 FEBRUARY 1674

War The Third Anglo-Dutch War is ended by the Treaty of Westminster with the English as victors. Under this pact, the American Dutch colonies are returned to England.

13 JUNE 1674

Colonial Affairs Philip Carteret is reinstated as governor of New Jersey, but Edmund Andros disputes his authority.

29 JUNE 1674

British Policy The Duke of York receives a patent reconfirming his title to all the land area lying between the Delaware and Connecticut Rivers, as well as the Maine territory between the Kennebec and St. Croix Rivers. The duke names Sir Edmund Andros as his governor general.

29 JULY 1674

British Policy The Duke of York reconfirms Philip Carteret's authority in the New Jersey area.

10 NOVEMBER 1674

War Sir Edmund Andros, deputy of the Duke of York, accepts the surrender of New York territory.

4 DECEMBER 1674

Westward Movement French Jesuit explorer Father Marquette establishes a mission at what is now Chicago.

OTHER EVENTS OF 1674

Colonial Affairs John, Lord Berkeley, sells his share of the New Jersey proprietorship for £1000 to John Fenwick who is an agent for fellow Quaker Edward Byllinge. Quaker leader George Fox had toured the colonies in 1673 and returned to England full of enthusiasm for the idea of a colonial Quaker commonwealth. This purchase initiates the organized appearance of the Quakers on the American scene.

Exploration French explorer LaSalle obtains a patent from King Louis XIV to build forts, trade with the Indians and explore the Mississippi River.

14 FEBRUARY 1675

Colonial Affairs Quaker William Penn obtains the West Jersey rights of Edward Byllinge. John Fenwick also later transfers his Jersey rights to Penn.

8 JUNE 1675

Indians Plymouth colonists try and execute three Wampanoag Indians who are implicated in the murder of an Indian who accused King Philip, chief of the Wampanoags, of conspiracy against the settlers.

20-25 JUNE 1675

War King Philip leads an Indian attack against

A battle at Hadley in King Philip's War.

COLONIAL CURRENCY

The colonial currency system was anything but systematic; it was a veritable hodgepodge. Of all the items in short supply in the American colonies, British currency was the most scarce. Parliament had instituted a policy of sending no British money to America, insisting that the colonial agricultural exports be paid for only in British goods. Nevertheless, some British money did work its way into the colonies via the British military garrisons, who paid colonial merchants in British money, but this money soon returned to England in payment of colonial debts.

The colonial need for a medium of exchange, particularly in the back country, led to the use of such commodity currency as wampum, corn, rice, wheat, tobacco, beaver skins and musket balls, which were all accepted as legal currency at various times. Most of the hard currency in circulation was foreign money, procured through trade with the West Indies, or injected into the economy with seaport purchases by pirates and privateers who had captured Spanish or French vessels. The most frequently used foreign coins were Spanish—the "piece of eight" or milled dollar, and the reale, worth one-eighth of the dollar. Although the Spanish dollar was considered the standard colonial currency, its value was usually denoted in terms of British shillings and pence. Also in circulation were French crowns, Portuguese moidores, and Dutch ducats. To add to the confusion, each colony set its own arbitrary value on the foreign coinage.

In 1652, Massachusetts defied the British edict and established its own colonial mint, which produced oak-tree, willow-tree, and pine-tree shillings for the next 30 years. England finally banned this colonial currency in 1684; but in 1690, Massachusetts began to issue bills of credit, or paper money, for use in government transactions in anticipation of tax revenues and therefore redeemable only when the taxes were collected. But the need was great and the bills of credit were soon widely accepted as legal tender in all private and business transactions. Other colonies followed suit, but when some failed to receive adequate tax revenues, their paper money depreciated rapidly. Great Britain sought to alleviate this predicament by its 1764 ban on all colonial paper money, causing a widespread economic crisis. The colonial currency problem was one of the causes of the Revolutionary War.

FOUNDING A NATION 986-1787

Swansea in retaliation for the Plymouth execution of three Wampanoag Indians, thus initiating King Philip's War. The pressures of colonial expansion have adversely affected the Indians over the course of the century to culminate in this fierce conflict that will rage on for over a year.

28 JUNE 1675

War After soldiers from Boston and Plymouth unite to form a joint military force to oppose King Philip, they attack the principal fort of the Wampanoags at Mount Hope with little success.

14 JULY 1675

War The Nipmuck Indians unite with the Wampanoag forces of King Philip to attack the settlement of Mendon, beginning a series of Indian attacks on the southern frontier of the English colonies.

2-4 AUGUST 1675

War The combined Wampanoag-Nipmuck Indian force led by King Philip attacks the settlement of Brookfield, Massachusetts.

19 AUGUST 1675

War King Philip leads the Wampanoags and Nipmucks in an attack against the settlement of Lancaster, Massachusetts.

1 SEPTEMBER 1675

War The Wampanoag and Nipmuck Indians attack the Connecticut River settlements of Deerfield and Hadley in Massachusetts. The Deerfield settlers are able to repulse this attack from their stockades and the Indians retreat, burning crops and outlying buildings as they withdraw. The Deerfield settlers are to suffer two more such attacks on 12 and 18 September.

2 SEPTEMBER 1675

War The Wampanoags and Nipmucks led by King Philip attack the Massachusetts settlement of Northfield.

9 SEPTEMBER 1675

War The New England Confederation officially declares war on King Philip, with each of the colonies required to provide a quota of men for the combined military force.

12 SEPTEMBER 1675

War Indians attack Falmouth, Maine. Farther south, they conduct a second raid on Deerfield, Massachusetts, where they are again repulsed.

18 SEPTEMBER 1675

War The Indian forces led by King Philip achieve a decisive victory at Bloody Brook, two miles from Deerfield. They massacre 64 of Deerfield's finest men, who are carrying food supplies to Hadley. In the wake of this disaster, Deerfield is abandoned and the survivors move south. A 1677 attempt to rebuild

Deerfield is thwarted by the Indians; but in 1682 the tenacious settlers are able to rebuild Deerfield, this time erecting stronger fortifications.

27 SEPTEMBER 1675

Indians In the south, a united company of Marylanders led by Thomas Truehart and Virginians led by John Washington is unable to eliminate the bands of warring Susquehannock Indians who are massacring Virginia settlers in a relentless series of raids. Virginia Governor Berkeley is accused of conflict of interest when he fails to protect frontier settlers in not letting Sir Henry Chickerly lead a military force against the Indians. He is suspected to trying to protect the fur trade in which he has considerable business interests.

5 OCTOBER 1675

War The Indian forces of King Philip attack Springfield, Massachusetts.

16 OCTOBER 1675

War The forces of King Philip attack Hatfield, Massachusetts.

19 NOVEMBER 1675

War Josiah Winslow leads a combined colonial force in an attack against the Narragansett Indian stronghold near present-day Kingston, Rhode Island. While most of the Narragansett warriors are able to escape, over 300 Indian women and children are killed.

JANUARY 1676

British Policy The Duke of York refuses to grant New York colonists the right to convene a general assembly. He refuses to acquiesce to the popular demands for representative government because he fears such political activity will disturb the peace.

10 FEBRUARY 1676

War The harsh winter reduces the Indian forces under King Philip to starvation and in search of food they again attack the settlement of Lancaster, taking a number of captives.

12 MARCH 1676

War Indians attack Plymouth, Massachusetts.

29-30 MARCH 1676

War Indians attack Providence, Rhode Island.

2 MAY 1676

War Mary Rowaldson, who was taken captive by the Indians in their attack on Lancaster, is ransomed. She later writes a *True History* which narrates an account of her captivity.

10 MAY 1676

Indians Nathaniel Bacon, a recently arrived settler in Virginia, takes it upon himself to lead a company of frontiersmen to the Roanoke River where they resoundingly defeat a force of the Susquehannock Indians who have been beleaguering the settlers.

18 MAY 1676
War In King Philip's War, Captain William Turner leads a force of 180 men in a crippling attack against a large Indian group near Deerfield, Massachusetts.

26 MAY 1676
Colonial Affairs Nathaniel Bacon is declared a traitor by Virginia governor Berkeley and is arrested when he arrives to assume his elected seat in the House of Burgesses.

JUNE 1676
British Policy Royal agent Edward Randolph comes to Boston to monitor Massachusetts Bay Colony enforcement of the English navigation acts. His investigations turn up various shortcomings in Massachusetts, including a failure to enforce the navigation acts, religious intolerance as the motivation for executing English subjects, refusing the right of appeal to the Privy Council and refusing to swear allegiance to the Crown. This serves as further ammunition in the move to revoke the Massachusetts charter.

5 JUNE 1676
Colonial Affairs Nathaniel Bacon is released from arrest when he admits his guilt. He is pardoned by Virginia governor Berkeley.

12 JUNE 1676
War In King Philip's War, Captain John Talcott leads a combined force of Connecticut Valley colonists and Mohegan Indians in a decisive battle against King Philip's men at Hadley. Following this defeat and that at Marlboro, the Indians begin to surrender.

23 JUNE 1676
Colonial Affairs In Virginia, Nathaniel Bacon returns to his home county of Henrico and there assembles a group of 500 men. He leads them into Jamestown, meeting no resistance. Supported by this military force, he makes Governor Berkeley sign his commission. Subsequently the Virginia House of Burgesses passes a series of democratic legislative reforms.

11 JULY 1676
Colonial Affairs The Quintipartite Deed divides the New Jersey proprietorship into East Jersey, Sir George Carteret's domain, and West Jersey. The proprietory rights to West Jersey were sold in 1674 to Quaker Edward Byllinge. The signers of the deed on behalf of the Quakers include Byllinge and William Penn.

29 JULY 1676
Colonial Affairs Once more, Virginia Governor Berkeley declares Nathaniel Bacon a rebel and tries to form a military company to oppose him. Berkeley fails in this attempt and is forced to flee.

3 AUGUST 1676
Colonial Affairs Influential Virginia planters meet at the Middle Plantation and take an oath to support Bacon who is meanwhile fighting Indians on the Virginia frontier.

12 AUGUST 1676
War New England colonial forces shoot King Philip in the Assowamset Swamp after he has been betrayed. King Philip's wife and child are sold into slavery.

28 AUGUST 1676
War King Philip's War ends when the Indian resistance collapses with a final surrender.

SEPTEMBER 1676
Colonial Affairs In Maryland a brief rebellion is led by William Davyes and John Pate against the proprietory regime—objecting to the prevalent abuse of power and nepotism of the absentee proprietorship, and reflecting the rampant anti-Catholicism within the colony. This minor uprising is unsuccessful, and Davyes and Pate are hanged.

13 SEPTEMBER 1676
Colonial Affairs In Virginia, Nathaniel Bacon returns from his frontier Indian foray and drives Governor Berkeley's military force out of Jamestown.

19 SEPTEMBER 1676
Colonial Affairs Bacon burns Jamestown.

18 OCTOBER 1676
Colonial Affairs Nathaniel Bacon dies suddenly. After the loss of its leader, the rebel army disintegrates into a group of smaller bands which are picked off one by one by Governor Berkeley's forces. The rest surrender when they are promised amnesty.

8 NOVEMBER 1676
Colonial Affairs John Fenwick, the governor of West Jersey, is arrested by New York authorities for the illegal exercise of governmental powers.

JANUARY 1677
Colonial Affairs West Jersey Governor John Fenwick is extradited to New York under arrest. There he is fined £40 for the illegal use of governmental powers. He will later return to West Jersey to reassume the duties of governor.

29 JANUARY 1677
British Policy Royal commissioners John Berry and Francis Moryson come to Jamestown, Virginia, to conduct an inquiry into the rebellion led by Bacon.

10 FEBRUARY 1677
British Policy Virginia Governor Berkeley revokes the royal pardon which Colonel Herbert Jeffreys has brought for the rebels. In defiance of the Crown, Berkeley proceeds to execute 23 of the rebels.

13 MARCH 1677
Colonial Affairs *The Laws, Concessions* and *Agree-*

ments is published by the proprietors of West Jersey. William Penn is one of the main authors of this document, which promotes basic civil rights, including trial by jury, freedom of conscience and taxation with representation.

Colonial Affairs Massachusetts solidifies its authority over the Maine territory by buying out the heirs of Sir Ferdinando Gorges whose title to Maine is supported by the English Lords of Trade.

27 APRIL 1677
Colonial Affairs In Virginia, Colonel Jeffreys officially assumes control of the government, replacing Governor Berkeley who leaves Jamestown.

AUGUST 1677
Indians A fort is constructed at Pemaquid, Maine, by Sir Edmund Andros as a stronghold against Indian raids.

10 OCTOBER 1677
British Policy The Massachusetts general court passes legislation to enforce the English navigation acts.

3 DECEMBER 1677
Colonial Affairs In the Carolinas, the antiproprietory party led by John Culpepper establishes a revolutionary government to oppose Thomas Miller, a supporter of the proprietorship. Miller has illegally assumed the position of governor. Culpepper is tried for treason but acquitted.

12 APRIL 1678
War In Maine, Sir Edmund Andros formally makes peace with the warring Indians, thus bringing King Philip's War to an end. The costs have been high for both colonists and Indians in terms of lives and material losses. The power of the New England Indian tribes has been effectively broken. From this time onward, only the Maine Indian tribes maintain some degree of independence.

26 OCTOBER 1678
Colonial Affairs New York Governor Sir Edmund Andros names his own officials to assume the duties of defiant West Jersey Governor John Fenwick.

DECEMBER 1678
Exploration Frenchmen René Robert Cavalier, Sieur de la Salle, and Father Louis Hennepin pass by Niagara Falls in an exploratory trip from Canadian territory into the American interior.

5 APRIL 1679
Colonial Affairs Despite the official status of East Jersey Governor Philip Carteret, Governor Edmund Andros of New York encroaches on Carteret's domain by collecting customs duties on trade commodities arriving in the ports of New Jersey. This dispute over spheres of influence originates from the 1665 refusal of English colonists to recognize the authority of the

proprietorship of New Jersey. Instead the colonists opt for the legality of the land grants issued to them by then New York Governor Nicolls.

10 OCTOBER 1679
Colonial Affairs Virginia bans the importation of tobacco from Carolina. Thus Carolina is driven to use New England traders to ship their crops north before carrying them to Europe. This stratagem is employed to avoid compliance with the English navigation acts.

15 JANUARY 1680
Westward Movement French explorer La Salle erects Fort Crevecoeur on the Illinois River.

30 APRIL 1680
Colonial Affairs The conflicting claims of New York and New Jersey come to a head when East Jersey Governor Philip Carteret is abducted and forced to stand trial in New York. He is accused of the illegal exercise of governmental powers. The jury acquits him.

2 JUNE 1680
Colonial Affairs New York Governor Edmund Andros comes to a sitting of the East Jersey general assembly. Andros usurps executive power in East Jersey and dissolves the general assembly when it refuses to recognize him.

6 AUGUST 1680
British Policy The Duke of York validates the legal rights of the Quaker proprietors to their West Jersey territory.

SEPTEMBER 1680
British Policy The territory of New Hampshire is separated from Massachusetts by order of a royal commission.

OTHER EVENTS OF 1680
Settling French Huguenot colonists arrive to settle in Charles Town, Carolina. The proprietors of Carolina designate Charles Town as the seat of Carolina government.

1 FEBRUARY 1681
Colonial Affairs The rights of Sir George Carteret in East Jersey are sold by his heirs to William Penn and 11 fellow Quakers.

4 MARCH 1681
British Policy William Penn receives a charter from King Charles II making him the proprietor of a large land grant in the Pennsylvania area. The charter limits Penn's governmental powers, provides for a legislative assembly and gives the English Crown overriding powers in the matter of taxation, legal appeal and the repeal of laws.

APRIL 1681
Colonial Affairs Continuing popular discontent with

WILLIAM PENN, 1644-1718

William Penn, the founder of Pennsylvania, consistently made political choices and decisions based upon his deeply-felt Quaker beliefs. The net result of his service in the public arena is a heritage of humanitarianism, liberalism and religious tolerance. Penn was born in London, the son of Admiral Sir William Penn. His Oxford University education was cut short by expulsion for his nonconformist religious activities. After a continental tour and naval service in the English war with Holland, Penn studied law at Lincoln's Inn. In 1667, he experienced a sudden and overwhelming conversion to the Quaker faith. His active Quakerism led to confinement in the Tower of London. Penn's connection with the American colonies began when he became one of the Quaker trustees of West Jersey. The Jersey colony's charter of liberties, the enlightened *Laws, Concessions, and Agreements,* was composed largely by Penn. This charter emphasized civil liberties, religious freedom and even laid down a just course for purchasing Indian lands. This document was to be followed by his subsequent *Frame of Government* and *Charter of Liberties* for Pennsylvania. But Pennsylvania, granted to Penn by the English Crown in repayment of debts owed his father (and named for his father), became a "Holy Experiment." His Pennsylvania proprietorship was characterized by a liberal government incorporating religious tolerance and friendly relations with the Indians. At first Penn governed the colony through his deputy William Markham. In 1682 he traveled to America himself, for what turned out to be a short stay, but during this first visit he laid out the plan for the city of Philadelphia. After his return to England to settle boundary disputes with Lord Baltimore, Penn was accused for treason when his patron James II was deposed by William and Mary. In addition, Pennsylvania was removed from his power. After the 1694 restoration of his proprietorship of Pennsylvania, Penn developed a plan for the union of the American colonies and established public education in Pennsylvania. After a 15-year absence, he returned to Pennsylvania in 1699. In 1701 he had to return to England again in order to defend the interests of his colony. His last years were made difficult by money problems that landed him in debtors prison for a while, the dissolute behavior of his son, and the quarrels of his delegates in Pennsylvania. A stroke incapacitated him for the last six years of his life. Yet for all his political machinations, Penn had remained an active Quaker missionary, a prolific writer on political and religious themes, and, antithetically, a worldly courtier in the train of English monarchs and European aristocrats.

the proprietory rule of Maryland results in a second rebellion (the first was in 1676) led by Josias Fendall. Fendall meets with defeat. He is treated somewhat more leniently than the earlier rebels in that he is only fined and ordered into exile.

10 APRIL 1681
Colonial Affairs Deputy governor William Markham is sent to inform Dutch and Swedish settlers in the Pennsylvania territory of the proprietorship of William Penn.

11 JULY 1681
Colonial Affairs William Penn drafts a Conditions and Concessions that will regulate real estate transactions in the Pennsylvania territory.

21 NOVEMBER 1681
Colonial Affairs Samuel Jennings, the governor of West Jersey, calls together the first session of the West Jersey assembly in Burlington.

12 JANUARY 1682
Colonial Affairs A revised version of the Fundamental Constitutions is issued in the Carolina colony.

1 MARCH 1682
Colonial Affairs In defiance of New York Governor Andros, John Fenwick deeds most of the West Jersey land grant under his control to William Penn and other Quakers.

9 APRIL 1682
Exploration French explorer La Salle reaches the mouth of the Mississippi River and claims possession of the surrounding territory, which he names Louisiana, for the French monarch Louis XIV.

11 APRIL 1682
British Policy Royal agent Edward Randolph sends to English authorities a report highly critical of the Massachusetts Bay colony. He cites Massachusetts for ignoring English laws mandating religious tolerance and for refusing to enforce the navigation acts.

APRIL 1682
Colonial Affairs William Penn sends Pennsylvania surveyor general Thomas Holme to mark out the streets for the planned city of Philadelphia.

5 MAY 1682
Colonial Affairs In his *Frame for Government,* William Penn drafts a detailed plan for the Pennsylvania government. This is in fact an early constitution which provides for a representative assembly of limited powers—it can only accept or reject legislation originated by the governor's council. The assembly is a primitive form of bicameral government.

7 AUGUST 1682
British Policy Royal agent Edward Randolph submits a second report critical of Massachusetts to the English authorities.

13 AUGUST 1682
Settling Following the widespread promotion of settlement opportunities in Pennsylvania, a group of Welshmen arrives to settle on land northwest of Philadelphia. They are to be followed by a large wave of immigration to Pennsylvania from Germany, Ireland and Britain. Many of these people are Quakers.

24 AUGUST 1682
Colonial Affairs William Penn receives a grant for the lower territory of Delaware from the Duke of York. This grant which is of dubious legality assigns no rights of government.

FOUNDING A NATION 986-1787

27 OCTOBER 1682
Colonial Affairs William Penn comes to the Delaware River to formally accept the Delaware territory from the Duke of York's deputy.

2 NOVEMBER 1682
Colonial Affairs William Penn declares in the Delaware assembly that the Duke's Laws are to remain in effect until the people decide to initiate another judicial and legislative code.

4 DECEMBER 1682
Colonial Affairs The first session of the Pennsylvania assembly convenes in Upland, or present-day Chester. The business transacted at this session includes the enactment of a legislative code and the incorporation of Delaware settlements within the area of Pennsylvania.

17 DECEMBER 1682
Colonial Affairs The Delaware assembly enacts a proclamation of freedom of conscience.

OTHER EVENTS OF 1682
Slavery The Virginia slavery law of 1670, which disallows lifelong servitude for those slaves converted to Christianity before their arrival in America, is repealed. The 1670 law has limited the importation of slaves into Virginia.

8 FEBRUARY 1683
Colonial Affairs The Dutch West India Company grants to the Dutch city of Amsterdam a large tract of its holdings in the Delaware River region surrounding New Amstel.

14 MARCH 1683
British Policy The Duke of York validates the claim of 24 Quaker proprietors to the territory of East Jersey.

2 APRIL 1683
Colonial Affairs A revised Frame of Government for Delaware and Pennsylvania is signed by William Penn.

13 JUNE 1683
British Policy Royal agent Edward Randolph returns to England from Massachusetts to assist in developing policies to deal with the rebellious Massachusetts Bay Colony.

23 JUNE 1683
Indians William Penn and the Indians negotiate a peace treaty at Shackamaxon under the Treaty Elm.

28 AUGUST 1683
Colonial Affairs Thomas Dongan, an Irish Catholic, arrives in New York to replace Sir Edmund Andros as governor. Andros has been investigated and found innocent of corruption and illegal commerce with the Dutch.

6 OCTOBER 1683
Settling In Pennsylvania, a group of Mennonite families from the Rhineland led by Daniel Francis Pastorius founds the settlement of Germantown.

30 OCTOBER 1683
Colonial Affairs A general assembly of delegates for New York, Maine, Nantucket and Martha's Vineyard convenes and legislates the Charter of Liberties. This assembly has been called together under orders from the Duke of York by Thomas Dongan, the new governor of New York. Matthias Nicolls is chosen as speaker of the assembly and is primarily responsible for composing the Charter of Liberties, which insists on the consent of those on whom taxes are levied and calls for meetings of the general assembly at least every three years. The Duke of York approves the charter at the time but later fails to implement it.

MAY 1684
British Policy The third Lord Baltimore, Charles Calvert, sails back to England in order to resolve the ongoing boundary disputes of Maryland with the Virginia colony and with William Penn. While in England, Calvert is charged with pro-Catholicism and with obstructing the royal customs collectors in Maryland. Meanwhile the matter of the boundary lines remains unresolved until the surveying of the Mason-Dixon line in 1784.

21 JUNE 1684
British Policy The charter of the Massachusetts Bay Colony is revoked after royal agent Edward Randolph submits a series of highly critical reports to English authorities. This action ends the Massachusetts requirement of church membership for suffrage.

24 JULY 1684
Settling In an attempt to establish a settlement on the Gulf Coast near the mouth of the Mississippi River, La Salle sets out from France with a fleet of several ships carrying prospective colonists. When he arrives, he is unable to locate the Mississippi River. The French are eager to colonize the Louisiana territory to solidify control over the fur trade and to establish a staging area for attacks on the Spanish colonies.

30 JULY 1684
Indians New York Governor Thomas Dongan negotiates an extension of the peace treaty with the Iroquois Indians in Albany.

14 AUGUST 1684
Colonial Affairs William Penn sails back to England to try to settle the boundary dispute with Lord Baltimore and Maryland.

5 SEPTEMBER 1684
Colonial Affairs The final session of the New England Confederation meets in Hartford.

31 OCTOBER 1684
British Policy In Maryland Christopher Rousby, a royal customs collector, is murdered by acting governor and nephew of proprietor Lord Baltimore, George Talbot. Baltimore, who is in England, is held accountable and is fined £2500. Talbot is removed to Virginia where a sentence of death is passed two years later. This death sentence is commuted by the English king and Talbot is therefore ordered into exile for five years instead.

JANUARY 1685
Exploration La Salle disembarks at Matagorda Bay, Texas, and builds Fort St Louis. He then begins the overland journey to Canada. Two years later La Salle is murdered by his men.

6 FEBRUARY 1685
British Policy The Duke of York, proprietor of New York, becomes King James II of England. New York becomes a royal province with the accession of King James.

SEPTEMBER 1685
British Policy Joseph Dudley, a representative of the Massachusetts Bay Colony who came to London to protect American colonial interests, is appointed governor of Maine, Masssachusetts and New Hampshire by James II.

17 OCTOBER 1685
British Policy The English Lords of Trade invalidate the claim of Lord Baltimore to Delaware territory. Thus William Penn is formally recognized as having jurisdiction over Delaware.

18 OCTOBER 1685
External Affairs King Louis XIV of France revokes the Edict of Nantes, which guaranteed religious freedom to French Protestants. This action leads to increasing numbers of French Huguenot settlers coming to South Carolina and the other colonies.

MAY 1686
British Policy King James II names Sir Edmund Andros as governor general of the Dominion of New England. The English crown creates this new political entity—which eventually comprises all the colonies north of Pennsylvania—into order to consolidate English holdings in North America. By this action the separate colonies are deprived of their independent status and local political rights. The colonial legislatures are dissolved, and Andros and the local councils appointed by the king assume all of the judicial and legislative power.

29 MAY 1686
British Policy King James II declares invalid the Charter of Liberties passed by the 1683 general assembly of New York and other New England colonies. This charter had called for the consent of the governed in the matter of the taxes levied against them.

17 AUGUST 1686
Colonial Affairs The South Carolina settlement of Stuart Town, or Port Royal, is destroyed by a Spanish military force from Florida.

AUGUST 1686
Colonial Affairs New England governor Edmund Andros issues an order forbidding East Jersey ships from entering the Hudson River.

20 DECEMBER 1686
British Policy Sir Edmund Andros finally arrives in Boston to serve as governor of the New England colonies with the exception of Connecticut and Rhode Island. He now begins to organize the Dominion of New England to facilitate military cooperation among the colonies and to effectively enforce rigidly the navigation acts.

21 DECEMBER 1686
Ideas/Beliefs Governor Andros makes the unpopular demand that the Puritans share the Old South Meeting in Boston with Anglicans.

30 DECEMBER 1686
Colonial Affairs Rhode Island is absorbed into the Dominion of New England.

OTHER EVENTS OF 1686
Westward Movement Frenchman Henri de Tonty founds the settlement of Arkansas Post at the mouth of the Arkansas River in the lower Mississippi Valley.

JANUARY 1687
Colonial Affairs The general assembly of New York is officially dissolved by Dominion Governor Edmund Andros. The assembly convened for its first and last session in 1683. The political power now rests firmly in the grasp of the royal governor.

25 MARCH 1687
Ideas/Beliefs In Boston, New England Governor Edmund Andros orders that the Old South Meeting House be converted into an Anglican Church.

23 AUGUST 1687
Colonial Affairs In Ipswich, Massachusetts, clergyman John Wise leads resistance against the assessments imposed by Governor Edmund Andros. For this activity Wise is tried and fined. The town of Topsfield also refuses to acquiesce to taxation without representation.

1 NOVEMBER 1687
British Policy New England Governor Edmund Andros dissolves the assembly of the Connecticut colony, thus effectively setting himself up as the ruler of New York and all of the New England colonies. Although the Connecticut charter is hidden in the

FOUNDING A NATION 986-1787

Charter Oak, this ploy is unsuccessful in preventing the royal annexation.

OTHER EVENTS OF 1687
Ideas/Beliefs William Penn publishes *The Excellent Privilege of Liberty and Property,* which reproduces the Magna Carta and the text of other English laws on liberty and property.

14 FEBRUARY 1688
Colonial Affairs The Carolina colonial assembly denies the power of the proprietors to invalidate the Fundamental Constitutions of 1669. Rebellion appears imminent.

19 FEBRUARY 1688
British Policy Governor Edmund Andros suggests to the English crown that New York annex the territory of New Jersey.

17 MARCH 1688
British Policy Governor Edmund Andros limits New England towns to no more than one annual town meeting.

24 MARCH 1688
British Policy Governor Edmund Andros issues an order placing the militia of the New England colonies under his own direct control.

MARCH 1688
British Policy King James II orders the invalidation of the colonial charters for East and West Jersey. The Jersey territories are incorporated into the Dominion of New England.

APRIL 1688
Slavery The Quaker colonists in Germantown, Pennsylvania, issue a formal protest against the institution of slavery in the American colonies. This is probably the earliest antislavery tract in the colonies.

SEPTEMBER 1688
British Policy Concluding a series of generally peaceful administrations in Virginia, the legislature is again at odds with the governor, Lord Howard of Effingham. A list of grievances is presented by representatives of the Virginia assembly to King James II. Before the king can act on these matters, he is deposed by William and Mary.

10 AUGUST 1688
British Policy The president of Harvard College, Increase Mather, secretly leaves for England in order to express the discontent of New England colonists with the policies of Governor Andros to the Lords of Trade, and also to petition the crown for a renewal of the Massachusetts charter.

24 NOVEMBER 1688
British Policy The Maryland assembly records its disapproval of newly-appointed Governor William Joseph, who has been sent out from England by Lord Baltimore. The assembly does, however, submit to this authority. This marks the continuing popular opposition to the proprietory regime.

18 DECEMBER 1688
External Affairs King James II flees to France when he hears that William of Orange has been invited to invade England by influential English leaders. This forced deposition of James II is known as the Glorious Revolution. During his short reign, James II has antagonized almost all factions in England by his absolutist acts, his militant Catholicism and his disregard for the traditional civil liberties. This change of monarchs is to have almost immediate ramifications among the American colonists, who had similar objections to James II and his policies, as expressed by New England Governor Edmund Andros.

10 JANUARY 1689
British Policy In Pemaquid, Maine, when Governor Andros hears of the imminent arrival of William of Orange in England, he returns to Boston.

13 FEBRUARY 1689
External Affairs William and Mary of Orange are proclaimed king and queen of England by Parliament, thus ending a Catholic monarchy in a Protestant county and concluding the Glorious Revolution.
British Policy The unpopular English governor of Virginia, Lord Howard of Effingham, is removed from power by the new English monarchs. This action is hailed by the colonists.

APRIL 1689
Colonial Affairs Governor Andros is forced to barricade himself in the British fort at Boston when he is opposed by a rebellious group of colonists. This uprising has popular support, and Cotton Mather writes a manifesto justifying the actions of the rebels. Andros surrenders and is jailed, along with royal agents Dudley and Randolph.

20 APRIL 1689
Colonial Affairs The rebellious Massachusetts colonists establish a "Council for the Safety and the Conservation of the Peace."

26-27 APRIL 1689
Colonial Affairs Upon receiving news of the Boston rebellion against royal Governor Andros, the New York counties of Queens, Suffolk and Westchester oust the members of their royal government and elect their own colonial representatives to replace them.

1 MAY 1689
Colonial Affairs The Rhode Island Colony reestablishes the government mandated by its old charter. Connecticut is to follow the example of Rhode Island on 9 May, and Massachusetts on 24 May.

24 MAY 1689
Ideas/Beliefs The English Parliament enacts a Toler-

COTTON MATHER, 1663-1728

That Cotton Mather's 1685 book, the *Memorable Providences Relating to Witchcraft and Possessions*, probably helped to stimulate the hysteria leading to the 1692 Salem witchcraft trials, belies Mather's omniverous interests and basically eclectic though conservative religiosity. In 1721, this enthusiastic scholar and prolific writer published *The Christian Philosopher*, in which he sought to reconcile Newtonian physics with Puritanism.

Cotton Mather was born into a prominent Boston Puritan family. His father, Increase Mather (1639-1723), was a lifetime pastor of Boston's North Church, a president of Harvard College, an author of 130 books on all subjects and a pioneering American diplomat who obtained a liberalized charter for the commonwealth of Massachusetts. Cotton Mather's paternal grandfather was Richard Mather (1596-1669), an influential theologian, an author of the *Bay Psalm Book,* and the drafter of the Cambridge Platform, the basic organizing document of the Massachusetts Congregationalists. Cotton Mather's maternal grandfather was theologian and clergyman John Cotton (1584-1652), who helped to shape the Massachusetts Puritan oligarchy.

Precociously entering Harvard at the age of 12, Cotton Mather later studied medicine as his stammering seemed to preclude a career in the pulpit. But after he gained control over his speech defect, he was ordained as a minister, becoming his father's colleague and successor at North Church. Refused the presidency of Harvard in 1701, Mather helped to found Yale College as a bastion of Congregational education. Temperamental and at times almost unbearably pompous, Mather was a frequent figure of controversy. During the Salem witchcraft trials, he humanely advised prayer and fasting rather than the death penalty for the convicted. As a remarkable scholar and scientist, Mather published more than 440 books, tracts and papers on all subjects—ranging from religion and medicine to botanical experiments—leading to membership in the prestigious Royal Society. And his *Magnalia Christi Americana*, a New England ecclesiastic history, was a colonial landmark. Conversant in seven languages, he collected a library of nearly 4000 books, second only in size to that of Virginian William Byrd. Mather's life of tireless achievement and ceaseless investigation ended with his death at 65. His immense body of works remains a monument to the last and greatest of the Puritan intellectuals.

ation Act, which provides for limited freedom of religion for those outside the Church of England.

31 MAY 1689
Colonial Affairs Jacob Leisler, a trader formerly employed by the Dutch West India Company, captures the British garrison at New York. He leads an army of farmers from Long Island and Westchester seeking to establish a popular representative government.

6 JUNE 1689
Colonial Affairs After the Massachusetts colonial government is reestablished under the older charter, deputies are elected to the general court.

11 JUNE 1689
Colonial Affairs Lieutenant Governor of New York

Francis Nicholson quietly steals away to England, leaving Jacob Leisler's rebels in charge of New York. After seizing the royal customs house, they set up a de facto government which declares Jacob Leisler commander-in-chief.

25 JULY 1689
British Policy An order arrives from the English government for the return of Edmund Andros and his assistants to Britain to stand trial.

27 JULY 1689
Colonial Affairs In Maryland, the rebel Protestant Association led by John Coode captures the colony's capital of St Mary's from the proprietory government and establishes a new government under the auspices of William and Mary, after the surrender of Governor William Joseph to a 250-man force.

27 JULY-15 AUGUST 1689
Colonial Affairs In New York, Jacob Leisler calls the first assembly of representatives from the communities around New York City. A number of counties and towns decline to participate.

3 AUGUST 1689
Colonial Affairs In Maine, a combined French and Indian force captures the fort at Pemaquid.

22 AUGUST 1689
Colonial Affairs In Maryland, the Protestant Association led by John Coode calls a session of the colonial assembly. The assembly petitions the English crown to assume authority over the colony, ousting the proprietorship of Lord Baltimore. The Maryland assembly also chooses as its president Nehemiah Blakiston.

14 OCTOBER 1689
Colonial Affairs In the New York colony, Albany elects its own government, having declined to participate in Jacob Leisler's New York City government.

16 OCTOBER 1689
External Affairs Bringing with him military supplies and a plan to conquer the New England colonies, Count Frontenac returns to Canada as governor from France. This sets the stage for King William's War.

16 DECEMBER 1689
Ideas/Beliefs The English Parliament enacts a bill of rights as a statute law. Something like this English bill of rights will be incorporated in the American constitution some 100 years later.

22 JANUARY 1690
Indians At Onondaga, New York, the Iroquois Indians renew their allegiance to the English crown.

1 FEBRUARY 1690
British Policy English monarchs William and Mary

declare their support for the new Maryland government established by the Protestant Association, under the leadership of John Coode.

9 FEBRUARY 1690

War In the intercolonial phase of King William's War, Schenectady, New York, is burned by a combined force of French and Indians. The French and Indians follow with a series of attacks on towns in Maine, New Hampshire and Massachusetts. The attack on Schenectady persuades Albany to submit to Jacob Leisler's revolutionary New York government.

12 MARCH 1690

Colonial Affairs In the face of the French and Indian threat, the New Hampshire colony votes to reannex itself to Massachusetts.

APRIL 1690

Colonial Affairs In New York, a legislative assembly called by Jacob Leisler enacts a law banning the trade monopolies of the colony's merchants, noting that "all towns and places shall have equal freedom . . . and that the one place shall have no more privileges than the other." This expresses the genuinely democratic basis of Leisler's rebellion.

1 MAY 1690

War Delegates from Connecticut, Massachusetts, Plymouth and New York meet at Albany, New York. They vote to organize a joint military force to invade Canada, and to send a naval fleet up the St. Lawrence River. The resulting campaign proves a failure.

11 MAY 1690

War In a campaign of King William's War, Massachusetts colonists led by Sir William Phips capture the French garrison of Port Royal in Nova Scotia. The French are to win back their outpost a year later.

20 MAY 1690

War During the course of King William's War, a combined French and Indian force destroys the settlement at Casco, Maine. This is part of Canadian governor Frontenac's plan to conquer the New England colonies.

AUGUST 1690

War A combined colonial military force led by Fitz-John Randolph, traveling crosscountry to attack Montreal, is forced to turn back to Albany because of shortages of supplies and reinforcements.

6 OCTOBER 1690

Colonial Affairs In the Carolina colony, popular leader Seth Sothell captures the government at Charleston and forces Governor James Colleton into exile.

7 OCTOBER 1690

War Following up his conquest of Port Royal, Nova Scotia, Sir William Phips and his Massachusetts troops begin an unsuccessful siege of Quebec City.

24 NOVEMBER 1690

British Policy The English Lords of Trade appoint Colonel Henry Sloughter as governor of New England. Various bureaucratic and naval mishaps delay his departure for the American colonies.

DECEMBER 1690

Finance The Massachusetts assembly issues its first paper money in order to pay the salaries of its soldiers returning from the expedition against Quebec led by Sir William Phips.

8 FEBRUARY 1691

British Policy English Major Robert Ingoldesby arrives in New York leading a military force. Jacob Leisler contests on legal grounds the right of Ingoldesby to demand the surrender of the fort occupied by Leisler and his followers.

27 MARCH 1691

British Policy Frustrated by Leisler's opposition, English Major Ingoldesby captures New York's city hall.

29 MARCH 1691

British Policy Newly-appointed New England governor Henry Sloughter finally arrives in New York, and Jacob Leisler surrenders to him the next day.

30 MARCH 1691

British Policy Governor Sloughter calls for an assembly to convene, initiating royally-sanctioned representative government in New York. On 13 May, the assembly will reenact the 1683 Charter of Liberties.

10-27 APRIL 1691

Colonial Affairs In New York, Jacob Leisler and nine of his compatriots are tried for treason. Leisler and seven others receive the death sentence, although six of the rebels are eventually pardoned.

APRIL 1691

Colonial Affairs William Penn grants the Lower Counties, or Delaware, a separate government from that of Pennsylvania, and he appoints William Markham deputy-governor.

26 MAY 1691

Colonial Affairs Of the leaders of the New York rebellion, only Jacob Leisler and his lieutenant Jacob Milborne are hanged after they have been denied their legal right of appeal to the English crown. It is thought that they would have been pardoned, too, but for the insistence of New York's ruling families.

27 JUNE 1691

British Policy Maryland is declared a royal province by the English Lords of Trade and Sir Lionel Copley is named royal governor. Thus Lord Baltimore is deprived of his political powers in Maryland, although he is permitted to keep his property rights. Maryland is to remain under royal rule until 1715, when the proprietorship is restored.

SEPTEMBER 30, 1697

17 OCTOBER 1691
British Policy When Massachusetts fails to have its old charter reinstated, a new royal charter is granted, extending the territorial rights of the Massachusetts colony over Plymouth and Maine. This new Massachusetts charter institutes, among other provisions, a royal governor, a governor's council elected by the general court and suffrage dependent on property rather than religious persuasion.

8 NOVEMBER 1691
British Policy The English crown places the northern Carolina region, or Albermarle, under the authority of a deputy of the Carolina governor who stays in Charleston, South Carolina. This is the first time that the name "North Carolina" is employed.

18 MARCH 1692
British Policy Following the accession of William III to the English throne, Pennsylvania is declared a royal colony, and New York governor Benjamin Fletcher is designated governor of Pennsylvania, depriving William Penn of his proprietory powers. The Crown takes over Pennsylvania because the pacifist Quakers refused to involve themselves in the war against France and because William Penn had maintained friendly relations with former English monarch King James II.

4 APRIL 1692
Colonial Affairs Andrew Hamilton is named to organize a system of colonial postal offices, after Thomas Neale had received a patent from the English crown to establish an American postal system during the next 21 years.

MAY 1692
Ideas/Beliefs The jail of Salem, Massachusetts, is filled with witchcraft suspects (who eventually reach a total of 150), the result of a frenzy that grips the town after a group of young girls feign hysteria and accuse a family slave of bewitching them. Massachusetts Governor William Phips comes to Salem to set up a special court, with William Stoughton as judge, to try the accused. From June to September 22, 20 persons, 14 of them women, are executed before Increase Mather and Thomas Brattle help to bring the mania under control. In October, the remaining prisoners are released and the special court is dissolved.

10 MAY 1692
Ideas/Beliefs The Anglican church is designated as the official church of the Maryland colony. In 1696, Parliament will revoke this status.

13 AUGUST 1692
Colonial Affairs New Hampshire returns to its prior status of royal colony.

8 FEBRUARY 1693
Education In the Virginia colony, the College of William and Mary is founded in Williamsburg by James Blair for the purpose of educating Anglican

clergymen. This is the second oldest institution of higher learning in America.

4 OCTOBER 1693
Colonial Affairs New York governor Benjamin Fletcher calls a meeting of delegates from the American colonies in order to plan strategy for a war against the French. Little of importance is achieved at this conference.

10 FEBRUARY 1694
Colonial Affairs Francis Nicholson is named the new royal governor of the Maryland colony.

15 AUGUST 1694
Indians Colonial representatives from Connecticut, Massachusetts, New Jersey and New York sign a peace treaty with the Iroquois Indians in Albany in order to prevent any future alliance between the Iroquois and the French.

20 AUGUST 1694
British Policy The proprietory government is reinstated in Pennsylvania after more than two years as a royal colony. William Penn will assume governorship of the colony in 1699.

10 APRIL 1696
British Policy The English Parliament passes the Navigation Act of 1696 which limits all colonial trade activity to English-built vessels including those built in the English colonies; gives the colonial customs commissioners powers similar to those of English customs officers, including the right of forcible entry; demands the posting of bond on specific goods, even where plantation duties are collected; voids laws passed by colonial assemblies that counteract the Navigation Acts.

15 AUGUST 1696
War A French force led by Le Moyne d'Iberville captures the fort at Pemaquid on the Maine border.

OTHER EVENTS OF 1696
Slavery During the course of this year, extensive slave trading is initiated by New Englanders, after the Royal African Trade Company loses its monopoly in the slave trade.

8 FEBRUARY 1697
Colonial Affairs In England, William Penn presents a proposal to the Board of Trade calling for an intercolonial congress composed of delegates from each American colony and presided over by a president named by the king.

15 MARCH 1697
War A combined force of French and Indians conducts a raid against the settlement of Haverhill, Massachusetts.

30 SEPTEMBER 1697
War The inconclusive Treaty of Ryswick between

the English and French ends King William's War, restoring all colonial possessions as they were before the war.

OTHER EVENTS OF 1697

Ideas/Beliefs In the wake of the Salem witchcraft trials of 1692, official repentance is expressed by the Massachusetts general court, deploring the actions of the judges. One of the judges, Samuel Sewall, publicly confesses his guilt from his Boston church pew. The jurors sign a statement of regret and compensatory indemnities are offered to the families of those so unjustly executed.

7 JANUARY 1699

War A peace treaty at Casco Bay, Maine, between the Abenaki Indians and the Massachusetts colony concludes the Indian and French hostilities on the northern and western New England frontier.

6 JULY 1699

Colonial Affairs In Boston, Captain Kidd the pirate is captured and extradited to England to stand trial. He will be hanged on May 23, 1701.

30 NOVEMBER 1699

Colonial Affairs After a 15-year stay in England, Pennsylvania proprietor William Penn comes back to his colony.

OTHER EVENTS OF 1699

British Policy The English Parliament passes the Wool Act to protect the British wool industry from incursion by Irish wool producers and also from future competition from the American colonies. This legislation limits wool production in Ireland and forbids the export of wool from the American colonies, in both international and intercolonial trade.

17 JUNE 1700

Ideas/Beliefs The Massachusetts representative assembly enacts legislation ordering all Roman Catholic priests to vacate the colony within three months. Any Roman Catholic priest found in residence after that date is subject to trial as an "incendiary and disturber of the public peace and safety." The punishment for these offenses is set at life imprisonment or execution. There is fear of the revival of the Stuart monarchy and Catholicism.

24 JUNE 1700

Slavery Boston Judge Samuel Sewall publishes an early anti-slavery tract, *The Selling of Joseph.* Sewall's anti-slavery arguments, often based on Biblical sources, remain generally unacknowledged for over a century. Sewall also keeps a detailed diary of events occurring during the years 1674 to 1729, which is not published until the late 19th century.

OTHER EVENTS OF 1700

Population The total population of the American colonies is estimated at about 275,000 persons. This population is distributed widely over the rural areas in isolated farm settlements. The largest city is Boston with around 7000 inhabitants and New York City claims about 5000 residents.

Arts/Culture The Carolina representative assembly passes the first colonial library law which provides for the establishment and public financial support of a library in Charleston.

British Policy The English Parliament passes the Piracy Act which mandates the organization of special colonial courts to try and sentence those suspected of piracy.

Ideas/Beliefs The New York legislative assembly follows the example of the Massachusetts assembly in enacting a law that banishes Catholic priests from the colony.

Settling The French construct a fort at Makinac in Michigan to secure the French hold on the Mississippi River Valley to protect their route to the Louisiana territory from Canada. In the same year, a group of some 500 French Huguenot colonists arrives to settle in coastal Virginia.

26 MARCH 1701

British Policy The English Board of Trade advises the English crown to create royal colonies of all the American charter colonies.

8 MAY 1701

Colonial Affairs The general court of the Connecticut Colony decides to convene the May session in Hartford, alternating with the October session which sits in New Haven.

4 AUGUST 1701

Indians The French colonists in Canada negotiate a peace treaty with the Iroquois Indians and their Indian allies in the territory surrounding the French settlement at Montreal.

JUNE 1701

Ideas/Beliefs In London, King William III charters the Society for the Propagation of the Gospel in Foreign Parts to support the widespread missionary activities of the Anglican Church in the American colonies. In the years between 1702 and 1783 some 202 major missions are established and maintained by 309 Anglican missionaries. Despite this concentrated effort, Anglicanism never becomes the dominant religion of the colonies. The religious separatists and nonconformists—the Congregationalists, Quakers, Baptists, and Presbyterians—maintain their strength.

24 JULY 1701

Settling A French fort is built at Detroit by Antoine de la Mothe Cadillac in the Michigan territory. La Mothe names his settlement Fort Pontchartrain. (The name Detroit comes from the French word for the narrows, a feature of the waterway nearby.) The establishment of this fort marks the renewed interest of the French crown in maintaining a hold on the interior fur trade and protecting the route from Louisiana to Canada.

16 OCTOBER 1701
Education Yale College, first established as a Congregational collegiate school, is founded in Saybrook, Connecticut, to counter the increasing liberalism of Harvard College. Yale College will be moved to New Haven in 1745 and it becomes a university in 1887. The first degrees to graduating students are bestowed in 1716.

8 NOVEMBER 1701
Colonial Affairs The colony of Pennsylvania receives its first constitution, the Charter of Privileges, from proprietor William Penn. This document remains in effect until the American Revolution. It provides for a unicameral legislature and for the governor to have authority over the passage of laws with the consent of the legislature. The proprietor appoints the governor but continues to involve himself with the problems of Pennsylvania.

12 NOVEMBER 1701
Ideas/Beliefs The Carolina assembly passes the Vestry Act of 1701 which makes the Anglican Church the established church of the northern Carolina territory. This measure provokes active opposition from resident Quakers and other religious nonconformists, and their organized protest reflects the diversified nature of religion in the early Carolina Colony. The protest encourages the proprietors to revoke the Vestry Act in 1703.

OTHER EVENTS OF 1701
Life/Customs During this year, six women sit on a jury during a trial in Albany, New York. This reflects the improving status of women in the American colonies.
Colonial Affairs With the Charter of 1701, the Delaware territory is granted a government separate from that of Pennsylvania.
Education Increase Mather is removed as president of Harvard College, thus opening the way for liberal and rationalist erosions of Puritanism.
Colonial Affairs The New York assembly endorses a stance of neutrality toward French colonists in Canada. This neutrality policy is to remain in effect until 1709.

8 MARCH 1702
External Affairs Queen Anne ascends the English throne.

17 APRIL 1702
Colonial Affairs The colonies of East and West Jersey are united and designated the royal province of New Jersey, to be under the authority of the New York governor. The sessions of the New Jersey representative assembly are to convene alternately in Burlington and Perth Amboy. New Jersey becomes a royal colony when the proprietors cede their rights in the territory to the English crown. The governor of New York maintains authority over New Jersey until 1738.

4 MAY 1702
War The War of the Spanish Succession, known in the American colonies as Queen Anne's War, begins when England declares war on France to prevent the union of France and Spain after the death of Charles II of Spain. This war is also played out in the colonies in a series of confrontations of the English and the colonists against the French, the Indians and the Spanish. Queen Anne's War rages on until 1713.

11 JUNE 1702
Colonial Affairs The newly designated governor of New Hampshire and Massachusetts by the English Crown, Joseph Dudley, arrives in Boston to assume his duties.

10 SEPTEMBER 1702
War During the course of Queen Anne's War, the Carolina legislature decides to organize a military expedition to capture the Spanish colony in St. Augustine, Florida, before the French can bring in additional soldiers and material to fortify the settlement.

SEPTEMBER 1702
War The Spanish settlement of St. Augustine is looted and burned by a force of Carolina colonists led by Governor James Moore.

DECEMBER 1702
War Although the settlement of St. Augustine has fallen to Carolina forces, the fort at St. Augustine remains impervious to their attacks.

OTHER EVENTS OF 1702
Settling The French Fort Maurepas, originally built in 1699 on Biloxi Bay by Iberville, is moved to Fort Louis on the Mobile River.
Ideas/Beliefs Influential Puritan thinker Cotton Mather, author of some 400 works, publishes his most important book, *Magnalia Christi Americana, or, The Ecclesiastical History of New England, 1620-1698*. This volume mixes fact and fable in a descriptive advocacy of the Puritan theocracy. During the same year, Cotton Mather founds the Society for the Suppression of Disorders, a quasi-vigilante committee intended to decrease public blasphemy, cursing and the frequenting of bawdy houses. Mather makes a practice of collecting the names of disreputable young men who are then warned off by the committee.

To the south, the Anglican Church is officially established in the Maryland colony through the enactment of the Act of Establishment by the representative assembly. Two such earlier acts have been voided by the English Board of Trade and Plantations but this time the act is confirmed through the assiduous agency of Dr. Thomas Bray, the Bishop of London's commissary. Taxes for the support of Anglican clergymen are to be levied on all free men, male servants and slaves of both sexes over the age of 16. The royal governor of Maryland is to name the clergymen. Active opposition to this act is led by Quakers and Roman Catholic colonists.

12 MAY 1703
Colonial Affairs The colonies of Connecticut and Rhode Island agree on a mutually designated common boundary line. This boundary is affirmed by the English Crown in 1728.

JUNE 1703
Indians At Casco, Maine, the Abenaki Indians of New England conclude a peace treaty with Massachusetts Governor Dudley. Before two months pass, a ten-year period of hostilities between the Indians and the English colonists will break out.

10 AUGUST 1703
War During the course of Queen Anne's War, the Abenaki Indians attack a number of English settlements in the Maine territory.

OTHER EVENTS OF 1703
Settling A French Jesuit post is established at the junction of the Kaskaskia and Mississippi Rivers to further secure the French control of the Mississippi River valley.
Finance The South Carolina assembly mandates the issuance of paper money to pay colonial soliders for their attack on the Spanish settlement at St. Augustine, Florida.

28-29 FEBRUARY 1704
War During the course of Queen Anne's War, the Abenaki Indians and French soldiers attack and destroy the western frontier settlement of Deerfield, Massachusetts. With the massacre of 50 Deerfield colonists and the abduction of some 100 more, this defeat is the low point of Queen Anne's War for the American colonists.

24 APRIL 1704
Arts/Culture The first regularly issued newspaper in the American colonies, the *Boston News-Letter,* is published by Massachusetts colonist John Campbell. The *News-Letter* will be issued weekly until the time of the American Revolution.

6 MAY 1704
Ideas/Beliefs The South Carolina representative assembly passes legislation to ban non-Anglicans from being elected as delegates to the assembly. This act is later declared void by the English crown in 1706.

18 JUNE 1704
British Policy The English crown issues a currency regulation limiting the value of a piece of eight to six shillings in all of the American colonies.

1-28 JULY 1074
War During the course of Queen Anne's War, Colonel Benjamin Church leads a military force of New England colonists in a successful attack against the French settlements of Minas and Beaubassin in Acadia (Nova Scotia). The destruction of these villages achieves the elimination of supply sources for the Abenaki Indians who have been conducting a series of raids on New England settlements. The New Englanders also gain control of the profitable Acadian fishing industry.

18-29 AUGUST 1704
War During the course of Queen Anne's War, a combined force of French and Indians attacks and defeats the English colony of Bonavista on Newfoundland.

OCTOBER 1704
Arts/Culture Boston schoolmistress Sarah Kemble Knight begins her *Private Journal* which will cover the period until March 1705. During these months she makes an unaccompanied round trip from Boston to New York. This classic travel narrative records Knight's astute observations of unusual characters and incidents encountered on her trip. The book will not be published until 1825. Knight is later to be a teacher of Benjamin Franklin.

22 NOVEMBER 1704
Colonial Affairs The first Delaware assembly convenes in New Castle. The Charter of 1701 has granted Delaware the right to have a government separate from that of Pennsylvania, although the two colonies share the same governor until the time of the American Revolution. (Delaware was formerly known as the "Lower Counties" of Pennsylvania.)

OTHER EVENTS OF 1704
War During the course of Queen Anne's War, a combined force of South Carolina colonists and friendly Indians led by Governor James Moore attacks and levels 13 of 14 Spanish missions in the Appalachian Indian territory. This opens the way to the French territory in Louisiana. But the Choctaw Indians prevent the Carolina forces from reaching the French settlements. Meanwhile in Canadian territory, New England forces carry on an unsuccessful siege of the French bastion at Port Royal.
Ideas/Beliefs In North Carolina the Second Vestry Act is passed. This legislation makes the Anglican Church the official religious institution of the colony. This measure excites the opposition of the Quakers who have been banned from holding public office. The Quakers are successful in persuading the proprietors of North Carolina to remove Deputy Governor Cary from office. Convicted of high crimes and misdemeanors, Cary flees to Virginia where he is captured. In the Maryland colony, Roman Catholic religious rites are permitted only within private dwellings. This policy remains in effect until the time of the American Revolution.
Settling The French erect Fort Miami at a portage to guard the route from Canada to the Mississippi River

via Lake Erie and the Maumee and Wabash Rivers. French Huguenot immigrants establish the settlement of Bath, close to the Pamlico River in North Carolina.

EVENTS OF 1705

British Policy The English Parliament passes a trade act expanding the number of colonial products that are to be exported only to English ports. Rice and molasses are added to the list of enumerated articles, as are naval stores—pitch, tar, rosin, turpentine, hemp. Parliament also establishes bounties, or subsidies, for the export of naval stores from the American colonies.

Slavery The Virginia Black Code of 1705 restricts the travel of slaves and provides severe penalties for miscegenation. This fifth revision of the slavery code proclaims slaves to be real estate. In the same year, the New York assembly enacts legislation to deal with runaway slaves. The death penalty is prescribed for all slaves caught beyond a line 40 miles north of Albany. In Massachusetts, marriage between blacks and whites is declared illegal.

Settling The French establish Fort Vincennes on the Wabash River, thus strengthening their chain of interior outposts.

Education The Virginia assembly enacts legislation requiring all apprenticed orphans be taught reading and writing skills by their masters.

Arts/Culture In London, Robert Beverley publishes the *History of Virginia,* an account of the early history of Virginia that achieves wide circulation in England and France. In this book Beverley presents an attractive vision of plantation life. He also enumerates social customs and describes in detail sports such as hunting.

17 JANUARY 1706

Life/Customs Benjamin Franklin is born in Boston, one of the 17 children of the devoutly Christian Josiah Franklin.

MARCH 1706

Ideas/Beliefs The first presbytery of the Presbyterian church is founded in Philadelphia by Francis Makemie. The first Presbyterian synod in the American colonies will be established in 1718. Makemie is later known as the father of Presbyterianism in the colonies.

10 JUNE 1706

Ideas/Beliefs The English crown revokes the South Carolina legislative enactment banning non-Anglicans from election to the South Carolina assembly.

24 AUGUST 1706

War During the course of Queen Anne's War, French soldiers and Spanish colonists from St. Augustine and Havana combine forces to attack the South Carolina settlement of Charlestown. The Carolina settlers are able to beat back the attack.

30 NOVEMBER 1706

Ideas/Beliefs Following the example of North Car-

olina, the South Carolina representative assembly makes the Anglican church the established church of the colony.

OTHER EVENTS OF 1706

British Policy At Yorktown, Virginia, the first important colonial customhouse is erected. Yorktown has been designated the port of entry for New York, Philadelphia and other northern cities. Because of the inconvenient location of the customhouse and the colonial opposition to English customs regulations, many merchants bypass the Yorktown customhouse.

Ideas/Beliefs In Boston, Cotton Mather publishes *The Good Old Way,* in which he decries the lessening of Puritan influence in the American colonies. Mather observes that the colonists have lost respect and reverence for clergymen and do not offer them as great financial support as in the past.

6 MARCH 1707

External Affairs In England, Queen Anne endorses the Act of the Union, which combines England, Scotland and Wales into the United Kingdom of Great Britain.

21 SEPTEMBER 1707

War During the course of Queen Anne's War, the Abenaki Indians attack the English settlement at Winter Harbor, Maine.

OTHER EVENTS OF 1707

Ideas/Beliefs In Philadelphia the first session of the Baptist Association meets, with delegates from five churches attending. A New York court tries and acquits Presbyterian Francis Makemie. This judicial decision marks the end of the prosecution of Protestant dissidents in the colony of New York.

Slavery The mechanics of Philadelphia band together to object to the competition to their craft provided by the use of hired black slaves.

Arts/Culture John Williams publishes *The Redeemed Captive,* a best-selling book in the colonial era. This narrative of the author's captivity by Indians is part of a popular colonial literary genre.

29 AUGUST 1708

War During the course of Queen Anne's War, a combined force of French Canadians and their Indian

A view of Philadelphia, 1707.

allies attacks the settlement at Haverhill, Massachusetts. They massacre all the settlers.

14 OCTOBER 1708
Ideas/Beliefs The Connecticut General Court enacts the Saybrook Platform. Adopted by the Congregational churches of the Connecticut colony, the platform institutes a form of church government resembling the Presbyterian system and moving away from the more localized nature of Massachusetts Congregationalism.

21 DECEMBER 1708
War During the course of Queen Anne's War, a combined force of French and Indians captures the English settlement at St. John's on Newfoundland. This victory gives the French control over the North Atlantic coastline.

OTHER EVENTS OF 1708
British Policy The English Parliament enacts a currency act that establishes fines for those guilty of offering illegal exchange rates, above those legally mandated, for foreign coins.
Colonial Affairs William Penn is forced to mortgage his interests in the Pennsylvania colony to trustees. The unethical dealings of Penn's steward Philip Ford have reduced him to penury.
Arts/Culture A colonist writing under the pseudonym of Ebenezer Cook publishes *The Sot-Weed Factor, or a Voyage to Maryland*. This imaginative satirical work describes the political organization and the notable social customs and quirks of Maryland colonists.

3 SEPTEMBER 1709
Settling The Carolina proprietors grant a tract of 13,500 acres to two agents representing Swiss and German Palatinate emigrants. This land grant encourages the increased immigration of Swiss and German settlers into the American colonies.

OTHER EVENTS OF 1709
British Policy The Parliamentary Act of 1709 allows the privileges of natural-born subjects to foreigners who swear loyalty to the English crown and partake of the sacrament. This law is repealed in 1711, as more liberal naturalization laws are already in effect in the American colonies.
War During the course of Queen Anne's War, the colonies of New England and New York combine to plan strategy. They plan an attack on the French fortress at Quebec by sea, and an attack on Montreal by land. This plan is not carried any further when the English refuse to participate.
Industry The Connecticut general assembly grants the first colonial mining company charter to a Simsbury, Connecticut, copper mine. Ore from this operation is exported to England. During the American Revolution, the mine will be used to imprison Loyalists.
Ideas/Beliefs The Quakers erect a meeting house in

QUAKERS

The most individualistic of all the seventeenth–century Protestant sects that originated in England, the Quakers—or Religious Society of Friends, as they were officially known—were the most persecuted of all the religious groups who arrived in America. In the Massachusetts Bay Colony, the Puritans greeted them with relentless harassment, even executing a number of Quakers who returned to the colony after banishment. Except for Rhode Island, the other colonies also passed rigorous statutes against the Society of Friends. They were named Quakers because of the physical trembling that sometimes occurred when believers saw the "inward light"—a direct spiritual communication from God. What made the Quakers so abhorrent to the other established religions probably was the fact that the Quaker faith was an intensely personal experience that eliminated all features of an organized religion, including ornate churches, the clergyman and the formal liturgy. All Quakers were lay preachers who gathered at meetings where the sometimes lengthy silence was broken by anyone who felt moved to speak or to pray aloud. Their nonviolence was characterized by their refusal to bear arms in wartime. They also refused to swear oaths. Hence, Quakers had to be granted special exemptions in order to occupy political office, and they did not serve in the military. Their individualism was also apparent in their plain dress and manners—they used the informal "thee" instead of the formal "you." Their strong humanitarian values led to active implementation of social improvements. Owing to Quaker influence, the city of Philadelphia had some of the best and most humane schools, hospitals, prisons and mental institutions in colonial America. The Quakers also advocated friendly relations with the Indians and strenuously opposed slavery. The most famous of the colonial Quakers was William Penn who, in 1682, founded Pennsylvania as a Quaker refuge, although the colony was opened to all religious beliefs. Despite their relatively small numbers, the invincible faith and resolute self–discipline of the Quakers led them to have an inordinately beneficial influence on the American social and political scene.

Boston. This reflects the growing liberalization of religious attitudes in the Massachusetts colony. In Philadelphia, the Quakers establish the first home for the treatment of mental illness in the American colonies. In 1751, this home is incorporated as the Pennsylvania Hospital.

APRIL 1710
Education The South Carolina representative assembly passes legislation establishing a free school in Charleston.

21 JUNE 1710
British Policy The newly appointed governor of Virginia, Alexander Spotswood, disembarks in Jamestown. He brings with him the authority to extend the common-law English civil right of habeas corpus to the Virginia colonists.

16 OCTOBER 1710
War During the course of Queen Anne's War, a combined British and colonial military force under

MARCH 23, 1713

Colonel Francis Nicholson and Sir Charles Hobby attempts to besiege the French stronghold at Port Royal (Nova Scotia) for a third time. This time the attack is successful and the English later rename the settlement Annapolis, in honor of Queen Anne.

OCTOBER 1710
Settling Three thousand German refugees from the Palatinate settle near Livingston Manor in New York's Hudson River valley in order to produce naval stores. This colony subsequently fails and the settlers follow Conrad Weiser first to the Schoharie Valley, then to the Mohawk Valley, and finally to Berks and Bucks counties in Pennsylvania. Another group of over 650 Swiss and German Palatines led by Baron Graffenried has settled New Bern on the Neuse River in North Carolina.

OTHER EVENTS OF 1710
British Policy The English Parliament enacts legislation that makes the postmaster general of London also the postmaster general for all the English colonies. The Post Office Act institutes an American colonial postal system, with a deputy postmaster located in New York City.

Settling The French move their Biloxi settlement to the location of present-day Mobile, Alabama.

Education In New York City, the Trinity School is established by the Society for the Propagation of the Gospel. This marks the parallel establishment of parochial and private schools along with the movement for free public schools.

Indians Colonel Peter Schuyler takes five Iroquois Indian chiefs to London to expose them to the imperial splendors of the royal court of Queen Anne.

JUNE 1711
War In the course of Queen Anne's War, Colonel Francis Nicholson calls a meeting of New England governors at New London, Connecticut, to cooperate on strategy to combat the French in Canada. They plan to attack French Quebec from the St. Lawrence River and Montreal from Lake Champlain.

30 JULY 1711
War Carrying colonial soldiers, a fleet of British warships sets sail from Boston to attack Quebec. The mission is never completed, owing to the mismanagement of the leaders of the expedition.

22 SEPTEMBER 1711
War The Tuscarora Indian War breaks out with the massacre of North Carolina settlers on the Roanoke and Chowan Rivers. This war will continue into 1713.

OTHER EVENTS OF 1711
Slavery In England the South Sea Company is organized. This British trading corporation will receive the right to import black slaves into the North American Spanish colonies under the terms of the 1713 Treaty of Utrecht. This provision, known as the Assiento, also allows the South Sea Company to send

one merchant ship a year to the Spanish colonies.

Ideas/Beliefs In the North Carolina Colony, Cary's Rebellion breaks out in opposition to the institution of the Anglican Church as the official religious establishment of the colony.

Education In Boston, a complaint against the excessive teaching of the classical languages of Latin and Greek in the free schools is entered into the town record.

28 JANUARY 1712
War In the Tuscarora Indian War, the militias of North and South Carolina, aided by Indian allies, attack the Tuscarora Indians on the Neuse River. Three hundred of the Tuscaroras are killed in this assault.

APRIL 1712
Slavery A black insurrection takes place in New York City and the militia is called out to quell the rebellion. In the aftermath of the incident, 21 blacks are executed.

9 MAY 1712
Colonial Affairs The Carolina territory is separated officially into the two colonies of North Carolina and South Carolina. Each colony is accorded its own governor. This first governor of North Carolina is Edward Hyde. Before this time, a common government for the entire territory was situated in Charlestown. The geographical distance between the colonial centers necessitated the institution of two governments.

7 JUNE 1712
Slavery The Pennsylvania representative assembly enacts legislation banning the import of slaves into the Pennsylvania Colony.

14 SEPTEMBER 1712
Colonial Affairs King Louis XIV of France grants French trader Antoine Crozat a trade monopoly in the Louisiana territory. This monopoly remains in effect until 1717.

OTHER EVENTS OF 1712
War In the Tuscarora Indian War, the Indians attack the settlement of 650 Palatine Germans at New Bern, North Carolina, on the Neuse River. They very nearly destroy the settlement and the German colonists are scattered over the southeastern territory of North Carolina.

Industry In Massachusetts, Nantucket whaler Christopher Hussey is the first American known to capture a sperm whale. Up to this date, whalers had kept close to shore. But the capture of this sperm whale encourages deep–water whale hunts and long voyages. By 1715, Nantucket is a whaling center with six ships devoted to hunting sperm whales.

23 MARCH 1713
War The capture of the Tuscarora Indian stronghold of Fort Nohucke by South Carolinian forces ends the hostile activities of the Tuscarora Indians. The

FOUNDING A NATION 986-1787

Tuscaroras escape northward to join the Iroquois Indians as the Sixth Indian Nation.

26 MARCH 1713
Slavery In the series of negotiations concluding Queen Anne's War, England's South Sea Company is permitted to transport 4800 slaves per year for a duration of 30 years into the Spanish colonies in North America. This document, known as the Assiento, also allows the English the right to send one merchant ship a year to the Spanish settlements for trade.

11 APRIL 1713
War The Treaty of Utrecht ends Queen Anne's War. This pact grants the French North American territories of Acadia (Nova Scotia), Hudson Bay and Newfoundland to England, while the French maintain control of Cape Breton Island and of the islands in the St. Lawrence River. The ambiguous delineation of the limits of the Acadia and Hudson Bay territory is to lead to subsequent hostilities between the French and English.

11 JULY 1713
War The New England Abenaki Indians negotiate a peace treaty with Massachusetts Governor Dudley at Portsmouth.

OTHER EVENTS OF 1713
British Policy The English Trade Act of 1705 expires in 1713. This act had enumerated articles to be shipped from the American colonies only to British ports. The list of items included rice, molasses, sugar, tobacco, indigo, cotton, ginger, some dyewoods and naval stores, with bounties applying to the naval stores. Despite the expiration of the Act of 1705, the bounties continue on the naval stores for another 11 years, and the subsidy on hemp continues for an additional 16 years.
Colonial Affairs A mutual boundary line is designated between the Connecticut and Massachusetts Colonies. This border is confirmed by the representative assemblies of each colony.
Settling After their settlement at Livingston Manor fails, the German Palatinate refugees are led from the Hudson River valley to the Schoharie River by Conrad Weiser.
Industry In Gloucester, Massachusetts, shipbuilder Captain Andrew Robinson designs and constructs a schooner, a specifically American type of sailing ship.
Arts/Culture Bostonian Thomas Brattle leaves an organ to the Anglican King's Chapel. It is unusual for colonial churches to have organs, since instrumental music is banned from Puritan church services and most of the other congregations are not wealthy enough to be able to purchase organs.

1 AUGUST 1714
External Affairs Queen Anne is succeeded by King George I on the English throne.

OTHER EVENTS OF 1714
Ideas/Beliefs In a public sermon, Boston clergyman

Cotton Mather testifies to his belief in the Copernican theory of the universe. The Coperican theory places the sun at the center of the universe, with the earth orbiting it. Many conservative thinkers of this era still support the older Ptolemaic theory of the universe, which places the earth at its center.
Life/Customs Tea is first introduced to the American colonies. At this time the most popular non-alcoholic colonial beverage is hot chocolate, and coffee is also consumed occasionally. The American colonists are quick to adopt the customs fashionable in continental European and English circles, although there is generally a time lag of several years.
Industry Virginia Governor Alexander Spotswood founds an ironworks on the Rapidan River. He imports German colonists to furnish labor for operating the blast furnaces.
Arts/Culture New York Governor Robert Hunter writes and publishes *Androboros,* a play satirizing contemporary politics. This is the first drama to be both composed and published in the American colonies.

15 APRIL 1715
Indians Instigated by the Spanish, the Yamassee Indians massacre several hundred Carolina settlers. The subsequent establishment of the Georgia colony in 1732 is designed to push the southern Indians farther away from settled Carolina areas.

MAY 1715
British Policy The proprietorship of Maryland is restored to Charles, the fourth Lord Baltimore, and the Maryland Charter of 1632 is also reinstituted. This concludes 24 years of royal rule of the Maryland colony. During the period of royal rule, Lord Baltimore had been allowed to keep his property rights in the Maryland territory.

OTHER EVENTS OF 1715
Ideas/Beliefs In North Carolina, the Anglican legislative majority passes the Third Vestry Act, designating Anglicanism as the official religion of the colony. The previous attempts to establish the Anglican church in this position in 1701 and 1705 have been voided by the Carolina proprietors. This time, the Society for the Propagation of the Gospel aids greatly in facilitating the passage of the act.
Slavery In the North Carolina colony, black slaves are denied the right to have separate religious meeting houses.

JANUARY 1716
Indians South Carolina settlers, with the help of Cherokee Indians, attack and defeat the Yamassee Indians in the region northwest of Port Royal. The conflict between the Yamassee and Lower Creek Indians and the Carolina settlers has resulted from the increasing incursion of South Carolina settlers into Yamassee territory, with the granting of large coastal land tracts for the purpose of cattle farming, as well as from what the Indians perceive as unfair trading practices.

These factors have motivated the Yamassee and Lower Creek Indians to carry out a series of devastating raids on the Carolina traders west of the Savannah River. The South Carolina victory over the Yamassee leads to subsequent victories against the Creek Indians during the course of the spring.

6 JUNE 1716
Slavery The first black slaves arrive in the French territory of Louisiana. They are brought in ships owned by the Company of the West.

OTHER EVENTS OF 1716
Westward Movement Virginia Governor Alexander Spotswood heads an exploratory expedition that follows the James River up across the Blue Ridge Mountains and into the Shenandoah Valley. The intent of this expedition is to open up the interior region of the Virginia colony to new settlement. The group of men accompanying Spotswood is known as the Knights of the Golden Horseshoe.
Colonial Affairs In the South Carolina colony, the assembly elections are mandated to be held in the local parishes instead of in Charlestown.
Arts/Culture In Williamsburg, Virginia, the first theater in the American colonies is built. This structure becomes the Williamsburg town hall in 1745.

EVENTS OF 1717
Industry After 1717, American colonial trading vessels are allowed to sail in the waters of the French West Indies to carry back inexpensive French molasses. This molasses is used in the distillation of rum in New England. Rum becomes an important product of New England industry.
Settling Scots–Irish immigration begins to the American colonies, spurred by the higher rents set by Anglo–Irish landlords. Some emigrate to the New England colonies, but the majority head for western Pennsylvania between the Allegheny Mountains and the Susquehanna River. Pennsylvania is also the destination of a great influx of German settlers, including such religious sects as Dunkers, Mennonites and Moravians. Also in 1717 the colonial outposts in the Illinois territory are absorbed into the Louisiana colony, under French control.
British Policy By royal proclamation, all pirates who surrender themselves to the authorities will be pardoned. A large group of pirates centered on Providence Island in the Bahamas takes advantage of this amnesty. the following year Edward Teach,· better known as Blackbeard, dies in an attack by Virginia colonists. With the virtual elimination of piracy, colonial trade can be conducted freely and profitably.
Finance French King Louis XIV grants a trade monopoly in the Louisiana territory to Scottish financier John Law and his Company of the West. Based on his prospects in the area, Law organizes the Mississippi Company and issues public shares in 1718. Wild speculation in the shares of the Mississippi Company ensues despite attempts at governmental regulation.

27 SEPTEMBER 1718
Colonial Affairs A Carolina coastal expedition captures pirate Stede Bonnet and his crew. Bonnet is tried and hanged on December 10.

NOVEMBER 1718
Settling The French city of New Orleans is founded by Louisiana governor Jean Baptiste le Moyne, Sieur de Bienville, as part of an ambitious program of French expansion along the Mississippi River. New Orleans is settled by immigrants from Canada and France. The French also erect forts upriver at the mouths of the Kaskaskia (1720) and Illinois Rivers (1726), as well as on the Missouri River (1723). French colonists from Canada eventually emigrate to the Mississippi River valley in the area of the Illinois territory. The early successes of the French in colonizing this territory are to give way to competition with Carolina settlers and to repeated attacks by the Chickasaw, Natchez and Yazoo Indians on the French settlements.

OTHER EVENTS OF 1718
British Policy The English Parliament passes an act fixing the term of service for English convict servants sent to the American colonies, particularly to Maryland and Virginia, in commutation of the death sentence and other penalties. Lesser crimes require seven years of service, felonies require 14 years, and a number of more serious crimes require lifelong service.
Colonial Affairs South Carolina colonists build forts at present-day Columbia and Port Royal to furnish protection against attacks by the French and Spanish.
Indians The Tuscarora Indians negotiate peace with the North Carolina colonists.
Settling In the Texas territory, the Spanish found the city of San Antonio.

MARCH 1719
Life/Customs In the New Jersey colony, the legislative assembly passes a statute regulating the institution of marriage. This law forbids the marriage of persons under the age of 21 without the consent of their parent or guardian. This act is called for by the not infrequent enticement of minors into secret marriages.

NOVEMBER 1719
Colonial Affairs After the colony of South Carolina suffers through Spanish and French attacks and the Yamassee Indian War, all of which weaken the power of the proprietorship, rebellious colonists institute a revolutionary government and eject Robert Johnson, the proprietory governor. James Moore is appointed interim governor and the South Carolina colony becomes a royal colony. The proprietors are allowed to keep their land rights in the area.

OTHER EVENTS OF 1719
Settling The French erect Fort Quiataon on the Wabash River to guard the route from Canada to the French settlements in the Mississippi River valley. Colonists from Northern Ireland and Scotland settle in

FOUNDING A NATION 986-1787

Londonderry, New Hampshire, and initiate the cultivation of potatoes in the colonies.
Colonial Affairs In Pensacola, Florida, the Spanish settlers surrender to French forces led by Louisiana Governor de Bienville.

MARCH 1720
Life/Customs In Philadelphia, William Smith and Hannah Travis are found guilty of theft and are sentenced to death. With the remarkable increase in colonial wealth since 1700 and the social instability resulting from the numerous colonial wars, the crime rate has also grown. The death penalty is a fairly standard punishment for theft during this era.

OTHER EVENTS OF 1720
Population The estimated total American colonial population is 474,000. The three largest cities are Boston with 12,000 residents, Philadelphia with 10,000 and New York City with 7000.
Finance The "Mississippi bubble" bursts after two years of wild speculation in the stock of the Mississippi Company, which received a French monopoly for trade in the Louisiana territory. Many investors are ruined while a few emerge rich from the debacle.
Settling In a continuing program of intensive expansion in the Mississippi River Valley, the French erect a fort on the Mississippi River at the mouth of the Kaskaskia River. In the same year they construct the fortress of Louisbourg on Cape Breton Island to regulate traffic into the St. Lawrence River. They also build Fort Niagara to protect the territory surrounding the lower Great Lakes and to serve as a bulwark against Iroquois Indian attacks.
Arts/Culture A German religious sect, the Dunkers, establishes the Ephrata Cloister outside of Philadelphia; their hymn books are copied and illuminated by women members. In 1730, Benjamin Franklin will publish the *Ephrata Hymnbook,* which is a compilation of musical pieces written mostly by Johann Conrad Beissel, one of the first colonial composers to have his works published. The German Dunkers customarily sing hymns in multipart harmony while other colonial religious groups sing in unison.

MARCH 1721
Settling A group of about 260 German colonists arrives in the French colony of Louisiana.

29 MAY 1721
British Policy The English Crown proclaims South Carolina a royal colony and appoints Francis Nicholson as governor. The proprietors of South Carolina do not surrender their proprietory charter until 1729, and seven of the eight proprietors sell their land holdings for £2500 each. Lord Carteret, the eighth proprietor, trades his land claim for a grant south of the Virginia border.

OTHER EVENTS OF 1721
British Policy The appointment of Sir Robert Wal-

pole as the English Chancellor of the Exchequer initiates a period of benign neglect of the American colonies. Walpole's trade policies, or the lack of them, result in the negligent enforcement of the navigation acts.
Life/Customs The government of France releases 25 prostitutes from jail and sends them to the Louisiana territory. This is to help relieve the scarcity of women in the region and to tempt the French Canadian settlers away from their Indian paramours.
Education French missionaries establish Jesuit College in the Illinois territory at Kaskaskia. Reportedly, its library has an impressive collection of books, including many volumes of French philosophical works.
Arts/Culture In his *Christian Philosopher,* Mather provides the first detailed colonial explanation of Isaac Newton's theory of physics, as it appeared in Newton's *Principia Mathematica* (1687). Newton's hypotheses had already been introduced to America, at shorter length, by James Logan in 1708. In the same year, the Massachusetts General Court revokes the censorship of publications in the Massachusetts colony.

4 JUNE 1722
Settling In the French territory on the Gulf Coast, some 250 prospective German settlers disembark at the site of Mobile, Alabama.

23 OCTOBER 1722
Ideas/Beliefs In an important advance for the cause of Anglicanism in the American colonies, three influential Connecticut Congregationalist clergymen—Daniel Brown, Timothy Cutler and Samuel Johnson—leave for England intending to be ordained as Anglican ministers. The three have been associated with Yale College.

OTHER EVENTS OF 1722
British Policy In a series of additional trade acts, the English Parliament adds copper, beaver and other furs to the list of enumerated items to be exported only to England. Parliament also removes hemp, lumber and naval stores from the list of items subject to import duties. In the same year, Parliament passes a currency regulation permitting the minting of copper coins by the American colonies.
Indians Virginia Governor Alexander Spotswood negotiates a peace treaty with the League of Six Indian Nations. According to the terms of this pact, the Iroquois and other tribes agree not to cross the Blue Ridge Mountains or the Potomac River unless Virginia gives them leave to do so. The Iroquois League has maintained amicable relations with the English colonists and hostile relations with the French, since the French have frequently sided with Indians tribes hostile to the Iroquois. The Iroquois League has been an indispensable ally of the English colonists. The Iroquois Indians have helped to protect the western frontier of the English colonies during a time of ambitious French territorial expansion in the Mississippi River valley. In the Maine territory, Lovewell's War be-

tween the Abenaki Indians, instigated by French Jesuit Father Râle, and the English colonists breaks out. This war is to go on for three years.

Settling In the Spanish settlement of San Antonio, Texas, the Alamo is built as a Franciscan mission.

Colonial Affairs New Jersey colonist Daniel Coxe publishes a plan for the political unification of the American colonies.

APRIL 1723

Arts/Culture In Boston, the construction of Old North Church, also known as Christ Church, is begun. The earliest Georgian-style church in the New England colonies, it is designed by William Prince, who has been influenced by the London church designs of Christopher Wren. The Georgian architectural style is to gain wide popularity in the American colonies. The Old North Church will be the site of the warning communicated to Paul Revere.

OTHER EVENTS OF 1723

Indians In Williamsburg, Virginia, at William and Mary College, Brafferton Hall is constructed to provide space for the first permanent Indian school in the American colonies. The endowment for the school has been provided by English scientist Robert Boyle.

Life/Customs In Philadelphia, a petition is presented to the Pennsylvania assembly requesting action on the problem of intermarriage between blacks and whites. In 1723, Philadelphia is also the destination of Benjamin Franklin, who decides to leave Boston.

Settling Continuing their program of intensive expansion in the Mississippi Valley territory, the French erect a fort on the north bank of the Missouri River. In the English colonies, a group of German Palatinate refugees led by Conrad Weiser arrives in Bucks County, Pennsylvania.

Education The Maryland representative assembly mandates public schools in all counties of the colony.

EVENTS OF 1724

War In northern New England, Lovewell's War, otherwise known as Dummer's War, climaxes in a bloody massacre of Maine settlers by French Jesuit missionary Father Râle and his Abenaki Indian allies. The English colonies of New England have erected a chain of northern forts to protect them from French expansionism and from Indian incursions, but these fortifications are of little use against this raid.

Settling The French erect Fort Vincennes on the lower Wabash River to protect the route from Canada to the French settlements in the Mississippi River valley and Louisiana. In Vermont, the first permanent settlement is established when Massachusetts colonists found Fort Dummer at the site of present-day Brattleboro to protect the Massachusetts frontier from French and Indian incursions.

Agriculture The introduction of irrigation into the cultivation of rice in the southern colonies greatly increases harvest yields. In New England Paul Dudley publishes a work on fruit trees, thus becoming the first American horticulturist.

THE SLAVE TRADE

By the time of the Revolutionary War, one of every six Americans was a black slave. According to various estimates, a total of from 10 to 24 million blacks were transported to the New World in order to be sold into slavery. Of these, about 3 million ended up in North America. Probably one-fifth of the blacks perished from the unparalleled torments of the voyage, which could last up to ten weeks. On the ships they were packed as tightly as "books upon a shelf" in the hellhole below decks. The water was impure and food inedible, if available at all. Many of those who became weak or sick were thrown overboard, and others committed suicide by jumping into the sea, rather than submit.

In Africa few of these blacks were captured by Europeans. Most of them were kidnapped by neighboring or enemy tribesmen, who sold them to Moslem traders in exchange for such goods as rum, codfish, salt and Spanish money. The slave ships, operating under the flags of all nations, plied the profitable triangular trade route. They departed New England ports with a cargo or rum, trinkets, firearms, and "African iron"—iron bars used in Africa as currency. Landing at trading posts along the West African coast, the masters of the slave ships bartered these material cargos for human cargo, branding the Africans before they were forced into the holds. When the dreadful "middle passage," or journey to the West Indies, ended, the surviving Africans were delivered to slave dealers, and then the vessels loaded up with the agricultural products of the Caribbean plantations for the final leg of the voyage north to New England. The slave trade greatly enriched Northeastern merchants, who invested their profits in factories, mines and transportation, thus initiating the Industrial Revolution.

The first 20 blacks were landed in 1619 at Jamestown, Virginia, to be sold as indentured servants. The slave trade did not become an important component of colonial American commerce until late in the 17th century. It was then that the Southern plantation system became firmly established. The success of the plantations in producing cash crops of tobacco, indigo, rice, cotton and sugar for the export trade led to an ever-increasing demand for additional hands to work the fields.

In the face of growing moral objections, all of the states had forbidden the importation of slaves by 1803, and Congress extended the ban nationwide in 1808. The American black slave population was thenceforth maintained and increased by the smuggling of slaves and by the "breeding" of those already in America. The domestic phase of the slave trade was conducted from the auction block, where slaves were sold like livestock with little regard for familial ties. The slave trade was finally ended with the 1863 Emancipation Proclamation.

Colonial Affairs The Rhode Island colony institutes property ownership requirements for the right to vote.

Slavery In New Orleans, French Louisiana Governor de Bienville establishes a code to regulate the activities of blacks. At the same time, all Jewish settlers are exiled from the Louisiana Colony.

20 FEBRUARY 1725

Indians In Wakefield, New Hampshire, Indian fighter Captain John Lovewell leads an attack against a group of Indians. Lovewell's men take 10 Indian scalps, in the first recorded instance of scalping by colonists. In Boston, the scalps bring a bounty of 100 pounds each.

OTHER EVENTS OF 1725

Slavery The population of black slaves in the American colonies is estimated at about 75,000. In the same year, slaves are granted the right to have a separate Baptist church in Williamsburg, Virginia.

Indians The flourishing illegal fur trade is controlled by strictly enforced measures. English colonial traders are prohibited from purchasing furs trapped by Indians living in French territory, just as French traders are forbidden from bartering for furs with Indians living in territory claimed by the English. As an example to the numerous scofflaws, several Albany fur traders are found guilty and sentenced for dealing in black market furs.

Arts/Culture In Boston, physician Nathaniel Ames begins the publication of the *Astronomical Diary and Almanac.* Ames continues to publish his almanac until the time of the American Revolution. Ames' almanac may have been the prototype for Benjamin Franklin's *Poor Richard's Almanac,* which begins publication in 1732. In New York City, William Bradford begins publication of the first New York newspaper, the *New York Gazette.* This paper is published regularly until 1745.

British Policy The Virginia legislative assembly enacts a statute forbidding the shipment of North Carolina tobacco from Virginia seaports. The English Board of Trade overrules this legislation.

Settling New England colonists erect Fort Oswego on Lake Ontario to meet the challenge of the recently-built French Fort Niagara, which extends French control over the territory of the lower Great Lakes. The New Englanders also build a series of forts along the northern boundary to protect them against attacks by the Abenaki Indians, who support the French as a result of intensive Jesuit missionary activity.

EVENTS OF 1726

Ideas/Beliefs The first college in the mid–Atlantic colonies is founded when Irish-born Presbyterian minister William Tennent establishes Log College at Neshaminy in Bucks County, Pennsylvania. Tennent is to be a strong influence in the training of evangelist preachers who will carry the message of the Bible throughout the colonies during the religious revival movement known as the Great Awakening during the decades of the 1730s and the 1740s. In New Jersey, the son of William Tennent, Gilbert Tennent, begins to preach to Presbyterians at New Brunswick. Gilbert Tennent becomes an important preacher in the religious revival movement in the mid-Atlantic colonies. He will later travel around New England in the company of evangelist George Whitefield. The galvanizing sermons of Theodore Frelinghuysen, a German-born minister of the Dutch Reformed Church in the Raritan Valley, New Jersey, also mark him as one of the originators of the Great Awakening. The foremost proponent of the religious revival movement in New England will be Jonathan Edwards.

Settling In a program of intensive expansion in the Mississippi River Valley, the French erect a fort on the Mississippi at the mouth of the Illinois River.

Life/Customs In Philadelphia, mobs of poor people riot in the center of the town after ripping down the pillory and stocks and burning them. The Pennsylvania governor quells the disturbance with necessary force. Other such riots are to reoccur in Philadelphia in the years that follow—one in 1729 and another in 1738.

FEBRUARY 1727

War Tensions run high and hostilities follow between the English and Spanish settlers in the North American colonies when the year-long Anglo-Spanish War breaks out. The Carolina settlers use the war as an excuse to attack Spanish settlements; and the Spanish protest the earlier series of forts constructed by Carolina colonists on the Altamaha, Santee, and Savannah Rivers.

19 SEPTEMBER 1727

Arts/Culture The first newspaper in the Maryland colony, the *Maryland Gazette,* begins publication in Annapolis.

OTHER EVENTS OF 1727

External Affairs in England, King George II ascends the throne, succeeding King George I.

Indians Dr. Cadwallader Colden publishes his account of the Iroquois tribes, the *History of the Five Indian Nations.* A Scottish-born physician, Colden has also served as lieutenant governor of the New York colony and has published various scientific articles on medical subjects. He is credited with introducing the Linnean system of botanical classification into the American colonies.

Arts/Culture In Philadelphia, Benjamin Franklin organizes the Junto Club, a "mutual improvement" association with a membership largely of artisans. This culturally influential society formally opposes slavery and other inhumane practices. In 1731 its members are to found the first colonial public library. Later, the American Philsophical Society is to develop from the Junto Club.

Settling Discouraged by the decreasing availability of land in the northern colonies, German and Scottish-Irish immigrants begin to pour into the Valley of Virginia.

9 MARCH 1728

War During the course of the Anglo-Spanish War, a military force of English settlers from the South Carolina colony conducts an expedition deep into Spanish territory in Florida to destroy a Yamassee Indian village close to the Spanish settlement at St. Augustine.

OTHER EVENTS OF 1728

Life/Customs The drinking of alcoholic beverages is

so prevalent in the American colonies that 2,124,500 gallons of rum are imported in 1728, supplementing the considerable colonial production of this drink.

In Louisiana, a group of prospective wives for the French settlers arrives in the territory. These ladies have been preceded by women who were former prisoners released from jail and the later arrivals are of a higher social status. They become known as "casket girls" because they are given dresses in caskets as a gift for their immigration.

To the north, Boston begins to ban horses and carriages from its common, a 48-acre reservation established in the center of the town in 1634. Originally intended as a communal pasture and a military parade ground, the common now becomes a fashionable public park where ladies and gentlemen promenade during late afternoons.

Ideas/Beliefs In New York City, Jewish colonists erect the first American synagogue on Mill Street, and a Hebrew school is later added to the edifice. Since 1628, the Jews have had their religious services in a rented building.

In Philadelphia, Benjamin Franklin publishes a prayer manual entitled *Articles of Faith and Acts of Religion,* in which he underlines the importance of reason as an element of religious faith. His pragmatic approach downplays the role of formal religious doctrines.

Colonial Affairs In the Virginia colony, Colonel William Byrd is the commissioner overseeing the determination of the boundary line between Virginia and North Carolina. His diary of day-to-day events during the process of the survey is the basis for his *History of the Dividing Line,* not to be published until 1841.

25 JULY 1729

British Policy After the continuing agitation of rebellious colonists who object to their proprietary rule, North Carolina becomes a royal colony when its original proprietary charter is surrendered to the English crown. The complaints of the colonists have included those of inadequate governmental protection against the Yamassee Indian attacks and the suppression of liberal election laws passed by the colony's representative assembly. The English crown buys out the proprietors for £17,500. Of the South Carolina territory that comes under royal control, the southern portion will later become Georgia when the crown issues the Charter of 1732 to James Oglethorpe and others. Of the original Carolina Proprietors, only Lord Carteret keeps his eighth of the grant. The English Parliament confirms the establishment of North Carolina and South Carolina as royal provinces in 1730.

OTHER EVENTS OF 1729

Colonial Affairs The second riot in three years occurs in Philadelphia when a mob of economically disadvantaged colonists breaks into the private garden of the mayor of Philadelphia and plunders the plants.

Ideas/Beliefs The Rhode Island colony practices discrimination against immigrants based on national origin. All incoming settlers, except those from England, Ireland and the English Channel islands of Jersey and Guernsey, must post a £50 bond before they are allowed to enter the colony.

In Boston, master mason Joshua Blanchard erects the Old South Meeting House, replacing the original 1670 structure. in the era preceding the American Revolution, the church becomes a meeting place for revolutionaries.

In Rhode Island, Irish-born philosopher and Anglican bishop George Berkeley arrives in Newport where he prepares his plans for founding a college in Bermuda for the purpose of educating blacks. He regards his Bermuda school as a prototype for a system of similar colleges throughout the American colonies. An important pioneering idealistic philosopher, Berkeley also founds a Literary and Philosophical Society and writes *Alciphron,* a refutation of Deism, during his stay in the colonies. His Bermuda project is never realized and Berkeley returns to England in 1731.

British Policy The English Parliament renews its bounties on naval stores—pitch, tar, rosin, turpentine, hemp, masts, yards and bowsprits—exported from the American colonies. In many cases the new bounties are lower than those set by the earlier 1705 act regulating the trade of naval stores. These bounties on the naval stores continue until 1774, although the hemp bounty lapses in 1741 and is reinstated in 1764.

Indians Following a period of intensive expansion, the French settlements in the Mississippi River valley are attacked by a combined force of Chickasaw, Natchez and Yazoo Indians. These continued hostilities by the Indians against the settlers eventually lead to the limitation of French colonization activity to the Louisiana Valley area.

Arts/Culture In Philadelphia Benjamin Franklin purchases and begins publication of *The Pennsylvania Gazette.* He buys the newspaper from Samuel Keimer, who began publication in 1728 under the title *Universal Instructor in All Arts and Sciences and Pennsylvania Gazette.* Through Franklin's astute business sense and his editorial skills, the *Pennsylvania Gazette* becomes the most popular newspaper of the colonial era. In 1821 the *Pennsylvania Gazette* is transformed into *The Saturday Evening Post,* a journal that continues publication through the 20th century. In the same year, Franklin also publishes his pamphlet, the *Modest Enquiry into the Nature and Necessity of a Paper-Currency.*

Boston jurist and Puritan Samuel Sewall finishes his personal diary of the era from 1674 to 1729. This book will not be published until 1879. Sewall's is the most complete surviving account of day-to-day life during these formative years, excluding 1677-1685, and it is a valuable source for social historians. Sewall has also published an earlier work, the influential antislavery tract, *The Selling of Joseph* of 1700.

Settling The French dispatch Chaussegros de Lery to build a chain of forts along the Ohio River in order to bar the increasing westward expansion of the English colonies. The British lack a decisive policy on this issue although the English crown has been advised, some eight years earlier, to take action to "interrupt the French communication from Quebec to the Mississippi River."

EVENTS OF 1730
Colonial Affairs The Virginia representative assembly passes legislation enacting the Tobacco Inspection Law. This statute mandates the quality inspection at seaports of tobacco bound for export. In the same year the former royal governor of the Virginia colony, Alexander Spotswood, is designated deputy postmaster general for the American colonies.

British Policy The English Parliament allows the export of rice from South Carolina to other countries in Europe besides England, but only to those ports that are south of Cape Finisterre at the northern reaches of Spain.

Settling In the Maryland colony, the town of Baltimore is established. The land for the settlement has been bought by the Maryland legislature. Baltimore becomes an important seaport for the interior regions of the colony as the rich yields of the grain and tobacco harvests pass through its harbor. Two earlier attempts to found a town named after Lord Baltimore had failed.

Industry The first commercial kiln for firing stoneware is established in New York City and the city subsequently becomes a pottery manufacturing center.

Life/Customs Newport, Rhode Island, becomes a popular vacation destination for the wealthy citizens of the colonies, who travel to the spa from as far away as the Carolinas and even the West Indies. The social status of Newport is enhanced by its cultural advantages—the Philosophical Society is founded there in 1730. Some years later, Newport is also to become an important mercantile town, as the center of the "triangular trade"—rum produced in New England distilleries is exchanged for black slaves from Africa, and the slaves are then traded for sugar and molasses from the West Indies.

Arts/Culture In Philadelphia, Andrew Hamilton completes a Georgian design for the Old State House, better known as Independence Hall. The construction of the building is not completed until 1753.

23 JANUARY 1731
Colonial Affairs In the Louisiana territory, trade rights in the region return to the French Crown, with the surrender of the charter of John Law's Company of the West. The corporation had held the trade monopoly since 1717, after receiving it from Antoine Crozat, a French trader who had been in possession of the concessions since 1712. With his exclusive right to trade on the Mississippi River and to develop the Louisiana territory, Scottish financier Law had become embroiled in the "Mississippi bubble," a speculative venture that collapsed in 1720 and ruined Law along with many others. Law had died in Europe in 1725.

OTHER EVENTS OF 1731
Settling The French erect a fort at Crown Point on Lake Champlain to guard the southern approaches to the St. Lawrence River against British and Iroquois Indian attacks.

Slavery An English royal order forbids the implementation of duties on imported slaves by the colonial legislatures.

Arts/Culture In Pennsylvania, the Junto Club led by Benjamin Franklin founds the Library Company of Philadelphia. This is the first circulating, or public, library in the American colonies. The establishment of the library reflects the growing literacy in the colonies, aided considerably by the widespread institution of public and private schools in the era preceding the American Revolution, as well as the increasing cultural amenities of such urban centers as Philadelphia.

22 FEBRUARY 1732
Life/Customs George Washington is born at Bridges Creek in the Virginia Colony. He is one of the 10 children of a well-to-do planter.

26 FEBRUARY 1732
Ideas/Beliefs In Philadelphia, the first and only Catholic church in the American colonies in the era before the American Revolution celebrates its first mass. In the other colonies, such as Maryland, Catholics are forced to practice church rituals in private houses.

28 FEBRUARY 1732
Settling The promoters of the proposed Georgia Colony buy out Lord Carteret's eighth share in the original Carolina grant.

20 JUNE 1732
Settling The trustees for the South Carolina land area between the Savannah and the Altamaha Rivers receive an English royal charter for the territory that will become known as the Colony of Georgia. Originally part of the South Carolina proprietorship, this territory came to the English crown when the proprietors were forced to give up their holdings in 1729. The Georgia charter grants the trustees the right of settlement in this area for a period of 21 years. The document also allows freedom of conscience to everyone except Catholics and it permits individual land grants of no more than 500 acres. This charter remains in effect until 1752, when Georgia becomes a royal colony. Foremost among the 20 trustees are James Edward Oglethorpe and John Viscount Perceval, later the first Earl of Egmont. Oglethorpe, a humanitarian, is particularly interested in recruiting settlers from English debtors' prisons and the colony is also to be a haven for persecuted Protestants. The geographical location of the new colony is of strategic importance, as it will protect South Carolina from attacks by Spanish colonists from Florida and by French settlers from Louisiana.

19 DECEMBER 1732

Arts/Culture In Philadelphia, Benjamin Franklin begins the publication of *Poor Richard's Almanac*, a compilation of weather predictions, epigrams, and proverbs. Franklin's almanac soon becomes the most popular of the various colonial almanacs, selling around 10,000 copies per year. Part of the success of the almanac is due to the fact that Franklin issues it in three regional editions, with corresponding adjustments of local meteorological and geographical data. Franklin's inventiveness is apparent in his creation of the character of Poor Richard, a homespun philosopher and commentator, and in his composition of a number of the witty sayings included in the almanac. He will continue to write for the almanac until around 1748, and he publishes it until 1757; after that time another publisher continues to issue the almanac.

OTHER EVENTS OF 1732

British Policy The English Parliament passes the Hat Act, banning the import of hats from one American colony to another; allowing the manufacture of hats only by those craftsmen who have undergone a seven-year apprenticeship; permitting each hat-making shop only two apprentices each; and forbidding the use of black apprentices. This act is passed to help support London felt-makers who are undergoing economic difficulties because of French competition and who now fear added competition from the growing hat-making business in the northern colonies. In the American colonies, the enforcement of this parliamentary law is lackadaisical.

Colonial Affairs The American colonial postal system is finally extended to the southern colonies under the leadership of former Virginia governor Alexander Spotswood as deputy postmaster general.

Settling The Scottish-Irish immigrants who originally settled in western Pennsylvania, begin to move down the Shenandoah Valley into Virginia, North Carolina, South Carolina and Georgia.

Transportation The first regularly-scheduled public stagecoach line begins operation between Burlington and Amboy, New Jersey. Connections may be made by boat from Amboy to New York and from Burlington to Philadelphia.

Life/Customs In Philadelphia, what is probably the first colonial publically-supported almshouse is founded by the Quakers, who are involved in a number of other humanitarian works.

13 JANUARY 1733

Settling The proprietor of the Georgia Colony, James Edward Oglethorpe disembarks in Charleston, South Carolina, accompanied by 130 prospective colonists. Oglethorpe also brings with him the new Georgia charter. Georgia is the last of the original 13 colonies to be established.

12 FEBRUARY 1733

Settling Under the authority of the 1732 royal charter granting him and 19 other trustees the Georgia territory, and after procuring the permission of the indigenous Creek Indians, James Edward Oglethorpe founds the city of Savannah. The trustees of the Georgia colony enforce strict regulations banning the import of slaves and of brandy and rum during the first years of the new colony. The original charter stipulation limiting individual land grants to 500 acres is broadened in 1740 to allow individual land grants of 200 acres. The prohibitions on rum importation and the slave trade are repealed in 1742 and 1749 respectively.

17 MAY 1733

British Policy The English Parliament passes the Molasses Act which sets heavy duties on all molasses, rum and sugar imported to the American colonies from Caribbean islands other than those under British control. The purpose of this act is to protect English West Indies planters from foreign competition. As were the earlier trade acts, this law is difficult to enforce. A group of West Indian planters has lobbied actively for the passage of this act. They have suffered severe economic setbacks since American merchant vessels have been permitted to purchase lower cost sugar and molasses for the rum trade from the French and Dutch islands of the West Indies.

JULY 1733

Settling Some 40 Jewish colonists are allowed to enter the newly–formed Georgia colony by its proprietors. These new inhabitants settle in Savannah.

5 NOVEMBER 1733

Arts/Culture In New York City, the *New York Weekly Journal* commences publication. Edited by John Peter Zenger, the newspaper is funded by a group of influential citizens who oppose New York Governor William Cosby and support the cause of the Popular Party. The *Journal* will continue publication until 1751.

OTHER EVENTS OF 1733

Life/Customs In its first widespread outbreak in the American colonies, an influenza epidemic rages through New York City and Philadelphia.

Industry Around this time, the pottery kilns of German settlers in the Pennsylvania Colony begin to produce a simple utilitarian tableware made of a porous reddish clay. The use of such redware dishes was widespread throughout the colonies, and the pieces originating from the Pennsylvania–German potters were often inscribed with sgraffito and homespun sayings and verses.

17 NOVEMBER 1734

Ideas/Beliefs German-born New York newspaper publisher John Peter Zenger is arrested and put in prison. He will be imprisoned for ten months before his case goes to trial. As editor, Zenger is held responsible for the polemical articles written by his reporters for the *New York Weekly Journal* and he is accused of seditious libel by New York Governor William Cosby.

DECEMBER 1734

Ideas/Beliefs In Northampton, Massachusetts, Congregationalist clergyman Jonathan Edwards preaches a series of stirring sermons that initiate the Great Awakening in the New England colonies. This religious revival movement is to sweep the American colonies during the next decade. Thousands of people are converted, a process often accompanied by emotional outbursts, screaming and physical tremors. As an aftermath of the Great Awakening, the conservative clergy and wings of the old Puritan churches lose ground as the Baptists, Methodists and Presbyterians grow in power and influence. In the 1740s, the best known revivalist preacher is English evangelist George Whitefield.

OTHER EVENTS OF 1734

Colonial Affairs In New York City, the Popular Party is the victor in an aldermanic election, aided greatly by the endorsement of the *New York Weekly Journal* edited by John Peter Zenger.

Education South Carolina colonist William Bull receives a medical degree in Europe. He is the first of some 40 colonial physicians to be educated abroad, mainly at the University of Edinburgh, at private English classes, or at the Universities of Paris and Leyden.

8 FEBRUARY 1735

Arts/Culture In Charleston, South Carolina, the first opera in the American colonies is produced. Presented at the Courtroom, the opera is *Flora; or, The Hob in the Well,* by Colley Cibber.

AUGUST 1735

Ideas/Beliefs After ten months of imprisonment, New York newspaper editor John Peter Zenger finally comes to trial. Accused of seditious libel by New York governor William Cosby, Zenger is ably defended by Philadelphia lawyer Andrew Hamilton who sways the jury by suggesting that the newspaper passages under consideration are not libelous because they are true. Zenger's acquittal is a milestone on the road toward freedom of the press.

10 DECEMBER 1735

Ideas/Beliefs During a return trip to England, Georgia proprietor James Edward Oglethorpe meets John and Charles Wesley, who are students at Oxford University. Impressed by their fervent evangelicism, Oglethorpe issues an invitation for them to visit the Georgia colony. They accept and soon set sail for the colonies, arriving in February of the next year.

OTHER EVENTS OF 1735

British Policy The English Parliament allows the export of rice from Georgia to other countries besides England, but only to those ports south of Cape Finisterre at the northern boundary of Spain. This privilege has already been accorded to South Carolina since 1730.

Settling French colonists arrive from Canada to set-tle French territory in the Illinois area of the Mississippi River Valley. To the east, in a series of fortifications on the southern Georgia frontier, James Oglethorpe establishes Fort Okfuskee on the Talapoosa River. In the same year, the trading post and fort of Augusta, Georgia, is founded on the shores of the Savannah River.

Slavery New York colonist John van Zandt horsewhips his black slave so severely that the man dies. Van Zandt is administering punishment for a violation of the city curfew. A coroner's jury considers the cause of death and attributes it to "a visitation of God." This incident reflects the tense racial relations in the New York colony, where blacks compose 20 percent of the total population. In this era the newspapers record the not infrequent lynchings of blacks for rape, theft and other crimes.

Ideas/Beliefs Led by Augustus Gottlieb Spangenberg, the Moravians attempt a collectivist experiment at Savannah, Georgia. The Moravians are members of an evangelical Protestant sect originating in the Moravian region of Czechoslovakia and Bohemia. Distinguished by the high quality of their religious music, the Moravians uphold tenets of personal service and Christian unity. An important Moravian colony will be founded at Bethlehem, Pennsylvania.

Finance In Charleston, South Carolina, the first American fire insurance company is founded. Named the Friendly Society for the Mutual Insurance of Houses Against Fire, the company enters bankruptcy five years later when a fire sweeps through Charleston, destroying half of the buildings there.

Life/Customs The status of women in the American colonies records further advances as more and more colonists attain positions of economic security and even wealth. According to contemporary newspaper accounts, increasing numbers of women are leaving their husbands for reasons of marital incompatibility. In the same year, the New England colonies are swept by a devastating scarlet fever epidemic.

Transportation The fact that between them Boston and Salem own some 25,000 tons of shipping stock is testimony to the rapid growth of the American colonial shipbuilding industry and mercantile establishment.

5 FEBRUARY 1736

Ideas/Beliefs English evangelist preacher John Wesley and his brother Charles arrive for a visit in Savannah, Georgia, in response to an invitation issue by Georgia proprietor James Edward Oglethrope. They remain for a drawn-out visit before they return to England. Although originally a branch of the Church of England, Methodism is characterized by an emphasis on personal revelation. During the era of the Great Awakening, the Methodist creed was spread throughout the American colonies by itinerant preachers who held services in informal settings, including private houses, barns and even pastures. Evangelism will make wide gains in the American colonies with the electrifying preaching tours of English religious revivialist George Whitefield during the years between 1738 and 1770.

OTHER EVENTS OF 1736
Settling In the recently created colony of Georgia, Scottish immigrants establish the settlement of New Inverness near the mouth of the Altamaha River.
Agriculture The South Carolina colony passes an act encouraging the production of silk.

9 MARCH 1737
Life/Customs In Boston, a group of reformers attacks and destroys a bawdy house on the waterfront. The prostitutes who inhabit such houses are accused of lewdness and dissoluteness, and are warned against displaying themselves in the windows on the Sabbath.

17 MARCH 1737
Life/Customs In Boston, the first municipal celebration of St. Patrick's Day is held by the newly-established Charitable Irish Society. Up to this time St. Patrick's Day has been celebrated only in a religious context. Municipal celebrations of the holiday are initiated in Philadelphia in 1780 and in New York in 1784, where it is jointly sponsored by Catholics and Presbyterians.

OTHER EVENTS OF 1737
Indians Thomas Penn employs professional walkers to pace out the boundaries of the land tract granted to William Penn by the Delaware Indians—a territory that is comprised of the land area a man can walk across in a day and a half. Penn's walkers pace off 66.5 miles. This tactic infuriates the Delaware Indians.
Finance Connecticut colonist John Higley mints the first colonial copper coins in his own furnace on Hopmeadow Brook in Simsbury. These Higley pennies bear the words, "I am good copper" and "Value me as you will."
Colonial Affairs In the New England colonies, a border dispute between Massachusetts and New Hampshire commences. This disagreement will continue from some 150 years before it is finally settled.
Ideas/Beliefs Methodist preacher John Wesley is brought before a Savannah, Georgia court and charged with inserting unauthorized hymns and psalms into the Anglican church service when he publishes *A Collection of Psalms and Hymns.* A number of the selections in his book are adaptations from the German Moravian *Gesangbuch.* Wesley is soon to return to England. In Boston, the *Narrative of Surprising Conversions* by Jonathan Edwards is published. This volume is an account of the Great Awakening religious revival movement.
Arts/Culture The New York City Trinity Church is the recipient of the first church organ constructed in the American colonies. The instrument is made by Moravian organ builder Johannes Klemm.

In the American Midwest a building is erected at Cahokia, Illinois. Later to be transformed into the Cahokia County Courthouse, it is constructed of up-

right posts driven into the ground and chinked with clay. Today it is the oldest continuously existing building in the US.

7 MAY 1738
Ideas/Beliefs English Methodist evangelist George Whitefield arrives in Savannah, Georgia on the first of his seven trips to the American colonies. A close early associate of John and Charles Wesley, he later breaks with them because he will not repudiate Calvinism. His electrifying sermons attract throngs of listeners wherever he goes, from New England to Georgia. Whitefield is a primary proponent of the colonial Great Awakening, a series of mid–eighteenth–century religious revivals.

21 DECEMBER 1738
Settling The Virginia legislative assembly establishes the new western cities of Augusta and Frederick on the other side of the Blue Ridge Mountains.

OTHER EVENTS OF 1738
Colonial Affairs The colony of New Jersey finally receives the privilege from the English Crown of having a governor separate from that of New York. (New Jersey and New York have shared the same governor since 1702.) Lewis Morris is appointed the first royal governor of New Jersey.
Industry Near Savannah, Georgia, Huguenot potter Andrew Duché discovers a clay for making Chinese-style porcelain (a process discovered in 1708 by Bottger of the German Meissen porcelain factory). Duché travels to England in 1743 taking a load of the clay with him. He signs an export contract with the Bow and Worcester porcelain factories for Unaker Virginia china clay, also known as Cherokee clay. Duché is able to amass a considerable fortune from his clay and porcelain business.
Education In Massachusetts, Harvard professor Isaac Greenwood concludes his career of teaching natural science. John Winthrop succeeds him in the chair of mathematics at Harvard College, initiating a teaching career that will span some 41 years. After Benjamin Franklin, Winthrop is the most important scientist in the American colonies. In 1746 he will present the first laboratory demonstration of electricity and magnetism. He also introduces the study of Newtonian fluxions. The importance of his own observations on the earthquake of 1755 ranks him as one of the founders of seismology.
Life/Customs In Philadelphia, a riot results from the proclamation of the city fathers that fishing in the Schuylkill River will be restricted.

In Massachusetts, at the funeral of Governor Belcher's wife, over 1000 pairs of gloves are given away as funeral gifts. A customary practice of the colonial era, the funeral gifts were often mourning rings. Clergymen and doctors frequently accumulated thousands of such items during a lifetime of service.

9 SEPTEMBER 1739
Slavery A black insurrection takes place in South

Carolina when a group of blacks sets out on a journey to St. Augustine, Florida, and liberation. They kill any whites in their path. Reportedly, the blacks were encouraged to rebel by Spanish missionaries. The violence results in 44 black deaths and 30 white deaths. This is the most serious of the three black uprisings that occur in South Carolina during 1739. The second uprising takes place in Stone Creek, South Carolina, and the third occurs in St. John's Parish in Berkeley County.

19 OCTOBER 1739

War As a result of their struggle for commercial supremacy, England declares war on Spain and the War of Jenkins' Ear is waged until 1742. This declaration of war is provoked by a series of incidents in the Americas—particularly the mistreatment of English merchant seaman Robert Jenkins; border disagreements in Florida; other Spanish naval hostilities related to the English conduct under the terms of the Assiento of the Treaty of Utrecht (1713); and the English logging activities in the Honduras. There is widespread outrage when Robert Jenkins reports to the House of Commons that the Spanish have lopped off his ear as a punishment for suspected smuggling activites. After the declaration of war, Georgia Governor James Oglethorpe encourages Georgia and South Carolina colonists to join the war against the Florida Spaniards. The Spaniards counter by attempting invasion of these colonies. The War of Jenkins' Ear will merge with the War of the Austrian Succession (1740-1748), of which King George's War (1743-1748) is the American phase.

OTHER EVENTS OF 1739

British Policy The English Parliament removes sugar from the list of enumerated items that are to be exported only to England. American colonists may now send refined sugar to ports south of Cape Finisterre, at the northern boundary of Spain.

Exploration French explorers Pierre and Paul Mallet travel upstream to the headwaters of the Arkansas River. Here they first sight the Rocky Mountains.

Settling By this date, Georgia proprietor James Edward Oglethorpe has competed a series of military fortifications in the new colony, with posts on the islands of Amelia, Cumberland, St. Andrew's and St. Simon's. Oglethorpe has also established the settlement of Augusta on the Savannah River and Fort Okfuskee on the Talapoosa River. In addition to these settlement advances, Oglethorpe has been particularly successful in reaching peace accords with the Creeks and other regional Indians.

Labor The trustees of the Georgia Colony set maximum wages scales for servants and laborers.

Industry The Salem County, New Jersey, glass designer and manufacturer Caspar Wistar builds a large glass factory in Allowaystown. Using the skills of immigrant glassblowers from Germany, the factory will remain in operation for 41 years, producing some of the finest artifacts of early American glassware. in the same year Wistar also erects another New Jersey factory for the production of window and bottle glass.

JANUARY 1740

War During the course of the War of Jenkins' Ear, Georgia leader James Oglethorpe, with the aid of Cherokee, Chickasaw and Creek Indians, invades the Spanish territory in Florida and captures Fort San Francisco de Pupo and Fort Picolata on the San Juan River.

Slavery A plan to revolt by black slaves is revealed in Charleston, South Carolina. Fifty slaves are hanged.

25 MARCH 1740

Life/Customs In Savannah, Georgia, the cornerstone is laid for the Bethesda Orphanage, the oldest surviving such structure in the American colonies. The orphanage is founded through the agency of English evangelist preacher George Whitefield. In 1769, during Whitefield's last visit to the colonies, the orphanage will be converted into Bethesda College.

MAY-JULY 1740

War During the War of Jenkins' Ear, the Georgian and Indian forces led by James Oglethorpe unsuccessfully lay siege to the Spanish settlement at St. Augustine, Florida. Oglethorpe is forced to withdraw when his forces are threatened from the rear.

30 JULY 1740

Industry In New Jersey, Caspar Wistar's second glass factory—one specializing in window and bottle glass—begins operations, employing the skills of Belgian glassblowers brought over from Europe. This factory becomes one of the first successful worker cooperatives in the American colonies.

5 AUGUST 1740

Colonial Affairs The new boundary line between the colonies of Massachusetts and New Hampshire, and the new boundary line between Maine and New Hampshire are confirmed by the English government.

16 DECEMBER 1740

External Affairs Frederick II of Prussia invades Silesia after the October death of Emperor Charles VI. The European alliances formed as a result of this action eventually lead to a union of France and Spain against England in King George's War, known in Europe as the War of the Austrian Succession. As was the case with preceding European wars, this war is also waged in the colonial territories of the European combatants.

OTHER EVENTS OF 1740

British Policy The English Parliament passes an act permitting the naturalization of immigrants to the American colonies after seven years of residence. Those who become naturalized citizens of one colony automatically become citizens of the other 12 colonies. Quakers and Jews are to be excepted from the customary oaths.

Settling The famine in Ireland gives an added momentum to Irish immigration to America, mainly to the Shenandoah Valley area, as well as to the colonies of Virginia, Georgia and the Carolinas.

Colonial Affairs The land grants permitted to Georgia settlers by the royal charter of 1732 are increased from 500 to 2000 acres. This gradual liberalization of land restrictions also allows seven-year tenancies on new land. In the same year, three dissident members of the Georgia colony—Hugh Anderson, David Douglass and Patrick Taiffer—publish a book severely critical of the arbitrary leadership of James Edward Oglethorpe entitled *A True and Historical Narrative of the Colony of Georgia*.

Finance The Massachusetts Colony initiates a land bank, which issues notes based on land mortgages. The English Parliament dissolves the bank in 1741.

28 FEBRUARY 1741

Slavery Panic occurs in New York City as a result of a burglary and a series of fires. Rumors rapidly spread throughout the city that the blacks and poor whites are plotting to seize power. Although little real evidence is produced for this theory, 101 blacks are convicted, 4 whites and 18 blacks are hanged, 13 blacks are burned alive and 70 blacks are banished.

1 JUNE 1741

Idea/Beliefs The religious revivalist methods of the Great Awakening cause a schism in the Presbyterian church. The church splits into the Old Side and the New Side, and in time separate synods are organized by each faction. In 1758, the two factions reunite.

OTHER EVENTS OF 1741

Colonial Affairs The English crown grants the colony of New Hampshire its own governor. New Hampshire has shared a governor with the Massachusetts colony since 1682. The first royal governor of New Hampshire is Benning Wentworth.

Settling In the Pennsylvania Colony, a Moravian settlement is founded at Bethlehem on the Lehigh River by immigrants who left the Georgia colony when their settlement there failed. These colonists are joined by a new group of Moravians from Europe led by Count Zinzendorf.

Exploration Sponsored by Russian Tsar Peter the Great, Danish navigator Vitus Bering leads an expedition to survey the coast of Alaska and the Aleutian Islands, opening the territory to Russian fur–traders.

Labor Labor unrest occurs in Boston when the ship–caulkers decide not to accept notes in payment of their salary. In the same year, the journeymen bakers of New York City go on strike.

Industry In this year, the Massachusetts fishing fleet centered in Marblehead numbers 60 boats, while that of Gloucester numbers 70 vessels. The total fishing fleet of all the New England colonies is estimated at some 1000 boats.

OTHER EVENTS OF 1743

War In the War of Jenkins' Ear, in punishment for Spanish raids on Georgia settlements in 1742, Governor James Oglethorpe leads a retaliatory foray against the Florida Spanish settlements around St. Augustine.

Slavery New Jersey itinerant Quaker clergyman John Woolman begins a series of sermons pointing out the evils of slavery and pleading for racial equality. His antislavery ideas are later published in *Some Considerations on the Keeping of Negroes*.

Arts/Culture Inspired by the example of the Royal Society of London, the first official scientific society in the American colonies is founded in Philadelphia by Junto Club members and Benjamin Franklin. The first president of the American Philosophical Society is Thomas Hopkinson and the secretary is Benjamin Franklin. Franklin is to become president of the society in 1769, when the organization is reorganized. He remains president until his death in 1790. Membership in the society is limited to those who have distinguished themselves in the areas of science, philosophy and literature.

Life/Customs Benjamin Franklin has been so successful at his various business ventures of publishing, printing and bookselling that he is able to retire at the age of 37. Henceforth he will devote himself to scientific inquiries and public service.

15 MARCH 1744

External Affairs After signing the Second Family Compact with Spain, France joins the Spanish war effort against England. Known in the American colonies as King George's War, and in Europe as the War of the Austrian Succession, this conflict is to last until 1748. Hostilities between the French and English in the North American colonies are to escalate.

OTHER EVENTS OF 1744

War During the course of King George's War, the French unsuccessfully attack the British garrison at Port Royal, Nova Scotia.

Indians In a treaty negotiated in Lancaster, Pennsylvania, with commissioners from the colonies of Maryland, Pennsylvania and Virginia, the Six Nations of the Iroquois League grant to the English colonies their lands in the northern Ohio territory, a region also claimed by the French.

Westward Movement Pennsylvania fur–traders, led by George Croghan and Conrad Weiser, begin to expand their posts in the Ohio territory.

Arts/Culture Distinguished for the high quality of their church music, the Moravian community of Bethlehem, Pennsylvania, founds a Collegium Musicum for the performance of compositions by Bach, Haydn, Mozart and others. The Moravians have organized a symphony orchestra to perform these works, as well as chamber music groups. This musical society will develop into the Philharmonic Society in 1820. A number of talented composers and musicians rise from the Moravian ranks during the eighteenth century, foremost among whom is John Frederick Peter.

16 JUNE 1745

War During the course of King George's War, a

PIRACY AND PRIVATEERING

The line drawn between piracy and privateering was a tenuous one at best. What in peacetime was considered an act of piracy became privateering—a perfectly legal naval strategy against the enemy—during wartime. The American sealanes were filled with a tempting flow of mercantile traffic that attracted the attentions of pirates, many of whom were former privateers who had continued to ply their trade long after the military exigency had faded. New England's Boston-based Dixey Bull, who had the dubious distinction of being the first American buccaneer, had no claims to the quasi-official status of privateer. Beginning in 1631, his raids terrorized Massachusetts coastal communities. Great Britain began the practice of privateering in American waters during its colonial wars with France and Spain by authorizing the colonial governors to issue letters of marque and reprisal to those daring mariners prepared to capture enemy ships. The captains and crews of the privateering vessels were allowed to split the enemy prizes among themselves. In the era before large national navies, the privateers were a necessary adjunct to military success. During the Revolutionary War, some 1100 privateers operated on the American behalf, seizing a total of 600 British ships, of which 16 were men of war. This activity was so lucrative that the newly established continental navy was sorely pressed to attract experienced recruits for its low–paying positions.

Among the most notorious pirates in the colonial era was the Englishman, Captain William Kidd. Operating from New York, Kidd reportedly turned pirate after he was dispatched on a privateering voyage to capture pirates. The lack of prizes led his crew to mutiny and led Kidd to change his flag. After Kidd was hanged in 1701, legends persisted, as they did for the other pirates, of immense buried treasurers. of equal notoriety was Edward Teach, known as Blackbeard. Blackbeard also was originally an English privateer in Queen Anne's War. At one time, he commanded a group of five ships manned by 400 bloodthirsty cutthroats who preyed on shipping in the West Indies and along the coastline of the American South. Although protected by the Carolina governor in return for a share of the booty, Blackbeard was eventually killed by an expedition initiated by Alexander Spotswood.

During the War of 1812, the United States again made heavy use of privateers against Great Britain. Some 1700 vessels served the American side and, to the fury of the British, even instituted a blockade of the British Isles. The French pirate brothers operating off the Louisiana coast, Jean and Pierre Lafitte, assisted Andrew Jackson at the Battle of New Orleans. For this they were pardoned, but subsequently resumed piracy activities off the Texas coast before they mysteriously disappeared. Piracy in American waters was ended by the United States Navy in 1827. But the United States refused to sign an 1856 international accord banning privateering, and both sides in the Civil War employed privateers. After that the practice died out.

The Siege of Louisbourg, 1745.

AUGUST 1745

War During King George's War, the French and their Indian allies execute a series of raids on the English settlements in the Maine territory.

28-29 NOVEMBER 1745

War During King George's War, the French attack and burn the English settlement at Saratoga in the northern region of the New York colony. They also assault the fort at Albany. These attacks are in retaliation for the activites of New York trader William Johnson who has persuaded the Iroquois Indians to wage war against the French.

OTHER EVENTS OF 1745

Arts/Culture Selections from the essays of French political philosopher Montesquieu are reprinted in various American periodicals; the subsequent reissuing of writings from his *Spirit of the Laws* in the *Boston Gazette* is to have a substantial influence on the content of the American Constitution. Montesquieu advocates a system of checks and balances in government.

By 1745, some 22 newspapers have been established in the American colonies; this contributes considerably to the increase in literacy among colonists.
Indians In Texas, the Franciscan fathers begin the long-term scholarly project of recording the early history of the territory. The Franciscans produce books on missionary techniques, as well as on the ethnography and language of the Texas Indians. This project will conclude in 1763.

28 MAY 1746

Colonial Affairs The English Parliament confirms the boundary between the colonies of Massachusetts and Rhode Island.

OTHER EVENTS OF 1746

Labor In the Georgia Colony, Savannah carpenters strike for better working conditions.

MAY 1747

Education Classes begin at Princeton College. Or-

New England force led by William Pepperell, combined with a fleet commanded by Sir Peter Warren, besieges for six weeks and finally captures the French fortress of Louisbourg on Cape Breton Island. Louisbourg guards the approach to the St. Lawrence.

OTHER EVENTS OF 1748

ganized in Elizabethtown, New Jersey the previous year, the College of New Jersey is founded as a Presbyterian school. During the rest of the 18th century it is to remain a bulwark of conservatism in the face of the schism in the Presbyterian Church. The school is moved to Newark in 1747 and to its final location of Princeton in 1756. This is the fifth of the nine American colleges to be founded before the Revolutionary War.

OTHER EVENTS OF 1747

Westward Movement The Virginia-based Ohio Company is organized by Thomas Lee to open up the western territories to eventual settlement.

Ideas/Beliefs In Boston Jonathan Mayhew, one of the first New England clergymen to dispute the theological doctrine of the Trinity, becomes the pastor of West Church. Mayhew's liberalism and support of Arminianism—which advocates free will, tolerance, and the ability of men to work for their salvation—provoke controversies with the more conservative Jonathan Edwards. The humanistic religious beliefs of Mayhew bring him the support and friendship of James Otis, John Adams and other radical patriots.

Labor In New York City, the first legal society in the American colonies is established with the organization of the New York Bar Association. The bar association is founded by New York attorneys to provide a unified front against the attacks of Lieutenant Governor Cadwallader Colden. Later the New York Bar Association is to lead resistance in the colony to the Stamp Act.

Agriculture The colony of South Carolina sends its first export shipment of indigo to England.

13 MAY 1748

British Policy The English Parliament passes a trade act placing a bounty of six pence per pound on indigo imported from the American colonies.

18 OCTOBER 1748

War The Treaty of Aix-la-Chapelle concludes King George's War and restores the colonies as they were before the war. The fortress of Louisbourg, which guards the approach to the St. Lawrence River, and Cape Breton Island are returned to the French. To alleviate the distress of the New England colonists who fought so hard to capture Louisbourg, the English crown agrees to bear the costs of the expedition. With the outbreak of the French and Indian War only seven years later, it becomes apparent that the Treaty of Aix-la-Chapelle is only a truce.

20 OCTOBER 1748

Westward Movement Led by Hugh Parker and Thomas Cresap, the traders of the Ohio Company reach the Ohio territory.

OTHER EVENTS OF 1748

Westward Movement After expanding their trading

BENJAMIN FRANKLIN, 1706-1790

Benjamin Franklin was the universal man of the 18th century. In Franklin were epitomized the essential features of the Age of Enlightenment—an era characterized by reason, pragmatism, and optimism. The international fame he gained made him the most famous man alive during his last decades. His reputation was based not only on his career as a distinguished scientist and a noted man of letters, but also on his successes as an inventor, statesman and diplomat. His achievements are all the more remarkable since, aside from two years of formal schooling, he was largely self-educated. In later years, his contributions were to bring him honorary degrees from Harvard, Yale and Oxford, among others. Born in Boston the youngest son of the 17 children of candle-maker Josiah Franklin, he was first apprenticed to his father and later to his brother James, a printer. Disagreements with his brother led to his escape to Philadelphia at the age of 17, where he continued in his trade. Franklin was fired by a passion for self-improvement, seen not only in his omniverous reading, his teaching himself of French, Italian and Spanish, and his step-by-step plan to reach moral perfection; but also in his practical inventions, including the lightning rod, bifocals and the Franklin stove; as well as in his initiation of civil and social projects—including a municipal police and fire force, the first circulating library in America, the American Philosophical Society, a city hospital, the University of Pennsylvania and a profitable and efficient national postal system. His success as a businessman—as a printer, a newspaper publisher and the issuer of *Poor Richard's Almanac*—achieved through the application of hard work and thrift, allowed him to retire in 1743 to devote himself to science. His studies of electricity brought him international renown. Although Franklin did not actively seek political office, he felt it his civic duty to serve the public when called to do so. His last 36 years were chiefly given to politics and diplomacy. Among his notable efforts were the presentation of a plan of union at the Albany Congress; his service as a colonial agent in London where he facilitated the repeal of the Stamp Act; his contributions to the second Continental Congress; his diplomatic mission to France to solicit military and financial aid for the revolutionary cause; his important part in the peace negotiations and his participation in the Constitutional Convention. After his 16 years of residence in London and 9 years in Paris, Franklin truly became a citizen of the world. His path through life was eased considerably by an ability to make friends, influential and otherwise; and his wit, skepticism, humanism and commonsense enabled him to communicate effectively with all social levels.

---

posts in the area of the Ohio River valley, the agents for the Pennsylvania legislature, George Croghan and Conrad Weiser, are able to negotiate the loyalty of the Ohio River Valley Indians. In the same year, frontiersmen from the Virginia colony found Draper's Meadows, the first permanent settlement west of the Allegheny Divide.

Indians In order to win over the support of the Iroquois Indians, the French establish a Sulpician mission in the territory of the New York Colony at the site of present-day Ogdensburg.

FOUNDING A NATION 986-1787

1 JANUARY 1749
Colonial Affairs New Hampshire Governor Benning Wentworth makes a land grant for the establishment of the township of Bennington, Vermont. This land area is also claimed by the colony of New York.

16 MARCH 1749
Westward Movement The English Privy Council grants 200,000 acres of land in the territory between the Ohio and the Great Kanawha Rivers and the Allegheny Mountains to the Ohio Company, with the stipulation that this area must be settled and a fort erected.

19 MAY 1749
Westward Movement The Ohio Company receives a royal charter from King George II. The company receives an additional grant of 500,000 acres along the upper Ohio River.

JUNE 1749
Settling The English, who have power over Nova Scotia, claim that their authority in this region also extends to the Gaspe Peninsula and New Brunswick. To solidify these British territorial claims, Lord Halifax dispatches more than 2500 colonists to Nova Scotia to establish the settlement of Halifax.

12 JULY 1749
Westward Movement The Colony of Virginia grants 800,000 acres west of the Virginia-North Carolina border to the Loyal Company. This company was organized by John Lewis and Dr. Thomas Walker, aided by John Robinson, the president of the Virginia council, and his son John.

AUGUST 1749
Arts/Culture In the realm of theatrical arts, Thomas Kean and Walter Murray establish the first American repertory acting company in Philadelphia. The company is to present Elizabethan plays as well as more contemporary works by English dramatists such as Addison, Congreve and Dryden in New York, Williamsburg, Fredericksburg and Annapolis. The premiere performance of the company stars Kean in the title role of *Richard III*.

26 OCTOBER 1749
Slavery With the permission of the English Parliament, the trustees of the Georgia colony revoke their prohibition on slavery in the colony, in effect since the founding of the Georgia colony. This move of Parliament marks the legal recognition of slavery in the colonies and the inauguration of the plantation system in the South. In addition, the Georgia legislature passes a stipulation requiring a ratio of four black males to each white servant.

13 NOVEMBER 1749
Education In the Pennsylvania Colony, an academy is established in Philadelphia by 24 of the city's leading citizens. The founding of this educational institution has been suggested by a pamphlet on education by Benjamin Franklin, who is subsequently chosen the first president of the trustees. The Pennsylvania proprietors donate $15,000 to the school in 1753 and two years later it is reorganized as the College, Academy, and Charitable School of Philadelphia. The University of Pennsylvania will eventually develop from this school.

OTHER EVENTS OF 1749
Westward Movement Alarmed by the English incursions into the Ohio River Valley, the French fortify their settlement at Toronto; and they also dispatch Celeron de Bienville from Lake Erie to reclaim the Ohio River Valley for the French. During his southward expedition, de Bienville erects lead plates documenting the claims of the French at the mouth of each major river.
Agriculture Such a severe drought occurs in the New England colonies that they are forced to import hay for their livestock from Pennsylvania and even from England.

22 JUNE 1750
Ideas/Beliefs In Massachusetts, clergyman Jonathan Edwards is dismissed from his Northampton church when he decides to reject the liberal halfway covenant. He travels westward to the frontier town of Stockbridge where he becomes pastor to a small group of settlers and also a missionary to the indigenous Indians.

OTHER EVENTS OF 1750
British Policy The English Parliament passes the Iron Act which bans the construction of rolling and sheeting mills, steel furnaces, and tilt–hammer forges in the American colonies. This act also permits the duty-free export of American pig and bar iron into England under certain conditions. This act is designed to limit the growth of the iron-finishing industry in the colonies, which would compete with the English iron industry. The act also seeks to ensure a steady supply of colonial pig and bar iron the English iron and steel industry.
Settling By this time the interior of Connecticut and Massachusetts are so fully settled that expansion now turns toward the north; in the years preceding the Revolutionary War some 94 new towns are founded in Maine, 100 in New Hampshire, and 74 in Vermont. All the best lands are also taken in New York, so the immigration originally directed to this area now veers to Pennsylvania and to the southern colonies.
Westward Movement The Virginia-based Ohio Company dispatches frontiersman and Indian trader Christopher Gist to survey its new holdings along the upper Ohio River. Gist explores as far west as Pickawillany. This westward movement results in the construction of a trading post at Cumberland, Maryland. Gist will also penetrate the Kentucky region some 18 years before Daniel Boone, guide George Washington

to the Ohio Valley to confront the French, and lead General Braddock to Fort Duquesne. In the same year, Thomas Walker passes through and names the Cumberland Gap on his way toward the Kentucky region.

Transportation Pennsylvania colonist Jacob Yoder develops a flatboat for the transportation of goods and passengers along the inland waterways. During this decade, the Conestoga wagon, which is suitable for frontier travel, first makes its appearance in the Pennsylvania colony. Both modes of travel will facilitate the settlement of western territories.

Industry A considerable candle-making industry is initiated in the Rhode Island colony. The candles are made of spermaceti supplied by the flourishing colonial whaling industry.

MARCH 1751

Colonial Affairs While a member of the Pennsylvania Assembly, Benjamin Franklin draws up a plan to unite the English colonies of New England, New York, Pennsylvania and Maryland. The plan will be presented officially before colonial authorities at the Albany Congress of 1754.

OTHER EVENTS OF 1751

British Policy The English parliament passes the Currency Act, which bans the New England colonies from issuing paper money.

Settling A group of German Moravians buys 100,000 acres of North Carolina land near the Yadkin River. Scottish-Irish immigrants settle along the western foothills of the Appalachian Mountains and erect posts along the rivers flowing into the Tennessee River.

13 JUNE 1752

Indians The Treaty of Logstown, enacted between the colony of Virginia and the Delaware and Iroquois Indians, claims for Virginia the territory south of the Ohio River. The pact also permits the Ohio Company to erect a fort in the territory under consideration and to settle the region.

4 JULY 1752

British Policy The trustees of the Georgia Colony convene for their last meeting. After this final session, the authority over the colony passes to the English crown and Georgia officially becomes a royal colony.

JULY 1752

Westward Movement In an attempt to gain back control over the Ohio River valley, the French attack and overcome the English trading post of Pickawillany.

OTHER EVENTS OF 1752

Westward Movement Fur trader John Finley travels downstream along the Ohio River as far as Louisville, and then explores the Kentucky territory.

Life/Customs Pennsylvania Hospital, the first general hospital in the colonies, is founded in Phila-

delphia by Thomas Bond. Before 1752, pesthouses had been established in Boston (1717), Philadelphia and Charlestown.

APRIL 1753

Westward Movement In an attempt to strengthen the French hold on the Ohio River valley, the New governor of Canada, Marquis Duquesne de Menneville, mandates the erection of Fort Presque Isle at present-day Erie, Pennsylvania; Fort Le Boeuf at the portage to French Creek; and Fort Venango at the fork of French Creek and the Allegheny River.

10 SEPTEMBER 1753

Indians At the Winchester Conference, the Indians revoke the 1752 Treaty of Logstown with Virginia, permitting land and settlement rights to English colonists south of the Ohio River. Instead, the Delaware and Iroquois Indians join forces with the French, who also lay claim to the Ohio territory.

31 OCTOBER 1753

Westward Movement Apprehensive over the new French fortifications in the Ohio territory, Virginia Lieutenant Governor Robert Dinwiddie sends 21-year-old George Washington to determine French intentions and to formally protest the French erection of the forts. Guided by frontiersman Christopher Gist, Washington travels to Fort Venango and Fort le Boeuf. He does not return to Virginia until January 1754 to report his findings.

12 DECEMBER 1753

Westward Movement After a two-week trek from Virginia into the Ohio territory, George Washington delivers the demand of Virginia Lieutenant Governor Dinwiddie that the French withdraw from the Ohio River valley to the French commander at Fort le Boeuf. The French disregard this demand.

OTHER EVENTS OF 1753

Colonial Affairs Benjamin Franklin and William Hunter are appointed joint postmasters general for the American colonies. Franklin and Hunter are able to increase the efficiency of the colonial postal system. Franklin will remain in this office until 1774.

Westward Movement As allowed in the Treaty of Logstown, Ohio Company representative Christopher

Baltimore in 1752.

FOUNDING A NATION 986-1787

Gist cuts a road through the wilderness to Red Stone Creek on the Monongahela River. He encourages 11 other families to accompany him to establish a new settlement along Red Stone Creek. A group of Bethlehem, Pennsylvania, Moravians settles a large land tract in the western foothills of North Carolina.

JANUARY 1754
Westward Movement George Washington returns to Virginia from his mission to the French forts in the Ohio River valley area. In his report to Lieutenant Governor Robert Dinwiddie he states that the French are determined to claim the Ohio territory and that they will resist removal with military force.

FEBRUARY 1754
Westward Movement To resist French claims in the Ohio River valley, Dinwiddie orders Captain William Trent to erect a fort at the fork of the Allegheny and Monongahela Rivers. The French capture that location and instead build their own Fort Duquesne there.

17 APRIL 1754
War The French capture the forks of the Ohio River, ending the attempts of English settlers to colonize the Ohio territory for the duration of the French and Indian War.

28 MAY 1754
War In the opening salvos of the French and Indian War (1754-1763), known in Europe as the Seven Year's War, George Washington leads 150 Virginians to victory over a French exploratory party while en route to occupy the new French Fort Duquesne. Washington erects Fort Necessity at Great Meadows and, aided by reinforcements, fights off a larger French military force led by Coulon de Villiers.

24 JUNE 1754
War At the Albany Congress called during the French and Indian War to negotiate a treaty with the Iroquois Indians against the French, the delegates from the New England colonies, Pennsylvania, Maryland, and New York hear the proposal of Pennsylvania delegate Benjamin Franklin that they consider his plan for a union of the English colonies in America.

3 JULY 1754
War In the French and Indian War, George Washington is finally forced to surrender Fort Necessity in the Ohio territory to the numerically superior French forces led by Coulon de Villiers.

10 JULY 1754
Colonial Affairs The colonial delegates at the Albany Congress approve Benjamin Franklin's "Plan of the Union," with amendments by Thomas Hutchinson of Massachusetts. This plan proposes a union of all American English colonies, excluding Georgia and Nova Scotia, under one president general named and salaried by the English Crown. A grand council elected by the individual colonial assemblies is to have

Washington's retreat from Great Meadows, 1754.

legislative power, subject to the approval of the president general and the English crown. The president and council are to have authority over new land purchases and Indian relations. When this plan is later presented to the individual colonial assemblies and to England, it is rejected by them.

9 AUGUST 1754
British Policy In response to the "Plan of the Union" passed by the Albany Congress, the English Board of Trade proposes a looser union, with one commander-in-chief for the English colonies and a commissioner of Indian affairs.

OTHER EVENTS OF 1754
Westward Movement The Connecticut-based Susquehanna Company buys a large tract of land in the Wyoming Valley on the upper Susquehanna River from the Six Nations of the Iroquois League. This territory is also claimed by the heirs of William Penn.
Education Chartered by King George II, King's College is founded in New York, the sixth of the nine colleges to be established before the Revolutionary War. Dr. Samuel Johnson serves as the first president and tutor of the college. The school suspends activities during the revolutionary years and then reopens in 1784 as Columbia College.

20 FEBRUARY 1755
War English General Edward Braddock, accompanied by two regiments of English troops, arrives in Virginia to assume the post of commander-in-chief of all the English forces in the American colonies. Soon after his arrival, General Braddock arranges a conference of the royal governors of Maryland, Massachusetts, North Carolina, New York, Pennsylvania and Virginia in Alexandria, Virginia, in order to develop a common strategy for an attack on the French forts at Crown Point, Duquesne, Niagara and Nova Scotia.

14 APRIL 1755
War Leading 1400 English soldiers, General Brad-

dock sets out, accompanied by Lieutenant Colonel George Washington at the head of 450 colonial soldiers, for Fort Duquesne to challenge the French in the Ohio territory. In an attempt to win over the Indians to the English cause, Braddock has appointed Sir William Johnson as Indian commissioner.

6-13 JUNE 1755
War English Admiral Edward Boscawen forms a naval blockade against the French. But the French fleet bringing reinforcements is able to slip through and to resupply the French forces with goods and men. This delays the planned foray against the French Fort Niagara led by Massachusetts Governor William Shirley.

19 JUNE 1755
War Colonels Robert Monckton and John Winslow lead 2000 New England colonists and some British soldiers against the French Fort Beauséjour in Nova Scotia. After a two-week siege, the English forces capture the fort.

30 JUNE 1755
War By this date, the territory surrounding the Bay of Fundy is under the control of English forces.

JUNE 1755
War General Braddock has a road cut through the wilderness from Fort Cumberland to the Monongahela River to accommodate the advance of the English troops against the positions of the French in the Ohio territory.

9 JULY 1755
War The combined English forces under General Braddock and colonial forces under Lieutenant Colonel Washington meet a force of some 900 French and Indians eight miles from Fort Duquesne, in the Ohio Territory. The French and Indians surround the British forces and defeat them in the Battle of the Wilderness. Braddock is mortally wounded and Washington leads the survivors back to Fort Cumberland. Massachusetts Governor William Shirley replaces Braddock as commander-in-chief of the English forces. This defeat also drives the early English settlers on the Monongahela River back east again.

5 SEPTEMBER 1755
War The governor of Nova Scotia, Colonel Charles Lawrence, orders all those Acadians who refuse to swear allegiance to the English Crown expelled from the colony. He fears they will support the French.

8 SEPTEMBER 1755
War Leading a force of some 3500 mostly New England colonists and 400 Indians, Sir William Johnson has been able rapidly to erect Fort William Henry on Lake George, to meet the expected French attack. In the Battle of Lake George, the forces led by Johnson defeat 1400 French and Indians led by Baron Dieskau. Johnson is unable to proceed to the planned

target of Crown Point because of poor morale among his men. In spite of his failure to capture Crown Point, Johnson has succeeded in turning away the French at the boundaries of the English colonies.

8 OCTOBER 1755
War Some 6000 Nova Scotia Acadians who have refused to take a loyalty oath to the English Crown begin to leave their homes. They are eventually distributed among the 13 colonies to the south. Their settlements around the Bay of Fundy are razed by the English. Eventually a considerable number of Acadians find their way back to Nova Scotia.

24 OCTOBER 1755
War Massachusetts Governor Shirley abandons his attempt to conquer the French fort at Niagara. Shirley leaves behind a garrison of 700 men at Oswego.

OCTOBER 1755
Agriculture In the Virginia colony, the tobacco crop fails because of extended drought conditions. Since 1662, tobacco shares have been used to pay Anglican clergymen. The amount of tobacco salary has been attuned to market prices. Now the colonial legislature changes the medium of salary into currency. The clergy are to object, and the English Privy Council will uphold their objection in 1759.

DECEMBER 1755
War As a protection against Indian attacks out of French Fort Duquesne, the colonial assemblies are persuaded by George Washington to construct a series of forts from the Potomac River across the headwaters of the James River and the Roanoke River to Fort Prince George in South Carolina.

OTHER EVENTS OF 1755
Ideas/Beliefs Rather than vote funds for military defense, some Quaker delegates withdraw from the Pennsylvania legislative assembly.

9 JANUARY 1756
Indians Peter Wraxhall, secretary to Indian commissioner Sir William Johnson, advocates that all future land transfers from Indians to colonists require the approval of the Indian commissioner. This advice reflects the belief of Wraxhall and Johnson that land frauds are the main cause of Indian turmoil.

16 JANUARY 1756
External Affairs The French and Indian War, or the Seven Years War, spreads to Europe with the formation of a new pact between England and Prussia.

APRIL 1756
Indians Sir William Johnson, appointed Indian commissioner in April 1755 by General Braddock, is reappointed in this position as Commissioner for the North, or the New England Indians.

1 MAY 1756
External Affairs In response to the recent English

and Prussian alliance, the French negotiate a pact with Austria.

11 MAY 1756
War Louis Joseph, Marquis de Montcalm, arrives in Canada to command the French forces.

15 MAY 1756
External Affairs The English declare war on France, initiating the European stage of the French and Indian War, the Seven Years War.

23 JULY 1756
War John Campbell, Earl of Loudoun, arrives in the American colonies to lead the British forces against the French, now commanded by Montcalm.

14 AUGUST 1756
War Montcalm successfully leads the French forces against the English forts of Oswego and George, and destroys them.

31 AUGUST 1756
War General Webb is forced to give up the Mohawk Valley to the numerically superior French forces. The settlers in this area relocate to Schenectady and Albany.

OTHER EVENTS OF 1756
British Policy The English Admiralty invokes the Rule of 1756, which asserts that neutral parties may not be permitted to carry on trade during wartime that is forbidden to them in peacetime.

Settling Philadelphia merchant Samuel Hazard and surveyor Lewis Evans suggest the establishment of a new colony in the Ohio territory. This proposal is superseded by that of Benjamin Franklin—namely, that the English Crown found two new colonies, one south of Lake Erie and the other on the banks of the Scioto River.

29 JUNE 1757
War William Pitt is chosen Britain's Secretary of State, and in order to deal with the lack of English success in the French and Indian War, he establishes a policy of unlimited warfare, of reinforcements to the American colonists, and of financial subsidies to England's European allies. This policy leads to rapidly increasing taxes and of governmental borrowing to support the war effort.

27 JULY 1757
Colonial Affairs Benjamin Franklin arrives for a five-year stay in London. He is present in the British capital as an agent for the Pennsylvania assembly.

JULY 1757
Westward Movement English colonists erect Fort Loudoun on the Little Tennessee River. This post is intended to serve as an advance settlement to facilitate friendly relations with the Cherokee and Creek Indians.

9 AUGUST 1757
War French forces under Montcalm capture and burn the English Fort William Henry on Lake George. The English commander of the forces stationed there, Lieutenant Colonel George Munro, surrenders to the French only to be attacked by the Indians. Munro is able to lead some 1400 survivors to safety at Fort Edward.

OTHER EVENTS OF 1757
British Policy The English Parliament amends the Iron Act of 1750 to allow the unrestricted duty-free import of American colonial bar and pig iron into England.

MAY 1758
Indians The Cherokee Indians begin a series of raids on settlements located in the Virginia Colony's frontier region. These raids continue for over a year and they are countered with retaliatory raids by the settlers.

30 JUNE 1758
War Commander of the English forces, the Earl of Loudoun, gathers a large military force at Halifax in preparation for an attack on the French fortress at Louisbourg. This move is ordered by British Secretary of State William Pitt. When Loudoun hears that the French Navy has arrived at Louisbourg, he gives up the attack plan. In addition to this setback in Halifax, Loudoun's efforts are also discouraged by the failure of the colonial assemblies to provide support for the war effort.

1 JULY 1758
War James Abercromby, who has replaced Loudoun as the leader of the English forces in America, gathers some 12,000 soldiers at Lake George in preparation for an attack on French Fort Ticonderoga. To defend the fort, French commander Montcalm, leading only 3000 men, decides on the strategy of constructing barricades to defend the ridge outside the fort. Abercrombly leads a frontal attack and meets with a devastating defeat. The French lose only 377 men to the 1944 lost by the British.

26 JULY 1758
War A force of 9000 English soldiers and 500 colonists led by Major General Jeffrey Amherst and Brigadier General James Wolfe, on a fleet of 40 ships commanded by Admiral Edward Boscawen, attacks and is able to capture the French fortress of Louisbourg, which protects the approach into the St. Lawrence River.

27 AUGUST 1758
War English forces led by Colonel John Bradstreet capture the French Fort Frontenac at the site of present-day Kingston, Ontario.

AUGUST 1758
Indians The New Jersey colonial assembly founds

the first Indian reservation in the American colonies. Established on a 3000-acre tract at the present-day village of Indian Mills in Burlington County, the reservation of Edge Pillock becomes home to some 100 Unami Indians who try to develop a self-supporting community.

18 SEPTEMBER 1758
War After his resounding defeat by Montcalm at Fort Ticonderoga, English commander James Abercromby is removed from authority and replaced by Major General Jeffrey Amherst, the victor at Louisbourg.

24 SEPTEMBER 1758
War The British naval force bringing reinforcements to the beleaguered English forces is destroyed en route by a hurricane.

OCTOBER 1758
Indians The Pennsylvania Colony negotiates the Treaty of Easton with the Indians in the western region of the colony. According to this agreement, Pennsylvania will not found any new settlements west of the Allegheny Mountains.

25 NOVEMBER 1758
War The French are forced to blow up their own post at Fort Duquesne when Brigadier General John Forbes approaches on a newly-constructed road from the southeast. When the news of the French abandonment of Fort Duquesne reaches the colonies, settlers defy the Treaty of Easton and throng the military roads cut through the wilderness to reach the Monongahela and Youghiogheny Valleys, where they intend to establish new homes.

OTHER EVENTS OF 1758
Education In Philadelphia, a school for blacks is founded by an Anglican missionary group named the Associates of Dr. Bray. This group is closely related to the Society for the Propagation of the Gospel in Foreign Parts. In the same year, Jonathan Edwards becomes president of the College of New Jersey, later Princeton University.

28 MAY 1759
War English Rear Admiral Durell lands a troop of soldiers on the Île-aux-Coudres in the St. Lawrence River in preparation for General Wolfe's advance up the river with the main body of soldiers.

16 JUNE 1759
War General James Wolfe, leading a force of some 9000 men, sails in a fleet commanded by Rear Admiral Charles Saunders up the St. Lawrence River.

25 JUNE 1759
War The English troops led by Rear Admiral Durell advance to the Île d'Orleans in the St. Lawrence River near Quebec to await the arrival of the main force led by General Wolfe.

27 JUNE 1759
War General Wolfe arrives and lands part of his men on the Île d'Orleans, and sends some under Colonel Robert Monckton to Pointe Levis across the river from Quebec.

9 JULY 1759
War General Wolfe sends Brigadier General George Townshend to occupy the north shore of the St. Lawrence River above Quebec.

25 JULY 1759
War A force of 2000 English soldiers led by Brigadier General John Prideaux and 100 Iroquois Indians led by Sir William Johnson capture the French Fort Niagara. This successfully completes the first stage of the strategy planned by England's William Pitt. After the capture of Fort Niagara, new settlers pour into the region.

26 JULY 1759
War General Amherst leads a numerically superior English force against the French Fort Carillon at Ticonderoga, and the French are forced to blow up their own fort to prevent it from falling into English hands.

27 JULY 1759
War French commander Montcalm attempts but fails to burn the British fleet anchored near Quebec.

31 JULY 1759
War Outnumbered by the English forces led by Amherst, the French blow up their Fort St. Frederick at Crown Point and retreat down the Richelieu River. On the same day, the English forces of General Wolfe unsuccessfully attempt to storm the French position at Quebec.

10 AUGUST 1759
Colonial Affairs The English Privy Council disallows the Virginia Act of 1755, reenacted in 1758, transforming the salary of Anglican clergymen from tobacco, because of crop failure, into currency. This action of the Privy Council has been instigated by the objections of the clergy. This revocation leads some clergy to sue for back pay. The most famous case is that of James Maury in November 1763; although the judge will disallow the 1758 act, the jury is impressed by the logic and eloquence of his attorney, Patrick Henry.

25 AUGUST 1759
War At Quebec, British General James Wolfe sends a force led by Brigadier General James Murray to attack the French forces above Quebec; when they return unsuccessful, he decides to lead the main attack himself.

12-13 SEPTEMBER 1759
War At Quebec, General Wolfe secretly ferries his troops in small boats during the night, so that they can scale the cliffs of the Plains of Abraham. Instead of waiting for reinforcements, French leader

FOUNDING A NATION 986-1787

Montcalm decides to lead his force of 4500 against the English force of 9000 commanded by Wolfe. The English win the battle and both Wolfe and Montcalm are killed.

18 SEPTEMBER 1759
War After losing the battle of the Plains of Abraham, Quebec surrenders to the English.

OCTOBER 1759
Indians The Cherokee Indian war begins in the southern colonies. These hostilities will extend into 1761.

26 DECEMBER 1759
Indians In an attempt to end the Indian raids on frontier settlements, South Carolina Governor Lyttleton negotiates a peace treaty with the Cherokee Indians. In this pact, the Indians are to deliver those individual responsible for the raids.

19 JANUARY 1760
War Cherokee Indians unsuccessfully attack Fort Prince George in South Carolina to rescue Indians held hostage by Governor Lyttleton to ensure compliance with the conditions of the peace treaty concluded in December 1759. Frustrated by the failure of their attack, the Indians resume their raids on the southwestern frontier settlements.

16 FEBRUARY 1760
War The Indian hostages held in Fort Prince George by South Carolina Governor Lyttleton are slain in retaliation for the renewed raids of the Cherokees, thus breaking the peace treaty of December 1759. This action on the part of the colonists leads to a renewal of the devastating attacks on the western settlements.

20 MARCH 1760
Life/Customs A severe fire rages out of control through the city of Boston.

1 APRIL 1760
War In the French and Indian War, General Jeffrey Amherst sends aid to the beleaguered forts protecting the western frontier of Virginia and the Carolina colonies. The relief is of little help, and the ferocious Indian attacks continue unabated.

28 APRIL 1760
War In a second battle on the Plains of Abraham at Quebec, the French forces are victorious over the British. The defeated British under General James Murray withdraw into the city of Quebec, which they manage to hold until the arrival of the British fleet.

16 MAY 1760
War English reinforcements arrive at Quebec, causing the French forces to withdraw.

7 AUGUST 1760
War Isolated by the relentless Indian raids on the western settlements, the English garrison at Fort Loudoun on the Little Tennessee River undergoes a period of starvation and finally surrenders to its Indian attackers.

10 AUGUST 1760
War The defeated English troops from Fort Loudoun, led by Captain Demere, are massacred while on the march back to safety at Fort Prince George.

1 SEPTEMBER 1760
War British forces led by William Haviland march north from Crown Point on Lake Champlain to seize the French post of Chambly.

6 SEPTEMBER 1760
War The English forces led by General Amherst arrive from Lake Ontario at Lachine, in preparation for the final attack on the French at Montreal.

8 SEPTEMBER 1760
War Faced at Montreal with the massed English forces, now joined by a detachment led by Governor James Murray, the Governor of Canada, Pierre Francois de Rigaud, Marquis de Vaudreuil, surrenders the province of Quebec, or New France, to the English.

26 OCTOBER 1760
External Affairs George III becomes king of England.

29 NOVEMBER 1760
War The French outpost of Detroit is surrendered by its commander Beletre to English forces led by Major Robert Rogers. The Indians of the region subsequently ask the English to drop the prices on goods traded to the Indians and to supply them with ammunition.

OTHER EVENTS OF 1760
Population The population of the 13 colonies is estimated at 1,600,000.
Slavery The South Carolina legislature completely bans the slave trade within the boundaries of the colony. This policy is disallowed by the English crown.
Industry The shipbuilding industry continues to flourish in the American colonies, as by this year one-third of the total English shipping stock has been constructed in America. It is possible to build ships in the colonies at 20 to 50 percent below European shipbuilding costs.
Arts/Culture Pennsylvania-born history painter Benjamin West travels to Italy to study art. He is the first of a stream of American artists to sample the cultural amenities of Europe. After three years in Italy, West settles in London where King George III becomes his patron. In London West welcomes and encourages American artists studying abroad. The greatest of the colonial and federal period artists enjoy the considerable benefits of West's sponsorship and technical guid-

ance. Among them are Ralph Earl, Gilbert Stuart, John Singleton Copley, John Trumbull, Thomas Sully, Charles Wilson Peale, Washington Allston and Samuel Morse.

24 FEBRUARY 1761

Revolution: Approach Boston lawyer James Otis delivers a rousing speech before the Massachusetts superior court, questioning the constitutionality of the writs of assistance, or general search warrants, allowed to customs officials by the colonial courts in 1751.

MAY 1761

Colonial Affairs James Otis is elected to the Massachusetts general court.

9 SEPTEMBER 1761

Indians In a conference with the Indians at Detroit, the English refuse to acquiesce to their demand that the English supply the Indians with ammunition and with lower-priced trade goods. This stubborn policy of the British is to lead to further conflict with the Indians who are fired by the Delaware Prophet, an Indian mystic of the upper Ohio River region. These hostilities will culminate in the rebellion led by Pontiac, chief of the Ottawa Indians.

13 OCTOBER 1761

Westward Movement English Colonel Henry Bouquet issues a proclamation banning any new settlement west of the Allegheny Mountains. The intent of this order is to enforce the terms of the 1758 Treaty of Easton between the colony of Pennsylvania and the western Pennsylvania Indians, in which Pennsylvania agreed not to settle the western territory. But the capture of Fort Duquesne from the French by the British in November 1758 had led to an influx of settlers into the region, in disregard of the Treaty of Easton.

2 DECEMBER 1761

British Policy The English Secretary of State for the Southern Department, Lord Egremont, issues a declaration requiring royal approval of all land grants within present Indian territory.

9 DECEMBER 1761

British Policy The English government issues a decree that American colonial judgeship appointments are subject to the approval of the crown.

OTHER EVENTS OF 1761

War English Colonel Grant ends the series of devastating Indian raids on the western frontier settlements of the southern colonies by forcing the Cherokee Indians to seek peace.
Slavery The English Crown disallows the Virginia-mandated duty increase on imported slaves.

2 JANUARY 1762

External Affairs During the course of the Seven Years War, England declares war on Spain, who is preparing to ally herself with the French and Austrians.

15 FEBRUARY 1762

War The British conquer Fort Martinique, the main French port in the West Indies, and then St. Lucia and Grenada. Later in the year, Britain will also overrun the Spanish colonial outposts of Cuba and of Manila in the Philippines.

12 AUGUST 1762

War After a two-month siege of Havana by British forces, the Spanish Cuban colony finally surrenders.

3 NOVEMBER 1762

War In the secret Treaty of Fontainebleau, French monarch Louis XV deeds to Spain all French territory west of the Mississippi River and the Isle of Orleans in Louisiana to compensate Spain for her losses at the hands of the British. The French are anxious to bring an early end to the Seven Years War. On the same day, France signs a preliminary peace pact with the English at Fontainebleau.

OTHER EVENTS OF 1762

Revolution: Approach Boston Lawyer James Otis issues his first political tract, *A Vindication of the Conduct of the House of Representatives* (Massachusetts), in which he enumerates the legal rights of the American colonies as provided for in the British constitution.
Transportation The Pennsylvania colonial government has the route surveyed for a proposed canal from the Susquehanna River at Middletown to the Schuylkill River at Reading. This canal is intended to open up trade with the gradually expanding western territories. Such trade might otherwise go to Baltimore. This ambitious public works project is delayed until 1791.
Western Movement After receiving a charter from the Connecticut Colony, the Susquehanna Company commences to settle the territory of Pennsylvania's Wyoming Valley, in spite of the protests of the Pennsylvania colony.

10 FEBRUARY 1763

War The Treaty of Paris concludes the colonial and European phases of the Seven Years War. Under this pact, France gives up Acadia (Nova Scotia), Cape Breton, the St. Lawrence River islands and Canada to the British. France is allowed to maintain fishing rights off Newfoundland and to keep the islands of St. Pierre and Miquelon. In addition, France gives to England all her territory east of the Mississippi River, excluding the city of New Orleans. In return, the French get back their Caribbean islands of Guadeloupe, Martinique and St. Lucia. Spain is given back Cuba, in return for her territory in East and West Florida.

7 MAY 1763

Indians The secret plan of Pontiac, chief of the Ottawa Indians, to seize Detroit from the British with a surprise attack, is betrayed. This leads Pontiac to elect the path of all-out warfare, with devastating effects for the British garrisons west of Niagara—the Indians destroy them all by late June. This active hostility of the Indians is the immediate result of the British refusal to agree to the demands of the Indians for lower-priced trade goods and for ammunition.

16 MAY 1763
War The western British garrison of Fort Sandusky is destroyed by the rebellious Indian forces led by Chief Pontiac.

25 MAY 1763
War A second British western post, Fort Saint Joseph, is destroyed by Pontiac's forces.

27 MAY 1763
War The British western force of Fort Miami is destroyed by the Indian forces of Chief Pontiac.

1 JUNE 1763
War The British western garrison of Fort Ouiatenon is destroyed by the rebellious forces of Chief Pontiac.

8 JUNE 1763
British Policy After the Treaty of Paris, the head of the British Board of Trade, William Petty, Lord Shelburne, is appointed the task of developing a policy for dealing with the American territories gained from France. Shelburne formulates a strategy that sets the Appalachian Mountains as a dividing line between colonial settlements and an Indian reservation. The sole exception to this boundary is a settlement planned for the upper Ohio River area. Some Indian settlement is to be allowed east of this demarcation line. Three new colonies are to be established in the recently gained territory—Quebec, East Florida and West Florida.

16 JUNE 1763
War The British western garrison of Fort Venango is destroyed by the forces of Chief Pontiac.

18 JUNE 1763
War The western English post of Fort Le Boeuf is destroyed by rebellious Indians led by Chief Pontiac.

20 JUNE 1763
War The western British garrison of Fort Duquesne is destroyed by Chief Pontiac's followers.

13 JULY 1763
War General Jeffrey Amherst suggests to Colonel Henry Bouquet that the Indian rebellion led by Chief Pontiac can be countered by spreading smallpox among the Indians by means of infected blankets. Bouquet points out that this stratagem might also prove dangerous to English soldiers.

29 JULY 1763
War British troops arrive to reinforce the besieged

English garrison at Detroit under the command of Major Henry Gladwin. Detroit is able to resist the rebellious Indian forces of Chief Pontiac for some five months.

31 JULY 1763
War At the Battle of Bloody Ridge, English forces led by Major Henry Gladwin out of Detroit are turned back by the rebellious Indian forces led by Chief Pontiac.

2-6 AUGUST 1763
War At Bushy Run near present-day Pittsburgh, Pennsylvania, Colonel Henry Bouquet attacks and defeats the rebellious Indian forces of Pontiac, who have been besieging Fort Pitt. On 10 August Bouquet is able to relieve the garrison at Fort Pitt.

2 SEPTEMBER 1763
British Policy The English government replaces Lord Shelburne, who had been named to formulate a policy for the newly-acquired territory in the American colonies, with the Earl of Hillsborough. This action by the government is influenced by word of renewed Indian discontent and is motivated by a desire to avoid further conflict with the Indians.

9 SEPTEMBER 1763
Westward Movement The Mississippi Company, led by George Washington, requests the English crown to grant it 2.5 million acres in the area of the fork of the Ohio and Mississippi Rivers. This land is to go to Virginia militia members as bounty grants to repay them for service in the French and Indian War.

7 OCTOBER 1763
British Policy King George III of England signs the Proclamation of 1763. This document is an amended version of the earlier Shelburne plan for the disposition of newly-acquired American territories, revised somewhat by Shelburne's successor, the Earl of Hillsborough. This more restrictive version not only disallows any English settlement west of the demarcation line of the Appalachian Mountains, but also requires all colonists already settled in those regions to return east; any purchase of Indian land west of the Appalachians is strictly forbidden; and a military commander is to govern the Indian territory. The same document also establishes English law as the governing judicial code in Quebec. The French settlers there consider this an arbitrary and inequitable measure.

5 NOVEMBER 1763
Colonial Affairs Patrick Henry is the attorney for the defense in the case of Virginia clergyman James Maury, who is suing the Virginia colony for back pay based on the proposition that the Virginia Act of 1758, replacing Anglican clergymen's original pay of tobacco with currency, is null and void. By the eloquence of his rhetoric and the logic of his arguments, Henry sways the jury to his side, against the advice of the judge. During the course of the trial, Henry pre-

sents the theory of a mutual compact between the governed and the ruler—a compact that has been broken by the actions of the ruler, who consequently loses all right to claim the loyalty of his subjects.

NOVEMBER 1763
War Chief Pontiac ends his unsuccessful five-month siege of the British garrison at Detroit.

13 DECEMBER 1763
Indians A mob of settlers from Donegal and Paxton, Pennsylvania, attack the non-belligerent Indians of Lancaster County. The settlers have been motivated to this extreme action by the persistent attacks by Indians on the frontier settlements of the Pennsylvania colony in the face of legislative inaction and a failure to provide protection to the frontiersmen. The Pennsylvania assembly mandates the arrest of the "Paxton Boys" and their Philadelphia trial. The rebellious frontiersmen ignore the order and begin a march east. Benjamin Franklin defuses the crisis by convincing the Paxton Boys to drop any idea of doing battle, in favor of posting a formal protest. By taking this action, they are to receive greater proportional representation for the western settlements in the Pennsylvania legislature, thus resulting in greater governmental attention to their needs.

DECEMBER 1763
Colonial Affairs An organization of Suffering Traders is created by Indian commissioner Sir William Johnson's agent George Croghan and two Pennsylvania merchant companies to procure compensation for losses suffered from Indian raids. This group is later to organize the Illinois Company and the Indian Company.

OTHER EVENTS OF 1763
British Policy The English Parliament reduces the bounties on indigo, a staple crop of the southern colonies and a dye used in the woolen industry.
Colonial Affairs The Indiana Company is formed as a result of the activities of the "Suffering Traders." This company lasts until 1767. In the same year, the four-year task of surveying the boundary line between Pennsylvania and Maryland is begun by Jeremiah Dixon and Charles Mason, English astronomers. Indicated by a series of milestones, this boundary will be known as the Mason and Dixon Line.

5 APRIL 1764
British Policy The Sugar Act, known in Parliament as the American Revenue Act, is passed in England. The earlier British trade acts, including the Hat, Wool and Iron Acts, were designed essentially to protect British commerce from colonial competition—creating in effect a monopoly for British industry. Enforcement of these trade acts has been at best sporadic and at worst impossible. The Sugar Act is notable in that it marks the end of a strictly commercial British relationship with her American colonies and initiates a policy of raising revenue. At this time England is car-

rying a large war debt from the French and Indian War; the Sugar Act seeks to alleviate the expenses of administering a greatly enlarged colonial territory. Specifically, the Sugar Act imposes new or higher duties on additional imports, including textiles, coffee, indigo and wines; it increases duties on foreign refined sugar. The act also doubles the duties on foreign trade goods reshipped to the colonies from England; adds additional goods to the list of enumerated items; and forbids the import of French wines and foreign rum. This act and other legislation enacted at the same time become known as the Grenville Acts, named after the British Chancellor of the Exchequer. On the same date, another Grenville measure is passed to reorganize the inefficient American customs system so that the trade laws can be enforced effectively. This act institutes a vice admiralty court in Halifax, Nova Scotia, with jurisdiction over all of the American colonies.

10 APRIL 1764
Colonial Affairs The Parson's Cause concludes when the Virginia general court rules against the Anglican clergy. James Maury had sued the colony for back pay after England disallowed Virginia's change of the clergy's pay from tobacco to currency, but defense attorney Patrick Henry successfully questioned the authority of Britain to revoke colonial statutes. The English Privy Council later supports this finding.

12 APRIL 1764
War English Colonel John Bradstreet signs peace treaties with a number of rebellious Indian tribes at Presque Isle near Detroit. Chief Pontiac is to continue his resistance for another two years.

19 APRIL 1764
British Policy The Currency Act is the third Grenville measure to be passed by the British Parliament. This act further provokes the colonies to protest by prohibiting them, and specifically Virginia, from issuing legal tender paper money. A similar currency act has been in effect for the New England colonies since 1751. This act serves to create a common grievance uniting the more commercial northern colonies with the agricultural southern colonies. And not only is the Currency Act a severe deflationary measure, but it also threatens to destabilize the colonial economy.

24 MAY 1764
Revolution: Approach The Grenville measures are protested at a Boston town meeting where James Otis first introduces the issue of taxation without representation, and he also suggests a united colonial response to the parliamentary acts.

12-13 JUNE 1764
Revolution: Approach The Massachusetts House of Representatives organizes a committee of correspondence to communicate with the other 12 colonies in the expression of their common grievances against the Sugar Act.

FOUNDING A NATION 986-1787

LOYALISTS

The Revolutionary War was not just a war for national independence; it was also a civil war. About one-third of the American population refused to join the patriot cause, instead remaining loyal to the English Crown. Such divided allegiances pitted neighbor against neighbor and even family members against each other. In one of the most ferociously fought battles of the war, that of King's Mountain in North Carolina, the soldiers on both sides were all Americans, except for the Englishman commanding the British force. Although the majority of British sympathizers came from the wealthy and land-owning classes, there were Tories, as they were disparagingly called, in all social milieus. In Georgia and South Carolina, the Loyalists were in the majority, and their influence was also strong in New Jersey, New York and Pennsylvania, but weak in Connecticut, Massachusetts, Maryland and Virginia. When the Declaration of Independence made the pro-British stance treasonous, some 80,000 Loyalists left the country, about half of them emigrating to Canada where they were assisted with a new start, but an even greater number stayed to take the oath of allegiance to the United States and to hope for a British victory. Loyalists refusing to take the oath faced employment restrictions, triple taxation, tarring and feathering, banishment, and even the threat of execution if they attempted to return. From 30,000 to 60,000 Loyalists served in the British Army during the war, while others acted as spies, guerillas, privateers and counterfeiters of continental currency. Still other remaining Loyalists provided the British forces with material and financial assistance. In 1777, the Continental Congress mandated the confiscation of Loyalist property to help finance the war. New York State, for instance, raised over $3.6 million from the sale of Loyalist lands. Many of those Loyalists who emigrated to England became dependent on the British government for financial help, and in the peace treaty ending the war Great Britain stipulated the restoration of Loyalist property. This condition was largely ignored, as American hostility toward Loyalists remained intense during the years that followed the Revolution. The United States kept anti-Tory laws on the books until the end of the War of 1812.

---

10 JULY 1764
British Policy The English Board of Trade accepts the proposal submitted by George Croghan, Sir William Johnson and Indian Commissioner for the Southern District Colonel John Stuart for the subdivision of the frontier territories into trade districts overseen by commissioners. But it becomes impossible to enforce the plan when the governors of the southern colonies refuse to control illegal trade activities. In the frontier territories of the northern colonies, Sir William Johnson's order to transact all trade at Detroit and Mackinac leads to a decline in the English fur trade as the French traders on the other side of the Mississippi River are able to procure skins from those Indians who are unwilling to travel to Detroit and Mackinac.

20 JULY 1764
Colonial Affairs A British royal order proclaims the

present-day Vermont region west of the Connecticut River and north of the Massachusetts Colony to be part of the territory of the New York colony.

23 JULY 1764
Revolution: Approach Boston lawyer James Otis publishes his views on taxation without representation in *The Rights of the British Colonies Asserted and Proved*, a response to the issue of the limits of British power raised by the passage of the Sugar Act.

AUGUST 1764
Revolution: Approach Boston merchants agree among themselves to boycott British luxury imports including lace and ruffles. This action initiates the effective resistance policy of nonimportation. The other colonies eventually follow the lead of the Boston merchants and join in this coordinated political action.

SEPTEMBER 1764
Revolution: Approach Boston mechanics follow the example set by the merchants and state their intent to boycott leather working–clothes manufactured outside of Massachusetts, thus widening the social boundaries of the nonimportation movement. The nonimportation policy is adopted by New York, the first of the other colonies to do so.

17 NOVEMBER 1764
War The Indian war of Chief Pontiac ends when the Indians surrender to British forces on the Muskingham River in the Ohio territory.

22 DECEMBER 1764
Revolution: Approach In the *Providence Gazette*, Rhode Island Governor Stephen Hopkins publishes "The Rights of the Colonies Examined." The issuance of this political analysis is approved by the Rhode Island assembly.

OTHER EVENTS OF 1764
Colonial Affairs A second American postal district is established with headquarters in Charleston, South Carolina, for the territories south of the Virginia colony. The Bahamas are also included in this postal district.
Industry Peter Hasenclever, a Prussian iron-monger, establishes ironworks in New York and New Jersey.
Education The Baptist school of Rhode Island College is founded by Baptists in Providence, Rhode Island. (This is the seventh of the nine colleges to be established before the Revolutionary War.) Rhode Island College is renamed Brown University in 1804.

22 MARCH 1765
Revolution: Approach In passing the Stamp Act, the English Parliament sets its first direct tax on the American colonies. The intent of this act is to raise adequate funds, together with the revenues from the 1764 Sugar Act, to support at least one-third of the total cost to the British of maintaining a military or-

ganization in the colonies. About £300,000 a year needs to be raised from the colonies. To be put into effect on November 1, 1765, the act mandates a tax on all printed materials, including almanacs, broadsides, pamphlets, newspapers, legal documents, licenses, insurance policies, ship's papers and even playing cards and dice. The revenues from the act are to be paid to the English Exchequer for the defense of the American colonies. Americans are to be appointed the stamp agents to collect the revenues. Again, the vice-admiralty courts are to have jurisdiction over the enforcement of the act, as are the colonial common-law courts. Unlike the civil courts, the vice-admiralty courts have no jury. The passage of the Stamp Act meets with almost universal colonial opposition. The main objections raised are those to direct taxation of the colonies by Parliament, and the likelihood that this tax will usher in others, as well as to the all-encompassing application of the tax. The fact that the act primarily affects the most powerful segments of colonial society—lawyers, publishers, merchants, shipowners, real estate owners, speculators and tavern owners—adds greatly to the force of the opposition. The jurisdiction of the vice-admiralty courts over the enforcement of the Stamp Act excites fears of the erosion of the basic civil right of trial by jury. Adding to the unpopularity of the act is its timing. It is to be imposed during an era of economic downturn and strict currency regulations, provoking speculation that the underlying motivation of the British is to intentionally weaken the colonial economies. Foremost among the political doctrines cited by opponents to the Stamp Act is that of the unfairness of taxation without representation, an issue already raised by James Otis in 1764 in reference to the Sugar Act. Maryland lawyer Daniel Dulany also seeks to prove the illegality of the Stamp Act by invoking a variation of the taxation without representation argument that distinguishes between internal and external taxation.

24 MARCH 1765

Revolution: Approach The Quartering Act goes into effect in the American colonies. This English law requires the colonies to provide quarters or housing for British troops stationed in the American colonies. It also requires the colonists to keep the soldiers supplied with food and other necessities. This act is to be effective for the two years following its institution. The Quartering Act has been enacted on the strong recommendation of the British military commander in the colonies, General Thomas Gage. This act serves to broaden the colonial discontent already provoked by the Grenville Acts of 1764—The Sugar Act and the Currency Act. A supplement to the Quartering Act is passed in 1766, which mandates the housing of British soldiers in unoccupied buildings, inns and taverns.

3 MAY 1765

Education In Philadelphia, the first medical school in the American colonies is founded by Dr. John Morgan and Dr. William Shippen, Jr. This school

will later become the College of Physicians and Surgeons, a subdivision of the University of Pennsylvania.

29 MAY 1765

Revolution: Approach Newly-elected member Patrick Henry presents the seven Virginia Resolutions to the House of Burgesses—a speech that ends, "If this be treason, make the most of it"—with a warning to King George III to note the fates of Julius Caesar and Charles I, two other notable tyrants. The resolutions assert that only the Virginia assembly has the legal power to tax Virginia residents, as the colony has received from England the long-standing privilege of governing its own internal affairs. After much debate and further consideration of the Virginia Resolutions, the House of Burgesses votes to delete the more radical clauses and passes a version that reaffirms the right of the Virginia colony to self government and its opposition to the principle of taxation without representation. Patrick Henry's original resolutions receive widespread publicity in colonial circles as they are published in the newspapers of the other colonies.

6 JUNE 1765

Revolution: Approach The Massachusetts general court votes to support a measure proposed by James Otis to convene an intercolonial meeting to plan strategy to oppose the Stamp Act.

8 JUNE 1765

Revolution: Approach The Massachusetts assembly sends out a circular letter to the other colonial assemblies, proposing an intercolonial congress to meet in New York City in October to coordinate colonial opposition to the Stamp Act.

JULY 1765

Revolution: Approach Spurred by the widespread opposition to the Stamp Act, a number of underground organizations which call themselves the Sons of Liberty are formed in various colonial towns. Often founded and led by men of wealth and influence, these groups will frequently use violence as a tool to force the resignation of the stamp agents and to force merchants to cancel orders for English trade goods.

2 AUGUST 1765

Revolution: Approach Upon receipt of the circular letter from the Massachusetts assembly proposing an intercolonial congress in October to oppose the Stamp Act, South Carolina accepts the invitation immediately, followed by the formal acceptance of the Rhode Island, Connecticut, Pennsylvania and Maryland assemblies. The assemblies of Delaware, New Jersey and New York take no official action, but delegates are informally elected to represent colonies at the congress. The remaining four colonies issue no acceptance and elect no delegates to attend the meeting.

15 AUGUST 1765

Revolution: Approach Andrew Oliver, the stamp

FOUNDING A NATION 986-1787

agent for Boston, is forced under threats of violence to resign from his position. Similar incidents occur in the other colonies, resulting in the resignation of all stamp agents before the Stamp Act becomes effective on November 1.

26 AUGUST 1765

Revolution: Approach In Boston, in a continuing series of protests against the imposition of the Stamp Act, the house of the currency comptroller is looted; the records of the vice-admiralty court are destroyed; and the library and house of Massachusetts Chief Justice Thomas Hutchinson, brother-in-law of resigned stamp agent Andrew Oliver, is plundered by a group of the Sons of Liberty activists.

7–25 OCTOBER 1765

Revolution: Approach The Stamp Act Congress convenes in New York City, with representatives from Connecticut, Delaware, Maryland, Massachusetts, New Jersey, New York, Pennsylvania, Rhode Island and South Carolina to consider concerted colonial opposition to the Stamp Act. Moderate rather than radical elements prevail at the congress, as evidenced by Pennsylvania attorney John Dickinson's "Declaration of Rights and Grievances," a series of resolutions petitioning King George III and the English Parliament for the repeal of the Stamp Act and the Acts of 1764. This declaration cites taxation without representation as a violation of the basic civil rights of all British subjects, and maintains that taxes may be instituted on colonial residents only by colonial legislatures. The jurisdiction of the vice-admiralty courts over the enforcement of the Stamp Act is specifically abhorred. Petitions opposing these injustices are prepared by the delegates for presentation to King George III and both houses of Parliament before the conclusion of the Stamp Act Congress on October 25.

28 OCTOBER 1765

Revolution: Approach In a renewal of the nonviolent nonimportation policy in opposition to the Stamp Act, New York's leading citizens sign a resolution which forbids the purchase of English trade goods until the Stamp Act is repealed by Parliament and the trade provisions of the 1764 Sugar Act are revised.

31 OCTOBER 1765

Revolution: Approach Some 200 New York merchants join the nonimportation pact initiated by leading New York citizens in opposition to the Stamp Act and the 1764 trade acts.

1 NOVEMBER 1765

Revolution: Approach The Stamp Act goes into effect in the American colonies. Business throughout the colonies is virtually suspended as almost all colonists refuse to use the stamps. Even the colonial courts close rather than use the stamps. Rhode Island Governor Stephen Hopkins refuses to implement the act and hence the Rhode Island courts are able to re-

main open. Business is later resumed, though, but without the use of the stamps, in flagrant violation of the legislation. In New York City a riotous mob buries an effigy of "Liberty," harasses British soldiers, burns the royal governor in effigy, and plunders houses, before it is suppressed by more law-abiding residents.

NOVEMBER 1765

Revolution: Approach The nonimportation movement spreads to Pennsylvania, as over 400 Philadelphia merchants agree to boycott English imports until the repeal of the Stamp Act and the revision of the 1764 trade acts.

9 DECEMBER 1765

Revolution: Approach Two hundred and fifty Boston merchants join the nonimportation movement, in an attempt to force the repeal of the Stamp Act and the revision of the 1764 trade acts. That this nonimportation policy is highly effective can be seen from the steep decline in English exports to the American colonies, and the organization in England of a merchants' committee to lobby for the parliamentary repeal of the act.

13 DECEMBER 1765

British Policy The British commander of all English military forces in America, General Thomas Gage, requests the New York assembly, through New York royal Governor Sir Henry Moore, to comply with the Quartering Act and to provide housing and supplies for his troops.

OTHER EVENTS OF 1765

Revolution: Approach The passage of the Stamp Act evokes a series of articles by John Adams in the *Boston Gazette*. Adams later rewrites the articles and they are republished in 1768 as *A Dissertation on the Canon and Feudal Law*.

Indians Indian Commissioner for the Southern District Colonel John Stuart reaches a preliminary agreement with the Chickasaw and Choctaw Indians to consider the high–tide line as the boundary of the Florida colonies.

Ideas/Beliefs The North Carolina assembly passes the Establishment Act, an addendum to the Vestry Act of 1715. This legislation, making Anglicanism the official religion of the colony, sets the salary of the clergymen and grants the royal governor of the colony authority over the appointment of clergymen. The British government approves this act, despite its earlier opposition to the Vestry Acts. Eventually, the Establishment Act proves counterproductive in that it lessens the prestige of the Anglican church when the local parishes oppose the governor's power over the appointment of clergymen.

14 JANUARY 1766

British Policy The English Parliament convenes and immediately begins to reconsider the repercussions of the Stamp Act. Former Chancellor of the Exchequer

Grenville advocates enforcement of the act by military force, while William Pitt supports the repeal of the Stamp Act, citing the principle of taxation without representation.

17 JANUARY 1766
British Policy A committee of English merchants working for the repeal of the Stamp Act presents a petition to Parliament citing the increase in merchant bankruptcies resulting from the colonial nonimportation movement.

JANUARY 1766
Revolution: Approach Having met to consider the request of General Thomas Gage for New York compliance with the Quartering Act, the New York assembly refuses to grant complete compliance. Since New York is Gage's headquarters, the New York assembly asserts that the Quartering Act is placing an unfairly heavy economic burden on the colony.

3 FEBRUARY 1766
British Policy In its consideration of the Stamp Act, Parliament calls before it all of the colonial agents to present their views.

11 FEBRUARY 1766
Revolution: Approach The county court of Northampton, Virginia, declares the Stamp Act unconstitutional.

13 FEBRUARY 1766
British Policy Pennsylvania agent Benjamin Franklin testifies before Parliament against the Stamp Act. He cites the heavy costs borne by the colonies during the French and Indian War with minimum recompensation from England and the continuing colonial expenditures on military expeditions against the Indians. Franklin also notes that the colonial assemblies lack sufficient specie to pay for the use of the stamps required in expediting the business of government. In addition, Franklin offers a distinction between internal and external taxation (1765), warns that the use of military power to enforce the Stamp Act might lead to open revolution, and concludes by supporting the repeal of the Stamp Act.

5 MARCH 1766
Colonial Affairs The first Spanish governor of the Louisiana territory, Don Antonio Ulloa, arrives to assume the duties of his new position in New Orleans.

18 MARCH 1766
British Policy King George III signs a bill fully repealing the Stamp Act. The repeal is to become effective 1 May. On the same day that the Stamp Act is revoked, the English Parliament passes the Declaratory Act, which asserts that the British government has complete power to legislate any laws governing the American colonists "in all cases whatsoever." In America, this law goes almost unnoticed in the flurry of rejoicing that greets the repeal of the Stamp Act.

MARCH 1766
Settling The Illinois Company is organized by the "Suffering Traders."

17 APRIL 1766
Westward Movement English Auditor General of North America Cholmondely declares that the royal Proclamation of 1763 does not revoke previous land grants in the western frontier territories. This opinion stimulates real estate speculators to press for the recognition of their claims.

26 APRIL 1766
Colonial Affairs News of the official repeal of the Stamp Act is greeted by celebration in New York and the immediate relaxation of the nonimportation policy. In its enthusiasm for repeal of the act, the New York legislature later votes to commission statues to be erected in honor of George III and of William Pitt.

24 JULY 1766
Indians After nearly three years of rebellion, Chief Pontiac finally signs a peace treaty with Sir William Johnson at Oswego. Pontiac is to keep his word and he maintains allegiance to the English until his death by foul play some three years later when an Indian allegedly bribed by a British trader kills him.

10 AUGUST 1766
Revolution: Approach The tension between British troops and New York colonists who have refused to comply with the Quartering Act results in an incident of violence. Some British soldiers destroy a liberty pole, an assembly point erected by the Sons of Liberty, resulting in a skirmish between armed citizens, including members of the Sons of Liberty and English soldiers brandishing bayonets. The leader of the Sons of Liberty, Isaac Sears, is wounded.

1 NOVEMBER 1766
British Policy Following the repeal of the Stamp Act, Parliament revises the 1764 trade acts. The duty on molasses is reduced and applied to all molasses imports, of both foreign and British West Indian origin. Sugar duties on British West Indian imports are eliminated. This modification of the trade laws also requires the passage through English ports of all colonial exports bound for northern European countries.

15 DECEMBER 1766
Revolution: Approach Voting again on the Quartering Act, the New York assembly refuses to appropriate any funds to provide housing and supplies for British soldiers stationed in the New York colony. The legislature is suspended by the English crown on December 19.

OTHER EVENTS OF 1766
Westward Movement Trader Benjamin Cutbird penetrates far into the western hinterland when he travels to the Mississippi River along the Tennessee-Kentucky border. He then voyages down the

FOUNDING A NATION 986-1787

Mississippi River to New Orleans to sell his furs. This trip beyond the western frontier precedes the explorations of Daniel Boone by one year.

Ideas/Beliefs The Methodist religion is officially instituted in the colonies, as an offshoot of the Anglican church. This first Methodist church is organized in New York by Philip Embury. Methodism is spread throughout the colonies by preachers such as Francis Asbury and Devereux Jarratt in the South.

Education Queens College is founded by the Dutch Reformed Church in New Jersey. It is the eighth of the nine colleges to be established before the Revolutionary War. Queens College is renamed Rutgers University in 1825.

Arts/Culture The first permanent theater, the Southwark, is erected in Philadelphia. The premiere performance at the Southwark Theater is *Katherine and Petruchio*, based on Shakespeare's *Taming of the Shrew*. In 1767 *The Prince of Parthias* by American colonist Thomas Godfrey is the first native play to be professionally presented at the Southwark.

JANUARY 1767
British Policy English Chancellor of the Exchequer Charles Townshend, actual leader of the British government by virtue of Prime Minister Lord Chatham's ill health, opposes the distinction made by American colonists, as well as by Lord Chatham (William Pitt) between internal and external taxation. Townshend serves notice that he is designing a new revenue instrument that will override the authority of the colonial legislative assemblies. The February 1767 reduction of the British real estate tax, which will result in a £500,000 shortfall in English internal revenues, forces an implementation of Townshend's planned American revenue acts.

6 JUNE 1767
Colonial Affairs In a motion of belated compliance with the 1765 and 1766 Quartering Acts, the New York Assembly votes to appropriate £3000 to pay for housing and necessary supplies for British soldiers stationed in the New York Colony. Unaware of this appropriation, the English Parliament votes to revoke the legislative powers of the New York assembly, to become effective October 1, 1767. The royal governor of New York does not enforce this parliamentary order because of the New York assembly appropriation passed on June 6.

29 JUNE 1767
British Policy The English Parliament passes the Townshend Acts, a new series of external taxes on the American colonies, including import duties on such goods as glass, lead, paints, paper and tea. The projected income from these duties is to help pay for the military defense of the American colonies, as well as for the governmental and judicial administration of the colonies. To enforce the new import duties effectively, the colonial supreme court justices are empowered to issue writs of assistance, additional vice-admiralty courts are instituted, and a colonial board of customs commissioners directly responsible to the English Treasury Board is established in Boston. The Townshend Acts are to become effective on November 20, 1767.

4 SEPTEMBER 1767
External Affairs The English Chancellor of the Exchequer, Charles Townshend, dies. He is succeeded by Lord North.

11 SEPTEMBER 1767
Indians The Secretary of State for the Southern Department, Lord Shelburne, proposes the abolition of the Indian Department, the removal of military detachments from the Indian lands, and the establishment of the three new colonies of Upper Ohio, Illinois, and Detroit, which will open the west to settlers. This proposal is not implemented.

28 OCTOBER 1767
Revolution: Approach In response to the impending imposition of the Townshend Acts, a Boston town meeting decides to reinstate the nonimportation movement in an attempt to force the British to retract these new measures. The colonists compose a list of English luxury items that are not to be purchased after the end of the year.

OCTOBER 1767
Indians Northern Indian Commissioner Sir William Johnson allows all licensed traders to transact business north of the Ottawa River and Lake Superior.

5 NOVEMBER 1767
British Policy The American colonial customs commissioners appointed by King George arrive in Boston.

20 NOVEMBER 1767
British Policy The Townshend Revenue Acts go into effect in the American colonies.

2 DECEMBER 1767
Revolution: Approach Pennsylvania attorney and legislator John Dickinson writes *Letters From a Farmer in Pennsylvania to the Inhabitants of the British Colonies*. First published in the *Pennsylvania Chronicle*, the *Letters* later appear in pamphlet form in the other colonies and in England in 1768. The *Letters* furnish in effect a constitutional basis for the widespread colonial opposition to the English trade acts. While Dickinson agrees that England has the legal power to regulate colonial trade, he denies the parliamentary authority to impose taxes to raise revenues from colonial sources. Dickinson also severely criticizes the parliamentary suspension of the New York assembly for its failure to comply with the Quartering Act. Dickinson insists that this action places all of the other colonial assemblies in jeopardy. This essay proves an immensely influential force in shaping colonial opinion.

29 DECEMBER 1767
Revolution: Approach A New York City open meet-

ing chooses a committee to design a policy that will enhance New York industry and lessen reliance on English imports of both necessities and luxury items. Again, this action is taken in opposition to the widely criticized Townshend Acts imposed by the British Parliament.

DECEMBER 1767

Westward Movement Frontiersman Daniel Boone makes his first exploratory trip beyond the Appalachian Mountains. He travels along the present West Virginia-Kentucky border, without going into Kentucky proper.

OTHER EVENTS OF 1767

British Policy The English Parliament passes a trade act requiring all goods not enumerated in the prior acts of 1705 and 1721 that are destined for European countries north of Cape Finisterre to be first shipped to England. This affects only a very small percentage of American exports since most of the colonial exports are already enumerated—including tobacco, rice, indigo, beaver skins and other furs. The non-enumerated items, including naval stores and pig and bar iron, are used almost exclusively in English manufacturing.

Science/Technology John Winthrop publishes an early study on the density of comets. A professor of mathematics and natural philosophy at Harvard, Winthrop has also issued his observations of and theories on sunspots (1739), on a transit of Venus and an eclipse of the moon (1740), a New England earthquake (1756) and on Halley's Comet (1759).

11 FEBRUARY 1768

Revolution: Approach With the approval of the Massachusetts assembly, Samuel Adams composes a circular letter, which seeks to communicate to the other colonial assemblies the steps taken by the Massachusetts general court to oppose the Townshend Acts. The circular letter also opposes taxation without representation and warns of the possibility that the English may try to make the American colonial governors and judges more independent of the colonists they govern. The letter concludes with a call for suggestions for united colonial actions against the British government.

FEBRUARY 1768

Revolution: Approach The Boston customs commissioners, hindered at every turn by the tactics of Boston agitators, formally request the British government for protective military forces. When they receive no response, they repeat their request.

MARCH 1768

Western Movement The first British Secretary of State for the Colonies, Lord Hillsborough, presents a new plan for the western territories. Accepted by the English cabinet, this plan calls for the return of control over the fur trade to colonial authorities; the limiting of Indian superintendents to the transaction of only imperial matters; and the shifting of the 1763

Daniel Boone protects his family.

DANIEL BOONE, 1734-1820

Daniel Boone is widely regarded as the archetypal frontiersman. Much of his reputation rests on the 19th century literary and artistic exploitation of his character and deeds—particularly in Lord Byron's *Don Juan*; in James Fenimore Cooper's Leatherstocking Tales for which he was the prototype; and in Horatio Greenough's allegorical sculptural portrait in the United States Capitol, where he is represented as a civilizing force struggling with a savage Indian warrior. Yet the facts of his life do not always support this legendary image. For instance, other frontiersmen explored Kentucky some 20 years before Boone traveled to the territory. And, during the course of his life, Boone held a series of political offices, a fact that receives little notice in the folk-tale version of his life. Born near Reading, Pennsylvania, to a Quaker family, Boone learned to hunt and trap at an early age. In 1750, the Boone family migrated to the North Carolina frontier, where he worked as a teamster and blacksmith. After his participation in General Braddock's disastrous 1755 campaign against the French at Fort Duquesne, he first traveled to the Kentucky territory through the Cumberland Gap in 1766-1767. Appointed an agent of the Transylvania Company, Boone led a group of settlers to Kentucky in 1775 to establish a fort at the site of Boonesborough. Made a militia captain and later a major, he was seized by Shawnee Indians and held captive for four months before his escape. After his return, he helped fight off an Indian attack on Boonesborough. In spite of the misfortunes of being robbed of $20,000 of Kentucky settlers' money entrusted to him for land purchases, and the voiding of his own land titles because of incorrect entry, Boone went on to fill the various public posts of legislative delegate, sheriff and deputy surveyor. In 1788 he moved to West Virginia, where he was named lieutenant colonel of Kanawha County and chosen as a legislative delegate. Around 1798 he moved to Missouri where he received a land grant and was appointed district magistrate. In 1810 he traveled back to Kentucky to pay off his outstanding debts there, a deed that afforded him great satisfaction. His last years were spent in Missouri. His apotheosis to myth is based on his activities as a frontiersman, Indian fighter and pioneer.

---

royal proclamation line farther west through the negotiation of Indian treaties.

Revolution: Approach A committee of Boston mer-

SAMUEL ADAMS, 1722-1803

Samuel Adams is reknowned as a firebrand of the American Revolution. Through his radical political activity and polemical writings, Adams sought to define and to keep alive the crucial issues of fundamental liberties, particularly those of the natural rights of man and of taxation without representation. Yet, as the revolutionary movement achieved success, the influence of Adams waned. Born into a prominent Boston family and cousin to John Adams, he graduated from Harvard to inherit the thriving family brewery business. Through incompetence or perhaps lack of interest he dissipated the entire estate, and was equally unsuccessful in his next venture as a Boston tax collector. Indeed, throughout his life, he and his family were forced to rely on the generosity of friends for the necessities of life. Adams' political effectiveness was motivated by a passionate belief in his cause. After membership in various political clubs, in 1765 he was elected to fill a vacancy in the Massachusetts legislative assembly, where he would also serve as clerk until 1774. He rapidly and skillfully attained a position of leadership, from which he made numerous speeches on topics such as American rights and the restriction of executive power. He led the opposition to the British Townshend Revenue Acts and helped to initiate committees of correspondence in the colonies. Adams also disseminated his ideas through his official papers and newspaper articles written under such pseudonyms as Candidus and Vindex. When the colonies threatened to settle back into an easy complacency after the 1770 repeal of the Townshend Acts, Adams effectively kept the controversies alive through an urgent stream of articles. He led the opposition to the 1773 Tea Act, and the resulting Boston Tea Party finally brought on the crisis. Elected to the first and second Continental Congresses, Adams favored immediate independence, and he was a signer of the Declaration of Independence. At first opposed to the federal constitution because it advocated a centralized government, Adams was eventually induced to support it by the proposed addition of the amendments. After the Revolutionary War, Adams returned to Massachusetts where he served as lieutenant governor and governor before his death in 1803.

chants meets to sign a stricter nonimportation pact, dependent on the implementation of similar agreements by mercantile groups in Philadelphia and New York.

21–22 APRIL 1768

British Policy   The English Secretary of State for the Colonies, Lord Hillsborough, sends an order to the American colonial governors denouncing the Massachusetts circular letter of Samuel Adams. Hillsborough commands the colonial governors to prevent the endorsement of the circular letter by their own colonial assemblies, even if they must dissolve the assemblies to achieve this end. This dispatch arrives too late for the governors to prevent legislative approval of the Massachusetts circular letter.

22 APRIL 1768

British Policy   Lord Hillsborough commands Massachusetts Governor Bernard to dissolve the new Massachusetts general court if the Massachusetts assembly refuses to revoke the circular letter penned by Samuel Adams.

APRIL 1768

Revolution: Approach   By the end of April, the legislative assemblies of Connecticut, New Hampshire, and New Jersey have supported the Massachusetts circular letter; the Virginia colony has issued its own circular letter urging support of the Massachusetts position.

New York merchants meet to institute a stricter nonimportation agreement to become effective October 1, 1768. The Philadelphia mercantile community also meets to try to achieve a similar accord, but they fail to do so.

7 MAY 1768

British Policy   The English Board of Trade supports the decision of New York royal governor Henry Moore not to enforce the 1767 parliamentary act revoking the legislative power of the New York assembly after they had finally complied with the Quartering Act. Nevertheless the Board of Trade declares all legislation enacted by the New York assembly after October 1, 1767 invalid.

17 MAY 1768

British Policy   Armed with 50 guns, the British frigate *Romney* arrives in Boston harbor in response to the call of customs commissioners for protection.

9 JUNE 1768

Revolution: Approach   A Boston customs official is shut up in the cabin of the *Liberty,* a sloop owned by Boston merchant John Hancock, while imported Madeira wine is being landed illegally without payment of the mandated duties.

10 JUNE 1768

Revolution: Approach   Boston customs officials order the seizure of John Hancock's sloop, the *Liberty,* for the flagrant violation of customs regulations. The *Liberty* is towed from her dock and anchored next to the *Romney,* a British 50-gun frigate sent to support customs officials. A rebellious mob attacks the customs officials on the wharf and also carries out protests before their houses.

11 JUNE 1768

Revolution: Approach   Threatened by violence from an angry mob opposed to the seizure of the *Liberty,* Boston customs officials escape to an island in Boston Harbor, Castle William, where they remain in safety.

15 JUNE 1768

Revolution: Approach   The threatened Boston customs officials on Castle William in Boston Harbor send out a dispatch requesting the intervention of English troops.

21 JUNE 1768

Revolution: Approach   Massachusetts Governor Ber-

OCTOBER 30, 1768

JOHN HANCOCK, 1736-1793

Thrust into the public eye by the seizure of his mercantile vessel *Liberty* for smuggling, John Hancock, the richest New Englander on the revolutionary side, was a patriot whose ambitions exceeded his abilities. Born in North Braintree, Massachusetts, the son of a poor clergyman, he was adopted by and became the heir, at the age of 27, of his uncle Thomas Hancock, Boston's wealthiest merchant. An important prelude to the American Revolution, the *Liberty* incident gained Hancock widespread popularity and instigated his entry into the political arena, under the tutelage of Samuel Adams. Hancock served as a Massachusetts general court member, a town committee head, and in a number of minor offices. Later he became president of the Massachusetts provincial congress and chairman of the committee of safety, earning him the distinction of being explicitly excluded from a general amnesty offered by the British. After serving as president of the Continental Congress and signing the Declaration of Independence, Hancock expected to be chosen commander in chief of the Continental Army, a post awarded instead to George Washington. Miffed by the frustration of his goals, Hancock fell out with Samuel Adams, whom he held responsible for blocking a congressional vote of thanks for his service. He then resigned the presidency of the Continental Congress and returned to Boston where he functioned less than brilliantly as a military commander and quite irresponsibly as the treasurer of Harvard College. Yet Hancock managed to sustain his popularity with the liberal dispensation of money. He was elected the first governor of the Commonwealth of Massachusetts. When the troubles leading to Shay's Rebellion surfaced, Hancock resigned the governorship, purportedly for reasons of health. After interim Governor James Bowdoin successfully repressed the rebellion, Hancock again returned to health, ran for and was reelected governor. He served in this position for nine terms before his death at the age of 56.

nard orders the assembly to delete from its records the resolution supporting the circular letter. The representatives debate the matter and conclude with a vote. The results of the poll support continued defiance.

1 JULY 1768
Revolution: Approach Massachusetts Governor Bernard dissolves the Massachusetts general court after the legislature defies his order to rescind the circular letter. The 17 delegates who did vote to revoke the letter are subsequently harassed by the Sons of Liberty and are voted out of their seats in the May 1769 election.

1 AUGUST 1768
Revolution: Approach Boston merchants sign a nonimportation pact that bans the import of all items enumerated in the Townshend Acts, as well as almost all other English goods except fishery supplies. The Townshend ban is to go into effect on January 1, 1769 until the Acts are repealed, and the other goods are to be boycotted for one year.

19 AUGUST 1768
Settling Of the 1400 colonists from Leghorn, Greece

and Minorca at New Smyrna, East Florida, led by Dr. Alexander Trumbull, the Minorcans rebel to protest working conditions. Two Minorcan leaders are executed. The New Smyrna colony is abandoned nine years later.

27 AUGUST 1768
Revolution: Approach In further support of the nonimportation movement, the mercantile community of New York agrees to cancel all orders for British goods submitted after August 15, and to import no English trade goods from November 1, 1768 until the Townshend Acts are repealed.

5 SEPTEMBER 1768
Revolution: Approach New York tradesmen agree to do no business with merchants who do not support the provisions of the New York nonimportation agreement.

13 SEPTEMBER 1768
Revolution: Approach Evoking the ploy of an imminent war with France, the Boston town meeting orders Boston residents to arm. The town meeting also asks the royal governor to call the Massachusetts general court back into session. This the governor refuses to do.

23-28 SEPTEMBER 1768
Revolution: Approach An unofficial provincial conference meets in Boston's Faneuil Hall, with delegates from 96 Massachusetts towns attending. On the agenda are the seizure of the *Liberty* by customs officials, and the call for Massachusetts residents to arm. After the delegates compose a list of grievances, they adjourn.

28 SEPTEMBER 1768
Revolution: Approach English warships arrive in Boston Harbor, bringing military reinforcements to support the authority of the customs officials. The Sons of Liberty react with threats of armed resistance.

1 OCTOBER 1768
Revolution: Approach Two regiments of English infantry from Halifax, Nova Scotia, are landed in Boston without incident and they are permanently billeted in the town in order to maintain order and enforce the customs laws.

14 OCTOBER 1768
Westward Movement The Virginia boundary is moved west by the Treaty of Hard Labor between southern Indian commissioner John Stuart and the Cherokee Indians. This pact implements the Lord Hillsborough plan of March 1768. Negotiated at Hard Labor, South Carolina, this treaty confirms the grants of Cherokee land within North Carolina, South Carolina and Virginia to the English crown.

30 OCTOBER 1768
Ideas/Beliefs In New York City, the Wesley Chapel,

107

the first Methodist church in the American colonies, is dedicated. This John Street edifice will be rebuilt in 1817 and again in 1840.

3 NOVEMBER 1768
Westward Movement The Indiana Company buys 1,800,000 acres from the Iroquois Indians in the territory southeast of the Ohio River.

5 NOVEMBER 1768
Westward Movement The Treaty of Stanwix between northern Indian Commissioner Sir William Johnson and the Iroquois Indians grants to the English Crown a large tract of land, including much of western New York state and the area to the west between the Ohio and Tennessee Rivers.

NOVEMBER 1768
Westward Movement The Creek Indians agree at Pensacola to the westward shift of the South Carolina border and to the establishment of the Georgia border at the Ogeechee River.

OTHER EVENTS OF 1768
Industry In Boston, a Mr. Michaelson establishes the first foundary for casting printer's type in the American colonies. This operation is unable adequately to supply the needs of colonial printers and publishers without additional imports from England, with the result that the Revolutionary War somewhat disrupts the issuance of colonial newspapers.
War In western North Carolina, the War of the Regulation (1768-1771), a frontier uprising against tidewater control, begins.

10 JANUARY 1769
Colonial Affairs The northern and southern colonial postal systems are linked as regular monthly boats sail to New York and Charleston from the transfer point between the two postal districts at Suffolk, Virginia.

JANUARY–FEBRUARY 1769
British Policy The English Parliament urges the bringing to trial of the inciters of rebellion in the American colonies.

10 MARCH 1769
Revolution: Approach Philadelphia merchants finally agree among themselves to support the intercolonial nonimportation movement. Effective April 1, they ban the import of nearly all British trade goods until the Townshend Acts are repealed.

30 MARCH 1769
Revolution: Approach Following the example of the Philadelphia merchants, Baltimore merchants join the nonimportation movement by banning the purchase of English goods until the repeal of the Townshend Acts.

APRIL 1769
Westward Movement After the negotiation of the recent treaties with the Indians, the Pittsburgh, Pennsylvania, land office is overrun by hordes of would-be purchasers of real estate in the western territories.

7 MAY 1769
Revolution: Approach George Washington presents a set of nonimportation resolutions composed by George Mason to the Virginia House of Burgesses. The resolutions oppose taxation without representation, the British interference with the Massachusetts and Virginia circular letters, and the parliamentary proposal to transport colonial malcontents to England for trial. In addition, Patrick Henry and Richard Henry Lee compose a proclamation to King George III.

13 MAY 1769
British Policy Faced by falling trade revenues caused by the American intercolonial nonimportation movement, the English Board of Trade notifies the colonial governors that the British government is considering revision of the Townshend Acts.

17 MAY 1769
Revolution: Approach Virginia royal Governor Botetourt dissolves the House of Burgesses in reaction to the Virginia resolutions drawn up by George Mason and presented by George Washington. The following day, the delegates meet informally in Williamsburg in the Raleigh Tavern to endorse the Virginia Association. This nonimportation agreement bans the import of nearly all English trade goods, of slaves, and of many European luxury items, until the repeal of the Townshend Acts.

7 JUNE 1769
Westward Movement Frontiersman and explorer Daniel Boone sights the Kentucky territory, after trekking into the western wilderness through the Cumberland Gap.

22 JUNE 1769
Revolution: Approach At an Annapolis, Maryland, informal convention delegates vote to form a nonimportation association similar to that established by the Virginia assembly, Maryland throws greater force behind its association by providing for the boycott of those refusing to agree to the compact. During the summer months of 1769, many harbor towns implement similar pledges.

JUNE 1769
Westward Movement The English Board of Trade is petitioned by the Vandalia Company, an Anglo-American syndicate, for permission to buy a 2,400,000-acre land tract in the western Virginia and eastern Kentucky region in order to found the new colony of Vandalia. The English crown endorses this plan in 1775.

16 JULY 1769
Settling In the California territory, Franciscan friar Father Junipero Serra founds the San Diego de Alcala mission, the first permanent Spanish settlement on the

west coast of America. Within the next 15 years, Serra will found eight more missions, extending as far north as San Francisco Bay.

18 OCTOBER 1769
Revolution: Approach The New Jersey assembly formally supports the nonimportation agreements passed by the New Jersey, New York and Pennsylvania merchants.

24 OCTOBER 1769
Revolution: Approach The merchants of Providence, Rhode Island, agree to support the intercolonial nonimportation movement until the repeal of the Townshend Acts. Newport, Rhode Island, signs a less stringent pact on 30 October which is tightened up under threat of boycott by Philadelphia and New York merchants.

7 NOVEMBER 1769
Revolution: Approach The North Carolina assembly meets informally to support the nonimportation pact of the Virginia Association.

27 DECEMBER 1769
Westward Movement The Grand Ohio Company is organized by Englishmen Samuel Wharton, Thomas Walpole, Lord Hertford and George Grenville. This company is able to procure a grant of 20 million acres from the English crown under the provisions of the Treaty of Stanwix.

OTHER EVENTS OF 1769
Indians Chief Pontiac is murdered in Cahokia, Illinois, by a Kaskaskia Indian in the pay of an English trader, according to some accounts.
Arts/Culture The American Philosophical Society, in existence since 1743, is reorganized as Benjamin Franklin, its first secretary, now becomes the president, a position he will retain until the end of his life. Situated in Philadelphia, the society first issues a periodical record of papers presented before it, the *Transactions,* in 1771.
Education Dartmouth College, a Congregationalist school, is founded. It is the last of the nine colleges to be established before the American Revolution. Named after Lord Dartmouth, it is originally founded as an Indian school by Eleazar Wheelock in Lebanon, Connecticut. The school is moved to Hanover, New Hampshire, in 1770.
Industry In Mannheim, Pennsylvania, Henry William Stiegel begins operations at his glassmaking factory. Designed and fabricated in a German tradition, Stiegel glass is one of the notable products of the colonial era.

19 JANUARY 1770
Revolution: Approach In an attempt to prohibit the posting of broadsides by British soldiers stationed in New York, the Sons of Liberty, led by Alexander McDougall, engage in a skirmish with soldiers on Golden Hill. Armed with swords and clubs, the colonists confront 30 to 40 British soldiers armed with bayonets. No fatalities result, although several participants are seriously wounded.

31 JANUARY 1770
British Policy In England, Lord Frederick North becomes prime minister, adding greater force to the movement for the repeal of the Townshend Acts. North opposes total repeal of the revenue acts which might indicate weakness on the part of the British government.

8 FEBRUARY 1770
Revolution: Approach The leader of the New York Sons of Liberty, Alexander McDougall, is arrested for his authorship of a broadside criticizing the New York assembly. Titled "To the Betrayed Inhabitants of the City and Colony of New York," the broadside was issued on December 1769. Refusing to post bond, McDougall remains in prison until April 29 when he pleads not guilty to the charges and is released on bail. This case never reaches the courts, as the colony's witness dies in the meantime.

5 MARCH 1770
Revolution: Approach A belligerent Boston mob confronts British soldiers stationed in the town and in an explosion of tensions, the soldiers fire their rifles pointblank into the crowd, killing three colonists, mortally wounding two and injuring six. The situation is defused when Massachusetts Governor Thomas Hutchinson agrees to the demand of Samuel Adams to withdraw British troops from the town to the islands in Boston harbor. Captain Thomas Preston who led the soldiers at the Boston Massacre and eight of his men are arrested for murder by the civil authorities on March 9, 1770. The case comes to trial in October.

12 APRIL 1770
British Policy The English crown approves the partial repeal of the Townshend Acts as proposed by Prime Minister Lord North, thus eliminating all duties on imports to the American colonies except tea. At

Paul Revere's drawing of the Boston Massacre.

the same time, the Quartering Act is allowed to lapse without renewal.

25 APRIL 1770

Colonial Affairs Although the waiving of the non-importation movement was dependent on the repeal of the Townshend Acts, the British refusal to remove the duty on tea motivates Boston to resist for a while the abandonment of nonimportation. The other colonies gradually begin to drop their nonimportation pledges.

MAY 1770

Colonial Affairs With the repeal of the Townshend Acts, the merchants of Albany, Providence and Newport decide to abandon nonimportation.

7-9 JULY 1770

Colonial Affairs After the repeal of the Townshend Acts, a poll of the residents of New York reveals support for the abandonment of the nonimportation pact, while maintaining a ban on the import of tea and other goods subject to a duty.

12 SEPTEMBER 1770

Colonial Affairs With the repeal of the Townshend Acts, the mercantile community of Philadelphia decides to abandon the nonimportation pact.

12 OCTOBER 1770

Colonial Affairs With the abandonment of nonimportation by Albany, Providence, Newport and Philadelphia after the repeal of the Townshend Acts, the residents of Boston finally agree to drop their own nonimportation policy.

18 OCTOBER 1770

Westward Movement Southern Indian Commissioner Colonel John Stuart negotiates the Treaty of Lochaber with the Cherokee Indians. This pact shifts the Virginia boundary line further west, adding nearly 9000 square miles to the area of the Virginia colony. This land includes the areas claimed by the Greenbrier Company and the Loyal Company.

OCTOBER–DECEMBER 1770

Colonial Affairs The case of the British soldiers responsible for the Boston Massacre comes to trial. Ably defended by colonial lawyers John Adams and Josiah Quincy, Captain Thomas Preston and six of his men are acquitted by the civil jury. Two other soldiers are found guilty of manslaughter, are punished with branding, and then are released. Radical activist Samuel Adams is able to exploit the Boston Massacre, and silversmith Paul Revere issues an engraving depicting the incident, but gradually the tension between England and her American colonies relaxes.

13 DECEMBER 1770

Colonial Affairs With the repeal of the Townshend Acts and the subsequent abandonment of nonimportation by many of the other colonies, South Carolina finally follows suit.

New York Sons of Liberty leader Alexander McDougall is called before the New York assembly to defend his publication of a broadside critical of the assembly in December 1769. He is found in contempt and imprisoned until April 29, 1771.

OTHER EVENTS OF 1770

Population The total population of the American colonies is estimated at 2,205,000 persons.

Arts/Culture In Virginia, Thomas Jefferson designs and builds his first house at Monticello. Inspired by classical Greek and Roman architecture, Monticello later is rebuilt completely. The creation of Monticello and the surrounding estate is a project that is to occupy Jefferson for the rest of his life.

Musical works by Boston composer William Billings are published in *The New England Psalm Singer, or American Chorister*. The most reknowned of the late 18th century native-born composers, Billings is to publish several other collections of his music in the following two decades.

15 JANUARY 1771

Colonial Affairs The North Carolina assembly passes the "Bloody Act" which makes rioters guilty of treason. The enactment of this legislation is instigated by the violent agitation of the Regulators led by Herman Husbands. Active since 1768, the Regulators represent the western frontier settlers of the interior territory. They protest the lack of equitable representation of the Piedmont region in the North Carolina assembly, and go even further in issuing charges of extortion and oppression against the politically powerful eastern part of the colony.

APRIL 1771

Westward Movement A hunting expedition sponsored by North Carolina judge Richard Henderson and led by Daniel Boone, accompanied by John Stuart and John Finley, returns from a trip through the Cumberland Gap and across the Licking, Kentucky, Green and Cumberland River Valleys.

16 MAY 1771

War North Carolina Governor William Tryon leads a group of 1200 militia into the western part of the colony to confront the rebellious Regulators at Alamance Creek near Hillsboro. Many of the Regulators lack firearms and Tryon's forces are able to overcome them. A leader of the Regulators, James Few, is executed on the battlefield on May 17, 1771, and 12 others are judged guilty of treason on June 17. Of these, six are executed. The other six defendants, along with some 6500 western North Carolina settlers in the Piedmont, are required to swear an oath of allegiance to the government of North Carolina. This course of events is indicative of the profound regional factionalism of the area. A similar protest movement, also known as the Regulators, had arisen on the South Carolina frontier, but the colonial assembly had been able to placate these rebels by the 1769 establishment of courts in the frontier territory.

OTHER EVENTS OF 1772

JULY 1771
Colonial Affairs With the abandonment of nonimportation by the other colonies after the repeal of the Townshend acts, Virginia is the last of the colonies to relinquish its own nonimportation policy.

AUGUST 1771
Westward Movement A Pennsylvania proprietory force is unable to dislodge the Connecticut settlers from the Wyoming Valley in Pennsylvania.

OTHER EVENTS OF 1771
Arts/Culture Benjamin Franklin begins work on his *Autobiography,* a work that is never to reach completion. Originally written for his son William, then the governor of New Jersey, the *Autobiography* is a rich compendium of the events of Franklin's life, as well as of shrewd observations on the literature, philosophy and religion of his day.

9 APRIL 1772
Westward Movement The British Attorney General and Solicitor General sends to George Croghan the amended Camden-Yorke opinion of 1757, which can be interpreted to allow for the legal purchase of Indian lands without patents from the English Crown. This gives added impetus to the activities of Pennsylvania land speculators, who rush to accumulate more acreage.

9 JUNE 1772
Revolution: Approach The British customs schooner *Gaspee* runs aground in Narragansett Bay off Rhode Island while pursuing another ship. Led by merchant John Brown, eight boatloads of men from Providence attack the *Gaspee,* set wounded Lieutenant William Duddingston and his crew ashore, and then burn the *Gaspee.*

JULY 1772
Finance The British banking system undergoes a crisis, resulting in the widespread reduction of credit. This affects the colonial economies in that many merchants are forced to liquidate their inventories. The

The burning of the *Gaspee,* 1772.

colonies enter a period of financial distress that will end in 1776 with the business boom produced by the Revolutionary War.

14 AUGUST 1772
Westward Movement The English Crown approves the Vandalia land grant. Although the Board of Trade fixes the boundaries of the new colony and drafts its charter in April 1773, the actual title to the territory is never conferred.

2 SEPTEMBER 1772
Revolution: Approach The English crown issues a proclamation offering a reward of £500 for the capture of those who burned the British customs vessel *Gaspee* on June 9. Those guilty are to be sent to England for trial, an announcement that disturbs even moderate colonists with its implication of the erosion of local self-rule. The king also appoints Rhode Island Governor Joseph Wanton, the Boston vice-admiralty judge, and the chief justices of Massachusetts, New York and New Jersey to serve as commissioners of inquiry to officially investigate the incident of the burning of the British customs vessel *Gaspee* in Narragansett Bay. The commissioners are to convene for two sessions in January 1773 and on May 17, 1773 with no result, owing to the hostility of the Rhode Island colonists. The commission is finally abandoned in June 1773.

28 OCTOBER 1772
Revolution: Approach Over the opposition of John Hancock and other influential patriots, Samuel Adams is able to issue a call for a Boston town meeting to take place at the beginning of November to consider the imminent threats to self–government in the colonies.

2 NOVEMBER 1772
Revolution: Approach At the Boston town meeting called by Samuel Adams, a 21-member committee of correspondence is appointed, with James Otis, Samuel Adams and Joseph Warren as chairmen, to make Boston's position known to other Massachusetts towns as well as to the other colonies. Other towns begin to organize committees of correspondence.

20 NOVEMBER 1772
Revolution: Approach The Boston town meeting endorses three radical proclamations issued by the newly created committee of correspondence, which are then transmitted to the other towns. Comprising these radical statements of principle are Samuel Adams' "State of the Rights of the Colonists," Joseph Warren's "List of Infringements and Violations of Those Rights," and Dr. Benjamin Church's "Letter of Correspondence." Church is subsequently unmasked as a British informer.

OTHER EVENTS OF 1772
Revolution: Approach Late in the year, London

agent for the Massachusetts Assembly Benjamin Franklin mails to Massachusetts Speaker of the House Thomas Cushing the original copies of six letters from then Massachusetts Chief Justice Thomas Hutchinson and provincial secretary Andrew Oliver to a member of the British government, Thomas Whately. Franklin was given the letters by Whately to demonstrate that misinformation from colonial sources has motivated some of the objectionable actions of the British. Franklin warns Cushing not to copy or publish the letters, but only to show the originals to involved Massachusetts colonists.

Slavery In the Sommersett case in England, the Chief Justice Lord Mansfield proclaims a slave free the moment he sets foot on English soil.

Westward Movement Settlers led by John Sevier and James Robertson from Virginia and North Carolina travel to the eastern territory of Tennessee, ceded to the English crown by the Six Nations of the Iroquois Indians. There they establish the Watauga Association. Formed to govern the area outside the established 13 colonies, the Watauga Association is the first local independent government in the American colonies. With the approval of the British, a committee of five elected delegates rules according to the articles issued by the Watauga Association.

Arts/Culture Maryland painter Charles Willson Peale paints the first full-length life-sized portrait of George Washington, showing him at the age of 40 and wearing the uniform of the French and Indian War. Washington will later pose for six other paintings by Peale. The versatile Peale, together with other members of his family, conducts a veritable factory of portrait painting and experiments in numerous other fields of endeavor. A number of Peale's 17 sons and daughters also become gifted painters in their own right.

12 MARCH 1773

Revolution: Approach Following the example of Massachusetts, the Virginia House of Burgesses delegates an 11-member correspondence committee, including Patrick Henry, Thomas Jefferson and Richard Henry Lee, to oversee communication with the other colonies in the common expression of their grievances against England.

27 APRIL–7 MAY 1773

British Policy The English Parliament passes legislation mandating the revocation of all export duties on English tea going to the American colonies. Nevertheless, the threepenny per pound import tax on tea remains in effect. This enactment is instigated by the desperate lobbying of the East India Company, which is teetering on the edge of bankruptcy in part because of the effective tea embargo by the American colonies.

10 MAY 1773

Revolution: Approach The Tea Act becomes effective. Aside from the retention of the threepenny tax, the act grants the East India Company the right to sell its tea directly to colonial agents or consignees, thus putting the East India Company in a position to undersell the law-abiding colonial merchants who have to purchase English tea through the agency of middlemen at higher prices.

JUNE 1773

Revolution: Approach Contrary to the warning of Massachusetts London agent Benjamin Franklin, Samuel Adams reads the Hutchinson letters to a secret meeting of the Massachusetts assembly, and subsequently has them copied and published.

8 JULY 1773

Revolution: Approach By this date, the colonies of Rhode Island, Connecticut, New Hampshire and South Carolina have formed committees of correspondence.

SEPTEMBER 1773

British Policy The English Parliament authorizes the East India Company to ship half a million pounds of tea to Boston, New York, Philadelphia and Charleston, consigned to a group of specifically chosen merchants.

16 OCTOBER 1773

Revolution: Approach In Philadelphia, a mass meeting is held to consider the implications of the new Tea Act. The colonists not only oppose the six-year-old threepenny import duty but also the virtual monopoly of the tea trade granted the East India Company by Parliament. The Philadelphians name a committee to procure the resignation of the tea consignees in the city.

5-6 NOVEMBER 1773

Revolution: Approach In Boston, a town meeting endorses the actions taken by Philadelphia colonists against the Tea Act. However, the Boston activists are unable to force the resignation of the Boston tea consignees, who include two sons and a nephew of Massachusetts Governor Hutchinson.

10 NOVEMBER 1773

Revolution: Approach In New York City, a broadside warns harbor pilots not to guide any vessels bearing tea into the harbor.

27 NOVEMBER 1773

Revolution: Approach In Boston, the first of the three ships bearing tea, the *Dartmouth,* arrives.

29 NOVEMBER 1773

Revolution: Approach A meeting of the New York Sons of Liberty condemns tea consignees as enemies of the colonists. The Sons of Liberty implement an embargo on tea and a boycott of the merchant consignees.

29-30 NOVEMBER 1773

Revolution: Approach Two mass meetings are held

in Boston to consider what actions should be taken on the issue of the shipload of tea now in Boston Harbor. The colonists decide to send the tea on the *Dartmouth* back to England without paying the import duty. Royal Governor Thomas Hutchinson opposes this motion and commands the harbor officials to let the tea ships out of the harbor only if their captains present proof that the tea duties have been paid. He is to repeat this command on December 16.

2 DECEMBER 1773
Revolution: Approach At Charleston, South Carolina, as the English ship *London* arrives bearing the tea bound for the city's merchant consignees, a mass meeting of activists the following day demands and receives the resignation of all tea consignees.

16 DECEMBER 1773
Revolution: Approach Some 8000 Bostonians meet in Old South Church to hear Samuel Adams, chairman of the gathering, receive the news that Massachusetts Governor Hutchinson will not allow the ships to leave Boston Harbor without the payment of the duty on the tea. During the night a group of activists disguised as Mohawk Indians board the tea ships and dump all 342 casks of tea into the water in what becomes known as the Boston Tea Party.

22 DECEMBER 1773
Revolution: Approach In Charleston, South Carolina, meeting no opposition, the royal customs commissioners board the tea ship *London* at the conclusion of the 20-day waiting period mandated by customs regulations and seize the tea for the nonpayment of the mandated duties. The tea is stored in government warehouses until American revolutionaries auction it off to raise money for the war effort.

25 DECEMBER 1773
Revolution: Approach Based on the information contained in the Hutchinson letters, published in June, the Massachusetts assembly petitions the English Crown for the removal of royal Governor Thomas Hutchinson and of Andrew Oliver. This causes a scandal in England. By now, Thomas Whately, who gave letters to Benjamin Franklin, has died. Whately's brother William accuses a John Temple of stealing and releasing the letters. This results in one duel and another one is planned when Benjamin Franklin hears of the turn of events. Franklin claims sole responsibility for sending the letters to Boston.

OTHER EVENTS OF 1773
Slavery Yale president Ezra Stiles and Congregational clergyman Samuel Hopkins promote the idea of colonizing West Africa with free American blacks.
Agriculture In Virginia, Philip Mazzei imports workers and materials from Italy in order to establish the culture of silkworms.

29 JANUARY 1774
British Policy A committee of the English Privy

Council meets to begin hearings on the Massachusetts petition for the removal of Governor Hutchinson and provincial secretary Andrew Oliver, based on the information revealed by the Hutchinson letters.

30 JANUARY 1774
British Policy Severely criticized for his role in the Hutchinson letters scandal, Benjamin Franklin is notified by the British government that he has been removed from his office as Deputy Postmaster General for America.

FEBRUARY 1774
Revolution: Approach By this time all of the American colonies except for North Carolina and Pennsylvania have formed committees of correspondence.

7 FEBRUARY 1774
British Policy The special investigative commission reports to the English Privy Council that the Massachusetts petition calling for the dismissal of Governor Hutchinson and Andrew Oliver is based on false charges.

31 MARCH 1774
Revolution: Approach In response to the continuing rebelliousness of the Massachusetts Colony, an angry Parliament passes a series of Coercive Acts. The first of these is the Boston Port Bill, to go into force June 1. The port bill forbids any shipping or trade in Boston harbor except for that involving military supplies and certain approved cargos of food and fuel. The bill also provides for the stationing of customs officials at Salem rather than Boston. If Massachusetts reimburses customs and the East India Company for the duties owed and the costs of the Boston Tea Party, only then will the port be reopened to all maritime traffic.

22 APRIL 1774
Revolution: Approach In New York, a private tea consignee secretly tries to unload a tea cargo in defiance of the colonial tea embargo. Disguised as Indians, members of the New York Sons of Liberty dump the tea into the water.

12 MAY 1774
Revolution: Approach A Boston town meeting calls for the reinstitution of the nonimportation policy against Great Britain to force repeal of the Boston Port Bill.

13 MAY 1774
British Policy The commander of all British forces in the American colonies, General Thomas Gage, arrives in Boston to replace Thomas Hutchinson as governor of Massachusetts. Four regiments of troops follow Gage to Boston.

17 MAY 1774
Revolution: Approach The citizens of Providence, Rhode Island, are the first to call for an intercolonial

congress to combat the Coercive Acts. This call is followed by one from Philadelphia on May 21, and another from New York on May 23. Instead of supporting Boston's call for immediate nonimportation, these cities advocate a discussion of possible common strategies at the proposed intercolonial congress.

20 MAY 1774
British Policy The English Parliament enacts another in the series of Coercive Acts, the Administration of Justice Act, which protects the royal officials of the Massachusetts colony by sheltering them from legal suits in the colonial courts. A trial can be transferred to England provided that the governor swears that the offense has been committed during the course of implementing British policy—such as suppressing a riot or collecting taxes—and that the defendant will not receive a fair colonial trial. The provincial council must agree to this change of venue.

The Massachusetts Regulating Act, passed on the same day by Parliament, effects radical alterations in the political structure of the colony. The Government Act virtually voids the Massachusetts charter by mandating the appointment of the members of the council, the chief justice and the superior judges by the king; and the appointment of the attorney general, the lower judges, justices of the peace and sheriffs by the royal governor. Juries are to be called by the sheriffs rather than chosen by the townspeople. Furthermore, the holding of town meetings and their agendas, aside from the annual election session, requires the written consent of the governor.

The third act passed by Parliament is the Quebec Act which mandates a permanent centralized civil governmental system in Canada. A council appointed by the king is to have power over legislation, subject to the king's veto, and Parliament is to have authority over all but local taxation. In addition, civil cases are to be tried without a jury and Catholics are granted freedom of conscience and basic civil rights. Finally, the southern boundary of Canada is extended to the Ohio River, encompassing the territory claimed by Connecticut, Massachusetts and Virginia. The American colonists object to the last provision most strenuously, leading to their classification of the Quebec Act as one of the "intolerable" measures.

24 MAY 1774
Revolution: Approach The Virginia House of Burgesses designates June 1, the day on which the Boston Port Act is to go into effect, as a day of fasting and prayer.

26 MAY 1774
Revolution: Approach Virginia Governor Dunmore dissolves the Virginia House of Burgesses.

27 MAY 1774
Revolution: Approach In an unofficial meeting at Williamsburg's Raleigh Tavern, the Virginia burgesses proclaim their support for an annual intercolonial congress. They dispatch copies of their resolution to the other colonial legislatures.

1 JUNE 1774
Revolution: Approach The Boston Port Act becomes effective and closes Boston Harbor to ship traffic and trade, until such time as the damages and duties for the Boston Tea Party are reimbursed to the East India Company and the English Crown.

2 JUNE 1774
British Policy Parliament enacts an amended version of the 1765 Quartering Act, now making it applicable to all of the American colonies and providing for the quartering of British troops in occupied houses, taverns and unoccupied buildings.

5 JUNE 1774
Revolution: Approach The Massachusetts Committee of Correspondence in Boston draws up a nonimportation pact, the Solemn League and Convenant, to become effective October 1, 1774.

15 JUNE-25 AUGUST 1774
Revolution: Approach Gradually, all of the American colonies, with the exception of Georgia, appoint delegates to the first intercolonial congress in Philadelphia in September.

6 AUGUST 1774
Ideas/Beliefs The founder of the Shaker movement in the American colonies, Mother Ann Lee, arrives in New York from Liverpool, England.

17 AUGUST 1774
Revolution: Approach Philadelphia attorney James Wilson issues an influential pamphlet, *Considerations on the Nature and Extent of the Legislative Authority of the British Parliament,* which advocates allegiance to the English king and rejects the power of Parliament over the colonies. Known as the dominion theory, this opinion is also espoused by Thomas Jefferson's *Summary View of the Rights of British America,* and John Adams' Novanglus "New England," letters of December 1774–April 1775, which propose the individual colonies as separate realms under the sovereignty of the British king.

27 AUGUST 1774
Westward Movement North Carolina Judge Richard Henderson and a group of his friends found the Transylvania Company for the purposes of land speculation in the Kentucky region and for settling Kentucky.

1 SEPTEMBER 1774
Revolution: Approach Governor Thomas Gage seizes the Massachusetts Colony's arsenal at Charlestown. Although thousands of militiamen rush to Charlestown, no violence ensues.

5 SEPTEMBER 1774
Revolution: Approach The First Continental Con-

gress with 56 delegates from all of the colonies except Georgia meets in Carpenters Hall, Philadelphia. This session will last until October 26, 1774. Conservative as well as radical delegates attend, and Peyton Randolph of Virginia is elected president.

17 SEPTEMBER 1774
Revolution: Approach The radicals from Massachusetts at the First Continental Congress are successful in having the Suffolk Resolves endorsed. Drawn up by Joseph Warren, adopted by a Suffolk County, Massachusetts, convention and delivered by Paul Revere to Philadelphia, the Suffolk Acts proclaim the Coercive Acts unconstitutional and "hence not to be obeyed;" advise Massachusetts citizens to form a tax collecting body and to hold the taxes in escrow until the Coercive Acts are repealed; promote the formation and arming of local militia units and advocate strict economic sanctions against England.

28 SEPTEMBER 1774
Revolution: Approach The conservative delegates to the First Continental Congress unite in supporting Pennsylvania delegate Joseph Galloway's "Plan of a Proposed Union between Great Britain and the Colonies." This plan, which is defeated by one vote at the congress, advocates local self rule and a central president-general appointed by the king, who also has veto powers over a legislative grand council elected by the colonial assemblies.

SEPTEMBER 1774
Revolution: Approach After the seizure of the Massachusetts arsenal at Charlestown, Governor Thomas Gage fortifies Boston Neck.

5 OCTOBER 1774
Revolution: Approach Following the adoption of the Suffolk Resolves, the Massachusetts Assembly, reorganized as a provincial congress, meets in Salem. This congress reconvenes later at Concord to elect John Hancock president and as head of a committee of safety to implement the organization of a colonial militia, and in particular the Minutemen.

10 OCTOBER 1774
Westward Movement Virginia forces win the battle of Point Pleasant at the mouth of the Great Kanawha River, thus ending the war of Governor Dunmore against the Shawnee Indians and eliminating danger to the new settlements in the Kentucky and Tennessee territory.

14 OCTOBER 1774
Revolution: Approach The First Continental Congress adopts a Declaration and Resolves opposing the Coercive Acts, the Quebec Act, the extension of the vice admiralty courts, the dissolution of the colonial assemblies, the maintenance of British troops in colonial towns during peacetime and all of the revenue acts since 1763. Ten resolutions enumerate the rights of the colonists, including those of "life, liberty and property," and the rights of the colonial assemblies to enact taxes and legislation, subject only to royal veto.

20 OCTOBER 1774
Revolution: Approach The First Continental Congress adopts the Continental Association, based on the Virginia Association. In execution of this association, the congressional delegates agree to implement a nonimportation policy, to discontinue the slave trade, and to embargo all exports to England, Ireland and the West Indies. These provisions are to be overseen by local committees, and violators are to be punished by boycott and publicity.

26 OCTOBER 1774
Revolution: Approach The First Continental Congress adjourns, with provisions for a second session of the congress on May 10, 1775 if the grievances of the American colonies against Britain have not been corrected by that date.

30 NOVEMBER 1774
Revolution: Approach Encouraged by Benjamin Franklin, Thomas Paine emigrates to America and settles in Philadelphia.

14 DECEMBER 1774
Revolution: Approach Warned by Paul Revere of a British plan to station troops at Portsmouth, New Hampshire, a group of Massachusetts militiamen led by Major John Sullivan successfully attack the arsenal of Fort William and Mary in Portsmouth and capture arms and ammunition. No lives are lost in this encounter.

OTHER EVENTS OF 1774
Westward Movement The Illinois and Wabash land companies are organized to purchase large tracts of western territory. Pennsylvanian James Harrod establishes Harrodsburg, the first permanent settlement in the Kentucky territory.
Slavery Rhode Island and Connecticut forbid the further importation of slaves.
Arts/Culture The foremost painter in the American colonies, Boston portraitist John Singleton Copley, emigrates to England among the early wave of Loyalists who foresee coming events.

19 JANUARY 1775
British Policy The colonial petitions and the Declaration and Resolves of the First Continental Congress are presented to Parliament. In a conciliatory move, Lord Chatham requests the immediate removal of British troops from Boston, but this motion is defeated.

23 JANUARY 1775
Revolution: Approach The Georgia Colony adopts a revised version of the Continental Association which mandates a nonimportation policy and a trade embargo against Britain to force repeal of the Coercive Acts of 1774.

THOMAS PAINE, 1737-1809

Ever a center of controversy, Thomas Paine was a professional radical and a revolutionary propagandist without peer. Born in England the son of a Quaker corsetmaker, Paine attended school until the age of 13 and then continued to intensively educate himself while pursuing various trades. His lobbying for better wages for excisemen led to his own dismissal and subsequent bankruptcy. Profoundly impressed by Paine, Benjamin Franklin sponsored his 1774 emigration at the age of 37 to Philadelphia, where he contributed articles on all subjects to the *Pennsylvania Magazine*. In 1776, Paine anonymously published his stirring *Common Sense*. This pamphlet advocated an immediate declaration of independence, and posited a special moral obligation of America to the rest of the world. An instant best-seller, both in the colonies and in Europe, *Common Sense* made Paine internationally famous. After enlistment in Washington's army as it retreated across New Jersey, Paine wrote the first of his 16 pamphlets entitled *The American Crisis*. Beginning with the words, "These are the times that try men's souls. The summer soldier and the sunshine patriot will, in this crisis, shrink from the service of their country," the pamphlet was read aloud to the troops during one of America's darker hours. It helped to raise morale and increase support for the revolutionary cause. In 1777 a grateful Congress appointed Paine as secretary to its committee on foreign affairs, and in 1781 he completed a successful mission to France to obtain financial aid and badly needed supplies. That idealism was his ruling motivation is proved by his donation of nearly a third of his salary to aid Washington's army. After the war, he retired to a confiscated Loyalist farm in New Rochelle given to him by the state of New York. There he continued his literary output and also designed an iron bridge. In 1787 Paine returned to Europe to see his bridge built and to fan the flames of revolution, unsuccessfully in England and successfully in France. Issued in 1791-1792, his *Rights of Man* advocated the role of government as protecting the natural rights of man and promoted the replacement of the British monarchy by a republic. For this the English found him guilty of treason. Welcomed in France by the revolutionaries, he was declared a citizen and elected to the legislative assembly. But the moderates lost power during the reign of terror and Paine, who supported imprisonment and banishment for Louis XVI, was forcibly confined in the Luxembourg Palais for the duration. Here he composed *The Age of Reason*, a Deistic work that earned him scorn for its atheistic implications. Finally released from jail through the efforts of James Monroe, Paine subsequently alienated America still further by his *Letter to Washington*, which unjustly accused the president and Gouverneur Morris of persecuting him. The 1802 return of Paine to America was greeted by a public outcry and social ostracism. He spent his last years in Bordentown, New Jersey, New York City and New Rochelle in ill health and penury.

1 FEBRUARY 1775

Revolution: Approach In Cambridge, Massachusetts, a second provincial congress convenes under John Hancock and Joseph Warren, and draws up a series of defensive measures to prepare the colony for a state of war.

British Policy In Parliament, Lord Chatham introduces a conciliation plan that recognizes the Continental Congress, advocates the assent of the colonists to all taxation and requires the American colonies to recognize the authority of Parliament. Again, this plan is rejected.

9 FEBRUARY 1775

British Policy Parliament declares the colony of Massachusetts to be in a state of rebellion.

26 FEBRUARY 1775

Revolution: Approach British forces land at Salem, Massachusetts, to capture the arsenal of the colonists, but they are repulsed with no casualties.

27 FEBRUARY 1775

British Policy Parliament endorses the conciliation plan of Lord North, which calls for the abolition of all but regulatory taxes on the American colonies and provides for the colonies to raise their own revenues for the common defense and the administrative costs of government and the judicial system.

10 MARCH 1775

Westward Movement The Transylvania Company sends Daniel Boone and 30 woodchoppers to cut the Wilderness Road from Fort Wautauga to the mouth of the Kentucky River.

17 MARCH 1775

Indians The treaty of Sycamore Shoals is negotiated between the Cherokee Indians and the Transylvania Company, whereby the Indians grant a land tract in the Kentucky territory to the company in return for $10,000 in goods.

22 MARCH 1775

British Policy Edmund Burke addresses Parliament

opposing the proposed New England Restraining Act and supporting conciliation with the colonies.

23 MARCH 1775
Revolution: Approach At the second meeting of the Virginia convention in Richmond, Patrick Henry opposes the arbitrary rule of Britain with a speech that closes, "Give me liberty or give me death."

30 MARCH 1775
British Policy King George III endorses the New England Restraining Act, which forbids the New England colonies from trading with any other countries except England after July 1, and also bans them from fishing in the North Atlantic after July 20. On April 13, the provisions of the New England Restraining Act will also be applied to Maryland, New Jersey, Pennsylvania, South Carolina and Virginia when Parliament hears that these colonies have ratified the Continental Association.

APRIL 1775
Revolution: Politics By April, the Continental Association, mandated by the first continental congress to enforce a nonimportation policy and trade embargo, is in effect in all 13 colonies.

1 APRIL 1775
Westward Movement In the employ of the Transylvania Company, Daniel Boone establishes the settlement and fort of Boonesborough on the Kentucky River.

14 APRIL 1775
Revolution: Approach Massachusetts Governor Gage receives a letter from Lord Dartmouth ordering him to use all necessary force to implement the Coercive and other acts, and to strike preemptively to circumvent further buildup of the colonial military machine.
Slavery The first abolition society in the American colonies, the Society for the Relief of Free Negroes Unlawfully Held in Bondage, is established in Philadelphia by Benjamin Franklin and Dr. Benjamin Rush.

18-19 APRIL 1775
Revolution: North General Thomas Gage orders Lieutenant Colonel Francis Smith to lead 700 British soldiers to Concord, Massachusetts, to destroy the colonial arms depot there. The Boston Committee of Safety sends Paul Revere and William Dawes to warn of the coming attack. Revere warns John Hancock and Samuel Adams in Lexington, and then rides on toward Concord with Dawes and Dr. Samuel Prescott. They encounter a British patrol which captures Revere, who is later released. Only Prescott is able to reach Concord. When Smith's forces reach Lexington, a standoff occurs between the British and some 70 armed minutemen. An unordered shot leads to the killing of eight Americans and the wounding of eight others. Smith proceeds to Concord where some arms

---

PATRICK HENRY, 1736-1799

Although his career encompassed the roles of influential statesman and of a brilliant self-educated lawyer, Patrick Henry's claim to immortality lies in his reputation as the greatest orator of the American Revolution—as a "forest-born Demosthenes." Born to a Virginia frontier farming family, Henry was educated at home. All of his early business ventures—as a part-owner of a store with his older brother, as a planter and once again as a store keeper—met with conspicuous failure. In 1760, he obtained a license to practice law. This vocation would finally bring him the success that had so far eluded him; in his first three years, he won most of his 1185 cases. Henry's eloquent defense in the "parson's cause" also brought him public acclaim and entry into politics. In his first term in the Virginia House of Burgesses, the radical Henry led a coalition of the frontier counties against the interests of the landed tidewater gentry. In his impetuous speech opposing the Stamp Act and its threat to individual liberties, Henry concluded with the stirring challenge, "If this be treason, make the most of it." This speech was equalled by his 1775 address to the Virginia legislature which ended, "Give me liberty, or give me death." After serving as a Virginia delegate to the First and Second Continental Congresses, Henry returned home to play an important part in drafting the new constitution of Virginia. Elected the first governor of Virginia, Henry was an active administrator who sent George Rogers Clark into the Northwest Territory in order to expel the British. He opposed the ratification of the new United States Constitution on the grounds that the resulting strong central government would threaten states' rights and individual liberties. After serving five terms as Virginia governor, Henry's failing health forced him to decline a number of important offices, including election to the United States Senate, the post of President Washington's secretary of state, the position of chief justice of the United States Supreme Court, reelection as Virginia governor and the position of minister to France. In a surprising and inexplicable reversal, in his last years Henry abandoned his lifelong antifederalist political philosophy and, in effect, became a fervent supporter of the now–declining Federalist party.

---

and supplies are destroyed. On the return to Boston, the British are beset by ever–increasing numbers of colonial militia, and only British reinforcements save Smith's troops from eradication. The colonial forces then begin a siege of Boston that lasts for nearly a

The Minutemen leaving home to fight.

The Battle of Lexington, April 19, 1775.

year. News of the Battles of Lexington and Concord reaches Philadelphia on April 24, Virginia on April 30, North Carolina on May 7 and South Carolina on May 8.

23 APRIL 1775
Revolution: North The Massachusetts Provincial Congress orders the mobilization of 13,600 colonial soldiers, appoints Artemas Ward commander–in–chief and requests aid from the other colonies.

10 MAY 1775
Revolution: North Ethan Allen, accompanied by Benedict Arnold, captures the strategic British garrison of Fort Ticonderoga and its rich arsenal of military supplies.
Revolution: Politics The Second Continental Congress convenes in Independence Hall in Philadelphia. After Virginian Peyton Randolph withdraws as president, John Hancock is elected to replace him. On May 15 a resolution is passed placing the colonies in a state of defense and on May 29 a measure is passed asking the colonists of Canada to join on the side of the American rebels.

12 MAY 1775
Revolution: North The British garrison at Crown Point on Lake Champlain is seized by Seth Warren and his men.

16 MAY 1775
Revolution: Politics The Massachusetts Provincial Congress drafts a constitution that is rejected by the popular vote.
Revolution: North Benedict Arnold destroys the British fort of St. John's in Canadian territory and then withdraws southward.

20 MAY 1775
Revolution: Politics The Mecklenburg County Resolutions, reputedly originating from North Carolina, are presented at the Second Continental Congress. They annul all British implemented and derived laws, sus-

BENEDICT ARNOLD, 1741-1801

The name of Benedict Arnold is synonymous with treachery. But although Arnold is inevitably cited as the would-be betrayer of West Point to the British, his earlier military successes, including various instances of conspicuous bravery, were so remarkable that he earned the respect and support of George Washington, leader of the Continental Army. Arnold was a fourth-generation American born in Norwich, Connecticut, to an influential New England family. He entered the military life at an early age when he ran away at 14 to fight in the French and Indian War. In an act that foreshadowed later events, he deserted the army and returned home alone through the wilderness when he had had enough of soldiering. Arnold carved a prosperous existence for himself and his family in New Haven, first as a druggist and bookseller, and later as a dealer in the West India trade. When news of the battles at Lexington and Concord reached him, Arnold immediately assembled the militia company he captained and volunteered to retrieve 80 cannons from Fort Ticonderoga. He had to share the Ticonderoga victory with Ethan Allen, and he later distinguished himself by capturing the British fort at St. John's and with his arduous march through the wilderness to attack Quebec. Arnold was able to thwart the British plan to invade England from Canada by his farsighted and resourceful construction of a naval fleet on Lake Champlain, and his commendable defense in the Battle of Valcour. When Congress promoted five junior officers over him, both Arnold and George Washington hotly protested, with no immediate result. But after Arnold's heroic attack on the British at Ridgefield and Norwalk, Connecticut, his clever ruse to capture Fort Stanwix and the important role he played in the defeat of Burgoyne at Saratoga, Congress advanced him to his rightful rank. In 1778, Washington appointed Arnold commander of Philadelphia after the evacuation of the British. There he was accused of improprieties. Arnold demanded and was granted a court martial which cleared him of most of the charges. During this period he initiated treasonous contact with the British with the aid of his second wife, Margaret Shippen, sending them important military information and finally planning to surrender West Point, of which he became commander. With the news of British agent Major Andre's capture, Arnold went over to the British. Before his departure for England in 1781, he conducted two brutal raids on American forces, one in Virginia and the other on New London, Connecticut. Various motivations have been ascribed for his treason—including an overly protective mother, his bitterness at being slighted by Congress and the Pennsylvania authorities, and a need for funds occasioned by the fact that Congress had not reimbursed him for monies he put out toward his military campaigns. In any case, rewards were not forthcoming from the British, who scorned him as a traitor and allowed him to die without ever fully paying him for his treason.

pend the royal government of the colony placing all power in the hands of the provincial congress, and brand those accepting royal commissions as traitors.

25 MAY 1775
Revolution: North British generals John Burgoyne, Sir Henry Clinton and Sir William Howe arrive in Boston to reinforce General Gage.

12 JUNE 1775

Revolution: North Massachusetts Governor General Gage imposes martial law, declaring the armed colonists and those helping them to be rebels and traitors, and offers pardons to all rebels who take an oath of allegiance to the crown. Samuel Adams and John Hancock are excepted from this pardon.

14 JUNE 1775

Revolution: Politics The Second Continental Congress decides to raise six companies of riflemen, and to authorize salaries for the soldiers of the Army.

15 JUNE 1775

Revolution: Politics By a unanimous vote of the Second Continental Congress, George Washington is appointed to head the Continental Army.

17 JUNE 1775

Revolution: North The Battle of Bunker Hill (actually on adjacent Breed's Hill) is fought outside of Boston. The British win but suffer heavy losses of men—1150, to the 441 lost by the colonists—while the Americans demonstrate their tenacity of purpose. The colonial leader, General Joseph Warren, is killed.
Revolution: Politics Congress appoints four major generals for the Continental Army—Charles Lee, Israel Putnam, Philip Schuyler and Artemas Ward.

22 JUNE 1775

Finance To raise money for the support of the army,

Congress votes to issue $2 million in bills of credit, or continental money.

3 JULY 1775

Revolution: North After a 12-day journey from Philadelphia, George Washington assumes formal command of the Continental Army of about 17,000 men in Cambridge, Massachusetts.

5 JULY 1775

Revolution: Politics Congress adopts the Olive Branch Petition written by John Dickinson, expressing colonial hopes of reconciliation to King George III and asking for his help in working for a restoration of peace.

6 JULY 1775

Revolution: Politics Congress adopts the Declaration of the Causes and Necessities of Taking Up Arms, written by Dickinson and Jefferson, which rejects independence but insists Americans would rather die than be enslaved.

25 JULY 1775

Revolution: Politics Dr. Benjamin Church is appointed the first surgeon general of the Continental Army. On October 4, 1775 he will be court martialled for "criminal correspondence with the enemy."

26 JULY 1775

Colonial Affairs Congress establishes a Post Office

A Revolutionary War enlistment poster.

FOUNDING A NATION 986-1787

The Battle of Bunker Hill, June 17, 1775.

Department with Benjamin Franklin as Postmaster General.

31 JULY 1775
Revolution: Politics Congress rejects the conciliation plan of Lord North, which it received on May 26.

1 AUGUST 1775
Life/Customs Thomas Paine publishes an article supporting women's rights in the *Pennsylvania Gazette,* of which he is editor.

23 AUGUST 1775
British Policy King George III refuses to receive the conciliatory Olive Branch Petition from the Second Continental Congress, and he issues a proclamation declaring the American colonies to be in a state of open rebellion.

18 OCTOBER 1775
Revolution: North British forces burn Falmouth, or present-day Portland, in Maine.

7 NOVEMBER 1775
Revolution: South Virginia Governor Dunmore institutes martial law in the colonies and starts to organize a Loyalist army. He loses the support of the planters, however, when he promises freedom to all blacks who leave their masters and join a regiment.

13 NOVEMBER 1775
Revolution: North American Brigadier General Richard Montgomery occupies Montreal, after his recapture of the British Canadian garrison of St. John's.

28 NOVEMBER 1775
Revolution: Naval The Second Continental Congress formally establishes an American Navy and adopts rules for its regulation. On 22 December, Esek Hopkins is named commodore of the Colonial Navy.

29 NOVEMBER 1775
Revolution: Politics Congress appoints a Committee of Secret Correspondence to establish relations with

and seek aid from friendly European nations. In December they hear through their agents that France may offer the American colonists support.

11 DECEMBER 1775
Revolution: South Virginia Governor Dunmore is defeated at Great Bridge by a combined force of 900 Virginians and North Carolinians.

23 DECEMBER 1775
British Policy King George III issues a royal proclamation closing the American colonies to all trade and commerce, effective March 1, 1776.

31 DECEMBER 1775
Revolution: North In the Battle of Quebec, the American forces led by Benedict Arnold and Richard Montgomery are driven back by the British.

1 JANUARY 1776
Revolution: South Virginia Governor Dunmore orders the shelling of the garrison at Norfolk.

5 JANUARY 1776
Revolution: Politics The assembly of the New Hampshire colony adopts the first state constitution.

9 JANUARY 1776
Revolution: Politics In Philadelphia, Thomas Paine publishes *Common Sense,* a highly effective propagandistic pamphlet that attacks the English crown and presents a clear and persuasive argument for colonial independence.

24 JANUARY 1776
Revolution: North American Colonel Henry Knox arrives in Cambridge, Massachusetts, with the 43 British cannons and 16 mortars captured by Ethan Allen at Fort Ticonderoga. The artillery have been transported cross country through the wilderness.

27 FEBRUARY 1776
Revolution: South A colonial force of North Carolina patriots resoundingly defeats a detachment of Scottish Loyalists at Moore's Creek Bridge near Wilmington. The colonists take some 900 prisoners.

3 MARCH 1776
Revolution: Politics The Continental Congress appoints Silas Deane as colonial agent to France, his assignment being to secure financial and military aid.

4-5 MARCH 1776
Revolution: North Led by General John Thomas, American forces capture Dorchester Heights, overlooking Boston Harbor. Now the patriots can place the artillery brought by Colonel Knox from Ticonderoga in place, to effectively enforce their siege of the British forces in Boston.

7-17 MARCH 1776
Revolution: North Led by General William Howe,

the British evacuate Boston. Howe's army and a group of 1000 Loyalists set sail on a fleet of troop-ships for Halifax, Nova Scotia.

14 MARCH 1776
Revolution: Politics The Continental Congress recommends a policy of disarming all loyalist American colonists.

19 MARCH 1776
Revolution: Naval The Continental Congress authorizes privateering raids on British shipping.

6 APRIL 1776
Revolution: Politics Congress proclaims the colonial ports open to all marine traffic excluding that of Great Britain and her possessions.

12 APRIL 1776
Revolution: Politics The North Carolina Provincial Assembly is the first to authorize her delegates to the Continental Congress to support independence of the American colonies from Great Britain.

13 APRIL 1776
Revolution: North After the evacuation of Boston by the British, George Washington leads the main part of his force to New York, thus anticipating the strategy of General Howe to secure New York City as his operational base.

1 MAY–5 JULY 1776
Revolution: North After a fruitless three-month siege of Montreal, American Brigadier General Benedict Arnold leads a part of his colonial forces southward to prepare for the defense of the Lake Champlain region. During the same period, the commander of the British forces in Canada, General Guy Carleton, prepares for an invasion of New England from the north.

2 MAY 1776
Revolution: Politics French King Louis XVI consigns one million dollars worth of arms and munitions to the American revolutionaries through secret agent Pierre de Beaumarchais. Soon thereafter, Spain also agrees to support the revolutionaries.

3 MAY 1776
Revolution: South British reinforcements led by General Cornwallis join General Clinton's forces off the Carolinas.

9-16 MAY 1776
Revolution: Naval Commodore of the colonial navy, Esek Hopkins successfully leads an attack on the British naval station in the Bahamas. The Americans occupy Nassau and capture a large military arsenal.

10 MAY 1776
Revolution: Politics The Continental Congress issues a resolution authorizing each of the 13 colonies to form a new provincial government.

15 MAY 1776
Revolution: Politics The Virginia delegation to the Continental Congress is authorized by its colonial assembly to support independence.

4 JUNE 1776
Revolution: South American General Charles Lee arrives from New York to command the colonial defense of Charleston, South Carolina.

7 JUNE 1776
Revolution: North During the American retreat from Canadian territory, General John Sullivan attempts an unsuccessful attack against the British at Three Rivers. Sullivan subsequently retreats to Fort Ticonderoga.
Revolution: Politics Virginia delegate to the Continental Congress, Richard Henry Lee, presents a formal resolution calling for independence. A final decision on this resolution is postponed until July 1.

11 JUNE 1776
Revolution: Politics The Continental Congress appoints a committee consisting of John Adams, Benjamin Franklin, Thomas Jefferson, Roger R. Livingston and Roger Sherman to compose a declaration of independence. The committee designates Jefferson to prepare the draft of the document.

12 JUNE 1776
Revolution: Politics Congress appoints a committee headed by John Dickinson to prepare a draft plan of confederation. The Virginia assembly endorses the first state bill of rights, drafted by George Mason, as part of the Virginia constitution.

27 JUNE 1776
Revolution: North Colonial traitor Thomas Hickey is publicly hanged in New York for conspiring to deliver George Washington to the British.

28 JUNE 1776
Revolution: Politics With a few changes by John Adams and Benjamin Franklin, Thomas Jefferson's draft of the declaration of independence is presented to Congress for consideration.
Revolution: South American forces under General Charles Lee successfully defend Charleston, South Carolina, against the British attack led by Generals Cornwallis and Clinton on Fort Moultrie. All of the ships in the British fleet are damaged, and the English are not to attempt operations here again for another two years.

JUNE 1776
Revolution: North A large British war fleet, led by General William Howe and Admiral Lord Richard Howe, sails into New York harbor, initiating an ambitious invasion plan.

FOUNDING A NATION 986-1787

2 JULY 1776
Revolution: Politics At the Continental Congress, 12 of the 13 delegations vote to support Richard Henry Lee's resolution for a declaration of independence. The New York delegation has been instructed to abstain from the vote by its colonial assembly.
Revolution: North At New York, British General Howe lands an army of 10,000 men on Staten Island unopposed. Through July and early August, British reinforcements keep arriving on Staten Island, until Howe finally commands a combined force of 32,000 men, of whom 9000 are German mercenaries.

4 JULY 1776
Revolution: Politics Congress formally endorses the Declaration of Independence. Copies of the document are then prepared and sent to all of the colonies. On 9 July, the provincial congress of New York will vote to endorse the document.

12 JULY 1776
Revolution: Politics John Dickinson presents his plan for the confederation of the 13 colonies to the Continental Congress.

20-21 JULY 1776
Indians In North Carolina, a force of Cherokee Indians attacks the settlement of Eaton's Station in the western part of the colony. In retaliation, the North Carolina militia destroys a neighboring Cherokee village.

1 AUGUST 1776
Revolution: North After the British defeat at Charleston, South Carolina, British General Clinton and his troops join the forces of General Howe on Staten Island.

2 AUGUST 1776
Revolution: Politics The parchment copy of the Declaration of Independence is signed in Philadelphia by most of the 55 members of the Continental Congress.

12 AUGUST 1776
Revolution: Politics In order to entice desertions from the British ranks, the Continental Congress enacts legislation granting free land as bounty to English deserters.

27-29 AUGUST 1776
Revolution: North In the Battle of Long Island, the British forces led by General Howe inflict a crushing defeat on Washington's army led by General Israel Putnam, General John Sullivan and General William Alexander. During the night Washington withdraws the colonial forces from Brooklyn Heights to Manhattan.

11 SEPTEMBER 1776
Revolution: Politics In a peace conference on Staten Island called by British General Howe, colonial repre-

The signing of the Declaration of Independence.

sentatives John Adams, Benjamin Franklin and Edmund Rutledge meet with Admiral Lord Howe to no avail, as Howe demands a revocation of the Declaration of Independence.

12 SEPTEMBER 1776
Revolution: North Rather than be trapped in lower Manhattan by the advancing British, Washington decides to evacuate New York City.

16 SEPTEMBER 1776
Revolution: North Before Washington withdraws his army from New York City, he prepares fortifications in upper Manhattan and repulses the British army led by General Howe in the Battle of Harlem Heights.

21 SEPTEMBER 1776
Life/Customs A widespread fire sweeps New York City, destroying nearly 300 buildings. New York, with a population of 22,000, is the second largest city in the colonies after Philadelphia, with 26,000.

22 SEPTEMBER 1776
Revolution: North Caught while spying on the British troops on Long Island, Captain Nathan Hale is executed by the British without the benefit of a trial. His famous last words reportedly are, "I only regret that I have but one life to lose for my country."

26 SEPTEMBER 1776
Revolution: Politics The Continental Congress appoints Silas Deane, Benjamin Franklin and Thomas Jefferson as diplomatic commissioners to negotiate treaties with European nations. Deane and Franklin travel to France, and Congress authorizes them to procure financial and military aid for the revolutionary cause. Jefferson will be replaced by Arthur Lee in December 1776.

3 OCTOBER 1776
Finance In order to help finance the war, Congress authorizes a domestic loan of $5 million at a four percent interest rate. Congress also authorizes the colonial commissioners in Paris to borrow up to £2 million.

9 OCTOBER 1776
Settling On the California coast, Spanish mission-

Franklin on his way to France, 1776.

ate the fort, leaving behind sorely needed munitions and supplies.

Westward Movement The North Carolina provincial congress extends the jurisdiction of the colony over the Watauga settlement, which is annexed as Washington County.

21 NOVEMBER 1776

Revolution: North After deciding to abandon the New York area, Washington moves his forces westward across the Hudson River and through New Jersey. He is joined by General Greene's forces at Hackensack and they retreat together toward the Delaware River with Cornwallis at their heels.

6 DECEMBER 1776

Revolution: North The naval base at Newport, Rhode Island, is occupied by a British force.

11 DECEMBER 1776

Revolution: North Washington leads his forces across the Delaware River near Trenton, New Jersey, into Pennsylvania.

aries establish the mission San Francisco de Asis, a settlement more familiarly known as Yerba Buena. In 1849, it becomes the city of San Francisco.

11 OCTOBER 1776

Revolution: North On Lake Champlain, the improvised colonial 83-gun fleet of Benedict Arnold is trounced by the professionally-manned 87-gun fleet commanded by British General Carleton. In a further confrontation at Split Rock on October 13, the surviving American ships are destroyed. Carleton occupies Crown Point, but soon abandons his plans to invade the American colonies from the north.

23 OCTOBER 1776

Revolution: North At New York, withdrawing before the advancing British forces of General Howe, Washington evacuates his main force from Manhattan Island, leaving behind a garrison at Fort Washington, and marches to White Plains.

28 OCTOBER 1776

Revolution: North In the Battle of White Plains, the British forces of General Howe inflict heavy casualties on Washington's army. Washington slips away westward to North Castle on November 1.

16 NOVEMBER 1776

Revolution: North The 13,000 British soldiers under General Howe capture the American garrison at Fort Washington, taking 2818 prisoners. The British lose 458 men.

19 NOVEMBER 1776

Revolution: North British General Cornwallis forces the American garrison at Fort Lee, New Jersey, commanded by General Nathanael Greene, to evacu-

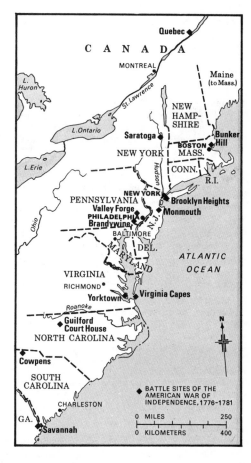

Washington crossing the Delaware.

12 DECEMBER 1776

Revolution: North   Fearing a British attack on Philadelphia, the Continental Congress flees to Baltimore,
where it will meet for the next three months.

13 DECEMBER 1776

Revolution: North   American General Charles Lee,
in charge of the troops from North Castle, is captured
by a British patrol at Basking Ridge, New Jersey.
General Sullivan assumes control of Lee's men and
joins Washington in Pennsylvania.

25–26 DECEMBER 1776

Revolution: North   In a surprise move on Christmas
Day, Washington leads 2400 of his men back across
the Delaware River for a successful attack on the Brit-
ish-Hessian garrison at Trenton, New Jersey under
Colonel Johann Rall. After an hour of battle, the Hessians surrender. Washington takes almost 1000 prisoners, while suffering only six casualties. This victory is
a major morale booster for the revolutionary cause.

31 DECEMBER 1776

Westward Movement   Virginia is petitioned by
George Rogers Clark to annex the Kentucky settle-
ments in danger of Indian attack. This move will also
circumvent the plans of Daniel Boone to organize
Kentucky as a separate state. It is Virginia's Kentucky
County until 1792, when it becomes a state.

3 JANUARY 1777

Revolution: North   George Washington achieves a
second important victory in defeating the British at
Princeton, New Jersey, and drives them, with heavy
losses, toward New Brunswick.

6 JANUARY 1777

Revolution: North   Washington establishes winter
quarters for the exhausted Continental Army in the
hills surrounding Morristown, New Jersey.

15 JANUARY 1777

Colonial Affairs   Independence is declared by the
residents of the New Hampshire Grants—the part of
the New Hampshire territory west of the Connecticut
River, which is also claimed by New York. The settlers establish the "republic" of New Connecticut.

12 MARCH 1777

Revolution: North   Since George Washington has
effectively cleared all but easternmost New Jersey of
British forces, the Continental Congress returns to
Philadelphia from Baltimore, where it reconvenes.

26 APRIL 1777

Revolution: North   British forces destroy an American storage depot in Danbury, Connecticut.

27 APRIL 1777

Revolution: North   In a vigorous battle, Benedict
Arnold defeats British forces at Ridgefield, Connecticut.

20 MAY 1777

Indians   In the Treaty of DeWitts Corner, the Cherokee Indians give up all of their territory in South
Carolina.

14 JUNE 1777

Revolution: Naval   Congress designates veteran seaman John Paul Jones as captain of the 18-gun vessel,
the *Ranger*. Jones is to raid the coastal towns of England.
Revolution: Politics   Congress   enacts   legislation
mandating a "United States" flag, displaying 13 stars
and 13 alternating white and red stripes.

17 JUNE 1777

Revolution: North   British General John Burgoyne
begins his planned invasion of the colonies from Canada with a combined force of 7700 men. Burgoyne
intends to travel down Lake Champlain and the Hudson River Valley to join up with General Howe in
New York City.

30 JUNE 1777

Revolution: North   The British forces of General
Howe leave eastern New Jersey for New York.

6 JULY 1777

Revolution: North   British General Burgoyne takes
Fort Ticonderoga from American General Arthur St.
Clair, who evacuates the fort leaving behind substan-
tial amounts of much-needed military supplies.

12 JULY 1777

Colonial Affairs   Renaming itself Vermont, the New
Connecticut "republic" adopts a constitution mandating manhood suffrage and banning slavery.

20 JULY 1777

Indians   In the Treaty of Long Island, the Overhill
Cherokee Indian cede all of their western North Carolina territory east of the Blue Ridge Mountains and
the Nolichucky River.

JOHN PAUL JONES, 1747-1792

John Paul Jones' command of the ship *Bonhomme Richard* in the naval battle against the *Serapis* reflects some essential features of Jones' character—he was audacious and tactically brilliant, but had little regard for the consequences that were to follow, or for human life. Although Jones had been compared as a naval leader to the likes of Lord Nelson, he was for most of his career a commander in search of a fleet, whether it be American, Russian, or Swedish. At heart, Jones was an adventurer. Born John Paul in Scotland to the family of a gardener, Jones entered the British maritime service at the age of 12. He rose through the ranks while serving on a series of merchant and slave ships. In two separate incidents, in 1770 and 1773, he was accused of causing the death of a crew member—the first by flogging, and the second by stabbing with a sword. Faced by legal action, he fled to Virginia, where he added "Jones" to his name, presumably to confuse pursuers. With the outbreak of the Revolutionary War, Jones volunteered for the American Navy, where he conducted himself commendably. With his first ship, the *Providence*, he raided British fisheries and seized 16 prizes. In 1777, Congress sent Jones to France on the *Ranger*. From France, he raided the British and Scottish coasts, taking seven prizes, including the British naval sloop *Drake*. Jones was then granted command of the *Bonhomme Richard* and a small fleet, sailing under the American flag but financed by the French. During further raids off the British Isles, he took 17 ships before he met the *Serapis* in a desparate and bloody battle. Outclassed in size and artillery, Jones lashed the two ships together and fought the British with muskets, while the continuous use of pumps kept the damaged *Bonhomme Richard* afloat. It was on this occasion that Jones stated the immortal words, "I have not yet begun to fight." After this exploit, Jones was received in Paris with adulation. Following an absence of over three years, he returned to America where he oversaw the construction of the ship, *America*, but his naval service to the United States was essentially over. He was appointed an agent to

France for the collection of prize monies, and he was awarded a congressional gold medal in 1787. After a spell in Empress Catherine's Russian navy, Jones spent his last two years in Paris in ill health. In 1905, Jones' alleged remains were brought from France to the American Naval Academy at Annapolis, Maryland, in order to be gloriously enshrined.

23 JULY 1777
Revolution: North Initiating his campaign to capture Philadelphia, British General Howe sets sail from New York with 15,000 men for Chesapeake Bay.

27 JULY 1777
Revolution: North French nobleman, 20-year-old Marquis de Lafayette arrives in Philadelphia to volunteer his services for the American revolutionary cause. Congress commissions him a major general in the Continental Army.
Revolution: Politics Settler Jane McCrea is murdered by Burgoyne's Indian allies. The news of this and other atrocities prompts colonists to enlist for military service in ever-increasing numbers.

29 JULY 1777
Revolution: North Hearing of the impending arrival of British General Burgoyne, American commander of the northern forces Philip Schuyler abandons Fort Edward, withdrawing down the Hudson River Valley. As Schuyler's men retreat, they fell trees across the wilderness road to impede the southward progress of Burgoyne's men.

3-6 AUGUST 1777
Revolution: North British forces led by Colonel Barry St. Leger unsuccessfully besiege Fort Stanwix

General William Howe.

MARIE JOSEPH PAUL, MARQUIS DE LAFAYETTE,
1757-1834

The 20-year old French aristocrat the Marquis de Lafayette, was stirred to support the American cause by a romantic idealism inspired by Rousseau's vision of a new and free society and by a desire for personal glory, as well as motivated by a wish to avenge his father's death at the hands of the British in the French and Indian War. Lafayette's offer to serve without pay as volunteer in the Continental Army was readily accepted by Congress in 1777. (He was eventually to spend some $200,000 of his own money to help the American cause.) Granted a commission as major general, Lafayette served on Washington's staff in the Battle of Brandywine, where he received a minor wound. His personal abilities, as well as political considerations, led Congress to reward him with the command of a division of Virginia light troops. Ever a loyal friend to Washington, he shared the deprivations of the severe Valley Forge winter with the common soldiers. An impractical strategy to conquer Canada with a small force in 1778 came to naught, but later in the same year Lafayette distinguished himself militarily at Barren Hill and in the Battle of Monmouth, as well as a liaison in the disastrous combined French-American attack on Newport, Rhode Island. After a leave in France, where he did much to advance the American cause, he returned to assist in the defense of Richmond. Lafayette was an essential actor in the successful plan to trap the British army under General Cornwallis at Yorktown. Lafayette demonstrated great military and diplomatic finesse during the Virginia campaign, and on his return to France, he was greeted with the acclaim he craved. His 1784 return visit to American also provoked wild enthusiasm from the populace, and Maryland conferred permanent citizenship on him. In the years preceding the French Revolution, Lafayette continued to actively support American interests in France—he was an invaluable ally of American minister to France Thomas Jefferson, helping him to gain most-favored-nation status for the United States in the French marketplace and in negotiating the postponed re-

payment of the American war debt. Although Lafayette supported the French revolutionary cause, he was imprisoned for five years and deprived of his estates. In 1794, Congress granted Lafayette his brigadier-general's pay of $24,424 and, some years later, a land grant in Louisiana. In 1824, his triumphal tour of America was an occasion of unequaled adulation, a tribute to the man as a hero and as a symbol of the American Revolution, now already receding into history.

in the Mohawk Valley, under the command of Colonel Peter Gansevoort.

4 AUGUST 1777
Revolution: North General Horatio Gates replaces General Philip Schuyler as the commander of the Continental Army of the North. Schuyler will be accused of negligence in October. He is later exonerated by a court martial.

6 AUGUST 1777
Revolution: North An American force led by General Nicholas Herkimer, coming to the aid of the besieged colonial troops at Fort Stanwix, is ambushed at Oriskany, New York, by a combined force of Loyalists and Indians led by Mohawk chief Joseph Brant.

16 AUGUST 1777
Revolution: North In the Battle of Bennington, Vermont militiamen led by General John Stark, aided by the Massachusetts troops of Colonel Seth Warner, eradicate a detachment of Burgoyne's men led by Lieutenant Colonel Friedrich Baum.

22 AUGUST 1777
Revolution: North British Colonel St. Leger ends his siege of Fort Stanwix when colonial reinforcements led by Benedict Arnold arrive. St. Leger withdraws his forces to Canada.

25 AUGUST 1777
Revolution: North In his campaign to capture Philadelphia, British General Howe disembarks at the head of Chesapeake Bay with 15,000 men.

9-11 SEPTEMBER 1777
Revolution: North In the Battle of Brandywine at Chadd's Ford, Pennsylvania, General Howe's British forces drive the 10,500 men led by George Washington toward Philadelphia.

19 SEPTEMBER 1777
Revolution: North Fearing an impending British invasion, the Continental Congress flees Philadelphia for a second time, relocating in Lancaster, Pennsylvania.

In the first Battle of Saratoga, American General Daniel Morgan and militia Colonel Henry Dearborn defeat General Burgoyne's forces at Freeman's Farm, near Saratoga, New York.

21 SEPTEMBER 1777
Revolution: North American General Anthony Wayne's forces are ambushed and routed in a bayonet

OCTOBER 17, 1777

JOSEPH BRANT, 1742-1807

Like a number of Indians before him, Mohawk war chief Joseph Brant was presented at the English court. Considered less a curiosity than a valuable ally, Brant, whose Indian name was Thayendanegea, consorted with the likes of Boswell and had his portrait in full regalia executed by society painter George Romney in this, his first, trip to London.

Brant rose to eminence through his association with colonial Indian superintendent Sir William Johnson, who had taken Brant's sister Molly as a common-law wife. At 13 Brant joined Johnson in his French and Indian War campaign. Some six years later Brant entered Eleazar Wheelock's Indian school in Lebanon, Connecticut, where he studied for two years. He went on to become a missionary's interpreter and later to assist in the translation of a number of religious books, including the *Book of Common Prayer* and the *Gospel According to St. Mark,* into the Mohawk language. An Anglican convert, Brant would found a Mohawk church in his final years.

During the rebellion of Chief Pontiac, Brant joined the Iroquois forces on the British side. Made secretary to the new superintendent of Indian affairs, Brant supported the British during the American Revolution. Granted a captain's commission, Brant returned from his trip to England to lead raiding forays, often together with British forces, against the settlers of the Mohawk Valley, southern New York state, and northern Pennsylvania. This reign of terror culminated in the Cherry Valley Massacre, when Brant lost control of the Seneca warriors under his command. At the close of the war, he helped the United States commissioners to negotiate peace treaties with the various Indian tribes, but he failed to achieve a land settlement for his own tribe. After he persuaded the British governor of Canada to grant the Mohawks land along Lake Ontario, he visited England again on a diplomatic mission to negotiate indemnification for the Iroquois. During his last years, he protected his Mohawk people from land speculators and sought to improve their social welfare. In Brantford, Ontario, a town named after him, he is commemorated by a monument honoring him for his skills as a courageous leader, a hard working missionary and an adept diplomat.

The Battle of Saratoga, October 7, 1777.

at Bemis Heights, American General Horatio Gates, assisted by Brigadier General Benedict Arnold, General Daniel Morgan and General Ebenezar Learned, defeats the forces of General Burgoyne, inflicting 600 casualties, to only 150 colonial casualties.

17 OCTOBER 1777
Revolution: North By the terms of the "Convention of Saratoga," British General Burgoyne surrenders his force of 5700 to the revolutionary forces led by General Gates. After laying down their arms, the British are marched to Boston where they board ships for England, swearing not to serve again in the war against America. When news of the American victory at Saratoga reaches Europe, it encourages further support of the revolutionary cause.

General Horatio Gates.

attack by General Howe's soldiers at Paoli, Pennsylvania.

26 SEPTEMBER 1777
Revolution: North The British forces led by General Howe occupy Philadelphia.

30 SEPTEMBER 1777
Revolution: North The Continental Congress moves from Lancaster to York, Pennsylvania.

4-5 OCTOBER 1777
Revolution: North In the Battle of Germantown, Pennsylvania, which begins favorably for American forces, the British army led by Howe gains ascendancy and kills 700 of Washington's men, to their own loss of 534.

7 OCTOBER 1777
Revolution: North In the Second Battle of Saratoga

FOUNDING A NATION 986-1787

2 NOVEMBER 1777
Revolution: Naval Captain John Paul Jones sets sail on the *Ranger* across the Atlantic. He plans to harry English port towns and shipping traffic.

15 NOVEMBER 1777
Revolution: Politics The Continental Congress endorses the Articles of Confederation. The Articles will now be presented to the individual colonies for ratification.

16-20 NOVEMBER 1777
Revolution: North British forces capture Fort Mifflin and Fort Mercer, thus establishing their power over the Delaware River region.

NOVEMBER 1777
Settling San Jose, the first non-religious community in California, is established on the Guadalupe River.

17 DECEMBER 1777
Revolution: North The Continental Army led by George Washington enters winter quarters at Valley Forge, Pennsylvania.
Revolution: Politics France officially recognizes the independence of the American colonies. This move is prompted by the impressive American victory at Saratoga.

23 DECEMBER 1777
Revolution: Politics The Conway Cabal, a purported plot of army officers and a few members of Congress to replace George Washington with General Horatio Gates, is revealed. Public opinion supports Washington and Major Thomas Conway is forced to resign.

DECEMBER 1777
Revolution: North Inventor of the one-man submarine *Turtle* in 1775, David Bushnell lays a minefield of gunpowder kegs to harass British naval operations.

6 FEBRUARY 1778
Revolution: Politics In Paris, France and colonial agents negotiate and sign two treaties—one of alliance and one of amity and commerce. According to the terms of the treaties, the Americans are given leave to conquer Canada and Bermuda, while France is permitted to conquer the British possessions in the West Indies. Congress ratifies the pacts on May 4, and in July French ambassador Conrad Alexandre Gerard arrives in America to present his credentials.

17 FEBRUARY 1778
Revolution: Politics In response to the Franco-American treaties, Lord North presents a plan of conciliation with the colonies to the British Parliament.

23 FEBRUARY 1778
Revolution: North Prussian Baron von Steuben arrives to join the Continental Army at Valley Forge.

He is of inestimable assistance in the training and drilling of Washington's soldiers.

16 MARCH 1778
Revolution: Politics The British Parliament creates a British Peace Commission which has wide powers to negotiate with the American revolutionaries.

23 APRIL 1778
Revolution: Naval After taking two British prizes, Captain John Paul Jones completes a raid on the fort at Whitehaven, England, and burns a ship in the harbor.

24 APRIL 1778
Revolution: Naval In a naval battle off the coast of northern Ireland, John Paul Jones accepts the surrender of the British sloop *Drake,* which he then takes with him to Brest, France.

8 MAY 1778
Revolution: North General Henry Clinton is named to replace General Howe as commander of all the British forces in the American colonies. Clinton formulates a plan to withdraw British forces from Philadelphia, as he fears a blockade by French ships.

15 MAY 1778
Revolution: South Beginning a campaign to secure colonial authority over the western frontier territories, George Rogers Clark captures Cahokia on the Mississippi River with the aid of 150 Virginia volunteers.

30 MAY 1778
Revolution: North The settlement of Cobleskill, New York, is burned by some 300 Iroquois Indians. This action initiates a campaign of terror by Loyalists and Indians against frontier settlements, instigated by the British.

6 JUNE 1778
Revolution: Politics The British Peace Commission arrives in Philadelphia with offers that will be rejected by the Continental Congress who, encouraged by their recent French alliance, now insist on continued independence.

18 JUNE 1778
Revolution: North General Henry Clinton withdraws British forces from Philadelphia in order to march them across New Jersey to New York City. As the British leave the city, the Americans reenter it.

19 JUNE 1778
Revolution: North Breaking his winter camp at Valley Forge, Washington dispatches General Charles Lee to intercept the British forces under Clinton heading toward New York City.

27-28 JUNE 1778
Revolution: North In the New Jersey Battle of

The Battle of Monmouth.

Monmouth, Washington's men and the British forces led by General Clinton, fight to a standoff. Washington is furious with American General Charles Lee for ordering a retreat. Lee is to be dismissed from the army in 1780, after he is found guilty of disobedience in a court martial. After disengaging his army, Clinton continues his retreat to New York City.

JUNE 1778

Revolution: Politics The Secret Service, initially known as the "Headquarters Secret Service," is organized and placed under the command of Aaron Burr.

2 JULY 1778

Revoltuion: Politics Congress returns to Philadelphia.

3 JULY 1778

Revolution: North In a continuing campaign of terror, a force of Loyalists and Indians massacres settlers in the Wyoming Valley of northern Pennsylvania.

4 JULY 1778

Revolution: South George Rogers Clark captures the British garrison at Kaskaskia, at the junction of the Mississippi and Kaskaskia rivers.

8 JULY 1778

Revolution: North George Washington establishes headquarters for the Continental Army at West Point.

9 JULY 1778

Revolution: Politics The Articles of Confederation are signed by Continental Congress delegates from Massachusetts, Rhode Island, Connecticut, New York, Pennsylvania, Virginia and South Carolina. The delegates of the other colonies endorse the document over the course of the next 11 months.

Revolution: North A British naval force raids and burns Fairfield, Connecticut. Norwalk, Connecticut, is to meet the same fate.

10 JULY 1778

Revolution: Naval A French fleet of 18 vessels commanded by Count Jean Baptiste d'Estaing arrives at the Delaware Capes to find that the British have evacuated Philadelphia.

External Affairs France declares war against Britain.

20 JULY 1778

Revolution: South George Rogers Clark captures the British garrison of Vincennes on the Wabash River.

29 JULY 1778

Revolution: Naval The French fleet of Count d'Estaing arrives off Newport, Rhode Island.

8 AUGUST 1778

Revolution: North The Americans led by General John Sullivan and the French fleet of Count d'Estaing attempt an unsuccessful siege of the British garrison at Newport, Rhode Island. Their plans go awry when the arrival of Sullivan's land forces is delayed and a storm disturbs the naval operation.

26 AUGUST 1778

Revolution: Naval The storm-damaged French fleet

under Count d'Estaing sets sail for Boston for much-needed repairs.

7-17 SEPTEMBER 1778
Indians The Shawnee Indians attempt an unsuccessful siege of Boonesborough, Kentucky.

14 DECEMBER 1778
Revolution: Politics The Continental Congress appoints Benjamin Franklin the American diplomatic representative to France.

11 NOVEMBER 1778
Revolution: North Led by Major Walter Butler and Mohawk Chief Joseph Brant, a combined force of Loyalists and Indians massacres over 40 militia and settlers at Cherry Valley, New York.

27 NOVEMBER 1778
Revolution: Politics Disappointed in their efforts, the British Peace Commission sets sail on the return trip to England.

9 DECEMBER 1778
Westward Movement The colony of Virginia annexes all territory recently captured by George Rogers Clark as the County of Illinois. Captain John Todd is named governor of Illinois County.

10 DECEMBER 1778
Revolution: Politics New York attorney John Jay is chosen as president of the Continental Congress.

17 DECEMBER 1778
Revolution: South British forces under Colonel Henry Hamilton retake their western outpost of Vincennes.

29 DECEMBER 1778
Revolution: South The British initiate a vigorous southern campaign with the capture of Savannah, Georgia, from American General Robert Howe.

6 JANUARY 1779
Revolution: South Pushing northward from Florida, British forces led by General Augustine Prevost capture Fort Sunbury, Georgia, and attack Augusta, Georgia.

10 JANUARY 1779
Revolution: Naval The French present John Paul Jones with a dilapidated vessel, the *Duc de Duras*. This Jones refits, mounts with 42 guns, and renames *Bonhomme Richard* in honor of Benjamin Franklin.

29 JANUARY 1779
Revolution: South Augusta, Georgia, is captured by a British force led by Lieutenant Colonel Archibald Campbell.

3 FEBRUARY 1779
Revolution: South American forces led by General

JOHN JAY, 1745-1829

Diplomat, statesman and jurist, John Jay was the sole founding father who served in all the important national offices, except that of president, without ever actively seeking any of them. His sound judgment, moral rectitude, sense of duty toward his country and responsible attitude toward his work were rewarded by his appointment to a series of influential positions. Like many of the other early American conservatives, Jay came from a wealthy family. The son of a New York City merchant of French Huguenot origins, Jay spent a privileged childhood, educated by tutors and graduating from King's College. Admitted to the New York bar in 1768, Jay developed a lucrative legal practice. He entered public life with his 1773 appointment as secretary of a royal commission to settle a boundary dispute between New York and New Jersey. The beginning of the Revolutionary War ended Jay's days as a private citizen. Serving first as a member of New York's committee of correspondence and then as a delegate to the First and Second Continental Congresses, Jay represented the conservative interests of colonial merchants who feared independence because it could result in mob rule by the democratic majority. But with the Declaration of Independence, he threw his full support behind the new nation. As a member of the New York Provincial Congress, he helped to draft the state constitution and then as chief justice of New York he went on to interpret that constitution. In December 1778, Jay was elected president of the Second Continental Congress, a post he held until his 1779 appointment as minister plenipotentiary to Spain. Jay's first diplomatic assignment was a difficult one—he could neither persuade the Spanish to recognize American independence, nor to join in alliance nor to lend substantial funds. Summoned to Paris by Benjamin Franklin in 1782, he joined the American mission to negotiate peace with Great Britain. Jay was largely responsible for the American tack of conferring solely with the English, independently of the French. At the end of the war, Jay declined the post of minister to Great Britain and of minister to France, in order to return home to enjoy private life. But Congress had already tapped him as secretary of foreign affairs, a position he filled until the 1790 induction of Thomas Jefferson as secretary of state. During his term in this post, Jay negotiated treaties of commerce with Prussia and Morocco, tried to resolve the issue of the still-remaining British garrisons on United States territory, and tried to settle America's differences with Spain. His Jay-Gardoqui Treaty, allowing Spain exclusive navigation of the Mississippi River, was denounced and defeated. Realizing the inefficacy of his role under the Articles of Confederation, Jay was not just a vocal advocate of the new Constitution, but also a contributor of five of the *Federalist Papers*. Appointed chief justice of the United States Supreme Court, Jay presided over the formative first five years of the federal judiciary, his most important decision being in the case of *Chisholm v. Georgia*. A frequently consulted adviser of President Washington, Jay was assigned to negotiate a treaty with Great Britain settling Anglo-American differences persisting since the Revolutionary War. This treaty was denounced by some as a betrayal of France. After his resignation as Supreme Court chief justice, Jay served two terms as New York governor, from 1795 to 1801. Before opting for a 28-year retirement, he successfully promoted the abolition of slavery in New York state.

William Moultrie successfully defend Port Royal, South Carolina, against a British attack.

14 FEBRUARY 1779
Revolution: South Commanded by Colonel Andrew Pickens, American forces achieve a decisive victory over a Loyalist brigade at Kettle Creek, Georgia.

25 FEBRUARY 1779
Revolution: South Leading 150 men, Lieutenant Colonel George Rogers Clark forces the surrender of British Colonel Henry Hamilton at Vincennes, after manipulating the desertion of the Indians who form half of Hamilton's 500-man force.

3 MARCH 1779
Revolution: South In an unsuccessful attempt to recapture Augusta, Georgia, General John Ashe loses over 350 men to the British at Briar Creek.

1-30 APRIL 1779
Revolution: South A combined force of North Carolina and Virginia troops led by Colonel Evan Selby successfully attacks a series of Chickamauga Indian villages in Tennessee, in retaliation for Indian raids on colonial settlements.

10 MAY 1779
Revolution: South British forces capture and burn Portsmouth and Norfolk, Virginia.

1 JUNE 1779
Revolution: North British commander Henry Clinton leads 6000 men up the Hudson River to capture the unfinished American forts at Stony Point and Verplanck Point, but fails to reach his ultimate goal of West Point, New York.

16 JUNE 1779
External Affairs After France promises to help recover Spain's former possessions of Gibraltar and the Floridas, Spain declares war on England, while making no alliances with the American revolutionaries.

19 JUNE 1779
Revolution: South At Stono Ferry, American troops led by General Benjamin Lincoln unsuccessfully attack the rear of the British forces under General Prevost that are withdrawing from Charleston, South Carolina, to Savannah, Georgia.

5-11 JULY 1779
Revolution: North A force of Loyalists under New York Governor William Tryon inflicts a series of raids on Connecticut coastal towns, burning Fairfield, Norwalk and the ships anchored in New Haven Harbor.

10 JULY 1779
Revolution: North In an attempt to take the Loyalist stronghold at Castine, Maine, the naval forces of Massachusetts are destroyed in the Penobscot River by the British.

15 JULY 1779
Revolution: North American General Anthony Wayne recaptures Stony Point, New York with a surprise bayonet attack. He takes some 700 prisoners at a cost of 15 casualties.

14 AUGUST 1779
Revolution: Politics Congress approves a peace plan that contains the stipulation of independence, specifically defined minimum boundaries, complete British evacuation of the American territories, and free navigation on the Mississippi River.

19 AUGUST 1779
Revolution: North American Major Henry Lee drives the British from Paulus Hook, their last major garrison in New Jersey.

29 AUGUST 1779
Revolution: North At Newton (Elmira), New York, American forces led by Generals John Sullivan and James Clinton defeat the combined Indian and Loyalist forces under Major John Butler and Joseph Brant.

1–15 SEPTEMBER 1779
Revolution: North Following the victory at Newtown, New York, American General John Sullivan presses northwest to destroy some 40 Seneca and Cayuga Indian villages, along with their considerable food stores, in retaliation for their participation in the campaign of terror against frontier settlers.

3 SEPTEMBER–28 OCTOBER 1779
Revolution: South In a disastrous attempt to recapture Savannah, Georgia, held by British General Prevost, American ally Count Casimir Pulaski is killed, the commander of the supporting French fleet Count d'Estaing is wounded, and General Benjamin Lincoln withdraws his men after the allied forces lose 800 men, to 140 lost by the British.

23 SEPTEMBER 1779
Revolution: Naval Commanding the *Bonhomme Richard* and a fleet of one American and two French ships, John Paul Jones engages the British 44-gun frigate *Serapis* in battle off the east coast of England. Jones takes the *Serapis,* losing the *Bonhomme Richard* to fire, and the *Countess of Scarborough* is captured by the French vessel, the *Pallas.*

27 SEPTEMBER 1779
Revolution: Politics Congress names John Adams to negotiate peace with England. Congress also names its president John Jay as minister to Spain.

SEPTEMBER 1779
Revolution: South Spanish Governor Galvez of Louisiana captures the British gulf coast ports of Manhac, Baton Rouge and Natchez.

11 OCTOBER 1779
Revolution: North: British General Henry Clinton

evacuates the naval base at Newport, Rhode Island, in order to concentrate his efforts on the southern campaign.

17 OCTOBER 1779
Revolution: North Washington leads the Continental Army back into winter quarters at Morristown, New Jersey, where the soldiers will suffer through a worse winter than the previous one at Valley Forge. Low morale, low supplies, desertions and attempts at mutiny plague the American forces.

29 NOVEMBER 1779
Finance Congress makes its last issue of paper money. The sum of over $10 million brings the total since June 1775 to nearly $242 million.

26 DECEMBER 1779
Revolution: South British commander Henry Clinton embarks from New York City with 8000 men for Charleston, South Carolina.

1 JANUARY 1780
Revolution: South American patriots conduct a continuing guerrilla campaign against the British in the territory surrounding Augusta, Georgia.

15 JANUARY 1780
Revolution: Politics The Continental Congress establishes the court of appeals.

28 JANUARY 1780
Westward Movement In order to secure the trans-Appalachian territory of North Carolina from Indian raids, Fort Nashborough is founded on the Cumberland River. In 1782, the post is renamed Nashville.

1 FEBRUARY 1780
Revolution: South The British fleet carrying General Clinton's 8000-man army arrives from New York off Charleston, South Carolina.
Revolution: Politics New York cedes to Congress all of her claims to western lands.

1 MARCH 1780
Slavery The Pennsylvania assembly enacts legislation mandating the gradual abolition of slavery within the state.

14 MARCH 1780
Revolution: South The Spanish governor of Louisiana, Galvez, captures the port of Mobile.

18 MARCH 1780
Finance In a severe deflationary move, Congress passes the Forty To One Act, which provides that continental paper money will be redeemable at one-fortieth of face value.

8 APRIL 1780
Revolution: South British naval forces initiate the attack on Charleston, South Carolina, by sailing past the guns of Fort Moultrie and entering Charleston harbor. Washington sends Maryland and Delaware troops to the aid of the American forces in the Carolinas.

6 MAY 1780
Revolution: South At Charleston, South Carolina, Fort Moultrie falls to the British.

12 MAY 1780
Revolution: South In the heaviest American defeat of the Revolutionary War, American General Benjamin Lincoln surrenders Charleston, South Carolina, to the British forces under General Henry Clinton. The British lose only 255 men while capturing a 5400-man American garrison, four ships and a well-stocked military arsenal and store.

25 MAY 1780
Revolution: North Mutiny is threatened at Washington's winter camp near Morristown, New Jersey, after a severe winter accompanied by the radical deflation of continental money. The demands of two Connecticut regiments for full rations and immediate payment of salary five months in arrears are reinforced by their armed march through camp. Pennsylvania troops put down this rebellion and two leaders of the protest are hanged.

29 MAY 1780
Revolution: South British Colonel Banastre Tarleton's cavalry unit destroys a Virginia regiment at Waxhaw, South Carolina.

11 JUNE 1780
Revolution: Politics In a specially-called convention, the new Massachusetts constitution is endorsed. Its bill of rights asserts that "all men are born free and equal," a claim that also pertains to black slaves.

13 JUNE 1780
Revolution: South Congress commissions General Horatio Gates as leader of the Southern Army. Gates will lead the troops sent by Washington.

22 JUNE 1780
Revolution: South The American reinforcements dispatched by Washington arrive in North Carolina after an arduous march through states that sometimes deny them food rations and supplies.

23 JUNE 1780
Revolution: North In the Battle of Springfield, New Jersey, American forces led by General Nathanael Greene defeat the British.

11 JULY 1780
Revolution: North Led by the Count de Rochambeau, 5000 French soldiers supported by a powerful naval escort arrive in Newport, Rhode Island. Several weeks later a British fleet under Admirals Marriot Arbuthnot and George Rodney begins a blockade of Newport.

25 JULY 1780
Revolution: South American General Horatio Gates assumes formal command of the Southern Army at Coxe's Mill, North Carolina, and begins the slow advance on the British garrison at Camden, South Carolina.

3 AUGUST 1780
Revolution: North Benedict Arnold is appointed commander of West Point. Arnold has been secretly collaborating with British commander Henry Clinton since May 1779, giving him information on Washington's movements.

16 AUGUST 1780
Revolution: South At Camden, South Carolina, the American forces led by General Horatio Gates are overwhelmingly defeated by General Cornwallis. Nearly 900 American soldiers are killed and 1000 are taken prisoner. American ally Baron Johann de Kalb is also killed in this encounter.

18 AUGUST 1780
Revolution: South At Fishing Creek, South Carolina, American forces led by General Thomas Sumter are defeated by Colonel Banastre Tarleton. This opens the way for a British invasion of North Carolina.

8 SEPTEMBER 1780
Revolution: South British forces under General Cornwallis begin the invasion of North Carolina.

23 SEPTEMBER 1780
Revolution: North British Major John Andre is captured near Tarrytown, New York, carrying the plans for Arnold's surrender of West Point.

25 SEPTEMBER 1780
Revolution: North Hearing of Andre's capture, Benedict Arnold flees from West Point to the British vessel *Vulture* in the Hudson River. He is to become a brigadier general in the British Army.

2 OCTOBER 1780
Revolution: North After his conviction as a spy, British Major John Andre is hanged for his role in the treason of Benedict Arnold. As Andre was apprehended in civilian clothes, the Americans deny him the rights of a prisoner of war.

7 OCTOBER 1780
Revolution: South At Kings Mountain, North Carolina, a Loyalist force of 1100 men led by Major Patrick Ferguson is captured by a 900-man force of American frontiersmen led by Colonel Isaac Selby and Colonel William Campbell. The loss of his Loyalist reinforcements convinces British General Cornwallis to abandon his invasion of North Carolina.

10 OCTOBER 1780
Westward Movement Congress issues a resolution encouraging the states to cede their western territories to the Union. These territories will then be settled and admitted to the Union as states in their own right. On the same day, the Connecticut assembly votes to cede their western lands to the Union.

14 OCTOBER 1780
Revolution: South General Nathanael Greene, the second most talented American military leader after Washington, is appointed to replace General Horatio Gates, the loser at Camden, as commander of the Southern Army. Greene plans a strategy of harassing the British forces of Cornwallis in a guerrilla campaign.

4 NOVEMBER 1780
Revolution: Politics Congress requests the states to fulfill wartime quotas of flour, pork and hay in support of the common military effort.

20 DECEMBER 1780
External Affairs England declares war on The Netherlands.

1 JANUARY 1781
Finance Congress issues an additional $191 million in continental paper currency. By spring, this money will cease to have any value, and the American economy will move close to collapse.

3 JANUARY 1781
Revolution: North Mutinous Pennsylvania troops make camp near Princeton, New Jersey, and elect representatives to bargain with Pennsylvania state officials. Negotiations resolve the crisis, although over half of the mutineers will leave the army.

17 JANUARY 1781
Revolution: South In Cowpens, South Carolina, American General Daniel Morgan decisively defeats British forces under Colonel Banastre Tarleton.

20 JANUARY 1781
Revolution: North In Pompton, New Jersey, troops mutiny. They are suppressed on January 27 by General Robert Howe's 600-man force sent by Washington. Two leaders of the mutiny are executed.

JANUARY 1781
Revolution: South Spanish forces led by Don Eugenio Pourré capture the British post of Fort St. Joseph in the Illinois territory. The Spanish will later claim this region on the basis of Pourré's victory.

20 FEBRUARY 1781
Finance Congress appoints Robert Morris as superintendent of finance. He will formally take office on May 14 during a period of economic crisis. Through his extensive reoganization efforts and forthcoming loans and aid from France and The Netherlands, Morris is able to make some progress by the end of the year.

FOUNDING A NATION 986-1787

1 MARCH 1781
Revolution: Politics After Maryland's ratification of the Articles of Confederation on February 27, the Continental Congress declares the document in force. On March 2 Congress takes the new name of "The United States in Congress Assembled." Samuel Huntington of Connecticut remains in his post as president of the Congress.

15 MARCH 1781
Revolution: South In the Battle of Guilford Courthouse, North Carolina, British General Cornwallis achieves a Pyrrhic victory over the American forces of General Greene and General Morgan. Cornwallis suffers such severe losses that he abandons the campaign to establish British control over the Carolinas.

18 MARCH 1781
Revolution: South British General Cornwallis retreats to Wilmington wait for expected reinforcements from General Clinton.

2 APRIL 1781
Revolution: Naval While returning from France, American Captain John Barry's ship *Alliance* is attacked by the British privateers *Mars* and *Minerva*. Barry's skillful maneuvering forces the surrender of the British ships.

25 APRIL 1781
Revolution: South British General Cornwallis begins a campaign to conquer Virginia. Reinforcements bring his army up to 7500 men, as he conducts raids into the interior of Virginia, aided by Colonel Tarleton.

9 MAY 1781
Revolution: South Spanish forces conquer all of West Florida with the British surrender of Pensacola.

21 MAY 1781
Revolution: North In Wethersfield, Connecticut, George Washington and French General Rochambeau hold a conference to discuss common strategy. Rochambeau reluctantly agrees to Washington's plan for a joint attack on New York, with the aid of the French West Indian fleet led by Count de Grasse.

26 MAY 1781
Finance Congress approves Robert Morris' proposal for the creation of a national bank. But the Bank of North American will not be officially chartered until December 31.

29 MAY 1781
Revolution: Naval American Captain John Barry captures two British men-of-war, the *Atalanta* and the *Trepassy*, despite a mutinous crew and his own wounds.

4 JUNE 1781
Revolution: South British Colonel Tarleton is al-

most successful in seizing Virginia Governor Thomas Jefferson at Charlottesville.

10 JUNE 1781
Revolution: South The American forces under the Marquis de Lafayette in Virginia are reinforced by General Anthony Wayne's men. Baron von Steuben will join them on June 19. This combined force combats the Virginia raids of Benedict Arnold and General Cornwallis.

11 JUNE 1781
Revolution: Politics Congress decides to supplement John Adams as sole peace negotiator with the addition of a commission comprised of John Jay, Benjamin Franklin, Henry Laurens and Thomas Jefferson.

15 JUNE 1781
Revolution: Politics Congress revises its 1779 peace instructions to demand only United States independence and sovereignty. The other conditions are to be left to the discretion of the peace commissioners.

20 JULY 1781
Slavery Rebellious slaves in Williamsburg, Virginia, set fire to several buildings, as well as to the capitol.

1 AUGUST 1781
Revolution: South Concluding a series of raids in Virginia, British General Cornwallis arrives at the coastal settlement of Yorktown to establish an operational base in order to maintain communication by sea with General Clinton's New York forces.

10 AUGUST 1781
Revolution: Politics Congress names Robert R. Livingston as secretary for foreign affairs.

14 AUGUST 1781
Revolution: North Washington receives a letter from the Count de Grasse in the West Indies carrying the news that de Grasse is sailing his entire 28-ship French fleet carrying 3000 soldiers to the Chesapeake Bay area. Immediately, Washington decides to secretly abandon the planned attack on New York and to lead his and Rochambeau's men to Philadelphia.

30 AUGUST 1781
Revolution: South The French fleet of Count de Grasse arrives off Yorktown.

31 AUGUST 1781
Revolution: South Count de Grasse lands French troops at Yorktown, to join with Lafayette's American forces in blocking off retreat by land for Cornwallis.

1 SEPTEMBER 1781
Revolution: South The forces of Washington and Rochambeau reach Philadelphia.

5-8 SEPTEMBER 1781
Revolution: Naval A naval battle occurs off York-

town, Virginia, between the British fleet of Admiral Thomas Graves and the French fleet of Count de Grasse, with de Grasse the victor. On September 9 the Count de Barras arrives from Newport, Rhode Island, with French reinforcements.

6 SEPTEMBER 1781
Revolution: North Benedict Arnold loots and burns the American port of New London, Connecticut.

8 SEPTEMBER 1781
Revolution: South American forces led by General Greene are defeated at Eutaw Springs, South Carolina. Yet in spite of this and other defeats, Greene has been able to force the British back toward Charleston, regaining most of South Carolina for the Americans.

14-24 SEPTEMBER 1781
Revolution: South Count de Grasse sends French ships up Chesapeake Bay to transport the combined forces of Washington and Rochambeau to Williamsburg, Virginia.

28 SEPTEMBER 1781
Revolution: South The allied army of 9000 Americans under Washington and 7000 French under Rochambeau begins the siege of Yorktown, Virginia.

19 OCTOBER 1781
Revolution: South The siege of Yorktown ends with the British surrender of General Cornwallis, whose 8000 men lay down their arms. This event spells the end of British hopes of victory in America.

24 OCTOBER 1781
Revolution: South British reinforcements of 7000 men led by General Clinton arrive off Chesapeake Bay. Clinton turns back to New York when he hears news of the surrender at Yorktown.

Washington is unsuccessful in persuading the

Washington fires the first gun at Yorktown.

French to join in an attack on New York. De Grasse sails back to the West Indies, Rochambeau winters in Virginia, and Washington marches north to resume his New York campaign.

5 NOVEMBER 1781
Finance The Netherlands extends a large loan to the United States.

31 DECEMBER 1781
Finance The Bank of North America is officially chartered by Congress.

1 JANUARY 1782
Revolution: North The supporters of the British cause, the Loyalists, begin to leave America, mainly for Nova Scotia and New Brunswick. Among the first to leave are those from the New England states and New York. If they stay, the Loyalists fear legal charges of treason or collaboration, and property confiscation.

5 JANUARY 1782
Revolution: South British forces withdraw from Wilmington, North Carolina, as part of their plan to evacuate all of the American towns they have occupied during the Revolutionary War.

27 FEBRUARY 1782
Revolution: Politics In England, the House of Commons votes against waging any further war in America. On March 5 Parliament enacts legislation empowering the English Crown to negotiate peace with the United States.

7 MARCH 1782
Indians In Gnadenhutten in the Ohio territory, American militiamen massacre 96 Christian Delaware Indians in retaliation for Indian terrorist raids executed by other tribes.

20 MARCH 1782
British Policy Beset by the peace faction in Parliament, British Prime Minister Lord North resigns. He is succeeded on March 22 by Lord Rockingham, who seeks immediate and direct negotiations with the American peace commissioners.

4 APRIL 1782
British Policy Sir Guy Carleton is commissioned as the commander in charge of British forces in America, replacing General Henry Clinton. Carleton is to implement the new British policy of ending hostilities and withdrawing British troops from America.

12 APRIL 1782
Revolution: Politics Peace talks begin between Britain and America. British representative Richard Oswald meets in Paris with the only available American peace commissioner, Benjamin Franklin. John Adams is in The Netherlands conducting delicate negotiations, John Jay is in Madrid and Henry Laurens is

imprisoned in the Tower of London. Jefferson does not serve on the commission.

16 APRIL 1782
Revolution: North At Newburgh, New York, Washington locates American army headquarters.

19 APRIL 1682
Revolution: Politics John Adams' mission to The Netherlands concludes with the Dutch recognition of the independence of the United States. Released from prison by the British in exchange for General Cornwallis, Henry Laurens arrives in The Hague. He will not participate in the preliminary peace negotiations.

9 MAY 1782
Revolution: North Sir Guy Carleton arrives in New York to take over the command of the British forces in America from General Henry Clinton.

4 JUNE 1782
Indians In an aftermath of the March Indian massacre at Gnadenhutten, Colonel William Crawford is ambushed and killed by a combined Indian and Loyalist detachment in the Ohio territory near Lake Erie. Some of Crawford's men were implicated in the Gnadenhutten massacre.

11 JUNE 1782
Revolution: South British forces evacuate Savannah, Georgia.

20 JUNE 1782
National Congress officially adopts the Great Seal of the United States.

23 JUNE 1782
Revolution: Politics John Jay arrives in Paris from Madrid to join in the preliminary peace negotiations with the British.

19 AUGUST 1782
Revolution: South Combined Indian and Loyalist forces, continuing to execute raids on frontier settlements, attack and defeat a group of frontiersmen at Blue Licks near present-day Lexington, Kentucky, in Virginia's Fayette County.

25 AUGUST 1782
Indians Mohawk chief Joseph Brant leads raids on Pennsylvania and Kentucky territory frontier settlements, burning the village of Hannastown, Pennsylvania.

27 AUGUST 1782
Revolution: South In the last eastern seaboard engagement of the Revolutionary War, a skirmish occurs between American forces and British troops by South Carolina's Combahee River.

19 SEPTEMBER 1782
Revolution: Politics In Paris, British peace representative Robert Oswald is empowered to initiate formal peace negotiations with Franklin and John Jay. John Adams will not arrive until October 26.

8 OCTOBER 1782
International The Netherlands and the United States sign a treaty of commerce and friendship. John Adams has negotiated this treaty for the United States.

10 NOVEMBER 1782
Revolution: South In what will become the last battle of the Revolutionary War, George Rogers Clark retaliates against Loyalist and Indian forces for the Blue Licks defeat of Kentucky frontiersmen. Heading a detachment of riflemen, Clark leads an attack against the Shawnee Indian village of Chillicothe in the Ohio territory.

30 NOVEMBER 1782
Revolution: Politics In Paris, American and British representatives sign a preliminary peace treaty. Adams, Franklin, Jay and Laurens sign for the United States. The extremely favorable conditions include the British recognition of American independence, the specific boundaries of the United States territory, continued American fishing rights off the coast of eastern Canada, a validation of debts, a restoration of rights and property to American Loyalists, and the withdrawal of British forces from American territory.

14 DECEMBER 1782
Revolution: South British forces evacuate Charleston, South Carolina.

15 DECEMBER 1782
Revolution: Politics The French object to not being consulted by the Americans before the signing of the preliminary peace pact with the British. A diplomatic response by Benjamin Franklin averts a falling out between the allies.

24 DECEMBER 1782
Revolution: North French troops embark on the voyage home from Boston.

20 JANUARY 1783
Revolution: Politics Preliminary articles of peace are signed between England and France and between England and Spain. The preliminary peace treaty between England and the United States will not go into effect until Great Britain and France negotiate a settlement.

3 FEBRUARY 1783
International Spain recognizes the independence of the United States. Sweden and Denmark will follow the lead of Spain before the end of the month, and Russia will recognize America's independence in July.

4 FEBRUARY 1783
Revolution: Politics Great Britain officially declares an end to the hostilities in America.

10 MARCH 1783

Revolution: Politics An anonymous address is circulated to the officers of Washington's main camp at Newburgh, New York. Actually written by Major John Armstrong, the first Newburgh Address rebukes Congress for the failure to honor its promises to Continental Army soldiers and exhorts the veterans to defy Congress if accounts are not equitably settled. A meeting of officers is called for the following day.

11 MARCH 1783

Revolution: Politics General Washington forbids the unauthorized meeting of officers called by the anonymous Newburgh Address, and suggests a regular meeting of officers to discuss grievances on March 15.

12 MARCH 1783

Revolution: Politics Major John Armstrong issues the second anonymous Newburgh Address, which suggests that Washington himself supports the claims of the discontented officers.

15 MARCH 1783

Revolution: Politics Washington personally addresses the regular meeting of his officers at Newburgh, New York, advising moderation and patience, and promising expeditious congressional action on the salary and pension demands of the soldiers. A week later Congress allots the officers a lump sum equalling five years' pay each.

11 APRIL 1783

Revolution: Politics Congress formally proclaims an end to the Revolutionary War against Great Britain.

15 APRIL 1783

Revolution: Politics Congress ratifies the preliminary peace treaty negotiated in Paris by John Adams, Benjamin Franklin, John Jay and Henry Laurens.

26 APRIL 1783

Revolution: Politics Bound for Canada, some 7000 Loyalists set sail from New York. This mass emigration is prompted by the imminent departure of the British Army. This group brings to a total of some 100,000 Loyalists who have left for Europe or Canada since the years immediately preceding the Revolution.

13 MAY 1783

Life/Customs In a meeting at the headquarters of Baron von Steuben in Fishkill, New York, the Society of the Cincinnati is founded at the suggestion of General Henry Knox. This fraternal order of Continental Army officers with hereditary membership enrolls over 2000 men, and George Washington is chosen its first president.

13 JUNE 1783

Revolution: Politics The main part of Washington's Continental Army disbands. A small group of soldiers remain with Washington until the British army leaves New York.

FOREIGN VOLUNTEERS AND MERCENARIES

In the Revolutionary War, both sides augmented their military strength with foreign soldiers. While Great Britain hired Hessian mercenaries from the monarchs of the German states, the American Continental Army was reinforced by a series of individual European volunteers, many of them aristocrats.

That the Hessian mercenaries formed an indispensible part of the British war strategy is attested to by their sheer numbers. Estimates place the total of Hessians serving on American soil at one-third of the British forces. The American revolutionaries regarded their participation as a particular insult. The reputation of the Hessians as good fighters was blackened by their tendency to plunder and by their high desertion rates. After the end of the conflict, many Hessians remained in the United States to settle as farmers in the New Jersey, Pennsylvania and Maryland region.

Many of the foreign officers volunteering for service in the American Army were motivated possibly more by an adventuristic pursuit of glory than by political idealism. The stream of marquises and barons who arrive demanding rank over Americans was a persistent source of discontent among Continental Army officers. Yet, a number of these volunteers proved dependable and even invaluable allies, some of whom shared the deprivations experienced by the common soldiers at Valley Forge. France's young Marquis de Lafayette perhaps best epitomized the image of the foreign volunteer as a seeker of glory and a romantic idealist. Lafayette's record of loyal service was echoed by those of Johann Kalb, Thaddeus Kosciusko, Count Casimir Pulaski, and Baron Friedrick von Steuben.

Kalb, a self-styled baron of German peasant birth, was a brigadier general in the French army before he joined the American cause. Wounded 11 times in his attempt to save the day at the Battle of Camden in the Southern campaign led by General Horatio Gates, Kalb died after his capture by the British. The great Polish national hero Thaddeus Kosciusko was a skilled military engineer who directed the fortifications at the Battle of Saratoga and of West Point. His activity as General Nathanael Greene's chief engineer contributed to the success of the Southern campaign. The Polish Count Casimir Pulaski was recommended to George Washington by Benjamin Franklin. After serving as Washington's aide at the Battle of Brandywine, he later organized Pulaski's Legion, an officially-authorized independent cavalry corps that served with General Benjamin Lincoln's army in South Carolina. Pulaski died of a wound received during a cavalry charge on Savannah, Georgia. Baron von Steuben also arrived carrying Franklin's recommendation. Washington appointed him the acting inspector general in charge of training the Continental Army. This Prussian drillmaster transformed America's ragtag rebel force into a well-disciplined and effective unit. After service in the Battle of Monmouth, von Steuben was given the command of the Virginia force under General Greene and he played an essential role in winning the crucial Battle of Yorktown. He later became an American citizen, receiving a congressional pension and settling down on a New York State land grant of 16,000 acres.

24 JUNE 1783

Revolution: Politics Faced by a protest by dissatisfied and unpaid Revolutionary War veterans in Philadelphia, Congress relocates to Princeton, New Jersey, where it sits until November 3.

2 JULY 1783
British Polity An English order in council closes the British West Indies to trade with the United States.

8 JULY 1783
Slavery The Massachusetts Supreme Court proclaims the abolition of slavery in the commonwealth, as mandated by the Massachusetts Declaration of Rights of 1780.

3 SEPTEMBER 1783
Revolution: Politics The Treaty of Paris is signed by Great Britain and the United States in Paris, thus formally ending the Revolutionary War. On the same day, England signs a peace pact with France and Spain at Versailles. By the terms of this treaty, Britain cedes Florida to Spain.

7 OCTOBER 1783
Slavery The Virginia House of Burgesses enacts legislation granting freedom to those black slaves who served in the Continental Army during the Revolutionary War.

2 NOVEMBER 1783
Revolution: Politics In Rocky Hill, New Jersey, George Washington issues his "Farewell Address to the Army," and the following day all troops not yet furloughed are formally discharged from the army.

25 NOVEMBER 1783
Revolution: Politics The last of the British troops leave Manhattan, as George Washington and Governor George Clinton enter the city. By December 4, all British soldiers on Staten Island and Long Island are boarding ships for England.

26 NOVEMBER 1783
National Congress meets in Annapolis, Maryland, under a plan mandating alternate sessions in Annapolis and Trenton, New Jersey, for the interim.

4 DECEMBER 1783
Revolution: Politics As the last of the British troops board ships for home, George Washington takes leave of his officers at Fraunces' Tavern in New York City.

23 DECEMBER 1783
Revolution: Politics After a triumphant journey to Annapolis, Maryland, George Washington comes before Congress to resign officially his commission as commander in chief of the Continental Army.

26 DECEMBER 1783
British Policy A British order in council permits the importation of American manufactured goods to England on terms as favorable as those of prerevolutionary days.

31 DECEMBER 1783
Slavery By this time, the importation of black African slaves has been banned by all of the northern states.

OTHER EVENTS OF 1783
Education Noah Webster issues the first part of his "Blue-Backed Speller," *A Grammatical Institute of the English Language*. The remaining two volumes will come out by 1785. One of the best–selling American books of all time, Webster's "Speller" proves influential in standardizing pronunciation and spelling, in distinguishing American English from British English, and in uniting the disparate segments of American society through the powerful medium of a common language.

14 JANUARY 1784
Revolution: Politics Congress ratifies the Treaty of Paris, officially ending the Revolutionary War and initiating peace with Great Britain.

20 FEBRUARY 1784
Westward Movement The Tennessee Company is organized by the state of Georgia, with authority to make land grants to settlers in the Tennessee Valley region.

22 FEBRUARY 1784
Commerce Captain John Greene sails the ship *Empress of China* out of New York harbor, bound for the orient. The embarkation of this vessel marks the search by American merchants for new markets for United States exports, now that the English have closed the British West Indies to American trade.

1 MARCH 1784
Westward Movement Congress accepts an amended version of Virginia's cession of her western lands. On the same date, a congressional committee led by Thomas Jefferson presents a plan that proposes a temporary government in the western territories, to be followed by a division of the region into states that will enter the confederation as states equal with the original 13. Jefferson's proposal to ban slavery everywhere in the United States after 1800 is narrowly defeated. An amended version of this territorial ordinance is adopted on April 23, though it is never enforced.

8 APRIL 1784
British Policy British Lord Sydney notifies Canadian Governor-General Haldimand that British troops will not withdraw from garrisons on the Great Lakes until the United States complies with the conditions of the Treaty of Paris, specifically those dealing with the treatment of Loyalists and the repayment of debts.

30 APRIL 1784
Commerce In order to stabilize American trade and commerce, Congress requests the right to pass a navigation act. Most of the states resist such a measure.

7 MAY 1784

International Finally about to return to America from Europe, John Jay is designated as the new American secretary for foreign affairs, filling the position vacated by Robert R. Livingston in December 1783.

28 MAY 1784

Finance Congress officially creates a Treasury Board, which replaces the office of superintendent of finances, at the request of Robert Morris. The Treasury Board is to be governed by a panel of three commissioners. Samuel Osgood and Walter Livingston have already been named in January, and Arthur Lee will be added in July.

2 JUNE 1784

Westward Movement The North Carolina assembly cedes her western lands to the United States. This motion will be repealed on November 20, when the state of Franklin in this area seeks independent status.

26 JUNE 1784

Transportation Spain officially closes the lower Mississippi River to American navigation.

31 JULY 1784

Commerce Thomas Jefferson arrives in Paris where, together with John Adams and Benjamin Franklin, he will serve as a commissioner authorized to negotiate commercial treaties with European nations.

23 AUGUST 1784

Westward Movement Fearing the lack of a government for the western lands of North Carolina when cession is formally completed, the settlers of this region, led by John Sevier, gather in Jonesboro to plan the creation of the independent state of Franklin. Until 1789, Franklin tries but fails to gain admission to the Union. The territory is then reabsorbed into North Carolina. In 1790 the area will be organized as the Southwest Territory and in 1796 it is admitted to the Union as the state of Tennessee.

30 AUGUST 1784

Commerce Commanded by Captain John Greene, the *Empress of China* reaches the Chinese port of Canton after a voyage by way of Cape Horn. The rich cargo of tea and silks that she transports back in May 1785 will convince American merchants to enter the China trade in large numbers.

1 SEPTEMBER 1784

Westward Movement George Washington sets out in a tour of the western territories to survey possibilities for land development.

15 SEPTEMBER 1784

Westward Movement The Pennsylvania Council of Censors forces the state assembly to pass legislation restoring Connecticut settlers to their lands in Pennsylvania's Wyoming Valley, after violence resulting from the state's 1783 decision to oust the Connecticut settlers from their farms.

22 SEPTEMBER 1784

Settling In Alaska, the Russians establish their first permanent settlement on Kodiak Island at Three Saints Bay.

22 OCTOBER 1784

Indian Affairs In the Second Treaty of Fort Stanwix, the Six Nations of the Iroquois Indians give up all claims to the territory west of the Niagara River. The Ohio Indian tribes reject this pact.

1 NOVEMBER 1784

National Congress meets in Trenton, New Jersey. In this session, it designates commissioners to plan a federal district on the Delaware River and decides to move to New York until that site is ready.

Westward Movement In the Treaty of Augusta with the Creek Indians, Georgia expands her northern boundary west from the Tugaloo to the Oconee River.

24 DECEMBER 1784

Ideas/Beliefs In Virginia, James Madison publishes his *Remonstrances Against Religious Assessments,* which persuasively advocates the separation of church and state, a growing trend in the new nation.

11 JANUARY 1785

National Congress relocates to New York City, the new temporary capital of the United States, until the planned federal city is completed.

21 JANUARY 1785

Indian Affairs In a treaty negotiated at Fort McIntosh, the Chippewa, Delaware, Ottawa and Wyandot Indians cede nearly all land in the present-day state of Ohio.

24 JANUARY 1785

Commerce Congress appoints a committee headed by James Madison to persuade the individual states to grant greater power to the federal government to regulate foreign commerce. This effort meets with failure.

7 FEBRUARY 1785

Westward Movement The state of Georgia founds Bourbon County in the area of the present-day states of Alabama and Mississippi. The Spanish, who also claim this region, will order the Georgia commissioners to vacate this land in October.

24 FEBRUARY 1785

International Congress appoints John Adams as minister to England, where he will seek to negotiate commerce treaties and enforce the terms of the Treaty of Paris. Frustrated in his attempts, Adams will leave this post and return to the United States in April 1788.

8 MARCH 1785

National Congress appoints Henry Knox as secretary of war. This post has been vacant for two years since the resignation of General Benjamin Lincoln.

10 MARCH 1785
International Congress appoints Thomas Jefferson as minister to France, replacing Benjamin Franklin who wishes to return home to Pennsylvania.

28 MARCH 1785
National After an Alexandria, Virginia, conference of Virginia and Maryland commissioners seeking to regulate navigation on Chesapeake Bay and the Potomac River, the delegates adjourn to Mount Vernon with George Washington as their host. Here they quickly resolve the navigation issue and go on to draft an agreement recommending uniform commercial regulation, uniform currency and annual commercial conferences to their legislatures. They also agree to invite Pennsylvania to join their navigation pact. The larger importance of the Mount Vernon conference is that it demonstrates the willingness and ability of individual states to cooperate among themselves in matters of common interest.

5 MAY 1785
Indian Affairs In the Treaty of Dumpling Creek, the Cherokee Indians cede most of their territory to the "State of Franklin" (Tennessee). United States commissioners will void the terms of this treaty in November.

8 MAY 1785
Westward Movement Congress passes the legislation known as the Land Ordinance of 1785. This enactment provides for a rectangular survey dividing the northwestern territories into 6-mile square townships, which in turn are divided into 36 lots of 640 acres each, with one lot set aside for financing public education. A motion to set aside another lot to support the religion of the majority of the residents is narrowly defeated. The 640-acre lots are to be sold for $640 each.

23 JUNE 1785
Commerce Massachusetts forbids the export of United States goods in British vessels and doubles the import duty on all trade items transported in other than American ships. Many of the other states also enact discriminatory tariffs to encourage the development of American domestic industry.

11 JULY 1785
National The Massachusetts Legislature passes a resolution recommending a convention to revise the Articles of Confederation. Although this resolution is never presented to Congress, its passage marks the growing recognition of the individual states that a stronger central government is needed if the new nation is to survive and prosper.

20 JULY 1785
International Congress authorizes John Jay to negotiate with Spain's minister to the United States, Don Diego de Gardoqui, for free navigation on the Mississippi River. Jay's mission meets with defeat.

10 SEPTEMBER 1785
International Initially negotiated by John Adams, an American treaty with Prussia is concluded. This pact supports the principle of free trade and proclaims the practice of privateering illegal.

10 OCTOBER 1785
Westward Movement Spain orders Georgia to give up its claim to Bourbon County, a political unit it has established in the area of present-day Alabama and Mississippi.

28 NOVEMBER 1785
Indian Affairs The Treaty of Hopewell between United States commissioners and the Cherokees confirms the right of the Indians to their land in the Tennessee area. This pact voids the earlier Treaty of Dumpling Creek between the Cherokees and the "State of Franklin."

30 NOVEMBER 1785
International United States minister to Great Britain John Adams formally demands that the British relinquish their military posts along the Great Lakes and in Ohio—notably the forts at Detroit, Michilimackinac, Niagara and Oswego—as mandated by the Treaty of Paris.

5 DECEMBER 1785
National The Maryland Legislature endorses the proposals of the March Mount Vernon conference, and suggests that Delaware be invited to join the pact.

16 JANUARY 1786
Ideas/Beliefs The Virginia legislature adopts an Ordinance of Religious Freedom. Although this very same statute, written by Thomas Jefferson, had been voted down by the assembly in 1779, it now passes when reintroduced by James Madison. The main thrust of this act, which is later to become the model for the first amendment to the United States Constitution, is to guarantee that no man can be forced to attend or support any church, nor may he be discriminated against because of his religious preference.

21 JANUARY 1786
National The Virginia Assembly issues an invitation to the other states to attend a commercial conference scheduled for September.

15 FEBRUARY 1786
National A committee reports to Congress the need for a strengthened confederation, particularly to facilitate tax collections from the individual states. No action is taken on this recommendation.

20 FEBRUARY 1786
National The state of New Jersey refuses outright to

SEPTEMBER 26, 1786

submit to Congress the requisition voted on the states in September 1785. This incident serves to further point up the weaknesses of the Articles of Confederation.

22 FEBRUARY 1786
International In London, John Adams meets with the ambassador of Tripoli in order to negotiate a settlement that will end piracy on American shipping in the Mediterranean Sea and off the coasts of Portugal and Spain. These negotiations fail.

28 FEBRUARY 1786
British Policy In answer to the November 30, 1785 demand of John Adams, the British respond that they will not vacate their American military garrisons along the northwest frontier—including Detroit, Michilimackinac, Niagara and Oswego—until the Americans carry out the provisions of the Treaty of Paris in reference to the treatment of Loyalists and the collection of debts.

1 MARCH 1786
Westward Movement In Boston, Reverend Manasseh Cutler, General Rufus Putnam and General Benjamin Tupper organize the Ohio Company of Associates in order to purchase Ohio lands and to settle New England homesteaders on 1.5 million acres in the Ohio territory.

28 JUNE 1786
International In further negotiations to halt piracy on American commercial shipping, Thomas Barclay executes a treaty with Morocco in exchange for gifts valued at $10,000. But American representatives are not able to reach agreements with Algiers, Tripoli and Tunis until a decade later.

JUNE-AUGUST 1786
Finance The American post-war depression reaches a low point, caused by currency shortages, high taxes and persistent creditors, leading to issues of unstable paper currency by individual states.

7 AUGUST 1786
National A series of proposed amendments to strengthen the Articles of Constitution are presented to Congress. Among the proposals are one for a federal court system, one giving Congress control over domestic and foreign commerce, and two for greater authority to obtain quota payments from states. These proposed amendments are never presented to the states because Congress fears unanimous approval will not be forthcoming.

8 AUGUST 1786
Finance Congress adopts a coinage system based on the Spanish milled dollar. Originally proposed by Thomas Jefferson in July 1785, the coinage system mandates a gold piece valued at $10; a silver piece worth $1; a tenth of a dollar also in silver, and a penny in copper.

22-25 AUGUST 1786
Finance Representatives from some 50 Massachusetts towns convene in Hatfield to consider the problems resulting from economic depression that were not addressed by the latest session of the Massachusetts legislature—the steadily increasing number of farm and home foreclosures, and the popular calls for a paper-money issue. The Hatfield meeting protests against the inefficacy of the state government, high legal expenses, the judicial system and taxation. Although the delegates advise against violence, they are unable to enforce this decree.

29 AUGUST 1786
International Congress authorizes John Jay to conclude a commercial treaty with Spain, allowing the Spanish stipulation of no American navigation on the Mississippi River for 25 or 30 years. The fierce congressional debate and close vote on the navigation issue indicate that the required nine states will not ratify the pact. The negotiations are suspended and a treaty with Spain is not concluded until a decade later.

31 AUGUST 1786
Regional In Massachusetts, an armed mob prevents the session of the Northampton court in an aftermath of the Hatfield conference of 22-25 August. Similar incidents are soon to occur in Worcester, Concord and Great Barrington.

11-14 SEPTEMBER 1786
National Delegates from only five states attend the interstate commercial conference known as the Annapolis Conference at the invitation of Virginia. Chaired by John Dickinson, the group decides they do not have enough attendees to consider commercial reforms. Alexander Hamilton drafts an address to the states that calls a meeting in Philadelphia for May 1787 to discuss needed political as well as commercial reforms. A congressional committee will endorse this meeting in February 1787.

20 SEPTEMBER 1786
Regional An armed mob marches on the New Hampshire assembly in an attempt to force the enactment of a paper-money issue.

25 SEPTEMBER 1786
Finance In the Rhode Island case of *Trevett v. Weeden*, the state court rules that forcing a creditor to accept paper money in payment of a debt is unconstitutional as this action violates the property guarantees of the state charter.

26 SEPTEMBER 1786
Regional After Massachusetts Governor James Bowdoin sends 600 militiamen led by General William Shepherd to protect the state supreme court session in Springfield, an armed band of insurgents led by Daniel Shays, a former Revolutionary War captain and now a bankrupt farmer, confronts the state forces and causes the court to adjourn.

141

FOUNDING A NATION 986-1787

16 OCTOBER 1786
Finance Congress mandates the establishment of a United States mint.

20 OCTOBER 1786
Regional Fearful of the proximity of Daniel Shays' army to the federal arsenal in Springfield, Massachusetts, Congress authorizes Secretary of War General Henry Knox to raise a 1340-man army from Connecticut and Massachusetts, purportedly for Indian service.

30 NOVEMBER 1786
Regional An insurrection in eastern Massachusetts is quelled with the capture of rebel leader Job Shattuck.

26 DECEMBER 1786
Regional In Massachusetts, Daniel Shays assembles a new rebel force of 1200 men near Worcester and marches to Springfield to unite with the forces led by Luke Day. Together, these forces outnumber the state militiamen led by General Shepherd, who are guarding the federal arsenal. Massachusetts Governor Bowdoin immediately calls for the short-term mobilization of a 4400-man force to deal with the insurrection.

5 JANUARY 1787
Regional The North Carolina supreme court rules that a court has the power to annul an act passed by the state legislature.

18-19 JANUARY 1787
Regional The newly activated Massachusetts militia force of 4400 men led by General Benjamin Lincoln assembles to combat the insurgents led by Daniel Shays in Springfield.

26 JANUARY 1787
Regional Daniel Shays leads his rebel force of 1200 men in an unsuccessful attack against the federal arsenal at Springfield, Massachusetts.

27 JANUARY 1787
Regional General Benjamin Lincoln arrives in Springfield and moves on to chase the rebels northward.

4 FEBRUARY 1787
Regional In an attack on Shays' insurgents at Petersham, Massachusetts, General Benjamin Lincoln captures 150 rebels and forces Shays to flee for Vermont. By the end of the month, the uprising has been completely suppressed. In March, the Massachusetts legislature offers a pardon to all except Shays, Luke Day and two other leaders. Shays will be pardoned on June 13, 1788. This rebellion has the result of causing the state legislature to avoid direct taxation, to lower court costs, and to exempt household necessities and workmen's tools from the debt process. Shays' Rebellion is also an important factor in influencing the creation of a new federal constitution, since the states have seen how essentially powerless they are to prevent such incidents of violence.

21 FEBRUARY 1787
National Congress endorses the resolution of the Annapolis Conference calling for a constitutional convention in Philadelphia on May 14. In the meantime, the various states name delegates to the convention. Only Rhode Island is to abstain from the convention.

25 MAY 1787
National Although the constitutional convention is scheduled to commence on May 14, not enough delegates arrive to achieve a working quorum until May 25. George Washington is nominated president of the convention and William Jackson is made secretary. The floor leaders for the debates are Elbridge Gerry, James Madison, George Mason, Gouverneur Morris, Roger Sherman and James Wilson. Aside from Washington, 81-year-old Benjamin Franklin is the most respected public figure attending.

29 MAY 1787
National At the constitutional convention, Edmund Randolph proposes the Virginia Plan of Union, which advocates a new form of national government with a bicameral legislature representing the states proportionately, the lower house to be chosen by popular vote and the upper house from nominees proposed by the state assemblies; an executive chosen by the legislature; a judiciary named by the legislature; and executive veto powers over the legislature. This plan is debated until June 13.

15 JUNE 1787
National The small states tend to oppose the Virginia Plan, particularly its principle of proportional representation in both houses of the legislature. To address some of their criticisms, William Paterson introduces the New Jersey Plan, which proposes for Congress the powers of taxation, regulation of commerce, and the authority to name a plural executive and a supreme court. The debate following the presentation of the New Jersey Plan focuses on whether to amend the Articles of Confederation or to draw up an entirely new framework for a national government.

19 JUNE 1787
National The constitutional convention delegates vote to develop the type of government proposed in the Virginia Plan. Debates follow on the issue of proportional versus equal representation of states in the federal legislature.

13 JULY 1787
National Congress enacts the Northwest Ordinance, drafted by Nathan Dane, establishing a government in the area north of the Ohio River. Based on Thomas Jefferson's ordinance plan of 1784 and a congressional committee report of September 1787, the plan provides for the eventual establishment of a bicameral assembly, the creation of three to five states to be equal with the original states, freedom of religion, the right of trial by jury, public education and a ban on slavery.

The signing of the Constitution.

16 JULY 1787

National At the constitutional convention, Roger Sherman presents the Connecticut Compromise advocating proportional representation in the lower house of the legislature and equal representation in the upper house, or Senate. The convention now goes on to draw up a rough draft of the constitution.

6-10 AUGUST 1787

National At the constitutional convention, a series of debates occurs on the provisions of the draft constitution—the terms of office for the president and legislators; the powers of Congress to regulate commerce; the prohibition of bills of attainder and *ex post facto* laws and a prohibition of any action on the part of Congress in the area of slavery for a period of 20 years. Earlier, another compromise had been reached on slavery, when the representation of blacks in the house of representatives was mandated at three-fifths of their total population.

22 AUGUST 1787

Transportation Inventor John Fitch builds and tests the first steamboat on the Delaware River, before the delegates of the constitutional convention. Fitch's second improved model will reach a top speed of three miles per hour. On December 3, James Rumsey will demonstrate his steamboat on the Potomac River.

17 SEPTEMBER 1787

National Thirty-nine delegates to the constitutional convention vote to endorse the final form of the Constitution, prepared by Governeur Morris. The approval of nine states is needed to ratify the constitution.

28 SEPTEMBER 1787

National Having received the proposed Constitution on September 20, Congress votes to send the Constitution to the state legislatures for ratification, after defeating motions to censure the continental congress for exceeding its authority.

5 OCTOBER 1787

Westward Movement Congress appoints Arthur St. Clair the first governor of the Northwest Territory, as mandated by the Northwest Ordinance of July 13. Winthrop Sargent is appointed secretary for the territory.

27 OCTOBER 1787

National The advocates of the new Constitution, the Federalists, begin to publish articles supporting ratification of the new constitution. Signed "Publius," the first of these articles appears in New York's *The Independent Journal*. Written by Alexander Hamilton, James Madison and John Jay, 77 essays are eventually published and finally compiled as *The Federalist* papers.

7 DECEMBER 1787

National Delaware becomes the first state to ratify the new constitution, followed by Pennsylvania on December 12 and by New Jersey on December 18.

TESTING A UNION

1788–1865

MARCUS CUNLIFFE
Professor of History, The George Washington University

TESTING A UNION 1788-1865

The dates 1783 and 1865 mark the resolution of the two most serious crises in American history. Each represents the end of what could be seen as, in both, an internal struggle or family conflict. The Peace of Paris in September 1783, brought a formal end to the War of Independence, waged against Great Britain by her thirteen mainland colonies in North America. The fighting had begun in 1775 and dragged on for more than six years, culminating with the last major engagement (and a Franco-American victory) at Yorktown, Virginia, in October 1781. In April 1865 the surrender of Robert E. Lee's Confederate Army to Ulysses S. Grant at Appomattox Court House (also in Virginia) proved the last important military event of the Civil War, or Brothers' War, or War Between the States. For four years the slave–holding states of the lower and middle South, led by their president, Jefferson Davis, had striven to demonstrate on the battlefield their right and capacity to secede from "Lord North" and become a separate nation, the Confederate States of America.

In both of these protracted, painful contests a great American leader had emerged, to become a figure of international renown. George Washington of Virginia was the prime hero of the Revolutionary era. Abraham Lincoln of Illinois, assassinated in his moment of triumph (or rather of characteristically informal ease, while enjoying a comedy at Ford's Theatre in Washington, D.C.), was to stand even higher in American esteem. According to every poll of American presidential popularity conducted during the 20th century, Lincoln and Washington have been the preeminent pair.

The two men are of course very different. Yet the gap between them has often been taken as a measure of the successful evolution of the young nation during a mere fourscore years. George Washington was raised according to the style of an English country gentleman—though with special Virginia overtones. He rode to hounds, became a colonel, married an heiress, acquired a handsome estate (at Mount Vernon) and—in common with other Virginia gentry—dispensed hospitality with calculated benevolence to the voters when he sought a seat in the colony's legislature. "Honest Abe," on the other hand, was a frontier boy of obscure family and no formal education whose father kept moving west in search of forever elusive prosperity. Lincoln, self-taught, ungainly, wry, yet movingly eloquent when the occasion called for such behavior, seemed to show that, far from demeaning the austere integrity of a George Washington, he was in truth fulfilling the new nation's promise, that the seeds of greatness were in every man.

The two men were in fact not so utterly different in that they were exemplars of a novel breed of human being, flourishing in the New World. For after all, neither was college-educated; each had to fend for himself in a restless, competitive society, and each combined modesty with a simple directness of character that made others pay attention.

Whatever the relationship of these two men, there is no doubt that for an optimistic and patriotic American the period from 1788 to 1865 was an era of extraordinary growth and achievement. Having successfully defied the wealth, numbers and military and naval strength of Britain, the Americans won diplomatic recognition as a sovereign people. Again in conflict with the Mother Country (1812-14), the United States once more indicated that conquest by a European power was practically impossible. Indeed in the final battle of the War of 1812 (sometimes called a second War of Independence), General Andrew Jackson inflicted a crushing defeat at New Orleans on an army of British veterans.

During the 1780s a momentous change was made in the governmental structure of the United States. The thirteen original states were operating under the aegis of the Articles of Confederation. Under this decentralized regime it was possible to conceive of "these United States" as a rather loose plural bundle—a group of semi-nations instead of a single national entity. Responding to bold initiatives from George Washington and others, the Continental Congress sanctioned a constitutional convention, which met at Philadelphia in 1787. The convention, chaired by Washington and attended by such luminaries as the elderly Benjamin Franklin and the youthful James Madison, devised an entirely new frame of government, which created a separate executive branch and a bicameral legislature, and which in general considerably increased the potential authority of the Federal Government.

The 1787 constitution, debated in state conventions, was ratified the following year and took effect in 1789, with Washington as first president. He held office during the onset of the world crisis brought about by the French Revolution. In France, Louis XVI was deposed and guillotined. The Republic was then overturned by Napoleon Bonaparte, who proclaimed himself emperor. In 1815 Napoleon's Empire at last crashed in ruins at the Battle of Waterloo. The United States did not remain altogether immune to the fire and fury of the Napoleonic wars. Partisan politics, neither anticipated nor welcomed by the founding fathers, appeared to divide the young country during the 1790s. Washington's successor, President John Adams of Massachusetts, had a rough passage at the hands both of "Democratic Republicans" who made Thomas Jefferson their leader, and of Alexander Hamilton and other "Federalists" nominally of his own party.

Nevertheless the contrast with France was remarkable. Washington retired from the presidency after two four-year terms, thus establishing what was to become an almost inviolable American political custom. Napoleon, on the other hand, replaced the Bourbon monarchy with a new autocratic dynasty—that of his own family. Despite the party conflicts of the 1790s, there was a peaceful transfer of political rule from Adams to Jefferson in the election of 1800. Thereafter, presidential elections engrossed public attention (perhaps in part because there were then no other sporting or other rival distractions); sometimes, as with Andrew Jackson, the winning candidate was accused by opponents of all kinds of wicked acts and intentions; but the process was basically peaceful and uncorrupt. When European visitors came to Washington, D.C. (the nation's capital after 1800) they were astonished to discover how easy it was to gain admission to the White House, and how accessibly direct the various presidents were.

True, except in time of war or comparable emergency, the Federal Government played no very prominent part in the life of the people. Except temporarily, during the Civil War, federal taxes were negligible. Revenue was raised through land sales and import duties. By European standards the regular army and navy were minuscule. Before the Civil War, turnpikes, canals, railroads and various other schemes for "internal improvement" were undertaken not by the national government but through state and local initiative. Jeffersonians and Jacksonians, members of what would become recognized as the Democratic party, were convinced that the nation's well–being actually depended upon such minimal interference. In the words of their slogan: "That government is best which governs least." The naysayer Henry David Thoreau of Massachusetts amended this in in his essay *Civil Disobedience* (1849) to read: "That government is best which governs not at all."

Thoreau was not the only American intellectual to regard individual liberty as the final test of the worth of a society. Some Americans, including John Quincy Adams (son of John Adams) and the Whig spokesmen Henry Clay and Daniel Webster, envisaged a somewhat greater role for the national government. None however advocated a level of central direction comparable to that of France or Prussia. And while state-rights sentiment remained strong and became a special feature of Southern argument (as in the pronouncements of John C. Calhoun of South Carolina), there was also an intense attachment to the idea of union: namely, that the United States was ultimately a single nation, bound together in perpetuity. Such was the adamant opinion of John Marshall, Chief Justice of the U.S. Supreme Court from 1800 to 1835. The crucial majority decisions of the Marshall Court affirmed the authority of the Court itself to determine constitu-

tionality, and asserted that in disputes over jurisdiction, the nation necessarily took precedence over a state or a section. This was not so much "statism," on the European model, as a concern for the enlargement of socio-economic opportunity for the greatest number of people. John Marshall's latter-day Federalism earned him the suspicious dislike of Jefferson and of Jackson. Jackson was relieved, when death at last removed Marshall, to be able to replace him with a more congenial appointee, Roger B. Taney of Maryland, who was to serve as Chief Justice for another long span, terminated by his own death in 1864. Yet on some economic issues Marshall and Taney reasoned on not dissimilar lines; both sought the most effective "release of energy" in order to generate growth.

Marshall and Taney alike were, to put the matter in broader terms, aligned with multitudes of their fellow-countrymen in being proudly American: proud, that is, of the nation's republican-democratic ideology. James Madison, who was to follow Jefferson from 1809 to 1817 in the "Virginia dynasty" of presidents, had expressed some of the crucial features of American republicanism in his contributions to the *Federalist Papers* (1787-88). In repudiating British control the colonists had repudiated monarchy. They had turned to the alternative mode, republicanism, whose historical lineage stretched from the finest epochs of ancient Greece and Rome down through the splendors of mediaeval and Renaissance Italy; and through the sturdy evolution of the Swiss cantons, the Netherlands and the Cromwellian interlude of 17th–century England. Most commentators, however, suggested that while republics were in theory preferable to monarchies, they were less practical. The conventional wisdom

Jackson on his way to Washington.

Chief Justice John Marshall.

held that republics operated best in small, mercantile communities, but did not last long: they were crushed by larger, more warlike monarchical societies. "Democracy," too, was generally regarded as a form of government (of all, by all) conceivable only in such restricted environments as a single town, but as fundamentally unsound.

The brilliant counter-argument of Madison was that such views were out of date, at least in relation to republicanism. Madison claimed that large federal structures on the American model were stronger than small traditional republics. An Athens or a Venice could be torn apart by class struggles or by family feuds: in the United States, Madison insisted, such contests would cancel one another out. Faction would be recognized and contained. The American republic would, he said, be a "representative" government, not a "pure" democracy. Citizens would elect other people to hold office for limited periods of time, whereas in a hypothetical "democracy" every citizen would be actively engaged in running affairs.

The distinction between republic and democracy has been repeated now and then since Madison's day, mostly by conservatives. But in the early and mid-19th century the two words became almost synonymous. As a republican democracy the United States had no titles of rank or other forms of hereditary privilege. It had no established church. By 1829, when Andrew Jackson of Tennessee was inaugurated as president, white adult male citizens could vote and hold office in nearly every state without having to own property. No other sizeable nation had gone so far toward honoring the principle that the country belonged to its inhabitants, and that officials, whether elected or appointed, were the servants and not the masters of the public. Other laws and customs were correspondingly rational and humanitarian, at least in relation to the Europe of the age. The obvious exception was the persistence of chattel slavery in the Southern states. Slavery had been terminated in the Northern states, either outright (as in Massachusetts in 1780) or by various schemes of gradual emancipation (for example in Pennsylvania in 1780 and in New York, in 1785). Anti-slavery societies were among the most active of the mass of reform movements (temperance, peace, women's rights etc.) that characterized Jacksonian America. And, in the North as well as in the South it was widely believed that the actual living conditions of black slaves in the South's plantation economy were better than those of the "white" or "wage slaves" laboring in British or Northern mills and mines.

Such consolations seemed to be borne out by the census figures. The first federal census was taken in 1790, and repeated every ten years. The population in 1790 (to the nearest thousand) was 3,930,000, including 698,000 slaves and 60,000 free blacks. Thereafter, population doubled about every 24 years. By 1820 it was 9,638,000. The figure in 1840 was 17,069,000; in 1860 it was 31,443,000. After the ending of slave importation in 1808 the proportion of black to white

inhabitants dropped; in 1860 there were fewer than four million slaves. But the black population had continued to increase at a rate which—according to defenders of slavery—proved the basic adequacy of black diet and housing.

The other side of the story will be discussed shortly. It would be hard, though, to disagree with the significance of the statistics for white immigration. Millions of Europeans "voted with their feet" by quitting their homelands in search of the farms and jobs apparently guaranteed by New World abundance. About a quarter of a million arrived between 1790 and 1820. The tempo then increased sensationally. Sixty thousand immigrants poured in in the single year 1832; 105,000 in 1842; 372,000 in 1852. Some joined the jostling crowds of the port cities. By 1820 New York had 124,000 inhabitants, Philadelphia 113,000, Baltimore 63,000, Boston 43,000 and New Orleans 27,000. In 1860 the respective figures were: New York, 1,080,000; Philadelphia 566,000; Baltimore 212,000; Boston 178,000; New Orleans 169,000. Chicago, which did not even exist until the 1830s, was by 1860 a great railroad center, surpassing its older Middle-Western rivals, St. Louis and Cincinnati.

Immigrants and native-born, city-dwellers and farmers, were drawn west by the thousands and then the millions. The process was speeded by the vast territorial acquisitions of the Louisiana Purchase in 1803 and those resulting from the Mexican War of 1846-48, which carried the domain of the United States to the Pacific. A simple and effective pattern had been determined through such early legislation as the Northwest Ordinance (1787). New western areas would be organized as territories and become eligible for statehood, joining the original thirteen on equal terms, when their population reached some such modest figure as 60,000.

By 1860 the United States had 9000 miles of railroad, appreciably more than the whole of Europe. Its merchant navy was second in tonnage only to that of Great Britain and American vessels traded with every corner of the world. Southern cotton was an essential item in the economy of Europe. For many Europeans, American tobacco was almost as essential. The special features of American economic activity were demonstrated at London's Great Exhibition in the Crystal Palace in 1851. Among the much-discussed American exhibits were cheap clocks, sewing-machines, Yale locks, Colt revolvers and McCormick reapers: examples of an innovatively mass-oriented technology. National pride was even more gratified in 1851 when the yacht *America* easily beat a British contender in what was to be the first race of the America's Cup. There seemed no limit to the victories of democratic, spread-eagle "go-aheadness."

We must, however, take note of other, less rosy interpretations of American history between the Revolution and the Civil War. Some of these express the revisionist and radical mood of many historians in the 1960s and 1970s. Some were voiced, for instance by Charles A. Beard, during the Progressive era of the

Meriwether Lewis.

early 20th century. Some have a much older pedigree.

It has often been pointed out, for example, that the conventional record ignores the American Indian, or Native American, at whose expense white settlement was carried out. Again, chattel slavery may have been defended as an economic necessity, given the insatiable world demand for raw cotton. But such justifications are difficult to reconcile with Jefferson's fine words in the preamble to the Declaration of Independence that "all men are created equal." The retention and expansion of plantation slavery created, in the barbed words of the Irish poet Thomas Moore, a "piebald polity" of "slaving blacks and democratic whites." Racial prejudice more or less excluded even free blacks from any but a marginal role in the life of the nation. Nor of course were women regarded by Jefferson and his contemporaries as being equal with men. They were denied the basic democratic right to vote; and though reforms improved matters in mid-century, their property rights were also restricted. The women's rights movement launched by Elizabeth Cady Stanton at Seneca Falls, New York, in 1848, had made little headway by the end of the Civil War.

Historians have also recently cast a cold eye on the conventional accounts of American economic democracy. They have argued that rich Americans tended to remain rich and poor ones to remain poor, especially when they were immigrants. The opportunities of the underpriviledged to better themselves may, it is suggested, have been quite circumscribed; for every self-

made Abraham Lincoln or Peter Cooper there were platoons of Americans whose ambitions were never realized. The founding of hundreds of colleges, often under the impetus of religious denominations, used to be evinced as proof of the nation's zeal for education. So was the spread, under local and state auspices, of common school systems like that in Massachusetts, tirelessly promoted in the 1840s by Horace Mann. A contrary interpretation is that antebellum education tended to sacrifice quality for quantity; that too many colleges were founded, and too few truly well-based grade schools; and that educators of the Mann type, consciously or not, were producing a docile, industrious working class, literate enough to perform the tasks of the American economy yet not educated, so to speak, beyond their station.

Further evidence could be drawn from American popular culture, in the shape of fiction and melodrama. Novels or plays that found favor portrayed decent, hard-working "democratic" young men and women. But their heroes and heroines were nearly always white and Protestant. Racially or religiously mixed marriages were unthinkable, or at least led to disaster. Anti-Irish and anti-Catholic feeling, dully embodied in the Know-Nothing nativist political organization of the 1850s, re-emphasized the old impression that America, while nondenominational and nonestablished, was nevertheless at heart a Protestant nation. To judge from popular literature or from expressions of religious sentiment, the ideal American was a Protestant native-born male, who might begin poor but who through his own enterprise rose into the ranks of the respectable and prosperous. Along the way he made a suitable marriage. He prided himself on his independent views, but (according to the observations of the Frenchman Alexis de Tocqueville and the American writer James Fenimore Cooper) he was actually a conformist. He mistrusted unorthodox behavior of any kind, including that of the abolitionists. He responded to "the tyranny of the majority." He believed in republican democracy, and liked to denounce the despotic nations of the world. But he was not unduly disquieted by the perpetuation of slavery in the United States, or by other manifest inequalities of condition.

This middling person prided himself, too, on the peaceable, humanitarian quality of American life. He thought, for example, that American penal codes and institutions were more sensible and less harsh than those of Europe. Yet he tolerated an extraordinary amount of violence and a much higher homicide rate than that of other civilized nations. A cynic might say this was the democracy of the Colt revolver, nicknamed the "great equalizer." Our average John Doe was proud, too, of the absence of military display. There was no conscription except during the latter half of the Civil War. On the other hand, the United States could be denounced (by such peace advocates as Elihu Burritt) as a highly belligerent nation, which after the Revolution engaged in two major foreign wars (with Britain and Mexico), that could and should have been avoided, and which, partly out of excessive greed for territorial expansion, was continually involved in Indian wars. This eagerness for expansion had ironical consequences. Madison had suggested that the Republic would grow in strength as it grew in area. But with mounting North-South tension over the status of slavery in the Western territories, the opposite tendency seemed in the ascendant. Every accession of territory, every new admission to statehood seemed to increase the grounds for suspicion and anger between the free states and the slave states. The huge accessions of the 1840s merely exacerbated the crisis-atmosphere of the 1850s; undeclared civil strife in Kansas was a prelude to the Civil War itself.

In this conception, prevalent in some foreign accounts (Frances Trollope, *Domestic Manners of the Americans*, 1832,; Charles Dickens, *American Notes*, 1842, and *Martin Chuzzlewit*, 1843-44), the United States was frantic, materialistic, brutal, chauvinistic and unstable. Its Constitution, said the eminent British historian Thomas B. Macaulay in 1857, was "all sail and no anchor." The republic was therefore doomed.

The testimony of Americans themselves occasionally sounded just as pessimistic. Consider the diary comments of Sidney George Fisher, a Philadelphia gentleman, in 1844:

> Taking the government, the social influences, . . . & the unhealthiness of this country together, . . . it certainly is the most God-forsaken region that civilized beings were ever compelled to dwell in. If you go to the South you have disease, the heat of Africa, mosquitoes, slavery, ferocious & vicious manners, and low & degraded standards of morals and opinion; if you go to the North you find the cold of Iceland during half the year, a society without refinement or elevated feelings, absorbed in money-getting & living without social intercourse in selfish isolation, and democracy with its mobs, riots, demagogues & corruption. Which of the two to choose is difficult to determine.

The two societies, of course, came to blows at the end of the 1850s. The "great experiment" reached an apparent climax in disaster: a civil war that took a million lives, North and South, in battlefield casualties and disease or illness attributable to combat. The Prussian general Helmuth von Moltke is said to have dismissed the sequence of Civil War battles—indecisive, despite their terrible toll of casualties—as the struggle of mere "armed mobs," thrown into the fray by mediocre West Point professionals or by inexperienced civilians dressed up as generals. Were Bull Run and Antietam, Fredericksburg and Chancellorsville, Chickamauga and the Wilderness and the Crater, scenes in the last act of an American tragedy, with elements of farce?

Neither a wholly optimistic nor a wholly pessimistic assessment of these decades is adequate. It is necessary to take account of both. One useful gauge is the condition of other nations at the time. In that context the United States in general comes out well. True, Americans were sometimes aggressive, materialistic, nationalistic, and racially and sexually biased. But so were British, French, German, Italian, Russian and other peoples, who often fell far below their own proclaimed standards of virtue. True, much in American life was raw and unsophisticated. But crudity was a consequence of a refreshing lack of conventionality, at any rate among Americans of "Western" temperament. Moreover, some aspects of American culture were comparatively nonmaterialistic; The Transcendentalists, as represented by Ralph Waldo Emerson or Margaret Fuller, were people of almost painful integrity, who made the majority of European intellectuals appear frivolous and hypocritical.

Emerson was one of those who was worried by the lack of social cohesion in his own country. Perhaps he contributed to the fragmentation by urging people to avoid "movements" and to cherish their separate individuality. But when the Civil War came he was stirred to discover the elements of sacrificial patriotism in the nation. Americans, it turned out, were not hopelessly self-absorbed. Hundreds of thousands of them, North and South, were prepared to face danger and death, for years if need be. This is a main reason why the battles of the Civil War were so hard-fought. Substantial numbers on both sides believed they were fighting for a cause. They may have been wrong-headed, but it cannot he said that they were half-hearted. The Confederates strove for states' rights, and to uphold slavery: an uncomfortable pairing that made theirs the "Lost Cause." The North stood for Union and for ending slavery: a combination that ultimately prevailed and acquired moral force. Pessimists, foreign and domestic, were proved wrong. The Union was preserved, and became a better place when chattel slavery was abolished. Immigrants in greater numbers than ever before, on the restoration of peace declared their preference for the Great Republic over the facts of material and spiritual existence in their own countries.

They did not find paradise. The United States had never been Eden. A considerable element of luck may have entered into the reckoning. The Stars and Stripes flew over an immense and rich domain, acquired with comparative ease. America after independence benefited immeasurably from the inflow of energetic young immigrants; from the availability of foreign capital; from unprecedented advances in medicine, engineering and other branches of science and from the ideological power of republican democracy. Yet in 1865 a reasonable observer might conclude that the United States, if fortunate, deserved much of its good fortune. Some American boasts remained unfulfilled. Several items on democracy's agenda had not yet been reached. There were, however, quite good grounds for believing that the agenda was still the basic order of business for the United States.

CHRONOLOGY

2 JANUARY 1788
National In ratifying the new Federal Constitution, Georgia becomes the fourth state to do so and the third state to ratify unanimously.

9 JANUARY 1788
National The fifth state to ratify the Constitution is Connecticut. The state's constitutional convention, which convenes on January 4, votes 128 to 40 for ratification. On the same day, the Massachusetts convention gathers to consider ratification of the Constitution.

6 FEBRUARY 1788
National The Massachusetts convention votes to ratify the Constitution. The strong Antifederalist forces, led by Samuel Adams and John Hancock, are persuaded to support the document after the Federalists effect a compromise by proposing amendments to the Constitution guaranteeing civil liberties. This move influences the convention to support ratification unconditionally, 187 votes to 168, and to recommend nine amendments, the most important of which grants to the states those powers not reserved for the Federal Government.

27 FEBRUARY—26 MARCH 1788
Slavery The Massachusetts legislature receives a petition from liberated blacks, led by Prince Hall, instigated by a notorious Boston incident in which free blacks were violently seized and transported to the West Indian island of Martinique. After consideration of this protest, the Massachusetts Assembly enacts a forceful bill to declare the slave trade illegal and to provide for monetary damages for any victims of such kidnappings.

24 MARCH 1788
National The Constitution is rejected by a popular referendum in Rhode Island, 2945 to 237 against ratification. Rhode Island had refused to send a delegation to the Philadelphia constitutional convention of 1787. Subsequently the state's rural legislators had rejected a state convention to consider ratification, a move strongly supported by the mercantile and professional factions of Rhode Island. The Federalists refuse to participate in the popular referendum of March 24 and a state convention to consider ratification of the Federal Constitution will not be called until January 1790.

7 APRIL 1788
Westward Movement Rufus Putnam of the Ohio Company of Associates conducts a group of pioneers to the Ohio territory. At the mouth of the Muskingum River, they found the settlement of Muskingum. This name is later changed to Marietta, in honor of Marie Antoinette of France. The establishment of Marietta marks the beginning of the settlement of the Northwest Territory, as provided for by the Northwest Ordinance of 1787.

28 APRIL 1788
National Maryland becomes the seventh state to support the new Federal Constitution by voting for ratification, 63 to 11.

23 MAY 1788
National South Carolina becomes the eighth state to support ratification of the Constitution by a vote of 149 to 73.

2 JUNE 1788
National The Virginia convention meets to consider ratification of the Constitution. Powerful Antifederalist forces led by Patrick Henry and George Mason oppose endorsement. The strategy of the Antifederalists is also supported by Richard Henry Lee's *Letters of the Federal Farmer*, which calls for a bill of rights and a lower legislative house organized on a more democratic basis. The Federalist, or pro-Constitutional faction, is led by James Madison.

17 JUNE 1788
National The New York convention meets in Poughkeepsie to consider ratification of the Constitution, with the Antifederalists led by New York Governor George Clinton in the majority. Federalist leader Alexander Hamilton is able to postpone the proceedings of the convention until the news of ratification by New Hampshire and Virginia arrives. This will prove to be a successful strategy.

21 JUNE 1788
National With the vote of New Hampshire for ratification of the Constitution, 57 to 46, the Federal Constitution is formally adopted by the United States. Along with its vote for ratification, the New Hampshire convention proposes 12 amendments to the Constitution.

25 JUNE 1788
National Although the Constitution is now technically in effect, the support of the Virginia convention is still considered essential. In spite of the forceful opposition of Antifederalists Patrick Henry and George Mason to the Constitution, James Madison is successful in gaining adequate support. The

close vote on June 25, 89 to 75, does finally endorse ratification, though with the proposed addition of a bill of rights, as well as 20 other alterations.

2 JULY 1788

National The president of the Congress, Cyrus Griffin of Virginia, formally announces the Constitution of the United States to be in effect, as it has now been ratified by the required nine states.

8 JULY 1788

National Congress appoints a committee to prepare procedures for the coming change in government. A blueprint is also prepared for the procedures of electing representatives to the first bicameral congress under the new Constitution and for choosing electors for the first president of the United States.

15 JULY 1788

Westward Movement In the Northwest Territory capital of Marietta, former Revolutionary War general Arthur St. Clair is officially installed as the first governor of the Ohio area.

26 JULY 1788

National The New York state constitutional convention, after rejecting a plea for conditional ratification of the new Federal Constitution, votes 30 to 27 for unconditional ratification. The New Yorkers also recommend the addition of a bill of rights.

2 AUGUST 1788

National The North Carolina state convention decides to postpone its ratification of the new Federal Constitution until a bill of rights and other specific amendments are officially incorporated.

17 AUGUST 1788

Westward Movement In the Ohio region, the town of Losantiville is established at the junction of the Ohio River and the Great Miami River by land speculator John Cleve Symmes and a group of settlers from New Jersey. In 1790, the town will be renamed Cincinnati in honor of the Society of the Cincinnati, an organization of Revolutionary War veterans.

13 SEPTEMBER 1788

National Under President Cyrus Griffin, Congress officially chooses New York City as the temporary seat of the soon-to-be-formed new government. Congress also issues detailed directives for the choosing of presidential electors on January 7, 1789, the guidelines for choosing the president on February 4, 1789 and the date for the first sessions of the new Congress on March 4, 1789.

25 SEPTEMBER 1788

National Congress presents 12 proposed amendments to the Constitution to the states.

2 OCTOBER 1788

National The Congress under the Articles of Confederation is forced out of its suite in New York City's Federal Hall, when renovations to prepare the building for the incoming new government are undertaken.

OCTOBER—DECEMBER 1788

Commerce A continuing downward plunge in commodity prices is finally halted, thus paving the way for the reinstatement of pre-Revolutionary prosperity.

1 NOVEMBER 1788

National The Congress under the Articles of Confederation adjourns, leaving the United States with no central government until the first week of April 1789, when the new Congress under the Constitution achieves its first quorum.

16 NOVEMBER 1788

National Satisfied by the September 25 submission of 12 proposed amendments to the Constitution by Congress, North Carolina calls a second state convention to consider ratification of the Constitution.

21 NOVEMBER 1788

National The North Carolina constitutional convention votes for ratification of the Federal Constitution, 194 to 77.

23 DECEMBER 1788

National The state of Maryland proposes the cession of a ten-square-mile land tract on the Potomac River to the United States for a federal town and seat of the national government. This area will become the District of Columbia.

OTHER EVENTS OF 1788

Westward Movement The inconclusive Jay-Gardoqui Treaty of August 29, 1787 between the United States and Spain is the source of much dissent in the western territories of Kentucky and Tennessee. James Wilkinson, formerly implicated in the Conway Cabal of 1777, accepts bribes from the Spanish at New Orleans and agrees to work for the secession of his home territory of Kentucky from the Union in order to ally it politically with Mexico. John Sevier is working for similar ends in Tennessee. The intrigues of Wilkinson, Sevier and other western conspirators seeking secession are motivated by a desire to gain access to Spanish harbor facilities. This threat of separating the lower Mississippi Valley from the United States persists until Pinckney's Treaty of 1795, also known as the Treaty of San Lorenzo, grants Americans the right of free navigation on the Mississippi River and documents Spanish recognition of American western boundary claims.

Arts/Culture The *Miscellaneous Works of Freneau* is published. Philip Freneau is considered America's finest poet to date, and the volume includes such notable examples of his work as "The Indian Burying Ground," "The Hurricane," "To the Memory of the Brave Americans" and his best-known work, "The Wild Honey Suckle."

In England, George Hepplewhite's *Cabinetmaker*

and Upholsterer's Guide is published. This volume becomes the bible of native American furniture makers who use and adapt many of Hepplewhite's designs for pieces in the Federal and Greek Revival styles—the preferred styles of the new nation.

An uncontrollable fire rages through the city of New Orleans, leveling most of the buildings in the old French and Spanish styles of architecture. In 1794 a second fire will complete the destruction of these edifices. After the 1803 purchase of the Louisiana Territory by the United States, much of the city will be rebuilt in the then fashionable Federal and Greek Revival architectual styles.

7 JANUARY 1789
National In all of the 11 ratifying states except New York, presidential electors are chosen either by citizens eligible to vote or by the state legislatures. (In Massachusetts for example, eight electors are appointed by the state legislature from a total of 24 candidates, while two more electors are chosen directly by the people.) Once chosen, the electors are at liberty to vote for whomever they choose.

9 JANUARY 1789
Indian Affairs The governor of the Northwest Territory, General Arthur St. Clair, signs the Treaty of Fort Harmar with the Ohio Indians. This pact renews the Treaty of Fort McIntosh.

23 JANUARY 1789
Education Father John Carroll founds Georgetown University, the first Catholic college in the United States. In 1805, the Jesuits will assume management of the university.

4 FEBRUARY 1789
National In the first presidential election, the newly-chosen electors cast their ballots, which will not be counted until 6 April. Meanwhile the election of senators and representatives will proceed in an orderly fashion in the separate states.

2 MARCH 1789
Arts/Culture The Pennsylvania legislature repeals a law banning the performance of stage plays. This liberalized attitude toward the dramatic arts will spread throughout the eastern seaboard. The frequent attendance of George Washington at New York's John Street Theater serves to endow the theater with an even greater aura of respectability.

4 MARCH 1789
National In New York City, the first Congress under the new Constitution convenes. With only 8 senators and 13 representatives on hand, Congress is unable to achieve a quorum. The rest of the delegates are still en route to New York. Of the members of the first congress, 54 were also delegates to the Philadelphia Constitutional Convention of 1787 or delegates to the state ratifying conventions, and only 7 of them had failed to support ratification.

1 APRIL 1789
National With 30 of a total of 59 members present, the House of Representatives reaches a quorum and begins operation. Pennsylvania representative Frederick Augustus Muhlenberg is chosen speaker of the house.

6 APRIL 1789
National With 9 of 22 senators on hand, New Hampshire's Senator John Langdon is selected as temporary presiding officer. Langdon proceeds to count the presidential ballots cast by the electors on February 4. George Washington has been elected President unanimously with 69 votes; and John Adams is Vice President with 34 votes. Messengers are dispatched to inform Washington and Adams of the election results.

8 APRIL 1789
National The first item on the agenda of the House of Representatives is the raising of revenue for the new government.

14 APRIL 1789
National The secretary of the new Congress, Charles Thomson, arrives at Mount Vernon to inform George Washington of his election as President.

15 APRIL 1789
Arts/Culture In New York City, John Fenno begins publication of the *Gazette of the United States*. This Federalist newspaper becomes the first administration's organ. In 1790 it will be moved to Philadelphia, where it will be renamed the *United States Gazette*.

16 APRIL 1789
National Leaving Mount Vernon, George Washington begins his eight-day journey to New York City in order to head the new government.

21 APRIL 1789
National Vice President John Adams arrives in New York. After taking his oath of office, he takes his seat as the presiding officer of the Senate.

23 APRIL 1789
National George Washington arrives in New York City.

30 APRIL 1789
National On the balcony of New York's Federal Hall, George Washington is inaugurated as the first President of the United States. Robert Livingston, chancellor of the state of New York, administers the oath of office. Washington then retires to the senate chamber to deliver his Inaugural Address, thus initiating a new tradition. Probably written by James Madison, Washington's oration urges the "preservation of the sacred fire of liberty."

7 MAY 1789
National Concluding the inaugural festivities, the first inaugural ball is held in George Washington's honor.

TESTING A UNION 1788-1865

GEORGE WASHINGTON, 1732-1799

Although George Washington would become probably the best known and the most honored individual in America's history, there is no denying that he would suffer from what later generations would call "an image problem." "First in war, first in peace" he undoubtedly was and would remain, but somehow he failed to remain "first in the hearts of his countrymen." Perhaps this is because most Americans would come to think of him almost entirely in his later years—elderly, upright, formal, aloof—and as an "indoor" man. Perhaps if they knew more about George Washington's early years, as an "outdoor" man, then more Americans could warm up to their Founding Father.

For the fact is that Washington's early life was far more like a Huck Finn's than that of the white-marble aristocrat. True, he came from a fine old English family, and his father was a prosperous planter, iron-foundry owner and trader. But George—born in Westmoreland County, Virginia, on February 22, 1732—only spent about eight years in school; not only did he never go to college, but he was never as well read in traditional culture as were, for example, such men as Thomas Jefferson. Instead, young George enjoyed the life of the country gentry—hunting, fishing, boating, riding. At one point in his teens he wanted to go off and join the British Navy, but his mother talked him out of it; instead, he became a surveyor, which meant that he continued to spend much of his time outdoors tramping through the Virginia wilds. Then, between 1753-58, Washington served as an officer in the British Army and again, he campaigned and fought in quite arduous conditions in what was then the American frontier. Long before George Washington was known to his fellow colonists he was known to Indians as Caunotaucarious, "The Towntaker." And long before he would enjoy the victories of his later career, he suffered various defeats—surrendering Fort Necessity (south of what was later Pittsburgh) to the French, being spurned by his first love.

When Washington retired from military service in 1758, he was still only 26, and he undoubtedly began to live a more domesticated life. He married Martha Dandridge Custis, a wealthy widow with two children, he supervised his estate at Mt. Vernon (which he did not fully inherit until 1761) and he participated in the social life of a person of his station. But again, this involved a great deal of outdoor, practical activities whether supervising the farming and construction activities (and the slaves) and fishing and foxhunting. His years of service in the Virginia legislature also came with the obligations of his class. It was all the more unexpected, then, that this American "aristocrat" became one of the most militant advocates of using force to gain independence from the "despotism" (his own word) of his English relatives. Washington attended the first two Continental Congresses, and it was at the second, in June 1775 that he was elected commander-in-chief of the Revolutionary army—and simultaneously entered into that final phase of his life where his career became inseparable from his nation's chronology. Again, though, most Americans would not know of the theme of near-despair that ran through his years of combat, the physical hardships endured (and not only during the winter at Valley Forge) and the sheer aggravations of holding his troops and generals together. When the war ended, Washington did not retire to a drawing room but went right back to his farming and land-holdings. His years as President—which many of his contemporaries and some

students since regard as crucial to the survival of the United States—undoubtedly fixed the image of Washington as something of a marble statue. In fact, they were often trying times, and it was probably his past as a frontiersman that helped him more than any college course would have. It was typical, too, that his final activity was a horseback ride through a storm that led to the cold that in turn led to his death.

Ideas/Beliefs In Philadelphia, the American branch of the Church of England is reorganized as the Protestant Episcopal Church, and the *Book of Common Prayer* is revised accordingly.

12 MAY 1789

Life/Customs In New York City the Society of Saint Tammany, an Antifederalist fraternal organization, is established by a group of laborers, tradesmen and political activists headed by William Mooney. Named satirically after the Delaware Indian chief who welcomed William Penn, this society becomes in the late 19th century a powerful democratic political machine under Boss Tweed.

1 JUNE 1789

National Congress passes its first act, which mandates the procedure for administering oaths of public office.

4 JULY 1789

Finance In order to raise revenue, Congress passes the first Tariff Act. To become effective August 1, the bill sets a protective tax of 8.5 percent on some 30 enumerated items. Imports arriving on American ships are to be taxed at a rate 10 percent lower than those coming in on foreign ships.

14 JULY 1789

International In Paris, the French Revolution begins with the fall of the Bastille. This event is witnessed by American minister to France Thomas Jefferson.

20 JULY 1789

Finance In a further move to raise revenue, Congress passes the Tonnage Act, which mandates a tax of 50 cents per ton on foreign ships entering American ports.

27 JULY 1789

National The first executive department organized by Congress is that of Foreign Affairs. It will be renamed the Department of State on September 15, and Thomas Jefferson is appointed its head. Pending Jefferson's delayed return from France, John Jay carries on the affairs of state until March 1790.

7 AUGUST 1789

National Congress establishes the War Department and on September 12 will name Henry Knox to the post of Secretary of War.

2 SEPTEMBER 1789

National Congress establishes the Treasury Department and on September 11 will name Alexander Hamilton to the post of Secretary of the Treasury.

22 SEPTEMBER 1789
National Congress establishes the office of Postmaster General under the Treasury Department and on September 26 will name Samuel Osgood to the post of Postmaster General.

24 SEPTEMBER 1789
National Congress passes the Federal Judiciary Act, creating a six-man Supreme Court with a chief justice and five associate justices. The act also provides for an attorney general, and for a judicial system of 13 district courts and 3 circuit courts.

25 SEPTEMBER 1789
National Congress formally submits 12 proposed amendments to the Constitution to the states for ratification. Of these amendments, the first ten will be ratified and officially appended to the Constitution in 1791 as the Bill of Rights.

26 SEPTEMBER 1789
National Congress names Edmund Randolph Attorney General and appoints John Jay as Chief Justice of the Supreme Court. In addition, Thomas Jefferson is officially named Secretary of State and Samuel Osgood becomes Postmaster General. As Jefferson is still in France, John Jay will also manage the State Department until March 1790.

29 SEPTEMBER 1789
National Congress establishes the 1000-man United States Army, composed of one regiment of eight infantry companies and one battalion of four artillery companies. These forces are already on hand, since they have been guarding the frontier and overseeing public lands during the last months of the confederation congress. With this final business completed, Congress adjourns.

15 OCTOBER 1789
National George Washington begins a tour of the New England states.

20 NOVEMBER 1789
National New Jersey becomes the first state to ratify the Bill of Rights.

21 NOVEMBER 1789
National Won over by the proposed amendments to the Constitution, North Carolina becomes the 12th state to ratify the Constitution, 184 to 77.

26 NOVEMBER 1789
Life/Customs The first national Thanksgiving Day is established by a congressional resolution and by George Washington's proclamation. Intended to formally offer thanks for the Constitution, the holiday is opposed by Antifederalists who maintain Washington's proclamation violates states' rights.

18 DECEMBER 1789
Westward Movement The state of Virginia agrees to release the counties of the Kentucky territory from her jurisdiction.

21 DECEMBER 1789
Westward Movement Three Yazoo land companies—named after Georgia's Yazoo River—purchase 25.4 million acres of western lands from the Georgia legislature for $207,580. Most of this area is claimed by Spain.

22 DECEMBER 1789
Westward Movement The North Carolina legislature passes a second act of cession, deeding its western lands to the United States. This grant will be formally accepted by the Federal Government on 2 April 1790.

DECEMBER 1789
National The state of Virginia cedes a land tract on the Potomac River, including the community of Alexandria, to the Federal Government for the planned federal district and national capital. Maryland ceded land in the same area in 1788.

OTHER EVENTS OF 1789
Commerce On New York City's Bowery, German immigrant and fur trader John Jacob Astor buys his first piece of real estate. Astor's New York real estate holdings and fur business eventually become a commercial empire that enables him to help finance the War of 1812. Astor's is the first of the great American fortunes—at his death in 1848 he will leave a $30 million estate, part of which will endow the New York Public Library.
Arts/Culture The first American novel is published: William Hill Brown's *The Power of Sympathy; or The Triumph of Nature* advocates the education of women, while exposing "the dangerous consequences of seduction."
Life/Customs Some 200 Connecticut farmers in Litchfield County organize a temperance group, forswearing all alcoholic refreshment during the farming season. This movement will not gain national force until the 1826 founding of the American Temperance Society.

14 JANUARY 1790
Finance Secretary of the Treasury Alexander Hamilton presents to Congress his first report on public credit. Hamilton breaks down the debt inherited from the Confederation to establish a foreign debt of $11,710,379 (owed mostly to France and Holland), a domestic national debt of $40,414,086, and estimated state debts of $25 million. In order to place the new nation on a sound fiscal footing, Hamilton recommends funding the national debt at par, allowing creditors to exchange depreciated securities for new, interest-bearing funds at face value, thus providing a bonanza to speculators and provoking the ire of debtors and agrarian groups who had been forced to sell their securities at a discount to

ALEXANDER HAMILTON, 1755-1804

The archetypal Federalist, Alexander Hamilton throughout his extraordinary career as a founder of the American nation fought for the maintaining of a strong central government. Although his party was to decline in influence at the end of his life, his ideas were ahead of their time. He was born out of wedlock in the West Indies, probably on January 11, 1755, and early showed himself an intelligent and articulate lad. Sent to the mainland by a friendly minister in 1773, he attended King's College (later Columbia), where he encountered and joined the rising tide of rebellion against Britain. He joined the Revolutionary army in 1775 and proved himself an outstanding officer in the battles of Princeton, Monmouth, and Yorktown. By the time of that last battle in 1781 he had become a friend and confidant of George Washington and of the Marquis de Lafayette.

After the Revolution, Hamilton began a legal practice while continuing his political activities. By 1784 he had become, along with Aaron Burr, one of New York City's most prominent lawyers and the founder and director of the Bank of New York. Along with Washington, Hamilton had become unsatisfied with the weak authority of the Articles of Confederation; he was among those instrumental in calling for a Constitutional Convention and participated in the deliberations in 1787. Though the final draft was by no means to his satisfaction—a conservative, he wanted a stronger central government—he became the most active promoter of ratification, writing the *Federalist Papers* (along with James Madison and John Jay) to interpret and popularize the new Constitution.

After the success of the often stormy fight for ratification, Hamilton was appointed to Washington's first cabinet as Secretary of the Treasury in 1789. He moved quickly to establish a firm financial basis for the new country, to pay its debts, and to institute taxes and protective tariffs. But his Federalist philosophy and his support of the rather anti-French Jay Treaty gained him the enmity of Jefferson and the growing Republican party,

whose attacks finally led Hamilton to resign in 1795.

Hamilton was always an activist, a strong advocate for his beliefs rather than the masterful compromiser Washington was; thus Hamilton later contributed to dividing his party by opposing John Adams for the presidency, and contributed to his own fate by his attacks, however justified, on Aaron Burr. In 1800 Hamilton worked for the election of his old opponent Jefferson when he was tied with Burr for the presidency in the House. After Hamilton also contributed to Burr's defeat as New York governor in 1804, the outraged Burr challenged him to the duel in which Hamilton was shot on July 11, 1804. He died the next day in New York.

speculators. The proposal of James Madison to discriminate between the original buyers of the securities and their later holders is defeated by the House on February 22, three to one. Hamilton also advises $21.5 million of the states' Revolutionary War debts be assumed by the Federal Government. This move is favored by the New England states, who have the greatest unpaid debts, and opposed by the southern states which have already arranged to repay their debts. The Southern opposition is led by Virginia's chief congressional representative, James Madison. The South also fears the tremendously increased national debt that will result in heavier taxation and that the federal assumption of state debts will further increase federal power, while decreasing that of the states. The House defeats the assumption proposal on April 12, 31 to 29.

11 FEBRUARY 1790
Slavery The Society of Friends presents to Congress the first petition calling for the abolition of slavery.

1 MARCH 1790
Population Congress passes the Census Act, which calls for a periodic census of the inhabitants of the United States. The first census, completed on August 1, shows a total population of 3,929,625, including 59,557 free blacks and 697,624 enslaved blacks. (Although blacks account for 19.3 percent of the total population, they are counted as only three-fifths of a person for the purposes of apportionment, as mandated by the Constitution.) Massachusetts is the only state to report no slaves. Philadelphia is the largest city with 42,000 inhabitants, followed by New York with 33,000, Boston with 18,000, Charleston with 16,000 and Baltimore with 13,000. Virginia is the most populous state, with over 820,000 inhabitants; Massachusetts, Pennsylvania and North Carolina each have over 400,000; South Carolina, Connecticut, New Hampshire and New Jersey are in the 200,000 range; Delaware, Georgia and Rhode Island each have less than 100,000. For purposes of voting, only free white males with a specific state-determined tax-paying ability are enumerated. In 1790, most of the population leads a rural agrarian existence, with relatively little industrial activity at this early date.

MARCH 1790
Westward Movement A large group of French royalists, driven abroad by the French Revolution, founds

SEPTEMBER 25, 1790

a settlement at Gallipolis on the Ohio River, attracted by the lavish promises of Joel Barlow, the European agent for the Scioto Company, a land speculation organization. The subsequent failure of the Scioto Company will leave the settlers stranded, without supplies and in possession of questionable land claims. This will open the Scioto Company to accusations of fraud.

22 MARCH 1790
National Thomas Jefferson finally returns from France to fill the office of Secretary of State, allowing John Jay to devote his full energies to heading the Supreme Court.

26 MARCH 1790
National Congress passes the Naturalization Act, mandating a two-year residency requirement for new citizens.

4 APRIL 1790
National Congress creates the Revenue Marine Service, later known as the Coast Guard, under the aegis of the Treasury Department. The purpose of the Coast Guard is to increase revenues by policing contraband trade and smuggling activities.

17 APRIL 1790
Life/Customs In Philadelphia, Benjamin Franklin dies at the age of 84. His funeral on April 21 draws 20,000 mourners, the largest American public gathering to date.

25 MAY 1790
Ideas/Beliefs Led by the Reverend Elhanan Winchester and Dr. Benjamin Rush, Universalists convene in Philadelphia. An anti-Trinitarian doctrine evolves from this meeting which holds that Jesus was only a human intermediary between man and God, rather than the son of God.

26 MAY 1790
Westward Movement Congress creates a government for the Territory South of the River Ohio (Tennessee) and appoints William Blount governor. These western lands, ceded by North Carolina in 1789, were formerly part of the "State of Franklin," which governed itself independently from 1785 to 1788.

29 MAY 1790
National Rhode Island becomes the last of the 13 states to endorse the Constitution, despite strong Antifederalist forces opposing ratification. A boycott by the other New England states helped to persuade Rhode Island to join the mainstream.

31 MAY 1790
Arts/Culture President Washington signs the first Copyright Act to protect plays, books and maps for a period of 14 years, with the right of renewal for another 14 years. The passage of this act is mainly due to the unrelenting activity of Noah Webster on its behalf.

20 JUNE 1790
Finance Through skillful negotiation, Alexander Hamilton is able to work out a compromise establishing the federal capital on the Potomac River, instead of in Philadelphia, in exchange for James Madison's aid in obtaining enough southern votes to pass the provision mandating the assumption of the states' debts by the Federal Government.

10 JULY 1790
National The House of Representatives votes, 32 to 29, to locate the planned national capital on a ten-square-mile site along the Potomac River, with the exact place to be chosen by President Washington. Philadelphia is designated the temporary capital.

26 JULY 1790
Finance The House of Representatives votes, 34 to 28, to adopt Alexander Hamilton's assumption plan, mandating the assumption of the states' Revolutionary War debts by the Federal Government.

4 AUGUST 1790
Finance Congress passes the Funding Act, which empowers the Treasury Department to issue bonds bearing six percent interest in exchange, at par, for Revolutionary War bonds in order to fund the national debt.

7 AUGUST 1790
Indian Affairs In New York's Federal Hall, Secretary of War Henry Knox signs the Treaty of New York with Creek Indian chief Alexander McGillivray, the son of a Scottish trader and an Indian mother. Knox also makes McGillivray a brigadier general. In this treaty, the Creek Indians of the Southwest recognize United States sovereignty over part of their territory. But soon thereafter, the Spanish increase their support of McGillivray to the extent that the Creeks resume their attacks on American frontier settlements.

10 AUGUST 1790
Commerce Captain Robert Gray sails his ship *Columbia* into Boston harbor, concluding the first American voyage circumnavigating the globe. During the three-year trip, the *Columbia* carried furs to Canton, China, and tea from China to America.

15 AUGUST 1790
Ideas/Beliefs In England, Father John Carroll is consecrated the first Roman Catholic bishop of the United States. Pope Pius VI chooses Carroll for this post and chooses Baltimore as the site of the first American see. Carroll, who founded Georgetown University the previous year, will become the first archbishop of Baltimore in 1811. His efforts to gain greater autonomy for the American Catholic Church mark him as the most important leader in the American Catholic establishment.

25 SEPTEMBER 1790
Finance As an aftermath of the federal assumption

of the states' war debts, the Massachusetts legislature repeals the state excise tax.

18 OCTOBER 1790
Indian Affairs In the first of a number of United States expeditions against the western Indians, the forces led by General Josiah Harmar are defeated in a battle with the Ohio Indians near Fort Wayne. With these hostilities, a five-year-long Indian war begins in the Northwest Territory.

28 OCTOBER 1790
International Great Britain and Spain negotiate the Nootka Sound Convention, which reinforces the British claims for holdings in the Oregon region, disputed by the United States.

6 DECEMBER 1790
National Congress moves from New York to the temporary capital of Philadelphia, until the new federal district on the Potomac River is ready.

14 DECEMBER 1790
Finance In a second report on public credit to the House of Representatives, Alexander Hamilton presents a plan for a Bank of the United States, which will take over the mechanism of funding the national debt under the Assumption Act of July 26, as well as establish credit for the new nation.

16 DECEMBER
Finance The Virginia resolutions, drafted by Patrick Henry, oppose Alexander Hamilton's plan for the federal assumption of state debts on the basis that it supports monied interests, subordinates the agricultural to the commercial interests, and is unconstitutional.

21 DECEMBER 1790
Industry In Pawtucket, Rhode Island, Samuel Slater begins production in the first American cotton mill, using new cotton cording and spindle mill machinery. This Arkwright machinery was a closely-held British trade secret, but after close observation in England, Slater was able to construct and assemble the machinery from memory in America. The machinery is operated by children of four to ten years old. Slater's segmentation of the production process into simple tasks permits his child workers to outproduce experienced adult laborers. This marks the beginning of the Industrial Revolution in the United States.

OTHER EVENTS OF 1790
Life/Customs The Society for Alleviating the Miseries of the Public Prisons, headed by Tenche Coxe, William Howard and Benjamin Rush, successfully lobbies for improvements in the Pennsylvania prison system. The changes implemented include adequate clothing, more privacy, religious instruction, separation of prisoners by type of crime and protection of prisoners from exploitative guards. In Philadelphia's Walnut Street Prison, the Pennsylvania system of prison management is introduced, instituting a solitary confinement policy in order to effect "moral regeneration" through "enforced meditation." The rest of the states follow the Auburn penal system, in which prisoners may interact during the day but sleep in separate cells at night.
Arts/Culture Production begins on *Dobson's Encyclopedia,* a deluxe American 18-volume edition of *Encyclopedia Britannica.* Incorporating unique typefaces and specially prepared engravings, the complete encyclopedia will finally be issued after seven years. It will be widely regarded as a triumph of the American publishing industry.

In New York City, Scottish immigrant furniture maker Duncan Phyfe opens his cabinet–making shop. Phyfe's exquisite standards of workmanship permit him to ask and receive prices as high as $25 for chairs and $300 for pier tables.
Transportation The first leg of the Philadelphia-Lancaster Turnpike is opened. The commercial success of this early 61-mile toll road leads to the widespread construction of toll roads, particularly in the New England and Middle Atlantic states. The hard-surfaced Philadelphia-Lancaster Turnpike will be completed in 1794.

5 JANUARY 1791
Black Experience In Charleston, North Carolina, free blacks present to the state legislature a formal protest against the banning of black-initiated lawsuits and the ban on black testimony in the courts. The legislature rejects the document.

10 JANUARY 1791
National Though not yet a state, Vermont ratifies the United States Constitution.

28 JANUARY 1791
Finance As requested by Congress, Alexander Hamilton presents a report on the organization of a national mint for the issuance of currency.

25 FEBRUARY 1791
Finance President Washington signs the bill chartering the Bank of the United States, only after calling for written opinions from his cabinet officers on the constitutionality of the measure. On February 15, Thomas Jefferson submitted his opinion which held the bill unconstitutional on the basis of the yet unadopted Tenth Amendment, insisting that the incorporation of a bank was not one of the special powers delegated to Congress. Alexander Hamilton's February 23 opinion supported the constitutionality of the measure, arguing that the planned bank was covered under the congressional power to collect taxes and regulate trade. These differing philosophies of constitutional interpretation are known as Jeffersonian strict constructionism and Hamiltonian loose constructionism, or the theory of implied powers. Although not entirely convinced by either view, Washington supports Hamilton's opinion as he feels the president should support the directly involved cabinet official.

SEPTEMBER 29, 1791

3 MARCH 1791

Finance On the recommendation of Alexander Hamilton, Congress passes the revenue-raising Whisky Act, setting an excise tax on distilled liquors and stills. This levy, creating 14 revenue districts, is strenuously opposed by those most affected by it, the backwoods farmers who dispose of surplus grain by distilling it. The state legislatures of Maryland, North Carolina and Virginia pass resolutions protesting the Whisky Act.

4 MARCH 1791

National Vermont enters the Union as the 14th independent state. Vermont has a population of about 85,000.

30 MARCH 1791

National President Washington personally selects the site for the proposed federal district and United States capital on the Potomac River. The chosen site includes the already existing communities of Georgetown, Maryland, and Alexandria, Virginia.

Transportation Construction is begun on the Knoxville Road, an early turnpike linking Virginia's Wilderness Road to the settlement of Knoxville in the Territory South of the River Ohio. The Knoxville Road will serve to facilitate settlement of the frontier regions.

7 APRIL 1791

National President Washington begins a two-month tour of the southern states.

15 APRIL 1791

National Official ceremonies are held at the site of the 70-square-mile planned federal district on the Potomac River. Construction of the White House will begin in 1792, and work on the United States Capitol begins in 1793.

26 APRIL 1791

Indian Affairs In the Treaty of Holston River, the Cherokee Indians cede most of their land holdings in the upper Tennessee River Valley to the United States Government, in return for the promise that the rest of the Cherokee lands will remain the sole property of the Indians, free of further demands by the Federal Government.

MAY—JUNE 1791

National Thomas Jefferson and James Madison conduct a tour of New York and New England in order to organize Antifederalist political factions in support of their opposition to Washington's Federalist administration. The Jefferson-Madison forces will later unite as the Republican (at first, the Democratic-Republican) party, while the supporters of the Washington administration will organize as the Federalist party. These emerging political alignments reflect the issues of the Jefferson-Hamilton feud. While Jefferson favors a democratic agrarian society based on the individual freeholder and opposed to a strong centralized government, Alexander Hamilton supports a diversified industrial society governed by a strong central government of the elite.

12 JUNE 1791

Slavery Inspired by a slave rebellion on the West Indian island of Haiti, a group of slaves revolt in the Spanish colony of Louisiana.

4 JULY 1791

Finance The newly-organized Bank of the United States begins a subscription drive to raise capital.

16 JULY 1791

Black Experience Black mathematician and scientist Benjamin Banneker is named one of the three commissioners appointed to survey the site for the planned federal capital on the Potomac River. In 1754, Banneker constructed the first clock made entirely in America, and in 1791 he will begin publication of a widely-distributed almanac.

10 SEPTEMBER 1791

Westward Movement The governor of the Northwest Territory, General Arthur St. Clair, leads an expedition northward from Fort Washington near Cincinnati in order to found the Ohio region forts of Hamilton, St. Clair, Jefferson, Greenville and Recovery. The construction of these forts is called for by the repeated attacks of the Ohio Indians on frontier settlements.

29 SEPTEMBER 1791

Transportation The Pennsylvania legislature char-

BENJAMIN BANNEKER, 1731-1806

Among the many once-forgotten individuals of American black history, Benjamin Banneker has received recognition in recent years as a mathematician, astronomer and surveyor who helped lay out the nation's capital. Banneker was born to a recently freed black family on November 9, 1731 in what would become Ellicott City, Maryland. During his long career as a farmer, he taught himself mathematics, experimented with mechanical devices (once making an unusual clock of his own design) and spent many hours observing and calculating the movements of the heavenly bodies. He published his own almanac in 1791 and it remained in print for over a decade. He also published a treatise on bees and calculated the life cycle of the 17-year locust. His skills as a mathematician came to the attention of Major Andrew Ellicott who in 1791 enlisted Banneker's help in surveying the Territory of Columbia, soon to be developed as the new capital of the United States. But it was also a simple fact that this same nation would not allow Banneker to share any of the privileges and rights of citizenship, and although he was hardly an activist, Banneker once wrote a famous letter to Thomas Jefferson in which he mildly reproved that eminent spokesman for "the rights of man," asking Jefferson to "embrace every opportunity to eradicate that train of absurd and false ideas and opinions which so generally prevail with respect to us [blacks]." Known as "the sable genius" to his contemporaries, Banneker never married and his reputation soon faded, but he had planted seeds that would eventually blossom into the abolition of slavery and the freedom of all black Americans.

159

ters a company to build a canal between the Schuylkill and Susquehanna Rivers.

OCTOBER 1791
International The first British minister to the United States, George Hammond, arrives in America.

31 OCTOBER 1791
National In Philadelphia, the emerging Jefferson-Hamilton feud is fueled by the publication of a partisan newspaper supporting Jeffersonianism. The *National Gazette* is edited by poet Philip Freneau.

4 NOVEMBER 1791
Indian Affairs Near the site of Fort Wayne, a force of Ohio Indians from the Maumee and Wabash River areas defeats an expeditionary force under General Arthur St. Clair, governor of the Northwest Territory.

26 NOVEMBER 1791
National President Washington consults with the heads of the government departments on foreign and military matters. This gradually leads to the accepted practice of regular cabinet meetings.

5 DECEMBER 1791
Commerce Alexander Hamilton presents a report on manufacturers to Congress, which calls for a tariff system to protect American industry, an agricultural bounty system and federal aid for public works projects such as roads and canals. Hamilton's intent is to encourage the growth of American industry and agriculture.

12 DECEMBER 1791
Finance In Philadelphia, the main office of the Bank of the United States opens its doors for business. Additional branches of the bank will be established in America's leading cities. The bank serves as the fiscal vehicle of the Federal Government. The gold and silver held by the Bank of the United States backs the American currency system.

15 DECEMBER 1791
National The Virginia legislature ratifies the Bill of Rights, thus bringing the number of ratifying states to three-quarters. This causes the first ten amendments to the United States Constitution to go into effect.

OTHER EVENTS OF 1791
International Great Britain seeks to validate her claims to the Oregon territory in the area of Nootka Sound by dispatching George Vancouver to explore the region.

Ideas/Beliefs Thomas Paine publishes the first part of his *Rights of Man,* a pamphlet violently attacking monarchy and supporting democracy. In the same year, John Adams' *Discourses of Davila* are published; these writings express Adams' conservative ideal of a classical utopian society, ruled by an elite of the rich, powerful and politically talented. This aristocratic monarchistic social philosophy is moti-

---

ROADS

In the early years of the nation, the construction of passable roads, and later of canals, was an essential prerequisite for the development of industry and commerce. This web of routes also served to draw the widespread settlements and separate states together into a semblance of national unity. And finally the roads were necessary to accommodate the growing wave of pioneers striking out for western regions.

Around the turn of the century, the state of even the most frequently travelled roads was abysmal. One survivor of a 1796 Baltimore to Philadelphia journey described the highway as characterized by "an aspect of savage desolation (with) chasms to the depth of six, eight, ten feet. . .at numerous intervals." The immense costs of road construction led to early experiments with the building of turnpikes, or toll roads, which were paid for by the users and not by the general taxpayers. In 1785, the state of Virginia financed the construction of the first American toll road. But it was the Lancaster Turnpike, a 63-mile hard-surfaced road from Philadelphia to Lancaster, Pennsylvania, costing $465,000 in private investments, that became a profitable venture. This success encouraged numerous private companies, as well as local governments, to build over 10,000 miles of turnpike during the next 50 years. The states often subsidized the building of turnpikes, which could cost as much as $10,000 per mile, through tax abatements or grants. Despite such advantages, many toll roads eventually had to be taken over by local communities, because of poor management and high original costs. As the focus shifted to railroad construction, many turnpikes of the earlier era fell into disuse and disrepair.

The Federal Government occupied an ambiguous position in this surge of road building. Early on, it supported the construction of the Cumberland Road, also known as the National Road, which eventually reached from Cumberland, Maryland, to Vandalia, Illinois. But later such projects met with presidential opposition, from James Monroe and then Andrew Jackson, to direct federal financing of roads. Their objections were based on constitutional grounds and on the justification that such federal projects unfairly benefited one region of the nation at the expense of other areas.

But Henry Clay's 1824 "American System," which proposed a national economic development plan based on a federally financed network of roads and canals, coupled with protective tariffs to encourage American industry, received widespread popular support. The government, however, remained unmoved for the rest of the 19th century, and most roads, even the well-travelled Oregon and Santa Fe Trails, remained unsurfaced potential mud holes, rutted with wagon tracks. It was the advent of the automobile that finally forced the Federal Government to commit itself to a road-building program.

---

vated by his fear of oppression by a democratic majority. It is understandably unpopular with the general public, and Adams' eight years as vice president of the United States are passed in an aura of resentment and mistrust. Also in 1791, the vice-president's son, John Quincy Adams, publishes his *Publicola* papers in Boston; the *Publicola* papers also oppose the democratic principles upheld by Tom Paine.

Arts/Culture American naturalist William Bartram

publishes an account of his botanizing expeditions throughout North and South Carolina, Georgia, and East and West Florida. Bartram's *Travels* will be highly valued by such European writers as Chateaubriand, Wordsworth and Coleridge; and the book also becomes a seminal document of romanticism, helping to inspire its interest in American landscape.

In Massachusetts, Boston clergyman and historian Jeremy Belknap founds the first American historical association, the Massachusetts Historical Society. The goal of the society is to collect and preserve significant documents of American history.

12 JANUARY 1792

International South Carolina Federalist Thomas Pinckney is appointed the first minister of the United States to Great Britain. Pinckney departs with instructions to obtain favorable commercial terms for American trade. On the same day, Congress confirms the appointment of Gouverneur Morris as minister to France. Morris is already in France, where he has been a witness to the French Revolution.

JANUARY 1792

Ideas/Beliefs The second part of Tom Paine's political pamphlet, *The Rights of Man,* is issued. This tract supports the revolutionary cause and argues that power should rest in the will of the democratic majority.

21 FEBRUARY 1792

National Congress passes the Presidential Succession Act, providing for the succession of the president pro tempore of the Senate and then the speaker of the House in case of the removal, death, resignation or disability of both the president and vice-president. Thomas Jefferson's attempt to place the secretary of state next in the line of succession is defeated by the Federalists; this proposal is finally incorporated into the Presidential Succession Act in 1886.

5 MARCH 1792

Indian Affairs Following his November 1791 defeat by the Ohio Indians, General Arthur St. Clair, governor of the Northwest Territory, is replaced as the military commander of the troops in the Ohio territory by General Anthony Wayne.

2 APRIL 1792

Finance Congress passes the Coinage Act, establishing a national mint in Philadelphia, mandating a decimal system of coinage, and setting the ratio of silver to gold in the United States dollar at 15 to 1. Astronomer and mathematician David Rittenhouse is appointed the first director of the mint.

APRIL 1792

Slavery At the Kentucky constitutional convention, Presbyterian clergyman David Rice unsuccessfully tries to exclude slavery from Kentucky. A second attempt, in 1799, to abolish slavery from Kentucky also fails.

8 MAY 1792

Indian Affairs Faced with the growing Indian hostilities in the Northwest Territory, Congress passes the Militia Act which authorizes the states to draft all able-bodied free white men between the ages of 18 and 45 into militia brigades.

11 MAY 1792

Discovery On a second voyage of circumnavigation of the globe, Boston Captain Robert Gray discovers the 1214-mile-long Columbia River in the Washington-Oregon territory. Gray names the river after his ship. The Columbia River will not be explored overland until the 1805 Lewis and Clark Expedition.

17 MAY 1792

Finance The New York Stock Exchange is organized by 24 brokers who gather at the Merchants Coffee House.

1 JUNE 1792

Westward Movement Kentucky becomes the 15th state to enter the Union, with a state constitution providing for male suffrage, slavery and a bill of rights.

18 JULY 1792

Life/Customs In Paris, John Paul Jones, the naval hero of the Revolutionary War, dies at the age of 45.

21 AUGUST 1792

Finance In Pennsylvania, the whisky excise tax of 1791 is protested at a Pittsburgh convention. Republican leader Albert Gallatin heads a committee to draft a series of resolutions opposing the tax, and the convention seeks to determine legal means to circumvent the tax. Opposition to the whisky excise tax is strong throughout the South, especially in central North Carolina.

29 SEPTEMBER 1792

Finance In reaction to the Pittsburgh proclamation opposing the whisky excise tax, President Washington issues a proclamation warning against avoidance of the tax and insisting that the tax will be collected as provided for in the law.

2 OCTOBER 1792

National At Mount Vernon, President Washington meets with Secretary of State Thomas Jefferson in an unsuccessful attempt to mediate an end to the feud between Jefferson and Alexander Hamilton. The quarrel has been fueled by a series of articles in the opposing partisan journals, the Jeffersonian *National Gazette* and the Hamiltonian *Gazette of the United States*. Hamilton accuses Jefferson of opposing the Constitution and the Washington Administration and of being the source of political intrigue undermining the government.

10 OCTOBER 1792

Regional The Virginia legislature enacts a bill

providing for the appointment of presidential electors, and for the division of the state into election districts.

13 OCTOBER 1792
National In Washington, the cornerstone is laid for the President's Palace, later known as the White House. Designed by James Hoban in imitation of the Irish mansion of the Duke of Leinster, this is the first public building to be erected in the new capital. The White House will be completed in time for John and Abigail Adams to take residence in 1800; burned by the British during the War of 1812, it will be rebuilt by Hoban.

1 NOVEMBER 1792
National A general election takes place to choose presidential electors for the nation's second presidential election.

5 NOVEMBER 1792
National In Philadelphia, the second Congress reconvenes for its second session.

5 DECEMBER 1792
National In the second presidential election, George Washington is reelected president with 132 electoral votes, and John Adams is reelected vice–president with 77 electoral votes. Antifederalist George Clinton of New York receives 50 electoral votes.

OTHER EVENTS OF 1792
Slavery Virginia statesman George Mason leads opposition to slavery in the state. Mason terms slavery a disgrace to mankind and compares it to a slow poison corrupting future politicians. In the same year, Denmark becomes the first nation to abolish the slave trade.

Life/Customs In England, Mary Wollstonecraft publishes her *A Vindication of the Rights of Women*. Her attack on the inferior status of women will be widely read and discussed in American intellectual circles, leading to some changes in attitude toward women.

9 JANUARY 1793
Transportation In Philadelphia the first balloon flight in America is made by Frenchman Jean-Pierre Francois Blanchard. (Eight years earlier Blanchard had crossed the English Channel by balloon.) Witnessed by President Washington, the balloon rises to a height of 5812 feet in 46 minutes.

21 JANUARY 1793
International In Paris, French revolutionaries guillotine Louis XVI and Marie Antoinette. The news of this action, as well as of France's later declaration of war on England, is to temper the original enthusiasm of the Jeffersonian Antifederalists for the French revolutionary cause.

23 JANUARY 1793
Finance Repeated unsubstantiated charges of corrup-

EARLY PRESIDENTIAL ELECTIONS AND
CONGRESSIONAL CAUCUSES

For all their wisdom, the founding fathers failed to foresee the rise of the political party system in the new nation. Thus, the framers of the Constitution had outlined a system in which the electors voted for president and vice–president indiscriminately. The candidate who received the majority of votes became president, and the one with the second highest number of votes became vice–president. It was a situation fraught with potential difficulties, but recognition of this was slow to dawn, as George Washington was nominated to his two terms in office informally, and elected unanimously.

When Washington announced his retirement in 1796, the presidential candidates then came to be chosen by congressional caucus. The caucus (a word probably derived from the Algonquian Indian term for counselor) was a long-standing American tradition. Since the early 1700s, wealthy Bostonians had been meeting in caucus clubs to endorse candidates for local elections. The 1796 election was the first between two opposing political parties. In secret congressional conferences, the Federalists nominated John Adams and Thomas Pinckney for president and vice–president, while the Democratic-Republicans chose Thomas Jefferson and Aaron Burr as presidential and vice–presidential candidates. The electors chose Adams as president and Jefferson as vice–president—resulting in the awkward situation of having political foes serving as leaders in the same administration. The 1800 tied election between Thomas Jefferson and Aaron Burr sent the decision to the House of Representatives, and led to the 12th Amendment to eliminate the ambiguities in presidential election by requiring separate ballots for the president and vice–president.

From 1796 to 1824, the president and vice–president continued to be nominated by the congressional caucus method. But popular sentiment began to oppose congressional caucus nomination as being undemocratic. By 1824, the selection of the two highest officials in the land by secret caucuses of senators and representatives had been decried by nationwide rallies of Andrew Jackson's supporters, who sought a more open method of candidate selection. The last congressional caucus took place in 1824; and in the 1828 presidential election, Andrew Jackson successfully waged the first modern-style campaign, thanks to the expert organizational abilities of Martin Van Buren of the Albany Regency, a New York state party machine. In 1831 the small Anti-Masonic party, with its Baltimore party convention, initiated the national convention system of choosing presidential candidates. From then on, political parties took over and American public servants would have to deal with them.

---

tion and mismanagement against Alexander Hamilton's conduct as Treasury Secretary culminate in a set of resolutions calling for an official inquiry into the condition of the Treasury. Hamilton will present two reports, on February 4 and February 13, to the House defending his actions. A subsequent February 28 call censuring Hamilton does not pass the House. Discontent with the Washington administration's fiscal policies is magnified by a crisis in real estate and stock speculation. Hamilton's opponents claim congress is dominated by monied interests, and they seek a return to "genuine republicanism."

SEPTEMBER 18, 1793

1 FEBRUARY 1793
International The revolutionary government of France declares war on Great Britain, as well as on Spain and The Netherlands. This declaration causes a number of Antifederalist supporters of the French cause to withdraw their support.

12 FEBRUARY 1793
Slavery Congress enacts a Fugitive Slave Act, mandating the right of a slaveowner to recover a runaway slave. This bill implements the provisions of Article IV, Section 2 of the Constitution by establishing the mechanism for the recovery of fugitive slaves.

18 FEBRUARY 1793
National In reaching a judgment in the case of *Chisholm v. Georgia,* the United States Supreme Court rules that a citizen of one state may indeed sue another state in a federal court, as provided for in Article III, Section 2 of the Constitution. This decision will lead in 1798 to the 11th Amendment, repealing this section of the Constitution.

4 MARCH 1793
National George Washington begins his second term as president of the United States, and John Adams begins his second term as vice–president. Washington's five-man cabinet includes Thomas Jefferson as Secretary of State, Alexander Hamilton as Secretary of the Treasury, Henry Knox as Secretary of War, Edmund Randolph as Attorney General, and Timothy Pickering as Postmaster General.

8 APRIL 1793
International Citizen Genêt (Edmond-Charles-Edouard Genêt), the minister from the French Republic to the United States, arrives in Charleston, South Carolina. Before he sets off to present his credentials in Philadelphia, Genêt commissions four privateering ships and sends them to raid British ships traveling along the American coast. Genêt also initiates expeditions against Spanish and British territories.

18 APRIL 1793
International Citizen Genêt sets out from Charleston, South Carolina, on the 28-day trip to Philadelphia. During his journey, he is greeted warmly by the American populace.

22 APRIL 1793
International President Washington issues a proclamation of neutrality on the part of the United States in the war that has erupted between the French Republic and England. He also warns American citizens to avoid involvement in the hostilities. Washington issues the neutrality proclamation after consulting with his cabinet on American obligations under the 1778 treaty with France. Although both Hamilton and Jefferson favor neutrality, Hamilton sides with Britain and Jefferson with France. James Madison questions the president's authority to issue such a proclamation without congressional approval.

9 MAY 1793
International The French republican government orders the seizure of ships of neutral nations carrying supplies to enemy (British, Spanish and Dutch) ports.

18 MAY 1793
International Having finally reached Philadelphia, Citizen Genêt presents his diplomatic credentials to President Washington, who receives him coolly.

5 JUNE 1793
International Secretary of State Thomas Jefferson conveys to Citizen Genêt a communication from President Washington warning the French minister that his actions have infringed American neutrality. Genêt agrees to issue no more military commissions on United States soil, and to order the four French privateers out of American waters. Yet, Genêt subsequently goes back on his word by arming still another privateer. When Genêt is again warned by the United States not to send out this vessel, he threatens to go directly to the American people, over the head of the president. He then orders the privateer out to sea.

8 JUNE 1793
International Great Britain orders the seizure of neutral vessels, including American ships, carrying provisions to French ports.

31 JULY 1793
National Thomas Jefferson submits his resignation as Secretary of State to President Washington, to become effective December 31. Washington has become more heavily dependent on Federalist Alexander Hamilton for advice on foreign affairs. Jefferson is to assume the leadership of the antifederalist Democratic-Republican party.
Exploration In Boston, Captain Robert Gray arrives on his ship *Columbia* from his second voyage of circumnavigation of the globe. On this trip he discovered the Columbia River in the American Pacific Northwest.

2 AUGUST 1793
International President Washington's cabinet decides to ask the government of the French Republic to recall its minister, Citizen Genêt, as Genêt's conduct has threatened American neutrality in the war between France and England. But when the Jacobins then come to power in France and send Joseph Fauchet as minister to the United States, carrying orders for Genêt's arrest, Genêt asks for and is granted political asylum in the United States. He will become an American citizen and marry the daughter of New York Governor George Clinton.

18 SEPTEMBER 1793
Arts/Culture In the planned federal capital on the Potomac River, President Washington lays the cornerstone for the Congress House, or United States Capitol, in a ceremony incorporating Masonic rites. Designed by William Thornton in the classical Palla-

TESTING A UNION 1788-1865

dian style, the north wing is completed by James Hoban and others in time to accommodate the House of Representatives and the federal courts in 1800. After destruction by the British in the War of 1812, the Capital wing will be rebuilt by Benjamin Latrobe in 1810, and the building will be completed by Charles Bulfinch in 1827.

6 NOVEMBER 1793
International A British order in council calls for the seizure of any neutral vessels carrying exports from the islands of the French West Indies. The enforcement of this order leads to the British capture of American ships, and the impressment and imprisonment of their crews. These hostile actions are to bring Britain and the United States dangerously close to war.

25 NOVEMBER 1793
Slavery In Albany, New York, a group of slaves rebel and set a series of devastating fires in the city.

31 DECEMBER 1793
National The resignation of Thomas Jefferson as Secretary of State becomes effective. Jefferson will be succeeded in this position by Edmund Randolph on January 2, 1794.

OTHER EVENTS OF 1793
Education Rhode Island textile industrialist Samuel Slater organizes a Sunday School in order to teach the basic skills of reading, writing and arithmetic to the children who labor in his Pawtucket factory. And the newly-chartered Williams College in Massachusetts sets entrance requirements that accept knowledge of the French language as an acceptable substitute for the classical languages of Latin and Greek.
Arts/Culture In Litchfield, Connecticut, Elihu Hubbard Smith publishes an important early anthology, *American Poems, Selected and Original,* which mainly includes the literary efforts of the Connecticut Wits. Formed to celebrate American literary independence, this group includes Joel Barlow, Timothy Dwight, Lemuel Hopkins and John Trumbull.
Ideas/Beliefs Itinerant Quaker minister John Woolman publishes his humanitarian essay, *A Word of Remembrance and Caution to the Rich,* which calls for sweeping social reforms, including the abolition of slavery. In 1898, The British socialist group, the Fabians, will reprint Woolman's tract, referring to him as "the voice in the wilderness, the John the Baptist of the gospel of socialism."
Transportation The 27-mile Middlesex Canal is built, linking Boston with the Merrimack River. A horse-pulled barge is charged $3.50 to travel its length.

2 JANUARY 1794
National In President Washington's cabinet, Virginian Edmund Randolph, formerly Attorney General, becomes Secretary of State.

EDMUND RANDOLPH, 1753-1813

One of the "Virginia Dynasty" that was largely responsible for founding the United States and guiding it through its early years, Edmund Randolph was a member of the distinguished Randolph family that also produced Thomas Jefferson (whose mother was a Randolph). Edmund was born near Williamsburg, Virginia, on August 10, 1753. After studies at the College of William and Mary he read law and briefly served in the Revolutionary army before becoming the attorney general of Virginia in 1776. Three years later he served in the Continental Congress.

Elected governor of Virginia in 1786, Randolph was a prominent member of the state's delegation to the Constitutional Convention the following year. Although he refused to sign the final document, he came eventually, like Alexander Hamilton, to favor ratification as better than nothing. He joined Washington's first cabinet as attorney general in 1789. In that capacity, despite his ties to Jefferson, he threaded a narrow neutral path between the Federalists in power and the growing opposition of Jefferson, between the supporters of Britain and of France, and the factions for and against the Jay Treaty. Jefferson broke with Washington and resigned as secretary of state in 1794, and for over a year Randolph filled that post as well. It was a difficult and thankless position, and Randolph resigned in 1795 after accusations—later proven erroneous—that he had made improper political offers to France.

Randolph returned to a prosperous legal career in Virginia. His last appearance on the national scene was in 1807, when he stood against his old friend Jefferson and successfully defended Aaron Burr in his trial for treason. In this effort Randolph was aided by Chief Justice Marshall's determination to see that President Jefferson would not obtain the guilty verdict he so clearly wanted. Randolph died in 1813.

---

3 JANUARY 1794
International In answer to the British orders in council of November 3, 1793, calling for the seizure of neutral ships carrying French West Indian exports, James Madison presents seven commercial resolutions in the House of Representatives. These resolutions seek remedies against any nations threatening American shipping and trade. After much discussion, none of the resolutions are passed.

13 JANUARY 1794
National Congress orders the addition of two more stars and stripes to the American flag by May 1, 1795 in recognition of the admission of the states of Vermont and Kentucky to the Union.

FEBRUARY 1794
Indian Affairs In Quebec, the British governor of lower Canada, Sir Guy Carleton, guarantees a delegation of Indians the return of their lands in the Northwest Territory in Ohio if the Indians promise to help Britain in a war with the United States.

28 FEBRUARY 1794
National Swiss-born Pennsylvanian Albert Gallatin

OTHER EVENTS OF 1794

is barred from his elected seat in the United States Senate on a residence technicality fabricated by Federalists who take exception to Gallatin's opposition to the whisky tax. In 1795 Gallatin will be elected to the House of Representatives, becoming a founder of the Democratic-Republican party and President Jefferson's Secretary of the Treasury in 1801.

5 MARCH 1794
National Congress submits to the states for ratification the 11th Amendment to the United States Constitution. Designed to limit federal judicial authority over the states, this move is instigated by the 1793 case of *Chisholm v. Georgia,* in which the Supreme Court had ruled that a citizen of one state could in effect sue another state. The 11th Amendment repeals the section of the Constitution that permits such legal suits. The 11th Amendment will be officially ratified on January 8, 1798.

22 MARCH 1794
Slavery Congress passes a bill banning slave trade with foreign nations.

27 MARCH 1794
National Congress authorizes the establishment of the United States Navy.

19 APRIL 1794
National Congress endorses President Washington's appointment of the Chief Justice of the United States, John Jay, as envoy to Great Britain with the mission of negotiating a commercial treaty with England.

24 APRIL 1794
Life/Customs The Pennsylvania legislature revises the state criminal code, abolishing capital punishment for all offenses except murder.

1 MAY 1794
Labor In Philadelphia, the Federal Society of Journeymen Cordwainers (shoemakers) is organized. This is America's first trade union.

27 MAY 1794
International James Monroe is appointed the American minister to France, replacing Gouverneur Morris, whose recall the French have requested because of his royalist sympathies and meddling. On the same day, John Quincy Adams is appointed. minister to The Netherlands.

1 JUNE 1794
International Protected by a French fleet, a large convoy of American ships carrying provisions to famine-stricken France is encountered by a British fleet under Admiral Sir Richard Howe. Although Howe defeats the French, the American convoy is able to escape safely during the heat of the naval battle.

5 JUNE 1794
International Reinforcing President Washington's

1793 neutrality proclamation, Congress passes the Neutrality Act to forbid American citizens from joining the military service of foreign powers and to ban the fitting and provisioning of foreign armed vessels in American ports.

JULY 1794
Finance In the Monongahela Valley of western Pennsylvania, the Whiskey Rebellion breaks out among backwoods farmers who oppose the collection of the federal excise tax on liquor and stills by violent actions such as burning tax collectors' houses, and tarring and feathering revenue officers.

7 AUGUST 1794
Regional During the course of the Whiskey Rebellion, President Washington issues a proclamation directing the insurgents to return to their homes, at the same time calling out a combined Virginia, Maryland, New Jersey and Pennsylvania 12,900-man militia force to put down the insurrection.

20 AUGUST 1794
Indian Affairs At the Battle of Fallen Timbers in northwest Ohio alongside the Maumee River, General Anthony Wayne decisively defeats a 2000-man Indian force, effectively ending Indian hostilities in the region. In October, Wayne will construct Fort Wayne at the headwaters of the Maumee River.

24 SEPTEMBER 1794
Regional During the course of the Whiskey Rebellion, President Washington issues a second proclamation ordering the suppression of the insurrection by the militia led by Henry Lee. Faced with the sizable military force, the insurgents return home quietly, thus ending the rebellion in mid-November. Two hundred rebels are arrested, 25 are tried for treason and two are convicted but later pardoned.

19 NOVEMBER 1794
International Special American envoy John Jay successfully concludes a commercial treaty with Great Britain. Jay's Treaty, as it is commonly known, mandates the withdrawal of British forces from their military forts in the Northwest Territory by June 1, 1796, in exchange for American settlement of pre-Revolutionary War debts owed to British citizens. The commercial provisions of Jay's Treaty open British East Indian and West Indian ports to American vessels, and place British trade with the United States on a most–favored–nation basis. Boundary disputes and the question of compensation for illegal maritime seizures by the British are to be brought before joint commissions. The problem of the British impressment of American ship crews is not addressed. The terms of Jay's Treaty will not be made known in the United States until March 1795.

OTHER EVENTS OF 1794
Transportation The 61-mile macadam Philadelphia-Lancaster Turnpike is completed. Its financial success

as a toll road will lead to the construction of many other toll roads. In the same year, another of the nation's earliest canals is constructed in South Hadley Falls, Massachusetts.

2 JANUARY 1795
National Former Postmaster General Timothy Pickering is appointed Secretary of War in President Washington's cabinet, succeeding Henry Knox.

5 JANUARY 1795
International France announces that it is aware of Jay's Treaty with Great Britain.

7 JANUARY 1795
Regional The corrupt Georgia legislature sells 35 million acres in the Yazoo River territory (including most of Alabama and Mississippi) to four land speculation companies for a nominal sum. The following year, a newly-elected Georgia legislature will invalidate the Yazoo land sale. The confusion over claims caused by this repudiation of the original sale will lead to a congressional investigation and an 1810 Supreme Court decision ruling that the state of Georgia could not revoke its original act.

29 JANUARY 1795
Immigration Congress passes the Naturalization Act, which mandates a five-year residency in the United States before citizenship will be granted.

31 JANUARY 1795
National Alexander Hamilton resigns as President Washington's Secretary of the Treasury. He is succeeded in this post by Oliver Wolcott, Jr. Hamilton will continue to advise Washington on major policy issues.

3 MARCH 1795
Westward Movement In the Ohio territory, the French settlers of Gallipolis finally receive clear title to their lands. The French had been persuaded to emigrate by the Scioto Company's misleading claims that the Ohio region was already a settled area.

APRIL 1795
International America's minister to Great Britain, Thomas Pinckney, is appointed special envoy to Spain.

24 JUNE 1795
International By a narrow margin and after a lengthy debate, the Senate ratifies Jay's Treaty of 19 November 1794 with Great Britain. The treaty has been the object of much controversy, with factions from both the North and the South, and from both the Federalists and Democratic-Republicans opposing it on the basis of its specific details dealing with their interests.

19 JULY 1795
Westward Movement In the Northwest Territory the

Connecticut Land Company buys in northeast Ohio, the Western Reserve, a large tract of land along the banks of Lake Erie. The company agent, Moses Cleaveland, makes preparations for the arrival of settlers. In 1796, he will lay out and name the city of Cleaveland (to become Cleveland about 1830).

3 AUGUST 1795
Indian Affairs In the Northwest Territory General Anthony Wayne signs the Treaty of Greenville with the 12 Ohio Indian tribes, whom he had decisively defeated in August 1794 at the Battle of Fallen Timbers. The Indians cede large tracts of their lands in the eastern part of the territory and a specific boundary is set, separating the remaining Indian lands from those of the settlers.

14 AUGUST 1795
International President Washington signs Jay's Treaty of November 19, 1794 with Great Britain, although the Democratic-Republicans in the House of Representatives have tried to block the treaty by voting against the appropriations necessary for enforcing its provisions. Washington sets an important precedent by exerting his executive prerogative, since the agreement of both houses of Congress is not required to validate the treaty.

19 AUGUST 1795
International Secretary of State Edmund Randolph resigns from his post under suspicion of corruption—charges that are never proven. Washington suspects Randolph of having intrigued with the French to block the implementation of Jay's Treaty. Randolph will be succeeded by Timothy Pickering in December.

5 SEPTEMBER 1795
International The United States signs a treaty of peace and amity with the Dey of Algiers, agreeing to pay tribute to the Barbary pirates who have been preying on American commercial shipping in the Mediterranean Sea and off the coasts of Spain and Portugal. The agreement sets an immediate American payment of $1 million for the ransom of 115 seamen, to be followed by a series of annual tribute payments.

27 OCTOBER 1795
International The American minister to Great Britain and special envoy to Spain Thomas Pinckney signs the Treaty of San Lorenzo with Spain, resolving the question of the southern and western boundaries between the United States and Spanish territory, setting them at the 31st parallel and the Mississippi River. Americans are also allowed free navigational access to the Mississippi River and the three-year right to deposit cargo at the port of New Orleans.

10 DECEMBER 1795
National Timothy Pickering, formerly Secretary of War, succeeds Edmund Randolph as Secretary of State. In January, James McHenry will become the new Secretary of War, completing President Washing-

ton's reorganization of his cabinet to include only Federalists. Alexander Hamilton, no longer a cabinet officer, will continue to exert a powerful influence on Pickering, McHenry and Secretary of the Treasury Oliver Wolcott, Jr. When John Adams becomes the second president of the United States, he will retain the same cabinet.

15 DECEMBER 1795
National The Senate rejects the nomination of John Rutledge, appointed by President Washington to head the Supreme Court, succeeding John Jay. The Senate opposes the choice of Rutledge because of his strong opposition to the adoption of Jay's Treaty. John Jay has resigned as chief justice of the Supreme Court in order to conclude his political career as the governor of New York State.

OTHER EVENTS OF 1795
Ideas/Beliefs Vermont Judge Nathaniel Chipman promotes a study of history emphasizing social forces instead of military events.
Transportation In Boston, the first primitive railroad in the United States is constructed. The wooden-railed inclined tramway runs on the slope of Beacon Hill.

1 JANUARY 1796
National President Washington nominates Oliver Ellsworth, the author of the Connecticut Resolutions at the Constitutional Convention, as chief justice of the United States Supreme Court, after his earlier appointment of John Rutledge has failed to receive Senate confirmation. Ellsworth's appointment will be confirmed on March 4.

27 JANUARY 1796
National Maryland army surgeon and former Washington aide James McHenry is appointed Secretary of War, succeeding Timothy Pickering.

JANUARY 1796
National Robert Randall is charged with trying to coerce members of the House of Representatives on behalf of Great Lakes fur traders. The House concludes that any such attempts to influence House members for private gain rather than the public good are to be considered instances of contempt.

15 FEBRUARY 1796
International American minister to France James Monroe is informed by the French foreign minister that Jay's Treaty with Great Britain annuls all previous French treaties with the United States.

18 FEBRUARY 1796
Regional The newly-elected Georgia legislature invalidates the Yazoo land sale of January 1795 by the previous corrupt state legislature.

29 FEBRUARY 1796
International After Great Britain has accepted the Senate's amendment of Jay's Treaty, President Washington declares the treaty in effect. This diplomatic move brings France and the United States to the brink of war.

8 MARCH 1796
National In the case of *Hylton* v. *United States,* the Supreme Court rules a 1794 carriage tax an indirect tax, and hence constitutional. This case is important in that this is the first time the court rules on the constitutionality of an act of Congress.

15 MARCH 1796
International The Senate unanimously endorses the October 27, 1795 Treaty of San Lorenzo with Spain.

22 APRIL 1796
National In a decision on treaties, the Supreme Court finds that all such pacts made under the Constitution are federal law, and hence they take precedence over any conflicting state laws.

30 APRIL 1796
National Overriding vehement Democratic-Republican opposition, the House of Representatives votes an appropriation to carry out the provisions of Jay's Treaty. The legislators have been swayed by the persuasive oratory of Federalist Fisher Ames on April 28.

18 MAY 1796
Westward Movement Congress passes a Land Act which mandates the survey of all public lands in the Northwest Territory, and permits the public auction sale of these lands at a minimum price of $2 per acre in minimum tracts of 640 acres each. Purchasers may have one year to pay, thus initiating a credit system. Since most settlers cannot afford the minimum purchase cost, land speculators are the prime beneficiaries of this legislation.

1 JUNE 1796
Regional Slave-holding Tennessee is admitted to the union as the 16th state. Former governor of the state of Franklin, John Sevier, is chosen the first governor of Tennessee. In a partisan Federalist move, Tennessee is permitted only one delegate to the United States House of Representatives for the next four years.

29 JUNE 1796
Indian Affairs In Colerain, Georgia, a treaty is signed with the Creek Indians.

11 JULY 1796
Westward Movement Following the withdrawal of British forces from their frontier posts under the provisions of Jay's Treaty, American Captain Moses Porter occupies the fort at Detroit with 65 men.

JULY 1796
International France proclaims that it will capture

and search all ships of neutral nations bound for British ports.

22 AUGUST 1796
International American minister to France James Monroe is notified by Secretary of State Timothy Pickering that he will be replaced by Charles C. Pinckney because he has failed to defend Jay's Treaty between the United States and Great Britain. When Pinckney tries to present his credentials on December 7, the French foreign minister states that the French government will not receive Monroe's successor until French "grievances have been redressed." Thus Pinckney is forced to return to the United States. On the same date, in compliance with Jay's Treaty, British forces evacuate their American frontier post of Fort Michilimackinac.

17 SEPTEMBER 1796
National President Washington publishes his Farewell Address in Philadelphia's *Daily American Advertiser,* announcing his planned withdrawal from politics and presenting his reasons for deciding against running for a third term in office. The Farewell Address also enumerates the achievements of the Washington administration, warns against the divisiveness of a party system, advises of the importance of a stable public credit system, warns against permanent foreign alliances, and cautions against an over-powerful military establishment. The Farewell Address is written with the help of James Madison and Alexander Hamilton, and is never actually delivered orally.

29 OCTOBER 1796
Exploration New England Captain Ebenezer Dorr sails the *Otter* into Monterey Bay. His is the first American ship to sail along the California coastline.

4 NOVEMBER 1796
International The United States signs a treaty with Tripoli, seeking an end to the costly raids of the Barbary pirates on American commercial shipping in the Mediterranean Sea and off the coasts of Spain and Portugal. In order to halt the seizure of American vessels and the imprisonment of American seamen, the United States agrees to pay ransom, large commissions and annual tribute. The Senate will ratify this treaty on June 7, 1797.

NOVEMBER 1796
Regional Tennessee voters choose Andrew Jackson as the new state's first delegate to the United States House of Representatives.

15 NOVEMBER 1796
International Relations between France and the United States deteriorate further as French minister Adat announces the suspension of diplomatic relations between the two nations.

7 DECEMBER 1796
National In the nation's third presidential election, Federalist candidate John Adams wins the presidency with 71 electoral votes, and Democratic-Republican candidate Thomas Jefferson gains the vice presidency with 68 electoral votes. The 13 candidates also include Federalist Thomas Pinckney who receives 59 votes, Democratic-Republican Aaron Burr who receives 30 votes, Samuel Adams with 15 votes, and Oliver Ellsworth with 11. The results of this election demonstrate the rising power of the Democratic-Republican party because of widespread dissatisfaction with Jay's Treaty between the United States and Great Britain.

OTHER EVENTS OF 1796
National Pennsylvania Representative Albert Gallatin leads the effort to create the Committee of Ways and Means in the United States House of Representatives. One of the founders of the Democratic-Republican party, Gallatin goes on to win the leadership of the party, and he will later become Treasury Secretary in the administrations of Presidents Jefferson and Madison.
Commerce Former Revolutionary War director of finance Robert Morris and James Greenleaf organize a syndicate for speculation in Washington real estate. The financial dealings of Morris will lead to a three-year term in debtor's prison.
Life/Customs Amelia Simmons publishes the first American cookbook, *American Cookery . . . Adapted to this Country and All Grades of Life.*

1 JANUARY 1797
Regional The capital of New York state is moved from New York City to Albany.

27 FEBRUARY 1797
International Secretary of State Timothy Pickering presents a report on the losses inflicted on American trade and shipping by the hostile actions of the French on vessels of neutral nations. Angered by Jay's Treaty, the French government had also refused to accept the credentials of new American minister to France Charles C. Pinckney in December 1796.

4 MARCH 1797
National John Adams is inaugurated as the second president of the United States, with Thomas Jefferson as vice–president. The cabinet of Adams, held over from Washington's second administration, includes Timothy Pickering as Secretary of State, Oliver Wolcott, Jr. as Secretary of the Treasury, James McHenry as Secretary of War, Joseph Habersham as Postmaster General and Charles Lee as Attorney General.

10 MAY 1797
National The first ship of the new United States Navy, the *United States,* is launched. The commander of the frigate is John Barry.

15 MAY 1797
International President Adams calls the first special session of Congress in order to consider the worsen-

JOHN ADAMS, 1735-1826

In the heady years before the American Revolution, the brilliant, witty and crusty John Adams was one of the most significant philosophers and planners of the coming new nation. As its second President, however, he was not able to master the factionalism of a growing two-party system as well as did his predecessor, George Washington.

Adams was born in Braintree, Massachusetts on October 30, 1735, the son of a distinguished family in the area, one that would remain distinguished well into the 20th century. After an outstanding career at Harvard he read law and settled in Braintree to practice in 1758. The focus of his interest soon shifted to Boston, where a group of lawyers met to discuss the problems of British domination and the ideals of liberty. By 1768, when he moved to Boston, Adams was already known for his newspaper articles and for his protest of the Stamp Act. Nonetheless, his commitment to justice led him to a successful defense of British soldiers after the Boston Massacre of 1770.

His growing radicalism got Adams thrown out of the Governor's Council in 1773; the following year he was a delegate to the first Continental Congress, where he became a major voice for independence and helped edit Jefferson's Declaration of Independence in 1776. His writings continued through the Revolution, laying the groundwork for the government to come. He was an envoy to the peace conference that produced the Treaty of Paris in 1783. Two years later he was in Britain as the U.S. minister, meanwhile writing on constitutional theory; these writings were important to the deliberations of the Constitutional Convention.

In 1789 Adams became the first Vice-President and heir apparent to George Washington. A confirmed Federalist, he nonetheless tried with some success to stay above partisan politics. Elected president by a narrow margin over

Jefferson (who thus became vice-president), Adams began his term trying to cement the divided Federalist Party while conciliating the Jeffersonian Republicans. It was an impossible task. In trying to build the national army and navy for the inevitable conflict with Britain or France, Adams ran afoul of the states' rights Republicans; and the Federalists on his cabinet, especially Hamilton, worked against him in promoting more active war preparations. In 1798 he signed the Alien and Sedition Acts, which virtually prohibited criticism of the government; the Acts, widely condemned, were the beginning of the end of the Federalist Party.

With a diplomatic masterstroke in 1800 Adams prevented war with France. But the country had turned against him; in the election that year he lost to Jefferson. Adams retired to the life of the elder statesman and to putting the final touches on grooming his son, John Quincy Adams, for the Presidency. He died on July Fourth, 1826, the same day as Jefferson, the 50th anniversary of the signing of the Declaration.

ing French-American crisis. Adams informs Congress of the expulsion of America's minister to France, Charles C. Pinckney, and assures Congress of projected negotiations, while recommending defense measures.

31 MAY 1797

International President Adams appoints a three-man commission, consisting of Charles C. Pinckney, John Marshall and Elbridge Gerry, whose assignment is to negotiate a treaty of commerce and amity with France.

1 JUNE 1797

International Secretary of State Timothy Pickering reports that 300 American vessels have been captured by the French on the high seas.

24 JUNE 1797

International Apprehensive of a war with France, Congress passes a bill calling for an 80,000-man militia force to be in a state of constant readiness should hostilities break out.

26 JUNE 1797

Agriculture New Jersey inventor Charles Newbold receives a patent for his cast–iron plow. Fearing that the plow will contaminate the soil, farmers refuse to purchase it.

8 JULY 1797

National The United States House of Representatives votes to impeach Tennessee Senator William Blount for conspiring to instigate a war with Spain and for stirring up the Cherokee Indians to attack both the United States and Spanish possessions. The Senate expels Blount, but will dismiss the charges against him on January 14, 1799.

28 AUGUST 1797

International The United States signs a treaty with Tunis in order to end the costly attacks of the Barbary pirates on American commercial shipping in the Mediterranean Sea and along the coasts of Spain and Portugal. In order to ensure the safety of its vessels and seamen, America agrees to an even higher tribute than that promised in the treaty with Tripoli. This pact will not be ratified until January 10, 1800.

7 SEPTEMBER 1797
National In Baltimore, Maryland, the U.S.S. *Constellation* is launched, adding considerably to the strength of the new United States Navy. This frigate is armed with 36 guns.

4 OCTOBER 1797
International The three-man American peace commission of Elbridge Gerry, John Marshall, and Charles C. Pinckney arrives in Paris.

18 OCTOBER 1797
International In Paris, the American peace commission is approached by three agents of French foreign minister Talleyrand. As a precondition for negotiating a treaty, they suggest a large American "loan" to France and a $240,000 bribe to Talleyrand. This incident, known as the XYZ Affair (referring to the three French agents), evokes the alleged reply from Charles C. Pinckney, "Millions for defense, but not one cent for tribute." While Pinckney and John Marshall leave Paris, Elbridge Gerry is forced to stay by Talleyrand's threat of a French declaration of war if he also leaves. The XYZ Affair results in an undeclared naval war between the United States and France from the years 1798 to 1800.

21 OCTOBER 1797
National In Boston, the U.S.S. *Constitution,* later known as *"Old Ironsides,"* is launched. This 44-gun and 1576-ton naval frigate is to serve gloriously in the undeclared naval war with France, in the Tripolitan War, and in the War of 1812. After serving as a training ship in the later 19th century, the *Constitution* will be rebuilt in 1925 to be anchored in Boston Harbor as a national historic relic.

8 JANUARY 1798
National The 11th Amendment to the United States Constitution is ratified. It forbids suits against a state by a citizen of another state or of a foreign nation.

17 JANUARY 1798
International In Paris, speaking for the American diplomatic commission to France, John Marshall formally rejects the bribes requested in exchange for the French presence at the negotiating table. The American commission also reiterates its protest against French interference with American commercial shipping. With an unsatisfactory French reply on March 18, the negotiations end.

19 MARCH 1798
International President Adams informs Congress of the failure of the American negotiations with France.

THE AMERICAN LANGUAGE

The separate evolution of the American language, as distinct from the English language, began as soon as the first English settlers landed on the North American coastline. Here, in this primeval wilderness, they saw entirely new animals and plants for which they had no names. Also, they immediately came in contact with an entirely alien culture, the indigenous Indian population, who spoke unknown languages, practised unique customs and employed exotic artifacts. This situation led to the rapid assimilation of such Indian words as *hickory, moccasin, moose, mugwump, opposum, raccoon, squash, squaw, toboggan, wigwam* and *woodchuck*. The English vocabulary of the American colonists was further augmented as they began to move inland from their coastal settlements. Now they came into contact with the outposts of the Spanish and French missionaries and traders. The Spanish enriched the American language with such words as *alfalfa, bronco, lasso* and *stampede*. And the words from French roots included *bayou, cache, chowder, gopher, picayune, portage* and *pumpkin*. And each of the growing numbers of national groups who joined the increasing American population added words from their own language. Distinctive words such as *boss* and *scow* come from the Dutch, and *dunk* and *noodle* come from German. The black slaves introduced such native African words as *gumbo* and *voodoo*.

The rapidly changing conditions of American colonial society encouraged the American language to adapt words from a multiplicity of cultures. Finally, by the time of the Revolutionary War, the colonial form of the English language had become so altered that it became the frequent butt of anti-American satires in the British press. American pioneer linguists focused attention on these differences, as in 1816 when John Pickering published his *Vocabulary* listing Americanisms; and in 1828 when Noah Webster issued his landmark edition of *An American Dictionary of the English Language*. During the early era of the new nation, the distinctively American idioms, dialects and regionalisms became a source of national pride, reflecting a pleasure in the uniqueness of the American language, comparable to the uniqueness of the American republic.

---

3 APRIL 1798
International President Adams releases to Congress the XYZ Affairs correspondence. American public knowledge of the unsavory details of the XYZ affair leads to a sharp rise in anti-French sentiment.

7 APRIL 1798
Regional The Mississippi Territory is created by an act of Congress, comprising parts of the present states of Alabama and Mississippi. The boundaries of this new territory will extend northward to Tennessee in 1804 and in 1812 southward to include West Florida.

3 MAY 1798
National Congress creates the Department of the Navy, independent of the War Department. Previously all naval activities had been overseen by the unsatisfactory administration of the War Department. This is part of President Adams' vigorous policy of strengthening the national defenses, while still follow-

ing an officially peaceful route with the French.

21 MAY 1798
National Benjamin Stoddert is named Secretary of the Navy.

28 MAY 1798
International Congress authorizes President Adams to order the commanders of American naval warships to seize any French armed ships interfering with American commercial shipping. Congress authorizes President Adams to raise a 10,000-man volunteer army for a period of three years.

6 JUNE 1798
Finance Congress enacts a bill abolishing the imprisonment of debtors, thus legally ending this form of punishment in the United States.

13 JUNE 1798
International Congress passes legislation suspending commerce with France and her dependencies.

18 JUNE 1798
National The divisive atmosphere and war fears caused by the French crisis lead the Federalists to pass legislation strengthening the Federal Government. The resulting Alien and Sedition Acts are intended to effectively silence any political opposition; on this date, Congress passes the first of the four Alien and Sedition Acts. The Naturalization Act requires a residency of 14 rather than five years by Aliens before they become eligible for United States citizenship. This act will be repealed in 1802, with a reinstatement of the 1795 naturalization law.

25 JUNE 1798
National Congress passes the second Alien and Sedition Act. The Alien Act authorizes the president of the United States to deport any potentially dangerous or treasonable alien during peacetime. This act will expire in 1800.

2 JULY 1798
National George Washington is named commander–in–chief of the United States Army; Alexander Hamilton will be designated the second in command and inspector general.

6 JULY 1798
National Congress passes the third Alien and Sedition Act. The Enemy Aliens Act permits the wartime arrest, imprisonment and banishment of any aliens subject to any enemy power.

7 JULY 1798
International Congress repeals the treaties of 1788 with France.

11 JULY 1798
National Congress passes legislation to establish the Marine Corps.

11 JULY 1798
National Congress passes the fourth of the Alien and Sedition Acts. The Sedition Act declares any anti-government activity, including the publication of "any false, scandalous and malicious writing," a high misdemeanor, punishable by fine and imprisonment.

16 JULY 1798
National Congress establishes the Marine Hospital Service, an organization that will later develop into the United States Public Health Service.

12 SEPTEMBER 1798
Ideas/Beliefs Benjamin Franklin's grandson Benjamin Franklin Bache, who edits the Philadelphia Democratic–Republican newspaper the *Aurora,* is arrested for violating the Sedition Act. He is charged with libeling President Adams. Bache's arrest evokes a wide-ranging protest against all of the Alien and Sedition Acts. Other Democratic–Republican editors and printers prosecuted in this partisan manner are James Thomas Callender, Matthew Lyon and Dr. Thomas Cooper. When Thomas Jefferson becomes president, he pardons all those convicted under the Sedition Act, and Congress restores all fines paid, with interest.

12 OCTOBER 1798
Regional In a reorganization of the Mississippi Territory, the territorial capital is located at Natchez, and the boundaries of the territory are spelled out in detail.

16 NOVEMBER 1798
National The Kentucky state legislature adopts a set of resolutions drafted by Thomas Jefferson. The resolutions strongly protest the usurpation of power by the Federal Government under the unconstitutional Alien and Sedition Acts. Jefferson insists that the Union is a compact among sovereign states, and therefore the states have a right to determine the unconstitutionality of the Alien and Sedition Acts. A second set of Kentucky Resolutions will be endorsed on November 22, 1799.

International On the high seas, British naval forces board the *Baltimore,* a 20-gun American frigate, to seek deserters from the Royal Navy. The British impress a number of the vessel's sailors.

20 NOVEMBER 1798
International The American schooner *Retaliation,* commanded by Lieutenant William Bainbridge, is seized by the French off the Caribbean island of Guadeloupe. Bainbridge and his 250-man crew will remain prisoners of the French until February 1799.

24 DECEMBER 1798
National The Virginia state legislature adopts the Virginia Resolutions, composed by James Madison. Like the Kentucky Resolutions of November 16, these resolutions also oppose the unconstitutional practice of power by the Federal Government, as exerted in the Alien and Sedition Acts.

TESTING A UNION 1788-1865

31 DECEMBER 1798
National In the case of *Calder* v. *Bull*, the Supreme Court rules that the constitutional prohibition against *ex post facto* laws applies to criminal laws only.

30 JANUARY 1799
International Congress passes the Logan Act, which makes it illegal for any private American citizen to conduct diplomatic negotiations with foreign governments. This legislation is prompted by the 1798 trip of Philadelphia Quaker Dr. George Logan to Paris in order to avert war with France by engaging in peace discussions with French foreign minister Talleyrand.

7 FEBRUARY 1799
Regional In Bethlehem, Pennsylvania, federal marshals arrest John Fries, the leader of a taxpayers rebellion. Fries had raised a force of several hundred men in Bucks, Montgomery and Northampton counties in order to protest the direct federal tax implemented by the acts of July 9 and 14, 1798 to raise revenue for the anticipated war with France. Tried twice, Fries will be convicted of treason both times. Although sentenced to death, he will be pardoned by President Adams.

9 FEBRUARY 1799
International In the undeclared naval war with France, American Captain Thomas Truxton, commanding the U.S.S. *Constellation*, captures the French frigate *L'Insurgente* off the island of Nevis.

18 FEBRUARY 1799
International President Adams nominates William Vans Murray as the new American minister to France, following French foreign minister Talleyrand's communication that he will now receive an American emissary with respect. Alexander Hamilton's pro-war Federalist faction is unable to sway Adams from this course of conciliation.

23 FEBRUARY 1799
Life/Customs Congress passes the first national quarantine act. This legislation mandates the assistance of federal officials for municipalities trying to enforce quarantine regulations.

25 FEBRUARY 1799
International At the insistence of Alexander Hamilton, President Adams nominates Patrick Henry and Oliver Ellsworth, two Federalists, as ministers plenipotentiary to France to accompany newly appointed minister to France William Vans Murray, to reopen peace negotiations. Henry declines because of his age, and North Carolina Governor William K. Davie is named to replace him. Ellsworth and Davie will be dispatched to France to join Murray on October 16.

29 MARCH 1799
Slavery The New York state legislature passes a gradual emancipation law.

5 MAY 1799
International French foreign minister Talleyrand is notified of President Adams' intent of reopening peace negotiations.

6 JUNE 1799
Life/Customs In Virginia, Revolutionary War patriot, orator, and statesman Patrick Henry dies at his Charlotte County plantation.

15 JUNE 1799
National The Federalist legislature of New Hampshire issues the New Hampshire Resolutions, rebutting the Kentucky Resolutions of November 16, 1798 and the Virginia Resolutions of December 24, 1798.

9-10 NOVEMBER 1799
International The French Directoire government is abolished by a coup d'état that establishes Napoleon Bonaparte as first consul, the virtual ruler of France.

22 NOVEMBER 1799
National The Kentucky legislature issues an additional Kentucky Resolution, drafted by Thomas Jefferson, in response to the repudiation of the earlier resolution (of November 16, 1798) by a number of northern states which insist that the federal judiciary is the sole arbiter of constitutionality. This resolution again insists on the right of states to nullify federal laws.

2 DECEMBER 1799
National The Sixth Congress meets for its first session. This will be the last Congress to have a Federalist majority.

14 DECEMBER 1799
Life/Customs George Washington dies suddenly at the age of 67 at Mount Vernon from a pulmonary disorder following exposure during a snowstorm horseback ride. The universal respect accorded to Washington is demonstrated by the honors paid to his memory in England, and by Napoleon Bonaparte's proclamation of a week of mourning in France.

26 DECEMBER 1799
Life/Customs General Henry "Light Horse Harry" Lee delivers a eulogy for George Washington in Congress, in which he describes Washington as "first in war, first in peace, first in the hearts of his countrymen."

OTHER EVENTS OF 1799
Westward Movement The Russian Czar grants the Russian American Company a virtual monopoly of trade in the northern Pacific region. The company establishes its headquarters at Sitka, Alaska.
Labor In Philadelphia, the Federal Society of Cordwainers (shoemakers) calls a nine-day strike of its members. This is the first such organized labor action in the United States. The strike ends when the cordwainers are granted their requested wage increases.

2 JANUARY 1800

Slavery The free blacks of Philadelphia present a petition opposing slavery, the slave trade, and the Fugitive Slave Act of 1793, to Congress, which lets the petition expire in committee.

10 JANUARY 1800

International Congress ratifies the treaty of August 28, 1797 with Tunis.

1 FEBRUARY 1800

International In the undeclared naval war with France, the American frigate U.S.S. *Constellation* engages in an indecisive battle with the French vessel *La Vengeance*.

8 MARCH 1800

International Napoleon Bonaparte receives the American peace commissioners William Vans Murray, Oliver Ellsworth, and William R. Davie with courtesy. Formal peace negotiations are to begin in April.

3 APRIL 1800

Life/Customs Congress authorizes the franking privilege for Martha Washington, allowing all mail sent and received by the president's widow to be carried postage free. Also extended to Revolutionary War veterans, franking becomes so widespread that a revision of the practice is soon called for.

4 APRIL 1800

Finance Congress passes the first Federal Bankruptcy Act, applying only to merchants and traders. This legislation permits the release of Robert Morris from debtors' prison. This law will be repealed on December 19, 1803.

24 APRIL 1800

Arts/Culture The Library of Congress is established by an act of Congress. The 1815 purchase of Thomas Jefferson's 7000-volume library will form the nucleus of the collection.

APRIL—MAY 1800

National In a series of congressional party caucuses, the presidential and vice–presidential candidates are nominated for the election of 1800. The Federalists choose John Adams and Charles C. Pinckney, and the Democratic-Republicans choose Thomas Jefferson and Aaron Burr.

29 APRIL 1800

International In a case involving the American mercantile vessel *Polly,* a British court accepts the principle of a "broken voyage." According to this principle, American trading vessels may carry cargos from the French West Indies to France if, en route, the cargos are landed at American ports and duty is paid on them.

6 MAY 1800

National Convinced that he is the victim of a Cabinet conspiracy in which Timothy Pickering and James McHenry are working in collusion with Alexander Hamilton for Adams' defeat in the 1800 presidential election, President John Adams requests the resignation of his Secretary of War James McHenry, to be effective May 31.

7 MAY 1800

Westward Movement Congress divides the nine counties of the Northwest Territory (Ohio) into two parts, bisected by a line running north from the junction of the Kentucky and Ohio Rivers. The sparsely settled western portion becomes the Indiana Territory, with a capital at Vincennes and William Henry Harrison as governor. The eastern region, known as the Northwest Territory, has a capital at Chillicothe.

10 MAY 1800

Westward Movement Congress passes the public Land Act of 1800, also known as the Harrison Land Act as it is sponsored by Governor William Henry Harrison of the Indiana Territory. The bill creates the new district public land offices, provides for liberal credit terms for land purchases, and for smaller–sized tracts—of a minimum of 320 acres. This legislation spurs a surge of speculative real estate purchases.

12 MAY 1800

National President Adams dismisses Secretary of State Timothy Pickering from office because of suspicion that he is conspiring with Alexander Hamilton to defeat John Adams in the 1800 presidential election.

13 MAY 1800

National President Adams appoints Virginia Federalist John Marshall to replace Timothy Pickering as secretary of state.

12 JUNE 1800

National Samuel Dexter of Massachusetts is appointed the new secretary of war, replacing James McHenry.

JUNE 1800

National The Federal Government moves from Philadelphia to the permanent federal capital of Washington, on the Potomac River. Washington is the first planned capital city in the world.

30 AUGUST 1800

Slavery In Virginia, a planned slave rebellion led by a slave named Gabriel Prosser is revealed. Prosser and 37 others are seized and tried on April 30, 1804. Prosser is hanged.

30 SEPTEMBER 1800

International The Treaty of Morfontaine, more commonly known as the Convention of 1800, is signed by the French consulate and by American peace commissioners William Vans Murray, Oliver Ellsworth, and William R. Davie. This pact restores normal diplomatic relations between the two nations and effectively ends the undeclared naval war. The treaty of 1778 is officially annulled and the question of French compensation for the seizure of American vessels is left to future negotiations. The convention will go into effect on December 21, 1801.

1 OCTOBER 1800
International In the secret Treaty of San Ildefonso, Spain cedes Louisiana to France at the command of Napoleon Bonaparte, who envisions a French colonial empire on the North American continent. This land transfer does not become known to the United States until May 1801.

19 OCTOBER 1800
International The Dey of Algiers forces American Captain William Bainbridge to carry the Dey's emissary to Constantinople in the vessel *George Washington.*

17 NOVEMBER 1800
National Congress convenes for its first session in the new federal capital of Washington. John and Abigail Adams move into the new presidential palace, later known as the White House.

3 DECEMBER 1800
National In the presidential election of 1800, the incumbent Federalist candidates John Adams and Charles C. Pinckney are opposed by Democratic-Republicans Thomas Jefferson and Aaron Burr. The ballots will not be counted until February 11, 1801. The main issues of the campaign center around the Alien and Sedition Acts, the increased federal taxation to support a defense build-up, the reduction of trade with France, and the British impressment of American seamen.

OTHER EVENTS OF 1800
Population The census of 1800 indicates a 35 percent population increase to a total of about 5.3 million, including 1 million blacks, of whom nine-tenths are enslaved. Virginia remains the most populous state with 900,000 inhabitants.
Agriculture Pennsylvania horticulturist John Chapman, better known as the legendary Johnny Appleseed, begins distributing young apple trees and seeds to settlers traveling to Ohio, as well as personally scattering appleseeds and Swedenborgian religious tracts in the Ohio River Valley. In the latter part of his 50-year career as Johnny Appleseed, Chapman will tend and prune the mature apple trees.

20 JANUARY 1801
National President Adams nominates Federalist John Marshall as chief justice of the Supreme Court, after John Jay has declined to serve in the position for a second term. The appointment of John Marshall is one of Adams' last official acts. Congress will approve Marshall's appointment on January 27; Marshall will take his oath of office on February 4, while still secretary of state.

11 FEBRUARY 1801
National The ballots are counted for the presidential election of 1800, revealing a Jefferson–Burr tie, with each candidate receiving 73 votes. John Adams receives 65 votes, Charles C. Pinckney receives 64 votes, and John Jay receives one vote. The tie constitutionally tosses the decision into the House of Representatives.

17 FEBRUARY 1801
National Following an all-night session of 36 ballots and a deadlock, the House of Representatives chooses Thomas Jefferson as president of the United States. Although the Federalist caucus backs Burr, Alexander Hamilton considers Jefferson "the lesser evil," and hence uses his influence to deliver the presidency to Jefferson. Aaron Burr becomes vice–president. These difficulties in selecting the president result in 1804 in the 12th Amendment to the Constitution, which mandates separate balloting for the president and vice–president. The final result of the 1800 election is that the Federalists lose the legislature and executive branch, but retain power in the judicial branch of government.

AARON BURR, 1756-1836

History has not decided and may never decide on the case of the brilliant and erratic Aaron Burr. Was his argument with Alexander Hamilton, which led to a fatal duel, justifiable? Was he a traitor who planned to set up a new country in the West with himself as king? Was he a misunderstood political genius or, as Hamilton wrote, "a dangerous man and one who ought not to be trusted with the reins of government?" These are strong words indeed, concerning a man who very nearly became president.

Burr was born to a distinguished family in Newark, New Jersey, on February 6, 1756. He established an outstanding record at the College of New Jersey (later Princeton) of which his father had been president. After some law studies he joined the Revolutionary Army in 1775, where he made a notable name as a fighter and retired in 1779 as a colonel. Returning to law, he entered the New York Bar in 1782 and within a few years was, with his rival Alexander Hamilton, one of the most successful lawyers in New York City. His skill and sagacity as well as his considerable personal charm brought him wealth, though he was apt to spend lavishly. In 1789 he became Governor Clinton's attorney general; two years later he was elected to a term in the U.S. Senate.

Returning to New York politics in 1797, he began to build a Republican political machine in opposition to Hamilton's Federalist one. His machine had sufficient power to give Burr a presidential bid in 1800. He tied with Jefferson in the electoral vote, and the election was thrown into the House. At that point, uncharacteristically, Burr made no effort for his cause and Jefferson was chosen, Burr becoming vice–president. During his term, Burr's penchant for intrigue made him a number of enemies, led by Hamilton, who with Jefferson's agreement squelched Burr's bid for New York governorship in 1804. Enraged, Burr challenged Hamilton to a duel and in July 1804 killed him (Hamilton apparently did not even aim at Burr).

Burr's final act as vice–president in 1804-5 was to preside over Jefferson's unsuccessful attempt to impeach Justice Chase; Burr's handling of the proceedings in the Senate was commended for its fairness. He left office in 1805 to some acclaim. But he had already begun plotting his historic scheme to invade Mexico. To that end, over the next two years he enlisted the help of various prominent people, raised a private army, made two trips West and landed in court a couple of times, only to be acquitted. Gradually his activities became notorious; in 1807 he was formally indicted for treason in Virginia. The ensuing trial was undoubtedly used by Chief Justice John Marshall to strike at his enemy Jefferson; the conduct of both Marshall and the President in the matter was far from creditable. In any case, Burr and his henchmen were acquitted, but by that time there was considerable public outcry against Burr.

For five years Burr traveled in Europe, petitioning Napoleon and anyone else who would listen to finance his Mexican invasion plans. The schemes became wilder, more distinctly treasonable; he seemed even to plan to set himself up as king of a new country, and perhaps wanted to incite Europe to war on America. He returned penniless to New York in 1812. After years of law practice and personal setbacks he died there in 1836, denying to the end that he had done anything traitorous.

The duel between Burr and Hamilton.

27 FEBRUARY 1801

National Congress passes the Judiciary Act, which reduces the number of Supreme Court justices from 6 to 5, sets up 16 circuit courts, and increases the number of judicial officials, including marshals, attorneys and clerks. On the same date, the District of Columbia is placed under the jurisdiction of Congress.

3 MARCH 1801

National Under the terms of the new Judiciary Act, President Adams makes several last–minute judicial appointments of "midnight judges" in order to ensure Federalist control of the courts. He also names Hugh Barclay as federal marshal of the western district of Pennsylvania. The opposition to President Adams' last judicial appointments will lead to the 1803 case of *Marbury* v. *Madison*.

4 MARCH 1801

National Thomas Jefferson is inaugurated as the third president of the United States. His is the first inauguration to be held in the new national capital of Washington. In his Inaugural Address, President Jefferson calls for a government of limited powers, operating economically, supporting states' rights, acquiescing in majority decisions, preserving civil liberties, and avoiding "entangling alliances" with foreign nations. In his cabinet, Jefferson will have James Madison as Secretary of State; Samuel Dexter as Secretary of the Treasury, to be succeeded by Albert Gallatin; Henry Dearborn as Secretary of War; Benjamin Stoddert as Secretary of the Navy; Joseph Habersham as Postmaster General; and Levi Lincoln as Attorney General.

14 MAY 1801

International Increasing his demands for tribute from the United States, Pasha Yusuf Karamanli of Tripoli declares war on the United States. In spite of his predisposition for peace, President Jefferson decides to take up the challenge and send naval warships into the Mediterranean Sea. This war will last into 1805.

1 AUGUST 1801

International In the war with Tripoli, The U.S.S. *Enterprise,* commanded by Captain Serret, seizes the corsair *Tripoli.*

6 AUGUST 1801

Ideas/Beliefs At a Presbyterian camp meeting in Cane Ridge, Kentucky, the religious Great Revival of the West begins.

16 OCTOBER 1801

International Robert R. Livingston, who has been newly named American minister to France, sets sail for Europe.

7 DECEMBER 1801

National The Seventh Congress meets for its first sessions with 18 Democratic–Republicans and 14 Federalists in the Senate, and 69 Democratic–Republicans and 36 Federalists in the House of Representatives. The Democratic-Republican party has made striking gains in the 1800 election.

8 DECEMBER 1801

National President Jefferson delivers his first annual message to Congress in written form, reflecting his dislike of ceremony. This precedent will continue until 1913.

8 JANUARY 1802

National President Jefferson asks Congress to repeal the Judiciary Act of February 13, 1801, which is widely regarded by the Democratic-Republican party as a piece of partisan Federalist legislation.

Finance As mandated by Jay's Treaty, a specially appointed commission finds that in settlement of the Revolutionary War financial claims of British citizens—of both colonial Loyalists and the English mercantile establishment—the United States owes $2,664,000.

TESTING A UNION 1788-1865

THOMAS JEFFERSON, 1743-1826

The plain stone obelisk on the hill below his beloved Monticello reads as Thomas Jefferson asked: "Here lies buried/Thomas Jefferson/author of the Declaration of Independence/of the Statute of Virginia for religious freedom/ and father of the University of Virginia." He left out a few things: he was a farmer, lawyer, family man, statesman, scientist, architect, linguist, philosopher, inventor, amateur musician, founder of the Library of Congress and (most tellingly omitted), president of the United States. For the rest, perhaps he was being modest; as for his presidency, he was omitting his least enjoyed endeavor, though one he pursued as passionately and brilliantly as he did everything else.

Jefferson was born into a distinguished farming family in Albermarle County, Virginia, on April 13, 1743. An avid student from his youth, he graduated from the College of William and Mary in 1762 and then studied law, being admitted to the Virginia bar in 1767. He soon became involved in local politics and was elected to the House of Burgesses. Bringing his wide knowledge of history and law to the rising tide of the independence movement, Jefferson became a noted pamphleteer and a member of the Continental Congress in 1775. His reputation for eloquence and wisdom made him the choice to draft the Declaration of Independence, which was adopted on July 4, 1776. In that document and in his ensuing public life Jefferson proclaimed himself for the natural rights of men and opposed to any artificial privilege.

During the Revolution, Jefferson, no military man, served in the Virginia legislature and became governor in 1779. After a frustrating tenure in that office he retired in 1781 to his estate, Monticello, which over the years he was to build and tinker with endlessly; during this period he also began work on a natural history of Virginia which would gain him laurels as a scientist. He returned to public life after the death of his wife in 1783, becoming a member of the Continental Congress. In 1784 he went as minister to France; there he observed and reported home the French Revolution, applauding its democratic aims while deploring its methods. He returned home in 1789 to find the Constitution completed. Worried about its centralizing of power, he approved it uneasily and agreed to be Washington's secretary of state. In that office he began his opposition to the Federalist's anti-French tendencies, their national bank, their catering to the wealthy.

Jefferson ran a close second to John Adams in the 1796 election, thus becoming by the procedure of the time vice–president (and giving a good indication of why that procedure was eventually changed). Throughout his term he resisted many of the administration's efforts, especially the oppressive Alien and Sedition Acts. In the Kentucky Resolution of 1798 Jefferson proposed that the states have authority to reject federal laws they deem unconstitutional (under the later name of nullification, this well-intentioned idea was later to divide the Union). The Acts helped doom Adams; Jefferson won the presidency in 1800, but only by narrowly defeating Aaron Burr in an election decided in the House.

As president, Jefferson stemmed a conservative tide that had dominated the country; nonetheless, he did so in a diplomatic and conciliatory fashion, thus setting vital American precedent for the peaceful transfer of power from one ideology to another. Yet Jefferson was simultaneously among the most beloved and most damned of all American presidents. The most significant and popular act of his tenure was the Louisiana Purchase of 1803; he also began the Lewis and Clark expedition during his first term. His suppression of the pirates in Tripoli beginning in 1801 was widely approved, giving him an easy reelection in 1804. His second term was marred by the controversy with ex–Vice-President Aaron Burr and by the embargo on exports to Europe. Jefferson, fearing a revolt, repealed the embargo in 1808.

Jefferson left office and returned to Monticello in 1809. The country soon forgot the turmoil of his second term and saw him admiringly as "The Sage of Monticello." His last great effort was a labor of love, the founding of the University of Virginia; the campus he designed was the masterpiece of his architectural career. Lying on his deathbed in 1826, he would wake and ask what day it was; he wanted to hold out until July Fourth, and he got his wish; a few hours later, John Adams, likewise determined, died in Boston. It was the 50th anniversary of the signing of the Declaration of Independence.

29 JANUARY 1802

Arts/Culture President Jefferson appoints John James Beckley the first Librarian of Congress. Beckley was formerly the clerk of the House of Representatives.

6 FEBRUARY 1802

International In recognition of the May 14, 1801 declaration of war on the United States by the Pasha of Tripoli, Congress passes legislation authorizing the arming of merchant ships in order to defend American interests in the Tripolitan war. By doing so, Congress in effect admits that a state of war exists between the two nations.

FEBRUARY 1802

Finance Newly appointed Secretary of the Treasury Albert Gallatin proposes federal aid for the building of roads, suggesting that in the Ohio Territory one-tenth of the proceeds from public land sales be used for the construction of roads from the Atlantic seaboard towns to the Ohio River. This requested increase in federal expenditures, however, is atypical of President Jefferson's fiscal policy of retrenchment, as implemented by the assiduous and far-seeing Gallatin. Gallatin is able to make good Jefferson's promise of a significant reduction in the national debt (from $83 million in 1801 to $57 million in 1809), in spite of the heavy costs of the Tripolitan war and of the Louisiana Purchase. Jefferson's financial policy also calls for the repeal of all internal taxes, cuts in defense expenditures and a congressional system of appropriations for designated uses.

8 MARCH 1802

National Congress repeals the Judiciary Act of February 13, 1801.

16 MARCH 1802

National Congress enacts legislation establishing the United States Military Academy to be located at West Point, New York. This site was selected by George Washington. The academy will open officially on July 4.

27 MARCH 1802
International The Treaty of Aliens among France, England, Spain and The Netherlands ends the European hostilities, offering American shipping a temporary respite from trade restraints.

6 APRIL 1802
Finance Congress abolishes all excise duties, including the controversial whiskey tax.

14 APRIL 1802
National Congress nullifies the Naturalization Act of June 18, 1798 that was part of the Alien and Sedition Acts. The Naturalization Act of 1795, which required five years of residency in order to render an alien eligible for American citizenship, is reinstated.

24 APRIL 1802
Regional The state of Georgia seeks to extricate itself from the aftermath of the Yazoo land fraud of 1795 and the state's 1796 invalidation of the sale of these lands, by ceding the lands in question to the United States. The Federal Government will seek to end the controversy over land claims by granting 5 million acres to the holders of Yazoo land warrants. This move will be blocked in Congress, and in 1810 the issue will come before the Supreme Court in the case of *Fletcher* v. *Peck*. Chief Justice John Marshall will rule that the state of Georgia could not revoke its original act, since to do so would constitute a breach of contract. In 1814, Congress will be forced to award the Yazoo land claimants, most of them real estate speculators, $4.2 million.

29 APRIL 1802
National Congresses passes a new Judiciary Act, restoring to six the number of Supreme Court justices, providing for one session a year of the Supreme Court and establishing a system of six circuit courts, each to be presided over by a Supreme Court justice.

30 APRIL 1802
Westward Movement Congress passes the Enabling Act, which permits any territory organized under the Ordinance of 1787 to become a state. This legislation refers specifically to the Northwest Territory (Ohio), which can now begin to elect delegates to a state constitutional convention. The precedent set by Ohio will be followed for the admission of the rest of the states.

APRIL 1802
International Having learned of the secret transfer of Spanish Louisiana to French sovereignty, President Jefferson is immediately concerned over the danger to the United States posed by an aggressive neighboring power that may close the Mississippi River to American commercial navigation. The president instructs Robert R. Livingston, the United States minister in Paris, to negotiate for a land tract on the lower Mississippi River for use as a port, or to obtain a permanent guarantee of free navigation and the right of deposit.

3 MAY 1802
National The new federal capital of Washington is incorporated as a city by an act of Congress, with a mayor to be appointed by the president and a council to be elected by local property owners.

4 JULY 1802
National The new United States Military Academy officially opens at West Point, New York.

11 AUGUST 1802
International American and Spanish diplomatic representatives sign a convention that provides for a commission to settle the claims of the inhabitants of both nations against each other.

16 OCTOBER 1802
International The Spanish officials at the port of New Orleans, now part of the French territory of Louisiana, forbid American traders from depositing their cargo there, thus revoking a concession granted in the October 27, 1795 Treaty of Lorenzo between the United States and Spain. The goods shipped by American traders down the Mississippi River are customarily transferred to ocean-going vessels at the port of New Orleans. This serious disruption of American commerce poses a significant economic threat, motivating the 1803 decision of President Jefferson to attempt to purchase New Orleans and West Florida.

29 NOVEMBER 1802
Regional The Ohio state constitutional convention, meeting at Chillicothe, approves a constitution in preparation for the application of the territory for statehood.

6 DECEMBER 1802
Finance In his annual message to the second session of the Seventh Congress, President Jefferson reiterates his policy of achieving governmental economy.

12 JANUARY 1803
International President Jefferson names James Monroe as minister plenipotentiary to France, to negotiate together with American minister to France Robert R. Livingston for concessions in the Louisiana Territory. Monroe is given specific instructions to attempt to purchase New Orleans and West Florida for the $2 million approved by the congressional appropriations committee. Monroe will be permitted to pay as much as $10 million if necessary.

JANUARY 1803
Westward Movement In a message to Congress, President Jefferson requests an appropriation to finance a western expedition with the goal of establishing friendly relations with the Indians and extending American internal commercial boundaries. Congress grants the president's request.

24 FEBRUARY 1803
National In the case of *Marbury* v. *Madison*, the

Supreme Court rules an act of Congress null and void when it conflicts with the provisions of the United States Constitution. This decision, written by Chief Justice John Marshall, establishes the principle of judicial review. The plaintiff in the case, William Marbury, had been appointed by President John Adams as a justice of the peace of the District of Columbia during the last hours of Adams' presidency. Under orders from President Jefferson, Secretary of State James Madison had refused to deliver the signed commission to Marbury and to three other last minute Federalist appointments, who join with Marbury in his legal suit. Chief Justice Marshall dismisses the suit on the grounds that the court lacks the jurisdiction to issue the requested writ of mandamus, since the applicable section of the 1789 Judiciary Act empowering the court to do so is in fact unconstitutional. In employing this strategem, Marshall avoids an open conflict between the executive and judiciary branches of government. Marshall thus strengthens the concept of the balance of power among the three branches of the Federal Government.

1 MARCH 1803

Regional Ohio enters the union as the 17th state. Since the Northwest Ordinance of 1787 outlawed slavery in the territory, Ohio is the first state in which slavery is illegal from the beginning.

3 MARCH 1803

Westward Movement Congress passes legislation providing for the sale of all uncommitted public lands in the Mississippi Territory.

12 APRIL 1803

International American minister plenipotentiary to France, James Monroe, arrives in Paris to pursue negotiations for purchases and concessions in the Louisiana territory. Monroe hears from American minister to France Robert R. Livingston that on the previous day French foreign minister Talleyrand had inquired how much the United States would be willing to pay for the entire Louisiana territory. Napoleon Bonaparte had abandoned his grand scheme for a North American colonial empire after the costly rebellion led by Toussaint L'Ouverture in Haiti and in face of the impending resumption of war with England.

19 APRIL 1803

International Spain restores to American traders the right of deposit at the port of New Orleans.

2 MAY 1803

International In Paris, American envoys James Monroe and Robert Livingston sign a treaty of cession with the French. For approximately $15 million the United States purchases the entire Louisiana territory. The cost of the territory is $11,250,000, while the remaining $3,750,000 covers the debts owed by France to American citizens. The United States government assumes these debts. This acquisition doubles the land area of the United States, adding some 828,000

JOHN MARSHALL, 1755-1835

By the year 1788 the United States *had* a Constitution; it was to become the task of John Marshall, as Chief Justice of the Supreme Court, to determine the path along which the nation was to *use* that great document. Marshall was born to a rustic but politically active family near Germantown, Virginia, on September 24, 1755; his father was an early admirer of their neighbor, George Washington. Largely self-taught, convivial of manner and informal in attire throughout his life, Marshall joined the Revolutionary Army, where he saw action at Monmouth and Stony Point and spent the bitter winter of 1777 at Valley Forge. After the war he attended a few lectures on the law and joined the Virginia bar in 1780.

As his practice prospered, Marshall entered the political life of Virginia. As a member of the Assembly he headed the successful effort to ratify the new Constitution. His growing prominence led to several offers of cabinet posts in the Washington and Adams administrations, all of which he declined; but in 1799 he entered Congress and the following year was named secretary of state. In 1801 he accepted John Adams' nomination as Chief Justice of the Supreme Court.

In the ensuing 35 years of his tenure, Marshall, in a number of epochal decisions, was to establish the definitive workings of the Constitution in and on government. His first years, however, were not promising; he ran afoul of Jefferson in the President's attempt to impeach Justice Chase and to convict Burr of treason—in both cases neither man acted with his usual sagacity. But in the *Marbury v. Madison* decision of 1803 the Chief Justice established once and for all the Supreme Court as the final authority in interpreting the Constitution. This principle, known as "the power of judicial review," means that the courts may strike down legislation deemed unconstitutional. Marshall went on in a series of landmark decisions to strengthen the power of the central government (he was generally a Federalist in his philosophy) and to favor a broad interpretation of the Constitution— what it *implied* rather than stated—as opposed to a narrow and literal interpretation. Marshall died in his 80th year on July 6, 1835.

---

square miles between the Mississippi River and the Rocky Mountains. Although the Mississippi River and the Gulf of Mexico are set as the eastern and southern boundaries of the purchase, the other boundaries are not defined, leaving the status of West Florida and Texas unclear. Although the Louisiana Purchase is not provided for in the United States Constitution, President Jefferson and the Democratic-Republican Congress take a broad-constructionist stand, involving implied powers, on the issue. The treaty with France will be approved by the Senate, 24 to 7, on October 20, 1803. The 13 states that will be carved out of this territory are Arkansas, Colorado, Iowa, Kansas, Louisiana, Minnesota, Missouri, Montana, Nebraska, North Dakota, Oklahoma, South Dakota and Wyoming.

23 MAY 1803

International American naval Commodore Edward Preble, an able organizer and efficient administrator, is appointed commander of the Mediterranean Squadron, which has been assigned the task of waging the Tripolitan war.

7 JUNE 1803
Westward Movement In the Indiana Territory, Governor William Henry Harrison signs a treaty with nine Indian tribes for the cession of the Indian lands around Vincennes along the Wabash River, beyond the boundary established by the August 3, 1795 Treaty of Greenville. A second treaty will be signed on August 7.

31 AUGUST 1803
Exploration The government–sponsored transcontinental expedition led by Meriwether Lewis and William Clark sets out down the Ohio River. This three-year journey of exploration and discovery to the Pacific coast and back will add significantly to the sum of scientific knowledge, prove the feasibility of an overland route to the West Coast, and stimulate a wave of western settlement.

31 OCTOBER 1803
International In the Tripolitan war, the American frigate *Philadelphia* is captured by the enemy in Tripoli Harbor, where the vessel has run aground on a reef. The Tripolitans will convert the frigate to their own use.

30 NOVEMBER 1803
International Spanish officials formally complete their cession of the Louisiana territory to France, as mandated by the October 1, 1800 Treaty of Ildefonso.

9 DECEMBER 1803
National Congress passes the 12th Amendment to the United States Constitution. This Amendment provides for the election of the president and vice president on separate ballots. This move is prompted by the tie in the Jefferson-Burr election of 1800. The 12th Amendment will now be sent to the states for ratification.

20 DECEMBER 1803
Regional In a ceremony at New Orleans, the United States takes formal possession of the Louisiana territory from French officials. Representing President Jefferson, Mississippi Governor William C. Claiborne and Army Commander in Chief James Wilkinson receive control of the territory.

OTHER EVENTS OF 1803
International Late this year, hostilities are renewed between Great Britain and France. This continuance of their fierce naval warfare is again accompanied by the resumption of their harassment of neutral vessels, and American commercial shipping will suffer accordingly.

5 JANUARY 1804
National In the House of Representatives, members of the Jeffersonian Democratic-Republican party begin to investigate a Federalist associate justice of the Supreme Court, Samuel Chase, for alleged biased conduct in the trials of publisher James Thomas Callender under the Sedition Act, and of the leader of a Pennsylvania taxpayer's rebellion, John Fries.

15 FEBRUARY 1804
Slavery New Jersey passes legislation calling for the gradual emancipation of the slaves within the state.

16 FEBRUARY 1804
International In the Tripolitan war, American naval Lieutenant Stephen Decatur wins a stunning victory by sailing his ketch *Intrepid* into Tripoli harbor and daringly recapturing and burning the frigate *Philadelphia,* seized by the Tripolitans more than three months previously when the vessel ran aground on a reef.
National Alexander Hamilton reportedly comments of Aaron Burr, candidate for the governorship of New York state, that he is "a dangerous man, and one who ought not to be trusted with the reins of government."

25 FEBRUARY 1804
National In the first regular congressional caucus, the members of the Democratic-Republican party unanimously nominate Thomas Jefferson for a second term as president and New York's George Clinton for vice president.

12 MARCH 1804
National The Senate impeaches New Hampshire federal district judge John Pickering. He is ruled guilty of unlawful decisions, intoxication and profanity. Although evidence is presented at the trial proving Pickering's insanity, he is still held responsible for high crimes and misdemeanors. Pickering's impeachment and the investigation of Supreme Court Justice Samuel Chase are part of President Jefferson's continuing conflict with the Federalist judiciary.

26 MARCH 1804
Westward Movement Congress passes the Land Act of 1804, which reduces the minimum price for public lands to $1.64 per acre and which permits the

The Louisiana Purchase, April 30, 1803.

TESTING A UNION 1788-1865

sale of 160-acre tracts, or quarter sections. Credit terms are also liberalized, as payment for the land may now be made in installments over ten years.

On the same date, Congress also passes legislation creating the Territory of Orleans in the southern region of the Louisiana Purchase, in the area of the present-day state of Louisiana west of the Mississippi River. The rest of the Louisiana Purchase lands are organized as the District (later the Territory) of Louisiana.

25 APRIL 1804
Regional In the New York state election, former Vice–President Aaron Burr is defeated in his race for governor. Burr's candidacy had been supported by the Essex Junto, a separatist movement of New England and New York Federalist extremists. The principal moderate Federalist leader, Alexander Hamilton, played a decisive role in securing Aaron Burr's defeat at the polls.

29 APRIL 1804
International In the Tripolitan war, American Commodore Edward Preble captures two enemy vessels.

14 MAY 1804
Exploration The Lewis and Clark Expedition leaves St. Louis, beginning a journey westward up the Missouri River. The group travels on a keelboat and two pirogue boats.

18 MAY 1804
International Napoleon Bonaparte becomes emperor of France. In the Paris coronation ceremony, Napoleon snatches the crown from the hands of Pope Pius VII and crowns himself and his consort Josephine. This act of self-aggrandizement leads Russia, Austria and Sweden to join in a coalition with Great Britain against France and the Napoleonic States.

7 JUNE 1804
National Aaron Burr sends a letter to Alexander Hamilton, demanding an explanation for Hamilton's alleged slurs on Burr's character, as reported in the New York press.

11 JULY 1804
National The quarrel between Aaron Burr and Alexander Hamilton culminates in a duel at Weehawken, New Jersey. Alexander Hamilton deliberately misfires in advance of Burr, who then aims with deadly purpose. Hamilton is fatally wounded and dies ten hours later in New York City.

13 AUGUST 1804
Westward Movement In the Indiana Territory, Governor William Henry Harrison purchases the land between the Wabash and Ohio Rivers from the Delaware Indians.

18 and 27 AUGUST 1804
Indian Affairs Indiana Governor William Henry Harrison signs two treaties at Vincennes for the cession of the Indian lands north of the Ohio River and south of the tract ceded in the June 7, 1803 Treaty of Vincennes.

AUGUST—SEPTEMBER 1804
International In the Tripolitan war, American Commodore Edward Preble bombards the city of Tripoli from his warship in a series of five unrelenting attacks.

25 SEPTEMBER 1804
National The 12th Amendment to the United States Constitution is ratified. This Amendment spells out the procedures for electing the president and vice-president, specifying separate electoral ballots for each office.

1 OCTOBER 1804
Regional William C. Claiborne becomes governor of the Territory of Orleans, thus inaugurating American government of the former Spanish and French region. The seat of government is the port of New Orleans.

27 OCTOBER 1804
Exploration Near present-day Bismarck, North Dakota, the Lewis and Clark Expedition prepares to spend its first winter in the wilderness of the American West. The explorers encamp at a Mandan Indian village on the banks of the upper Missouri River.

3 NOVEMBER 1804
Indian Affairs In St. Louis, Indiana territorial Governor William Henry Harrison negotiates a treaty with the Fox and Sauk Indian tribes for the transfer of five million acres in the present-day Wisconsin region to the United States. The Indians are granted the right to stay on the land as long as it remains in the public domain.

29 NOVEMBER 1804
Arts/Culture Wealthy New York merchant and philanthropist John Pintard, along with New York City Mayor DeWitt Clinton, Judge Egbert Benson and botanist Dr. David Hosack, establishes the New York Historical Society. John Pintard is also credited with encouraging the earlier establishment of the Massachusetts Historical Society and similar organizations in other New England areas. This provision for the permanent preservation and cataloging of the nation's significant historical documents and records is an essential contribution to scholarship.

5 DECEMBER 1804
National In the first presidential election carried out under the procedural regulation of the newly ratified 12th Amendment to the Constitution—which mandates separate ballots for the offices of president and vice-president—incumbent President Thomas Jefferson is opposed by Federalist candidate Charles Cotesworth Pinckney. Jefferson wins a second term in office, with

162 electoral votes against the 14 cast for Pinckney. George Clinton is elected vice president, also with 162 votes, against the 14 cast for his opponent, New York's Rufus King. In the congressional races, the Jeffersonian Republicans gain an undisputed majority.

OTHER EVENTS OF 1804

International In the renewed hostilities between the French and English, the harassment of United States neutral shipping by the British is reinstituted, leading to an increased public antipathy toward the British, a decrease in anger against the French.

National The Federalist party, greatly diminished in influence and power since the 1800 election debacle following the unpopular implementation of the Alien and Sedition Acts and by the death of Alexander Hamilton, feels threatened by the Louisiana Purchase because the incorporation of this territory into the United States could radically upset the balance of power. The reactionary New England arm of the Federalist party, the Essex Junto, going so far as to express secessionist sentiments, puts forth a plan for a Northern Confederacy, to be formed of the southern New England states, New York and New Jersey. The election of Aaron Burr as New York's governor was central to this scheme. This move is opposed by the more moderate Alexander Hamilton before his death.

Ideas/Beliefs In the Louisiana Territory, the French-instituted Napoleonic legal code is maintained. It will serve as the model for the legal code of the state of Louisiana. The rest of the states follow the common-law and statutory law system originating from England.

11 JANUARY 1805

Westward Movement The Indiana Territory is divided to form the new Michigan Territory. The Michigan Territory includes the area of the Lower Peninsula and the eastern region of the Upper Peninsula. General William Hull is named governor and Michigan's capital is located at Detroit.

JANUARY 1805

International The Napoleonic Wars continue to disrupt American commercial shipping everywhere on the high seas. Both the British orders in council and the French Berlin and Milan Decrees bar neutral vessels from entering enemy harbors, or from entering the harbors of allies of the enemy.

Exploration A government-sponsored scientific expedition to explore the lower Red River and the Ouachita River returns to Natchez, Mississippi, after successfully completing its mission. Begun in October 1804, the expedition to the old Southwest was led by Scottish-born scientist and Mississippi planter William Dunbar, who was assisted by Dr. George Hunter. Dunbar's important reports back to President Jefferson made the first mention of features such as the mineral wells at Hot Springs, Arkansas.

11 FEBRUARY 1805

Exploration On the Lewis and Clark Expedition, wintering in a Mandan Indian village near the site of present-day Bismarck, South Dakota, Meriwether Lewis acts as a midwife at the birth of Sacajawea's child. Also known as "Birdwoman," the 16-year-old Shoshone Indian guide is the wife of the expedition's interpreter, Frenchman Touisaint Charbonneau.

1 MARCH 1805

National The Senate dismisses the charges against Supreme Court Justice Samuel Chase, who had been impeached by the House of Representatives for partisan conduct unbecoming to a judge. Chase retakes his seat on the bench, although with a considerable loss of credibility. The failure of the case against Chase discourages later administrations from attempting to use the impeachment process to limit the power of the federal judiciary for political reasons.

2 MARCH 1805

Regional Congress enacts legislation confirming the Spanish and French Louisiana land grants and transforming the Louisiana District into the Louisiana Territory with its capital at St. Louis. As a territory, Louisiana will follow the mandated pattern of townships and sections.

4 MARCH 1805

National Thomas Jefferson is inaugurated for his second term as president of the United States, and New York's George Clinton is inaugurated as vice–president. In his inaugural address, Jefferson notes the end of internal taxes, which have been replaced by consumption taxes on imported luxury items. Jefferson also asks support for a federally-financed public works program.

In his second administration, President Jefferson's cabinet includes James Madison as Secretary of State, Albert Gallatin as Secretary of the Treasury, Henry Dearborn as Secretary of War, Jacob Crowninshield as Secretary of the Navy, Gideon Granger as Postmaster General and Robert Smith as Attorney General.

7 APRIL 1805

Exploration After wintering near Bismarck, South Dakota, the Lewis and Clark Expedition resumes its journey, traveling northwest up the Missouri River.

26 APRIL 1805

Exploration The Lewis and Clark Expedition reaches the mouth of the Yellowstone River.

26-29 APRIL 1805

International In the Tripolitan war, a small American land invasion force captures the port city of Derna in Tripoli. William Eaton, the United States consul in Tunis, had led a rabble army from Egypt, supplemented by Lieutenant Presley, N.O. O'Bannon and seven marines, to a victory that signals a turning point for America in the Tripolitan War.

25 MAY 1805

Labor In Philadelphia, a strike led by the nation's

oldest labor union, the Federal Society of Journeymen Cordwainers (shoemakers), is suppressed and the leaders are arrested for criminal conspiracy for the purpose of increasing their wages, under an English common law doctrine. This is the first time an employer has made an appeal to the judicial system during the course of a strike against him.

26 MAY 1805
Exploration The Lewis and Clark Expedition first sights the Rocky Mountains. After an unsuccessful attempt to cross the mountain range by way of the Jefferson River, they take an overland route over the continental divide at Lemhi Pass.

MAY—SEPTEMBER 1805
Regional Aaron Burr tours the Mississippi Valley region and meets with General James Wilkinson, the commander of American forces in the area.

4 JUNE 1805
International A peace treaty ends the war between the United States and Tripoli after the Americans have installed the Pasha's brother on the throne. In order to get back his throne, Pasha Yusuf grants the American Navy the right to sail the Mediterranean Sea unmolested, while the United States agrees to pay $60,000 in order to ransom the crew of the *Philadelphia*. This is to be a one-time payment, and Tripoli gives up any right to demand further tribute from the United States. Congress will ratify this treaty on April 12, 1806.

13 JUNE 1805
Exploration The Lewis and Clark Expedition reaches the Great Falls of the Missouri River.

23 JULY 1805
International American trade with the islands of the French West Indies is imperiled as Great Britain invokes its Rule of 1756, which bans ships of neutral nations from trading during wartime in ports that they do not normally frequent in peacetime. Up to this time, American traders had been able to successfully employ the stratagem of breaking a journey between French ports or between the ports of her allies with a stop in a neutral American port. In the *Essex* case, British Judge Sir William Scott declares that a trading voyage by a neutral vessel will be considered a continuous one between enemy ports, unless the shipper can prove he had originally intended to end the voyage in an American port. Under this ruling, Great Britain justifies its seizure of many American commercial vessels.

9 AUGUST 1805
Exploration General James Wilkinson commissions Lieutenant Zebulon Montgomery Pike to explore the territory of the Louisiana Purchase, and specifically to search out the sources of the Mississippi River. On his first expedition, Pike leaves St. Louis with a party of 20 men that he leads into the Minnesota region,

which he mistakenly takes to be the source of the Mississippi River. Pike will return from this expedition on April 30, 1806.

10 OCTOBER 1805
Exploration After crossing the continental divide, the Lewis and Clark expedition reaches the westward flowing Snake River. In canoes of their own manufacture, the party will float down the Snake River and enter the Columbia River on October 17.

7 NOVEMBER 1805
Exploration In the Oregon region, the Lewis and Clark expedition sights the Pacific Ocean near the mouth of the Columbia River. They build Fort Clatsop near the site of present-day Astoria, Oregon, and spend the winter there.

9 DECEMBER 1805
National The Ninth Congress convenes with a decisive Democratic-Republican majority in both houses. In the Senate, there are 27 Democratic-Republicans to seven Federalists; in the House, there are 116 Democratic-Republicans to 25 Federalists.

OTHER EVENTS OF 1805
Arts/Culture Mercy Otis Warren, sister of James Otis, publishes her three-volume history of the American Revolution, the *Rise, Progress and Termination of the American Revolution*. This is the earliest account of the era written by an American. Although Warren's history is provocative, clever and full of anecdotes, it is also marred by a partisan antifederalist bias that portrays Warren's old friend John Adams in an unfavorable light. The work is imbued with a patriotic tone typical of those years.

In Philadelphia, painter Charles Willson Peale founds a public art gallery, the Pennsylvania Academy of Fine Art—the oldest still–existing arts institution in the nation. The New York Academy had been established in 1801, but it lasted for only four years.
Commerce New England merchant Frederick Tudor ships a cargo of ice to the French island of Martinique in the Caribbean Sea. The ice not only serves as ballast on the trading vessel, which will load up by West Indian products at the destination port, but it will also find a ready market at the end of the voyage. Ice becomes a lucrative export item for many New Englanders trading with India and other countries of the Far East.

25 JANUARY 1806
International Secretary of State James Madison delivers a report to Congress on the continuing British interference with the commercial shipping of neutral nations, including America, and on the British policy of impressing American seamen, in the context of the Napoleonic wars. Madison's report will give rise to a new wave of anti-British feeling.

JANUARY 1806
Arts/Culture Connecticut-born grammarian, lex-

APRIL 18, 1806

IMPRESSMENT

Impressment was one of the emotionally charged issues that eventually led to the outbreak of hostilities between the United States and Great Britain in the War of 1812. The seizure of American merchant seamen by British Royal Navy captains was more a matter of exigency and opportunity than of official policy. This practice began toward the end of the 18th century and continued through the years of the European Napoleonic wars. During this era British sailors were fleeing the Royal Navy, which offered harsh discipline, low pay and poor food, in droves—some estimates place the number of deserters at 2500 annually. A goodly proportion of these deserters found employment on the more amenable American commercial trade vessels. The urgent need for replacement sailors led British captains to stop American and other neutral vessels, not only to search them for contraband in violation of the British maritime orders in council, but also to search for British deserters among the merchant marine crews. In doing so, Great Britain claimed only the legal right to seize British deserters, but in actuality the British all too often seized any likely seaman who could not prove with documents that he was a native-born American. With these actions, the British denied the right of English sailors to become naturalized American citizens. In a series of humiliating incidents, some 10,000 men were impressed from American commercial ships. The claims of the wrongfully seized Americans occupied nearly 90 percent of the correspondence of the American diplomatic mission to London, and eventually only 1000 impressed sailors were proved to be British deserters. The issue of impressment reached a climax with the widely publicized 1807 *Chesapeake-Leopold* incident, in which the British seized three Americans after firing broadsides at the *Chesapeake*. The resulting public outcry was skillfully exploited by the American prowar faction. Despite the importance of the impressment issue as a cause of the War of 1812, the 1814 Treaty of Ghent ending the war, negotiated by United States envoys anxious for peace almost at any cost, made no mention of impressment. Yet, despite the absence of a specific treaty provision, after 1815 no more British vessels stopped American merchant marine ships in order to seize sailors.

---

icographer and Federalist journalist Noah Webster issues his modest *Compendius Dictionary of the English Language*. With this volume, Webster has retreated from his earlier efforts to Americanize the English language, although other nationalistic linguists continue to press the cause. Webster does include such Americanisms as "belittle," "caucus," "sot" and "sprig," but the basic intent of this work is to formulate a standardized English language in the United States. His compromises with the mother tongue will become the accepted standards of language. Some 20 years later Webster will publish his most ambitious work, *An American Dictionary of the English Language*.

JANUARY—MARCH 1806
Exploration In a second winter in the wilderness, the Lewis and Clark Expedition settles at Fort Clatsop in Oregon, organizing their scientific, geographic, ethnographic and meterological notes of observations

made while on their journey. They also complete and refine the maps depicting their important discoveries.

12 FEBRUARY 1806
International Following James Madison's report on the British naval hostilities against American commercial shipping, the Senate issues a resolution condemning these actions as "an unprovoked aggression" and a "violation of neutral rights." This proclamation has little effect on moderating British actions.

29 MARCH 1806
Westward Movement Congress passes legislation authorizing the construction of the federally-financed Cumberland Road from Cumberland, Maryland, to the village of Zanesburg, Virginia, on the Ohio River. A new charter is granted to Zanesburg, renaming it Wheeling, now in the state of West Virginia. The road is to eventually reach as far as Vandalia, Illinois. The Cumberland Road will facilitate the flow of pioneers into the West, as well as increase commerce along its route.

18 APRIL 1806
Commerce Congress passes the Nicholson Act, also known as the first Nonimportation Act. To become effective on November 15, the act forbids the importa-

---

NOAH WEBSTER, 1758-1843

Although he was a man of extraordinarily wide knowledge and influence, the genius of Noah Webster as a lexicographer was to be so enduring that his name became practically synonomous with the word *dictionary*. Webster was born in West Hartford, Connecticut, on October 16, 1758. After gaining a degree from Yale in 1778 he pursued law studies while teaching in Goshen, New York. Dissatisfied with the texts available for schoolchildren, Webster wrote a series of books—a speller, grammar, and reader—that were collected as *A Grammatical Institute of the English Language*, completed in 1785. These books were an immense success in Webster's time and were to be in use into the 20th century.

Because of his school texts, Webster began campaigning for better copyright protection for authors in America, and these efforts took him into public life, where he was to make the acquaintance of Washington and other leaders and to become a friend of Benjamin Franklin. In 1787 Webster established the *American Magazine* in New York, beginning a career of several years as a political writer in support of the Federalist party.

But in his publishing ventures found little success and Webster turned to writing and lectures in an extraordinary range of fields—economics, medicine, politics, science and meteorology—all of which prepared him for his last and greatest work as a pioneer writer of dictionaries. His first short dictionary appeared in 1806. After 20 more years of labor there appeared in 1828 the monumental two volumes of *An American Dictionary of the English Language*, soon to be acclaimed as the greatest dictionary in the language. During his writing of this work Webster had become involved with higher education and helped found Amherst College in Massachusetts. Pursuing his scholarly interests and revising his work to the end of his life, Webster died in 1843.

tion from England of a long list of enumerated items that can also be produced in America or imported from other countries. On the list are brass, hemp, flax, tin and various types of woolen textiles. President Jefferson will suspend the act on December 19, but it will be reinstated two years later.

16 MAY 1806
International During the course of the Napoleonic wars, British foreign minister Charles James Fox proclaims a naval blockade of European coastal ports from Brest to the mouth of the Elbe River. This blockade further disrupts American commercial shipping.

19 MAY 1806
Education A New York City school introduces the Lancastrian system of education, which promotes the use of pupil-teachers who learn from more advanced pupil-teachers, or from a master-teacher. The pupil-teachers then instruct less advanced students. The founder of the system, Englishman Joseph Lancaster, will come to the United States to supervise this new educational method. The Lancastrian–school concept will be widely accepted because its low cost makes it an attractive alternative to the tax-consuming public school system.

30 MAY 1806
Life/Customs Former Tennessee supreme court judge Andrew Jackson kills lawyer Charles Dickinson in a duel over a personal insult. This unfortunate event will become a political liability when Jackson runs for president some 20 years later.

MAY 1806
International On the advice of Congress, President Jefferson sends Maryland's William Pinkney to London as a special diplomatic envoy. Pinkney is to assist American minister to England James Monroe with negotiating a treaty with the British. The president instructs Monroe and Pinkney to seek an end to the British impressment of American seamen, a restoration of the American-West Indian trade on the principle of the "broken voyage" and British indemnity payments for illegal seizures of American ships.

15 JUNE 1806
Exploration The Lewis and Clark Expedition begins an ascent of the western slope of the Rocky Mountains on their journey back to St. Louis. When the party descends on the other side of the continental divide, they will separate into three smaller groups in order to explore the western territory more intensively.

15 JULY 1806
Exploration In a second expedition commissioned by General James Wilkinson, Lieutenant Zebulon Montgomery Pike leaves Fort Bellefontaine leading a party to explore the Southwest, especially in the area of New Mexico and Colorado.

On the Lewis and Clark Expedition, the small group led by William Clark reaches the Yellowstone River, which it will follow downstream to its junction with the Missouri River.

20 JULY 1806
National On Blennerhassett's Island in the Ohio River, Aaron Burr joins with Irish adventurer Harman Blennerhassett to prepare a military expedition of some 80 participants who will travel on 10 boats. Burr's intentions are unclear, but it is believed that he is planning to annex territory in the West, either from the Louisiana Purchase area or by capturing Spanish lands in the Southwest and Mexico.

27 AUGUST 1806
International In London, American minister James Monroe and special envoy William Pinkney open negotiations with Lord Holland for an end to the British interference with American commercial shipping. The American threat of the Nonimportation Act does not move the British, and the American negotiators are unable to fulfill their instructions. The treaty that will finally result does not cover the essential issues of impressment and indemnity.

AUGUST 1806
Ideas/Beliefs In Massachusetts, a group of five Williams College students establishes the first American society for foreign missionary work, "The Brethren." The goal of the society is to facilitate American missionary work in other countries.

23 SEPTEMBER 1806
Exploration The Lewis and Clark Expedition ends its epic two-year journey across the American western wilderness to the Pacific coast in the Oregon area and back. With its return to St. Louis, the successful expedition proves the feasibility of an overland route to the Pacific coast.

21 OCTOBER 1806
National Congress passes legislation to develop an organizational and legal framework for the governance of the military forces of the United States.

15 NOVEMBER 1806
Exploration During his second exploratory expedition for General James Wilkinson in the American Southwest, Lieutenant Zebulon Montgomery Pike spots a distant mountain peak with looks "like a small blue cloud," in the Colorado foothills of the Rocky Mountains. This mountain will be named Pike's Peak in his honor. Pike's party will be captured by the Spanish, later to be released unharmed.

21 NOVEMBER 1806
International During the Napoleonic wars, Napoleon Bonaparte issues the Berlin Decree in response to the British naval blockade of the European coastline from Brest northward to the Elbe River. The Berlin Decree declares the British Isles in a state of block-

ade, forbids commerce and communication with them and orders the seizure of all ships and cargo headed for or coming from Great Britain.

27 NOVEMBER 1806
National After General James Wilkinson reveals the Aaron Burr conspiracy to carve out an empire in the American Southwest and Mexico, President Jefferson issues a proclamation warning American citizens against joining any illegal expedition against the Spanish. Apparently unaware of Wilkinson's betrayal and Jefferson's proclamation, Aaron Burr leads his expedition down the Mississippi River to a point 30 miles above Natchez. Here he is informed of the recent developments and escapes toward Florida.

2 DECEMBER 1806
Slavery President Jefferson sends Congress a message asking for a ban on all slave importations to the United States, to become effective January 1, 1808.

31 DECEMBER 1806
International In London, American minister James Monroe and special envoy William Pinkney sign a treaty with the British designed to alleviate British harassment of American commercial shipping. As the British make no concessions on the essential issues of impressment and indemnity, and a negligible compromise on the West Indian trade issue, the treaty is a failure of American diplomacy. When President Jefferson receives the treaty in March 1807, he will suppress it.

OTHER EVENTS OF 1806
Finance President Jefferson orders the United States Mint to cease coining the silver dollar. The silver dollar will not be reissued until 1836.
Transportation Congress passes legislation authorizing the construction of yet another wilderness route. The Natchez Road is to run some 500 miles from Nashville, Tennessee, to Natchez, Mississippi, following an old Indian trail.
Exploration A government-sponsored expedition led by Thomas Freeman results in the first accurate map of the lower Red River, in present-day Louisiana.

JANUARY 1807
Arts/Culture In New York, the series of essays titled *Salmagundi; or the Whim-Whams and Opinions of Launcelot Longstaff, Esq., and Others* begins publication. These satirical social and political pieces in the 18th–century style of English writers Addison and Steele are written by Washington Irving, William Irving and James Kirk Paulding. *Salmagundi* marks the beginning of the Knickerbocker school of writers, a group of New York authors whose works were characterized by realism, humor and a preference for native American subject matter.

7 JANUARY 1807
International In the Napoleonic wars, a British order in council bars all commercial shipping in the coastal waters of France and her allies. This order is in response to Napoleon's Berlin Decree of November 21, 1806, which created a naval blockade around the British Isles.

22 JANUARY 1807
National President Jefferson formally notifies Congress of Aaron Burr's conspiracy.

19 FEBRUARY 1807
National In Alabama, the fleeing Aaron Burr is captured and arrested for the misdemeanor of forming and leading an expedition against Spanish territory.

2 MARCH 1807
Slavery On the recommendation of President Jefferson, Congress passes legislation prohibiting the importation of any more slaves into the United States after January 1, 1808.

30 MARCH 1807
National In Richmond, Virginia, the arrested Aaron Burr is brought before the federal circuit court presided over by Supreme Court Chief Justice John Marshall.

MARCH 1807
International President Jefferson receives the Monroe-Pinkney treaty of December 31, 1806, negotiated between the United States and Great Britain. This treaty is a dismal failure for American diplomacy since Britain has made no concessions on the urgent problems of impressment and indemnification for damages to American commercial shipping. Jefferson is so dismayed by the terms of this pact that he never submits it to Congress.

20 MARCH 1807
International President Jefferson sends new instructions to American special envoy William Pinkney and American minister to Great Britain James Monroe, advising them to use the 1806 Monroe-Pinkney treaty as a basis for reopening negotiations on British interference with American commercial shipping.

22 JUNE 1807
International A volatile incident that brings the United States and Great Britain to the brink of war occurs when the British 52-gun frigate H.M.S. *Leopold* tries to stop the American 39-gun frigate U.S.S. *Chesapeake* just outside the three-miles limit off Norfolk, Virginia. The British commander insists that four men on the *Chesapeake* are British deserters and demands their surrender. When American Commodore James Barron refuses to acquiesce, the British open fire, killing three, wounding 18, and forcibly removing the four alleged British deserters. Only one of the four men is later proven to be a British deserter; he is hanged.

24 JUNE 1807
National In the Richmond, Virginia, federal circuit court, Aaron Burr is indicted for treason, although the

TESTING A UNION 1788-1865

charge on which he had originally been arrested was a misdemeanor.

25 JUNE 1807
International Napoleon Bonaparte signs the Tilsit Agreement with Czar Alexander I of Russia, thus strengthening the French political position in Europe and prolonging the Napoleonic wars, which have affected American commercial shipping adversely.

2 JULY 1807
International In response to the *Leopold-Chesapeake* incident of June 22, President Jefferson issues a proclamation calling for all British warships to vacate the territorial waters of the United States.

3 AUGUST 1807
National In the Richmond, Virginia, federal circuit court, the treason trial of Aaron Burr begins. The verdict will be issued on September 1.

17-21 AUGUST 1807
Transportation The voyage of the steamboat *Clermont* from New York City up the Hudson River to Albany and back again inaugurates the era of commercially successful steamboat navigation. The trip from New York to Albany takes 32 hours. Designed by Robert Fulton, with the financial backing of Robert R. Livingston, the *Clermont* is a 150-foot paddlewheel vessel driven by a Watt engine that travels at a rate of five miles per hour. President Jefferson will encourage Fulton in his other experiments with submarines and torpedoes. The first steamboat, invented by John Fitch, had been demonstrated on the Delaware River in 1787, but lacked the reliability of its descendant.

1 SEPTEMBER 1807
National In Richmond, Virginia, the treason trial of Aaron Burr ends with the acquittal of Burr and his associates. Presiding judge and Supreme Court Chief Justice John Marshall interprets the United States law on treason strictly, finding that Burr was not actually present when an overt act was committed. Before he can stand trial on other charges facing him, including one for Alexander Hamilton's murder, Burr jumps bail and escapes to Europe, where his plans to overthrow President Jefferson and to unite France and England against the United States are snubbed.

17 OCTOBER 1807
International In response to President Jefferson's July 2 proclamation ordering all British warships to quit American waters, the British announce their intention to enforce even more rigorously their policy of impressing American seamen.

26 OCTOBER 1807
National In Washington, the Tenth Congress convenes. The Democratic-Republicans have a decisive majority in both houses, with 28 to 6 Federalists in the Senate, and 118 to 24 Federalists in the House of Representatives.

Robert Fulton's steamboat, *Clermont*.

15 NOVEMBER 1807
Commerce The American Non-Importation Act of April 18, 1806 becomes effective. The act bars a long list of British imports from the United States. Its threatened use has failed to secure any concessions from the British in the matter of the harassment of American commercial shipping.

17 DECEMBER 1807
International Napoleon Bonaparte issues the Milan Decree, in answer to the British orders in council of November 11. This countermeasure rules that all ships obeying the British orders in council and all ships searched by the British will be held as "denationalized," and hence subject to seizure and confiscation by the French.

18 DECEMBER 1807
Commerce President Jefferson sends a message to Congress asking for an embargo on all trade and commerce with foreign nations. The Federalist faction fails to block this measure and the Embargo Act passes the Senate on the same day, 22 to 6. On December 21 it will pass the House of Representatives, 82 to 44.

22 DECEMBER 1807
Commerce The Embargo Act becomes law. The act essentially bans all trade with foreign countries and specifically it forbids all American ships to set sail for foreign ports. The United States vessels plying the coastal trade are required to post a bond double the value of the ship and its cargo in order to guarantee that the cargo is destined for another American port. The Embargo Act does not actually state that imports arriving on foreign ships are banned; rather, the provision that no foreign ships can carry cargos out of American ports has the same effect. This law is widely protested in states with sizeable maritime interests, as in New England. The destructive effect on the New England economy will lead to a surge in smuggling activities, especially from Canada. Those American ships at sea when the Embargo Act is passed remain abroad and continue their trade activities, with the cooperation of the British. Both the British and French eventually suffer little from the Embargo Act. For British merchants, American competition is re-

moved and they turn to South America for imports. The French use the embargo as an excuse to seize those American ships that remain abroad. In New England, the widespread trade losses outweigh the stimulation to regional industry; and the act ends by harming America more than the English and French. The Embargo Act will be reinforced by the Embargo Acts of January 9 and March 12, 1808.

1 JANUARY 1808
Slavery According to Article I, Section 9 of the United States Constitution, Congress has been banned from passing any legislation affecting the foreign slave trade before 1808. On this date, a congressional law, passed on Marcy 2, 1807, forbidding the importation of slaves into the United States becomes effective. As recommended by President Jefferson, the African slave trade law calls for the forfeiture of the importing ship and its slave cargo. The state that makes the seizure is to dispose of the slaves.

9 JANUARY 1808
Commerce The Embargo Act of December 22, 1807 is supplemented by an additional Embargo Act, to be followed by a third Embargo Act on March 12. These Embargo Acts prove relatively ineffective, as smugglers carry on an active trade across the Canadian border, as well as at sea using ships that remained abroad after the passage of the first Embargo Act.

12 MARCH 1808
Commerce The third Embargo Act is passed by Congress, reinforcing the first two Embargo Acts. By the end of 1808, contrary to President Jefferson's expectations, the Embargo Acts will nearly destroy the American shipping industry, as well as impose severe economic hardships on the New England States, which depend on trade in large amounts of perishable goods and manufactured goods. The Embargo Acts also lead to the virtual demise of small New England seaports such as Newburyport, Massachusetts, and New Haven, Connecticut. The Southern States are not as seriously affected because their staple exports, including cotton, tobacco and wheat, can be stored for long periods of time. Nor does the embargo achieve its ultimate goal of causing the British to cease their policy of harassing American commercial shipping.

6 APRIL 1808
Transportation Secretary of the Treasury Albert Gallatin presents to the Senate his *Report on the Subject of Public Roads and Canals.*
Commerce In New York City, John Jacob Astor incorporates the American Fur Company, with himself as the sole stockholder. Astor forms the company in order effectively to compete with such successful fur traders as the North West Company. One result of the Lewis and Clark Expedition is that it has opened up vast new areas to the lucrative fur trade in the region west of the Mississippi River. By 1828, Astor will control the fur trade in the United States, with his 1810 establishment of the Pacific Fur Company and

his 1811 establishment of the South West Fur Company, with Montreal merchants as partners.
Arts/Culture In Philadelphia, James N. Barker's *The Indian Princess, or La Belle Sauvage* is performed. This play, the first having an Indian theme to be staged in the United States, portrays incidents from the life of Pocahontas—a story that is to provide subject matter for many subsequent dramatic compositions during the course of the 19th century.

17 APRIL 1808
International Napoleon Bonaparte issues the Bayonne Decree, which orders the seizure of any American vessels entering the harbors of France, Italy and the Hanseatic League ports. Napoleon justifies this decree by accepting the American Embargo Acts as having jurisdiction, therefore making any United States vessels in European ports in violation of those acts, or making any such ships British vessels operating under false registration. In other words, Napoleon is supposedly supporting President Jefferson's Embargo Acts by confiscating American vessels violating the acts. This interpretation makes any suspect ships fair game. The French will enforce the Bayonne Decree strictly during the next two years, resulting in their seizure of some $10 million worth of American cargos and ships.

12 JULY 1808
Arts/Culture In St. Louis, *The Missouri Gazette* is published, thus becoming the first newspaper west of the Mississippi River.

16 JULY 1808
Commerce In St. Louis, western fur traders Manuel Lisa, William Clark of the Lewis and Clark Expedition, Pierre Chouteau and others incorporate the Missouri Fur Company in order to compete for the thriving fur trade in the newly opened up American interior. Manuel Lisa already runs a trading post at the junction of the Bighorn and Yellowstone Rivers.

OCTOBER 1808
International In an attempt to settle the *Chesapeake-Leopold* controversy following the incident of June 22, 1807, Great Britain dispatches George Rose to the United States as a special envoy empowered to discuss reparation payments. The controversy does not reach a satisfactory resolution, however, until November 12, 1811, because the British persist in demanding the withdrawal of President Jefferson's July 2, 1807 proclamation ordering the vacating of American territorial waters by British warships.

10 NOVEMBER 1808
Indian Affairs The Osage Indians, the most important southern Sioux tribe in the western territory, sign the Osage Treaty with the United States. According to this pact, the Osage cede all their lands in present-day Missouri and Arkansas north of the Arkansas River to the United States. This treaty will be ratified by Congress on April 28, 1810, and the Indians will move to

TESTING A UNION 1788-1865

a reservation in present-day Oklahoma along the Arkansas River.

7 DECEMBER 1808

National Following the precedent set by George Washington, Thomas Jefferson refuses to run for a third term as president. He supports as his successor James Madison, who was nominated for the office by a Democratic-Republican congressional caucus. Madison is opposed by two rebellious factions of the Democratic-Republican party. James Monroe is chosen a presidential candidate by the southern "Old Republicans," led by John Randolph and John Taylor. Monroe removes his name from the race. The Eastern Republicans, provoked by the disastrous economic results of the Embargo Acts on New England, name Vice–President George Clinton as their presidential candidate. The waning Federalist party puts forward the team of Charles Cotesworth Pinckney and Rufus King—the same candidates they ran unsuccessfully four years ago. The national election on December 7 is a victory for the Jeffersonian Democratic-Republicans. James Madison is elected president with 122 electoral votes to 47 for Federalist candidate Pinckney and 6 for George Clinton; however, Clinton is reelected vice–president with 113 electoral votes against 47 votes for Federalist candidate Rufus King. In the congressional race, the Federalist party gains seats in the House of Representatives, but it is unable to reach a majority. The widespread popular opposition to the Embargo Acts brings Federalists into power on the New England state level.

OTHER EVENTS OF 1808

Education In Baltimore, Maryland, the earliest legal periodical in the United States is established. Founded by professor of rhetoric at the University of Maryland John Elihu Hall, the journal is to continue publication until 1817.

Arts/Culture In New Orleans, the opera house, Theatre d'Orleans, is constructed at a total cost of $100,000. This edifice marks the ascendancy of New Orleans to the status of opera capital of the United States. In the same year, New York City makes a significant advance as an American art center with the establishment of the New York Academy of Fine Arts, whose European tendencies attract the patronage of New York's upper classes. Robert R. Livingston, American minister to France, serves as the Academy's first president.

9 JANUARY 1809

Commerce Congress passes the Enforcement Act, which is designed to halt smuggling activities and other illegal avoidance of the Embargo Acts. The Enforcement Act mandates the strict enforcement of the Embargo Acts, along with harsh penalties for evasion of the acts, including the authorized seizure of any goods suspected of being export cargos in violation of the Embargo Acts. In the New England states, already severely economically depressed as a result of the

acts, popular antagonism to the Embargo and Enforcements Acts leads to town meetings attacking the embargo as pro-French and anti-British.

1 FEBRUARY 1809

Commerce Former Secretary of War and State, Senator Timothy Pickering of Massachusetts calls for a New England convention to nullify the embargo. A Federalist and former member of the secessionist New England Essex Junto, Pickering has vigorously opposed the Democratic-Republican policies of the Jefferson administration and has supported the British cause.

20 FEBRUARY 1809

National In the case of *United States v. Peters,* also known as the Olmstead Case, Supreme Court Chief Justice John Marshall hands down a decision supporting the power of the national government over that of the state governments. Although the case involved the nullification of a federal court order by the state of Pennsylvania, the decision is also applicable to the proposals current in the New England states to try to rescind the Embargo Acts. The Embargo Act itself will be upheld later in 1809 in a Massachusetts federal district court by Federalist Judge John Davis. The appeal of this decision will never reach the Supreme Court.

23 FEBRUARY 1809

National Connecticut Governor John Trumbull delivers an address to the state legislature in which he maintains that the Embargo Acts constitute an unconstitutional exercise of power by the Federal Government, infringing on the rights of the states and on the civil liberties of the people. As the New England state legislatures concur in questioning the constitutionality of the Embargo Acts, the New England governors will refuse to supply militia in order to help enforce the embargo.

1 MARCH 1809

Commerce Faced with unrelenting widespread opposition to the Embargo Acts, President Jefferson signs the Non-Intercourse Act, which repeals the Embargo Acts, effective March 15. The act reopens all overseas commerce to American shipping, except that of France and Great Britain. But should either France or Great Britain, or both, halt their interference with neutral shipping, then trade may resume with these nations also, upon presidential proclamation.

Westward Movement Congress establishes the Territory of Illinois, which has been formed from the western portion of the Indiana Territory. The Illinois Territory includes the present-day states of Illinois, Wisconsin and eastern Minnesota.

4 MARCH 1809

National In Washington, James Madison is inaugurated as the fourth president of the United States, and George Clinton is again inaugurated as vice–president. President Madison's cabinet includes Robert Smith as

Secretary of State, Albert Gallatin as Secretary of the Treasury, William Eustis as Secretary of War, Paul Hamilton as Secretary of the Navy, Gideon Granger as Postmaster General, and C.A. Rodney as Attorney General. Thomas Jefferson retires to private life at Monticello, his home near Charlottesville, Virginia. Jefferson's financial estate has been reduced considerably by his 44 years of public service.

19 APRIL 1809

Commerce President Madison issues a proclamation reinstituting trade with Great Britain, thus effectively suspending the Non-Intercourse Act. Madison's move is based on the assurances of the British minister to the United States David M. Erskine who informs Secretary of State Robert Smith that the British orders in council relating to American shipping will be revoked on June 10, 1809. Unfortunately, Erskine has no authority to make any such assurances.

22 MAY 1809

National In Washington, the 11th Congress convenes for its first session, with 28 Democratic-Republicans and 6 Federalists in the Senate, and 94 Democratic-Republicans to 48 Federalists in the House of Representatives. Although the party lines of the Senate have remained unaffected by the 1808 election, the Federalists have doubled their numbers in the House, thanks to widespread popular opposition to the Embargo Acts.

30 MAY 1809

International In London, British foreign secretary George Canning rescinds the Erskine Agreement of April 19 with the United States and orders the return of Erskine to England. This action is to lead, in turn, to the August reinstatement of the Non-Intercourse Act against Great Britain by President Madison.

JUNE 1809

Transportation The *Phoenix*, a seagoing steamboat, completes the first ocean voyage made by a steam-powered vessel. Designed by John Stevens, the *Phoenix* travels from Hoboken, New Jersey, to the sea, and around southern New Jersey to the Delaware River near Philadelphia. The *Phoenix* is to travel successfully on the Delaware River for six years. One of America's most successful inventors, Stevens was an ardent advocate of American patent law. The inventor of a screw propeller in 1802, he later went on to develop the railroad in New Jersey, to invent the Stevens plow, and to found the Stevens Institute of Technology.

27 JUNE 1809

International President Madison appoints John Quincy Adams the United States minister to Russia.

2 JULY 1809

Indian Affairs The remarkable warrior, statesman and chief of the Shawnee Indians, Tecumseh, along with his brother The Prophet, starts a campaign to

---

JAMES MADISON, 1751-1836

Of that group of great men who forged the American dream on paper and then proceeded to forge it in reality, James Madison was the last to become president. He held that office for eight difficult and ultimately triumphant years, but his countrymen would remember him first as "Father of the Constitution." Madison was born in Port Conway, Virginia, on March 16, 1751, and studied at the College of New Jersey (later Princeton), graduating in 1771. There he read the philosophers of the European Enlightenment who were later to help form his ideas. He entered political life in Virginia, where in the state convention of 1776 he voted for independence and helped write a new state constitution. After desk service during the first part of the Revolution, Madison was elected to the Continental Congress; in his years there his ideas concerning government took shape, his central concept being the *separation of powers,* creating a system of checks and balances within a government.

Madison returned to Virginia to serve in the legislature. Dissatisfied with the weak authority of the Articles of Confederation, he insisted on the need of a new constitution. When the Convention met in 1787 it was his theories that were most central to the deliberations, and which were largely embodied in the final document. As a member of the first House of Representatives he added a vital element to the Constitution by sponsoring the Bill of Rights during Washington's Presidency. From his perspective in the House, Madison began to dislike the direction the Federalists were taking. Madison and Jefferson became partners in forming an opposition party, soon to be called the Republicans (and later Democrats). Madison left Congress in some disgust in 1797, returning to his estate, Montpelier, and the joys of his marriage to the delightful Dolley.

Distressed by Adams' signing of the Alien and Sedition Acts, Madison, as a member of the Virginia legislature, wrote a resolution that called for states' rights in rejecting federal law deemed unconstitutional. He worked actively for the campaign of Jefferson in 1800 and became Jefferson's secretary of state. Madison was elected President in 1808 with the Republican party already showing divisive strains over the problems with Britain, which had been violating American neutrality on the sea for some years. As a believer in limited government, Madison was reluctant to build up the national army and navy, but the young "war hawks" of his party in Congress forced his hand: war was declared on Britain in 1812. For some time there was furious resistance to the war at home and serious setbacks in the fighting—the most humiliating point came in 1814, when the government fled and British troops burned the Capital. But then the tide turned; in October of the same year Britain gave up and the Treaty of Ghent was signed on Christmas Eve, 1814.

Now perceived as the victorious leader of the country's first war, Madison had a most pleasant end to his second term. The new nation had survived serious problems from within and had proved its mettle in war; the country looked as if it might endure after all. Satisfied by the election of his friend James Monroe, Madison left office in 1817 and settled into a long retirement as an active elder statesman in Virginia. He died in 1836.

---

establish a defensive confederacy of Indian tribes to resist the westward progress of American settlers, who in the past seven years have acquired over 30 million acres of Indian lands north of the Ohio River. The British government of Canada reportedly backs the efforts of Tecumseh.

9 AUGUST 1809
Commerce Because of the British annulment of the Erskine agreement of April 19, 1809, President Madison reinstates the Non-Intercourse Act of March 1, again banning all American trade with England and France as long as those nations continue to harass neutral shipping.

30 SEPTEMBER 1809
Indian Affairs The governor of the Indiana Territory, William Henry Harrison, signs the Treaty of Fort Wayne with the Indians of the southern Indiana region. In this pact, the Indians cede three additional tracts of land along the Wabash River to the United States.

OTHER EVENTS OF 1809
Arts/Culture Under the pseudonym of Diedrick Knickerbocker, Washington Irving publishes his *History of New York,* a humorous account of 17th and 18th century New Amsterdam. This best-selling book is to bring Irving American and European acclaim as a 'leading man of letters in the United States.
Industry The Boston Crown Glass Company incorporates. The act of incorporation frees the business from taxes and grants its employees a waiver from military service. The company has been in operation since 1792 when it produced the first successful American window glass of such high quality that it was deemed superior to European imports.

16 MARCH 1810
Regional Supreme Court Chief Justice John Marshall hands down a decision in the case of *Fletcher v. Peck,* involving the claims arising from the Georgia Yazoo land fraud. The questionable 1795 sale of western Georgia lands to real estate speculators by corrupt legislators had been rescinded by the subsequent state legislature, resulting in a number of land claim cases. The unanimous opinion of the Supreme Court is that the original sale must be regarded as valid, under the law of contracts. This is the first decision in which the Supreme Court nullifies a state law on the basis of its unconstitutionality. This decision allows the original purchasers of the Yazoo lands to receive some $4 million from the Federal Government, to which Georgia had ceded the lands in question in 1802.

23 MARCH 1810
International In France, Napoleon Bonaparte signs the Rambouillet Decree which mandates the seizure, confiscation and sale of any American ships in French ports. The Rambouillet Decree, published on May 14, is to be retroactive to May 20, 1809.

1 MAY 1810
Commerce With the expiration of the Non-Intercourse Act pending, Congress passes Macon's Bill No. 2, which authorizes President Madison to reopen trade with Great Britain and France, but stipulates that he may restore non-intercourse with either nation, if the one should revoke its policy of interfering with American shipping before March 3, 1811 and the other nation does not follow suit within three months. The bill also forbids French and British warcraft from entering American territorial waters. In Congress, Federalists oppose the passage of the bill. And the French are to regard its passage as favoring Great Britain.

23 JUNE 1810
Commerce Fur–trading magnate John Jacob Astor founds the Pacific Fur Company in order to extend his influence over the fur resources of the Pacific Northwest. In April 1811, the Pacific Fur Company will found the trading post and village of Astoria at the mouth of the Oregon River, in order to tranship furs to Canton, China. During the War of 1812, Astor will lose his key Astoria post.

12 JULY 1810
Labor In New York City, the trial of the members of Journeymen Cordwainers (shoemakers) begins. The cordwainers are accused and convicted of illegal conspiracy for having used a strike to enforce their demands for a higher salary. Each members is fined $1 plus costs. The setback to early trade unionism has a precedent in the 1806 trial of Philadelphia cordwainers, who were also found guilty of conspiracy for strike activities. In both cases, the court interpreted labor strikes as conspiracies, holding that an act lawful in itself can be considered illegal if perpetrated through a conspiracy. This interpretation of strikes as conspiracies will not be overturned until an 1842 Massachusetts Supreme Court decision.

5 AUGUST 1810
International When Napoleon Bonaparte hears of Macon's Bill No. 2 of May 1, he instructs French foreign minister Duc de Cadone to inform the United States that after November 1 France will rescind its Berlin and Milan Decrees if the United States will declare non-intercourse against Great Britain, unless the British have already withdrawn their orders in council. When the Duc de Cadone conveys Napoleon's message to American minister John Armstrong, he changes the wording to imply that the Berlin and Milan Decrees have already been cancelled. On the same day, in contradiction to his message to the Americans, Napoleon deceptively signs the Decree Trianon, which orders the seizure of all American ships that anchored in French ports between May 30, 1809 and May 1, 1810.

26 SEPTEMBER 1810
International American settlers living in the western portion of Spanish West Florida, the possession of which has been in dispute since the Louisiana Purchase, rise up in rebellion against their Spanish rulers, seizing the fort at Baton Rouge and declaring the re-

gion between New Orleans and the Pearl River to be the Republic of West Florida, seeking annexation to the United States.

1 OCTOBER 1810
Agriculture In Pittsfield, Massachusetts, the Berkshire Cattle Show, organized by Elkanah Watson, opens. From this will develop the first permanent agricultural association in the United States and the American tradition of country fairs.

27 OCTOBER 1810
International President Madison announces the United States annexation and military occupation of the western region of Spanish West Florida. The annexed area, between the Mississippi River and the Perdido River, is declared part of the Territory of Orleans, which will become the state of Louisiana in 1812.

2 NOVEMBER 1810
International Believing that the Berlin and Milan Decrees, which legalize French interference with neutral shipping, have actually been rescinded by Napoleon Bonaparte as stated in the Cadone letter of August 5, President Madison releases a proclamation reinstating American trade with France and forbidding American trade with Great Britain, effective February 2, 1811, if the British do not withdraw their orders in council within three months. But Madison has been misled by the French, and the French continue to harass American shipping. The Americans will remain unaware of this deception until September 1811, and meanwhile this American move results in an intensification of hostilities between the United States and Great Britain.

OTHER EVENTS OF 1810
Population In the third national census, the United States population is recorded at 7,239,881, marking a gain of nearly 2 million inhabitants, or 36.4 percent since 1800. Of this total, 1,378,110 Americans are blacks and all but 186,746 of those are slaves. With the 1803 admission of Ohio, the number of states in the Union has reached 17.

Transportation New Yorker Cornelius Vanderbilt begins his career as a shipping magnate with the initiation of regular ferry service between Staten Island and Manhattan. Vanderbilt will go on to control ferry lines between New York and New Jersey, across Long Island Sound, and on the Hudson River. By mid-century he will establish a bimonthly shipping route between New York and San Francisco by way of a connecting land route across Nicaragua, and a regular passenger and freight service between America and Europe. At the same time, he will build his railroad holdings into an empire.

Also in 1810, aeronauts A.R. Hawley and Augustus Post will complete an 1173-mile balloon flight from St. Louis to Canada.

Arts/Culture In Boston, Johann Christian Gottlieb Graupner founds the Boston Philharmonic Society, the first regular orchestra in the United States. The orchestra will play its last performance in 1824 at Boston's Pantheon. In 1799, Graupner had marked another American first when during the Boston performance of the play *Oroonoko* he made up in blackface, thus presenting one of the earliest known performances of black minstrelsy.

15 JANUARY 1811
International In a secret session, Congress adopts a resolution authorizing the United States to extend its sovereignty over Spanish East Florida if the inhabitants agree to the annexation, or if a foreign power tries to occupy the territory.

2 FEBRUARY 1811
Settling In the California region, a group of Russian settlers lands at Bodega Bay, north of San Francisco, in order to establish Fort Ross which will become the center of an agricultural colony and a trading post for sea otter furs. In 1841, John Augustus Sutter will purchase Fort Ross.

20 FEBRUARY 1811
Finance Congress votes against renewing the charter of the first Bank of the United States, due to expire on March 4. Secretary of the Treasury Albert Gallatin has strongly endorsed renewal of the charter, but he faces strong foes in the "Old Republicans" faction who regard the bank as an unconstitutional Federalist imposition; in those who find the fact that two-thirds of the bank stock is owned by British citizens a dangerous situation; and in those who advocate the development of state-chartered banks. The intense congressional debate over this issue ends in a tie vote in the Senate, and the vote of Vice–President Clinton against the charter settles the matter. The failure to renew the bank charter will prove an unwise move, as the War of 1812 will require the kind of financing facilitated by the Bank of the United States.

2 MARCH 1811
International Congress supports the reinstatement of the non-intercourse policy against Great Britain, as spelled out in the Non-Intercourse Act of March 1, 1809. The Madison administration makes this move based on deceptive communications from the French relaying the information that Napoleon has rescinded his Berlin and Milan Decrees, which in fact he has not done. Over a year will pass before Great Britain rescinds her orders in council relating to neutral shipping. Meanwhile, the reinstatement of the American non-intercourse provokes the British to renew their blockade of New York and to follow an even harsher policy of impressing American seamen.

4 MARCH 1811
Finance The Bank of the United States is dissolved.

2 APRIL 1811
National James Monroe is named Secretary of State.

TESTING A UNION 1788-1865

12 APRIL 1811

Settling Under the sponsorship of John Jacob Astor, a group of colonists from New York led by Captain Thorn establishes the first permanent American settlement in the Pacific Northwest—Fort Astoria at the mouth of the Columbia River. After traveling around Cape Horn on the ship *Tonquin,* the group had landed at Cape Disappointment, Washington.

1 MAY 1811

International Off Sandy Hook, New York, the British 38-gun frigate *Guerrière* stops the American brig *Spitfire,* and seizes a native-born American seaman. This impressment arouses a public outcry.

16 MAY 1811

International In the wake of the *Guerriere-Spitfire* incident of May 1, Captain John Rodgers of the 44-gun American frigate *President* has been ordered to protect American shipping off New York harbor. The *President* chases and engages a vessel thought to be the British frigate *Guerriere,* but which turns out to be the British 20-gun corvette *Little Belt.* The *Little Belt* is disabled, with nine seamen killed and 23 wounded.

MAY 1811

International American minister to Great Britain William Pinkney sets sail for the United States, leaving a diplomatic impasse between England and America.

31 JULY 1811

Indian Affairs Fearful of the Indian confederacy being formed by Shawnee chief Tecumseh and his brother The Prophet, the frontier settlers of Vincennes in the Indiana Territory issue a call for the destruction of the main Indian village on the Tippecanoe River.

11 SEPTEMBER 1811

Transportation In Pittsburgh, Pennsylvania, the first American inland steamboat the *New Orleans* sets sail down the Ohio River. After an eventful four-month journey down the Mississippi River, the vessel reaches New Orleans. This run initiates regular riverboat service on the Mississippi River between New Orleans and Natchez. The fare for the downstream trip is $18, and for the upstream trip it is $25.

19 SEPTEMBER 1811

International The new United States minister to France, Joel Barlow, arrives in Paris to clarify the issue of the French nullification of the Berlin and Milan Decrees relating to American commercial shipping. French foreign minister Duc de Bassano will show Barlow the Decree of St. Cloud, apparently signed by Napoleon Bonaparte on April 28, 1811, rescinding the Berlin and Milan Decrees effective November 1, 1810. As it turns out, the Decree of St. Cloud has never been published, nor has it been officially dispatched to the American government, thus giving it no diplomatic import.

26 SEPTEMBER 1811

Indian Affairs In the Indiana Territory, Governor William Henry Harrison leads a 1000-man military force out of Vincennes, headed for the Indian capital at the junction of the Tippecanoe and Wabash Rivers. The goal of the expedition is to eradicate the settlement and to thwart the confederacy plans of Shawnee chief Tecumseh, who has traveled to the Southwest to seek allies among the Creek Indian tribes. The expeditionary group will erect Fort Harrison 65 miles north of the Vincennes in late October.

1 NOVEMBER 1811

International In the matter of the *Little Belt* affair of May 16, British minister to the United States Augustus John Foster is notified by the American Government that the United States is prepared to reach a friendly agreement on the incident, provided that Great Britain rescinds her orders in council affecting American commercial shipping. The British will not accept the American offer of compensation, but they will present a counter offer to settle the *Chesapeake* incident of June 22, 1807.

4 NOVEMBER 1811

National In Washington, the 12th Congress convenes. The midterm elections of 1810 have drastically altered the political alignment of both houses. The prevalent popular nationalism and pro-war sentiment have swept the "War Hawks" into office, replacing the old generation of appeasers and peace-seekers. Among the new Democratic-Republicans who advocate expansionism and nationalism are South Carolina's John C. Calhoun, William Lowndes, and Langdon Cheves; New York's Peter B. Porter; Kentucky's Richard M. Johnson and Henry Clay; and Tennessee's Felix Grundy and John Sevier. Although the War Hawks are in a numerical minority, they achieve great influence in the House of Representatives. Henry Clay is elected Speaker of the House; Calhoun, Grundy and Porter gain control of the foreign relations committee; and Cheves is chosen chairman of the naval committee. The northwestern War Hawks will call for the conquest of Canada, while the Southerners call for the annexation of all of Florida.

5 NOVEMBER 1811

National In his message to Congress, President Madison calls for increased preparations for the national defense in face of the continued British and French harassment of American commercial shipping.

7 NOVEMBER 1811

Indian Affairs In the Indiana Territory, the Indians led by The Prophet carry out a successful surprise attack on the 1000-man force led by Governor William Henry Harrison. In the hard–fought Battle of Tippecanoe, Harrison's men are able to repulse the Indians despite heavy losses. After razing the Indian village, Harrison's troops withdraw southward to Fort Harrison. Despite the indecisive aftermath of the battle, the frontier settlers acclaim it as a great victory over the menacing Indians, adding to the influence of the congressional War Hawks. The British in Canada withdraw their support of Tecumseh and The Prophet. Nevertheless, anti–British sentiment on the frontier has been fueled with bellicose calls to expel the British from Canada.

12 NOVEMBER 1811
International Secretary of State James Monroe accepts the offer of the British to settle the *Chesapeake* incident of June 22, 1807.

20 NOVEMBER 1811
Transportation The construction of the Cumberland Road begins. Also known as the Old National Road, this paved highway will connect Cumberland, Maryland with Wheeling (West Virginia) on the Ohio River. The road will be completed to Wheeling in 1818, and subsequent extensions will carry it first to Columbus, Ohio, and finally to Vandalia, Illinois, in 1840. The Cumberland Road will be the main route along which settlers will travel to colonize the Far West.

OTHER EVENTS OF 1811
International British King George III is declared insane, leading to the regency of his son, George IV.

11 FEBRUARY 1812
Regional In Boston, Governor Elbridge Gerry signs a Massachusetts law redistricting Essex County in time for the state senatorial election in order to ensure a Jeffersonian Democratic-Republican majority in the state legislature. The rearrangement of the Essex County voting districts without regard for geography results in an odd salamander-like shape that suggests to a contemporary cartoonist the word "gerrymander." This procedure will be adopted by other partisan legislatures from time to time.

14 MARCH 1812
National Congress authorizes a bond issue of $11 million in order to provide financing for the defensive military preparations requested by President Madison in his November 5, 1811 message to Congress. This is the first of six such war bond issues to take place by 1815. The lack of a national bank becomes a severe disadvantage when the mechanics and costs of financing the war become apparent.

1 APRIL 1812
Commerce President Madison recommends to Congress a 60-day embargo. The War Hawks faction of the Democratic-Republican party regards this embargo as the "prelude to armed conflict."

4 APRIL 1812
Commerce The embargo becomes law, altered by moderate congressional Democratic-Republicans who still hope to resolve America's problems with Great Britain peacefully. The embargo is to be effective for 90 instead of the 60 days advocated by the War Hawks.

10 APRIL 1812
National Congress empowers President Madison to call up 100,000 militia from the states and territories for six months' service.

International The British Foreign Office notifies the United States that the British orders in council affecting American commercial shipping remain in effect, since the French have not actually rescinded their Berlin and Milan Decrees affecting neutral shipping.

APRIL 1812
Indian Affairs In the northwest region, the peace between the Indians and settlers following the Battle of Tippecanoe ends, as the Indians begin another series of raids on the frontier settlements, while Tecumseh himself remains on the defensive. The regional pro-war faction realizes that a war with Great Britain will inevitably lead to open war with the Indians.

20 APRIL 1812
National Vice President George Clinton dies.

30 APRIL 1812
Regional The Territory of Orleans enters the Union as the state of Louisiana, bringing the total number of states to 18 and adding 75,000 to the population of the United States. New Orleans, the state capital, is America's fifth most populous city.

14 MAY 1812
Regional Congress formally incorporates Spanish West Florida, until recently the Republic of West Florida, into the Mississippi Territory. The area comprises the land south of the 31st parallel between the Mississippi and Perdido Rivers.

18 MAY 1812
National In a congressional caucus of southern Democratic-Republicans, President James Madison is nominated for reelection and John Langdon is nominated as vice presidential candidate. When Langdon refuses the nomination, Elbridge Gerry will be nominated for the vice presidential post on June 8.

29 MAY 1812
National In Albany, New York, a Democratic-Republican caucus of New York legislators, supported by the Federalists, nominates Lieutenant Governor De Witt Clinton as the anti-war fusion candidate for president of the United States.

1 JUNE 1812
War of 1812 Motivated by the apparently unyielding position of Great Britain on neutral shipping—specifically the impressment of seamen, interference with trade, and the blockade of American ports—as well as by British encouragement of Indian hostilities, President Madison sends a message to Congress asking for a declaration of war against Great Britain.

3 JUNE 1812
War of 1812 Concluding that war is inevitable, the

TESTING A UNION 1788-1865

British Governor General of Canada Sir George Prevost calls Shawnee Indian chief Tecumseh to a meeting at Amherstburg in present-day Ontario, across from Detroit.

4 JUNE 1812
War of 1812 The House of Representatives, in a vote of 79 to 49, supports President Madison's declaration of war on Great Britain.
Regional The original Louisiana Territory is renamed the Missouri Territory, since the former Territory of Orleans now is named the state of Louisiana. The Missouri Territory includes all of the original Louisiana Purchase area except for the state of Louisiana.

16 JUNE 1812
International In London, British Prime Minister Lord Castlereagh proclaims the suspension of the British orders in council affecting neutral shipping, to be effective June 23. This move is motivated by worsening economic conditions in Britain, due largely to the American policy of non-intercourse, and the effectiveness of Napoleon Bonaparte's continental system.

18 JUNE 1812
War of 1812 Unaware of the major concession made by Great Britain in suspending its orders in council affecting neutral shipping, the United States Senate votes 19 to 13 in favor of war with England, with the western and southern states in the majority. Except for Vermont, the New England states and other maritime and commercial states such as New York, New Jersey and Delaware vote for peace. The opponents to the war are to call it "Mr. Madison's War."

19 JUNE 1812
War of 1812 President Madison officially proclaims the United States to be in a state of war with Great Britain.

23 JUNE 1812
War of 1812 Unaware of the United States declaration of war, Great Britain officially suspends the orders in council affecting neutral shipping.

26 JUNE 1812
War of 1812 In a letter to American London envoy Jonathan Russell, President Madison instructs him to negotiate an armistice based on the condition of the suspension of the British orders in council affecting neutral shipping and of an end to the British policy of impressing American seamen.

In Massachusetts, Governor Caleb Strong declares a public statewide fast in order to protest the war, while the state legislature issues a statement proclaiming the war to be against the public interest and stating that the state will provide military forces only for defensive purposes.

30 JUNE 1812
War of 1812 Congress authorizes an issue of $5 million in war bonds, in order to help finance the conflict.

1 JULY 1812
War of 1812 In order to raise additional funds for the war, Congress sets increased tariffs on import items.

2 JULY 1812
War of 1812 In Connecticut, Governor John Cotton Smith refuses to provide militia forces to the Federal Government. Massachusetts will take the same step on August 5. The American side in the War of 1812 is at a severe disadvantage because of its inexperienced and poorly equipped army, and because of the vigorous opposition of the New England states to the war.

17 JULY 1812
War of 1812 In the western campaign against Canada led by American General William Hull, the United States port of Michilimackinac surrenders to the British without a shot fired, encouraging the Indians led by Tecumseh to ally themselves to the British. This Indian move alarms General Hull who has led a 2200-man force across the Detroit River to occupy Sandwich.

19 JULY 1812
War of 1812 The British attack the American naval base at Sacketts Harbor, New York, on Lake Ontario, but they are driven back by the artillery of the ship *Oneida*, under the command of Lieutenant Melancthon T. Woolsey.

8 AUGUST 1812
War of 1812 In the western campaign against Canada, General William Hull withdraws his 2200-man force from Canada, retreating to Detroit. Hull feels his line of communication with Ohio is threatened by the new alliance of the Indians, under Tecumseh, with the British, and he fears the strength of British General Isaac Brock's 2000-man Canadian army.

13 AUGUST 1812
War of 1812 In the naval phase of the war, the British man of war *Alert* is captured by American Captain David Porter, on the vessel *Essex*.

15 AUGUST 1812
War of 1812 At the site of present-day Chicago, Indians massacre the American garrison as it evacuates Fort Dearborn. The fort is burned the following day.

16 AUGUST 1812
War of 1812 Fearing an Indian massacre of civilian settlers, American General William Hull surrenders Detroit to General Isaac Brock without a shot fired. This capitulation gives the British power over the Lake Erie-Lake Michigan region. On March 26, 1814 General Hull will be found guilty of cowardice and neglect of duty by a court martial, but his death

penalty will be commuted because of his fine Revolutionary War record.

17 AUGUST 1812

National In New York City, the Federalist party holds a secret 11–state convention that decides to support the candidacy of De Witt Clinton for president. Clinton was also the May 29 choice of the New York state Democratic-Republican caucus.

19 AUGUST 1812

War of 1812 In the Atlantic off Nova Scotia, Captain Isaac Hull, commanding the 44-gun frigate U.S.S. *Constitution,* engages the British 38-gun frigate *Guerrière* in a half-hour naval battle. The *Guerrière* is decisively defeated and so disabled that the vessel must be blown up. This victory, after the fall of Detroit, serves to raise the low American morale.

23 AUGUST 1812

War of 1812 Following his capture of Detroit, British General Isaac Brock reaches Fort George at the mouth of the Niagara River, facing the American forces commanded by General Stephen Van Rensselaer at Fort Niagara across the river.

29 AUGUST 1812

War of 1812 British Prime Minister Lord Castlereagh rejects the peace proposals of American envoy Jonathan Russell, who declares that the United States is willing to negotiate an armistice if the British will cease their impressment policy and naval blockades, and will agree to indemnities for past incidents.

17 SEPTEMBER 1812

War of 1812 William Henry Harrison is commissioned brigadier general and given command of the American northwest army, with orders to retake Detroit.

21 SEPTEMBER 1812

International In order to strengthen the allied British and Russian effort against Napoleon, Czar Alexander I of Russia offers to mediate in the war between Great Britain and the United States.

30 SEPTEMBER 1812

War of 1812 From Halifax, Nova Scotia, British Admiral Sir John Borlase Warren conveys an offer of armistice and negotiation to the American government. This peace–feeler will have no result, although on October 27, Secretary of State James Monroe will respond to Warren that the United States will agree to an armistice and negotiations if the British will suspend the impressment of American seamen.

4 OCTOBER 1812

War of 1812 At Ogdensburg, New York, American forces defeat the British.

9 OCTOBER 1812

War of 1812 On Lake Erie, American Lieutenant

Jesse Duncan Elliott surprises and captures two British vessels, the *Detroit* and the *Caledonia.*

13 OCTOBER 1812

War of 1812 American General Stephen Van Rensselaer leads his 600-man force across the Niagara River to capture Queenston Heights, Ontario. British General Isaac Brock is killed in the action, but the Americans are defeated by the 1000-man British force when the New York state militia refuses to come to Rensselaer's aid on the grounds that their commission does not require them to proceed beyond the boundaries of the state.

17 OCTOBER 1812

War of 1812 In a naval encounter 600 miles off the Virginia coast, American Captain Jacob Jones' 18-gun sloop of war *Wasp* defeats the British 18-gun brig *Frolic,* with only 10 casualties to the 90 suffered by the British.

25 OCTOBER 1812

War of 1812 Off the Madeira Islands, Captain Stephen Decatur's 44-gun frigate *United States* captures the British 38-gun frigate *Macedonian* and tows this prize intact into the harbor of New London, Connecticut.

19 NOVEMBER 1812

War of 1812 At Plattsburg, New York, American General Henry Dearborn, in command of the largest single American force, leads his army against Montreal. Dearborn's militia forces refuse to cross the Canadian border, and he is forced to turn back.

2 DECEMBER 1812

National In the presidential election, James Madison is reelected to a second term as president, defeating New York's antiwar candidate De Witt Clinton by 128 to 89 electoral votes. Elbridge Gerry is chosen vice–president, defeating his Federalist opponent Jared Ingersoll by 131 to 86 votes. But the Federalists double their strength in Congress, following a sweeping victory in the Northeast.

24 DECEMBER 1812

International In Poland, The United States minister to France, Joel Barlow, dies, ending the American negotiations with Napoleon.

26 DECEMBER 1812

War of 1812 The British Admiralty officially announces a naval blockade of Chesapeake and Delaware Bays. The blockade will effectively bar all commercial vessels from the mid-Atlantic coastal waters. During the course of the blockade, British Rear Admiral Sir George Cockburn will conduct a series of raids along the upper Chesapeake Bay coastline.

29 DECEMBER 1812

War of 1812 In a naval engagement off the Brazilian coast, American Captain William Bambridge's *Con-*

stitution destroys the British 38-gun frigate *Java.* The performance of the *Constitution* during this vicious fight gains for her the nickname *"Old Ironsides."*

13 JANUARY 1813
National John Armstrong is named President Madison's Secretary of War, replacing William Eustis. Armstrong was the author of the 1783 Newburgh Addresses, and later was Jefferson's minister to France.

22 JANUARY 1813
War of 1812 In the Battle of Raisin River, at Frenchtown at the western end of Lake Erie, American General James Winchester's Kentucky militia force is decisively defeated by a combined British and Indian force under Colonel Henry A. Procter. Some 500 Americans are taken prisoner and 400 others are killed in the battle or massacred by the Indians after Procter departs.

20 FEBRUARY 1813
Regional New Hampshire-born Major General Lewis Cass is appointed governor of the Michigan Territory, a post he will fill for 19 years.

24 FEBRUARY 1813
War of 1812 In a naval engagement off the coast of 'Guiana, South America, the American 18-gun sloop *Hornet,* under the command of Captain James Lawrence, sinks the 20-gun British sloop *Peacock.*

4 MARCH 1813
National James Madison is inaugurated for his second term as president of the United States and Elbridge Gerry is inducted as vice–president. In Madison's cabinet are James Monroe as Secretary of State, Albert Gallatin as Secretary of the Treasury, John Armstrong as Secretary of War, William Jones as Secretary of the Navy, Gideon Granger as Postmaster General, and William Pinkney as Attorney General.

8 MARCH 1813
International President Madison names Secretary of the Treasury Albert Gallatin and Delaware Senator James A. Bayard as special peace commissioners to join American minister to Russia John Quincy Adams in St. Petersburg at the invitation of Czar Alexander I, who has offered to mediate between Great Britain and the United States in the War of 1812. Bayard and Gallatin will arrive in St. Petersburg on July 21.

11 MARCH 1813
War of 1812 President Madison formally accepts the offer of Czar Alexander to mediate between Great Britain and the United States. The British, however, reject the Czar's offer.

27 MARCH 1813
War of 1812 Captain Oliver Hazard Perry arrives in Presque Isle (Michigan), where he will supervise the construction of a flotilla of two brigs, a schooner and three gunboats from materials transported over land

and inland waterway from Philadelphia, by way of Pittsburgh, in preparation for the naval battle for Lake Erie.

15 APRIL 1813
War of 1812 American forces led by General James Wilkinson capture the Spanish fort at Mobile being used by the British. The Americans will occupy the Mobile region of West Florida between the Pearl and Perdido Rivers.

27 APRIL 1813
War of 1812 From Sackett's Harbor, New York, a combined American military and naval force headed by General Henry Dearborn and Captain Isaac Chauncey, seeking to obtain control of Lake Ontario, raids and captures the 600-man British garrison at York (present-day Toronto). There the Americans set fire to the government buildings in what is the capital of Upper Canada. In addition, one British ship is destroyed, another is captured, but 320 Americans, including General Zebulon Pike, are killed or wounded in the explosion of a powder magazine. This incendiary destruction will serve as a motivation for the British to burn Washington in 1814.

1-9 MAY 1813
War of 1812 In northwestern Ohio, Shawnee Indian chief Tecumseh and the British lay siege to the American post of Fort Meigs, which is successfully defended by General William Henry Harrison.

24 MAY 1813
National In Washington, the 13th Congress convenes. Among the freshmen congressmen is Daniel Webster of New Hampshire. In the Senate are 27 Democratic-Republicans to 9 Federalists, and in the House of Representatives are 112 Democratic-Republicans to 68 Federalists. As a result of the most recent national census, 36 new seats have been added to the House. Of these new representatives, 32 are Federalists.

26 MAY 1813
War of 1812 The British extend their naval blockade of the Chesapeake and Delaware Bays southward to the mouth of the Mississippi River. From their naval station on Chesapeake Bay, the British also extend their blockade to the ports of New York, Charleston, Port Royal and Savannah. In addition, they conduct raids and bombardments on coastal settlements along the southern Atlantic Coast.

27 MAY 1813
War of 1812 In an American attack on Fort George, near the mouth of the Niagara River, Lieutenant Colonel Winfield Scott ·with a 4000-man force captures the 1600-man British garrison under General John Vincent. The British withdraw from Lake Erie. This action permits American Captain Oliver Hazard Perry to surreptitiously remove five naval vessels from the Black Rock shipyard and to take them to Presque Isle

SEPTEMBER 18, 1813

in order to reinforce the flotilla under construction.

28-29 MAY 1813
War of 1812 In the Battle of Sackett's Harbor near the mouth of Lake Ontario, American General Jacob J. Brown successfully turns back a British attack force led by Sir George Prevost, governor general of Canada.

1 JUNE 1813
War of 1812 In a naval battle 30 miles off Boston Harbor, the American 38-gun frigate *Chesapeake,* with an inexperienced and mutinous crew commanded by Captain James Lawrence, is captured by the British 52-gun frigate *Shannon* commanded by Captain P.V.B. Broke. The mortally wounded Captain Lawrence exhorts his crew with the words, "Don't give up the ship"—to become the rallying cry of the American Navy. The *Chesapeake* will be towed into Halifax as a prize. The capture of the *Chesapeake* is a blow to American morale.

6 JUNE 1813
War of 1812 Near Hamilton, Ontario, at Stoney Creek, the retreating British General John Vincent commands his 700-man force in an attack on the 2000-man pursuing American force. The British capture two American generals, William H. Winder and John Chandler, and force the Americans to fall back to Fort George. The Americans will be forced to abandon the recently won Lake Erie on June 9.

6 JULY 1813
War of 1812 In a reorganization of the American military command, General Henry Dearborn is replaced as commander of the northeastern frontier forces by General James Wilkinson. In a related move, General Wade Hampton has been put in charge of the Lake Champlain force on July 3.

2 AUGUST 1813
War of 1812 In Ohio, the British attack on Fort Stephenson on the Sandusky River is turned back by a successful defense led by Major George Croghan.

4 AUGUST 1813
War of 1812 On Lake Erie, Captain Oliver Hazard Perry floats the heavy ships of his newly constructed American flotilla into deep waters off the island of Put-in-Bay, while the British blockading squadron is in another part of the lake.

14 AUGUST 1813
War of 1812 In a naval engagement off the coast of Great Britain, the British 21-gun brig *Pelican* captures the American 20-gun sloop *Argus,* under the command of Captain W. H. Allen. In its privateering career, the *Argus* has captured 27 British merchant vessels.

30 AUGUST 1813
Indian Affairs In the opening engagement of the

Commodore Perry at the Battle of Lake Erie.

Creek War near Mobile, the Mississippi Valley Creek Indians led by William Weatherford, who is also known as Chief Red Eagle, attack Fort Mims, massacring nearly half of the 550 people in the fort and burning many others to death. The news of this incident motivates Andrew Jackson, major general of the Tennessee militia, to call up a 2000-man volunteer army.

5 SEPTEMBER 1813
War of 1812 At Sackett's Harbor on Lake Ontario, Secretary of War John Armstrong arrives to coordinate a combined attack on Montreal led by General James Wilkinson and General Wade Hampton.

10 SEPTEMBER 1813
War of 1812 In the three-hour bloody naval Battle of Lake Erie, American Captain Oliver Hazard Perry leads his makeshift 10-vessel fleet to victory over the 6-vessel British squadron commanded by Captain Robert H. Barclay. Perry sends to General William Henry Harrison the immortal message, "We have met the enemy and they are ours." This decisive battle gives the United States control over Lake Erie.

18 SEPTEMBER 1813
War of 1812 With the loss of British supremacy over Lake Erie, British General Henry A. Procter is forced to evacuate Detroit, over the protests of Tecumseh. The British also leave Malden, with the

197

TESTING A UNION 1788-1865

American forces of General William Henry Harrison in hot pursuit.

5 OCTOBER 1813
War of 1812 In the Battle of the Thames, north of Lake Erie, American General William Henry Harrison overtakes the retreating British and Indian forces led by British General Henry Procter and Tecumseh. The British are decisively defeated, and Tecumseh's death leads to the collapse of the Indian confederacy and their support of the British.

25 OCTOBER 1813
War of 1812 In the American campaign to take Montreal, General Wade Hampton fights the Battle of Chateaugay against a smaller British force, but then withdraws his army to Plattsburg, New York, abandoning the drive on Montreal. Secretary of War John Armstrong has informed him that the American Army is going into winter quarters.

3 NOVEMBER 1813
Indian Affairs In the Creek War in the Mississippi Valley, General John Coffee leads a Tennessee militia force in the destruction of the Indian village of Talishatchee.

4 NOVEMBER 1813
War of 1812 British Prime Minister Lord Castlereagh sends President Madison a letter offering direct negotiation for an end to hostilities between Great Britain and the United States. Madison accepts the offer at once, nominating John Quincy Adams, J. A. Bayard, Henry Clay, Albert Gallatin and Jonathan Russell as peace commissioners.

9 NOVEMBER 1813
Indian Affairs In the Creek War, Major General Andrew Jackson destroys the Indian village of Talladega in present-day Alabama, killing more than 500 Indian warriors.

11 NOVEMBER 1813
War of 1812 In the campaign against Montreal, American General James Wilkinson's expeditionary force is soundly defeated by Colonel J.W. Morrison's British force at Chrysler's Farm, some 90 miles southwest of Montreal. On November 13, Wilkinson will enter winter quarters at French Mills on the Salmon River.

16 NOVEMBER 1813
War of 1812 The British Admiralty extends its naval blockade of the American coast to include Long Island. Now only the New England ports north of New London, Connecticut, remain open to commercial shipping.

9 DECEMBER 1813
War of 1812 In a message to Congress, President Madison calls for an embargo forbidding all trade with the British. New England and New York mer-

chants have been provisioning the British in Canada and off the East Coast. After congressional passage, the war embargo becomes law on December 17.

10 DECEMBER 1813
War of 1812 A British advance forces the Americans under Brigadier General George McClure to evacuate Fort George. As they leave, the Americans burn the village of Newark (Niagara-on-the-Lake) and part of Queenston.

18 DECEMBER 1813
War of 1812 In retaliation for the American burning of Newark, the British under Colonel John Murray take Fort Niagara from the Americans, sending their Indian allies to plunder the town of Lewiston, New York, and vicinity. Fort Niagara will remain under British control until the end of the war.

29-30 DECEMBER 1813
War of 1812 A 1500-man British force led by General Gordon Drummond burns Buffalo, New York, and the nearby strategically important Black Rock Navy Yard, destroying both ships and stores.

30 DECEMBER 1813
War of 1812 Bearing a truce flag, the British schooner *Bramble* arrives in Annapolis, Maryland, carrying peace dispatches from England.

22 JANUARY 1814
Indian Affairs In the Creek Indian War, Tennessee militia forces are repulsed at Emuckfaw. The militia will also suffer defeats at Enotachopco Creek on Jaunary 24 and at Calibee Creek on January 27.

25 JANUARY 1814
War of 1812 Congress modifies the embargo forbidding trade with the British when the embargo's strict enforcement results in famine among the inhabitants of Nantucket Island, off the Massachusetts coast.

27 JANUARY 1814
War of 1812 Congress passes legislation authorizing a United States Army of 62,773 men. At this time the effective strength of the regular army stands at about 11,000 men. Madison's proposal to conscript 100,000 men is denied by Congress. During the War of 1812, the militia is used only as a last resort. Secretary of War John Armstrong divides the United States into nine military districts and he will go on to remove such ineffectual leaders from command as General James Wilkinson (on March 24) and General Wade Hampton (on May 1), for their part in the failure of the campaign to take Montreal.

9 FEBRUARY 1814
National George W. Campbell is appointed Secretary of State, replacing Albert Gallatin who has been named a peace commissioner to England.

24 MARCH 1814
War of 1812 Although American General James

Wilkinson is acquitted by a court of inquiry for his conduct in the Montreal campaign, he is replaced by Major General Jacob Brown who, along with newly promoted Brigadier General Winfield Scott, is to head the military operations in the Niagara region.

27 MARCH 1814

Indian Affairs In the Creek Indian War, Tennessee militia forces led by Andrew Jackson and his subordinate General John Coffee achieve a decisive victory over the Creeks and their Cherokee allies at the Battle of Horseshoe Bend, on the Tallapoosa River in Alabama. This defeat effectively destroys all Indian resistance, thus ending the Creek War.

28 MARCH 1814

War of 1812 In the Pacific Ocean off Valparaiso, Chile, the American 32-gun frigate *Essex* under Captain David Porter is captured by the British ships *Phoebe* and *Cherub* after a three-hour naval battle. Two-thirds of the American seamen are killed or wounded, although 13-year old Midshipman David Farragut, later a Civil War naval hero, survives. Before its capture, the *Essex* has seized or destroyed more than 40 merchant and whaling ships in the Atlantic and southern Pacific Oceans.

31 MARCH 1814

Commerce In a message to Congress, President Madison recommends the repeal of the Embargo and Non-Importation Acts. This legislation has failed to achieve its purpose, and the repeal is supported by New England, despite the newly developing industries that have been protected by the acts.

6 APRIL 1814

International In France, Napoleon Bonaparte is overthrown, freeing the British to concentrate solely on the American war. Some 14,000 veterans of the Duke of Wellington's Napoleonic campaigns will be sent to fight the War of 1812.

14 APRIL 1814

Commerce With the overwhelming endorsement of the Senate and the House, the Embargo Act and the Non-importation Act are officially repealed. In order to protect the new American manufacturing industries, the repeal bill guarantees war duties for two years after peace is declared.

25 APRIL 1814

War of 1812 In order to support their new offensive thrust, the British extend their embargo to New England. The blockade proves to be an effective economic measure that will cause shortages, speculation and price inflation, and will bring the United States Treasury close to bankruptcy, because of the severe drop in customs duties revenues. The Americans retaliate by privateering off the British coast. By summer, American privateers will have captured 825 British vessels.

29 APRIL 1814

War of 1812 Off the Florida coast, the American sloop of war *Peacock* captures the British brig *Epervier,* which is carrying $120,000 in hard currency.

1 MAY 1814

War of 1812 Recently promoted American Major General George Izard replaces General Wade Hampton at Plattsburg, New York.

6 MAY 1814

War of 1812 British forces destroy Fort Oswego, New York.

22 MAY 1814

War of 1812 Andrew Jackson is promoted to major general of the United States Army.

3 JULY 1814

War of 1812 In the northern campaign, American General Jacob Brown captures Fort Erie.

5 JULY 1814

War of 1812 In the northern campaign, the Battle of Chippewa is fought 16 miles north of Fort Erie. The outnumbered American forces under General Winfield Scott inflict a decisive defeat on the British forces led by General Sir Phineas Ball.

22 JULY 1814

Indian Affairs In the Treaty of Grenville, the Delaware, Miami, Seneca, Shawnee and Wyandot Indians made peace with the United States. The treaty also requires the Indians to declare war on the British.

25 JULY 1814

War of 1812 In the most violent battle of the war, American General Jacob Brown's 2600-man force engages 3000 British soldiers led by Generals Riall and Drummond in an indecisive five-hour conflict at the village of Lundy's Lane, near Niagara Falls. At the end of the battle, the Americans withdraw to Fort Erie.

2 AUGUST 1814

War of 1812 The British forces of General Drummond begin a siege of Fort Erie, the refuge of a 2000-man United States military force.

8 AUGUST 1814

War of 1812 In the Flemish town of Ghent, peace discussions begin. The American peace commissioners are John Quincy Adams, J.A. Bayard, Henry Clay, Albert Gallatin and Jonathan Russell. The British are represented by Lord Gambier, Henry Goulburn, and William Adams. Each side will alter its demands, depending on the most recent news from the field of battle.

9 AUGUST 1814

Indian Affairs Part of the Creek Indians sign the Treaty of Fort Jackson, ceding two-thirds of their lands in southern Georgia and in the eastern Mississippi Territory, some 20 million acres in all, to

TESTING A UNION 1788-1865

the United States. In this pact they also agree to vacate the southern and western regions of Alabama.

19 AUGUST 1814
War of 1812 A 4000-man veteran British expeditionary force under General Robert Ross lands at Benedict, Maryland, southeast of Washington, D.C. The goal of the force is to seize and destroy the gunboats under the command of Commodore Joshua Barney in the Patuxent River, and to conduct raids on Washington and Alexandria.

22 AUGUST 1814
War of 1812 In Maryland's Patuxent River, American Commodore Joshua Barney blows up his flotilla of gunboats, to prevent their capture by the approaching British fleet under Rear Admiral Sir George Cockburn.

24 AUGUST 1814
War of 1812 Near Washington, D.C., the British force under General Robert Ross routs a 7000-man American force at the Battle of Bladensburg, witnessed by President Madison and most of his cabinet. The American force withdraws to Georgetown. The defense of the Potomac district is in the inept hands of General William H. Winder.

24-25 AUGUST 1814
War of 1812 General Ross' British force marches unopposed on Washington, as the United States Army and government officials flee to Virginia. In retaliation for the earlier American burning of York (Toronto), the British set fire to the Capitol, the White House and most government buildings, as well as a number of private houses. Secretary of the Navy William Jones orders the destruction of the American navy yard. A storm forces the British to withdraw and board their waiting ships on the Patuxent River.

27 AUGUST 1814
War of 1812 President Madison and several of his cabinet officers return to the smoking ruins of Washington. The president names James Monroe as interim Secretary of War, replacing John Armstrong who is largely held responsible for the capture and burning of Washington.

1 SEPTEMBER 1814
War of 1812 A British military force lands at the mouth of Maine's Castine River, and moves on toward Bangor after capturing Castine.

11 SEPTEMBER 1814
War of 1812 On Lake Champlain, American naval commander Captain Thomas McDonough soundly defeats a larger British squadron under Captain Downie. This halts the joint land and water British offensive from Canada led by General Sir George Prevost. The Americans gain control of Lake Champlain, and Prevost retreats to Canada in disarray, leaving behind large amounts of supplies.

12-14 SEPTEMBER 1814
War of 1812 Under the command of General Samuel Smith, Baltimore effectively defends itself against a joint land and water attack by the British. British General Robert Ross is mortally wounded, and the British fleet under Sir Alexander Cochrane unsuccessfully bombards Fort McHenry from beyond a line of sunken ship hulks. The British withdraw, and on October 14 their army will sail for Jamaica. The bombardment of Fort McHenry inspires Francis Scott Key to write the "Star Spangled Banner."

17 SEPTEMBER 1814
War of 1812 In the continuing siege of Fort Erie by the British, American General Peter B. Porter successfully leads a 1600-man raid to destroy the British batteries. As a result, British General Drummond will withdraw his forces.

17 OCTOBER 1814
Regional The Massachusetts legislature issues a call

The capture of the city of Washington by the British, August 24, 1814.

for a convention of the New England states in order to discuss their "public grievances and concerns," and to propose amendments to the United States Constitution. The convention will meet in secret session in Hartford, Connecticut, on December 15.

21 OCTOBER 1814
Arts/Culture In order to replace the books in the Library of Congress, burned by the British on August 25, Congress authorizes the purchase of Thomas Jefferson's personal 7000-volume library.

5 NOVEMBER 1814
War of 1812 The Americans evacuate and blow up Fort Erie, finally abandoning their plan to invade Canada.

7 NOVEMBER 1814
War of 1812 In opposition to the orders issued by Secretary of War James Monroe, General Andrew Jackson captures Pensacola, as part of his plan to invade Spanish Florida.

26 NOVEMBER 1814
War of 1812 A 50-ship British fleet carrying 7500 veteran soldiers under Sir Edward Pakenham sets sail from Jamaica. The goal is an attack on New Orleans, and the eventual British control of the Mississippi River.

1 DECEMBER 1814
War of 1812 General Andrew Jackson arrives in New Orleans, yet unaware of the powerful British invasion fleet sailing across the Gulf of Mexico for New Orleans. When Jackson hears of the British move, he will set up his main defense at Baton Rouge in order to repel the British attack by way of the Mississippi River.

13 DECEMBER 1814
War of 1812 In the New Orleans campaign, the British fleet from Jamaica enters Lake Borne, 40 miles east of New Orleans. As the British disembark, American General Andrew Jackson proclaims martial law in New Orleans and rushes his main force from Baton Rouge to New Orleans.

15 DECEMBER 1814
Regional In Hartford, Connecticut, the Hartford Convention secretly convenes, with 26 Federalist anti-war delegates from Connecticut, Massachusetts, New Hampshire, Rhode Island and Vermont. All of the delegates, except those from New Hampshire and Vermont, are elected by their state legislatures. George Cabot, the moderate leader of the Massachusetts delegation, presides over the convention, assisted by Massachusetts delegate Harrison Gray Otis. The convention will adopt a series of states' rights proposals addressing their grievances, covering military conscription, federal revenues used for state defense, an interstate defense pact, a prohibition of embargos of more than two–months duration, a requirement of a two-thirds vote of both houses of Congress in order to declare war, restrictions on foreign imports, restrictions on the admission of new states to the union, a ban on nationalized citizens holding federal civil office, and a limitation to one presidential term. The Hartford Convention's proposed amendments to the Constitution include the apportionment of direct taxes, and representation among the states according to the population of free persons in each. News of the Treaty of Ghent and of Andrew Jackson's New Orleans victory will bring an end to the convention on January 5, 1815. The Hartford Convention will become an object of public derision, as well as an excuse for its opponents to levy unfounded charges of conspiracy, sedition and treason.

23-24 DECEMBER 1814
War of 1812 In New Orleans, American General Andrew Jackson stalls the British advance on the city with a 5000-man night attack, supported by bombardment from the 14-gun schooner *Carolina*. This action gives Jackson time to complete an elaborate system of breastworks and fortifications five miles outside the city in a dry canal bed.

24 DECEMBER 1814
War of 1812 In Europe, American and British peace commissioners sign the Treaty of Ghent, ending the War of 1812. The pact provides for the release of prisoners; for the restoration of all conquered territory except West Florida, which remains in American hands and for an arbitration panel to resolve United States-Canadian boundary disputes. The treaty does not address such maritime issues as impressment, blockades, indemnities, the right of search and visit, or the military control of the Great Lakes. Nor is the British demand for a neutral Indian buffer state in the northwest considered. Such issues are either left unresolved or postponed.

OTHER EVENTS OF 1814
Industry In Waltham, Massachusetts, Boston textile manufacturer Francis Cabot Lowell establishes the first factory enclosing power cotton spinning and weaving machinery in the same building. Lowell invented a power loom of his own after covertly observing similar machinery in operation in Great Britain. His Waltham Boston Manufacturing Company will be followed by his establishment of subsequent cotton textile factories in the city of Lowell, named for him. His paternalistic attitude toward his factory workers will draw national attention.

1 JANUARY 1815
War of 1812 At New Orleans, British commander Sir Edward Pakenham leads an attack against the American fortifications around the city. Under General Andrew Jackson, the American artillery proves superior, and the British are forced to withdraw in order to await reinforcements.

5 JANUARY 1815
Regional Having drafted a set of states' rights pro-

posals, the New England Federalists meeting at the Hartford Convention since December 15, 1814 wind up their deliberations and disband. The intent of the convention was to increase the power of the New England industrial and commercial interests in the face of the growing agrarian interests of the West and South, as represented by the nationalistic War Hawks in Congress.

8 JANUARY 1815
War of 1812 Two weeks after the signing of the Treaty of Ghent, the Battle of New Orleans is fiercely fought. Unaware that peace has been declared, British General Sir Edward Pakenham leads his 5300 seasoned veterans in a frontal assault against General Andrew Jackson's entrenched 4500-man army of Tennessee and Kentucky sharpshooters, who employ the long rifle. Scorning lucrative offers from the British, French pirate and smuggler Jean Lafitte aids the Americans. In the half hour battle, 2036 British soldiers are killed or wounded, with Pakenham and two other generals among the dead. The United States casualties include eight killed, and 13 wounded. Although the battle has no military value, this is the most spectacular land victory of the war for the Americans, and it serves to make Andrew Jackson a national hero, as well as to restore the badly battered American national pride.

15 JANUARY 1815
War of 1812 Fifty miles off Sandy Hook, New York, a British naval squadron captures the American frigate *President,* commanded by Commodore Stephen Decatur.

20 JANUARY 1815
Finance President Madison vetoes a bill to create a second national bank, as proposed in the House of Representatives on January 7 and in the Senate on January 20. Madison's objection is not based on philosophic differences but rather on the practical aspects of undercapitalization and inadequate powers granted to the bank.

6 FEBRUARY 1815
Transportation In New Jersey, inventor and steamboat designer John Stevens is granted the first American railroad charter. Stevens plans to construct a railway from Trenton to New Brunswick—a project that is never actually to be developed. Stevens will not build a track for an early locomotive until 1826.

7 FEBRUARY 1815
National Congress authorizes a three-man board of navy commissioners, and the position of Secretary of the Navy to oversee the Navy Department.

11 FEBRUARY 1815
War of 1812 The news of signing of the Treaty of Ghent, on December 24, 1814, formally ending the War of 1812 between the United States and Great Britain, finally reaches America.

The Battle of New Orleans.

17 FEBRUARY 1815
War of 1812 The Senate unanimously ratifies the Treaty of Ghent, and President Madison officially declares the war over.

20 FEBRUARY 1815
War of 1812 Still unaware that peace has been declared, the American frigate *Constitution* captures the British sloops of war *Cyane* and *Levant* off the Portuguese coast.

27 FEBRUARY 1815
National In order to return the United States Navy to a peacetime status, Congress mandates the sale of the navy's gunboat flotilla and the docking of the Great Lakes warships.

3 MARCH 1815
National President Madison requests a standing army of 20,000 men, but the House of Representatives, in a vote of 70 to 38, decides to set the number of men at 10,000, with two major generals and four brigadier generals.
International Congress passes legislation authorizing hostilities against the Dey of Algiers, who has reinstated the plunder of American shipping during the War of 1812. Insisting that he had not been receiving enough tribute from the United States, the Dey dismissed the American minister and had declared war on the United States.
Commerce Congress authorizes a national policy of trade reciprocity with all nations.

23 MARCH 1815
War of 1812 Off Africa's Cape of Good Hope, the American sloop of war *Hornet* seizes the British sloop of war *Penguin.* The news of peace has not yet reached the *Hornet.*

10 MAY 1815
International In New York, Captain Stephen Decatur takes command of a ten-ship fleet setting sail for Algiers. His mission is to end the raids of the Barbary pirates on American commercial shipping in the Mediterranean.

MAY 1815
Arts/Culture In Boston, the first issue of the *North*

MARCH 14, 1816

American Review, edited by Connecticut-born historian Jared Sparks, is published. Intended to raise the standards of American literature and criticism, the *Review* will become a widely respected scholarly journal.

17 JUNE 1815
International In the Mediterranean Sea, American Captain Stephen Decatur captures the Algerian 44-gun frigate *Mashouda,* killing the renowned Algerian Admiral Hammida. Two days later Decatur will capture the 22-gun brig *Estido,* then tow both ships into Algiers harbor, and threaten to bombard the city.

30 JUNE 1815
International The forceful actions of Captain Decatur lead the Dey of Algiers to sign a treaty in which he agrees to cease hostilities against American shipping, to free all American prisoners without ransom, and to end all demands for tribute payments from the American government.

3 JULY 1815
Commerce Representatives of the United States and Great Britain sign a joint commercial convention, nullifying discriminatory duties and permitting the United States to trade with the British East Indies, although no concessions are made in regard to United States trade with the British West Indies.

26 JULY 1815
International In North Africa, Captain Stephen Decatur has Tunis sign a treaty, in which it agrees to halt interference with American commercial shipping in the Mediterranean and to cease tribute demands from the American government. Tunis is also required to make restitution for the American vessels it allowed the British to seize as prizes during the War of 1812.

JULY-SEPTEMBER 1815
Indian Affairs The Treaties of Portage des Sioux are signed, effectively ending all Indian resistance in the Old Northwest, and freeing the territory below Lake Michigan for settlement.

5 AUGUST 1815
International In North Africa, Captain Stephen Decatur exacts a treaty from Tripoli, receiving a guarantee of the cessation of raids on American commercial shipping in the Mediterranean, the release of American prisoners without ransom and the dropping of all demands for American tribute. Tripoli must also compensate the United States for American vessels seized by Great Britain as prizes, with the cooperation of Tripoli, during the War of 1812.

4 DECEMBER 1815
National Following the mid–term elections, the 14th Congress convenes for its first session. In the Senate are 25 Democratic-Republicans to 11 Federalists, and in the House are 177 Democratic-Republicans to 65 Federalists. Henry Clay is reelected Speaker of the House. It is interesting to note that, despite the professedly agrarian and states' rights position of the Democratic-Republican party, the Democratic-Republicans over the past few years have come to adopt formerly Federalist positions as to protective tariffs, national roads and public works, and a second national bank and a national currency, as well as other issues. At the same time, the Federalists, especially those participating in the Hartford Convention of December 15, 1814, have demonstrated a propensity for formerly Democratic-Republican ideals, particularly those of states' rights and civil liberties.

5 DECEMBER 1815
Finance In his message to the 14th Congress, President Madison requests authorization of a national public works program. He also advises that serious consideration be given once again to the creation of a second Bank of the United States, to succeed the first bank that was allowed to lapse in 1811. Madison proposes this move because the state banks are not capable of restoring a uniform national currency. In his message, Madison also asks for improvements in the military forces and for the establishment of a national university.

8 JANUARY 1816
Finance In face of the postwar national financial chaos and soaring inflation, John C. Calhoun introduces a congressional bill for the organization of a second Bank of the United States. The bill calls for a capitalization of $50 million and for presidential power to suspend hard currency payments. The bill has been forged in the House through the Democratic-Republican leadership of Calhoun and Henry Clay. Calhoun and Clay have now reversed their former objections to a national bank on constitutional grounds, basing their present advocacy on the pressing need for a strong and uniform national currency, and on the constitutional power of congress to regulate the currency. Daniel Webster, however, continues to oppose the creation of a national bank, arguing against the need for currency reform in face of the current legislative provisions existing for a gold and silver currency. According to Webster, congressional action against the banknote issues of suspended state banks can solve the currency problems.

14 MARCH 1816
Finance The bill to create a second Bank of the United States passes the House of Representatives, 80 to 71. Opposing the bill are 33 Democratic-Republicans and 38 Federalists. The bill also passes the Senate, 22 to 12. In its final form, the bill creates a national bank with a capitalization of $35 million, of which $7 million is contributed by the government. As a condition of receiving its 20-year charter, the bank is to pay a bonus of $1.5 million to the Federal Government, and the president is to name 5 of its 25 directors. The bank receives the privilege of holding government funds without paying interest for their use. The central office of the bank will be in Philadelphia and will open on January 1, 1817, with William Jones as its first president. The

TESTING A UNION 1788-1865

unprofessional conduct of Jones will lead to a reorganization, followed by the capable management of Langdon Cheves and then of Nicholas Biddle.

16 MARCH 1816
National The Democratic-Republican congressional caucus chooses Secretary of State James Monroe over Georgia's William C. Crawford, by a vote of 65 to 54, as its presidential candidate.

20 MARCH 1816
National In the Virginia legal case of *Martin v. Hunter's Lessee,* the Supreme Court rules in this matter of appellate jurisdiction that the 1789 Judiciary Act constitutionally supports the right of the Supreme Court to review decisions by state courts.

11 APRIL 1816
Black Experience In Philadelphia, Blacks establish the African Methodist Church, the first Black church in the United States to be completely independent of white churches. Clergyman Richard Allen is ordained as the church's first bishop.

27 APRIL 1816
Commerce Congress passes the Tariff Act of 1816, with the support of John C. Calhoun and Henry Clay. The Tariff Act perpetuates the protective duties set during the War of 1812 in order to shelter developing American industries that are now facing competition from abroad during the postwar era. With import duties of 15 to 30 percent on cotton, textiles, leather, paper, pig iron, wool and other goods, the chief beneficiaries of the legislation are the new American textile and iron industries.

10 MAY 1816
Commerce In Wisconsin, the post of Fort Howard is founded at Green Bay, as a center of the Illinois Territory fur trade.

6 JUNE 1816
Science/Technology A meteorological phenomenon occurs. Ten inches of snow fall in the Berkshire Mountains in Massachusetts, and in Vermont and New Hampshire. This is the year in which there is "no summer" in New England. In July and August, a half inch of frost will cover Vermont and New Hampshire, wreaking havoc on agricultural crops. This cold weather effect is attributed to volcanic eruptions in Indonesia.

11 JUNE 1816
Science/Technology Baltimore, Maryland, becomes the first American city to institute a gas company for the purpose of street lighting. The Gas Light Company of Baltimore will illuminate the city at night through the use of coal gas.

JUNE 1816
Westward Movement In the Indiana Territory at Corydon, a convention meets to draft a constitution for a state government, as authorized by Congress.

9 JULY 1816
Indian Affairs In a treaty with the Cherokee Indians, W.L. Lovely effects the cession of Indian lands in northern Maine to the United States.

27 JULY 1816
Indian Affairs In Spanish-held East Florida, a United States government military expedition destroys Fort Apalachicola at the request of the state of Georgia. The fort had become a refuge for runaway slaves and hostile Indians, both of whom were sheltered by the Seminole Indians.

22 OCTOBER 1816
Finance Secretary of War William H. Crawford is named to the post of Secretary of the Treasury, replacing Albert Gallatin whom President Madison has named American minister to France.

4 DECEMBER 1816
National In the election, James Monroe is elected president over his Federalist opponent Rufus King, by receiving 183 to 34 votes. Daniel D. Tompkins is chosen vice president. The Federalists lose seats in Congress, remaining influential only in the states of Connecticut, Massachusetts and Delaware.

11 DECEMBER 1816
Westward Movement Indiana is admitted to the Union as a free state, with slavery forbidden. The 19th state has its capital at Corydon.

13 DECEMBER 1816
Finance In Boston, the first savings bank in the United States, The Provident Institution for Savings, is chartered.

20 DECEMBER 1816
Finance In Congress, John C. Calhoun proposes a bill setting aside the $1.5 million bonus paid to the United States government by the second Bank of the United States, for the purpose of a public works fund. Lame–duck President Madison opposes this move.

28 DECEMBER 1816
Black Experience In Washington, Presbyterian clergyman Robert Finley founds the American Colonization Society. This organization's goal is to resettle freed blacks in Africa. The eventual result of this program will be the establishment of the African republic of Liberia.

OTHER EVENTS OF 1816
Arts/Culture John Pickering publishes *Vocabulary,* a dictionary of some 500 indigenous American words and phrases. In spite of continuing vocabulary and spelling alterations, American English is never to achieve independence from British English, so fervently hoped for by the nationalistic partisans.

JAMES MONROE, 1758-1831

Before he became the fifth president, James Monroe was a successful diplomat for his country, and indeed he was wonderfully diplomatic in all his public service. But though his Presidency began resolving partisan clashes into an "Era of Good Feeling," it was to be clouded at its end by the first rumblings of a far more divisive confrontation to come. Monroe was born in Westmoreland County, Virginia, on April 28, 1758. After two years at the College of William and Mary, he joined the Revolutionary Army in 1776. During the next few years he saw much action, spent the terrible winter of 1777 at Valley Forge, and was seriously wounded. Returning to Virginia to study law in 1780, he met Thomas Jefferson, who was to become his lifelong friend and mentor. During the next decade he served in the Virginia House and in the Confederation Congress; in 1790 he was elected to the U.S. House of Representatives, where he joined Madison and Jefferson's Republican efforts to combat the growing conservatism and the pro-British inclinations of the Federalists. Appointed minister to France in 1794, Monroe was quickly recalled for working against Washington's policies. He was elected governor of Virginia in 1799.

In 1800 Jefferson gained the White House; three years later he named Monroe as an envoy to bargain with Napoleon concerning American rights on the Mississippi; France had just taken over Louisiana from Spain. The delegates, to their surprise, found themselves being offered the whole place; moving quickly before Napoleon changed his mind, Jefferson snapped up Louisiana at a bargain price, thus vastly expanding the country.

After further diplomatic missions Monroe returned to politics in Virginia for some years before being named secretary of state by Madison. In that post he helped bring the war with Britain to its successful conclusion; by the end of the fighting he was secretary of war as well as of state. In the election of 1816, with the support of Madison and Jefferson, Monroe was easily elected president. He turned his diplomatic abilities first to resolving the conflicts within his own party and with the declining Federalist party; the Era of Good Feeling began, and Monroe hoped for an end of partisan strife in the country. On the foreign front he managed to turn an embarrassing invasion of Florida by Andrew Jackson into a victory when Spain ceded the area in 1818. In 1823 he proclaimed what came to be called the Monroe Doctrine, which stated America's opposition to colonization of or foreign interference with all of South America.

But the good feelings could not last. The great moral dilemma of the nation, slavery, was beginning its slow rise toward the tragic climax of the Civil War. The issue was the new state of Missouri—slave state or not? The Missouri Compromise staved off the problem for a while, but hardly resolved it, and the bitterness brought by the controversy created new divisiveness in Monroe's second term—it would take much more than diplomacy to deal with slavery. Monroe left office in 1825 and died in New York City in 1831.

1 JANUARY 1817

Finance In Philadelphia, the second Bank of the United States opens its doors for business, as mandated by legislation passed on March 14, 1816. Before the expiration of the bank's 20-year charter in 1836, some 25 branch offices will augment its operations throughout the United States. For the first two years of its existence, the bank is managed by William Jones, who proves to be an incompetent administrator.

8 FEBRUARY 1817

Transportation Congress passes John C. Calhoun's proposal to set aside the $1.5 million bonus to the Federal Government from the Bank of the United States, as a fund for federally financed public works projects, such as roads and canals. New England Federalists oppose the bill, fearing its impetus to westward expansion.

1 MARCH 1817

Westward Movement Congress authorizes the Mississippi Territory to hold a convention in order to draft a state constitution, in preparation for Mississippi entering the union.

3 MARCH 1817

National Despite his support for a federally-subsidized public works program, President Madison vetoes the Bonus Bill passed by congress on February 8. In this, his last official act, Madison does not accept the implied powers interpretation of the Constitution adopted by John C. Calhoun, but rather the president insists that a constitutional amendment is required to legally permit the involvement of the Federal Government in internal improvements.

Westward Movement The Alabama Territory, with a capital at St. Stephens near Mobile, is organized from the eastern part of the Mississippi Territory.

Transportation The steamboat *Washington*, designed by Henry Shreve, initiates a commercial route on the Ohio and Mississippi Rivers, between Louisville and New Orleans.

4 MARCH 1817

National James Monroe is inaugurated as the fifth president of the United States, and New York's Daniel D. Tompkins becomes the nation's sixth vice president. In Monroe's cabinet are John Quincy Adams as Secretary of State, William H. Crawford as Secretary of the Treasury, Isaac Shelby as Secretary of War, B.W. Crowninshield as Secretary of the Navy, R.J. Meigs as Postmaster General and Richard Rush as Attorney General. In his Inauguration Address, Monroe expresses his support for a standing army, an ade-

TESTING A UNION 1788-1865

quate navy, and the protection of American industry. The Democratic-Republican party has in effect adopted the nationalistic principles of the waning Federalist party.

15 MARCH 1817
Transportation With the enthusiastic support of Governor De Witt Clinton, the New York state legislature authorizes the construction of the Erie Canal, a $7 million project to be financed by the state. The planned toll waterway will give New York City access to the West, by way of the Hudson River and proposed canal between Albany and Buffalo, challenging Canadian supremacy in trade on the Great Lakes. The ground will be broken for this project on July 4, and "Clinton's ditch" will open in 1825.

28-29 APRIL 1817
International In order to avoid a threatened naval armaments race between Great Britain and the United States on the Great Lakes, American Secretary of State Richard Rush and Britain's minister to the United States Charles Bagot conclude the Rush-Bagot Agreement. Both nations agree to limit the number of their naval vessels on the Great Lakes and on other inland waterways. The mutual demilitarization of the lakes and the Canadian frontier will be a drawn-out process that continues into the last third of the 19th century. On April 16, 1818 the United States Senate will unanimously approve the pact, giving it the status of a treaty.

12 JULY 1817
National The Boston *Columbian Sentinel* dubs the Monroe presidency as the "era of good feeling," a reaction evoked by the enthusiastic reception of Monroe by both Federalists and Democratic-Republicans as he travels the Northeast and Midwest during the summer. This characterization of the era is somewhat misleading, despite the aura of overriding nationalism, as political factionalism is on the increase, instigated by the underlying economic problems and sectional differences.

27 SEPTEMBER 1817
Indian Affairs In a treaty with the United States, the Ohio Indians give up four million acres of their remaining lands in northwestern Ohio.

8 OCTOBER 1817
National South Carolina congressman and war hawk John C. Calhoun is named Secretary of War.

NOVEMBER 1817
Indian Affairs The First Seminole War begins with the raids of the Seminole Indians along the Florida-Georgia border in retaliation for the destruction of Fort Apalachicola on July 27, 1816 by a United States expeditionary force.

1 DECEMBER 1817
National In Washington, the 15th Congress convenes. As a result of the last election, the Senate is composed of 34 Democratic-Republicans to 14 Federalists, and the House of Representatives has 141 Democratic-Republicans to 42 Federalists.

2 DECEMBER 1817
National In his first annual message to Congress, President James Monroe supports the view that the United States Constitution grants Congress no authority to institute a public works program.

10 DECEMBER 1817
Westward Movement Mississippi enters the union as a state; Mississippi allows slavery. The eastern portion of the original Mississippi Territory has been separately organized as the Alabama Territory.

26 DECEMBER 1817
Indian Affairs In Florida, during the course of the First Seminole War, General Andrew Jackson replaces General Edmund Gaine in the command of the United States expeditionary force to the region to pacify the hostile Seminole Indians. Secretary of War John C. Calhoun instructs Jackson to do whatever is necessary to end the conflict.

6 JANUARY 1818
Indian Affairs During the course of Florida's First Seminole Indian War, General Andrew Jackson sends a letter through Tennessee congressman John Rhea to President Monroe suggesting that he can capture Spanish Florida for the United States in a 60-day military campaign. President's Monroe's failure to respond to the letter will be taken by Jackson as a sign of tacit approval for his proposed plan.

8 JANUARY 1818
Westward Movement Congress receives the first of several petitions calling for the admission of Missouri to the union as the 21st state.

18 MARCH 1818
National Congress passes the first Pension Act, which provides lifetime pensions for the veterans of the Revolutionary War.

25 MARCH 1818
International In Congress, Speaker of the House Henry Clay delivers a three-hour speech calling for United States recognition of a number of revolutionary governments in South America, which have recently liberated their nations from Spanish colonial rule. Clay's resolution is defeated because Congress fears this foreign policy initiative would confuse its concerns with wresting Florida from Spain.

4 APRIL 1818
National Congress limits the number of stripes on the American flag to 13 again, and orders only new stars to be added for each new state.

7 APRIL 1818
Indian Affairs In his First Seminole War campaign,

General Andrew Jackson seizes St. Marks, Florida, where he has Scottish trader Alexander Arbuthnot and English trader Robert Armbrister arrested for inciting the Seminole Indians. Both men are courtmartialed and executed on April 29. Jackson's actions in this affair will excite public outcry and provoke a congressional call for Jackson's censure, but will result in no action by the government.

20 APRIL 1818
Commerce In approving a new protective tariff bill, Congress postpones scheduled reductions in textile duties and increases the levies on iron imports.

24 MAY 1818
Indian Affairs In his First Seminole Indian War campaign, General Andrew Jackson seizes the Spanish post of Pensacola, Florida, effectively ending the war.

20 JUNE 1818
Regional The Connecticut state legislature rescinds the property requirement for voting, becoming the first eastern state to liberalize suffrage in this way.

23 AUGUST 1818
Transportation In Buffalo, New York, the steamboat *Walk-in-the-Water* departs on a trip across Lake Erie, headed for Detroit. It is the first such vessel to offer service on the Great Lakes. Three years later it will become lost in a storm and sink.

19 OCTOBER 1818
Indian Affairs In a treaty with the United States, the Chickasaw Indians sign over all their lands between the Mississippi River and the northern part of the Tennessee River.

20 OCTOBER 1818
International In London, American minister to Great Britain Richard Rush and American minister to France Albert Gallatin sign the Convention of 1818 with England. This pact clarifies the settlement reached in the December 24, 1814 Treaty of Ghent. The Convention of 1818 fixes the border between the United States and Canada along the 49th parallel from Lake of the Woods to the continental divide. No boundary is established west of the Rocky Mountains, and for the next ten years the Oregon region is to be open to the settlers and maritime traffic of both nations. The pact also allows American fishermen the right to fish the waters off Labrador and Newfoundland, and it renews the commercial convention of 1815.

28 NOVEMBER 1818
International Secretary of State John Quincy Adams officially informs the Spanish government in Madrid that General Andrew Jackson's military expedition into the territory of Spanish Florida has been an act of self-defense on the part of the United States, since Spain, by sheltering hostile Indians and runaway slaves, has virtually supported aggression against the United States. Adams further informs Spain that if she is unable to effectively govern and control her Florida possessions, she should cede this area to the United States.

3 DECEMBER 1818
Westward Movement The area of the Illinois Territory south of 42°31' N enters the union as Illinois—a free state and the 21st state. The state capital of Illinois is the Mississippi River town of Kaskaskia. The northern part of the Illinois Territory is added to the Michigan Territory.

JANUARY 1819
Finance The first serious American financial panic occurs as a result of the curtailment of credit and the 1817 congressional order mandating the resumption of payments in hard currency. In the years since the end of the War of 1812, the national financial situation has been characterized by commodity inflation, land speculation, overextended manufacturing investments and the unwise policies of the second Bank of the United States. The South and the West are particularly hard hit. In a number of western states, including Kentucky, Illinois and the Missouri Territory, legislation is passed to alleviate the desperate situation of debtors. The financial panic, which will extend through the end of the year, sees the collapse of a number of state banks and the foreclosure of large tracts of western real estate by the Bank of the United States.

12 JANUARY 1819
National Congress fails to endorse a report sponsored by Henry Clay, condemning Andrew Jackson's conduct in the First Seminole War in Florida.

26 JANUARY 1819
Westward Movement A resolution is introduced in Congress to reorganize Arkansas County of the Missouri Territory as the Arkansas Territory. John W. Taylor's amendment to this resolution, banning slavery from the new territory, is defeated on February 18.

2 FEBRUARY 1819
National In an appeal of the case *Trustees of Dartmouth College v. Woodward,* Supreme Court Chief Justice John Marshall issues the opinion that a private corporate charter is a contract and therefore cannot be revised or broken by a state. This decision disallows the 1816 New Hampshire state legislature alteration of the 1769 royal charter of Dartmouth College. The broad result of this decision is that business growth is encouraged, since corporations are thus ruled free of state control.

13 FEBRUARY 1819
Westward Movement In Congress the Missouri Bill is introduced, permitting the Missouri Territory to draft a state constitution and to prepare for statehood. New York Representative James Tallmadge proposes two antislavery amendments to the Missouri Bill, one

banning the further introduction of slavery, and the other declaring children born to slaves after the admission of Missouri to be free at the age of 25. Tallmadge's amendments will pass the House of Representatives on February 17, but will be defeated in the Senate on February 27.

17 FEBRUARY 1819
National In the case of *Sturges v. Crowninshield,* the Supreme Court finds that a state bankruptcy law passed after the sealing of a contract violates the contract clause of the United States Constitution.

22 FEBRUARY 1819
International In Washington, the Adams-Onis Treaty is signed, in which Spain cedes East Florida to the United States and renounces any claims to West Florida, already annexed by the United States. The United States renounces its claims to Texas and assumes responsibility for the $5 million of debts owed by Spain to American citizens. And finally, the boundary between the United States and Spanish territories is set. The Senate will ratify the treaty on February 25, and again on February 22, 1821, after Spanish delays.

2 MARCH 1819
Westward Movement Arkansas County of the Missouri Territory is reorganized as the Arkansas Territory. The territorial capital is located at Arkansas Post on the Mississippi River.
Immigration Congress passes legislation regulating immigration, specifically mandating ships' captains to provide descriptive lists of the passengers brought in on each voyage.

3 MARCH 1819
Slavery Congress enacts legislation setting a $50 reward per slave for informers reporting the illegal importation of slaves into the United States. The president is also empowered to return to Africa any slaves captured under the provisions of this act. The smuggling of slaves has become a profitable and widespread activity.

6 MARCH 1819
National In the case of *McCulloch v. Maryland,* which involves the taxation of the Baltimore branch of the Bank of the United States by the state of Maryland, the Supreme Court finds that states may not tax an agency of the United States, including the federal bank, thus upholding the principle of federal sovereignty. In Chief Justice John Marshall's opinion, the court also upholds the right of Congress to create the bank, under the Hamiltonian doctrines of "implied powers" and "loose construction."

5 MAY 1819
Ideas/Beliefs In Baltimore, Maryland, William Ellery Channing delivers a sermon entitled "Unitarian Christianity" at the ordination of Jared Sparks. Channing's sermon underlines the schism—between the Unitarians and traditional Christians.

24 MAY-20 JUNE 1819
Transportation The steam-assisted sailing ship *Savannah* sets out from Savannah, Georgia, for Liverpool, England, in the first transatlantic passage of a steamship. After 80 hours of the steam engine's use, the *Savannah's* coal supply is exhausted, and wind power is used to complete the voyage.

19 JUNE 1819
Regional Massachusetts agrees to allow the District of Maine to petition for separate statehood in December.

JUNE 1819
Exploration Secretary of War John C. Calhoun commissions Major Stephen H. Long to lead a two-year exploratory expedition from Pittsburgh, Pennsylvania, on June 6, 1820, to the area south of the Missouri River. With his group of scientists and soldiers, Long will spend the winter at Council Bluffs and explore the eastern Rocky Mountains after passing through the plains which he names the Great American Desert.

14 DECEMBER 1819
Regional Alabama enters the Union as the 22nd state, with its capital at Huntsville and as a slaveholding state.

23 JANUARY 1820
Regional The bill for the admission of Maine as a state is passed by the House of Representatives. Since Maine will be admitted as a free state, this will upset the balance between the number of free and slave states, achieved by alternately admitting slave and free states.

6 FEBRUARY 1820
Black Experience The ship *Mayflower of Liberia* sets sail for Sierra Leone from New York. Traveling aboard are 86 free blacks who have decided to emigrate to the West African British colony which has openly received freed blacks and fugitive slaves for the past 30 years.

17 FEBRUARY 1820
Slavery The Senate passes the Missouri Compromise measure. Illinois Senator Jesse B. Thomas has proposed a compromise amendment to the proposal to combine the admission of Maine as a free state, with the admission of Missouri as a slave state, thus maintaining the balance between free and slave states in the union. The Thomas Amendment calls for a prohibition on slavery in the western territory of the Louisiana Purchase north of the line 36°30'.

28 FEBRUARY 1820
Slavery The House of Representatives rejects the February 17 compromise measure passed by the Senate, and will go on to pass its own slavery prohibition bill, incorporating the restrictive amendment proposed by New York Representative John W. Taylor on January 26, 1819.

3 MARCH 1820
Slavery The Missouri Compromise becomes official with the proposed admission of Maine as a free state and of Missouri as a slave state, and with the exclusion of slavery from the Louisiana Purchase north of 36°30'. This move has been made possible by the Senate's reinsertion of the Thomas Amendment for the Taylor Amendment, and the subsequent passage of the compromise bill by the House on March 2.

6 MARCH 1820
Westward Movement Congress enacts legislation enabling the inhabitants of the Missouri Territory to draft a state constitution.

15 MARCH 1820
Regional Maine is admitted to the union as the 23rd state, with its capital at Portland, and with a ban on slavery. Maine has been a part of Massachusetts, but its separation was called for by the rapid increase in its population since the War of 1812.

30 MARCH 1820
Westward Movement A group of New England missionaries arrives on the Hawaiian Islands, to be greeted by King Kamehameha II.

24 APRIL 1820
Westward Movement Congress passes the Public Land Act, which reduces the minimum price from $2.00 to $1.25 per acre, and reduces the size of the minimum purchase from 160 to 80 acres. Although the act abolishes the use of credit for western land purchases, it is intended to enable settlers to purchase land. Yet, as with the earlier land acts, real estate speculators are the chief beneficiaries of this legislation.

15 MAY 1820
Slavery Congress passes legislation making the trade in foreign slaves an act of piracy. The punishment for this activity is increased from the forfeiture of the involved vessels to include the death penalty for any American citizens found guilty of engaging in such smuggling activities.
National Congress passes the Tenure of Office Act, which limits the length of specified political appointments to a four-year term. This measure contributes to the principle of rotation in office.

14-15 JULY 1820
Exploration On the Long expedition, Edwin James leads two other group members on an ascent of a mountain on the eastern fringe of the Rocky Mountains. First noted by Zebulon Pike in 1806, the peak is named for James, but remains popularly known as Pike's Peak.

19 JULY 1820
Black Experience In the constitution drafted by the inhabitants of the Missouri Territory, free blacks and mulattoes are barred from the future state. This dis-

criminatory clause will meet with opposition when the constitution is presented to congress on November 14 for approval.

26 SEPTEMBER 1820
Life/Customs Legendary explorer, Indian fighter and pioneer Daniel Boone dies in Missouri at the age of 85.

18 NOVEMBER 1820
Discovery While on a sealing expedition, Connecticut's Nathaniel B. Palmer, captain of the sloop *Hero,* reports the sighting of a land mass south of Cape Horn, in what is possibly the first discovery of Antarctica.

6 DECEMBER 1820
National In the presidential election of 1820, President Monroe is reelected by 231 electoral votes to 1 for John Quincy Adams. Vice–President Daniel D. Tompkins is also returned to office with 218 votes.

26 DECEMBER 1820
Westward Movement In the Spanish town of San Antonio, Texas, Moses Austin asks for permission to settle 300 American families in Texas.

DECEMBER 1820
Finance In response to the financial panic of 1819 and the subsequent economic depression, the Kentucky "Relief Party" is formed to press for assistance for delinquent debtors. Henry Clay will oppose the Relief Party, and Andrew Jackson will support it. The Clay faction will develop into the Whig party, while Jackson's followers will become known as the Democrats.

17 JANUARY 1821
Westward Movement Missouri's Moses Austin receives from the government of New Spain a large grant in Texas and permission to bring in 300 American families. After Austin's July death, the grant will be taken over by his son Stephen F. Austin, who will later found a settlement in the lower Brazos River region.

24 FEBRUARY 1821
International Mexico declares its independence from Spain.

2 MARCH 1821
National In a second Missouri Compromise vote, Congress agrees to admit Missouri into the union on the condition that the state constitution will not try to limit the rights of citizens, specifically free blacks, as guaranteed by the United States Constitution. This compromise has been negotiated by Speaker of the House Henry Clay. The Missouri legislature will agree to this provision on June 26.
Finance Congress passes the Relief Act, which permits price adjustments on unpaid-for western land purchases.

TESTING A UNION 1788-1865

3 MARCH 1821
National In the case of *Cohens v. Virginia*, the Supreme Court reaffirms its 1816 decision on *Martin v. Hunter's Lessee,* which holds that the higher federal court has the authority to review decisions of the state courts.

5 MARCH 1821
National President Monroe and Vice–President Daniel Tompkins are inaugurated for their second terms in office. Monroe keeps on the same cabinet.

15 APRIL 1821
Regional President Monroe appoints General Andrew Jackson as the first governor of the recently acquired Florida territory.

1 JUNE 1821
Education The first women's collegiate-level school in America is established with Emma Willard's founding of a female academy in Waterford, New York. The Waterford Academy for Young Ladies is later moved to Troy, New York, where it will later become known as the Emma Willard School.

1 JULY 1821
Regional Governor Andrew Jackson officially receives the Florida territory from the Spanish. As no provisions have yet been made for a territorial government, Jackson will act as a quasi-military commander.

10 AUGUST 1821
Westward Movement Missouri officially enters the union as the 24th state, with its capital at Jefferson City. Its addition as a slave state brings the total of free and slave states to 12 each. The first United States Senator from Missouri is Thomas Hart Benton, who will occupy this position for the next 30 years.

1 SEPTEMBER 1821
Westward Movement In Independence, Missouri, William Becknell leads a wagon train of goods out toward Santa Fe, New Mexico, thus initiating the trade along the route that will become known as the Santa Fe Trail. Becknell will arrive in San Francisco on November 16.

4 SEPTEMBER 1821
International Czar Alexander I of Russia claims all of the American Pacific coast north of the 51st parallel, which crosses at the northern end of Vancouver Island and bisects the Oregon territory claimed by both Great Britain and the United States. This imperial order also closes the surrounding waters to the commercial shipping of other nations.

10 NOVEMBER 1821
Regional The New York state constitutional convention extends suffrage by abolishing nearly all the property qualifications for the right to vote. Free blacks, however, are not benefitted by this legislation. The liberalized suffrage movement is led by Martin

Van Buren at the head of the Albany Regency, a radical faction of the Democratic-Republican party.

DECEMBER 1821
Slavery In the case of *Hall v. Mullin,* the Maryland state supreme court rules that a bequest of property to a slave by his master entitles the slave to freedom by implication, since a slave cannot legally own property.

OTHER EVENTS OF 1821
Slavery In West Africa, the republic of Liberia is founded by the American Colonization Society as a haven for freed American slaves. In Mt. Pleasant, Ohio, Quaker Benjamin Lundy begins publication of one of the nation's earliest abolitionist journals, *The Genius of Universal Emancipation.*
Arts/Culture James Fenimore Cooper issues his second novel, *The Spy,* the success of which will establish his reputation as a romantic writer on American themes.

8 MARCH 1822
International President Monroe sends a special message to Congress proposing United States recognition of the new Latin American republics that have recently achieved independence. Among them are Colombia, Peru, Argentina and Mexico. Henry Clay has been pressing for such recognition since 1818, but President Monroe has delayed recognition until after the ratification of the Florida treaty with Spain and the cession of this formerly Spanish region to the U.S.

20 MARCH 1822
Westward Movement In St. Louis' *Missouri Republican,* veteran fur trader William Henry Ashley publishes an advertisement calling for 100 young men to ascend the Missouri River to its source in order to there develop the fur trade. The nearly 200 adventurers who respond to the ad will in due course found the Rocky Mountain Fur Company, and their exploratory expeditions under Ashley's leadership will help to open up the Far West.

30 MARCH 1822
Regional Congress enacts legislation to combine East and West Florida into the Florida Territory. This territorial organization replaces the military government of the region under General Andrew Jackson.

29 APRIL 1822
Transportation Congress passes the Cumberland Road Tolls Bill, calling for the institution of a system of tolls in order to finance repairs to the Cumberland Road. President Monroe will veto the bill on May 4, basing his denial on the belief that the Federal Government lacks jurisdiction over public improvements. Monroe will recommend a constitutional amendment that will provide Congress with such authority.

4 MAY 1822
International Congress appropriates $100,000 in

JANUARY 27, 1823

FREE BLACKS: THE LIBERIA SOLUTION

The increasing numbers of free blacks in the United States during the early 19th century presented a unique social problem that led to an idiosyncratic solution—the creation of the African republic of Liberia. The 1810 national census counted a total of 200,000 free blacks. Few of them were to receive the opportunity and education to achieve the national status of Benjamin Banneker, the remarkable mathematician and astronomer, later appointed a District of Columbia commissioner by George Washington. Nor did the utopian approach of social reformer and feminist Fanny Wright meet with success: her 1825 Nashoba community, established in Tennessee, in order to purchase and educate slaves, and then to allow them to earn their freedom, collapsed in 1828.

The insurrection organized by Denmark Vesey crystallized the worst fears of many white Americans. Vesey had bought his freedom after winning a $1500 lottery, and went on to become a prosperous and influential Charleston, South Carolina carpenter. His planned massive rebellion, inspired by that of Toussaint l'Ouverture in Haiti, was betrayed in 1822 by an informant, and resulted in the imposition of severe black codes throughout the slave states.

The 1816 formation of the American Colonization Society was a culmination of the efforts of numerous anti-slavery societies to promote the resettlement of free blacks in their ancestral home of Africa. Free blacks occupied a shadowy zone in American society—denied citizenship, and a likely source of rebellion, they were considered by many to be unassimilable into the larger white society. Among the prominent public figures supporting the colonization plan were Thomas Jefferson, James Monroe, Henry Clay, and Daniel Webster.

With government and private funds, the colonization society purchased a large land tract in West Africa in 1821. Settlement began the next year, and Liberia's capital city was named Monrovia, after President James Monroe. Although some 15,000 blacks had gone to Liberia by 1870, many more blacks preferred to remain in America, where they had been born and which they now considered their home.

This American solution to the black problem ironically paralleled the earlier European solution for many of its social outcasts—resettlement in New World colonies. The colonization of Liberia marked the ambiguous attitudes of Americans toward blacks—it was an uncomfortable accommodation of abolitionist idealism to the realities of racial prejudice.

order to establish diplomatic missions in the independent Latin American nations, at the discretion of President Monroe.

30 MAY 1822
Slavery In Charleston, South Carolina, a black informer reveals a plot led by freed Black Denmark Vesey for a massive slave uprising. Of the conspirators, 130 blacks and 4 whites are brought to trial. Of these, 35 blacks, including Vesey, will be hanged. The four whites will be jailed and fined. A far-reaching result of this rebellion will be the institution of a strict system of slave control throughout the lower Southern states.

19 JUNE 1822
International The United States formally recognizes the republic of Gran Colombia, headed by South American independence hero Simon Bolivar. This nation includes the present-day countries of Venezuela, Ecuador and Panama within its borders.

20 JULY 1822
National The Tennessee state legislature nominates Andrew Jackson as its presidential candidate for the 1824 election. This action by a state legislature marks the end of the system of selecting presidential candidates by congressional party caucuses. The demise of partisan politics, with the end of the Federalist party, has made a new system of nomination necessary. This popular method of nomination heralds the approach of Jacksonian democracy.

24 JULY 1822
International In a strongly worded diplomatic note, the United States protests the Russian Czar's September 4, 1821 claim to the American Pacific coast, threatening the possibility of war if the Russians attempt to assume physical control of the region.

3 SEPTEMBER 1822
Indian Affairs The Fox and Sauk Indians sign a treaty with the United States that permits them to live on territory ceded to the Federal Government. These lands are in the Wisconsin Territory and Illinois.

27 OCTOBER 1822
Transportation In New York state, a 280-mile section of the Erie Canal is opened, linking Rochester and Albany.

18 NOVEMBER 1822
National The Kentucky state legislature nominates Henry Clay as its presidential candidate in the 1824 national election.

NOVEMBER 1822
International At the Congress of Vienna, the Holy Alliance of Austria, France, Prussia and Russia agree to support Spain in her attempt to recover her former New World colonies. Great Britain breaks with the Holy Alliance over this issue.

12 DECEMBER 1822
International The United States officially recognizes the independent nation of Mexico, headed by Emperor Agustín de Iturbide.

JANUARY 1823
Finance Wealthy Philadelphian, diplomat, and writer Nicholas Biddle is appointed to manage the second Bank of the United States. Under Biddle's expert stewardship and sound money policies, the bank will prosper until the 1836 expiration of its charter.

27 JANUARY 1823
International The United States formally recognizes

211

LITERATURE: AMERICAN ROMANTICISM

In the decades following the Revolutionary War, conscientious attempts were made to develop a distinctly American form of literature. But despite this nationalistic bias, the dominant writers of the era—Washington Irving and James Fenimore Cooper—found themselves part of a larger European literary and artistic movement, that of Romanticism. And ironically, most American writers sought assurances of their success abroad. Irving and Cooper, especially, were accorded widespread European fame.

In the colonial era, the American literary output had been dominated by religious works, and during the Revolutionary period by political works. The writers of the post-revolutionary era turned their attention to works of romantic fiction. The dominant movement of the 19th century, Romanticism was characterized by a striving for liberty, both individual and social; a revolt against classical rationalism; an idealization of nature; the primacy of imagination and an appreciation of the faraway and exotic. Politically, revolutions were romantic, as were utopian societies, social reform movements, and abolitionism. Accordingly, European intellectuals regarded America as the epitome of all that was romantic.

In literature, romanticism was characterized, in both Irving's and Cooper's work, by an emphasis on remote subject matter—remote to the authors in time, social circumstances, and place. The native American subject matter fitting this idea were the colonial era, the Revolutionary era and the frontier. Thus, Washington Irving chose to write about the legendary and picturesque colonial era in his humorous *Knickerbocker's History of New York* (1809) and in various pieces in *The Sketchbook*, composed during his English and European sojourn that lasted from 1815 to 1832.

The prolific James Fenimore Cooper also based the most popular of his 39 full–length novels on remote subject matter. His adventurous *Leatherstocking Tales*, including *The Pioneers* (1823), *The Last of the Mohicans* (1826), *The Prairie* (1827), *The Pathfinder* (1841) and *The Deerslayer* (1841) portray the suspenseful life of fictional frontier hunter and fighter Natty Bumppo, who participates in the epic struggle resulting from advance of civilization on the primeval wilderness. Like Irving, Cooper too spent seven of his busiest years as a writer, from 1826 to 1833, in Europe.

It has been noted that the predilection of Irving, the son of a well-to-do New York City merchant, and Cooper, who grew up on an immense manorial estate, for the past was a form of escapism informed by a nostalgic longing for the earlier and less democratic era of American history. Both Irving and Cooper, conservatives at heart, found little to admire in the bustling materialism of the present. But to future generations they appeared to have struck the first chords of the American experience.

the independent nations of Chile and Argentina.

18 FEBRUARY 1823
Westward Movement Mexico's Emperor Agustín de Iturbide reconfirms the land grant made by the government of New Spain to the late Moses Austin, made transferrable to his son Stephen F. Austin. This tract along the Rio Brazos in Texas will become home to the 300 American families brought in by Austin in 1825.

FEBRUARY 1823
National In the case of *Green v. Biddle*, the United States Supreme Court rules that a contract between two states is constitutionally just as valid as a contract between two private parties.

3 MARCH 1823
Transportation Congress enacts legislation authorizing the construction of lighthouses and beacons for the improvement of the nation's harbors.

17 JULY 1823
International Secretary of State John Quincy Adams informs the Russian minister to the United States that the "American continents are no longer subjects for any new European colonial establishments," thus directly challenging the Russian imperial decree of September 4, 1821, claiming the American Pacific coast from Oregon to Alaska. The United States and Russia will sign a treaty resolving this issue on April 17, 1824.

20 AUGUST 1823
International British foreign secretary George Canning sends a formal note to American minister to Great Britain Richard Rush, suggesting the possibility of joint Anglo-American action against proposed hemispheric intervention by the Holy Alliance to help Spain regain her former colonies. The United States will initially regard this British initiative with favor.

10 SEPTEMBER 1823
Transportation In New York State, the Champlain Canal linking the Hudson River and Lake Champlain is opened to inland commercial traffic.

9 OCTOBER 1823
International In the Polignac Agreement between Great Britain and France, France renounces all intentions of assisting Spain to regain her former colonies in the New World.

7 NOVEMBER 1823
International In a cabinet meeting, Secretary of State John Quincy Adams voices his objections to the proposed alliance with the British in order to counter European intervention in the New World. Adams convinces President Monroe to pursue a policy of independent United States action.

1 DECEMBER 1823
National In Washington, the 18th Congress convenes, with Massachusetts Representative Daniel Webster taking a seat in the House. Henry Clay is again elected Speaker of the House.

2 DECEMBER 1823
International In his annual message to Congress, President Monroe presents the Monroe Doctrine, proclaiming that the Americas will no longer be the subject of European colonization; that the American political system differs essentially from European gov-

ernmental systems; that the United States would consider dangerous the attempt of any European nation to extend its political systems to the Western Hemisphere; and that the United States will not interfere with any existing European colonies in the New World, or interfere in European internal affairs, or participate in European wars of foreign interest.

14 FEBRUARY 1824

National With only 66 of the 216 Democratic-Republican Representatives participating, a "rump" or minority congressional caucus nominates Secretary of the Treasury William H. Crawford, despite a September 1823 paralytic stroke, as a presidential candidate in the 1824 national election. This is the last time the congressional caucus procedure will be used to nominate a presidential candidate.

15 FEBRUARY 1824

National In a Boston political gathering, Secretary of State John Quincy Adams is nominated a presidential candidate in the 1824 national election. The last of the five candidates to be nominated, Adams initially holds the strongest position since he benefits from the dissension among the western and southern candidates. The other New England states will soon follow in endorsing Adams.

FEBRUARY 1824

Westward Movement "Mountain Man" Jedediah Strong Smith, a guide for William Ashley's Rocky Mountain Fur Company, leads a group of explorers through Wyoming's South Pass. This wide gateway through the Rocky Mountains, originally discovered in 1812, has remained virtually unused until now. South Pass will provide the route for the later 19th–century Oregon Trail migrations to the Far West.

1 MARCH 1824

Transportation In New Jersey, work is begun on the Morris County Canal which will link New York City with the Delaware River at its junction with the Lehigh River.

2 MARCH 1824

Transportation In the case of *Gibbons v. Ogden,* Supreme Court Chief Justice John Marshall rules that a monopoly granted by the New York state legislature for steamboat navigation between New York and New Jersey is unconstitutional because only the Federal Government has jurisdiction over interstate commerce.

4 MARCH 1824

National Andrew Jackson, who has already been nominated as presidential candidate by the Tennessee legislature on July 20, 1822, is now endorsed by a Harrisburg, Pennsylvania, nominating convention. The Pennsylvanians also tap John C. Calhoun for the vice–presidential position.

19 MARCH 1824

National In the case of *Osborn v. Bank of the*

United States, Supreme Court Chief Justice John Marshall holds that the state of Ohio cannot tax the Bank of the United States. Ohio state auditor Ralph Osborn and other state officials who had seized bank assets had been assessed damages and they had appealed this earlier decision. Marshall finds that if an agent of a state executes an unconstitutional statute, he will be personally liable for damages resulting from his enforcement of the act. In this opinion, Marshall denies the state the protection of the 11th Amendment in such cases.

30-31 MARCH 1824

Commerce In a debate in the House of Representatives, Henry Clay defends the protectionist features of the proposed Tariff of 1824. He defines as the American system this combination of protective tariffs and internal improvements, including the construction of transportation routes intended to expand domestic trade and industry, thus decreasing American dependence on foreign imports. On April 1-2 Daniel Webster will deliver a speech supporting the principle of free trade.

17 APRIL 1824

International Russia and the United States sign a treaty in which Russia agrees to 54°40′ as the southern limit of its American West Coast claims, and removes its ban on the commercial shipping of other nations in its territorial waters.

30 APRIL 1824

Transportation Congress passes the General Survey Bill, authorizing the federal surveying and cost estimates for proposed national road and canal routes, important for military, postal and commercial purposes.

7 MAY 1824

Regional Under the new constitution of Mexico, the state of Texas and Coahuila is organized. This region is home to several thousand officially-sanctioned American settlers, as well as numerous unofficial squatters.

22 MAY 1824

Commerce Congress adopts the Tariff Act of 1824, vigorously promoted by Henry Clay to protect American industry. This legislation raises rates on wool, cotton and iron; and sets duties on such previously untaxed items as linen, silk, glass and lead.

26 MAY 1824

International The United States extends diplomatic recognition to the recently liberated Empire of Brazil.

17 JUNE 1824

Indian Affairs The Bureau of Indian Affairs is established as a subsidiary of the War Department.

26 JUNE 1824

Finance In the case of *Bank of United States v.*

TESTING A UNION 1788-1865

Planter's Bank of Georgia, the Supreme Court decides that a state that becomes party to any banking or business venture, is liable to legal suit as a part of that commercial venture.

4 AUGUST 1824
International The United States extends diplomatic recognition to what will be the short-lived Central American Union—a coalition of present-day Costa Rica, Guatemala, Honduras, Nicaragua and El Salvador.

14 AUGUST 1824
Life/Customs America's invaluable Revolutionary War ally, the Marquise de Lafayette, arrives in New York at the invitation of President Monroe for what will be a year-long triumphal tour of the nation to visit battle sites, to stay with Jefferson at Monticello, and to assist at the dedication of the Bunker Hill Monument.

3 OCTOBER 1824
International The United States and Gran Colombia sign a commercial and friendship pact.
Education In Troy, New York, the Rensselaer School of Theoretical and Practical Science is established. The school is remarkable for its innovative curriculum of science and engineering courses, rather than the customary fare of classical studies.

1 DECEMBER 1824
National In the presidential election, none of the candidates gains a majority. Andrew Jackson receives 99 electoral votes; John Quincy Adams, 84; William H. Crawford, 41; and Henry Clay, 37. Hence the election is thrown into the House of Representatives, who must choose among the top three candidates on February 9, 1825. John C. Calhoun, however, has been chosen vice–president, with 182 electoral votes.

DECEMBER 1824
Slavery The Indiana legislature passes a fugitive slave act which allows justices of the peace to rule on claims in fugitive slave cases, with both the claimant and fugitive possessing the right to a jury trial. This bill will be invalidated in 1850.
Exploration Great Salt Lake is discovered by fur trapper and scout Jim Bridger.

3 JANUARY 1825
Ideas/Beliefs In Indiana, Scottish mill owner Robert Owen buys the 20,000-acre former George Rapp estate in order to establish a model community at New Harmony. This pioneering utopian experiment will fail some two years later, after having consumed most of Owen's fortune.

31 JANUARY 1825
Transportation In Maryland, the Chesapeake and Ohio Canal Company is chartered.

9 FEBRUARY 1825
National In the House of Representatives, the unre-solved presidential election is decided. John Quincy Adams receives the votes of 13 states, to Andrew Jackson's 7, and William Crawford's 4. Adams' victory is made possible by the support of Henry Clay, raising the accusation of a "corrupt bargain," by Jackson and his supporters when Adams later appoints Clay his Secretary of State. A major result of the 1824 election is the schism in the Democratic-Republican party. The Adams-Clay faction will become known as the National Republicans (or the Whig party in the 1830s), and the pro-Jackson faction keeps the Democratic-Republican name, to become the Democratic party after 1828.

FEBRUARY 1825
Indian Affairs On John C. Calhoun's advice, lame–duck President Monroe institutes a federal policy of transferring the Indians on the lands east of the Mississippi River to territories in the American West.

12 FEBRUARY 1825
Indian Affairs In Georgia, Creek Indian chief William McIntosh signs the Treaty of Indian Springs, ceding all Creek lands in the state to the United States, and agreeing to vacate the state by September 1, 1826. The other Creek Indians repudiate the pact, calling McIntosh a traitor and killing him.

3 MARCH 1825
Transportation A federal survey to mark the Santa Fe Trail, linking the Missouri River and New Mexico, is authorized by Congress.

4 MARCH 1825
National John Quincy Adams is inaugurated as the sixth president of the United States, with John C. Calhoun as his vice–president. The members of the Adams cabinet will be Henry Clay as Secretary of State, Richard Rush as Secretary of the Treasury, James Barbour as Secretary of War, S.L. Southard as Secretary of the Navy, John McLean as Postmaster General, and William Wirt as Attorney General. Adams' stated policy of avoiding political patronage will cost him important support.

7 MARCH 1825
National On the day that Henry Clay is appointed Secretary of State, Joel R. Poinsett is nominated as America's first minister to Mexico. Poinsett's appointment will be confirmed the following day.

24 MARCH 1825
Westward Movement The Mexican state of Texas-Coahuila officially declares itself open to American settlers.

4 JULY 1825
Transportation Construction is recommenced on the Cumberland Road in order to extend it westward from Wheeling, West Virginia, through Ohio. From Wheeling onward, the route will be named the National Road.

JOHN QUINCY ADAMS, 1767-1848

John Quincy Adams was groomed from his youth by his father, John Adams, to become president of the United States. Appropriately enough, he was elected to the office but, ironically enough, in his long and brilliant career in public office it was only as president that he did not excel. Adams was born in Braintree, Massachusetts, on July 11, 1767, and was educated first in Europe while accompanying his father's diplomatic journeys; returning to America, he received a Harvard degree in 1787, read law and began practice in Boston. By then he was already one of the most learned men of his time, an extraordinary linguist who, it was said, could write English with one hand while translating into Greek with the other.

Adams was to be no isolated intellectual, however. Washington appointed him minister to the Netherlands in 1794, and his father sent Adams to Germany in 1797. In 1803 he ran successfully for the Senate. Still nominally a Federalist, he soon showed his sympathies for the rising Republican movement by supporting Jefferson's ill-fated embargo, which position eventually got him recalled from the Senate. After an interval of teaching at Harvard, he went to Russia as a minister in 1809 and to England in 1815. Meanwhile, he was head of the American delegation that negotiated the Treaty of Ghent, ending the war with Britain in 1814.

His success as a diplomat made him a clear choice as James Monroe's secretary of state in 1817. In that position he was instrumental in forming the Monroe Doctrine and in gaining Florida from Spain, at which time he pressed the Spanish to agree to American claims above the 42nd parallel to the Pacific; the latter achievement, entirely his own, has been called "the greatest diplomatic victory. . .in the history of the United States."

Running for President in 1824, Adams won fewer popular votes than Andrew Jackson; the election was decided in the House after Henry Clay threw his vote to Adams. When Adams then made Clay his secretary of state, Jackson took up the cry of "bargain and corruption" that would hound Adams throughout his term. But this was far from his only problem; his ambitious programs for strengthening the central government, controlling public lands and improving national transportation routes ran afoul of states' rights interests. Behind all the troubles loomed the specter of slavery, and the South's fear that the North would outlaw it (which is just what Adams planned, though he was too practical to push for immediate abolition). Adams lost the Presidency to Jackson in 1828; two years later he began his long and distinguished career in the House, where he fought against slavery until his death in 1848. He had carried on a tradition of scholarship and service that would endure in his descendants to make the Adams family one of the most distinguished in American history.

19 AUGUST 1825
Indian Affairs In Prairie du Chien, Wisconsin, the Chippewa, Iowa, Potawami, Sauk and Fox, Sioux and Winnebago tribes will sign a treaty among themselves, setting their territorial boundaries in order to avoid further intertribal bloodshed. The negotiations for the pact have been arranged by the Federal Government, at the request of the Chippewa and Sioux.

OCTOBER 1825
National The Tennessee legislature nominates Andrew Jackson as its presidential candidate in the 1828 national election.

26 OCTOBER 1825
Transportation The Erie Canal, linking New York City with the Great Lakes, is completed. Its official opening at Buffalo will greatly encourage the commercial growth of New York City and of the other cities along the canal's route. Connecting the Hudson River with Lake Erie by way of the Mohawk River, channels in Lake Oneida and short stretches of other rivers, the Erie Canal is 363 miles long, making the water route from New York City to Lake Erie 550 miles long.

5 DECEMBER 1825
International Diplomatic negotiations are concluded with the Central American Union for a treaty of amity and commerce. The Senate will unanimously endorse the pact on December 29.

National In Washington, the 19th Congress convenes. The Federalist party no longer exists at the national level, and the Democratic-Republican party has split into a pro-Adams administration and an anti-Adams administration faction. In the House of Representatives, 105 support the administration and 97 oppose it; in the Senate, 26 support the administration and 20 oppose it.

6 DECEMBER 1825
National In what is the first annual presidential message to Congress, President John Quincy Adams proposes a national program of internal improvements and reforms. In addition, he urges government support for the establishment of a national university, and for arts and sciences, including the erection of a national astronomical observatory in Washington.

TESTING A UNION 1788-1865

CANALS

With the 1825 completion of the Erie Canal, the great era of canal building began in the United States. Combined with the surge of road building, the construction of these inland waterways helped to open up many new territories to commerce and settlement. The Erie Canal was the most important, but not the first canal to be built. Previously, short canals had been dug to bypass the falls of New England rivers; three such canals, including the South Hadley Canal, had already been constructed in Massachusetts. In 1800, Charleston, South Carolina, had been linked to the Santee River by way of the Santee and Cooper Canal; and in 1808, the Middlesex Canal connected Boston with the Merrimac River and with the inland textile mills.

The savings in transportation costs were dramatic. Compared to the fees for wagon portage at $100 a ton, canal barge transportation cost $12 a ton. Mules pulled the flat-bottomed barges along the four-foot deep, 363-mile-long Erie Canal at the rate of a mile and a half an hour. During its first year of operation, the Erie Canal saw 7000 barges travel its course from Albany to Buffalo. The thousands of new immigrants who had worked on building the Erie Canal, remained to establish towns along its route. The heavy flow of goods along the Erie Canal and the Hudson River made New York the nation's busiest seaport, as well as America's financial center. The building of the canal also furnished untried American engineers with invaluable experience in the construction of such major transportation projects.

The boom in canal building initiated by the financial success of the Erie Canal led to the construction of some 3000 miles of inland waterways by the 1840s. The major projects linked Philadelphia and Pittsburgh, and connected the Great Lakes with the Mississippi River by way of the Illinois and Michigan Canal. The increased traffic between the Midwest and the East made such cities as Cleveland and Toledo, Ohio, major ports on the Great Lakes.

But the Erie Canal was unique in achieving a profit. Most of the other canals eventually failed because their construction required an insurmountable debt that could not be repaid from users' fees. The new age of the railroad brought an end to the role of canals in the commercial growth and westward expansion of the nation.

26 DECEMBER 1825
International President Adams requests that Congress allow United States representatives to attend, as consultants, Simon Bolivar's Panama Congress, called in order to promote a general Latin American confederation. After heated debate, Congress will vote to send United States envoys only as observers. Neither of the two chosen representatives will actually attend the June 1826 Panama Congress, as one will die on the way and the other will arrive too late.

6 JANUARY 1826
National In Washington, the first issue of the *United States Telegraph* comes out. This anti-Adams administration newspaper is supported by pro-Jacksonian forces in the Senate and House, and its publication marks the deep factionalism that mars Adams' term in office.

24 JANUARY 1826
Indian Affairs In the Treaty of Washington, Georgia's Creek Indians cede a smaller tract to the United States than negotiated in the February 12, 1825 Treaty of Indian Springs. The Creek Indians must vacate their western Georgia lands by January 1, 1827.

13 FEBRUARY 1826
Life/Customs In Boston, the American Society for the Promotion of Temperance is founded by an all-male group of clergymen and laymen. The first society opposing the consumption of alcoholic beverages had been founded in 1808 in New York's Saratoga County.

8 APRIL 1826
National Along the Virginia bank of the Potomac River, Secretary of State Henry Clay and Jackson supporter John Randolph fight a duel over Randolph's accusation that Clay had made a "corrupt bargain" in throwing his support to John Quincy Adams in the 1825 presidential election. As both men misfire, no blood is shed.

26 APRIL 1826
International In Washington, a treaty of amity, commerce and navigation is signed with Denmark.

2 MAY 1826
International The United States extends diplomatic recognition to the republic of Peru.

4 JULY 1826
National On the 50th anniversary of the Declaration of Independence, founding fathers and former presidents Thomas Jefferson, 83, and John Adams, 91, die. Jefferson dies first at Monticello in Virginia, after having queried during the night, "Is it the Fourth?" John Adams dies some four and one-half hours later in Quincy, Massachusetts, murmuring, "Thomas Jefferson still survives." This event symbolizes to many God's divine approval of the United States.

2 AUGUST 1826
National In Boston's Faneuil Hall, Daniel Webster delivers a eulogy on John Adams and Thomas Jefferson, whose common death concludes the revolutionary epoch of American history.

22 AUGUST 1826
Westward Movement Jedediah Strong Smith leads the first overland expedition from Great Salt Lake, Utah, to California by way of the Cajon Pass, arriving in San Diego on November 27.

12 SEPTEMBER 1826
National In Batavia, New York, former Freemason William Morgan disappears under unusual circumstances after having disclosed some of the order's secrets. Suspicions that the Freemasons have abducted and killed him lead to the formation of the Anti-Masonic party, the earliest American third party.

7 OCTOBER 1826
Transportation In Quincy, Massachusetts, the first American railroad is completed. The three–mile long metal track from the Quincy granite quarry to the Neponset River accommodates horse-drawn wagons.

NOVEMBER 1826
National In the national mid–term elections, the anti-administration Jacksonians win a majority in both houses of Congress.

10 JANUARY 1827
Commerce A bill is introduced in Congress by the advocates of protectionism calling for higher duties on imported woolen goods. The Tariff of 1824 has failed to eliminate British competition in textiles. The bill will pass the House of Representatives on February 10, but it will be rejected on February 28 in the Senate when Vice–President John Calhoun casts a tie-breaking vote against the measure.

2 FEBRUARY 1827
National In the case of *Martin v. Mott,* the Supreme Court finds that constitutionally the President alone has the final power to determine whether the state militias should be mobilized in the national interest.

17 FEBRUARY 1827
Indian Affairs Georgia Governor George M. Troup calls up the state militia to oppose Federal Troops who have been dispatched to western Georgia to bar the premature surveying of the Creek Indian lands which were ceded in the January 24, 1826 Treaty of Washington, but whose transfer has not yet officially taken place.

28 FEBRUARY 1827
Transportation In Maryland, the Baltimore and Ohio Railroad is chartered by the state to carry passengers and freight. The railroad will also receive a charter from Virginia on March 8.

13 MARCH 1827
National In the case of *Ogden v. Saunders,* the Supreme Court rules that a contract made after the passage of a bankruptcy law is controlled by the provisions of that law.

8 MAY 1827
Westward Movement In present-day Kansas, the location is chosen for Cantonment Leavenworth, later Fort Leavenworth, in order to provide protection for the thriving commercial trade along the Santa Fe Trail.

MAY 1827
Transportation In Pennsylvania, the Mauch Chunk gravity railroad is constructed. The nine-mile line runs from the Carbondale coal mines to the Lehigh River.

2 JULY 1827
Commerce In a Columbia, South Carolina, meet-ing, Thomas Cooper, the president of South Carolina College, opposes protective tariffs as favoring the interests of the industrial North over those of the agricultural South.

30 JULY 1827
Commerce In Harrisburg, Pennsylvania, a convention of some 100 delegates from 13 states meets to call for higher tariffs. Despite the February defeat of the tariff bill in the Senate, there is a strong popular movement promoting such protectionist policies in order to shelter the American wool industry, as well as the producers of such goods as hemp, flax and hammered bar iron and steel.

6 AUGUST 1827
Commerce Envoys of Great Britain and the United States sign a mutual pact renewing their 1818 commercial treaty and continuing their joint occupation of the Oregon region. The Senate will ratify this treaty on February 5, 1828.

15 NOVEMBER 1827
Indian Affairs The Creek Indians sign a second treaty, ceding the rest of their western Georgia lands to the United States.

3 DECEMBER 1827
National After the mid–term elections, the 20th Congress convenes with significant gains for the Jacksonian forces. In the House, they number 119 to 94 for the pro-Adams forces, and in the Senate, 26 to 20.

24 DECEMBER 1827
Commerce Congress reviews the protectionist recommendations of the July 30, Harrisburg Convention, but the controlling Jacksonian forces oppose endorsement of the recommendations.

12 JANUARY 1828
International Mexico and the United States sign a treaty setting their common boundary line along the Sabine River, as established in the treaty of 1819 with Spain. The Senate will approve this pact on April 28.

31 JANUARY 1828
Commerce In the House of Representatives, the anti-administration Jacksonians introduce a new tariff bill calling for extremely high duties on a number of import goods and raw materials, including iron, hemp and flax, while eliminating some of the protection for the New England wool industry. The Jacksonians are exploiting the tariff issue raised by the July 30, 1827 Harrisburg Convention in order to embarrass President Adams politically when the bill is rejected as they fully expect it to be. Debate will begin on this measure on March 4.

21 FEBRUARY 1828
Indian Affairs In Oklahoma, Indian linguist Sequoyah and Elias Boudinot found the *Cherokee Phoenix,* the first American newspaper to be published in

an Indian language. Sequoyah had invented an 86-symbol written version of the Cherokee language in 1821, thus allowing thousands of Cherokees to learn to read and write in their own tongue.

24 MARCH 1828
Transportation In Pennsylvania, the state legislature votes to assist with the construction funding of a proposed railroad between Philadelphia and Columbia. This is the first instance of a publicly sponsored project of this nature.

21 APRIL 1828
Arts/Culture After more than 20 years' labor, Noah Webster finally publishes his *American Dictionary of the English Language*. This monumental volume contains some 70,000 definitions—12,000 more than any other English language dictionary—and it includes numerous words derived from the other American immigrant languages and from the various Indian languages.

19 MAY 1828
Commerce The "Tariff of Abominations," as it will come to be known, originally proposed on January 31, is signed into law by President Adams, thus thwarting the Machiavellian plans of the congressional Jacksonians to discredit Adams by the bill's defeat. After heated debate, the coalition of Southern and Middle Atlantic states led by Martin Van Buren and Vice-President John Calhoun voted down all attempts by New Englanders to amend the more flagrant provisions of the bill. Nevertheless, when the legislation came to a vote, the New Englanders surprisingly supported the bill, as it promoted the protection of American industry. The tariff passed the House, 105 to 94, on April 23 and the Senate, 26 to 21, on May 13.

24 MAY 1828
Commerce Congress passes the Reciprocity Act, which mandates the nullification of all discriminatory import duties on trade with reciprocating nations.

4 JULY 1828
Transportation Ground-breaking ceremonies are held for the Baltimore and Ohio Railroad, with the assistance of Charles Carroll, the only surviving signer of the Declaration of Independence. On December 22, 1829, the first completed section of rail will open for passenger service in a horse-drawn excursion train. The line will begin conversion to steam power on August 30, 1830. On the same day, President Adams inaugurates the construction of the Chesapeake and Ohio Canal.

16 OCTOBER 1828
Transportation The Delaware and Hudson Canal is opened for service. Running from Honesdale, Pennsylvania, to Kingston, New York, the canal will permit the transportation of anthracite coal from northeastern Pennsylvania to the industrial centers of New York and New England.

Daniel Webster.

3 DECEMBER 1828
National After a virulent, name-calling presidential campaign, Andrew Jackson is chosen president, with the invaluable support of New York's Albany Regency leaders Martin Van Buren and William L. Marcy. Jackson receives 178 electoral votes to the 83 received by incumbent President John Quincy Adams. John C. Calhoun is elected Jackson's vice-president, defeating Richard Rush, Adams' running mate.

12 DECEMBER 1828
International The United States signs a treaty of peace and navigation with Brazil. The Senate will ratify the pact on March 10, 1829.

19 DECEMBER 1828
Commerce The Tariff of May 19 is opposed as unconstitutional, oppressive and unjust by eight resolutions issued by the South Carolina legislature. The resolutions are accompanied by the essay, "South Carolina Exposition and Protest," anonymously written by Vice-President John C. Calhoun, who advocates state sovereignty and the doctrine of nullification by a single state. The Georgia legislature will protest the tariff on December 30, as will Virginia and Mississippi in February 1829.

20 DECEMBER 1828
Indian Affairs The Georgia legislature enacts a bill

declaring the laws of the Cherokee Indians to be null and void after June 1, 1830.

OTHER EVENTS OF 1828
Arts/Culture   Painter and naturalist John James Audubon issues the first volume of his *Birds of America*, an engraved series of 1065 birds shown in their natural habitats. This five-volume portfolio will not be completed until 1838.

9 JANUARY 1829
Westward Movement   The House of Representatives defeats a bill advocating the establishment of a territorial government and the construction of an American fort in Oregon. During this year, the American Society for Encouraging Settlement of Oregon Territory is founded in Boston.

4 MARCH 1829
National   Andrew Jackson is inaugurated as the seventh president of the United States, and John Calhoun is inaugurated as vice–president. In his low-key Inaugural Address, Jackson calls for economy in government, the support of states' rights, a fair Indian policy, and a reorganization of the federal civil service. He does not address the burning issue of the tariff, the national currency system, the Bank of the United States or public works projects.

In the rambunctious reception at the White House that follows the ceremony, Jackson's enthusiastic supporters crowd into the mansion, leaving muddy footprints on the satin-covered chairs.

In President Jackson's cabinet are Martin Van Buren as Secretary of State, Samuel D. Ingham as Secretary of the Treasury, John H. Eaton as Secretary of War, John Branch as Secretary of the Navy, John M. Berrien as Attorney General, and William T. Barry as Postmaster General. But Jackson mainly will rely for advice instead on his unofficial "kitchen cabinet," including Andrew J. Donelson, Duff Green, Isaac Hull, Amos Kendall, and William B. Lewis.

The Jackson administration will also introduce the "spoils system" into national politics. But Jackson is to employ patronage for partisan purposes only moderately, as he removes only nine percent of the incumbent federal office holders during his first term.

23 MARCH 1829
Indian Affairs   The Creek Indians receive a message from President Jackson ordering them either to conform to the laws of Alabama or to relocate across the Mississippi River.

29 JULY 1829
Indian Affairs   In the Michigan Territory, the Chippewa, Ottawa and Potawatomi Indians cede lands to the United States.

8 AUGUST 1829
Transportation   In Pennsylvania, the *Stourbridge Lion*, the first steam–powered locomotive in America, is run on the Delaware and Hudson Canal Company's

ANDREW JACKSON, 1767-1845

Jackson was the first President with no connection to the Virginia Dynasty, the first self-made man with no trace of the aristocrat, the first who came to fame primarily as a military man and the first to gain office largely by the slinging of mud. Nonetheless, from that unpromising resume came a great President, one who forever marked the office with the force of his personality and his carrying on of the Democratic (formerly Republican) party legacy of Jefferson.

Jackson was born along Waxhaw Creek in South Carolina on March 15, 1767. By the age of 20 he had read enough law to be admitted to the bar; he moved to Nashville, Tennessee, and his practice soon prospered in that frontier town. Falling in love with Rachel Donelson Robards, he married her on a mistaken assumption that her previous marriage had been dissolved; the problem was eventually resolved by a second and legal marriage, but the irregular aspect of the whole affair was to pursue the couple for the rest of their lives and be the cause of several conflicts, including one duel in which Jackson killed his opponent. Rising quickly in local politics, Jackson was elected to the U.S. House in 1796 and the Senate the following year, but was soon forced by financial problems to resign in favor of a Tennessee superior court position. Over the next few years he established a reputation as a fair, if not particularly learned, judge; as always, he was guided mainly by his convictions and intuitions. In 1804 he began a long retirement to his estate, The Hermitage, near Nashville. At the outbreak of the War of 1812 he was an eager volunteer; as a tough officer he acquired from his troops his classic nickname, "Old Hickory. He gained national adulation as the hero of New Orleans in 1815; in the last battle of the war, his men inflicted 2000 casualties on the British to his own 16. His sights already on the Presidency, he mounted a more or less unordered invasion of Spanish Florida in 1817 that began as an embarrassment but resulted in Spain's ceding Florida.

In the Presidential election of 1824 Jackson won the

TESTING A UNION 1788-1865

popular vote but was defeated in the House when Henry Clay swung his vote to John Quincy Adams. Over the next four years, Jackson put together a wide–ranging coalition to oust Adams and the old order of aristocratic politicians he represented. After a campaign marked by much mudslinging on both sides, Jackson won by a landslide in 1828. He proceeded first to effect a wholesale cleaning out of Adams men in the government, replacing them with his own appointees and thereby setting an unhealthy precedent for the "spoils system" in American politics. A steadfast Unionist, Jackson threatened military force to combat Calhoun's nullification efforts in South Carolina. Nonetheless, Jackson was concerned enough with states' rights to squelch the Bank of the United States in his second term (which began a currency crisis tthat led to a panic in 1837). His foreign efforts proved less ambigously successful; he settled problems with Britain and France and widely recognized the independence of Texas, delaying for a time the slavery question that arose with each new state.

Retiring to The Hermitage in 1837, Jackson remained an active elder statesman. As he died in 1845, his last words were strange and prophetic: "I expect to see you all in heaven, both white and black."

track from Carbondale to Honesdale. This British-made engine travels at a rate of 10 miles per hour. The first American-built engine will run in South Carolina the following year, leading to the inauguration of scheduled passenger service on December 25, 1830.

25 AUGUST 1829

Regional The Mexican government rejects the offer of President Jackson to purchase Texas, where thousands of American settlers now live. The United States will persist in its negotiations on this topic.

2 DECEMBER 1829

Slavery Mexican President Guerrero proclaims Texas exempt from the Mexican anti-slavery decree of September 15.

8 DECEMBER 1829

National In his first annual message to Congress, President Jackson again raises the issue of the constitutionality of the Bank of the United States. He also proposes the sharing of surplus federal revenue with the state governments.

29 DECEMBER 1829

Westward Movement Connecticut Senator Samuel A. Foot introduces a resolution calling for temporary restrictions on western public land sales. This resolution will later lead to the 1830 Webster-Hayne debate over states' rights and federal sovereignty.

18 JANUARY 1830

National Senate response to the Foot Resolution of 29 December 1829 begins when Thomas Hart Benton of Missouri charges that powers in the Northeast want to slow prosperity in the West.

12-27 JANUARY 1830

National Robert Y. Hayne of South Carolina sup-ports Benton's stand in the Senate and begins a debate over the issues with Daniel Webster of Massachusetts. It soon becomes apparent that the real subject under discussion is not the sale of the vast lands of the American West, but that of states' rights versus federal power. This sets Southern Senators against Northern Senators; Hayne and Webster eventually argue the origin and nature of the Constitution. Hayne supports state sovereignty and nullification. Webster

LANDSCAPE PAINTING: THE HUDSON RIVER SCHOOL

Just as the writers and linguists of the early American republic sought to develop a truly American literature and language, so did this urge extend to the visual arts. The most profound expression of this nationalism was found in landscape—a realm of painting hitherto held in low regard. The early 19th century focus on nature and landscape was an integral part of the larger Romantic movement, influential in Europe as well as in America. The romantic attitude saw nature as the source of man's knowledge and inspiration—it was the mind of God made visible and the embodiment of man's freedom. The nation's landscape was regarded as uniquely American in that it was a primeval paradise, analogous to the Garden of Eden. European culture was represented by architectural monuments and classical ruins, while America possessed equally ancient remains in her primeval forests, awesome mountains, unspoiled lakes and picturesque waterfalls. Furthermore, while education in the classics, world history and literature was required to paint and appreciate European-style history paintings, the American landscape as subject was democratic in that it required of the painter and audience only a deeply-felt individual experience of the beauties and terrors of nature. Not only was the landscape evocative of emotional states, it also conveyed moral lessons: sunlight was seen as the emanation of God's divine power, and the eternal cycle of birth, death and rebirth could be inferred by the juxtaposition of young saplings, mature trees and decrepit stumps.

The American landscape painters who expressed these ideas were known as the Hudson River School, because of their summer sketching expeditions to the Hudson River Valley, as well as to New Hampshire's White Mountains, the Berkshires and the "Arcadian vales" of the Connecticut River Valley. During the winters the artists retired to their studios to work up dramatic and typical panoramas by combining details from their summer sketches.

English-born Thomas Cole painted his visionary landscapes as seen through the haze of memory, erasing and reconstituting the details of the actual sites according to conventional formulas. A more objective observation of nature was the interest of Asher Brown Durand; he let the actual landscape determine the composition of the painting and the actual weather conditions determine the light and atmospheric effects employed. The New England paintings of Cole, Durand, Thomas Doughty, John F. Kensett and many others were later succeeded by Frederick Church's and Albert Bierstadt's panoramas of the unique topographic wonders of the Far West. These canvas visions served as an idealistic contrast to the less rarified social realities of broken Indian treaties, rampant land speculation, widespread pioneer settlement and inevitably the leveling of those spectacular wilderness forests.

responds with what some have called the greatest American oration ever recorded. He centers his remarks on the nature of the Union, emphasizing that states derive their power from the Constitution and that the national government reigns over the people. He further declares that disputes between state and federal governments are settled by agencies designated for this purpose in the Constitution. In his ringing climax to his defense of the Union, Webster concludes, "Liberty and Union, now and forever, one and inseparable!"

12 MARCH 1830
Finance The Supreme Court considers state loan certificates in the case of *Craig v. Missouri*. It declares that the certificates, intended for circulation, are bills of credit and therefore unconstitutional.

31 MARCH 1830
National The Pennsylvania legislature nominates Andrew Jackson for president. Several states endorse his nomination.

6 APRIL 1830
Ideas/Beliefs Based on his visions and translations of messages on golden tablets, Joseph Smith organizes the Church of Latter-Day Saints (Mormons) at Fayette, New York. Smith publishes his *Book of Mormon* this same year. After early persecution, his religion will become one of the most powerful in America.

International Mexico passes the colonization law to block United States citizens from any further colonizing in the Texas territories. The law also prohibits U.S. citizens from importing black slaves to that area.

13 APRIL 1830
Civil War: Approach At a dinner on the anniversary of Thomas Jefferson's birthday, President Andrew Jackson deliberately challenges the Southerners present by toasting, "Our Federal Union—it must be preserved!" Vice–President John Calhoun returns the toast with his challenge: "The Union—next to our liberty, the most dear!"

20-29 MAY 1830
International Congress reduces duties on tea, coffee, salt and molasses.

21 MAY 1830
National The Foot Resolution, which inspired the Webster-Hayne debate, is tabled.

27 MAY 1830
National President Jackson vetoes the Maysville Road bill which would add federal support to build a 60-mile road in Kentucky. He argues against federal subsidies for roads and canals when they are limited to individual states and not part of larger systems of improvement. He thus concedes to states-righters in the South without losing the support of others who generally favor internal improvements. In a few days,

JOHN C. CALHOUN, 1782-1850

John C. Calhoun came to national attention as a fiery nationalist and ended his life as an apostle of Nullification, sectionalism, and the virtues of slavery. Calhoun was born on his family's settlement along the Savannah River in South Carolina on March 18, 1782. After graduating from Yale in 1804 he briefly practiced law, but after a fortunate marriage brought him wealth he established a plantation in South Carolina. He entered the state legislature as a Republican in 1808 and two years later was elected to the U.S. House, where he quickly allied with the "war hawks" who successfully agitated for war with Britain. After the war he promoted various nationalistic issues including a standing army and a national bank. His extraordinary gift for oratory made him a powerful figure in the House.

Becoming Monroe's secretary of war in 1817, Calhoun labored to strengthen military organization and to promote his growing presidential ambitions. He became Adams' vice–president in 1824 and the same for Jackson in 1828. But events back home were claiming his attention; distressed by damaging government tariffs, South Carolina and other Southern States were proclaiming the right of states to nullify federal law. In a long series of essays, Calhoun was to become the champion and theorist of Nullification; though he always hoped to prevent a total rupture of the Union, his ideas helped to bring about that tragedy.

Estranged from Jackson, Calhoun resigned the vice–presidency in 1833 and joined with Henry Clay to effect a compromise tariff in the Senate, thus defusing the nullification issue for a time. After a period as an anti-Jackson Whig, Calhoun shifted to the Democratic party and kept up his writings supporting nullification and promoting slavery as an economic necessity and a positive moral good. After being Tyler's secretary of state and fighting unsuccessfully for the annexation of Texas as a slave state, Calhoun was elected to the Senate in 1845 and there continued his efforts on behalf of Southern regional rights until his death in 1850. He would later be considered one of the principal prophets of the Confederacy.

TESTING A UNION 1788-1865

on May 31, he will approve the Cumberland Road bill, the only large land-route construction project during his years in office.

28 MAY 1830
Indian Affairs President Jackson signs the Indian Removal Act, granting authority to move Eastern Indians to Western lands. His goal is to take possession of Indian lands east of the Mississippi.

29 MAY 1830
Settling The Preemption Act is adopted to protect squatters from land speculators and claim jumpers. Any settler who cultivated public land during the previous 12 months can purchase up to 160 acres of land at $1.25 per acre. This act will be renewed in later years.

15 JULY 1830
Indian Affairs At Prairie du Chien, Wisconsin, Indians, including the Sioux, Sauk and Fox, sign a treaty to give the United States most of what is now Iowa, Missouri and Minnesota.

28 AUGUST 1830
Transportation The first locomotive built in America, Peter Cooper's "Tom Thumb," runs from Baltimore to Ellicott's Mills on the Baltimore and Ohio Railroad, laid down just a few months before. In addition, New Jersey's first railroad, the Camden-Amboy, was chartered earlier this year.

SEPTEMBER 1830
National The Republican convention at Hartford, Connecticut, nominates Henry Clay for President.

15 SEPTEMBER 1830
Indian Affairs The Choctaw Indians sign a treaty at Dancing Rabbit Creek. They transfer nearly 8 million acres of their land east of the Mississippi to the United States. In exchange they receive land in what is now the state of Oklahoma.

5 OCTOBER 1830
International Secretary of State Martin Van Buren has been meeting with British Minister Sir Charles Vaughan in Washington to negotiate trade agreements with the British West Indies. President Jackson proclaims that US trade with this area is reopened.

DECEMBER 1830
Slavery A schooner, the *Comet,* leaves Alexandria, Virginia, en route to New Orleans, but is wrecked off the Bahamas. British authorities declare that the slaves aboard are free; this creates a lingering point of conflict between the two countries.

6 DECEMBER 1830
National President Jackson delivers his annual message. He again attacks the Bank of the United States and refuses to finance internal improvements through the distribution of surplus federal revenue to states.

HENRY CLAY, 1777-1852

Although his career came long before the era of film and recording, the striking figure and stirring oratory of Henry Clay have remained in the nation's memory. Indeed, his impact on American history was stronger than that of some of the people who beat him for the presidency, the office he most coveted and, sadly for his country, never won. Clay was born in Hanover County, Virginia, on April 12, 1777. Though he had little formal schooling, he became a law clerk in Richmond in 1792; in four years he had studied enough law to be admitted to the bar, and the following year he moved to Lexington, Kentucky, to begin his practice.

Clay soon became the most famous criminal lawyer in the state, but his increasing involvement in public issues took him to the legislature in 1803 and to the U.S. Senate in 1806 and 1809—both times filling out unexpired terms. In 1810 he ran successfully for the U.S. House of Representatives, where soon becoming speaker of the House, he joined the "war hawks" who pressed Madison to declare war on Britain. At the end of the war Clay joined the commission that negotiated the Treaty of Ghent.

Now setting his sights on the presidency, Clay began a series of attacks on his chief rival, Andrew Jackson. In 1824 he worked in the House against Jackson to effect the election of John Quincy Adams as President; when Clay thereafter was appointed secretary of state, Jackson took up the cry of "bargain and corruption" that helped put him in the White House four years later. After a frustrating tenure in the cabinet and the defeat of Adams in 1828, Clay retired until 1831, when he was elected to the Senate; there he became the most vocal opponent of Jackson's policies and an unsuccessful candidate to unseat Jackson in 1832.

The most fervent of unionists, Clay helped defuse the South Carolina nullification turmoil over tariffs in 1833. He was passed over by the anti-Jackson Whig party for the 1840 Presidential nomination, but became the Whig candidate in the next election. Perceived by the country as an abolitionist, Clay was tripped up by the Texas annexation question; Polk was elected, certainly the wrong man for those troubled times. Spurned by the Whigs in 1848, Clay returned to the Senate and resumed his efforts to preserve the Union and gradually to eliminate slavery. In the midst of these efforts he died in Washington in 1852. If any president in that era could have prevented the Civil War, it would likely have been Henry Clay.

7 DECEMBER 1830

National As the split between President Jackson and Calhoun continues to grow, the President and his advisors decide to publish an administration newspaper. They choose Francis P. Blair of Kentucky to edit the *Washington Globe,* and the first issue appears on this day. Another paper, Duff Green's *United States Telegraph,* which has a loan from the Bank of the United States, soon becomes an anti-administration publication.

OTHER EVENTS OF 1830

National Several states revise their constitutions to provide broader suffrage and greater representation.
Settling The town of Chicago is planned at the site of Fort Dearborn, which has been a federal post for 27 years. Western movement continues as Jedediah Strong Smith and William Sublette of the Rocky Mountain Fur Company lead the first group of covered wagons from the Missouri River to the Rockies.
Immigration A new wave of German immigrants begins after the attempted revolution in Germany fails.
Arts/Culture Louis A. Godey begins publishing *Godey's Lady's Book* in Philadelphia. It is the first successful women's magazine. He later hires Sarah Hale to edit the popular magazine; she continues with the publication until her retirement in 1877 at the age of 90. The magazine features colored plates of women's fashions, articles by famous writers, and helps define morality and taste. It eventually has a circulation of 150,000.
Industry A woolen mill based on the Waltham system opens in Lowell, Massachusetts. It attracts the daughters of rural farmers with assurances to their parents about well–supervised dormitory living.
Ideas/Beliefs Sylvester Graham, an activist in the temperance movement, begins to advocate a particular diet based on vegetables and whole wheat. He claims the diet will help calm the sex drive.

1 JANUARY 1831

National In Boston, William Lloyd Garrison, among the more radical of the abolitionists, begins publishing *The Liberator,* a newspaper dedicated to the abolition of slavery. He vows to continue publishing the paper until slaves are freed.

JANUARY 1831

Ideas/Beliefs Joseph Smith and his followers in the Mormon Church move temporarily to Kirtland, Ohio.

15 JANUARY 1831

Transportation The "Best Friend" is the first American-make locomotive to actually carry passengers. It runs from Charlestown to Hamburg on the South Carolina Railroad. Later this year, Isaac Dripps invents a device that will become standard on locomotives—the cowcatcher.

3 FEBRUARY 1831

Industry A new Copyright Act is passed and provides far more generously for authors than a previous law of 1790.

15 FEBRUARY 1831

National Vice–President John Calhoun exacerbates the growing breach between himself and President Jackson by publishing letters related to what Calhoun perceived as Jackson's misconduct during the Seminole War in 1818. Jackson had burned Seminole villages and seized Spanish forts until Spain agreed to sell the Florida area. For military desertion, Jackson advocated whippings after the first two attempts and execution if a soldier tried again. Angered by Calhoun's move, Jackson chooses Van Buren as his successor to the presidency.

5 MARCH 1831

Transportation A locomotive with a four-wheeled truck, the "West Point," makes a first trip on the South Carolina Railroad.

18 MARCH 1831

Indian Affairs The Supreme Court rules against the Cherokees in *Cherokee Nation v. Georgia.* The Indian tribe is trying to prevent Georgia from applying its laws in Indian territory where gold has recently been discovered. The court rules that the Cherokees are a "domestic dependent" and not a foreign nation and therefore cannot sue in Federal courts.

5 APRIL 1831

International The United States completes final negotiations on a commercial treaty with Mexico. The Senate approves it a year later.

7 APRIL 1831

National Secretary of War John Eaton resigns from President Jackson's cabinet and starts a series of resignations. The cabinet is split between those who support Calhoun and those who support Van Buren as the next presidential nominee. What started as a social feud against Eaton's wife, Peggy O'Neale, became a political issue. As a former barmaid, O'Neale is not accepted socially by Mrs. Calhoun nor by other cabinet members' wives. Only Van Buren, a widower, supports her. Jackson stubbornly tries to have her accepted and even tries without success to raise the issue at a cabinet meeting. Van Buren sees the split as a weakness in the administration and offers to resign. Hearing this, Eaton resigns first. By August 8 all cabinet members except Postmaster General William T. Barry have been replaced. Van Buren becomes minister to England, and Eaton becomes governor of Florida, thereby ending the Washington social feud. Notable in the new cabinet are Attorney General Roger B. Taney of Maryland and Secretary of War Lewis Cass of Ohio.

26 APRIL 1831

Regional The New York legislature finds that pov-

COTTON AND SOCIETY

The southern agricultural system centered on cotton presented a remarkable example of how economic needs came to dictate social patterns in 19th century America. In the years before the Revolutionary War, the southern planters had developed the profitable culture of tobacco, rice, indigo, sugar and cotton for the export market. But after the war, the bottom fell out of the tobacco and indigo markets, leading to the dissolution of many plantations. In many cases, the slave-labor forces became economic liabilities to their owners; indeed, the future survival of slavery and of the plantation system appeared uncertain.

But this trend was dramatically reversed by Eli Whitney's 1793 invention of the cotton gin. By 1815, cotton had become the dominant southern crop for export to the newly built textile mills in the North, as well as to eager mill operators all over Europe. But the social results of the cotton economy were devastating to southern Indians and blacks. In fertile Georgia and the Gulf states, the Indians were unfeelingly dispossessed of their ancestral lands and were forced to move across the Mississippi River. This westward push of the Indians would continue throughout the century. By the 1830s, hundreds of land speculators and would-be planters had thronged into Alabama and Mississippi to obsessively clear the land of wilderness forests in order to plant cotton. This monumental task was achieved by the use of slave labor, imported from the coastal states. Thus, the now immensely profitable cultivation of cotton led to the perpetuation and expansion of slavery in the United States. After the 1808 national ban on the foreign slave trade, the South turned to breeding slaves to meet its own domestic needs as well as those of the newly opened up western regions. Slave-breeding became a highly profitable venture on its own. The 7000,000 slaves counted in the 1790 census expanded to 4 million slaves in 1860. At the same time, the plantation system was revived. As enormous quasi-feudal estates, the plantations consisted of fields, orchards, barns, slave quarters and work houses. In the interests of self-sufficiency, the plantations raised their own food and livestock, and even had their own blacksmiths to make and repair agricultural tools. The privileged whites who presided over these plantations led aristocratic lives of leisure, based on chivalric values.

Before the Civil War, the Cotton Kingdom extended from South Carolina to Texas and Arkansas; cotton accounted for almost two-thirds of the nation's exports. The Civil War and the emancipation of the slaves eventually had little result on cotton production. After the war, the planters turned instead to sharecroppers and tenant farmers, many of them former slaves, and the cotton output soon equalled and then surpassed the pre-war yields.

erty is not a crime and abolishes prison terms for debtors.

30 JUNE 1831
Indian Affairs Black Hawk, the proud leader of the Sauk and Fox Indians, reluctantly agrees to move from tribal lands to an area west of the Mississippi.

4 JULY 1831
International William C. Rives, the United States minister to France, concludes a treaty in Paris to settle spoliation claims from the Napoleonic Wars, pending since 1815. Previous attempts to settle the claims for depredations on American commerce during the wars were halted by French counterclaims of violations of commercial agreements in the Louisiana Treaty. America will pay $300,000; France will pay $5 million.
Arts/Culture Dr. Samuel Francis Smith's song *America,* written to the tune of *God Save the King,* is sung for the first time in Worcester, Massachusetts.

AUGUST 1831
Ideas/Beliefs Joseph Smith chooses Independence, Missouri, as the Mormon Holy City of Zion.

9 AUGUST 1831
National A public meeting in New York City nominates John C. Calhoun for president.

21 AUGUST 1831
Slavery Nat Turner, a pious but radical slave preacher, leads an uprising of slaves in Southampton County, Virginia. About 70 whites are killed before soldiers put down the rebellion. Turner is executed along with 12 of his followers, and about 100 blacks are killed in a search for Turner.

26 SEPTEMBER 1831
National The Anti-Masonic Party holds the first national nominating convention with a platform and delegates from the 13 states. The party first appeared in New York during the previous year as a reaction to investigations of Freemasonry members in public office. The party nominates William Wirt of Maryland for president and Amos Ellmaker of Pennsylvania for vice-president. The Anti-Masonic Party is the third party in the nation and will merge with the Whigs in 1836.

30 SEPTEMBER—7 OCTOBER 1831
National Those endorsing free trade meet in Philadelphia to send a message to Congress. Albert Gallatin drafts this statement.

26 OCTOBER 1831
National A protective tariff convention begins in New York.

5 DECEMBER 1831

National John Quincy Adams, the ex-president from Massachusetts, takes a seat in the House of Representatives. He will serve until February 23, 1848.

12 DECEMBER 1831

National The National Republican Party holds a convention in Baltimore. It soon nominates Henry Clay of Kentucky for President and John Sergeant of Pennsylvania for Vice President.

John Quincy Adams begins a long-term stand in favor of abolition. In the House of Representatives he presents 15 petitions delivered from Pennsylvania which call for abolishing slavery in the District of Columbia.

OTHER EVENTS OF 1831

Transportation The first steamboat to make a trip on the upper Missouri River is the *Yellowstone,* owned by the American Fur Company.

9 JANUARY 1832

Finance Although the charter of the Bank of the United States will not expire for four more years, the bank applies to Congress for an extension now because of heavy criticism of its conservative policies, especially by those in the West.

International Promoting something he calls his "American System," Henry Clay introduces a resolution in the Senate that would alter foreign trade. He hopes to abolish duties on foreign goods that do not compete with American goods.

21 JANUARY 1832

Slavery The Virginia assembly debates abolition, and Thomas Jefferson Randolph, the grandson of Thomas Jefferson, presents an old Jeffersonian plan endorsing gradual emancipation. Later, Thomas Dew publishes *Review of the Debate in the Virginia Legislature of 1831 and 1832,* emphasizing a pro-slavery stand.

3 MARCH 1832

Indian Affairs In *Worcester v. Georgia,* the Supreme Court finds that the Federal Government has jurisdiction over Indians and their territories within a state. An 1830 Georgia law had required all white citizens living in Cherokee country to have a state-granted license for doing so and to swear allegiance to the state. The court rules this law unconstitutional because Indian nations can make treaties, and these, according to the Constitution, are the highest law in the land. The court declares, therefore, that the laws of Georgia "can have no force" within Cherokee boundaries. Georgia refuses to acknowledge the court's decision and finds support with President Jackson who declares, "John Marshall has made his decision, now let him enforce it!"

24 MARCH 1832

Indian Affairs As part of Jackson's continuing effort to move Indians, the Creek tribe signs a treaty

NAT TURNER'S REBELLION

Since the 1790s when slaves had successfully rebelled in Santo Domingo and slaughtered 60,000 people, Southerners realized that their own slaves might rise up against them. From 1820 to 1831 many slave revolt conspiracies developed, especially along the coast where blacks outnumbered whites; of these, Nat Turner's rebellion in 1831 most frightened white Southerners. When Turner was born in 1800 (the same year as John Brown) his mother feared the strange markings and bumps on his forehead and attempted to kill him. He grew to be an unusual, especially bright boy; Turner's master increased the boy's self-esteem by having him recite the Bible in front of guests. Turner became a slave preacher in Southampton County, Virginia. Gradually, by fasting, meditation and reading the Bible, Turner began to build a kind of religious revival justifying uprising. He believed God had chosen him to lead blacks to freedom. Turner had studied the history of Denmark Vesey whose 1822 revolt failed when a loyal house servant exposed his plan. Turner used only field–hand blacks to plan and begin the revolt. He hoped others would join them.

On 22 August Turner and about 70 recruits began a two-day rampage. They killed Turner's master and about 70 others. Some decapitated children (some of the slaves might have been drunk); Turner himself killed only one white. Many blacks chose not to join Turner because they sensed the futility of his effort. Indeed, the revolt was soon crushed. Turner managed to escape and hid out in the woods for 30 days before being caught. In the search to find him, 100 Virginia slaves were slaughtered. Turner was hanged. His uprising had been the most serious in the country to date. It so shook Southern States that they passed more stringent laws related to slaves, increased censorship against abolition, and made military preparations to halt further uprisings.

to cede their territory east of the Mississippi River to the United States.

6 APRIL—2 AUGUST 1832

Indian Affairs The Black Hawk War begins when Black Hawk leads a group of Sauk Indians across the Mississippi River into northern Illinois. They take one village and hope to regain their ceded lands throughout that area and in the Wisconsin territory. Fighting continues until August 2 when the Indians are clearly defeated. Among the soldiers who serve in this war are Abraham Lincoln and Jefferson Davis.

1 MAY 1832
Westward Movement A wagon train leaves from Fort Osage on the Missouri River under the leadership of Captain Benjamin Louis Eulalie de Bonneville. He takes the group to the Columbia River and continues to explore the West for three years. This year, the Oregon Trail becomes the main route for settlers headed for the Oregon Territory. The trail begins at Independence, Missouri, on the Missouri River and runs through the Platte and Snake river valleys to the mouth of the Columbia River. Nathaniel Wyeth guides a group of New Englanders over the Trail to establish a post on the Columbia. James Hall's publication, *Legends of the West,* encourages many others to try their luck in the West.

9 MAY 1832
Indian Affairs In Payne Landing, Florida, a group of 15 Seminole chiefs sign a treaty that cedes their lands in Florida to the United States. They agree to move west of the Mississippi River.

16 MAY 1832
International The United States signs a treaty of peace and commerce with Chile at Santiago.

21-22 MAY 1832
National The Democratic Party, formerly the Democratic-Republican Party, gathers in Baltimore to hold its first national convention. Those attending unanimously back Jackson; they repeatedly nominate him for a second term and choose Martin Van Buren for the vice-presidency. They do not adopt a platform. Jackson and Van Buren needed a two-thirds majority to win the nomination, and this method will prevail at later Democratic conventions.

10 JULY 1832
Finance President Jackson vetoes a bill that would recharter the Bank of the United States. His Vice-President, Van Buren, has long opposed Nicholas Biddle, the conservative head of the bank whose policies seem to favor corporations and a moneyed aristocracy. Jackson wants such a government-owned institution to have limited operations, mostly confined to deposit. The bill to recharter passes the Senate on June 11 and the House of July 3. On July 13, with a Senate vote of 22 to 19, that body fails to override the veto.

13 JULY 1832
Exploration An exploring party led by Henry Schoolcraft finds the source of the Mississippi River at Lake Itasca, Minnesota.

14 JULY 1832
National Congress adopts the Tariff Act of 1832. Although more moderate than that of 1828, it still leaves the South dissatisfied. Textiles and iron still require high duties; these are seen to benefit the Northeast.

2 AUGUST 1832
Indian Affairs The Black Hawk War ends when the Illinois militia slaughter warriors. Black Hawk finds shelter with the Winnebagoes, but he surrenders on August 27.

21 SEPTEMBER 1832
Indian Affairs The Sauk and Fox Indians sign a treaty which requires them to stay on lands west of the Mississippi River.

14 OCTOBER 1832
Indian Affairs The Chickasaws follow the Sauk and the Fox. They agree to give the United States all of their land east of the Mississippi River.

26 OCTOBER 1832
Regional Mississippi adopts a new state constitution that makes many offices elective.

19-24 NOVEMBER 1832
Civil War: Approach A special state convention meets in South Carolina, one of the most outspoken of the Southern states, and on November 24 adopts an ordinance that nullifies the Tariff Acts of 1828 and 1832. On November 27, the South Carolina legislature adopts measures to enforce this ordinance—even allowing for military preparations and secession if the Federal Government resorts to force.

5 DECEMBER 1832
National Andrew Jackson wins an overwhelming victory for the Democrats and is re–elected President. Voters on the frontier and on farms respond to the principal campaign issue of the Bank; they regard it as representative of Eastern control. (Bank head Nicholas Biddle had actually written and circulated campaign literature in support of Clay.) Jackson wins 219 electoral votes to Clay's 49.

10 DECEMBER 1832
Civil War: Approach President Jackson issues a proclamation—after reinforcing the Federal forts off Charleston—warning the people of South Carolina that no state can secede from the Union "because each secession . . . destroys the unity of a nation."

12 DECEMBER 1832
National Vice–President Calhoun is successful in his race for the Senate. On December 28 Calhoun resigns from the vice–presidency. Wanting to distribute surplus revenue from public lands equally among the states, Henry Clay introduces a bill which is passed by both the House and the Senate for this purpose. President Jackson will pocket veto it.

13 DECEMBER 1832
Regional Robert Young Hayne, who debated Daniel

Webster over states' rights related to the Foot Resolution, becomes governor of South Carolina.

18 DECEMBER 1832

International At St. Petersburg, the United States and Russia sign a treaty for commercial agreements.

27 DECEMBER 1832

National In another effort to reduce tariff duties, Gulian Verplanck of New York introduces a bill in Congress.

OTHER EVENTS OF 1832

Civil War: Approach The New England Anti-Slavery Society is founded to work for abolition.

Westward Movement Thomas Larkin opens the first store in Monterey, California.

Transportation A horse-drawn streetcar first carries passengers in New York. A canal running from Cleveland, Ohio, to Portsmouth on the Ohio River is completed. Work begins on the Wabash Canal which will connect the Ohio River in Indiana with Lake Erie in Toledo; the canal, a total of 459 miles, will be completed in 1853.

Education In Boston, Samuel Gridley Howe opens the Perkins Institute, the first major school for the blind. In Cincinnati, Lyman Beecher begins teaching as a professor of theology at Lane Seminary.

Arts/Culture Horatio Greenough receives a commission to sculpt a statue of George Washington for the rotunda in the Capitol building. It will be placed there in 1842.

1 JANUARY 1833

Life/Customs The first issue of *Knickerbocker Magazine* appears in New York City; it will be the country's most popular and influential literary magazine until it ceases publication in 1859.

16 JANUARY 1833

Civil War: Approach In the uproar that follows President Jackson's proclamation against secession (December 5, 1832), the South Carolina legislature defies "King Jackson" and even raises a volunteer unit to repel any "invasion." Jackson then asks Congress to adopt a "force bill" to enable him to enforce the provisions of the Tariff Acts of 1828 and 1832.

12 FEBRUARY 1833

Civil War: Approach Henry Clay, always anxious to work out a compromise that will save the union, draws up a new tariff bill that is presented to the House of Representatives. The bill includes a gradual cutback in tariffs, which pleases the South. The battle grows as Calhoun argues against the "force bill" on February 15-16 and brings the nullification issue back into question.

16 FEBRUARY 1833

National In *Barron v. Baltimore*, the Supreme Court rules that actions of state governments are not subject to the Bill of Rights in the Constitution.

SLAVERY—A PATERNALISTIC SYSTEM

In the antebellum South, about 350,000 white families were slaveholders. The other 1,750,000 were subsistence farmers who did not own slaves. Of the slaveholders, only about seven per cent had more than ten slaves, yet all slaveholders in the South eventually operated in a pattern of paternalism that developed from a continuing relationship between slaveholder and slave.

Many Southerners regarded slavery as "our burden," as they had the job of "civilizing" Africans, and this attitude developed into a pervasive set of relations. Because the slave trade had been closed since 1808 and the slave population could not be replaced, slaveholders had a large stake in maintaining their slaves. (By the year 1860 nearly all slaves had been born in the South.) Slaveholders tried to see that slaves had little communication with slaves elsewhere, hoping they would identify with their own plantation and be less likely to run away. Slaveholders did not freely choose to be paternalistic, but were forced into such a system because they knew that slaves could resist. They had to make and hold to bargains, hoping for consistent work habits and a personal bond. By using methods of resistance—not working as hard or deliberately breaking tools—slaves earned the right to set limits. They could put constraints on slave holders, such as demanding that they only work certain hours and have Sundays off. They could negotiate what they regarded as proper punishment and adequate food. The paternalistic system gave slaves an opportunity to defend themselves against overseers and encouraged them to create a culture, including religion and pastimes.

As the system developed, it placed constraints on both slaveholders and slaves. The slaveholder could no longer act as the unquestioned dictator, arbitrarily selling individual slaves or families. The slaves, for their part, were forced into reconciling themselves to their situation. They used short-lived revolts and day-to-day resistance to improve their conditions. Slaves' patterns of resistance helped define what crops would be successful in the South. The area would become prosperous from cotton, which required that slaves work in a group under an overseer, but the South would perpetually underproduce livestock, which required too much individual care and which was too easily stolen.

Slavery was more than a system of labor; it was a mode of production and a form of society, out of which grew a legal system, social patterns, and an ideology. The system itself was based on racism, and by discriminating against blacks and excluding them from schools, slaveholders prevented poor whites from relating to blacks. The paternalistic relationship grew not from a medieval model of regarding slaves as born to their position, but from a capitalist ideology that everyone has the right to bargain. Eventually, the system of paternalism that white slaveholders developed to maintain slavery helped cause its demise. Because slaves regarded themselves as people with a right to bargain, more and more of them came to realize that they also had a right to freedom.

---

20 FEBRUARY 1833

Civil War: Approach The Senate passes the "force bill" with a vote of 32-1. On February 26, the House of Representatives passes Henry Clay's Compromise Tariff by a vote of 149-47. On March 1, the House passes the "force bill," and the Senate in turn passes the tariff. President Jackson signs them both within 24 hours. The confrontation with nullification is averted.

2 MARCH 1833
National With backing from Calhoun and Clay, a resolution in the House of Representatives states that the Bank of the United States can continue as a safe place of deposit for government funds. Jackson, however, wants the funds withdrawn and feels his re-election is an indication that Americans agree with him. On March 19 Jackson consults his cabinet members on the matter, and on April 3 his Attorney General Roger B. Taney supports the legal basis for removing deposits and distributing them to selected state banks. Not all cabinet members agree with Jackson.

4 MARCH 1833
National Andrew Jackson's second term begins as he is inaugurated. Martin Van Buren is inaugurated as his vice-president. Jackson's cabinet includes Secretary of War Louis Cass and Attorney General Roger B. Taney.

20 MARCH 1833
International The United States signs a commercial treaty with Siam at Bangkok.

1-3 APRIL 1833
Regional Meeting at San Felipe de Austin, a group of Americans who live in the Texas territory hold a convention and vote to separate Texas from Mexico.

1 JUNE 1833
National Because his cabinet cannot agree over the removal of government deposits in the Bank of the United States, President Jackson reorganizes the cabinet. Secretary of the Treasury Louis McLane becomes Secretary of State and William J. Duane becomes Secretary of the Treasury. But when Jackson instructs Duane to remove the deposits, he too is reluctant. On July 10 Duane writes to Jackson opposing such a move.

6 JUNE 1833
Regional President Jackson begins a tour of the Atlantic Coast States. He starts with Virginia and goes as far as New Hampshire.

1 AUGUST 1833
Labor Journeymen shoemakers in Geneva, New York, strike for a wage increase. They are successful, but their action will lead to an 1835 court case, *The People v. Fisher,* on the legality of strikes.

28 AUGUST 1833
Slavery Great Britain no longer allows slavery in her colonies. America is more and more becoming an isolated nation in this regard.

3 SEPTEMBER 1833
Arts/Culture The first issue of a successful penny newspaper, The New York *Sun,* appears in New York City. Its editor is Benjamin H. Day.

SAMUEL HOUSTON, 1793-1863

A man who could function as effectively within the Cherokee Indian society as he could within the U.S. Senate, Sam Houston captured the American imagination and played an important role in early Texas history. Houston spent his childhood in Tennessee and lived with the Cherokees for a time after his widowed mother died. He fought in the Creek campaign under Andrew Jackson, but returned to Tennessee after being seriously wounded. He practiced law in Nashville and soon was elected to represent Tennessee in Congress. Popular with his constituents, Houston was elected governor of that state in 1827, but resigned abruptly in 1829 when his wife left him. He returned to live with the Cherokees, became a government post trader, and drank heavily for a time.

By 1836, he had found his way to Texas and led the volunteers who defeated Mexican President Santa Anna at San Jacinto. This was the decisive event to guarantee the Texas territory's independence from Mexico, and Texans quickly elected the vigorous and dramatic Houston—he sometimes wore Cherokee dress in public—as president of their republic. Houston used his contacts in Washington to have Texas admitted to the Union in 1845. He was immediately elected U.S. senator and served until 1859 when he became governor of Texas. He was destined not to have the job for long. Always independent, he refused to take an oath supporting the Confederacy after the start of the Civil War and was removed from office. Houston died before his Texas was again united with all the other states, but his energetic personality became memorialized in his burgeoning namesake city, Houston, Texas.

---

10 SEPTEMBER 1833
National President Jackson announces to his cabinet that on October 1 the government will no longer use the Bank of the United States for its deposits. Some, including Secretary of the Treasury Duane, refuse to agree with the plan.

18 SEPTEMBER 1833
National President Jackson submits to the cabinet a document drafted by Attorney General Roger Taney which lists reasons for removing government deposits from the Bank. In doing so, Jackson indicates that the role of the cabinet is to be his personal organ.

21 SEPTEMBER 1833
International The United States signs a commercial treaty with the Sultan of Muscat.

23 SEPTEMBER 1833
National When Secretary of the Treasury Duane persists in refusing to carry out the removal of government funds from the Bank of the United States, President Jackson replaces him with Roger B. Taney.

26 SEPTEMBER 1833
National Roger Taney, now Secretary of the Treasury, orders the first removal of government funds from the Bank of the United States, to be placed in the Girard Bank of Philadelphia by transfer. During the next few months, funds are transferred to 23 other state banks which become known as "pet banks."

DECEMBER 1833
National Lucretia Mott helps to organize the Female Anti-Slavery Society in Philadelphia. She becomes the organization's first president.

3 DECEMBER 1833
National President Jackson makes his annual message to Congress and assumes the responsibility for removing government deposits from the Bank of the United States. He claims he was justified in this action because the Bank took a partisan position during the election of 1832. On December 11 the Senate asks to see a copy of the paper Jackson earlier read to his cabinet. Claiming that the executive branch is independent of the Senate, Jackson refuses.

6 DECEMBER 1833
National In Philadelphia, the American Anti-Slavery Society is organized due primarily to the efforts of Arthur and Lewis Tappan, wealthy New York City merchants, and Theodore Weld, a prominent abolitionist minister. Weld, through his writings and speeches, will continue to play a major role in convincing many Americans of the necessity and justice of abolishing slavery. The abolition movement is growing in other ways. In St. Louis, Elijah P. Lovejoy begins publishing an anti-slavery newspaper, the *Observer*. William Lloyd Garrison confers with English abolitionists in England, and John Greenleaf Whittier publishes an abolition tract, *Justice and Expediency*.

26 DECEMBER 1833
National Henry Clay introduces two resolutions in the Senate. The first censures the Treasury and Taney's "unsatisfactory and insufficient" explanation for removing deposits from the Bank of the United States. The second censures President Jackson for assuming authority and power beyond what the Constitution allows him.

OTHER EVENTS OF 1833
Settling Between this year and 1837, people throughout the United States are wildly speculating in land, canals, roads, banks, buildings and planting cotton. They hope to reap profits with new settlers.
Industry Samuel Preston invents a machine to peg shoes.
Agriculture The first successful grain reaper drawn by a horse is patented by Obed Hussey.
Labor All of the trade unions of New York join together to form the General Trades Union. Its first president, Ely Moore, is then elected to Congress.
Education The town of Peterborough, New Hampshire, is the first to establish a tax-supported library, provided according to state law. The first American co-educational college, Oberlin, opens in Oberlin, Ohio. It is also the first to admit blacks. Meanwhile, in Canterbury, Connecticut, Prudence Crandall tries to admit black girls to her private school; the Connecticut legislature hastily passes a state law against educating blacks who are not Connecticut residents; Crandall is jailed; the school closes in 1834.
Ideas/Beliefs Massachusetts becomes the last of the states to sever the connection between church and state with the disestablishment of the Congregational Church.

3 JANUARY 1834
International Stephen F. Austin goes to Mexico City to present a resolution from American settlers in Texas stating their desire to separate from Mexico. The Mexican government arrests Austin and holds him in prison for eight months.

29 JANUARY 1834
Labor Workmen along the Chesapeake and Ohio Canal are rioting because their called strike for a closed shop was met with violence. President Jackson issues orders to Secretary of War Louis Cass to dispatch troops to quell the riots. This is the first time Federal troops are used in a labor dispute.

15 FEBRUARY 1834
International In Madrid, the Van Ness Convention settles claims between the United States and Spain.

28 MARCH 1834
National The Senate adopts the two resolutions introduced by Henry Clay on December 26, 1833 to censure President Jackson and the Treasury after the removal of government funds from the Bank of the United States.

4 APRIL 1834
National Jackson's supporters in the Senate push through their own resolutions to sustain the administration's bank policy.

14 APRIL 1834
National The name "Whig" is formally adopted for a new U.S. political party after Henry Clay mentions it approvingly in a Senate speech. This month the name appears in *Nile's Register* although it has been in use for at least two years. Among those anti-Jackson forces who come together to form the party are former members of the National Republican Party, those who support states' rights and John Calhoun's nullification stand, Democrats who disagree with Jackson over the Bank of the United States, Southern planters and Northern industrialists. After 1836, members of the Anti-Masonic party will join as well. Clay and Daniel Webster are prominent leaders.

15 APRIL 1834
National President Jackson formally protests the Senate's approval of Clay's censure resolutions. Jackson claims that the Senate has charged him with an offense that might bring about impeachment, yet he has not been given an opportunity to defend his actions. Jackson sends another message to members of the Senate on April 21 in order to gain their good will.

TESTING A UNION 1788-1865

7 MAY 1834
National Refusing to accept President Jackson's power to question its authority, the Senate declines to include his message in the official record of their proceedings. Not until January 16, 1837, mostly due to the efforts of Senator Thomas Hart Benton, will the resolution of censure be expunged from the Senate Journal.

15 JUNE 1834
Settling N. J. Wyeth, the fur trader, establishes the first settlement in Idaho at Fort Hall on the Snake River. Fort Hall becomes a major stop on the Oregon Trail.

24 JUNE 1834
National Many in the Senate continue to oppose President Jackson's policies; they refuse to confirm Roger B. Taney as Secretary of the Treasury.

28 JUNE 1834
Finance With the adoption of the Second Coinage Act, the ratio of silver to gold changes from 15 to 1 to nearly 16 to 1. This move undervalues silver, driving it from circulation and causing a shortage of coins.

30 JUNE 1834
Indian Affairs Congress establishes the Department of Indian Affairs to administer Indian territory west of the Mississippi River.

4 JULY 1834
National An anti-slavery society meeting at the Chatham Street Chapel in New York is disrupted by a pro-slavery mob. The mob is angry because blacks and whites are sitting together in the audience. Rioting continues for eight days until July 12 with many churches and houses destroyed in the melee.

OCTOBER 1834
National Individuals who favor slavery go on a rampage in Philadelphia, the birthplace of anti-slavery societies. Rioters destroy approximately 40 houses belonging to blacks.

28 OCTOBER 1834
Indian Affairs The United States Government demands that Seminole Indians leave Florida, as called for in provisions of the Treaty of Payne's Landing, signed in 1832.

1 NOVEMBER 1834
Transportation Another railroad is completed. This one runs from Philadelphia to Trenton, New Jersey.

2 DECEMBER 1834
International President Jackson's annual message to Congress includes comments on the spoliation agreement with France. According to a treaty signed on July 4, 1831, France was to make annual installments for spoliations committed against United States subjects during the Napoleonic wars. The French have not made the first payment, and President Jackson recommends reprisals on French property.

OTHER EVENTS OF 1834
Labor The General Trades Union of New York, organized in 1833, calls together a National Trades Union, to include all crafts.

Transportation Regular steamboat service between Chicago and Buffalo begins on a weekly basis. Elsewhere, canals are increasingly used for transportation. The Delaware and Raritan Canal from New Brunswick to Trenton, New Jersey, is completed. The Portage Railroad, using both canals and railroads, opens between Philadelphia and Pittsburgh.

Agriculture Cyrus McCormick patents his horse-drawn grain reaper. It provides the basic model for every successful reaper to follow.

Ideas/Beliefs A group of protesters opposed to Roman Catholics burn the Ursuline convent in Somerville, Massachusetts, near Boston. Albert Brisbane, an American who has been studying under Fourier in France, returns to the United States to introduce the concept of Fourierism, a philosophy used as the basis for cooperative communities. Reverand Jason Lee of Boston establishes a Methodist mission in Oregon on the Willamette River to work with Indians there.

Arts/Culture George Bancroft publishes the first volume of his *History of the United States from the Discovery of the American Continent*. He will continue working on the history and will publish Volume X in 1874. Jared Sparks publishes another popular history book, the first volume of *The Life and Writings of George Washington*. At Richmond, Virginia, the first issue of the *Southern Literary Messenger* appears.

JANUARY 1835
National The Whig party encourages legislative caucuses in the states of Massachusetts and Tennessee. Massachusetts nominates Daniel Webster for the presidency and Tennessee nominates Hugh L. White. By promoting several different candidates, Whigs hope to prevent a Democratic majority and have the election transferred to the House of Representatives.

Finance With a final payment, the national debt is paid off, and Congress must now decide how to allocate surplus revenue.

30 JANUARY 1835
National Richard Lawrence abruptly fires two pistols at President Jackson as he is leaving the House of Representatives chamber. The president is unharmed because both of Lawrence's pistols misfire. Judged insane, Lawrence is committed to a lunatic asylum.

3 MARCH 1835
Finance The growing country has a growing need for money. An act of Congress provides for United States mints in New Orleans; Charlotte, North Carolina and Dahlohega, Georgia.

25 APRIL 1835
International France finally appropriates monies to pay for America's spoliation claims, but does so on the condition that President Jackson apologize for or explain his December 1834 call for reprisals. President Jackson refuses and, in his annual message on December 7, states, "The honor of my country shall never be stained by an apology from me for the statement of truth and the performance of duty."

20 MAY 1835
National Meeting in Baltimore, the Democratic National Convention nominates current Vice-President Martin Van Buren for President and Colonel Richard M. Johnson for Vice-President. The Democrats attempt to achieve a regional balance with Van Buren being from New York and Johnson from Kentucky.

30 JUNE 1835
International President Santa Anna of Mexico is rapidly turning toward a centralist position and expects to rule over all Mexicans, including Texans. This worsens relations between American settlers and the Mexican government. William B. Travis leads a group of colonists to seize a Mexican fort at Anahuac. Later in the fall other clashes occur and Texans will hold conventions to oppose centralized authority and plan to resist Santa Anna.

JULY 1835
International Wanting to expand the country, President Jackson authorizes the purchase of Texas, but Mexico refuses to sell the territory.

6 JULY 1835
National Chief Justice of the Supreme Court John Marshall dies. On December 28 President Jackson names Roger B. Taney to succeed him. Many Senators oppose the former slaveholder and refuse to confirm his appointment until March 15, 1836.
National A mob in Charleston, South Carolina, burns the abolitionist literature that a local post office has impounded. The abolitionist tracts had come from New York and lead Alfred Huger, the Charleston postmaster, to request that anti-slavery societies be prohibited from sending their literature through the mails. Huger's appeal is rejected. Postmaster General Kendall publicly replies that he lacks official authority to bar such mail, but unofficially he recommends that local postmasters do just that. He states, "We owe an obligation to the laws, but a higher one to the communities in which we live." Frightened by slave uprisings such as that of Nat Turner, Southern states are beginning to pass prohibitory laws against abolitionist propaganda. A Georgia law passed this year provides the death penalty to anyone publishing material that could lead to slave insurrections. Abolitionist writers and agents are expelled by nearly all Southern states, and in South Carolina, Governor George McDuffie urges the legislature that, "the laws of every community should punish this species of interference by death without benefit of clergy."

10 AUGUST 1835
National A group of citizens in Canaan, New Hampshire, demonstrate that Northerners as well as Southerners can have strong prejudice against blacks: they burn the Noyes Academy to the ground because it enrolls 14 black students.

13 SEPTEMBER 1835
Civil War: Approach James G. Birney's letter to fellow abolitionist Gerrit Smith indicates their strengthening attitudes. Birney writes, "The antagonist principles of liberty and slavery have been roused into action and one or the other must be victorious. There will be no cessation of strife until slavery shall be exterminated or liberty destroyed."

21 OCTOBER 1835
Civil War: Approach An angry pro-slavery mob interrupts when the English abolitionist George Thompson is scheduled to address the Female Anti-Slavery Society in Boston. The mob parades William Lloyd Garrison through the streets with a rope around his neck to express their disgust with his extreme views on slavery. And in Utica, New York, people meeting to organize an anti-slavery society are attacked by a mob (said to be led by a judge and a Congressman).

29 OCTOBER 1835
National A radical wing of the Jacksonian Democrats, sometimes known as the Equal Rights Party, meets at Tammany Hall in New York City. Here, at a primary meeting they earn the name "Loco-Focos" when they refuse to endorse a ticket carried by regular Democrats. After an adjournment, they remain in the hall to continue meeting. When their opponents turn out the gas lights, the Equal Rights men simply pull out candles and light them with the new friction matches called "loco-focos." They go on to develop a platform and choose their own ticket. They are urban dwellers, and many have been associated with the Workingmen's Party. The "Loco-Focos" split with regular Democrats over banking and currency questions. They feel Jackson's policies are inflationary and work against the financial interests which seek corporation charters from the legislature. The New York *Evening Post* provides a voice for their views against monopolies, special privileges, direct taxes, Jeffersonian strict construction and free trade.

NOVEMBER 1835
Indian Affairs The Seminole Indians in Florida resist their scheduled removal to the West, thereby setting off the Second Seminole War. It will last until August 14, 1843. Osceola leads the Indians in this war until he is captured in 1837.

7 DECEMBER 1835
National Responding to the outbreak of violence over abolitionist activities and the Charleston, South Carolina, request for federal assistance to prevent mail circulation of antislavery publications, Jackson uses his annual message to recommend just such a law.

TESTING A UNION 1788-1865

15 DECEMBER 1835
Civil War: Approach Santa Anna, President of Mexico, proclaims a unified constitution for all territories of Mexico. The North American settlers in Texas announce that they intend to secede from Mexico rather than give up their "right" to slavery, which Mexico had abolished.

16 DECEMBER 1835
National Meeting at Harrisburg, Pennsylvania, in a state convention, the Anti-Masonic Party nominates William Henry Harrison of Ohio for president and Francis Granger of New York for vice-president. Pennsylvania Whigs also endorse Harrison.

28 DECEMBER 1835
Indian Affairs In a major action of the Second Seminole War, General Wiley Thompson and his troops are massacred at Fort King, Florida. Also on this day, Major Dade and 100 of his men are killed at Fort Brooke, Florida.

29 DECEMBER 1835
Indian Affairs The Cherokees sign a treaty at New Echota to surrender all of their lands east of the Mississippi River in exchange for $5 million, some funds for transportation, and land in the Indian Territory. They will move there by 1838.

OTHER EVENTS OF 1835
Civil War: Approach The Unitarian leader William Ellery Channing begins openly to advocate the abolition of slavery. He publishes *Slavery,* an anti-slavery pamphlet which will be followed by two others.
Labor A court case results from the Geneva, New York strike of August 1, 1833. Strikes are declared illegal by a New York court in *The People v. Fisher.*
Education By this time, lyceums have become a popular method of local adult education and entertainment; held in town halls usually, they attract speakers on politics, natural history, literature or such subjects; by now some 3000 lyceums exist throughout the USA, with the largest concentration in New England and Ohio.
Arts/Culture In Brussels Alexis de Tocqueville publishes *Democracy in America.* It will become a classic depiction and analysis of the new country and its people.

JANUARY 1836
Civil War: Approach In Philadelphia James Birney edits the first issue of the *Philanthropist,* an anti-slavery newspaper.

11 JANUARY 1836
Civil War: Approach Abolitionists present petitions to Congress in an attempt to abolish slavery in the District of Columbia. Calhoun refuses to accept the petitions and calls them "foul slander" of the South.

15 JANUARY 1836
International President Jackson again calls for re-prisals against France for not making good the spoliation claims assigned in the treaty of July 4, 1831; he also offers a carefully phrased conciliation in response to France's 1835 demand for an apology.

27 JANUARY 1836
International Great Britain intervenes to aid in the smooth payment of spoliation claims between France and America. Finally, on May 10, President Jackson will announce that France has paid four installments.

15 FEBRUARY 1836
Finance The Bank of the United States obtains a state charter in Pennsylvania because it has failed to secure a renewed charter as a national bank. On March 1 it officially becomes the Bank of the United States of Pennsylvania.

23 FEBRUARY 1836
Civil War: Approach President Santa Anna raises an army of 6000 men to defend his idea of a unitary state. He leads 3000 men in a siege on the Alamo. There 187 Texans hold off the assault until March 6 when the Mexicans overwhelm the fort, killing all in William Travis's garrison, including Davy Crockett. The heroic defense of the Alamo, however, inspires the North American settlers to develop their own goals for governing the territory.

1 MARCH 1836
Regional A group of Texas settlers meet in Washington, Texas, to discuss Santa Anna's call for a central government. On March 2 they adopt a declaration of independence from Mexico, and draw up a constitution. On March 4 they name Sam Houston commander of their army.

11 MARCH 1836
National The Senate begins what will become a routine reaction to abolitionist petitions: they hear petitions, then reject them.

17 MARCH 1836
Civil War: Approach A constitution which formally legalizes slavery is officially adopted by Texas.

27 MARCH 1836
International Santa Anna continues his assault on Texas settlers. His troops massacre approximately 300 soldiers led by Captain James Fannin, who is trying to defend Goliad. Santa Anna continues to sweep through American settlements and by mid-April he will reach Galveston Bay.

20 APRIL 1836
Regional Congress establishes the Wisconsin Territory in the western portion of the Michigan Territory. The area's first newspaper, the *Dubuque Visitor,* begins publication on May 11.

21 APRIL 1836
Civil War: Approach Under General Sam Houston,

Texans defeat the Mexicans and capture Santa Anna at the battle of San Jacinto. The Texans ratify their own constitution, elect Sam Houston as President, and send an envoy to Washington to demand annexation to the United States or recognition of the independent Republic of Texas. Since they intend to legalize slavery in any case, the debate that follows in Congress once again pits pro-slavery Southerners against anti-slavery Northerners.

25 MAY 1836
International In the House of Representatives, John Quincy Adams declares that the country should not annex Texas if such an action would risk a war with Mexico.

26 MAY 1836
Civil War: Approach Despite the strong objection of John Quincy Adams, Southern members of the House of Representatives get a majority to vote for a "gag" resolution, one that declares that all petitions or papers that in any way involve the issue of slavery should be "laid on the table"—that is, there should be no discussion. The House of Representatives will continue to vote such a "gag rule" at the outset of every session until 1844, but instead of burying the issue of slavery it only sharpens the differences between the two sides.

15 JUNE 1836
National The 25th state, Arkansas, is admitted to the Union as a slave state.

23 JUNE 1836
Finance The Deposit Act, also known as the Surplus Revenue Act, is adopted and provides for one or more banks in each state to hold public deposits. It also provides a procedure for excess revenue in the national government; any amount over $5 million will be distributed among the states.

1 JULY 1836
Regional The Senate adopts a resolution to recognize the Texas territory. The House follows with a similar resolution on July 4. Although sympathetic to Texans, President Jackson feels obligated to honor the United States' obligations to Mexico and to maintain neutrality. Fearing a war with Mexico, he waits until March 3, 1837 to nominate Alceé La Branche to be chargé d'affaires in Texas. The annexation of Texas remains a controversial issue for the next nine years.

11 JULY 1836
Finance Because more and more different types of paper money have become acceptable tender, inflation and land speculation have skyrocketed. In 1832 land sales amounted to $2,623,000: by 1836, they have increased to $24,877,000. President Jackson issues a Specie Circular mandating that only gold and silver be used by buy government lands. Actual settlers or residents of the state in which the land is purchased will be permitted to use paper money until December 15.

12 JULY 1836
National An angry pro-slavery mob in Cincinnati destroys the type James Birney uses to print his anti-slavery newspaper, the *Philanthropist*.

SEPTEMBER 1836
Regional In a popular vote, settlers in the Republic of Texas determine that they want annexation by the United States.

1 SEPTEMBER 1836
Western Movement A wagon train of missionaries and their wives reaches Walla Walla at the Columbia and Snake Rivers. They have been led by Dr. Marcus Whitman through the South Pass. This is the first group to make the overland journey with a number of women.

22 OCTOBER 1836
Regional Sam Houston is sworn in as the first President of the Republic of Texas.

7 DECEMBER 1836
National Martin Van Buren wins 170 electoral votes to William Henry Harrison's 73 and is elected president. Van Buren ran on the Democratic ticket and had agreed to follow President Jackson's policies. Whigs had hoped to throw the election into the House of Representatives by nominating several favorite sons, but their strategy fails. None of the four candidates for vice-president receive a majority, and for the first and only time in the country's history, that election goes into the Senate. On February 8, 1837 they elect the Democratic nominee Richard M. Johnson to serve with Van Buren.

OTHER EVENTS OF 1836
National Interest in the abolition movement grows, and approximately 500 abolitionist societies are now active in the North. Their activities continue to cause violence and controversy. In Granville, Ohio, a meeting of the Ohio Anti-slavery Society ends in riotous fighting incited by ruffians reportedly hired by some of the town's "respectable" citizens.
International Following the failure of his military coup in Strasbourg, Louis Napoleon takes exile in the United States.
Slavery In a move that strikes a blow for Northern abolitionists, the Massachusetts Supreme Court rules that any slave brought within the state's borders by a master can be regarded as freed.
Transportation Construction begins on the Illinois and Michigan Canal. It will connect the city of Chicago with the Illinois River and the Mississippi system of transportation. Meanwhile, the first load of grain shipped from Chicago to Buffalo is ready to move along the Erie Canal.
Education Mark Hopkins takes over the presidency of Williams College in Williamstown, Massachusetts. William Holmes McGuffey publishes his *First Reader* and *Second Reader*, the first of his *Eclectic Readers*, which will become classic schoolbooks in America.

TESTING A UNION 1788-1865

Ideas/Beliefs Ralph Waldo Emerson publishes an essay, "Nature," which sets forth some of the ideas shared by his friends including Bronson Alcott and George Ripley who are meeting in a group that will come to be known as the "Transcendentalists."

26 JANUARY 1837
National Michigan, the 26th state, joins the Union as a free state.

FEBRUARY 1837
Immigration The Supreme Court upholds a New York State law regarding immigrants. In *New York v. Miln* the court finds that any ship captain involved in interstate or foreign trade must supply reports on each of his passengers brought into the country.

FEBRUARY 1837
Arts/Culture Fifty-six British authors petition Congress requesting copyright protection in the United States.

11 FEBRUARY 1837
Finance Ruling in *Briscoe v. the Bank of Common-*

RALPH WALDO EMERSON, 1803-1882

In the middle decades of the 19th century, America was blessed with several of its most important writers, writers who still loom like thunder clouds above the others' windy fields of words. Ralph Waldo Emerson was one of these few.

Emerson was born in Boston in 1803 but although his family belonged to the "Brahmin caste of New England," they were not really rich. However, his father was already deeply involved in the new theology changing the soul-thoughts of America. The week Emerson was born, William Ellery Channing proclaimed his revolutionary creed that "God is love." Oddly enough, this extraordinarily simple thought released an entire age from the narrow bonds of Calvinism and sternhearted determinism. Emerson became a preacher in the Unitarian Church but left to pioneer the still more remote frontiers that the controversial new theology was opening up. Settling in Concord, Massachusetts, he became the acknowledged leader of the "transcendentalists" and introduced such radical thinkers as Margaret Fuller to his highminded circle of friends, which included Bronson Alcott, Nathaniel Hawthorne, and Henry David Thoreau. A later historian has called Concord at this time, a "rustic Weimar." Emerson also maintained strong ties across the ocean from his visits to lecture there. Among his British friends he could count Wordsworth, Coleridge and, in particular, Thomas Carlyle.

Emerson published his first essay in 1836. Called "Nature" it contained the seeds of his subsequent ideas, ideas that would eventually spread beyond the boundaries of America. He continued to write prolifically all the rest of his long life. He was also famed for his great eloquence. He was sometimes called "the Columbus of Modern Thought," Walt Whitman said of him: "an author who has through a long life and in spirit, written as honestly, spontaneously and innocently, as the sun shines or the wheat grows—the truest, sanest most moral, sweetest literary man on record." Whitman was speaking of a peer.

---

wealth of Kentucky, the Supreme Court finds that any bank owned by a state may issue bills of credit.

12 FEBRUARY 1837
Finance In one of the first indications of the coming Panic of 1837, a mob of unemployed workers demonstrate against high rents and the high prices of food and fuel by ransacking flour warehouses in New York.

14 FEBRUARY 1837
Transportation In a blow against transportation monopolies, the Supreme Court rules in *Charles River Bridge v. Warren Bridge* that one bridge company cannot hold control over transportation routes.

MARCH 1837
Agriculture The price of cotton falls by nearly one half on the New Orleans market. A major cotton house, Herman Briggs and Company of New Orleans, closes, a victim of the unstable financial condition in the country.

1 MARCH 1837
Finance Many members of Congress are against the Specie Circular of July 11, 1836 which requires that land be paid for in gold or silver. They adopt a bill to rescind it, but President Jackson, who issued the Specie Circular, simply pocket vetoes the bill.

3 MARCH 1837
Civil War: Approach On his last day in office, President Jackson recognizes the independent Lone Star Republic of Texas. Jackson has been avoiding this decision for many months, not wanting to aggravate the problems that already separate the South and the North. This leaves a union of 13 free states and 13 slave states, but of the large territories that remain to be converted into states, only one—Florida—is controlled by slaveholders, while three non-slave territories still exist. A movement to admit Texas as a "slave territory" to balance out these free territories is defeated.
National Congress acts to increase the number of Supreme Court justices from seven to nine.

4 MARCH 1837
National Martin Van Buren is inaugurated as the eighth president and the second Democrat to hold the office. Fellow Democrat Richard M. Johnson becomes vice-president. Van Buren's cabinet includes Secretary of State John Forsyth, Secretary of the Treasury Levi Woodbury, Postmaster General Amos Kendall and Attorney General B.F. Butler.

On this same day Jackson reiterates his policies one final time as he publishes his farewell address. The document (which was originally drafted by Taney) appeals to the different regions of the country to place their loyalty to the Union above all else. He condemns monopolies, speculation and paper currency.

MARCH—MAY 1837
Finance Economic problems have been developing

MARTIN VAN BUREN, 1782-1862

Van Buren originated the use of political patronage while in New York state but never used it effectively enough while President to win more than one term in office. Born in Kinderhook, New York, the son of a farmer and tavern keeper, Van Buren completed public school at 14 and began clerking in a local law office. He was admitted to the bar in 1803 but quickly took more interest in politics than in law. Beginning in 1813, he held a number of positions—state senator, state attorney general, U.S. senator and governor of New York. He led a political machine in Albany that pioneered the use of patronage and used it to support Andrew Jackson for President. Van Buren became Jackson's secretary of state and later his vice–president. Democrats recognized Van Buren as Jackson's protégé and nominated him for President in 1836. He won easily.

A severe depression began two months after Van Buren's inauguration and thwarted his efforts to aid farmers, artisans, laborers and small businessmen. Hoping to help the economy, he established a ten-hour day for federal workers and tried to make cheap land available to farmers, but conservative Democrats and Whigs opposed his plans in Congress. Van Buren was more successful in his peaceful stance toward both Canada and Mexico. He avoided confrontations except with the Indians; he continued Jackson's policy of forcing them westward and ordered General Winfield Scott to use any necessary military force to move the Cherokees. Van Buren was renominated for President in 1840, but economic problems made him vulnerable. Detractors accused him of being a crafty politician who disregarded the common man, yet some of these same people had blocked the legislative plans he introduced to help the economy. He lost the election to William Henry Harrison and retired to Kinderhook, where he maintained an interest in politics. In 1848, Van Buren headed the Free Soil ticket for President and took enough votes from Cass to give Taylor the victory. Never a strict party man, Van Buren later rejoined the Democratic party he had helped shape and then eventually supported Abraham Lincoln in the secession crisis.

all during Jackson's administration and grow worse during this period. Following a time of wild land speculation and inflation, credit shrinks due to several causes: the Specie Circular issued by President Jackson in 1836, payments withdrawn from various depository banks for distribution to states under the Surplus Revenue Act and English banks calling loans in.

10 MAY 1837

Finance New York banks stop making payments in specie and begin the Panic of 1837. Other banks in Baltimore, Philadelphia and Boston soon follow, and 618 banks fail this year. The effects of the panic, including substantial unemployment, especially in the Southern and Western states, will continue for the next seven years.

10 JUNE 1837

Industry The state of Connecticut passes the first law in the country to provide for general incorporation.

4 AUGUST 1837

Regional The Republic of Texas petitions the United States for annexation to the country. This formal request is denied on August 25 chiefly because the United States wants to avoid the slavery question in Texas.

31 AUGUST 1837

Education At Harvard College Ralph Waldo Emerson gives a Phi Beta Kappa oration, "The American Scholar."

5 SEPTEMBER 1837

Finance Addressing a special session of Congress, President Van Buren advocates a specie currency and criticizes state-chartered banks. He hopes to have the government sponsor depositories independent of state banks for federal funds. During the next few years additional bank failures will help build dissatisfaction with state banks and lead to the acceptance of an independent Treasury.

14 SEPTEMBER 1837

Finance A bill to provide for an independent Treasury is introduced in the Senate and passed on October 4. It moves to the House of Representatives and is tabled on October 14.

2 OCTOBER 1837

Finance Numerous bank failures result in suspension of the fourth installment of surplus revenue distribution among states.

12 OCTOBER 1837

Finance In an attempt to improve the financial situation, Congress authorizes the use of treasury notes. They are not to exceed $10 million.

7 NOVEMBER 1837

Civil War: Approach Elijah Lovejoy, publisher of an abolitionist newspaper in Alton, Illinois, is killed by a mob. He had continued to proclaim his anti-slavery views even after his printing press had twice been thrown into a river.

4 DECEMBER 1837

Civil War: Approach The second session of the 25th Congress convenes, but the "gag rule" regarding abolitionist petitions is not immediately renewed. Protests, especially from former President John Quincy Adams, have made the issue a controversial one, and Representative William Slade from Vermont takes advantage of this lull in the "gag rule" to present anti-slavery petitions. An angry debate follows and Southern representatives threaten to promote an amendment to protect slavery or to recommend the expediency of dissolving the Union. Eventually, on December 19, a coalition of Northern and Southern Democrats adopt an even stricter "gag" resolution with a vote of 122-74. The rule will be renewed each year in Congress until 1844, despite opposition from Adams, Joshua Gidding from Ohio and other Northern legislators.

8 DECEMBER 1837
National Wendell Phillips, who will become a great abolitionist orator, delivers his first abolitionist speech following the brutal murder of Elijah Lovejoy.

25 DECEMBER 1837
Indian Affairs Fighting in the Second Seminole War, General Zachary Taylor defeats a group of Seminoles at Okeechobee Swamp, Florida.

29 DECEMBER 1837
International William Lyon Mackenzie has been trying to lead an insurrection in Canada for the past few months. He has some aid from American sympathizers and has taken refuge on Navy Island, located on the Canadian side of the Niagara River, where he is attacking the Canadian frontier. He has leased the *Caroline,* a small American steamboat, to transport supplies. Canadians board the *Caroline* and set it afire, but in overpowering the crew, they kill American Amos Durfee, setting off violent anti-British feelings.

OTHER EVENTS OF 1837
National The American Peace Society becomes an active group, following the example of peace societies in other countries. It is against all wars, whether defensive or offensive.
Immigration Arriving in Illinois from Norway, Ole Rynning believes other Scandinavians would benefit from following him. His book, *True Account of America for the Information and Help of Peasant and Commoner*, will be published in 1838 and results in a surge of Scandinavian immigrants after 1840.
Agriculture In Vermont John Deere starts what will become a huge farm machinery company with the manufacture of steel-faced plows.
Education Horace Mann, who has been working as a Massachusetts legislator to increase public support for schools, becomes the first secretary of the new Massachusetts Board of Education. He will improve school buildings and curriculum, and introduce uniform training for teachers. With Mann's support, Lowell Mason introduces singing into the Boston schools both to provide students with music instruction and to increase their breathing capacity. Mann collects statistics on Massachusetts schools and issues his first *Annual Report* on education. Mann's ideal of a public education system open to all children will become the model for the American system of education. Elsewhere, Ohio adopts a system of free common schools based on a report filed by Calvin Stowe with the state legislature. Stowe had studied the Prussian system of education. In the Western part of Massachusetts Mary Lyon opens the Mount Holyoke Female Seminary, the first institution founded to provide women with higher education. In 1893 it will be chartered as Mount Holyoke College.

3-12 JANUARY 1838
National Responding to abolitionists who want to abolish slavery in the District of Columbia and elimi-

nate slave trading across state lines, John C. Calhoun introduces resolutions into the Senate that will affirm slavery as a legal institution. The Senate adopts the resolutions that reaffirm the compact theory of the Union and the role of the Federal Government to "resist all attempts by one portion of the Union to use it as an instrument to attack the domestic institutions of another." The Senate also resolves that the institution of slavery should not be interfered with and that attempts to abolish slavery in the District of Columbia could be construed as attacks on institutions of slaveholding states. The Senate refuses, however, to automatically approve any annexation that might expand the nation's entire slave territory.

5 JANUARY 1838
International President Van Buren reacts to the destruction of the American steamship, the *Caroline,* by Canadian militiamen on December 29, 1837. The incident has exacerbated Anglophobe feelings in the United States, and the President urges neutrality. He warns American citizens not to assist the Canadian revolutionaries who had leased the *Caroline.* Van Buren posts members of the militia along the Canadian frontier with General Winfield Scott in command. The Canadian rebels will cease their attempts at insurrection on January 13 and will surrender their weapons to the United States militia.

15 FEBRUARY 1838
Civil War: Approach In defiance of the new "gag rule" adopted on December 19, 1837, Representative John Quincy Adams introduces 350 petitions against slavery into the House. The petitions are all laid on the table.

16 FEBRUARY 1838
Education In one of the first instances of voting rights for women, the Kentucky legislature grants school suffrage to widows who have children of school age.

26 MARCH 1838
Finance For the second time, the Senate passes a bill to establish an independent Treasury. It will be defeated in the House of Representatives on June 25, 1838, largely because of disagreements between Democrats. The Loco-Focos support Van Buren's plan for an independent Treasury, but the conservative Democrats side with the Whig opposition. Such a treasury would allow the United States government the exclusive right to care for its own monies.

19 APRIL 1838
Life/Customs A new Massachusetts law attempts to bring the use of alcohol under some control: Liquor cannot be sold on a retail basis except in quantities of 15 gallons.

17 MAY 1838
Civil War: Approach A pro-slavery mob grows angry because of the anti-slavery meetings held in Phila-

delphia's Pennsylvania Hall. They burn it to the ground.

21 MAY 1838
Finance Congress rescinds President Jackson's Specie Circular of July 11, 1836.

29 MAY 1838
International Anti-British feelings have remained strong and sometimes violent since the destruction of the steamship *Caroline*. A group of American citizens sympathetic to Canadian rebels board the Canadian steamship, the *Sir Robert Peel,* which is on the American side of the St. Lawrence River, and burn it. Other Americans begin to organize secret "Hunters Lodges" along the Canadian frontier with the express goal of overthrowing the British government in Canada.

12 JUNE 1838
Regional Separating land off from the western portion of the Wisconsin territory, Congress establishes the Iowa territory.

7 JULY 1838
Transportation Congress designates all parts of the rapidly expanding railroad system as postal routes.

13 AUGUST 1838
Finance With slightly more gold and silver available, New York banks are able to once again make payments in specie. Other banks soon follow, but in 1839 banks in Pennsylvania must again suspend specie payments. Not until 1842 will specie payments be fully resumed.

18 AUGUST 1838
Exploration With six ships under his command, Charles Wilkes begins what will be a four-year voyage to gather scientific information about the Pacific and Antarctic oceans.

OCTOBER 1838
Indian Affairs Some Cherokee Indians are still living in Georgia. Federal Troops remove them and force them to travel westward on a route that will become known as the "Trail of Tears."

12 OCTOBER 1838
Regional Having been turned down by Congress, the Texas Republic formally withdraws its offer of annexation to the United States. Mirabeau B. Lamar succeeds Sam Houston as President of Texas in December 1838 and advocates a foreign policy of independence from the United States. He appoints diplomatic agents to European countries and will negotiate treaties with France, Holland, Belgium and Great Britain. The British are especially pleased to deal with Texas as an independent power because it provides a limit to the potential power of the United States. They hope to use Texas as a source of cotton and as an outlet for their manufactured goods. Iron-

ically, some of the most prominent Britons who support Texas independence are abolitionists who hope that Texas will forfeit slavery in return for a British loan.

OCTOBER—NOVEMBER 1838
National As a new President, Van Buren has not built a base of support. During Congressional midterm elections, he loses control of the Senate and of the House of Representatives.

7 NOVEMBER 1838
Regional A rising young Whig, William H. Seward, becomes Governor of New York.

21 NOVEMBER 1838
International A few of the American parties intent on overthrowing the British government in Canada are making their way into the Canadian frontier. President Van Buren issues a second proclamation to follow up his January 5 plea for neutrality, and he orders swift reprisals against those Americans who break with the idea of neutrality. Border incidents with Canada will have almost completely ceased within the next few months.

3 DECEMBER 1838
National As Joshua Giddings, a Whig from Ohio, takes his seat in the House of Representatives, he becomes the first abolitionist in Congress.

11 DECEMBER 1838
National The House of Representatives adopts a new "gag rule"; this year it becomes known as the "Atherton gag" because Charles Atherton of New Hampshire proposed the resolution. The House will continue to adopt a rule prohibiting the discussion of slavery each year until 1844.

OTHER EVENTS OF 1838
National The Underground Railroad is organized by abolitionists to provide black slaves with an assisted route of escape to the North and to freedom.
Life/Customs Edward Hoyle publishes his *Improved Edition of the Rules for the Playing of Fashionable Games.* It will become the handbook for card games for several generations.
Transportation A steamship, the *Great Western,* begins offering service between New York and Bristol, England.
Ideas/Beliefs The Unitarian leader William Ellery Channing publishes *Self Culture* and provides Americans with an alternative to strict Calvinist theology. Channing promotes the "doctrine of self-improvement."

JANUARY 1839
International Governor John Fairfield of Maine asks the state legislature to appoint a land agent and send some forces to help him resolve disputes over lumbering in the Aroostook River area. Since 1783, the United States and Britain have argued over bound-

aries in this area, imprecisely defined in the Treaty of Paris. Both countries submitted the problem to the King of the Netherlands, but his compromise of 1831 was accepted only by Great Britain. America continued to ignore British land grants to settlers in the area. During the past few months Canadian lumberjacks have begun operations in the region. The Maine legislature appoints Rufus McIntire as a land agent with the power to expel Canadians.

12 JANUARY 1839
Industry In Mauch Chunk, Pennsylvania, anthracite coal is first used to smelt iron.

7 FEBRUARY 1839
Civil War: Approach The Senate is debating slavery, and Henry Clay, who hopes soon to run for President as a Whig, attempts to appeal to both Northern and Southern conservatives. He believes they identify those in the Whig party with abolitionism, so he condemns abolitionists, claiming they have no constitutional right to interfere with slavery where it already exists. He also claims they are willing to risk a civil war.

12 FEBRUARY 1839
International Canadians refuse to leave the disputed Aroostook area and arrest land agent Rufus McIntire. This begins what becomes known as the Aroostook War. Although both Maine and New Brunswick mobilize their militia, the conflict is never officially declared and no one suffers any bloodshed. Congress even authorizes raising 50,000 men to fight and a $10,000,000 budget for military expenses, but General Winfield Scott, sent to the area by President Van Buren, is able to arrange a truce with New Brunswick. Great Britain agrees to let a boundary commission settle the dispute. In 1842 the Webster-Ashburton Treaty will determine the present boundary.

20 FEBRUARY 1839
Life/Customs Congress acts to forbid dueling in the District of Columbia.

11 APRIL 1839
International The United States signs a treaty with

The Underground Railroad.

Mexico to provide arbitration of claims made by American citizens.

AUGUST 1839
Civil War: Approach The Spanish slave-ship, *Amistad*, carrying 53 African slaves between two Cuban ports, is taken over in a mutiny led by Cinque, one of the slaves. They kill the captain and the crew except for two who are forced to navigate the ship to North American waters, where a United States warship brings the *Amistad* into a Connecticut port. Spain immediately demands that the slaves be turned back to Spaniards, but Americans force the case into the courts. Eventually it will be taken all the way to the Supreme Court, where John Quincy Adams argues for their right to be freed. In March 1841 the Supreme Court will rule this way, and Cinque and the others are returned to Africa.

25 SEPTEMBER 1839
International France becomes the first European country to sign a treaty with Texas as an independent power.

13 NOVEMBER 1839
National Abolitionists enter the political arena in an organized way. Those of moderate views hold a convention at Warsaw, New York, and form the Liberty Party. For President, they nominate James G. Birney, a former Kentucky slaveholder, now of New York, who is one of many converted to abolitionist views by Theodore Dwight Weld. For Vice-President, they nominate Thomas Earle of Pennsylvania. The Liberty Party does not agree with William Lloyd Garrison's more radical views and would never advocate the dissolution of the Union. Prominent members Gerrit Smith of New York and Salmon P. Chase of Ohio lead the party in its strongest platform issue against the annexation of Texas.

4 DECEMBER 1839
National Whigs meet in a national convention at Harrisburg, Pennsylvania. Leaders plan to unite in the support of one candidate. Henry Clay has been a leading contender, but his views on the protective tariff and other issues have made political enemies. Instead of choosing Clay, the Whigs nominate William Henry Harrison, a man without experience in public service, but also a man without political enemies. In addition, Harrison already has a somewhat exaggerated national reputation as a military hero from the Battle of Tippecanoe (November 1811). Even though Clay led the first ballot, he had agreed to withdraw from the race if necessary for "union and harmony." When he did so, this convention became known by that phrase. Whigs choose states'-righter John Tyler as their vice-presidential candidate. Still operating as a coalition rather than a recognized party, the Whigs have no set platform, but are simply organized around their opposition to Democrats.

OTHER EVENTS OF 1839
Westward Movement Choosing a strategic site on

the route travelers use to cross the Sierra Nevada mountains, John Sutter founds a Swiss settlement on land that is now Sacramento, California.

Life/Customs Mississippi becomes the first state to allow women the right to control their own property; here, they are no longer required to have guardians take legal responsibility for any property they might own. In Cooperstown, New York, Abner Doubleday determines the first set of rules for the game of baseball. The first business periodical in the country, *Hunts' Merchants' Magazine,* begins publication.

Industry Erastus B. Bigelow develops a working power loom that weaves two-ply ingrain carpets. His invention provides the basis for what will become a major corporation.

Transportation One man begins an express package service between Boston and New York: William F. Harnden loads packages into a carpet bag and rides the railroads for fast delivery.

Agriculture Congress appropriates $1000 to distribute free seeds. Meanwhile, D. S. Rockwell invents a corn planter, drawn by horses, that can plant two rows at one time.

Education Since the 1820s, different individuals have attempted to establish normal schools for teacher training based on the model of such schools in Prussia. This year, through political work in the state legislature and fund raising from private individuals, Horace Mann, as Secretary of the Massachusetts Board of Education, starts the first public normal school in the country. Cyrus Peirce, a well-known teacher who was responsible for integrating the Nantucket schools, becomes the first principal of the normal school in Lexington, Massachusetts. It enrolls only young women. Peirce must play the role of teacher, substitute parent, janitor and organizer of a model school for practice teaching. He sleeps only a few hours per night. In Boston, the will of John Lowell has provided for an institute to offer general education to the public. Benjamin Silliman presents the first lecture at this, the Lowell Institute.

Ideas/Beliefs Joseph Smith moves his Mormon followers to establish a town at Nauvoo, Illinois.

12 JANUARY 1840

Finance The Independent Treasury bill once again passes in the United States Senate. Now it must also pass in the House of Representatives.

19 JANUARY 1840

Exploration The first national marine exploring expedition, led by Charles Wilkes, sights the continent of Antarctica. Part of the continent is named Wilkes Land in honor of the captain.

31 MARCH 1840

Labor President Van Buren issues an executive order that establishes a ten–hour work day for federal employees involved in public works jobs.

1 APRIL 1840

National The abolitionist Liberty Party holds its first national convention in Albany, New York. By now the membership in various abolitionist and anti–slavery societies in the United States is over 150,000. The convention confirms the November 1839 nomination of James G. Birney of New York for president and Thomas Earle of Pennsylvania for vice-president. Birney is the first anti–slavery candidate for President.

5 MAY 1840

National The Democrats hold their national convention in Baltimore, Maryland. They agree to renominate President Van Buren, but many oppose the renomination of vice-president Richard Johnson. The party decides to leave that choice up to individual states. They do choose a platform. They become the first major party to introduce the slavery question by opposing congressional interference with that institution. They also oppose federal expenditures for internal improvements and a national bank. They adhere to strict constructionist doctrine of the Constitution and are the last Democratic convention in the antebellum era to affirm adherence to the principles in the Declaration of Independence.

30 JUNE 1840

Finance With a vote of 124-107, the House of Representatives finally passes the Independent Treasury Act, as those who follow Calhoun reunite with the Democratic party. Those Southerners who support

---

HARRIET TUBMAN, c. 1820-1913

Tubman was an escaped slave who believed so strongly in her right to liberty that she risked her life repeatedly to help other slaves reach the North. Born to two slaves in Maryland, she was first named Araminta, only later assuming the name "Harriet." She worked as a field hand and was forced by her master to marry a fellow slave, John Tubman. In 1849 she made her way to the North and she soon became active in the so-called underground railroad, the network of individuals—white and black, free and slave, committed abolitionists and the merely sympathetic—who worked from about 1840 to 1861 to help slaves escape from the South. Harriet Tubman made at least 19 trips back to the South and led other slaves North—sometimes "encouraging" them with a loaded pistol, it was said. In 1857 she was able to get her own parents up to New York; altogether she was credited with leading at least 300 blacks to freedom.

Illiterate but possessed of great natural skills in planning, she came to know many of the prominent abolitionists and was probably one of few who knew about John Brown's plans to raid Harper's Ferry. Illness prevented her from joining him there. During the Civil War, she served as a nurse, cook and laundress to the Union Troops in South Carolina; she also was said to have gone behind Confederate lines as a spy on occasion. On one expedition with troops, she helped free 750 slaves. After the war, she lived in Auburn, New York, where she worked to help children and the elderly, using the profits from her autobiography for her causes. Harriet Tubman's actions helped to sharpen the conflict between the North and South, but her own life became a vindication of the need to end slavery.

states' rights work with hard-money Democrats from the North to push the bill through despite continued opposition from Whigs. Calhoun and his followers go with the North on this issue because they fear what they sense as the growing aspirations of the Whigs.

4 JULY 1840

Finance With a signature from President Van Buren, the Independent Treasury Act becomes law. It allows the government exclusive responsibility over its own funds and provides for government depositories to hold funds. According to the act, all government transactions will be made in specie payments after June 30, 1843. Subtreasuries for deposits are established in Boston, New York, Philadelphia, Washington, Charleston, St. Louis and New Orleans.

7 JULY 1840

National The presidential campaign is underway. Daniel Webster is stumping in the Whig campaign for Harrison and Tyler. On Stratton Mountain, Vermont, he addresses 15,000 people. The Whigs are using campaign methods and devices that will become common in later American elections. They cleverly change a derisive Democratic remark about Harrison into an entire campaign theme. One of the Democratic newspapers, the Baltimore *Republican,* suggested on March 23 "that upon condition of his receiving a pension of $2000 and a barrel of cider, General Harrison would no doubt consent to withdraw his pretensions, and spend his days in a log cabin on the banks of the Ohio." Whigs develop what becomes known as the "Log Cabin and Hard Cider" campaign as they use these symbols to portray Harrison as a sturdy man of the frontier. They enthusiastically employ campaign hats, placards, effigies, floats and transportable log cabins with barrels of cider. They sing "Tippecanoe and Tyler too," including the refrain, "Van, Van is a used up man." Thus they focus the election solely on the basis of personality and ignore discussions of leading issues. Whigs portray Van Buren as a man of aristocratic, extravagant taste. Eventually the campaign deteriorates into exaggerated misrepresentation, abuse and irrelevancy. It also marks the beginning of a distinct two-party political system in America.

NOVEMBER-DECEMBER 1840

International Although the tensions between America and Great Britain have lessened somewhat, there are many who remember the destruction of the American steamship, the *Caroline,* in 1838. In New York, a Canadian deputy sheriff, Alexander McLeod, is arrested and charged with killing Amos Durfee during the burning of the *Caroline.* On December 13 the British minister to the United States demands that McLeod be released immediately. On December 26 Secretary of State John Forsyth refuses, claiming that New York courts have jurisdiction over McLeod, who will await trial for nearly a year.

13 NOVEMBER 1840

International The Republic of Texas signs a com-

SAMUEL MORSE, 1791-1872

Talented as both an artist and an inventor, Morse's electromagnetic telegraph revolutionized long–distance communication. Born to a cultured family, Morse was the son of Rev. Jedidiah Morse, often referred to as the "father of American geography." He graduated from Yale in 1810 and then went to England to study art extensively for four years. He returned to America and achieved moderate success as a portrait painter in Boston, Washington and New York. On his return from a second trip abroad in 1832, Morse met Charles T. Jackson who showed him a device which could conduct electricity over long distances.

Back in New York, as a professor of painting and sculpture at New York University and founder of the National Academy of Design, Morse experimented with such a device for three years. By 1835 he had a working model for an electric telegraph. Then he worked for several more years with assistance from Joseph Henry, Leonard Gale and Alfred Vail to perfect his design. Morse expanded on previous codes to devise his own code of dots and dashes, corresponding to electric signals of long and short duration, to represent letters and numbers. In 1843 Congress voted $30,000 to construct a telegraph line from Baltimore to Washington. Morse completed the line the following year and sent the first message, "What hath God wrought?" The U.S. Government would not buy rights to the telegraph, so Morse formed his own company. After many lawsuits over his rights to royalties, Morse became wealthy and famous throughout the world. He was also known for introducing daguerreotypes in America and for pioneering the submarine cable telegraph.

mercial treaty with Great Britain, which recognizes Texas's independence.

2 DECEMBER 1840

National After six months of "Log Cabin and Cider" campaigning, William Henry Harrison defeats Martin Van Buren in the presidential election. Harrison receives 234 electoral votes to Van Buren's 60. John Tyler becomes vice-president. Abolitionist James G. Birney receives just over 7000 popular votes which came from every free state except Indiana. This election gives Whigs a majority in Congress. The Whig victory marks the first time since 1800 that a coalition has defeated the political party in power.

OTHER EVENTS OF 1840

National Many American Abolitionists attend a worldwide Anti-Slavery Convention held this year in London. Much to their indignation, American women delegates are not allowed to take delegates' seats. William Lloyd Garrison walks out with them in protest. This action will lead delegates, including Lucretia Mott and Elizabeth Cady Stanton, to consider their own status as citizens and eventually organize conferences focused on women's rights.

International William Ladd publishes *An Essay on a Congress of Nations.* He wants Congress to develop a set of principles that will govern international law and to set up an international court.

APRIL 4, 1841

ELIZABETH CADY STANTON, 1815-1902

Injustice to women in the antislavery movement led Elizabeth Cady Stanton to become a leader for women's rights. A native of Johnstown, New York, she married the abolitionist lawyer, Henry Brewer Stewart, and moved to Boston. There she met other abolitionists, Frederick Douglass, John Greenleaf Whittier and Lydia Maria Child. In 1840, Stanton was a delegate to an international slavery convention in London with her husband, but she, Lucretia Mott, and other women delegates were excluded from the convention floor. Upon returning to America, Stanton moved to Seneca Falls, New York. Here, isolated from her Boston reform friends and still indignant over the London convention, she organized the first American women's rights conference with Lucretia Mott in 1848. Stanton wrote a declaration of 18 legal grievances, including a call for national women's suffrage—a goal that would not be achieved for 70 years.

From 1852 Stanton worked closely with Susan B. Anthony to promote women's legal, political and industrial rights. A powerful orator, she was the first woman to speak to the New York legislature and convinced them in 1860 to grant women the right to their own wages. She served as president of the National Woman Suffrage Association from 1869–90 and then as president of the National American Woman Suffrage Association from 1890–92. Stanton sometimes accepted the support of eccentrics such as the spirtualist and free-love advocate, Victoria Woodhull, who hurt her cause, but her skill as a journalist always stood in her favor. She wrote articles for the New York *Tribune* and for Amelia Bloomer's paper, *The Lily.* From 1868–70 she edited a militant feminist magazine, the *Revolution.* In the 1880s Stanton helped write the first three volumes of *History of Woman Suffrage* and in 1898 published a retrospective on womens' rights, *Eighty Years and More.* Throughout her life, Stanton advocated liberal divorce laws, coeducation, less restricting clothing for women and more liberal religion. A mother of seven, she was a prolific writer, and one of the busiest lecturers of her time because she knew that her goals would not come easily.

Life/Customs A group of reformed drunkards founds the Washingtonian Temperance Society in Baltimore.

Ideas/Beliefs Prominent Mormon Brigham Young travels to England to speak about the Mormon Church. His message is so convincing that between now and 1846 approximately 4000 English converts to Mormonism will emigrate to Nauvoo, Illinois.

Arts/Culture The group known as the "Transcendentalists," including Ralph Waldo Emerson and George Ripley, that has been meeting to discuss philosophy and literature, begins to publish their own journal, *The Dial,* in Boston. Margaret Fuller, a member of the group, is the first editor. Richard Henry Dana, Jr. first publishes *Two Years Before the Mast.*

4 MARCH 1841

National William Henry Harrison is inaugurated as the ninth President and the first Whig to hold this position. John Tyler becomes vice-president. Harrison makes an inaugural address that demonstrates his lack

of political experience and indicates that he will defer to the leaders of Congress. On March 5-6 Harrison appoints his Cabinet members, including Secretary of State Daniel Webster, Secretary of the Treasury Thomas Ewing, Secretary of War John Bell, and Attorney General John Crittenden. Harrison had originally offered the Secretary of State position to Henry Clay who refused it. Aside from Webster, most Cabinet members are Clay supporters.

9 MARCH 1841

Slavery The Supreme Court rules on the *Amistad* case involving 53 black mutineers from a Spanish slave ship who had been taken into United States custody. The Court upholds the lower court decision to free the blacks and allow them to return to Africa.

4 APRIL 1841

National The rigors of the presidential campaign and the cold he caught while outdoors for his inauguration prove too stressful for 68-year-old William

---

WILLIAM HENRY HARRISON, 1773-1841

Given the odd distinction of holding the presidency for only one month, Harrison is better remembered for the military exploits which helped put him into office. The son of Benjamin Harrison, who signed the Declaration of Independence, Harrison was raised in Charles City County, Virginia, and attended Hampden-Sydney College. He joined the army in 1791 and fought against Indians in the Northwest Territory; he soon became secretary of the territory, then territorial delegate to Congress. From 1800 to 1812 he served as governor of the territory and tried to obtain as much land as possible, often using bribes and whiskey to encourage Indians to sign treaties until they had turned over most of what is now Indiana, Michigan and Illinois. He helped spread disease and alcoholism throughout the Indian ranks, but they fought back in one last grand effort of resistance under two brothers, Tucumseh and the Prophet. In 1811 Harrison marched against Tecumseh's Shawnee Village on the Tippecanoe River and a few months later repulsed the Prophet's warriors. He then defeated a British commander at the Thames River in the Ontario wilderness to help win the War of 1812.

Harrison exaggerated his exploits to advance his political career. He served in the U.S. House of Representatives and then in the Senate. He became better known, and a group of Anti-Mason Whigs nominated him for president in 1836. Whigs regarded Harrison as a compromise candidate between Clay and Webster, and he won the 1840 nomination with Webster's support. An enthusiastic campaign followed, portraying Harrison and Tyler, both Southern aristocrats, as simple frontiersmen. The campaign ignored issues and used the slogan "Tippecanoe and Tyler too," along with pictures of cider and log cabins to appeal to popular notions. Harrison was swept into office. But just a month after his inauguration—held outdoors on a cold, rainy day during which he caught a cold—the "old hero" died of pneumonia. Harrison's presidency might have been a good one; he chose brilliant men, including Daniel Webster, to serve in his cabinet. As if to carry out a family responsibility, his grandson Benjamin Harrison became President 48 years later.

Henry Harrison. After only one month in office, he dies of pneumonia. Vice-President John Tyler becomes the first American to succeed to the presidency.

Civil War: Approach When Tyler declares a Sunday as a "day of national prayer" for the deceased Harrison, various speakers use the occasion to speak out on the issue of slavery. One minister in the South is reported as taking the occasion to preach on "current wild notions of equality."

9 APRIL 1841

National The Whigs as a group have never solidly endorsed Tyler. Now that he is president, he openly differs with them on both practical issues and constitutional principles. In a public address, he promises to follow strict construction principles in changing government fiscal structure. Much of Congress disagrees with him, and they label his supporters as "the Corporal's Guard."

10 APRIL 1841

Arts/Culture Horace Greeley begins to publish the New York *Tribune*. As editor of this newspaper, Greeley will become one of the most influential people in the country.

19 MAY 1841

Ideas/Beliefs The Unitarian preacher Theodore Parker delivers a landmark sermon in South Boston, "On the Transient and Permanent in Christianity."

7 JUNE 1841

Finance Henry Clay introduces a complete fiscal proposal in the Senate with the support of other Whigs. He wants to repeal the Independent Treasury Act, set up a new government bank, increase tariffs, and distribute proceeds from the sale of public land to individual states.

28 JULY 1841

Finance The Senate passes the Fiscal Bank Bill with a vote of 26-23. This is a Whig proposal to incorporate a new fiscal organ in the District of Columbia. It would be called the Fiscal Bank of the United States and is understood by most to be simply a revival of the Second Bank of the United States. The bill will pass the House of Representatives on August 6, but on August 16 President Tyler will veto it as unconstitutional. On August 19 the Senate will not be able to override the veto.

13 AUGUST 1841

Finance According to the wishes of Clay and other Whigs, the Independent Treasury Act is repealed. They hope to continue in their fiscal policies and follow this by establishing a national bank. During the next five years they prevent Democrats from reestablishing a subtreasury system. Instead, the Secretary of the Treasury has jurisdiction over public funds and uses state banks for deposits. This system is not regulated and operates at the discretion of the Secretary.

JOHN TYLER, 1790-1862

In April 1841 when William Henry Harrison died after only one month in office, most legislators were not ready to accept Vice-President Tyler as the first person to succeed to the presidency. Tyler was a tall, soft–spoken man, the son of an aristocratic farming family near Richmond, Virginia, who had been put on the Whig ticket solely to capture Southern votes for Harrison. Because he believed in both states' rights and a strict interpretation of the Constitution, neither the Democrats nor the Whigs cared for his views. Tyler made matters worse by remaining so faithful to his "principles" that he failed to win allies or accomplish much in office. Many took to calling Tyler "his accidency."

Tyler had been a firm states' rights Democrat when he began his political career in 1811 as a state legislator and then as a U.S. Representative. As governor of Virginia (1825-27) and as a U.S. Senator (1827-36), he opposed Andrew Jackson's policies relating to the Missouri Compromise and fiscal matters so strongly that he became a Whig. Once he was president, his lack of commitment to Whig policies was obvious, and that party's leader, Henry Clay, refused to support him. After Tyler's second veto of a national bank measure, his entire cabinet, except for Daniel Webster, resigned. Tyler was an expansionist and did manage to set the stage for the annexation of Texas. He favored a joint resolution which was accepted by Texas just a few days before he left office in 1844. A small faction of Democrats had nominated Tyler for reelection, but he withdrew when he realized he had no chance to win. When the Civil War seemed imminent, Tyler worked unsuccessfully for a last–minute reconciliation at a conference in Washington. He was eventually elected to the Confederate House of Representatives, but died before taking his seat.

---

19 AUGUST 1841

Finance A system of uniform bankruptcy law begins throughout the nation. A person can now voluntarily declare bankruptcy. The law will be repealed on March 3, 1843, but during its three-year tenure 33,737 people will take advantage of it.

3 SEPTEMBER 1841

Finance Congress adopts a second Whig–sponsored bank bill; this one is designed to satisfy President Tyler's objections to the first by providing for state offices of the bank only by state consent. On September 9 President Tyler vetoes this bill as well. On September 10 the Senate fails to override the veto.

4 SEPTEMBER 1841

Settling The Distribution-Preemption Act is passed. It is a combination of Thomas Hart Benton's preemption scheme and Clay's goal to distribute proceeds from the sale of public lands. After individuals have settled public lands, they may purchase them for a minimum price. If tariff rates rise above 20 percent, the distribution provision will be rescinded.

11 SEPTEMBER 1841

National President Tyler's veto of the bank bills angers his cabinet members. Except for Secretary of

State Daniel Webster, they all resign. Almost without exception, the departing Cabinet members publicly charge Tyler with changing his former commitment to support a bank bill, even though the record does not show he had supported it in the way they suggest. Tyler makes new Cabinet appointments, but these will change often during the next few years. Most conspicuous will be the appointment of John C. Calhoun as Secretary of State on March 6, 1844, an indication that Southerners will have more and more influence in the Democratic party.

OCTOBER 1841

Regional Only adult males who own land and their eldest sons are allowed to vote in Rhode Island. More than half of the adult males in this state do not fit into that category, and a group of them hold a convention to demand that they be given suffrage. They draw up a constitution that will be ratified in December by a majority of adult males who vote on it.

12 OCTOBER 1841

International A court in Utica, New York, acquits Alexander McLeod, the Canadian deputy sheriff accused of murdering Amos Durfee in the burning of the American steamship, the *Caroline*. New York Governor William Seward has planned to pardon him if necessary in order to prevent tension between America and Canada.

7 NOVEMBER 1841

Slavery Both pro-slavery and anti-slavery Americans become very excited when a group of slaves being taken from Hampton Roads, Virginia, to New Orleans successfully mutiny and take control of the United States ship, *Creole*. They sail it into Nassau, a British port, where except for those accused of murder, they are immediately freed.

16 DECEMBER 1841

Westward Movement Senator Lewis Linn of Missouri introduces a bill that will encourage immigration to Oregon. He wants to provide military protection along the route between Missouri and Oregon and to give land grants to males over 18 years old. The bill never passes, but serves to make the British apprehensive about America's expanding control over territory.

OTHER EVENTS OF 1841

Westward Movement The first large group to emigrate to California travels over the Oregon Trail, the Humbolt River and the Sierra Nevada Mountains. The 48 wagons in the party reach Sacramento.

Ideas/Beliefs Largely as an outgrowth of discussions by the Transcendentalists, George Ripley and the Brook Farm Association set up a cooperative living experiment, the Brook Farm Institute of Agriculture and Education 9 miles from Boston. It attracts Nathaniel Hawthorne and Charles A. Dana. Meanwhile, in Ohio, the Marlboro Association establishes the first Fourierist community in the country.

ANTEBELLUM BLACK CHRISTIANITY

Because white slaveholders preferred to perceive blacks as similar to children who needed both protection and instruction, they often took responsibility for indoctrinating their slaves with moral and religious teaching. They encouraged the "saving" of blacks' souls and often had them sit in the balconies of white churches, where New Testament teachings would encourage them to be "meek" and submissive. Slaves saw some logic in conversion to Christianity as they could gain additional sympathy from their masters. It also gave them a way to order the world and to interpret injustice and evil.

Blacks soon realized that they could have their own churches, and more importantly, their own preachers. The black preacher could deliver emotional, articulate, embellished sermons in a call-and-response style that gave everyone a chance to join in, to experience a poetic uplift. Black Christianity grew into a powerful mixture of European Christianity, as taught by the whites, and African religion, customs, magic and mythology. Although some officials limited the movements and activities of black preachers after Nat Turner's rebellion, other whites supported them completely, and there are many reports of black preachers ministering to whites. Talented black preachers could successfully move between varied groups: from field hands who spoke dialect to house servants to free blacks and even to white congregations.

Both blacks and whites alike appreciated the slave spirituals as one of the most distinctive aspects of the religion. Blacks could release themselves in singing beautiful spirituals, making themselves, if only for a while, free of their masters and of their toil. Their talent for improvisation and their deep religious feelings combined to give the songs a rich intensity. One white woman who heard her slaves singing at a "praise meeting" called their song "mostly a sort of weird chant that makes me feel all out of myself when I hear it way in the night." They also sang for survival, often putting coded messages into songs in order to share news, plots or information about slave rebellions. This religion and music contributed a great deal to both 19th and 20th century American culture. The style of black preachers almost certainly defined part of Southern American oratory, and the slave spirituals formed the basis for two unique American musical forms—the blues and jazz.

Arts/Culture Ralph Waldo Emerson publishes his first series of *Essays*. A young writer, Edgar Allan Poe, becomes associate editor of *Graham's Magazine,* founded this year in Philadelphia. Poe will be recognized here for his criticism.

24 JANUARY 1842

Civil War: Approach Citizens in the northeastern Massachusetts town of Haverhill have John Quincy Adams submit a petition to Congress that requests the peaceful dissolution of the Union.

1 MARCH 1842

Civil War: Approach The United States Supreme Court rules, in *Prigg v. Commonwealth of Pennsylvania,* that a Pennsylvania law forbidding the seizure of fugitive slaves in that state is unconstitutional. But the opinion goes on to state that the enforcement of fugitive slave laws is entirely a federal responsibility, so various Northern states use this as a loophole and adopt personal liberty laws.

4 MARCH 1842
Finance Ruling in *Dobbins v. Commissioners,* the United States Supreme Court finds that a state cannot impose a tax on the salary earned by a federal officer.

21-23 MARCH 1842
National Abolitionist Representative Joshua Giddings, an Ohio Whig, presents several resolutions to the House following the controversy over the *Creole* mutiny and subsequent British freeing of slaves from that American vessel. Secretary of State Daniel Webster, among others, has demanded that the British return the slaves because they were the "property" of American citizens. Giddings, however, disagrees and opposes both slavery and the shipment of slaves in America's coastal trade. This angers Southern Representatives who are able to garner a healthy majority to vote censureship of Giddings in the House. On March 23 Giddings resigns his seat. In April voters in his home district will reelect Giddings; he will return to his seat in the House on May 8.

30 MARCH 1842
National Congress adopts the highly protective Tariff Act of 1842 which raises rates to the same level determined by the Tariff Act of 1832.

31 MARCH 1842
National After 40 years' work in public service, Henry Clay submits his resignation to the Senate. The Whigs have lost control of Congress, as shown by the failure of their programs, and Clay wants to help build the Whig party to prepare for the election of 1844. He will return to the Senate in 1849.

18 APRIL 1842
Regional The opponents of the established Rhode Island government and constitution, which only allows the vote to landowning males, hold their own election and elect Thomas W. Dorr as Governor. His followers control most of northern Rhode Island and, based on their own constitution, they declare their own right to vote. The old government reelects Samuel King as Governor, and Rhode Island is run under a dual government. The Rhode Island General Assembly calls out the state militia to remove Dorr's government. Both Dorr and King appeal to President Tyler for assistance. On May 18 the Dorrites unsuccessfully attempt to take the Rhode Island state arsenal. Dorr and his followers flee the state and then return; Dorr is tried on June 25, 1844 and sentenced to life in prison. He will be released a year later.

MAY 1842
Exploration Colonel John C. Frémont heads an expedition to explore the Rocky Mountains in southern Wyoming. He will make a national reputation for himself as he begins what will be a four-year journey.

National Because President Tyler has alienated the Democratic party, former President Van Buren realizes that he may again be in the running for that office. He visits Henry Clay in Kentucky where the two men almost certainly agree to leave the Texas annexation issue out of the future presidential campaign.

10 JUNE 1842
Exploration Lieutenant Charles Wilkes has led his exploration team over 90,000 miles during the past four years in the Pacific and Antarctic oceans. He returns to New York City.

25 JUNE 1842
National Congress passes the Reapportionment Act. After March 3 members of Congress will be elected according to districts, with each state having the number of districts that corresponds to their quota of representatives.

9 AUGUST 1842
International Many disputes between the United States and Britain are settled with the signing of the Webster–Ashburton Treaty. Secretary of State Daniel Webster has been working since he first took office to settle the question of the northeastern boundary. On June 13 he began meeting in Washington with Lord Ashburton, Alexander Baring, and included state commissioners from Maine and Massachusetts and even President Tyler in negotiations. The United States receives about 7000 of the 12,000 square miles in dispute between the two countries. This settlement allows the British to maintain their transportation and military route between New Brunswick and Quebec. The United States government pays $150,000 to both Massachusetts and Maine for the land they claim to have lost in the compromise. The treaty provides America with navigational rights on the St. John River, crucial to Maine's economic development, and agreements on mutual extradition. The British agree to give the U.S. the area south of a line from Lake Superior to the Lake of the Woods. (In 1866 the rich Mesabi iron deposits will be discovered in this area.) Lord Ashburton writes an official apology that puts the *Caroline* affair to rest.

26 AUGUST 1842
Finance Congress defines the fiscal year as beginning on each July 1.

11 SEPTEMBER 1842
International A group of Mexican soldiers invade the Texas Republic and capture San Antonio. Hostilities will continue into 1843.

3 OCTOBER 1842
Settling To create public interest in his mission in the Oregon territory, Marcus Whitman sets off to make a winter journey to Boston and Washington.

20 OCTOBER 1842
International Commodore Thomas Jones of the

United States Navy mistakenly believes that the British are about to seize California and that the U.S. is at war with Mexico. He assaults Monterey and hoists the American flag there. In a short time, he realizes his error, apologizes to Mexico, and leaves.

DECEMBER 1842
Life/Customs A political exile from Hesse, Dr. Charles Frederick Ernest Minnegerode, reportedly cuts, sets up and trims a tree for the first time in this country to celebrate Christmas.

30 DECEMBER 1842
International Daniel Webster advises President Tyler to take a stand on the Hawaiian islands. In a message to Congress Tyler warns that the United States would not approve of any power trying to take control of the islands. In 1843 he will send a diplomatic representative to Hawaii.

OTHER EVENTS OF 1842
Civil War: Approach An accused fugitive slave, George Latimer, is seized by authorities in Boston. Abolitionists in that city force authorities to let them buy his freedom from his Virginia owner.
Westward Movement A major party of 130 people in 18 wagons heads for the Oregon territory from Independence, Missouri. The newly appointed Indian Agent for that territory, Dr. Elijah White, leads the party to Whitman's mission in Walla Walla.
Life/Customs In New York City, P. T. Barnum opens his American Museum to the public.
Labor Massachusetts Chief Justice Lemuel Shaw rules in *Commonwealth v. Hunt* that a trade union is a lawful organization; further, a union is not responsible for the illegal acts of individuals, and a strike that might occur in a closed shop is a legal act.
Transportation A canal between Cincinnati and Toledo, Ohio, is completed.
Agriculture In Buffalo, New York, the first grain elevator in the country is built.
Education Francis Wayland, the president of Brown College, publishes *Thoughts on the Present Collegiate System in the United States.* He advocates that students be allowed to elect their own courses of study.

JANUARY 1843
Life/Customs Dorothea Lynde Dix addresses the Massachusetts Legislature on the harsh treatment of the insane. She publishes her address and continues investigations that will lead to significant reforms.

3 FEBRUARY 1843
Settling The Senate passes the Oregon Bill, introduced by Lewis Linn of Missouri in 1841, to encourage immigration to the Northwest. It will not pass in the House of Representatives.

APRIL 1843
Regional Following the Dorr rebellion of disenfranchised residents who want the vote, Rhode Island adopts a new constitution with more liberal suffrage.

DANIEL WEBSTER, 1782-1852

Known as the greatest orator of his generation, Webster often relied on his keen knowledge of Constitutional law to emphasize his point of view. A native of New Hampshire, Webster graduated from Dartmouth College in 1801 and began practicing law in 1805. Beginning in 1813 he served two terms in Congress and then moved his law practice to Boston. With an eye toward New England shipping interests, he argued before the Supreme Court against state intervention in private and corporate property. Webster also gained fame as a powerful public orator at Plymouth in 1820, at Bunker Hill in 1825, and at the deaths of Jefferson and John Adams in 1826. From 1827-41 Webster served in the Senate where, as a spokesman for New England's manufacturers, he supported protective tariffs.

Webster disagreed with President Andrew Jackson over the Bank of the United States and joined with Henry Clay to form the Whig party. He became one of three Whig candidates for the presidency in 1836, but failed to win the nomination in later years. As Secretary of State to William Henry Harrison, Webster was the only cabinet member who did not resign when Tyler succeeded to the presidency and broke with the Whig party. Webster served until he had completed the Webster-Ashburton Treaty with Great Britain in 1843. Webster returned to the Senate and opposed the Mexican War, but came to view disunion as a greater evil than slavery. Ignoring his New England abolitionist constituents, he supported the Compromise of 1850 because he valued the preservation of the Union over his own popularity. Although he lost some popular support, many in his party still respected Webster. He served as Millard Fillmore's Secretary of State until his death at age 70.

The dispute between the two separate governments of the state will eventually be decided in the Supreme Court in 1849.

MAY 1843
Exploration John C. Frémont leaves Missouri on his second expedition. He will cross the Rocky Mountains into the Snake and Columbia River valleys and then explore California's central San Joaquin Valley. He will return to Missouri in July 1844.

2 MAY 1843
Settling Settlers in the Oregon territory hold a meeting at Champoeg and complete the preliminary work of forming their own government.

8 MAY 1843
National Daniel Webster resigns from his position as Secretary of State. He is the last of the Cabinet originally appointed by President William Henry Harrison to do so. Abel P. Upshur takes over the job on July 24.

22 MAY 1843
Westward Movement One thousand Easterners leave from Independence, Missouri to settle in the Oregon territory. This marks the beginning of a large migration westward.

TESTING A UNION 1788-1865

JUNE 1843
International American delegates travel to London to meet with others at the World Peace Conference.

17 JUNE 1843
Regional Daniel Webster delivers a stirring oration at the dedication of the Bunker Hill Monument in Charlestown, Massachusetts.

5 JULY 1843
Settling The Oregon settlers meeting at Champoeg adopt a constitution modeled on the laws of Iowa. It will serve for a provisional government until the United States establishes jurisdiction over the area. This month a convention in Cincinnati calls for 54°40' as the American line in that territory.

14 AUGUST 1843
Indian Affairs The Second Seminole War ends after years of deliberate massacres against the Seminoles in Florida.

23 AUGUST 1843
International Mexico's President Santa Anna warns the United States that he would consider the American annexation of Texas as tantamount to a declaration of war against Mexico. Following the Mexican invasion of San Antonio, Texas, British and French ministers have arranged a truce between the countries. American powers are worried about the growing close alliance between Texas and European countries and so are showing a renewed interest in annexing Texas.

30-31 AUGUST 1843
National The anti-slavery Liberty party holds a national convention in Buffalo, New York. Delegates unanimously nominate James G. Birney of Michigan for president and Thomas Morris of Ohio for vice-president. Their platform denounces the extension of slave territory, but takes no firm stand on the annexation of Texas.

16 OCTOBER 1843
Regional Secretary of State Abel Upshur reports to Isaac Van Zandt, the Texas minister at Washington, that the United States wants to discuss negotiations for the annexation of Texas. Sam Houston, Texas president, declines the proposal because he realizes that opposition from Northerners in the Senate could result in rejection, and he does not want to risk losing Great Britain's support.

OTHER EVENTS OF 1843
International The United States is protecting its interest in the Hawaiian Islands. It sends a diplomatic agent, George Brown, there to act as commissioner and refuses to join Great Britain and France in supporting the independence of the islands.

Civil War: Approach In Vermont, the state assembly acts to block execution of the Fugitive Slave Act of 1793.

Ideas/Beliefs The country's major Fourierist community, the North American Phalanx, is organized in Red Bank, New Jersey. In New York City, German Jews organize the B'nai B'rith. Unitarian Theodore Parker publishes his translation of DeWette's *Critical and Historic Introduction to the Old Testament*.

Arts/Culture Sculptor Hiram Powers finishes his work "Greek Slave."

16 JANUARY 1844
Regional Knowing that Sam Houston is hesitant to negotiate America's annexation of Texas, Secretary of State Upshur asks the United States representative in Texas to assure Houston that the required two-thirds of the Senate will approve an annexation treaty.

MARCH 1844
Exploration John C. Frémont's expedition crosses through the Sierra Nevada Mountains to arrive at Sutter's Fort in Sacramento.

6 MARCH 1844
National John C. Calhoun becomes Secretary of State after the February 28 death of Abel Upshur in a gun explosion on the warship *Princeton*.

27 MARCH 1844
Arts/Culture Springfield, Massachusetts, a growing city on the Connecticut River, now has a daily newspaper, the Springfield *Republican*. Samuel Bowles, Jr. is the first editor.

4 APRIL 1844
Ideas/Beliefs The Fourierists are at their peak in membership. At a large meeting in Clinton Hall, New York, they elect George Ripley of Brook Farm as their president. Among vice-presidents are Horace Greeley, Charles A. Dana and Parke Godwin.

12 APRIL 1844
Civil War: Approach A treaty agreeing to the American annexation of Texas, negotiated by John C. Calhoun, now Secretary of State, is signed and President Tyler submits it to the Senate on April 22.

27 APRIL 1844
National Van Buren and Clay, who both hope to run for president, publish letters (in separate newspapers) that oppose the annexation of Texas. Van Buren's letter makes Andrew Jackson switch his support to James K. Polk. After Clay receives the Whig nomination he will qualify his letter by saying that he would be happy to see annexation without war. He loses the support of some Southerners, and Democrats will use the statement to describe Clay as an opportunist.

1 MAY 1844
National The Whig National Convention unanimously supports Henry Clay for president. They choose Theodore Frelinghuysen of New Jersey for vice-president. The Whig platform makes no statements about Texas annexation nor about a national bank.

OTHER EVENTS OF 1844

6-8 MAY 1844
National Increasing conflicts between native–born American Protestants and immigrant Catholics result in violent clashes between these groups now and on July 5-8 in Philadelphia. About 100 people are injured and 20 killed. This year the American Republican Party is supporting a platform that prohibits Catholics from holding office or voting; they manage to elect a nativist mayor in New York City.

27-29 MAY 1844
National The Democrats meet at Baltimore and nominate James K. Polk for president. Polk wins only after the eighth ballot and is the first "dark horse" candidate for the presidency, filling the role when Van Buren cannot win enough supporters. Anti-slavery man Silas Wright of New York refuses the nomination for vice-president, and the Democrats then choose George M. Dallas of Pennsylvania. Their platform stresses the "reannexation" of Texas and the "reoccupation" of Oregon. By choosing the campaign motto, "Fifty-Four Forty or Fight," the Democrats intensify the Anglo-United States dispute over the Oregon boundary. On these same days, those Democrats who support President Tyler also meet in Baltimore. He accepts their nomination but withdraws from the campaign on August 20.

8 JUNE 1844
Civil War: Approach The Texas annexation treaty is rejected by the Senate, where anti-slavery forces convince a majority that admitting a slave state will simply lead to another confrontation between the South and the North.

27 JUNE 1844
Ideas/Beliefs Joseph Smith, leader of the Mormons, is killed by a mob in Nauvoo, Illinois. Brigham Young becomes head of the church.

3 JULY 1844
International Caleb Cushing negotiates the Treaty of Wang Hiya, the first treaty between America and China. It opens five ports for trading by American merchants and gives legal rights to those Americans living in China.

13 AUGUST 1844
Regional A newly ratified constitution in New Jersey allows only white male citizens to vote.

3 DECEMBER 1844
National Following the urging of John Quincy Adams, the House of Representatives votes to rescind the gag rule of 1836 that prohibits discussion of anti-slavery petitions. This same day President Tyler delivers his fourth annual message and asks Congress to annex Texas.

4 DECEMBER 1844
Civil War: Approach James K. Polk defeats Henry Clay for the Presidency. Polk is virtually an unknown politician, but his somewhat aggressive-expansionist

---

UTOPIAN MOVEMENTS

In a time characterized by reform—temperance, anti-slavery, education—many people became interested in the basic reform of day-to-day living. Deliberate communities and many attempts at utopianism flowered. One of the earliest in this country was Robert Owen's New Harmony experiment of the 1820s. Many such communities had already appeared in France and England. In fact American Albert Brisbane went to France to study the philosophy of Charles Fourier and then worked to spread the word in this country. The great increase in utopianism in America during the 1840s was the first strong evidence that not all was well in the country—not everyone was getting what democracy had promised. Deliberate communities became popular because they gave people a place to go, a structured society where all would be regarded as equal, all sharing.

Some experimented with open marriage, shared spouses or rather simple methods of marriage and divorce, such as the statement, "I divorce thee." Many tried communal child rearing. Certainly the success of the Mormons and the Shakers was the most conspicuous, and others soon followed. Frances Wright, a Scotswoman who had shocked Americans in the 1820s by giving public lectures, was influenced by Robert Owen. Vigorously anti-slavery, she bought 680 acres near Tennessee and founded Nashoba, a colony for free blacks and others. Nashoba had no organized religion and no sexual taboos. Wright soon learned that social reforms didn't work well in the wilderness. She moved to New York and began publishing her own newspaper instead. Other prominent examples of communities included the Transcendentalists' Brook Farm experiment near Roxbury, Massachusetts, and the Midwestern communities of Amana and Oneida. Many of the communities established newspapers to put forth their philosophies, and these sometimes attracted donations from those supporters who could not actually join. But too often the communities did not have enough money, enough leadership or enough experience at farming to be successful. One of the most well-known examples of disillusionment with communal living experiments was Nathaniel Hawthorne's response to the Brook Farm community—his novel, the *Blythedale Romance*. The longest lived communities had strong leaders—Joseph Smith of the Mormons, John H. Noyes of Oneida, Barbara Heynemann of Amana—or a commitment to produce a product that would provide a steady income. Oneida and Amana produced such quality goods that their names are still associated with silver and appliances.

---

views on acquiring Texas, Oregon and California strike a receptive chord among Americans. He owes his very nomination, in part, to the fact that the more obvious Democratic candidate, Martin Van Buren, had earlier in the year published a letter opposing the annexation of Texas. James Birney of the anti-slavery Liberty party wins 62,300 popular votes, and thereby contributes to Clay's defeat.

12 DECEMBER 1844
Regional Anson Jones succeeds Sam Houston as president of Texas.

OTHER EVENTS OF 1844
Civil War: Approach The Baptist Church cannot

agree on the question of slavery. It splits into the Northern and Southern conventions.

Ideas/Beliefs Amos Bronson Alcott, who recently ran the experimental Temple School in Boston, founds a utopian community called Fruitlands near the rural community of Harvard, Massachusetts. His daughter, Louisa May, will later write about their idyllic family life in *Little Women*. Ralph Waldo Emerson publishes his second series of *Essays*.

23 JANUARY 1845
National Congress acts to establish a uniform election day for all presidential elections. They will take place on the first Tuesday following the first Monday in November in all states.

3 FEBRUARY 1845
Regional The House of Representatives passes a bill that would set up a government for Oregon with a northern border of 54°40'. The Senate refuses to consider the bill because it would prohibit slavery.

20 FEBRUARY 1845
National Congress has passed a law that would prevent the Treasury from paying for ships that President Tyler ordered. He vetoes this bill. Then on March 3, in an unprecedented action, Congress overrides the veto.

28 FEBRUARY 1845
Civil War: Approach The House of Representatives and the Senate, acting on the proposal of President-elect Polk, adopt a joint resolution for the annexation of Texas. This is essentially a procedure to bypass the requirement of a two-thirds vote of the Senate alone, traditionally used to ratify a treaty. The resolution also authorizes the President to negotiate a new treaty with Texas, one that could be approved by either procedure, but the President does not immediately exercise this choice.

MARCH 1845
International Mexico agrees in a preliminary way to recognize Texas as an independent Republic, but their discussions related to this sort of treaty cease when Texas learns of the February congressional annexation resolution. In addition, Mexico severs diplomatic relations with the United States on March 28.

3 MARCH 1845
National Florida, the 27th state, joins the Union as a slave state. The Postal Act reduces postage rates to five cents per one–half ounce for 300 miles. It also provides for government subsidies to steamships which carry mail.

4 MARCH 1845
National James Knox Polk is inaugurated as the 11th President and the third Democrat to hold this office. His inaugural address reaffirms the Democratic platform in proclaiming that the United States has "clear and unquestionable" title to Oregon and that the an-

---

JAMES K. POLK, 1795-1849

Polk became the first U.S. President to pledge himself to only one term. He then set out to achieve his powerful goals of expansion during that term. Born in Mecklenburg County, North Carolina, Polk grew up in Tennessee and graduated at the top of his 1818 class at the University of North Carolina. He was admitted to the bar in 1820 and three years later began a rapidly advancing political career—first in the Tennessee legislature, then in the U.S. House of Representatives, serving as Speaker of the House from 1835-39, then as governor of Tennessee. Democrats nominated Polk for president in 1844 as the first "dark horse" candidate for that office because they had split over Van Buren and Cass. His carefully worded platform included the "reannexation" of Texas and the "reoccupation" of Oregon. In fact he lusted after both of these territories and even before Mexico showed any hostility toward the United States, Polk was suggesting to his cabinet that they had a right to declare war because of financial claims against Mexico. But then he incited war by sending troops into territory that had historically been ruled by Mexicans. With almost no debate in Congress, Polk had money for both soldiers and guns. When the war ended in 1848 with the Treaty of Guadelupe Hidalgo, Americans had won a tremendous territory for only 18 million dollars.

Polk worked doggedly to achieve his other goals of reducing the tariff, settling the Oregon boundary dispute and re–establishing the independent treasury. His health collapsed at the end of his term and he died at his home in Nashville three months after leaving office. Some considered Polk the one great president between Jackson and Lincoln because he achieved his program of expansion in such a short time. Others regarded him as a narrow-minded and obstinate man whose goals could have been accomplished by more conventional means that would not have intensified the controversies between North and South.

---

nexation of Texas is a matter between those countries only. James Buchanan becomes Secretary of State and historian George Bancroft becomes Secretary of the Navy.

6 MARCH 1845
International Following President Polk's references to Texas annexation in his inaugural address, the Mexican minister at Washington protests and demands his passports.

MAY 1845
Exploration John C. Frémont begins his third expedition to the West.

28 MAY 1845
Civil War: Approach President Polk believes Texas will agree to annexation, so he simply decides to treat it as a state, even though it remains Mexican territory under international law. Polk sends a detachment of the United States army, led by General Zachary Taylor, to the southwestern border of Texas to guard the state against an "invasion" from Mexico.

15 JUNE 1845
Regional Secretary of State James Buchanan guaran-

OTHER EVENTS OF 1845

tees protection by United States Troops if Texas consents to the terms of annexation. This same day President Polk orders General Zachary Taylor to move to a point on or near the Rio Grande to be able to defend Texas. Taylor stops on the Neuces River near Corpus Christi on July 31.

23 JUNE 1845
Regional Texas holds a special session of its congress to vote for annexation to the United States. A convention on July 4 in San Felipe de Austin accepts the terms that Texas be admitted to statehood immediately without a time of territorial status and that not more than four states would be formed from its territory. Texas is to maintain control over its public lands and the Missouri Compromise line of 36°30′ will extend into the Texas territory.

JULY 1845
National An article credited to John L. O'Sullivan, the editor of an expansionist magazine, *The United States Magazine and Democratic Review*, appears in that publication and uses the term "manifest destiny" for the first time. In complaining about other countries interfering with the annexation of Texas, O'Sullivan described "our manifest destiny to overspread the continent allotted by Providence for the free development of our yearly multiplying millions." The term will be borrowed by other publications.

12 JULY 1845
International Secretary of State James Buchanan wants to settle the dispute with Great Britain over the Oregon territory. He offers to extend the 49th parallel for the boundary. The British minister, Pakenham, refuses the offer on July 29, but requests the United States to reconsider on December 27.

AUGUST 1845
Regional Agrarian unrest over leases dating back to Dutch and English rule in the Albany, New York, area is creating problems. An anti–rent war broke out in 1839-40 when heirs of Stephen Van Rensselaer tried to collect $40,000 in back rent. Residents are revolting against the patroonship system, and farmers disguised as Indians are attacking the militia called out by the governor to keep the peace. A deputy sheriff is murdered this month and Delaware County is now under martial law.

10 OCTOBER 1845
National Secretary of the Navy George Bancroft oversees the formal opening of a naval academy at Fort Severn, Annapolis, Maryland.

17 OCTOBER 1845
Regional President Polk appoints Thomas O. Larkin to be the United States consul in Monterey. Polk wants Larkin to encourage Californians to favor annexation and, based on European interest in Texas, asks Larkin to block any foreign powers trying to secure California.

10 NOVEMBER 1845
International The President commissions John Slidell, to negotiate a settlement with Mexico that will not only attempt to pay off Mexico for Texas but also to purchase New Mexico and California from Mexico. Polk instructs Slidell to pay $5 million for New Mexico and $25 million for California in exchange for Mexican approval of the Texas boundary at the Rio Grande River.

2 DECEMBER 1845
National President Polk makes his first annual message to Congress and his opinions are clear: he claims all of Oregon and will not tolerate any future European colony or dominion on the continent without North American consent. He also recommends revisions of the tariff and restoration of the Independent Treasury. His elaboration of the Monroe Doctrine becomes known as the "Polk Doctrine."

16 DECEMBER 1845
International Even though the president of Mexico refuses to receive envoy John Slidell because of hostile public opinion against this agent who did not have the full consent of Congress, a Mexican general leads a military takeover of the government on the excuse that the president was planning a treasonable action.

29 DECEMBER 1845
National Texas joins the Union as the twenty-eighth state.

OTHER EVENTS OF 1845
National Two factions of the Democratic party in New York state are in open conflict this year as they run opposing candidates in races for the state legislature. The radical wing of the party is called the "Barnburners" by their opponents who compare them to the Dutch farmer who got rid of his rats by burning the barn. The other wing is known as the "Hunkers," from the Dutch word *hunkerer*, in this case, one who "hunkers" or "hankers" after office. Eventually the Barnburners will withdraw and join the Free-Soilers because of their anti-slavery views.

Westward Movement John C. Frémont publishes *The Report of the Exploring Expedition to the Rocky Mountains in the Year 1842 and to Oregon and Northern California in the Years 1843-44* and greatly increases interest in the West.

Immigration Beginning this year potato famines in Ireland force great numbers of Irish immigrants to try to find better lives in America. The migration will continue for the next several years with about 1.5 million people immigrating.

Industry The town of Lawrence, Massachusetts, located on the Merrimack River, is founded to manufacture woolens. It is just a few miles away from the successful mill town of Lowell.

Transportation A great clipper ship, the *Rainbow*, is built and launched by John W. Griffiths in New York. It ushers in the era of huge clipper ships.

Ideas/Beliefs Just as the Baptist church has split

TESTING A UNION 1788-1865

FACTORIES AND THE CHANGING STRUCTURE OF THE FAMILY

Early American factories, such as textile mills in Waltham and Lowell, could be built and operate successfully not just because of an industrial revolution—that had happened years before in England—but because of a new organization of labor. Many New England families had worked their land so much and divided it over generations that they now found their farms could support fewer and fewer of their children. They needed other ways to earn money. The factories had a major impact on the family. They caused a separation between work life and home life, and work life became demarcated by the clock. In the case of the Lowell factories that thrived by the 1850s, the worklife became the geographical location of the homelife as well. The family no longer functioned as a unit of production, but as a unit of consumption. Children were, like their parents, simply regarded as workers, although smaller and not as efficient at the work. Many people resisted mass education because they were more interested in preparing their children to enter factories. Parents either needed the extra income from their children's work or felt that work in the factories would help the children get ahead.

Gradually people became accustomed to the factories. Their early complaints of having to work by a clock and having supervisors who turned clocks back to get more work eventually evolved into the struggle to reduce the number of hours to the workday. Controversy over the factories and the beginnings of worker resistance were sped up by the depressions of the 1830s and 1857, which caused the first widespread unemployment. Suddenly people realized that they were vulnerable to industrial depression. This was not simply like a drought or hard times that they might have anticipated as farmers—it marked the end of self-sufficiency.

over the slavery question, the Methodist Episcopal church now splits as well into Northern and Southern conferences when their Bishop James O. Andrew of Georgia is asked by the General Convention to choose between his slaves or his position.

Arts/Culture Margaret Fuller publishes *Woman in the Nineteenth Century,* a collection of her essays on the role of women in America. Edgar Allan Poe publishes a collection, *The Raven and Other Poems,* which makes him famous.

5 JANUARY 1846
Regional The House of Representatives passes a resolution to end the Anglo-American joint occupation of the Oregon country. In debating the resolution, Representative Robert C. Winthrop of Massachusetts refers to "the right of our manifest destiny to spread over this whole continent."

12 JANUARY 1846
International John Slidell's report on his unsuccessful attempt to negotiate with the President of Mexico reaches President Polk. The following day Polk orders General Zachary Taylor to move from the Nueces River to a position on or near the left bank of the Rio Grande River. Taylor's "Army of Observation" now

has nearly 3500 troops, about one–half of the United States Army.

27 JANUARY 1846
Regional A party led by John C. Frémont arrives in Monterey, California. He will stay in the area until March 9, when he is asked by local authorities to move further north.

12 FEBRUARY 1846
International The new Mexican President, General Mariano Paredes, refuses to receive envoy John Slidell, who then returns to the United States.

19 FEBRUARY 1846
Regional Texas formally installs a state government at Austin.

27 MARCH 1846
National Representative Andrew Johnson of Tennessee introduces a bill that would provide for free homesteading, but the House defeats it.

28 MARCH 1846
International General Taylor takes his troops onto the left bank of the Rio Grande, always recognized as Mexican territory, on the orders of President Polk. There, across from Matamoros, Americans begin building fortifications. Mexicans opposite them are doing the same.

SPRING 1846
Ideas/Beliefs Beginning now and continuing through the summer, 12,000 Mormons move from Nauvoo, Illinois, to Council Bluffs on the Missouri River.

12 APRIL 1846
International A Mexican general, Pedro de Ampudia, who commands the forces at Matamoros, warns General Taylor to retire his position beyond the Nueces River or, he warns, "arms alone must decide the question."

13 APRIL 1846
Transportation The Pennsylvania Railroad receives a charter.

24 APRIL 1846
International Despite Mexico's evident desire to find some face-saving way of negotiating its way out of an armed conflict, President Polk persists in seeking an excuse for war. It comes when a small Mexican cavalry unit inflicts a few casualties on United States troops blockading a Mexican town. On April 26 General Taylor reports to Washington that "hostilities may now be considered as commenced."

25 APRIL 1846
National President Polk plans his war message to Congress, based on Mexico's refusal to meet with Slidell and her unpaid claims to United States nationals.

27 APRIL 1846
International President Polk signs a Congressional resolution to end the Anglo-American joint occupation of Oregon, thereby terminating the treaty of 1827. Polk insists that the British make a formal proposal to fix the boundary at 49°N.

3 MAY 1846
International Mexican forces attack Fort Texas, constructed by Taylor's men. En route to relieve the fort, Taylor defeats a group of Mexicans at Palo Alto on May 8 and then followed the numerically superior retreating Mexicans to attack again at the Battle of Resaca de la Palma on May 9. One report of this battle holds that the Americans lost 39, with 83 wounded, and the Mexicans lost 262 with 355 wounded and 150 others captured. It makes Taylor a popular hero.

13 MAY 1846
Civil War: Approach At the request of President Polk on May 11, Congress approves a declaration stating that "By the act of the Republic of Mexico, a state of war exists between that Government and the United States." Congress authorizes the recruitment of 50,000 soldiers and $10 million to fight the war. In the debate leading up to the declaration of war and in the months to follow, it is clear that the war with Mexico is yet another divisive issue between the North and the South: Southerners tend to support the war as they see it leading to more territory to be worked by slaves, while Northerners oppose the war for that very reason.

18 MAY 1846
International General Taylor crosses the Rio Grande to occupy Matamoros.

MAY—JUNE 1846
International President Polk orders blockades of Mexican ports located on the Pacific Ocean and at the Gulf of Mexico. On June 3 Colonel Stephen Kearney is instructed to occupy Santa Fe, and then move on to California.

6 JUNE 1846
International There has long been simmering a dispute between the United States and Great Britain over the border between the Oregon Territory and Canada. President Polk, anxious to gain support for the widening war with Mexico, submits to the Senate a British treaty that extends the international boundary along latitude 40° to Puget Sound and then to the ocean through the Juan de Fuca Strait. In return for Southern support for the treaty, President Polk agrees to reduce certain tariffs. The Senate will ratify the treaty on June 15.

14 JUNE 1846
Regional North American settlers in California, long seeking to break away from the rule of Mexico, proclaim the Republic of California, also called the Bear

CITIZEN RESISTANCE TO THE MEXICAN WAR

Americans as a whole never shared President Polk's enthusiasm for the Mexican War. Some, of course, supported him. They felt that the United States' way of living and governing should be shared with others, especially those of an "inferior" race. Others looked at the lush, varied lands of California and New Mexico with the desire to explore, settle and start commercial developments. Following the congressional declaration of war in 1846, major rallies and demonstrations took place in cities such as New York, Indianapolis and Philadelphia, and thousands rushed to volunteer, mostly for the pay and for agressive adventure in a distant land. As Walt Whitman wrote, it was time for the world to see that "America knows how to crush, as well as how to expand."

But opposition to the war was just as strong and came from many fronts. Some anti-slavery Congressmen, including Joshua Giddings of Ohio, feared that the war was just a way of extending slavery, and they voted against every war measure. Others felt strongly that the United States had no right to be in an area that had always belonged to Mexico, and they found different ways to protest. Henry David Thoreau chose to spend time in jail rather than pay his Massachusetts poll tax and contribute to the war; this experience provided the basis for his classic essay, "Civil Disobedience." Poet James Russell Lowell published satirical anti-war poems in a Boston newspaper, and in *The Liberator*, abolitionist William Lloyd Garrison actually reported that he wished for America's defeat. Congregational, Quaker and Unitarian churches publicly denounced the war, and Rev. Theodore Parker urged resistance to enlistment and manufacturing weapons.

Some of the most telling resistance came from enlisted men themselves. Nearly half were recent immigrants who were there for the money and perhaps for social advancement, but too many soon learned that promises of advance pay and other inducements to enlist were frauds. They became tired of pointless killing, ashamed of fellow soldiers who ransacked towns, drinking, raping and killing civilians. Many deserted, and the end of the war saw a total of 9207 deserters. None of these men would share the glory of victory with President Polk and his generals.

Flag Republic because of the flag they raise over Sonoma. John C. Frémont arrives on June 25 and settlers will give him command on July 5.

17 JUNE 1846
National James Russell Lowell publishes the first of his "Biglow Papers" in the *Boston Courier* to voice his opposition to the war with Mexico.

19 JUNE 1846
Life/Customs The first match baseball game in the United States occurs in Hoboken, New Jersey, when the New Yorks beat the Knickerbockers, 23-1.

26 JUNE 1846
Agriculture Great Britain repeals the Corn Laws and thereby increases American exports.

7 JULY 1846
Regional Commodore John Sloat lands at Monterey

TESTING A UNION 1788-1865

and claims possession of California for the United States. He hoists an American flag.

6 AUGUST 1846
Regional Congress authorizes a state government for Wisconsin.
Finance Congress readopts the Independent Treasury Act, first in effect in 1840.

8 AUGUST 1846
Civil War: Approach President Polk asks Congress to appropriate $2 million to help purchase territory from Mexico in negotiations that he assumes will follow any fighting. The appropriation bill comes to the House where it is amended to include what is known as the Wilmot Proviso, so named after an otherwise obscure Pennsylvania Representative, David Wilmot, who introduces the amendment. Using words taken verbatim from the Northwest Ordinance of 1787, the Wilmot Proviso states that "neither slavery nor involuntary servitude shall ever exist in any part of" the territories that might be acquired from Mexico. The House passes the appropriation with this amendment, but the lines between Northerners and Southerners are once more sharply drawn. The Senate will adjourn before acting on this bill.

13 AUGUST 1846
International Commodore David Stockton has succeeded Commodore Sloat and joins with John Frémont to take Los Angeles. On August 17 Stockton will declare that the United States has annexed California and will establish himself as governor of the area.

15 AUGUST 1846
Regional The first newspaper in California, the *California*, begins publication in Monterey.
International Colonel Kearney arrives in Las Vegas and announces the annexation of New Mexico by the United States. On August 18 he will occupy Santa Fe and then set up a temporary government there.

14 SEPTEMBER 1846
International General Santa Anna becomes commander-in-chief of the Mexican army.

20-24 SEPTEMBER 1846
International General Taylor battles fiercely for four days in Monterrey, Mexico and takes the city.

22 SEPTEMBER 1846
International A group of Mexican Californians led by Jose Maria Flores revolt against the United States. They conquer San Diego and Los Angeles and shortly control all of California south of San Luis Obispo. Flores is acting as governor.

5 NOVEMBER 1846
Regional The Navy orders Commodore Stockton to recognize Kearney as governor and commander-in-chief of California.

16 NOVEMBER 1846
International General Taylor captures Saltillo, the capital of Coahuilla, Mexico.

25 NOVEMBER 1846
International Colonel Kearney crosses into Southern California where the Mexican–Americans are in control, but he defeats them at San Pascual on December 6 and occupies San Diego on December 12.

12 DECEMBER 1846
International The United States signs a treaty with the government of New Granada in what is now Bogota, Colombia, which guarantees America transit rights over the Isthmus of Panama yet also guarantees New Granada sovereignty.

28 DECEMBER 1846
National The free state of Iowa joins the Union as the 29th state.

29 DECEMBER 1846
International General Taylor is now occupying the capital of Tamaulipas—Victoria.

OTHER EVENTS OF 1846
Regional Anti–rent wars in New York state lead to legislation that restricts the duration of farm leases by replacing perpetual leases with fee-simple leases. These issues are included in a more liberal constitution adopted by the state.
Education Louis Agassiz comes from Switzerland to America where he will become foremost in the fields of zoology and geology. He lectures at the Lowell Institute in Boston and becomes a professor at Harvard College.
Arts/Culture Herman Melville gains instant success when he publishes *Typee*, a dreamy tale of travel in Polynesia.

3 JANUARY 1847
International General Winfield Scott, who has taken command of the Gulf expedition in Mexico, orders 9000 men from General Taylor's force to assault Vera Cruz.

10 JANUARY 1847
International Kearney, now a general, takes Los Angeles after two skirmishes near the San Gabriel River. These end the hostilities in California, and on January 13 the remaining Mexican forces in the area sign the Treaty of Cahuenga with Captain Frémont.

16 JANUARY 1847
Regional Commodore Stockton believes that he, and not General Kearney, has the power to set up a civil government in California and appoints Frémont as Governor.

The Oregon Bill, which excludes slavery in that territory through the restrictions of the Northwest Ordinance, passes in the House of Representatives. On March 3 the Senate will table it.

5 FEBRUARY 1847
National General Taylor has growing disagreements with President Polk and believes he must protect himself politically and militarily. He defends his views and actions in a New York newspaper on January 22 and then disobeys orders to communicate with General Scott and moves west.

13 FEBRUARY 1847
Regional General Kearney acts on orders to establish a new government in Monterey while Fremont still acts as governor in Los Angeles.

15 FEBRUARY 1847
International The House of Representatives approves a bill for negotiations to purchase territory from Mexico. The bill includes the Wilmot Proviso.

19 FEBRUARY 1847
Civil War: Approach The Senate takes up the appropriation bill with the Wilmot Proviso, and ends up passing the former without the latter. The House then approves the Senate version of the appropriation bill, so that the question of slavery within the territories remains open. But during the Senate's debate on the Wilmot Proviso, John Calhoun introduces four resolutions that attempt to provide justification for the Southern position. Essentially Calhoun argues that Congress has no right to limit existent or prospective states in matters of laws pertaining to slavery. Furthermore, since slaves are like any property that might be taken into a territory, Congress has the obligation to protect slavery. Calhoun's doctrine effectively sets aside the Missouri Compromise of 1820, and although the Senate in no way endorses it, the doctrine is in the air.

22-23 FEBRUARY 1847
International The Battle of Buena Vista takes place after General Taylor refuses Santa Anna's demand for surrender. General Taylor's 4800 men are mostly inexperienced volunteers, yet they soundly defeat Santa Anna's equally untrained 15,000 men. Santa Anna will return to Mexico City.

28 FEBRUARY 1847
International Colonel Alexander Doniphan heads across desert wastes from El Paso toward Chihuahua and defeats an army at Sacramento. He occupies Chihuahua the following day.

3 MARCH 1847
Life/Customs Congress approves adhesive postage stamps. They will go on sale in New York on July 1. On this same day Congress adopts gas lighting fixtures for the Capitol and its grounds.

9 MARCH 1847
International General Scott's force lands near Vera Cruz. It is the most powerful fortress of the time in the Western Hemisphere. The city cannot bear attacks from both land and sea and Scott takes it on March 29.

8 APRIL 1847
International General Scott leaves Vera Cruz and heads in the direction of Mexico City. He will defeat Santa Anna's men at Cerro Gordo on April 18, take Jalapa on April 19 and Puebla on May 15.

16 APRIL 1847
Ideas/Beliefs Leaving most of the Mormons at Council Bluffs, Brigham Young takes a small group of followers to look for suitable land in the West.

31 MAY 1847
Regional General Kearny appoints Richard B. Mason to be governor in California and then leaves with Captain Frémont and Commodore Stockton to straighten out their conflicts in Washington.

6 JUNE 1847
International Nicholas P. Trist, appointed by President Polk to arrange a peace with Mexico, begins negotiations through Charles Bankhead, a British minister.

24 JULY 1847
Ideas/Beliefs Brigham Young and his followers arrive at the valley of the Great Salt Lake; he establishes the State of Deseret, which is now Utah.

20 AUGUST 1847
International General Scott is moving closer to Mexico City. After his forces take Contreras and Churubusco, Santa Anna asks for an armistice.

27 AUGUST 1847
International Peace negotiations begin between Mexican and American representatives but end in failure. The armistice ends on September 7.

SEPTEMBER 1847
National The Native American Party holds a meet-

Landing the troops at Vera Cruz.

ing in Philadelphia and supports war hero General Zachary Taylor of Louisiana for president. They nominate Henry Dearborn of Massachusetts for vice-president.

8 SEPTEMBER 1847
International General Scott takes Molino del Rey after a day-long battle. On September 23-13 he also takes Chapultepec although seriously outnumbered. Then on September 13-14 Scott marches victorious into Mexico City after a whirlwind campaign since landing at Vera Cruz in May.

NOVEMBER 1847
National The abolitionist Liberty party holds a convention in New York and nominates John P. Hale of New Hampshire for president and Leicester King of Ohio for vice-president. Hale will later withdraw in deference to Martin Van Buren.

22 NOVEMBER 1847
International Nicholas Trist, who has been recalled to Washington, receives word that the Mexican government is now ready to negotiate the terms of peace. He agrees to take part.

29 NOVEMBER 1847
Indian Affairs Oregon Indians kill Marcus Whitman, his wife, and a party of settlers.

6 DECEMBER 1847
Regional Abraham Lincoln takes his seat in the House of Representatives for Illinois.

14 DECEMBER 1847
National Senator D. S. Dickinson of New York introduces a resolution in the Senate to support "popular sovereignty," which would allow territorial legislatures to rule on slavery in those territories.

22 DECEMBER 1847
National Abraham Lincoln makes his first speech in the House and sharply disagrees with President Polk over the Mexican War.

29 DECEMBER 1847
Civil War: Approach Senator Lewis Cass of Michigan, in a letter to A. P. Nicholson, a Tennessee politician, sets forth the doctrine that slavery should be left to the decision of the territorial government. Because Cass is an influential politician—he plans to run for president in 1848—his proposal is given serious consideration. It will become known as the doctrine of "popular sovereignty" and will attract many supporters anxious to sidestep either the constitutional or the moral issues of slavery.

OTHER EVENTS OF 1847
Immigration A great number of immigrants from the Netherlands begin to settle in the Midwestern states.
Labor The state of New Hampshire passes a law

Scott's entry into Mexico City.

that limits workers to a 10-hour day.
Agriculture S. Page receives a patent on his revolving disc harrow, and Cyrus McCormick opens a new reaper factory in Chicago.
Ideas/Beliefs Henry Ward Beecher takes over the ministry at Brooklyn's Plymouth Congregational Church.
Arts/Culture Henry Wadsworth Longfellow publishes *Evangeline*.

24 JANUARY 1848
Regional A New Jersey mechanic named James Marshall is building a sawmill for Johann Sutter and discovers gold in the American River, about 40 miles from Sutter's Fort, which is the site of present-day Sacramento, California. The news spreads quickly and provides the impetus for the California gold rush.

31 JANUARY 1848
National Captain John C. Fremont is found guilty of the charges placed by General Kearney: mutiny, disobedience and prejudicial conduct. He is dismissed from the army. President Polk approves most of the sentence, omitting mutiny, but restores Fremont to duty. Frémont eventually resigns and the situation causes opposition between Polk and Thomas Hart Benton, who is Frémont's father-in-law.

2 FEBRUARY 1848
Civil War: Approach The United States signs the Treaty of Guadalupe Hidalgo, ending the war with Mexico. The United States gets over 500,000 square miles that include what will become the states of California, Nevada, Utah, most of New Mexico and Arizona, and parts of Wyoming and Colorado. Texas is also conceded to the United States, with the boundary at the Rio Grande. The United States will pay $15 million and an additional $3.25 million in claims of the Rio Grande. This makes the United States a transcontinental republic, but it also opens up new land to be disputed by pro- and anti-slavery forces.

15 FEBRUARY 1848
Arts/Culture Benjamin Baker writes a play, *A Glance at New York*, which starts a vogue for plays that portray city life. His central character Mose the foreman will appear later as *Mose in Philadelphia*.

MARCH 1848
Civil War: Approach The Senate ratifies the Treaty of Guadalupe Hidalgo, and President Polk gets an appropriation bill to pay Mexico—but without the Wilmot Proviso.

23 MARCH 1848
National While speaking in the House of Representatives, John Quincy Adams dies at the age of 81.

APRIL 1848
Transportation With a growing population in the West, the Pacific Mail Steamship Company is founded to follow a route across the Isthmus of Panama and deliver mail in that area.

MAY 1848
Ideas/Beliefs A flock of seagulls from the Great Salt Lake devour a swarm of locusts that threaten the new Mormon settlement.

22-26 MAY 1848
National The Democrats hold their national convention in Baltimore. Polk had pledged himself to only one term and declines to run again. The Democrats nominate General Lewis Cass of Michigan for president and General William O. Butler from Kentucky for vice-president. Their platform criticizes all efforts to bring the slavery question before Congress.

29 MAY 1848
National Wisconsin, a free state, joins the Union as the 30th state.

2 JUNE 1848
National An abolitionist group called the Liberty League holds a meeting in Rochester, New York, and nominates Gerrit Smith of New York for president and Charles E. Foot of Michigan for vice-president.

7-9 JUNE 1848
National The Whigs hold their national convention in Philadelphia and choose among three contenders for the presidential nomination: Henry Clay, General Zachary Taylor and General Winfield Scott. Taylor's popularity has soared because of the Mexican War and the Whigs choose him. They nominate Millard Fillmore of New York for vice-president. The Whig platform is simply an advertisement of General Taylor's military reputation.

13 JUNE 1848
National Representatives of labor organizations hold a meeting at Philadelphia to nominate their own candidates for the presidential election. They choose Gerrit Smith of New York for president and William S. Waitt of Illinois for vice-president.

22 JUNE 1848
National The Barnburners, who have left the Democratic party, hold their own convention in Utica, New York, and nominate Martin Van Buren for president and Henry Dodge of Wisconsin for vice-president.

4 JULY 1848
Arts/Culture Building begins on the Washington Monument with the laying of a cornerstone.

12-19 JULY 1848
Lucretia Mott and Elizabeth Cady Stanton are the two main organizers of the first American women's rights convention held at Seneca Falls, New York. The two women have previously worked successfully to pass a New York law allowing a married woman to have control over her own property. The convention attracts both men and women. Among Stanton's resolutions are declarations that all people are equal, women must be educated in the laws, women should have suffrage and women should be free to speak in public without incurring the wrath of their families.

9 AUGUST 1848
National A coalition of anti-slavery groups assembles in Buffalo, New York, to form the Free Soil party. It nominates Martin Van Buren for president and Charles Frances Adams of Massachusetts for vice-president. Charles Sumner and Salmon P. Chase of Ohio are among those attending. The Free Soil party platform opposes slavery and upholds the substance of the Wilmot Proviso. It also favors internal improvements and free homesteads to settlers. Its campaign slogan is "Free soil, free speech, free labor, and free men."

14 AUGUST 1848
Civil War: Approach President Polk signs the bill organizing the Oregon Territory without slavery. The bill has passed with the support of Southern Senators, who clearly are willing to concede Oregon to the "free-soilers" with the understanding that other territory belongs to the slaveholders.

19 AUGUST 1848
National The New York *Herald* is the first publication to report the discovery of gold.

7 NOVEMBER 1848
Civil War: Approach General Zachary Taylor, a Whig and hero of the Mexican War, is elected president. Taylor is a slaveholder but is not especially committed to the principle of slavery. Millard Fillmore is elected vice-president. The Free Soil candidate Van Buren wins 291,263 popular votes and noticeably contributes to Taylor's victory by taking Democratic votes.

5 DECEMBER 1848
National President Polk confirms the reports of the gold discovery in California.

15 DECEMBER 1848
International The United States and Great Britain sign a postal treaty in London.

22 DECEMBER 1848
Civil War: Approach Southern congressmen hold a

255

caucus to discuss the slavery question and how to protect the rights of slaveholders.

OTHER EVENTS OF 1848

International President Polk wants to purchase Cuba from Spain and is willing to pay $100 million. The leader of America's peace movement, Elihu Burritt, calls an international congress in Brussels where delegates agree to support a court of arbitration.

Civil War: Approach The Vermont legislature agrees in a resolution to prohibit slavery in territories and to abolish it in the District of Columbia. Meanwhile, the Alabama legislature adopts a platform stressing the responsibility of Congress to protect people and their property in territories.

Immigration The failure of a revolution in Germany starts a great German migration to the United States, while a Swedish migration begins into the Mississippi Valley, and Andrew Carnegie arrives from Scotland.

Life/Customs The nation's first department store is built on Broadway in New York City.

JANUARY 1849

Life/Customs Amelia Bloomer begins publishing *The Lily*, a journal supporting temperance and women's rights. She advocates clothing reform to improve women's health and freedom of movement. The "Bloomers" outfit consists of long tunics over full harem pants, but causes too many jeers in public to become a lasting fashion.

7 FEBRUARY 1849

Immigration The Supreme Court denies the right of New York and Massachusetts to charge a tax on each entering alien.

12 FEBRUARY 1849

Regional San Franciscans gather to set up a temporary government for their region.

28 FEBRUARY 1849

Regional The first gold seekers arrive at San Francisco aboard the ship, *California*. Thousands more will follow by land and sea from all parts of the United States and from other countries as distant as China and Australia. By the end of this year, the population of California will swell to 100,000.

3 MARCH 1849

National Congress establishes the Home Department which will become the Department of the Interior. The Department begins setting policies on Indians, public lands and settlements to meet the demands of those in the West who want to exploit the land.

4 MARCH 1849

National President Polk signs an act setting up a territorial government for Minnesota. Slavery is prohibited there.

5 MARCH 1849

National Zachary Taylor is inaugurated as the 12th

IMMIGRANTS

Up to 1825, less than 10,000 new immigrants came to the United States each year. By the late 1840s, revolutions in Europe and the devastating potato famine in Ireland sent people to this country by the hundreds of thousands. Immigration increased steadily during the 1850s, and by 1860, one-eighth of America's 32 million people were foreign born. Most came packed into old sailing ships, and many of these were quarantined upon arrival because they carried the plague. In June, 1847, 84 ships arrived, and each carried some typhus—made worse for those on board from lack of food and foul conditions in the ships' holds.

Immigrants formed the basis for company towns that grew around mills in Rhode Island, Connecticut, New Jersey and Pennsylvania. Companies had families sign contracts which pledged each member of a family to work for a year. They had no choice but to live in tenement slums and to buy all their goods in over-priced company stores; their pay came in company scrip. Most immigrants also confronted religious prejudice and an extreme American ethnocentrism. The nativist political movement wanted to restrict voting rights and citizenship for immigrants and others wanted to keep them out of schools. Massachusetts, for instance, passed the first law promoting integrated education in the 1850s not because of an overwhelming desire to include blacks, but because they believed that Irish immigrants so disliked blacks that they would stay away rather than attend school with them. Certainly some of the problem was economic: immigrants were so hungry and so needed money that they would work in factories for less money than native Americans. Sadly, neither the new immigrants, the working class activists nor the oppressed blacks in the country seemed able to assist or understand each other.

---

president. He is the third and last Whig to hold this office. Millard Fillmore becomes vice-president.

10 MARCH 1849

Civil War: Approach The Missouri legislature states that "the right to prohibit slavery in any territory belongs exclusively to the people thereof."

Arts/Culture A riot erupts in New York where a British actor named Macready is performing at the Astor Place Opera House. Crowds are angry because of the theater's snobbish dress requirements and because Macready makes scornful comments on the vulgarity of Americans. As if to prove his point, the rioters shatter the theater windows with bricks, clubs and stones. Twenty-two people are killed and thirty-six injured when troops are called in.

17 MAY 1849

Regional A fire in St. Louis, Missouri, destroys more than 400 buildings and 27 steamships.

11 AUGUST 1849

International President Taylor forbids Americans from making filibustering trips into Cuba.

1 SEPTEMBER-13 OCTOBER 1849

Civil War: Approach A California constitutional

ZACHARY TAYLOR, 1784-1850

Taylor was the first American to become president without previous political experience, but the skills that made him a popular war hero failed to make him a distinctive president. A native of Virginia, Taylor grew up near Louisville, Kentucky, and was commissioned as a first lieutenant in 1808. He then held several frontier posts—fighting in the War of 1812 and in Indian wars, both in the Northwest Territories and Florida. His major reputation as a soldier resulted from his leadership in the Mexican war. America and Mexico both claimed the land between the Rio Grande and the Nueces River, and by May 1846 war seemed inevitable. Taylor's force of 5000 had moved to the Rio Grande and before war was even declared they defeated an army nearly three times their size. Taylor then took Monterrey where hundreds of men and horses died; one soldier described the scene as "slippery with. . .foam and blood." Moving against orders, he pushed on to defeat Santa Anna at Buena Vista in February 1847. Taylor's stocky build and strong endurance in battle earned him the nickname, "Old Rough and Ready." Officers respected him because he never hesitated to expose himself to enemy fire.

Taylor had nearly won the war single-handedly, and Whigs immediately decided he was the person who could unite their party. Taylor won the presidential election in 1848 against Lewis Cass, but his only real platform had been his good intentions; once he was in office they could not make up for his lack of political experience. Taylor appointed three different cabinet members who were charged with corruption. He never developed any real policies to organize the new Mexican Territory, to cope with problems following the rush to California goldfields, or to solve conflicts over the Mormons. His free-soil views made him oppose measures that would become the Compromise of 1850, negotiated by so many as a reasonable response to the slavery conflict. On July 9, 1850, before Taylor made a final decision on these measures, he died suddenly after less than one and one-half years in office. Some, including Vice-President Millard Fillmore, who would eventually sign the measures, were almost relieved. In fairness to Taylor, he had little time to develop his abilities as president. His skill as a commander in battle was, however, verified by such men as Abraham Lincoln, Ulysses S. Grant and Jefferson Davis, all of whom served under him.

convention meets at Monterey. Their drafted constitution prohibits slavery and is ratified on November 13 by popular vote. Californians then ask for admission into the Union.

4 DECEMBER 1849
Civil War: Approach President Taylor urges Congress to admit California as a state. Southern Congressmen balk at the idea of another free state—this will leave the slave states in a minority. There is talk again among some such as Calhoun of secession, but Taylor says he will crush secession even if he himself has to take to the field again. Election of a Speaker for the House of Representatives further exacerbates divisions between House members. After three weeks of turbulance and 63 ballots, Georgian Howell Cobb is elected Speaker on December 22.

20 DECEMBER 1849
International The United States signs a treaty of friendship, navigation and trade with the Hawaiian Islands.

OTHER EVENTS OF 1849
Westward Movement The Pacific Railroad is chartered in Missouri with plans to link St. Louis and Kansas City. A stagecoach line opens to carry mail between Independence, Missouri and Santa Fe.
Industry The first successful American watch company begins production in Roxbury, Massachusetts; known as the American Horologe Company, it will later become the Waltham Watch Company.
Transportation Transatlantic packet lines now sail regularly from New York to Liverpool. Improved ship design has shortened average travel time to 33.3 days, down from an average of 39 days around 1820.
Education Several new colleges are founded by religious groups. The United Brethren charter Otterbein University in Westerville, Ohio. The Baptists found William Jewell College in Liberty, Missouri and the Presbyterians found Austin College in Huntsville, Texas. Elizabeth Blackwell graduates from Geneva College, Geneva, New York, as the first woman in America to receive a medical degree.
Ideas/Beliefs Henry David Thoreau publishes "Civil Disobedience," an essay that grew out of his refusal to pay taxes supporting the Mexican War. He advocates citizen action to protest unjust government deeds. In Rochester, New York, Margaret and Kate Fox begin the Spiritualism movement. Within a few months, at least six publications dealing exclusively with spiritualism appear, launching what will become a national cult. Many people regularly hold seances.
Arts/Culture The Great Chinese Museum opens in New York City. It displays the everyday details of Chinese life, including the dress of all classes, paintings, home furnishing and models of pagodas, bridges and temples.

29 JANUARY 1850
Civil War: Approach The aging Senator Henry Clay, who has dedicated his career to preserving the Union, is annoyed at the extremists from both the South and North who threaten to resort to force. He offers to the Senate a series of resolutions that he hopes all sides can agree on. From these resolutions will eventually come the Compromise of 1850. The resolutions involve admitting California as a free state on the grounds that this is its people's own wish; meanwhile, no decision will be made at this time in regard to slavery in the other territory gained from Mexico, but the clear implication is that it will later be made according to the settlers' wishes. Other topics in Clay's resolutions include a strict new fugitive slave law and the barring of trade in slaves—but not slavery itself—from Washington, D.C.

5-6 FEBRUARY 1850
Civil War: Approach In opening the Senate debate on his resolutions, Clay pleads for a compromise by

TESTING A UNION 1788-1865

both sides in his last great speech. But the strongest advocates of both sides oppose compromise. Senator William Seward of New York argues that "there is a higher law than the Constitution which regulates our authority" while Senator John Calhoun of South Carolina argues that not only must the North concede the right of extending slavery, but it must also "cease the agitation of the slave question." Calhoun is so ill that his speech is read for him by Senator James Mason of Virginia. (Calhoun will die on March 31.)

7 MARCH 1850
Civil War: Approach The decisive speech on the compromise of Clay's resolutions is made by the Senator from Massachusetts, Daniel Webster, long a political opponent of Clay and a moral opponent of slavery. "I speak today for the preservation of the Union," he begins, and he proceeds to argue that the North must be ready to accept even slavery for this cause. Webster does not convert everyone immediately, but the spirit of compromise is now abroad.

19 APRIL 1850
International America and Great Britain sign the Clayton-Bulwer Treaty and agree that the projected canal across Central America will be neutral. Neither government will attempt to control any part of Central America and they will both act as protectors to the area.

27 APRIL 1850
Transportation The Collins Line launches the *Atlantic,* one of four steamships that will offer transatlantic service in competition with Great Britain's Cunard Line.

8 MAY 1850
National Clay's resolutions have been referred to a Senate committee of seven Whigs and six Democrats. They now report two compromise bills: the first is an "Omnibus Bill" to cover the territories, and the second prohibits the slave trade in the District of Columbia.

3-12 JUNE 1850
Civil War: Approach Leaders from nine Southern states convene in Nashville, Tennessee, to discuss the issues of slavery and states' rights. Although some delegates openly advocate secession, the moderates prevail. The convention ends when they adopt several modest resolutions, but one calls for extending the Missouri Compromise line of 36°30' all the way across the new territories to the Pacific coast.

9 JULY 1850
National President Taylor, who has opposed Clay's compromise measures, dies of cholera and Vice-President Millard Fillmore assumes the office. Fillmore will appoint Daniel Webster Secretary of State.

9-12 SEPTEMBER 1850
Civil War: Approach Congress adopts five bills based on the original resolutions of Henry Clay, and they come to be known as the Compromise of 1850. The bills include the following: California is admitted to the Union as a free state; the territories of New Mexico and Utah are organized without any restriction on slavery; Texas, also not restricted as to slavery, has boundaries set, with Texas being reimbursed $10 million by the United States government for relinquishing claims to land that is now New Mexico; slave trade in the District of Columbia is abolished after January 1, 1851; a new Fugitive Slave Act provides federal jurisdiction to strengthen the act of 1793. The bill that continues to give Northerners the most trouble is the strict Fugitive Slave Act. President Fillmore signs all the acts.

SEPTEMBER 1850
National A convention of Whigs in Syracuse splits over the Compromise of 1850. A group of conservatives led by Francis Granger hold their own convention, condemning Senator Seward's radical position and supporting Fillmore's. Eventually they will gain control of the American nativist group in New York.

20 SEPTEMBER 1850
Transportation Senator Stephen A. Douglas's efforts

FEBRUARY 15, 1850

MILLARD FILLMORE, 1800-1874

Fillmore is often forgotten as a president because he was surrounded by men such as Henry Clay, John C. Calhoun and Daniel Webster, who excelled in the tradition of classical debate. Yet he was a moderate and sensible man whose calm leadership was a welcome change after Zachary Taylor's rambunctious presidency. Fillmore was born in Cayuga County, New York. He left home at an early age to learn tailoring and woolcarding and managed to educate himself. At 19, he began to study law while teaching school and was admitted to the bar in 1823. He practiced law in Aurora, New York, and then in Buffalo. He was soon elected to the state Assembly and successfully advocated an act that ended imprisonment for debtors. Elected to U.S. Congress in 1833 and reelected for three more terms as a Whig, Fillmore became prominent in that party. In 1844 he ran unsuccessfully for the New York governorship in a close race that split proslavery and antislavery forces.

In 1848 he ran as the vice-presidential candidate with Zachary Taylor. Once in office, he presided with a calm impartiality over the fiery debates on the Compromise of 1850. Taylor had threatened to veto the compromise, but when he died on July 9, 1850, Fillmore became President. Fillmore than used patronage to pressure House members to vote for the compromise. He made Daniel Webster Secretary of State and sent Commodore Perry to Japan in 1852 to sign a treaty opening that nation to western commerce. Fillmore wanted to make the Whigs a national party based on moderate conciliation between North and South, but he failed to win the nomination for a second term because the party had split. In 1856, Fillmore hoped the Know-Nothing movement could unite North and South, and ran for President with their party, but he never had the stature or following to regain the office on his own merits. Later, he opposed Lincoln's administration and Andrew Johnson's reconstruction policies, but he simply retired to a quiet life in Buffalo where he became president of the Buffalo Historical Society.

result in a federal land grant to Illinois, Mississippi and Alabama to build a railroad between Chicago and Mobile.

28 SEPTEMBER 1850
Life/Customs Congress abolishes flogging in the Navy, yet it is still legal for schoolteachers to resort to flogging and other painful punishments to make their young charges behave in class

OCTOBER 1850
National The nation responds to the new Fugitive Slave Act. On October 21 the Chicago City Council refuses to endorse it, and on October 30 a meeting of New Yorkers resolves to sustain it.

11-18 NOVEMBER 1850
Civil War: Approach Southern leaders reconvene in Nashville, and since the more extreme delegates hold the majority, there is much talk of the South's right to secede.

13-14 DECEMBER 1850
Civil War: Approach A state convention in Georgia votes its desire to remain in the Union—but declares that the state will secede if the Compromise of 1850 is not observed by the North.

21 DECEMBER 1850
International Chevalier Hulsemann, the Hungarian charge d'affaires to the United States, writes a letter of protest against an 1848 message of support sent by President Taylor to those attempting a revolution in Hungary. Secretary of State Webster replies that the United States has a right to interest in European revolutions, especially when "events appeared to have their origin in those great ideas of responsible and popular government on which the American constitutions themselves are founded."

OTHER EVENTS OF 1850
Immigration Those Europeans wanting to come to America can now buy steerage for as little as $10, but conditions en route are atrocious. Immigrants who live in New York City do not find conditions much better. There are now 18,456 people living in only 8141 cellars in the city.

Slavery The phrase "sold down the river" enters American language from a reference to slavery: Those slaves on older plantations were supposed to regard their lives as better than those in their families who might have been sold into work further down the Mississippi River, in the Deep South, cut off from home.

Agriculture The Brooklyn Institute imports eight pairs of English sparrows to rid shade trees of caterpillars. The sparrows multiply so successfully that by 1890, the city of New York will import starlings to prey on the sparrows in Central Park.

Arts/Culture Nathaniel Hawthorne publishes *The Scarlet Letter*, which immediately becomes a best seller. All of 4000 copies are sold in the first ten days, probably because it discusses the daring subject of adultery. Herman Melville writes a novel, *White-Jacket*, to reveal the poor conditions and inhumane treatment sailors receive on United States warships. *Harper's Magazine* begins serializing the novels of Dickens, Thackeray, and Eliot, often paying more than English publishers.

15 FEBRUARY 1850
Civil War: Approach A mob of blacks, angry over the new Fugitive Slave Law, rescue Shadrach, an accused fugitive, from a Boston jail. On February 18 President Fillmore insists that the law must be followed by both officials and citizens. Many northerners are angry about this law that requires only an affidavit from a claimant to prove ownership. It allows great power to commissioners authorized to arrest fugitives for pay, but the accused fugitives themselves cannot have a trial by jury and cannot speak in their own behalf. Marshals who fail to hold slaves can be sued, and citizens who conceal or rescue fugitives are subject to harsh fines and imprisonment. Yet resistance to the law is strong and Southern slave–holders traveling in free states to find runaways could be mobbed or

259

TESTING A UNION 1788-1865

jailed for kidnapping. Other rescues to gain national attention this year include that of Rachel Parker in Baltimore, Thomas Simms in Boston, Jerry in Syracuse and Christiana in Pennsylvania.

3 MARCH 1851
Finance Congress authorizes the coinage of three-cent silver pieces.
National The postage rate drops to three cents for a half–ounce to travel up to 3000 miles.

25 APRIL 1851
International Filibustering expeditions are a continuing problem in Cuba. Those in the South who hope to annex Cuba want to stimulate a rebellion against the Spanish rule. President Fillmore makes another proclamation against such actions.

19 MAY 1851
Transportation The first train to travel the 483 miles of the Erie Railroad arrives in Dunkirk, New York, from New York City. The Great Lakes and New York City are now connected by rail.

2 JUNE 1851
Life/Customs The state of Maine passes a law prohibiting the sale and manufacture of intoxicating beverages.

5 JUNE 1851
Civil War: Approach *Uncle Tom's Cabin,* by Harriet Beecher Stowe, begins to appear as a serial in the *National Era,* an anti-slavery paper published in Washington, D.C.

9 JUNE 1851
Regional San Francisco is growing quickly with the gold rush, but that area's crime is also increasing. Groups of citizens band together and are encouraged by leading citizens to enforce laws.

23 JULY 1851
Indian Affairs Representatives of the Sioux Indians meet with representatives of the United States government to sign the Treaty of Traverse des Sioux. The Sioux give up all of their land in Iowa and most of their land in Minnesota.

3 AUGUST 1851
International General Narcisco Lopez, a Cuban refugee, ignores President Fillmore's proclamation against filibustering in Cuba and leads a group of Americans to start what he hopes will be a revolt against Spanish rule in that country. On August 3 they land about 60 miles from Havana, but fail to incite an uprising. Fifty of the American volunteers are captured and executed on August 16. Anti-Spanish riots follow in New Orleans, and a mob destroys the Spanish consulate there. Lopez is publicly garroted in Havana, and about 80 of his American supporters are imprisoned in Spain. They are not released until Congress agrees to pay $25,000 to Spain.

THE GOLD RUSH

John Marshall's discovery of gold at Sutter's Mill in Sacramento, California set off an influx of hopeful adventurers, prospectors and merchants who would provide the stimulus to growth in the far West. The romance of possible riches in unsettled territory lured over 40,000 prospectors to California in two years. Shipping companies began transporting passengers, freight and mail from New York City to the Isthmus of Panama. There, they crossed land by mule and canoe, and boarded a Pacific ship to take them to San Francisco. This was a dangerous route. Crossing Central America meant the risk of yellow fever, and many travelers died. Other routes were across the continent, with the risk of cholera, starvation or Indian attack, and the safest—a slow sail around Cape Horn.

Most gold seekers came without wives or families. They were generally young men willing to undergo the difficult work of digging mine shafts, building flumes and shoveling tons of gravel. Between 1849 and 1853, they added more than $200,000,000 to American gold circulation and caused an inflation in the 1850s. The gold attracted not just Americans, but also Mexicans, Chileans, Chinese, Hawaiians and Australians and Frenchmen abandoning their native country after the revolution of 1848. Foreign sailors often jumped ship in San Francisco to head for the goldfields. San Franciscans at first took pride in their diverse population, but before long, Americans felt less generous about sharing their potential wealth with foreigners. They gradually prohibited all but American miners in camps, and they usually ran the Chinese out first.

Many of those who did not find fortune in goldfields went into businesses that serviced miners. Agriculture, commerce, transportation and industry grew rapidly. Wells Fargo company was among the most successful express companies. One young forty-niner, a physician named Hugh Glenn, never tried mining or medicine in California. Instead, he made money enough in the freighting business to start wheat production in the Sacramento Valley. He soon had 50,000 acres and harvested more than one million bushels in a single year. Others followed with even larger farms, and began shipping their crops by sea. Cattle ranchers in Southern California made fortunes by selling their beef at inflated prices to the miners who had no other sources of meat. Collis P. Huntington, Charles Crocker, Mark Hopkins and Leland Stanford all used profits made as merchants during this period to create the Central Pacific-Southern Pacific Railroad empire, which took over the Western segment of the transcontinental railroad and controlled California. Surviving monuments to their fortunes include Stanford University and the Huntington Art Gallery and Library.

In 1858, ten years after the California discovery, gold was also discovered in what is now Denver, Colorado, setting off a rush of people to that area. Pike's Peak had a rush in 1858-59, and the Comstock Lode near Virginia City netted $300 million in gold and silver beginning about this same time. Gold discoveries caught the imagination of American writers as well as prospectors. Bret Harte and Mark Twain were among those who built reputations writing about the excitement of the gold rush. They knew it was shaping part of America.

---

22 AUGUST 1851
Transportation America has a growing reputation for making better and faster ships. One of its yachts,

America, wins an international race sponsored by the Royal Yacht Society of England. The United States will continue to win this race every year until the final race in 1937.

18 SEPTEMBER 1851

Arts/Culture Henry J. Raymond edits the first issue of the *New York Daily Times*. This newspaper will become the *New York Times* in 1857.

8 OCTOBER 1851

Transportation New York City and Albany are now connected as the Hudson Railroad opens.

22 OCTOBER 1851

International President Fillmore enjoins Americans against participating in further military exploits in Mexico.

1 DECEMBER 1851

National Congressional elections indicate that many Southerners feel the Compromise of 1850 is an acceptable alternative to secession. Unionists win elections in Mississippi, South Carolina and Alabama. In the North, however, radicals gain a triumph with the election of abolitionist Charles Sumner of Massachusetts to the United States Senate.

5 DECEMBER 1851

International Louis Kossuth, the Hungarian patriot who tried to lead a revolution against the Hapsburgs in 1848, visits the United States and receives a hero's welcome in New York.

24 DECEMBER 1851

National A huge fire in the Library of Congress leaves 35,000 volumes in ashes. This represents two-thirds of the Library's collection and included many of the books originally donated by Thomas Jefferson in 1815.

OTHER EVENTS OF 1851

Exploration Lieutenant William Lewis Herndon makes an expedition to explore the Amazon River.
International Sixty delegates travel from America to attend an international peace conference in London.
Slavery The Supreme Court, in *Strader v. Graham*, rules that slaves returning to Kentucky from Ohio must be governed by Kentucky law.
Transportation Donald McKay sets a record for clipper ship travel from New York to San Francisco that will never be bettered. His *Flying Cloud* makes the trip in 89 days, 8 hours.
Ideas/Beliefs Horace Greeley publishes a serial version of Karl Marx's *Revolution and Counter Revolution* in the New York *Tribune*.
Arts/Culture Herman Melville publishes *Moby Dick*, a novel which captures some of the romance, power and mysticism many Americans feel for the sea. Stephen Foster publishes one of his songs that will become popular both in America and in Europe—the sentimental "Old Folks at Home."

JANUARY 1852

National A rather amorphous group called "Young America," which evolved from the Democratic party in the 1840s, is highlighted in the first of a series of articles by George N. Sanders. These appear in the movement's organ, *Democratic Review*. Younger men such as Stephen A. Douglas are leaders of the group which espouses a philosophy of a romantic, yet aggressive nationalism, manifest destiny and strong support for European revolutions. Sanders lays out a program of American expansion to the south, free trade and United States assistance to republican revolutionaries in foreign countries.
International President Fillmore approves of a plan to send Commodore Matthew C. Perry to Japan. That country has been almost completely isolated since the early 17th century when it began barring outsiders. Perry will leave on November 24 with four ships and hopes to agree on permission to trade in some Japanese ports, assistance for shipwrecked Americans and arrangements for ship repairs in Japan.

5 JANUARY 1852

Regional Business representatives from 11 Southern states meet in New Orleans in the first of many conventions to discuss the economics of their area.

6 FEBRUARY 1852

National The Supreme Court rules, in *Pennsylvania v. Wheeling Bridge Company*, that Virginia does not have the right to bridge a navigable stream that lies only within state boundaries.

20 FEBRUARY 1852

Transportation Completion of the Michigan Southern Railway enables a train to arrive in Chicago from the East.

MARCH 1852

Civil War: Approach The complete novel, *Uncle Tom's Cabin, or Life Among the Lowly*, by Harriet Beecher Stowe, is published in Boston. Within a year it will sell over one million copies, and its critical portrayal of slave life serves to arouse both Northerners and Southerners.

13 MARCH 1852

Arts/Culture A great American symbol is born with the first appearance of Uncle Sam in *Diogenes, His Lantern*, a weekly comic publication in New York.

1-6 JUNE 1852

National The Democrats hold their National Convention in Baltimore. After 49 ballots, they nominate Franklin Pierce of New Hampshire for president and William R. King of Alabama for vice-president. Their platform reconfirms the Compromise of 1850 as the best and final solution to the slavery problem, and they oppose any more congressional discussions.

16-21 JUNE 1852

National The Whigs also hold their National Con-

TESTING A UNION 1788-1865

HARRIET BEECHER STOWE, 1811-1896

Stowe's novel, *Uncle Tom's Cabin*, stirred the American conscience over the slavery issue and thereby changed history. Born to the remarkable Beecher family in Connecticut, Stowe's father was a minister of strong Calvinist views; her mother died when the girl was only four. The family had black servants, and their washerwoman, Candace, was one of the young girl's special influences. She early came to question her father's strict religion and was extremely close to her brother Henry, a man of broad interests. In 1832, the father took his family to Cincinnati where he was to head a new theological seminary, and in 1836 Harriet married Calvin Stowe, a professor of Biblical literature at this school. She had tried a little writing and her husband encouraged her to continue, but she devoted the next 14 years to raising six children. The seminary was a center of the antislavery movement in that area; once, too, Stowe visited a plantation in nearby Kentucky and caught a glimpse of slave life. In 1850 she went with her husband to Maine where he took on a position at Bowdoin College, and now she gave in to the urgings of her family to write something about the slavery issue that was so bothering many of her circle.

The result was *Uncle Tom's Cabin, or Life Among the Lowly*, which began to appear as a serial in the *National Era*, an abolitionist periodical, on June 5, 1851. By the time the last installment had appeared on April 1, 1852, a Boston publisher had brought the completed novel out in two volumes; within a week, 10,000 copies were sold, and within a year, 300,000. Soon 1,500,000 copies were sold in England. Adapted for the stage, it became one of the most popular plays of all time, yet Stowe did not profit from dramatic versions or from "pirated" editions. Literary critics pointed out that the book lacked the literary values of important works, and the South condemned it for what it insisted were distortions, but Stowe had written the first American novel to portray blacks as serious protagonists. She was treated as a celebrity in the North and throughout Europe. Her second antislavery novel, *Dred, A Tale of the Great Dismal Swamp* (1856), was widely read. After the war, she continued to publish, but she never matched the success of *Uncle Tom's Cabin*. Then again, few books could have matched that work's impact on history.

vention in Baltimore. Their party is growing even more divided than the Democrats and they require 53 ballots to nominate General Winfield Scott of New Jersey for president and William A. Graham of North Carolina for vice-president. Their platform also accepts the Compromise of 1850. They reaffirm states' rights and support internal improvements for rivers and harbors. A strong Whig leader, Henry Clay, who originally organized the party, dies in Washington on June 29.

3 JULY 1852
Finance The activity and growth in California require that Congress act to establish a branch of the United States mint in San Francisco.

11 AUGUST 1852
National Members of the Free Soil party meet in their national convention at Pittsburgh. They nominate John P. Hale of New Hampshire for president and George W. Julian of Indiana for vice-president. Their platform soundly condemns both slavery and the Compromise of 1850, claiming, "Slavery is a sin against God and a crime against man." They further support free homesteads for settlers and easy entry to this country for immigrants.

24 AUGUST 1852
Arts/Culture A popular stage play is made from Harriet Beecher Stowe's novel, *Uncle Tom's Cabin*. The sentimental story, inspired by the Fugitive Slave Act of 1850, now reaches even more people with its message of the brutality and injustice of slaves' lives.

24 OCTOBER 1852
National Daniel Webster, who has resigned as Secretary of State, dies in Marshfield, Massachusetts. Much of Massachusetts mourns Webster, whom they call their "greatest statesman."

26 OCTOBER 1852
Civil War: Approach The new antislavery Senator from Massachusetts, Charles Sumner, submits a resolution against the Fugitive Slave Act, and then he attacks the law over and over again in a four-hour speech.

2 NOVEMBER 1852
National Democrat Franklin Pierce defeats General Winfield Scott for the presidency. Pierce receives 254 electoral votes to Scott's 42. The Free Soil candidate, Hale, wins only about 156,000 popular votes, an indication of the decline of his party. Whigs have less and less power because the Southerners who continue to support the Union have now joined the Democrats.

NOVEMBER-DECEMBER 1852
National As both the Free Soil and the Whig Parties decline, the American, or Nativist party begins to attract more supporters. Originally founded as a secret society, it soon becomes known as the "Know-Nothing" Party because members claim to know nothing about its workings. Its members oppose Catholics and foreigners; the party will be at its strongest in the next few years.

OTHER EVENTS OF 1852
Civil War: Approach Leaders of the pro-slavery movement publish *The Pro-Slavery Argument*, a collection of essays.
Life/Customs The first American intercollegiate rowing match is held between Yale and Harvard at Lake Winnipesaukee in New Hampshire. Growing concern over alcohol consumption results in new prohibition laws in Massachusetts, Vermont and Louisiana.
Labor A convention of journeymen printers held in Cincinnati results in the founding of the National Typographical Union.
Transportation Pittsburgh and Philadelphia are now

Dred Scott and his wife.

connected by rail with the completion of the Pennsylvania Railroad, but Pennsylvania deliberately adopts a different gauge than that used by railroads in New York to prevent New York's Erie Railroad from extending through Pennsylvania to Ohio.

Education Massachusetts, the state that has led the country in establishing and improving public schools, passes the first compulsory school attendance law in the country. Many of those who oppose child labor in the textile mills and in other factories have supported the bill.

21 FEBRUARY 1853
Finance Congress passes the Coinage Act of 1853. To keep smaller coins in circulation, it establishes a subsidiary silver system which reduces the amount of silver in all coins smaller than the dollar. It also now allows the minting of $3 gold pieces.

2 MARCH 1853
National Congress adopts an act to set off the Washington Territory from the northern part of the Oregon Territory.

4 MARCH 1853
Transportation Congress passes the Army Appropriation Act which provides $150,000 for an extensive survey on possible transcontinental railroad routes. The War Department will conduct the survey to determine the most practical route.

National Franklin Pierce of New Hampshire is inaugurated as the 14th President and the fourth Democrat to hold the office. He is the first president to give his inaugural address from memory, and he promises fully to support the Compromise of 1850. He also pledges to gain new territories by peaceful means. William R. King becomes vice-president and takes his oath of office in Cuba, a country President Pierce hopes to annex. Among Pierce's Cabinet members are Secretary of State William Marcy, Secretary of the Treasury James Guthrie, Secretary of War Jefferson Davis and Secretary of the Interior Robert McClel-

land. His choices for diplomatic appointments are all expansionists, including the new minister to Great Britain, James Buchanan.

18 APRIL 1853
National Less than one month after his inauguration, vice-president William R. King dies. Pierce will be without a vice-president nearly the whole of his term in office.

19 MAY 1853
International James Gadsden receives instructions from President Pierce to negotiate a settlement with Mexico over some disputed property that goes back to the Treaty of Guadalupe Hidalgo in 1848. Both America and Mexico have an interest in the area along the southern border of present-day Arizona and New Mexico, south of the Gila River in the Mesilla Valley. The United States especially wants to acquire the property because it provides the best location for a projected railroad route from Texas to California.

31 MAY 1853
Exploration The Second Grinnel Arctic expedition begins under the command of Dr. Elisha K. Kane. He leaves from New York on the brig *Advance* and will go further north than any sailing vessel before him, all the way to Cape Constitution.

JUNE 1853
International In order to promote a popular image of the United States as a democracy, Secretary of State William Marcy instructs all American diplomats abroad to be modest in their dress while in court. They are to appear in the "simple dress of an American citizen."

8 JULY 1853
International The special expedition commanded by Commodore Matthew Calbraith Perry reaches Yedo Bay, Japan. The United States is interested in the trading and commercial potential of Japan and wants to make arrangements for American nationals who might be shipwrecked in the area. Since the Japanese have been isolated for nearly one and one-half centuries, they are distrustful of Perry. On July 14 he presents them with a letter from President Fillmore to a representative of the Emperor, and then he leaves to allow time for the government to consider the situation and reply. He will return in February 1854 for a favorable response.

30 DECEMBER 1853
International James Gadsden signs a treaty with the Mexican government. For a price of $15 million, Mexico agrees to cede to the United States a rectangular strip of territory along the present-day southern border of Arizona and New Mexico, all together about 29,640 square miles. The land provides part of an ideal route for a railroad to the Pacific Ocean. This treaty also gives the United States the right to protect that area when it is being used. The Senate will ratify

TESTING A UNION 1788-1865

this treaty on June 29, 1854 after further negotiations reduce the purchase price to $10 million.

OTHER EVENTS OF 1853
Life/Customs Mrs. Amos Bronson Alcott, who has assisted her husband in organizing the Fruitlands community, presents a petition with 73 other women to the Massachusetts Constitutional Convention to urge suffrage for women. Policemen in New York City begin wearing uniforms and official caps. The Police Departments in Boston and Philadelphia will soon follow with similar uniforms.
Transportation The Baltimore and Ohio Railroad now extends as far as Wheeling, located on the Ohio River. Meanwhile, ten railroad lines that run between Albany and Buffalo merge to form the New York Central Railroad.
Ideas/Beliefs Norwegians who have settled in Wisconsin establish the Norwegian Evangelical Church of America.
Arts/Culture Harriet Beecher Stowe's novel, *Uncle Tom's Cabin*, has now sold 1,200,000 copies. Many criticize her work, claiming that her brutal depiction of slavery is exaggerated. She writes the *Key to Uncle Tom's Cabin* to verify her sources of factual evidence in writing the original novel.

4 JANUARY 1854
Civil War: Approach A national competition for the lucrative transcontinental railroad route has been underway for some time. Senator Stephen A. Douglas of Illinois, hoping to have the route pass through the Great Plains region, supports a bill that he hopes will win over proponents of the southern route (promoted, among others, by Jefferson Davis, now Secretary of War under President Pierce). Douglas agrees to divide the central territory into two, the Kansas Territory and the Nebraska Territory; the assumption is that one will be settled by pro-slavery people and the other by anti-slavery people. Since Douglas endorses the concept of "popular sovereignty," which means that the settlers will be able to decide for themselves about slavery, the bill effectively repeals the Missouri Compromise of 1820, as both Kansas and Nebraska lie above latitude 36°30′. The debate that follows pits pro-slavery Southerners against anti-slavery Northerners.

16 JANUARY 1854
Civil War: Approach In the debate over the Kansas-Nebraska Act, Senator Archibald Dixon of Kentucky suggests an amendment to the bill that would formally repeal the Missouri Compromise. The following day, on January 17, Senator Charles Sumner of Massachusetts also suggests an amendment—to reaffirm the Compromise.

18 JANUARY 1854
International William Walker, an American filibuster, establishes himself as president of a new republic, Sonora, made up of the Mexican states Sonora and Baja California. He will be tried in the United States for breaching neutrality in the area.

FRANKLIN PIERCE, 1804-1869

A charming but indecisive politician, Pierce was a man overwhelmed by his times. He became President in the same year that Harriet Beecher Stowe published *Uncle Tom's Cabin*, a dramatic book that reflected the dramatic period Pierce confronted. Born in Hillsborough, New Hampshire, Pierce's father had been governor of that state. He attended Bowdoin College, began to practice law in 1827, and by 1829 was elected to the state house of representatives. He soon moved into the U.S. House of Representatives and then in 1837 became the youngest member of the U.S. Senate. After a rather undistinguished career there, Pierce resigned in 1842 to appease his wife who disliked Washington life. He then continued to support the Democrats and was appointed a U.S. district attorney. Pierce's vocal support of the compromises of 1850 gained him favorable attention in the South, and Democrats nominated him as a compromise candidate at their 1852 convention. With a split in the Whig party, Pierce easily won the presidency against his former Mexican War commander Winfield Scott, but was unprepared for the difficulties facing the nation.

A "dough face" Democrat, a Northerner with Southern principles, Pierce tried to appease the South when he made his Secretary of War Jefferson Davis responsible for major policy decisions. His support of the Kansas-Nebraska Bill of 1854 led to the expansion of slavery and bloody confrontations between settlers in Kansas. Few supported Pierce for renomination, and he retired to New Hampshire. There, he supported Lincoln at the beginning of the Civil War, but became so critical of the President's actions that he himself became unpopular even in his home state. Pierce died with few admirers.

---

24 JANUARY 1854
Civil War: Approach A group of Democrats publish "The Appeal of the Independent Democrats in Congress, to the People of the United States" in strong opposition to the Kansas-Nebraska Act. Signers include Salmon P. Chase, credited with writing the document, and Charles Sumner. They call the bill a slaveholders' "plot," and the document will contribute to the organization of the Republican Party.

28 FEBRUARY 1854
Civil War: Approach At Ripon, Wisconsin, anti-slavery opponents of the Kansas-Nebraska bill meet and recommend forming a new political party, the Republican Party. In the months that follow, other meetings in various Northern states join in the formation of the new party.
International In Havana, Spanish officials stop the American packet ship, *Black Warrior*, which runs between New York and Mobile. They find an error in the ship's papers and impose a fine, but apologize in 1855.

31 MARCH 1854
International Commodore Perry has returned to Japan bearing gifts of a miniature railroad and telegraph as evidence of advanced civilization in the Western world. He induces the Japanese to sign the

Treaty of Kanagawa which opens the ports of Shimoda and Hakodate for trade with U.S. ships.

26 APRIL 1854

Civil War: Approach Eli Thay organizes the Emigrant Aid Society in Worcester, Massachusetts, to encourage anti-slavery supporters to settle in Kansas and thus "save" it as a free state. Relatively soon, about 2000 people go under the auspices of this project. In 1855 the Society is renamed the New England Emigrant Aid Company and has founded many communities, including Lawrence, Kansas, but its activities also lead to the forming of secret societies aimed at establishing slavery in Kansas.

26 MAY 1854

Civil War: Approach After much debate, the Kansas-Nebraska Act has already passed in the House, and now passes in the Senate at 1:10 A.M. It creates two new territories with "squatter" or "popular sovereignty," passes with a clear majority, and is signed by President Pierce. The territories can be admitted with or without slavery, and Stephen A. Douglas seems to have sponsored this bill for three major reasons: he believes in self-government; he wants Southern support for his political ambitions; and he wants to build a transcontinental railroad along a central route. Many Northerners denounce the Act. In particular, Northerners threaten to stop obeying the Fugitive Slave Law of 1850. On this same day, Wendell Phillips and others lead an anti-slavery mob to attack a Federal court house in Boston where an accused fugitive slave, Anthony Burns, is held. They are thwarted by authorities, but call attention to the case, and 50,000 citizens turn out a few days later to watch Burns walk to a ship headed for Virginia.

31 MAY 1854

International President Pierce enjoins Americans not to take part in filibustering expeditions in Cuba.

5 JUNE 1854

International The United States and Britain have been trying to settle disputes over fishing privileges in the Atlantic Ocean. In Washington, representatives of both countries sign a Reciprocity Treaty that allows the United States to fish along the coast of Canada, including New Brunswick, Nova Scotia and Prince Edward Island. The Canadians, in turn, are allowed to fish along the United States coastline as far as the 36th parallel. Both countries receive duty-free entry for agricultural goods and other commodities. The treaty will stay in force until the United States annuls it in 1866.

JULY 1854

Regional The Federal Government opens a land office in the new Kansas territory to distribute property. Pro-slavery forces there are already taking claims and fighting each other with little regard for any laws.

6-13 JULY 1854

Civil War: Approach In Michigan, anti-slavery men

STEPHEN DOUGLAS, 1813-1861

Although he was overshadowed by a greater politician from his state of Illinois, Douglas was a very good politician who helped shape national affairs. Born in Vermont, Douglas moved westward to Illinois where he became a lawyer and then a judge by age 28. He was active in the Democratic Party and by 1847 he was elected to the U.S. Senate. Douglas supported the acquisition of territories and worked to reach compromises between the North and South. He thus asked that the South, and any new territories or states, be allowed to choose to maintain slaves if the white citizens so desired. Douglas became popular with the strong Southern wing of his party, and in 1852 he was nominated for president. He lost, but remained in the Senate, constantly trying to keep the issue of slavery from upsetting all other issues. His approach to the Kansas-Nebraska Bill of 1854 was to espouse "popular sovereignty," the concept that residents of each state or territory should be allowed to vote for or against slavery. But he ended up antagonizing both parties—Republicans, because they had organized expressly to protest slavery, and fellow Democrats, because they saw no reason to put slavery to the vote over and over again.

When he ran for Senator in 1858 against a little-known fellow Springfield lawyer, Abraham Lincoln, Douglas continued to straddle the issue in a famous series of debates. He won the Senate seat but his own prominence and arguments made Lincoln into a national figure. As his party's candidate for President in 1860, he again found himself competing against Lincoln. Douglas campaigned vigorously throughout the nation, but sensed that Lincoln would probably win and actually began to ask the electorate to accept the coming results and work to preserve the Union. After his loss—due more to the split in his own party than to Lincoln's popular support—Douglas continued to work for compromise. After the firing on Fort Sumter, Douglas went to the White House to endorse publicly Lincoln's call for volunteers. He then went

TESTING A UNION 1788-1865

to the Northwest Territory to rally support for Lincoln, and on this trip he contracted typhoid fever. He died on June 3, 1861, his final words asking his sons to support the Constitution while the Civil War the "Little Giant" had tried so hard to avert raged on.

meeting to join the new Republican Party demand that both the Kansas-Nebraska Act and the Fugitive Slave Law be repealed. The party is made up of Whigs, Free-Soilers and anti-slavery Democrats. Similar meetings are held in Ohio, Wisconsin, Indiana and Vermont. Leaders of the party include Charles Sumner, George Julian, Salmon P. Chase and Whigs Edward Bates and Orville Browning.

19 JULY 1854
Civil War: Approach The Wisconsin Supreme Court declares the Fugitive Slave Act unconstitutional and frees a Mr. Booth who had been convicted of rescuing an accused runaway.

4 OCTOBER 1854
Civil War: Approach Abraham Lincoln gives a speech in Springfield, Illinois, that soundly condemns the Kansas-Nebraska Act, yet acknowledges the rights of Southerners and supports gradual emancipation. He will give the same speech in Peoria, Illinois, and his reputation will begin to spread throughout the region.

7 OCTOBER 1854
Regional President Pierce appoints Andrew H. Reeder, a Pennsylvania Democrat, to be the first territorial governor in Kansas.

18 OCTOBER 1854
International United States European ministers Buchanan, Mason and Soule meet in Ostend, Belgium, to discuss American acquisition of Cuba. The ministers decide that the United States needs to annex Cuba for the security of slavery and that if Spain refuses to sell the island it should be taken by force: They write, "we shall be justified in wresting it from Spain, if we possess the power." The document becomes known as the Ostend Manifesto. It arouses the ire of both Northerners and the Spanish who already resent Pierce's policy of expansion.

NOVEMBER 1854
National The Know-Nothing party of native–born Protestants holds a national meeting in Cincinnati. They want to exclude Catholics and foreigners from public office and want a 21-year resident requirement for citizenship.

29 NOVEMBER 1854
Regional In a Congressional election, J. W. Whitfield becomes the Representative from Kansas when 1600 armed ruffians cross the border from Missouri to vote for a pro-slavery candidate.

OTHER EVENTS OF 1854
Education Part of the need for public education of

adults is filled when the Boston Public Library and New York's Astor Library open this year.
Arts/Culture Henry David Thoreau publishes *Walden*.

9 JANUARY 1855
International An American-born British banker, Joshua Bates, acts as an umpire in the 1841 case involving slaves who mutinied on the *Creole* and were released by the British. Bates awards $119,330 in damages to the United States.

16 JANUARY 1855
Regional The first territorial legislature of Nebraska meets at Omaha City.

10 FEBRUARY 1855
Immigration Congress acts to ensure citizenship rights to those children born to United States citizens abroad. In addition, foreign-born women who marry American citizens can also be citizens.

3 MARCH 1855
International The Ostend Manifesto is published in America and public reaction is so negative that Secretary of State William L. Marcy refuses to support it.
Transportation At the suggestion of Secretary of War Jefferson Davis, Congress appropriates $30,000 to introduce camels into the deserts of the Southwest. Thirty-three camels will arrive from Egypt.

30 MARCH 1855
Civil War: Approach Elections for a territorial legislature are held in Kansas. Several thousand pro-slavery Missourians, called "Border Ruffians" because they are armed, cross into Kansas and vote, thus electing a pro-slavery legislature. The election is recognized by Reeder, the federal governor of the territory, because he fears further violence.

5 JUNE 1855
National The Know-Nothing Party holds a national council meeting in Philadelphia, and Southerners seize control.

2 JULY 1855
Civil War: Approach The pro-slavery Kansas legislature meets in Pawnee and not only adopts an extremely strict series of pro-slavery laws, including severe penalties for anti-slavery agitation and oaths for officeholders, but also expels the anti-slavery legislators.

31 JULY 1855
Regional President Pierce removes Governor Reeder ostensibly because he has been speculating in the Kansas land that he is supposed to protect, but his real mistake was opposing the pro-slavery legislature. Pierce will now install Wilson Shannon of Ohio, a strong pro-slavery man.

4 AUGUST 1855
Civil War: Approach A group of free-state support-

OTHER EVENTS OF 1855

ers meet at Lawrence in the Kansas territory and call for their own constitutional convention, given the fraudulently elected legislature.

3 SEPTEMBER 1855
International William Walker, who has previously tried to set up his own state in Mexico in 1853, now exploits a civil war currently in progress in Nicaragua. He takes advantage of the divided country and declares himself as dictator, managing to rule for two years. Some Northerners believe that Walker is supported by a slaveholding plot to extend slavery, but he is actually backed by the Accessory Transit Company which is interested in travel routes across the Central American isthmus.

5 SEPTEMBER 1855
Civil War: Approach The anti-slavery colonists in Kansas hold a convention at Big Springs and ask for admission to the Union as a free state. They declare that the territorial legislature is illegal.

1 OCTOBER 1855
Civil War: Approach Once again J. W. Whitfield is elected by "Border Ruffians" and pro-slavery men as the Congressional Representative for the Kansas Territory. But on October 9 anti-slavery supporters independently elect former governor Andrew Reeder to be the Congressional delegate.

23 OCTOBER-12 NOVEMBER 1855
Civil War: Approach Free-soil Kansans hold a convention of their own in Topeka and adopt a constitution that outlaws slavery. (But they will also adopt a law that bars all blacks from Kansas.) A virtual civil war now exists, with frequent clashes between the pro-slavery and anti-slavery elements in Kansas.

26 NOVEMBER-7 DECEMBER 1855
Civil War: Approach Approximately 1500 "Border Ruffians" come into Kansas after some shootings and small skirmishes along the Wakarusa River. The Missourians who have crossed the border planned to attack the anti-slavery town of Lawrence but refrain when they learn that the town is well defended. Governor Shannon intervenes to stop what is known as the Wakarusa War.

8 DECEMBER 1855
International President Pierce issues a proclamation against William Walker's filibustering expedition in Nicaragua, yet he will accept Walker's emissary next year.

15 DECEMBER 1855
Regional The free-soil people of Kansas approve the Topeka constitution (and the law banning blacks).

OTHER EVENTS OF 1855
Regional Abolitionist Salmon P. Chase is elected governor of Ohio.
Immigration Approximately 400,000 immigrants arrive in New York City this year.

Slavery Former slave Frederick Douglass publishes his autobiography, *My Bondage, My Freedom*. He describes the "peculiar Institution" of which he is a self-proclaimed graduate.
Life/Customs More states adopt prohibition laws against liquor: New Hampshire, Delaware, New York, Michigan, Iowa and the Nebraska Territory. Women's rights activist Lucy Stone agrees to marry Henry Blackwell when he convinces her that they can work more effectively for the cause if they work together. Their marriage ceremony is conducted by Thomas Wentworth Higginson and includes statements about the inequities between men and women. They have no obedience clause, they will retain their personal property, and each will have the freedom to travel alone.
Transportation John Augustus Roebling builds another beautiful suspension bridge, this one over Niagara Falls. Further west, Lake Superior and Lake Huron are connected by a canal, the Sault Ste. Marie, also known as the "Soo." A railroad now complete across the Isthmus of Panama has been built with United States financing. It will allow an alternative route to the West.
Education The Elmira (New York) Female College is established; it is the first institution of higher educa-

---

FREDERICK DOUGLASS, 1817-1895

Douglass, a former slave who eventually advised President Lincoln, became the most famous black American of his era. He was born in 1817 on a Maryland plantation, the son of a black woman, Harriet Bailey, and an unknown white man. (Douglass later adopted his own surname from the hero of Scott's *Lady of the Lake*.) Reared as a field hand and houseboy, Douglass became literate because the wife of his master defied the law and taught him to read. He escaped and made his way to Massachusetts in 1838 where he found work as a laborer. After giving a spontaneous speech at a meeting of the Anti-Slavery Society he was employed in 1841 by that organization to lecture for the abolitionist cause. An eloquent handsome man, Douglass became so prominent through his lectures and the publication of his autobiography that he feared he would be seized as a fugitive slave. He went to England until he could raise enough money to buy his own freedom.
In 1847 Douglass returned to the United States and founded an abolitionist newspaper, the *North Star*. Because he came to believe that wiping out slavery was probably going to require resorting to violence, he fell out with one of his early supporters, William Lloyd Garrison. When the war broke out, Douglass saw it simply as a crusade to abolish slavery, but he could never persuade Lincoln to define his goals that decisively. Douglass did persuade Lincoln to use blacks as soldiers, however, and personally recruited many. He urged Lincoln to give them the same pay and promotion opportunities as whites. Douglass later accepted government appointments, including the ambassadorship to Haiti in 1889, and added to his reputation through his autobiographical writings. He served as an inspiration to later generations of blacks, and in his advocacy of passive resistance yet violence in retaliation against violence, Douglass anticipated the modern civil rights movement.

267

tion to grant academic degrees to women. Mrs. Carl Schurz, who studied the kindergarten methods of Friedrich Froebel in Germany, organizes the first American kindergarten. It is a German-speaking school, located in a Watertown, Wisconsin home.

Henry Barnard of Connecticut begins reporting on kindergartens and other educational issues in his *American Journal of Education*. The respected journal will be published until 1882; it helps give form to the education profession as more individuals make life-time commitments to teaching careers.

Arts/Culture A manuscript copy of William Bradford's *History of Plymouth Plantation* is discovered in the library of the Bishop of London. The Massachusetts Historical Society will publish the document in 1856. Walt Whitman publishes his controversial collection of poems, *Leaves of Grass*.

1 JANUARY 1856
Life/Customs Adhesive postage stamps have been available since 1847. Now Congress makes their use obligatory.

15 JANUARY 1856
Civil War: Approach The free-soil Kansans elect their own governor, Charles Robinson, and their own legislature. On January 24 President Pierce condemns this as an act of "rebellion" since the Federal governor approved the pro-slavery legislature.

24 JANUARY 1856
Regional The Georgian Senator Robert A. Toombs travels north to Tremont Temple in Boston where he defends slavery in an oration.

2 FEBRUARY 1856
National Congress is breaking down more distinctly into groups of those for and against the Kansas-Nebraska Act. Members of the House of Representatives take two months to elect a speaker, finally choosing Nathaniel Banks of Massachusetts.

11 FEBRUARY 1856
Civil War: Approach President Pierce makes a special proclamation to warn both the "border ruffians" and the free state men in Kansas to stop their fighting, but he clearly supports the pro-slavery element in the territory.

22 FEBRUARY 1856
National The Know-Nothing Party (now known as the American Party) holds its annual conference in Philadelphia. It nominates for president Millard Fillmore and for vice-president Andrew J. Donelson of Tennessee. The party stays with a strict nativist platform, and they attack the emerging "Black Republicans" as a threat to the Union.

4 MARCH 1856
Civil War: Approach The anti-slavery government in Topeka, Kansas, petitions Congress for admission

WALT WHITMAN, 1819-1892

Whitman was the first American poet of world stature. He was born on Long Island, New York, to a Quaker family. By the age of 13, Whitman was a printer's assistant in Brooklyn, and as he progressed up to printer and then editor, he took an active role in Democratic Party politics and wrote short stories and a novel. Editor of a Democratic Party paper, the Brooklyn *Daily Eagle*, from 1846, he spoke out so strongly against the party's position on slavery that he was fired in January 1848. He went to New Orleans, then returned to Brooklyn and a career in journalism, but he was also writing the poems that he published at his own expense in 1855 as *Leaves of Grass*. Although the public did not know what to make of these joyous and impassioned poems, some perceptive critics recognized him as a true poet; slightly enlarged editions appeared in 1856 and 1860, both receiving the same mixture of popular rejection and critical recognition.

When the Civil War began, Whitman was writing for New York newspapers, but he began to visit the Broadway Hospital as a volunteer aide to the sick and wounded from the war, and he also began to write poems influenced by the war. On hearing that his brother had been wounded, Whitman rushed to Virginia; the brother recovered, but Walt (as he called himself from 1855) had seen enough of the horrors of the war to decide he would do something. He stayed in Washington, and earning some money by copying documents for an army paymaster, he devoted many hours to nursing the wounded, both Northerners and Southerners. He bought them fruit, candy and stationery and even assisted in operations. He added to his income by writing for newspapers. He also took a clerk's job in the Department of the Interior in March 1865, but he was dismissed that very June for his scandalous poems and opinions.

During his years in Washington, Whitman never met Lincoln, but he had seen the President around town occasionally. After Lincoln's death, Whitman wrote "When lilacs last in the dooryard bloom'd," and added this to a collection, *Drum-Taps*; a second poem about Lincoln, "O Captain! my Captain!" appeared in a sequel.

JULY 4, 1856

In 1873 Whitman suffered a stroke that left him partially paralyzed, and he lived out his final years in Camden, New Jersey. His poetry never attained its earlier peaks, but he lived on the meager earnings from his revisions of *Leaves of Grass,* other books and occasional articles. He attracted numerous disciples and many literary lights of the day—especially those from England, where his reputation had always stood higher than in America. Eventually, however, "the good gray poet" as he was called, came to be honored by his countrymen.

to the Union. Republicans in Congress support them, but Stephen Douglas introduces a bill that would admit Kansas as a state only after a new constitutional convention is held.

21 APRIL 1856
Transportation The first railroad bridge is constructed between Rock Island, Illinois, and Davenport, Iowa, crossing the Mississippi River.

19 MAY 1856
Civil War: Approach Charles Sumner, the Senator from Massachusetts and an outspoken anti-slavery man, gives a vituperative speech against the pro-slavery elements in the Senate. Three days later, as Sumner is sitting at this Senate desk, a South Carolina Representative, Preston Brooks, beats Sumner unconscious with a cane for insulting Brooks's uncle, Senator Andrew Butler. It will be three years before Sumner fully recovers, but he is regarded as a martyr by Northern abolitionists—while many Southerners praise Congressman Brooks.

21 MAY 1856
Civil War: Approach In Kansas, pro-slavery men attack Lawrence, center of the anti-slavery settlers, and kill one man. In retaliation, a band of anti-slavery men, led by the fiery abolitionist John Brown, kills five pro-slavery men in a night massacre at Pottawotamie Creek. The problems in Kansas have given the territory a commonly used name: "Bleeding Kansas."

JUNE 1856
National The Democrats meet in their National Convention at Cincinnati. They nominate neither Pierce nor Stephen Douglas, both hopeful candidates, because each of the men are too much identified with the problems in Kansas. Instead, after 17 ballots, they choose James Buchanan of Pennsylvania for president and John C. Breckinridge of Kentucky for vice-president. Again their platform supports the Compromise of 1850 and the Kansas-Nebraska Act, calling it "the only sound and safe solution of the slavery problem." At the same time, a group of Know-Nothings from the Northeast who are against slavery have separated themselves from the main wing of their party and hold a convention in New York. They choose John Frémont of California for president and W. F. Johnston of Pennsylvania for vice-president. Their motto becomes "Free territory and Free Kansas."

17-19 JUNE 1856
National The new Republican Party holds its first National Convention in Philadelphia. It nominates

John Frémont of California for president and William L. Dayton of New Jersey for vice-president. Their platform favors a railroad to the Pacific and admission of Kansas as a free state.

3 JULY 1856
Civil War: Approach The House of Representatives votes to admit Kansas as a state with its anti-slavery Topeka constitution, but the Senate rejects this, so the issue is left open when Congress adjourns.

4 JULY 1856
Civil War: Approach Federal troops from Fort

JOHN FRÉMONT, 1813-1890

Frémont was a celebrated Western explorer who could never live up to the hopes others had for him in politics and the military. Son of a French immigrant who had run off with an American woman, Frémont was born in Georgia and became an officer in the U.S. Topographical Corps. He conducted daring, even foolhardy, expeditions and wrote vivid descriptions of the Rockies, the Oregon Trail, California and other regions which made him something of a national hero. By revealing the possibilities for routes, settlements, railroads, forts, farms and mines, Frémont appealed to the expansionist spirit of the 1830s and 1840s, and he personally believed that North American settlers had a right to all these lands. While in California in the 1840s, he openly encouraged Americans to provoke a war with Mexico and fought to take land from Mexico once war broke out. Then, in a quarrel with General Kearney over authority, Frémont was courtmartialed in 1847-48 and found guilty of mutiny. President Polk remitted the penalty, but Frémont resigned from the army and led a disastrous expedition of his own to California, losing 11 men in a winter passage. Frémont found gold on previously acquired land in California and soon became rich. Elected a Senator from California, he served a year and in 1856 was given the new Republican Party's first nomination for the presidency. Frémont lacked the political skills to overcome the Democrats' attack on his illegitimacy and lost to Buchanan.

When the Civil War began, Frémont raised money in Europe to buy English arms for the Union. He was made a major general in charge of the Department of the West and took up his post in St. Louis in July 1861. In August he issued a proclamation declaring the property of disloyal Missourians confiscated and their slaves emancipated. Lincoln modified this declaration and removed Frémont from command, but the radical antislavery Republicans in Congress forced Lincoln to give Frémont a new command in western Virginia. After a defeat there by Stonewall Jackson and his subsequent refusal to serve under General Pope, Frémont was relieved of his command in June 1862. He had become something of a rallying figure for the radical Republicans who supported him against Lincoln in the summer of 1864, but Fremont had sense enough to withdraw that September. He tried unsuccessfully to rescue his failing California property and then got involved in railroads. In 1873 he was found guilty of swindles, and he declared bankruptcy. It was a sad climax to a once glorious career, and its anticlimax came in 1890 when, feeling sorry for the poor old man, the army restored him to the rank of major general—but Frémont died before he could enjoy the pension.

TESTING A UNION 1788-1865

AMERICA'S OWN LITERARY FORMS

As the United States stretched its geographical boundaries in the 19th century and began to establish more and more colleges, Americans grew less dependent on European education, writing and culture. They developed a sense of their particular way of life and soon were reading their own literature. Edgar Allen Poe, Nathaniel Hawthorne, and Herman Melville soon became as popular as Charles Dickens. Each of these writers had a particular contribution not only to American literature, but to general literary forms as well.

A complex man, Poe was one of America's most gifted writers. As a critic for *Burton's Gentleman's Magazine* and *Graham's Magazine* in the 1840s his judgements of poetry and fiction affected literature throughout the world. In 1844 Poe published *The Raven and Other Poems* and he was to achieve fame as a fiction writer as well. He mastered the art of writing short stories and created the detective or mystery story. Typical of his stories were "The Masque of the Red Death" and "The Fall of the House of Usher." Both pull the reader into a beautiful, yet grotesque world.

Nathaniel Hawthorne helped establish the American short story as an important art form. His *Twice-Told Tales* won him critical success in this genre. Hawthorne's masterpiece, *The Scarlet Letter,* which used symbolism and allegory to explore guilt and suffering, has been called the first American psychological novel. Some viewed his work as a criticism of democracy, yet Hawthorne saw pain and suffering as an inescapable part of life.

Hawthorne's friend, Herman Melville, spent some time on a whaler and then lived in Polynesia before he wrote *Typee* (1846), *Omoo* (1847) and *Redburn* (1849), all popular travel romances. Ironically, Melville's greatest work, *Moby Dick,* was not well received in its day. Readers found the book's symbolism confusing. Melville was one of democracy's harshest critics. *Moby Dick* seemed to warn that there were no guarantees for human progress, that good and evil are always with us and that our purpose in the world is to ally with good against evil in the search for truth. Poe, Hawthorne and Melville each enriched literature in his own way.

Leavenworth, Kansas, disperse the Free-state legislature in Topeka.

20 JULY 1856
Ideas/Beliefs A major migration of Mormons from Florence, Nebraska, to the Great Salt Lake begins; it will become known as the Handcart Migration.

18 AUGUST 1856
International In a sweeping gesture, Congress acts to authorize United States annexation of any small guano island that is unclaimed by other governments. In 1857, they will annex Jarvis Island and Baker's Island, located in the mid-Pacific, and in 1858, Howard's Island as well.
Regional Governor Shannon of the Kansas Territory resigns. On September 9, President Pierce appoints John W. Geary to succeed him. Geary used Federal Troops on September 15 to stop an army of nearly 2500 "border ruffians" who are about to march on Kansas.

17 SEPTEMBER 1856
National The Whig Party holds its National Convention at Baltimore and simply nominates the same candidates chosen by the American party, Millard Fillmore and Andrew Donelson. Their platform warns against the increasing sectionalization of political parties.

21 SEPTEMBER 1856
Transportation The Illinois Central Railroad is now complete. It runs between Chicago and Cairo, Illinois.

4 NOVEMBER 1856
National James Buchanan, the Democratic candidate, defeats John Frémont, the Republican candidate, for the presidency in a contest that is fought quite openly along the lines of South versus North, pro-slavery versus anti-slavery. Buchanan wins 14 slave states and 4 free states, Frémont wins 11 free states, and Fillmore wins 1 free state. The Whig Party is quickly falling apart as sectionalism increases.

OTHER EVENTS OF 1856
International Commodore Perry publishes the *Narrative of the Expedition of an American Squadron to the China Sea and Japan Performed in the Years 1852, 1853, and 1854.*
Slavery South Carolina's governor James H. Adams fears that plantation owners and farmers in his state will not have enough slaves and publicly argues for the repeal of the 1807 law that prohibited the slave trade into this country.
Industry The Western Union Telegraph Company is established to take advantage of the increasing system of telegraph wires across the country. The potential of the whaling industry becomes obvious when a ship, the E L B Jenney, returns to New Bedford, Massachusetts, after four and one–half years out and displays 2500 barrels of sperm oil.

12 JANUARY-15 FEBRUARY 1857
Regional The pro-slavery legislature of the Kansas Territory calls a session in Lecompton. They pass a bill calling for a census and for an election of delegates to a constitutional convention. The Territorial governor, Geary, originally was sympathetic with the pro-slavery forces, but now he only hopes to establish impartial justice and free elections. Even so, he vetoes this bill, and the convention then repasses it.

15 JANUARY 1857
Civil War: Approach Abolitionist William Lloyd Garrison is more and more supportive of disunion; he wants in no way to be associated with slavery. Garrison is one of the main speakers at a Massachusetts Disunion Convention held in Worcester. Their slogan becomes, "No union with slaveholders."

21 FEBRUARY 1857
Finance Congress acts to make foreign coins no longer valuable as legal tender.

JAMES BUCHANAN, 1791-1868

Buchanan built a political career on his ability to appease both the North and the South, but by the time he became president such an approach made him ineffectual. A lawyer by training, he had become a Jacksonian Democrat in 1824. He denounced slavery as a moral and political evil, but then admitted that if the slaves were to rise up in revolt, he would aid his fellow whites. As a Representative and then a Senator from his native state of Pennsylvania, Buchanan was a solid party man. He served as President Polk's Secretary of State and handled the negotiations over Texas and Oregon that balanced the demands of the proslavery and antislavery forces. As ambassador to England in 1854, he claimed that the U.S. had the right to take Cuba from Spain rather than allow it to become "Africanized." Such a claim (officially disowned) was recognized by Northerners as an expression of proslavery sentiments, but it made Buchanan acceptable to Southerners and he got the Democratic nomination for president in 1856.

Buchanan won on a platform of non-interference, but later supported the proslavery forces—fully endorsing the Dred Scott decision and trying to admit Kansas with its proslavery Lecompton constitution—and the Union disintegrated around him. When the Democratic Party split in 1860, Buchanan tried to appear to be supporting Douglas but his words and actions actually brought him closer to Breckenridge. And when Lincoln won, Buchanan passed his four months as a truly "lame duck" President—still claiming to be against secession yet unable to take decisive action against secessionists, wanting to preserve the Union but unable to reinforce Fort Sumter. Finally in January 1861 he sent a ship to supply the fort, but he was still trying to avoid hard decisions by advocating a national referendum on whether the President should call out the militia. When he turned over the government to Lincoln in March, war was inevitable. Buchanan retired to his estate in Pennsylvania and publicly supported Lincoln. Had he been able to act more decisively, it most certainly would have brought on a war sooner, and Buchanan, not Lincoln, would have been the war President.

3 MARCH 1857
International Congress passes the Tariff Act of 1857. The average duties on goods are lowered to 20 percent.

4 MARCH 1857
National James Buchanan is inaugurated as the 15th President and the fifth Democrat to hold the office. His inaugural address echoes the Democratic platform, supporting the policy of noninterference with slavery in the states and popular sovereignty in territories. While condemning violence over slavery, he offers no solution to the problem. John C. Breckinridge is sworn in as vice-president. Among Buchanan's Cabinet are Secretary of State Lewis Cass and Secretary of the Treasury Howell Cobb.

Regional Governor Geary's efforts at non-partisanship in the Kansas territory eventually cause him to lose favor with the Pierce administration, and he resigns.

6 MARCH 1857
Civil War: Approach The Supreme Court hands down its decision in the case of *Dred Scott v. Sandford*, and a majority declare that the Missouri Compromise of 1820 is unconstitutional. Scott is a black man whose owner took him from the slave state of Missouri into the free state of Illinois and territory north of the latitude 36°30′ and then back to Missouri. Scott sued for his freedom, and the state Supreme Court overruled a lower court's decision in favor of Scott. Each of the United States Supreme Court justices writes an opinion, but that of Chief Justice Roger Taney is cited for the majority. The Court rules that Scott had never ceased to be a slave and so could not be considered a citizen with the right to sue in a federal court. The most far-reaching impact of the decision comes from the claim that Congress has no right to deprive citizens of their property—such as slaves—anywhere within the United States. Justices John McLean and Benjamin Harris dissent and maintain that free blacks are citizens. An outburst of protest from Northerners and Republicans greets the decision.

21 MAY 1857
International The rule of filibuster William Walker in Nicaragua comes to an end when armies of other countries and forces hired by Cornelius Vanderbilt confront him. (Vanderbilt now controls the Accessory Transit Company which originally supported Walker's exploits, and has since been ignored by him.)

26 MAY 1857
Regional Robert J. Walker of Mississippi becomes the new governor of the Kansas Territory. In an inaugural address, he pleads for cooperation and promises to see that any constitution submitted to the territory will have a fair vote.

18 JUNE 1857
International Japan and America sign an agreement that will allow United States ships to trade in port of Nagasaki.

24 AUGUST 1857
Finance The New York branch of the Ohio Life Insurance and Trust Company fails and signals the beginning of a commercial and financial panic that will be known as the Panic of 1857, as 4932 businesses fail this year. Conditions will improve by 1859.

11 SEPTEMBER 1857
Ideas/Beliefs A Mormon fanatic named John D. Lee is angry over President Buchanan's order to remove Brigham Young from the governorship of Utah. Lee arouses a band of Indians to help him massacre 120 California–bound emigrants in Mountain Meadow, Utah.

5 OCTOBER 1857
Regional Kansas Territory governor Robert Walker

ROGER TANEY, 1777-1864

A former slave owner, Roger Taney became Chief Justice of the Supreme Court and issued the Dred Scott decision which served to widen the gap between North and South. Born in Maryland to a prosperous, slave-owning family, Taney was admitted to his state's bar in 1799 and by 1827 was Maryland's attorney general. A Democrat and supporter of Andrew Jackson, Taney was made attorney general of the United States by President Jackson in 1831, and in 1836 became Chief Justice. Taney handed down numerous decisions that bore on economics and slavery. He usually came down on the side of local control, states' rights, *laissez-faire* capitalism—essentially supporting the position that Southerners should be allowed to run their plantation economy as they saw fit. One of his most important decisions came in 1851, in *Strader v. Graham*, where Taney ruled that the status of a slave was governed by each state's laws, so that if a slave voluntarily returned to a slave state after living in a free state that individual could again be treated as a slave. This case anticipated his decision in the Dred Scott case of 1857.

Justices took sides in this case along sectional issues, and Taney asserted the most extreme position. He not only ruled that Dred Scott himself was still a slave but that no black person descended from a slave could be a citizen and that the Missouri Compromise, or for that matter any Congressional prohibition of slavery, violated the Constitution. Taney's decision provoked a bitter national debate and led to a split within the Democratic Party, thus contributing to Lincoln's victory.

Once the war began, Lincoln essentially ignored Taney and the Supreme Court and proceeded to run the government as he saw fit. When Taney ruled that the Federal Government had no right to suspend the right of habeas corpus in pursuit of those favoring the Confederate cause, Lincoln asserted that the Constitution gave him that right in cases where rebellion affected public safety. But Taney had been forced to administer the oath of office to Lincoln in March 1861, and when Taney died in October 1864, President Lincoln attended his funeral.

---

strictly supervises the territorial elections. Thousands of fraudulent votes cast by the pro-slavery party are discarded by the territorial secretary, Frederick P. Stanton of Tennessee. After final counting of ballots, the Free State Party wins a majority in both houses.

19 OCTOBER-8 NOVEMBER 1857
Civil War: Approach Those attending a constitutional convention held at Lecompton, Kansas, realize that a strictly pro-slavery constitution could not pass a general vote. The convention drafts an article on slavery which will be submitted to popular vote, without submitting the entire constitution. No matter how the vote on this article turns out, the constitution will legalize property in slaves then in Kansas. Many in the North denounce the convention because it gives an obvious advantage to the pro-slavery forces. Governor Walker complains to President Buchanan who approves of the convention in the interest of party unity.

NOVEMBER 1857
International Filibuster William Walker returns to

Nicaragua on yet another expedition, but the United States Navy arrests him and returns him to America.

8 DECEMBER 1857
National President Buchanan makes his annual message to Congress and requests troops to calm Mormon disturbances in Utah. He also reaffirms his belief in the legality of the proposed Kansas constitution. On the following day, fellow Democrat Stephen Douglas publicly opposes the constitution in the Senate.

21 DECEMBER 1857
Civil War: Approach In Lecompton, Kansas, the Free State Party members refuse to vote in the constitutional convention and the pro-slavery constitution is approved.

OTHER EVENTS OF 1857
Regional In New York City, John O'Mahoney forms the Fenian movement, a secret Irish revolutionary group, and Peter Cooper founds the Cooper Union, providing education for the working class.
Civil War: Approach Hinton Rowan Helper publishes *The Impending Crisis of the South*. Helper uses statistics from the 1850 census to suggest that slavery has improverished great numbers of Southern whites. Sixty–eight members of the House of Representatives endorse the book, but it is banned in the South.
Transportation The last length of track is laid to connect New York City and St. Louis by rail. All across the country people gather in railroad celebrations. The Pennsylvania Railroad eliminates competition in transportation through that state when it purchases the main canal system there.
Arts/Culture James Russell Lowell edits the first copy of the *Atlantic Monthly*, and George William Curtis edits the first copy of *Harper's Weekly*.

4 JANUARY 1858
Regional The Lecompton, Kansas, constitution, which was approved on December 21, 1857, comes up for a second vote. This time the pro-slavery men do not vote and the constitution is rejected.

2 FEBRUARY 1858
Civil War: Approach Even though Kansas has rejected the pro-slavery constitution, President Buchanan asks Congress to admit Kansas to the Union as a slave state with the Lecompton constitution intact. Stephen Douglas bitterly opposes the President and speaks on February 3 to condemn the constitution as a violation of the principle of popular sovereignty.

23 MARCH 1858
National Stephen Douglas does not have enough supporters to outnumber the President on the issue of the Lecompton constitution, and the Senate votes to admit Kansas as a state under it.

1 APRIL 1858
National The House of Representatives amends the

Kansas bill to provide for resubmitting the Lecompton constitution for a new popular vote.

4 MAY 1858
National Representative William B. English of Indiana, a moderate Democrat, sponsors a compromise bill that would admit Kansas to the Union if the Lecompton constitution is ratified by Kansas.

11 MAY 1858
National Minnesota, the 32nd state, enters the Union as a free state.

16 JUNE 1858
Civil War: Approach The Republican Party of Illinois nominates a former one-term Representative, Abraham Lincoln, to challenge the incumbent Senator, Stephen A. Douglas. Although personally opposed to slavery, Douglas has tried to straddle the issue in order to hold the Democratic Party together, but his promotion of popular sovereignty—that is, allowing each territory or state to decide the issue for itself—has only antagonized many staunch pro-slavery Democrats from the South. Lincoln, however, chooses to meet the issue head on, and in his acceptance speech at the convention he asserts, "I believe this government cannot endure permanently half slave and half free."

18 JUNE 1858
International The United States and China sign a treaty of peace, friendship and commerce.

29 JULY 1858
International The first American consul to Japan, Townsend Harris, completes an agreement between the two countries which opens additional ports for trade, grants residence rights to Americans and establishes diplomatic representatives at the capitals of each country. This agreement will become the basis of Japan's trade relations for other foreign powers during the rest of the century.

2 AUGUST 1858
Civil War: Approach With the addition of the English Act of May 4 the Lecompton constitution is submitted for a third time to Kansans, who reject it, and therefore reject immediate statehood for their right to decide about slavery in their territory. Kansas will not be admitted to the Union until 1861. The disturbances in Kansas have given the Republicans a powerful campaign issue while disrupting the Democratic party. They have also encouraged Southern extremists.

16 AUGUST 1858
International President Buchanan and Queen Victoria communicate greetings across the new Atlantic cable.

21 AUGUST-15 OCTOBER 1858
Civil War: Approach Lincoln and Douglas meet in towns across Illinois in a series of seven debates. Although Lincoln is little known outside Illinois and Douglas is a national figure desperately trying to placate his own party, the debates help to define the most pressing issue confronting the nation. Lincoln takes a strong stand against slavery on moral, social and political grounds, while Douglas defends not slavery as such but the right of Americans to vote their preference. Douglas will be elected Senator by the Democratic majority in the Illinois legislature, but Lincoln emerges on the national stage as an articulate and respected spokesman for the anti-slavery position.

SEPTEMBER 1858
Civil War: Approach A group of students from Oberlin College, led by one of their professors, suc-

---

WHALING

Whaling provided a substantial portion of the nation's economy before the Civil War. Early American settlers first saw Indians in canoes killing porpoises and right whales with stone weapons. They quickly took to it as well, chasing whales in small boats, often with Indians aboard as harpooners. By 1700 the sale of whale oil and bone for corset stays provided the principal support for Quakers on Nantucket Island, off the coast of Cape Cod. Soon they had depleted the Gulf of St. Lawrence and the waters between the Azores and Virginia. Like Yankee fishermen, the whalers shared the profits of their work and became most excited when they found entire schools of whales.

Experienced with foreign trade, Yankees made excellent seamen. Whalers from Nantucket and New Bedford, Massachusetts, by the early 1800s accounted for four-fifths of the world's whaling. They went out on longer and longer trips in their roomy boats with bluff-like bows. They hunted throughout the Pacific and Indian Oceans and eventually traveled in the Arctic Ocean and Bering Strait. An average voyage lasted three years. Whaling was not a totally male business. Mrs. Martha Smith, for instance, successfully carried on a Long Island shore whaling station after her husband's death.

Whaling operations were severely curtailed when Confederate cruisers destroyed many whalers during the Civil War. About the same time, a freeze-up in the Bering Strait paralyzed still more ships. For a while steamers from San Francisco hunted whales with bomb harpoons and therefore reduced many of the hazards of the hunt. But the 1859 discovery of oil near Titusville, Pennsylvania meant that kerosene would take the place of whale oil in lamps and the great days of New Bedford and Nantucket were over.

An American whaler.

cessfully rescues John, an accused fugitive slave, and helps him travel to Canada.

9 OCTOBER 1858
Transportation The new Overland Mail stage completes its first trip from San Francisco on the West Coast. The stage reaches St. Louis, Missouri, after 23 days and 4 hours. A westbound stage left at the same time and arrives in San Francisco after 24 days, 20 hours.

AUTUMN, 1858
Regional Gold is discovered in the Kansas Territory on Cherry Creek, about 90 miles from Pike's Peak in an area that is part of present-day Colorado. The discovery launches a new gold rush.

25 OCTOBER 1858
Civil War: Approach Senator William H. Seward currently hopes to be the Republican candidate for President. He speaks at Rochester, New York, on the sectional controversy: "It is an irrepressible conflict between opposing and enduring forces, and it means that the United States must and will, sooner or later, become either entirely a slaveholding nation or entirely a free-labor nation." Throughout the autumn, Republicans win more and more seats in Congress.

6 DECEMBER 1858
International President Buchanan delivers his annual message and urges Congress to give him the authority to purchase Cuba and establish a "temporary protectorate" over northern Mexico.

OTHER EVENTS OF 1858
Regional Frederick Law Olmstead begins work to design Central Park in New York City.
Life/Customs The Ladies Christian Association is formed in New York. This organization will eventually become the Young Women's Christian Association.
Transportation In Chicago, George M. Pullman begins building sleeping cars for use on railroads. The first ones will be used on the Chicago and Alton Railroad.
Agriculture Lewis Mill receives a patent on a modern mowing machine, and Charles Wesley March receives one for a harvester which can gather grain into bundles.
Ideas/Beliefs The financial panic continues. This year 4222 businesses fail. Many people hope religion might help them accept or change economic problems, and a religious revival sweeps the country. In New York City, construction begins on the great Catholic edifice, St. Patrick's Cathedral.
Arts/Culture Mathew B. Brady sets up photography studios in both New York and Washington.

14 FEBRUARY 1859
National Oregon, the 33rd state, joins the Union as a free state.

7 MARCH 1859
Civil War: Approach The Supreme Court reverses a decision of the Wisconsin Supreme Court in *Ableman v. Booth* and rules that state courts may not free Federal prisoners. Booth had been convicted in a Federal court for having rescued a fugitive slave, and in upholding this conviction, the United States Supreme Court confirmed the constitutionality of the Fugitive Slave Act of 1850. The Wisconsin legislature declares that "this assumption of jurisdiction by the federal judiciary . . . is an act of undelegated power, void, and of no force." Although in this instance it is an anti-slavery state defying the Federal authority, this is yet another case of a state asserting its rights. The Federal Government rearrests and imprisons Booth.

4 APRIL 1859
Arts/Culture The song *Dixie* is first sung publicly in Mechanics Hall in New York City. Dan D. Emmett wrote *Dixie* for Bryant's Minstrels.

12 MAY 1859
Civil War: Approach The annual Southern Commercial Convention, an organization designed to promote economic development, meets in Vicksburg, Mississippi. After many years of considering the issue of reopening the African slave trade, the convention votes to approve the following: "In the opinion of this Convention, all laws, State or Federal, prohibiting the African Slave Trade, ought to be repealed." The Southerners feel the Federal Government should play a role of positively protecting slavery.

JUNE 1859
Regional A huge deposit of silver is discovered in what will be called the Comstock Lode, located near present-day Virginia City, Nevada. It is the first major discovery of silver in the United States and adds fuel to the rush of people to the goldfields near Pike's Peak in the Kansas Territory. The slogan "Pike's Peak or Bust" becomes popular.

5 JULY 1859
Regional Kansas hold another constitutional convention, this one at Wyandotte. By July 29 those attending have completed the draft of a constitution that prohibits slavery.

27 AUGUST 1859
Regional Edwin L. Drake strikes oil while drilling a well near Titusville, Pennsylvania. This will be the first oil well in the country and marks the beginning of what will become a major industry.

SEPTEMBER 1859
Agriculture Midwesterners want better methods of shipping their ever–increasing grain crops. In Chicago, they organize the Merchants Grain Forwarding Association.

4 OCTOBER 1859
Civil War: Approach Kansans vote to ratify the

anti-slavery Wyandotte constitution. The popular vote is 10,421 to 5,530.

16-18 OCTOBER 1859

Civil War: Approach At Harper's Ferry, Virginia (now West Virginia), John Brown, one of the most radical of the abolitionists, leads an armed group (5 blacks, 16 whites, including his 3 sons) that seizes the Federal arsenal. Although this is the first action in his vague plan to establish a "country" for fugitive slaves in the Appalachians, there is no armed support from outside people. Within 24 hours Brown and 4 other survivors are captured by a force of United States Marines led by Colonel Robert E. Lee. (Buchanan had put a price of $250 on Brown's head; Brown had put a price of $2.50 on Buchanan's.) Brown felt he had been foreordained by God to break up slavery—he hoped for a massive slave insurrection, but if he failed at that, he knew that he could shock and stun people enough to cause a sectional blow-up, perhaps start a civil war, and in that war slavery might die. Within six weeks Brown is tried for criminal conspiracy and treason, convicted and hanged. Although most Northerners condemn the way that Brown went about his plan, Southerners note that many Northerners admire Brown and his goals. They see Brown's raid as confirming their worst fears about the violence and upheaval that would prevail if blacks are not held firmly down.

28 NOVEMBER 1859

International Great Britain signs a treaty to give up its land in the Central America isthmian area that could cause friction with the United States. It cedes the Bay Islands to Honduras and two months from now will give the Mosquito Coast to Nicaragua. Then the United States and Great Britain will be on equal footing in the area.

2 DECEMBER 1859

Civil War: Approach John Brown is hanged in the public square of Charlestown, Virginia. He leaves a last note indicating that only by using blood can the country be rid of slavery.

5 DECEMBER 1859

National Sectionalism is now so pervasive in the House of Representatives that choosing a Speaker has taken two months. (At one point, someone puts forward the resolution that one of the 68 Representatives who endorsed Hinton Helper's study, *The Impending Crisis in the South* would not be fit for consideration.) Finally, New Jersey's William Pennington, a conservative Republican, is elected.

14 DECEMBER 1859

Slavery Georgia acts to maintain its slave population. A new state law no longer allows a will or deed to grant freedom to slaves after an owner's death.

17 DECEMBER 1859

Slavery In another move to maintain the number of

JOHN BROWN, 1800-1859

Regarded by some as a genius and by others as a lunatic, the abolitionist John Brown is among the most controversial figures in American history. From an old New England family with a tradition of opposing slavery, Brown was writing as early as 1834 of his intention to devote his life to abolishing slavery. Though he worked at various jobs—the wool business, surveying, postmaster—this was his real concern. In 1855 he deliberately moved to Kansas with his five sons in order to bring that territory into the Union as a free state. Insisting that he acted as an instrument of God, Brown led an 1856 attack that killed five proslavery men in retaliation for raids and murders by their side.

With support from leading abolitionists, Brown then conceived of a plan for establishing a stronghold in the Appalachian Mountains where escaped slaves and freed blacks could take refuge and then lead an armed uprising throughout the South. He rented a farm near Harper's Ferry, Virginia, and from this base he launched an attack with 21 men on October 16, 1859. He seized the town and the U.S. Armory there, but the local militia kept them under siege until a troop of U.S. Marines, led by Robert E. Lee, assaulted the engine house where Brown and his followers were making their last stand. Ten of them were killed, and the wounded Brown was captured. Tried and convicted of treason, Brown was hanged in Charlestown on December 2. If his raid failed, Brown's eloquent defense during the trial convinced many Northerners that the abolition of slavery was a noble cause that required drastic, possibly violent action. His last prediction that "much bloodshed" would follow proved to be right. Although his violent tactics were not approved by many (and were discreetly disowned by the prominent abolitionists who had encouraged him), Brown became something of a martyr. He inspired the words to a marching song that was the unofficial anthem of the Union troops, "John Brown's Body Lies A'mouldering in the Grave."

---

slaves in Georgia, the state legislature declares that any black indicted for vagrancy can now be sold.

19 DECEMBER 1859

Slavery In his annual message to Congress, President Buchanan opposes increasing foreign slave trade. He will use all lawful means to stop illicit trafficking in slaves, yet he also pledges to support United States merchant ships against detention and search, effectively giving them immunity from British patrols.

OTHER EVENTS OF 1859

Life/Customs Students from Amherst College in Amherst, Massachusetts, and from Williams College in Williamstown, Massachusetts, meet in Pittsfield to play the first intercollegiate baseball game.

Industry A general store on Vesey Street in New York City opens and signals the beginning of what will grow to be the Great Atlantic and Pacific Tea Company.

Agriculture John F. Appleby improves on the mechanical grain binder by adding a self-knotting feature.

Arts/Culture John Rogers creates a work of group sculpture entitled "Slave Auction."

TESTING A UNION 1788-1865

2 FEBRUARY 1860
Civil War: Approach Jefferson Davis, the Senator from Mississippi, presents a set of resolutions to the Senate to affirm that the Federal Government cannot prohibit slavery in the territories but must actually protect slaveholders there. But Davis is less interested in getting the whole Senate's approval than that of the Democratic members, for he is anticipating the forthcoming Democratic party convention and presidential election: Davis wants to commit the Democratic party against Stephen Douglas and his concept of popular sovereignty.

22 FEBRUARY 1860
Labor A major strike in Lynn, Massachusetts, shoe factories results in higher wages for workers.

27 FEBRUARY 1860
Civil War: Approach Abraham Lincoln speaks to the Young Men's Central Republican Union and describes the power of the Constitution in controlling slavery in territories.

19 MARCH 1860
Regional Elizabeth Cady Stanton appears before the New York State legislature to promote the cause of women's suffrage.

3 APRIL 1860
Transportation The Pony Express mail service begins and thrives before the transcontinental telegraph line is in operation in 1861. Riders cover the route between St. Joseph, Missouri, and Sacramento, California, in about 8 days.

23 APRIL-3 MAY 1860
Civil War: Approach The Democratic party holds its convention in Charleston, South Carolina. When the pro-slavery platform is rejected, delegates from eight Southern states depart. But the remaining delegates are unable to agree on a candidate, so the convention adjourns.

9 MAY 1860
National Former members of the American and Whig parties meet in Baltimore to form the Constitutional Union party. They nominate John Bell of Tennessee for president and Edward Everett of Massachusetts for vice-president.

14 MAY 1860
International The United States receives the first Japanese diplomat to visit a foreign state.

16-18 MAY 1860
Civil War: Approach In Chicago, the Republican party, on its third ballot, nominates Abraham Lincoln as its presidential candidate. To gain the nomination, Lincoln has had to present himself as fairly moderate on the question of slavery, and the party's platform declares only that it is for prohibiting it in the territories but against interfering with slavery in the states.

18-23 JUNE 1860
Civil War: Approach The Democratic party reconvenes, this time in Baltimore, and after another walkout by the anti-Douglas forces, he is nominated for the presidency.

22 JUNE 1860
National Congress passes the Homestead Bill, but President Buchanan vetoes it because he fears Congress does not have the power to give land to individual citizens.

28 JUNE 1860
National Those Southern Democrats who left the convention in Charleston meet in Baltimore. They nominate current Vice-President John C. Breckinridge of Kentucky for president on a platform that calls for the protection of the right to own slaves. They nominate Joseph Lane of Oregon for vice-president.

JULY-OCTOBER 1860
Civil War: Approach In the presidential campaign the issues are reduced to slavery and sectionalism. Extremists on both sides do little except to fan the fears of people, North and South. Of the candidates only Stephen Douglas even bothers to travel to all sections in an attempt to broaden his appeal, but even he soon realizes that his cause is lost due to the split

---

THE LYNN SHOEWORKERS' STRIKE

During the 19th century, the coastal town of Lynn, Massachusetts, about ten miles north of Boston, was transformed. Lynn's residents had been able to live in an economy based on three sources: farming, fishing and some shoemaking. Most residents worked at the varied tasks according to weather, season and inclination. But the 1830s brought an influx of factory stitching machines to replace shoemaker artisans. Gradually citizens became dependent on the factories for livelihood.

When wages were cut in the 1840s, workers there began to organize and put out an articulate newspaper called the *Awl*. The Panic of 1857 closed many factories and lowered wages even further. In 1859 men made only $3 per week and women made $1 per week—both worked 16 hour days. In 1860 workers called meetings with factory owners who refused to attend. They organized a strike for Washington's birthday that would be the largest in the country prior to the Civil War. Three thousand shoemakers met and divided into committees—some would post the names of scabs, some watched to stop possible violence and others made certain that shoes would not be finished by workers in other towns. Shoemakers throughout Massachusetts, New Hampshire and Maine joined the strike and stopped work as well. Six thousand men and women marched through Lynn in a blizzard. They carried American flags and banners, such as, "American ladies will not be slaves. . .We Dare Battle for the Right, Shoulder to Shoulder with our Fathers, Husbands and Brothers." One and one-half weeks later, other workers joined for a total of 10,000 marching through the city. Finally in April the manufacturers offered higher wages, but still refused to recognize the union. Although workers would have to deal with the factory as individuals, they had won one of the first major battles in the country.

within his own party. Various Southern spokesmen make it clear that secession will follow if Lincoln is elected.

12 SEPTEMBER 1860

International The filibuster William Walker, who has led a rather infamous life as a military adventurer, makes yet another expedition—this time to Honduras where he is executed by a firing squad.

6 NOVEMBER 1860

National Abraham Lincoln is elected President with a clear majority of the electoral college votes but only a plurality of the popular votes. Although Lincoln has deliberately muffled his message of attacking slavery, there is no mistaking the fact that for the first time in its history the United States has a president of a party that declares that "the normal condition of all the territory of the United States is that of freedom." Within days of Lincoln's election Southern leaders are speaking of secession as an inevitable necessity, yet some, such as Alexander H. Stevens, give anti–secession speeches and urge state legislatures to support the Constitution.

3 DECEMBER 1860

National President Buchanan makes his final annual message to Congress, stressing that states have no legal basis for secession, yet neither does the Federal Government have the basis to prevent such action.

6 DECEMBER 1860

National The Speaker of the House of Representatives appoints the Committee of Thirty-three to address the problem of sectionalism.

20 DECEMBER 1860

Civil War: Approach South Carolina, long a leader in threatening secession, holds a state convention that votes to secede from the Union. Meanwhile, Congress convenes and in an effort to work out some compromise each house appoints a special committee. A member of the Senate's committee, John J. Crittenden of Kentucky, has introduced a series of proposals on December 18. The chief proposal calls for a constitutional amendment that restores the Missouri Compromise line across the continent and for all time. Although Crittenden's proposals and various others will eventually be brought before both houses, they will prove to be ineffectual in the face of events. Members of President Buchanan's Cabinet are quitting in December to protest either his actions or inaction.

26 DECEMBER 1860

Civil War: Approach Robert Anderson, a major in command of the Federal forts in the harbor of Charleston, South Carolina, moves his entire force to the larger and more defensible of the two, Fort Sumter.

27 DECEMBER 1860

Civil War: Approach South Carolina state troops seize both Fort Moultrie and Castle Pinckney.

28-29 DECEMBER 1860

Civil War: Approach A delegation from South Carolina comes to Washington and demands that President Buchanan remove all Federal Troops from Charleston.

30 DECEMBER 1860

Civil War: Approach South Carolina state militia take over the Federal arsenal at Charleston.

31 DECEMBER 1860

Civil War: Approach President Buchanan, who has always been sympathetic to the Southern position on slavery and states' rights, cannot accede to the Southerners' demand that he remove Federal Troops from Charleston. He announces that Fort Sumter will be defended "against all hostile attacks, from whatever quarter," and authorizes preparation of a relief expedition by sea. In Illinois, President-elect Lincoln tries to avoid taking any position that will exacerbate the situation, but at the same time he has made himself clear: "Let there be no compromise on the question of extending slavery."

OTHER EVENTS OF 1860

Education Elizabeth Peabody opens an experimental English-speaking kindergarten in Boston, Massachusetts. She will close it in just a few years, but in 1862 Nathaniel Allen will open the first American kindergarten as part of a larger school in West Newton, Massachusetts. This kindergarten will operate for at least 20 years.

Arts/Culture Dime novels are first published. They quickly become a popular form of entertainment.

3 JANUARY 1861

Civil War: Approach The state of Georgia takes over Federal Fort Pulaski.

9 JANUARY 1861

Civil War: Approach A state convention in Mississippi votes to secede from the Union. An unarmed supply ship sent by President Buchanan to the Federal garrison of Fort Sumter in Charleston Harbor, South Carolina, is fired on by a battery in the harbor. The ship retreats.

10 JANUARY 1861

Civil War: Approach Florida secedes from the Union.

11 JANUARY 1861

Civil War: Approach Alabama secedes from the Union.

19 JANUARY 1861

Civil War: Approach Georgia secedes from the Union.

26 JANUARY 1861

Civil War: Approach Louisiana secedes from the Union.

THE NORTH AND SOUTH
ON THE EVE OF THE WAR

A comparison of resources between the North and the South at the outset of the Civil War might at first suggest that the outcome of the conflict was inevitable—and immediate. In population the North numbered some 22,000,000 people (in 23 states and seven large territories) while the South had just over 9,000,000 (in 11 states); more to the point, some 3,500,000 of the South's people were black slaves, so they had only about 1,140,-000 males between the ages of 15 and 40—compared to the North's 4,000,000 eligible males. The economy of the North was far more varied and industrialized than that of the South; in fact, the South had essentially a one-crop agrarian economy—cotton, mostly raised by slave labor. The North not only raised far more food crops than the South, but it had over five times the manufacturing capacity and ten times the available work force. The North had some 70 percent of the country's railroad mileage, 96 percent of the rail equipment, and 81 percent of the bank deposits. All this meant that the North had the means to continue and increase its supply of war matériel, while the South simply lacked the capacity ever to catch up. Nearly all of the country's weapons factories were in the North as were factories that made the components of ships. The South would immediately set out to buy weapons and ships and other needed materiel from abroad—England and France in particular—but the North's blockade very quickly began to cut off the South from any commerce (and eventually, as supplies of all kinds became scarce, a crippling inflation would take over the Confederacy).

But this imbalance was not all that it seemed on the surface; other elements seemed at least as crucial. The Regular Army of the United States had only about 16,000 men when the war began; many of these were Southerners and many of them defected—not the least of these being a certain Robert E. Lee. Meantime, a large proportion of the U.S. Navy was also Southerners and most of these went over to the Confederate Navy—including 200 officers alone. Both sides were thus immediately dependent on volunteers, and certainly at the outset Southerners were at least as quick to volunteer as were Northerners. Moreover, the North had one critical handicap at the outset: in order to win it was going to have to physically invade the South, occupy its territory, and subdue a population of millions. All the South had to do was bar the door and hold on. Beyond that advantage, the South seemed to possess more fighting spirit and the largely farm-bred Southern youths on the whole rode, marched and shot better than their Northern counterparts. Southerners also had an advantage in morale (at least if the slavery issue were ignored): they saw themselves as defending their hearth and home against an invasion of an unwanted oppressor.

Once the war began, the South achieved prodigious advances in production and arming. But as the Confederate government began to come apart at the center—never agreeing on how to raise the needed revenues, let alone whether to draft black males—and the blockade increasingly cut off the South from imports of all kinds, the advantages of the North in manpower, production capacity, armaments and such areas proved critical. But as has been pointed out, at the outset at least, the South's chances were probably better than those of the embattled American colonists who took on imperial Britain.

29 JANUARY 1861
National Kansas admitted as a slave-free state to the Union, becoming the 34th state.

4 FEBRUARY 1861
Civil War: Approach At a convention in Montgomery, Alabama, delegates from the seceding states—currently Alabama, Florida, Georgia, Louisiana, Mississippi, South Carolina—meet to form the provisional government of the Confederate States of America. Meanwhile, in an effort to forestall hostilities, a peace convention, called by Virginia, meets in Washington. The convention fails in its attempts to propose compromise legislation.

9 FEBRUARY 1861
Civil War: Approach The Confederate Provisional Congress elects Jefferson Davis President and declares that laws of the U.S. Constitution not inconsistent with the new Confederate Constitution are to remain in force.

13 FEBRUARY 1861
National The counting of electoral votes completed, Abraham Lincoln is officially designated the new President.

18 FEBRUARY 1861
The Confederacy In Montgomery, Alabama, Jefferson Davis is inaugurated President of the Confederate States of America. "Dixie," the unofficial anthem of the South, is played at the ceremonies.

22 FEBRUARY 1861
National President-elect Lincoln, warned in Baltimore of a plot on his life, journeys by a secret train to Washington.

23 FEBRUARY 1861
The Confederacy Texas secedes from the Union.

2 MARCH 1861
National The Territories of Nevada and Dakota are divided from the Territory of Utah.

4 MARCH 1861
National Abraham Lincoln is inaugurated president of the United States, with Hannibal Hamlin as his vice-president. In spite of his personal anti-slavery convictions, Lincoln in his first inaugural address is generally conciliatory, stating, "I have no purpose . . . to interfere with the institution of slavery." Nonetheless, he warns, "No state, on its own mere action, can get out of the Union." Thus, if war is to come, it will come over secession, not slavery. Lincoln concludes: "The mystic chords of memory will yet swell the chorus of the Union, when again touched, as they surely will be, by the better angels of our nature."

11 MARCH 1861
The Confederacy The Confederate Congress adopts

JEFFERSON DAVIS, 1808-1889

As President of the Confederacy Davis had neither the military nor political skills necessary to lead the beleaguered South to victory. He graduated from West Point with Robert E. Lee and saw a little action in the Black Hawk Indian War of 1832, but Davis never became an experienced combat soldier. He left the army, and after his young wife—who was Zachary Taylor's daughter—died of malaria, Davis immersed himself in running a plantation back home in Mississippi. He came to identify with the whole Southern plantation mentality: the social system it valued—including slavery, pride in one's state and a feeling that the South must be allowed to choose its own way. In 1845 Davis married into an upperclass family and was also elected to the U.S. House of Representatives. Then, as a Senator and as Franklin Pierce's Secretary of War, he advocated expanding slavery, but remained opposed to secession and hoped for some sort of compromise.

With the election of Lincoln, Davis went along with his own state and the South, and on January 21, 1861, he formally withdrew from the Senate. He hoped to command the armies for the South, but soon became the Confederacy's President—mainly because the delegates could not agree on any other candidate—and was inaugurated on February 18. Davis confronted a tremendous challenge. Confederate states were not only unprepared for war, they also lacked resources for large-scale military enterprises, and the blockade soon cut off prospects of earning money or buying supplies abroad. In addition, Davis saw himself as leading a truly united South but he was constantly opposed by states'-righters who could not agree to let their central government in Richmond have the right to conscript troops or the power to tax.

Davis's ill health and hot temper exacerbated his problems. He quarreled with most Confederate leaders and with his generals. One of his most controversial moves was to suggest that the Confederate government purchase 40,000 slaves and put them into the military. After their service, they would be freed. Although desperately short of men, Southerners could not justify emancipating slaves, and the idea never gained favor. The Confederate cause seemed doomed from the outset, but even as military resistance was collapsing during the winter of 1864-65, Davis persisted in hoping for a peace. By April 3 Davis and his government were fleeing from the capital. Captured by a Federal cavalry unit on May 10 near Irwinville, Georgia, Davis was at first kept in irons and then given comfortable quarters to share with his second wife. Although charged with treason, he was released on bond on May 13, 1867. His home, health and fortune

gone, Davis recuperated in Europe and then settled on the Gulf of Mexico to write his account of the Confederacy. He refused to request a pardon from the Federal Government so could not take up the seat in the Senate that Mississippi wanted to vote him. It was typical of the honor that his fellow Southerners would extend to Davis, and typical of his own sense of honor that he had to decline it.

a Constitution based on the U.S. Constitution but stressing states' rights and protecting slavery.

11 APRIL 1861
The Confederacy Having been informed by President Lincoln that provisions are on the way to Federal Fort Sumter, South Carolina demands the immediate surrender of the garrison.

12 APRIL 1861
Civil War The war begins when South Carolina forces, under the direction of General Beauregard, fire on Fort Sumter. The Union commander there, having suffered no casualties but lacking supplies, surrenders on April 13.

15 APRIL 1861
National President Lincoln, declaring not war but rather a state of "insurrection," calls for 75,000 volunteers for three months' service.

17 APRIL 1861
The Confederacy In the wake of Fort Sumter, other Southern states will secede; this day Virginia becomes the eighth.

19 APRIL 1861
National The first casualties of the war occur when Union troops are stoned by a secessionist mob in Baltimore; four are killed. (Nonetheless, Maryland and three other slave-holding states—Kentucky, Missouri and Delaware—are to remain loyal to the Union.) President Lincoln orders a blockade of Southern ports. Gradually choking Southern supply imports, the blockade will be an increasingly significant element of Northern strategy.

20 APRIL 1861
The Confederacy After much consideration, Robert E. Lee resigns his U.S. Army commission and assumes a commission for the Confederacy.

6 MAY 1861
The Confederacy Arkansas secedes from the Union.

13 MAY 1861
International England proclaims neutrality in the conflict, dashing Southern hopes for a foreign ally; France and Spain soon make similar declarations.

20 MAY 1861
The Confederacy North Carolina secedes from the Union.

Jefferson Davis and his cabinet.

TESTING A UNION 1788-1865

ABRAHAM LINCOLN, 1809-1865

Lincoln led the Union through its most difficult period and emerged a mythical hero. Many stories of his early life were true: the barely literate father, the log cabin home, the stepmother who encouraged his bookish side, a total of only about one year in school, work in the village store and reading law on his own. But Lincoln was also upwardly mobile. In 1834 he was elected to the Illinois legislature; by 1836 he was a licensed attorney; by 1837 he settled in Springfield, the state capital; in 1842 he married Mary Todd, who came from a relatively higher class; in 1847 he went to Washington to serve in the House of Representatives. There, although he had previously not taken a strong stand on slavery, he voted for the Wilmot Proviso, prohibiting slavery in territory acquired in the Mexican War, and he proposed prohibiting slavery in Washington. Such stands contributed to the loss of his seat after one term. Lincoln returned to Springfield and built up his law practice. He began to give speeches in a straightforward, down-to-earth style and gained supporters. He switched from the Whig Party to the new Republican party and as early as 1856 received some votes for its vice-presidential nomination.

His 1858 debates against Stephen Douglas for the Senate gave him a national reputation, and he became the Republican candidate for president in 1860. Lincoln avoided provocative statements, but even before he became president, Southern states began to secede. In his inaugural address he tried to assure the South that he was not intent on doing away with slavery in those states where it already existed. But when he gave the order to defend the besieged Fort Sumter, either side might have fired first.

Congress would not meet until July, so Lincoln fought the war during its opening months with executive orders. Later he had to bypass Congress to pursue the enemy and cajole his Cabinet to make them see his points. The armed forces were not organized for a war of such ambitious extent and Lincoln himself took an active role: he outlined strategies and tactics for campaigns, prepared specific orders, concerned himself over logistics of supply, followed day–to–day movements with maps and even chased his generals to their tents in the field to make his points, all the while persuading the home front to supply still more youths for the armed forces. Problems on the home front seemed as demanding as those of the battlefields. Lincoln suspended the writ of habeas corpus in order to detain thousands of individuals without any solid charges, and he allowed some publications to be suppressed, but he also tolerated verbal criticism and acts of protest that went far beyond the accepted politics of the day. Northern abolitionists attacked him for not pursuing the issue of slavery single–mindedly enough and Copperheads attacked him for pursuing the war in the first place. But he never lost sight of the true goal of the war: to restore the United States of America to its previous condition—a union of separate but equal states.

Some accused Lincoln of being a dictator, and he was almost denied the nomination for a second term. That would have saved his life. He was not without flaws, but it would be hard to imagine a real human being who could have managed the presidency better during such a war, which was by definition a time of irreconcilable stresses and strains. Lincoln, with his great spirit to match his tall height, worked through the storm like a lightning rod for a nation's passions and frustrations.

21 MAY 1861
The Confederacy Richmond, Virginia, is designated capital of the Confederacy.

3 JUNE 1861
Civil War: East Federals under General George McClellan defeat Rebels in a minor action in Phillipi, Virginia.

8 JUNE 1861
The Confederacy Tennessee secedes from the Union, the 11th and final state to do so.

11-19 JUNE 1861
National Loyalists form a Unionist government in western Virginia.

2 JULY 1861
National President Lincoln authorizes suspension of the privilege of *habeas corpus* in exceptional cases.

21 JULY 1861
Civil War: East In the first battle of Bull Run, near Manassas, Virginia, inexperienced Union Troops under General Irvin McDowell are routed by Confederates under Generals J. E. Johnston and P. T. Beauregard. For leading a valiant stand of his troops that turns the tide of battle, Southern General Thomas J. Jackson is dubbed "Stonewall." Part of the reason for the Union defeat is poor generalship; the North delayed the attack too long, allowing the South to gain reinforcements. The Union will have leadership problems for some time to come.

22 JULY 1861
National In a conciliatory move toward the South, resolutions in the U.S. Congress state that the war is being fought "to preserve the Union," and not specifically to abolish slavery. Not until the following year will abolition become an overt goal of the war.

5 AUGUST 1861
National To aid in financing the war, the U.S. Congress passes the first income tax law. Governmental calls for volunteers increase steadily and the stated length of service has changed from three months to two years.

10 AUGUST 1861
Civil War: Trans-Mississippi Union Forces are defeated at Wilson's Creek, Missouri.

30 AUGUST 1861
National In Missouri, where the majority of citizens are Unionist but there is a large Confederate element, Union General J. C. Frémont institutes martial law and declares the slaves of secessionists are freed. Still trying to be conciliatory, Lincoln on September 2 countermands the order and transfers Frémont.

13 SEPTEMBER 1861
Civil War: Naval In the first significant naval action of the war, Union Lieutenant J. H. Russel makes a dar-

---

THOMAS JACKSON, 1824-1863

A grave man of military genius, "Stonewall" Jackson's actions during the Civil War made him one of the most admired American soldiers. Orphaned as a child in Virginia, he went to West Point with little previous education, but managed to graduate 17th in his 1846 class. He immediately gained distinction in the Mexican War and was made a major. In 1852 he resigned his commission to become a professor of military tactics and natural philosophy at Virginia Military Institute where his reputation was that of a stern task-master. By 1861 the 36-year-old Jackson had settled into a life largely focused on his membership in the Presbyterian Church.

When the war broke out, Jackson was ordered to take some of his cadets to Richmond and then trained infantry at Harper's Ferry. Promoted to brigadier general by June, he took his units to the first battle at Bull Run, and they held off such a crucial Union assault that a fellow general, Bernard Bee, was reported as saying, "There is Jackson standing like a stone wall." Bee intended this to describe the whole unit, but the name "Stonewall" became attached to Jackson. He was promoted to major general and in March 1862 led the Army of the Shenandoah Valley in a march up the Valley. Greatly outnumbered, Jackson deployed his troops with such intelligence and speed that he was able to keep the major Union forces in northern and western Virginia from attacking Richmond. In August 1862 Jackson led 20,000 men over 50 miles in two days and then played a crucial role in defeating General Pope at Second Bull Run. Now advancing into Union territory in Maryland, Jackson distinguished himself at Sharpsburg in September and at Fredericksburg in December.

In April 1863, then a lieutenant general, Jackson joined Lee to confront Hooker's Union forces along the Rappahannock. On May 1 the Confederates were forced back toward Chancellorsville, and the next day Jackson led his men in a daring march around to the rear of the Union troops. Jackson struck before sunset and forced the enemy to retreat, but as he was returning to his own lines in the twilight he was mistakenly shot by a Confederate soldier; he died of pneumonia on May 10, 1863. Jackson's reputation had become a mainstay of the Confederate struggle. Yet his evangelical piousness kept him separate from fellow officers and made him almost a martinet in the discipline he imposed on troops. Posterity has judged his tactics—speed, surprise, deception, pursuit, and maneuvering to avoid confronting any large force—as the strategy of a great general.

---

ing raid on a Southern navy yard in Pensacola, Florida, and burns a Confederate privateer.

4 OCTOBER 1861
Civil War: Naval Construction is authorized by the U.S. Navy for an armored warship, the *Monitor.*

21 OCTOBER 1861
Civil War: East Another Union defeat is suffered at Ball's Bluff, near Leesburg, Virginia, where some 1900 Northern soldiers die.

1 NOVEMBER 1861
National President Lincoln, searching for a more effective leader for the Union armies, retires aging General Winfield Scott and names General George B. McClellan general-in-chief.

7 NOVEMBER 1861
Civil War: Naval In a significant victory, the Union fleet captures two Rebel forts on Port Royal Sound in South Carolina. These forts will become bases for attacks along the coast.

20 DECEMBER 1861
National A number of so-called Radical Republicans, members of Lincoln's party who are critical of his conciliatory attitude toward the South and his assumption of almost dictatorial powers, set up in Congress a Joint Committee on the Conduct of the War to oversee the President.

OTHER EVENTS OF 1861
Education Yale University establishes the first organized graduate department in the nation and awards the country's first Ph.D. degrees.

11 JANUARY 1862
National President Lincoln improves the effectiveness of the War Department by replacing Secretary Simon Cameron with Edwin M. Stanton.

27 JANUARY 1862
Civil War President Lincoln issues General War Order #1, calling for a general Union offensive. General-in-Chief McClellan ignores this order.

30 JANUARY 1862
Civil War: Naval The Union turreted ironclad ship, the *Monitor,* is launched.

6 FEBRUARY 1862
Civil War: West Beginning a large flanking movement from the West by Union forces, General Ulysses S. Grant and Commodore Andrew J. Foote initiate a campaign against Southern strongholds in the Mississippi valley, taking Fort Henry on the Tennessee River.

8 FEBRUARY 1862
Civil War: West Union forces led by General Ambrose E. Burnside capture a Rebel stronghold at Roanoke Island, North Carolina.

16 FEBRUARY 1862
Civil War: West After a four days' siege, Confederate Fort Donelson, near Nashville, Tennessee, falls to forces under General Grant.

22 FEBRUARY 1862
The Confederacy The Confederate Constitution and Presidency are declared "permanent" and no longer "provisional."

23 FEBRUARY 1862
National Andrew Johnson is appointed by President Lincoln as military governor of the Unionist parts of Tennessee.

TESTING A UNION 1788-1865

25 FEBRUARY 1862
Civil War: West Confederate forces evacuate Nashville, the capital of Tennessee, in the face of advancing Union forces under Grant.

9 MARCH 1862
Civil War: Naval In an historic naval battle, the first between two fully armored warships, the Federal *Monitor* and the Confederate *Merrimac* (called the *Virginia* since it had been encased in iron) fight off Hampton Roads, Virginia. The *Merrimac* finally withdraws after five hours of fighting; on May 11 it is blown up to prevent its capture.

11 MARCH 1862
National Frustrated by the inaction of McClellan, Lincoln removes him as general–in–chief of the Union Armies but leaves him at the head of the Army of the Potomac.

23 MARCH 1862
Civil War: East Confederate General Stonewall Jackson begins his Shenandoah Valley Campaign in Virginia; over the next two months he will successfully tie up Federal Troops needed for the Peninsular Campaign.

4 APRIL 1862
Civil War: East Beginning the Peninsular Campaign against the Confederate capital of Richmond, the Union Army of the Potomac advances toward Yorktown, Virginia, on the peninsula between the James and York Rivers.

6-7 APRIL 1862
Civil War: West On April 6 Confederate Forces under General A. S. Johnston attack Grant's army at Pittsburg Landing, Tennessee, beginning the Battle of Shiloh. Grant has not prepared adequate defenses and the first day of fighting ends with the Union close to defeat. Federal reinforcements arrive during the night and on April 7 Federals force the Rebel army to withdraw after a furious day of fighting. Casualties are staggering on both sides—13,000 for the Union and 11,000 for the South—and Union forces are too exhausted to pursue the retreating Rebels.

11 APRIL 1862
Civil War: West Fort Pulaski in Georgia, which commands the approaches to Savannah on the coast, falls to Union Forces.

25 APRIL 1862
Civil War: Naval Union Admiral Farraguut occupies New Orleans, Louisiana.

4 MAY 1862
Civil War: East After a month's siege, the Union Army of the Potomac under McClellan occupies Yorktown, Virginia, as part of the Peninsular Campaign toward Richmond.

The Monitor versus the Merrimack.

5 MAY 1862

Civil War: East The Army of the Potomac takes Williamsburg, Virginia, after a stubborn rear-guard action by retreating Confederates.

14 MAY 1862

Civil War: East Having reached White House, a town 20 miles from the Confederate capital of Richmond, Virginia, Federal General McClellan settles down to await reinforcements despite overwhelming Union superiority.

20 MAY 1862

National President Lincoln signs the Homestead Act, which allows citizens to acquire up to 160 acres by settling on public land for five years and paying $1.25 per acre.

31 MAY-1 JUNE 1862

Civil War: East Confederates under General Joseph E. Johnston attack an isolated part of McClellan's Army of the Potomac in the Battle of Seven Pines (or Fair Oaks) near Richmond. A fortuitous arrival of Union reinforcements prevents a disastrous defeat. The battle is inconclusive, though the Rebel forces at length retire, and is costly to both sides. Southern General J. E. Johnston is badly wounded.

2 JUNE 1862

The Confederacy General Robert E. Lee takes command of the Confederate Armies of Northern Virginia.

19 JUNE 1862

National An act of Congress forbids slavery in Federal territories (but not in the states).

26 JUNE-2 JULY 1862

Civil War: East In a series of engagements called the Seven Days' Battles, Confederate General Lee attempts to drive McClellan off the peninsula and away from Richmond. The Union Army of the Potomac finally withdraws to Harrison's Landing on the James River and the Confederates pull back to protect Richmond. The Peninsular Campaign, which might have taken Richmond and ended the war, is over.

1 JULY 1862

National Congress passes the Pacific Railway Act, authorizing construction of the first transcontinental railroad. The Union Pacific, building west, and the Central Pacific, building east, will connect in Utah in 1869.

2 JULY 1862

National Lincoln signs the Morrill Act, granting land to states for establishing agricultural colleges.

11 JULY 1862

Civil War Still searching for an effective supreme commander, Lincoln names General Henry W. Halleck as general in chief. Grant is left in command of the Army of West Tennessee.

THE SOLDIERS' LIFE

On both sides the recruiting posters painted a dashing view of the soldiers' life: pleasant evenings around the campfire, singing the rousing military songs of the day—the North's "Tenting Tonight" or "The Battle Hymn of the Republic"; the South's "Dixie" or "Bonnie Blue Flag"; there were sentimental songs, too—"Just Before the Battle, Mother," and "Aura Lee," among others. And then, the recruiters went on, came the glories and triumphs of battle gallantly waged.

The reality was of course otherwise. It was long periods of inactivity, boredom, incessant drill and frequent forced marches of 20 to 30 miles a day. Sanitary conditions were poor and only later in the war was it seen that cleanliness could reduce the appalling number of deaths from disease. Pay was less than $15 a month for both sides most of the war and Southern soldiers were chronically short of clothing and shoes. The Federal soldier usually ate more or less adequately, the Southern army spent much of the war on the edge of starvation. Thus most of the time the soldiers were exhausted, dirty, close to sickness and, in the South, cold and hungry as well. For everyone, always, there was the gnawing of fear.

There were relaxations, naturally, most notably the traditional ones of the soldier—drink, gambling, and prostitutes. Games such as baseball were organized, and foraging among civilians for food and supplies was pursued almost as a sport. Not infrequently, fighting men of opposing sides would fraternize, stepping across the lines to gamble, joke and barter before the shooting started again.

Given these conditions in addition to the inhuman horror of battle, it is not surprising that the desertion rate was high, about 10 percent on both sides during the war (and much higher in the South near the end). What is surprising, though, is that on both sides morale was generally high, cowardice was rare and again and again the soldiers fought with astonishing determination and courage.

---

22 JULY 1862

National Resigned to the necessity of war, aware of growing abolitionist sentiment in the North, and in response to his own deeply-felt convictions, President Lincoln submits to his surprised Cabinet the first draft of the Emancipation Proclamation, which orders the freeing of slaves within the Confederacy only. Although the Cabinet's response is not unfavorable, Lincoln is persuaded to keep the proclamation quiet until Union fortunes improve in the war.

30 JULY 1862

Civil War: Homefront A Cincinnati paper coins the term "Copperhead" to denote Southern sympathizers, of which there are many among Democrats in the North.

9 AUGUST 1862

Civil War: East Confederate General Stonewall Jackson defeats Union forces at Cedar Mountain, Virginia.

18 AUGUST 1862

Indian Affairs A Sioux uprising flares in Min-

ROBERT EDWARD LEE, 1807-1870

A man of magnificent presence, Lee came to epitomize the cavalier tradition in the Confederate Army although his military achievements alone never justified his mythical place in Civil War history. Lee was the son of "Lighthorse" Harry Lee, a revolutionary cavalry officer and a Virginia governor; but his father's business failures and early death meant that Lee was raised in genteel poverty. He graduated second in the 1829 class at West Point and took routine posts as an army engineer officer. He served in the Mexican War in 1846, supervised construction of Fort Carroll in Baltimore Harbor and then acted for a short time as superintendent of West Point. In 1855 he was transferred to the 2nd Cavalry Division and spent some time in Texas. Lee happened to be in Washington when John Brown carried out his raid at Harper's Ferry and was assigned to lead the Federal Troops that put down this "rebellion."

As the North and South moved rapidly toward a major confrontation, Lee had little sympathy for the arguments justifying either slavery or states' rights, but realized that his first loyalty was to his home state. When Virginia voted to secede, Lee resigned his commission. He hoped not to have to fight against the Union, but by June 1861 Jefferson Davis had appointed him a general and his personal military advisor. Lee helped organize defenses of the Atlantic coast, but his first true field command came in June 1862, at 55 years old, when he was named to head the Army of Northern Virginia. McClellan's troops were invading Richmond and Lee moved quickly and decisively, collaborating with Stonewall Jackson, to force them to withdraw. His troops went on to defeat General Pope's army at Second Bull Run. Lee next moved his force into Maryland during two weeks which cost the Federals some 27,000 casualties and cost the outnumbered Confederates some 13,000. He defeated Burnside's troops at Fredericksburg in November and also Hooker's Union forces in May 1863 at Chancellorsville, but lost Stonewall Jackson from a wound in this battle. Lee then reorganized the Confederate Army in Virginia and erred in placing too many inexperienced officers over too many

unfamiliar units. He tried to move north but was turned back at Gettysburg, Pennsylvania, in July with casualties of 28,000. Lee's subsequent offer to resign his command was rejected. In May 1864 he defeated Grant in the Wilderness Campaign, but then the long campaign at Petersburg began—dragging on month after month as Lee's units suffered casualties, malnutrition, exhaustion and desertion. Confederate Forces elsewhere were also in retreat. In February 1865 when Lee was named general-in-chief of all Confederate armies, it was virtually an empty title and command. Lee was forced to evacuate Petersburg and Richmond on April 2-3 and eventually surrendered on April 9 at Appomattox Court House, Virginia.

Up to this point, Lee would have been known as a superb commander in a lost war, but from the time he rode to Appomattox on his horse, Traveller, the mythical Lee began. Grant contributed greatly by his generous terms and sensitive treatment—he refused to take Lee's sword—but Lee inspired such idealism. He was paroled home and officially indicted for treason but never brought to trial. Lee urged his troops and all Southerners to accept the outcome and get on with rebuilding their homeland; he himself accepted the presidency of the small, destitute Washington College (later Washington and Lee University). A man of faith, dignity and patience, Lee was one of the few heroes who owes his greatness to his actions in defeat.

nesota, led by Chief Little Crow. It will be suppressed by Colonel Henry Sibley in September.

22 AUGUST 1862
National In response to Horace Greeley's editorial of August 20, "A Prayer of Twenty Millions," which urges emancipation, President Lincoln (in spite of already having written the preliminary Emancipation Proclamation) replies, "My paramount object. . .is to save the Union, and it is not either to save or to destroy slavery."

30 AUGUST 1862
Civil War: East Union Forces under General Pope are defeated in the Second Battle of Bull Run near Manassas, Virginia, by Southern Generals Jackson, Lee and Longstreet.

4-7 SEPTEMBER 1862
Civil War: East Lee's Confederates cross the Potomac in preparation for the Maryland Campaign, a general invasion of the North toward Washington.

15 SEPTEMBER 1862
Civil War: East Confederates under Jackson take Harper's Ferry, Maryland, capturing an immense body of equipment and prisoners.

17 SEPTEMBER 1862
Civil War: East McClellan's Federals meet Lee's advancing army in the Battle of Antietam, Maryland. In the bloodiest day's fighting of the entire war, both sides lose over 10,000 men in killed and wounded. Though the result is essentially a draw, Lee's invasion of the North is halted and the Rebels pull back into Virginia. The cautious McClellan does not pursue

Manassas after the evacuation.

Lee. The battle revives flagging Northern hopes and subdues Southern sympathizers in European governments.

23 SEPTEMBER 1862
Civil War: Home Front Lincoln's Emancipation Proclamation is published in Northern newspapers.

5 NOVEMBER 1862
Civil War President Lincoln relieves McClellan as head of the Army of the Potomac and replaces him by Ambrose E. Burnside, with disastrous results.

24 NOVEMBER 1862
The Confederacy Confederate President Davis appoints General Joseph E. Johnston as commander of the Army in the West.

13 DECEMBER 1862
Civil War: East In spite of an overwhelming advantage, Burnside's Federals are routed at Fredericksburg, Virginia, by Lee. The Union suffers over 12,000 casualties to the South's 5000.

DECEMBER 1862-2 JANUARY 1863
Civil War: West Union and Rebel forces fight to a costly draw in the battle of Murfreesboro, or Stone's River, Tennessee. The Union advance toward the vital rail center of Chattanooga is checked for the time being.

Lincoln on the Antietam battlefield.

OTHER EVENTS OF 1862
Life/Customs The first enclosed baseball field opens in Brooklyn, New York.

1 JANUARY 1863
National The Emancipation Proclamation takes effect. Although historically a monumental step in ending slavery, it actually frees no slaves at this time, since it applies only to areas *not* under Union control, and exempts the four loyal slave states and areas of the South under Federal occupation. The Confederacy views the proclamation as confirming its view of Lincoln as a hypocritical anti-Southern abolitionist.

25 JANUARY 1863
National Lincoln replaces the incompetent General Burnside with General Joseph Hooker as head of the Army of the Potomac.

30 JANUARY 1863
Civil War: West Federal General Grant begins his Vicksburg Campaign to open the Mississippi River to the Union.

24 FEBRUARY 1863
National The Arizona Territory is formed from part of the New Mexico Territory.

3 MARCH 1863
National The Idaho Territory is formed from parts of four other Territories. Congress charters the National Academy of Sciences. The first national Conscription Act is passed, demanding enrollment in the army of males between 20 and 45 (substitutes or payment of $300 can be used for exemption).

30 APRIL 1863
Civil War: West In the Vicksburg Campaign, General Grant moves his troops across the Mississippi.

1 MAY 1863
Civil War: West Grant defeats a Rebel force at Port Gibson, Mississippi.

2-4 MAY 1863
Civil War: East Lee's Army at Chancellorsville defeats the Union Army of the Potomac under Hooker in a major Southern victory, but one of the South's most effective leaders is lost when Stonewall Jackson is mortally wounded by his own men during a night reconnaissance. Both sides lose over 10,000 casualties in the fighting.

2 MAY 1863
National Copperhead Clement L. Vallandigham is arrested in Ohio for condemning the Federal war effort. He is later courtmartialled, but his sentence is commuted to banishment by Lincoln.

14 MAY 1863
Civil War: West Union Generals Sherman and McPherson defeat J. E. Johnston's Confederates and occupy Jackson, Mississippi.

TESTING A UNION 1788-1865

16-17 MAY 1863
Civil War: West Continuing the Vicksburg Campaign, Grant defeats Confederates at Champion's Hill and Big Black River, Mississippi.

22 MAY 1863
Civil War: West Grant besieges Vicksburg, Mississippi.

1 JUNE 1863
Civil War: Homefront The anti-Lincoln Copperhead Chicago *Times* is suppressed by order of General Burnside, but the order is revoked on June 4 by Lincoln.

20 JUNE 1863
National Pro-Union West Virginia is admitted as the 35th state, its constitution mandating gradual emancipation of slaves.

24 JUNE 1863
Civil War: East General Lee and the Army of Northern Virginia cross the Potomac at Harpers Ferry. Planning a general invasion of Pennsylvania, Lee heads toward Gettysburg.

25 JUNE 1863
Civil War: East At odds with general of the army Halleck, Hooker resigns his command and is replaced by General George G. Meade, who desperately begins organizing the Army of the Potomac for the impending confrontation.

1-3 JULY 1863
Civil War: East The Battle of Gettysburg, one of the most devastating of the conflict and the turning point of the war, sees the Southern Army defeated by the superior numbers and strong defensive positions of the Union Army. On the third day Lee, in one of his rare mistakes, orders the disastrous attack on impregnable Union lines that comes to be known as "Pickett's Charge" (though that general did not lead it). The South withdraws having lost nearly 28,000 casualties to the Union's 23,000. Never again will the South have the strength to mount an offensive into the North.

4 JULY 1863
Civil War: East Lee's defeated army begins its retreat to Virginia.
Civil War: West The siege of Vicksburg, Mississippi, ends with Grant coolly demanding "immediate and unconditional surrender" and getting it (thus acquiring the occasional nickname "Unconditional Surrender" Grant). Over 29,000 Rebel troops surrender with the city, giving the Union control of the Mississippi River and splitting the Confederacy north to south.

8 JULY 1863
Civil War: Trans-Mississippi Port Hudson, Mississippi, the last major Confederate stronghold on the Mississippi River, surrenders to the Union forces after a six-week siege.

13-16 JULY 1863
Civil War: Homefront Resentment of the Union Conscription Act boils over into violence as New York sees four days of draft riots, a largely Irish-American mob pillaging property and lynching blacks. The riots are quelled by Federal troops.

9 SEPTEMBER 1863
Civil War: West A Confederate Army under General Braxton Bragg evacuates the vital rail center of Chattanooga, Tennessee, and the city is occupied by Federals under General W. S. Rosecrans.
International Britain begins actions that will eventually prevent delivery of the "Laird Rams"—ships built in England for the Confederacy.

19-20 SEPTEMBER 1863
Civil War: West Another of the great battles of the war breaks out at Chickamauga, Georgia, between the armies of Rosecrans and Bragg. On the second day a mistake in orders leads to the shattering of the Union line; only a desperate stand by Federals under General George H. Thomas (henceforth known as the "Rock of Chickamauga") prevents a total rout. The Federal army withdraws defeated to Chattanooga, where they are besieged by Bragg. Casualties are 16,000 for the Union, 18,000 for the South.

3 OCTOBER 1863
National President Lincoln proclaims the last Thursday in November as Thanksgiving Day.

16 OCTOBER 1863
Civil War: West Lincoln places Union forces in the West under General U. S. Grant, who then replaces the defeated Rosecrans with Thomas in Chattanooga.

19 NOVEMBER 1863
National President Lincoln delivers his Gettysburg Address, dedicating a military cemetery on the bloodstained Pennsylvania battlefield. He prophesies that the "honored dead" of both sides "shall not have died in vain," that there will be "a new birth of freedom; and that government of the people, by the people, for the people, shall not perish from the earth." With less accuracy, he also predicts, "the world will little note, nor long remember, what we say here." The Address is to become one of the immortal utterances of human history.

23-25 NOVEMBER 1863
Civil War: West In an almost unprecedented maneuver, the Union Armies under General Grant sweep up the mountains over enemy strongholds and drive Bragg's Confederates away from Chattanooga, ending their siege. Having split the South vertically by conquering the Mississippi, the Union is now ready to march through Georgia to the sea and split the Confederacy horizontally.

BLACKS IN THE WAR

The situation of blacks during the Civil War might be described at best as "ambiguous," especially to the extent that the attitude of most Northerners to them was ambivalent. Although slavery was undeniably at the heart of the issues that led to the war, even many of the leading abolitionists seemed more concerned with the concept of "slavery" than with black people: Many abolitionist societies did not even accept black members. When the war actually broke out, the official position of the Federal Government was that secession and rebellion were the causes; Lincoln, who was personally and profoundly antislavery, wisely soft-pedaled the issue of slavery at first to avoid alienating pro-union slave-holding border states.

Yet as soon as the war started, blacks volunteered to fight for the Union—and were immediately rejected. There were several reasons: some whites sincerely felt it wasn't "appropriate" for blacks to be expected to fight a "white man's war"; many including Lincoln still worried about offending the border states; and many (also including Lincoln) frankly thought that blacks wouldn't make good soldiers. As the Union army moved into Confederate territory, some slaves took refuge in the Union camps; some officers allowed them to stay—but others returned them to their Southern owners. And when Union General John Frémont declared all slaves in his Missouri command to be freed, President Lincoln himself canceled Frémont's order and removed Frémont himself from his post. Finally, in July 1862, the Federal Congress passed two crucial acts: (1) the Confiscation Act, which declared free all slaves whose owners aided the Confederacy; and (2) the Militia Act, which authorized President Lincoln to use blacks as soldiers. Yet Lincoln continued to avoid this, instead limiting them to serve only as laborers, kitchen personnel, nurses, scouts or even spies.

It was the Emancipation Proclamation that changed this. Publicly announced in September 1862, formally proclaimed on January 1, 1863, the Proclamation contained a little-noted announcement: Lincoln finally agreed to use blacks in the army and navy. Before the war ended, some 180,000 blacks served in the Union Army, while another 30,000 were in the Union Navy (about one-quarter of that navy, in fact). But black soldiers were in segregated units, usually under white officers; there were only about 100 black officers, and until 1864, all blacks received only about half the pay of white servicemen. Yet despite their treatment, blacks fought gallantly in several campaigns; about 68,000 black soldiers and sailors were killed or wounded; 21 blacks won the Congressional Medal of Honor. It was President Lincoln who, referring still ambivalently to the blacks as a "physical force," would say: "Keep it and you can save the Union. Throw it away, and the Union goes with it."

The South at least had the virtue of not being ambivalent about their black population; the mythical image of the carefree, grateful slave had long worn thin, especially after John Brown's revolt, and most Southerners feared the potential power of armed blacks. Thus, though the Confederacy was desperately short of manpower, the idea of using blacks as soldiers was long resisted. Finally, in 1865, Jefferson Davis proposed and the Confederate Congress approved an act calling for 300,000 slave-soldiers—who would be promised their freedom in return for service. The South now was forced in its own extremity to recognize its dependence on blacks.

3 DECEMBER 1863
Civil War: West In the wake of Chattanooga, Southern forces withdraw from Knoxville, leaving Tennessee under Union control.

8 DECEMBER 1863
National Looking beyond the recent victories toward the end of the war, Lincoln issues a Proclamation of Amnesty and Reconstruction, offering pardon to Confederates who take a loyalty oath.

OTHER EVENTS OF 1863
Civil War Desertions among the armies of both sides average about 10 percent.
Labor A pioneering labor union is formed, the Brotherhood of Railway Locomotives Engineers.
Arts/Culture Still little recognized as a poet, Walt Whitman works as a hospital volunteer, writing heart-rending letters about his experiences. Herman Melville and William Cullen Bryant publish wartime poems. Artist James MacNeil Whistler causes a sensation in Paris with his painting, *Little White Girl.*

14 JANUARY 1864
Civil War: Trans-Mississippi Union General William T. Sherman occupies Meridian, Mississippi. In a foretaste of his tactics in Georgia and the Carolinas, he destroys supplies, buildings and railroads.

19 JANUARY 1864
National Arkansas, a Union slaveholding state, adopts a new anti-slavery constitution.

17 FEBRUARY 1864
Civil War: Naval In the first submarine attack of the war, the tiny Southern semi-submersible *H. L. Hunley* sinks a Federal ship in Charleston Harbor with a torpedo, but herself goes down with all hands.

20 FEBRUARY 1864
Civil War: West Union attempts to take Florida flounder when Federals are beaten at the Battle of Olustee.

10 MARCH 1864
Civil War After his victory in Chattanooga, General

Troops liberating slaves.

TESTING A UNION 1788-1865

U. S. Grant is named to succeed General Halleck as commander of the Union armies.

12 MARCH 1864

Civil War: Trans-Mississippi   Federal General N. P. Banks begins moving his flotilla up the Red River in Louisiana, the goal being Shreveport.

8 APRIL 1864

Civil War: Trans-Mississippi   The Union Red River Campaign is halted by Confederates at Sabine Crossroads, Louisiana, and Banks retreats toward the Mississippi River, his ships handicapped by low water.

12 APRIL 1864

Civil War: West   Confederates under Nathan Bedford Forrest take Fort Pillow on the Mississippi River, massacring a number of black soldiers, who by now are numerous in the Union army. The slaughter causes considerable outcry in the North.

17 APRIL 1864

Civil War   Until this point there have been frequent

COMMUNICATIONS AND THE WAR

Of all the many ways in which the Civil War became the first modern war, perhaps none was more striking, more influential, than the role played by communications. At many levels, the war involved communications, and the new technologies employed by the armies were only the most tangible and obvious forms. For the first time, the telegraph was available to allow the government in its capital to communicate directly with its commanders in the field and to allow commanders in their field headquarters to communicate with lower echelons; in battles like Fredericksburg telegraph wires were strung behind the lines to speed the results of the fighting to the generals. (Incidentally, the telegraph eliminated the previous fastest means of communication in America up to that time—the Pony Express, which had been introduced only in April 1860, was discontinued by the end of 1861 once the Atlantic and Pacific coasts were connected by the telegraph lines.) Railroads also moved information as well as troops and supplies; the Union's superiority in railroads, and their success in gradually cutting off the South from their own, was a major element in its victory. And the balloons that Thaddeus Lowe persuaded Lincoln and the Union army to employ were not only used for visual observations of the enemy's positions; Lowe sent telegraph messages from them on occasion, and photographs—such as the panoramic views of the Confederate defenses of Richmond—were also taken from balloons.

Photography, then in its youth, was perhaps the most powerful means of communication to emerge in the Civil War. The most famous images are those recorded by Mathew Brady; before the war he was known for his static if insightful portraits of the great and prosperous; in the war he traveled all over hauling his cumbersome equipment for the awkward wet-plate process so as to capture the brutality of battles. And Brady was only one of many who recorded and communicated the war, both to his contemporaries and to future generations. What *The New York Times* said of Brady's pictures might be applied

to all these photographs of the Civil War: "Brady has done something to bring home to us the terrible reality and earnestness of war. If he has not brought bodies and laid them on our dooryards. . .he has done something very like it."

Most Americans did not get to see that many photographs during the war itself, but they were kept fully informed by the newspapers and periodicals of the time. No war up till then had been so totally "covered" and the new technologies of the telegraph and printing allowed news of the war to reach Americans quickly. (The very role of "war correspondent" had only been invented in the Crimean War of 1853-56.) A small army of correspondents, many from overseas, milled about the battlefields and sent their accounts to a hungry public. As Oliver Wendell Holmes said at the time: "Only bread and newspapers we must have. . .Everything else we can do without." And the millions of words were supplemented by the thousands of illustrations drawn by artists who followed the progress of the war and sketched the fighting for the newspapers and magazines such as *Harper's Weekly*; Thomas Nast and Winslow Homer were only two of the best known artists who communicated the effects of the war to a waiting public.

And in a still broader sense, the Civil War involved communications. It is a commonplace today to claim that wars result from a lack of communications, but this cannot be said of the Civil War: the North and South had been communicating their goals and intentions for decades through speeches, articles, books, sermons, resolutions, editorials and every other verbal means. In the North and South, newspapers played a crucial role in preparing their publics for war; journalists such as Horace Greeley in the North or Robert Barnwell Rhett and James Hammond in the South deliberately and overtly rallied their readers to the cause. Meanwhile, books had been appearing for decades that also prepared readers for the coming struggle; *Uncle Tom's Cabin* is only the best known, but the South had its propagandists, too—men such as George Fitzhugh, who in *Sociology for the South* (1854) and *Cannibals All!* (1857) gave intellectual arguments to support the South's cause. And the Abolitionists of the North were nothing if not articulate and communicative; for years they promoted their cause in newspapers, periodicals, books and speeches.

The Civil War, in fact, was fought for decades by verbal communications: the many acts of Congress, the countless speeches, the various "compromises"—these were all attempts to confine the conflict to words. Once the fighting itself was underway, this kind of communication was exposed as ineffectual, and new forms took over. Newspaper communiqués, as mentioned, were among the most significant. But private citizens also began to communicate as never before. Because most participants were accessible by land, letters were easily exchanged; the Civil War would produce a vast and moving literature of correspondence and diaries: many Americans, both those at home and those on the front lines, kept revealing journals (of which Mary Chestnut's is simply among the best known). And even before the war was over, Americans from every walk of life were publishing their personal accounts of the war—nurses, spies, officers, foot soldiers, all had something to say. And once the war ended, there was a virtual flood of books about every aspect of the war by every possible participant and witness. Truly, the Civil War was a war of communications.

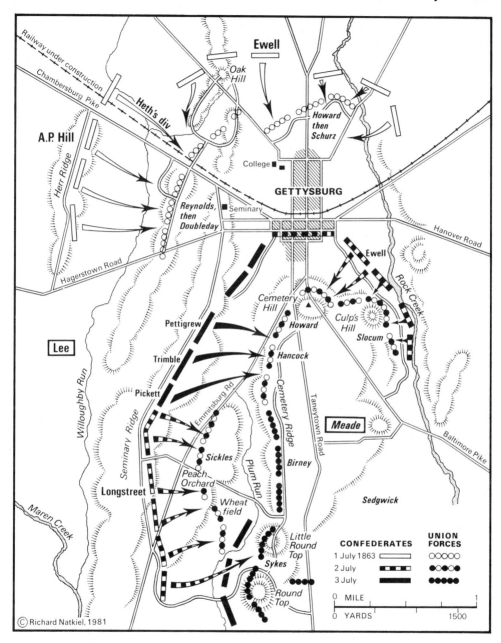

Railway under construction

Chambersburg Pike

Ewell

Oak Hill

Heth's div

Howard then Schurz

A.P. Hill

Her Ridge

College ■

Reynolds, then Doubleday

Seminary ■

GETTYSBURG

Hagerstown Road

Hanover Road

Ewell

Cemetery Hill

Howard

Culp's Hill

Slocum

Lee

Rock Creek

Pettigrew

Trimble

Hancock

Willoughby Run

Pickett

Emmitsburg Rd

Seminary Ridge

Cemetery Ridge

Taneytown Road

Meade

Baltimore Pike

Sickles

Plum Run

Birney

Peach Orchard

Longstreet

Wheat field

Sedgwick

Maren Creek

Little Round Top

Sykes

Round Top

CONFEDERATES		UNION FORCES
1 July 1863 ▭		○○○○○
2 July ■▫■▫		●○●○●
3 July ■■■■		●●●●●

0 MILE 1

0 YARDS 1500

© Richard Natkiel, 1981

prisoner exchanges between North and South, but this day General Grant tightens the knot on the South's declining manpower by ordering a halt to exchanges. The tactic is effective, but it condemns many Union prisoners to slow death in overcrowded Southern camps—by now, the South has little food to spare for prisoners of war.

3 MAY 1864
Civil War: East Grant and Mead with 100,000 men cross the Rapidan River in Virginia, moving toward Lee (with 60,000 men) and Richmond.

4 MAY 1864
Civil War: West General Sherman moves his Union

army of 110,000 men out of Chattanooga, Tennessee, toward the forces of J. E. Johnston in Georgia, whose army numbers just over half Sherman's. Sherman's immediate goal is Atlanta.

5-6 MAY 1864
Civil War: East Grant's and Lee's armies battle in the tangled woods of the Wilderness in Virginia. Two days of bloody fighting are inconclusive, and hundreds of wounded burn to death in brush fires during the night. Grant decides to try to move around Lee toward Richmond, but Lee anticipates the move.

8-12 MAY 1864
Civil War: East Grant, trying to run around Lee, arrives at Spotsylvania, Virginia, to find the Confederates waiting for him. Five more days of inconclusive fighting ensue before both sides sink exhausted into their trenches. Inexplicably, the wounded of both sides are left to die between the entrenched lines. Grimly determined to wear down Lee at whatever cost, Grant writes to Halleck, now chief of staff, on May 11, "I propose to fight it out on this line if it takes all summer."

13–15 MAY 1864
Civil War: West Sherman's superior forces defeat Johnston at Resaca, Georgia, on the road to Atlanta. Johnston executes the first of several skillful withdrawals that preserve his forces.

15 MAY 1864
Civil War: East Federal forces under General Sigel are defeated by Jubal Early, ending a Union effort to sweep the Shenandoah Valley of Virginia, part of a broad Union offensive.

26 MAY 1864
National The Territory of Montana is formed from part of the Territory of Idaho.

31 MAY 1864
National Radical Republicans, opponents of Lincoln within his own party, nominate their own Presidential candidate, General John C. Frémont, in Cleveland.

3 JUNE 1864
Civil War: East Lee repulses the Union army at Cold Harbor, Virginia, as Grant hurls several futile attacks on impregnable Confederate defenses. One Confederate general says of the carnage, "This is not war, this is murder." It is a horrible failure of Union leadership, and Grant later admits his mistake. In the campaign Grant has lost over 60,000 casualties (12,000 on this day alone), equal to Lee's total strength; the South has lost 25-30,000. But given their declining manpower, the Confederate losses are far more critical, and Grant well knows it.

7 JUNE 1864
National The Republican (or Union) Party, in con-

vention at Baltimore, Maryland, nominates Lincoln for President, with Tennessee's Andrew Johnson as his new vice–president. Johnson, a Southern War Democrat (many Democrats being against the war), is expected to broaden the appeal of the ticket. On the whole, Lincoln's chances look poor.

10 JUNE 1864
The Confederacy The Confederate Congress widens the army age limits to between 17 and 50.

15-18 JUNE 1864
Civil War: East Grant is repulsed by Lee in an attempt to take Petersburg, Virginia, "the back door to Richmond." Grant settles into a siege of the city.

19 JUNE 1864
Civil War: Naval The Confederate ocean-going raider *Alabama,* which has taken over 60 Union ships, is sunk off Cherbourg, France, by the U.S.S. *Kearsarge.*

27 JUNE 1864
Civil War: West Sherman's Union forces are repulsed by Johnston at Kenesaw Mountain, Georgia.

30 JUNE 1864
National Congress passes the Internal Revenue Act, increasing taxes to finance the war.

2-13 JULY 1864
Civil War: East Confederate forces under General Jubal Early raid Maryland, heading for Washington, D.C.

4 JULY 1864
National Congress passes the Immigration Act, permitting immigration of contract labor. Lincoln pocket-vetoes the Wade-Davis Reconstruction bill, a Radical Republican measure that would place reconstruction in the hands of Congress.

5 JULY 1864
National Journalist Horace Greeley receives peace overtures from the Confederacy. Lincoln sends Greeley on a peace mission to Canada later in the month, but it comes to nothing—the North unequivocally demands the abolition of slavery, and the South refuses.

14 JULY 1864
Civil War: East Union General Lew Wallace (later the writer of *Ben Hur*) slows up Jubal Early at Monacacy, Maryland, enabling reinforcements to reach the poorly defended capital. Early penetrates the District of Columbia on July 11, but turns back without a fight.

17 JULY 1864
Civil War: West Though Johnston's skillful retreats have saved his army from annihilation by Sherman, Confederate President Davis replaces General

Johnston with the impulsive John B. Hood, who vows to take the offensive.

22 JULY 1864

Civil War: East Hood attacks Sherman outside Atlanta and is turned back with heavy losses. A second attack fails on July 28.

30 JULY 1864

Civil War: East Hapless Union General Burnside again shows his mettle in directing a gigantic mine explosion into the defenses of Petersburg. The resulting attack is a debacle, with nearly 4000 Union casualties to minimal ones for the defenders. Burnside is soon dismissed for the second and final time.

5 AUGUST 1864

Civil War: Naval With the famous phrase, "Damn the torpedoes! Full speed ahead!"—or something to that general effect—Federal Admiral David Farragut leads his flagship into Mobile Bay, Alabama. On August 23 the port is taken and closed to Southern blockade runners, further choking the South's critical supply line.

29 AUGUST 1864

National The Democratic National Convention, meeting in Chicago, nominates General McClellan, former head of the army, as its presidential candidate. The Democratic party is generally conciliatory to the South and includes many Copperheads. McClellan rejects a peace plank in the platform but declares Lincoln's conduct of the war a failure. Lincoln now has running against him two generals whom he previously sacked.

2 SEPTEMBER 1864

Civil War: West Sherman occupies Atlanta after the previous day's withdrawal by Hood. Much of the city is burned. The fall of Atlanta lifts Northern morale and improves Lincoln's election chances.

19 SEPTEMBER 1864

Civil War: East Federals under General Sheridan are victorious over Jubal Early in Winchester, Virginia. As with Grant's campaign, Union casualties are far higher than Confederate. Sheridan again beats Early on September 22.

19 OCTOBER 1864

Civil War: East Sheridan defeats Early again at Cedar Creek in the Shenandoah, driving the Confederates from the Valley. Since it is a major Southern supply source, Sheridan lays waste the area.

28 OCTOBER 1864

Civil War: Naval The last Confederate ram, the *Albemarle*, is sunk on the Roanoke River in Virginia.

31 OCTOBER 1864

National Nevada is admitted to the Union as the 36th state.

DAVID FARRAGUT, 1801-1870

Farragut led the most exciting naval maneuvers of the Civil War. He came from one naval family and was essentially adopted by another American naval hero, David Porter. As a youth, Farragut sailed under Porter, who in the War of 1812 made the 12-year-old Farragut "master" of a seized ship; in a fierce battle that followed, Farragut was taken prisoner, but was eventually released. He spent the next five decades in the Navy, but was too independent and undiplomatic to gain a high reputation among fellow officers.

When the Civil War broke out, the Federal Government decided that New Orleans had to be taken so as to have clear passage up and down the Mississippi. In January 1862, Farragut—now 60 years old—got himself appointed to command the squadron assigned to take possession of New Orleans. He sailed from Hampton Roads on February 2, and after assembling his fleet off the mouth of the Mississippi, he began the attack in April. Failing to silence the guns of the two forts guarding the approaches, he defied his orders and had his fleet make a run past their guns. He lost three ships, but proceeded to defeat the Confederate Fleet guarding New Orleans and took the city. Farragut suddenly became the most admired officer in the U.S. Navy; Lincoln approved a Congressional resolution to thank him and saw that he was promoted to rear-admiral.

After missions in Vicksburg and Port Hudson, Farragut got the assignment he had been waiting for in January 1864: to capture the Confederate Forces around Mobile Bay. On August 5 Farragut began the assault against the two defending forts with four ironclads and 14 wooden ships. When one of his ships, the *Tecumseh*, was hit by a torpedo and sank, his fleet became confused and hesitated. "Torpedoes ahead!" Farragut was warned; he was high up on the main rigging of his flagship and called out, "Damn the torpedoes—full speed ahead!" His fleet took the bay, and the North became ecstatic. A new rank of vice-admiral was created for Farragut and wealthy New Yorkers gave him a purse of $50,000. After the war, Europeans received his goodwill tour with great admiration. While visiting a Portsmouth, New Hampshire, navy yard, Farragut had a heart attack and died. His success came from his aggressive approach: he accepted that there would be losses, but refused to consider the possibility of defeat.

---

8 NOVEMBER 1864

National Abraham Lincoln wins the Presidential contest by less than half a million votes.

16 NOVEMBER 1864

Civil War: West Sherman begins his march across Georgia to Savannah and the sea. Along the way he destroys everything in his path and encourages his men to forage for food.

29 NOVEMBER 1864

Indian Affairs Federal Troops under Colonel Chivington massacre Cheyennes in Sand Creek, Colorado, ending an uprising.

30 NOVEMBER 1864

Civil War: West In an effort to sever Sherman's

TESTING A UNION 1788-1865

OTHER EVENTS OF 1864

National "In God We Trust" appears on U.S. coins for the first time. In his presidential campaign, Lincoln coins the phrase. "it was not best to swap horses while crossing the stream."

Civil War Union prisoners are sent to Andersonville Prison in Georgia, which will become the most notorious of the war—thousands die of disease, exposure, and starvation. Meanwhile, Confederate desertions increase to over 50 percent by the end of the year.

International The French install puppet Emperor Maximillian of Austria on the throne of Mexico.

Industry Bessemer steel is first made in the U.S. in Michigan.

Labor Unionism spreads with the organization of the Cigar Makers and Iron Moulders.

9 JANUARY 1865

National A pro-Union convention in Tennessee adopts anti-slavery amendments to the state constitution.

15 JANUARY 1865

Civil War: West A joint Union land and sea operation takes Fort Fisher on the North Carolina coast, closing another Confederate port to blockade-runners.

16 JANUARY 1865

Civil War: West Sherman's army begins a campaign north through the Carolinas, one that will cause even more destruction than in Georgia.

1 FEBRUARY 1865

National The U.S. Congress proposes the 13th Amendment, which prohibits slavery.

3 FEBRUARY 1865

National President Lincoln meets in a peace conference with Confederate Vice–President Stephens and others on a ship off Hampton Roads, Virginia. The Southern demand for autonomy deadlocks the talks.

4 FEBRUARY 1865

The Confederacy Belatedly, Robert E. Lee is named Commander in Chief of the Confederate Army. Lee knows as well as anyone else that the cause is now hopeless.

17 FEBRUARY 1865

Civil War: West Columbia, South Carolina, is almost completely destroyed by fire; whether the blaze is started by Sherman or departing Confederates is unclear. Sherman occupies Charleston on February 18.

22 FEBRUARY 1865

Civil War: West The last open Confederate port falls to the Union in Wilmington, North Carolina.

2 MARCH 1865

Civil War A request for negotiations from Lee is rejected by Lincoln, who demands surrender before negotiation.

supply line, Hood attacks Thomas at Nashville, but the Confederates are turned back with heavy losses. Over the next two days Hood's army is all but destroyed.

6 DECEMBER 1864

National Salmon P. Chase, a Radical Republican who has resigned as Secretary of the Treasury after disagreements with Lincoln, is appointed by the President as Chief Justice of the Supreme Court. It is a wise and conciliatory move on Lincoln's part.

22 DECEMBER 1864

Civil War: West Entering Savannah unopposed after a Confederate withdrawal on December 20, Sherman completes his march eastward to the sea, bisecting the South horizontally.

3 MARCH 1865
National The Freedmen's Bureau is founded by Congress to aid former slaves.

4 MARCH 1865
National Abraham Lincoln is inaugurated for his second term, with Andrew Johnson as his vice–president. Lincoln's address closes memorably: "With malice toward none; with charity for all. . .let us strive on to finish the work we are in; to bind up the nation's wounds. . .to do all which may achieve and cherish a just and lasting peace."

13 MARCH 1865
The Confederacy With the South desperate for manpower, President Davis signs a bill allowing slaves to enlist; those who do are to be freed.

19-20 MARCH 1865
Civil War: West Sherman's army defeats Confederates at Bentonville, North Carolina.

25 MARCH 1865
Civil War: East Lee tries to break out of Grant's siege at Fort Steadman, near Petersburg, but is badly defeated.

27-28 MARCH 1865
National In conference with Generals Grant and Sherman, President Lincoln deplores further bloodshed and urges the offering of generous surrender terms to the Confederacy.

1 APRIL 1865
Civil War: East In the last important battle of the war, Sheridan routs a Confederate assault at Five Forks, Virginia.

2 APRIL 1865
Civil War: East Lee withdraws his army from Petersburg, ending the six–months' siege, and advises President Davis to move the Confederate government out of Richmond.

3 APRIL 1865
Civil War: East Union troops enter Petersburg and Richmond.

5 APRIL 1865
Civil War: East President Lincoln arrives in Richmond and tours the city; at one point he sits in Jefferson Davis's chair with almost boyish excitement.

7 APRIL 1865
Civil War: East Having virtually surrounded Lee's army, Grant formally requests a surrender. Lee, his forces depleted and facing starvation, asks Grant for terms.

8 APRIL 1865
Civil War: East Lee surrenders to Grant at Appomattox Court House, Virginia. As Lincoln requested, the terms are generous: Confederate officers

and men are free to go home with their own horses and officers may retain sidearms; all equipment is to be surrendered.

11 APRIL 1865
National In his last public address, President Lincoln urges reconstruction in the spirit of generous conciliation. He voices similar sentiments to his Cabinet on the morning of April 14.

14 APRIL 1865
National While watching a comedy at Ford's Theater in Washington, President Lincoln is mortally wounded by actor and Southern patriot John Wilkes Booth. Lincoln dies early the next morning at the age of 56. He is the first President to be assassinated. Secretary Seward is stabbed by a co-conspirator.

15 APRIL 1865
National Three hours after Lincoln's death, Andrew Johnson takes the oath of office as President.

18 APRIL 1865
Civil War: West Confederate General J. E. Johnston surrenders to Sherman in North Carolina. Minor resistance will continue in the South for several weeks.

26 APRIL 1865
National Assassin John Wilkes Booth is cornered and shot to death near Bowling Green, Virginia.

27 APRIL 1865
Regional Steamships not infrequently explode in this era, and the worst ship disaster in U.S. history occurs in an explosion of the *Sultana* on the Mississippi; 1700 people die, most of them Union soldiers returning from Southern prisons.

29 APRIL 1865
National Commercial restrictions are removed from most parts of the South, except Texas, by order of President Johnson.

2 MAY 1865
Civil War: Aftermath Jefferson Davis has gone into hiding. It is presumed he has taken part in Lin-

The assassination of Lincoln.

TESTING A UNION 1788-1865

coln's assassination. Johnson offers a $100,000 reward for his capture. This delights Republicans. It suggests that the tailor from Tennessee will take a hard line against the Southerners.

4 MAY 1865
Civil War: Aftermath One by one the theaters of war are closed. The end of all resistance east of the Mississippi is effected when General Richard Taylor surrenders to General Edward R.S. Canby.

10 MAY 1865
Civil War: Aftermath Jefferson Davis is captured in Georgia. He is put in jail to await trial. He will be pardoned in 1868 when Johnson, in one of his last acts in office, grants amnesty to all Southerners.

13 MAY 1865
Civil War: Aftermath General Kirby Smith surren-

ders Confederate forces west of the Mississippi. All organized resistance now comes to an end. Reduction of the Federal Army had already begun April 13. From figures provided by the Senate it has been estimated that there were approximately 2,324,516 Union soldiers enlisted for the war. About 360,000 were killed. In the Confederate Army there were at least 1,000,000 enlisted and 135,000 dead. Cost to the Union side was $6,189,908 and to the Confederate side roughly half that figure.

29 MAY 1865
Reconstruction Johnson begins to put his own reconstruction plan into effect. He prefers to call it "Restoration." The essential difference between his plan and the subsequent one which Congress will devise is the lack of protection for civil rights for blacks. Johnson's sees the Southern states as part of a federation, whereas the reconstruction plan devised piecemeal by Congress will attack them as having committed "state suicide," as needing to be punished for their rebellion, and requiring a strong Northern hand to prevent excesses toward freed blacks. Johnson names a provisional governor for North Carolina to help reorganize and prepare the state for re–entry into Congress. It is one of the first acts in the long struggle for what Johnson calls "restoration" and Congress calls "reconstruction."

2 JUNE 1865
Civil War: Aftermath The last naval act of the war takes place at Galveston, Texas, as Confederates surrender their one remaining seaport. Of 471 ships and 2455 guns in active service during the war, only 29 vessels and 210 guns will be active by December.

6 JUNE 1865
Reconstruction Missouri fulfills the presidential conditions for ratification of a new state constitution and is readmitted to the Union. President Johnson offers amnesty to all prisoners of war who will take an oath that they never fought against the Union voluntarily. Once the oath is taken they are released.

13 JUNE 1865
Reconstruction Johnson names provisional governors for six states: Alabama, Georgia, Mississippi, Florida, South Carolina and Texas. The governors are empowered to arrange for conventions to meet the lenient presidential requirements for readmission to the Union. Congress itself will not reconvene until December; thus at first the states receive no guidelines from a Congress which will insist upon some rather harsh conditions for readmission.

1 JULY 1865
National All southern ports which have been closed to foreign shipping because of the war are now opened by executive decree.

5 SEPTEMBER 1865
Reconstruction South Carolina repeals its ordinance of secession, declaring it null and void.

DECEMBER 12, 1865

THE FIRST MODERN WAR

The Civil War has occasionally been labeled "the first modern war." Just what are the credentials it offers for such a claim, desirable or otherwise? On the most literal level, there were quite a number of "firsts" in weaponry and technology that would indeed seem to point the way to modern warfare. Most soldiers fought the war with a mixed arsenal of weapons, many of which dated back to at least the American Revolution—and some even to much earlier wars—and many of the basic developments had in fact appeared well before the Civil War started. These included such breakthroughs as the percussion cap, replacing the flintlock; breechloading small-arms as well as artillery; rifled bores for more accurate shooting; and even repeating rifles: all these received their major trials-by-fire in the Civil War, however. But the first machine gun used in combat, the Williams Gun—invented by a Captain Williams of the Confederate Army—can claim a solid first, while the Gatling Gun that later served armies as a mechanical machine gun was developed during the Civil War, although it did not see much action in it. Simple rockets and crude hand grenades were also used at times but neither of these were invented during the war nor did they count much in its outcome.

At sea, there were several notable anticipations of modern naval warfare, of which the first use of ironclads is only the best known. Equally crucial for modern ships was the revolving turret of the *Monitor*. Submarines were neither invented in the Civil War nor were they used for the first time in a war. (The American David Bushnell had tried to sink a British ship from his submarine during the Revolution.) But the Confederates worked hard at perfecting a submarine, and even though their best effort went down with the Union ship it sank in 1864, they showed what might be done in future wars.

There were other important applications of new technology that looked ahead to the future, too. Thaddeus Lowe was by no means the first to fly in lighter-than-air balloons, but he was the first to use these craft for doing reconnaissance work on enemy positions. Likewise, the telegraph had been around for some years, but the Civil War was the first war in which it played a crucial role. So, too, railroads were already enjoying a robust adolescence, but it was during the Civil War that they found themselves making a major contribution. Barbed wire entanglements were also used for the first time in the Civil War, as were land and water mines.

But beyond such weaponry and technology, the Civil War saw the beginnings of several innovations in tactics and strategy that would come to characterize modern warfare. On the one hand, there was the first extensive use of trenches, while on the other there were the flexible maneuvers of commanders such as Sheridan and Sherman: the battles of the American Civil War are still studied by those preparing for possible wars. The naval blockade of the South was so thorough and relatively successful that it, too, would influence modern states in their conduct of war.

And what the blockade also represented was another of the Civil War's major claims on the future: perhaps it is redundant, but as well as the "first modern" it is sometimes called the "first total" war. This refers to the fact that it was not fought on remote fields by fairly small armies—and often at pre-arranged times—but rather involved the mobilization of large segments of both sides' people and economies for an extended period. Once this concept of "total war" is understood, many other elements of the Civil War begin to reveal their modernity: the demand for "unconditional surrender," for instance or the almost incredible casualties borne by both sides. And perhaps the most modern of all its characteristics is the fact that the Civil War is the war that left the double-barrelled legacy of war as "hell" and war for a "noble cause."

24 NOVEMBER 1865
Reconstruction In an ominous move, Mississippi establishes the Black Codes, thus formalizing what all Southern States have begun to do informally: the Black Codes forbid blacks to testify against whites; blacks without work can be arrested for vagrancy and hired out to any employer requesting their help; public schools will be separate if there are any at all. Blacks cannot serve on juries, bear arms or hold large meetings. A Chicago newspaper voices Northern reaction: "We tell the men of Mississippi that the men of the North will convert. . .Mississippi into a frog pond before they will allow such laws."

1 DECEMBER 1865
Reconstruction The writ of habeas corpus, suspended by Lincoln under the press of war, is restored by presidential decree.

4 DECEMBER 1865
National The thirty-ninth Congress convenes. It is the first session since Lincoln's death. All Confederate states, with the exception of Mississippi, have formally accepted presidential requirements for readmission to the Union and representation in Congress. In every case all–white delegations are returned ready for the roll call. Among the delegates are four Confederate generals, many colonels, and many members of the Confederate congresses. With unsurpassed arrogance, Georgia sends Alexander H. Stevens, the former Vice-President of the Confederate States, as one of its delegates. Although only six northern states have laws relating to black suffrage, northern congressmen are furious. Led by the intractable but "gloriously triumphant" Thaddeus Stevens, the House simply omits the southerners from the roll call, effectively denying them admittance. It then proceeds to discuss punishment for the rebellious South which according to Radical Republican Charles Sumner has committed "state suicide."
Reconstruction The House votes to establish a Joint Committee on Reconstruction, called the Committee of Fifteen. Ultimately there will be nine Republican representatives and six Democratic Senators, and they will vote for their proposals on strict party lines.

5 DECEMBER 1865
Finance Secretary of the Treasury Hugh McCulloch proposes retirement of "greenbacks."

12 DECEMBER 1865
Reconstruction The Senate agrees to a joint committee on Reconstruction. William P. Fessenden of Maine will be named chairman of the Senate committee.

TESTING A UNION 1788-1865

14 DECEMBER 1865
Reconstruction The uncompromising, pro-black Thaddeus Stevens of Pennsylvania is named head of the Committee of Fifteen.

18 DECEMBER 1865
National Secretary of State Seward announces that the necessary number of states, 27 in all, have ratified the Thirteenth Amendment to the Constitution. The Amendment has two sections:
1. "Neither slavery nor involuntary servitude, except as punishment for crime whereof the party shall have been duly convicted, shall exist within the United States, or any place subject to their jurisdiction.
2. Congress shall have power to enforce this article by appropriate legislation."

24 DECEMBER 1865
Regional The Ku Klux Klan is formed in Tennessee by Thomas M. Jones, James R. Crowe and others. It starts out as one of many secret societies set up to terrorize blacks. Its methods become ever more vicious as whites become more sure that they will rid themselves of northern troops and return to their old two-tiered system, with blacks on the bottom. Unable to feel the new winds of industry and technology sweeping the country, the Ku Klux Klan sets its goal on racial repression.

25 DECEMBER 1865
Industry Chicago opens the Union stockyards and changes the business patterns of the prairies.

OTHER EVENTS OF 1865
National Congress mandates free delivery of mail in larger cities.
Life/Custom Beards become fashionable just after the war. Interest in baseball mushrooms with the formation of 91 clubs within the National Association.
Arts/Culture *The Nation,* a liberal weekly magazine, is founded. Mark Twain publishes "The Celebrated Jumping Frog of Calaveras County," and Walt Whitman publishes the war poems of *Drum Taps*.

Union soldiers at Appomattox Court House.

Abraham Lincoln, the rail splitter.

FORGING A
NATION

1866–1900

S. L. MAYER
Former Professor of International Relations, University of Southern California

FORGING A NATION 1866-1900

The period of 35 years from the end of the Civil War to the era of Theodore Roosevelt was the crucible of the nation's history, in which the strains which rent America in the 20th century were forged. Although the Union had been preserved, it had been done at the expense of the agricultural South to the benefit of the burgeoning, newly industrial East. The West, which had allied itself to eastern industrial interests in the cause of anti-slavery, now found itself, apart from certain key industrial centers such as Chicago, tethered to the defeated South, for the Midwest as well as the prairies and mountains beyond it were cattle and wheat lands, dependent upon the growing chain of railroads for their survival. Railroads, which provided the wheels of the industrial machine that eventually wore down the Confederacy, also brought goods to market. The markets were in the East, and the sources of beef and bread which fed it were in the West. The owners of the railroads were, for the most part, in New York, financed by two sources: the first, the Federal Government, which gave the railroads free land to build on and exploit; the second, the banks, led by J.P. Morgan, who acted as the banker's banker. To have an account at the House of Morgan, located at the corner of Broad and Wall Streets in New York, it was necessary to have a million dollars, the rough equivalent of 20 million dollars today. Otherwise, one had to bank at the Dime, or any of the small banks which were supported by the big banks, that were supported by Morgan. Morgan, a ruthless and cunning financial genius, tied the entire country to his own interests. His bank had more capital than even the Federal Government, to which it occasionally denied loans because of lack of collateral.

Morgan was not alone. With his colleagues who owned the railroads—Commodore Vanderbilt, Jay Gould, C.P. Huntington, Leland Stanford, James J. Hill, E.H. Harriman and the others—he controlled the fortunes of the West, which needed the railroads to sell its produce. If the railroad rates went up, the West suffered. If the rates went down, it prospered. Utilizing their great power, the rail moguls, backed by Morgan, kept the rates up.

The defeated South, dependent as ever on cotton, was occupied by Union troops, in some states, until 1877, under Reconstruction. The fundamental principle of Reconstruction made sense. To bind up the nation's wounds, Lincoln had said, it was necessary to lend the South a helping hand. Had Lincoln lived, perhaps it would have happened that way. But under weak and pliant presidents, well-meaning, like the impeached Andrew Johnson, or uncaring, like Ulysses S. Grant, the South became bitter and resentful. Blacks leaped into high public office. Others tried their hand at farming, given the opportunity for free land which Reconstruction allowed. Had Reconstruction been without scandal, honestly administered and selflessly allowed to proceed, the advance from slavery might have gone forward smoothly, for the well-being of the South, as the nation, depended upon the well-being of all its citizens. But corrupt carpetbaggers, scalawags as well as blacks, made the very name of Reconstruction hated by Southern whites, and when it finally ended, not untypically in the election fraud of 1876-77, the worst aspects of the old Confederacy rose from the ashes of defeat to gain a bitter revenge. The Ku Klux Klan succeeded in grasping the fruits of emancipation from all Southern blacks. Poll taxes robbed them of the vote, and fear, corruption and profligacy on their own part robbed many of them of their land. By the 1880s the Southern cotton economy again prospered, producing double the amount of cotton produced in 1860, but blacks became exploited tenant farmers, only a small step away from the slavery from which they had so recently emerged. Poor whites were equally impoverished. A few large landowners in the South prospered, as they had done before the Civil War. But most of the Southern people were in a vitiated condition, and the region's progress would be retarded for generations.

In politics, most Americans had little to choose from between the two political parties. The Republicans represented Morgan, the industrialists like Andrew Carnegie, czar of steel, John D. Rockefeller, emperor of oil, and their ilk, plus the railroad interests. The Democrats were the party of the defeated South, representing, for the most part, large Southern landowners, as well as immigrant minority groups in the North. The Republicans usually won. In the 35 years from the end of the Civil War to the first Age of Roosevelt, Democrats were in office for eleven years. The first, Johnson, was emasculated from the start and driven from office in disgrace. The other eight years were under Grover Cleveland, a former Mayor of Buffalo, who gained office because of a split in the Republican Party, and was driven from it by scandal and the Panic of 1893, the last Great Depression of the 19th century. Neither Democrat accomplished very much, although both tried. Even some of the Republicans made an effort, an attempt to

Cornelius Vanderbilt, financier.

Immigrant Landing Station, Ellis Island, N.Y.

break the political log-jam, but when one did, when Rutherford B. Hayes attempted to reform the Civil Service, he did not have the chance to run again. The bosses of the Republican Party dumped him in favor of the more pliant James Garfield. It was not that Cleveland or Garfield, or his successor, Chester A. Arthur, or Benjamin Harrison, or William McKinley were terrible men. They could not help it if their parties were unrepresentative of most of the American people.

But the very character of the American people was rapidly changing. Millions of immigrants from western, southern and eastern Europe poured into industrial America to provide the cheap labor which was needed to build the industrial machine of the East and subsequently, the Midwest. First came the Germans and Irish, then the Italians and Greeks, then the Poles, Hungarians and Russians, all of them crowded into hideous slums, all of them poorly paid, fed, and housed, all of them discriminated against by Americans whose ancestors came to the United States in earlier times. The strength of the Republican Party lay in the small towns and farms of America, where people shuddered at the thought of these huddled masses yearning to breathe free, and hoped that they would never meet any of them. Shadowy organizations, mirroring the "ideals" of the Ku Klux Klan—anti-foreign, anti-Catholic, anti-Semitic—grew in the North, and their aims were similar: to deny civil rights to the immigrant whites as the Klan had done to the native blacks. Groups such as Tammany Hall in New York befriended the immigrants in exchange for their franchise, and political machines burgeoned in most of the major cities of the Northeast and Midwest. The immigrants would arrive from Castle Garden, and later from Ellis Island, be offered housing and even a job by Tammany, and then vote the way the precinct captain or ward heeler wanted once they became citizens. But if they wanted to make it out of the slums, they had to do so on their own. Despite the intense prejudice against them, many did. Immigrants pro-

vided the human fuel the steel and rail barons needed, but they did not go South. There, sufficient cheap labor already existed—the poor whites and the blacks. All provided the vitality which built modern America.

The political log-jam could not, however, hold for long. Many groups, like the Grangers, sought to create a political force which would drive both parties from office. The best chance came with the formation of the Populist Party, which wanted to ally the forces of the Southern, rural whites with the farmers and ranchers of the Midwest and West. It could have been, and to an extent, was, a major political force. Springing from almost nowhere, it made a good showing in the election of 1892, helping Cleveland back into office, drawing from some of the natural voting power of the Republicans. When the Panic of 1893 occurred, it seemed likely that the Populists could win office, with both parties in disfavor and retreat.

But the Populists had grave weaknesses. They, too, were anti-immigrant, anti-Catholic, anti-black, and anti-Semitic. Therefore they could not draw for support on the "hyphenated Americans," who were their natural allies. And their leadership lacked vision, and occasionally tended toward madness. Their banner was stolen by a young Democrat from Nebraska, whose presence became a lightning rod for the farmers of the South and West. William Jennings Bryan, a 36-year-old barnburner of a stump speaker, embraced most of the Populist program of a ten-hour day and government regulation of the railroads and utilities under the banner of "free silver." It was his contention that, stated in more modern terms, the money supply was too tightly controlled by the gold standard, which linked the dollar to the amount of gold held by the Federal Government. Each and every dollar in the United States was backed by an equal amount of gold, and was redeemable in gold. Actually, much of the currency was in gold. Bryan contended that the free coinage of silver, at the then-prevalent ratio of 16:1 against gold, would provide more money for the workers and farmers, would thereby increase the money supply, and free millions from a lifetime of grinding poverty. Of course, silver miners in Colorado and other Western states supported this program. This simplistic formula won Bryan the Democratic nomination for President in 1896. The Democratic Convention, and the public, thrilled to the acceptance speech of "the Boy Orator of the Platte" when he announced: "You shall not press upon the brow of labor this crown of thorns. You shall not crucify mankind upon a Cross of Gold."

It looked as if Bryan was a shoo-in against the laconic William McKinley, who satisfied himself and his party by making occasional bland pronouncements from the front porch of his Ohio homestead, while Bryan criss-crossed the country in a frenzy of energy and oratory in the first American whistle-stop campaign. But big business backed McKinley, and when the business cycle turned upward in September, people returned to work, and Bryan's oratory became repetitive. In modern terms, Bryan peaked too early. If the election had been held in September, he would have won. But American presidential elections always take place in November, and McKinley, supported by middle class townspeople, won. Most of the blacks and many of the immigrants could, but did not, vote. But the real loser was Populism. The party soon foundered and collapsed. Bryan, who had embraced

William Jennings Bryan.

much of their program, was to run twice more for president, running his losing streak to three, a record never to be equalled. But the long reign of Morgan was to draw slowly to a close when Theodore Roosevelt was nominated for vice-president to run with McKinley in 1900. When McKinley was shot by an anarchist in 1901, the Republican Progressive, Theodore Roosevelt, became the president, a prospect feared by McKinley's political boss, Marc Hanna, himself a Cleveland multimillionaire. That "damned cowboy," as Hanna had called him, was a patrician who loved the West, a Harvard man who wanted to fight the monopolies (or "trusts," as they were then known), an Eastern aristocrat who was bound and determined to fight the Morgans and win. He inherited the mantle of Populism, and turned the country in another direction.

Theodore Roosevelt had been Assistant Secretary of the Navy when the Spanish-American War broke out in 1898. He resigned his position to fight with his Rough Riders in Cuba. The war was short, and in six weeks the United States seized an overseas empire to join the imperial rush for colonies which other industrialized states had begun decades and even centuries earlier. By chance or by design, the United States annexed the Philippines, Guam, Puerto Rico, and, in the excitement, Hawaii, which Cleveland had spurned four years before. To defend it, and the new American protectorate, Cuba, made independent in 1901, the U.S. would need a navy. American industrial power and foreign policy, turned inward from the War of 1812 until 1898, turned its face outward toward the Caribbean and the Pacific at the turn of the century, and Roosevelt, who embodied this spirit of imperial vigor, became the president. American isolationism was at an end, and with it the stranglehold Eastern big business held over the country. There was enough wealth in the country to be shared by more than the very few, and Roosevelt's Progressivism would eliminate some of the gravest abuses of the post-Civil War era. He promised much, delivered some, but, more importantly, galvanized the wider public behind a genuinely popular program of reform and nationalism.

It was that spirit of nationalism, created during the era of immigration and industrialization, which molded a new America. In the years following Appomattox, the United States ceased to be an ex-British colony, with a post-colonial economy, largely dependent upon Britain for its industrial products and protected from Europe by the Royal Navy. The country also ceased to be composed chiefly of people of British and African stock. Although the melting pot never really happened, even in those years, it was a European stew of nationalities, all of whom had one aim in mind—a better life and a freer life for themselves and their offspring. Although throughout the period few shared this good life, all shared the dream of it. The dream spurred the establishment of scores of new colleges and universities, especially the state universities established by land grant after 1862. It spurred the inventions which were soon to change America and

Theodore Roosevelt.

the world. Thomas Edison's electric light bulb, invented in 1879, became commonplace within 25 years, ending the era of gaslight and shadow. Edison also invented the phonograph and moving pictures. Alexander Graham Bell invented the telephone in 1876, which entered almost ten percent of American homes within three decades. And there were many other innovations that changed America and the world in those years: the refrigerated railroad car, barbed wire, which fenced in much of the West, Louis Sullivan's early skyscrapers, steel bridges. American cities began to rival those of Europe, and were certainly better lit and more modern, if not safer. Chicago, a village in the 1830s, razed to the ground by the Great Fire of 1871, had more than a million inhabitants by 1900. Other new cities arose from the prairies: Cleveland, Buffalo, Detroit, Minneapolis, Milwaukee. Older river towns grew to become metropolises: St. Louis, Cincinnati, Pittsburgh, Louisville, all at least in part created by the railroads which linked their people and products to the world beyond through Baltimore, Washington, Philadelphia, Boston and New York.

In all these developments the South was left behind. Only a few universities were established. Immigration scarcely affected the plantation economy. Industrialization, apart from one or two centers, was something Southerners read about with a mixture of fear and disdain. The failure of Reconstruction was to leave the nation still divided, both in character and wealth, until after World War II. But the West was transformed. The last of the Indian Wars opened the Rocky Mountain area to mining booms, new ranches and farms, oil speculation and a population boom, as

the remaining Indians were herded into reservations. California, admitted as a state in 1850, was joined by many others, which became populated in much the same manner. Although the mineral booms were usually short-lived, most emigrants to the West stayed to settle the land so that by 1900 there were only two territories left in the West which had not yet reached statehood. These new states, all dependent upon rail links, helped to create the Rooseveltian political revolution, and the cities of the West, like San Francisco and Denver, began to rise and make their voices heard.

Behind this political change lay major social change as well. Trade unions were formed and socialists demanded even greater reforms than Roosevelt, Bryan, or the Populists envisaged. The Haymarket Riots and Pullman Strike in Chicago had reverberations throughout the country. The warning was clear. If reforms were not at hand, there were darker and more radical forces which could have gained widespread popularity. If unorganized labor made the capitalists rich, organized labor could take it all away if the industrial workers, mainly immigrants, were not given a chance to share the newly created national wealth. The miracle of America was its ability to stifle revolution by reform. Every American shared the dream, and by 1900 every American was beginning to see his or her opportunity to realize it.

America's coming of age by 1900 was marked by the establishment of symphony orchestras in every major city, art galleries the equal of many in Europe, opera companies, vaudeville, restaurants, parks and other civilized ameneties. In 1865 the United States was trying to recover from a violent civil conflict, the most bloody in its history, before or since. But culturally, apart from a few distinguished authors, it was a backwater; industrially, a midget. By 1900, however, it was the world's third largest producer of steel, the world's greatest exporter of agricultural produce and one of the world's leading industrial powers. Soon it was to possess one of the world's largest navies. America did not know its own strength, and the world did not know of it. America in the Victorian Age was a nation of quiet, pleasant, safe small towns, a nation of farms and ranches, and vast, largely untapped resources available to most of its citizens. Above all, it was a land of boundless opportunity, and millions from Europe and Asia flocked to its shores to participate in this great social experiment. Secure behind its moat of great oceans, America was given the chance to develop its resources and its people without interference from foreign powers. Its isolation led to its rapid growth. It was ironic that the very inventions which Americans helped to develop would narrow the gap between itself and Europe and would hasten the end of its isolation. This vibrant and self-confident nation wished to play no role on the world stage which it entered by stealth or by chance in 1898. But by 1900 its adolescence was over. In little more than a generation the United States had become a world power.

CHRONOLOGY

19 FEBRUARY 1866
Reconstruction The authority of the Bureau of Refugees, Freedmen and Abandoned Lands is extended and expanded by an Act of Congress. The Freedmen's Bureau had been formed by Lincoln in the spring of 1865. Congress has become increasingly concerned over the condition, treatment and rights of blacks. Reacting to the nefarious Black Codes with which the South is attempting to subjugate the blacks, Congress strengthens the powers of the bureau, giving it jurisdiction over anyone depriving blacks of their civil rights. The bureau is also to continue to give relief in the form of food, clothing and shelter to those in need. To northern dismay, including moderate John-

---

RECONSTRUCTION

The Civil War had put the Union to the test and the Union had passed. There would be no secession and no slavery. But between slavery and equal rights there was room and the forces colliding over these issues were fierce and unforgiving. First of all, encouraged by presidential expressions of leniency, southern leaders produced a set of vicious regulations known as the Black Codes. These were the laws which before the war had applied to "slaves. . ." Now they were shifted without modifications onto "ex-slaves. . ." The Confederates also sent "lily-white" delegations to the convening Congress. Congress was in no mood to readmit them without some change in their attitude. First they would have to meet conditions. Among these were that each State should ratify the Thirteenth Amendment abolishing slavery and the new Fourteenth Amendment guaranteeing civil liberties. After that representatives could be elected to Congress. Meantime the South was divided into five military districts under the command of the Army; the Freedmen's Bureau was extended into peacetime to dispense money and aid to the needy. The Federal Government had abrogated powers to itself greater than any granted to it before. Under the protection of Federal Troops, blacks and whites began to build strong and essentially just structures within which to live. Businesses emerged out of the wreckage, schools sprouted like mushrooms in warm rain. Blacks and landless whites voted and held public office. Patrician whites and "rednecks" bided their time. They accepted the terms for readmission. By 1870 the procedures had all been completed and most Federal Troops were removed from southern soil. The South then proceeded to dismantle "Reconstruction" with unseemly haste. By 1877 the process was complete. The entire South had settled into a pattern of segregation and "white supremacy."

Underlying Reconstruction lay principles important to modern civilized nations: civil rights, racial equality, federal powers. These issues remained essentially unexamined. But the currents of the times favored freedom and these currents would ultimately carve their way back into the "unreconstructed" South.

---

son supporters, the president vetoes the bill. He explains that it is unconstitutional, since it expands federal jurisdiction in states which have not been permitted representation in Congress. In his view the states have been legitimately restored to the Union and should be seated. If Johnson had maintained his stance at this constitutional level, he might have rallied congressional support. Instead he went on to clarify his position: the freedmen, he explained, should manage "through their own merits and exertions." Johnson's veto is met with boos and hisses. Congress will override on 10 July 1866.

22 FEBRUARY 1866
National A group of Johnson supporters, called "copperheads" by disgusted radicals, marches to the White House to show its delight in Johnson's veto. In the light of a candle, Johnson puts on such an extraordinary performance that Washington concludes he must have been drunk. Says John Sherman, Senator from Ohio: "There is no true friend of Andrew Johnson who would not be willing to wipe out that speech from the pages of history." First he reads from a prepared text, then he ad–libs, vilifying his Republican opponents, calling them traitors. When egged on by the crowd, he names Thaddeus Stevens and Charles Sumner as two of the traitors. The crowd loves it, but it is to be a turning point in Johnson's fortunes. His behavior this evening decisively erodes his support in Congress, leaving the field to men who have neither links nor sympathies with the Southern white cause.

2 MARCH 1866
Reconstruction Congress accepts a resolution from the Joint Committee on Reconstruction which dictates that Confederate states will not be seated in Congress until admitted by the authority of Congress itself. However it still does not produce guidelines for procedures which will have to be followed in order to achieve congressional approval.

2 APRIL 1866
Civil War: Aftermath Johnson declares an end to war in ten states: Alabama, Arkansas, Florida, Georgia, Louisiana, Mississippi, North Carolina, South Carolina, Tennessee and Virginia.

9 APRIL 1866
Reconstruction The Civil Rights Bill of 1866 is enacted by Congress. Noting the flagrant breach of the spirit of the Thirteenth Amendment by southerners who have been slowly forcing blacks back into a condition bordering on slavery, northerners propose to

buttress the amendment with the Civil Rights Bill. It grants full citizenship to all persons born on United States soil (Indians, not taxable, excepted). All citizens are to have equal rights to enforce contracts, to sue, to give evidence, to buy property—in effect to have all the civil laws a full citizen is entitled to. It is moderate although precise in tone. If Johnson accepts it, he might regain some of his lost leadership. Rutherford B. Hayes, later to become President himself, but now a Congressman, writes: "If he signs, the

---

PRESIDENT JOHNSON'S OWN "RESTORATION" PLAN

Having taken advantage of the nine–month absence of Congress from Washington, Johnson proceeded to put his own Reconstruction Plan, or Restoration Plan, as he preferred to call it, into effect. Following Lincoln's lead and his own southern sympathies, Johnson favored leniency to all but the hard core of civil and military leadership, and some patricians with taxable property over $20,000 against whom he seemed to hold a grudge. All such men would be disenfranchised until further notice. Unlike Lincoln, who already had had second thoughts about peace terms, Johnson could make up his mind on an issue only once, and when circumstances required rethinking, Johnson was unprepared to try. The terms of Johnson's plan were fairly mild considering the intractability of the rebels. He proposed amnesty for all who would swear allegiance to the Union. Only 10 percent of the enfranchised population need take the oath, he decreed. The proclamation was worded in an ugly fashion which offended many: "Amnesty and pardon with restoration of all rights of property, except as to slaves." States were then expected to convene conventions which would repudiate the Confederate debt, declare secession null and void and ratify the Thirteenth Amendment abolishing slavery. Nothing was said about civil rights for blacks. Once all that had been accomplished the states would elect officials and send representatives to Congress. Johnson decided that it was unconstitutional for the President or Congress to abolish slavery by fiat. As soon as each state ratified the Thirteenth Amendment its military governor would be removed; Johnson's plan was slightly more severe than anything Lincoln had spoken of, but it was still unacceptable to Congress.

---

chances are that a complete rupture will be avoided. Otherwise, otherwise." To the dismay of all parties, Johnson vetoes the bill. Johnson arms himself with some sound constitutional arguments: it will diminish the rights of states to make their own laws, it will weaken the limits to federal power. It will provide "security for the colored race, safeguards which go infinitely beyond any that the General Government has ever provided for the white race." Congress, still reluctant to challenge the President directly, nonetheless overrides the veto by one vote. The galleries erupt in noisy glee. The Executive will now be bypassed in all essential federal considerations. In an intense power struggle Congress has come out on top.

30 APRIL 1866
Reconstruction Congress gets proposals from the Joint Committee on Reconstruction. Senator William

P. Fessenden has modified Northern demands, some of which the North has its own selfish motives for modifying. Full male black suffrage, for instance, would give the South a great number of new voters, which, if the South has enough sense to accept, will tip power away from the North. However the South is not prepared to give the vote to black voters. Keeping the South out of competition for the great new prizes offered to industry is something that pleases many Northern congressmen who are closely allied to industrialists bent on exploiting the natural resources which through railroad, inventions and technology are suddenly within their reach. Once the South has rejected the moderate proposals, radical Republicans are authorized to bring in their more severe procedures.

BLACKS

Usually when a war is over, people are free to go home. In 1865 the four-million black population of America was merely free. There were no homes to go to. Some fortunate blacks had already bought their freedom, some were well-educated, some were highly skilled craftsmen whose talents would be in great demand; others were able construction workers, farmers and the like. Most were unskilled field laborers, with little prospects of any kind. Very few had been taught essential managerial skills. Whatever their talents, without money or protection, they were set adrift into a hostile society made desolate by war. Their immediate and primary goal was to preserve their independence through education and power. And they made the most of every opportunity. With generous help from northerners they founded at least nine institutions for higher learning, including Howard and Fisk Universities, and Tuskegee Institute. It is estimated that four thousand schools were reaching black students of all ages within five years of the end of the war. Teaming up with "carpetbaggers" and "scalawags" in the days of Reconstruction, blacks held almost every political state office, high and low. Two blacks, Blanche K. Bruce and Hiram R. Revels, became U.S. Senators. Blacks, like other Americans, educated and uneducated, had an instinct for politics. They served with the usual mixture of intelligence, greed, corruption and concern for the public weal found in all democratic situations. Moving north into the big cities, they teamed up with the growing labor movement and actively protested discrimination. Their persistence set an example for other oppressed minorities.

Blacks early made important contributions to American society: Dr. Daniel Hale Williams performed the first open heart surgery. A black, Jan E. Matzeliger, invented the mechanical lasting machine which overnight changed the shoemaking industry. Blacks started newspapers and magazines and became writers and painters of national renown. But it is in music that they surpassed all others. Black music has spoken of resentment without weakness, patience without despair, joy without compromise. It has become the authentic, earthy sound of America.

---

16 MAY 1866
Finance Congress authorizes a new coin. It will be nicknamed the "nickel."

16 JUNE 1866
Reconstruction Congress proposes the Fourteenth

FORGING A NATION 1866-1900

Amendment. So far the Thirteenth Amendment has freed the slaves and the Civil Rights Act of 1866 has buttressed civil laws to protect freedmen. But Congress is still uneasy about readmitting the rebellious states to full representation. Lurid stories of ugly treatment of blacks by whites fill the newspapers. The Joint Committee on Reconstruction, led by the radical Republicans, now brings forth the Fourteenth Amendment to provide constitutional definitions of civil rights.

THE FOURTEENTH AMENDMENT

The major guarantees provided by the Fourteenth Amendment are:
1. All persons born or naturalized in the United States are citizens of the United States and of the state in which they reside. No law can be made which will infringe the basic protections granted to all United States citizens.
2. All males twenty-one or over (except Indians, not taxed) have the right to vote. If this right is denied to anyone, then the total vote is to be reduced by a similar number. [This section has never been applied.]
3. No person who has taken the oath to support the Constitution and has then gone on to support the rebellion shall have the right to civil or military office in United States government.
4. The Union debt "shall not be questioned." The Confederate debt on the other hand is declared null and void. It is forbidden to states to redeem it.

Johnson actively works against the amendment, telling Southerners they have no obligation to ratify it since it cannot validly be applied to States which are unrepresented in Congress. Union-oriented Tennessee ratifies the amendment almost at once and by July is readmitted to the Union. The others refuse ratification. Pushed to the wall, Congress finally clarifies its position: ratification of the Fourteenth Amendment by each Southern state is to be a condition for re-admission into Congress.

---

1 JULY 1866
Finance In a move to get the states out of the business of issuing their own currency, Congress imposes a 10 percent tax on all State bank notes. The move dries up state money and brings about an acceptable national currency.

19 JULY 1866
Reconstruction Tennessee ratifies the Fourteenth Amendment. It is the first state to do so.

24 JULY 1866
Reconstruction Tennessee is restored to full partnership in the Union.

30 JULY 1866
Reconstruction Race riots have been reported in the South over the introduction of black male suffrage into the Louisiana Constitution. In the subsequent violence which erupts in New Orleans, 48 blacks are killed and at least 160 more are wounded. Moderate Northerners are incensed at the Southerners and turn their support from President Johnson, who increasingly appears to be the spokesman for some of

the least attractive Southern ideals.

14 AUGUST 1866
National President Johnson organizes the National Union Party in a feeble effort to offset the power of Thaddeus Stevens in Congress; however, his uncouth behavior alienates his supporters as he makes a political tour of the country. Meanwhile, clashes occurring between blacks and whites in the South lead even the moderate northerners to distrust southern promises so that the Union Party never gets strong support. Radical Republicans will sweep the next election.

20 AUGUST 1866
National President Johnson proclaims an end to insurrection in Texas. Then, ignoring the war going on against the Indians, he declares that peace, order and tranquility have been returned to the country.
Labor The unexpectedly fast growth of big business has brought unsafe and unhealthy conditions into factories, mills, mines and railroads. Responding to the growing crisis, workers meet for a National Labor Congress in Baltimore, Maryland. From this meeting develops the National Labor Union which will begin to focus the nation's attention on needed guidelines, safeguards and restraints. But it will be many decades before the working man or woman is secure against exploitation under the nation's laws.

NOVEMBER 1866
National Preparing to return to Congress, representatives find that elections have provided anti-Johnson majorities in both houses. Congress will be sovereign over states and before the President. While strong men rule Congress the weakness in this turn of events is not a threat to the country. Exults Thaddeus Stevens, vitriolic leader of the opposition to Johnson: "No government official, from President and Chief Justice down, can do any act which is not prescribed and directed by legislative power."

17 DECEMBER 1866
National In *Ex Parte Milligan*, the Supreme Court judges that: "Martial law can never exist where the courts are open and in the proper and unobstructed exercise of their jurisdiction." This is intended to set a limit on the military powers authorized by the Federal Government. However Congress will find ways to retain the military protection it has provided for black civil rights which southern courts are attempting to curtail.

21 DECEMBER 1866
Indian Affairs The ongoing war against the Indians leads to constant skirmishing. General Patrick E. Connors, expressing the exasperation that whites feel over the Indian question, declares that Indians living north of the Platte River "must be hunted like wolves." Organizing a three-column march on the area known as Crazy Woman's Fork of the Powder River in the Black Hills of Dakota, his orders are to attack and kill every male Indian over the age of 12. The Sioux de-

fend their traditional hunting grounds. On December 21 they defeat Colonel William Judd Fetterman at Fort Kearney on the Bozeman gold trail in Montana Territory. Eighty whites are killed and settlers are predictably furious.

8 JANUARY 1867
Reconstruction Suffrage is granted to blacks in Washington, DC. In a continuing battle over blacks' v. states' rights, Johnson, siding with the states, vetoes the bill on the grounds that each state must enfranchise its own citizens. Congress, as it now regularly does, overrides the veto.

31 JANUARY 1867
National By an act of Congress, suffrage is granted to all males over 21 in all United States territories.

1 MARCH 1867
National Nebraska is the 37th state to be admitted to the Union.
Reconstruction By this date the Fourteenth Amendment has been rejected by 12 out of the 37 states. Ten of these 12 are southern states. Congress and the North generally sees this as unrepentant backsliding. The North still looks upon the Civil War as a fight for black freedom as well as for Union, and finds that freedom plainly does not exist without civil rights legislation to protect it. Southerners still cherish the view that the war was fought purely over the question of secession. Although Northerners have not yet really come to grips with black suffrage themselves, still the ungentlemanly haste with which the Fourteenth Amendment is dismissed by the South angers the men of strong principle in Congress. To them the South appears to be rushing straight back to its pre-war social arrangements.

2 MARCH 1867
Reconstruction The First Reconstruction Act is passed by Congress over Johnson's veto. Congress explains that there are "no legal State governments or adequate protection for life or property," since Congress itself has declared that Southern state governments are "provisional only." Now the vanquished states, excluding Tennessee, which had been accepted back into the Republic, are to be divided into five military districts under federal control. Each will be governed by a general to be appointed by the president. The military government will have powers to try and punish offenders, thus maintaining order which seems to be tenuous at best. A condition for readmission demanded by Congress is ratification of the Fourteenth Amendment granting suffrage to black males. Whites who led the rebellion are still restricted from voting, but poor and landless whites are not.
National In his unremitting chipping away at presidential powers, Johnson's implacable foe, Thaddeus Stevens, steers the Tenure of Office Act through Congress. The President is now denied the power to remove officials from office who have been appointed or approved by Congress. This act, whose constitu-

tionality remains in doubt, will become the basis for impeachment proceedings against Johnson. The egregious act will be only slightly modified, and will not be removed from the statute books until 1926. Continuing their pressure upon the President, Congress passes the Command of the Army Act. All military orders from the president must go first through the General of the Army, who is at this time General Grant. The president, as Supreme Commander, and in the absence of Congress, has been dealing directly with military governors of the South.
Industry Northern industry begins to exact protection for itself by urging Congress to pass the Wool and Woolens Act which increases tariffs on imports.
Finance Congress removes excise taxes imposed during the war, and exempts incomes under 1000 dollars from taxation.

4 MARCH 1867
National Fortieth Congress convenes. In another move to weaken presidential control over Reconstruction, Congress has arranged to convene in March instead of allowing the usual nine months between sessions. Once again a minor move proves decisive in establishing congressional authority. The President will no longer be on his own in Washington for the best part of a year.

5 MARCH 1867
Reconstruction In Virginia, one thousand black votes are discounted. Blacks are testing both the Reconstruction Act and white goodwill, and find both wanting.

11 MARCH 1867
Reconstruction Acquiescing to the will of Congress, the president appoints commanders for the five military districts carved out by the First Reconstruction Act; 20,000 troops, including black militia, are sent South. Under their protection over 700,000 blacks and over 6000 whites are registered. Many of the whites are landless people who have been prevented from voting in previous years. Coalitions of blacks and southern whites, "scalawags," as they are contemptuously called, elect representatives sensitive to their needs. With the army also come thousands of northerners ready to help, or according to their nature, to loot the South. These are disparagingly called "carpetbaggers" since they seem to have all their possessions in a large cheap bag made of carpet material. Actually many of these come south with the highest of motives and do extremely well for the needy. The Freedmen's Bureau, for instance, will authorize $5,000,000 for black education, which will fall mostly to "carpetbaggers" to furnish. Food, shelter and technical help are also provided. Corruption plays a large part in these postwar years, but does not negate the heroic quality and genuine highmindedness of a great part of the work of Reconstruction.

23 MARCH 1867
Reconstruction Seeing the need to bolster the

powers of the first Reconstruction Act, Congress, over the expected presidential veto, passes a second one. Since the states have made no move to call constitutional conventions, the five military governors are empowered to initiate proceedings. The black vote is to be protected at all cost and blacks may be elected representatives to these conventions. Ultimately blacks will be represented in formulating all state constitutions.

30 MARCH 1867
International The United States acquires Alaska. In a treaty executed with the greatest of secrecy, Secretary of State Seward arranges to buy the "large lump of ice" for two cents an acre for a total cost of $7,200,000. The territory is seemingly barren, but is rich in furs and fish. America is also happy to rid itself of "one more monarch from this continent." It is the first bit of land the Russians have ever parted with. The deal completed, Johnson sends troops to take possession even before Congress ratifies the treaty. Some disgruntled congressmen refer to the purchase as "Seward's Folly" but all are prepared to accept its essential logic. The territory is put under the control of the Treasury Department since that office regulates the primary source of wealth Alaska appears to provide: furs and fish. Thus by default no proper governmental body is set up and the fur industry becomes a lucrative government monopoly, a situation which would lead to trouble later on. It is not until 1896 that gold is found in the Klondike region bringing first the miners, but soon enough the settlers.

19 JULY 1867
Reconstruction The Third Reconstruction Act is passed by Congress over a presidential veto. Some southern states have found that they can repudiate the civil rights form of government that northerners wish to impose simply by staying away from the polls, because Congress has stated that a majority of half the registered voters are required to ratify their constitutions. In its Third Reconstruction Act, Congress declares that a majority of those voting will now suffice to effect ratification and readmission.

5 AUGUST 1867
National Secretary of War Stanton, in a general cabinet meeting, has told President Johnson that military governors of the south are answerable to Congress and not to the president. He claims that the correct chain of command is through the Commander of the Army and then to the House of Representatives. Johnson is outraged at this rank insubordination and requests the resignation of his secretary of war. Under usual circumstances, a president has every right to work with Cabinet officers of his own choice, but now Congress has tied the president's hands with the Tenure of Office Act, and claims Johnson has no right to fire his Secretary. The request for Stanton's resignation will ultimately lead to serious impeachment proceedings in a test of executive versus congressional

powers. Stanton refuses to resign, believing that Reconstruction policies of the radical Republican stamp are in jeopardy. Ignoring Stanton, Johnson nominates General U.S. Grant to the post, in spite of the fact that Grant has been steadily moving over to the radical camp, and Johnson distrusts him in any case. Stanton, under protest, transfers all documents and keys to Grant, then awaits the reconvening of Congress in November when his resignation and the General's appointment will have to be reviewed by that body. Meanwhile Johnson takes advantage of the absence of Congress to dismiss military governors and replace them with more lenient men of the president's own stamp.

28 AUGUST 1867
International The Midway Islands in the Pacific are annexed by the United States. Captain William Reynolds of the *Lackawanna* is put in charge of occupation formalities.

9 OCTOBER 1867
Regional General Lovell H. Rousseau of the United States Army takes formal possession of Alaska territory. The Treaty has been ratified by Congress on June 20.

25 NOVEMBER 1867
National The impeachment of President Johnson is formally proposed by the Judiciary Committee of the House of Representatives on grounds of "high crimes and misdemeanors." The vote is 5 to 4 to begin trial proceedings. Once before in January 1867 a resolution had been introduced in Congress to investigate the acts of the President. An obsessive congressman from Ohio, James M. Ashley, had introduced the resolution, but he made such a ridiculous case that although the resolution passed, it was soon voted down for lack of interest and evidence. The new impeachment resolution would carry more weight, but the outcome would be the same. The famous third attempt will be led by Thaddeus Stevens early the following year.

4 DECEMBER 1867
Agriculture Oliver Hudson Kelley, an obscure young clerk in the government's Agriculture Department, resigns his job to found the Patrons of Husbandry. It begins as a secret society with the usual rituals and trappings, but will ultimately become the voice of the farmer across the land, and will tangle successfully with the formidable railroad cabal. The Grange, as it will subsequently become named, starts out as an educational, social, non-political society which even admits women. At first it attracts few members but when it undertakes to challenge the Goliaths of industry, suspicion dissipates and only six years after its slow inception at Fredonia, New York, the Grange Movement has enrolled 858,000 members into its ranks.

10 JANUARY 1868
National The Senate Committee on Military Affairs

releases its report which exonerates Stanton in his struggle with Johnson over dismissal from office.

THE CHISOLM TRAIL

Jesse Chisolm was a half-breed—half Scot and half Cherokee. He is remembered for having traced out the most famous of all cattle trails, the legendary Chisolm, named after him. The trail was begun in 1867 when Chisolm mapped out the flattest route between south–central Kansas and his own place on the Canadian River. The Chisolm had supplanted the earlier Shawnee Trail, which had led to St. Louis and the earlier shipping points to eastern markets, by the time that Joseph McCoy offered forty dollars a head for cattle arriving at his new town, Abilene, Kansas. Sometimes as many as 28 herds would start the trail in a day, each herd numbering somewhere between 1000 and 3000 head of cattle. Usually the ratio of cowboys to cattle was one for every 250 animals. There were also horses, of course, with extras in case of rustlers or other disasters. The herd would be led by a pair of longhorns who instinctively took the lead in the arduous trek. Some bovine leaders were used over and over again, although horses and cattle were usually shipped east indiscriminately. The trail from the Texas Panhandle to the booming Kansas railhead took roughly four dangerous months. Crossing the Red River and Indian Territory, struggling against the harsh weather conditions and the dust and the rustler, took stamina and courage. Sometimes at the Red River, waiting for waters to recede from some storm in the headwaters, as many as 60,000 animals might be milling on the shore, anxious about crossing. Merely to separate the animals into their own herds would cause trouble and delays. The plaintive lullabies of cowboys on the watch marked the trail at night. Cowboys were not singing for their women, but to calm the skittish longhorns who were apt to stampede at the drop of a frying pan. The opening of the Chisolm Trail marked the beginning of the Ranger's frontier. When, 20 years later, the railroad had spread its tentacles north and south from the transcontinental line, it signaled the end of the Chisolm. The Ranger frontier was officially declared dead in the mid-1880s.

11 JANUARY 1868

National Grant asks to be relieved of his post, having been apprised of the penalties for violation of the Tenure of Office Act: $10,000 fine and five years in prison, although it was unlikely that such a popular hero would have been so ill-used.

13 JANUARY 1868

National By a vote of 35 to 6, the Senate refuses to concur with Johnson's suspension of his Secretary of War and his replacement by Grant. The Tenure of Office Act is used as grounds for refusal.

14 JANUARY 1868

National Grant turns the office of Secretary of War back to Stanton without giving Johnson a chance to put someone else in his place. Johnson, as might be expected, is furious at what he deems betrayal by his Commander of the Army.

5 FEBRUARY 1868

International Archduke Maximilian and his Empress Carlota have refused to leave their loyal troops and elect to remain in Mexico. The bulk of the French Army leaves, less than 10,000 men staying to fight a last ditch battle against Mexico's Republican President Juárez.

21 FEBRUARY 1868

National For the second time Johnson dismisses his Secretary of War over Reconstruction policies. Seeking to mitigate the consequences of military rule in the South, Johnson has ordered commanding officers to report directly to him and not through his increasingly radical Secretary of War, nor through the Commander of the Army, General Grant, a man who disagrees with the President on matters pertaining to Reconstruction. Congress has deliberately sought to weaken the President through the Command of the Army Act (1867) and the Tenure of Office Act (1867). However, Johnson decides to test the constitutionality of the Tenure of Office Act on the Stanton issue. After a long search he has found a weak, boozy general, Lorenzo Thomas, from Delaware, to accept the high office. All other men of reputation have, in one way or another, refused the heady offer. Stanton informs Thomas that "I want some time for reflection, I don't know whether I shall obey your orders or not." Docilely, Thomas leaves to await Stanton's wishes. Both Johnson and Stanton report their several moves to Congress. Charles Sumner sends his famous message to Stanton, "Stick," and most others support the sentiment. Stanton barricades himself in his office, preparing for a long siege. Later, over a bottle of whiskey, genial General Thomas is induced to abandon the scene of conflict.

22 FEBRUARY 1868

National Thaddeus Stevens drafts a formal resolution of impeachment. As spokesman for the House Reconstruction Committee he has decided Congress can now build a case against the president on the grounds that he has violated the Tenure of Office Act as well as besmirching Congress and behaving crudely toward the country's representatives. Thaddeus Stevens, a man whose "speech was with him at times a cat-o-nine-tails," who has taunted and tangled with his stubborn, rough diamond of a president, now takes on this last most bitter battle. "Old Thad" is frail, too sick to walk to the House. He is carried into Senate chambers each day on a wooden armchair. But his vitriolic eloquence is as harsh as ever. In a bitter bit of melodramatic business he offers his resolution on a Saturday because it is Washington's birthday. When the resolution is to be passed by Congress, that august body sets the clock back to February 22 so that the 13th President may be brought to trial on the birthday of the exemplary first president.

24 FEBRUARY 1868

National Ben Butler and Thaddeus Stevens are two of the seven chosen to steer impeachment proceedings. Johnson never appears at his trial. He is ably represented by Henry Stanberry, the former Attorney General, who has resigned to take on the precedent-making case. Grounds for impeachment will be the vague "high crimes and misdemeanors." Nine of the 11 articles of impeachment relate to the Tenure of Office Act, two to the general tone of Johnson's behavior toward Congress.

5 MARCH 1868
National The Senate chambers are arranged for the awesome trial. The Senate will sit as the jury; the House will act as the prosecutor; the Supreme Court, in the person of Chief Justice Chase, will be the judge. Scalpers get exaggerated amounts for gallery seats. Police roam the tense halls of the Capitol. All the unhappiness and disappointments relating to Reconstruction are now projected onto the stolid, well-meaning, though partisan, president and much malice is intertwined with the proceedings. People such as the dying Thaddeus Stevens, who believes blacks will soon be disenfranchised if something drastic is not done, add vehemence to the drama. Stevens warns that anyone voting to acquit will be "tortured on the gibbet of everlasting obloquy."

13 MARCH 1868
National The impeachment trial of President Andrew Johnson formally begins. It is a precedent-setting occasion, one upon which rests the future of the American form of government: will a balance of powers among the three phases of government be maintained or will the legislative absorb all initiatives and the government become essentially a parliamentary body?

16 MARCH 1868
National The strategic vote indicating whether the thrust against Johnson will succeed or fail is scheduled for this day. It is to be on Article XI, an omnibus article referring to Johnson's behavior toward

Andrew Johnson's Impeachment Trial.

THE IMPEACHMENT TRIAL OF
ANDREW JOHNSON

The trial of President Andrew Johnson had no precedent in history. The arraignment of the chief officer of the Republic was made by the representatives of Congress and held before the Chief Justices of the Supreme Court presiding in Senate chambers. The House, led by Thaddeus Stevens, acted as prosecutor. The Senate was the jury. The trial began on March 5, 1868, and ended for lack of evidence with the dismissal of all charges on May 26 of the same year.

The trial centered on the legality of the dismissal of Secretary of War Stanton under the Tenure of Office Act. The country was aghast at the spectacle of their President on trial, and enthralled by unfolding events. Inside the Capitol, proceedings went on with careful and cool deliberation. Eleven articles of impeachment were drawn up, nine relating to the Tenure of Office Act, and the other two relating to Johnson's uncouth behavior toward Congress. As the trial continued, pressure mounted for impeachment. Threats of retaliation and party excommunication were made. Tension within the sacred halls of Congress reached fever pitch. When the crucial vote was taken, seven Republicans had voted against impeachment. Honorable men, of strong principles, they knew what the consequences would be. They were denounced as traitors and found political life closed to them thereafter.

What went almost unnoticed in the fury of the times were the consequences threatening the form of the Republic. Had Johnson been impeached, the elegant experiment in the new form of government would have ended before it had scarcely begun. The American system of balance of power between the Judiciary, the Executive and the Legislative branches would have been irrevocably diluted. Congress would have faded into little more than a Parliament. Given the luxuriant mix of the American population, it is unlikely that a parliamentary system would have long survived.

Congress and also toward the Office of the President. Nine Democrats, three Johnson Conservatives, and six Radical Republicans are committed to acquittal. Johnson needs only one vote more to prevent a two-thirds majority out of the 54 senators required for impeachment. It is the vote of Edmund G. Ross, a young Radical Republican from Kansas, upon which Johnson's fate now rests. Ross is the only undecided senator left. "It hangs in an even balance," writes Garfield just before the voting takes place. Ross is warned that a vote for acquittal will spell political ruin. Twenty-four votes are recorded before Ross's name is called. Right up to the very last moment the pressure for impeachment has been so intense that Ross himself does not know whether he will have the courage to stand up for his principles. As he tells of that excruciating moment later, he "looked down into my open grave. Friendships, position, fortune, everything that makes life desirable . . . were about to be swept away by the breath of my mouth." In the almost unbearable tension his faltering voice is heard saying softly: "Not guilty." Everyone is aware that Ross's vote effectively ends the trial in Johnson's favor. Stevens laments that in the future no president would "be again removed by peaceful means." And for little over a century he remains correct in his prophecy. It is one of the essentially stabilizing factors in American government that its chief executive officer cannot be removed from office on the whims of a volatile and oddly mixed population. As for Ross, his prediction will turn out to be accurate: "Kansas repudiates you as she does all perjurers and skunks," telegraph his constituents, and he will never again be elected to national office.

APRIL 1868
Indian Affairs The treaty of Fort Laramie brings to an end the First Sioux War.

20-21 MAY 1868
National The Republican National Convention gathers in the bustling new cattle town, Chicago, to nominate the next candidate for president. The vastly popular General Grant succeeds on the first ballot. Putting Schuyler Colfax of Indiana on the ticket as Vice-President reflects the westward trend of North American population. At this time the Republicans are the popular party and Republican presidents will outnumber Democrats until the turn of the century.

28 MAY 1868
National The final vote for acquittal formally ends the impeachment trial of President Andrew Johnson.

1 JUNE 1868
National James Buchanan dies.

22 JUNE 1868
Reconstruction Arkansas meets Congressional standards for readmission to representation in Congress.

25 JUNE 1868
Reconstruction Alabama, Florida, Georgia, Louisiana, North Carolina and South Carolina meet Congressional standards and in the "Omnibus Act" are all readmitted to representation in Congress. This leaves Texas as the only state still to meet readmission standards. It will not do so until March 30, 1870, when it is readmitted.

Labor The 8-hour day for government employees is made federal law by an act of Congress. Some states have enacted 8-hour-day laws; however these have been relatively ineffectual. Although this new act covers only government employees, it will slowly have an effect on the working hours of the rest of industry.

4 JULY 1868
National The Democratic Convention meets in New York City to nominate Horatio Seymour from New York for President and the equally unprepossessing Francis P. Blair for Vice-President.

15 JULY 1868
International A national outpouring of love and admiration greets President Benito Juárez as he returns to Mexico to restore republican government after a five-year guerrilla war against Napoleon III and his representative Archduke Maximilian. Maximilian is captured and executed.

25 JULY 1868
National The Territory of Wyoming is created by act of Congress. Western lands are becoming increasingly populated and people begin to want the protection of a structured government.

28 JULY 1868
International A treaty between the United States and China is concluded, establishing policies of commerce and friendship. One of its principal purposes is to protect the right of both Chinese and whites to migrate freely from one country to another for trade or even settling. Monthly steamers will plow back and forth between San Francisco and Hong Kong making firmer commercial ties possible and making Chinese immigration easier. The man who has achieved this treaty is Anson Burlingame, a former ambassador to China. He had gained such a reputation for fairness and friendliness to the Chinese while serving as United States ambassador that upon the end of his term of duty, the Chinese have asked him to become their representative to the Western Powers. The first thing that Burlingame notices upon his arrival in San Francisco after accepting the offer is that the Chinese do not have a flag. He puts a dragon, the symbol of empire, on a field of yellow, the imperial color. He thus creates the Chinese Imperial flag.

Reconstruction Secretary of State Seward announces ratification of the Fourteenth Amendment. The Amendment grants full citizenship to blacks and all others born in the United States or naturalized (always excepting Indians). Representatives to Congress will be apportioned among the several states according to their respective populations. None can hold national office who, having previously taken an oath to uphold the Constitution, has subsequently fought against the United States. All public debts incurred by the United States are to be paid, but the government will not assume, nor allow states to assume, the debts of the insurrectionists.

SEPTEMBER 1868
Reconstruction Georgia expels blacks from its legislature. Military rule is instantly reimposed upon the state and earlier admission to representation in Congress is revoked. Ratification of the Fourteenth Amendment is now made obligatory before representation in Congress will be allowed.

21 OCTOBER 1868
Regional An earthquake strikes the city of San Francisco causing over $3,000,000 in damage.

3 NOVEMBER 1868
National It is a landslide victory for General Ulysses S. Grant and Schuyler Colfax. They win by 214 electoral votes over 80 for Seymour and Blair. How-

ever, Grant's popular majority is not so huge, only 309,594 out of 5,715,000 votes cast. This indicates that blacks, under the protection of Federal Troops, have cast a decisive 700,000 votes for the Republican party.

3 DECEMBER 1868
Reconstruction The trial for treason of Confederate President Jefferson Davis begins in Richmond, Virginia. The charge will be dropped on February 15, 1869 in consequence of Johnson's proclamation of general amnesty.

25 DECEMBER 1868
Reconstruction In one of his last acts in office, President Andrew Johnson proclaims general amnesty to all parties in the Rebellion. Whether it was a War of Secession, as the South believed, or a War for the Emancipation of Blacks, as many Northerners believed, it is now ended.

12 JANUARY 1869
National Sensing the changes taking place across the nation, and gearing up for oncoming elections, special interest groups begin to meet in national conventions to press for their rights. Particularly alarmed by the direction race relations are taking in North and South alike, blacks make their first attempt to organize on a national level. They form the National Convention of Colored Men and name their Civil War hero, Frederick Douglass, president.

19 JANUARY 1869
National The American Equal Rights Association meets in Washington DC. It is the beginning of an organized women's movement. Susan Brownell Anthony is elected president.

2 FEBRUARY 1869
Science/Technology James Oliver patents the chilled iron plow. This plow improved on John Deere's original round–bladed plow. After 12 years of searching, Oliver produces a tool made of a body of good iron with a hardened surface to which was fitted a cutting edge of tempered steel. The edge can be removed for sharpening. The blade will help make homesteading possible on the hard prairie, where temperatures range from 100 degrees in summer to 40 below in winter.

24 FEBRUARY 1869
Industry Under rising pressure from industrialists, the Morrill Tariff Act is enacted by Congress to protect U.S. manufacturers even though they are not in a particularly vulnerable position. More costly imports impose additional burdens on the poor.

27 FEBRUARY 1869
Reconstruction The Fifteenth Amendment is proposed by Congress. Increasingly worried about violence in the South, but reluctant to bring about more stable conditions by increasing army control, Congress resorts to another constitutional amendment.

These recent amendments will apply to all United States citizens, although they emerge out of the immediate needs of the black freedmen of the South. The Fifteenth Amendment is in two sections: "1. The right of citizens of the United States to vote shall not be denied or abridged by the United States or by any State on account of race, color or previous condition of servitude. 2. Congress shall have power to enforce this article by appropriate legislation." Despite an already active agitation on the part of women, the word "sex" is omitted.

4 MARCH 1869
National Ulysses S. Grant, the hero of the Civil War, is inaugurated as the 18th President of the United States. He is the second Republican to hold the office and will serve two terms.

10 MARCH 1869
Arts/Culture Charles W. Eliot is inaugurated President of Harvard University. By upgrading requirements and introducing the elective system and other reforms, Eliot will affect the entire structure of American higher education. Ultimately the curriculum emphasizes wider professional and business interests as well as the traditional classical and liberal arts studies.

18 MARCH 1869
Finance The Public Credit Act is adopted by Congress. The Act stipulates that payment of government bonds be made in gold. The so-called "Ohio Idea,"

Ulysses S. Grant.

ULYSSES S. GRANT, 1822-1885

U. S. Grant, with a name to match his country's, was like his country in many ways: trusting, excessive and commanding. His trust would lead him to put his faith in scoundrels; his excessiveness would lead to intemperate drinking on the one hand and on the other to a single-mindedness of purpose which would stand his country in good stead during the Civil War when he was in command of the Union army; his sense of command would lead him inexorably to the White House.

Grant was born to farmer folk and was fortunate to be appointed to West Point where he graduated 21st in a class of 39, although the lad with the non-intellectual bent was deemed the best horseman. He fought in the Mexican War but resigned his commission soon after. Already drinking heavily, he seemed destined for obscurity when the Civil War erupted. Reenlisting, he rose rapidly to the rank of Brigadier General. He showed himself to be a capable leader, his understanding of the immediate exigencies of single maneuvers blending well with his grasp of the overall picture. Grant had energy, daring and iron determination, although compassion was often lacking: his strategy of attrition sacrificed 72,000 of his own men in two months but it got him to Richmond. Ultimately it got him Lee's surrender.

In 1868 the Republicans chose as their presidential nominee the popular national hero, whose contact with politics was almost non-existent. Grant was not fitted for the awesome office of the President in which he served two terms. A singlemindedness permitted on the field of battle was inappropriate in the White House, and subtleties of national importance escaped him. The country needed a man of vision to help prevent southerners from sliding into the divisive doldrums of white supremacy, and the northerners from entering the technological age like a bunch of Barbary pirates. Grant, the embodiment of government by neglect, was not the man. Scandal among his most intimate associates tarnished his great career. He spent his last years trying to make money, characteristically lost in a friend's fraudulent venture. He wrote his *Personal Memoirs*, one of the best military biographies, to pay his debts. Finishing it four days before he died of cancer of the throat, it earned his wife half a million dollars.

which was a pro-inflationary plank in the Democratic platform, had backed the printing of more "greenbacks." Congress repudiates the paper–money solution, but does not resolve the currency argument—for instance, what to do with the $356,000,000 in still–circulating "greenbacks."

10 APRIL 1869
National The number of judges on the Supreme Court rises to nine from seven in the Judiciary Act as amended by Congress.
Indian Affairs The Board of Indian Commissioners is created by an Act of Congress. Although it is supposed to supervise all federal spending for tribes, the Board will be just another link in the long chain of official betrayal of the Indians.

10 MAY 1869
Transportation The first rail line to cross the continent is completed. As a Union Pacific engine bumps

"cowcatchers" with the engine from the Central Pacific Railroad, the news is flashed by telegraph and the nation celebrates from coast to coast. Aside from America's tapping of its own vast resources, a railroad network will be the single most influential factor in the emergence of the new industrial age.

15 MAY 1869
National Inspired by a patchwork quilt of political successes across the country in the form of voting rights and election to public office, women form the National Woman Suffrage Association. This group will press for voting rights at the federal level. Elizabeth Cady Stanton is elected president.

13 JULY 1869
Immigration Riots against the Chinese take place in San Francisco. Chinese laborers have come into the United States in increasing numbers. Not speaking the language, and willing to work extremely well for the lowest wages, the Chinese call forth great anger from competing groups of laborers. They are discriminated

THE FIRST SIOUX WAR

The war began innocuously enough. In 1866 the Army, seeking to build some forts along the Bozeman Trail, sent scouts to survey for sites. The Bozeman Trail was an important route to the gold fields of Virginia City in Montana Territory. It also ran through some of the very best hunting grounds of the Sioux Indians. The Sioux and their Cheyenne allies, led by Chief Red Cloud, decided to defend these rich and sacred hunting grounds. Nonetheless, the Army proceeded to build forts along the trail. Forts Kearney and Smith were put under siege by the Sioux. The Indians continued their ferocious attacks on trespassers. In 1866 Captain William Fetterman and 80 men were annihilated. The Army arranged for large convoys through the dangerous land. In 1868 Custer led a dishonorable charge against a peaceful Indian village. Chief Black Kettle and his unprepared men, women and children were barbarously massacred. Once again the Indians fought victoriously and in the Treaty of Fort Laramie of 1869 the Army finally agreed to abandon Forts Kearney, Reno and Smith. The government also agreed to furnish food and some other supplies to the Indians if they would remain on their reservation. Land east of the Bighorn and north of the Platte River was designated Indian land. As in all Indian victories, white reaction was bitter and intense. Gold fever and land fever clouded white judgement. Baiting Indians into open resistance, then relentlessly tracking them down, remained unofficial government policy. Indians were increasingly restricted to their reservations, but often these did not offer subsistence living. The Indians tended to stay put in winter, receiving what few supplies filtered to them through the sticky fingers of corrupt Indian agents. In early summer their nomad instincts and hunting patterns reasserted themselves and brought the Indians into conflict with the Army, settlers and trespassers once again. The whites, as a rule, echoed General Sheridan's sentiments: "The only good Indian is a dead Indian." If, like General George Crook, an army man began to deal fairly, he could be dismissed overnight. The Treaty of Fort Laramie brought an end to the First Sioux War, but not an end to genocidal skirmishes.

FORGING A NATION 1866-1900

against in their social life, beaten up at work and often involved in bloody riots such as this one in San Francisco.

1 SEPTEMBER 1869
National Riding a rising tide of public opinion, the National Temperance Convention meets in Chicago to form the Prohibition Party.

6 SEPTEMBER 1869
Industry In one of the worst of a continuing series of industrial disasters, 108 miners are killed in a coal mine accident in Avondale, Pennsylvania. The miners all die by suffocation.

24 SEPTEMBER 1869
Finance This day will become known as Black Friday. Despite President Grant's refusal to cooperate with stock manipulators Jay Gould and James Fisk, Jr., they spread the word that he will prevent the sale of government gold. Grant himself has been led to believe the sale would harm farmers and small businessmen. Wining and dining him, Gould and Fisk reinforce him in this idea. The price of gold rises to panic-causing heights as the gold necessary for day-

to-day business operation goes out of the reach of small merchants. Slow-thinking Grant finally realizes the disastrous nature of the scheme and belatedly orders release of $4,000,000 in gold. This offsets a cornering of the market, and bullion plunges from 162 to 135. Small and large investors are caught in the aftermath of the ruinous adventure, and a tarnished Grant emerges as a crony of crooks.

10 DECEMBER 1869
National In keeping with the ever–greater freedom allowed the pioneer women of the West, Wyoming Territory passes the first law in the United States giving women the right to vote.

22 DECEMBER 1869
Reconstruction Because of the dismissal of blacks from its State Legislature, Georgia has been denied representation in Congress. Georgia has become emboldened by its previous readmission to Congress and once freed of iron federal control has reasserted its genuine social attitudes by denying blacks a place in state politics. Congress has responded by reintroducing military rule, forbidding admission to Congress, and now insists that Georgia must ratify the Fifteenth Amendment before it will be accepted to full state-

Central Pacific Railroad construction camp.

THE FIRST TRANSCONTINENTAL RAILWAY

Finally the nation turned its concentrated gaze away from the South and began to look longer and farther into the West. And 1869 gave them something to celebrate: the completion of the first transcontinental rail line. The costs of the project had been staggering. The Federal Government agreed to pay $16,000 per mile across the 300 ice- and snow–bound miles that chopped through the Rocky Mountain heights. In addition, for each mile built, the two rail companies, the Central Pacific and the Union Pacific, received 12,800 acres of choice public land on each side of the tracks; 25,000,000 acres were placed in the hands of the promoters. Not content, the directors of both corporations made extra millions by setting up their own contracting companies and awarding themselves the lucrative subcontracts. It was estimated later, when the dishonorable proceedings surfaced in the Credit Mobilier Scandal, that Oakes Ames and his crew made off with close to $73,000,000 for $50,000,000 worth of work. Leland Stanford's Central Pacific worked eastward and Oakes Ames' Union Pacific moved westward. Each worked with crews of 10,000 men, the Central Pacific using primarily low-wage, tea-drinking and incredibly hard-working Chinese laborers. One spectacular day they were able to construct ten miles of track. Five hundred miles snaked over an altitude of 5000 feet and 200 miles crawled over 6500 feet. Ten spikes held each rail, 400 rails covered a mile. Each mile required 40 cars to carry 400 tons of rail, timber, food and fuel. The Central Pacific brought its materials, including locomotives, 12,000 miles on the swift if short-lived Clipper ships, by way of Cape Horn.

Once the project was well underway, the Central Pacific built 690 mountainous miles and the Union Pacific an easier 1085. The project caught the imagination of the country. On May 10, 1869 a glittering crowd of dignitaries, laborers and hangers-on gathered at Promontory Point in Utah to celebrate the laying of the last tie. Five states sent symbolic gold and silver spikes to be knocked in by a silver hammer made for the occasion. Two locomotives faced each other across the last tie. Western Union eagerly kept its lines open. After two inglorious swipes at the last golden spike, someone unknown to history hammered it in. The two engines moved together and gently bumped cowcatchers. The news had been tapped from coast to coast and the nation was already celebrating. "U.S. annexed," claimed a San Francisco paper.

hood. Georgia's behavior points to the true nature of Southern Reconstruction. It is only while Federal Troops keep control of the situation that the white population accepts black participation on a somewhat equal level. There is not sufficient tolerance to preserve an interracial society once troops are withdrawn.

4 JANUARY 1870

Labor A telegraph operators' strike spreads throughout the country. Although the union movement has grown slowly, considering the conditions under which workers are forced to labor, membership has reached 300,000 now and people are becoming aware that a single person is not on equal footing with the million–dollar industries they might like to bargain with.

10 JANUARY 1870

Industry The Standard Oil Company of Ohio is in-

corporated in Cleveland. It is the beginning of the Rockefellers' great oil ventures. With a million dollars in capital, the Rockefellers organize two refineries in Cleveland and a sales force in New York City.

26 JANUARY 1870

Reconstruction Virginia is granted readmission to the Union, and thus to representation in Congress, after accepting the Fifteenth Amendment.

7 FEBRUARY 1870

Finance The Supreme Court, in *Hepburn v. Griswold,* decides that the Legal Tender Act cannot be applied retroactively. Thus debts contracted prior to adoption of the acts of 1862 and 1863 cannot be redeemed by treasury notes issued under the acts.

9 FEBRUARY 1870

National The first National Weather Bureau is established by Act of Congress. It is designated as part of

INVENTIONS, 1865-1869

In the first five years after the Civil War some basic innovations shifted the country out of a way of life which had lasted almost from the beginning of time and made necessary an entirely new gathering of social forces. The discovery of the uses of oil and the creation of a pipeline system started things off. Steel rails made railroads a viable transport system which contributed to revolutionary shifts in travel and merchandising. George Westinghouse's air brake and George M. Pullman's luxury sleeping cars made travel safer and more comfortable. William Davis patented and built a refrigerator car for delivery of fish and fruit, though its development fell to Gustavus F. Swift who began use on a large scale to ship dressed beef out of Chicago. The principle was simple enough: cold air blown across ice and circulated throughout the car. Small merchants along the railroad tracks were put out of business, and fortunes were made by the big shippers. Andrew S. Hallidie invented an underground continuous cable and mechanical gripper. It made electric trains and cable cars possible in hilly cities such as San Francisco. Indeed, San Francisco will be the first to put the device into operation in 1873. Meantime, in 1866, across the Atlantic a cable was laid between England and the United States, bringing the two countries closer. I.W. McGaffey was first to apply the suction principle in his mundane but gratefully received vacuum cleaner. Although not immediately put to any great use, the Hyatt brothers of Albany, N.Y. patented the celluloid process. The brothers also patented the less revolutionary, but nonetheless welcome, composition billiard ball, which earned a $10,000 prize and meant the game need no longer be played with ivory balls. And Thomas A. Edison invented the electric voting machine, although it was not used until 1892 because, as a politician kindly explained, it interfered with the patronage system. More importantly, John Oliver's chilled steel plow helped settle the prairie, and L.H. Wheeler's windmill modifications took advantage of the mindnumbing winds of the great plains to make homesteading possible in areas otherwise uninhabitable. Last but not least, the left-handed Christopher L. Sholes provided the right-handed world with a typewriter. His pattern of lettering has remained essentially unshakeable ever since.

the Signal Corps. On July 1, 1891 it will be transferred to the Agriculture Department; on June 30, 1940 it will be merged into the Commerce Department.

12 FEBRUARY 1870

Regional Utah Territory, following Wyoming's lead, grants full suffrage to women. Women in the West have a great deal more freedom than had been granted to those in the East. Out in the prairies and mountains of the new frontier women can hold office, and jobs once open only to men are increasingly available to women. Land-grant colleges begin to open their doors to women and even sports such as fishing attract the newly liberated sex.

23 FEBRUARY 1870

Reconstruction Mississippi is granted readmission to Union and representation in Congress after accepting congressional directives including the Fifteenth Amendment. The State will grow increasingly violent, chalking up 63 black murders in two months and giving impetus to Benjamin Butler's Force Act of 1871 which seeks to curb such violence with legislation.

25 FEBRUARY 1870

Black Experience Hiram R. Revels, the first black to be elected to the U.S. Senate, takes his seat. Revels is a black moderate, although his maiden speech in Congress is a plea to block admission of Georgia until proper safeguards for blacks have been put into effect. Revels is a free black, a minister of the African Methodist Episcopal Church. He studied at a Quaker Seminary and graduated from Knox College. He travelled the midwest and joined the Union Army in 1864. Later he became one of the thousands of service-oriented "carpetbaggers" who returned to help the freedmen. Settling in Natchez, Mississippi, he soon found his way into the political stream. Rising swiftly, he is appointed to a vacant Senate seat. Ironically, Revels is appointed to the unexpired term of Jefferson Davis. When he walks into Congress on this fateful Friday afternoon the audience in the galleries stands up and cheers.

30 MARCH 1870

National Secretary of State Hamilton Fish proclaims ratification of the Fifteenth Amendment which guarantees suffrage to all citizens born or naturalized in the U.S.

Reconstruction Texas is readmitted to union after having hurdled all congressional obstacles.

25-27 MAY 1870

International The Anti-British Irish group called the Fenians continue their ineffectual raids across the Canadian border despite careful watch by U.S. and Canadian authorities. The leaders of the adventure are jailed but when released are given a great parade in New York City. The terrorist organization continues to be regarded as heroes by the Irish immigrant populations on the East coast of the United States.

31 MAY 1870

Reconstruction The Ku Klux Klan Act of 1870, also called the Enforcement Act, is adopted by Congress. Congress seeks to enforce the Fifteenth Amendment in a last-ditch effort to stem mounting backlash from newly enfranchised southern whites. Whites have been turning on the blacks who have been running governments for their own benefit, and by using terrorist tactics are getting the reins of government

---

BENJAMIN BUTLER, 1818-1893

Benjamin Butler was a general in the Civil War and collided roughly with the Southern rebels, but he came into his own during the days of Reconstruction. He was a pragmatic politician, more interested in the spoils of office than in high-flying ideals. Nevertheless he attached himself to the radical Republicans as they attempted to rebuild the wounded nation, and was a staunch defender of black civil rights all the way down to the final sellout in 1877. Butler, with Charles Sumner and Thaddeus Stevens, helped push through much Reconstruction legislation.

Butler began his career as a lawyer in Massachusetts. Perhaps characteristically, he stood out as a criminal lawyer. He rose to the rank of general in the war, during which he served as Governor of New Orleans. There he won the undying enmity of the South with his so-called "woman order" which declared that if a woman should insult a Union soldier—which they were wont to do with great vehemence—she would henceforth be treated as "a woman of the town plying her vocation." Butler was nicknamed "The Beast" for this bit of hyperbole, but he never erased his antagonism for the Bourbon South from his heart. Butler tended to play on people's emotions: once when pushing through one of the last Reconstruction bills, the Ku Klux Klan Act, he brought a bloody shirt into Congress; it was one purporting to be from a carpetbagger who had been unjustly whipped. "Waving the bloody shirt" became a famous figure of speech after that, to denote the kind of macabre emotionalism for which Butler was duly famous. Voters loved his shrewd, inflammatory rhetoric. With Thaddeus Stevens he led the unsuccessful battle to impeach President Andrew Johnson. Later he became the spokesman in the House for President Grant, a person sympathetic to the essentially practical politician. When Butler attached himself to men of high ideals he helped infuse their battles with fire and iron. Left to his own devices, he tended to choose programs of a dubious nature. He was a fighter, but unless the times handed him one, he was a fighter without a cause.

---

back into their own hands. Under pressure from Senator Ben Butler, who cannot forget his wartime stay in the South, Congress enacts legislation which authorizes a person to sue should he be deprived of his rights by another.

15 JUNE 1870

International President Grant, in his usual blunt manner, forces the resignation of his Attorney General Ebenezer R. Hoar. It is a disgraceful and ineffectual effort to garner votes for Grant's scheme to annex the Dominican Republic. Southerner Amos T. Akerman of Georgia replaces Hoar.

KU KLUX KLAN

As Southern society struggled to integrate blacks into its wobbly structures, diehard whites banded together in secret societies. They called themselves by childishly romantic names: Knights of the White Camellia, Society of the White Rose. The most durable and the most chilling was the Ku Klux Klan.

The Klan was started in Pulaski, Tennessee in 1866 by six ex-Confederate soldiers wishing to form a secret social group. Searching for a fraternity-like three-letter name, they struck upon the word *kyklos*, Greek for "circle." Liking the sound, they added Klan for alliterative purposes and the KKK was born. Soon dens and klaverns bubbled up, and in a grand meeting in Nashville in 1869 the Invisible Empire of the South was formally established, complete with Grand Wizard, and lesser officers known as Grand Dragon, Fury, Titan, Hydra, Nighthawk. Their uniform was the ludicrous all-hiding sheet.

At first the members were fairly restrained. They tended to ride around in sheets scaring the superstitious and drawing a certain amount of laughter from otherwise puzzled citizens. But intimidation proceeded under the cloak of anonymity and soon, emboldened, their acts became ever more vicious. In fact, members behaved so despicably that in 1869 its own officers formally disbanded the group. However, nothing could now stop the terrifying troops. Night rides turned to numbing horror: whippings, mutilations, burnings, lynchings. The North was revolted and Congress attempted to legislate against secret societies, but the Ku Klux Klan Acts of 1870 and 1871 had no teeth and were later declared unconstitutional.

As the withdrawal of Federal Troops proceeded, the Klan stepped up its terrorism unopposed. By the end of Reconstruction in 1877 the Klan had enforced its will. Because of the vicious policing by the Ku Klux Klan it would be almost a century before the South would recover from its wound.

---

22 JUNE 1870

National Congress establishes the Department of Justice, thus acknowledging growing responsibilities of the Attorney General.

Finance Special Commissioner of Revenue David A. Wells meets with the fate accorded all Grant's more honorable associates, being dismissed from office for advocating needed reforms.

30 JUNE 1870

International In a tie vote of 28 to 28 the Senate refuses to approve Hamilton Fish's treaty of annexation of the Dominican Republic submitted by Grant on January 10. The treaty had originally been written by Orville Babcock, Grant's private secretary. To an astonished Foreign Relations Committee Grant explained: "Babcock has returned, as you see, and has brought a treaty of annexation. I suppose it is not formal, as he has no diplomatic powers; but we can easily cure that." Grant never forgave Charles Sumner, the chairman of the Foreign Relations Committee, for leading the opposition to annexation.

8 JULY 1870

International The Senate consents to signing of the United States and Great Britain's treaty for the suppression of the African slave trade, still a lucrative business worldwide.

14 JULY 1870

National The Internal Revenue and Tariff Act of 1870 is adopted by Congress. Rates are lowered and duties removed from only a few items. Excise taxes are eliminated. Overall it is a victory for a protectionist Congress under pressure from industrialists. High tariff walls are a great disappointment to European manufacturers.

International Clarifying the Monroe Doctrine as it is to be applied now and in the future, Secretary of State Hamilton Fish declares that territory in the Western Hemisphere belonging to a European power cannot be handed over to a second European power but must be set free with no strings attached.

24 JULY 1870

Transportation The first railroad car to have traveled from the Pacific coast arrives in New York.

1 AUGUST 1870

Regional Women use their voté for the first time in the United States in an election in Utah territory.

4 AUGUST 1870

Reconstruction As if playing a game of follow the leader, Virginia, Tennessee, Texas and Mississippi are coerced by white supremacists back into Democratic governments. Democrats now regain control of the North Carolina legislature. Now that northern control is being relinquished, southerners will lose no time in revenging themselves on the "carpetbaggers" and the "scalawags," both black and white, who have been in control of governments under federal protection. All pretense of conforming to the Thirteenth, Fourteenth or Fifteenth Amendments begins to peel away, and the politics of terror supplants civil rights as the custom of the South. There is little fight left in Congress for Reconstruction. The great crusader Thaddeus Stevens is dead. Almost alone, bitter Ben Butler, who has never forgotten his days as Governor of New Orleans during the war, carries the banner of Reconstruction with his Ku Klux Klan Bill designed to enforce the Fifteenth Amendment.

3 OCTOBER 1870

National Secretary of the Interior Jacob D. Cox, in advocating restraint in the use of the nation's natural resources, runs afoul of industry's rapacious "robber barons." Cox is pressured to resign by a Congress paid well to cater to the whims of industrial giants.

4 OCTOBER 1870

National The first solicitor General of the U.S. is appointed by President Grant. He is Benjamin H. Bristow.

12 OCTOBER 1870

National General Robert E. Lee, beloved Com-

PRESIDENT GRANT'S POLITICS OF CEREMONY, LOYALTY AND SCANDAL

Scandals and intrigues besmirched the beloved if slow-witted general, although Grant himself did not seem to have profited especially from the mindboggling shennanigans. His simple soldier's sense of personal loyalty blinded him to the higher need for loyalty to one's country required in managing affairs of state. Many of Grant's personal friends were scoundrels, and most of his staff were. Still, Grant threw the protective mantle of the presidency around each one.

Under the influence of Radical Republicans who thought the Federal legislature should govern the country, Grant viewed his office as largely ceremonial, and did not propose to originate policies, but rather to carry out the will of Congress. Even a year earlier, when men of greater stature still peopled Congress, this might have been a reasonable tack to take. Now, however, Congress was in the hands of "pragmatic" politicians, those interested in the spoils of office and who saw profit in a president open to any suggestion.

In the term of Grant's eight years, the corruption that whirled around the Executive Office astonished the nation. Close associates, family and friends were all embroiled in unsavory activities. His Vice-President, Schuyler Colfax, was ruined by the Credit Mobilier bribery scandal. He stubbornly reappointed his brother-in-law Casey to a second term as Collector of Customs after being informed of outrageous misconduct in office. His private secretary, Orville Babcock, had a finger in almost every scurrilous scheme in Washington.

Grant was to watch without noticeable anguish the careful dismantling of all Reconstruction policies and take no action as a mesh of white supremacy laws was laid over the South. The groundwork for development of some important constitutional advances had been laid in the early days of Reconstruction, but because of his policy of benign neglect nothing came of these ideas for almost another century.

In a farewell speech to Congress, Grant, in his own defense, explained: "It was my fortune, or misfortune, to be called to the office of Chief Executive without any previous political training. Under such circumstances, it is but reasonable to suppose that errors of judgement must have occurred."

mander in Chief of the Confederate Army, dies at Lexington, Virginia. He is 63.

8 NOVEMBER 1870
Reconstruction Missouri follows North Carolina's lead in dismantling Reconstruction; in a coalition of liberal Republicans and Democrats, the State elects its own anti-Radical Republican Governor, Benjamin G. Brown.

5 DECEMBER 1870
National The Forty-first Congress convenes with every state represented. Not since 1860 have all the states gathered at the Capitol.

21 FEBRUARY 1871
Regional A territorial form of government is tried in the District of Columbia. It is not successful and will

be changed when the present system is adopted in 1878.

28 FEBRUARY 1871
Reconstruction Congress enacts a law which provides for federal supervision of elections in any city over 20,000 population. This law will be put into operation in the South to help enforce the Fifteenth Amendment.

3 MARCH 1871
National President Grant reluctantly gets around to forming a Civil Service Commission. It is mostly cosmetic to appeal to voters without seriously cutting into the patronage system of government. However the federal bureaucracy is growing by leaps and bounds and a merit system is becoming ever more desirable. Reformers clamor for a more just system, but President Grant does not like to tamper with a system which gives so much comfort to his friends.

Indian Affairs The Indian Appropriation Act of 1871 is accepted by Congress. George Washington had initiated a policy toward the Indian tribes which recognized them as "distinct, independent, political communities," and "domestic dependent nations." Thus essentially they were to be regarded somewhat as States, with the Federal Government having ultimate sovereignty. The Indian Appropriation Act reverses this policy. Tribes will no longer be regarded as independent entities with treaty-making powers; rather, Indians are declared wards of the State. With an eye on elections, Grant devises an astonishing Peace Policy:

A COW TOWN AND ITS MARSHAL

Abilene, Kansas, was the first and the wildest of the legendary Wild West towns. It boasted saloons, brothels and gambling joints, although for sleeping and eating, cowboys had to retire, sometimes in the hundreds, to their chuckwagons. The town attracted the most unsavory elements of society to prey on the transient cowpokes ready for a wild time after their long, extremely dangerous journeys up the Chisolm Trail from Texas. Marshalls were appointed to control the volatile situation and the most famous marshall of that first cowtown of the West was "Wild Bill" Hickok. Hickok had been a "bad man" himself, having chalked up some 43 killings before he threw in with the law. The dandy of the prairie shot only two people while marshall of Abilene, one of them a friend of his, a policeman. Hickok was a snappy dresser, a former Union Army scout and a gambler. He used two pearl-handled pistols and was known as the fastest draw in the West. He preferred to keep a firm hand on his town from the round table in the gambling den. He held his office for eight months at $150 per month but killing the policeman discouraged the Abilene townsfolk, who felt that he had been too quick on the draw. They also felt that they had had enough of cattle. After replacing Hickok, they put an ad in the newspaper requesting that cattlemen no longer use Abilene as their destination point for shipping to eastern markets. In 1872 the Texas drovers headed for Wichita and Ellsworth. Abilene took the sterner road to homesteading and respectability.

whole reservations are divided among a number of squabbling religious groups in an incongruous move to police, pacify and educate the prosecuted nomads. Attempts to clean up corrupt Indian agencies meet with defeat. Two years later, under President Hayes, the religious groups will be ousted and the lucrative Indian agencies and trading posts will sink back into the spoils system of government.

9 MARCH 1871

National Charles Sumner is forced off the Foreign Relations Committee because of Grant's fury over his reluctance to back annexation of the Dominican Republic.

7 APRIL 1871

Transportation In the Illinois Railroad Act, a commission is set up with powers to fix maximum rates on railroad and warehouse use; it also forbids all discrimination that favors giant corporations over small businesses. These early and just attempts to regulate the giant interstate corporations now spreading like octopi across the nation will in 1886 be thwarted by an odd interpretation of the Fourteenth Amendment. In a Supreme Court decision the Court will rule that a corporation is a person under the meaning of the amendment and therefore cannot be deprived of property, meaning in this case profits, except by due process. This decision will be applied against states, curtailing their regulatory powers. It will be an austere decision since there is yet no national regulatory body to police enormous industries such as railroads, oil, steel and coal.

20 APRIL 1871

Reconstruction The Ku Klux Klan Act of 1871 is pushed through a torpid Congress by the indefatigable Ben Butler. Its purpose is to provide appropriate legislation to support and enforce the Fourteenth Amendment. The Act authorizes the President to suspend writ of *habeas corpus* and to enforce the Fourteenth Amendment by the use of Federal Troops. By 1877, when the last Federal Troops are removed from southern soil, the Fourteenth Amendment will become virtually inoperative.

1 MAY 1871

National The Supreme Court reverses an earlier decision and in *Knox v. Lee* declares the Legal Tender Act constitutional. In 1862 when the United States government was in need of credit it passed the Legal Tender Act which authorized $450,000,000 in treasury notes. These became known as "greenbacks" and were legal tender for all transactions except import duties and interest on the public debt. On February 7, 1870 in *Hepburn v. Griswold* the Supreme Court, with only seven members, declared the Act unconstitutional; the same day the decision is rendered, Grant, with uncharacteristic speed, names two new justices to the Court's empty seats. Four days later the Court agrees to reargue the case. Whether this is a deliberate case of "packing the court" is uncertain,

but the original decision is reversed and the Act is now declared constitutional. The first decision was made on grounds that congressional powers had been exceeded and creditors deprived of property without due process. The second decision is grounded in the constitutional powers granted to Congress to coin money and wage war. The 1871 Supreme Court decision finds that Congress may impair contracts, but the states cannot. Thus payment of debts contracted before 1862 can be made in greenbacks, now designated as fully legal tender. Greenbacks are inflationary and thus seem desirable to creditors; they tend to fluctuate and do not always reflect their face value.

MAY 1871

International The United States attempts to get a favorable treaty with strategic Korea by using force. Naval vessels bombard and destroy five Korean forts but retire emptyhanded.

8 MAY 1871

International The Treaty of Washington is formalized between the United States and Great Britain. The Treaty provides for a joint commission to settle fishing and boundary disputes. Arbitration will also be used to settle outstanding claims of many millions of dollars against Great Britain for the damage inflicted upon United States shipping by British vessels during the Civil War; five arbitrators are appointed by Brazil, Great Britain, Italy, Switzerland and the United States. The question of San Juan Island off the coast of Washington and British Columbia is to be adjudicated by the German Emperor.

24 MAY 1871

International The Senate consents to the provisions of the Treaty of Washington, which have been worked out by the able Secretary of State Hamilton Fish.

8 JULY 1871

Regional William "Boss" Tweed is exposed in a series of articles published in the *New York Times*. Tweed will be brought to trial and held responsible for taking up to $200,000,000 in fraudulent contracts, kickbacks, false vouchers and other corrupt practices which have brought New York City to the verge of bankruptcy in six short years. Jay Gould, of the Black Friday 1869 gold scandal, is one of the signatories to Tweed's million dollar bail bond.

2 OCTOBER 1871

Regional Stepping up pressure on the Mormons and their "special institution," the Federal Government arrests leader Brigham Young for practicing polygamy.

8 OCTOBER 1871

Regional Fire almost obliterates Chicago. Damage is estimated at $196,000,000; 250 people are killed in the blaze; 98,000 persons are made homeless; and 17,450 buildings are consumed. Among precious objects destroyed is the original of Lincoln's Emancipation Proclamation. Due to the same conditions of

FORGING A NATION 1866-1900

WILLIAM "BOSS" TWEED, 1823-1878

William Tweed was chief of the Department of Public Works for New York City but his popular title of "Boss" really described his role in history. He was an example of a new breed of political leader that emerged during the last third of the 19th century to take advantage of the soul-destroying conditions in the big cities. Cities had to cope with an influx of immigrants by the thousands unprepared for a new life and language; with the hard core unemployed beginning to be accepted as a permanent part of an industrial society; with the disappointed and broken coming back from their adventures in the arid plains and unproductive mines of the West; with the workers in factories and mills where conditions were swiftly degenerating into something close to slavery; and finally with the ruthless thieves and grafters that perennially prey on the hopeless. The "Bosses" created a political machine to deal with the misery, and they ruled with a firm hand. In return for asking no questions, they arranged for small but important favors to be given to their desperate constituents.

Tweed himself had been a mechanic before his shrewd machinations brought him to power. With a small gang of friends he maneuvered some favorable legislation through a compliant New York State legislature. The result: money poured into the City of New York's treasury. Then through a combination of fraudulent contracts, kickbacks, false vouchers and other corrupt practices, the "Tweed Ring" managed to bring the city to the verge of bankruptcy within the short span of six years. The "Ring" ultimately was exposed by a dissatisfied associate and Tweed was apprehended, convicted and sent to jail for 12 years. Tweed was the only one of the "Ring" tried and convicted. The others all fled the country with their ill-gotten gains. Allowed to escape, Tweed made his way to Cuba and from there to Spain. In 1876 he was sent back to the States where he related the extraordinary procedures he had used to milk the city. He expected immunity in return for the confession. Instead he was returned to jail where he died April 12, 1878.

Tweed was a man of his time, a time laced with greed and corruption. It had seemed, for a while, that Tweed, in his single-minded attachment to graft, was invulnerable. As it turned out he was merely one of the more flamboyantly acquisitive "bosses" of the age.

---

prevailing drought, in one of the least publicized and most devastating fires on record, the community of Peshtigo, in northern Wisconsin, is engulfed in flames. Six hundred people die and over 2000 square miles of virgin forest are turned to charcoal and ashes.

24 OCTOBER 1871
Regional Race riots erupt in Los Angeles, California, against the Chinese. Fifteen laborers are lynched in the ongoing violence which has begun to characterize opposition to Oriental immigration. Aside from vicious racial antipathy, there is also the fact that the Chinese work harder, better and longer for less money than anyone else. They are also sober and clean.

2 FEBRUARY 1872
National By an act of Congress, beginning in 1876 congressional elections will be synchronized to fall on the first Tuesday after the first Monday in November.

17 FEBRUARY 1872
International The Senate refuses to ratify a treaty with the Samoan Islands which would give the United

---

THE CHICAGO FIRE

Purportedly it was Mrs. O'Leary who lived on De Koven Street who milked that restless cow in the fateful early morning of October 8, 1871 and started one of the most devastating fires any city ever had. Like her fellow citizens, she was not taking any special precautions against the perilous conditions brought on by a year-long drought. She brought a lighted kerosene lamp with her into the tinder-dry barn. The uneasy cow kicked over the lamp, it seems, and so began the monstrous blaze. Within minutes it had licked its way through the wooden barn. Soon a strong west wind fanned it farther and the parched city was engulfed in a tidal wave of incandescent all-consuming destruction. In a day and a night it ate its way through 2124 acres of property, reducing 17,450 buildings to ashes or calcined material, caused damage in the realm of $196,000,000, killed 250 people and left 98,500 homeless. The city was bailed out by state loans and the homeless refugees were helped by over $3,000,000 in contributions which poured in from all over the world. It was a measure of the vigor of Chicago that it took almost no time to recover and, like the legendary Phoenix, grow anew and stronger from the ashes.

States the right to install a naval coaling station on Pago Pago and at the same time become "protector" of Samoa. The Senate is unwilling to face up to an emerging imperialism in America's foreign policy. Not until the 1880s, when James G. Blaine becomes Secretary of State, is the country steered into this natural big-power role.

22 FEBRUARY 1872
National Meeting in Columbus, Ohio, the National Labor Convention nominates David Davis of Illinois for President and Joel Parker of New Jersey for Vice-President. Labor is beginning to try its strength in the political arena in an effort to restrain the repressive activities of big business. The Prohibition Party convenes to begin its campaign for country-wide attention. The party nominates James Black of Pennsylvania for President.

1 MARCH 1872
Conservation Pressed by a growing agitation for conservation of the badly exploited natural resources of the country, Congress begins to reverse its wholesale giveaway programs and creates Yellowstone Park as a public preserve in Wyoming.

1 MAY 1872
National The Liberal Republicans, splintering off from the Radical Republicans who have dominated the party since the war, meet in Cincinnati to nominate a candidate who might derail Grant from a second term. The leaders are Charles Sumner, Carl Schurz, Gideon

Welles, E. L. Godkin, Charles Francis Adams and Horace Greeley, the editor of the New York *Tribune*. Incongruously, the convention chooses Greeley as its standard–bearer. It is an ill–advised choice, and not all members of the new party are happy about it. Carl Schurz, who has been chairman of the convention, leaves to organize a third Republican Party, splintering off from the splinter liberals to nominate an even less likely candidate, William S. Groesbeck, for President.

22 MAY 1872

Reconstruction The Amnesty Act is adopted by Congress. Under the Fourteenth Amendment many Southerners have been forbidden to hold elective office. This Act will remove restrictions from all but a few hundred former Confederate leaders.

23 MAY 1872

National The Workingmen's national convention meeting in New York throws its votes as a block be-

---

THE AMERICAN COWBOY

The heyday of the American Cowboy lay between 1867 and 1887 when the beef cattle industry became big business. One rail line linked East with West and the cowboy emerged as the unlikely knight of the prairie.

From 1769 to 1848 aristocratic Spanish families sent their second sons to be missionaries in the New World. They settled in lush Spanish California, where, contrary to Spanish law, they began to teach their superb horsemanship to their peons, in order to put them to guarding huge herds of cattle. As eastern markets increased their demand for hides and tallow, cattle grew in value. Soon cattle ranches spread across into U.S. territory and American boys quickly learned to handle the animals with skill and daring.

A cowboy's tightfitting shirt and trousers, floppy black vest and wide-brimmed hat harked back to the Spanish grandee. Much cowboy jargon did, too. Rodeo originally meant the roundup. Chaps came from *chaparreras*, the leather protection against the chaparral bush; lariat, from *la reata*, a twisted rawhide rope; *dar la vuelta* became "dally," to stop an animal by wrapping a rope around its horns.

On the arduous drives to the raucous railroad towns of booming Kansas, the cowboy stolidly faced searing desert heat, bruising hail, Indian raids, rattlers, rustlers, hunger, thirst and the terrifying stampede. For this he usually received a lowly 25 dollars a month. It took two months' pay to buy a pair of cowboy boots. He also cared for ranches sometimes larger than many eastern states, fattening indestructible Texas longhorns on the green gold of the prairies, all the while living a life of dignified loneliness. The cowboy became a most engaging folk hero. His legend spawned whole industries of exhibitions and rodeos, of books, magazines, photographs, firearms, fashions and songs.

Railroads finally crisscrossed the West and the great demand for the cowboy was over. He did not disappear, however. Righteously rowdy, bowlegged and lovelorn, independent and eminently able, he walked out of the austere landscape of prairie and plain into the imagination of the world.

---

hind Grant for a second term.

5–6 JUNE 1872

National The Republican National Convention is still dominated by Radical Republicans as it meets in Philadelphia, Pennsylvania. Present are the first black delegates to a presidential convention. Three of their number give speeches endorsing President Grant, who is elected on the first ballot. Grant could boast that his country, under his hands–off policies, is in good shape: he has reduced the national debt; gold is at 114; the Treaty of Washington bodes fair to settle some long–standing injustices which have been rankling many citizens; some strong anti–Ku Klux Klan legislation has been enacted; Grant has declared a Peace Policy toward the Indians; and receipts from the usually corrupt Post Office have sbstantially increased. If one does not look too closely into most of these boasts, it appears to be a strong position to campaign from. Besides which, no other man can compete with the affectionate hold Grant has on the nation. Scandals may swirl around him like tornadoes, but the beloved old soldier manages to remain unscathed by the worst of them.

6 JUNE 1872

National With an eye on elections, Grant's administration makes some token reductions in duties by declaring a ten percent cut on all major imported items.

10 JUNE 1872

Reconstruction Declaring that it is time for Southern Republicans, meaning blacks, to stand on their own feet, Liberal Republicans effect the end of the Freedmen's Bureau. The nation is becoming tired of bailing out a situation which must be kept in place with bayonets and one which promises no change. It is a sad day for blacks and another milestone in the dismantling of Reconstruction.

9 JULY 1872

National The Democratic Party meets in Baltimore, Maryland, and nominates Horace Greeley for President, thereby sowing the seeds of its own defeat in November. Greeley is an inauspicious choice because he has long been vociferously opposed to Democratic policies. An eloquent supporter of eccentric causes, Greeley has made enemies in most political places. The Democrats decide to cash in on his national reputation. In any case they have no candidate who could bring disparate factions of the party together nor one of the stature to challenge war hero Grant.

4 SEPTEMBER 1872

National The Credit Mobilier scandal erupts in the press. During the building of the cross–continental railway, which was done with considerable government money, Massachussetts Representative Oakes Ames and other directors of the Union Pacific Railroad formed a company and then awarded themselves the rich construction contracts. During the life of the company, named Credit Mobilier of America, mil-

FORGING A NATION 1866-1900

Blacks are elected to Congress for the first time.

lions of dollars were siphoned into the pockets of the directors and their friends. In order to forestall congressional investigations, Ames distributed shares to congressmen, Cabinet officers, even to Vice–President Schuyler Colfax.

14 SEPTEMBER 1872
International Under the Treaty of Washington the United States is awarded $15,500,000 on its *Alabama* claims resulting from damages inflicted by British vessels during the Civil War.

21 OCTOBER 1872
International Arbitrating the United States–Canada dispute over islands off the British Columbia–Washington Territory coasts, the German Emperor William I awards the San Juan Islands to the United States. The Emperor has been asked to arbitrate under the 1871 Treaty of Washington.

5 NOVEMBER 1872
National U.S. Grant wins a second term by a landslide 286 electoral votes to 66 for Horace Greeley. Grant receives 3,597,132 votes to Greeley's 2,834,125. Greeley, at home with the felicitous phrase, is out of his depth in the mudslinging and dirty games of a presidential contest. During the election, Susan B. Anthony, Vice–President–at–large of the National Woman Suffrage Association, casts a vote in New York State. She is arrested and fined

THE CREDIT MOBILIER SCANDAL

In September 1872, the New York *Sun* began a series of articles exposing a lucrative scandal with ramifications that reached to the highest levels of government. During the building of the transcontinental railway, millions of dollars were dispensed by the United States government. Massachusetts Representative Oakes Ames and the other directors of the Union Pacific Railroad formed a company and named it "Credit Mobilier of America." To this company they awarded all the construction contracts. Some estimate that $73,000,000 was paid to Credit Mobilier for work worth closer to $50,000,000. In order to forestall congressional investigations, Oakes Ames, taking advantage of his position in Congress, distributed 160 shares to congressmen, Cabinet officers, and even to Vice-President Colfax, or as he so succinctly put it, "where it would do the most good." Some of the contracts paid $341.85 on each $100 share and some of the lucky beneficiaries of Ames' generosity paid only par value, if anything at all. Vice-President Schuyler Colfax and Grant's second term Vice-President Henry Wilson, James G. Blaine and many otherwise honorable men were badly damaged politically by the greedy scheme. Ames admitted it was a "diamond mine" and the *Sun*, in a bit of hyperbole considering the nature of other swindles in the Grant administration, called him the "King of Frauds." The House proposed to expel Ames, but finally settled on February 28, 1873 for a vote of censure. Leland Stanford's Central Pacific Railroad Company adopted the same procedures but their schemes were never exposed.

$100. She objects, citing the Fourteenth Amendment which states that the vote cannot be denied to born or naturalized citizens on basis of race or color. It is a stand–off: Anthony never pays the fine but not until

---

HORACE GREELEY, 1811-1872

Horace Greeley was a brilliant editor, a leader of opinion and an ex-officio statesman. He is best known as an editor, particularly as the editor who initiated the *New Yorker*, the sophisticated literary news magazine, and the nationally respected New York *Tribune*. He was a prolific writer and essayist, steering his own idiosyncratic course through innovative ideas stirring his country. He introduced Charles Fourier's socialistic doctrines, espoused vegetarianism and spiritualism, and challenged women's suffrage. He opposed the use of alcohol, theaters, divorce. Greeley had opinions on most subjects, but the one that made him nationally renowned was his anti-slavery stand. He helped elect Lincoln and then pressed the President to declare emancipation. His famous "The Prayer of Twenty Millions" warned of dire perils in putting off the fateful decision. After a trip to the West which captivated his imagination he wrote: "Go West, young man—go West." He himself did not emigrate, but did set up a model town, Greeley, Colorado, complete with model irrigation system. Greeley was one of the founders of the Republican Party and served out a vacancy in Congress for three months, during which time he introduced a bill to give free land to settlers.

Always in the midst of controversy, Greeley was instrumental in forming the Liberal Republican Party in 1871, in a vain attempt to defeat Grant. He was given the party's nomination. His old enemies, the Democrats, also nominated Greeley as their standard bearer, having no one else of national reputation willing to run. He was then drawn into a personal campaign for which he was ill prepared. The Republicans venemously vilified the unfortunate editor: "I was assailed so bitterly," he recounted, "that I hardly knew whether I was running for the presidency or the penitentiary." The campaign and the death of his wife left him a broken man. Before the year was out Greeley died of "brain fever."

1920 will the Twentieth Amendment be adopted guaranteeing women's right to vote.

Regional William "Boss" Tweed is convicted on all counts of defrauding the city of New York of some $200,000,000. He is sentenced to twelve years in jail. His cohorts escape abroad with their share of the loot and are never punished. Oddly enough, when "Boss" Tweed escapes to Spain in 1876 he is sent home by that country's government. Tweed dies in jail in 1878.

9 NOVEMBER 1872
Regional A fire in Boston rages for three days, killing 13 and causing an estimated $75,000,000 in property damage in 65 acres.

12 FEBRUARY 1873
National Congress passes the Coinage Act of 1873. Gold-standard advocates lobby successfully for demonitizing silver. The silver dollar is dropped as a coin, although a special coin continues in use for trade in the Orient. It is not by chance that the gold–standard advocates push legislation through Congress

New York workers strike for the eight-hour day.

FORGING A NATION 1866-1900

GOLD, SILVER AND COPPER MINING IN THE WEST

Mining had started out easy: you dipped your pan in likely water, carefully sifted the sand away and were left with gold. This kind of mining was called "placer" from a pleasing Spanish word meaning "submarine plain." And much of the West was opened by gold–seekers intent on filling a small bag full of gold dust and moving on. But placer gold soon ran out and at that point mining became big business. Huge capital investments were required to develop the deep tunnel mine, and such capital was not given to the irresponsible, half-crazy solitary wanderers of the West. A new breed of high–stakes capital investors stepped in. Of all the big strikes, none surpassed the Comstock lode, and within the Comstock, no single find ever surpassed the Big Bonanza which four Irishmen found following a hunch in 1873. Digging down 1167 feet, the silver seekers hit the top of an incredible ore body. It was a solid 600 by 400 by 70 feet of silver. The U.S. Geological Survey explained ecstatically: "No discovery which matches it has been made on this earth from the day when the first miner struck a ledge with his crude pick until the present." The partners extracted some $1,500,000 a month during the first five years and by the time the veins ran out, $135,800,000 had been produced from the silvery ground. With deep tunnels, mining became dirty and dangerous. Often working over a thousand feet beneath the surface in sweltering heat, without proper ventilation, with the new unpredictable dynamite, accidents were frequent. Every day in some big mines a person was disabled, every month a man killed. Accidents where an entire shaft was blown to small pieces became almost commonplace. Owners merely covered the tunnel with quicklime before sending down a new group. Strikes spread and grew vicious. They were dealt with by immigrant strikebreakers, and by State and Federal militia. As silver and gold supplies dwindled, "red metal" twinkled its way to the top. In 1882 a miner in Butte, Montana bought the wornout Anaconda silver mine and set his face to the future. By 1892 Anaconda was supplying the world with 100,000,000 pounds of processed copper a year.

at this time: rich silver strikes in Nevada are already making silver available in quantity. Later, when silver is mined on a large scale, the money issue becomes political, as pro–inflationary groups allied to the mine owners press for silver coinage. The 1873 Act becomes known as the "Crime of 1873" and unsubstantiated charges of a gold conspiracy persist for two decades.

18 FEBRUARY 1873
National The House Committee investigating the Credit Mobilier Scandal finds Massachusetts Representative Oakes Ames guilty of bribery and recommends his expulsion from Congress. Although guilty of corruption as charged, Ames had to his credit that he, more than any other person, had instigated the building of the transcontinental railroad. Whether it was public opinion that came to his defense or the fact that so many congressmen and high government officials were implicated in the scandal, in the end Ames is merely censured.

3 MARCH 1873
National The Timber Culture Act authorizes grants of an additional quarter of a section (160 acres) to a homesteader who will agree to plant trees on a quarter of his land. By virtue of this legislation, 65,292 homesteaders receive 10,000,000 acres of land. In the harsh conditions of the plains, small farms of a quarter section are not liable to survive a drought, and thousands of acres are needed for cattle and sheep ranches. The Timber Culture Act remains in effect for 15 years.

National In the so–called "Salary Grab" Act, Congress increases its salaries by 50 percent and doubles both the President's salary and that of the Justices of the Supreme Court. To add insult to injury the increase is made retroactive for two years. The Act is met with strong opposition in the country. The public is deeply disgusted with the venal ways of its representatives. Congress will be forced to repeal the raises which it has granted to its own members. On the same day, Congress passes the Coal Lands Act which offers public coalbearing lands to anyone who can pay $10 to $20 an acre. Not more than 160 acres are permitted per person and 320 acres per group. All such acts which limit the purchase of land grants are circumvented by fraudulent means, and rich acreage is easily transferred to cagey profiteers sometimes for as little as a glass of beer.

4 MARCH 1873
National Ulysses S. Grant is inaugurated for his second term as President of the United States. Henry Wilson is his Vice–President.

14 APRIL 1873
National In its first interpretation of the controversial Fourteenth Amendment, the Supreme Court in *Slaughter Houses* cases finds that the amendment does not give federal jurisdiction over all civil rights; that it is designed specifically to protect black rights and not to protect property rights even when these are threatened by unfair monopolistic practices.

1 MAY 1873
National The Post Office issues one–cent post cards.

AUGUST 1873
Agriculture Grasshopper plagues have devastated western farms. Droughts have exacerbated the harsh conditions under which farmers struggle for survival. In debt to banks and merchants for seed, tools and machinery, farmers are forced to sell their land. In increasing numbers they become part of the rootless masses swelling the teeming factory cities, their dream of an independent life dissipating like water on the acid plains. Farms need to consolidate into bigger units in order to steer through the vagaries of weather in the unirrigated plains.

18 SEPTEMBER 1873
Finance The failure of the respectable brokerage

CORRUPTION IN RECONSTRUCTION SOUTH, NORTHERN INDUSTRY AND NATIONAL POLITICS

Americans were intoxicated with their new–found freedom and luck, and did not notice when excess became corruption. Corruption in the last third of the 19th century was of a special order because an entirely new social structure, one of capital and technology, was being developed without the guiding restraints of law. Dangerous precedents of a dubious sort were set and corruption became as acceptable as apple pie.

Stories of fraud in the Reconstruction South make lurid reading. Senator Patterson of South Carolina said it for all: "There are five more years of good stealing in South Carolina." Henry C. Warmoth managed to make an $8000 salary add up to $1,000,000 in four years. A Louisiana chief justice sold a state–invested $2,000,000 railroad to friends for $50,000. Blacks and whites alike, suddenly put in charge of city and state treasuries, found no curbs placed on greed. Corruption in the industrial North was as staggering. It was said of John D. Rockefeller, and was equally true of several other industrial barons, that he owned the best legislatures that money could buy. Jay Gould's attempt to corner the gold market involved officials all the way up to the vice–president. Grant's Secretary of the Treasury took 50 percent on all collections, racking up $213,000 in one year. Scandal was endemic to the Post Office and the Navy, and impeachment procedures were begun against Secretary of War William Belknap for selling Indian trading posts. The $4,000,000 Whiskey Ring scandal touched high and low in the Republican Party, including Grant's private secretary, Orville Babcock, already involved in most other big scandals. In the cities, new organizations like Tammany Hall were invented to deal with new conditions. Thieves like "Boss" Tweed of New York bilked the city out of $200,000,000 in less than six years. In the West, buying timber, farm and mining land under "dummy" names was common practice. Illegal rebates from railroads served to consolidate some companies into giants while forcing other middle-sized merchants into bankruptcy. Selling a barren tract of land to settlers or salting a played–out mine with gold nuggets made easy money. The exuberant young society agreed on one point; a citizen's value could be judged by one standard alone: money.

firm of Jay Cooke and Company precipitates the country into a five–year depression. The Panic of 1873 causes 5000 businesses to fail in the first year and 10,478 will close before the country turns a corner in 1879. The Panic of 1873 is essentially the result of years of over–trading, over–production, over–speculation, over–issues of paper money and inflated prices. The economy has been running at fever heat for 12 years and a letdown is inevitable. The failure of Cooke is merely the snowball that starts the avalanche, it is not in itself responsible for the conditions that lead to the disaster. Unforeseen problems in financing the Northern Pacific Railroad, a projected second transcontinental line, wrecks the otherwise honorable company. Thirty–seven banks and brokerage houses close the same day as Cooke. Two days later the Stock Exchange closes for an unprecedented 10 days. Other railroads and banks are soon

forced to shut down, affecting the fortunes of thousands of merchants and farmers. The Panic is a psychological watershed in the fortunes of the country. Some part of the continent's unbridled optimism leaks away forever. In its place the need for cooperation emerges as a necessary factor in the affairs of both management and labor.

20 SEPTEMBER 1873

Finance The Stock Exchange closes its doors for 10 days, and the Secretary of the Treasury releases $26,000,000 in greenbacks which are marked for recall by January 1874. The total circulation of the paper money is now $382,000,000.

CHICAGO BECOMES THE HEART OF THE PRAIRIES

Before the advent of railroads, Chicago had already become the busiest port in America. It could handle more ships, docked at its throbbing port, than the next six most active ports of the nation combined. When Chicago opened its Union stockyards on December 25, 1865 it was one more milestone in the irrevocable transformation of America. With the building of the railroads, particularly with the laying of the transcontinental tracks, Chicago, centered as it was on the prairie, came into its own. After Joseph McCoy had inspired the ranchers of Texas to send their cattle to the Abilene railhead and from there to ship east, Chicago overtook Cincinnati, Ohio, as the foremost meat processing capital. The refrigerated railroad car would help consolidate the meat business and make Chicago the meatpacking center also. But it was after the homesteaders turned the green gold of the buffalo grass into the amber gold of grain, with the planting of the hardy Turkey Red strain of wheat, that Chicago became the true heart of the nation. It was an artificial heart transplanted into the prairie to fill the gargantuan demands of big business. Companies expanded to fill needs which their own consolidations brought about, and farming turned into big business as land, no longer a source of independence and subsistence, became one more speculative natural resource.

27 OCTOBER 1873

Indian Affairs General E.R.S. Canby is killed while negotiating with the Modoc Indians of Oregon. This tribe has refused to return to their Klamath Reservation and have found sanctuary in the lava beds of eastern Oregon. These caves and passageways provide shelter and protection from the white hunters, and the Modocs are able to resist their relentless pursuers. Finally General Canby and two civilian Peace Commissioners meet with the tribe which is led by Chief Kintpuash, called by the whites Captain Jack. Unhappy with the way negotiations are proceeding the Indians open fire and kill Canby and one of the commissioners. Thus begins another "Indian War." The tribe is hunted with full Army attention until Chief Kintpuash and his braves are captured. The Chief and six of his warriors are treated as ordinary criminals and hanged for murder at Fort Klamath. The rest are transferred to a reservation in the Dakotas.

FORGING A NATION 1866-1900

BARBED WIRE

In 1874, Joseph F. Glidden, an Illinois farmer, changed the face of the Great Plains with a simple, even humble invention: barbed wire. The vast area had remained essentially unsettled, open to roving herds of buffalo and cattle because there was not enough cheap timber to provide for fences. With the advent of barbed wire the herds could be kept off farm land; free range became private pasture land; cowboys became settled ranchers and farmers felt secure. The change to the new way of life was not easily made. "Fence cutter" wars began between cattlemen and sheepmen, between ranchers and cattle thieves, between Indians and cowboys, with farmers against them all. Water holes, roads, even whole towns were fenced in. Free movement was inhibited as thousands of miles of steel wound legally and illegally across the prairie. The cowboy was fenced in, and the geography of the Great Plains was redrawn by the prickly coils of the lowly barbed wire.

---

31 OCTOBER 1873
International The American steamer *Virginius*, illegally flying the American flag and said to be carrying men and munitions destined for the insurgents in Cuba, is captured by a Spanish gunboat. Eight Americans and ultimately 53 passengers and crew are taken into custody and executed before the Spanish Government can intervene. Secretary Hamilton Fish negotiates for compensation and Spain agrees to pay $80,000 in damages to American families.

20 JANUARY 1874
National Under great pressure from a shocked nation, Congress repeals the "Salary Grab" Act of 1873. It leaves intact raises for the President and Supreme Court Justices but forgoes raises for itself.

21 JANUARY 1874
National Morrison R. Waite succeeds Salmon P. Chase as Chief Justice of the Supreme Court.

8 MARCH 1874
National Millard Fillmore dies in Buffalo, New York. He is 74.

11 MARCH 1874
Regional The Potter Law, Wisconsin legislation initiated by the Grange movement, regulates railroad freight rates within the State. It is achieved against massive resistance by lumber and railroad interests.

23 MARCH 1874
Regional Legislation in Iowa, initiated by the growing Grange movement, regulates rail freight rates within the State.

14 APRIL 1874
Currency The Legal Tender Act, the so-called Inflation Bill, passes the House. It adds $18,000,000 of greenbacks to circulation, and validates $26,000,000 authorized in 1873, bringing the total paper circulation to $400,000,000. President Grant will veto the bill the

following week, but by June Congress passes the new bill bringing total notes to $382,000,000.

15 APRIL 1874
Regional In Arkansas, settling the two-year-old dispute over who is governor, President Grant recognizes fellow Republican Elisha Baxter, thus averting a small war. Rival claimant Democrat James Brooks has barricaded himself in the State House and some skirmishes lead to several lives lost. Brooks peaceably turns over the State House to Baxter upon Grant's order, but upon Hayes' inauguration to the Presidency and his promised withdrawal of federal troops, one of

---

THE BUFFALO

The buffalo was the economic basis for Indian culture. The animal provided meat, clothes and tents for human survival. The Indian picked off the buffalo in a symbiotic arrangement that threatened neither group. When the first white man arrived on the Great Plains, huge herds, estimated at 12,000,000 animals, covered Kansas and Texas sometimes as far as the eye could see. Then one day the indefatigable "iron horse" puffed its way across the plains. It was clear that without the herds, and oddshaped beast the land could be settled—if only the gentle animals would disappear. And disappear they did. Incredible as it seems today, in the two years between 1872 and 1874 the wandering herds were hunted to all but extinction. "Buffalo Bill" Cody led the hunt, but soon professional hide-hunters, big game hunters, wild west tours, poured in to take part in the astonishing slaughter. The Army winked at the butchery, figuring it would help keep the Indians on their reservation. Richard Dodge describes the carnage he saw in 1873: "Where there were myriads of buffalo the year before there were now myriads of carcasses." The air was foul with sickening stench, and the vast plain, which only a short twelvemonth before teemed with animal life, was a dead, solitary, putrid desert. Henry M. Stanley, the intrepid reporter, explained it all: "But half a continent could not be kept as buffalo pasture and hunting ground."

---

the first acts of the white supremacist southern Democrats will be to try to get rid of Baxter.

22 APRIL 1874
Currency Grant vetoes the Legal Tender Bill as being too inflationary.

8 MAY 1874
Regional Massachusetts is the first state to adopt a 10-hour day law for women. Public demand for reform of substandard working conditions is increasing daily.

16 MAY 1874
Regional When the Williamsburg Dam breaks in Massachusetts it floods the Mill River Valley, causing millions of dollars of property damage and 100 deaths.

4 JULY 1874
Regional A steel arch bridge across the Mississippi

NOVEMBER 4, 1874

John D. Rockefeller, Sr.

River at St. Louis is completed. It is built by James Buchanan Eads and is the first to span the great river. It takes seven years to complete and is the inspiration for further such construction.

JULY 1874

Life/Customs The Chautauqua Movement is begun by Lewis Miller and John H. Vincent. Vincent is a Methodist clergyman, and the movement begins as a summer training of Sunday School teachers. Lewis Miller is an Ohio industrialist who agrees to finance the establishment at Lake Chautauqua, New York. The movement subsequently changes its emphasis to include subjects of greater interest to a people grappling with the new age and draws nationally known speakers such as Mark Twain to its meetings.

17 SEPTEMBER 1874

Reconstruction Governor William P. Kellogg, a notorious carpetbagger, loses the Louisiana election in 1872 by 10,000 votes to native–born Liberal Republican–Democrat candidate John McEmery. With the backing of the Custom House Ring, an especially corrupt group, the election is fixed to appear as if Kellogg has won by 18,000 votes. President Grant sends troops to support Radical Republican Kellogg whom he recognizes as the legitimate governor. For three years Louisiana is in turmoil. Vicious white supremacists clash in bloody battles with some of the most blantantly corrupt carpetbag politicians of the postwar South. In the fall of 1874 White Leaguers attack Kellogg's people in a violent fight on the streets of New Orleans. Kellogg barricades himself in the state capitol and waits for Federal Troops to rescue him. Later, after another fixed election returns Radical Republicans to power, Grant sends the South's arch–enemy General Philip Sheridan to prop up the regime with his bayonets.

4 NOVEMBER 1874

National For the first time since 1860, Democratic majorities are returned to the House of Representatives.

Regional Samuel J. Tilden becomes governor of New York. It is he more than anyone who is responsible for breaking up the incredible "Tweed Ring." By analyzing the bank accounts of some Ring mem-

FORGING A NATION 1866-1900

bers he amasses the necessary proof of the extent of the larceny. In order to bring the corrupt politicians to trial, Tilden has first to get rid of the corrupt judges that prevent prosecution. He manages to get the impeachment of some of them and can proceed against Tweed. His energetic and successful reforms bring him to public attention and to the New York Governorship. In 1877 the rapidly rising, reform–minded lawyer has a chance at the Executive Office in the uniquely contested presidential election.

18–20 NOVEMBER 1874

National Delegates from 17 states meet in Cleveland, Ohio to form the Women's Christian Temperance Union. Other organizations formed this year include the Young Men's Hebrew Association and in November the Greenback Party is organized in Indianapolis. It mainly attracts farmers who favor inflationary money over gold because it helps them to pay their debts. The Social Democratic Workingmen's Party is also organized in America this year. The Social Democrats base themselves on the economic theories of the German Socialist Ferdinand LaSalle. LaSalle is a social evolutionist and advocates a political approach to reform. Capitalism has become twopronged: on the one hand, it believes in freedom and sees this as freedom from legislative restraint. On the other hand, it is clear that there is a need to curb unbridled greed and dishonest maneuverings merely to leave anything at all for future capitalists. In the same way labor has two prongs: first there is the need for relief from increasingly oppressive practices in factories and mines and in general working conditions. The second is the fact that it is becoming ever more apparent that two classes are emerging in classless America, the rich and the poor, and unless action is taken, the American dream of independent and socially mobile citizens will come to an abrupt end. The Social Democrats inject a new issue into this already complicated scene: Will reform be brought about by legislation and public opinion, or will government have to take over the activities of private enterprise to ensure a fair distribution of the incredible wealth of the nation? The debate is never clearly articulated. The fight is usually more bloody than eloquent. The distinctively American contribution to the controversy will emerge in the 1880s when Samuel Gompers begins to organize the American Federation of Labor.

7 DECEMBER 1874

Regional In a last-gasp attack on the Vicksburg, Mississippi courthouse, blacks attempt to prevent ouster of a carpetbag sheriff. Approximately 75 blacks are killed in the battle before the crowd is dispersed.

14 JANUARY 1875

Currency The Specie Resumption Act is passed by Congress. It provides for exchange of gold for legal tender beginning January 1, 1879. Meanwhile the number of greenbacks still circulating will decrease to $300,000,000.

30 JANUARY 1875

International In a treaty with Hawaii, the United States agrees to allow imports of Hawaiian goods, primarily sugar, duty free. The treaty also declares that no third power can acquire Hawaiian territory.

1 MARCH 1875

Reconstruction The Civil Rights Act is pushed through Congress. It states that no citizen can be denied equal use of public facilities such as conveyances, inns, or restaurants on the basis of color. In addition no one may be arbitrarily prevented from jury service.

3 MARCH 1875

National The Tariff Act of 1875 passes Congress. Tariff rates are raised 10 percent to pre–1870 level.
Finance Congress authorizes the minting of a silver 20–cent piece. It is discontinued May 2, 1878.

15 MARCH 1875

Ideas/Beliefs Archbishop John McCloskey of New York is invested as the first American Cardinal. Investiture takes place in St. Patrick's Cathedral of New York.

18 MARCH 1875

International The Senate ratifies a reciprocity treaty with Hawaii, allowing duty-free imports from the is-

---

MARY BAKER EDDY, 1821-1910

Mary Baker Eddy was 57 when in 1879 she founded the Church of Christ, Scientist, an authentically American religion. Within 50 years, her system, almost completely distinct from most orthodox sects, had 2370 churches and groups and reached around the world. Mrs. Eddy was a frail woman, for a long time weak and indecisive, but with a deep interest in matters spiritual. The Reverend Enoch Cosser, who tutored her for some six years, described her as an "intellectual and spiritual genius." She was well educated although she had little inclination for a formal profession. In her childhood at 12 years of age she had cured herself of a bad fever through prayer and at 45 she cured herself again the same way: "The spiritual significance [of the Bible] appeared . . . and the Principle and rule of Spiritual Science and metaphysical healing—in a word Christian Science."

In 1875 she published the basic text of the movement: *Science and Health with a Key to the Scriptures.* In 1876 she organized the Christian Science Association which three years later became the Church of Christ, Scientist located in Boston. Mrs. Eddy had surrounded herself with a group of devoted followers and in spite of quarrels among them she became a shrewd and effective organizer. The Church is grounded in a set of rules entitled the Church Manual which she developed so it would never depend on her own or another's charismatic leadership, and this is one reason for its extraordinary survival. Mrs. Eddy went on to found the *Christian Science Monitor*, a successful daily newspaper which has maintained its high tone and standards to this day. Mrs. Eddy actively led her Church and demonstrated the power of spiritual healing until her death in 1910.

lands, and agreeing that no third power may acquire Hawaiian land.

30 MARCH 1875

National In *Minor v. Happersett,* the Supreme Court finds that the Fourteenth Amendment does not prevent a state from setting up suffrage requirements. A time-bound interpretation of the privileges and immunities clause deprives women of the voting rights otherwise guaranteed to all United States citizens.

1 MAY 1875

National The Whiskey Ring scandal surfaces into public view. Scandal after scandal has laced Grant's easygoing administration. Perhaps the one that spreads furthest in the country is the Whiskey Ring. Although the ring was not confined to St. Louis, it was there that the corruption reached its greatest depths. It is led by John McDonald, a personal friend of President Grant and now a supervisor in the internal revenue in that city. Through blackmail and threats, Republican officials large and small have been snared into cooperation with the leaders, and shakedowns of millions from distillers and government taxes have occurred. The Chief Clerk of the Treasury is involved and so is Orville Babcock, Grant's personal secretary. Thirty-two distillers in Milwaukee, St. Louis and Chicago are found to be involved, but the corruption has spread like a cancer and there is no way to catch all the men implicated in the fraud. Although Babcock is saved from conviction by intercession from his protector Grant, the faithful President realizes that Babcock is too much of a liability to stay on as personal secretary to the man who holds the highest office in the land.

3 MAY 1875

National The United States becomes a member of the Universal Postal Union.

31 JULY 1875

National Andrew Johnson dies. He is 66.

JULY 1875

Ideas/Beliefs Dwight Lyman Moody begins evangelistic revival meetings in the East. Moody is one of the greatest of nineteenth–century evangelists. In the 1870s he leads some formidable meetings attracting thousands by his sweetness of soul and passion for the Gospels. One of his disciples says that he "reduced the population of hell by a million souls."

1 SEPTEMBER 1875

Labor A conviction of murder leads to the breakup of the Irish miners' group known as the "Molly Maguires." The Mollies are an outgrowth of the unsanitary and unsafe conditions in which miners are forced to work. Miners are badly paid and harassed into long working hours. Mine operators are able to buy off government officials who might have come to the miners' aid, and public opinion is still ensnared by the idea that somehow it is his own laziness or moral weakness that brings a laborer into such distressing conditions. The Mollies take matters into their own hands. They begin to organize in the anthracite mines of Pennsylvania, where some of the most severely exploited white workers in the country can be found. They resort to the ruthless tactics of terror using murder, intimidation, property damage and the like to bend contractors, "bosses" and strikebreakers to their will. The uniform they adopt is women's clothes and they call themselves the Molly Maguires after the secret and sinister Irish terrorist organization which they take as their model. The Mollies are finally exposed when a coal boss hires a detective to infiltrate the group's inner circle. The leaders are brought to trial and the group dissolves. However once the public no longer has the bloody doings of the Mollies to fulminate against they turn their attention to the inexcusa-

THE LAST SIOUX WAR

The Paha Sapa section of South Dakota's Black Hills was a sacred part of the Sioux reservation which had been ceded to the Indians in the Treaty of 1868 made with Chief Red Cloud. In 1874 the intrepid Indian hunter Lieutenant Colonel George Custer trespassed into the holy grounds following reports that there was gold in the hills. And gold he found. Foreseeing the predictable reaction, he broadcast his find, inevitably enticing golddiggers to the area. The government attempted to purchase the land but the Indians refused to leave. The Indians were then ordered to return to their reservations, without recompense of any kind, and without regard to whether the passage was possible in advancing winter weather. General George Crook was ordered to round up recalcitrant bands north of the Platte River. His first encounter was with a band of Cheyennes heading toward an Indian agency to surrender. George Crook was later known and trusted by the Indians for his dealings, but in this instance he attacked without provocation. The braves fought hard and were fortunately reinforced by heroic young Crazy Horse and his band. Crook retreated to fortifications on the Platte River. Left no choice, the Cheyennes threw in with the Sioux to endure together the bitter last fights against white encroachments.

As spring 1876 came, General Crook once again advanced north of the Platte into Indian hunting grounds in central Montana. Again he was stopped by the fierce Crazy Horse and his Oglala band at Rosebud Creek.

On June 25 a three-pronged attack on the Sioux and Cheyenne encampment at the Little Bighorn River was turned into a massacre when Lieutenant Colonel Custer disobeyed orders and contacted the enemy prematurely. He and 250 of his men were killed. Custer had incautiously attacked some 2000 to 4000 braves.

Some have called the Battle of Little Bighorn Custer's Last Stand, and some have cynically called it the Indians' Last Stand, because the nation was so revolted by the defeat that it tacitly concurred in the extinction of the Sioux nation. Army efforts were savage and successful. By May 1877 hunger had forced Crazy Horse to surrender. That September, in a well choreographed fight in a guard room, the brave hero was bayoneted to death. The Sioux were squeezed into the intolerable conditions of the reservations and never seriously threatened the white settlers again. It was 1877 and the Sioux Wars were over.

ble working conditions, and protest for reform begins to find energetic backing.

OCTOBER 1875
Indian Affairs The government attempts to buy some of the Indian lands north of the Platte but the Indians refuse the money. They are then told to return to their reservations nonetheless, and forfeit these lands ceded to them by treaty in 1868. The Second Sioux War erupts violently and treacherously. It will continue through the winter, but by spring and summer stepped–up attacks by the Army, led by General George Crook and incited by Lieutenant Colonel George A. Custer, bring the Indians to final defeat.

12 OCTOBER 1875
Regional Rutherford B. Hayes, an anti-greenback advocate, is elected Republican governor of Ohio.

17 NOVEMBER 1875
Ideas/Beliefs A branch of the Theosophical Society is founded in New York by Helena Petrovna Blavatsky or "H.P." as she prefers to be called. The main objects of the society are: first, to begin to establish the universal brotherhood of humanity, molding public opinion away from strictly national views; second, to promote study of comparative religion and philosophy; third, to take more interest in the realms of "occultism." Belief in reincarnation was central to Blavatsky's thinking and the idea was first introduced by her into American thought. Madame Blavatsky is a charismatic woman who has a profound effect upon many of her contemporaries. The poet W. B. Yeats is one of her disciples, as are the famous religious leaders Annie Besant, Krishnamurti, Rudolf Steiner and Alice Bailey

22 NOVEMBER 1875
National Vice-President Henry Wilson dies.

4 DECEMBER 1875
Regional William "Boss" Tweed, convicted of cheating New York City out of some $200,000,000, is helped to escape from jail and gets away to Cuba.

15 DECEMBER 1875
National The House enthusiastically passes an anti-third term resolution in an attempt to discourage any ambitions Grant, or more likely his wife, might have.

OTHER EVENTS OF 1875
Agriculture Luther Burbank uses crossbreeding and selection on a commercial scale. He develops new strains of plant life, including berries, fruits, vegetables and grains.
Ideas/Beliefs A new method of medicine is developed by Dr. Andrew T. Still in Kirksville, Missouri. He calls it osteopathy. Mary Baker Eddy, founder of Christian Science, publishes *Science and Health*.

FEBRUARY 1876
National Contractor Caleb P. Marsh charges that

Secretary of War William W. Belknap has offered him control over trading posts at Fort Sill in Indian Territory. Belknap has informed Marsh this should be worth $12,000 to the contractor. Belknap expects money in return for the favor. Subsequent investigation shows that Belknap has received at least $24,450 for trading post privileges. Impeachment proceedings will be initiated against the Secretary.

MARCH 1876
Indian Affairs General Crook encounters Cheyenne Chief Two Moons and Oglala warrior Crazy Horse at Rosebud Creek, north of the Platte River. In a fierce battle the Oglalas force Crook's withdrawal.

2 MARCH 1876
National Impeachment proceedings are voted against Secretary of War William W. Belknap by Congress. Belknap has been found to be taking bribes in return for lucrative trading posts in the Indian Territory. Grounds for impeachment are malfeasance in office. Belknap resigns and Grant, with unseemly haste, accepts his resignation the same day. By this deft maneuver Belknap successfully avoids prosecution. The trial without his presence continues, but the resolution for impeachment is dismissed on the grounds that there is no jurisdiction over Belknap since he is no longer in office.

10 MARCH 1876
Science/Technology The telephone, for which Alexander Graham Bell has received a patent on March 7, now functions.

27 MARCH 1876
National In *United States v. Cruikshank* the Su-

ALEXANDER GRAHAM BELL, 1847-1922

Alexander Graham Bell was one of those immigrants whose contributions to their new land modified it beyond recognition. Bell was an inventor, a teacher, a physicist. The son and grandson of speech teachers, he was educated at the Universities of Edinburgh and London where he studied elocution. He subsequently emigrated to the United States by way of Canada. There he worked on a phonetic alphabet for the Mohawk Indian language. By 1872 he had settled in Boston, invited to work with deaf-mutes by the Board of Education. He opened a school to train teachers for the deaf and fell in love with a deaf girl whom he later married. The mechanics of speech patterns and the nature of sound fascinated him all his life. Later he founded the American Association to Promote Teaching of Speech to the Deaf. In that felicity of forms that fate often shapes, Alexander Graham Bell invented the mechanism to transmit vocal sound waves over wire: the telephone was in effect an extension of hearing. Through diligence and accident the miracle was made: on March 10, 1876 his assistant Thomas A. Watson in an adjoining room suddenly heard over the wire the excited message: "Mr. Watson, come here. I want you." Bell set up a company the following year and soon the country was well on its way to instant communication.

---

preme Court finds that the Fourteenth Amendment does not protect blacks from individual action infringing on their rights, only from state action. The interpretation weakens the hand of those who are still struggling to protect black civil rights in the South from white supremacists. Essentially it renders the Enforcement Act of 1870 and the Ku Klux Klan Act of 1871 inoperative. In *United States v. Reese* the Supreme Court finds that the Fifteenth Amendment does not confer rights to suffrage; it merely forbids some specific restrictions.

2 APRIL 1876

Life/Customs National League baseball plays its first official game. Jim O'Rourke gets the first hit, and Boston beats Philadelphia, six to five.

17 MAY 1876

National Cleveland, Ohio hosts the Prohibition Party's National Convention. General Green Clay Smith of Kentucky is nominated for President and Gideon T. Stewart of Ohio for Vice-President.

18 MAY 1876

National Indianapolis, Indiana hosts the Greenback Party's National Convention. Peter Cooper of New York is nominated for President and Samuel F. Cary, Ohio, for Vice-President.

6 JUNE 1876

Ideas/Beliefs The United States branch of a Masonic

THE CENTENNIAL EXPOSITION

The Centennial Exposition was opened by President Grant in Philadelphia in May 1876. Congress had appropriated $2,000,000, Pennsylvania $1,000,000 and Philadelphia $1,500,000 toward the exposition at Fairmont Park. There was much in the way of native art and foreign culture to examine, but the focus of the fair was Machinery Hall, a 1402-foot by 360-foot wooden building that covered 13 acres. In it was a display of American inventions of the past decades, including the telephone, the typewriter, the mimeograph and the 2500 horsepower Corliss engine later bought by George Pullman for his sleeper-car factory. Of this astounding piece of machinery William Dean Howells wrote: "The Corliss engine does not lend itself to description. . . . It rises loftily in the centre of the huge structure, an athlete of steel and iron with not a superfluous ounce of metal on it; the mighty walking beams plunge their pistons downward, the enormous flywheel revolves with hoarded power that makes all tremble, the hundred life-like details do their office with unerring intelligence." Howell worried about the power of machinery over men but, he wrote, "For the present America is voluble in the strong metals and their infinite uses." In the six months the Fair was open, just under 10,000,000 people wandered awestruck through the beautiful grounds, some 274,000 a day. They paid $3,800,000 just for admissions. All 38 States exhibited, and countries as far away as China and Egypt participated in the lavish International section. It was a fitting celebration marking the end of the first hundred years of the United States.

GEORGE ARMSTRONG CUSTER, 1839-1876

Custer's is a remarkable and puzzling story. He graduated at the bottom of his class at West Point and his conduct in the Civil War was flamboyant, theatrical and impulsive. He designed his own uniform of velveteen and gold braid and wore his blond hair long. Distinguishing himself for gallantry at the Battle of Aldie in 1863, he was made instant brigadier general and by age 25 was commanding the Third Cavalry Division as a major-general. He was the "Boy Hero" of the savage Civil War battles, and the Confederate flag was tendered to him when Lee surrendered. He remained in the army after the war, going west to track down Indians. In 1867 he was courtmartialed for deserting his post. In a curious episode nine years later, Custer went to Washington to testify against his civilian superior Secretary of War Belknap in his trial on charges of corruption relating to Indian trading posts. Custer made undiplomatic accusations against Belknap, intemperate ones against the President's brother and wild ones against President Grant himself. Grant personally stripped him of all commands. "Honor," said a cavalry private, "weighed lightly in the scale against the 'Glorious' name of George A Custer."

Nonetheless, the erratic and intemperate soldier was reinstated in time to take part' in a three-pronged attack on the Sioux at the Battle of Little Bighorn in 1876. Acting in an unprofessional manner, Custer disobeyed written orders and paid no heed to reports of the extent of the enemy encampment. Dividing his own small number, he left himself with 250 men. Attacked by Chief Gall, Chief Two Moons and Crazy Horse leading somewhere between 2000 and 4000 Indian braves, he was quickly annihilated. Custer's death might have dropped into oblivion instead of the history books, had it not been for its national repercussions. The nation was infuriated and the Army finally freed to wage all-out war. Within a year, thanks to Custer's last stand, the Sioux were a broken, defeated nation.

Order is organized by Dr. Walter Fleming with the help of Charles T. McClenachan. It is called the Imperial Council of the Ancient Arabic Order of Nobles of the Mystic Shrine.

16 JUNE 1876

National Cincinnati, Ohio, hosts the Republican National Convention. Rutherford B. Hayes of Ohio is nominated for President and William A. Wheeler, New York, is nominated for Vice-President.

17 JUNE 1876

Indian Affairs The Army launches an all-out attack on the Sioux and their new allies, the Cheyennes. The cold weather has passed; a three-pronged maneuver is planned by General Sheridan to trap a large Indian army camping on the Little Bighorn River. General George Crook will lead the southern prong. The second column will be led by Colonel John Gibbon marching east from Fort Ellis, Montana, and the third prong will be under the command of Brigadier General Alfred H. Terry moving west from Fort Lincoln in Dakota territory. Among his men is Lieutenant Colonel George A. Custer and the doomed Seventh Cavalry. On June 17, Crook unexpectedly encounters the enemy; 1500 Indian allies under Crazy Horse's command engage Crook on Rosebud Creek. The Indians are forced from the field, but Crook withdraws to resupply and regroup. Terry and Gibbon are unaware of the fateful engagement. The two columns meet on the Yellowstone River near Rosebud Creek. Terry then sends the Seventh Cavalry under the command of George Custer to ride down Rosebud Creek, cross the headwaters of the Little Bighorn River, then return downstream. Meanwhile Gibbon will march upstream and between them they plan to catch the Indians in a two–pronged attack. Noting Custer's individualistic approach to war, Terry gives Custer written instructions not to attack before Gibbon is in an agreed position.

20 JUNE 1876

Indian Affairs Custer finds the Indian encampment. Scouts warn him that it contains between 2000 to 4000 warriors. They also warn him that the enemy is aware of his presence. Chief Two Moons of the Cheyennes, Chief Gall and Crazy Horse are more than ready for a fight.

25 JUNE 1876

Indian Affairs Custer ignores both instructions and warnings. He divides his troop of 600 men into three battalions. Captain Frederick Benteen is ordered to take three companies on a scouting mission in the south. Major Marcus Reno is ordered to attack the Indians with 112 men. Custer retains five companies to support Reno's attack. Reno follows orders, is instantly overwhelmed, but manages to extricate himself and his men. He is fortunately joined by Benteen who has returned from his useless scouting mission. Meanwhile Custer takes the brunt of the Indian attack and has no way to help Reno. Chief Gall, Crazy Horse and Chief Two Moons direct their forces against the hated Custer. Whether they knew it was their arch-foe or not, they make sure no white man escapes from

The Battle of the Little Bighorn, June 25, 1876.

OTHER EVENTS OF 1876

General George A. Custer.

this battle. Only the half-breed scout Curley and a horse belonging to Captain Keogh escape alive. The U.S. Army in a sentimental gesture gives orders that no one may ride the horse again.

26 JUNE 1876
Indian Affairs The country is infuriated at the news of the humiliating defeat at the hands of the Indians and at the loss of a national hero. The Indians will pay heavily for their victory.

29 JUNE 1876
National St. Louis, Missouri hosts the Democratic National convention. Samuel J. Tilden, New York, is nominated for President and Thomas H. Hendricks, Indiana, for Vice-President.

25 JULY 1876
Currency A bill to issue unlimited coinage of silver is brought into the House by Richard P. Bland of Missouri.

1 AUGUST 1876
National The 38th state to join the Union is Colorado. The impeachment trial against Secretary of War William W. Belknap is dismissed on grounds he is no longer in office and Congress has no jurisdiction over him.

SEPTEMBER 1876
Indian Affairs Sitting Bull escapes to Canada. Sitting Bull had not fought at the Battle of Little Bighorn, but had been a medicine man at the encampment. However all Sioux are now to be rounded up

and either killed or forced onto reservations. Sitting Bull remains safe under the protective eye of Canadian authorities. In 1881 he returns to the United States where he tours peacefully in wild west shows. In 1890 he is murdered in one last act of treachery at Wounded Knee, South Dakota.

7 NOVEMBER 1876
National In the presidential election, Tilden gets a majority of the popular votes, but disputes over fraudulent election practices and electoral votes will throw the final decision to Congress and Hayes will be declared the winner in March 1877.

23 NOVEMBER 1876
Regional William 'Boss' Tweed is sent back to New York by Spanish authorities as a courtesy to the United States. Spain does not have an extradition treaty with the United States.

12 DECEMBER 1876
National The first amendment relating to prohibition is proposed by Henry W. Blair of New Hampshire.

13 DECEMBER 1876
Currency House passes bill introduced by Richard P. Bland authorizing unlimited coinage of silver in a ratio of 16 silver to one gold. Senate takes no action. The bill will be revived in 1877 and 1878 before it is adopted.

OTHER EVENTS OF 1876
Arts/Culture Olmstead completes his first big com-

Democratic Party presidential candidates, 1876.

333

FORGING A NATION 1866-1900

mission: the magical Central Park in New York.

2 JANUARY 1877

Reconstruction One by one the Republican carpet-bag and scalawag governments are coming to an end in the South. The Ku Klux Klan and other gangs persist in their terrorist tactics. Whippings, tar–and–featherings, incendiarism drive northerners away. Federal Troops no longer can prevent large–scale intimidation.

29 JANUARY 1877

National The Electoral Commission Bill is passed by Congress. By this measure a Commission of 15 is set up to decide the outcome of the disputed election of Rutherford Hayes and Samuel J. Tilden. The House appoints three Democrats (the House has been Democrat since 1875) and two Republicans. The Senate, which is still Republican, appoints three Republican justices and two Democrats. The decisive vote is promised to an independent who is elected to the United States Senate before he can take his place on the commission. The deciding vote is then given to a New Jersey Republican, Justice Joseph Bradley. All the decisions of the Commission will henceforth be divided eight to seven along party lines.

1 MARCH 1877

Agriculture The Grange Movement wins two significant cases before the Supreme Court. In *Peik v Chicago and Northwestern Railroad Company,* the Supreme Court declares for Granger interests by finding that a state has the power to regulate intrastate and interstate traffic which originates within its boundaries. And in *Munn v Illinois,* on the same day, the Supreme Court declares for Granger interests by finding that a state has power to legislate warehouse and intrastate rates. Both cases are designed to restrain railroads from gouging small or independent merchants, often putting them out of business with the discrepancies between long and short haul charges and warehouse rates. This practice of rate fixing has originated with Rockefeller who offers his huge freight business to the railroad which will give him the best deal. It effectively demolishes his competition, sets a precedent for other uncontrolled giants also unrestrained by regulatory laws, and morally distasteful as it is, for a while becomes part of the dogma relating to the growth of American capitalism. Later the Supreme Court will reverse itself and knock down even these puny regulations. But not for long. With the enactment of the Interstate Commerce Act of 1887 and the Anti-trust Act of 1890 greater precision will

---

THE TILDEN—HAYES ELECTION COMPROMISE

The election compromise was called the Great Swap. At best it was a compromise which averted armed conflict. At worst it was a sell-out of black civil rights.

At midnight on election night it was clear that Tilden had won. He was well on the way to piling up his 4,300,000 votes, while Hayes received 4,036,000 a difference of some 264,000 votes. But there was a catch. Tilden was still one little vote short of the necessary electoral majority. If it could be shown that the Democratic votes from Florida, Louisiana, South Carolina and Oregon were fraudulent because of intimidation and other illegal practices, then Hayes could have the election. A vicious contest ensued, bringing the country to the very edge of civil war. Two sets of votes were returned from each of the four states. One set was achieved through fraud, the other through intimidation. A special commission of 15 was set up to determine the count. The Commission was made up of eight Republicans and seven Democrats and its strictly party-line vote was a foregone conclusion. But how to make a Hayes victory palatable to the South? A swap. First, Republicans agreed to pull out the last Federal troops policing the South; second, they would appoint a Southerner to the Cabinet; third, they would share Southern patronage with local politicians; and fourth, they would subsidize Southern railroad and other industries. Only slightly uneasy about abandoning 4,000,000 black citizens to the mercies of white supremacy, the Republicans asked for verbal assurance that the blacks would be treated fairly. The Southerners, a bit more realistic, extracted a written and signed statement from Hayes that he would keep his side of the bargain.

RUTHERFORD BIRCHARD HAYES, 1822-1893

Although it would have happened without him, the mild reformer and able administrator Rutherford B. Hayes was the man who arranged the end of Reconstruction.

Hayes was born in New England, where he received his education, including a degree from Harvard Law School. He moved to Ohio to practice law and soon became city solicitor for Cincinnati. His political career was growing strong when it was interrupted by the Civil War. Hayes served ably and bravely, retiring ultimately as a major-general of volunteers. He was immediately elected to Congress on the Republican ticket where he served two terms, leaving to become governor of Ohio. His reputation as a hard–money man and a sound administrator brought him to national attention and he won his party's nomination in 1877. The election was a sordid affair, a sorry chapter in American history. It is sometimes called the Great Swap. Hayes' claim to victory was angrily contested, and the country teetered toward violence on a national scale. To prevent this, a compromise was arranged which gave the executive office to Hayes in return for concessions to white southern Democrats. Hayes was taunted as "His Fraudulency" or "Boss Thief" and sometimes referred to as Rutherfraud Hayes.

As President he began to make a dent on civil service reform, much to the disgust of Republicans and the opposition of the Democrats who wished to prevent adoption of a merit system until some of their own people were admitted to the patronage jobs. Hayes tried his hand at other reforms, too. He ousted the darling of New York Bosses and future President of the United States, Chester A. Arthur, from his position as Collector of Customs of the Port of New York. These small efforts at cleaning the Augean stables of political patronage only served to weaken the Republican party. Hayes was honest, but dull, hampered by virtue; his wife, nicknamed Lemonade Lucy, served no alcohol in the White House and social occasions, important as the oil in the machinery of government, became occasions of anguish. After his first term expired, Hayes did not run for renomination.

be given to defining the parameters of acceptable industrial practices.

2 MARCH 1877
National The Senate President announces the election of Rutherford B. Hayes as President of the United States and William A. Wheeler as Vice-President.

3 MARCH 1877
Westward Movement The Desert Land Act is enacted by Congress to encourage development of arid lands by farmers who have found quarter sections of 160 acres unprofitable in the Great Plains and Southwest. This act offers any person paying 25 cents an acre an entire section, or 640 acres, if he irrigates some part of his claim in three years. If in that time he can prove irrigation of the land, he need pay only one dollar more per acre and the land is his. It is estimated that 95 percent of the claims made under this act are fraudulent and end up in the hands of the big cattle ranchers. To prove irrigation, an owner, in the presence of the appropriate official, might merely dump a pail of water on the dry earth.

5 MARCH 1877
National Rutherford B. Hayes is inaugurated 19th President of the United States. He takes the oath of office privately, Saturday, March 3, to avoid having to do so on a Sunday. Public ceremonies are performed on Monday to cries of "Rutherfraud President," and "eight to seven," and the like.

APRIL 1877
Transportation In an ominous move which will

Rutherford B. Hayes.

have violent repercussions come summer, the four great trunk lines of the East get together and call off their ruinous rate war. Then, taking advantage of the desperate straits labor is in because of the ongoing depression, the four agree to fix rates among themselves and cut wages by 10 percent.

10 APRIL 1877
Reconstruction South Carolina turns Democrat as Federal Troops withdraw by order of President Hayes, according to his preelection promise to the southerners. Southerners have a "gentlemen's agreement" among themselves to fight their battles now within the Democratic Party.

24 APRIL 1877
Reconstruction The last Federal Troops still policing the South are withdrawn from New Orleans by order of the President. The South, as southerners say, is "redeemed." Although Reconstruction has not achieved its primary goal of black civil rights, and although state governments have mired down in some extravagant corruption, nonetheless Reconstruction has some notable achievements to its credit. By providing money and skills it has helped rebuild the war-wrecked South and established many services not there before the war, such as hospitals, and asylums. Perhaps the most effective and lasting of Reconstruction achievements is the development of a strong public school system.

17 MAY 1877
National Grant begins a post-presidential ceremonial trip around the world.

JUNE 1877
Indian Affairs The Nez Percé battle the Army in Idaho. Chief Joseph is defeated by Colonel Nelson Miles as he tries to reach the safety of Canada with his whole tribe of men, women and children, sick, wounded and elderly. Trapped 30 miles from freedom, the tribe is forced onto a malarial Oklahoma reservation where many succumb to the harsh conditions.

1 JUNE 1877
Arts/Culture The Society of American Artists is founded by sculptor Augustus Saint-Gaudens and fellow artists. Artists are finding what industrialists already know and what many other Americans are discovering: that joining together in groups makes all effort more endurable and ultimately more profitable. Joining has become a sign of the times—the Knights of Columbus, the Elks, the Moose, the Sons and the Daughters of the American Revolution, the Masonic Lodges, rising religious groups, labor unions, fellowship orders, professional organizations—all reflect a characteristically American response to social needs. As Henry James wrote in 1879: "The best things come, as a general thing, from the talents that are members of a group; every man works better when he has companions working in the same line, and yield-

ing the stimulus of suggestion, comparison, emulation. Great things of course have been done by solitary workers: but they have usually been done with double the pains they would have cost if they had been produced in more genial circumstances."

14 JUNE 1877
National The first Flag Day commemorates the 100th anniversary of the first flag of the United States.

21 JUNE 1877
Labor Ten members of the violent reformist Irish miners' society, the Molly Maguires, are hanged for murder. The Society, infiltrated by Pinkerton detectives, is severely weakened and soon forced to disband.

14 JULY 1877
Labor The great strike of 1877 begins as workers walk out on the Baltimore and Ohio Railroad. Railroad unions demand better working conditions, protest recent 10 percent cuts in pay, the second since the depression began, and demand redress for their many grievances. Strikes spread to other railroads from New England to the Mississippi and soon from the Atlantic to the Pacific. All the great cities are pulled into the struggle which is finally settled by militia and Federal Troops. But it serves notice that labor and capital are on a new footing, that until reconciling social ideas are brought to bear, conflict between the two forces will be sanguinary, wasteful and titanic. Sympathetic strikes of factory workers and miners engulf industry. Overnight the nation grinds to a halt. Sympathetic strikes are a novelty and speak of a growing understanding of the distress shared by industrial workers.

16 JULY 1877
Labor Violence reerupts at Martinsburg, West Virginia. State militia has been ordered to guard railroad property on the B & O to prevent a train from being moved. Instead the train is derailed. Soon the entire line, yards, tracks, roundhouses are in the strikers' hands. President Hayes orders the men back to work. The local militia refuses to fire on the strikers but the Secretary of War sends Federal Troops to break up the strike. It is the first time since Jackson that Federal Troops have been used against civilian Americans. Violence continues unabated across the country.

20 JULY 1877
Labor In Baltimore nine strikers are killed and several wounded when State militia fire point blank at a crowd trying to prevent them from reaching the railway station, which is in the hands of angry strikers. In four days of rioting, 50 more people are killed.

21 JULY 1877
Labor In Pittsburgh, where railway property is concentrated, a large number of sympathy strikers and general populace support the railroad workers. They are attacked by State troops when the Pennsylvania militia, attempting to clear a street, is met by volleys of stones. The militia fire into the crowd, which then fires back. In the battle which ensues the militia secures itself in a roundhouse from which it is ultimately forced by fire. At one time a wall of fire three miles long destroys installations. About 2000 freight cars are burned and nearly $10,000,000 in property damage is sustained by the rail companies. All night long the strikers riot, turning from sullen, desperate working men into a monstrous mob, looting shops, burning buildings, often attacking people and property which have no other connection with the railroads than proximity.

26 JULY 1877
Labor In Chicago a strike turns into a bloody massacre when an unorganized gathering is attacked by police aided by cavalry. Nineteen people are killed.

31 JULY 1877
Labor Inspired by the railroad workers, strikes have spread to most other industries in the two hot weeks of July. Meanwhile under intense pressure from state and federal governments the railroad strikers have been forced to settle. Most railroad men return to work without substantial increases or betterment of working conditions. Sympathizing strikes in coal mines have spread, and by the end of July, 40,000 coalminers are on strike in Scranton, Pennsylvania. These workers are more fortunate than the railway workers: after almost a month of violence and looting, the mine owners cave in, offering a 10 percent raise, and agree to other demands made by the unions. Order is restored, but not before the strike has spread through most of the coal-producing states. From this inauspicious beginning a cohesiveness is formed among workers that has not existed before. The strikes have been dramatic lessons in the power of employers and the powerlessness of the single working person or even small groups. The labor movement, which has begun to weaken during the depression, membership having fallen from 300,000 to 50,000, finds new energy in the explosive events of the summer of 1877.

29 AUGUST 1877
Ideas/Beliefs Brigham Young, the fanatic leader of the Mormon Church in Utah Territory, dies. From now on the Church will begin to negotiate with the rest of the world. The Federal Government will not accept Utah Territory as a full-fledged state unless it forbids polygamy. Now that Brigham Young has gone, the necessary steps will be successfully taken.

5 NOVEMBER 1877
Currency Richard P. Bland reintroduces his bill for monetization of silver at the ratio of 16 to one (gold). Silver strikes in Nevada, Utah and Colorado are bringing increased pressure from mine owners for silver coinage. The Senate takes no action.

23 NOVEMBER 1877
International Under the Treaty of Washington, the

American Halifax Fisheries Commission gives Great Britain $5,500,000 for North Atlantic fishing privileges.

OTHER EVENTS OF 1877

Science/Technology   George B. Selden, one of many working on the combustion engine, develops a 2-cycle "gasoline carriage." Curiously enough, Selden is a patent lawyer, and yet he fails to get a patent until 1895. By then it is too late because when Henry Ford and others begin to manufacture automobiles, Selden's claim is submerged in the modifications and advances made since his time and he is unable to lay claim to his discovery. Meanwhile, Thomas Edison patents the phonograph, which he had invented ten years earlier but had not gotten around to perfecting while he concentrated on his incandescent light.

10 JANUARY 1878

National   The Women's Suffrage Amendment is introduced into Congress by Senator A.A. Sargent. The battle for a woman's right to vote will be arduous, vicious and long, but the words used in the final Amendment adopted in 1920 will be those in Senator Sargent's proposal of 1878.

14 JANUARY 1878

Transportation   In *Hall v Cuir*, the Supreme Court finds that railroads need not provide equal accomodations to all passengers regardless of race.

17 JANUARY 1878

International   A treaty between the United States and Samoa is ratified by Congress. The harbor of Pago Pago will be given to the United States Navy for use as a fueling station. Ratification by Congress demonstrates a growing interest in events in the world outside the continental United States.

22 FEBRUARY 1878

National   The Greenback and Labor Reform parties pool their strength and unite into the Greenback Labor Party. The party will press for more greenbacks and free coinage of silver, restrictions on Chinese immigration and fewer working hours for labor. Twenty-eight states are represented at the Convention, 800 delegates being present. During this election year the party garners 1,060,000 votes and sends 14 representatives to Congress. In 1880 the party endorses woman's suffrage and in 1884 Benjamin F. Butler, the old Reconstructionist, will be its candidate for President.

28 FEBRUARY 1878

Currency   The Bland-Allison Act is passed by Congress. Deflation of currency has reached its lowest point since the Civil War. Meanwhile silver has been found in great abundance in the West and miners team up with pro-inflationary farmers and workers to press for unlimited use of silver in coins. The Bland-Allison Act provides for silver coinage but the number is restricted to monthly purchases between $2,000,000 and $4,000,000. The conservative Secretary of the Treasury keeps his purchases to the $2,000,000 minimum to avoid unhealthy inflation and, in any case, the country comes out of the depression by the following year, thus removing some of the silverite pressure.

MAY 1878

Regional   A massive epidemic of yellow fever sweeps through the South. It is brought to New Orleans from Havana and spreads rapidly, the more so as people already infected flee the area and spread the germs far and wide. Louisiana, Mississippi, Alabama and Tennessee are the hardest hit, but the epidemic reaches as far north as Cincinnati. Twenty-four thousand cases are reported in New Orleans alone, with 4000 fatalities. Ultimately the virulent fever claims 14,000 lives before it subsides for the winter. The next year it will break out again, but its former power has been weakened by winter's cold; New Orleans, now enforcing a rigid quarantine, reports only 41 cases. Help pours into the stricken areas from all over the world, Americans themselves donating some $400,000 in cash and generously sending doctors and nurses, clothing and supplies.

3 JUNE 1878

Conservation   The Timber and Stone Act is passed by Congress. By permitting the cutting of timber on public land the act will ostensibly increase the acreage of farmland. Because farmers tend to work extensively rather than intensively, the land is eroding cataclysmically. New land is needed as soil becomes exhausted from overuse and bad management. However, the Timber and Stone Act achieves other goals. Most of the timbered land goes to timber interests. Only one-sixteenth of lands given to small claimants becomes farm land. Some of the richest forests ever seen by man are sold for $2.50 an acre.

11 JUNE 1878

Regional   The District of Columbia receives a permanent constitution by Act of Congress. Ironically, in the capital of the bastion of freedom, residents will have no direct voice on either local or national matters.

18 JUNE 1878

National   The United States Life-Saving Service is established by Act of Congress. It is the first such government organization in the world. The bill is brought forward by Representative S.S. Cox of New York and the service is made a subdivision of the Treasury Department.

11 JULY 1878

National   President Hayes, with the consent of the Senate and with Democratic support, removes the suave Chester A. Arthur from his post as Collector of Customs for the Port of New York, one of the most lucrative patronage posts of all. This is the beginning of Hayes' attempt to reform the civil service system which is badly in need of change. However, Hayes runs afoul of "Boss" Roscoe Conkling on this matter

FORGING A NATION 1866-1900

LAND, LUMBER AND BUSINESS

Forest and farm land were fast becoming big business. Forest land was called pine land if two or three of the valuable white Norway pines were to be found on an acre. In Northern Wisconsin and on out to the Pacific Coast, acres with 16 to 20 fully matured trees could commonly be found. Pine is straight-grained, light and strong. Being resinous, it resists bug infestation and rot and floats easily in the rivers and streams. Demand for Wisconsin pine grew as whites settled the Plains. Indians were forced to cede their primeval forests as early as 1836. Starting in 1831 with Daniel Whitney's sawmill in Wisconsin, mills appeared almost overnight. By 1890 there were 1033 sawmills with an annual cut of approximately 4,000,000,000 board feet. A mill could consume 200,000 board feet a day. At 20,000 board feet an acre, one mill could chew up 10 acres or 400 large logs a day. In 1857 some 2500 lumbermen found work in Wisconsin; by 1873, 7500 could find work, 1200 at the Knapp and Stouts mill alone. This company, following the national trend, was quick to see the benefits of vertical organization, and was consolidating smaller businesses and outlets into its own structure. Lumbermen were necessarily strong and courageous; they either died in the dangerous work or got rich. A good raft pilot could clear $1000 in a season, and many invested their money in down–river finishing mills. At first the river provided the means of getting timber out of the forest. Boards were cut into 12-16 foot strips, then cribs of 12-20 boards were built. Seven cribs made a "rapids piece." These were then floated together into rafts. As the rivers widened, rafts were consolidated into ever-larger units. Rafts of 120 cribs, or two-thirds of an acre, were common. Once steamboats began to pull the rafts they were known to reach three to four acres apiece. Log jams could be terrible. In 1869 on the Chippewa, boards backed up for 15 miles, crumbling like matchsticks into stacks 30 feet high. Dams and slides were built to control the mammoth jams which resulted from uncoordinated dumping into tributary rivers.

Fortunes were made in the early days of the lumber business when land was given out almost free and there were few restrictions on forest management and no conservation regulations of any kind. The railroads soon threw in their lot with lumber interests and changed the industry, expanding its seasons beyond the winter months and making accessible prime timber growing far from river banks. Between 1890 and 1900, Wisconsin lumber was a $70,000,000 business and one-fourth of all the State's wages went to lumbermen. It was thoughtless exploitation of a vulnerable resource. Some of the devastation can still be seen in what is called the Wisconsin Cutover where today nothing grows at all.

and does not do much more than weaken the Republican party.

15 OCTOBER 1878

Industry In what will amount to a complete revolution in the American way of life, Edison establishes the Edison Electric Light Company in New York City. Although Edison won't find the answer to the incandescent light for another year, he knows he is on the track and it is only a matter of time. J. P. Morgan and other financiers are eager to invest in any invention of Edison's and back the company which plans to produce electricity on a large scale for public and private use. Once the light bulb is developed, other companies are quickly formed to cash in on the electrical bonanza. But guided by Financier J. P. Morgan, a master of the vertical organization, the Edison Company soon eats up all its rivals and becomes the General Electric Company. The only one to hold out is the Westinghouse Company, established by the inventor George Westinghouse in 1886. To forego further competition the two companies come to agreements on the division of patents and territories. No laws prevent monopolies or such unfair competition, so that small companies simply go under.

27 OCTOBER 1878

Life/Customs "Western George" L. Leslie was once

THE NEZ PERCE WAR

By the 1870s the Nez Percé Indians were reduced to a small reservation at Lapwai in northeastern Oregon. Their chief was a great statesman and fighter whom the whites called Chief Joseph. He is remembered as the "Red Napoleon" for his daring and skill in battle. Final trouble for the Nez Percés broke out in 1877. Joseph had sadly agreed to go to an even smaller reservation because gold had been found in the area ceded to him by treaty. Through the usual methods of trickery and bribery, agents had managed to wrest a dubious document purporting to sign away this Indian land. The Indians objected that the documents held no binding force because they had not been signed by the chiefs. But to no avail. Wishing to avoid a suicidal fight, Joseph agreed to retreat to the smaller reservation. On the way, several young braves, unhappy with the way things were going, attacked settlers along the Salmon River, killing 19. Troops instantly counterattacked but were defeated by the desperate Indians; 34 soldiers were killed, two Indians died. Now began one of the great epics of Indian history. Chief Joseph saw no way of coming to terms with the Army. His only hope was to escape with his tribe to Canada. Afraid to let them go, the Army pursued them with ruthless, wasteful vengeance. At the Battle of Clear Water, General Howard was defeated and the Indians captured his artillery and pack train. Sustained by this victory, the Nez Percés proceeded through the Bitterroot Mountains. At Big Hole Basin in Montana, the Indians defended themselves against a surprise attack by Colonel John Gibbon, killing most of the white infantry. In the Bear Paw Mountains, just 30 miles from the Canadian border, Colonel Nelson Miles, a veteran of many Indian battles, trapped the Indians. His troops vastly outnumbered Chief Joseph's tired band.

Pursued by the Army, which was freshly reinforced at each stage, the Indians had carried their wounded, their women, children and old people with them. They had managed to cover 1300 miles before their pursuers stopped them at the very gates of freedom. The Indians had had five major engagements with the enemy, but had lost the important one, the last. They were sent to the malaria-ridden reservations of Oklahoma, where most were unable to endure the harsh conditions. Later, remnants of the tribe, once their spirits had been broken, were permitted to return to Washington Territory.

thought to have been responsible for four-fifths of all American bank robberies, although perhaps many of these robberies are attached to his name merely to enhance a legend. By far the biggest of his hauls is the $3,000,000 burglary of the Manhattan Institute for Savings. Two of his accomplices are brought to trial for this heist, but "Western George" is never caught.

5 NOVEMBER 1878
National In the mid-term elections, control of both houses of Congress reverts to the Democratic Party. Members from the new Greenback Party are seated.

9 DECEMBER 1878
Finance Greenbacks reach face value on Wall Street. They can be redeemed one–for–one for gold for the first time since 1862.

DECEMBER 1878
Indian Affairs The Dull Knife Campaign in Wyoming Territory is a remarkable effort on the part of the Northern Cheyennes to break out of the dreadful malaria-ridden reservation in Oklahoma where they are concentrated. Under the leadership of Morning Star, also known as Dull Knife, they manage to escape. In an heroic, if doomed, attempt to reach Montana Territory and their rich hunting grounds, they fight off capture for many months, suffering great hardships in their fight for freedom. Many die in battle. Finally forced to surrender to the pursuing Army, they are returned to the unhealthy reservation, nevermore to attempt rebellion.

OTHER EVENTS OF 1878
Industry George Eastman begins manufacture of photographic dry plate.
Science/Technology Albert A. Michelson measures distances by light wave–lengths. He uses his own invention, an interferometer, to grasp the enormous interplanetary distances he is measuring.

1 JANUARY 1879
Finance Greenbacks have reached a face value with gold. The public has confidence in the government's ability to redeem paper in specie, which will be done for the first time since 1861. When specie payments begin, as authorized by Congress in 1875, there is no great demand for the coinage.

25 JANUARY 1879
National The Arrears of Pensions Act is passed by Congress. It authorizes back-payment of military pensions beginning from the day of discharge. If the veteran is dead, payments will be made to the family.

ANDREW CARNEGIE, 1835-1919

As much as any man, Andrew Carnegie created the new era of finance capitalism.

Born in Scotland, Carnegie emigrated to the United States when he was 13. He worked as a bobbin boy in a cotton factory, but brilliant, hardworking and highly competitive, he soon climbed the economic ladder. Making money in various enterprises, he hit the big time when a farm of his returned oil. Carnegie understood well in advance of most the beauty of consolidation. He could foresee the results of owning the sources of raw materials, the means of transportation and production, and the manufacturing outlets. Carnegie made sure he did. Iron fields, steamships, railroads, oil, everything he needed he got. By aggressive manipulation he coerced his competitors to choose between ruin and selling to him. He started a gigantic steel mill on the Monongahela near Pittsburgh, and later bought the Homestead works which got caught in the much publicized strikes during the labor unrest of the 1890s.

He got Congress to enact protective legislation, took advantage of inadequate policing by state and federal governments, and by 1880 had fulfilled his ambition: he had monopolized the steel industry.

Eventually, he retired to Scotland. There he proceeded to divest himself of an estimated $350,000,000 of his $400,000,000 fortune before his death. His name still tops a brilliant roster of institutions, including the Carnegie Endowment for Peace and the Carnegie Institute of Technology.

Carnegie brought out the paradoxes of his times. In the name of competition he did as much as anyone to crush it. Ruining thousands of his fellow Americans, he spoke happily of his respect for "Individualism." He wrote of the sanctity of the "Accumulation of Wealth," and saw no need to protect the social structures usually held dear by free people. His privately owned companies were richer than most nations, and he had absolute control over the lives of his workers. Nonetheless he spoke of his vast empire as if it were just a local hardware store on Main Street. The contradictions he brought to the surface tantalize and bedevil all discussions about capitalism to this day.

Andrew Carnegie, capitalist extraordinary.

FORGING A NATION 1866-1900

STEEL

In 1860 the United States produced approximately one million tons of pig-iron. By 1900 production had jumped to 36,000,000 tons and the country was first in the world in the manufacture of iron and steel products.

The mining of iron began in the Appalachians in early colonial times. The industry moved steadily westward until in the 1840s it reached spectacular deposits in northern Michigan. Forty years later, the extraordinary Mesabi range on Lake Superior offered up its easy-to-mine and extremely pure treasure. Coal and iron were brought to the centrally located smelters of Chicago where the first steel rails were rolled in 1865. With steel rails the railroads could expand like so much ribbon. Other smelters began to flourish in Pittsburgh and other mid-west cities. By the 1880s the coal and iron deposits of the Southern Appalachians were exploited and Birmingham could claim to rival Pittsburgh.

The Kelly-Bessemer and open hearth processes, electricity and chemistry all contributed to the gigantic growth of the industry. The open hearth process produced superior steel and by 1880 became the predominant method of manufacture.

Mill life for the workers was hard in the extreme. It was not unusual for the fiery furnaces to claim 200 deaths a year in a single factory. Neither state nor federal governments concerned themselves with workers. Usually they had been bribed into passivity by mill owners. Labor had not yet devised the means to deal with the new industrial giants.

At first steel mills grew strong in the almost genial competition of pre-Civil War days. Alexander Holley and Abram S. Hewitt of New York pioneered the new technological processes, sharing their knowledge throughout the spreading industry. When Andrew Carnegie and his men came on the scene, vertical organization took over, crushing out competition like so much pig-iron. Carnegie ended up with most of the industry in his hands. The added efficiency was in some ways admirable. By 1890 the United States made more steel than Great Britain and by 1900 the country made more than Germany and Great Britain combined. Although American raw materials combined with American labor produced the American steel, $400,000,000 in profits went to Carnegie. In 1901 Carnegie sold his company to a J.P. Morgan combine, capitalized at $1,400,000,000, which called itself United States Steel. It was America's first billion-dollar corporation.

15 FEBRUARY 1879
National By an act of Congress women lawyers are given the right to practice before the Supreme Court.

1 MARCH 1879
National Since the Democrats have gained control of Congress, they have been working to repeal the Enforcement Acts of 1865 and 1874 which have given the President power to use Federal Troops in elections to prevent infringement of civil rights. The acts are aimed at the South, and now that Democrats are back in power pressure mounts for repeal. Democrats attach a rider to the Army Appropriations Act. Passage of the rider will weaken the power of government to offer protection against infringement of civil rights. It will also weaken Executive power. Hayes, with the help of Radical and Liberal Republicans, successfully vetoes the bill. He does so on four subsequent occasions. By meeting the challenge from Congress head on, Hayes begins to restore Presidential independence which has been lost by Johnson during the bitter battles over Reconstruction in the late 1860s.

11 MARCH 1879
Immigration Congress passes a bill to restrict Chinese immigration. President Hayes vetoes it on the grounds that it violates the Burlingame Treaty of 1868.

7 MAY 1879
Regional Feeling against "cheap Chinese labor" is running so high in California that when the State is adopting a new constitution, a clause is inserted and accepted which forbids employment of any Chinese laborers. The man behind the clause is the very popular unemployed Californian Denis Kearney whose Workingmen's Party is strictly based on racial issues. His speeches always begin and end with "The Chinese must go." He usually delivers his rabble-rousing rhetoric in vacant lots in San Francisco. He and his followers become known as "Sandlotters."

28 JUNE 1879
Regional The Mississippi River Commission is authorized by an act of Congress. It consists of seven members appointed by the President. Its purpose is to improve navigability of the immense and ever-shifting river.

JUNE 1879
Black Experience Beginning to feel the inexorable pressure of white rule, blacks suddenly panic, sell their small holdings and by the thousands cross the Mississippi heading toward St. Louis. It is a mysterious move, exacerbated by lurid tales of Indians coming to attack. The mass of migrants, some 7000 by August, camps in hot, dusty Kansas which, a poor State, valiantly comes to their aid, providing food and shelter and also their nickname: "the exodusters." The Mayor of St. Louis warns them against coming to his city, explaining he cannot provide for them. It is a feverish, uncoordinated exodus which climaxes in summer and dies down by the end of the year.

SEPTEMBER 1879
Indian Affairs The Ute Indians turn on a dictatorial Indian agent, ambush a military force, and set upon the agency. They are quickly subdued. Under provisions of a "treaty" the entire Ute nation is forced onto the Utah reservation. To leave reservations becomes exceedingly dangerous. The white population is in an ugly mood toward Indians since Custer's ill-fated military maneuvers of 1876. A directive has gone out to either kill or get unconditional surrender from all Indians. When the veteran Indian fighter General George Crook negotiates a surrender with the Apaches, he is dismissed overnight.

THE NOBLE ORDER OF THE KNIGHTS OF LABOR

The first national labor union, the Noble Order of the Knights of Labor, was founded in 1869 by Uriah S. Stephens. Stephens was a tailor, and his union grew out of a craft approach to labor's problems. However, it soon opened its doors to all comers, men and women, skilled and unskilled, white and black. Only gamblers, liquor dealers, lawyers and bankers, "all whom God abjures," were excluded. The aims of the union were noble and vague: "To secure to the toilers a proper share of the wealth they create; more of the leisure that rightfully belongs to them; more of the rights and privileges and emoluments of the world. . . ." Through cooperation and arbitration and political activity, the union strove to get the eight–hour day, abolition of child labor, better wages, better working conditions. The growth of the union matched the tipping of ever more Americans into the industrial pool of poverty as land became scarce, dreams more difficult to fulfill, and immigration reached staggering heights. When Terence Powderly took over as Grand Master in 1878 the union had a membership of 50,000. He began to shape it into a political force. In 1882 the Knights helped to get Congress to enact the Chinese Exclusion Act, and in 1885 they took credit for an act forbidding importation of contract labor. Later they were instrumental in passage of the Interstate Commerce Act and the Sherman Anti-trust law. Allying themselves with farmers in the South, they helped overthrow entrenched backward–looking Bourbon regimes. But it was the Knights' victory over Railroader Jay Gould in 1884 that gave them national popularity. The powerful entrepreneur sat down with labor executives as equals, and rescinded an order to cut wages. The following year the union jumped to 700,000 members. In 1886, the Noble Order was caught in the Haymarket tragedy. Although the order was not responsible in any way for the bombing, an easily swayed public was confirmed in its fear that labor was infiltrated by foreign saboteurs, and the political intentions of the organization were called into question. By 1890 the Knights had fallen to 100,000 members and declined steadily thereafter.

19-21 OCTOBER 1879

Science/Technology Thomas A. Edison finds that a thread of carbonized cotton in one–millionth of an atmosphere will burn for 45 hours without overheating. His dream of an incandescent lightbulb is within reach. He will now proceed to test 6000 other possible vegetable fibers which he has in his well-stocked laboratory at Menlo Park, New Jersey. He finally settles on carbonized bamboo which he finds lasts for 1000 hours. Nine years later tungsten will satisfactorily replace carbonized bamboo. Edison immediately puts his invention to practical use. By the following year the Edison Electric Light Company begins to light up New York City.

12 FEBRUARY 1880

Regional Far west of the Mississippi, south of Kansas, Arkansas and Missouri, are some two million acres of Indian territory, ceded to them by treaty in 1866. Not all this land is as lush and salubrious as envious would-be settlers describe, but some of it is rich enough to attract trespassers rolling westward. Cattle ranchers begin to fence in prime land and covetous outsiders begin to press for opening of the forbidden territory. President Hayes issues a warning against illegal settlers, ordering them to refrain from inciting the Indians by usurping their lands. It is only a staying gesture. The land will be turned over to settlers in 1889.

MARCH 1880

Ideas/Beliefs At the request of an advance group in Philadelphia, Commissioner George Railton and seven women come to organize the American branch of the Salvation Army. The Army is a philanthropic and evangelical organization which holds that self-sacrifice is one's supreme duty, and that the reality of sin can be offset by the reality of redemption through good works. Its cheery brass bands become known in every nation of the world and its helping hands will reach

THOMAS ALVA EDISON, 1847-1931

Thomas Alva Edison was born into one of the most intensely inventive times in history, and Edison was the man for his time. He claimed he was an inventor and not a discoverer, because, as he explained: "In a discovery there must be an element of accident, while an invention is purely deductive." Long hours and infinite patience characterized his working methods. But this was not all: he also set up a dream laboratory, Menlo Park in New Jersey. It contained every material and chemical then known to man. He could order up parts or whole machines at will, and could design and have built any object he could imagine.

Thomas Edison was born on February 11, 1847 in Milan, Ohio. Although there was nothing in his background to account for his dazzling genius, he was all his life inventive in both practical and mechanical ways. As a child he was taught at home by his schoolteacher mother and by 12 years he was selling newspapers on a railroad route to finance his experiments.

At 21 he took a job in a brokerage house in New York. True to form, he made some elegant changes in the stock tickers. He sold the rights for an astonishing $40,000 and set himself up as a freelance inventor, a fulltime profession one could not have claimed in any other period in history. For the next five years, he patented a new invention almost every month.

Edison was slightly deaf and, when on the trail of an idea, often irascible. He was a little stooped, and usually unkempt, wearing a chemist's white coat, smoking long cigars, his fingers burned and stained by his chemicals, his hair dirty from oils and dust. His baby face belied the intensity of his dreams. He could go for days without eating or sleeping if he were on the verge of a solution. On the day he married Mary Stilwell, he went back to his laboratory for the night, quite forgetting his bride.

His ideas were the basis of whole industries; mere modifications became another's wealth. From among his hundreds of important inventions, the electric light bulb and its subsequent supply system, the gramophone and the "kinetoscopic," or motion picture, are perhaps his most refreshingly revolutionary productions. He was without doubt the most inventive man in American history.

FORGING A NATION 1866-1900

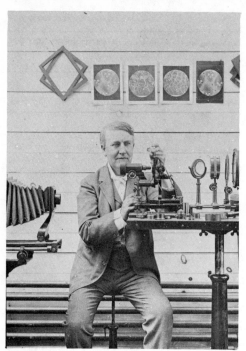

Thomas A. Edison in his laboratory.

out to hundreds of thousands of people in desperate need.

1 MARCH 1880
National In *Strauder* v. *West Virginia* the Supreme Court finds it unconstitutional to exclude blacks from jury duty. The Court bases its findings on the Fourteenth Amendment.

8 MARCH 1880
International President Hayes warns that any canal across the Isthmus of Panama will be strictly under United States control.

18 MARCH 1880
The Frenchman Ferdinand de Lesseps is asked to testify before a House committee regarding the French Canal Company which is building the Panama Canal. De Lesseps assures the House that France has no official connection with the canal.

APRIL 1880
National The National Farmers Alliance, also called the Northern Alliance, is organized by Milton George. In 1892 it will help to form the People's Party, also called the Populist Party. The farmers' plight has taken on the proportions of catastrophe in the face of high tariffs, flood and drought, unfair railroad rates and high interest on loans and mortgages.
Regional Wabash, Indiana, is the first town to be completely lit by electric light. In a public demonstra-

tion Wabash installs Charles F. Brush's arc lamp system which had already been tried the year before in Cleveland and San Francisco. However Thomas A. Edison's invention of the more versatile incandescent lightbulb, and J. P. Morgan's financing of the Edison Electric Light Company, doom Brush's system.

8 JUNE 1880
National James A. Garfield of Ohio is nominated as Republican candidate for president on the 36th ballot, besting General Grant in a fight for the nomination. The convention is split between Roscoe Conkling and other Stalwart followers of Grant, and those that follow the popular leader James G. Blaine. When the two finally stop fighting they pool their votes to back Garfield. The Stalwarts manage to get their man, the urbane Chester A. Arthur, onto the ticket as the vice-presidential nominee. During the convention Senator Blanche K. Bruce of Mississippi is temporarily made presiding officer, thus becoming the first black chairman of a major political convention.

9 JUNE 1880
National In Chicago the National Convention of the Greenback Labor Party nominates James B. Weaver for president and B. J. Chambers of Texas for vice-president.

17 JUNE 1880
National The Third National Convention of the Pro-

THE SALVATION ARMY

One of the noblest groups to respond to the needs created by an industrial society was the Salvation Army, founded in 1865 in England by William Booth. Booth was concerned with spreading the Gospel to counteract the materialism dominating the Industrial Society. The idea caught on and in 1880 the group was reorganized into a disciplined body with Booth made "General." Soon the organization, basing itself on good works, spread throughout the world. It established social centers from which to preach its evangelical message. These centers directly helped local populations and served to invent new ways to reach those in greatest need. Training schools for Army volunteers were also begun to meet the needs of new recruits. After the reorganization of 1880, members began to wear uniforms, and were formed along quasi-military lines.

The Army's doctrine asserted the reality of sin and the promise of redemption. It upheld self-sacrifice as a person's supreme duty. It saw itself as at war with the forces of evil, forces most visible in the slums and poverty-stricken areas of the industrial world. Among the most familiar and endearing aspects of the Salvation Army were its street bands which have delighted many over the years.

The United States branch of the Army was established in 1880 by Commissioner George Railton and seven women members. Later Commander Evangeline Booth, daughter of the founder, was put in charge. (In the Army women have absolute equality with men.) She served ably, helping the organization to prosper, enabling it to expand its philanthropic work in war and peace.

hibition Party nominates Neal Dow of Maine for president and A.M. Thompson of Ohio for vice-president.

24 JUNE 1880
National The Democratic National convention picks General Winfield S. Hancock of Pennsylvania for president and William H. English of Indiana for vice-president. There is little to choose between the Republican platform and the Democratic one, now that black Reconstruction is out of the way. Both weakly advocate civil service reform, both are in favor of exclusion of Chinese immigration. Both advocate high protective tariffs. In the 15 years since the end of the Civil War, a fundamental shift from an agrarian to an industrial/technological society has taken place. Finance capital has found its way and industry has blossomed. But social forms and judicial restraints lag far behind. Solutions worked out for small businesses or feudal societies no longer apply to impersonal corporations of continental size. Laborer, farmer, city dweller, politician flounder in paradoxes presented to them by new needs. Cherished values and protections of free men are being lost just when a promised better world seems within grasp. Now, when the nation could have profited from vigorous public debate, Congress is dominated by rascally, small-minded men.

3 JULY 1880
International In a move to support national independence movements in Morocco, major European nations and the United States meet in Madrid and agree to prevent Moroccan territory from being "protected" by outside powers.

2 NOVEMBER 1880
National James A. Garfield wins the presidency by 214 to 155 electoral votes. Chester A. Arthur becomes vice-president. It has been an ugly, personal campaign and the passions inflamed by the very men who should set the standards for rational debate will have serious repercussions before the year is out.

17 NOVEMBER 1880
International The Chinese Exclusion Treaty is

Republican National Convention, Chicago, 1880.

FORGING A NATION 1866-1900

signed by China and the United States. It permits the United States to restrict but not exclude immigration of Chinese laborers.

20 DECEMBER 1880
Regional To a glittering New York, new glitter is added when an entire mile of Broadway is lit by the Brush arc–light system.

OTHER EVENTS OF 1880
Science/Technology George Eastman patents a roll of film for cameras. Development of the camera for home use proceeded apace in the following years. By 1885 a box camera with film sealed inside was put on the market. The camera and film both had to be sent back to the Eastman Company in Rochester, New York, for developing of the film. By 1891 Eastman had perfected a daylight loading camera, and the first pocket Kodak was in use by 1895. Meanwhile the Kampfe Brothers of New York City invent the safety razor, beginning the slow change to do-it-yourself shaving. And an all-purpose house paint is manufactured in Cleveland by the Sherwin-Williams Company to a standard formula.

Life/Customs By order of the Irish Land League the Irish are forbidden to supply British land agent Captain Charles Boycott with any provisions. It is from this event that the word "boycott" originates, and it

will soon be adopted as a tactic by American labor.

19 JANUARY 1881
Industry In 1866 the Western Union Telegraph Company had taken over the United States and American Telegraph Companies to control some 75,000 miles of wire and to forge the new pattern of monopoly which would subsequently dominate the industry. In 1881 financiers Jay Gould and William H. Vanderbilt direct their Western Union to gobble up American Union and Atlantic– and Pacific–coast companies thus consolidating and maintaining the monopolistic character of the business. Consolidation is admittedly efficient and makes for greater profits, but by cutting out competition it will call forth its own modifying backlash. Movements to offset raw efficiency and simple profit motives with rules of fair play begin to take on a political character.

24 JANUARY 1881
National In *Springer v. United States,* the Supreme Court finds that income tax laws are constitutional. The Court argues that the Federal Income Tax Law of

1862 was not enacted as a restricted tax such as those on real estate or slaves had been, and so did not come under Article I, Section 8 of the Constitution which bars a non–uniform tax.

19 FEBRUARY 1881
Regional   Kansas is the first state to prohibit the sale of liquor.

22 FEBRUARY 1881
National   President Hayes, whose wife is nicknamed Lemonade Lucy because she serves no alcohol in the White House, decrees that no alcoholic beverages are to be sold at military posts.

3 MARCH 1881
National   With a bow to the fact that many businesses have expanded to become national enterprises, Congress authorizes a central registration agency for the protection of trademarks.

4 MARCH 1881
National   James A. Garfield is inaugurated president and Chester A. Arthur becomes vice–president of the United States.

5 MARCH 1881
National   James G. Blaine is appointed secretary of state, a victory for the "Half–breed" faction of Congress. It leads to a bitter split in the party. President Garfield stirs up another hornets' nest when he appoints Judge William H. Robertson to the lucrative

---

CLARA BARTON, 1821-1912

One of several positive institutions that came out of the Civil War was the American Branch of the Red Cross, and this is most directly attributed to Clara Barton. Born in rural Massachusetts, Barton had been a school teacher and then was working as a clerk in the United States Patent Office when the war began. She volunteered to help care for the wounded soldiers and soon recognized the need not only for medical nursing but also for supplies and support for morale. Going to Union camps and even to battlefields, Barton became known among the troops as "the angel of the battlefield." By 1864 she was officially appointed the "lady in charge" of the hospitals of the Federal Army of the James. Lincoln asked her to lead the search for the many missing Union men, and in 1865 she went to Andersonville, the site of the Confederate prison in Georgia, to identify and mark the graves of the thousands of Union dead. When the war ended, Barton turned to lecturing on her experiences, and finding herself in Europe during the Franco-German War in 1870, she worked at the front with the International Red Cross. Growing out of an organization started in 1863, the Red Cross impressed Clara Barton as the instrument to achieve her goals, and on returning to the United States she worked to establish the American National Red Cross. It was 1881 before she obtained formal recognition from the President and she was to serve as its head until 1904. During these years she was influential in extending the organization's activities beyond the casualties of wars to those suffering in floods, famines, fires and other disasters.

JAMES ABRAM GARFIELD, 1831-1881

James A. Garfield was born in a log cabin on a farm in Ohio. His was a constant struggle with poverty, but by 1856 Garfield had graduated from Williams College, a student of ancient languages and literature. Within a year he was principal of the Eclectic Institute of Hiram showing early his leadership abilities.

He served honorably during the Civil War, and was made a major-general of volunteers for his intelligence and bravery in battle. In 1863 he resigned his commission to become an Ohio representative to Congress, where he joined Thaddeus Stevens, Charles Sumner and Ben Butler in the exciting Radical Reconstruction battles of post-Civil War days. Garfield was a pious man, a strong, melodic speaker, and became a hardworking member of important committees dealing with the intractable problems of the freedmen. In the 1870s, the Republicans were mired in petty-minded politics and corruption. Garfield played along with the trivialities of the time. He was a Republican member of the Electoral Commission, the famous "Eight to Seven" which resolved the Hayes-Tilden 1876 dispute. As Senator from Ohio he went to the 1880 Republican Convention which became deadlocked over a third term for General Grant. Conkling's Stalwarts, backing Grant, were fighting Blaine's Half–breeds. Finally on the 36th ballot the two agreed to compromise on Garfield if Conkling could have Chester A. Arthur thrown in as vice-president. It was a disgusting spectacle degrading the office of president, unworthy of the officials elected to some of the highest posts in American political life. Passions were inflamed and subsided slowly.

On July 2, 1881 Garfield was on his way to Williams College in Massachusetts when he was shot in the back by Charles J. Guiteau. Fatally wounded, Garfield lingered on through the hot summer. He died on September 19, 1881. Garfield had been a self-denying, good man. The entire nation was saddened by the tragedy of his death. In Europe, the Royal Courts observed a day of mourning, the first ever for a citizen of a republic.

---

position of Collector of Customs for the Port of New York. Judge Robertson is a political opponent of New York Senator Roscoe Conkling, who considers himself in control of New York's patronage system.

16 MAY 1881
National   New York Senators Roscoe Conkling and Thomas Platt stall on the appointment of James G. Blaine for secretary of state. They then proceed to make a tactical error: both resign to protest the appointment. They are surprised and dismayed when the New York Legislature refuses to reelect them. Conkling's "Stalwart" Republicans lose much of their political clout. One benefit to the country from this distasteful encounter is that the Executive Office retrieves some of the power lost in the early days of Reconstruction. However, passions have been stirred and the subsequent assassination of President Garfield is directly related to this unseemly squabble carried on in public at the highest levels of government.

21 MAY 1881
Ideas/Beliefs   The American Red Cross, a branch of the International Red Cross, is organized by Clara

FORGING A NATION 1866-1900

Barton who has been working with the parent group in Europe. Clara Barton is made president of the American branch.

24 JUNE 1881

International Secretary of State James G. Blaine, protecting United States interests in the Western Hemisphere, sends strong letters to European ministers asking them to refrain from making guarantees to Ferdinand de Lesseps and his company organized privately to build the Panama Canal.

2 JULY 1881

National On a hot summer day while waiting for a train to take him to New England, President James A. Garfield is shot by a madman at the station in Washington D.C. Crying "I am a Stalwart and Arthur will be President!" Charles Guiteau fatally wounds the President, although he lives out the summer, dying on September 19. Guiteau is a smalltime "Stalwart" who expected a small job after Republicans won the national elections. He has not been offered any position, and stirred up by Roscoe Conkling's ugly fight over Blaine's appointment as secretary of state, Guiteau blames Garfield for his own failure to get a job. Guiteau is apprehended on the spot and hanged after a trial, a year later, on June 30, 1882. The public's interest in Civil Service Reform and removal of the

The shooting of President James A. Garfield.

spoils system stems from this day's tragedy.

4 JULY 1881

Black Experience Tuskegee Normal and Industrial Institute is founded by black leader Booker T. Washington in Alabama. Tuskegee is the base from which Washington rises to national prominence. He is a new kind of leader, non-revolutionary, anxious to better his people but without violence or conflict. At Tuskegee Institute he advocates an education limited to vocational skills. Whites respect Washington because he seems to express their racial predisposition. Many blacks follow him, hoping he will help them to a toehold on American society, no matter how tenuous. Others believe he betrays his race into third–class citizenship. Washington becomes the center of black controversy. Washington's simple, yet effective, leadership counsels slow but steady progress and slow but sure acceptance within the American structure. Only in the 1880s is the South beginning to abandon its dependence on cotton and starting to diversify into fruits, vegetables, timber, coal and steel. Tentative moves have been made to invite northern capital into southern territory to help develop its industrial potential. Soon Birmingham will rival Pittsburgh as a steel center. Booker T. Washington methodically helps to prepare blacks for a place in the industrial sun.

24 AUGUST 1881

Science/Technology The United States Government establishes a scientific observation post in northern Greenland. Lieutenant Adolphus W. Greeley is put in charge of the expedition. He is to remain there, with 24 others, for two years, making observations for a multi-national undertaking. In 1883 a relief party will fail to reach Greeley's expedition. On June 22, 1884, eight survivors are rescued just as their final rations of mosses, lichen and seal skin have given out.

19 SEPTEMBER 1881

National President James A. Garfield dies. Doctors have been most diplomatically uninformative during his last days, and no official determination has been made as to whether Garfield is fit to carry on the office of the president as he lies dying in bed. His death causes an international outpouring of grief, and a day of mourning is declared in the Courts of Europe, the first time ever for a citizen of a Republic.

20 SEPTEMBER 1881

National Chester A. Arthur is inaugurated 21st President of the United States. He is an old–time professional spoilsman, a good friend of "Boss" Roscoe Conkling. The news of his rise to the highest office in the land causes apprehension. However, Arthur manages to keep himself independent of Roscoe's discredited "Stalwarts." Considering his background as Collector of Customs for the Port of New York, and considering his friendship with some of the more unsavory characters of his time, Arthur will serve as a fairly honest if not necessarily distinguished President. In the process he will alienate and weaken his party which is held together by some overly pragmatic spoilsmen. He paves the way for the first Democratic President since the inception of the Civil War.

17 NOVEMBER 1881

Labor Under the steadying hand of Samuel Gompers, the Federation of Organized Trades and Labor Unions of the United States is formed. It is a forerunner of the American Federation of Labor, the characteristically American entrant into the labor reform movement. Gompers' group will serve to de-mystify union activities, ridding itself of all the old rituals and trappings of secret societies beloved of the 19th century. It will offer an alternative to violent political action and to socialist ideas of government operation of industry. Gompers will help to unite labor groups and steer them to immediate and socially acceptable goals.

22 NOVEMBER 1881

International James G. Blaine, putting his charismatic energies into the office of Secretary of State, launches the Pan-American movement with an invitation to Latin American nations to meet in Washington in 1882. However, when Garfield dies, Half–breed Blaine tenders his resignation to old Stalwart Chester Arthur who accepts it. Congress is not ready to shoulder international responsibilities. Blaine's initiative is not followed up by his successor.

1 DECEMBER 1881

International In one of his last acts in office, Secretary of State James G. Blaine declares that the Hawaiian Islands are part of the American system and

---

CHESTER A. ARTHUR, 1830-1886

Chester A. Arthur was the New York darling of the Stalwart faction of an increasingly corrupt Republican Party. Urbane, goodlooking, his blond hair and muttonchop sideburns always curled and combed, his clothes always in the very height of fashion, he wandered smoothly in and out of the drawing rooms of power. Thanks to Senator Roscoe Conkling's patronage, he was given the post of Collector of Customs for the Port of New York, an office well known for its temptations. When Conkling and Blaine hotly contested the 1880 Republican presidential nomination, dark horse James Garfield got the compromise nod for president but Conkling's friend Chester Arthur was given the vice-presidential slot. Conkling and other Republican bosses liked genial, gentleman Arthur. He was a clubman with refined tastes and an easy way of making firm friendships. His early career was marked by larceny and loyalty to corrupt men of the Conkling stamp. Apprehension greeted the news of his accession to the Executive Office. He did not distinguish himself as president but he did put corruption aside and initiated some badly needed civil service reforms, tangling, in the process, with his old Stalwart allies. Arthur lived through a time of incredible changes without seeming to notice any of them. He is probably one of the least distinguished of American Presidents.

FORGING A NATION 1866-1900

thus come under the intent of the Monroe Doctrine. Blaine is the first post-Civil War politician to recognize the need for an American foreign policy.

2 JANUARY 1882
Industry John D. Rockefeller organizes the Standard Oil Trust to circumvent the laws of individual States which set limits to the running of his organization. The trust is the brainchild of a Rockefeller lawyer named Samuel C. T. Dodd. It is immediately successful and becomes the example upon which other large corporations will model their organizations. In 1884 the cottonseed trust will be formed; in 1885 the linseed oil trust; by 1887 lead, whisky, cordage, wire nails and plate glass industries all form trusts. Sugar organizes as a trust in 1887, and soon employs 25,000 of the 30,000 workers in the industry. In 1888 the

Standard Oil Trust will surface in a Senate investigation; four years later the Ohio Supreme Court declares it illegal. In 1899 smelters and coal producers combine. The Sherman Anti-trust Law of 1887 is passed largely to try to deal with this spiderweb that is strangling free competition and individual initiative. The law serves to bring the issue to public debate. However, for the next three to four decades the Supreme Court unravels whatever Congress or the President knits. Only when Theodore Roosevelt becomes President will firm steps be taken to legislate the place of trusts in a free society.

15 JANUARY 1882
National The Star Route mail frauds capture public attention as the post office scandal unfolds in the courts. The existence of illegal practices in the Post Office has been common knowledge for some time. The Star Route frauds surface once dissatisfaction with government employee corruption begins to sweep the country. The crime is simple enough: there are several post office delivery and pickup routes which do not have much business. By augmenting their figures, budget requests are drawn up for larger amounts than necessary. Routes that otherwise are unprofitable make money by phony scheduling of frequent trips. It is alleged that 134 routes have made $622,808 on $143,169 worth of mail business. Another 26 routes have received $530,319 for an actual $65,216 of legitimate expenses. On the official schedule these routes were marked with a star, hence the poetic name of the scandal. The Star Routes trial went on for two years. Republican Senator S. W. Dorsey of Arkansas was indicted and other Senators and officials were found to be part of the gang. Exposure forced the resignation of Thomas J. Brady, Second Assistant Postmas-

---

SAMUEL GOMPERS, 1850-1924

Samuel Gompers became the most influential labor leader in American history. More than any other one person, he served to steer labor through the rapids of industrial turbulence in the last decades of the 19th century. His leadership could be said to have prevented the country from choosing class warfare as the only solution to its economic woes.

Gompers was born in England but emigrated with his family to America when he was 13. He knew firsthand the poverty of New York's tenements, working with his father in a tenement "sweat shop." He listened to endless discussions between the ideologists as to whether to follow Karl Marx and educate people toward abolishing private ownership, or Ferdinand Lassalle and use political means to achieve a non-capitalist society. The young immigrant kept his own counsel, but when the time came to act, he helped to provide a singularly American response to the immediate needs of American industrial workers. His American Federation of Labor was trade unionism without political goals, working merely to improve the conditions of workers in a no-nonsense American way. "Our labor movement has no system to crush," he said, and in the great industrial struggles ahead, Gompers maintained this stance always. Except for one year when he was ousted by a socialist move to capture the organization, the energetic little man remained securely in charge of the A. F. of L. for 40 years. And where the Knights of Labor—the A. F. of L.'s early rival—had shied away from using the strike, Gompers had no such squeamishness about using this formidable weapon. For him the strike and the boycott were both of value in his struggle to protect the rights and lives of workers.

Gompers was indefatigable in his efforts on behalf of the new working class in America. Dignified, a trifle stout as he aged, he wielded his pen with elegance. He represented the A. F. of L. at the Paris Peace Conference in 1918. He engaged in forming the Pan-American Federation of Labor. He steered his union clear of political movements agitating workers and met union opposition implacably and yet generously. The center of vicious controversy all his life, he maintained his straight and narrow path with constancy, achieving without revolution victories which indeed created a better life for millions. In the process, he protected (some say strengthened) the fabric of a free republic.

Labor leader Samuel Gompers.

A frontier homestead in Aberdeen, South Dakota, 1882.

ter-general. However given the lax standards of the times it is not surprising to learn that no one was ever convicted.

2 FEBRUARY 1882
Ideas/Beliefs Bowing to a growing interest in fraternal groups, the Roman Catholic church permits organization of the Knights of Columbus.

MARCH 1882
Regional Because of extensive timber cutting and soil exhaustion, violent flooding on the Mississippi sweeps away vast amounts of property and renders 85,000 homeless.

22 MARCH 1882
National In a move aimed directly at the Mormon Church, the Edmunds Act is passed by Congress. It prohibits polygamists from voting or from holding public office. Five commissioners are appointed by the President to oversee elections.

31 MARCH 1882
National Congress votes special pensions for the widows of Presidents Polk, Tyler and Garfield, setting a precedent for the future.

4 APRIL 1882
National President Chester A. Arthur courageously vetoes the Chinese Exclusion Act, saying it violates the Burlingame Treaty.

6 MAY 1882
National Overriding the President's veto, Congress enacts the Chinese Exclusion Act. The Bill excludes Chinese laborers for 10 years.

15 MAY 1882
Industry A Tariff Commission is authorized by Congress. Its nine members are to be appointed by the President. John L. Hayes, Secretary of the National Association of Wool Manufacturers, a not exactly disinterested party, is named chairman. Tariffs remain a protective device to help American business, much to the disappointment of the rest of the world and in spite of the harrowing costs to farmers and laborers.

22 MAY 1882
International A treaty of friendship and commerce is signed by Korea and the United States which will be ratified by the Senate on February 13, 1883. Korean independence from China, Russia and Japan is recognized as desirable to the United States.

JUNE 1882
Labor Severe strikes engulf the Iron and Steel industry. The Amalgamated Association of Iron and

Steel workers is able to hold out until September and a freight handlers strike disrupts rail transportation for several weeks.

26 JULY 1882
National The United States announces that as of March 16 it has agreed to accept the provisions of the Geneva Convention of 1864 for improving the care of the wounded in wartime.

2 AUGUST 1882
National Congress authorizes a $19,000,000 "pork barrel" Rivers and Harbors Bill for public works. Arthur vetoes the bill and his veto is sustained.

3 AUGUST 1882
Immigration For the first time, Congress acts to re-

THE INVENTION OF THE TRUST

In 1882 a lawyer on his staff named Samuel C.T. Dodd came to John D. Rockefeller with a plan—a trust. Rockefeller's usual procedure had been to buy out his competitors, once he had weakened them sufficiently, paying them in Standard Oil stock. In the future he would exchange the stocks for "trust certificates of ownership." Rockefeller held the stocks in trusteeship and in return managed the huge conglomerate as one of nine trustees. The trust, a holding company, could be incorporated under the easy-going laws of New Jersey, which permitted a New Jersey corporation to own and vote stock in any other corporation in any other state. The Standard Oil Company of New Jersey undertook responsibility for Rockefeller's new organization. It centralized control of the management of the growing number of state–chartered companies that Rockefeller was buying up. Thus he had created the biggest monopoly and effectively evaded anti-monopoly laws. The final arrangements of the trust, worked out over several years, included 14 companies and controlled 26 more. It was capitalized at $70,000,000 and paid dividends annually from 30 to 48 percent. A quarter of the shares was owned by Rockefeller.

The trust provided the necessary legal tool to surmount barriers put by states to regulate corporations within their jurisdiction. The form was instantly copied by corporations in copper, steel, tobacco, sugar, rubber, leather and farm machinery, all of which were capitalized over $50,000,000. In the 1880s and early 1890s roughly 5000 companies consolidated into 300 trusts or corporations, over half in just one four-year period. A mere six groups owned all but 40,000 miles of the nation's railroads. Only one percent of manufacturing concerns had an annual output of over $1,000,000, but this one percent produced 38 percent of all manufactured goods, and 33 of these combines topped the $100,000,000 mark.

Consolidation was made at the expense of competition, although in the name of a "person." The public was outraged, although a little late. The first moves to restrain the giants were made by Congress in 1887 when the Interstate Commerce Department was established. In 1890 the Sherman Anti-trust law was passed. Both were weakly supported by the executive and further weakened by Supreme Court decisions. But they reflected a growing national concern and would find their strength in the following century.

---

strict immigration on a selective basis. Standards are not very stringent but the bill will bar paupers, convicts and the insane. The bill also puts a modest 50-

---

JOHN PIERPONT MORGAN, 1837-1913

John Pierpont Morgan was a banker, the son of a banker and through his own abilities the most formidable of all American financiers. His hand was in almost every major American enterprise undertaken in the last third of the 19th century and the early years of the 20th.

Morgan began at the top working as lawyer and banker in his father's international banking firm of J. S. Morgan and Company, and for his father's equally astute banking partner, George Peabody. But young Morgan was a creative genius in his own right. He did more than anyone to initiate the new era of finance capitalism—buying, holding, merging, helping to reorganize vertically and horizontally entire industries such as steel, railroads, coal, steamships and electricity. In 1896 The Morgan House was able to bail out the United States government by donating $62,000,000 to help restore gold reserves. Morgan formed the first billion dollar company in America, the United States Steel Company, a combination of several companies including giant Carnegie Steel, capitalized at $1,400,000,000. Morgan made a satisfying $62,000,000 in commissions on the deal.

J. P. Morgan was a handsome man who admired handsome men and beautiful women. His homes, one of which is now a museum in New York, were filled with exquisite objects brought from around the world, particularly the manuscripts which were his first love. He was a generous benefactor of the Metropolitan Museum of Art and the American Museum of Natural History. Morgan was a man born to rule. He never met his match until he collided with Theodore Roosevelt over the trust issue. "The Congress of the United States," said Teddy, seeing the trust problem clearly, "is not at the mercy of the State of New Jersey." The House of Morgan was not severely discommoded by the new rules that government set up. It was a little like closing the door once the horse had bolted.

---

cent tax on all immigrants. Between 1860 and 1900 roughly 14,000,000 immigrants come to America; between 1881 and 1890 approximately 5,246,613 foreigners settle in the United States.

4 SEPTEMBER 1882
Industry Thomas A. Edison's Pearl Street steam-powered central station begins to supply electricity and New York begins to sparkle with an incandescent glow. New York's glamorous mix of skyscrapers and electric lights will become one of America's most awe-inspiring and endearing sights.

5 SEPTEMBER 1882
Regional The first parade is held in New York City to honor the observance of Labor Day. In 1894 Congress will declare the first Monday in September National Labor Day and a legal holiday. It is a sign that the labor movement and the status of labor are becoming central to the nation's concerns. America is becoming a nation of employees but these employees as yet do not have the minimum subsistence protec-

tion given in the past to slaves.

7 NOVEMBER 1882
Regional Grover Cleveland has moved from color-less lawyer to vigorous "Veto Mayor" of Buffalo. Now by a landslide he becomes Democratic Governor of New York. His election reflects the reemergence of Democratic power in the nation, and a marked division in Republican ranks. Two years later Cleveland, like some great clipper ship nosing into harbor, will head into the White House, a spectacular rise by a most unspectacular man.

11 DECEMBER 1882
Industry For the first time a theater is lit by Edison's incandescent lights. He uses 650 bulbs in the Bijou Theater in Boston for a performance of Gilbert and Sullivan's opera, *Iolanthe.*

OTHER EVENTS OF 1882
Labor New York prohibits the manufacture of cigars

IMMIGRATION

In 1869 it was claimed that the transcontinental railroads could not have been built without immigrant labor. That year the number of immigrants reached 352,569. Fifteen years later, in 1884, 1,514,816 new Americans arrived. By 1880 the population of the United States reached 50,100,000, of which 6,600,000 were foreign born. Between 1881 and 1890, 5,246,613 immigrants stepped onto American shores. During the Civil War the Union Army scouted abroad for young men willing to be paid to fight Union battles. Later, when the railroads were being built, foreigners, mostly Chinese and Irish, contracted for the backbreaking, not to mention strike-breaking, labor. The railroads themselves subsequently sent scouts abroad to encourage people to come and settle the plains and prairies. Forests, deserts, mountains and farmland, all offered opportunity for the lucky immigrant, many of whom got wealthy beyond their wildest dreams. Immigrants are often thought of as newcomers to an already established society, but immigrants created the psyche of the American nation over many generations. While there was free land to be had, the immigrants were largely from Northern Europe: Great Britain, Germany, Scandinavia, Ireland. When the population flow was diverted from farm and forest to the poverty-stricken, over-crowded cities, it was the Italians, Russians and Eastern Europeans who provided the greatest number of newcomers. The Chinese Exclusion Act of 1882 put an end to cheap Chinese labor which had caused some ugly racial riots in the West. In 1885, pressed by vigorous reform movements, the Contract Labor law was passed. It was aimed at stopping the practice of importing strike-breakers. In 1888 provision was made to deport undesirable aliens.

By the end of the century immigration had become a political issue of national proportions. The "immigrant," said the powerful industrialist Henry Clay Frick, "however illiterate or ignorant he may be, always learns too soon." Despite the dreadful suffering and hideous conditions which prevailed for many, for hundreds of others America did indeed become the Promised Land, if not for themselves, at least for their children.

---

in tenement houses. These little factories in rooms where whole families sleep and eat have come to be known as "sweat shops." Grover Cleveland signs the bill into law. But the Supreme Court knocks it down on the grounds that "It cannot be perceived how the cigarmaker is to be improved in his health or his morals by forcing him from his home and its hallowed associations and beneficent influences to ply his trade elsewhere." The ruling had a profound effect on Theodore Roosevelt who had seen the one–room dwellings. Later he wrote in his *Autobiography*: "It was this case which first waked me to a dim and partial understanding of the fact that the courts were not necessarily the best judges of what should be done to better social and industrial conditions. The judges who rendered this decision were well-meaning men. They knew nothing whatever of tenement-house conditions; they knew legalism, not life. This decision completely blocked tenement-house reform legislation in New York for a score of years . . . It was one of the most serious setbacks which the cause of industrial and social progress and reform ever received." So ended Samuel Gompers' first attempt to offset the rapidly growing practice of the "sweat shop."

16 JANUARY 1883
National In December 1882 the Senate passed the Pendleton Civil Service Act. Now the House votes it

---

CIVIL SERVICE REFORM

Lincoln had already put his finger on the danger inherent in the spoils system of government, whereby government jobs were regularly filled by the party in power, rather than on merit. It is "going to ruin republican government," Lincoln prophesied. Scandal pervaded the Civil Service system almost from the start. Job security became the security to make money out of the job by whatever means available before the return of the opposing party doomed one to departure. Enormous amounts of time were consumed in dispensing patronage. Charles Sumner, the highminded Senator from Massachusetts, had already introduced a bill in 1864 to reform the Civil Service and Representative Jenckes of Rhode Island tried to initiate reforms along British lines in 1867. Support for Civil Service reform was forthcoming from major reformers of the time, such as E.L. Godkin of *The Nation* and Senator Carl Schurz of Ohio. In 1871 Grant recommended that changes "in the manner of all appointments," be instituted, and a Civil Service Commission was duly set up, but it was a cosmetic affair, designed to offset reformers and prepare for elections. It made no serious attacks on needed reforms. At all times efforts to clean up, even to police, the Civil Service met with opposition from the buccaneering spoilsmen of both major parties. Master spoilsman of them all, Roscoe Conkling, said: "When Dr. Johnson defined patriotism as the last refuge of a scoundrel, he ignored the enormous possibilities of the word reform." Hayes supported moves toward reform but it was the unlikely old darling of Gould, Fisk and Conkling, Chester A. Arthur who, on becoming President, signed the Pendleton Act into law and brought the merit system into the Civil Service.

---

into law. The Pendleton Act authorizes reform of the Civil Service. This has been a scandalous and time-consuming aspect of government for some time. The number of federal employees has grown enormously and Republicans do not relish the loss of such extensive patronage to the merit system. Democrats do not wish to agitate too vociferously for reform until some of their own people have been placed in the patronage slots. The Pendleton Act establishes a bi-partisan, three-man commission which will draw up and administer competitive examinations and thus begin the process of filling civil servant jobs on a merit basis rather than on party affiliation. The act has been drawn up by Dorman B. Eaton who is Secretary of the Civil Service Reform Organization. It is introduced by Senator George H. Pendleton of Ohio. Among its provisions the act forbids kickback contributions to political parties. At first only 14,000, or approximately 12 percent of all federal employees, are covered by the act, and only future employees. But the Executive is empowered to extend the new rules. By 1900, at least 100,000 jobs have been absorbed into the system and the number continues to grow in the following century.

15 FEBRUARY 1883
Regional In Cincinnati, flooding on the Ohio River crests at 62 feet and four inches. Flood damage is estimated in the millions in the worst floods the country has yet seen. Although Cincinnati is hardest hit, floods cause damage all along the Ohio River. The new menace of flooding is caused by indiscriminate cutting of trees, and the wasteful farming methods which are eroding the rich topsoil of America. Pressure for better education on the subject is already being made by reform groups and farmers' organizations.

27 FEBRUARY 1883
Life/Customs The first practical cigar-rolling machine is patented by Oscar Hammerstein, who is also an operatic impresario. He is the grandfather of the famous 20th-century librettist Oscar Hammerstein III.

3 MARCH 1883
National Congress authorizes construction of three steel cruisers and one dispatch boat. It is the beginning of what will be known as the Steel Navy. Construction will be completed in 1887. It begins the long process of modernization of the United States Navy, which at this point consists solely of wooden ships and has fallen to 12th place among naval powers. The "Mongrel" Tariff Act is adopted by Congress. It provides for reductions of five percent on some items, but increases other tariffs, wool among them, in spite of the recommendations of a special congressional committee which suggests lowering tariffs on some items.

24 MARCH 1883
Regional Telephone service is put into operation be-

tween Chicago and New York.

26 MARCH 1883
Life/Customs William K. Vanderbilt gives the most expensive ($250,000) fancy dress ball ever given. Twelve hundred guests vie for invitations, including the arbiter of society, Alva Astor. From now on the grandson of the old ferryboat captain sets the standards for ostentatious extravagance, and his style of living becomes the best example for the economic theory of conspicuous consumption.

A STEEL NAVY FOR THE UNITED STATES

After the Civil War, the United States Navy was allowed to disintegrate into "rot, rust and obsolescence." By 1870 the Navy was down from 700 vessels to 200, all but 52 in mothballs. The Department itself fell on evil times under Grant's Secretary of the Navy George M. Robeson when graft and corruption were an acknowledged fact of Navy life. Then in 1883, inspired by Secretary of the Navy William E. Chandler and supported by Chester A. Arthur, Congress authorized the building of three steel ships, a tentative but most important first step toward an up-to-date Navy. This was followed, in August 1886, with authorization for further steel vessels. Great credit for reorganization and modernization went to Secretary of the Navy William C. Whitney who coordinated the necessary means of production and helped develop native steel mills to supply the necessary heavy steel plates, and in the process made the United States Navy independent of European steel sources. On March 16, 1889, on the eve of battle with the Germans over jurisdiction over Samoa, the American Navy was crushed into broomsticks by a hurricane. After this disaster the thrust toward modernization found increasing public support. Young Congressman Henry Cabot Lodge, later a strong advocate for imperial power, took up the cause, saying "Sea power is essential to the greatness of every splendid people." By the time Whitney left office in 1886, 22 vessels had either been built or authorized. By 1900 the United States Navy was among the most modern of the navies, ranking third among world sea powers. America was beginning to look beyond the old western land frontier, out over the waves, and the United States Navy was ready to take it overseas.

---

24 MAY 1883
Regional The beautiful Brooklyn Bridge is opened with great fanfare by President Chester A. Arthur and Governor Grover Cleveland. The Bridge was begun in 1869 and has a span of 1595½ feet which is half again longer than any suspension bridge yet built. Two stone towers with caissons 78 feet deep hold four woven cables, each of which can carry 18,000 tons. New Yorkers are convinced that the Brooklyn Bridge is the eighth wonder of the world.

21 SEPTEMBER 1883
International Telegraph connection is made between Brazil and the United States.

15 OCTOBER 1883
National The Supreme Court finds the Civil Rights

MAY 14, 1884

Act of 1875 unconstitutional. The 1875 act had given equal rights to blacks in public places. The Court argues that the act, which was passed as enabling legislation for the Fourteenth Amendment, cannot constitutionally protect blacks from individual infringement of their civil rights, but only from state action. Exception is made for interstate travel and where the act relates to jury duty.

22 OCTOBER 1883
Life/Customs New York is host to the first New York Horse Show. One hundred sixty-five exhibitors show 299 horses including fire-engine, police and draft horses. The show is a great success and becomes an annual event, but work animals are soon excluded and the program is limited to classes that do not remind the new–rich visitors of their backgrounds among the laboring masses.

18 NOVEMBER 1883
International Canadian and United States railroads meet and agree to eliminate conflicting time systems. Four zones each 15 degrees wide are established for the North American continent. In 1918 Congress gives supervision of national time zones to the Interstate Commerce Commission.

4 DECEMBER 1883
Customs/Beliefs The Sons of the American Revolution is organized in New York.

OTHER EVENTS OF 1883
Arts/Culture Benjamin Franklin Keith opens the first of over 400 theaters in Boston, Massachusetts. Keith began in vaudeville and provides the best vaudevillian entertainment, which is to say some of the very best entertainment to be had in the country. Vaudeville is the cradle for most successful actors and actresses of the early 20th century, and shapes the tone of theater for many decades. Keith dies in 1914 before vaudeville itself is killed by the impact of Edison's newfangled moving pictures.

9 FEBRUARY 1884
Regional A tornado kills 700 people as it crashes across the South.

14 FEBRUARY 1884
Regional The Ohio River again floods, causing extensive damage along its banks, particularly in Cincinnati, where the flood crests at 71 feet, the highest ever recorded.

3 MARCH 1884
Finance The Supreme Court finds that Congress has legitimate power to make treasury notes, the so–called "greenbacks," legal tender even in peacetime.
Regional Severe riots occur in Cincinnati over the question of lax administration of justice. Gathering in front of the jail, a mob grows to disordinate proportions and then begins ransacking gun shops for arms. Soon the city is thrown into complete disorder. State

militia is sent into the city to restore order but rioting is not quelled for six days. At least 45 people are killed and 135 wounded before peace is restored.

4 MARCH 1884
Regional Iowa state adopts laws prohibiting the sale of alcohol.

APRIL 1884
Labor The Hocking Valley coal miners strike over wages and working conditions. Public sympathy is at first with the badly used miners but subsequent violence by an enraged minority turns this sympathy away. The miners are starved into submission.

14 MAY 1884
National The Anti-Monopoly Party is the first of several reform parties to organize and convene on a national basis this election year. Old Republican Reconstructionist and Union General Benjamin Butler is nominated for president. Butler has already been a Radical Republican and a Northern Democrat. The party is responding to the apparent need for legislation at the federal level to regulate gigantic trusts, combines and monopolies which are creating a powerful network of a few interlocking companies working to forestall competition, legislation or regulation. The Anti-Monopoly Party backs several other reform measures, including a graduated income tax.

CARL SCHURZ, 1829-1906

Carl Schurz was one of several distinguished reform politicians of the 19th century. His career spanned turbulent times and his concerns coincided with the nobler aspirations of his fellow countrymen.

Schurz was born in Germany, where he went to college. During his student years, revolution broke out and after severe fighting he managed to escape to Switzerland. Characteristically brave, he returned to free his college professor from jail and help him escape the country. Schurz finally made his way to America where he studied law, settling in Missouri, engaged in politics. During the Civil War he participated bravely in most major engagements, resigning as major-general once hostilities had come to an end. Schurz had been a staunch abolitionist and after the war was a fair-minded Reconstructionist. He advocated leniency toward Southern States but with some legislative safeguards. A highminded, incorruptible man, Schurz served as Senator from Missouri and later as Secretary of the Interior. In 1872 he helped form the Liberal Republican Party over which he presided. In 1884 he was instrumental in forming the Mugwumps, whose bolt from Republican Blaine propelled Democrat Grover Cleveland into the White House. Although Blaine was a good politician, he had a reputation for shoddy entanglements, and had made some implacable enemies. Cleveland shone with the kind of honesty that Schurz felt would serve to make for honest government.

Schurz did as much as anyone to form an American sociopolitical conscience. He was an influential editor and writer, affecting the currents of public opinion. As a politician of national renown, he brought disparate minority concerns into the mainstream of national politics.

FORGING A NATION 1866-1900

28 MAY 1884
National The Greenback Party meets in Indianapolis, Indiana, and nominates old Republican Reconstructionist and Union General Benjamin Butler for president. The party will later merge with the Anti-Monopoly Party to become the Populist Party.

17 MAY 1884
Regional By an Act of Congress the laws pertaining to Oregon are broadened to apply to Alaska. Gold has been found in Alaska and gold–seekers are trekking up to the snowbound territory. The need to establish some form of government is obvious although statehood is not yet an option.

6 JUNE 1884
National The Republican Convention is held in Chi-

THE WEALTHY

"Those who are most successful in acquisition of property," pontificated Andrew Carnegie, "are the very men who are able to handle it in the way most useful to society." To prove his point, the wealthy set about using their wealth for all the world to see.

The Vanderbilts led the way with their $3,000,000 imitation Château de Blois on Fifth Avenue. Soon the Astors and others followed suit and American streets began to look like some ostentatious nightmare. A second, summer castle was called a "cottage" and to build one in Newport became the goal of millionaires. Vanderbilt's grandson, William, built his for $11,000,000. But it was in the fancy balls that the newly rich outdid themselves, entrancing and dismaying the world. In 1866 it is estimated that those who had prospered during the Civil War gave some 600 balls at a cost of some $7,000,000 in New York alone, and that sometimes a single one reached $100,000. Less than 20 years later fortunes were counted in the millions. By then Mrs. William Astor had taken it upon herself to crown herself "Queen of the Four Hundred." It was the number that supposedly fit into her ballroom. William K. Vanderbilt changed all that, starting with the most expensive fancy dress ball ever given, a $250,000 affair for 1200 guests. The hostess matched her dress to live white doves which fluttered around her throughout the evening.

But others prepared to match and outmatch. In Philadelphia a $75,000 debutante ball with thousands of imported live butterflies enthralled the guests. The doomed butterflies flew around in all their exquisite beauty until, tired, they fell to their glamorous deaths drowned in champagne glasses and crushed beneath satin slippers. Classier and more permanent was the dinner at which a sand trough was placed down the center of the Vanderbilt's dinner table. Each guest was given a little sterling silver pail and shovel and told to dig. The trough was filled with loose diamonds, emeralds and rubies. The occasion that topped them all was the party given for 100 well-bred dogs, whose pedigrees mostly outshone their masters'. The menu was leaked to the press: liver and rice, fricassee of bones, shredded dog biscuits. The desolate victims of the industries providing the profits for these graceless affairs were justly upset, although they might have felt better had they known that the dogs got into a free-for-all and dogs and owners had gone home badly bitten.

---

cago. On the fourth ballot the ever–popular "Plumed Knight" James G. Blaine is nominated for president and General John A. Logan of Illinois for vice-president. Disgusted by the nomination of the politically tarnished James G. Blaine, several reformers and Liberal Republicans bolt the party.

16 JUNE 1884
National Liberal Republicans convene in New York City and agree to support the Democratic candidate should he be sufficiently liberal. George William Curtis is Chairman of the dissident group among whom are some of the Republican Party's most illustrious names: Senators Carl Schurz, Missouri; Charles Sumner, Massachusetts; Lyman Trumbull, Illinois; and General N. P. Banks, Massachusetts. Chief among reasons for the bolt is the nomination of James G. Blaine for president. His ethics while Senator and Speaker of the House are questioned and for all his popularity among the rank and file, he has made some implacable foes, such as Roscoe Conkling, among the spoilsmen and Charles Sumner and Carl Schurz among the Liberals. Nor is he noted for his perspicacity in identifying the deeper issues that are dragging the country into open class warfare. The splinter group is dubbed the Mugwumps, an Algonquin word for "Big Chief," whose political connotation lies somewhere between egghead and big-wig. The formation of the Liberal Republican Party indicates another deep change in American politics. Agrarian economics had lasted well into Grant's tolerant administration; now as the country suffers from dire poverty and increasing labor unrest, an intense debate develops over bigness, trusts, combines, monopolies, working conditions, women's rights, farmers' needs, immigration, tariffs and finally imperialism. These issues begin to move out of small well-meaning reform groups into the central political arena. The nation's exuberant search for treasure is supplanted by a search for meaningful responsibility.

27 JUNE 1884
National As part of the Department of the Interior, Congress creates the United States Bureau of Labor. This much-needed department will begin to supply some vital statistics which will serve to sort out legitimate needs and prove legitimate grievances.

11 JULY 1884
National The Democratic Party holds its national convention in Chicago. It nominates Grover Cleveland for president and Thomas A. Hendricks, Indiana, for vice-president. Grover Cleveland has hardly had time to become sullied by politics. Elected in 1882 to governorship of New York State by an extraordinary majority of 190,000 votes, his nomination for president is never seriously contested. Furthermore, the Republican Mugwumps have agreed to back the Democrats should they nominate a liberal-minded candidate. Cleveland, an honest and able administrator, fills the bill.

23 JULY 1884

National The Prohibition Party gathers momentum as it holds its fourth National convention in Pittsburgh. John P. St. John of Kansas, which is a dry state, is nominated for president and William Daniel, of Maryland, is nominated for vice-president.

1 AUGUST 1884

National Every four years the presidential campaigns of the two major parties seems to sink to a lower level. Neither party has undertaken to confront the main issues convulsing the country. Instead a great deal is made of Blaine's "Mulligan letters." These supposedly incriminating letters were written by Blaine to a friend and disavow his having had a part in the great Credit Mobilier Scandal. In one letter Blaine requests a reply to this effect from his friend Fisher. The missive ends with "Burn this letter." The

Immigrants landing at New York's Castle Garden in 1884.

letter surfaces, of course, and causes incalculable damage to Blaine's career. In this campaign Democrats chant:

> Burn this letter! Burn this letter!
> Kind regards to Mrs. Fisher!

Meanwhile Cleveland, it seems, has sired an illegitimate child. With characteristic honesty, he admits the fact. During the campaign Republicans heckle him:

> Ma! Ma! Where's my Pa?
> Gone to the White House
> Ha! Ha! Ha!

CORNELIUS VANDERBILT, 1794-1877

Cornelius Vanderbilt was one of the first American capitalists, a new, if incredibly successful, subdivision of society which rose partially out of business initiatives taken by Vanderbilt himself.

Vanderbilt was born on Staten Island, New York, and started in business at an early age. At 16 he bought a sailboat and began to ferry freight and passengers between Staten Island and New York. From this humble beginning he developed a fleet of floating carriers plying the world. He was given the nickname "Commodore" which he proudly used ever after. By 1862 he had seen the possibilities in a new kind of carrier, the railroad, and had turned the full brunt of his energies onto that industry. Vanderbilt and railroads became synonymous, like Rockefeller and oil, or Carnegie and steel. Within 12 years he had enlarged his fortune tenfold, to close to $100,000,000. He controlled the mammoth New York Central which had some 14,000 miles of track, the largest in one combine. Later his wheeling and dealing in rolling stock would be ably and avariciously carried on by his heirs. It was William H. Vanderbilt who, reminded by a reporter that he had a responsibility to the public, replied "The public be damned." The Vanderbilt family was also credited with initiating the era of conspicuous consumption for which the plutocracy of the late 19th century is justly famous.

---

26 AUGUST 1884

Science/Technology The linotype machine to set type is patented by its inventor, Ottmar Mergenthaler. It will be built the following year and sold for its first use to Whitelaw Reid's New York *Tribune*.

OCTOBER 1884

International The International Prime Meridian Conference meets in Washington D.C. The conference chooses Greenwich, England to mark the prime meridian for the world.

6 OCTOBER 1884

National The Reverend Samuel D. Burchard makes a speech in support of James G. Blaine for President. Later Blaine will claim that this speech cost him the election. The minister applauds the fact that Blaine is not part of the Democratic Party which he alliteratively thunders is the Party of "Rum, Romanism and Rebellion." The phrase rolls so mellifluously off the tongue that Blaine lets it slide by without rebuke. When the Irish Catholics hear of the tasteless phrase it is too late for Blaine to disavow it.

4 NOVEMBER 1884

National Grover Cleveland is elected president. He garners 4,911,017 popular votes to Blaine's 4,848,334; Butler gets 175,370 for his Populists and St. John 150,369. Thomas A. Hendricks is elected vice-president. Blaine loses crucial New York by 1149 votes out of the 1,125,000. Electoral votes go to Cleveland 219 to 182. Cleveland is the first Democrat to be elected president since James Buchanan, 1857-1861.

Regional One of the most influential of new socially conscious politicians will be Robert "Bob" La Follette. He is elected from Wisconsin to his first term in Congress.

8 NOVEMBER 1884

Arts/Culture Samuel Sidney McClure initiates the first newspaper syndicate in the United States. He calls it the McClure's Syndicate. The Civil War has sparked an interest in newspapers which has not subsided with the return to peace. The use of far–flung correspondents, an idea begun during the war, is continued afterward, helped by the telegraph. Advertising, new printing methods, innovative approaches, such as those initiated by Joseph Pulitzer, help propel newspapers into the forefront of information distribution and the molding of public opinion.

16 DECEMBER 1884

Regional The World's Industrial and Cotton Centennial Exposition of 1884-85 is opened in New Orleans. The Fair turns out to be a third larger than the great Philadelphia Centennial Fair at Fairmont Park. Austria, Belgium, England, France, China and Japan all send impressive displays. South America takes an active part and each department of the United States government supplies an exhibit. The wonder of the fair still lies in the variety and ingenuity of American products. The Fair is a coming–out party for the South which has begun to bestir itself and address the prospect of taking an active part in the tumultuous industrial growth of the nation.

OTHER EVENTS OF 1884

Arts/Culture A ten-story building called the Home Life Insurance Building is constructed in Chicago. It is the world's first true "skyscraper." Designed by William Le Baron Jenne, it adopts use of a new principle of steel skeleton upon which floors and walls are hung. The invention of the steel skeleton is one of the biggest steps ever made in architecture. Flexible and free, the new way of building can be applied to any structure. But until now, walls have been made of self-supporting masonry, thickening at the base as structures soared higher. Jenne releases the walls by hanging them to the steel frames just like floors. Structurally the "skyscraper" is now free to go as high as it can go.

29 JANUARY 1885

International The Senate decides not to ratify the 1884 treaty which authorizes the building of a canal across Nicaragua. The canal issue is plagued with doubts and indecisions. Americans are still reluctant to shoulder responsibilities outside the continental domain. The Federal Government is not yet a strongly defined entity, people being still more closely identified with their states. Gradually a change is taking place and some people see far enough into the murky future to make intelligent preparations for predictable circumstances. Secretary of the Navy Whitney has brought his prestige to bear on building a steel navy. Commodore Stephen Bleecker has instigated a navy training school and Secretary of State Blaine is slowly turning the nation's attention to events in Hawaii, the Philippines, Korea, Puerto Rico and Cuba.

21 FEBRUARY 1885
Regional The Washington Monument is dedicated in Washington D.C. Begun on July 4, 1848, it has taken 36 years to complete. It reaches 585 feet and 5⅛ inches. Eight hundred and ninety-eight steps, or a less exhausting elevator ride, will get a person to the top. The monument costs $1,300,000 to build.

26 FEBRUARY 1885
Labor The Contract Labor law is enacted by Congress because contract labor has become industry's way of breaking a strike. Immigrants, contracting in good faith, are set to breaking up unions and thus weaken labor's bargaining power. Fighting among the workers serves to render them all ever more powerless. Belatedly responding to the situation, Congress enacts the Contract Labor Law which forbids a future employer from contracting abroad for immigrant labor in return for passage to America.

3 MARCH 1885
National Special Delivery is inaugurated by the United States Post Office. After exposure of the Star Route Frauds in 1882, the Post Office is trying to police itself, and the savings are being passed along to the public in better service.

4 MARCH 1885
National Grover Cleveland is inaugurated 22nd president of the United States and Thomas A. Hendricks is 21st vice-president.

13 MARCH 1885
Regional President Cleveland warns settlers to stay off Indian lands in Oklahoma. These are not particularly desirable tracts and the government has waged a harsh war to round up the nomadic Indians and fence them onto these acres. However, the land is coveted by whites and by the end of this decade will be settled by the strongest and most persistent of them.

1 JULY 1885
International Acting on a joint resolution of Congress made on March 3, 1883, the United States unilaterally abrogates the fisheries reciprocity section of the 1871 Treaty of Washington.

23 JULY 1885
National General Ulysses S. Grant, two–term President of the United States and beloved hero of the Civil War, dies at 63. Grant dominated the political scene for the hinge decades when "business" was transforming itself into "industry" and the country was shaping an entirely new destiny. His laissez–faire policies enabled the distinctive industrial shape of the American nation to take place, although his benign neglect of social forces left some permanent scars. For two days and nights a line a mile long files past the body as it lies in state in City Hall in New York. On the rainy funeral day thousands throng the streets to pay their last respects and to see the magnificent funeral cortege. General Hancock leads the march. Among the military groups are the battalion from Virginia which Grant defeated, followed symbolically by his own battalion. President Cleveland and a glittering

RAILROADS

From the invention of steel rails in 1865 to the advent of the gasoline engine in 1893, railroads transformed and dominated American life. Railroads created new concepts of bigness, new patterns of industry, new forms of freedom.

In 1865 when the first steel rails were manufactured, there were about 35,000 miles of steam railroads, most of them east of the Mississippi. These lines were independently owned and operated. Between 1874 and 1887 another 87,000 miles were laid; by 1900, with a capital investment of $11,000,000,000, there were some 200,000 miles in operation. However, through mergers and consolidations, only six groups owned all but 37,977 miles.

To encourage the building of railroads the Federal Government gave 158,293,377 acres of prime farmland, rich timberland and substantial waterways to the railmen. In addition the government lent them some $60,000,000. States and municipalities equalled and surpassed this amount again and again, in loans and outright donations. The country was intoxicated with the prospects in railroads. To help settle the new lands through which the tracks wound, railroad companies sent scouts abroad to bring immigrants to the New World. At one time there were over 1000 agents scouring Europe and Russia for settlers.

"Great" is usually attached to the names of the men who built the railroads, men like Vanderbilt, Morgan, Harriman, Gould, Hill, Stanford, Huntington, but their behavior was often more piratical than exemplary. They were fierce and ruthless men, unscrupulous in competition with each other and with everyone else. Soon railroads came to dominate the business community, making or breaking merchants at will. It was said that no man dared enter into a business in which railroads would be used unless he had previously consulted a railroad manager.

By the 1880s the public began to protest the fact that these largely publicly funded enterprises were being run purely for private gain and without regard for the public weal, at which point the government moved slowly to regulate the industry.

As the silver tracks wound across the nation, America became transportation–dependent, and, uncanny as it may seem, the ground beneath the new age became transportation, as up until 1865 it had been land.

FORGING A NATION 1866-1900

group of 500 celebrities ride behind the hearse. Standing beside the bier at the tomb are ex-Presidents Arthur and Hayes, Generals Sherman and Sheridan, Admiral Porter and, poignantly, the Confederate Generals Gordon, Buckner and Fitzhugh Lee. A vine from Napoleon's grave, taken from his island of exile, is planted on Grant's tomb. The irony of pairing the despot Napoleon with the stolid fighter for Union and freedom is missed by more than a few. From Grant's success, millions made their first steps toward a civilized life of freedom, and thanks to men like Grant, the United States has remained the bastion of freedom standing against just such oppressors as Napoleon.

17 AUGUST 1885
Regional Responding to public protest, Congress tries to curb abuses in the management of public lands in the West over which government supervision has been erratic and not particularly public spirited. Large holdings have been allowed to accumulate in private hands, Indians have been ignominiously forced out, and now, without authorization, public lands are being fenced off, including the strategic and life-giving water holes. This permits ever greater concentrations of land, often owned by railroad and cattle men. The powerful land speculators show no wish to compromise. For giving them a slight tap on the wrists, President Cleveland's Land Commissioner, W. A.J. Sparks, is forced to resign. On August 17 Cleveland orders all illegal fences removed. Meanwhile conservation movements are growing, moved by the devastation wrought by thoughtless farming methods and wanton timber cutting. For the first time the public foresees an end to what had seemed only ten years before an absolutely boundless and bounteous cornucopia of natural resources.

25 NOVEMBER 1885
National Vice-President Thomas A. Hendricks dies. He is not replaced.

OTHER EVENTS OF 1885
Science/Technology Furnaces to burn garbage are put into use in many cities. Garbage disposal emerges as a public problem requiring some immediate solutions. It has been found that when fed to the pigs garbage may cause trichinosis, a disease which can easily be transmitted to people. Garbage left untended adds to health hazards. In the Midwest it cannot easily be dumped into rivers and lakes. It is one more example of the growing need to develop social forms to meet social needs.
Ideas/Beliefs The American Economic Association is established. A number of young economists have become disillusioned with the premises standing behind the philosophy of economic determinism or "laissez-faire." They claim that policies arising from such views are "unsafe in politics and unsound in morals." The organization is the first economic group to argue that the state must contribute actively in the way of "positive aid" to maintaining the just progress of its citizens. There is ample precedent for these

A Currier and Ives view of coast-to-coast rail travel.

FEBRUARY 9, 1886

GROVER CLEVELAND, 1837-1908

According to the judgment of history it would seem that Grover Cleveland was the most distinguished of the least distinguished American Presidents. Grover Stephen Cleveland belonged to a family come to America in 1635. He studied law in Buffalo, New York, and remained there during the Civil War, supporting his mother. Always interested in politics, he joined the Democratic party, although Erie County was predominantly Republican. In 1881 he was nominated reform Mayor of Buffalo from where he caught the attention of the New York State political machine. Only a year later he had won the governorship by an unprecedented 192,854 votes.

Cleveland was a massive, unimaginative man, able in administration, honest in government. His appearance was dignified, even stern, but he had a little-known other side which included a taste for crude company, brawls and barrooms. He admitted to fathering an illegitimate child.

In 1884, over opposition of the spoilsmen of his party, he won the presidency. He added thousands of jobs to the Civil Service, tried to stop annexation of Hawaii, vetoed 413, or two-thirds, of the bills which crossed his desk, and weathered violent labor unrest without contributing anything of importance to the situation.

The portly president was defeated in the 1888 elections, people being tired of "avoirdupois and cussedness," but won a second term in 1892. During his first term the 49-year-old bachelor married his young ward, the 23-year-old Frances Folsom, which brought some luster to an otherwise dreary White House.

Cleveland was unable to understand the power inherent in the presidency and the need for statesmanship in the highest office in the land. He ran the nation as if it were just another big city in need of a good scrubbing.

economists to draw upon. The government has been dispensing aid to help railroad expansion; it has given vast tracts of land to cattlemen, timbermen, miners and settlers; earlier it had established the Freedmen's Bureau to help newly enfranchised whites and blacks adjust to a new society; it had also funneled large amounts of capital to aid in rebuilding southern industries. Thomas Jefferson had already articulated government responsibility to provide minimal education to insure for an enlightened citizenry, that is, a citizenry able to cast an intelligent vote. The public has found it hard to let go of a familiar dream: that of a country of independent merchants and farmers, free to move at will, out of debt, with leisure to pursue the things of the spirit. However, the new economists contend that unless concerted efforts are made to prevent further degradation of the new class of workers, the dream will turn into the nightmare of class warfare. Andrew Carnegie, Woodrow Wilson and Henry C. Adams are among the 186 founding members.

19 JANUARY 1886
National The Presidential Succession Act is enacted by Congress, partly in response to growing outbreaks of violence across the country. Congress provides for succession in the event of removal, resignation, death or the inability of the president or vice-president to function in office. Succession will proceed through the Cabinet in the order of the creation of those offices. The act remains unmodified until 1947.

7 FEBRUARY 1886
Regional Riots amounting to a small war occur against the Chinese in Seattle, Washington. At least 400 aliens are forcibly ejected from their homes. Federal Troops are required to restore order.

9 FEBRUARY 1886
National General Winfield S. Hancock dies. He is one of three candidates for President who die this year. Horatio Seymour dies on February 12 and Samuel Tilden on August 4. Vice-President Thames Hendricks had died in late 1885 and on November 12,

THE AMERICAN FEDERATION OF LABOR

The most stable and most profoundly middle-of-the-road union America has ever known has been the American Federation of Labor. It has given a uniquely American tone to the labor movement, keeping itself clear of the anachronisms of simple craft unionism and the time-consuming ideologies of trade union socialism. From the beginning, founding members such as Adolph Strasser, president of the Cigarmakers' International, and Samuel Gompers, president of the American Federation of Labor for 41 years, moved away from political discussion toward pragmatic goals which involved improving the workers' lot.

The American Federation of Labor grew out of a gathering of national unions in Pittsburgh in 1881. They formed a Federation of Organized Trades and Labor Unions on a rough analogy with the Federal government. As it modified its shape it drew from the example of industry and formed into separate and autonomous unions, drawing only on skilled workers, set up in vertical and horizontal combinations within industries. These then consolidated into the larger federation which acted on their behalf. Municipal charters were granted to deal at a city level, and state charters to deal with state situations. From its inception the American Federation of Labor proposed to use the strike fiercely and fearlessly, and priority was given to the strike fund. Perhaps the most important goal the federation set itself was the continual protection of the right to collective bargaining by representatives of one's own choosing. It was the fundamental principle upon which the federation rested. It created a measure of equality when federation officials sat down to negotiate with executives of industrial empires. The impersonal corporation which had been declared a "person" by the Supreme Court, was faced with a "person" equally impersonal, and not nearly so vulnerable as a single individual.

By the time the federation turned into the 20th century it had half a million members. It has been instrumental in achieving the eight-hour day, the five- and six-day week, factory inspection, workmen's compensation, compulsory education, outlawing of the injunction and much more. The invention of the purely economic union created a purely American solution to labor's conflicting demands for equality, equity and upward mobility. The federation has done much to better working conditions while the larger social questions still remain open for further debate.

FORGING A NATION 1866-1900

1886 Chester A. Arthur breathes his last.

14 FEBRUARY 1886
National The Morrison Tarriff Bill reducing tariffs is introduced in the House. But in the protectionist climate which still dominates Congress the bill is defeated.
Industry The California orange groves, on the way to becoming big business, send their first trainload of the fruit to eastern markets.

6 MARCH 1886
Labor The Knights of Labor strike against Jay Gould's Missouri-Pacific railroad system. Over 9000 strikers tie up some 5000 miles of track. The strike lasts into May but the workers are forced by hunger to return without any noticeable gains. Strikes are getting to be bigger and ever more violent. The number of workers out in this bumper year is 610,000 and property damage amounts to $33,580,000. Capital, having siphoned off incredible profits, can last longer than strikers who are only now beginning to under-

stand the power and strategy of strike and union. In this one railroad strike, which tied up commerce from the Atlantic to the Pacific, $900,000 was lost in wages and $3,000,000 was lost to the company.

22 APRIL 1886
National Grover Cleveland, in the first presidential message relating to Labor, suggests government serve as arbitrator in industrial disputes.

1 MAY 1886
Ideas/Beliefs In concerted demonstrations, labor groups, including the all-embracing Knights of Labor, the Black International anarchists, the Socialist unions and the trade unions join in strikes and demonstrations for an eight-hour day. Between 40,000 and 60,000 workers take part.

3 MAY 1886
Ideas/Beliefs An attack on strikebreaking workers at the McCormick Reaper Manufacturing Company which has been on strike since February draws police

The Haymarket Square Riot of May 4, 1886, Chicago.

who fire on the crowd. Six people are killed and at least a dozen are wounded. Anarchist August Spies takes advantage of the crowd's explosive feelings to call a meeting at Chicago's Haymarket Square to protest "the latest atrocious act of the police." "Revenge! Workingmen! To Arms!" say headlines in leaflets circulated during the night.

4 MAY 1886

Ideas/Beliefs About 1300-1400 people gather in Chicago's Haymarket Square. The meeting begins in an orderly fashion, although some speeches are inflammatory. The police, 180 strong, arrive to disperse the throng which is just breaking up owing to the rain. At this point teamster Samuel Fielden is speaking. From somewhere a bomb is thrown into the midst of the police. Seven officers are killed and more than 50 others severely wounded. No one seems to know who committed the dreadful crime. Terror grips the country as it becomes known that terrorist anarchist groups, bent on the destruction of all governments, have branches in all major industrial cities. It is estimated that 7000 persons may be members. Eight anarchists, including Samuel Fielden, are arrested for murder.

10 MAY 1886

National In one of its most important rulings ever, the Supreme Court in *Santa Clara County* v. *Southern Pacific Railroad* rules that a corporation is a person under the Fourteenth Amendment and therefore cannot be deprived of profits or other rights without due process. The effect of this is to give corporations the privileges of citizenship without demanding the moral responsibility expected of a person.

19 JUNE 1886

Ideas/Beliefs The trial of the Haymarket anarchists begins under Judge Joseph E. Gary. August Spies, Albert Parsons, Samuel Fielden, Michael Schwab and four others are arraigned on charges of conspiring to kill. They are subsequently found guilty on the grounds that it is not necessary to have planned a murder for members of a conspiracy to be murderers or accessories before the fact. The trial is not solidly based, but in the aftermath of the ugly deed it is deemed necessary to blame the crime on someone and these men are well known for their inflammatory rhetoric. The actual criminals are never discovered.

29 JUNE 1886

Labor Approval is given by Congress for the incorporation of trade unions. Because of peaceful political participation of trade unions in the regular channels of government, Congress is becoming responsive to the national needs of industrial workers.

30 JUNE 1886

National A Division of Forestry, to be part of the Department of Agriculture, is approved by Congress. The government is showing itself to be responsive to public as well as private pressures.

3 AUGUST 1886

National Congress authorizes the construction of two iron-clads, a cruiser and a torpedo boat, in its ongoing program to modernize the Navy.

20 AUGUST 1886

Ideas/Beliefs Found guilty of conspiring to kill, eight anarchists are sentenced by Judge Joseph E. Gary in the Haymarket case. August Spies, Albert Parsons, Adoph Fisher, George Engel are sentenced to death. Samuel Fielden and Michael Schwab are given life sentences. Oscar Neebe is sentenced to 15 years. Louis Lingg hangs himself. In 1893 Democratic Governor J. P. Altgeld becomes so convinced of the bias and injustice of the trial and the innocence of the prisoners that he pardons the three still in prison. Because feelings are still intense, he ruins himself politically by doing so.

4 SEPTEMBER 1886

Indian Affairs Geronimo, the last of the Indian Chiefs to give himself up, is taken by veteran Indian hunter General Nelson A. Miles, and sent to a reservation in Florida.

16 SEPTEMBER 1886

Regional The Convention of Anti-Saloon Republicans is held in Chicago, Illinois. The transformation from reform group to political activists is a sign of the times.

25 OCTOBER 1886

National In *Wabash, St. Louis and Pacific Railway Company v. Illinois,* the Supreme Court, taking upon itself economic responsibility well beyond any given to it heretofore, declares that a state cannot regulate even that portion of interstate commerce that takes place within its own borders. This annuls the States' legislative powers over trusts, railroads, holding companies and other combines. Responding quickly, Congress will seek powers at the national level, because a dangerous vacuum has been created into which neither state nor federal governments can react. Congress will pass the historic Interstate Commerce Act the following year.

28 OCTOBER 1886

National The Statue of Liberty is dedicated in New York Harbor amid great rejoicings. Grover Cleveland presides over parades and parties given to honor visiting French and other dignitaries.

8 DECEMBER 1886

Labor The American Federation of Labor is organized out of the Federation of Trades and Labor Unions by Samuel Gompers and Adolph Strasser in Columbus, Ohio. It will be the cutting edge of the Labor Movement for the next several decades. The Knights of Labor having taken part with the anarchists in the eight-hour day movement, although in no way involved in the Haymarket affair, have had their reputation nonetheless irreparably tarnished.

FORGING A NATION 1866-1900

Pioneers going West via covered wagon in 1886.

20 JANUARY 1887

International The Senate ratifies renewal of its 1875 treaty with Hawaii. The treaty guarantees the United States sole rights to build a naval base at Pearl Harbor.

3 FEBRUARY 1887

National In order to avoid an impasse as in the Hayes–Tilden dispute, the Electoral Count Act is signed into law. Each state will now be absolute judge as to the validity of its votes. Congress will take part only if a state is unable to reach a decision or if the decision is obviously irregular. A decision by the two houses of Congress voting together will be final. Should the two houses disagree, then state–certified electors will have the final decision.

4 FEBRUARY 1887

National The Interstate Commerce Act of 1887 is passed by Congress and signed into law by Grover Cleveland. It is one of the most important pieces of legislation affecting the economy to be enacted in the nineteenth century. In the 1886 case of *Wabash, St. Louis and Pacific Railroad v. Illinois*, the Supreme Court has reversed an earlier finding which supported State jurisdiction over interstate commerce within its own borders. This has left a significant void. Interstate commerce, including railroads, is totally unregulated and behaving in a manner deleterious to the community, dangerously undermining national solidarity. Responding to public pressure, Congress enacts the Interstate Commerce Act. A five–man

commission is created to see that rates are just and "reasonable;" to forbid double–tiered rates for long and short hauls on freight carriers; to stop discrimina-

---

THE BIRTH OF AMERICAN IMPERIALISM

In 1886 Josiah Strong published a book which would have a profound effect on the course of international affairs. Called *Our Country*, it was a mix of racism, patriotism, chauvinism, avarice and millenial expectations, but sunk within the ridiculous trappings was an important question which no one missed: When and how would America begin to look beyond its continental boundaries to the world beyond? Josiah Strong was influenced by Herbert Spencer's economic theories of "survival of the fittest." These theories had done much to rationalize the thrust to bigness in the last two decades of business. Josiah Strong shifted their application from the limited boundaries of the continental United States to the world. Strong decided, rather arbitrarily, that the Anglo-Saxons had been selected by God to lead the world, so that any interference with their leadership would simply be thwarting God's will, or, the "survival of the fittest." By this means he got to the root point of his thesis: America had a right and a duty to become an imperial power. Strong articulated something that was stirring in the national psyche. Four years later a more reasoned and realistic appraisal of the issue of imperialism was made by Alred Thayer Mahan, the American naval officer-historian. In 1890 he published his monumental *The Influence of Sea Power Upon History 1660-1783*. Through his careful arguments on the necessity for American sea power he undertook to lead the nation into the uncharted realms of world power.

AUGUST 10, 1887

tory rates between competitive and non–competitive localities and to stop the practice of pooling. The act is weakened, for a time, by the Supreme Court, which is baffled by the question of what constitutes "reasonable rates" and who is to decide. However, subsequent rulings combined with Executive initiative and an active public opinion will give government effective regulatory oversight.

11 FEBRUARY 1887
National Cleveland vetoes the Dependent Pension Bill passed by Congress in January. Cleveland approves pensions on an individual basis and has approved more and also disapproved more than his predecessors. Pension expenditures in 1885 had been $56,000,000. By 1888 they will have increased to $80,000,000. Braving the wrath of the Grand Army of the Republic, Cleveland balks at New Hampshire

---

THE GRANGERS

In the two decades of their early history, the Grangers were among the first to organize and to take on Moloch-like industries such as the railroad empires which, in the years after the Civil War, were chewing up small independent farmers and producers.

The unlikely group that accomplished this then seemingly impossible task was organized by an obscure young clerk in the government's Agriculture Department. Seeing the need for some form of cooperation among the farmers in order to protect themselves from all manner of despoilation, Oliver Hudson Kelley, in the manner of the times, founded in 1867 a secret society called Patrons of Husbandry. The organization soon had Granges, that is meeting places, across the country and members found strength in cooperation. Their single greatest accomplishment was enactment of the so-called Granger Laws which in 1877 were upheld by the Supreme Court. In the precedent-setting cases the Court found that the several States have the power to regulate maximum rates even over interstate commerce and established as principle the concept that States are empowered to act to regulate businesses within their borders when such businesses involve "a public interest."

The Granger Movement brought Northerners and Southerners together into one national union which helped to heal sectional wounds. It was instrumental in raising the Department of Agriculture to Cabinet level and obtained rural delivery and parcel post services. It admitted women to its membership and fought for women's suffrage. Conservation and pure food laws were also among its goals.

In the end, the Grangers failed to keep up their militant momentum and by 1880 85 percent of their million-and-a-half members had fallen away and the Grange settled into a social and educational role. However, the Grangers' early recognition of the dangers of unprecedentedly large industries going totally unregulated would not soon be forgotten by a grateful society. The Grangers set an example for subsequent formal and informal organizations of laborers and producers to work together. Later, after the bitter and dangerous industry-labor disputes of the last decades of the century, this cooperation would bring some measure of equilibrium back into the social order.

Senator Henry Blair's bill which would provide a pension to honorably discharged veterans who have served a minimum of 90 days in the Army. The only condition is that they be manual laborers who, at the time, are unable to earn a living. Later, when the country is deeper into industrial poverty, the bill will pass as hidden relief.

8 FEBRUARY 1887
Indian Affairs The Dawes Severalty Act is passed by Congress. It provides for 160 acres to be given individually to each Indian family. The land is to be held in trust by the Federal Government to prevent sale for a minimum of 25 years. The act is well intentioned, hoping to help the Indians adjust to the new world. Indians are often tricked or forced into sale of their land. This act is to correct such abuses.

2 MARCH 1887
Agriculture Taking a much-needed step toward developing a science of agriculture, Congress enacts the Hatch Act. The object is to help farmers prevent continuing destruction of their land. Crude farming methods, bad management, new machinery, one–crop planting, extensive rather than intensive farming, over–grazing of cattle, have contributed to eroding the rich top soil which has begun to blow and wash away in alarming proportions. Millions of acres will be left unsuitable for cultivation unless action is taken. The Hatch Act begins to reverse the destructive process by providing funds for agricultural experimental stations to be located in most states. Farming techniques, crop diseases, crop uses and abuses will be studied by these new establishments.
International The United States in 1885 unilaterally abrogated the articles pertaining to the fishing settlement with Canada which had been agreed to in the Treaty of Washington. In retaliation, Canadians now harass American fishermen in an effort to regain their privileges. Newspapers play up the outrages, and talk of war is heard. A commission is set up by Cleveland to consider the entire issue. Meanwhile a *modus vivendi* is reached by Canadians for rights in their ports, and the tempest in a teapot dies down.

3 MARCH 1887
National The Tenure of Office Act of 1867 is repealed by Congress. Grover Cleveland has fought to restore executive privilege in this regard. In an 1886 message to the Senate, he has insisted on the president's power under the Constitution to suspend or remove appointees from office. Repeal of the act is a move toward reestablishing the independence and authority of the executive branch of government.

10 AUGUST 1887
Transportation In Chatsworth, Illinois, 100 people are killed and hundreds more are injured when a burning bridge collapses under the weight of a crossing train. The bridge had been screened by a knoll so the engine driver had no warning. It is estimated that accidents to American railroad employees or passengers

FORGING A NATION 1866-1900

exceed the number killed in the same period in the Boer War.

6 DECEMBER 1887
National In a bold speech Grover Cleveland tackles the tariff issue. He begins his speech by saying: "It is a condition which confronts us, not a theory." He then proceeds to plead for a radical reduction of tariffs on the necessities if not the luxuries of life. Reverse reform is felt by some to be a vital need because there is an accumulation of surplus revenue which is causing anxiety. Some people wish to make the most of the beguiling excess but others feel tariff protection is subsidizing some businesses at the expense of the public.

OTHER EVENTS OF 1887
National Free delivery of mail is provided in all communities of 10,000 or over.
Conservation In one of his first acts in what will be a lifetime struggle for conservation of the public's natural resources, Theodore Roosevelt organizes the Boone and Crocket Club for the protection of big game. Although he is often pictured as a great hunter, Roosevelt was opposed to needless slaughter.

15 FEBRUARY 1888
International The fishing dispute between Canada and the United States comes to an end with the Bayard–Chamberlain Treaty signed in Washington. The Senate refuses to ratify the treaty, partly because it provides for reciprocal tariffs which are still anathema to high–tariff industrialists, but the two countries proceed on an amicable basis, generally following the provisions of the treaty anyway.

19 FEBRUARY 1888
Regional A cyclone twists through Mount Vernon, Illinois, destroying the city and killing 35 people. Dramatic destruction in the form of floods, twisters, insect plagues is haunting the settlers of the Midwest.

22 FEBRUARY 1888
National The first party to convene in this election year is the Industrial Reform Party. Meeting in Washington, D.C., it nominates Albert E. Redstone of California for president and John Colvin of Kansas for vice–president. Although little more than a lobby, the party helps to focus political attention on the central economic issues of the day.

FEBRUARY 1888
Regional In a local municipal election in Louisville, Kentucky, the secret ballot is introduced into the United States electoral system for the first time. It is called the Australian system, or "Kangaroo voting,"

A storefront in frontier Coburg, Nebraska.

since Australia has been using the secret ballot since 1858. Henry George, the famous advocate of the single tax, has also been a proponent of the secret ballot. Most Americans happily adopt the system as their own, although South Carolina holds out until 1950.

12 MARCH 1888

Regional The Great Blizzard of 1888 strikes an unprepared Atlantic Seaboard. The center of the disaster is New York City. For 36 hours snow falls and cuts the city off from the nation, paralyzes transportation, causes $25,000,000 in damages and kills 400 people. Travel in and out of the city is not possible in the knee–high snowfall. Offices and shops are shut, supplies dwindle to dangerous lows, walking in the deep snows causes many deaths from exhaustion. Roscoe Conkling, the politician, is just one such victim of the unaccustomed exertion. But there is no other form of locomotion. The city is virtually at a standstill for 48 hours before clearing is achieved and the city returns to normal.

15 MAY 1888

National The national convention of the Equal Rights Party meets in Des Moines, Iowa. The Midwest and West are sympathetic to women's rights partly because the manner of living in the open country breaks down artificial behavior patterns. Some territories such as Utah and Wyoming already have women's suffrage. Next year Wyoming will insist that it be allowed to enter the Union as a state with this article in its constitution intact and will be allowed to do so.

16 MAY 1888

National The Union Labor Party convenes in Cincinnati, Ohio. The party selects A.J. Sweeter of Illinois for president, and Charles E. Cunningham of Arkansas for vice–president. This is one of several parties now forming to support the cause of the new militant American laborers.

17 MAY 1888

National Similarly named and similarly motivated, the United Labor Party holds its national convention in Cincinnati, Ohio. Robert H. Cowdrey of Illinois is nominated for president, and W.H.T. Wakefield of Kansas for vice–president.

4 JUNE 1888

Regional New York State replaces death by hanging with electrocution as the preferred form of capital punishment. Governor Hill signs the bill which will take effect on January 1, 1889.

5 JUNE 1888

National The Democratic Party holds its national convention in St. Louis, Missouri. Grover Cleveland is renominated by acclamation for the presidency with Allen G. Thurmand of Ohio for vice–president. Vice–President Thomas A. Hendricks had died in the first year of his term and had not been replaced.

13 JUNE 1888

Labor Congress establishes a Department of Labor. The department is not yet given cabinet status, but the move reflects a growing social response to forces endangering the rights and privileges of citizens of a republic.

25 JUNE 1888

National The Republican Party holds its national convention in Chicago. Benjamin Harrison of Indiana is nominated for president on the eighth ballot and Levi P. Morton of New York for vice–president. It adopts a platform favoring a high tariff and becomes the party of the big industrialists. The issue of protection will be the central one of the campaign. Although tariff walls seriously hurt farmers, small merchants and the general populace, the judicial application of money to legislative palms keep tariffs creeping ever higher. Manufacturers buy in a free world market and

SOUTHERN ALLIANCE

Springing up in the Southwest, the Southern Alliance evolved out of myriad groups fighting against the injustices inflicted upon farmers at this time. The country was changing from an agriculturally based one of independent yeoman farmers into a manufacturing country with employees making up the bulk of its citizens. The farmers were being badly used. Forming into ever larger groups, the southern and southwestern organizations finally merged into the National Farmers' Alliance and Industrial Union, usually referred to as the Southern Alliance. The alliance welcomed just about everybody that was not "obnoxious to the Constitution." There was a long list of "obnoxious" people: railroad officials, bankers, cotton buyers, real estate dealers and "any person who keeps a store, who buys and sells for gain." Shortsightedly, it excluded blacks although a Northern Farmers' Alliance admitted them, and an independent Colored Farmers' Organization, a million members strong, had emerged by 1888.

The Southern Alliance advocated against land syndicates and crop futures speculation; it pressed for government control of railroads and for interstate commerce regulation. It experimented with cooperatives and instituted its own exchanges for supplying low–cost farm foods to help farmers get out of debt. Seeing the difficulty of challenging the Exchange, the group promoted the idea of government warehouses, in which farmers could store goods and borrow against 80 percent of their value. These ideas later became reality in the Warehouse Act of 1912, and in the Commodity Credit Corp Act of 1933.

In 1889 the less radical Northern Alliance and the evangelistical Southern Alliance attempted to combine. However, separate interests kept them apart, such as Northern prosperity and Northerners' concern with synthetic foods such as margarine. Also the Southern Alliance's three–times–larger membership, exclusion of blacks and secret rituals led the forthright Northerners to shy away from a merger. The Knights of Labor and the Grange sympathized with the Southern Alliance which became the chief spokesman for the embattled farmers and set the tone of Southern politics for many years to come.

FORGING A NATION 1866-1900

sell in a protected national one. Farmers buy in a high tariff market and are forced to sell in the free world market. The Republicans also back generous use of the accumulating tariff revenues for Civil War veterans. Cleveland has vetoed the Arrears Pension Act and lost much Grand Army of the Republican support. Cleveland has also routinely agreed to return to the South the Confederate battle flags captured by the Union Army, to which Republicans object. Old wounds are opened and organized veterans force Cleveland to revoke the Battle Flags order. (The flags will be returned by Theodore Roosevelt in 1905.) Thirteen Republicans vie for the presidential nomination. Although he has repeatedly, and it would seem sincerely, requested that his name be kept off the list, the perenially popular James G. Blaine has loyal supporters who keep his votes coming right to the end, on the eighth and last ballot. McKinley's name is also among the list of candidates who survive to the last vote although he too has asked that his name not be used. The able if somewhat aloof Benjamin Harrison gets the nod. Candidate John Sherman, who led the balloting at the top of the list with 229 votes, insists that the unlikely Harrison has won because of an unsavory party deal made with the New York delegation.

13 JULY 1888
International Secretary of State Thomas F. Bayard invites the Latin American nations to an inter–American conference. He has the backing of Congress for this move. The conference is scheduled to be held in Washington the following year.

29 JULY 1888
Regional Once again the South is swept by an epidemic of yellow fever. Breaking out in in Jacksonville, Florida, 4500 cases are reported before the dreadful disease subsides. Over 400 people die.

15 AUGUST 1888
National The last of the year's many national conventions takes place in Philadelphia as the chauvinistic American Party convenes to nominate James L. Curtis of New York for president and James R. Gree. of Tennessee for vice–president.

1 OCTOBER 1888
Immigration Bowing to continued western pressure groups, Congress forbids the return to the United States of any Chinese laborers who have left the country.

21 OCTOBER 1888
National In a serious diplomatic gaffe, the British ambassador to Washington has responded to a letter asking for his advice on how to vote in the upcoming elections. Lord Sackville–West advises the writer to vote for Cleveland. The letter is purportedly from a naturalized citizen, British by birth. Actually it is written by a California Republican involved in campaign dirty tricks. Sackville–West has fallen into the trap. The letter is publicized in time to inflame the

Irish vote against Cleveland and does much to lose him the crucial New York electoral vote.

6 NOVEMBER 1888
National Cleveland receives the larger popular vote, 5,540,050 to Harrison's 5,444,337, but Republican Benjamin Harrison gets the important electoral vote—233–168 including crucial New York—to win the election. Levi P. Morton is elected vice–president and the Republicans gain a majority in the house.

9 FEBRUARY 1889
Agriculture Cabinet status is finally accorded the Department of Agriculture by an act of Congress. The move underlines the political significance implicit in the farm question. Farming is turning into big business. The nation will now try to come to terms with the new realities.

20 FEBRUARY 1889
International The Maritime Canal Company of Nicaragua is incorporated by Congress to build and operate a canal across that country. The company itself will be under U.S. control, but have no financial responsibility. Work is scheduled to begin October 22, 1889.

22 FEBRUARY 1889
National North Dakota, South Dakota, Montana and

BENJAMIN HARRISON, 1833-1901

Harrison came from a distinguished political family in which his great grandfather had been a signer of the Declaration of Independence, his grandfather had been ninth president of the United States, and his own father had been a member of Congress.

A man of sincere beliefs, Harrison enlisted in the Union Army when war broke out. He was a colonel until the end of hostilities, when he was breveted brigadier-general of volunteers for "ability and manifest energy and gallantry in command of brigades." Settling in Indianapolis, Indiana, the eloquent young lawyer became a leading member of the bar. For many years he pursued his law career but then began to take part in Garfield's campaign, later running successfully for the Senate himself. Garfield wished to appoint him to his Cabinet, but Harrison preferred to serve out his Senate term. Taking an energetic and intelligent part in many active committees, he had a say on most of the issues considered by Congress in his time. In 1887 he was defeated for the Senate, but the following year won the Republican nomination for president. He went on to defeat Grover Cleveland who had taken some unpopular if trivial stands.

Harrison was a reserved, dignified man whom many thought to be cold and aloof. However, he made loyal friends and his chief characteristic was thoroughness; it took him far. During his term as president, the McKinley (high) Tariff Bill was passed as was the controversial Silver Bill of 1890. He supported modernization of the Navy and pressed reform of the Civil Service. Otherwise his presidency claims no great distinguishing features and except in a litany of presidents his term of office is usually forgotten.

Washington are all admitted to statehood in an Omnibus Bill signed by President Cleveland.

2 MARCH 1889

Industry The first anti–trust law is passed by Kansas. In a memorable move, Kansas challenges the might of the giant trusts and their unabashed privileges. They have come to control the economic life of the nation simply by default. Maine, Michigan and Tennessee follow suit this same year. In May, New Jersey offsets the gains thus made by passing a law authorizing incorporation of "holding companies" within its boundaries. Since New Jersey laws must be respected in other states, this regulation will be used to circumvent their anti–trust laws. South Dakota, Kentucky and Mississippi pass anti–trust laws in 1890, demonstrating the growing national concern over mergers, monopolies, trusts, holding companies and pools, all corporate means for evading social responsibility. The U.S. Congress, sensing the new mood in the country, passes the Sherman Anti–Trust Law of 1890. Then eight more states pass strengthening anti–trust legislation in 1891. The intent of the country is obvious, but New Jersey's holding company legislation weakens enforcement as Rockefeller's Standard Oil Company of New Jersey is quick to demonstrate. Subsequent rulings by the Supreme Court tie the hands of both the executive and legislative branches of government. Sensing a new ally, industry will shift its rearguard legal battles from Congress to the Supreme Court, which is deeply imbued with late–19th–century laissez–faire Spencerian doctrine. Supreme Court Justice Oliver Wendell Holmes—speaking for the minority Justices—will look elsewhere for relief: Theodore Roosevelt does much to challenge the most dictatorial assumption of power over the economy which the Supreme Court now takes upon itself as it proceeds to deny validity to legislative and executive action.

4 MARCH 1889

National Benjamin Harrison is inaugurated as 23rd president of the nation and Levi P. Morton as vice–president.

15 MARCH 1889

International The Samoan Islands have been in the throes of civil war ever since 1878 when the Hayes Administration arranged a treaty giving the United States a coaling station on Pago Pago. The German Navy has cruised the area and German interests have ranged alongside the forces fighting King Malietoa of the Samoan Islands, whom the Americans are backing. Although the British are interested in the outcome, they have not yet taken sides, but now things have reached a point whereby both the United States and Germany might become directly involved. The Germans have unilaterally put the Americans and British under military law. With the independence of Samoa obviously threatened, warships from the three great powers congregate in the harbor of Apia in

order to influence the outcome of negotiations between America and Germany, negotiations which are deteriorating rapidly. Vessels from the three countries are anchored in the bay when, on the eve of what seems to be unavoidable conflict, a hurricane smashes all but one to bits. Only the British corvette *Calliope* manages to avoid the reefs and get to the safety of the open sea. Subsequently the three big powers, Germany, Great Britain and the United States, meet on April 29, 1889, restore King Malietoa to the throne, put general administration back into his hands, but retain the power to appoint the presiding justice of the one–man Supreme Court.

22 APRIL 1889

Regional Responding to public pressure, land in Oklahoma formally ceded to the Indians is opened to white settlers by government decree. When the signal is given, some 50,000 people rush in to claim their lots. The government has paid $4,000,000 for about 2,000,000 acres of the Indians' "Beautiful Land."

OKLAHOMA SOONERS

Responding to public pressure, on April 22, 1889, great tracts of Oklahoma Territory, land formally ceded to the Indians, were opened to white settlers by government decree. Official start for the land grab was set at 12 noon. Marshals aided by cavalry ringed the border keeping the eager from jumping the gun. Rumors had it that friends of the marshals had already gone into the territory during the night to stake out their claims in the area designated Guthrie City. Like a pack of dogs straining to be let loose on the fox, eager settlers waited on horseback and buggy to make the rush for the previously well-surveyed Indian land which ranchers, squatters and trespassers had been coveting for some time. Once the government had paid $4,000,000 for the 2,000,000 acres, then the gun could sound that April morning and the rush was on. Guthrie had been claimed two hours ahead of schedule, as rumor had had it. Later these people were euphemistically called "Sooners" and Oklahoma the Sooner State. Lawyers dotted the area to register applications. By sunset the allotted 2,000,000 acres were all claimed, with both Guthrie and Oklahoma City well established. Towns of 10,000 were laid out and 50,000 people were encamped on the torn and littered land. However, by the end of the following day, orderly municipal governments were set up. Supplies remained scarce for some time, causing some hunger in the new boomtowns.

Oklahoma Territory had been highly touted by the "boomers," those drifters who followed the boomtowns of railroaders and miners. Indians already knew that arid and malarial conditions prevailed in many places. It was not long before many settlers were forced to withdraw. By the end of the year a stable population of 60,000 was reported in the census.

This curious land grab practice was repeated next year in a similar rush made on Sioux Indian holdings in South Dakota. There, in mid-winter, 11,000,000 acres were opened to settlers who had surveyed their claims in more clement weather. Assembling at the border they waited for days for proclamation of the hour of entry. On February 10 notice arrived and by evening the land was dotted with cabins and shacks which served notice of claims.

FORGING A NATION 1866-1900

This famous "Oklahoma Land Rush" is only the first of several such organized land settlements arranged by the government.

29 APRIL 1889
Regional Centennial celebrations reach a picturesque high in New York City, where a reenactment of Washington's inauguration takes place. Beginning at the small port of Elizabethtown in New Jersey, a thrilling escort of gaily festooned ships leads President Benjamin Harrison to New York following Washington's original route. New York has planned three days of festivities with political and social dignitaries invited. Madison Square is the scene of a gigantic open–air concert and the Metropolitan Opera House of an elaborate dinner. More than 50,000 people take part in a grand parade; another 75,000 romp through a series of animated scenes from history. Flowers are strewn along Harrison's path as had been done for Washington. Exquisite arches have been designed by Stanford White. One of these is subsequently translated into stone in Washington Square, where it still stands to commemorate this glorious day.

9 MAY 1889
National In an important bit of legislation in the battle between the people of the United States and the unpoliced industry, New Jersey amends its corporation laws. Now holding companies may be legally chartered in the state. Industry will use the law to evade the Sherman Anti–Trust Act of 1890.

13 MAY 1889
National Harrison appoints Theodore Roosevelt Civil Service Commissioner.

31 MAY 1889
Regional The dam holding the partly natural, partly artificial Conemaugh Lake, 78 miles southeast of Pittsburgh, breaks, destroying Johnstown, Pennsylvania. Inhabitants were warned of the likelihood of a break but the oft–repeated warnings were ignored again. The lake was 275 feet above Johnstown, at a distance of 18 miles. When at 3 o'clock in the afternoon the dam broke, the waters moved in a solid upright mass 40 feet high and reached the city in eight minutes, destroying it almost instantly. The river became clogged with bodies and debris, so that recoiling water and conflagration added to the terror. An estimated 5000 persons lost their lives, every family in Johnstown losing at least one relative. A probable $10,000,000 is sustained in property losses. The nation, responding with its usual generosity, sends some $3,000,000 in cash denotions and supplies. Pennsylvania gives $1,000,000 and New York City and Philadelphia each $500,000.

14 JUNE 1889
International A tripartite protectorate is set up to oversee Samoa. The United States agrees to the arrangement. The Senate will ratify the treaty on February 4, 1890.

2 OCTOBER 1889
International The First International Conference of American States meets in Washington, D.C. It establishes the International Bureau of American Republics in an attempt to form a customs union. The conference will last until April 19, 1890 but high–tariff industrialists block all meaningful progress.

2 NOVEMBER 1889
National North Dakota and South Dakota are both admitted to the Union as full–fledged states.

8 NOVEMBER 1889
National Montana is admitted to the Union.

11 NOVEMBER 1889
National Washington enters the Union. It becomes the 42nd state.

14 NOVEMBER 1889
Life/Customs The journalist for the New York

FARMS AND FARMING

For a long time Americans had imagined a nation in the pattern of New England stretching across the continent. Small, self-supporting farms would employ people's energies to keep them clothed, fed and, most important for a republic, independent. Small towns nearby would provide culture and companionship. Eighty-five percent of the people were farmers, and land constituted wealth. In 1860, 6,000,000 people worked in agriculture; only 4,000,000 worked in nonfarm enterprises. By 1900 the ratio was reversed, with 11,000,000 farm workers to 18,-000,000 in other occupations, and approximately one percent of Americans owned seven-tenths of all the wealth. The first American dream was about to shift drastically.

By 1860 there were 2,033,000 farms and by 1910, 6,-361,000. Acreage under cultivation had risen from 407,-212,000 in 1860 to 878,798,000 in 1910. Production had also risen dramatically, enabling the American farmer to feed the teeming cities. Production of wheat went from 173,000,000 in 1860 to 635,000,000 bushels in 1910. Corn went up from 838,000,000 to 2,886,000,000 bushels, and cotton from 3,841,000,000 to 11,609,000,000 bales. This very success glutted internal markets, and the farmer was forced to sell in the world's free centers. Soon he was dangerously in debt to Eastern bankers. Farms had to become hundreds, even tens of thousands of acres large in order to survive. Forty to 50 tractors moving abreast across a field was an awe-inspiring but increasingly familiar sight. It meant debt, dispossession and unemployment for thousands.

Farmers faced intractable problems: soil exhaustion, drought, frost, flood; over-expansion, over-production, high mortgage, interest, and railroad rates; isolation. Farm centers moved west, dislocating populations, becoming railroad dependent. But no matter how the individual farmer fared, American farming prospered, eventually stabilized, and began to solve its problems. It populated the prairies, it fed the cities and ultimately made a case for the kind of government aid first given to business and then to labor. It would take time, and another big shift in the American dream.

World, Nelly Bly, starts her trip around the world, challenging the fictitious Jules Verne and his 80–day voyage. Nelly Bly, a pseudonym for Elizabeth Cochrane, takes 72 days, six hours and 11 minutes. She will end her adventure on January 25, 1890. A fearless journalist, she later committed herself to an insane asylum in order to be able to write an accurate and factual account of the scandalous treatment given to the insane.

6 DECEMBER 1889
National Jefferson Davis dies in New Orleans.

25 JANUARY 1890
Labor Consolidating forces, workers from the weakening Knights of Labor and from the burgeoning American Federation of Labor form the United Mine Workers to battle the scandalous working conditions in the mines.

14 FEBRUARY 1890
National In a move to circumvent traditional congressional practice, Speaker Thomas B. Reed sets new rules. Henceforward he will count those present rather than only those answering the roll call. The old way had been a parliamentary move used to prevent a vote for lack of a quorum.

18 FEBRUARY 1890
National The American and the National women's suffrage groups consolidate into the National American Women's Suffrage Association. In most states women have been given "partial suffrage,"—that is, freedom to vote in state, municipal, school and other local elections. They now hold office in many states, but are completely blocked in the national sphere. Primarily this is because of southern obstruction. The South fears that women's vote will exacerbate their already unsettling problem with the black vote.

24 MARCH 1890
National Taking a most surprising stance, the Supreme Court reverses an earlier decision made in 1877 in the so–called Granger Cases. In *Chicago, Milwaukee, & St. Paul Railroad* v. *Minnesota* the Court rules that a State cannot set fees so as to deny a "reasonable profit" because it is thereby depriving a person of his rights under the Fourteenth Amendment. In this case the "person" is the scandalously mismanaged railroad corporations which Roscoe Conkling has argued are "persons" under the intent of the Amendment. It is a setback for the forces of social justice. The Supreme Court has unilaterally declared itself the sole arbiter of what is "reasonable profit." The delicate balance between judicial, executive and legislative powers is put seriously, if temporarily, out of kilter. It will take another decade before it begins to regain its equilibrium again.

28 APRIL 1890
National Still attacking the sovereignty of the States, the Supreme Court in *Leisy* v. *Hardin* rules unconstitutional state laws which forbid package liquor from entering the state on grounds that it interferes with gainful profit.

2 MAY 1890
Regional Oklahoma Territory is established by act of Congress.

27 JUNE 1890
National Harrison has appointed Grand Army Commander James "Corporal" Tanner as Commissioner of Pensions: "God help the surplus!" he exclaims gleefully as he takes office. During his office Congress passes the controversial Dependent Pension Act which provides pensions to unemployed manual laborers with a minimal 90 days service in Union forces. It also provides pensions for widows and orphans. Between 1891 and 1895 the number of pensioners rises from 676,000 to 970,000 providing much–needed relief to those caught in the depression

---

BOOKER T. WASHINGTON, 1859-1915

Booker T. Washington was born on a plantation and as a young teenager worked in a salt furnace and a coal mine. He rose to be spokesman for the blacks of America and counselor to two presidents. Taking advantage of opportunities offered by Reconstruction, he went to night school until he was about 16 then walked 500 miles to enroll in the Hampton (Virginia) Normal and Agricultural Institute, working as a janitor to pay his way. Following in his mother's footsteps, he became a schoolteacher. He was a tall, commanding, muscular man, with piercing black eyes that had dreams in them. But it was when he spoke that he was most impressive. He could have a cheering crowd on its feet in a matter of minutes. In 1881 he was assigned to head up the black Tuskegee Institute. Under Washington's guiding hand, Tuskegee went from a small shanty and a church with a budget of $2000 a year, to the foremost institute for vocational training for blacks in the country.

At Hampton, Washington had imbibed the "spiritual" virtues of hard work, honesty, perseverance, thrift and cleanliness. For the rest of his life he could not abide dust or dirt in any form. He seems to have absorbed other strictures with equal intensity, and as head of Tuskegee he proposed to instill them in his pupils, admonishing them to be polite, obey the law and stay clear of socializing with whites. A fellow black leader, Harvard Ph.D. W. E. DuBois, later wrote that Washington preached "a gospel of Work and Money to such an extent as apparently to overshadow the higher aims in life." Washington felt that blacks needed to learn vocational skills in order to survive economically. "I would set no limits to the attainments of the Negro in arts, letters or statesmanship, but I believe the surest way to reach those ends is by laying the foundation in the little things of life that lie immediately about one's door."

Washington became a national figure, a friend to the powerful. He financed some of the earliest court cases against segregation, and founded the National Negro Business League. Washington counseled a philosophy of compliant productivity, of safe and short-term goals for blacks. In a nation still scratching the scars of a Civil War, it was perhaps the best anyone could offer.

and receiving no other benefits from either industry or government for past services. By 1893 the veterans pension appropriation has risen from $81,000,000 to $135,000,000.

29 JUNE 1890

National Henry Cabot Lodge sponsors the Federal Elections Bill, better known as the Force Bill of 1890. It proposes federal supervision of federal elections in order to guarantee black male suffrage from state obstruction. Several states have introduced white supremacist "grandfather" clauses, whereby no person may vote unless he is a descendant of a person who voted before 1866. Other measures are also used to circumvent the Fifteenth Amendment. The Force Bill passes the House but fails in the Senate.

30 JUNE 1890

National Congress authorizes construction of three steelplated battle ships. These are designed to replace the wooden ships lost at Samoa and will help bring the United States Navy up to date.

2 JULY 1890

National One of the most important pieces of legislation of the last 25 years is introduced into the Senate by John Sherman of Ohio. It is the Sherman Anti–Trust Law drafted by George F. Hoar of Massachusetts and George F. Edmunds of Vermont. Passing with little opposition, it makes illegal "every contract, combination in the form of trust or otherwise, or conspiracy, in restraint of trade of commerce among the several States, or with foreign nations." Provision is made for the dissolution of those in existence. The ambiguous phrasing of the words "trust," "combination" and "restraint" will later be twisted to weaken labor unions. In *U.S.* v. *Debs* in 1894 the Supreme Court will declare that the provisions of the act covered labor unions and railroads as well as combinations of capital.
International The United States signs the International Act for the Suppression of African Slave Trade to which the Senate will consent on January 11, 1892.

3 JULY 1890

National Idaho enters the Union as the 43rd State.

10 JULY 1890

National Wyoming enters the Union as the first State to have women's suffrage. As a territory, Wyoming has already enfranchised women. The state then fought to keep its provision intact when it should become a state.

14 JULY 1890

National In a continuing battle over silver and gold coinage, passage of the Sherman Silver Purchase Act supplants the Bland–Allison Act of 1878. The Western pro–silver states make a trade with the Eastern protection–prone states, high tariffs in return for silver. The result is a bill which calls for government purchase of 4,500,000 ounces of silver each month. The treasury

is to issue legal tender notes in payment for the silver which are redeemable in either silver or gold; difficult to believe, the notes, once redeemed, are then sent back into circulation where they can be redeemed again for either gold or silver.

8 AUGUST 1890

National Beginning a long fight Congress responds to the Court's decision in the *Leisy v. Hardin* case. Congress adopts the Original Package Act and in the process upholds a State's right to subject merchandising of goods from another state to its own laws. Thus Kansas or other dry states may again forbid sale of out–of–state liquor within their jurisdictions. The Act will put out of business those instant packagers who have lined up along the borders of the dry states in order to do their business from across state lines.

30 AUGUST 1890

National By an Act of Congress, the Department of Agriculture may inspect pork destined for foreign markets. Diseased pork has caused outrage in European markets and embarrassment to America in its

---

ARCHITECTURE

American building of the late 19th century was eclectic, derivative and ostentatious. Some architects took advantage of new construction possibilities to build such grandiose structures as Grand Central Terminal in New York. It featured webbed wrought iron in an awesome glass vault and was an exuberant example of the grandeur of ancient Rome adapted to new uses. However, the best architects were hardly changing things at all. H.H. Richardson gained a reputation with his Trinity Church in Boston, but beautiful as it was, it offered nothing essentially new. In 1881 the respected firm of McKim, Mead and White, which featured Stanford White, designed the Boston Public Library based on designs of the 15th century Italian architect Alberti.

Meanwhile a truly revolutionary style of building never before seen in the world was developing out of new engineering opportunities and truly satisfying the exuberant needs of the times. This new style was to be called "skyscraper" and was exemplified in 1883 by the 16–story Monadnock Building in Chicago. The walls were masonry, some 15 feet thick at the base, but with the combination of elevators and steel framework a new architecture was being born. Complete steel-skeleton construction was first tried in the Jenney Building, also in Chicago. Floors and walls were both hung from the steel framework, freeing construction from the weight of masonry. It was the first true "skyscraper." Later Louis Sullivan would put his genius to the new form and in the Wainwright Building in St. Louis create one of the loveliest of the early tall buildings. Sullivan is sometimes called the "inventor of the skyscraper."

The man who was to do most to free private homes from the dead hand of Europe, shingle and gingerbread was Frank Lloyd Wright who completed his first commission in 1893: the Winslow house in Chicago. Using materials in a natural way, Wright sought to locate a home so as to make it an organic part of the landscape. Wright led the way into what might be called an American architecture: streamlined, functional, inventive and personal.

foreign relations. Inspection will serve to remove restrictions on imports of American pork into Germany, France, Italy, Belgium and Spain.

JANE ADDAMS, 1860-1935

Brilliant and hardworking, Jane Addams was in tune with the pragmatic thrust of her times: if you believe it, make it happen. Graduating in 1881 from one of the first women's colleges in the U.S., Jane Addams studied economics and sociology for the next few years both in America and in Europe. Yearning to sort out theory from practice, she planned and organized the settlement house in Chicago which was destined to be an example to the world: Hull House. In 1889 with Ellen Gates Starr, she set up a place where the poor and vulnerable could come for aid in coping with some of the elements of the society. While working exhaustively in her community, Addams continued her research and over the years produced some important sociological writings starting with *Democracy and Social Ethics* in 1902. Her imaginative yet practical work attracted national and international attention and her settlement house was copied extensively. In 1915 Addams was made Chairwoman of the International Congress of Women meeting in The Hague. World recognition came in 1931 when she received the Nobel Peace Prize, a fitting honor for her creative solutions to some of the most intractable social problems of her time.

---

2 SEPTEMBER 1890

Ideas/Beliefs At a meeting in Cooper Union, New York, the Single Tax National League, instigated and chaired by Henry George, adopts its single platform: a single tax to be levied on all property. Delegates have come from 30 states to adopt the singular platform.

25 SEPTEMBER 1890

Conservation Yosemite Park is created by an Act of Congress to prevent further depredations by hunters and timbermen on flora and fauna belonging to the nation.

29 SEPTEMBER 1890

National Congress provides for forfeiture of all unused land grants made to railroad companies as an inducement toward railroad construction.

1 OCTOBER 1890

National The McKinley Tariff Act is passed by Congress, raising tariffs to their highest point ever, although the Act is softened to include provision for reciprocity agreements with other nations. The Bill will help defeat Republicans at the mid–term Congressionnal elections in November and yet will become a slogan in McKinley's later bid for President in 1896: "Bill McKinley and the McKinley Bill."

4 NOVEMBER 1890

Regional The working population in South Carolina elect Democrat Benjamin Tillman governor. Done with Southern Alliance support, it is the first attack on the entrenched power of the aristocratic Bourbon Democrats. Southern politics, it has been agreed by all whites, will be played out within the confines of the Democratic Party. Tillman's Rednecks will be no more tolerant of blacks than the Bourbons.

DECEMBER 1890

Agriculture The Southern Alliance (sometimes called the Farmers' Alliance), the Farmers' Mutual Benefit Association and the Colored Farmers' alliance meets in Ocala, Florida, to see if there is some way to take joint action. Racial barriers are still too strong in the South and nothing important comes of the meeting.

1 MARCH 1891

National In 1881 the Supreme Court had upheld the validity of the federal income tax which the government had adopted as an expedient measure during the Civil War; the Court found that tax on income falls outside the constitutional meaning of direct tax since it does not require apportionment among the states in proportion to population. However, the amount of direct tax collected from other sources by the Federal Government during the Civil War is to be returned to the States, which is duly accomplished this first day of March.

3 MARCH 1891

National Congress establishes the Circuit Court of Appeals. It serves to relieve the Supreme Court of some of its appellate jurisdiction.

Immigration The office of Superintendent of Immigration is created by Congress. Immigration is increasing, frontier land is almost gone, depression threatens the land and job security in industry is non–existent.

Conservation Public opinion is increasingly effective in areas of national concern. Responding, Congress passes the Forest Reserve Act of 1891. Under its provisions, President Harrison will set aside 13,000,000 acres of public lands for a national forest reserve.

4 MARCH 1891

International Beginning to take a more responsible attitude in its relations with other nations, Congress adopts the International Copyright Act. Rights of foreign authors will hereafter be protected from piracy by American publishers. Despite its grandiose title, this act applies only to Great Britain, France, Belgium and Switzerland. Later it will be extended to most other countries.

14 MARCH 1891

National Eleven Sicilians are indicted for the murder of the Irish chief of police of New Orleans. During the trial there is the suggestion that these men are members of the sinister "Mafia" gang. Later they are forcibly taken out of jail and murdered by a mob. Incensed at this brutality to its citizens, Italy insists upon and receives $25,000 in financial recompense.

7 APRIL 1891

Labor Chalking up one gain at a time, labor gets an

FORGING A NATION 1866-1900

eight–hour day law passed in Nebraska.

14 APRIL 1891
National President Harrison starts off on a month–long tour of Southern and Western States.

19 MAY 1891
National Growing out of an enthusiastic meeting held in Kansas the year before, the vibrant, eclectic, reform–minded Populist Party is formed at the national level at an enthusiastic convention held in Cincinnati, Ohio. Although the party draws from many groups, its main strength lies in united support from labor and farmers. Government ownership of railroads is one of their important demands along with free coinage of silver. They back a graduated income tax; an eight–hour day; popular election of senators; the secret ballot; government ownership of telegraphs and

---

THE POPULIST PARTY

In increasing numbers during the late 19th century, small special interest groups were forming, then banding together, subsequently joining with others, and so proceeding until they had achieved their goals. Joining for political ends had supplanted joining for social purposes. Organizations of the most disparate elements combined, learned from each other, split apart like colliding atoms, only to merge again with other groups also seeking political life.

The Populists, also called the People's Party, was just such a grouping of individualistic, multi-faceted organizations although it drew its main strength from the merging of the farmers' interests with those of industrial labor. At their first exploratory gathering in Topeka, Kansas, in 1890 the golden–voiced Mary Elizabeth Lease, herself of Kansas, struck the keynote when she exhorted: "What you farmers need to do is raise less corn and more Hell!" She went on to explain her demands: "We want money, land and transportation. We want the abolition of the National Banks, and we want the power to make loans direct from the government. We want the accursed foreclosure system wiped out. . . We will stand by our homes and stay by our firesides by force if necessary, and we will not pay our debts to the loanshark companies until the Government pays its debts to us." Mary Lease spoke for many, but others equally eloquent spoke, too: James Weaver for his "greenbackers"; Ignatius Donnelly for Utopians; "Sockless" Jerry Simpson for the farmers. It was a colorful gathering filled with evangelistic fervor.

By 1892 the Populists had won the governorship and legislature of Kansas, taken control of four Midwestern states, and held their own national convention and nominated their own presidential candidate, James Weaver. As their numbers grew, so did their hopes of replacing the Democrats as the second major party, but when the Democrats nominated William Jennings Bryan for President in 1896 and adopted a platform of free silver coinage, the Populists found themselves effectively pushed aside. They, too, nominated Bryan, and with his loss, the rise of farm prices, and the Populists' own failure to attract urban-industrial supporters, the Populists collapsed as an organized party. Many of their concerns and reforms, however, were adopted by the other parties and by American society as a whole.

---

telephones and government warehouses where farmers could deposit grain against treasury notes. The Populist Party will hold a national convention in the presidential elections of 1892 and poll over 1,000,000 votes.

20 JULY 1891
Labor In Briceville, Tennessee, 200 convicts are returned to jail by state troops after forcing the miners there to surrender. Labor unrest is increasing in violence with every passing year. Although prices on many goods and services have gone down, many necessities remain high because of tariff walls and unfair railroad rates. Appalling working conditions do not change except through strife. As strikes reach ever larger proportions, state and federal troops are more often called in to quell them. Convict labor is being routinely used to break strikes.

24 AUGUST 1891
Science/Technology Indefatigable Thomas Edison receives a patent for his motion picture camera, which he calls a kinetoscope. Along with Thomas Armat's Vitascope it will produce the first true motion pictures in 1896.

22 SEPTEMBER 1891
Indian Affairs By presidential proclamation another 900,000 acres of Indian land in Oklahoma are opened for settlers. This is land owned by the Sauk, Fox and Potawatomie Indians. It is ceded to the United States by treaty although these treaties have since been found to be less than honest transactions. Said one

---

EARLY DEVELOPMENT OF MOTION PICTURES

In 1891 Thomas Edison was given a patent for a motion picture camera. The subsequent invention of the photographic gun by the Frenchman E.J. Marey, and then John Carbutt's development of celluloid film, led Edison to the next step, what he called a kinetoscope, better known as the peepshow, which was unveiled in 1893. The device used a continuous role of film, patented by George Eastman in 1880, but had a serious drawback: it could be seen by only one viewer at a time. In 1893 Edison and his band of technicians constructed a "film studio" in West Orange, New Jersey. The structure was built to pivot with the sun. Progress continued as Woodville Latham demonstrated a Pantoptikon in 1895. This device was a combination of the Kinetoscope and the Magic Lantern. At the same time the engagingly named Lumière family in France achieved the world's most advanced projector with their Cinematographe. Other modifications followed, until the American Thomas Armat demonstrated the Vitascope in 1896. This was the true prototype of the modern motion picture. The mechanism projected an image onto a screen. On April 23, 1896, the first commercial motion picture exhibition was held at Koster and Bial's Music Hall in New York. Edison will be the first to develop sound along with motion in his cameraphone, demonstrated in 1904. This was just the beginning; motion pictures in the 20th century will become a phenomenon requiring its own history.

Indian lamenting the loss of his lands: "They made us many promises, more than I can remember, but they never kept but one; they promised to take our land, and they took it."

16 OCTOBER 1891

International A war is threatened with Chile when American sailors ashore from the U.S.S. *Baltimore* are attacked by an angered mob. Two sailors are killed and several wounded. Chile finally negotiates a settlement paying $75,000 in indemnity to families of wounded and slain.

3 NOVEMBER 1891

Regional William McKinley is elected Governor of Ohio. McKinley has lost his seat as senator because of his high–tariff stance, but he has many powerful friends who help him win the governorship.

29 DECEMBER 1891

Science/Technology Thomas Edison is granted a patent for the first meaningful radio device. It transmits signals electrically without the use of wire.

OTHER EVENTS OF 1891

Science/Technology Whitcomb L. Judson patents a device he calls the "zipper." George E. Hale takes the first picture of the sun with his invention of the spectroheliograph.

1 JANUARY 1892

Immigration Ellis Island becomes the golden door for foreigners coming to live in America. More than half a million immigrants are arriving yearly and Castle Garden has become too small for such a multitude. Ellis will remain the legendary entrance to America for 62 years and will process over 20 million people before it closes on November 12, 1954.

29 FEBRUARY 1892

International The United States and Great Britain agree to submit to arbitration their controversy over seal–hunting in the Bering Sea. A Commission of representatives from Italy, France and Sweden is set up to look into the problem. Americans have claimed the Bering Sea as their own and have seized Canadian vessels for hunting in the open waters. The controversy will be resolved in favor of Great Britain in a decision agreed to August 15, 1893, when Canadian vessels will be free to go into the disputed area. Damages will be awarded to Britain. Hunting will be forbidden during certain times of the year.

MARCH 1892

Industry In a landmark decision The Standard Oil Trust is dissolved by the Ohio Supreme Court, which orders the Standard Oil Company of Ohio to sever its connections with the main company.

1 APRIL 1892

Labor Miners in the Coeur D'Alene silver mines in Idaho go on strike. The strike will last well into July

JAMES GILLESPIE BLAINE, 1830-1893

A colorful, influential figure in American politics for over 60 years, James G. Blaine took an active and forward-looking part in most of the issues confronting his country, from Reconstruction's bandaging of the national wounds of war to America's first wobbly steps into world affairs in the 1880s.

Settling in Maine, from 1854 his springboard into politics was the influential *Kennebec Journal* which Blaine owned and edited. Maine politics led him to the national arena and from 1863 to 1876 he was active in the House of Representatives. He then went on to the Senate where he served until he resigned in 1881 to become secretary of state under his friend James Garfield.

Blaine was admired and loved by his colleagues and by the public at large. Known affectionately as the "Plumed Knight," he was a leader in party councils and commanded a loyal following. Several times he came near to being nominated for president and he might indeed have won that office but for some dealings in which he had ungainfully profited from his position. The one time he did win his party's nomination was in 1884. The golden goal seemed well within his grasp but was lost by a single mellifluous phrase. In a speech at the Fifth Avenue Hotel on October 29, a Blaine supporter, the Rev. Dr. Samuel D. Burchard, rolled out the unfortunate sentence which referred to the Democrats as the party of "Rum, Romanism, and Rebellion." Blaine, occupied elsewhere, did not instantly disavow the unfortunate slander and his New York vote, heavily dependent on the Catholics, was lost. The trivial mischance cost him the presidency.

Blaine was active until the end of his life. He was a good secretary of state under both Garfield and Harrison, working ably for an enlightened foreign policy, particularly in respect to pan-American relations. He was a man of many parts, and though not a moral example, he was a forceful political personality on the side of common sense.

and will amount to a mini–guerrilla war.

19 APRIL 1892

Science/Technology The first American automobile is perfected by Charles E. Duryea and his brother Frank in Springfield, Massachusetts. It will have its initial public run on September 21, 1893. It is the first successful American–made automobile, although George B. Selden of Rochester, New York had achieved a working gasoline auto engine as early as 1879. However, his patent was not granted until 1895, causing legal controversy over patent rights. Modifications and advances will come rapidly one after another in the early decades of the 20th century.

Indian Affairs President Harrison opens another 3,000,000 acres of Oklahoma land to white settlers. The land belongs to Cheyenne and Arapaho Indians forced into Oklahoma territory at the end of tragic battles in the 1870s and 1880s.

5 MAY 1892

Immigration Registration of Chinese is now required by Act of Congress. Chinese must register within a year or be deported. The act is called the Geary Chinese Exclusion Act. It extends existing laws

FORGING A NATION 1866-1900

for another ten years.

4 JUNE 1892
National James G. Blaine resigns as Secretary of State. His hopes are now centered on the Republican presidential nomination.

10 JUNE 1892
National The Republican Party holds its national convention in Minneapolis, Minnesota. It renominates Benjamin Harrison for president on the first ballot with 535 votes. The perennially popular James G. Blaine loses with 183 votes and McKinley receives 182. Whitelaw Reid of New York is given the nomination for vice–president. Although the country is almost in a state of war over the industrial situation, the party's chief concern is high tariffs.

23 JUNE 1892
National The Democratic Party meets in Chicago and nominates former president Grover Cleveland for president and reform–minded Adlai E. Stevenson of Illinois for vice–president. Radical Democrats oppose high tariffs and push through a declaration that states: "The government has no constitutional power to impose and collect tariff duties, except for purposes of revenue only."

29 JUNE 1892
National The Prohibition Party convenes in Cincinnati, Ohio. General John Bidwell of California is nominated for president and James B. Cranfill of Texas for vice–president.

1 JULY 1892
Labor Strikes have been instituted against corporations all over the nation. Pennsylvania, Tennessee and Idaho have been severely hit. The most significant is called this day against Andrew Carnegie's Homestead Mill on the Monongahela River in Pennsylvania. The steel company, under the management of Henry Clay Frick, refuses to recognize the Amalgamated Association of Iron and Steel Workers which has been working amicably in the factory for some time. There is nothing for it but to strike. The main issue is whether labor will be permitted to bargain as a single unit, a corporation, or whether each individual worker will have to contract unprotected with the giant combine by himself. The Homestead strike lasts five months. Although the fight badly tarnishes Carnegie's good name, it ends with no gains for the strikers. It can merely claim to be the most vicious in industrial relations up until this time. However, lessons are becoming clearer: rules carefully worked out for agrarian societies will need to be brought up to date to meet industrial conditions.

2 JULY 1892
National The Populist Party, also called the People's Party, holds its first national convention in Omaha, Nebraska. James B. Weaver of Iowa, who has been a persistent fighter for minority causes, is nominated for

president, and James G. Field of Virginia for vice–president.

6 JULY 1892
Labor Some 5000 Homestead Steel workers battle 300 Pinkerton "detectives" brought in by Frick to break the strike. Hundreds are wounded and some 20 persons killed.

9 JULY 1892
Labor A thoroughly overwhelming force of 7000 state troopers is ordered to the Homestead Works by Governor Pattison of Pennsylvania.

11 JULY 1892
Labor Striking silver miners in Coeur d'Alene, Idaho, engage in violent struggle with strikebreakers.

14 JULY 1892
National Congress authorizes a $50–a–month pension for Civil War veterans wounded in service.

THE HOMESTEAD STRIKE

On July 1, 1892, the contract between Andrew Carnegie's Homestead Steel Mill and the Amalgamated Association of Iron and Steel Workers expired. Although industrial relations had been fairly smooth between them, Carnegie's manager Henry Clay Frick chose to take the opportunity to rid himself of the union. First he cut wages, then put forth other, secondary objections and finally refused to negotiate. By the time the contract expired, the workers were forced to vote for strike. Frick prepared for the showdown by hiring 300 Pinkerton guards to protect Homestead Steel. They were brought up the Monongahela River on two barges. Some 5000 men and women waited tensely to repulse them at the landing. By the time the fight was over more than 20 people were dead and all 300 Pinkertons were wounded. The successful strikers were willing to accept management terms, but Frick now refused to negotiate at all. Instead he got the governor to send in 7000 militiamen. The nation's sympathy was overwhelmingly with the union. Cleveland referred to "the tender mercy the workingman receives from those made selfish and sordid by unjust government favoritism." Desperate Republican politicians cabled Carnegie, happily ensconced in Scotland, to recognize the union, but to no avail. By July 15 the Homestead Mill went back into operation with strikebreakers under military guard.

In the midst of the appalling situation a young anarchist, Alexander Berkman, shot Frick twice in the abdomen and stabbed him several times. The iron man was treated but finished the day at his office and then triumphantly waited out the months until the strike was broken.

On November 14 it was over. In the short run, Homestead management had won, but in reality everyone had lost. Carnegie's reputation had suffered irreparably. Frick had been severely wounded and most of the workers lost their jobs to strikebreakers. But the country was beginning to understand the issues. The need for greater social action was apparent to all, especially to those who were to wield power in the future. They were being nurtured in the present industrial conditions without nostalgia for an agrarian past they had never lived.

23 JULY 1892
Indian Affairs Congress bans the sale of alcohol on Indian lands.
Labor In a controversial move federal troops are sent to the Coeur d'Alene mines in Idaho to force strikers back to work.

27 JULY 1892
National Congress authorizes a pension of eight dollars a month to survivors of the Indian Wars of 1832-1842 and the following week grants a $12–a–month pension to women who served as nurses during the Civil War.

28 AUGUST 1892
National The Socialist Party holds its national convention in New York. It nominates Simon Wing of Massachusetts for president and Charles H. Matchet of New York for vice-president.

30 AUGUST 1892
Life/Customs Cholera arrives in the United States for the first time. It is transmitted by an infection carried aboard the Hamburg-American Line's *Moravia.*

15 OCTOBER 1892
Indian Affairs Benjamin Harrison opens 1,800,000 acres of Indian reservation in Montana to white settlers. This is land belonging to the Crow Indians.

8 NOVEMBER 1892
National Grover Cleveland defeats Benjamin Harrison by 277-145 electoral votes. Adlai E. Stevenson is elected vice-president. Popular vote is Cleveland 5,554,414; Harrison 5,190,801. General Weaver's Populist Party comes in with a spoiler's strong 1,027,329 votes.

14 NOVEMBER 1892
Labor Without having gained anything tangible, workers are finally forced to call off their strike against the Homestead Mill.

2 DECEMBER 1892
Industry One of the most flamboyant and daring entrepreneurs of the early buccaneering industrial days, Jay Gould, dies of consumption at age 56. Responsible for the Black Friday gold scandal (September 24, 1869) which did much to precipitate the great depression of the 1870s, Gould was a wheeler-dealer in the railroad industry, gutting, merging, breaking, and building with equal skill. When he sat down with the Knights of Labor in an industrial dispute, his presence lent prestige and membership rose from 100,000 to 700,000 in one year. The union did not make any tangible gains, but for the first time Labor and Capital had met as equals. Gould, however, was not a benevolent employer. He was typical of the pre-Civil War individualist let loose onto an unregulated industrial age. "I can hire one half of the working class to kill the other half," he once said. At his death his personal estate was valued at $72,000,000.

4 JANUARY 1893
National Wishing to come to terms with the new Mormon Church, the Federal Government offers amnesty to all polygamists, on condition that in the future laws against polygamy are heeded.

16 JANUARY 1893
International John L. Stevens, United States ambassador to Hawaii, and powerful planters led by Sanford P. Dole, overthrow Queen Liliuokalani's autocratic government in Hawaii which had come to power in 1891 and upset the pro-annexationist movement. Dole sets up a revolutionary Committee of Safety and on January 17 occupies government buildings with the help of U.S. Marines. Stevens recognizes the new regime without permission from the State Department and blandly proceeds to negotiate a treaty of annexation with the new, if fragile, Hawaiian government.

17 JANUARY 1893
National Former President Rutherford B. Hayes dies at 70. He is buried in Fremont, Ohio.

1 FEBRUARY 1893
International The United States flag is raised over government buildings in Honolulu, Hawaii. Still without authorization from Washington, John L. Stevens declares Hawaii a United States protectorate.

15 FEBRUARY 1893
National John L. Stevens belatedly submits a Treaty of Annexation of Hawaii to the U.S. Senate.

20 FEBRUARY 1983
National With debts amounting to more than $125,000,000, the Philadelphia and Reading Railroads are relinquished to receivers. This is the first glimpse of the onrushing Panic of 1893. As the situation deteriorates rapidly, 74 railroads will fall into receivership this year, 600 banks will close, and 15,000 commercial houses will collapse.

1 MARCH 1893
National The creation of the rank of ambassador is authorized by Congress under the Diplomatic Appropriation Act. On April 3 Thomas F. Bayard will be the first person appointed ambassador in the U.S. foreign service. He is made ambassador to Great Britain.

4 MARCH 1893
National Grover Cleveland is inaugurated for his second term. Adlai Stevenson is vice-president.

9 MARCH 1893
International The Hawaiian Annexation Treaty is withdrawn from the Senate by President Cleveland pending further inquiry into the unorthodox events leading up to its submission. On July 17 Cleveland sends J. H. Blount to investigate the cause of the revolution. Blount's report finds the provisional Hawaiian government was established by force and external intervention.

FORGING A NATION 1866-1900

On December 18, 1893, President Cleveland tells Congress that the treaty will not be resubmitted. This is only a setback for the pro-annexationist movement.

10 MARCH 1893
Regional Fire rages through Boston killing many and causing $5,000,000 in damages.

13 APRIL 1893
International Commander J. H. Blount orders United States troops to leave Hawaii, thus putting an end to the brief American "protectorate" there.

15 APRIL 1893
National The gold reserve has fallen below the magic $100,000,000 mark causing even greater runs on the Federal Treasury. The issue of gold certificates is temporarily suspended.

PANIC OF 1893

There were many factors leading up to the Panic of 1893. British investors, heavily into railroads, had early sensed a weakness in the American economic system and had been unloading American securities. A failure two years earlier of the British banking house of Baring Brothers had merely accelerated the process. In February 1893 a major railroad, the Philadelphia and Reading, had gone bankrupt with debts of $125,000,000. Stocks kept falling, trusts collapsed, and thousands of farm mortgages were foreclosed. The Silver Purchase Act had badly drained gold reserves. By April 21, 1893, even with mammoth bail-outs by Eastern bankers, the nation's reserve had fallen below the magic $100,000,000 mark and it was apparent to almost everyone that disaster loomed; however, Cleveland could not get Congress to make a move until the decisive crash of June 27. He then called for a special session of Congress to convene August 7. The dangerous delay of over a month was due to the need for Cleveland to have a cancer removed from his mouth. This operation had to be kept secret for fear of precipitating an even worse crisis. In August, Cleveland forced repeal of the Sherman Silver Purchase Act and stemmed the tide. Even so, by the end of the year, gold reserves had fallen to $80,000,000 and the country was in the throes of one of the worst depressions of its history.

---

1 MAY 1893
Arts/Culture President Cleveland opens the World's Columbian Exposition in Chicago. The Fair commemorates the 400th anniversary of the discovery of America.

5 MAY 1893
National Panic is generated on the New York Stock Exchange as securities fall dramatically.

15 MAY 1893
National The Geary Exclusion Act—which effectively excludes Chinese from the U.S.—is found to be constitutional by the Supreme Court.

20 JUNE 1893
National Eugene V. Debs establishes the militant American Railway Union in Chicago.

26 JUNE 1893
National Putting his career in jeopardy, Governor John P. Altgeld of Illinois pardons the last three anarchists in jail from the Haymarket Square riot of May 4, 1886.

27 JUNE 1893
National Four years of deep depression begin with the crash of the New York stock market.

1 JULY 1893
National Cleveland undergoes surgery for cancer of the mouth. The operation is done on a friend's yacht in order to maintain absolute secrecy. Word of his illness might precipitate an even greater crisis than now exists in the nation. The operation is a success.

8 AUGUST 1893
National Finally taking a strong stand in the monetary crisis, in a special session of Congress Cleveland pleads for repeal of the Sherman Silver Purchase Act. Ultimately he will get the votes, but the Democratic Party is badly wounded in the ugly fight.

13 AUGUST 1893
Regional A fire in Minneapolis causes $2,000,000

EUGENE DEBS, 1855-1926

Eugene Debs was one of the most admired figures in the workers' movement during the closing years of the 19th century and well into the 20th. His career began quietly enough as a locomotive fireman. He then served a term as member of the Indiana State Legislature before becoming secretary and treasurer of the Brotherhood of Locomotive Firemen. But the times demanded action and in 1893 Debs responded by organizing the militant American Railway Union. A year later he led the membership in one of the most severe strikes in the turbulent history of the railroads: the strike against the Pullman Palace Car Company. Some 60,000 railway workers went out in the first two days. Spreading, the strike soon involved 20 companies in 27 States and Territories. Federal Troops were sent in to break the strike. Still unable to control the situation, Cleveland authorized an injunction against the Railroad Union on the grounds that it was obstructing the nation's mail. For ignoring the injunction, Debs ended up in jail for six months. For the union movement the use of injunction set a severe precedent which Labor would be burdened with ever after.

In 1897 Debs joined the Socialist Party and from then on identified the worker's struggle with the political one. He ran for president five times, once while serving a term in prison for alleged espionage. Never a fanatic ideologue, he saw relief for the worker in such practical solutions as municipal ownership of public utilities and is rather to be identified with the American Progressive movement than with revolutionary international communism.

For many years Debs edited the Socialist Party's weekly *Appeal to Reason*. He died one of the most respected members of the Socialist movement.

---

in property damage and renders 1500 homeless.

15 AUGUST 1893
International The killing of seals is forbidden within 60 miles of the Pribilof Islands by decision of the Bering Sea Arbitration Court.

24 AUGUST 1893
Regional A cyclone leaves 1000 dead and inflicts severe damage as it roars through heavily populated areas of Savannah and Charleston.

16 SEPTEMBER 1893
Regional More than 50,000 rush to settle the Cherokee Strip between Kansas and Oklahoma, 6,000,000 acres bought from the Cherokees for $8,500,000.

17 SEPTEMBER 1893
Regional Brunswick, Georgia, reports a severe epidemic of yellow fever.

2 OCTOBER 1893
Regional A cyclone ravages the Gulf Coast of Louisiana. Over 2000 are left dead by the disaster.

1 NOVEMBER 1893
National The Sherman Silver Purchase Act is repealed after a bitter congressional fight.

7 NOVEMBER 1893
Regional Women's suffrage is adopted in Colorado by popular vote.

OTHER EVENTS OF 1893
Ideas/Beliefs The Mormon Temple is dedicated at Salt Lake City, Utah. The huge, awesome structure took 40 years to build and cost somewhere up to $12,000,000.

8 JANUARY 1894
Regional Almost all the buildings of Chicago's Columbian Exposition are destroyed by fire, causing damage estimated at $2,000,000.

17 JANUARY 1894
National The United States Treasury offers a

Coxey's Army marches on Washington to protest unemployment.

FORGING A NATION 1866-1900

$50,000,000 bond issue to restore the gold reserve which continues to decline despite repeal of the Sherman Silver Purchase Act. Public response to the offer is dismal; most of the bonds are bought by banks.

30 JANUARY 1894
Regional The New York Senate appoints the Lexow Committee to investigate New York City scandals. The police department is under particular scrutiny. One police officer confesses that he bought his captaincy for $15,000.

8 FEBRUARY 1894
National By Act of Congress the Enforcement Act of February 28, 1871 is repealed. States now control elections, which leaves the white supremacist Solid South to do as it will in relation to the black vote. Mississippi is the first to take advantage of the situation with its "understanding" clause. Voters when challenged must answer questions about the Constitution.

13 FEBRUARY 1894
Labor A collapsed coal mine in Plymouth, Pennsylvania, caves in, burying 13 miners.

5 APRIL 1894
Labor Fierce riots break out among miners striking in Connellsville, Pennsylvania. Eleven men are killed. Riots underline the rotten conditions prevailing in the new mines. The romance that once surrounded the colorful individuals involved in early placer gold mining no longer exists in the hot, airless, dangerously deep shafts of commercial coal mining.

20 APRIL 1894
Labor Almost taking the country to the edge of civil war, 136,000 desperate coal miners strike at Columbus, Ohio, over wages. By the end of the year 750,000 workers will have gone on strike.

24 APRIL 1894
Labor In another tragic mine accident at Franklin, Washington, 37 men die.

30 APRIL 1894
National Jacob Sechler Coxey leads 400 people from Ohio to Washington, D.C. Known as Coxey's Army, the motley crew marches to protest unemployment; underlying that is their sense that the government refuses to legislate in favor of working people, but feels no such compunction to refrain from legislating in favor of large corporations. Arriving in Washington amid great applause from a waiting crowd, Coxey and his lieutenants are arrested for trespassing on the grass. The "army" melts away. Coxey's Army is only one of many such "armies" which gather to protest the problems of a society that no one seems to be able to manage fairly.

6 MAY 1894
National In *Regan v Farmers' Loan and Trust Company,* the Supreme Court rules that judicial review can determine reasonableness of rates, both those already set by legislature as well as by State commission. It is a sweeping decision, conceived out of the Spencerian laissez-faire philosophy which is being increasingly discredited in the legislative and executive branches of government.

11 MAY 1894
Labor Workers at the Pullman Palace Car Company call a strike. The autocratic company has reduced its payroll and substantially reduced wages without reducing rents in its model workers' homes, nor prices in its company stores.

31 MAY 1894
International In a unanimous decision, the Senate declares that Hawaii is to keep its own government and warns that any nation interfering with that government will be considered hostile to the United States. This will be a shortlived respite for the independent islands.

21 JUNE 1894
National Wiliam Jennings Bryan leaps into national

FREDERICK REMINGTON, 1861-1909

Although well known for his paintings, Frederick Remington is perhaps more deeply respected for his sculpture. He finished only 25 bronzes but these are treasured in many collections including the Metropolitan Museum of Art's.

Born in upstate New York into a well-off family, Remington went as a boy to military academy, and by 16 was ready to enter Yale as one of only two art students. But Remington was a self-confident, self-indulgent person and when his father died leaving him a small inheritance, he left college and headed to the romantic West. One day in 1881 when he was 20 years old, Remington was sitting on a bluff watching a train chug across the prairie. Noting the moment later he wrote: "I knew the wild riders and the vacant land were about to vanish forever and the more I considered the subject, the bigger *forever* loomed. . . I began to record some facts around me." He painted cowboys at the water hole, Indians scouting for friends, and sought to record in metal and color the legendary life of the Wild West. In all, Remington painted 2739 pictures and illustrated 147 books, eight of which he had written himself. He was widely reproduced in national magazines such as *Harper's Weekly.* Described as a "big, goodnatured overgrown boy," Remington was a friend of Roosevelt and followed him to Cuba at the outbreak of war. Working for capricious William Randolph Hearst, Remington opined that he could not find the war. "You furnish the pictures, I'll furnish the war!" Hearst wired his famous reply. Later Remington painted his old friend Theodore Roosevelt in his famous *Charge of the Rough Riders at San Juan Hill.*

Most of all Remington loved to paint and sculpt the horse, and there, perhaps, he was at his very best. He rode every day of his life until he reached some 300 pounds and his own beloved animal could no longer hold him. His final request was that his epitaph read: "He knew the horse."

prominence at the Democratic Silver convention in Omaha, Nebraska. Over a thousand delegates attend. Bryan's eloquence begins to fire great numbers of suffering voters to find consolation in his simplistic solution to their woes: free silver.

26 JUNE 1894
Labor To help the striking Pullman workers, Eugene Debs' American Railway Union calls a general sympathy strike of all railway workers. The fairminded Illinois Governor Altgeld maintains order with the state guard. The Railway Managers' Association refuses to negotiate with the strikers and hires 3600 deputy marshals to see that the strike is broken.

28 JUNE 1894
National In the midst of national labor chaos, Congress declares Labor Day a national holiday.

2 JULY 1894
Labor In a landmark move with longterm repercussions, the United States government issues an injunction against the railroad strikers on the grounds of "interference with interstate commerce and postal service." President Cleveland makes the move at the behest of U.S. Attorney General Olney. Richard Olney has his own reasons for wanting this: he had himself been a railroad director and a member of the Managers' Association; he is still an attorney for several railroads. The injunction orders Debs to call off the strike. That Pullman cars do not carry mail is disregarded by Cleveland. A possible alternative order to resume regular mail and passenger car service while the Pullman situation is negotiated is never tried.

3 JULY 1894
Labor U.S. troops are sent to Chicago to enforce the court injunction. Cleveland is determined to get the mail through. He declares that interference with the postal service is unconstitutional and that he will see that the lowliest postcard gets delivered if it takes the whole army to deliver it. Governor Altgeld protests the misuse of the Army to break a strike, claiming it violates the Constitution and interferes in the internal affairs of a state. Altgeld's fairmindedness throughout the strike will merely ruin his career in politics.

6 JULY 1894
Labor Two men are killed and several injured when railroad strikers are fired upon by troops in Kensington near Chicago.

10 JULY 1894
Labor A Federal Grand Jury indicts Eugene Debs for failing to comply with the injunction. On December 14 he will be sentenced to six months' imprisonment.

20 JULY 1894
Labor U.S. troops are withdrawn from Chicago, but not before extensive damage has been caused by mobs made angry by their presence. Fire alone causes some $3,000,000 worth of damage. These disorderly groups are not predominantly strikers but include the unemployed in general together with a goodly number of simple troublemakers.

3 AUGUST 1894
Labor The Pullman strike is broken, officially called off by the Railway union. No concessions have been made to the strikers, but the Labor cause has gained greater public understanding and sympathy. In the long struggle, many lives and an estimated $80,000,000 in property and wages have been lost.

18 AUGUST 1894
National The Bureau of Immigration is established by an Act of Congress. Also the Carey Act is adopted, which promises States up to 1,000,000 acres of public lands each if they will agree to irrigate them.

27 AUGUST 1894
National Against heavy opposition, the Wilson-Gorman Tariff Act passes Congress. The bill includes the first graduated income tax law. The Act is passed without Cleveland's signature, and it will be found unconstitutional by the Supreme Court in 1895.

1 SEPTEMBER 1894
Regional A hurricane whips a fierce fire through Hinckley, Minnesota, and nearby towns, killing 500 people and rendering thousands more homeless. Hinckley Station is burned to the ground while hundreds flee in a train.

4 SEPTEMBER 1894
Labor To protest the "sweat shops" and piece work, 12,000 tailors strike in New York City. The "sweat shops" have become a new symbol of social injustice.

13 NOVEMBER 1894
National Gold reserves are still declining and the United States Treasury offers its second $50,000,000 bond issue of the year. The silverites are right—the money is in short supply—but new deposits of gold will soon be discovered abroad, in Australia, Africa and elsewhere, which will help replenish depleted world treasuries. In 1890 two metallurgists, McArthur and Forrest, use cyanide in a process to extract gold from lowgrade ore. This process, which comes into wide use, will almost double gold production within eight years.

22 NOVEMBER 1894
International The United States and Japan sign a commercial treaty in Washington.

14 DECEMBER 1894
Labor Eugene Debs is sentenced to six months in prison for his part in the Railway Strike. His defense attorney is Clarence Darrow, in his first major case.

FORGING A NATION 1866-1900

14 JANUARY 1895
Labor Employees of the trolley railroad in Brooklyn, New York go on strike. Riots ensue which are eventually suppressed by the New York and Brooklyn militia.

21 JANUARY 1895
National In *United States v E. C. Knight,* the Supreme Court finds that the Sherman Anti-Trust Act is applicable only to monopolies involved in interstate trade. Ruling that a sugar combine is beyond the law, the Court draws a fine line between manufacturing and commerce. The Sherman Anti-Trust Act which was designed to regulate all forms of trusts is found to be invalid (even in such flagrant cases as this one, where one company is allowed to own 98 percent of the sugar refining business) on the grounds that it is manufacturing sugar within the boundaries of one state. This ruling will temporarily render the Sherman Act useless. Not until Theodore Roosevelt is elected President and undertakes to modify the power of the trusts will the Court substantially change its stance.

22 JANUARY 1895
Industry The National Association of Manufacturers is formed in Cincinnati.

8 FEBRUARY 1895
National The federal gold reserves are down to $41,000,000. Congress has refused to pass a bill whereby notes once redeemed in gold could not be reissued. The process is an "endless chain." In a move born of desperation, Cleveland makes a deal with J. P. Morgan to sell his syndicate about $62,000,000 at a premium of four–and–a–half percent. The syndicate is permitted to resell to the public at 118. Although Cleveland had no choice, his arrangement is looked upon by the country as a sellout to the bankers. Gold is hoarded in dangerous amounts, but the bankers control the market and are able to put a stop to the "endless chain" which Congress had done nothing to limit.

20 FEBRUARY 1895
International Congress endorses Cleveland's suggestion that he help arbitrate in the long–drawn–out dispute over the Venezuela–British Guiana border which has been contested since 1814. With discovery of gold in the area, the boundary line becomes an issue once again. Great Britain grandly refuses to accept U.S. arbitration on the grounds that the area "belonged to the Throne of England before the Republic of Venezuela came into existence."

24 FEBRUARY 1895
Spanish-American War: Approach Cuban insurgents revolt against Spanish rule. They are supplied with money by American sugar planters surreptitiously agitating for American domination of the island. They are also anxious to keep their plantations from being burned by the *insurrectos.* When the Cubans attack Spanish forces, General Weyler is sent from Spain to quell the revolt. Rounding up the population, he squashes them into *reconcentrado* camps so that he can more easily go after the guerrillas. Many sicken and die in the dreadful camp conditions. Sympathy for the Cubans is roused in the United States. Later fanned by the "yellow journalism" of Hearst and Pulitzer, and egged on by imperialists like Theodore Roosevelt and Henry Cabot Lodge, the country will be led into an adventure which will change its very nature.

5 MARCH 1895
National Starting the silver campaign for the year, a minority of the House Democrats back an appeal for free coinage of silver at the ratio to gold of 16 to one. The appeal is conceived by Representatives Richard Bland of Missouri and the captivating William Jennings Bryan of Nebraska. There will be several silver conventions this year, particularly in the South and West.

20 MAY 1895
National In *Pollock v Farmers' Loan and Trust Company,* the Supreme Court finds that the income tax clause of the Wilson-Gorman Tariff Act of August 27, 1894 is unconstitutional on the grounds that it is a direct tax on only a section of the country. The clause had stipulated an income tax on incomes over $4000.

MUSICIANS

American music, while tuneful, soulful and sometimes stirring, did not come into its own in the 19th century. However, the seeds of some of America's greatest music were sown at this time

In one of the first public uses of black music, Harrigan and Hart in 1877 wrote *Walking for Dat Cake* in imitation of the "cakewalks" of plantation time. Tapping black musical sources by white musicians would ultimately lead to America's most authentic music, a jealous marriage of black and white genius. Later Scott Joplin, a black from St. Louis, applied his classical training to black ragtime. He was one of the all–time great performers and composers of rag. In 1890 "Buddy" Bolden organized his famous band in New Orleans. He drew to his group most of the early great black musicians who together developed the sounds of jazz.

Composer Edward MacDowell, having studied in Europe for 12 years, became one of the first classical musicians to be taken seriously by Europeans. He used American themes, Indian and black, for his compositions as did classical composer George W. Chadwick, who drew on hobo tunes for his *Symphonic Sketches.*

The stirring marches of John Philip Sousa captured the hearts of Americans, especially *The Stars and Stripes Forever*, still a favorite marching tune.

Although the currents of great American music were running strong, they were running underground. On the surface, people were harmonizing to sentimental songs like *On the Banks of the Wabash.* It would be another 20 years before black music would surface into popular consciousness and several more before black and white strains merged into the intoxicating sounds of the 20th century.

Fifteen years earlier the Court had upheld the income tax as constitutional.

27 MAY 1895
Labor In *Re Debs* the Supreme Court turns the Sherman Anti-Trust Act against organized labor by declaring legitimate a federal injunction issued against railway strikers for hindering interstate commerce. The verdict handed down in the same year that the Sugar Trust is permitted total freedom of action causes howls of rage across the country.

12 JUNE 1895
Spanish-American War: Approach In a speech to the nation, President Cleveland asks that citizens refrain from giving aid and comfort to Cuban rebels. The "Yellow Press," riding a good thing, continues to fan the flames of imperialism.

20 JULY 1895
International Secretary of State Richard Olney sends an astonishing note to Lord Salisbury, Prime Minister and Foreign Secretary of Great Britain, proclaiming: "Today the United States is practically sovereign on this continent, and its fiat is law upon the subjects to which it confines its interposition. Why? . . . It is because, in addition to all other grounds, its infinite resources combined with its isolated position render it master of the situation and practically invulnerable as against any or all powers." Neither Canada nor Latin-America is pleased to hear the offensive note and Lord Salisbury ignores it. It is only when the first whisper of trouble between England and Germany surfaces that Great Britain adopts a conciliatory manner. Kaiser Wilhelm II sends a congratulatory telegram to President Kruger of the Boer Republic on repulsing a British attack on the territory. Foreseeing danger in alienating allies, on January 25, 1896 the Colonial Secretary Joseph Chamberlain will let it be known that conflict between Great Britain and America is unthinkable. It would be, he says, "an absurdity as well as a crime . . . The two nations are allied, and more closely allied in sentiment and interest than any other nations on the face of the earth."

18 SEPTEMBER 1895
Regional The Cotton States and International Exposition is held in Atlanta, Georgia. It is an effort on the part of the South to proclaim its participation in the industrialization of the country.

21 DECEMBER 1895
International Cleveland presents Congress with the belligerent correspondence between his Secretary of State and Lord Salisbury. He requests that a commission be set up to settle the boundary dispute between Venezuela and Great Britain. His tone is not conciliatory: when its report is made, Cleveland asserts, it will "be the duty of the United States to resist by every means in its power, as a willful aggression upon its rights and interests, the appropriation by Great Britain of any lands or the exercise of govern-

mental jurisdiction over any territory which after investigation we have determined of right belongs to Venezuela." That Great Britain could cause great hardship to the U.S. is clear in just their naval superiority. The public in both nations are aghast at the undiplomatic exchange. Congress gives authorization for the commission and allots $100,000 for its work. By this time the British are gently helping the Americans to come to an acceptable decision. On October 3, 1899 the boundary will be drawn substantially along the line laid down in the British claim, the big difference being that the mouth of the Orinoco will be given to Venezuela.

WINSLOW HOMER, 1836-1910

Winslow Homer was a contemplative in a world of action. He made a reputation as an illustrator, but as he put the case, "if a man wants to be an artist he should never look at pictures."

Born in Boston, Homer was the son of a hardware merchant; his mother painted flowers. Because of an obvious facility, Homer was apprenticed at 19 to a commercial lithographer. By the time he was 21 he was a successful freelance illustrator. Ultimately, he was able to make a living doing watercolor sketches, all the while concentrating on some deeper private quest of his own. "The Sun will not rise or set without my notice, and thanks" he once wrote. In 1884, the short, slim, easily exacerbated artist moved to tiny Prout's Neck on the coast of Maine. There, during the long isolated winters, he lovingly translated to canvas what his reverent watching meant to him. He was never overtly allegorical; however, his careful choice of subject, his attention to detail, deliberately painting everything "exactly as it appears," lent his canvasses an intensity that takes the viewer below the magnificence of nature into a silent, solemn world of wordless significance.

Homer lived to a ripe old age, seemingly delighted with his solitary ways. He died at 74, one of the great artists of the 19th century.

---

4 JANUARY 1896
National Utah enters the Union as the 45th State. Its constitution includes women's suffrage.

6 JANUARY 1896
National Gold reserves fall to dangerously low levels. Because the public had been so outraged at his previous arrangement with the banking establishment—whom Pulitzer in his New York *World* characterized as "Robber Barons"—Cleveland now authorizes a public subscription. It is a measure of renewed confidence in the country that the issue is completely bought up.

29 JANUARY 1896
Science/Technology For the first time X-rays are used in the United States for the treatment of breast cancer. The operation is performed by Dr. Emil H. Grube. The discovery of X-ray treatment for cancer had been made by Konrad Roentgen the previous year in Germany.

381

FORGING A NATION 1866-1900

10 FEBRUARY 1896
Spanish-American War: Approach Insurgents in Cuba are cruelly quelled when General Valeriano Weyler arrives from Spain. The "Yellow Press" quickly dubs him "the Butcher."

20 MARCH 1896
International Revolution breaks out in Nicaragua. U.S. Marines go to Corinto to protect U.S. citizens there.

6 APRIL 1896
Spanish-American War: Approach Congress favors granting belligerent status to Cuban revolutionaries and offers its services as arbiter to Spain, with independence for Cuba as the goal. Spain will reject this offer.
Life/Customs The first modern Olympic Games are held in Athens, Greece. Organized by the French Baron Pierre de Courbetin, the Games are held every four years except when war interrupts. In spite of the fact that the little band of U.S. contestants arrives at the site after a long ocean voyage and only just in time to answer the roll call, they win nine of the 12 events. James B. Connolly wins the hop, step and jump; he becomes the first Olympic champion in more than 15 centuries.

23 APRIL 1896
Science/Technology The first public showing of a moving picture is presented at Koster and Bial's Music Hall in New York City. A review in the *New York Times* proclaims it "all wonderfully real and singularly exhilarating." Included in the show are scenes of a turbulent coastline surf, two girls dancing, and a comic boxing act.

6 MAY 1896
National The "separate but equal doctrine" is held constitutional by the Supreme Court in the famous *Plessy v Ferguson* case, known popularly as the Jim Crow Car Law. The Court holds that as long as the facilities are equal, the fact that they are separate does not constitute infringement of civil rights. The doctrine will remain intact until May 17, 1954, when Chief Justice Earl Warren will argue that in the field of education separate facilities are inherently unequal.

27 MAY 1896
National The Prohibition Party meets in Pittsburgh and nominates Joshua Levering of Maryland for president and Hale Johnson of Illinois for vice-president.
Regional Heralded by 120 mph winds, a tornado ravages St. Louis and East St. Louis, killing 400 and destroying the homes of some 5000 persons.

16 JUNE 1896
National The Republican National Convention gathers in St. Louis. In a well-orchestrated convention that has cost Mark Hanna almost $100,000 to arrange, the uncontroversial and easily manipulated William McKinley is nominated for president. The

presidential campaign will cost up to $7,000,000 but Mark Hanna will see to it that it is worth every penny to big business. Almost lost in the discussion over the gold standard and the protective tariff are the new demands for annexation of Hawaii and for Cuban independence.

4 JULY 1896
National The Socialist Labor Party convenes in New York City. Charles H. Matchett of New York is nominated for president and Matthew Maguire of New Jersey is nominated for vice-president.

7 JULY 1896
National Chicago hosts the dramatic Democratic National Convention. Under the glass and steel roof of the Coliseum, 20,000 delegates gather in search of a leader. Their rallying cry is silver, free coinage at 16 to one. The convention is falling into bedlam when William Jennings Bryan rises to speak. Bringing all his hypnotic powers to cast a spell over the disorganized delegates, Bryan captures their attention almost immediately and holds it completely right through to the end when he thunders: "Having behind us the producing masses of this nation and the world, supported by the commercial interests, the laboring interests, and the toilers everywhere, we will answer their demand for a gold standard by saying to them: You shall not press down upon the brow of labor this crown of thorns, you shall not crucify mankind upon a cross of gold." Bryan returns to his seat amid a stunned silence. Then as he describes it later, "bedlam broke loose!" For over an hour the delegates shout and stomp, rejoicing in their new leader. Bryan has won the nomination.

22 JULY 1896
National Led by Senator Henry M. Teller, several Republicans bolt their party and covene in St. Louis to nominate Democrat William Jennings Bryan for president and Arthur Sewal for vice-president. The same day the Populist Party meets in St. Louis. These irrepressible reformers nominate William Jennings Bryan for president, since he is all they could ever hope for, but in order to maintain their independence from the Democratic Party and thereby preserve their own identity, they nominate the Southern demagogue farmer Thomas Watson for vice-president.

12 AUGUST 1896
Regional Gold is discovered in northwest Canada in Klondike Creek near Alaska. Thousands will rush to dig the precious metal; within two years there will be over 18,000 prospectors and "boomers" in the area and a year later 100,000 will be there.

2 SEPTEMBER 1896
National The Gold Democrats who have bolted their party when Bryan is nominated now hold a National Democratic Convention in Indianapolis and nominate John M. Palmer of Illinois for president and Simon B. Buckner of Kentucky for vice-president.

1 OCTOBER 1896

National Rural free delivery is established across the country by the Federal Post Office.

3 NOVEMBER 1896

National McKinley wins a vicious election campaign by a large electoral vote. Tactics have been exceedingly dirty. Workers have been told that they will not have jobs should McKinley lose. Business contracts have been made contingent on a McKinley win. Bankers, insurance companies, oil companies, all give liberally; Standard Oil alone gives $250,000. The wife of Republican Senator Lodge writes about the campaign to a friend in England: "The great fight is won and a fight conducted by trained and experienced and organized forces, with both hands full of money, with the full power of the press—and of prestige on the one side; on the other, a disorganized mob at first, out of which burst into sight and hearing and force—one man, but such a man! Alone, penniless, without backing, without money, with scarce a paper, without speakers, that man fought such a fight that even those in the East can call him a Crusader, an inspired fanatic, a prophet! It has been marvellous." Indeed Bryan's campaign had cost no more than an estimated $300,000 to the Republican's acknowledged $7,000,000, and party leaders, many of whom were against silver coinage, did not actively campaign for their nominee. Had Bryan been able to enlarge his own monetary concepts enough to include the powerful of his party, the outcome might have been different. The popular vote was 7,104,799 to Bryan's 6,502,925; Palmer of the National Democrats, 133,148; Levering for the Prohibition Party, 132,007; Matchett for Socialist Labor Party, 38,274.

William Jennings Bryan's "Cross of Gold" speech satirized.

FORGING A NATION 1866-1900

Regional Almost lost in the excitement of the Presidential election is the news that Idaho adopts women's suffrage as an amendment to the state constitution.

10 DECEMBER 1896
International Queen Liliuokalani, the recently deposed queen of Hawaii and affectionately referred to in the press as "Queen Lil," visits the United States, arriving in San Francisco.

OTHER EVENTS OF 1896
Arts/Culture The first comic strip, "The Yellow Kid," first appears in the New York *World*. The captivating kid is drawn by R.F. Outcault who puts captions on the boy's baggy yellow shirt. "The Yellow Kid" will give his name to an entire genre of journalism, the sensationalistic, jingoistic, "yellow journalism."

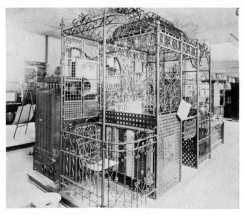
Early elevator car on exhibit.

The 1896 Republican National Convention in St. Louis.

JOURNALISM

During the Civil War Americans had become used to keeping abreast of the ongoing struggle through the newspapers. Their desire to know more about their new society continued into peacetime, revolutionizing accepted concepts of journalism. Several influential magazines and newspapers were established soon after the end of hostilities: the prestigious *The Nation* was founded by James Miller McKim, William Moss began the San Francisco *Examiner*, and the De Young family started the San Francisco *Chronicle*. Less than three years later the *Atlanta Constitution*, one of the foremost newspapers of the East, was begun by W.A. Hemphill. On his staff was Joel Chandler Harris, who wrote the Uncle Remus stories. In 1878 Joseph Pulitzer founded the St. Louis *Post-Dispatch*. This became one of the great American newspapers, educating new immigrants and crusading against corruption. Using the sensational headlines that had captured readers during the Civil War, Pulitzer extended sensationalism to peacetime problems. His papers were aimed at the new citizens of America, unfamiliar with customs and language. He no longer catered merely to the educated American. Almost singlehandedly, Pulitzer created a new style of journalism. Later he competed with William Randolph Hearst, buying the *New York World* which, while losing none of its crusading vigor, did fall into jingoistic sensationalism over the war with Spain. *The Ladies Home Journal*, begun in 1883, demonstrated a widening of women's horizons, as did *Cosmopolitan* founded in 1886. In 1895, Hearst bought the *New York Journal* in which he developed a rather crude sensationalism with none of the saving virtues of Pulitzer's social conscience. Nicknamed "Yellow Journalism" after a cartoon character, it played on people's emotions in a dangerous manner. Hearst's desire for American involvement in Cuba in 1898 was just one of his more lurid journalistic adventures.

Despite its excesses, American journalism of the last half of the century was a democratization of learning, a sharing of information which ultimately led to a more informed and closely knit society.

12 JANUARY 1897

National The National Monetary Conference meets at Indianapolis, Indiana. It sets up a commission to offer Congress a long–range monetary system based on the gold standard. With Bryan's defeat on the silver issue, and world gold reserves rising, the pressure is off the goldbugs. Wheat on the Chicago market has risen to $1.09 a bushel due to bad crops in Europe. This is bringing prosperity back to the farmlands. Announcement of the Klondike strike will siphon off some of the more boisterous and adventurous elements, thus further stabilizing society. In fact prosperity is returning to the country.

11 JANUARY 1897

International The Olney-Paunceforte Convention is signed by Great Britain and the U.S. in Washington D.C. It provides for arbitration for territorial disputes between the two nations. Parliament ratifies the treaty but the Senate refuses consent. Nonetheless the signing of the treaty cements relations between the parties.

2 FEBRUARY 1897

Regional The Pennsylvania State Capitol at Harrisburg is devastated by fire.

International Venezuela and Great Britain sign a treaty agreeing to settle their South American boundary dispute by arbitration.

21 FEBRUARY 1897

National In recognition of his untiring efforts on behalf of president-elect McKinley, Mark Hanna is given what he wants: A Senate seat. Appointed by Ohio Governor Bushnell, he replaces John Sherman, who reluctantly agrees to become secretary of state. Sherman has had a distinguished career, but his health is failing. He will soon be replaced.

2 MARCH 1897

National In one of his last acts as President, Cleveland vetoes the Immigration Bill which would make mandatory a literacy test for immigrants. Cleveland declares it a too "radical departure from our national policy."

WILLIAM JENNINGS BRYAN, 1860-1925

Born in the Midwest, William Jennings Bryan imbibed the agrarian dream and to the end, his approach to national problems remained rooted in this fast–fading vision. He studied law and began to take part in politics by speaking for Democratic candidates in the 1888 presidential campaign. His eloquence attracted immediate attention. Later in Congress it was not only his hard work that interested his fellow politicians, but his uncanny way with words. Speaking against repeal of silver purchase he was soon identified with the free-silverites, whose cause rallied the country in a massive struggle with Big Business.

Perhaps the high point of his career came during the 1896 Democratic convention. As a delegate–at–large, he wrote the party platform and then with eloquence defended the free silver position: "You shall not press down upon the brow of labor this crown of thorns; you shall not crucify mankind upon a cross of gold." The convention went crazy with excitement, and Bryan was nominated to run for president.

Bryan ran twice against the Republican William McKinley and twice lost. In 1913, in recognition of his help in the election of Woodrow Wilson, he was appointed secretary of state, from which position he worked hard to keep America out of war. Characteristically he tried to enlist as a private once war was declared with Germany, even though he was 57 at the time.

Bryan's remarkable career as spokesman for simple solutions to complex problems was crowned when he undertook to help the prosecution in the famous 1925 Scopes trial in Tennessee. Scopes was accused of teaching a theory which denied divine creation as taught in the Bible. Bryan, consistent to the end in his fundamentalist views, took a literal interpretation of the Scriptures. He lent his eloquence to the case, while Clarence Darrow spoke for the defense. Success, if such it could be called, went to Bryan and Scopes was found guilty; he was fined $100. Bryan died on July 25, 1925, only five days after the trial ended.

FORGING A NATION 1866-1900

William McKinley.

4 MARCH 1897

National William McKinley is inaugurated 25th president of the U.S. Garett A. Hobart is vice-president.

22 MARCH 1897

National In a change from its recent bias, the Supreme Court in *Trans-Missouri Freight*, finds that railroads are indeed subject to the Sherman Anti-Trust Law. The vote is a close 5-4, but it is a straw in the wind.

22 MAY 1897

Spanish-American War: Approach Responding to the hysteria whipped up by Hearst and Pulitzer newspapers, Congress appropriates $50,000 for relief of U.S. citizens in Cuba. The sensational press is doing what it can to get the country embroiled in a war with Spain. Day after day, headlines scream lurid tales of despicable atrocities never committed and engagements never fought. When the artist Frederick Remington on assignment for Hearst cables that he could find no trouble, Hearst cables truculently, "You furnish the pictures, I'll furnish the war!" War is good

business for the papers.

7 JUNE 1897

Spanish-American War: Approach John Sherman complains to Spain of General Weyler's brutality. Another element in American relations with Spain over Cuba is a sentimental public opinion which combines idealism with an "underdog complex" in a combustible combination which will be tinder for the coming conflagration.

16 JUNE 1897

International Secretary of State John Sherman and the Hawaiian Government sign a Treaty of Annexation, something that the planters on the islands have been wanting for some time. It has been particularly desirable since the tariff on sugar has gone up to 97 percent, causing serious financial loses. There are some 25,000 Japanese on the islands and Japan makes strong objections to annexation. Congress delays ratification, but the strategic significance of the islands becomes apparent to all during the struggle over the Philippines, and annexation will take place on July 7, 1898.

WILLIAM McKINLEY, 1843-1901

William McKinley, 25th president of the United States, was born in Ohio into a wealthy business family, his father being an iron manufacturer. As a young man, William served in the Union Army, at one time on the staff of future President General Rutherford B. Hayes. In 1865 he was breveted major of volunteers for gallant and meritorious services. After the war, McKinley studied law and joined the Republican Party, with whose policies he very strongly identified. In 1890 as Chairman of the House Ways and Means Committee he introduced one of the strongest high tariff bills ever passed by Congress. This measure, especially pleasing to American businessmen, led to McKinley's nomination for President on the 1896 Republican ticket. The popular slogan of the campaign was "Bill McKinley and the McKinley Bill." Running against the silver-tongued, silver coin advocate William Jennings Bryan, the Republican campaign, smoothly organized by Mark Hanna, won easily. Although McKinley won on the isolationist tariff issue, he presided over the Spanish American War which marked the end of continental isolation. McKinley himself did not harbor imperialist ambitions. He was in fact as mild mannered an imperialist as any pacifist would ever hope to see. However his administration arranged for U.S. control of the Philippines and of the Samoan Islands. Puerto Rico also fell under U.S. jurisdiction at this time.

In 1900 McKinley was reelected President for a second term with the irrepressible Theodore Roosevelt of New York as his running mate. By this time his views on high tariffs had changed substantially. Early in September, McKinley traveled about the country, including the West and Southern States. On September 5 he was in Buffalo, N.Y., to attend the Pan-American Expositon. There he gave a speech announcing new, lower tariff policies. The next day at a public reception, McKinley was shot in the abdomen by a Polish anarchist named Leon Czolgosz. He died eight days later.

Hawaiian Queen Liliuokalani.

7 JULY 1897

National The Dingley Tariff Bill passes Congress. Both houses are now strongly Republican, and Republicans have come to believe that protection is a foundation of American prosperity. The Dingley Bill raises tariffs higher than they have ever been raised before. The average is 57 percent, but on woolen goods the tariff is a crippling 91 percent, on sugar 97 percent (which affected busines interests in both Cuba and Hawaii), and on tobacco 119 percent.

14 JULY 1897

Regional In the first news of the incredible Klondike find, $750,000 in gold arrives in San Francisco aboard the *Excelsior*. The rush to the snowbound north is on. In the next three years, over 100,000 people make their difficult way to the frozen finds. About $10,000,000 will be shipped out each year until the mines dry up.

11 SEPTEMBER 1897

Labor Deputy sheriffs fire on coal miners striking in Hazleton and Latimer in Pennsylvania. Twenty men are killed. The coal miners' strike, which began in July, has engulfed Ohio and West Virginia as well as Pennsylvania. Before it is over at least 75,000 men are out on strike. The strike is one of the first unqualified labor successes, and demonstrates the new-found power of the United Mine Workers, an outgrowth of the American Federation of Labor. Workers win the almost legendary eight-hour day, semi-monthly pay, abolition of company stores, and miners will be allowed their own biennial conferences.

6 OCTOBER 1897

Spanish-American War: Approach Moderate Premier Sagasta is inaugurated in Madrid. He will recall the hated General Weyler, offer home rule to Cuba and end the concentration camps. However an honorable settlement is not what some people want. Pulitzer has been heard to remark that "he rather liked the idea of a war—not a big one—but one which would arouse interest and give him a chance to gauge the reflex in circulation figures." Under Secretary of the Navy Theodore Roosevelt writes to his friend Senator Lodge that "it would be everything for us to take firm action on behalf of the Cubans. It would be a splendid thing for the Navy, too." Looking back a year later McKinley explained his own weak leadership: "But for the inflamed state of public opinion, and the fact that Congress could no longer be held in check, a peaceful solution might have been had."

25 JANUARY 1898

Spanish-American War: Approach The U.S. battleship *Maine* arrives in Havana.

9 FEBRUARY 1898

Spanish-American War: Approach Señor de Lôme, Spanish Minister to the United States, is forced to resign. when a private letter he has written to a Cuban friend is published in Hearst's New York *Journal*. In the letter, de Lôme characterizes McKinley as feebleminded. Publication arouses great indignation in the U.S.

15 FEBRUARY 1898

Spanish-American War: Approach A ghastly explosion destroys the battleship *Maine* in Havana harbor, killing 260 of its crew. The disaster serves to fan the flames of war. "Remember the *Maine!*" becomes a battlecry. The cause of the explosion is never satisfactorily settled. The Americans claim it is caused by a mine, the Spaniards that it is an internal explosion. Thirteen years later the hull will be re-examined by American experts and the board of inquiry will claim it was an external explosion; however, the ship will be immediately towed out into deep water before anyone else can investigate, so that the verdict remains uncertain.

25 FEBRUARY 1898

Spanish-American War: Approach Continuing his preparations for war, Assistant Secretary of the Navy Theodore Roosevelt sends a highly confidential order to Commodore George Dewey, leader of the Asiatic Squadron, to go to Hong Kong. Dewey is to be prepared to attack the Spanish fleet in the Philippines should war be declared. This preparation will serve the American Navy well once hostilities begin.

28 FEBRUARY 1898

National The Supreme Court in *Holden v Hardy* up-

FORGING A NATION 1866-1900

holds the validity of the Utah statute which limits daily working hours in mining industries to eight. The Court finds that the freedom to contract must be modified when substantial inequalities in bargaining powers exist between tne two parties. This was important legislation for labor and sets precedent for future negotiations.

9 MARCH 1898
Spanish American War: Approach War fever is spreading across the country. Congress unanimously appropriates $50,000,000 "for national defense and each and every purpose connected therewith." The Navy is already well prepared, but the Army is scandalously disorganized.

19 MARCH 1898
Spanish-American War: Approach The battleship *Oregon* leaves San Francisco for Key West. The ship will play an important part in the Gulf of Mexico during the war, and the fact that it will take 67 days to round Cape Horn brings to urgent attention the need for a Central American canal.

27 MARCH 1898
Spanish-American War: Approach Following an antiwar policy in the face of great pressure for what

John Hay calls "a splendid little war," McKinley has the U.S. Minister to Spain instructed to demand the following: temporary truce with the Cuban rebels; revocation of the *reconcentrado* order, which concentrated civilians in camps; United States arbitration for a peaceful settlement; relief to be sent to Cuba.

28 MARCH 1898
National In a landmark decision, the Supreme Court finds in *United States v Wong Kim Ark* that U.S. Citizenship is without respect to race or color. In consequence, a child born in the United States cannot be deported under the Chinese Exclusion Act even though both parents are Chinese.

9 APRIL 1898
Spanish-American War: Approach Complying with the U.S. request, the Governor General of Cuba offers rebels armistice.

10 APRIL 1898
Spanish-American War: Approach The American Minister to Madrid cables that the Sagasta regime is ready to negotiate Cuban independence.

11 APRIL 1898
Spanish-American War: Approach McKinley de-

The battleship *Maine* in Havana Harbor, 1898.

APRIL 26, 1898

GEORGE DEWEY, 1837-1917

George Dewey devoted his life to the Navy. He graduated from the U.S. Naval Academy in 1858 and ably served his country during the Civil War. Rising steadily through the ranks, by 1896 he was a commodore when he requested sea service and was sent to the Pacific. Assistant Secretary of the Navy Theodore Roosevelt kept him abreast of preparations for war with Spain which he, Roosevelt, was instigating. Less than a month after being notified of the declaration of war, Dewey was completely prepared to successfully engage the Spanish fleet in the Pacific. In the seven-hour Battle of Manila Bay on May 1, he defeated the ill-prepared and outdated Spanish vessels without loss of American life. Dewey became a national hero and Congress reactivated the rank of Admiral for him, a rank held before by only two others: Farragut and Porter. As a further courtesy, Dewey was never retired but continued to serve as President of the General Board of the Navy until his death in 1917.

Admiral Dewey on board ship.

livers his "War Message" to Congress. Having decided that peace might split the Republican Party, the President is less than candid about Spanish response to peace initiatives. There are powerful forces agitating for war with Spain: Theodore Roosevelt in the Navy Department, Henry Cabot Lodge in Congress. The Confederate general Fitzhugh Lee, Consul in Havana, is anxious for U.S. intervention. Not least of those agitating for combat are Hearst and Pulitzer, who use their inflammatory newspapers to stir up public opinion in favor of war.

19 APRIL 1898
Spanish-American War: Approach A war resolution is adopted by Congress. Provisos include the recognition of Cuban independence from Spain and the demand that Spanish armed forces evacuate the island. The president is allowed to use American Armed Forces to put the resolutions into effect and finally Congress offers assurances that the U.S. is entirely uninterested in itself controlling Cuba but will "leave the government and control of the island to its people." The final component for war—a just and idealistic cause—is now firmly in place.

20 APRIL 1898
Spanish-American War: Approach The U.S. Minister to Madrid has his passport returned to him before he can deliver the U.S. ultimatum to the Spanish government.

21 APRIL 1898
Spanish-American War: Approach Spain breaks off diplomatic relations with the U.S.

22 APRIL 1898
Spanish-American War: Approach The Volunteer Army Act is passed by Congress. It authorizes organization for a 1st Volunteer cavalry, or "Rough Riders." Theodore Roosevelt will resign his post in the Navy to take up the commission of lieutenant colonel in the "Rough Riders," under the command of Colonel Leonard Wood. Meanwhile, a blockade of Cuban ports is put into effect by the U.S. Navy. The *Nashville* captures Spain's *Buena Ventura* in the first moves of war.

23 APRIL 1898
Spanish-American War: Approach McKinley calls for 125,000 volunteers.

24 APRIL 1898
Spanish-American War Spain declares war on the United States.

25 APRIL 1898
Spanish-American War The United States formally declares that a state of war with Spain has existed since April 21, when Spain broke off diplomatic relations.

26 APRIL 1898
National Secretary of State John Sherman, sadly se-

FORGING A NATION 1866-1900

nile, resigns his post. He is succeeded by William R. Day.

1 MAY 1898

Spanish-American War While all eyes are on Cuba, Spain's holdings in the Pacific come under unexpected attack in the Philippines. Admiral Dewey's Asiatic Squadron engages the Spanish fleet, which is anchored in Manila Bay under the command of the gallant Admiral Montojo. The Spaniards sail out of the harbor so as to cause no civilian casualties. The ensuing battle lasts seven hours. Spain's losses are 381 sailors and all its ships. There is no damage to U.S. vessels and only eight men are wounded. The United States, prepared to attack, has the advantage over the Spanish Navy which does not expect action, is old fashioned, poorly armed and badly trained. However, since most of the decisive battles in the Spanish-American war are naval, the outcome soon points to U.S. victory.

12 MAY 1898

Spanish-American War San Juan in Puerto Rico is bombarded by U.S. vessels under Admiral Sampson's command.
Regional A new constitution which allows disenfranchisement of black citizens under property and literacy tests is adopted by Louisiana.

19 MAY 1898

Spanish-American War Under the auspices of the Americans, Philippine guerrilla leader Aguinaldo arrives at Cavite from Hong Kong. The same day Admiral Cervera takes the Spanish fleet into Santiago Harbor, Cuba.

Spanish-American War transports at Tampa.

25 MAY 1898

Spanish-American War The first troopships take 2500 men to Manila. McKinley asks for 75,000 to enlist in the fight against Spain.

29 MAY 1898

Spanish-American War Commodore Winfield Scott Schley blockades the Spanish fleet in Santiago.

1 JUNE 1898

National The Erdman Arbitration Act is passed, making government mediation in railroad disputes legitimate. It also makes blacklists of union laborers illegal.

3 JUNE 1898

Spanish-American War In an unsuccessful attempt to block the exit of the Spanish fleet from Santiago Harbor by sinking his own ship, Lieutenant Richard P. Hobson and his men are captured and the *Merrimac* is destroyed.

10 JUNE 1898

Spanish-American War Beginning the invasion of Cuba, 647 Marines land at Guantanamo Bay.

13 JUNE 1898

National The War Revenue Act is passed, authorizing excise duties, taxes on tea, tobacco, liquor, and for the first time in U.S. history, on legacies. The Act also authorizes a bond issue of $200,000,000.

14 JUNE 1898

Spanish-American War Just under 17,000 American troops depart from Tampa, Florida, for invasion of Santiago. They are under the command of General William R. Shafter. The popular war brings about high spirits as the men sing lustily *There'll Be a Hot Time In The Old Town Tonight*.

20 JUNE 1898

Spanish-American War Enlarging the theater of war, Captain Henry Glass captures the island of Guam, which is under Spanish rule. When Glass fires on the island, a dispatch is sent to his ship with an apology for the discourtesy in not returning the salute, but, as the Spanish commander explains, there is no ammunition on the island. The Spanish commander has not heard of the war.

22 JUNE 1898

Spanish-American War Some 17,000 troops under General Shafter arrive at Daiquiri, about 15 miles from Santiago. One man is killed and four wounded as they take the town.

24 JUNE 1898

Spanish-American War Under the leadership of General Joseph Wheeler and Colonels Leonard Wood and Theodore Roosevelt, 1000 regular troops and "Rough Riders" are victorious in the first land battle of the war at Las Guasimas, Cuba.

American infantry prepare to attack San Juan Hill.

1 JULY 1898

Spanish-American War U.S. Troops suffer heavy casualties in the general engagements at El Caney and San Juan Hill. Under the command of the obese General Shafter who is suffering severely from the heat, American troops move through the jungle with a massive observation balloon floating overhead pulled along by four men, the Signal Corps thus signaling their position to the enemy at all times. At El Caney, 6653 U.S. troops suffer 441 casualties taking the position valliantly held by 600 Spaniards.

Meanwhile, across the San Juan River, a vanguard waits for ten minutes before the order is given to take the heights of Kettle Hill and Fort San Juan Hill. In that short time, a quarter of the Sixth Infantry is mowed down by Spanish fire. Impatient, Roosevelt spurs his horse up Kettle Hill before the bugle sounds the attack, but immediately the command is given and he is followed by the black Ninth and Tenth Regiments. By the end of the day, San Juan Hill is taken and Santiago lies below the weary conquerors. In all, 1572 Americans are left dead or wounded at the end of the eight–hour battle. Theodore Roosevelt has led the charge up the hill with gusto and valor. Two days later, the Fifth Corps has entrenched itself waiting for possible counter-attack. Roosevelt writes: "We are within measurable distance of a terrible military disaster."

3 JULY 1898

Spanish-American War Admiral Cervera is thwarted when he attempts to lead the Spanish fleet out of Santiago Harbor. Cervera is following orders from Madrid, orders which he has done his best to have changed since he knows that "the absolutely certain result will be the ruin of each and all of the ships and the death of the greater part of their crews." The Americans are amazed at the sight of the vessels in full sail, battle flags flying. Writes Captain John Philip: "The Spanish ships came out as gaily as brides to the altar." With the American fleet under the command of Commodore Schley, the battle lasts for four hours. The enemy fleet is utterly destroyed. Spanish dead or wounded are 474, prisoners: 1750. The U.S. has lost but one man dead and one other wounded.

4 JULY 1898

Spanish-American War Troops on their way to the Philippines raise the U.S. flag over Wake Island which is vacant at the time.

7 JULY 1898

International Even as the U.S. disclaims territorial ambitions regarding Cuba, Congress is finally getting around to what Henry Cabot Lodge calls "the outlying things." Amidst bitter opposition the Annexation of Hawaii Treaty is signed by McKinley. Democrats

FORGING A NATION 1866-1900

and anti-imperialists have delayed ratification, but the war has clearly demonstrated the strategic importance of the islands to the U.S.

8 JULY 1898
Spanish-American War Isla Grande, near Manila, is taken by Admiral Dewey.

10 JULY 1898
Spanish-American War General Shafter and his troops invade Santiago now that the Spanish fleet has been destroyed.

17 JULY 1898
Spanish-American War Santiago surrenders and General Shafter takes 24,000 Spanish prisoners. While the United States flag is raised over the House of Civil Government, the band plays the national anthem and the popular *Rally Round the Flag, Boys*. In the battle, 260 men have died and 1431 have been wounded.

25 JULY 1898
Spanish-American War After a brief struggle, General Miles occupies Guanica in Puerto Rico.

26 JULY 1898
Spanish-American War Three months after it begins, the "splendid little war" substantially ends when Spain requests peace terms. The request is made through the French ambassador.

30 JULY 1898
Spanish-American War President McKinley out-lines peace terms to Spain: Cuba is to be granted independence; Puerto Rico and an island in the Ladrones are to be given to the U.S.; Manila is to be occupied by the U.S. until further peace negotiations have taken place.

1 AUGUST 1898
Spanish-American War The War Department gets word that 4200 American soldiers are suffering from disease in Cuba. Over 3000 of them have yellow fever. The War Department belatedly orders the remaining healthy troops off the island. They are transferred first of all to Montauk Point, Long Island.

9 AUGUST 1898
Spanish-American War Coamo, in Puerto Rico, surrenders to the United States. The peace terms offered by President McKinley are formally accepted by the Spanish Government. A protocol is signed in Washington at 4:30 this afternoon.

13 AUGUST 1898
Spanish-American War Manila surrenders to Admiral Dewey and General Wesley Merritt, concluding hostilities between the United States and Spain. The total cost of the war has been $250,000,000; of the 274,000 men who took part in the war, 5462 died, although only 379 in battle. The rest succumbed to disease partly through the scandalous mismanagement of the Army. A further 1604 men were wounded.

1 OCTOBER 1898
Spanish-American War Peace negotiations begin in Paris.

Teddy Roosevelt and his victorious troops.

8 NOVEMBER 1898

Spanish-American War Mostly due to his brave and ebullient leadership in the war, and much to the irritation of party bosses, Theodore Roosevelt is elected Republican Governor of New York. Sharing his delight he writes: "I have played it in bull luck this summer. First, to get into the war; and then to get out of it; then to get elected."

10 DECEMBER 1898

Spanish-American War The Treaty of Paris is signed by the United States and Spain, formally ending the war. Spain cedes the Philippines to the U.S. for $20,000,000, ending almost 100 years of turbulent Spanish rule. McKinley declares the Philippines are "not to exploit but to develop, to educate, to train in the science of self-government. (The archipelago will not be set free until 1946.) Spain also gives over Puerto Rico and Guam. The defeated country assumes liabilities for $400,000,000 in Cuban debts while abandoning all claims to the island.

20 JANUARY 1899

International The Philippine Commission is appointed by President McKinley. It is headed by Jacob G. Schurman who will suggest U.S. rule of the islands until the Filipinos are ready for self-government. The move will prevent annexation by Germany which has moved its navy nearby. It will also transform the United States into a major power in the Pacific, bringing her, naturally, into conflict with Japan.

6 FEBRUARY 1899

International After a protracted struggle between imperialists and anti-imperialists, the Treaty of Paris is ratified by the Senate 57 to 27. The argument for ratification is led by Henry Cabot Lodge who contends that it will enhance national prestige, prevent foreign annexation, and constitute economic, strategic and civilizing advantages. The case against ratification is that it is contrary to U.S. tradition to acquire territory outside the continental area; that people of alien races will not easily be assimilated into the American

way of life; that the treaty is against the spirit of the Monroe Doctrine and will weaken the American belief in self-government. Anti-imperialists also contend that "the Constitution follows the flag," but imperialists argue that the people of these new acquisitions, even while being nationals, are not automatically endowed with the privileges of U.S. citizenship. Their actual status will be a vexing question not settled for some time.

14 FEBRUARY 1899

National Congress approves the use of voting machines for federal elections at the discretion of individual states.

2 MARCH 1899

International Congress authorizes an addition of 65,000 men to the regular Army and asks for 35,000 volunteers to help in the suppression of the Filipino rebellion led by Emilio Aguinaldo.

3 MARCH 1899

National Congress establishes the third Isthmian Canal Commission, under the chairmanship of Admiral John G. Walker. The first commission was established in 1895, the second in 1897. The purposes of all three have been the same: to investigate the various routes for a possible canal in Central America and the probable cost of such an undertaking. Also this day Congress authorizes increase in Navy appropriations for three battleships, three armed cruisers and six protective cruisers.

24 APRIL 1899

Labor Striking miners at Wardner, Idaho, demand $3.50 per day and the shutdown of company stores. The offer is refused and riots begin. On April 29 property is destroyed estimated at $250,000.

27 APRIL 1899

Regional Northern Missouri is ravaged by a tornado which kills over 40 and injures 100.

28 APRIL 1899

International Peace terms are requested by the Filipinos. The request is rejected by General Otis who demands nothing less than unconditional surrender.

18 MAY 1899

International The First Hague Peace Conference opens. After two months of debate, a Permanent Court of International Arbitration is established at the insistence of the United States. Its purpose: a place peacefully to adjust international disputes. The U.S. and Mexico together will be the first to use its facilities.

1 JULY 1899

Ideas/Beliefs The commercial travelers belonging to the Christian Commercial Men's Association of America organize the Gideons. The first Gideon Bible will be placed in Superior Hotel, Iron Mountain, Montana,

Insurgent prisoners at Manila, Philippines, 1899.

in November 1908.

19 JULY 1899
National Secretary of War Russel A. Alger resigns under fire for his part in the Spanish-American War for which the Army had been ill–prepared. Investigations have found military command inefficient, military training insufficient and provisions inadequate.

MARK TWAIN, 1835-1910

Mark Twain was born Samuel Langhorne Clemens in Florida, Missouri. The son of an unsuccessful lawyer, he spent his early life moving from place to place and ended his schooling by the time he was 12 when he was apprenticed to a printer. However, wandering had become part of his way of life, and he did not settle down until his mid–30s. Meanwhile, working on and around newspapers, he was inspired to write upon hearing the story of Joan of Arc. He began to study history and published early stories in the *Saturday Evening Post*. Around 1857 he took to the Mississippi riverboats, and ultimately received a pilot's license. One guesses from his writings that this was one of the best times of his adventurous life. Later, he went to work for his newspaperman brother in Nevada where he came in contact with the rollicking, romantic West that was to influence so many of his stories. It was about this time that he adopted his nom-de-plume, Mark Twain, a term stemming from riverboat calls meaning "two fathoms deep."

In 1867, Twain published his first book of stories entitled *The Celebrated Jumping Frog of Calaveras Country*. A tour of Europe the same year led to his popular *Innocents Abroad*. In 1876 he published the perennial favorite, *Tom Sawyer*. After a stint as editor at the Buffalo *Express*, Twain married and settled in Connecticut.

Twain went to the heart of American life for his inspiration, and wrote vividly of life on the Mississippi and the Wild West. He exaggerated for ludicrous effect, but kept a clean stiletto ready to cut into hypocrisy, pomposity, cruelty and snobbery. Underneath he was a serious thinker, and this is most evident in his masterpiece, *Huckleberry Finn*. In an age when the subject of race was almost taboo, Twain dealt sensitively with interpersonal relations among the prejudiced and unprejudiced. Whether he laughed or cut, Twain was always in touch with the realities of his country.

---

6 SEPTEMBER 1899
International Secretary of State John Hay requests U.S. Ambassadors to countries already having commerce, treaties and long–term leases with China to ask for an "open door" policy by which all nations receive equal treatment from China so as not to weaken the old giant by further carving out "spheres of influence." Early next year Russia, Germany, France, England, Italy and Japan will consent to this "open door" policy, thus preventing dismemberment of China.

4 OCTOBER 1899
International Additional warships and troops are dispatched to the Philippines at the request of Admiral George Dewey. By the end of August, 30,963

soldiers will be stationed there.

14 OCTOBER 1899
Life/Customs President McKinley takes a ride in a Stanley Steamer, the first President to ride in an automobile. In Cleveland the United States Post Office makes its first experimental mail collection in a motor vehicle using a Winton truck, although it will be 15 years before a motorized Post Office comes into being; meanwhile, Alexander Winton drives from Cleveland to New York, making the first long–distance trip by car. The *Literary Digest* publishes the following assessment of the burgeoning automobile industry: "The ordinary 'horseless carriage' is at present a luxury for the wealthy; and although its price will probably fall in the future, it will never, of course, come into as common use as the bicycle."

21 NOVEMBER 1899
National Vice–President Garret A. Hobart dies in Paterson, New Jersey.

24 NOVEMBER 1899
International The President of the Philippine Congress, the Filipino Secretary of State and the Treasurer are reported to be prisoners of General Otis in Central Luzon, an area which has just surrendered to the United States.

PAINTERS

The painters of the last half of the 19th century were some of America's greatest, such as Thomas Eakins and Winslow Homer. At the same time there were lesser painters who still reached heights of excellence and who produced a quicker response from an appreciative audience. For instance, by 1865 the gentle George Inness had come to be recognized as one of America's foremost landscape artists. The first major commission to be awarded to an American painter was given to John La Farge for a mural for the walls of Richardson's Trinity Church, Boston. While America's best painter, Thomas Eakins, struggled to make a go of his insistent realism, another son of America, James McNeil Whistler, was making his fame painting and shocking the artistic establishment of London. In 1877 he took the acknowledged dean of British critics to court for his remarks about a Whistler show; the painter won one farthing. However his subtle, soft painting of his mother, entitled *Arrangement in Gray and Black*, is still one of America's mysterious masterpieces. Another who drew on Europe, in his case for a satiny sophistication, was John Singer Sargent. Exhibition in 1884 of his skillful though unflattering portrait of Mme Gautreau, entitled *Madame X*, forced him to leave Paris. Michael Harnett with his *trompe l'oeil* fascinated a wide public, while America's most famous woman artist of the time was Mary Cassatt who was completely accepted by the Parisian art world although unrecognized in her own country.

American art of the 19th century was observant, reportorial, honest and penetrating. It was hypnotized by the grandeur of the American continent but seldom lost sight of one of the essential mysteries with which all painting ultimately deals, the human condition.

---

4 DECEMBER 1899

National In *Addyston Pipe & Steel Co.* v. *United States*, the Supreme Court finds that negotiations made between corporations to be rid of competition are violations of the Anti–Trust Law. The finding serves to strengthen the law which has been weakened by previous Court rulings and lack of Executive attention.

5 DECEMBER 1899

National Addressing the issue that the country has come to see as taking priority over all others, the intractable issue of trusts, the genial McKinley, in his third annual talk to Congress, declares: "Combinations of capital organized into trusts . . . should early claim the attention of Congress." Although it sounds innocuous enough, it is a bold statement for a Republican president to make, especially one whose election has been paid for by businessman Mark Hanna and his friends. Along with the *Addyston Pipe* finding by the Supreme Court the day before, the President's concern signals a revitalization of the conscience of the country. Even in an industrial economy, it will be found that social order will take precedence over the remorseless economic forces that have dominated the last three decades of the 19th century.

6 FEBRUARY 1900

National "Under no circumstances could I or would I accept the nomination for the vice–presidency," the energetic Theodore Roosevelt, presently governor of New York State, declares. He, as well as his enemies who are helping to steer him into the office, are aware that to be vice–president is essentially a meaningless task. The famous Boss Platt of New York is working hard to get him on the McKinley ticket. "I have come to watch Teddy take the veil," Platt will gloat on inauguration day. President–maker Mark Hanna is less enthusiastic: "Don't any of you realize," he shouts angrily at a backroom gathering, "that there's only one life between that madman and the Presidency?"

6 MARCH 1900

National The Social Democratic Party holds its national convention in Indianapolis, Indiana, nominating Eugene V. Debs of Indiana for president and Job Harrison of California for vice–president.

14 MARCH 1900

National The Gold Standard Act is ratified by Congress. The Act establishes a gold dollar of 25.8 grains, nine-tenths fine, and puts all forms of U.S. money on a parity with gold. There now exists a gold reserve of $150,000,000. To help with agrarian financial needs, national banks with capital of $25,000 and over are established in towns of 3000 or less population. The increase in the world's gold supply has taken the sting out of the gold issue.

24 MARCH 1900

Industry The New Carnegie Steel Company is incorporated in New Jersey in direct defiance of the Sherman Anti–trust Law which by this time has no teeth in it at all. Capitalization of the new corporation amounts to a dazzling $160,000,000. It is the largest and most controversial incorporation to date. In April, the largest quarterly dividend payment ever offered will be paid by the Standard Oil Company for the first quarter of 1900 amounting to $20,000,000. Only 15 percent of this sum is regular quarterly dividends; eighty–five percent is sheer profit.

12 APRIL 1900

International The Foraker Act confirms Puerto Rico as an unconsolidated territory of the United States. The system that Congress confers on its new subjects is substantially the same as England had subjected her Crown Colonies to prior to 1773. The president, with the advice and consent of Congress, appoints a governor and an executive council. The executive council appoints those under it. The legislature is made up of two houses; the executive council as the upper house, and 35 elected members in the lower house. The elective branch could refuse to appropriate funds, but other than that, the Puerto Ricans have hardly a say in their government. In 1916, the Jones Act will change the machinery of government to provide for an elective upper house. It will also make the Puerto Ricans citizens of the United States.

30 APRIL 1900

Regional By Act of Congress Hawaii is granted territorial standing in the United States.

Life/Customs The heroic Casey Jones dies at the throttle of his crashing "Cannonball," saving his passengers' lives by trying to slow it down. Ballads and folktales commemorate the dramatic act which catches the imagination of the country.

9 MAY 1900

National A splinter group breaking away from the main, the Populist Party convenes in Cincinnati, Ohio, and nominates Wharton Barker of Pennsylvania for president, and Ignatius Donnelly of Minnesota for vice–president. The main branch of the Populists meet at Sioux Falls, South Dakota, and nominate the ever–popular William Jennings Bryan for president and Charles A. Town of Minnesota for vice–president.

14 MAY 1900

National In *Knowlton* v. *Moore*, the Supreme Court finds that the inheritance tax which was levied for the first time in the United States under the War Revenue Act of 1898 is indeed constitutional.

Life/Customs Carrie Nation takes her anti–liquor campaign to the nation, leading a group of women through Kansas and inflicting damage and destruction on saloons and all liquor–selling establishments.

2 JUNE 1900

National The Socialist Labor Party meets in New York and nominates Joseph P. Maloney of Massachusetts for president and Valentine Remmel of Pennsyl-

FORGING A NATION 1866-1900

vania for vice–president.

19 JUNE 1900
National The Republican National Convention meets in Philadelphia, Pennsylvania. Under the deft management of Mark Hanna, McKinley is a shoo–in for a second term as president. Less likely is the nomination of Theodore Roosevelt for vice–president. "Teddy" has denied all desire for the office and needs only to stay away from the convention to have his wishes respected. Instead he attends complete with "Rough Rider" hat and kerchief and electrifies an otherwise dull meeting with his seconding speech for McKinley. Roosevelt agrees to accept the nomination given to him by acclamation.

20 JUNE 1900
International Desperate revolt against foreign domination breaks out in China. Each foreign minister has been given 24 hours to get out of Peking. When the German minister Baron von Ketteler objects, he is shot and killed. The rest of the diplomatic corps seeks refuge in the British legation where they are kept under siege for almost two months. The revolutionaries call themselves "righteous harmony fists" which is quickly translated to "boxers" and this episode is known as the Boxer Rebellion. Determined to rid the country of all "foreign devils" they are prevented from killing the besieged by the arrival on August 14 of a rescue force made up of 2500 Americans, 3000 British, 800 French and 8000 Japanese. The revolt having been squashed, United States Secretary of State John Hay sends a second note to all participating powers reiterating the need to protect Chinese territorial integrity and to "safeguard for the world the principle of equal and impartial trade with all parts of the Chinese Empire." All the foreigners could expect is proper cash indemnity for any actual losses and punishment of the revolutionaries. The United States receives $24,000,000, but five years later, more accurate accounting being made, it will be found that only $11,000,000 had been owed. America returns the extra monies which the Chinese, appreciative of the gesture, put into a fund to send students to American universities.

27 JUNE 1900
National The Prohibition Party holds its national convention in Chicago. Nominated for president is John G. Wooley of Illinois, and Henry B. Metcalf of Rhode Island is nominated for vice–president.

4 JULY 1900
National The Democratic National Convention meets in Kansas City to nominate William Jennings Bryan of Nebraska for president and Adlai E. Stevenson of Illinois for vice–president. The platform condemns imperialism and the Gold Standard Act of March 14. Although many smaller reform parties are active during this election, nonetheless the main fight is between the "Full Dinner Pail" of the Republicans

and the personality of the Democrats' charismatic, but overly fundamentalist William Jennings Bryan. Bryan has had a long run on the silver question, but prosperity and enough gold has made this issue virtually irrelevant. Bryan will turn his attention onto the "trusts" and capture a faithful following, but the energetic Roosevelt is more than his match. Roosevelt is already attacking the "trusts" with booming sincerity. "I am as strong as a bull moose," he exclaims enthusiastically. Bryan campaigns in 24 States and makes over 600 speeches pulling around him the Populists, the agrarians, and organized labor.

8 SEPTEMBER 1900
Regional A horrendous hurricane kills 6000 in Galveston, Texas, and causes damage to property in excess of $20,000,000. Winds blowing over 120 mph drive Gulf waters overland. Pandemonium ensues. Plundering and looting follow; thieves are even discovered with the ringed hands of the dead cut off since the fingers had become too swollen to remove the jewelry. Because of the horror involved in this tragedy, the first form of commission city government

An aging William Jennings Bryan wins new support.

is established, in Galveston. It aims to organize aid more efficiently in future catastrophes.

18 SEPTEMBER 1900

National The first direct primary in the United States is held in Minnesota. It creates great interest in the rest of the country which will soon adopt the system for most of its elective offices.

SEPTEMBER 1900

Science/Technology Doctor Walter Reed of the United States Army Medical Corps, researching the source of the yellow fever which has killed thousands of soldiers during the Spanish–American War, discovers the virus is transmitted by mosquitoes. The disease is virtually eradicated from Cuba by the following year.

6 NOVEMBER 1900

National McKinley wins the Presidential election for a second term. Popular vote: 7,219,530, against Bryan's 6,358,071. The electoral vote is McKinley 292, Bryan 155. Wooley, Prohibition: 208,914; Debs, Social Democrat: 87,814; Barker, Populist: 50,373; Malloney, Socialist Labor: 39,739.

WRITERS

The last half of the 19th century found its most sophisticated artistic expression in its prose. There were the high–adventure writers chronicling life in the West, such as Bret Harte whose *The Luck of Roaring Camp* brought instant recognition. Remorseless realism also won skillful adherents, such as Stephen Crane with his masterpiece *The Red Badge of Courage.*

There were already propaganda writers like Horatio Alger, who published his enthusiastically received *Ragged Dick*. It was one of 135 books Alger wrote in order to depict the life of children in the slums, but popularity came from his premise that virtue and hard work got a young lad to the top. Over 16,000,000 were sold. Edward Bellamy took a less rosy–colored look at society in his Utopian *Looking Backward*. His book sold 200,000 copies in two years. Henry Adams was among the first to tackle the problem of political corruption in his *Democracy*.

Wholesomeness took nothing away from the enchantment of Louisa May Alcott's writing. Her *Little Women* is probably still the most popular book ever written for girls. Louisa Alcott supported her family from her writings. Another woman whose writing endures is Sarah Orne Jewett. She depicted the life of a Maine country doctor in *The Country of the Pointed Firs*.

The master of the study of manners was the urbane Henry James. Born in New York City, James, along with his equally famous brother William, was educated by tutors both at home and abroad. He settled in England where later, disturbed by America's isolationism during the early years of World War I, he became a British subject. He was a most innovative writer, probing the conflicts and contrasts between Europe and America, perceptively digging for motive, and yet fully concerned with the struggle between an individual's need for growth and society's tendency to maintain a civilized status quo.

Nonfiction also had its exponents: Henry George created a cult with his *Progress and Poverty*. Francis Parkman wrote his monumental *Montcalm and Wolfe* and Alfred Thayer Mahan affected the future of American military might with his massive *The Influence of Sea Power upon History, 1660-1783*.

"The Bosses of the Senate" caricaturized.

EXPANDING RESOURCES

1901–1945

RICHARD C. WADE
Professor of History, City University of New York

EXPANDING RESOURCES 1901-1945

The 20th century dawned on a confident, optimistic America. The previous generation had occupied the West to the Pacific Ocean, had wrought a technological revolution that transformed American society, and had just finished what Secretary of State John Hay called a "splendid little war" with Spain, leaving the United States a world power. The business community commanded the heights of the new industrial system, and its power did not seem seriously threatened by internal protests. America was by most standards the world's success story of the 19th century.

The cost of creating what later observers would call a "modern" society was often high. The democratic fabric was strained; a rich land was mercilessly ravaged; working people were tied to long hours of work at inadequate wages; farmers knew many more bad years than good; only a few women escaped the daily drudgery of domestic work or exploitation on the job; whites demanded institutionalized deference from blacks. Even some of the successful could not survey the scene without a shudder. A whole generation of the famous Adams family, which had been, after all, among the nation's "founding fathers," found it impossible to adjust to the new society, and held a melancholy view of the future.

Yet not even the gloomiest prophet could foresee that in the first half of the 20th century the United States would witness two world wars and the deepest depression the country had ever known. Nor could even the most imaginative scientist forecast that August day in 1945 when the first atomic explosion, with all its ambivalence and terror, fundamentally altered the prospects of American society and of all of mankind. In 1900 all seemed so serene that Andrew Carnegie's assertion in 1886 that the United States was destined to become the most democratic and most advanced industrial nation in world history seemed assured. Abraham Lincoln's "last best hope of earth" had become the globe's first glimpse of the possibilities of a free modern society.

Indeed the first decades of the century seemed to vindicate the pervasive optimism. A "progressive" spirit which had been gathering force in the previous decades suddenly achieved national power. Even before the assassination of President William McKinley and the elevation of Theodore Roosevelt to the White House in 1901, there had been premonitions of change. The anti-trust movement had mobilized some business support against monopolies; middle class intellectuals complained of what they considered the excessive materialism of the new successful class; sporadic attempts to organize labor into trade unions reflected increasing working class discontent; and farmer distress had led to an agrarian political revolt culminating in the Populist movement in the 1890s.

Just as important was a sturdy reform movement arising in the nation's burgeoning cities. The 19th century created the nation's first "urban explosion" which produced the usual range of city problems—overcrowding, wretched housing, inadequate schools, high crime, endemic disorder, political corruption, rampant pollution of the air and water and the uncontrolled activity of real estate operators and development entrepreneurs. For a quarter of a century local reform movements in almost every large city addressed these problems. Occasionally they enjoyed spectacular successes; as often they endured defeat. By 1894 they established the National Municipal League, which brought together urban reformers from across the country for the first time and created a wide programmatic consensus to inform national policy.

Indeed, urban reformers had already created the context for the national progressive debate. They had fought the local monopolies that most intimately affected city dwellers, such as mass transit, gas and water "rings" and rigged municipal contracts. They had formulated all the arguments against national trusts in endless contests with the concentrated power and inordinate political influence of local business interests. The drive for the democratization of political processes had begun with the revolt against the almost universal corruption of local governments which Lord Bryce referred to as the most "conspicuous failure" of American democracy and which was immortalized in Lincoln Steffens's bestseller, *The Shame of the Cities*.

Progressives agreed that the central question of their time was how to control the power of concentrated wealth in a democracy. If they could agree on the analysis, they could not on a solution. The rampant power of naked industrial interests clearly threatened every notion of popular government. Yet the condition was new, and the answers were not easy to devise. Some, like Theodore Roosevelt, believed that the growth of industry with its great concentrations was inevitable and, generally, socially useful. But, if left uncontrolled, the new "plutocracy's" obsession with self–interest would prevail over public interest. Thus, Roosevelt argued, the Federal Government's power ought to be increasingly enhanced so that it was always greater than any private interest or collection of private interests. Others, like Woodrow Wilson, came to believe that the only effective control over concentrated economic power was to break up the trusts into smaller, presumably more competitive units, and let the marketplace contain the problems of "bigness." The country's democratic institutions, fortified by federal anti–trust legislation, would ensure the primacy of the public interest. The socialist response was more predictable. Since concentration and size were the hallmarks of a modern society, the obvious solution was for the Federal Government itself to own the means of production. The more orthodox, economists as well as businessmen, contended that the economic system was self–regulating and therefore, no matter how disturbing any particular situation appeared, government intervention would exacerbate rather than ameliorate the general problem. It would be better to permit natural private forces to determine winners and losers in a competitive society.

Progressivism also attempted to widen the democratic base of American politics. Some proposals were institutional and depended on state rather than national action. The secret ballot to protect the sanctity of the voter's choice, the popular initiation of issues by referendum and mechanisms to recall public office-holders all passed some legislatures. On the national level, two Constitutional Amendments were the perfect embodiment of the progressive spirit: the 17th, which required the election of United States Senators directly by voters rather than by state legislatures, and the 19th Amendment which extended the suffrage to women and, in one stroke, doubled the potential electorate. All these measures reflected the progressive maxim that, whatever the problem, the solution was more democracy. Later some historians minimized the impact of these changes because the next decade was to be a conservative period, but no one could deny that the American political process on every level was freer, more open and more democratic by 1920 than ever before.

Nor were the attempts to control concentrated wealth and widen democratic participation purely partisan matters. The progressive impulse energized both parties. Republicans in New York elected Charles Evans Hughes; in Wisconsin they chose Robert LaFollette. Democrats found Hiram Johnson in California and David I. Walsh in Massachusetts. The urban dimension perhaps can best be illustrated by the rise to party leadership of the Republican Theodore Roosevelt, a New Yorker and former city Police Commissioner, and of the Democrat Woodrow Wilson, governor of the nation's most urban state. Roosevelt's predecessor as president was a small town Ohioan; Wilson's predecessor as party leader was a national symbol of America's farmers.

The Progressive consensus was never better illustrated than in the presidential election of 1912. Three of the four parties courted progressive voters. The Democrats chose Wilson. The G.O.P. re-nominated its incumbent, William Howard Taft, whose modest claims to progressivism were sacrificed to the conservatism of his sponsors. Rejected by the Republican party, former president Theodore Roosevelt established his own Progressive Party. Eugene V. Debs continued to be the Socialist standard bearer. Taft ran a weak third, and, though Wilson got only 40 percent of the total, Progressives had every reason to believe the election conferred on him a strong mandate for change.

The reforms of the Progressive Era, mild by present standards, seemed radical enough to contemporaries. For the first time a loose harness was placed on corporate wealth; cities and states adopted labor, women and child protection laws; the consumer movement found a new generation of supporters and a modest income tax established an important new principle of federal financing. Most of all, the business community was placed on the defensive and its claim to be the "natural" leader of society suffered permanent damage. One opponent, unhappy with all this, referred to progressivism as a "contagion" that infected all parts of the country, raising "impossible hopes" of a "perfect" world.

The reform impulse declined in the country in the last years of its second decade. Perhaps it had run its course and had exhausted its energy. More likely, the war in Europe, which began in 1914 and which the United States entered in 1917, diverted attention from domestic change to a debate about America's role in world affairs. Initially, Wilson and most other Americans hoped and expected that the United States could avoid being drawn into the conflict, and the president pronounced the country's neutrality. Yet it was easier to pronounce than to pursue a neutral course. German submarine activity threatened to interrupt trade, especially with the Allies, and jeopardize the historic American commitment to "freedom of the seas." Moreover, as the conflict dragged on, Americans began to choose sides, dividing society along ethnic and political lines. In addition, financial and manufacturing interests increasingly tilted toward the Allied cause.

Wilson's own sympathies were, from the beginning, with Great Britain and its allies, but he had a profound fear of what American involvement might do to our own democratic institutions. In time, however, he began to fear even more the long term consequences to the United States of a German victory. When the Germans revived unrestricted submarine warfare in the spring of 1917, he chose to make the decision to enter World War I on the narrow question of freedom of the seas. Yet, in his war speech to Congress on April 2 he could not resist placing the action on higher grounds. "We shall fight for the things which we have always carried nearest our hearts—for democracy, for the right of those who submit to authority to have a voice in their own governments, for the rights and liberties of small nations, for a universal dominion of right by such a concert of free peoples as shall bring peace and safety to all nations and make the world at last free." The war, then, he envisaged was to be progressivism writ large.

America's involvement increasingly lost its progressive tinge. Ethnic differences became magnified as the war became increasingly anti-German; the civil liberties of those who opposed the war were regularly violated—and with court sanction; the felt need for national unity strained the pluralistic character of the country. To be sure, conducting a war required some federal planning of resources, and many progressives

U.S. troops attack at St. Mihiel.

looked on wartime necessities as an opportunity to further Washington's influence on the national economic system. Even though the war, despite its high casualties, was mercifully short for the United States, it sapped the idealism of the generation; by 1920, a victorious America refused to join the League of Nations—the logical, progressive result of the "war to end all wars."

The end of the war brought a cumulative disillusionment. The sacrifice of the conflict did not seem commensurate with a fragile and questionable peace; the resurgence of business power in the 1920s threatened to undermine the reforms so painfully erected in the previous generation and rampant materialism and hedonism seemed to reject the idealism and social consciousness of the progressive era. A college student poll which found Jesus Christ coming in third behind Henry Ford and Napoleon Bonaparte only fortified the fears of those who thought the country had lost its idealistic moorings. For two years the national best seller was Bruce Barton's *The Man Nobody Knows*, which, depicting Christ as the founder of the modern business system and the Apostles as a kind of corporate Board of Directors, signaled the return of values which reformers comfortably felt had been left behind in the 19th century.

Less visible in the 1920s was a demographic change which would affect not just a decade but the next two generations. The Census Bureau in 1920, in its awkward way, discovered that for the first time in American history more people lived in "urban places" than "rural places." Cities had always played a disproportionate role in the country's development; the new figures ratified the fact that the future lay in metropolitan America. Only a few social scientists noticed this moment of national passage, but its consequences would shape the next half century.

The social issues of the 1920s concealed the significance of this demographic change. The 18th Amendment made national prohibition the "law of the land"; Congress enacted increasingly discriminatory legislation against the new immigrants from Southern and Eastern Europe; the Ku Klux Klan, after resurrection in the South, spread to the Middle West; the dramatic Scopes Trial over the teaching of evolution in the schools revived the old science and religion controversy. Many contemporaries, as well as most subsequent scholars, viewed these social issues as the last stand of rural, small town America against an increasingly metropolitan society.

Actually, all these movements had profound roots in the burgeoning cities and never would have been adopted without urban support. The temperance movement flourished in new neighborhoods which voted to exclude saloons and liquor stores through the progressive device of local option. Settlement-house workers favored reducing the surge of unassimilated immigrants; the largest Klan meeting in American history took place in the southwest side of Chicago. What literary critics called the "revolt of the small town" succeeded only because it had numerous allies in the nation's expanding cities.

Nothing illustrates the new urban dominance better than the vaunted "prosperity" of the 1920s. It was wholly a metropolitan phenomenon. Everywhere skylines shot upward; over a million housing starts a year were concentrated almost exclusively in urban areas; governments built more than 600,000 miles of roads to accommodate the growing popularity of the automobile with its largely middle class ownership; old municipal boundaries could no longer contain the population growth and new suburbs sprouted up beyond the city limits. The "progress of the age" centered in the metropolis. The automobile, radio, movies, endless electrical appliances and the other symbols of American technological superiority reached the countryside only much later. Meanwhile metropolitan Americans enjoyed what seemed like a permanent prosperity.

The country's cultural life reflected the city's economic supremacy. The major literary figures, such as Sherwood Anderson, depicted the loneliness and "death–in–life" of small–town dwellers, or, like Sinclair Lewis, relentlessly satirized the mind and customs of the old America. While other authors surgically dissected urban living, they did so knowing that the country's future lay in the metropolis. Only in the new movie palaces could one find a benign view of the small town—and these theaters were all in the cities.

If metropolitan America was the major beneficiary of the prosperity of the 20s, it was its special victim in the Great Depression. The beginnings of the collapse are usually marked from the stock market crash in October 1929, but the harbinger can be found in the decline of housing starts in 1927; Chicago's teachers were being paid in scrip the next year. The spectacular antics and final ruin of the market concealed a larger malaise in the economy. The depression of the 1930s became "great" because it was the first urban depression in American history. Previous economic slumps had often been steep and involved great human suffering. But they had been relatively brief, seldom lasting more than a few years. Indeed, it was widely believed that, since they occurred periodically, depressions were an inevitable part of a successful capitalist system.

President Herbert Hoover acted on the historical expectation: the economy would plummet, but after a year or two it would bounce back. Washington should do little but watch the country "go through the wringer," meanwhile encouraging state and local governments, along with charitable institutions, to scrape together whatever resources they could find to tide their unemployed over until better days. In his darker moments Hoover believed that the depression had begun in Europe and spread to the United States, and that only a world recovery could bring the United States out of the slough. Always he clung to the notion that the Federal Government's proper response was retrenchment, restraint and patience.

The Great Depression, however, was different from

RICHARD C. WADE

A Missouri family feels the Depression.

any other. It did indeed reach the bottom in 1930–31, but it did not bounce back. It stuck. As months passed, industrial unemployment remained above 30 percent; industrial production stagnated; bankruptcies flourished; whole areas of the economy virtually shut down. The President tried to remain optimistic, if not cheerful. He kept saying that "prosperity is just around the corner"; in September 1931 he journeyed to Philadelphia to throw out the first ball of the World Series as a gesture of official confidence. But by 1932 it was clear that the "natural forces" which had cured economic hard times before were no longer operating.

It is hard even for Americans in the 1980s who have witnessed unemployment of over ten percent to comprehend the desperate conditions of 50 years before. No government agencies kept even approximate figures, but unemployment seldom fell below 25 percent; in some cities it was double that. Farmers armed themselves to prevent the foreclosure of mortgages. Sporadic rioting in cities accompanied evictions. Illness related to stress multiplied; suicides soared. In a grim joke, Amos and Andy, radio's favorite comedians of the era, had a hotel clerk ask a customer who sought a room, "Is it for sleeping or jumping?" There was starvation and unprecedented want. And as the months and years dragged on there was a dangerous shortage of hope that things would ever really improve.

Previous depressions had been borne largely by the poor and working class; the Great Depression was the middle classes' first prolonged experience of deep economic hardships. Homes, newly won in the previous decade, were lost; savings, prudently deposited in local institutions, disappeared in bank failures; college prospects for children dimmed; even food and clothing had to be husbanded. College professors, teachers, writers, artists, musicians and others accustomed

to genteel poverty found themselves bereft of public or private patrons. Is it any wonder that some people began to look around for a social system that could feed, clothe and shelter its citizens?

Franklin Delano Roosevelt, the governor of New York, probably shared some of Hoover's ideas in the 1920s. But by 1932 it was clear that the traditional response to hard times was inadequate. By then the states and municipalities had exhausted their funds, and constitutional limitations prevented further borrowing. Private charity had largely dried up. Only the Federal Government had the resources to meet immediate, desperate needs. During the presidential campaign of 1932, Roosevelt dutifully pledged to balance the national budget, but by the time of his inauguration he could say, referring to relief and other items, "We must act, and act quickly." The result was a large expansion of federal power in the nation's economic and social life.

The New Deal did not spring from a conspiracy of state planners or crypto–socialists or from a power–hungry president. It developed out of the intractability of 25 percent unemployment, a stagnant economy and the mounting desperation of millions. Roosevelt had no blueprint of the future in his hands. Indeed, his piecemeal, often contradictory New Deal programs attest to bewilderment rather than ideology. Nor did the New Deal usurp state and local rights. State and local governments simply could no longer cope with their most important immediate problems, much less plan for the future.

Roosevelt's first response was conservative; relief for the millions who could no longer take care of themselves or their families. Historians later would emphasize the New Deal "reforms"; but the possibilities of reform depended at first on meeting the more elementary demand of relief. That meant that the Federal Government accepted responsibility for what previously had been local responsibilities. Many of its relief programs were easily characterized as "make work," "boondoggling" and worse. Yet their design was to give a sense of dignity to those who received public aid. At its most trivial men raked leaves; at its best actors, musicians and scholars preserved their skills while performing public services for a pittance. At all levels, the haphazard relief effort conveyed to the depression's victims that their national government at least cared.

The New Deal's second response sought to reduce permanently insecurities present in the system even in prosperous years. It provided a minimum wage for those who had jobs; it provided workmen's compensation for those injured on the job; it provided unemployment insurance for those who were temporarily without jobs, and it provided Social Security for those too old or unable to work. A later president described these measures as "a safety net" for the needy. An unintended benefit of this federal legislation was the substantial improvement of the position of blacks and minorities who previously had to rely on states and localities for help. The new programs were color blind, and they especially reached into the South where institutionalized discrimination had afflicted blacks since the days of slavery.

The New Deal also came to the rescue of the besieged urban middle class. The Federal Deposit Insurance Corporation guaranteed modest bank savings. The Federal Housing Administration offered mortgages at below–market rates for prospective homeowners. Federal arts and writers projects permitted unemployed actors, scholars, musicians and photographers to practice and enhance their talent. The Federal Government also invaded education, hitherto the sanctified preserve of the states. It funded work-study programs to keep students in schools; it put young people to work on a host of useful local public enterprises. And in 1945, prodded by the sacrifices of the young in wartime, it established the G.I. Bill of Rights which opened higher education to a whole new generation of Americans, most of whose families had never even dared to think of college.

Middle class taxpayers were also relieved of the costs of expensive public works when the Federal Government funded the construction of new libraries, city halls, county court houses, subways, grade crossings, dams and public housing. What is now referred to as the "urban infrastructure" was first built at the end of the 19th century with local financing; the second generation of urban public works owed its construction to federal funding. Thus local governments could keep modest tax rates for property owners and enjoy substantial capital improvements at the same time.

The New Deal was a not wholly coherent, and certainly not ideological, approach to the problems it inherited. Instinctively it had followed the census returns of 1920. Its major figures understood the urban crisis better than the agrarian one. Many had been part of the urban reform movements which had sporadic successes in the previous decades. Without really quite knowing it, they forged a coalition of two groups that historically had been at odds. The relief programs for the poor and unemployed appealed to urban bosses and machines that could no longer service their inner city residents; and the reform programs nationalized proposals advanced by middle class municipal reformers for more than a generation. There was still hostility and rivalry on the local level, but when national issues arose, the boss and the reformer found the New Deal mutually satisfactory. This unlikely alliance lasted through four presidential elections and provided the Democratic party with a healthy electoral base for two decades.

Roosevelt's approach to persistent farm problems was less extensive and successful. Its major objective was to aid smaller farmers and to prop up farm prices. It tried many devices, some of which ran afoul of the Supreme Court. Though the Farm Security Administration's loans ultimately helped nearly a million marginal farmers, the New Deal left the dream of a rural America of family farmers as remote as ever. But no one could deny the accomplishment of the Rural Electrification Administration in bringing electric power to most of the nation's farms. Though historians often refer to the New Deal as a "labor–farmer coalition," it is important to note that a large number of midwestern Congressional districts in rural areas had returned to their traditional Republican moorings by the election of 1940.

The extension of Federal activity had its opponents both in the cities and on the farms. The resulting political debate made the decade the most contentious since the controversy over slavery in the 1850s. The Republican platform in 1936 rejected the entire New Deal, asserting that it had "dishonored American traditions" and the G.O.P. reaffirmed its "unalterable conviction that, in the future as in the past, the fate of the nation will depend, not so much on the wisdom and power of Government, as on the character and virtue, self–reliance, industry and thrift of the people." The Supreme Court, too, resisted, striking down some legislation as an unwarranted expansion of federal power. By 1940 and 1944, however, Republican presidential platforms and candidates, Wendell Willkie and Thomas E. Dewey, accepted the New Deal as an accomplished fact and confined their criticism to abuses rather than substance. Not until Barry Goldwater's nomination in 1964 and Ronald Reagan's election in 1980 was there a serious political questioning of the new social and governmental system forged in the desperation of the Great Depression.

The New Deal failed to end the nation's high unemployment and low productivity during the 1930s. Yet it preserved its basic economic system and protected essential human freedoms. At the end of the decade the United States was challenged by systems which had met their depression in much more drastic ways. The Nazis in Germany and the Fascists in Italy had handled unemployment by massive military buildups, and by the destruction of any fragile democratic roots that had managed to sprout in those two countries after World War I. Germany posed the most ominous threat. By the mid–1930s the three totalitarian countries of Germany, Italy and Japan had established the Axis, a kind of interlocking directorate of international aggression. And America, disillusioned with the consequences of the First World War, was reluctant to believe that even dictators would knowingly risk another blood bath.

From the beginning, Roosevelt was deeply suspicious of Hitler's aims, but the country's isolationist mood limited his statesmanship. As early as October 1937 he made a "quarantine" speech in Chicago which sought to warn aggressors. After war broke out in Europe in the fall of 1939 he threw American support increasingly behind the Allies. When France fell in 1940 and Britain stood alone, his anti–Axis view had few reservations. But American involvement in the war actually began halfway across the world at Pearl Harbor in a surprise Japanese attack on American naval and air forces. By 1942, the country which ten years before had been preoccupied with an economic depression was engaged in the largest war

U.S. ships burn at Pearl Harbor.

mankind had ever known.

The centralizing tendencies of the New Deal now seemed small next to the concentration of planning and control required by war. The allocation of all resources—from manpower and manufacturing to the rationing of meat and gasoline—was organized by Washington. If the New Deal had, in its last years, divided the country, Americans were almost unanimously behind the war effort. Once again, the emotions of war suppressed the country's customary pluralism. Japanese citizens were summarily interned in camps far removed from their homes; outspoken isolationists found few forums for their views. It took a threatened "march on Washington" to assure black workers decent access to wartime employment and most services remained segregated to the end.

Yet the country had never fought a war where the issues seemed so clear to contemporaries. It was widely believed to be a war of free men against totalitarianism. Even the awkward alliance with the Soviet Union did not greatly diminish this dimension. Thus, at the end, Americans viewed the outcome not just as the result of military or industrial supremacy, but somehow as a vindication of the whole national experience. The democracy promised in 1776 had now global application, and the moral qualities of the American system which had provided victory would elevate, if not redeem, the rest of the world in the next half century to come.

Day's end at Utah Beach, D-Day, 1944.

CHRONOLOGY

10 JANUARY 1901
Regional The famous Spindletop claim near Beaumont, Texas, brings in oil, the first drop in the mighty river of black gold to pour from the region.

21 FEBRUARY 1901
International Cuba adopts a constitution which follows the pattern of the United States.

25 FEBRUARY 1901
Industry The United States Steel Corporation is incorporated in the State of New Jersey. It is the first billion dollar corporation. The trend to combine into gargantuan organizations has accelerated rapidly in the past decade. Within the iron and steel industry more than 20 mergers have taken place in the last two years alone, and copper, sugar, meat, tobacco and oil have all become giant monopolies. By this time one per cent of the population owns seven–eighths of the wealth of the country. The United States Steel Corporation is formed by J.P. Morgan in defiance of the Sherman · Anti–trust Law. The primary reason is to buy out Andrew Carnegie for $250,000,000, at his own request. The gigantic trust is capitalized at $1,400,000,000, although actual assets are under $700,000,000. One–seventh of the total capitalization goes to the men who arrange the intricate deal. Morgan is said to have made $80,000,000. Although this is the biggest such merger, it is typical of the financial maneuvers of the day. They succeed as long as wages can be kept low through liberal immigration policies and prices high through tariff regulations.

2 MARCH 1901
National The Army Appropriations Act is passed by Congress. It includes the Platt Amendment which states that American troops will not withdraw from Cuba until the following conditions are included in their constitution: Cuba will not sign any agreement with a foreign power which will limit its independence; only the United States will be allowed to intervene to preserve Cuban independence and law and order; the Cubans agree to lease or sell naval stations to the United States. The Cubans temporarily accept their quasi–protectorate status on June 12 but in 1934 the amendment will be abrogated.

4 MARCH 1901
National William McKinley is inaugurated president for a second term; Theodore Roosevelt is vice-president.

23 MARCH 1901
International The leader of the Philippine rebellion against United States domination, Emilio Aguinaldo, is captured by American forces in Luzon.

9 MAY 1901
Finance In a titanic struggle for control of the Great Northern and Northern Pacific railroad lines, the Hill-Morgan group collides with the comparative newcomer Harriman and his associates Kuhn, Loeb and Company. Stock value soars from $100 a share to $1000 on May 9. As other stocks fall, panic results and a settlement is forced upon the two contestants in order to save the whole banking structure. Pooling their shares, including 78,000 of non–existent ones bought up in the frenzy of the fight, on November 13 they form a corporation in lenient New Jersey, capitalized at $400,000,000. Northern Securities Company, as it is called, almost monopolizes transportation between the Great Lakes and the Pacific Coast. It is also the corporation against which Theodore Roosevelt makes his first moves when as president he initiates his campaign to bring "Big Business" under the control of the Federal Government. "The Congress of the United States is not at the mercy of the state of New Jersey," Roosevelt states flatly. In February 1902 he will bring suit for dissolution of the monopoly, and in less than two years will have won the case. It signals a healthy new era in industrial relations.

27 MAY 1901
National Coming to grips with the issue of non-continental territories, the Supreme Court returns three verdicts in what are known as the Insular Cases. In *De Lima v Bidwell* the Supreme Court rules that Puerto Rico, no longer being a foreign nation, cannot have duties levied upon goods sent to the United States mainland. This same year, in *Dooley v United States*, this verdict is upheld on the principle that "the Constitution follows the flag." And in *Downes v Bidwell* the Supreme Court reverses itself and states that the Constitution does not apply immediately to annexed territorials but that the privileges of United States citizenship must be conferred specifically by Congress. On July 25 McKinley proclaims a free trade policy with the island, but the longer–term effect of these rulings on Puerto Rico is to allow duties to be levied against its imports. The Philippines, also a territory beyond the continental shores and with an alien population, is another direct target of the ruling.

6 SEPTEMBER 1901
National President McKinley is shot by Anarchist Leon Czolgosz as he attends a reception for the Pan-American Exhibition in Buffalo. At first it appears as if McKinley will recover from the attack, but on September 14 he dies of his wounds.

14 SEPTEMBER 1901
National President McKinley dies at 2:15 in the

morning. He is 58. Forty–two–year–old Theodore Roosevelt takes the oath of office at 3:00 in the afternoon. He asks McKinley's cabinet to stay on and temporarily allays the fears of Big Business and its political machine bosses at the rise to pre–eminence of the man they have thought to have been safely muzzled in the innocuous role of vice–president.

16 OCTOBER 1901
National In one of his first controversial moves as president, Roosevelt invites black leader Booker T. Washington to the White House. The South is incensed and reacts with violence against blacks. The visit will have alienated the South when, later, Roosevelt tries for a third term.

18 NOVEMBER 1901
International The Hay–Pauncefote Treaty is signed between Great Britain and the United States. It supersedes the Clayton–Bulwer Treaty of 1850 and authorizes the United States to build, operate and fortify a canal across the Central American Isthmus. The canal is to be open to all nations. The Senate ratifies the treaty on December 16.

28 NOVEMBER 1901
Regional Alabama adopts a new constitution which effectively disenfranchises blacks through its literacy and property tests, and for extraordinary circumstances, by way of its "grandfather" clause which states that a person cannot vote if his grandfather has not voted before him.

3 DECEMBER 1901
National In a 20,000–word message to Congress, Roosevelt announces that trusts need to be regulated "within reasonable limits." Unlike some of the more radical reformers, Roosevelt, a rich man himself, does not feel that money itself is evil or that large combinations are bad for the country. However, he advocates restraint under a new principle: "the public interest." Although later he would be called a "trust buster," and be heartily disliked by Big Business, Roosevelt is a fair–minded administrator, a man whose strong sense of justice does not obscure his understanding of the economic realities of bigness in a big country.

6 MARCH 1902
National The Bureau of the Census is created by an Act of Congress.

10 MARCH 1902
Industry Instigated by Roosevelt's vigorous campaign to bring the operations of Big Business within the reach of law, Attorney General Philander C. Knox invokes the Sherman Anti–trust Law to bring suit against Morgan and Harriman's Northern Securities Company, the New Jersey holding company for their western railroad combine.

12 MAY 1902
Labor Under the leadership of John Mitchell,

THEODORE ROOSEVELT, 1858-1919

From the heights of Mount Rushmore the face of Theodore Roosevelt looms gigantically over his countrymen. Of those four monolithic faces, his is perhaps the only one that seems to belong there: he wished to be, and was, a figure larger than life. Scholar, sportsman, soldier, naturalist and reformer president, his vision and courage helped transform America into a modern world power.

Born into an aristocratic family in New York City on October 27, 1858, the asthmatic and nearsighted youth built up his strength with sports and natural history outings. At Harvard he was a Phi Beta Kappa scholar and graduated in 1880, already working on the first of his many history books. After years of state politics he joined the U.S. Civil Service in 1889; there and later as a police commissioner in New York he proved to be a dynamic reformer and corruption-fighter. Named in 1897 as assistant secretary of the navy and already chafing for "a bit of a spar" with Spain, he soon got his war and his glory as a leader of the Rough Riders.

Roosevelt returned to popular acclaim and election as governor of New York state, where his liberal approach inspired exasperated Republican bosses to kick him upstairs—he became McKinley's vice–president in 1900. With McKinley's assassination six months later, the Republican old guard were appalled to find the "damned cowboy" their leader. The country called him "Teddy," a nickname he hated; at 42, he was the youngest President in American history.

During Roosevelt's two terms as President his efforts were astonishingly far-reaching and decisive. In the domestic sphere he reduced the booming power of business interests by busting some trusts and regulating others, often intervening on behalf of labor. An ardent conservationist, he doubled the number of national parks. As part of his "Square Deal" he regulated interstate commerce and initiated the Pure Food and Drug Act. Among his foreign initiatives, he began the Panama Canal (after some rather shabby diplomatic machinations), admitted Japan to world power and mediated the end of the Russo-Japanese War (for which he won the Nobel Prize in 1905). Saying "Speak softly and carry a big stick," he built up American armed forces and made sure the world

EXPANDING RESOURCES 1901-1945

noticed. He left office in 1909, beloved by his countrymen but estranged from conservatives in his party; his bid for the Republican nomination in 1912 was turned down and an independent campaign failed. But at his death in 1919 it was already clear that Teddy would be remembered as one of the great presidents; to many Americans he was already a face on the mountain.

140,000 United Mine Workers go on strike. Mitchell is willing to arbitrate, but the owners have refused. At this point, the railroad companies own most of the mines. Evading the law, the railroads have successfully eliminated all competition, mainly by their policy of selective rebates, and freight charges are excessively high, causing untold regional hardships. To this general complaint, the ill–paid miners have added grievances of their own: miners are compelled to live in company houses, at company rents, to buy only at company stores; they are often paid only in supplies from these stores, and are what has come to be called economic slaves. The owners refuse to recognize the UMW and refuse to negotiate. The strike will continue well into the fall, and by October the general public, particularly in the Northeast, becomes directly involved as the price of coal rises from $5.00 to $30.00 a ton. The owners complacently wait for the government to intervene on their behalf as it has so often in major strikes of the past. On July 17 George F. Baer, President of the Reading Coal and Iron Company, expresses their position in a famous message: "The rights and interests of the laboring man will be protected and cared for, not by the labor agitators, but by the Christian men to whom God in his infinite wisdom has given the control of the property interests of his country, and upon the successful management of which so much depends." Although the strike is more peaceful than usual, violence occasionally erupts. Without constitutional authority to intervene, Roosevelt waits out the summer, but by October the public is putting considerable pressure upon him to provide a settlement. Unsure of how to proceed, he summons the opposing groups to the White House for consultations; the owners retire in anger. Impatient with their recalcitrance, Roosevelt arranges to have the Army take over the mines and run them in the "public interest." Seeing that he is serious, J.P. Morgan agrees to negotiate. He meets with Secretary of War Elihu Root. On October 16 a Commission of Arbitration is formed to investigate the miners' grievances; in the meantime the men return to work. In March 1903 the Commission will recommend most of the provisions for which the miners had struck, including a permanent board of arbitration, at least token recognition of their union, higher wages, shorter hours and greater independence from the owners. Roosevelt's successful handling of the situation brings him great national popularity.

20 MAY 1902

International The United States withdraws its troops from the island as the first President of Cuba is installed.

2 JUNE 1902

Regional Oregon recovers some of its former political vigor, adopting the initiative and the referendum. Under the leadership of William S. U'ren the state will also adopt direct primary and recall of public officials. These are tools of government for which the Progressive movement has been long advocating. In the new political climate that Roosevelt has created with his "strenuous" efforts on behalf of social justice, Oregon is just one of many State governments which begin to experiment with reforms such as women's suffrage, primaries, labor legislation, minimum wage and workmen's compensation. The trend is to force government to be responsive to a wider section of the public than it has been for the past three decades.

17 JUNE 1902

Conservation Inspired by Roosevelt's concern for the land, the Federal Government passes the Newlands Reclamation Act which authorizes the building of irrigation dams across the West. During his term of office, Roosevelt also forms a 150,000,000–acre national forest preserve, and withdraws from sale 85,000,000 acres of prime Alaskan land until their mineral contents can be assessed. Roosevelt's concern for conservation will endear him to the country. Although a hunter himself, on one of his shooting expeditions the flamboyant president is reported to have refused to shoot a baby bear. The result of the head-line–grabbing incident is one of the most popular toys ever created: the Teddy Bear.

28 JUNE 1902

International Congress passes the Spooner or Isthmian Canal Act which authorizes the President to proceed with negotiations to buy rights from France for canal construction. Impatient to forge ahead at all costs, Roosevelt obtains these rights for $40,000,000 although the French lease is about to run out. The Colombians, through whose land it is proposed to cut the canal, would prefer to cut the French out of all negotiations, and in the ensuing ill–will the impetuous President will find it impossible to negotiate a treaty with Colombia. A revolt by the Colombian province of Panama in 1903 will bring a ten–mile–wide stretch of land to the United States through which the Panama Canal will be constructed.

1 JULY 1902

International The Philippine Government Act is passed by Congress. It authorizes a commission, picked by the president with the advice and consent of Congress, to run the islands and declares the inhabitants to be citizens of the archipelago, not the United States. On July 4, civil government is established by Presidential order.

11 AUGUST 1902

National Oliver Wendell Holmes is appointed Associate Justice of the Supreme Court. One of the Court's most respected Justices, Holmes, in his deliberations, will eloquently and effectively support the principle of the "public interest" as having priority over profits.

12 AUGUST 1902

Industry International Harvester Company, with capital of $120,000,000, is incorporated in New Jersey. Producing 85 percent of all farm machinery, it dominates the market. However, the moderate manner in which Harvester conducts business will be a helpful factor in getting the anti–Big Business groups to recognize that bigness is here to stay; that it is more a matter of placing Big Business within reach of the law than of breaking up the enormous industrial concentrations. In effect, the Robber Barons have served their purpose. It is becoming increasingly apparent that in a country as large as the United States, it will be necessary to have businesses of unprecedented size. The corollary, however, is that in a civilized nation, business, no matter how big, must conduct itself in a civilized fashion.

19 AUGUST 1902

National Taking his case to the nation, Roosevelt begins a trip around New England and the Midwest speaking out against the irresponsibility of trusts and monopolies. The electorate is widely enthusiastic, having agitated for relief from unregulated Big Business for some time.

15 SEPTEMBER 1902

International The United States and Mexico are the first two countries to use the new machinery for settling international disputes of the Permanent Court of Arbitration at the Hague. The dispute is over backpayment of interest.

OTHER EVENTS OF 1902

Arts/Culture Publication of Ida Tarbell's exposé of the oil monopoly, *History of the Standard Oil Company*, is begun in *McClure's Magazine*. It is one of the first of a series of investigative reports into current business practices and social situations. Others include *The Octopus* and *The Pit*, by Frank Norris, *The Shame of the Cities*, by Lincoln Steffens, *The Jungle* by Upton Sinclair and *The Iron Heel* by Jack London. These were electrifying works, carefully researched, and reported with restraint and courage. They will have a direct impact on the course of future political action.

22 JANUARY 1903

International The Hay–Herran Treaty relating to rights to the Panama Canal is signed by the Colombian chargé at Washington. Provisions include a 100–year lease on a 10–mile wide strip in the Panamanian province of Colombia. The price is $10,000,-000 and an annual rental of $250,000. The sticking point, however, is the issue of sovereignty of the proposed Canal Zone which in this treaty is to cede to the United States. On August 12 the Colombian government will reject the proposal. In one of his more myopic moments, Roosevelt will react with anger.

11 FEBRUARY 1903

National Reflecting popular support for Roosevelt's active campaign for social justice, Congress adopts the Expedition Act, which gives priority to the Attorney General's antitrust cases in the circuit courts.

14 FEBRUARY 1903

National The Department of Commerce and Labor is created by Act of Congress and signed into law by Roosevelt. It gives the Secretary Cabinet status, and is the 9th Cabinet office. George B. Cortelyou is named the first secretary of the department. In 1913 the office will be separated into two different departments.

The same day Congress authorizes centralization of the military, creating the General Staff of the Army.

19 FEBRUARY 1903

National The Elkins Act is passed by Congress. The Act carves out new ground by declaring illegal all rebates on published freight rates. However, staying within the powers granted under the Sherman Antitrust Act, the new Act does not extend to regulation of rates. Not until the Hepburn Act of 1906, enacted after more railroad scandals come to light, will the Federal Government be empowered to regulate most interstate transportation.

23 FEBRUARY 1903

National In *Champion v Ames* the Supreme Court upholds a federal law which prohibits lottery tickets from being sent through the mails from one state to another. In articulating the reasons for its findings, the Court addresses the issue of "federal police power" which is found to supersede the police powers of the States. The Court finds that, under the Interstate Commerce Act, federal powers include the power to prohibit as well as to regulate. The ruling will be the basis for later regulation of food, drugs and other items.

22 MARCH 1903

Labor The special commission set up by Roosevelt to settle the anthracite coal dispute recommends shorter hours, a 10 percent wage increase and an "open shop." The principle of the "open shop" will later be used against organized labor, but in this instance, when the owners adamantly refuse to recognize the United Mine Workers union, the decision precludes discrimination against union members.

23 MAY 1903

Regional Wisconsin is the first State to adopt direct primary elections. By 1948 all states will have adopted the system.

4 JULY 1903

International The first Pacific cable is laid between San Francisco and Manila. The first message is sent to the Philippines by President Roosevelt.

1 AUGUST 1903

Transportation Completing a 52–day cross–country

EXPANDING RESOURCES 1901-1945

drive, a Packard automobile arrives in New York having been driven from San Francisco, the first time an automobile has made the journey. By 1905 there will be some 80,000 cars chugging along the roads of America. A year later, Woodrow Wilson will state: "Nothing has spread socialistic feeling in this country more than the use of the automobile."

20 OCTOBER 1903
International The Joint Commission set up on January 24 by Great Britain and the United States to report on their Alaskan boundary dispute rules in favor of United States interests.

2 NOVEMBER 1903
International Instigated by a triumvirate of Panamanian businessmen, French agents of the Panama Canal Company and United States Army officers, Panama makes plans to secede from Colombia. In October, Roosevelt orders three ships of the United States Navy to steam toward the area. On November 2 they are ordered to prevent Colombia from landing troops in the Panamanian province.

3 NOVEMBER 1903
International The expected uprising of the Panamanians takes place at six in the evening with no bloodshed. The new government is organized during the night. The local fire department becomes the army. The lobbyist for the French Canal Company, Philippe Buneau–Varilla, is made Panamanian minister to Washington; Secretary Hay, with unseemly haste, will proceed to complete canal negotiations with him. Meanwhile, troops from the U.S.S. *Nashville* prevent Colombians from reaching Panama City.

4 NOVEMBER 1903
International Panamanian independence is declared.

6 NOVEMBER 1903
International Secretary Hay recognizes the new Panamanian government in the quickest recognition then given to a foreign country by the United States.

18 NOVEMBER 1903
International The United States and Panama sign the Hay–Buneau-Varilla treaty giving the United States permanent rights to a 10–mile–wide strip of land in return for $10,000,000 and an annual charge of $250,-000 after nine years. Although it appears at the time to be a mere technicality, the independence of Panama is guaranteed. Says Secretary of War William Howard Taft: "To the Spanish or Latin mind—poetic and sentimental, enjoying the intellectual refinements, and dwelling much on names and forms—it is by no means unimportant." Independence had been the sticking point in negotiations with Colombia, and there are those who believe that a bit of patience on Roosevelt's part would have meant more stability in the area for the long run. Years later Roosevelt was still proud of his "big stick" in the Caribbean, boasting: "I took the Canal and let Congress debate."

17 DECEMBER 1903
Life/Customs Orville and Wilbur Wright make the first four successful flights of a heavier–than air machine; Orville flies 120 feet in 12 seconds and Wilbur later flies 852 feet in 59 seconds. The airplane is flown at Kitty Hawk in North Carolina.

4 JANUARY 1904
International In *Gonzales v Williams*, the Supreme Court rules that Puerto Ricans are not aliens and may not be refused admission to the continental United States. This ruling does not give them the additional privileges of citizenship which will not be granted until 1917.

29 FEBRUARY 1904
International The seven–man Panama Canal Commission is appointed by Roosevelt to complete the Canal. With America becoming ever more intricately bound into the politics of the Atlantic and Pacific, the project has now more urgency than ever.

14 MARCH 1904
National In a landmark case, *Northern Securities Company v United States*, the Supreme Court finds that the company violates the Sherman Anti–trust Act. This is the first case that Roosevelt has undertaken in his campaign to bring Big Business within the restraint of law. His later reputation as a "trustbuster" will largely rest upon his vigorous participation in the outcome of this decision.

5 MAY 1904
National The National Convention of the Socialist Party meets in Chicago to nominate perennial candidate Eugene V. Debs of Indiana for president and Benjamin Hanford of New York for vice–president.

23 MAY 1904
Transportation North European steamship companies cut their steerage rates to $10. Up to 1,000,000 immigrants are arriving in the United States each year.

21 JUNE 1904
National The Republican Party holds its National Convention in Chicago. Theodore Roosevelt is enthusiastically nominated for president over some strong opposition from what he calls the "malefactors of great wealth," and Charles W. Fairbanks of Indiana is nominated for vice–president.

29 JUNE 1904
National The Prohibition Party holds its National Convention in Indianapolis, Indiana. The felicitously named Silas C. Swallow of Pennsylvania is nominated for president, and George W. Carroll of Texas for vice–president.

4 JULY 1904
National The Populist Party convenes in Springfield, Illinois, to nominate Thomas E. Watson of Georgia

ORVILLE AND WILBUR WRIGHT, 1871-1948 and 1867-1912

Aviation pioneers Orville and Wilbur Wright were archetypical American inventors—self-educated plucky individualists who astonished the world by doing what the great and educated said could not be done. As builders of the first successful heavier-than-air flying machine, they began not only the actuality but also the science of aviation.

Wilbur was born on April 16, 1867, in Millville, Indiana, and Orville on August 19, 1871, in Dayton, Ohio. They were sons of a minister with scientific leanings and a mother who inspired her children with an interest in things mechanical—the young Wrights, working always as a team, were inveterate builders and tinkerers from early childhood. By 1888 they had hand-built a large press and were in the printing business; a few years later they had established a bicycle shop and were successfully manufacturing their own designs. Neither brother attended college.

In the 1890s the Wright brothers keenly followed the progress of aviation experiments around the world. They began to examine critically the reasons for the invariable failure of these experiments and concluded that most of the theoretical bases for heavier-than-air flight were unsound. Near the end of the decade they developed their first aviation patent and began to experiment with kites. In 1900 they worked with gliders on the windy dunes of Kitty Hawk, North Carolina. Examining the results of these experiments, they built the first wind tunnel and tested over 200 wing designs. The result was the development of the modern science of aerodynamics and a stream of design innovations. Returning to Kitty Hawk in 1902 and 1903, they made hundreds of tests of new gliders.

Now they knew what was needed for powered flight. In 1903 they built a gasoline engine and designed a new airscrew. Then at Kitty Hawk, on December 17, 1903, with five witnesses present and Orville reclining on the airplane's wing, man truly flew for the first time. The next years saw a continuing series of experiments and slowly mounting attention from an incredulous world.

The brothers remained in the field thereafter as designers, builders and promoters. Wilbur died of typhoid in 1912, Orville in 1948. The Wright brothers had launched humankind into the air age; they were of that heroic generation of early 20th century inventors who were to awaken the world to the idea that perhaps nothing is impossible.

for president and Thomas H. Tibbles of Nebraska for vice–president.

6 JULY 1904

National The Democratic Party convenes in St. Louis, Missouri, to nominate the little–known New York Judge Alton B. Parker for president, spelling easy victory for the popular Roosevelt. Henry G. Davis of West Virginia is nominated for vice-president.

25 JULY 1904

Labor The long and bitter textile strike of some 25,000 workers in the mills of Massachusetts begins in Fall River. The struggle brings to national attention reprehensible conditions in the mills. The National Child Labor Committee is formed this year in order to bring some protection to children who, as young as 10 years old, are working long adult hours under the most difficult circumstances.

27 OCTOBER 1904

Transportation The first part of the underground and underwater railroad is completed in New York City. The subway has been under the supervision of Alexander Ector Orr and runs from City Hall to 145th Street. Meantime New York and New Jersey are being joined by the Morton Street Tunnel.

8 NOVEMBER 1904

National Theodore Roosevelt and his running–mate Charles W. Fairbanks defeat the Democrats by 2,500,000 votes. The electoral vote is 336 to 140. Missouri goes Republican for the first time since the Civil War.

6 DECEMBER 1904

National The Roosevelt Corollary is articulated for the first time by the president in his annual message to Congress. The principle states that since America, by way of the Monroe Doctrine, has forbidden foreign interference in the Western Hemisphere, the United States has a responsibility to insist on proper redress for wrongs inflicted upon a foreign state by any country within the U.S. sphere of influence. Says Roosevelt: "Chronic wrongdoing . . . may force the United States . . . to the exercise of international police power." The first occasion to test the Corollary will come early the following year, when the Dominican Republic reneges on its debts to Great Britain, which then has no recourse other than to use force to collect. Instead, Roosevelt places Americans in charge of Dominican revenues until the debt is discharged and the country out of danger of bankruptcy. This Corollary sets a dangerous precedent which will become all too burdensome to the United States and rankle badly in the South American nations. In 1930 it will be repudiated by the Department of State.

OTHER EVENTS OF 1904

Transportation New York is the first state to pass a speed law for automobiles: maximum speed in cities is 10 mph; 15 mph is allowed in small towns, and 20 mph in the country.

20 JANUARY 1905

International The Roosevelt Corollary to the Monroe Doctrine is tested when the United States begins supervision of the Dominican Republic's national and international debts. Although the Senate withholds approval of the protocol, Roosevelt reaches agreement with the Dominican government nonetheless. The Americans figure that if only 50 percent of all receipts are stolen by corrupt government officials, the government can stay in business; 90 percent is too much.

30 JANUARY 1905

National In *Swift & Co v United States*, the Su-

HELEN KELLER, 1880-1968

In a century full of wars Helen Keller became a world-wide symbol of another kind of victory, a victory over crushing personal handicaps, a victory gained with rare grace and determination to help others with similar problems. Keller was born to a prominent family in Tuscumbia, Alabama on June 27, 1880. Midway through her second year a serious illness left her blind and deaf; she quickly became wild and uncontrollable. Desperate, her father took her to a famous oculist who, while he held out no hope for a cure, advised him to try to educate Helen. A request to an institute for the blind in Boston brought to Alabama Anne Sullivan, who became governess and teacher of the difficult child. One day Anne Sullivan poured water over Helen's hand and wrote the word "water" in her other hand. The world of language came to the child in a flash. Within a few years she was reading and typing in braille and in 1890 began speech classes at the Horace Mann School for the Deaf. In 1904, still guided by Sullivan, Keller graduated with honors in English from Radcliffe College in Cambridge, Massachusetts.

Deciding to concentrate on promoting the treatment and education of the blind, Keller began a lifelong series of lectures, books and articles. She was instrumental in creating the first state commission for the blind, in Massachusetts, and successfully spread the idea throughout the country; she also promoted medical research on blindness. Frequently in need of funds in her early career, she and Sullivan during the 20s toured on a vaudeville circuit, and in 1918 she appeared in a film based on her life. In 1932 she started the Helen Keller Endowment Fund for the American Foundation for the Blind. Anne Sullivan died in 1936. Keller's secretary, Polly Thompson, became her new companion. Before her death in 1968 Keller's efforts were to bear fruit worldwide; perhaps more than any other single person she had shown the world the human potential of the blind.

preme Court rules unanimously in favor of the government in its attempt to break up the ill-famed "Beef Trust"; however the ruling fails to affect the strongly entrenched meat monopoly.

17 APRIL 1905
National In *Lochner v New York*, the Supreme Court finds unconstitutional a state law which limits maximum working hours for bakers. The Court holds that such a law interferes with the right to free contract and is an improper use of police powers. In his famous dissent Justice Holmes holds that the Constitution "is not intended to embody a particular economic theory, whether of paternalism . . . or of *laissez-faire*." The need for some legislative protection for the single worker in the face of the enormous power wielded by employers is becoming increasingly obvious.

8 JUNE 1905
International Roosevelt, sensing a great desire for peace in the world, urges Japan and Russia, which have been at war since February 1904, to negotiate. Inviting the two powers to Portsmouth, New Hampshire, the President displays statesmanlike skills

in aiding the belligerents to resolve their differences. Roosevelt takes a firm hand in the negotiations, although in July Secretary of War William Howard Taft makes a secret agreement with Japan's prime minister to keep his hands off the Philippines in return for Korea. In the final agreement signed at Portsmouth on September 5 Japan is given protection over Korea, and receives the South Manchurian Railway and the southern Liaotung Peninsula. Roosevelt adroitly prevents Japan from taking more than half of disputed Sakhalin Island and Russia receives economic restitution. Roosevelt will receive the Nobel Peace Prize for his mediation, and America's international reputation for justice and fair play will be much restored.

27 JUNE 1905
Labor The Industrial Workers of the World, a union, is organized in Chicago, as a more militant attempt to restore balance to the social structure of the nation. William D. Haywood is the active proponent of industrial unionism to offset the temperate craft unionism of the venerable American Federation of Labor. The IWW distinguishes the industrial laborer as a separate entity from other workers in the struggle for a more equitable share of American wealth. However the working segment of society, increasingly tipped into poverty, aware of the vast wealth consolidating into a few hands, is beset by unrest, inevitably feeling that resort to violence may be the only solution to Big Business practices unrestrained by social justice. But the voices for balance are becoming stronger, and side by side with militant unionism is a roused electorate which is experimenting with new forms to make government more responsive to the will of the people. The Senate, now the most blatant body resisting ongoing social adjustments to newly rising situations, will come under peaceful but effective attack through new experiments in initiative, referendum and recall which are being adopted in Western States.

6 SEPTEMBER 1905
Industry Continuing his campaign to restore social justice to the economic life of the nation, Roosevelt turns his big guns onto the insurance companies whose scandalous behavior has shocked the nation. Fifty-seven hearings will be conducted under the able direction of Charles Evans Hughes, whom Roosevelt has charged with the investigation. Many of the nation's richest men are found to be involved in penny-ante schemes to defraud small-policy holders. Exposure of the corrupt manner in which the companies operate will lead to many reforms.

8 NOVEMBER 1905
Industry The Chicago & North Western railroad installs electric lamps on its "Overland Limited," which runs from Chicago to California, the first railroad to do so.

18 APRIL 1906
Regional San Francisco is rocked by the most exten-

sive earthquake in United States history. Fire spreads and lasts for three days, destroying four square miles of the city. Over 500,000 people are made homeless, and some 500 people are killed.

21 MAY 1906
International The United States and Mexico come to an agreement over distribution of the waters of the Rio Grande which are being increasingly diverted into the United States for irrigation.

29 JUNE 1906
National Congress passes the Hepburn Act, which Roosevelt has strongly endorsed. It will give teeth to the Interstate Commerce Act by permitting regulation of rates charged by railroads, pipelines and terminals. The number of members on the Interstate Commission is raised from five to seven, and new accounting methods are introduced. In his persuasive way, Roosevelt ably creates a climate of opinion whereby the Hepburn Act passes through the usually unresponsive Senate, and by-passes the unlikely coalition of liberal Robert La Follette and rabble-rousing Ben Tillman who are demanding appraisal of railroad property in order to determine fair rates.

30 JUNE 1906
National Congress passes the Meat Inspection Act. Upton Sinclair's *The Jungle*, a lurid exposé of the disgusting procedures in the meat-packing industry of the time, has roused the wrath of the nation, Roosevelt included. The president has tried to reach an agreement with the meat packers to allow government inspection. Their adamant refusal and arrogant assumption that there is nothing he can do about it goads him to release a government report on the meat industry's practices, a report which has been ordered by Roosevelt after reading Sinclair's book. Overnight, meat sales drop in half and the suddenly repentant meat packers plead for government inspection in order to restore public confidence. Congress quickly enacts the needed legislation.

The same day Congress passes the Pure Food and Drug Act. The writers whom Roosevelt has called "muckrakers" have done a good, if sensational, job of exposing the wretched practices of the food and drug industries. Now, with Roosevelt's blessing, the new act is passed prohibiting adulterated or mislabeled food and drugs from interstate commerce.

3 AUGUST 1906
International Cuban President Tomas Estrade Palma asks for aid in quelling a rebellion. Roosevelt sends William Howard Taft to head a provisional government and maintain order. The United States will remain in charge of the island until February 1, 1909 when a new Cuban president is elected.

11 OCTOBER 1906
International The San Francisco Board of Education orders children of Oriental extraction to attend a purely Oriental school. Those "infernal fools in Cal-

---

MUCKRAKERS

In April 1906, Theodore Roosevelt felt exasperated enough to expostulate against the press and a new breed of writers who were busy exposing the evils of the society in which they lived. "Muckrakers," he called these men and women after the man in *Pilgrim's Progress* who was so used to watching the filth it was his job to scrape up that he could see nothing else. By the end of that year, thanks to just one of those "muckrakers," Upton Sinclair, and his novel *The Jungle*, the meat industry, one of the most scandalous of all, had so lost public confidence that it had been brought to beg for federal regulation of its infamous meatpacking procedures. Although she did not initiate the form, in 1903 Ida Tarbell's monumental investigation of the oil monopoly, *History of the Standard Oil Company*, was published by *McClure's* in serial form. The book did much to influence demand for subsequent trust legislation, and its success set the stage for serious writers to search out social injustices wherever they might be found. At the same time, newspapers and magazines seemed to have insatiable appetites for any and all exposures, the more sensational the better; between 1904 and 1910 some very lurid reading appeared in the press, answering to Roosevelt's irate description. However, among the sensationalism some serious investigative reporting of the highest order was to be found; for example, there were Thomas Lawson's *Frenzied Finance*, (1902); Charles E. Russell's *The Greatest Trust in the World* (1905); Ray Stannard Baker's *The Railroads on Trial* (1906); David Phillips' *The Treason of the Senate*, (1906) and Lincoln Steffens' *The Shame of the Cities* (1904).

A noticeable increase in social sense and conscience is discernible in these early years of the century; America was coming of age. For this welcome change, the "muckrakers" could take their share of the credit.

---

ifornia," explodes Roosevelt when he hears of the order. Anti-American feeling in Japan runs high, and Roosevelt, worried about the international consequences of the law, feels called upon to intervene. Inviting the Mayor of San Francisco to the White House, the President persuades him to rescind the order with the understanding that the White House will attempt to discourage Japanese emigration to the United States. This Roosevelt accomplishes diplomatically in his "gentleman's agreement" of 1907.

9 NOVEMBER 1906
International The first President to take a trip abroad, Roosevelt journeys to Panama to see for himself how the Panama Canal project is progressing. The Canal, begun this year, will take eight years to complete, at a cost of $375,000,000. Roosevelt travels the 17-day journey on the battleship *Louisiana*. The Canal will remain one of the proudest accomplishments of this most effective president.

26 JANUARY 1907
National Finally responsive to public anger at the blatant way some of the captains of industry have been corrupting public officials, Congress passes an act forbidding corporations from contributing to election campaigns for national office.

EXPANDING RESOURCES 1901-1945

THE AIRPLANE

On the morning of December 17, 1903, the shy, taciturn brothers, Wilbur and Orville Wright, made history. They had constructed their own four-cylinder, 12-horsepower, 200-pound gasoline engine and fitted it into their own design for a flying machine. Orville then proceeded to fly 120 feet in 12 seconds, and Wilbur managed 852 feet in 59 seconds. Between them, that matchless morning, they made one of man's oldest dreams come true.

By 1905, Wilbur flew a redesigned machine 24 miles in 38 minutes. And in 1908, demonstrating his airplane in France, he stayed aloft almost two hours covering 62 miles at an altitude of 361 feet. Meanwhile, others were following the daring young brothers. In July 1908, Glenn Curtiss, one of the few builders to steer the rough rapids of early airplane development, demonstrated serious competition with a plane which flew a mile. In July 1909, the Frenchman Louis Bleriot flew across the English Channel, and soon international flying meets became almost commonplace. At home, flying circuses became an accepted if still thrilling feature at country fairs. In 1911 Curtiss' seaplane was bought by the Navy, the beginning of an insatiable military interest in aircraft. And in 1913, Elmer A. Sperry demonstrated his gyroscope stabilizer which would later lead to instrument flying. The lure of transatlantic flying grew rapidly, culminating in Charles Lindbergh's historic 3735-mile odyssey from Roosevelt Field, Long Island to Paris on May 20-21, 1927. The journey took 33 hours and 39 minutes and the world would never be the same, nor as big, again.

25 FEBRUARY 1907

International The Senate ratifies Roosevelt's agreement made with the Dominican Republic whereby the United States will supervise Dominican customs until foreign creditors have been recompensed. The unusual arrangement springs from Roosevelt's Corollary to the Monroe Doctrine, which states that since the United States will not allow foreign military intervention within the Western Hemisphere in order to redress wrongs, America must properly see that justice is done in any way it deems proper.

26 FEBRUARY 1907

National Congress passes the General Appropriations Bill which increases salaries in the House and Senate to $7500. Cabinet members and the vice-president will get $12,000.
Immigration A commission on immigration is established by Congress to look into the problems created by the flood of unskilled immigrants arriving on American shores each year.

14 MARCH 1907

Immigration By Presidential order the United States excludes Japanese laborers from entering the country.
Conservation Members of The Inland Waterways Commission are appointed by Roosevelt. The Commission is to study and report on the rivers and lakes of the United States, their relation to forests, traffic congestion and other such matters. During Roosevelt's administration five national parks will be established, including Crater Lake in Oregon and Mesa Verde in Colorado. In addition, under the National Monuments Act of 1906 he sets aside 16 national monuments and creates 51 wildlife santuaries. Devil's Tower in Wyoming is the first monument to come under the Act.

21 MARCH 1907

International Following the Roosevelt Corollary wherever it leads, United States Marines are sent to Honduras to help quell a revolution there, and at the same time protect life and property. The resource-draining episode makes the Corollary less appealing to U.S. policymakers.

15 JUNE 1907

International The Second Hague Peace Conference, with 46 nations participating, meets to deliberate international regulations. At the instigation of the United States, the conference will forbid war as an instrument for collection of debts.

12 SEPTEMBER 1907

Transportation The *Lusitania*, the largest steamship in the world, sets a new speed record of five days and 54 minutes as it completes its maiden voyage between Queenstown, Ireland, and New York.

1 OCTOBER 1907

National Due to a shortage of currency from reckless over–capitalization of new enterprises, a downturn in the stock market has been heralding trouble since spring. Now the public, which has been investing heavily in Big Business, panics and makes runs on banks across the nation. In New York thousands converge on the Kickerbocker Trust Company which, after a day and a half, fails to meet its obligations, thus beginning the depression of 1907–08. Roosevelt asks his arch–enemy, the skillful financier J.P. Morgan, to come out of semi–retirement and manage the financial crisis. Morgan deftly steers the country out of financial trouble. He and his friends import $100,000,000 of gold from Europe to help shore up U.S. currency. But his financial wizardry does not include measures to offset the depression which follows, one which will last into the following election year. The Panic of 1907 is seen to be caused by the rigidity of the bond–secured currency system. Next year the entire banking system will come under review by a special banking commission headed by Senator Nelson W. Aldrich.

16 NOVEMBER 1907

National Oklahoma becomes the 46th State.

6 DECEMBER 1907

Industry In one of the worst mine disasters in United States history, 361 miners are killed when a coalmine explodes in Monongah, West Virginia.

16 DECEMBER 1907

International In a grandiose gesture to induce Japan and other Pacific nations to maintain the status quo there, Roosevelt sends the Great White Fleet of 16 battleships on a cruise around the world. The Fleet is under the command of "Fighting Bob" Evans, and will go to South America, Australia and Japan among its other stops. The imposing armada is received with enthusiasm, and the message that the United States is an important international power is not missed. After more than a year on its grand tour, the fleet returns home on February 22, 1909. The United States Navy, too, has learned some lessons, notably that it has been heavily dependent on foreign supplies. The Navy can see that in case of war, a more balanced distribution of vessels will be needed, one to include destroyer escorts and a supply network.

OTHER EVENTS OF 1907

Arts/Culture Frank Lloyd Wright completes the imaginative and exemplary Robey House in Chicago and reveals his genius for placing his constructions organically in their environments.

This same year Elinor Glyn publishes her romantic novel *Three Weeks*, which is banned in Boston. The book sells in the hundreds of thousands. Elinor Glyn is credited with coining the term "It" for sex appeal.

12 FEBRUARY 1908

Life/Customs The first round the world automobile race begins in New York City. It will proceed to Paris by way of Alaska and Siberia. Six cars participate, but only three reach the finish line: the German "Protos" driven by Lieutenant Koepens (who is penalized for having shipped his car to Seattle) and the American "Thomas Flyer" driven by George Schuster. The Italian "Zust" arrives two weeks after the winner.

2 APRIL 1908

National The Populist Party holds its National Convention at St. Louis, Missouri. It nominates Thomas E. Watson of Georgia for president, and Samuel W. Williams of Indiana, for vice–president.

30 APRIL 1908

Regional Heralding a trend, 267 Massachusetts towns and cities vote for local prohibition. Worcester, with its population of 130,000, is the largest city in the country to go dry.

10 MAY 1908

National The Socialist Party holds its National Convention in Chicago, Illinois. It nominates Eugene V. Debs of Indiana for president and Benjamin Hanford of New York for vice–president.

28 MAY 1908

National Congress enacts a bill which will regulate child labor in the District of Columbia. It is hoped that the law will set an example for the states.

30 MAY 1908

Finance Congress passes the Aldrich–Vreeland Act which frees banks to issue notes backed by commercial paper and bonds of state and local governments.

FRANK LLOYD WRIGHT, 1867-1959

In a career spanning over 70 years and more than 1000 works, architect and visionary Frank Lloyd Wright left to the world a legacy of buildings astonishing in their originality and fertility of invention; he also left his dream of a humanistic and democratic architecture that would lead people to live more at peace with one another and with nature. Wright was born on June 8, 1867, at Richland Center, Wisconsin, the son of a musician and preacher. He worked for years on the family farm and attended the University of Wisconsin. Though he never received an architecture degree, by 1888 he was an associate of progressive architect Louis Sullivan and by 1893 was in practice on his own in Oak Park, near Chicago.

After 1900 Wright became leader of the so-called Prairie School, which introduced a radical new approach to American home design—room flowed into room, interior into exterior, in simple, open designs stressing rows of windows and lines parallel to the ground. Wright had already developed his ideas of buildings designed around the human form and human doings, describing them with terms such as "organic architecture" and "the architecture of democracy." From early in the century Wright was among the most famous American architects, designing and building tirelessly. The 1904 Larkin Building in Buffalo was a pioneering business edifice; the 1906 Unity Temple in Oak Park later became a National Historical Landmark. In 1911 he built Taliesin, his home, school, and studio, in Wisconsin.

As Wright's reputation spread throughout both America and the world, he was able to select his commissions and make each of his buildings into an individual statement. Among his most notable works of the ensuing decades are the Imperial Hotel in Tokyo (1916-22)—which survived the great earthquake of 1923 (but later fell to the wrecker's ball); the Johnson Wax Company's administration building (1933-36) and research tower (1950); the house named Falling Water in Bear Run, Pennsylvania (1937); a Unitarian Church in Madison, Wisconsin (1947); and the Guggenheim Museum in New York City, the project on which he was still working when he died in 1959. Wright left many legacies including his home in Scottsdale, Arizona, Taliesin West, which became a major school of modern architecture and design; his plan for a mile-high skyscraper; his rhapsodic writings and inspiring drawings. But above all, by changing people's ideas about the nature of the space they might live and work in, Wright had helped change the spirit of his century.

At the same time, the arch–conservative Nelson W. Aldrich, is placed as head of the National Monetary Commission set up to review the nation's entire financial structure. So far, Roosevelt is successfully walking a middle line between such men as Aldrich on the one hand and the anti–business politicians like Bryan and Robert La Follette on the other.

16 JUNE 1908

National The Republican Party holds its National Convention in Chicago, Illinois. In 1904, Roosevelt has categorically stated that "On the fourth of March next I shall have served three and a half years, and this . . . constitutes my first term. The wise custom which limits the President to two terms regards the substance and not the form. Under no circumstances

EXPANDING RESOURCES 1901-1945

will I be a candidate for or accept another nomination." This statement will haunt him now in 1908 when his popularity throughout the country would have kept him in the White House for another term, the second to which he would have been elected on his own merits. However his enemies capitalize on the remark and somehow it has the force of law. "I would cut my hand off right there," says Roosevelt to a friend, pointing at his wrist. "if I could recall that written statement." Roosevelt's hand instead picks his successor, William H. Taft of Ohio, whose secret ambition is to be Chief Justice of the Supreme Court, to have "power without worry." Roosevelt feels that Taft will lead the party out of its 18th century business habits, habits which do not apply to 20th century conditions. James S. Sherman of New York is nominated for vice–president.

4 JULY 1908
National The Socialist Labor Party holds its National Convention in New York City and nominates Martin R. Preston of Nevada for president. Preston is serving a jail sentence for murder, and is in any case ineligible because of his youth. The Party will have to pick another candidate: August Gilhaus of New York. Nominated for the vice–presidency is Donald L. Munro.

7 JULY 1908
National The Democratic Party holds its National Convention in Denver, Colorado. William Jennings Bryan is once again nominated for president, and John W. Kern is nominated for vice–president.

15 JULY 1908
National The Prohibition Party, ever increasing in strength, nominates Eugene W. Chafin for president at its National Convention in Columbus, Ohio. Aaron S. Watkins of Ohio is nominated for vice–president.

14 AUGUST 1908
Black Experience Ugly race riots break out in Springfield, Illinois. Governor Charles S. Deneen declares martial law, but it does not stop the rioting. Several blacks are lynched.

1 OCTOBER 1908
Transportation Henry Ford introduces his famous Model T. Although it sells at an expensive $850, it is being mass–produced and will change the face of the nation. By 1926 the price will have gone down to $310 and be within the range of almost everyone.

3 NOVEMBER 1908
National William Howard Taft wins the election with an electoral vote of 321 to 162 for Bryan. Popular vote is Taft, 7,679,006; Bryan, 6,409,106; none of the other candidates poll over a half million votes. James S. Sherman is elected vice–president.

28 NOVEMBER 1908
Industry An explosion in the Marianna Mine at Monongahela, Pennsylvania, causes the supporting structure to collapse, killing 100 miners.

21 DECEMBER 1908
National Almost as if writing an epitaph for the business practices of the last 40 years, Andrew Carnegie testifies at Congressional tariff hearings: "Take back your protection; we are now men, and we can beat the world." The remark, however, will not change things substantially, and the bill that is ultimately signed by Taft has some of the highest tariffs ever.

OTHER EVENTS OF 1908
National In *Muller v Oregon* the Supreme Court rules that an Oregon law limiting the maximum hours a woman can work is constitutional and denies that it curtails the liberty of contract guaranteed by the 14th Amendment.

Arts/Culture The 47–story Singer Building is built in New York. By 1913, the 50–story Metropolitan Tower and the 60–story Woolworth Building will have been completed. The world–delighting New York skyline is coming into view.

This same year, led by Robert Henri, a group of young artists form what will be known as the "Ashcan School." The school includes George Luks, William Glackens, Everett Shinn and George Bellows. In a new departure for American art, which has been so largely dependent on landscape and figure, the group, centered in New York's Greenwich Village, proposes to paint the boisterous life of the cities of the 20th century.

4 MARCH 1909
National Plump, portly William Howard Taft is inaugurated 27th President of the United States. James S. Sherman is vice–president. Following on the tail of Roosevelt's radiant comet, Taft will find it hard to make a mark on the public mind. Although he will continue Roosevelt's policies of social justice and increased protection within the law, his bland, even boring, public manner will serve to alienate the electorate. A lawyer, Taft himself is more inclined to the judicial sphere and does not appreciate the value of public opinion. His headline–grabbing predecessor will hover over his administration, missed and remembered by all, while the 300–pound President plods ahead, sound but unsung.

23 MARCH 1909
Life/Customs In order to give Taft a fair chance at the presidency, the energetic Mr. Roosevelt undertakes a scientific expedition to Africa. The Smithsonian Institution agrees to sponsor the expedition and *Scribner's* will pay $50,000 for a description of his year. Roosevelt sails with his son and they will bag some 3000 large game, which they duly bring back stuffed for the Natural History Museum. Upon his return, Roosevelt will be given a hero's welcome by New York City. His popularity is undimmed, and spells trouble for the Republican Party.

JULY 27, 1909

WILLIAM HOWARD TAFT, 1857-1930

William Howard Taft once wrote, "Politics, when I am in it, makes me sick." Nonetheless, he came to be President of the United States, which post he endured as best he could for four years before finally settling down in the job he had wanted in the first place, Chief Justice of the Supreme Court. Taft was born in Cincinnati, Ohio, on September 15, 1857. After studies at Yale and the Cincinnati Law School he was admitted to the bar in 1880; he practiced law for a few years before becoming a superior court judge. President Harrison named him solicitor general in 1890, and in 1892 he returned to the bench as a circuit court judge.

In 1900 Taft began a highly successful four-year appointment as civil governor of the Philippines, with the mission of moving the colony toward self-rule. When Taft's acquaintance Theodore Roosevelt became president on the assassination of McKinley, the two men became close friends and political partners; soon Taft was Roosevelt's hand-picked, albeit reluctant, successor and, equally reluctantly, his secretary of war. With Roosevelt's popularity behind him, Taft rolled over William Jennings Bryan to become President in 1909.

But imposing as he was physically—the heaviest President ever—Taft lacked the political weight to carry forward the bold progressive programs of his predecessor; he often fumbled in mediating between the conservative and liberal wings of his party. In time Taft was abandoned by Roosevelt, who began planning to retake the presidency. Nonetheless, Taft's tenure did accomplish much trustbusting and some vital legislation, creating the parcel post system and overseeing the constitutional amendments for popular election of senators and a federal income tax.

By the 1912 Republican convention the two old allies were enemies, but the conservatives managed to nominate Taft over Roosevelt, who then ran on a third-party ticket, split the vote, and ensured the election of Woodrow Wilson. Finally, in 1921, President Harding appointed Taft to the job he had always wanted, Chief Justice. He thus became the only man to serve both in that office and as President, remaining on the Court until his death in 1930.

ADMIRAL ROBERT PEARY, 1856-1920

Pioneer explorer of Greenland and the Arctic, Robert Peary was denied his life's dream by a quirk of fate, but he would be remembered as the man who perhaps *should* have been the first to reach the North Pole. Peary was born in Cresson, Pennsylvania, on May 6, 1856; after graduating from Bowdoin College with an engineering degree in 1877, he became a navy engineer. Fascinated with the continent of Greenland, he went there in 1886; he and a partner, along with native carriers, made a difficult reconnaissance of the interior which fired his ambition to be first to cross the continent. But in 1889 this was achieved by a Norwegian, and Peary was for the first time scooped by fate.

Peary's Greenland expedition set off in 1891, making a difficult and important study of the continent which included a 1300-mile sled journey to the northernmost extent of the ice cap. With the acclaim this journey brought him, Peary turned his attention to the North Pole. He mounted a series of expeditions beginning in 1893, all of which failed to reach the Pole but each of which represented a gain in planning, knowledge and, not least, his own determination and endurance.

In 1908, now 52, Peary set out on what he knew was his last chance. He and his men, including a crew of Eskimos, used native dress and dogsleds as the most effective way of traveling and surviving. On April 7, 1908 Peary, a black assistant, Matthew Henson, and four Eskimos became, they were sure, the first human beings to stand on the North Pole. But on their return to civilization in September, they learned to their dismay that a former associate, Dr. Frederick A. Cook, had reached the Pole with a small group of Eskimos nearly a year earlier. It was a terrible blow to Peary, whose ambitions were as much personal as scientific.

The next few months saw a nasty public debate in which each party tried to discredit the other. Eventually both claims were validated by the scientific community, who lauded Peary's meticulous study of the area. Peary retired with the rank of rear admiral in 1911. He died in 1920, among the most famous of second-place finishers.

6 APRIL 1909
Life/Customs Robert E. Peary reaches latitude 90 degrees north, better known as the North Pole. Peary leaves the advance base with 18 companions, four of whom are Eskimos and one of whom is a black, Matthew Henson.

9 APRIL 1909
National Congress passes the Payne–Aldrich tariff bill. It is another high–tariff act which brings no relief to the country. Taft signs it with no sign of disapproval, and six weeks later, with clear lack of political savvy, claims that it is the best tariff bill ever passed by Congress. Although Taft will sponsor much legislation dear to Progressive hearts, this lack of political tact helps to lose him the liberal support of his party.

22 MAY 1909
Conservation The President authorizes 700,000 acres of land in Washington, Montana and Idaho to be opened to settlers.

1 JUNE 1909
Black Experience W.E.B. Du Bois founds the National Association for the Advancement of Colored People. The group is in direct opposition to Booker T. Washington's policy of restraint. Harvard–educated Du Bois advocates equality and equal opportunity for blacks, both intellectually and economically.

12 JULY 1909
National Congress proposes the 16th Amendment which would authorize an income tax.

27 JULY 1909
Transportation Orville Wright, who has been making thousands of flights, makes a new flight–duration record of 1 hour, 1 minute and 40 seconds. Meanwhile, two days before, the French aviator Louis Blériot has flown across the English Channel and is the first person to travel to England other than by sea. Although flying is capturing the public imagination, the first commercially built plane is manufactured only this year, by Herring–Curtis's Company, and

417

EXPANDING RESOURCES 1901-1945

sold to the New York Aeronautical Society. In three years only five planes will be sold.

27 SEPTEMBER 1909

Conservation President Taft puts aside 3,000,000 acres of oil–rich public land for conservation purposes. (The land includes Teapot Dome, Wyoming.) Though Taft follows Roosevelt's conservation policies with energy, he gets no public acknowledgement for his work.

13 NOVEMBER 1909

Industry In a continuing series of coalmine disasters, 259 miners are killed in an explosion at the St. Paul mine in Cherry, Illinois. Mine disasters reach their high number mostly through lack of safeguards in handling explosives, but also through lack of needed safety features. In the past five years there have been 84 catastrophes, with 2494 miners killed. In one month in 1907, 702 people died from mine accidents.

OTHER EVENTS OF 1909

Industry A major advance in plastic manufacturing is the production of bakelite, a process which was discovered earlier by Leo H. Baekeland.

Life/Customs W. C. Handy writes a campaign song for Boss Crump of Memphis, Tennessee. The song is the first blues to be written down, and will later be known as "Memphis Blues." Meanwhile "Buddy" Bolden, the famous New Orleans jazz musician, is put into an insane asylum. His band, which includes among other famous jazz artists Sidney Bechet and Joe "King" Oliver, will be taken over by cornetist Freddie Keppard.

7 JANUARY 1910

Conservation After a special congressional committee has vindicated Secretary of the Interior Richard A. Ballinger, Taft dismisses his accuser, Gifford Pinchot. Pinchot has been head of the Forest Service for some years, is a close friend of Roosevelt, and has been instrumental in getting Roosevelt's conservation measures started. In his zealous crusade for the preservation of natural resources, he has accused Ballinger of giving away part of the nation's land to a Morgan–Guggenheim syndicate. Since Taft does not wish to handle the delicate matter himself, it goes to Congress where it merely dredges up unwanted headlines. Pinchot is helped by the able Louis D. Brandeis and wins the battle of the newspapers, but Ballinger is not found to have done any wrong. Once again Taft loses, the public deciding that, in any case, he has not done as well as Roosevelt in the conservation of public lands. The record shows that Taft was the first to reserve oil–rich public lands including the notorious Teapot Dome lands which will feature later in public scandals during the Harding administration. Taft has gotten Congressional authority to reserve coal lands, and establishes a much–needed Bureau of Mines.

6 FEBRUARY 1910

Ideas/Beliefs The Boy Scouts of America are chartered in Washington, D.C., by William D. Boyce, who gets the idea from the English Boy Scouts established by Sir Robert Baden–Powell.

19 MARCH 1910

National Congress reorganizes its Committee on Rules in a successful attempt to liberate it from the firm hand of archconservative Speaker "Uncle" Joe Cannon. Henceforward the committee members will be elected by the House rather than appointed by the Speaker. The move has been undertaken by "insurgent" Republicans and Democrats after Cannon has rammed the Payne–Aldrich Tariff Bill through Congress, allowing 847 amendments which raised tariffs while withstanding the extreme pressure from the Progressives to liberalize them. Now Cannon is bypassed since he may no longer appoint, and the Speaker is ruled ineligible for membership on this committee.

26 MARCH 1910

Immigration An amendment to the Immigration Act of 1907 makes it no longer possible to admit criminals, paupers, anarchists and diseased persons into the United States. Some countries have been scouring jails and asylums and officially sending the inmates over to the U.S.

18 APRIL 1910

Ideas/Beliefs Suffragists are getting more numerous and more likely to be heard. Petitioning Congress for the vote, a vociferous group brings 500,000 names to their representatives. Grover Cleveland, writing earlier in the *Ladies' Home Journal*, fails to endear himself to the ladies when he states, as if he has a means of knowing: "Sensible and responsible women do not want to vote. The relative positions to be assumed by man and woman in the working out of our civilization were assigned long ago by a higher intelligence."

16 MAY 1910

National The Bureau of Mines is set up as part of the Department of the Interior.

18 JUNE 1910

National Congress passes the Mann–Elkins Act. It is Taft's major contribution to much–needed railroad reform. The Interstate Commerce Act and the Hepburn Act had both begun to tackle the diseased transportation network so vital to the vast nation. However there are still enormous combines which are draining the companies. The interlocking directorates, overtly engaged in political corruption, are matters of public concern. The Mann–Elkins Act proposes to give the Interstate Commerce Commission power to bring the railroads within the embrace of the law. The act sets up a Commerce Court consisting of five judges to hear only appeals from the Commission. The Commission itself is empowered to suspend rate raises for up to 10 months while it conducts an investigation on the need for the raise. Most important, the Commission can begin judicial proceedings against a railroad, not needing the Attorney General to initiate action. The Commission's jurisdiction is also extended to include telegraph and telephone companies.

25 JUNE 1910

National Congress establishes the postal savings system in response to public demand. The public has little faith in savings banks. The new system will pay two percent interest.

The same day Congress adopts the Publicity Act which requires representatives to report campaign contributions.

The Mann Act is adopted by Congress as a weapon to stop the importation of European girls to work in American bordellos. The Act is known as the "white slave traffic act" and prohibits the transportation of women across state lines for immoral purposes.

31 AUGUST 1910

National Beginning in August, Roosevelt has made a 5000–mile speaking tour of 16 states. Ostensibly it is non–political; however, the split between himself and Taft has widened and the Progressive Movement is anxious to induct him into their camp. At Osawatomie, Kansas, Roosevelt makes an important political speech, outlining his views. In it he advocates, in his famous phrase, "a square deal." Under the banner of what he names the New Nationalism he calls for fair play before the law, but additionally points out the need for "having those rules changed so as to work for a more substantial equality of opportunity and reward." He advocates regulation of the political activities of corporations whose current practices are distorting the moral fiber of the country. He advocates graduated income tax and inheritance taxes; he points out the need for federal regulation of labor, especially as regards women and children, but also the need for workmen's compensation legislation. He sees a place for a tariff commission made up of experts, and, of course, advocates a continuation of sound conservation measures, a policy which has always been dear to his heart. Says Roosevelt with his characteristic combination of bombast and perspicacity: "I stand for the square deal; property shall be the servant and not the master of the commonwealth." Roosevelt does not mention Taft, who is angered by the speech. Taft's own record on trust action, following in Roosevelt's pioneering footsteps, is an outstanding 67 bills and indictments in four years. Under his administration the Standard Oil Company will be dissolved and the Tobacco Trust broken up. Taft contemptuously comments on Roosevelt's speech that if they were to remove his skull they would find only "1912" inside. However, the speech will be a rallying cry for the Progressive Movement. And when the present leader of the insurgents, Robert La Follette, becomes sick, Roosevelt will quite naturally take his place.

8 NOVEMBER 1910

National For the first time since 1894 the country returns a Democratic Congress. It also sees the first socialist ever to sit in Congress, Victor L. Berger. In Duchess County, N.Y., young Franklin Delano Roosevelt is elected to the state senate.

21 JANUARY 1911

National Senator Robert La Follette helps to found the National Progressive Republican League to promote more responsive government at all levels. Senator Jonathon Bourne of Oregon is made president. The organization proposes to attract the men who find the Republican Party in the grip of overly conservative leaders like Aldrich and Cannon, and hopes to draw "insurgents" from both parties, in effect creating a third force in politics. The new League advocates the initiative, referendum and recall; direct primaries and direct election of delegates to conventions; and, naturally, more and stronger Progressive legislation. However, while the move tends to gather the Progressives together into one camp, it loses its leader when La Follette collapses on a speaking tour in February. Foundering, eyes will turn hopefully to the energetic Roosevelt, who declares: "My hat is in the ring." "Political emotionalists and neurotics," snorts Taft, his break with his mentor Roosevelt widening every day.

EXPANDING RESOURCES 1901-1945

As Wisconsin governor and U.S. Senator, Robert La Follette was among the most fiery and uncompromising of the progressive Republican reformers around the turn of the century. La Follette was born in Primrose, Wisconsin, on June 14, 1855. After graduating from the University of Wisconsin he studied law and was admitted to the bar in 1880; at that time he married another lawyer, Belle Case, who was his lifelong partner and advisor. After holding several local Wisconsin offices he was elected for three terms, beginning in 1885, in the U.S. House, where he was a competent and somewhat conservative Representative. Defeated in 1891, he spent the next two years in revising his political and social ideas until he had become a thorough progressive.

It took La Follette many years of Herculean labor to achieve his goal of the governorship, which he finally won in 1900. He immediately began to work for his programs—tax reform, direct-primary elections, and state control of the railroads—with a hostile legislature. After much campaigning, he got enough power in the legislature to enact his pathbreaking reforms, which came to be known as the "Wisconsin idea." The next step was the U.S. Senate, to which he was elected in 1905. In the Senate La Follette once again faced an uphill battle, and he pursued it tenaciously. Eventually the reforms he had created in Wisconsin appeared, due largely to his efforts, on the national scene—federal regulatory commissions, direct-primary elections, and the national income tax. Eventually he became dissatisfied with the pace of his own party's most visible progressive, Theodore Roosevelt, but his 1912 challenge to Roosevelt for the Presidential nomination came to naught.

La Follette was often supportive of the Wilson Presidency, but he broke with Wilson when it came to war with Germany; many of his constituents had German ancestry. After the war he joined with the isolationists in rejecting the League of Nations. In 1924 he ran as a progressive independent for the presidency, receiving almost 5 million votes. La Follette was then at the peak of his popularity, but the incessant struggles of his life had caught up with him, and he died in the summer of 1925.

7 MARCH 1911
International The United States orders 20,000 troops to the Mexican border. On November 20, 1910 revolution broke out against Dictator Porfirio Diaz. Diaz has been carving up the country for his friends, creating conditions for the poor as harsh as in any country in the world. Taft is not prepared to look beneath the surface and holds Diaz in esteem for his ability to keep "law and order." Taft writes that his respect for Diaz is occasioned also "for the reason that we have two billions American capital in Mexico that will be greatly endangered if Diaz were to die." Despite this lack of support from its neighbor, the Mexican revolution brings to power a gentle liberal named Francisco Madero. In subsequent efforts to keep the *status quo ante*, American diplomat Henry Lane Wilson helps the ruthless General Victoriano Huerta, friend of the landowners, to stage a coup d'etat. In 1913, Madero will be killed and Mexico left in subjection to Huerta, whom one historian calls "a super–gangster."

1 MAY 1911
National In *United States v. Grimaud*, the Supreme Court finds that the Federal Government, by reason of "administrative discretion," has authority over forest reserves. The Court witholds outright delegation of legislative power, but in effect takes overall authority away from the States.

15 MAY 1911
National The Supreme Court finds the Standard Oil Company in "unreasonable" restraint of trade. A new judicial principle, "the rule of reason," is articulated in this case.

29 MAY 1911
National In *United States v. American Tobacco Company*, the Supreme Court finds the American Tobacco Company violates the Sherman Anti–trust Act. However under the new principle of "rule of reason," the Court orders it reorganized rather than dissolved.

22 AUGUST 1911
National President Taft vetoes statehood for Arizona because it will permit recall of judges. Taft, a man of the law himself, feels this to be a threat to the judiciary. Arizona quietly removes the provision, at which point it is duly admitted to the Union. Safely in, the young state adopts recall of judges.

16 OCTOBER 1911
National The first National Conference of Progressive Republicans holds its convention in Chicago. Robert La Follette is nominated for president. The split between Taft and Roosevelt has become irrevocable, foundering on the unlikely shoal of an anti–trust suit. Taft's Attorney General has gone after the giant United States Steel Corporation in an effort to force it to disgorge some of its holdings, among which is the Tennessee Coal and Iron Company. Roosevelt himself had allowed the huge steel corporation to acquire this company. Roosevelt's enemies feel he may have sold out, or has been a fool at best. Roosevelt asks in exasperation what is gained "by breaking up a huge industrial organization which has not offended otherwise than by its size." He articulates the prevailing view that comes to dominate American society, that morality must be cast anew and new legislation is required to meet the new conditions.

OTHER EVENTS OF 1911
Industry In 1899 Clyde J. Coleman invented the electric self–starter. By February 1911 it has been perfected by Charles F. Kettering and is now demonstrated by General Motors. It will open a new era for the automobile.

6 JANUARY 1912
National New Mexico joins the Union as the 47th State.

12 JANUARY 1912
Labor Workers strike against sweatshop conditions

Strikers protest sweatshop conditions in the mills of Lawrence, Massachusetts.

in the mills of Lawrence, Massachusetts. Workers are protesting a cut in wages under a new law which has limited working hours. The strike will last two months. The militant Industrial Workers of the World will use the violent struggle to move into the East.

15 APRIL 1912

Transportation The steamship *Titanic* strikes an iceberg as it steams at full speed through dangerous waters. Because there are not enough lifeboats for all passengers, 1502 lives are lost at sea. Later this year the Federal Government will order all ocean–going vessels to contain enough lifeboats for all passengers. Since the first wireless message, which has been sent from New York to Chicago in 1909, the Federal Government has already ordered steamships to have radio equipment aboard for safety's sake.

17 MAY 1912

National The Socialist Party holds its National Convention at Indianapolis, Indiana, and nominates Eugene V. Debs for president and Emil Seidel of Wisconsin for vice–president.

5 JUNE 1912

International To protect American interests in Cuba, the United States sends marines. This is a deviation from Taft's new policy toward South America which has come to be called Dollar Diplomacy: Taft has said he wishes to substitute "dollars for bullets"

in his dealings with Latin America, with American capital bringing healthy reform to corrupt governments. The effect is too often to stabilize harsh and dishonest administrations and create long–lasting animosity toward the United States.

18 JUNE 1912

National The Republican National Convention is held in Chicago. The party is badly split between Taft, about whom the Conservatives are rallying, and Roosevelt, who is leading the Progressives in the absence of La Follete. The Taft forces manage to squeeze out 200 Roosevelt–leaning delegates and under the firm hand of party regulars such as Elihu Root and Warren Harding, the convention nominates Taft for a second term. Roosevelt tells his followers not to vote and they stalk off to form what at first is called the Bull Moose Party, in honor of Roosevelt's much used phrase "I am as strong as a Bull Moose." He tells his followers that he will accept their nomination for president if they will give it to him at a formal convention of the Progressive Party. The long–term result of the walkout is to drain most liberal elements out of the Republican Party.

2 JULY 1912

National Now that Roosevelt has split the Republicans, national interest focuses on the outcome of the Democratic Party's convention. Although Bryan still has a firm hold on his party, on the 46th ballot, a

EXPANDING RESOURCES 1901-1945

weary Bryan tosses his votes to New Jersey Governor Woodrow Wilson. Wilson had been president of Princeton University but tangled with wealthy alumni and retired. He has been taken up by New Jersey politicans anxious for a figurehead to mask their odoriferous ways. Wilson not only wins the governorship but then tackles New Jersey and attracts a national reputation through his clean and effective administration. The Democrats finally drop their obsession with silver and adopt policies indistinguishable from those of the Progressive Movement. Thomas R. Marshall of Indiana is nominated vice–president.

5 AUGUST 1912

National A third party is formed by Republican "insurgents" who follow Roosevelt off the convention floor. With evangelistical fervor, the party nominates Roosevelt for president. Hiram Johnson of California is nominated for vice–president. Johnson goes to the convention with a large sign reading:

I want to be a Bull Moose
And with the Bull Moose stand.
With antlers on my forehead
And a big stick in my hand.

24 AUGUST 1912

National The much–hoped–for parcel post system is authorized by Congress. It will go into service the following year.

4 OCTOBER 1912

National About to make a speech in Milwaukee, Roosevelt is shot from 6 feet away by a fanatic. The bullet slows as it goes through an overcoat, a glasses case, a folded (in this case fortunately long) speech, before penetrating to the lung. Although the wound was serious enough, still Roosevelt insists upon giving his speech before being taken to the hospital. The melodramatic gesture captures headlines as all his actions still tend to do. The tough outdoorsman will be well in two weeks. However he will never again be center stage. He has successfully articulated and acted upon the demands for social justice rising from the country in much the same egocentric, arrogant and high–handed manner used by his great antagonists. He has ably served to usher in a new age, ironically one that will have no place for such as himself.

5 NOVEMBER 1912

National Woodrow Wilson wins the election by a landslide 435 electoral votes to Roosevelt's 88 and Taft's 8. The popular vote is 6,293,454 for Wilson, 4,119,538 for Roosevelt and 3,484,980 for Taft, demonstrating that the Republicans might have won had they not split. Eugene Debs garners close to a million votes.

25 FEBRUARY 1913

National The 16th Amendment to the Constitution is adopted by the nation. The Supreme Court has earlier found that an income tax whose monies are not then reapportioned to the States is unconstitutional. The

---

J. PIERPONT MORGAN, 1837-1913

The piercing eyes, imposing nose, and imperious figure of J. Pierpont Morgan are still the popular image of the big-stakes banker. In his own time and after he was considered the prince of American financiers. Morgan was born into a prominent family of international bankers in Hartford, Connecticut, on April 17, 1837. After schooling in Boston, Switzerland, and Germany, he first worked for his father's bank in London. He shortly returned to New York and rapidly rose in financial circles. In 1895 he founded J.P. Morgan and Company, which was to become one of the premier banking houses in the world.

During the Civil War Morgan's house was very active, finally becoming dominant in government financing. But it was in the 1880s, when he turned his attention to railroads, that Morgan became widely known to the public. By the end of the century he had helped reorganize, and become the dominant power in, most of the railroad empires in America. In 1895 he formed a syndicate to bail out the national Treasury during a gold-reserve depletion crisis; though the syndicate resolved the crisis, its terms were widely perceived to be extortionary. It seemed to many that the government was at the mercy of private financiers.

Next came the turn of the steel industry. Morgan bought out a number of faltering companies and in 1901 formed United States Steel, the largest corporation in the world. By then Morgan dominated an incredibly far-reaching financial empire that included railroads, marine operations, steel companies, International Harvester, General Electric, American Telephone and Telegraph and many others. Altogether, Morgan and ten associates held 72 directorships in 47 major corporations.

Not surprisingly, the government and public became nervous at this concentration of power. A 1912 congressional investigation probed the extent of Morgan's interests; Morgan firmly, politely, and successfully denied everything, and the investigation led nowhere. He died shortly thereafter in Rome in 1913, leaving a large fortune and an enormous collection of art, manuscripts, and books which now grace the collections of the Metropolitan Museum of Art and the Morgan Library.

Amendment will provide the necessary legal basis for a graduated income tax.

1 MARCH 1913

National In a great victory for the anti–liquor groups led by the Anti–Saloon League, the Webb–Kenyon Interstate Liquor Act is upheld by Congress, overriding a Taft veto. The Act states that it is unlawful to ship liquor into a state which has made its sale illegal. This shores up state authority vis–a–vis the Federal Goverment.

Similarly, in what is known as the Minnesota Rate Cases, the Supreme Court this year validates an order by a state commission which regulates intrastate railroad rates. The Court finds that while Congress has exclusive authority over interstate commerce, a state may act independently as long as it does not act against federal laws. Many consider this a long overdue decision by the Court.

4 MARCH 1913

National The first Democratic President since

Grover Cleveland, Woodrow Wilson, is inaugurated as president. In his inaugural address Wilson says: "We have been proud of our industrial achievements, but we have not hitherto stopped thoughtfully enough to count the human cost, the cost of lives snuffed out, of energies overtaxed and broken, the fearful physical and spiritual cost to the men and women and children upon whom the dead weight and burden of it all has fallen pitilessly the years through. . . . The great government we loved has too often been made use of for private and selfish purposes, and those who used it had forgotten the people. . . . Our cry has been 'Let every man look out for himself, let every generation look out for itself,' while we reared giant machinery which made it impossible that any but those who stood at the levers of control should have a chance to look out for themselves." The speech makes a great impact. Wilson is a reformer, with a solid Democratic House, able to set about his reforms, which would successfully include the hitherto intractable tariff and banking systems before World War would usurp his full attention.

This same day Congress divides the Department of Commerce and Labor into two, giving both Cabinet status.

8 APRIL 1913
National President Wilson goes before a joint session of Congress to deliver a pointed tariff program. He is the first to address Congress in this manner since John Quincy Adams, and immediately gets popular approval. Congress, too, is impressed and predisposed to follow where he leads.

19 APRIL 1913
National Governor Hiram Johnson of California signs into law the Webb Alien Land–Holding Bill which excludes the Japanese from owning land. This will not help international relations and Wilson strenuously objects, as do the Japanese.

31 MAY 1913
National Riding the popular wave for governmental reform, the 17th Amendment is passed, establishing popular election of senators. Until now, senators have been chosen by state legislatures and have been unresponsive to the electorate. This amendment will weaken the state legislatures while strengthening popular control of the Senate.

26 AUGUST 1913
National Keokuk Dam is opened across the Mississippi River. It is the world's largest dam. The dam will serve to control flooding which is causing hardship along many rivers. In March, the Dayton Flood caused some $100,000,000 in damages as it rampaged through the Miami Valley in Ohio, killing at least 400 people on its way. And some 200 more were killed by flooding in Indiana. Later, in October, in Texas, $50,000,000 in damages and some 500 deaths are due to rampaging river waters. Flood control will become a major concern in the 20s as when,

WOODROW WILSON, 1856-1924

The intense and scholarly features of Woodrow Wilson might have belonged to a medieval church philosopher; he was one of the rare U.S. Presidents who possessed genuine idealism, sincere piety, and formidable intellect. Wilson was born in Staunton, Virginia, on December 28, 1856. After studying history at Princeton and law at the University of Virginia, he tried law practice in 1882 but soon gravitated back to his historical interests at Johns Hopkins in Baltimore. He earned his doctorate there and from 1885 held teaching appointments at Bryn Mawr, Wesleyan and finally Princeton. During this period he wrote a number of important books on government.

By the time the presidency of Princeton fell vacant in 1902, Wilson was the clear candidate for the position. His tenure produced a number of far-reaching reforms that resulted in the ascension of Princeton from a tired college to a major institution. But by 1909 Wilson was increasingly stymied by resistance to his reforms; when he was offered a chance at New Jersey's gubernatorial nomination, he took it. He proved to be an able campaigner and was swept into office by a landslide in 1910. As governor he was as effective a reformer as at Princeton, and his triumphs there brought him national attention and a shot at the 1912 Democratic presidential nomination, which he won on the 46th ballot. The campaign pitted Wilson's New Freedom against Theodore Roosevelt's New Nationalism, with incumbent Taft splitting the vote enough to give Wilson the victory. In the first two years of his term, Wilson pushed through all the programs he had promised—tariff reform, the Federal Reserve system, and the Federal Trade Commission. But larger problems were looming overseas. War broke out in Europe in 1914; desperately, Wilson worked for nearly two years to preserve American neutrality and to mediate between the combatant countries. In April 1917, at the beginning of his second term, after a series of German violations of U.S. neutrality, Wilson reluctantly asked for a declaration of war.

Wilson went on to lead the nation through the war. Even before the armistice he began to agitate for a fair and liberal settlement. When the chance came, though, at the Versailles Peace Conference of 1919, Wilson's efforts for an American initiative largely failed, though they won him the Nobel Prize for peace in 1920. Meanwhile, Wilson's idealistic dream of a League of Nations was meeting stiff resistance by isolationists back home. Faced by the impending Senate defeat of American membership in the League, Wilson began a nationwide tour to arouse public support. The tour accomplished little except to ruin his health; after a serious stroke in October 1919, Wilson was incapacitated just when he was most needed. The result was the defeat of the League. The ailing Wilson retired to seclusion in Washington, where he died in 1924. Like most people, he had fallen short of his aspirations, but the sincere vision and the historical implications of his aspirations made their failure more tragic than most.

among other projects, $32,000,000 is spent on five dams across the Miami River.

3 OCTOBER 1913

National Wilson has called Congress into a special session in order to tackle the tariff situation. Forcefully explaining the case, he says: "We must abolish everything that bears even the semblance of privilege or of any kind of artificial advantage and put our business men and producers under the stimulation of a constant necessity to be efficient, economical, enterprising, masters of competitive supremacy, better workers and merchants than any in the world." Congress is inspired and enacts the Underwood–Simmons Tariff Act, the first tariff reform since the Civil War. Duties are brought down on 958 articles, including food–stuffs, clothing and raw materials. Rates on cotton are cut 50 percent and on woolens over 50 percent. Congress will enact the graduated income tax law to make up the difference in revenues.

10 OCTOBER 1913

International Wilson presses an electric button in the White House setting off an explosion of the Gamoa Dike, which thus opens the Panama Canal for shipping.

10 DECEMBER 1913

International Elihu Root wins the 1912 Nobel Peace Prize for his work as Secretary of War.

23 DECEMBER 1913

Finance Wilson proceeds with the reform in banking that has been initiated by Roosevelt in 1907, and gets Congress to pass the Owen–Glass Federal Reserve Act, which provides a bank note currency which is more responsive to business requirements than heretofore. The Act creates 12 regional Federal Reserve Banks, and all national banks are forced to join the system by depositing from one half to two–thirds of their legal reserves in a common account. The Reserve Banks are pools open to member banks anywhere in the land. The Federal Reserve Banks deal only with the Treasury or with member banks. A

PANAMA CANAL

One of the most grandiose engineering feats of all time was construction of the Panama Canal begun in 1907 and finished only seven years later in 1914.

Once underway, Canal construction proceeded smoothly, but a long history preceded its completion. As early as 1523 Charles V of Spain, convinced that there was no natural waterway to the Pacific, made the first suggestion to build a canal. Ineffectual interest and effort continued into the 19th century until Spanish rule over Central American countries ended. In 1880, the Frenchman Ferdinand de Lesseps convened an international congress to draw up plans and to raise necessary loans. He managed to raise some $80,000,000 but corruption and extravagance doomed the project which lay dormant until the energetic President Roosevelt perceived how such a mighty undertaking would redound to American credit.

"Speak softly and carry a big stick," Roosevelt had been fond of saying, and in this instance the big stick was more than evident. With tacit American approval, Panama was induced to secede from Nicaragua, taking with it the most promising route across the Isthmus. The new republic was recognized with unseemly haste by the United States and a treaty for the canal was immediately forthcoming.

Built by the U.S. Army Corps of Engineers under the supervision of the competent Colonel G.W. Goethals, the Canal cost $366,650,000. Starting from the Atlantic side it runs for 11½ miles due south to Gatun Lake and then unexpectedly turns southeast, proceeding to the Pacific coast line. Its total length is 40.27 miles. Although much of the Panama Canal is at sea level, for 24 miles the Canal crosses the 164 square mile Lake Gatun. Ships are lifted 85 feet to its channel by a series of locks.

When the first ocean steamer passed through the Canal on August 3, 1914, a search that had lasted for centuries was ended. Even though it had had to be blasted out of bedrock, a waterway between the Atlantic and Pacific Oceans had at last been created.

Federal Reserve Board is created to manage the new network.

OTHER EVENTS OF 1913

Industry Henry Ford adopts the conveyor belt system used by the meat–packers. Putting the idea to work for cars, within 10 years he brings down the price of a Model T from $950 to $290. He also sets an example by paying his men $5 a day when many are making not much more than a week.

Labor About 150,000 garment–workers go on strike. The workers will win reduced hours and recognition of their union, plus an increase in their meager wages.

Life/Customs The glamorous dancing Vernon and Irene Castle make their debut in *The Sunshine Girl*. They capture the imagination of the country for almost a decade.

13 JANUARY 1914

Transportation In the United State Circuit Court the Wright Brothers win an important decision regarding airplane balancing patents. The loser is Glenn Curtiss.

4 FEBRUARY 1914
International Congress confirms George W. Goethals as first governor of the Permanent Civil Government of the Panama Canal Zone.

13 FEBRUARY 1914
Arts/Culture The American Society of Composers, Authors and Publishers, ASCAP, is organized by Victor Herbert and others at New York City. More than a hundred people join and name Herbert director.

9 APRIL 1914
International President Wilson has refused to recognize Huerta as the rightful President of Mexico on the grounds that he has not been elected by the people. When some sailors and officers from the American barge *Dolphin* go ashore at Tampico for supplies, they are promptly arrested, and as promptly released. Unable to leave the incident alone, Admiral Henry Mayo demands not only an apology but a humiliating "salute to the American flag" as well. This last, Dictator Huerta refuses to do and on April 11 breaks off diplomatic relations. There is great pressure from European powers for Wilson to recognize Huerta, since he is a strong ruler and may be able to keep peace, which is threatened by Pancho Villa and Venustiano Carranza. Foreigners, including Americans, are heavily invested in Mexico which is as rich in natural resources as any country in the world.

19 APRIL 1914
International In an uncharacteristically belligerent move, Wilson asks and receives from Congress the authority to use armed force to make Huerta comply to his wishes.

21 APRIL 1914
International The United States Navy is dispatched to Vera Cruz, Mexico and Marines take control of the city. Through this port Germany has been funneling arms for Huerta. Americans lose four men and 20 are wounded. Only the timely intervention of the "ABC Powers,"—the governments of Argentina, Brazil and Chile—as mediators, saves America from getting involved in war. However, stopping supplies for Huerta dries up a strong source of foreign aid and will be a factor in pressuring Huerta to resign and leave the country.

7 MAY 1914
Life/Customs Congress sends Wilson a bill providing that the second Sunday in May be known as Mother's Day. Wilson asks that the public display the flag on that day as a sign of "love and reverence for the mothers."

29 MAY 1914
Arts/Culture Edgar Lee Masters, who will later achieve popular renown through his *Spoon River Anthology*, publishes his first poems: *Reedey's Mirror*. This same year will see publication of Edgar Rice Burroughs' *Tarzan Of The Apes*, the first of his world-

---

HENRY FORD, 1863-1947

The career of Henry Ford was the quintessential success story of American myth: a man of ordinary birth who raised himself by his own bootstraps to a position of wealth and power. It is hard to avoid the conclusion that his greatness and his faults were inseparable: both came from his rugged individualism and his single–minded and intuitive genius as an engineer and industrialist; but it was also these qualities that often made him insensitive, bigoted and reactionary in his dealings with the outside world.

Ford was born to an Irish-American farming family in Greenfield Township, Michigan, on July 30, 1863. He was mechanically proficient as a child and after eight years of schooling became a machinist in various businesses. He moved to Detroit in 1891 to become an engineer with the Edison company; meanwhile, he began experiments with gasoline engines that led to his first—only four horsepower—automobile in 1896 and an improved version in 1899.

Ford founded the Detroit Automobile Company in 1899, his plans already moving toward concepts of mass production and of standardization of design and parts with which he was to revolutionize industry around the world. In 1903 he formed the Ford Motor Company and brought out the Model N. As his business grew he issued a series of popularly-priced designs culminating in 1908 in the innovative Model T, which has been called "the greatest single vehicle in the history of world transportation." Ford built his Model T until 1927; it brought the automobile to the common man and helped to transform the texture of American life.

As the company grew by leaps and bounds, Ford instituted his second profound innovation in 1913-14—the continuously–moving assembly line that changed his output from 248,367 cars in 1913-14 to 2000 cars *per day* in 1916. Soon sensing the dehumanization that threatened his workers, Ford more than doubled their pay in 1915. The acclaim this brought him at the time was later to be forgotten during his brutal struggle against unions; in 1941 Ford became the last major auto company to unionize.

After the 20s the company sank from first place, largely due to Henry Ford's autocratic and conservative control. His efforts in public life were marked by his social provincialism and anti-intellectualism; for example, in the 20s he issued several anti-Semitic diatribes. Ford slipped into retirement in the 40s; but despite the enmity of organized labor he died a popular folk hero in 1947.

---

famous series. And recitation of his own poems brings recognition to Vachel Lindsay whose incantatory *The Congo And Other Poems* is published this year. The power of Robert Frost is recognized when his *North of Boston* is published abroad.

28 JUNE 1914
World War I Archduke Francis Ferdinand, Crown Prince of Austria, is murdered by Gabriel Princips and some Pan–Slav fanatics in Sarajevo. The Austro–Hungarian Government sends an ultimatum to Serbia and five days later declares war. Russia begins to mobilize.

31 JULY 1914
Finance The London Stock Exchange, at this time

the most influential in the world, announces its closing due to war. The United States follows suit and for several weeks all other important exchanges will also close.

1 AUGUST 1914

World War I Germany declares war on Russia. The Kaiser has put his ponderous war machine into high gear and is marching on Belgium, aiming for France.

3 AUGUST 1914

World War I Germany declares war on France.

4 AUGUST 1914

World War I Standing by its treaties, Great Britain declares war on Germany as German troops roll into Belgium.

5 AUGUST 1914

America's Approach to War The United States makes a formal statement to the effect that it will remain neutral in the European wars, but offers its services as mediator in the mushrooming conflict.

This same day the United States signs a treaty with Nicaragua giving Americans the right to build a canal there, plus a 99-year lease on islands and a naval base. The price is $3,000,000. The treaty is the product of what Taft has created and calls Dollar Diplomacy. The policy proposes to substitute dollars for bullets.

6 AUGUST 1914

World War I Austria–Hungary declares war on Russia. The United States proposes that the belligerents stand by the 1901 Declaration of London which states that the open seas are neutral areas and neutral shipping is thus protected. This same day $5,000,000 in gold is shipped to Europe to aid Americans stranded there by war.

10 AUGUST 1914

America's Approach to War George Sylvester Viereck begins publication of his pro–German weekly newspaper, *The Fatherland*.

15 AUGUST 1914

International The Panama Canal is opened to shipping.

Writing to J. P. Morgan, Secretary of State William Jennings Bryan says that loans to belligerents goes against our policy of neutrality. But on October 15, the government declares it will not prohibit shipments of gold or extensions of credits nonetheless. On November 3 the Rockefeller Foundation will send the *Massapequa* loaded with food for Belgium, and the same month the *Jason* carries $3,000,000 in Christmas gifts for war victims.

19 AUGUST 1914

America's Approach to War Wilson proclaims complete neutrality and urges the United States to be "impartial in thought as well as in action . . . neutral

in fact as well as in name." Even Roosevelt, writing next month in *The Outlook* well after Belgium has succumbed, claims the United States has "not the smallest responsibility for Belgium" and he too advises neutrality. However, sentiment soon polarizes into pro–Allies, pro–German or pro–neutral. The pro–Allies side will form the legendary Lafayette Esquadrille of the French Air Force; some young Americans will join either the British Army or the French Foreign Legion and will serve as ambulance drivers in Allied contingents; still other Americans will provide welcome war relief organizations. President Charles W. Eliot of Harvard suggests "an offensive and defensive alliance with the entente powers, including Japan," but he refuses the Ambassadorship to England that might have brought that about sooner. As might be expected, the main body of German–Americans sides with the pacifists to advocate neutrality, and the erstwhile inflammatory Hearst newspapers and the Midwest's influential Chicago *Tribune* do, too. The Irish–Americans are vocally anti–British.

23 AUGUST 1914

World War I Japan declares war on Germany.

26 AUGUST 1914

World War I The Germans rout the Russians at Tannenberg, decisively weakening their importance to Allied victory.

2 SEPTEMBER 1914

America's Approach to War The Treasury Department establishes the Bureau of War Risk Insurance to provide up to $5,000,000 insurance for merchant ships and their crews.

5 SEPTEMBER 1914

America's Approach to War The president orders wireless stations be provided by the Navy for direct transatlantic communications. Wilson will permit German diplomats to use these facilities even if they encode messages. Arrogant German abuse of this naive courtesy on the President's part, later discovered by the British, may well be the decisive factor in Wilson's long delayed decision to go to war.

World War I In one of the most strategic battles of the war, the German juggernaut is stopped dead in its tracks by the French at the Marne. The Kaiser's strategy has been to grasp the entire continent in his iron fist before it can gather its forces, but now this decisive battle forces them to fall back to Aisne and dig trenches and settle down for the horrendous three-year stalemate that results. The Germans will be forced to step up submarine warfare in an attempt to break the British stranglehold on the high seas, thereby drawing the Americans directly into the conflict.

15 SEPTEMBER 1914

World War I The Russians are effectively knocked out of the fight as an important consideration in Allied

FEBRUARY 10, 1915

strategy by the German victory at Masurian.

26 SEPTEMBER 1914
National The Federal Trade Commission is set up to oversee regulation of corporations engaged in interstate commerce. The five-man commission proposes to oversee industrial corporations in a manner similar to that of the Interstate Commerce Commission over railroads.

15 OCTOBER 1914
National America comes of industrial age as the milestone Clayton Anti-trust Act is passed by Congress. Samuel Gompers will call this "labor's charter of freedom." It provides organized labor with the necessary legislation to balance its bargaining power vis-a-vis corporations. Most importantly it exempts unions from anti-trust laws; unions cannot be declared combinations in restraint of trade; the injunction will no longer be permitted to be used against unions; strikes, picketing and boycotting are made legal. Elsewhere in the Act, interlocking directorates are made illegal for corporations as is discrimination in setting prices which would effect a monopoly.

22 OCTOBER 1914
National The Revenue Act passes Congress. It imposes the first income tax on incomes over $3000 to offset loss of tariff money brought about through enactment of the Underwood-Simmons Act of 1913.

2 NOVEMBER 1914
America's Approach to War Great Britain responds to German naval tactics by declaring the entire North Sea a military area. Neutral ships bound for neutral ports will pass at their own risk, subject to search and seizure. Keeping the sea lanes open for commerce is an indispensable aspect of British strategy. The United States has begun to profit from European war needs and is sending cargoes to all belligerents including Germany which is getting its goods funneled through neutral countries. To stop this, on August 20, Britain, in its Order of Council, enlarges the list of goods it unilaterally considers contraband and therefore subject to search and seizure. Britain immediately begins to confiscate the contraband cargoes, although willingly paying for each shipload, and in the process causes no loss of life. British procedures will stand it in good stead with American businessmen who are making a good deal of money out of the war, and appreciate not being drawn into it further. Included in the list is cotton, now used in making munitions. On September 26, Bryan protests the Order in Council, but American leaders are beginning to appreciate the value of lightly leaning on the Allied side and by October 22 formally withdraw the United States' demand that Britain keep to the letter of the Declaration of London. Thereafter, Britain manages to contain the German fleet in harbor and dries to a trickle the flow of goods to the Central Powers. Smarting under the impact of the blockade, the Germans step up their submarine warfare with skillful use of their sinister U-boats. However, still hoping to induce America to come in on the side of the Kaiser, Germany will attack only warships during this first year of conflict.

23 NOVEMBER 1914
International The United States starts to disentangle itself from the Mexican morass by evacuating troops from Vera Cruz, Mexico. During the war, the Germans will play heavily on Mexican anti-American sentiment, funneling millions of dollars into the country trying to foment revolution there, and later, in the Zimmerman telegram debacle, even attempting to manipulate an outright declaration of war against the United States.

26 JANUARY 1915
Conservation Pursuing Roosevelt's policies, Congress establishes Rocky Mountain National Park. Roosevelt is never quite as magnanimous after his presidency as before and during, and never gives Taft nor Wilson credit for their labor and conservation initiatives.

28 JANUARY 1915
National Wilson vetoes a bill which would require immigrants to pass a literacy test.

The same day Congress passes legislation authorizing the United States Coast Guard. It will be charged with preventing contraband trade, will assist persons and vessels in distress and generally be useful to all maritime shipping.
America's Approach to War The *William P. Frye* with its cargo of wheat for Britain is torpedoed in the South Atlantic by the German Navy.

30 JANUARY 1915
America's Approach to War The good friend of Wilson, Colonel Edward M. House, sails to Europe on the Lusitania to try to mediate a peace settlement. Both sides still feel that they can get what they want and are in no mood to settle the conflict so quickly. Germany, for one, wants Poland and Belgium, and makes no bones about wishing to have the rest of Europe under its mailed fist. Its is becoming slowly but increasingly apparent that the Allies represent the civilized values dear to American hearts.

4 FEBRUARY 1915
America's Approach to War In retaliation for the blockade of its ports, Germany proclaims a war zone around the British Isles to offset their advantage of supply by neutral vessels.

10 FEBRUARY 1915
America's Approach to War Wilson warns Germany that the United States will hold it "to a strict accountability" for "property endangered or lives lost." German submarine warfare is taking a serious toll of neutral shipping, including American. German U-boat captains are in a predicament because they

cannot safely surface to follow the old rules of sea warfare which require giving the enemy ship a chance to get its crew and passengers into lifeboats, because the fragile U–boats are vulnerable themselves to small–caliber deck guns. Nonetheless, the president, in spite of pressure from the pacifists to go easy, will continue to hold Germany responsible for loss of life and property. Wilson is proceeding cautiously, but seems to be preparing the ground that should America's entry into the war become inevitable, it will be on the Allied side.

11 MARCH 1915
America's Approach to War Britain declares a blockade of all German ports. The British will stop all German vessels before they reach the North Sea or the English Channel.

30 MARCH 1915
America's Approach to War Wilson protests the blockade of German ports. His concern is for American shipping and neutral vessels destined for neutral ports. However since most of these vessels are carrying cargoes which will ultimately find their way to Germany, Britain refuses to budge.

4 APRIL 1915
America's Approach to War Germany makes a vigorous protest to the United States, claiming it must insist that Britain lift its blockade and permit America to proceed with its trade with Germany.

30 APRIL 1915
Conservation Out of 9481 acres in Teapot Dome, Wyoming, Wilson creates Naval Petroleum Reserve No. 3.

1 MAY 1915
America's Approach to War Without warning, the American tanker *Gulflight* is sunk by a German U–boat. Germany quickly offers to make reparations and promises not to attack again without warning, unless the enemy ship tries to escape. Germany refuses to abandon submarine warfare, which though decidedly dangerous, is the only maritime warfare it can successfully carry out.

7 MAY 1915
Approach to War The great ocean–going British passenger ship *Lusitania* is sunk without warning, losing 1198 of its 1924 passengers. There are 114 Americans aboard and the tragedy strikes home. According to the Germans, the vessel is carrying munitions, although the British deny this. Roosevelt calls it "murder on the high seas." The German Ambassador, Count von Bernstorff, had issued a warning on May 1, printed in the New York newspapers, that it was unwise to travel into a war zone on vessels carrying cargoes vital to the Allies.

10 MAY 1915
America's Approach to War Count von Bernstorff offers his condolences for the tragic loss of life upon the sinking of the *Lusitania*. The apology serves to rub salt in the wounds. However, not to be stampeded into war, Wilson in an ill–timed speech in Philadelphia says: "There is such a thing as a man being too proud to fight. There is such a thing as a nation being so right that it does not need to convince others that it is right."

13 MAY 1915
America's Approach to War Secretary of State Bryan sends the first *Lusitania* note to Germany. In it the United States demands disavowal of the attack on the *Lusitania*. Germany must also make immediate reparations. The note adds ominously that America will omit no word or deed which may be necessary to uphold the rights of its citizens anywhere in the world. Incredibly, Bryan then proceeds to tell the Austrian Ambassador that the note "means no harm, but had to be written in order to pacify excited public opinion. The Berlin Government therefore need not feel itself injured, but need only make suitable concessions if it desires to put an end to the dispute." The Bryan dispatch is soon in the hands of Foreign Secretary Zimmerman who has it by the time the American Ambassador appears to proffer the antagonistic missive. Zimmerman shows Bryan's dispatch and claims to call the bluff. In the aftermath, Bryan is forced to resign and the Germans never do disavow the attack or make reparations.

24 MAY 1915
Finance The Pan–American Financial Conference begins in Washington, D.C. under the chairmanship of Secretary of the Treasury William G. McAdoo.

8 JUNE 1915
America's Approach to War Bryan resigns on the grounds that as a pacifist he cannot sign the strong second *Lusitania* note which has been written by Wilson and other members of the Cabinet.

9 JUNE 1915
America's Approach to War Wilson sends his second *Lusitania* note. In it he demands an end to German procrastination over the sinking of the unarmed passenger vessel. Germany must make reparations and "prevent the recurrence of anything so obviously subversive of the principles of warfare." Wilson refuses to recognize the previously non–existent "war zone" set up by Germany around the British Isles. Wilson then goes on to say: "the lives of noncombatants cannot lawfully or rightfully be put in jeopardy by the capture or destruction of an unresisting merchantman." Bryan has strongly objected to this part saying: "a ship carrying contraband should not rely upon passengers to protect her from an attack—it would be like putting women and children in front of the army." (Sixty–three infants have drowned in the sinking of the *Lusitania*.) Germany will not give the asked–for pledges, but claims it will allow Americans to travel in well–marked neutral ships.

Last voyage of the *Lusitania*.

17 JUNE 1915

National The League to Enforce Peace is organized at Independence Hall in Philadelphia. William Howard Taft is made president. The League is a prototype of the later League of Nations, a natural idea for Americans to develop since they have successfully achieved their own union of states. It is not hard for American visionaries to imagine the formula working as well in Europe, with America included.

2 JULY 1915

America's Approach to War Erich Muenter, a German instructor at Cornell University, manages to explode a bomb in the U.S. Senate reception room. The next day he shoots J.P. Morgan for representing the British Government in war contract negotiations. Muenter is caught this time and jailed, but commits suicide three days later. The incident serves to excite war nerves.

15 JULY 1915

America's Approach to War Making a trivial mistake, Dr. Heinrich F. Albert, head of the German propaganda in the United States, leaves a briefcase on a subway in New York. A Secret Service agent retrieves it and proves the existence of an extensive espionage and subversive activities network spread across the country. German consuls, embassy staff, officials of the Hamburg–American Steamship Line and many German–Americans are implicated. (George Sylvester Viereck is among them.) Secretary of the Treasury William G. McAdoo releases the contents to the New York *World* and rouses the country to the ambiguities inherent in the neutralist position.

Germany agrees to make reparations for its U-boat attack on the American vessel *Nebraskan*.

21 JULY 1915

National The Supreme Court finds that the so-called "grandfather clause" added to the constitutions of Oklahoma and Maryland is unconstitutional. The clause states that anyone whose grandfather did not vote in an election cannot now vote. Aimed primarily at blacks, it cuts into immigrants' votes too.

America's Approach to War Wilson sends his third *Lusitania* note. In it he warns that future infringement of American rights will be deemed "deliberately unfriendly." The stand serves to steer the ship of state into dangerous currents which make war almost inevitable.

25 JULY 1915

America's Approach to War A German U-boat sinks the American vessel *Leelanaw* off the coast of Scotland. The ship is carrying flax.

27 JULY 1915

International Bringing nations ever closer together, wireless communications are set up between Japan and the United States.

28 JULY 1915

International Beginning a 19-year occupation, U.S. Marines land in Haiti to snuff out a revolution. Unlike some other American occupations, this one does not lead to better administrative arrangements nor long-lasting changes.

5 AUGUST 1915

International The Latin–American Conference meets to discuss conditions in Mexico which are quite unstable. Suspicion of American Dollar Diplomacy is strong, conditions among the poor are appalling and corruption is widespread. Pancho Villa has been causing havoc in the Mexican countryside. Argentina, Brazil, Bolivia, Chile, Guatemala and Uruguay join the United States to debate what can be done.

10 AUGUST 1915

America's Approach to War General Leonard Wood sets up a military training camp in Plattsburg, New York. It will begin training of civilians. This is the first of many such "Plattsburgs" which are set up on the initiative of Grenville Clark, Theodore Roosevelt Jr. and others. The first camp will train 1200 volunteers who will pay for their own travel expenses, food and uniforms. Wilson will not endorse the idea of "preparedness" until November 4, while Bryan and La Follette actively campaign against the policy, knowing that there is no longer a chance that America will come in on other than the Allied side. By the summer of 1916, 16,000 men will be in unofficial military training.

15 OCTOBER 1915

America's Approach to War United States bankers arrange a much-needed $500,000,000 loan to the British and French.

19 OCTOBER 1915

International Thanks to the good offices of the Latin–American Conference, Wilson is brought to recognize Carranza as President of Mexico. Carranza has objected to having to include revolutionaries Zapata and Villa in negotiations and thus irritated Wilson. But Carranza will not be able to police his land and Pancho Villa will continue to create a serious disturbance along the border areas.

7 NOVEMBER 1915
America's Approach to War Carrying 27 American passengers, the Italian liner *Ancona* is sunk without warning by an Austrian submarine.

25 NOVEMBER 1915
Regional The almost dormant Ku Klux Klan is revived in Atlanta, Georgia, by Colonel William J. Simmons.

30 NOVEMBER 1915
America's Approach to War Sabotage is suspected in the explosion at the DuPont munitions plant in Wilmington, Delaware.

4 DECEMBER 1915
America's Approach to War "To get the boys out of the trenches by Christmas," Henry Ford fits out a "peace ship." Pacifist Ford manages to make the gesture look slightly ludicrous by the time it is ready to leave, and no one of importance agrees to take part.

7 DECEMBER 1915
America's Approach to War Wilson asks for a standing army of 142,000 and a reserve of 400,000.

10 DECEMBER 1915
Transportation The one millionth Ford motorcar moves down the assembly line. This same year for a "jitney"—that is, a nickel—automobile owners offer rides. From this practice originates the taxicab. Soon there is regular intercity "jitney" service.

27 DECEMBER 1915
Labor The Iron and Steel Workers strike in East Youngstown, Ohio. They demand the eight–hour day and other concessions. Since their labor is vital, the strike will be soon settled in their favor.

7 JANUARY 1916
America's Approach to War In response to pressure from Wilson, Germany notifies the State Department that it will abide by strict international rules of maritime warfare.

10 JANUARY 1916
International In an attempt to embroil the United States in the turmoil in Mexico, General Francisco "Pancho" Villa forces 18 American mining engineers off a train and shoots them in cold blood.

24 JANUARY 1916
National The Supreme Court finds that a federal income tax is constitutional.

2 FEBRUARY 1916
America's Approach to War In a last-ditch attempt to eliminate overseas travel as a cause for American involvement in war, Representative McLemore introduces a resolution in Congress which asks Wilson to warn Americans not to travel on vessels owned by the warring nations. In a quick move to thwart any attempt to tie his hands, Wilson declares that Americans must have their rights protected and requests an immediate vote on the matter. A motion to table the resolution passes 175 to 135.

9 MARCH 1916
International Pancho Villa leads an attack of 1500 men into New Mexico and kills 17 Americans. Brigadier-General John J. Pershing with 6000 men will be ordered to pursue Villa into Mexico and to capture him. The subsequent two–year effort will result in failure.

15 MARCH 1916
America's Approach to War The Army Reorganization Bill passes the House. Meanwhile, the Senate has unanimously resolved to bring the army to full strength. On June 3 the National Defense Act will pass, authorizing a standing army of 175,000, and the National Guard, which will later go into battle intact, will reach 450,000. By the end of June, the House will pass a $182,000,000 army appropriation bill, the largest military budget so far.

24 MARCH 1916
America's Approach to War German U-boats sink the French vessel *Sussex* which is steaming through the English Channel. The ship is unarmed and three Americans lose their lives. On April 18, Secretary of State Lansing warns Germany that the United States will break off diplomatic relations unless these attacks are discontinued. American diplomatic notes are getting increasingly severe, and the general public is in sympathy with Wilson and his Cabinet.

23 APRIL 1916
National The Socialist Labor Party holds its National Convention in New York to nominate Arthur E. Reimer of Massachusetts for president and Caleb Harrison of Illinois for vice-president.

15 MAY 1916
International In a move that will keep them there until 1914, the U.S. Marines land in Santo Domingo to quell disorder.

9 MAY 1916
International Wilson orders mobilization along the Mexican border. This will lead Carranza to order U.S. troops out of Mexico.

7 JUNE 1916
National The Progressive Party meets in National Convention in Chicago. The delegates enthusiastically elect Theodore Roosevelt, who declines the nomina-

tion. He throws his votes behind Charles Evans Hughes in a move to restore unity to the Republican Party. However, the convention nominates John M. Parker of Louisiana for vice-president in a feeble move to demonstrate its independence. When the Progressives move back into the fold of the national parties, they will dissolve into the Democratic Party.

10 JUNE 1916
National The Republican Party holds its National Convention in Chicago to nominate the little–known Charles Evans Hughes of New York for president and Charles Fairbanks of Indiana for vice-president.

14 JUNE 1916
America's Approach to War While accepting German assurances that no more merchant vessels will be sunk without warning, Wilson leads a preparedness parade in Washington.

16 JUNE 1916
National While campaigning on the slogan "He kept us out of war," Wilson skillfully prepares the way for ultimate entrance on the Allied side. The country feels deep sympathy for his peace efforts and at the Democratic Convention in St. Louis, Missouri, Wilson is renominated enthusiastically for president. Thomas R. Marshall is renominated for vice-president.

21 JUNE 1916
International Carranza orders his troops to attack American soldiers on Mexican ground. At Carrizal 18 Americans are killed or wounded. The Mexicans warn that a repetition will result unless Americans leave Mexico. Americans refuse until order is restored along the border. Next month the two countries will submit to arbitration in an effort to avoid all-out war.

17 JULY 1916
Agriculture The Federal Farm Loan Act is passed by Congress. This bill, which has been advocated long and loudly by farmers, establishes a land bank system for maintenance and improvement loans to farmers.

21 JULY 1916
National The Prohibition Party holds its National Convention in St. Paul, Minnesota; to nominate Frank Hanly of Indiana for president and Ira D. Landrith of Massachusetts for vice-president.

16 AUGUST 1916
International Canada and the United States sign a treaty to protect migratory birds in North America.

1 SEPTEMBER 1916
Labor In a long-delayed move, Congress enacts the Keating-Owen Act which bars from interstate commerce any item made by child labor. Some states have already begun to tackle the child labor problem as children work 12 to 14 hours a day. South Carolina

this year has raised the age limit to 14 years for employment in mills, factories and mines. Still working for equity for labor, two days later the President signs into law the Adamson Bill which provides for an eight-hour day and time and a half for overtime on railroads.

7 SEPTEMBER 1916
National The Workmen's Compensation Act is enacted by Congress, bringing 500,000 Federal employees under its umbrella.

7 NOVEMBER 1916
National Wilson wins the election on his peace and preparedness platform. The Democrats retain control of Congress and Jeanette Rankin of Montana is the first woman elected to the House. However, women have still not been granted suffrage in most states.

18 DECEMBER 1916
America's Approach to War Wilson asks the warring powers to state their conditions for peace negotiations. Nothing comes of it because the Allies are suspicious of American motives.

17 JANUARY 1917
International The Virgin Islands are bought by the United States from Denmark for $25,000,000. The islands are important strategic bases guarding the Panama Canal.

22 JANUARY 1917
America's Approach to War Wilson appears before Congress and outlines a plan for a league of peace, an organization which would bring about an effective federation of peaceloving nations. In it he puts forth his conditions for American participation and asks that the present conflict be resolved in such a way as to leave no aftermath of bitterness in the hearts of the defeated, a not unprophetic wish: it is told that Hitler, then a mere wounded corporal, will burst into tears when he hears the terms of Germany's later surrender, and vows revenge on the spot. In a famous phrase Wilson asks for a "Peace without victory," a concept, however, unappealing to both warring factions. Although both sides long for peace, neither is willing to give up the prospect of victory at this point.

31 JANUARY 1917
America's Approach to War Germany declares that it will resume unrestricted submarine warfare. Neutral ships, armed or unarmed, sailing into a German war zone, will be attacked without warning.

3 FEBRUARY 1917
America's Approach to War Wilson breaks off diplomatic relations with Germany. Citing Germany's renewed submarine warfare as reason enough to intervene, Wilson says: "this government has no alternative consistent with the dignity and honor of the United States." The same day the American steamship *Housatonic* is sunk without warning.

EXPANDING RESOURCES 1901-1945

5 FEBRUARY 1917
Immigration The Immigration Act is passed over Wilson's veto. It provides for a literacy test for immigrants, and excludes Asiatic laborers other than Japanese.

19 FEBRUARY 1917
International American troops stationed along the Mexican border are recalled. General Pershing has already been ordered off the unsuccessful Pancho Villa hunt. Carranza will now concentrate on promulgating a Constitution for his country. The one he creates is the one still intact in Mexico. In the next few years, Carranza, Zapata and Villa will all be assassinated, victims of the unstable conditions surrounding Mexican politics at this time.

23 FEBRUARY 1917
National The Federal Board for Vocational Education is created by Congress when it passes the Smith-Hughes Act. The Act provides matching funds to states for trade and agricultural schools.

24 FEBRUARY 1917
America's Approach to War Wilson has permitted Germany use of its wireless transmission system, and Germany has been arrogantly, some say stupidly, taking advantage of the courtesy to send coded diplomatic notes. British Secret Service agents have recently intercepted a telegram from the German Foreign Minister Zimmerman to the German Ambassador in Mexico. They now turn the decoded missive over to Wilson, the contents of which constitute one of the most important factors in leading Wilson to declare war on Germany. Zimmerman, foreseeing war with the United States as inevitable, in his notorious Zimmerman Telegram, has instructed the German Ambassador to instigate Mexican entrance into war on the side of the Central Powers in return for New Mexico, Texas and Arizona. The British had held onto the note ready to present it to Wilson at the most propitious moment to attempt to push him over the brink and into war. His severing diplomatic relations with Germany seems to present the opportune moment. Wilson insists on verifying the incredible blunder for it makes him look particularly naive and foolish, but in the end the telegram is released to the public which responds with predictable anger.

26 FEBRUARY 1917
America's Approach to War Wilson asks Congress for permission to arm merchant ships to safeguard American lives and rights at sea. Pacifist Senator La Follette leads a filibuster against the authorizing legislation. "A little group of willful men have rendered the great government of the United States helpless and contemptible," says Wilson angrily. The Senate will subsequently adopt the cloture rule permitting a majority to terminate debate. Meanwhile, the Attorney General finds that the requested powers are inherent in the Presidency and on March 9 Wilson proceeds to issue the necessary directive.

2 MARCH 1917
International The Jones Act makes Puerto Rico part of United States territory, thus making its inhabitants U.S. citizens.

5 MARCH 1917
National Wilson is inaugurated President.

12 MARCH 1917
America's Approach to War The American merchant ship *Algonquin* is sunk without warning.

15 MARCH 1917
International News of the first revolution in Russia reaches America. The Czar has been forced to abdicate. The United States will recognize the new government formed by Aleksandr Kerenski on March 22.

18 MARCH 1917
America's Approach to War The *City of Memphis*, *Vigilante* and *Illinois*, all American ships, are sunk without warning. Three days later the American *Healdton* is sunk off the Dutch coast.

2 APRIL 1917
World War I Wilson asks Congress to declare war on Germany. "The world," he says in a famous phrase, "must be made safe for democracy." Two days later the Senate concurs and on Good Friday the House follows suit. The vote in Congress is overwhelmingly in favor of war.

18 MAY 1917
National The Selective Service Act authorizing registration and draft of all men between 21 and 30 for military service is passed by Congress. The first American soldiers will go abroad under John J. Pershing, commander of the American Expeditionary Force which lands in France on June 24. On July 4, Colonel Charles E. Stanton speaks at the tomb of Lafayette, the French hero of the American War of Independence, saying proudly: "Lafayette, we are here." These American soldiers will be dispersed among European contingents where they are most needed. Not until October 27 will an American soldier fire a shot in the horrendous trench warfare, and November 3 will see the first three Americans killed in action. The famous Rainbow Division, commanded by Colonel Douglas MacArthur and representing every state of the Union, will land on November 30. By the end of the year 180,000 American soldiers will have arrived in France, and by the end of the war 2,000,000 men will have landed, of whom some 1,300,000 will see action. Some 49,000 will be killed in action and another 230,000 wounded. Disease will take a greater toll than bullets, claiming 57,000 men. Colonel Roosevelt wishes to form his own division of "horse riflemen" but is refused by Army Chief of Staff Hugh L. Scott. Roosevelt never quite forgives Wilson.

4 JULY 1917
World War I The first training field for military air-

men is opened at Rantoul, Illinois. Ten days later the House appropriates $640,000,000 for the military aviation program. The army will begin the war with 55 planes and 4500 aviators. By war's end there will be some 16,801 aircraft in service.

10 AUGUST 1917

World War I Herbert Hoover is put in charge of the food program designed to increase food production and distribution as set up by the Lever Food and Fuel Control Act.

6 NOVEMBER 1917

Regional An important victory for women in their fight for suffrage is won when New York ratifies a constitutional amendment giving women the vote.
World War I The Bolsheviks overthrow the Kerenski government of Russia and will soon make peace with Germany. The United States does not immediately recognize the new government.

7 DECEMBER 1917

The United States declares war on Austria-Hungary.

OTHER EVENTS OF 1917

Arts/Culture The first Pulitzer prizes are given out by the Columbia School of Journalism. Among the winners are Laura E. Richards and Maude Howe Elliott for their biography *Julia Ward Howe*.

7 JANUARY 1918

National In *Arver v. United States*, the Supreme Court finds that conscription during war is authorized by the Constitution which gives Congress the power "to declare war . . . to raise and support armies." There are several challenges to the government's power to draft armies which become known as the Selective Services Law Cases.

8 JANUARY 1918

World War I Wilson sets forth his famous "Fourteen Points" for peace in the world. Most of these are specific to German borders, Polish, Turkish and Belgian sovereignty, war reparations and the like, but the final point will cause ripples in the international world for many years. It asks for "a general association of nations . . . under specific covenants for the purpose of affording mutual guarantees of political independence and territorial integrity to great and small states alike." This is an idea which seems quite natural to Americans but formidable and threatening to Europeans caught in their web of historical hatreds. Says Clemenceau, the French Prime Minister with whom Wilson will soon have to negotiate peace terms: "President Wilson and his Fourteen Points bore me. Even God Almighty has only ten!"

25 FEBRUARY 1918

National Muscle Shoals Dam is given a go-ahead by Wilson. It will span the Tennessee River and provide much-needed electricity for the war effort.

THE WOMEN'S SUFFRAGE MOVEMENT

The Women's Movement effectively began on July 19, 1848 when Elizabeth Cady Stanton and Lucretia Mott convened a woman's rights convention at Seneca Falls, New York. It was the first such convention in the world and would lead to one of the world's most peaceful revolutions.

It was Susan B. Anthony who gave direction to the movement. Forming and reforming, always under her influence, women's groups successfully campaigned for voting rights at all levels of government. And it was the 19th Amendment, first broached in 1869, and often called the Susan B. Anthony Amendment, which gave coherence to the movement for 50 years.

To their dismay, in the turbulent years after the Civil War, women had watched as the 14th Amendment gave black males the vote, deliberately excluding females. Women turned directly to the states for support and with careful strategy got some 15 to give them the ballot. From a position of strength they could begin their offensive on the Federal government.

National organizations were drawing some important women into their fold, and by 1920 the movement had grown to include the new class of working women, now a fifth of the total work force, who were no longer merely servants. Until Alice Paul appeared on the scene, tactics were fairly genteel. In 1914, Alice Paul, however, impatient with the government's delaying tactics, brought a militant element into the movement; soon the police, with Wilson's tacit approval, would respond with brutality. Women picketing the White House were roughly hauled off to jail, stripped naked and thrown into dirty cells with syphilitic prostitutes. Sometimes punishment for infraction of rules was severe, as in the case of Ada Davenport Kendall who, for protesting some injustice, was put on bread and water for 17 days in solitary confinement.

The main stumbling block facing the women was the "solid South" with which the politically shrewd Wilson declined to tangle; its own "illegal" constitutions had effectively disenfranchised black males and it was not now prepared to give black females the vote instead. However, under the joint leadership of the able Carrie Chapman Catt and the fiery Alice Paul, Wilson's compromising policies backfired and in 1918, thanks in part to the women's vote, a Republican Congress was returned to Washington. The new legislature agreed to submit the Amendment to the States for ratification so that grateful women might vote Republican in the 1920 Presidential election. Finally conflict centered on the decisive 36th State: Tennessee. To offset a Democratic Party defeat, Wilson pressed for ratification. At four in the morning on August 26, 1920, Tennessee delivered the needed 36th and last certificate to Secretary of State Colby. With Wilson's belated blessing, Colby hastily announced the historic decision.

The women, finally, had the vote.

3 MARCH 1918

World War I Russia, under its new Bolshevik government, signs a peace treaty with Germany.

21 MARCH 1918

World War I Realizing that they must make their move before Americans can get fully into the war, the German Army begins its final offensive on the West-

As commander of the American forces in Europe and his country's most famous World War I general, John J. Pershing helped to swing the tide of the war toward the Allied cause; but among military men he is also remembered as the architect of the modern American Army. Pershing was born near Laclede, Missouri, on September 13, 1860. In his youth he was an able student and a country schoolteacher; in 1882 he won admission to West Point, where he was an outstanding cadet and finished as president of his class. After West Point, Pershing languished in cavalry service in the Southwest as part of the government's ignoble mopping up of the last Indian resistance. From 1891 to 1895 he was a professor of military science at the University of Nebraska. After another year fighting Indians he moved to West Point as a tactics instructor.

Wishing to get back to field service, he found assignments to cavalry operations in Cuba during the Spanish-American War, where he won a reputation for great bravery, and then to the Philippines, where he successfully led American resistance to the Moro insurrection. As an official observer of the Russo-Japanese War in 1905, his dispatches gained the attention of President Roosevelt, who promoted him to brigadier general. He then saw service again in the Philippines and in Texas; while he was there dealing with Mexican border problems, his wife and three of his four children died in a fire. Thereafter Pershing became the stiff and taciturn man whom the world came to know. In 1916-17 he led the United States action that broke the power of Pancho Villa in Mexico.

When the United States joined the First World War in 1917, the Allies were near defeat. As commander of the American Expeditionary Forces, Pershing brought his gifts as a tactician and leader to help turn the tide. There he developed the methods of modern warfare that were models for the leaders of the next World War. After the German defeat in 1918, he returned to America as a hero and was promoted to general of the armies and chief of staff. He retired in 1924 and died in Washington in 1948.

ern front. Russia is out of the war and Italy has been effectively routed. Only token forces need be left to guard their rear. Germany has 207 divisions to the Allies' 173. Beginning the assault on the British lines between Arras and La Fere, the Germans force the enemy back up to 40 miles.

9 APRIL 1918
World War I The British are forced to withdraw from Ypres to Armentieres. In May the French Army, fighting between Noyon and Rheims, is equally unable to repulse German assaults.

14 APRIL 1918
World War I General Ferdinand Foch is made supreme commander of Allied forces, including the Americans. With General Pershing, he makes a special plea to Wilson to get more troops over quickly, even if untrained. The situation is desperate. Some 313,000 troops arrive in July.

28 MAY 1918
World War I In its first independent action, the 1st

Division helps to win the Battle of Cantigny. American troops are fresh, idealistic and surprisingly fearless in battle.

25 JUNE 1918
World War I In a battle which has lasted almost two weeks, the Marine Brigade of the U.S. 2nd Division captures Bouresche and Belleau Wood. The marines suffer 9500 casualties, almost 55 percent, but finally take the offensive in a hideous square mile of battle field.

17 JULY 1918
World War I The Allies halt the German's four-month drive in a fight known as the Second Battle of the Marne. The Germans have gotten out of the trenches and begun some strategic offensives. On July 15, they attack on both sides of Rheims, almost reaching their objectives within the next two days until, in the words of a German general, we "encountered American units." By July 18, Foch could order a counterattack at Soissons and later the German Chancellor could write: "On the 18th even the most optimistic among us knew that all was lost. The history of the world was played out in three days."

10 AUGUST 1918
World War I General Pershing is permitted by the

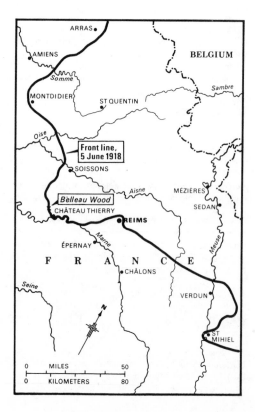

U.S. tanks advancing into France, 1918.

The costly Meuse offensive.

Allies to establish an independent American Army. He assumes command and makes Colonel George C. Marshall his operations officer. Meanwhile, 10,000 Americans join Japan in occupying Vladivostok on the Pacific, and some of Siberia. This will drag the Americans into the internal affairs of Russia as they side with the White Russians in the Archangel-Murmansk campaign which will last until May 1919.

14 SEPTEMBER 1918
World War I The strategic St. Mihiel salient is taken by the independent American forces under General Pershing. Some 15,000 Germans are made prisoner. There are nearly 8000 casualties.

26 SEPTEMBER 1918
World War I In the final major battle of the war, the Allies plan an offensive from Ypres to Verdun. Around 896,000 American troops join with 135,000 French soldiers in an attack on a sector between the Argonne Forest and the Meuse. In the largest battle fought up to this time, casualties will mount to 120,000. Meanwhile, up north, the Hindenburg line, Germany's last line of defense, is broken by the British and the collapse of the Central Powers is virtually assured.

3 OCTOBER 1918
World War I Germany forms a parliamentary gov-

American soldiers in the Meuse Valley, battleground for over a million Allied troops.

EXPANDING RESOURCES 1901-1945

ernment with Prince Max of Baden as its head, and by October 9, with collapse at the front, mutiny in the navy and revolution in Munich, the Kaiser abdicates. Germany begins peace overtures to Wilson on the basis of Wilson's Fourteen Points.

25 OCTOBER 1918
National Wilson calls for a Democratic Congress to be returned on election day in order to back his peace negotiations. It is ill-timed and unfortunately partisan.

30 OCTOBER 1918
World War I Austria sues Italy for an armistice, and on November 4 surrenders.

11 NOVEMBER 1918
World War I After a month of negotiations, the German government signs the armistice treaty at five in the morning, in a dining car in the forest of Compiegne. Hostilities cease six hours later and the victorious powers erupt into joyous celebrations. The war will have cost America $41,755,000,000; there will have been 130,174 deaths and 203,460 wounded.

4 DECEMBER 1918
International With a large contingent of historians, geographers, political scientists and economists, Wilson sails for Europe as head of the delegation to the Peace Conference. He takes with him Secretary of State Lansing, General of the Army Bliss, and his friend Colonel House. He does not include anyone from the now largely Republican Congress. Wilson might have served himself and his country better had he not lost himself in the petty details of day–to–day negotiations and maintained the high dignity of his office of President. He might also have done politically better to get Congress sympathetic to his interests. Wilson, nonetheless, speaks for the hopes of mankind and is greeted everywhere with great enthusiasm. He is known as "Wilson the Just."

18 JANUARY 1919
International The Peace Conference begins in Paris. Germany is prepared to sit down and negotiate a peace treaty based on Wilson's Fourteen Points. However, the Peace Conference begins without representa-

U.S. delegation to the Peace Conference in Paris.

Wilson with George Creel, Public Information head.

tives from the Central Powers present. In fact, rather than dignified representation at the peace table, the Germans will be at the mercy of the armistice which will be renewed each month for six months; the blockade (including foodstuffs) will remain in place for that time, and conditions will deteriorate severely in Germany, creating a residue of bitterness which will begin to raise havoc only a decade later.

29 JANUARY 1919
National The 18th Amendment to the Constitution is ratified when Nebraska agrees to the Prohibition measure on January 16. Prohibition of alcohol throughout the United States will come into effect January 16, 1920. Meanwhile, on June 29, the War Prohibition Act—placing some limits on the sale of alcohol—is extended to remain in effect until mobilization is completed. The law will be tested in the courts, but ultimately the Supreme Court will rule that the measure is a legitimate exercise of the war powers of government. On October 28, the Volstead Act will be passed to enforce Prohibition.

10 MARCH 1919
National In *Schenk v. United States*, the Supreme Court finds that the Espionage Act does not violate the First Amendment. In this case Holmes agrees with the majority that in war there exists the "clear and present danger" referred to in the Constitution. In any case, he adds, free speech is always under restraint. Under this ruling Eugene V. Debs is sentenced to ten years in prison for interfering with the draft. He will serve three years. In *Abrams v. United States*, Holmes will disagree with the majority which finds that distributing pamphlets expressing dissatisfaction with the American presence in Siberia falls under the 1918 Sedition Act. The eloquent Holmes, writing for the minority, states: "the best test of truth is the power of the thought to get itself accepted in the competition of the market."

15 MARCH 1919
Ideas/Beliefs The American Legion is formed in Paris by about 1000 delegates from units of the American Expeditionary Force.

4 JUNE 1919
National The proposal to adopt the 19th Amendment, which will enfranchise American women, is passed by Congress and goes to the States for ratification.

28 JUNE 1919
International The Peace Conference ends with the signing of the Versailles Treaty. Germany is asked to admit her guilt, to give up the rich Alsace-Lorraine and her overseas colonies, and to pay reparations of some $15,000,000,000. Although Pershing has wished to plunge right on into Berlin, Foch has prevailed and the Allies have not entered the conquered country until now when the German economic system is placed under Allied control. In effect, the Germans have experienced the bitter consequences of defeat but not seen the military might that effected it. Further trouble will accrue from clauses in the treaty that prevent German rearmament, and which provide for an indemnity of an indeterminate amount designed to keep the defeated nation perpetually poor. The final treaty does not follow closely Wilson's Fourteen Points, upon which Germany has agreed to negotiate peace. Later, Hitler will distort this fact to claim that Germany has been betrayed, not defeated.

Ultimately the issue dearest to Wilson's heart, the League of Nations, is accepted by all signatories. However, just because of the League issue, the Senate will never ratify the treaty.

1 JULY 1919
Transportation The first daily air mail service is established between Chicago and New York.

14 JULY 1919
International With the signing of the peace treaty, the embargo on trade to Germany is lifted and the United States resumes business relations.

31 AUGUST 1919
Ideas/Beliefs The Communist Party is formed in Chicago, Illinois. Party motto is "Workers of the world unite!" First members are mostly Russian.

3 SEPTEMBER 1919
National Instead of negotiating the Versailles Treaty and the League of Nations Covenant with the Senate, Wilson goes on a tour of the country to rouse public opinion in favor of the project. The President is already quite sick and proceeds against the advice of doctors but this technique of going over the head of Congress has worked for him successfully in the past. The League of Nations Covenant provides for an assembly of nations to "promote international co-operation and to achieve international peace and security." Membership is open to all nations. There would be an assembly of all members, and a council made up of permanent delegates from the five great powers plus four elected delegates. The machinery is substantially that adopted by the United Nations after World War II. There are many among the leaders of American

opinion who endorse the League, particularly Taft and Elihu Root, who began the notion with their "League to Enforce Peace." At this juncture both Lodge and Roosevelt back the Covenant as do labor unions and financial and industrial leaders; the country's leading intellectuals find it a surprisingly good idea. But Wilson does not attempt to rally their support and his rigidity manages to alienate most of his supporters. By the middle of 1919, enthusiasm for the league has badly eroded and Wilson collides in a bitter fight with the Senate.

9 SEPTEMBER 1919
Regional When 1117 of Boston's 1544 policemen go on strike, Governor Calvin Coolidge promptly hires new patrolmen. In a statement that propels him to national attention he declares: "There is no right to strike against the public safety by anybody, anywhere, any time."

25 SEPTEMBER 1919
National Already showing signs of exhaustion, Wilson suffers a stroke in Colorado. For some five weeks, the President of the United States is delicately balanced between life and death. Outside the family, only his doctor, his secretary Joseph Tumulty and, infrequently, Bernard Baruch are permitted to see him. His mind, it seems, is clouded, but there is no provision in the law for declaring a president unable "to discharge the powers and duties of the said office," even though the Constitution declares that in such a case the duties should devolve on the vice-president. In this instance it would have been the accommodating Thomas R. Marshall who would have taken hold of the reins of government. (As it is, his fame now rests on his quip: "What this country needs is a good five cent cigar.") By November 1, the president is again in control of his faculties, although he never fully recovers from the effects of arteriosclerosis and heart attack. Meanwhile, the Senate led by Lodge, brings a noble dream to an end by entangling the peace treaty in reservations, knowing that the rigid old man will never compromise.

19 NOVEMBER 1919
National The Senate refuses to ratify the Versailles Treaty by a vote of 55 to 39. The most popular war in American history comes to a squabbling end with opportunities lost and hopes foreclosed.

OTHER EVENTS OF 1919
Arts/Culture The Pulitzer Prize for literature is given to Booth Tarkington for his novel *The Magnificent Ambersons*. The story catches the life of three generations of one family in a fast-changing Indianapolis community. The privately printed and exemplary biography *The Education of Henry Adams* wins Henry Adams a Pulitzer Prize for biography. And this year Sherwood Anderson will publish his collection of short stories, *Winesburg, Ohio*.

Father Divine, the charismatic black evangelistic leader, establishes himself as a national force. His disciples believe him to be God incarnate, unable to die. Hidden in the clouds of religious rubble that surround him are some portentous social directives to his black community. He advocates racial and economic equality, black responsibility, black business, and carries his philosophy down into the details of everyday life. He forbids his followers to accept tips, telling them to insist on proper pay, rather than remaining dependent on others' generosity. His no-nonsense approach to black social philosophy will lay some of the groundwork for the black rights movement of the 60s.

1 JANUARY 1920

National The nation is caught in a war psychology without a war in sight. Taking advantage of the undirected emotion, Attorney General A. Mitchell Palmer turns it on what he sees as a "Red Menace." Without warrants or reason Palmer authorizes raids on private homes and labor headquarters across the country. In one night he pounces in 33 separate cities and arrests 4000 people. Many are Russians, some are Communists, but most are victims of Palmer's grab for fame. "Do not let the country see Red," pleads the sick Wilson at his first Cabinet meeting since his stroke. But Red is just about all Palmer can see. In Detroit, when 300 totally innocent people are arrested, they are held for a week, one day without food. In New England, too, hundreds are arrested without any foundation. Although Palmer finds no signs of imminent revolution, nor even much radicalism, he enjoys the public adulation his hysteria rouses for him in the country.

16 JANUARY 1920

National The 18th Amendment brings about a new era as it goes into effect at midnight. From this intentionally moral legislation will come some of the shadiest people and practices in American history. Not the least of the evils following upon its enactment will be the increase in alcoholism seen at all levels. Fortunately the Amendment has a built–in seven–year time span and will eventually be repealed, the only Constitutional Amendment to have this dubious honor.

28 FEBRUARY 1920

National The Esch-Cummins Transportation Act creates the Railroad Labor Board to supervise railroad regulation. The railroads, which have been run by the government during the war, are now returned to private ownership.

1 MARCH 1920

National In *United States v. United States Steel Corporation*, the Supreme Court finds that the large corporation is not an illegal monopoly.

2 MARCH 1920

Regional The maverick State of New Jersey tests the new Prohibition Amendment by declaring 3.5 percent beer legal. But later in the year, in the *National*

Prohibition Cases, the Supreme Court will declare such laws invalid.

1 APRIL 1920

Regional As part of the Red scare that is sweeping the nation, five members of the New York Legislature are expelled for being members of the Socialist Party. They will be legitimately re-elected, but once again they will be refused permission to sit in session.

5 MAY 1920

National In one of the least edifying examples of the nation's Red hysteria, Nicola Sacco and Bartolomeo Vanzetti are arrested on charges of robbery and murder of the paymaster at a shoe factory in Braintree, Massachusetts. On extremely tenuous evidence the two men will be convicted in 1921 and held in jail until August 23, 1927 when they will be executed. Their case, built on an unfortunately weak foundation, polarized the nation in a highly charged and essentially meaningless manner.

10 MAY 1920

National The Socialist Labor Party meets for its National Convention in New York City and nominates W.W. Cox for president and August Gilhaus of Brooklyn for vice-president.

14 MAY 1920

National The Socialist Party convenes in New York

SACCO AND VANZETTI

After World War I was over, the nation recoiled into itself. Foreigners, meaning people who had not yet arrived on American shores or who had only recently arrived, were looked upon with increasing suspicion. Social conditions were changing with extreme speed and scapegoats to blame for their unsettling results were easily found: the Reds. In this atmosphere on April 15, 1920, two men, taking the $15,000 payroll for their shoe factory from Boston to Braintree, Massachusetts, were set upon by five men in an automobile and shot dead. The payroll was stolen. Helpful witnesses claimed that two of the gangsters looked very Italian. Three weeks later, on this flimsy description, Nicola Sacco and Bartolomeo Vanzetti were arrested for murder. Both had alibis, Sacco's furnished by the Italian Consulate in Boston, but to no avail. Both were known locally to have anarchistic leanings. Sacco and Vanzetti were particularly swarthy looking Italian–born men, "dagos" and "sons of bitches," the less than fair-minded Judge Thayer was reported to have called them after the case came before him on May 31, 1921. The case polarized the nation. Many high–standing leaders of American thought deplored the "trial by atmosphere." Finally, more martyrs than men, the two prisoners were sentenced to death. For six years they remained in prison while people fought for their release. However, on August 22, 1927 they were both executed, their guilt or innocence not satisfactorily proved because of faulty investigation techniques based on presumption of their guilt. Ballistic tests since then suggest that Sacco had a pistol that was used in the killings, but the riddle remains as one of the archetypal cases of possible injustice due to prejudice.

City and nominates Eugene V. Debs for president and Seymour Stedman of Ohio for vice-president. Debs will run his campaign from jail.

4 JUNE 1920
National Congress passes the Army Reorganization Act which will establish a peacetime army of some 300,000 men.

5 JUNE 1920
National Only slightly dismantling the machinery of war, Congress passes the Merchant Marine Act which continues the wartime Shipping Board whose duties now will be to sell the fleet to private owners but then to operate all vessels not sold.

10 JUNE 1920
National Congress enacts the Water Power Act and creates the Federal Power Commission to regulate power plants. With numerous boards to oversee that necessary functions operate smoothly, the Federal Government has run the war in a fairly efficient manner. The country is now less of a federation and more of a unit than in past history.

12 JUNE 1920
National The Republican Party holds its National Convention in Chicago and nominates Warren G.

MARCUS GARVEY, 1887-1940

The career of Marcus Garvey was one of the more colorful and ambiguous episodes in the struggle of America's black citizens for equality in this century. He was born in Jamaica on August 17, 1887. After working as a newspaper editor in Jamaica he went to London in 1912; there he came under the influence of a half-black Egyptian nationalist named Duse Mohammed Ali and decided to promote a worldwide black movement with himself as leader. To that end he formed in 1914 the Universal Negro Improvement Organization in Jamaica, and from there took his cause to New York City in 1916.

Garvey attracted many followers in Harlem; within a few years he had established a newspaper, started a steamship line, promoted black businesses and fostered branch organizations around the country. By 1920, when he presided over an international convention in New York, he had millions of followers, most of them from among poorer blacks who responded to his gradiose oratory, outlandish uniforms, and militant black chauvinism.

But his movement faltered in the 20s after inept management led to the failure of many of the UNIA's business ventures; this helped fuel rising criticism of Garvey from the black upper classes. He was finally convicted on mail fraud charges in 1923; but before beginning his sentence he announced plans for a "Back to Africa" movement which proposed mass emigration of American blacks to Liberia. The plan was never implemented. In 1927 Garvey was pardoned by President Coolidge and deported to Jamaica, where he continued his efforts with indifferent success until his death in 1940. Though his movement accomplished few of its goals and had its naive aspects, Garvey is remembered as a powerful voice of black pride and a disturbing and prophetic figure on the American scene.

Harding of Ohio for president and Calvin Coolidge for vice-president. Harding is an old "pol" friend of the machine bosses. He will be thrust on the convention by the party leaders from what Harry M. Daugherty calls a "smoke-filled room." Explains Daugherty: "The convention will be deadlocked . . . some 12 or 15 men, worn out and bleary-eyed for lack of sleep, will sit down about two o'clock in the morning around a table in a smoke-filled room in some hotel and decide the nomination. When that time comes, Harding will be selected." And so it happens. When the "pols" try to choke another of the same ilk down the convention throat as nominee for vice-president, delegates insist on a man of higher caliber. For this reason, the taciturn and colorless Coolidge, who has nevertheless shown his firmness in Boston's policeman's strike, is chosen.

5 JULY 1920
National The Democratic Party holds its National Convention in San Francisco and nominates the little-known James M. Cox, Governor of Ohio, for president, and Franklin Delano Roosevelt for vice-president.

16 JULY 1920
National The Farmer Labor Party holds its national convention in Chicago and nominates Parley P. Christensen of Utah for president, and Max S. Hayes of Ohio for vice-president. The Farmer Labor Party has been formed the month before in Chicago. It will later join with La Follette's Progressive Party. Also formed this year is the American Farm Bureau Federation.

22 JULY 1920
National The National Convention of the Prohibition Party is held in Lincoln, Nebraska, to nominate Aaron S. Watkins of Ohio for president. (William J. Bryan finally has declined a nomination for the presidency.)

26 AUGUST 1920
National The 19th Amendment to the Constitution which gives women suffrage is enacted. To educate women in the ways of politics, the National League of Women Voters is organized this same year.

2 NOVEMBER 1920
National Harding wins by 404 electoral votes to the Democrats' ignominious 127. Harding wins a popular vote of 16,152,200; the Democrats win 9,147,353; From jail, Debs polls a substantial 919,799 votes.
Industry The first regular broadcasting service is initiated by station KDKA in East Pittsburgh, Pennsylvania.

OTHER EVENTS OF 1920
Life/Customs The Nobel Peace Prize is given to Woodrow Wilson. Wilson ends his final speech to Congress quoting Lincoln: "Let us have faith that right makes might, and in that faith let us dare to do our duty as we understand it."

EXPANDING RESOURCES 1901-1945

Arts/Culture The Pulitzer Prize for drama is given to Eugene O'Neill for *Beyond the Horizon*. This year glittering Broadway will also see his *Emperor Jones*. Although no Pulitzer prize is offered for the novel, publishing this year are Sinclair Lewis with *Main Street*, F. Scott Fitzgerald with *This Side of Paradise*, and Edith Wharton with *The Age of Innocence*. For this novel, however, Wharton will receive the Pulitzer the following year.

4 JANUARY 1921
National The War Finance Corporation is put back into operation to help badly depressed farm areas. Congress has had to override President Wilson's veto.

4 MARCH 1921
National The genial machine politician from Wisconsin, Warren Gamaliel Harding, is inaugurated 29th President of the U.S. "A great *looking* President," says his mentor Harry Micajah Daugherty. He lacks experience in international affairs at this crucial time when the world is still reeling from the effects of war, however, he represents the mood of the country which would like to avoid the burdens of international responsibilities. Harding has expressed himself and reflected his country in a speech given on May 14, 1920 in which he said: "America's need is not heroics, but healing; not nostrums, but normalcy; not revolution, but restoration; not agitation, but adjustment; not surgery but serenity; not the dramatic, but the dispassionate; not experiment but equipoise; not submergence in internationality, but sustainment in triumphant nationality." Like the national optimism which he effuses, his term will be short for he will die of apoplexy within two years.

2 APRIL 1921
Ideas/Beliefs Professor Albert Einstein arrives in New York to give a lecture on his new theory of relativity. The lecture at Columbia opens up a totally new way of thinking which will displace much scientific theory which has preceded it.

19 MAY 1921
National The country is inexorably moving from rural to urban as 51 percent of the population is found to be living in towns of 2500 or over. Some 800,000 immigrants arrive this year. To control the flow, Congress enacts the Emergency Quota Act. This bill permits entry on the basis of 3 percent of the nationality already in the United States in 1910, the total not to exceed 357,000. It is the first seriously restrictive immigration bill enacted by Congress. Others will follow.

27 MAY 1921
National Succumbing to the inevitable, Congress and the president agree to the Emergency Tariff Act which, as usual, increases tariffs. In this case one of the protected areas is farm products. While the act does little for the American farmer, Europe, strug-

WARREN G. HARDING, 1865-1923

Although almost totally incompetent, Warren G. Harding rose to the highest office in the land by a combination of backroom shenanigans, complex political tides and a stream of his own mellifluous rhetoric. His country would remember him affectionately as the worst president ever.

Harding was born on November 2, 1865 in Blooming Grove, Ohio. After gaining a small-college degree he tried and failed in several jobs before becoming in 1881 a partner in a newspaper. One of his rare successes, the Marion *Star* became a noted Ohio paper. In 1891 he married a local banker's daughter, Florence Kling DeWolfe; a formidable and ambitious woman, she drove his political career and also drove him into a series of extramarital liaisons that continued straight into the White House. During the same period he had the first of several nervous breakdowns. His position as a publisher as well as the stentorian fog of his rhetoric brought Harding into the ken of one Harry M. Daugherty, an Ohio Republican kingmaker. This dubious liaison soon led Harding to a seat in the Ohio State Senate in 1899, where he showed his political acumen by sponsoring no significant legislation whatever. Nonetheless, his backroom backslapping took him to the position, in 1902, of lieutenant governor, and in 1914, with Daugherty's help, he gained a seat in the U.S. Senate.

During his six years in the Senate, Harding demonstrated the same genial incompetence that had already brought him to high office. When he sponsored an absurd and unsuccessful bill to allow Theodore Roosevelt to raise a volunteer army during World War I, the grateful Roosevelt fixed on Harding as his next vice–president. When Roosevelt died before the election he left a muddled Republican situation that Daugherty, in the legendary "smoke-filled room" of the Convention, exploited to make Harding the nominee.

At that point the country was tired of war, tired of European entanglements, and tired of Woodrow Wilson, who himself was gravely ill. The citizenry noted Harding's imposing, handsome features: he undoubtedly *looked* like a president, and sounded like one, too; and he promised a "return to normalcy," whatever that meant. He was elected by a landslide. Among his cabinet appointments were a few good men and a few, including Daugherty, who would leave a legacy of corruption. Harding himself was not notably corrupt; rather, he was blindly loyal to corrupt cronies and innocently hypocritical—an ardent Prohibitionist on the first floor of the White House, he served bootleg hooch to his poker pals upstairs.

440

Under his nearly nonexistent leadership, corruption spread happily. But in the country the postwar economic crunch had started and Prohibition was increasingly resented. In mid–term Harding began to take some of the reins of command, but a sudden heart attack felled him in August 1923—perhaps mercifully, before the Teapot Dome and other scandals that sent two of his appointees to jail and left his administration as a blot on American history.

gling to get back on its feet, will be badly damaged by its shortsighted protectionism, an outcome of a new bipartisan farm bloc formed in Congress. The United States also rejects overtures from Russia to resume trade as long as Russia persists in Communism.

31 MAY 1921
National In a move that passes almost unnoticed, Secretary of the Navy Edwin Denby transfers the naval oil reserves at Elk Hills, California, and Teapot Dome, Wyoming, to Albert B. Fall's Department of the Interior. The move will have serious repercussions, which will unfold in one of the worst scandals of the decade.

10 JUNE 1921
National In an effort to bring order into the national accounts, Congress passes the Budget and Accounting Act. Two offices are set up: the Bureau of the Budget and the General Accounting Office. Charles D. Dawes is made director of the Budget Bureau; John R. Carl is named Comptroller General; both offices come under the Treasury Department.

20 JUNE 1921
National Alice Robertson of Oklahoma presides over the House of Representatives. She is the first woman to do so. Her session lasts 30 minutes.

25 JUNE 1921
Labor In an expression of respect and loyalty, Samuel Gompers is elected president of the American Federation of Labor for the 40th time. But organized labor will suffer during the coming years and starting with some 5,000,000 members in 1920, will dwindle to 3,444,000 by 1929.

30 JUNE 1921
National President Harding appoints William Howard Taft as Chief Justice of the Supreme Court. This has been the appointment that Taft has wanted above all others, including the presidency.

1 JULY 1921
Labor The economy has been deteriorating since the booming war years. Industry meets the crisis by cutting wages rather than hours. Working hours are usually 12-14 per day, with weekends included; in some industries such as steel, every two weeks there is what is called a "stretch-out" where workers are called upon to work 24 hours straight. Children and women fare no better. An attempt to protect children has been ruled unconstitutional by the Supreme Court in 1918. Now, in 1921, the New York Central cuts the

wages of some 43,000 employees by almost 23 percent, while the Railroad Labor Board authorizes a 12 percent cut; the clothing workers are forced to accept a 15 percent chop. U.S. Steel will decrease wages three times this year. During the same months some 20,000 businesses will fail causing massive unemployment. Figures released in August show 5,735,000 unemployed. Ford, which had earlier closed its plants because dealers were unable to sell cars, is the only industry to feel that a crisis is past as assets rise to $345,140,000.

2 JULY 1921
International President Harding signs a joint resolution of Congress declaring an end to war with Germany. Negotiations on reparations will continue for some time. The peace treaty will be signed in August. An end to war with Austria and Hungary will also be proclaimed.

21 JULY 1921
National Demonstrating his contention that air power is superior to sea power, former General William Mitchell orchestrates a display of concentrated bombing, sinking the German battleship *Ostfriesland*.

26 SEPTEMBER 1921
Labor Herbert Hoover presides over a national conference on unemployment. A corollary to the mass of workers without jobs is the spread of violence, led by a revitalized Ku Klux Klan. Blacks back from the war, are not as ready to submit to their previous condition of subservience. To prevent the newfound dignity from spreading, whippings, brandings, lynchings, tarrings become widespread. Women, too, are being pressured back into the home after a heady moment of freedom during the war. To help relieve the mounting labor tension, the Hoover Commission recommends a cut in prices instead of wages. This would serve to bring goods, which are increasingly hard to sell, within reach of a new, if less wealthy, group of consumers. The commission also recommends a job program. The following year Harding will intercede and press the steel industry to accept the eight-hour day.

2 NOVEMBER 1921
Ideas/Beliefs Margaret Sanger's National Birth Control League combines with Mary Ware Dennett's Voluntary Parenthood League to form the American Birth Control League.

12 NOVEMBER 1921
International Although it has backed away from the League of Nations and the World Court, America keeps its hands in the international scene by convening the Washington Armament Conference at the behest of Senator William Borah. Russia is not invited, but England, France, Italy and Japan attend. The subsequent treaty fixes the tonnage of ships over 10,000 tons displacement at a ratio of United States 5, Britain 5, Japan, 3, France and Italy each 1.67. France does

EXPANDING RESOURCES 1901-1945

GEORGE WASHINGTON CARVER, 1861-1943

In the tragic and paradoxical story of American race relations, the career of black chemist and botanist George Washington Carver is an instructive chapter. A natural scientific genius, Carver was among the most famous and influential scientists of his time, but was lauded by many whites because he was a genius who seemed to "know his place."

Carver was born into a slave family in Diamond Grove, Missouri, around 1861. Wishing to pursue his education, he studied where he could as a teenager. Denied admission because of his color to one college in 1885, he was accepted to Iowa's Simpson College in 1890, where he was a brilliant student and finally a faculty assistant. In 1896 he was invited by Booker T. Washington to come to Tuskegee Institute in Alabama; in the 47 years of his work there he would help to maintain that school as the preeminent black college in the country.

Carver turned his attention first to improving agricultural methods and the nutrition of black farmers in the South. His innovative ideas on changing the area's growing patterns from soil-depleting crops like cotton to crops such as peanuts and sweet potatoes came finally to national prominence in 1921, when he spoke of his ideas in the U.S. House of Representatives. There followed his famous experiments deriving an astonishing range of products from various crops, most notably peanuts. More than anyone else's, his research helped inspire an agricultural revolution in the South, to the great benefit of whites as well as blacks. At the same time, because of segregation he could not sleep in a white hotel or eat in a white restaurant. Among his many awards and commendations, including a fellowship in London's Royal Society of Arts, there were none from his government and few from the people of the South. He died at Tuskegee in 1943.

---

not agree to limit smaller vessels nor land armaments. All five powers agree not to build large vessels for ten years. One of the few agreements of the meeting which has largely been respected is not to use asphyxiating gases in war. The conference also defines the rights of all major powers in the Pacific. (Japan soon ignores the agreements and invades Manchuria. Besides diplomatic protest, nothing concerted is done about the infringement.) The United States has signed with the reservation that "there is no commitment to armed force."

23 DECEMBER 1921
Ideas/Beliefs Harding signs the order releasing Eugene V. Debs from prison. Harding changes the date of the pardon from December 31, 1921 to December 24 because "I want him to eat his Christmas dinner with his wife." The belated pardon frees Debs from a controversial ten–year sentence for supposedly seditious speeches delivered in 1918 against war; Debs has served two years and eight months.

OTHER EVENTS OF 1921
Arts/Culture The Pulitzer Prize for fiction is awarded to Edith Wharton for *The Age of Innocence*. This year sees the publication of such works as John

Dos Passos's *Three Soldiers*, but the popular bestseller is Rafael Sabatini's *Scaramouche*. It is also the year that James Joyce's *Ulysses* is published in Paris; some 500 copies that arrive at the American borders are seized by the U.S. Post Office.

9 FEBRUARY 1922
International The World War Foreign Debt Commission is established by Congress to settle the thorny problem of Allied war and postwar loans. Great Britain owes over $4 billion, France some $3 billion and Italy over $1,600,000,000. Other countries are indebted to the United States to a lesser degree, and some are indebted to Great Britain to the tune of $10,000,000,000. None will be able to pay the full amount. Blinking at reality, Wilson had insisted on full repayment. Later the Commission will settle for repayment of $11,500,000,000 at interest of just over 2 percent payable over 62 years. With Germany unable to pay agreed–upon reparations, the necessary money is unavailable. For the second time, Great Britain offers to remit debts and reparations due it on condition that the United States not hold it to repayment. Wilson adamantly refuses. A great deal of unnecessary anti-American feeling is generated, since Europeans feel that America has amply profited from the war, not only because it became America's war, but its manufacturers received lucrative contracts for war supplies and postwar relief. To many Americans, default merely reinforces their suspicions of all foreigners. Harding and Coolidge both will stand firm against canceling the debts. However, by 1925 deep cuts will have to be made, Mussolini's Italy being the first to receive relief, with 80 percent of its debt cancelled, followed the next year by France with 60 percent reduction granted. Meanwhile Germany, kept deliberately poor, is unable to pay either interest or debt so that in January 1923 French and Belgian troops will occupy Germany's Ruhr Valley, claiming it as part payment. American loans to Germany are subscribed, but too late to undo the damage of vengeful and uncoordinated international monetary policies.

18 FEBRUARY 1922
Agriculture The legislature responds to the anguish of the farmers and passes the Capper-Volstead Act which allows farmers to buy and sell cooperatively without running the risk of being prosecuted for violation of anti-trust laws. The law brings much–needed relief to embattled farmers who are being forced off their farms in increasing numbers. In the two years of the Harding Administration alone, there will be 300,000 farm foreclosures.

27 FEBRUARY 1922
National In a unanimous decision, the Supreme Court finds the 19th Amendment giving women suffrage to be constitutional.

7 APRIL 1922
National The secret Teapot Dome oil deal begins to

seep its way into fullfledged scandal when Interior Secretary Albert B. Fall leases some of its land to Mammoth Oil Company, owned by Harry Sinclair. Fall bypasses the proper channels of competitive bidding. A subsequent lease of a second naval oil reserve in Elk Hills, California, to Edward L. Doheny follows the same illegal procedure. On April 15 Senator John B. Kendrick of Wyoming, on a tip from a constituent, asks for Fall to explain to the Senate the seemingly inappropriate deal. The Congressional investigation which follows will take another two years to unfold before Fall, Sinclair, Doheny and others are tried for bribery and conspiracy.

26 MAY 1922
National The creation of the Federal Narcotics Control Board is signed into law by Harding.

22 SEPTEMBER 1922
National The Cable Act is passed by Congress. In future an American woman who marries an alien will not lose her citizenship; neither will a woman marrying an American automatically become an American citizen.

3 OCTOBER 1922
National The first woman to become a Senator is Rebecca L. Felton who is appointed by the Governor of Georgia to fill a vacancy caused by the death of Thomas E. Watson. The appointment is more symbolic than substantial, as the vacancy extends for only one day.

4 DECEMBER 1922
International The Second Central American Conference meets in Washington. Nicaragua and Honduras are in need of help in resolving their differences. The result is a treaty of neutrality and a revitalization of a Central American Court of Justice. America retains her right under the Roosevelt Corollary to intercede at will in South American affairs. U.S. troops will be sent to Nicaragua in 1926 to shore up the conservative Adolfo Diaz and will remain until 1933.

OTHER EVENTS OF 1922
Arts/Culture The luster of "King" Oliver's Creole Jazz Band, already one of the legendary great jazz groups of all time, shines even brighter as Louis Armstrong joins in as its new cornetist. The Pulitzer Prize for the best novel of the year goes to Booth Tarkington for his *Alice Adams.*
Life/Customs Radio chalks up several firsts this year: the first Presidential broadcast, when it carries President Harding's dedication of the Francis Scott Key Memorial in Baltimore; the first World Series broadcast and the first "network" broadcast, involving WJZ of New York City and WGY in Schenectady, New York.

4 JANUARY 1923
Ideas/Beliefs The French psychologist Emil Coué arrives in the United States and starts a health fad. His basic idea is self-suggestion. He recommends repeating each day: "Every day in every way I am getting better and better."

10 JANUARY 1923
International The last of the American troops stationed in Germany are withdrawn by Harding.

2 MARCH 1923
National The Senate begins its investigation of the Veterans' Bureau. Charles R. Forbes, head of the department, is accused of corrupt dealings with contractors in hospital building.

4 MARCH 1923
Agriculture Congress adopts the Intermediate Credit Act, the primary purpose of which is to give relief to farmers. The Act authorizes the Federal Reserve to add an intermediate credit bank to each of its districts in order to aid in financing agricultural cooperatives.

5 MARCH 1923
Regional Montana and Nevada enact old age pensions, providing up to $25 for qualifying people over seventy.

15 MARCH 1923
National Charles F. Cramer, assistant to Charles R. Forbes, head of the Veterans' Bureau, commits suicide. He is one of Harding's inner circle, one of the so-called Ohio Gang. His death bodes ill for the president. Jesse Smith, close friend to Attorney General Daugherty and an unethical Washington power-broker, has already committed suicide after being told to leave Washington by none other than Harding himself. "Colonel" Forbes will soon be forced to resign as director of the Veteran's Bureau.

9 APRIL 1923
National In *Adkins v. Children's Hospital* the Supreme Court finds that the minimum wage law for women and children which has been adopted in the District of Columbia is unconstitutional. Organized Labor is everywhere being weakened at this time. Attorney General Daugherty is overtly unsympathetic to Labor's rights. He uses the outlawed injunction and refuses to acknowledge even those rights guaranteed Labor by the Clayton Act. Labor is losing the ground gained under the shelter of Theodore Roosevelt's (and subsequent) administrations.

4 MAY 1923
Regional In what many regard as the beginning of the end of Prohibition, New York State disregards Harding's warnings and repeals its enforcement act. Bootlegging has become big business, and the enforcement act is being circumvented on all sides: "speakeasies," "moonshiners," "rumrunners," "highjacking" and "medicinal purposes" are only a few of the ways that alcohol gets to its "dry" destinations. Gangsters, with total disregard for the safety of their

customers, regularly "cut" their liquor, or unskillfully "convert" wood alcohol to be sold under fake labels. "Bathtub" gin is made at home, as is home-brewed ale and wine. During the Prohibition decade over 300,000 lawbreakers will be convicted under the Volstead Act, which seeks to enforce Prohibition at the Federal level.

20 JUNE 1923
National Harding, depressed and worried by the scandals that are bubbling up among his most trusted companions, begins a tour of the West and Alaska.

2 AUGUST 1923
National Upon his return from Alaska, President Harding, suffering from an attack of ptomaine poisoning, develops pneumonia. He seems to be recovering when he dies of an embolism, or what is then called apoplexy. Rumors will surround his death in a hotel in San Francisco, for now the scandals that discredit his administration erupt onto the front pages of the nation. Although nothing is ever proved to besmirch his personal reputation, nonetheless his closeness to those who deal dishonestly in their high positions will tarnish the good-natured Harding himself.

3 AUGUST 1923
National In a simple ceremony at 2:30 in the morning, conducted by his father, Calvin Coolidge is sworn in as 30th President of the United States. He is in Plymouth, Vermont, when the news reaches him. Later, upon being asked what he thought when he heard of Harding's death, he will reply: "I thought I could swing it."

13 AUGUST 1923
Labor United States Steel, under pressure from Harding for over a year, finally relents and institutes the 8-hour day. It is a milestone for Labor. The cut in hours will also help industry, which must roll back production in any case but has been nonetheless reluctant to cut working hours. Steelworkers are accustomed to work from 12 to 14 hours every day of the week. Other industries will follow U.S. Steel's lead.

15 SEPTEMBER 1923
Regional Oklahoma Governor J.C. Walton places the State under martial law in order to quell the rising terrorism of the Ku Klux Klan. The Klan, inevitably revitalized by depression conditions, is using terrorist tactics to affect the politics of mid-Western States.

25 OCTOBER 1923
National The Teapot Dome oil scandal is brought back to public attention as the diligent Thomas J. Walsh, Senator from Montana and chairman of the Senate subcommittee investigation, proceeds to unveil his findings of the past 18 months. His carefully built case will result in the conviction of Harry F. Sinclair, owner of Mammoth Oil, and later in the conviction of Secretary of the Interior Albert B. Fall, the first Cabinet member in history to go to jail.

CALVIN COOLIDGE, 1872-1933

Coolidge was born in Plymouth Notch, Vermont, on July 4, 1872, and attended Amherst College in Massachusetts. After reading law a while he joined the Massachusetts bar in 1897. Though his practice was successful he soon moved to politics as a Republican and over the years rose through a series of elected offices to become the mayor of Northampton (1909-1914), lieutenant governor in 1915 and governor in 1918. A quietly competent governor, he made a dramatic entrance into national headlines when he suppressed a Boston police strike in 1919. This widely-acclaimed action led directly to a position on the 1920 Republican ticket as Warren G. Harding's vice-president. They swept into office on a wave of anti-Wilson sentiment. Three years later came another dramatic turn in Coolidge's undramatic life—the death of Harding.

As President, Coolidge set out to deal with Harding's ex-appointees in the Teapot Dome and other scandals. He defended his party while zealously prosecuting the offenders, thus restoring a measure of respect to his office. It was a period of relative prosperity, between the disasters of war and Depression. Reelected in 1924, he was effective in his second term, stressing various economy measures, reducing income taxes and restoring relations with Mexico. Coolidge, in fact, strongly wished to pare down the burgeoning power of the presidency; to a large extent that led to his unassuming style. Meanwhile, his taciturn and often wry Yankee demeanor made him popular.

Coolidge spent much of his time seeking ways of promoting international peace, and helped reduce the crushing war reparations demanded by Germany. He supported the Kellogg-Briand Pact of 1928, which outlawed war; this was a noble effort, but the tide of history was soon to sweep it aside. In 1928 Coolidge announced, "I do not choose to run," and thereafter settled into a quiet retirement in Northampton, where he died in 1933. He had presided over a period of exciting but troubled prosperity, and he had handled it all tolerably well.

12 FEBRUARY 1924
Arts/Culture George Gershwin's innovative and ever–popular symphonic work *Rhapsody in Blue* receives its first performance.

18 MARCH 1924

National The Soldiers' Bonus Bill is passed by the House. It offers 20-year annuities for veterans and will cost $2,000,000,000. The Senate will concur on April 23, but Coolidge will veto it; Congress will override the veto.

26 MAY 1924

Immigration Still trying to control entrance into the country, Congress enacts a new Immigration law. The quota will be rolled back still further to admit only 2 percent of the nationality that was in the country in 1890. Japanese will be totally excluded. Canadians and Mexicans will be unaffected.

2 JUNE 1924

Labor A Child Labor Amendment is sent to the States for ratification. The country, led by the South, is still reluctant to circumscribe the work done by children. By 1950, still ten States short, only 26 will have ratified the Amendment and it will be dropped.

12 JUNE 1924

National The Republican Party convenes in Cleveland, Ohio, to nominate Calvin Coolidge for president and Charles G. Dawes of Illinois for vice-president.

4 JULY 1924

National The National Convention of the Conference for Progressive Political Action meets in Cleveland, Ohio, to nominate Robert La Follette, Senator from Wisconsin, for president. Burton K. Wheeler, Senator from Montana, will be nominated for vice-president.

9 JULY 1924

National The Democratic Party convenes in New York City and nominates John W. Davis of West Virginia (and the House of Morgan) for president and Charles W. Bryan of Nebraska for vice-president. Bryan is brother to the famous Populist leader William Jennings Bryan.

10 JULY 1924

National The Workers' Party convenes in Chicago to nominate William Z. Foster of Illinois for president

The Senate Investigation into Teapot Dome.

WILL ROGERS, 1879-1935

The bemused grin, rumpled cowboy clothes and down-home wisecrackery of Will Rogers made him one of the most beloved American figures of his time. He wanted to be and was the voice of the common man speaking out about the doings of the great and powerful—but the great and powerful loved him just as much as the common man did. He was born of prosperous Irish-Cherokee parents near Oologah, in what would become Oklahoma; prizing his Indian ancestry, he later said, "My ancestors didn't come over on the *Mayflower*—they met the boat." An indifferent student, he much preferred roping cows, and in 1898 he quit school to become a cowboy.

In 1902 Rogers became a "rope artist and rough rider" in various Wild West shows. It was in that capacity that he stumbled on his sense of humor in 1905: finding a New York audience laughing at his Southwestern drawl, he began to joke with them during his rope tricks; that technique, refined over the years, made him famous. In 1912 he appeared in his first Broadway show and went on to become a *Ziegfeld Follies* regular in the "teens and 20s." The staple of his act' was news commentary; for many years no development on the national scene was complete without its aphorism from Will Rogers. As examples: during the peace conference following World War I, Rogers observed, "The United States never lost a war or won a conference," and of Coolidge's bull market he said, "Two thirds of the people promote while one-third provide." Nonetheless, Woodrow Wilson was himself a fan and Calvin Coolidge a personal friend.

In the middle 20s Rogers began his daily syndicated newspaper commentaries on the news and held forth extensively on radio and on the lecture platform. Several of his movies, such as *State Fair* and *A Connecticut Yankee*, were great hits. Throughout his career he was a generous man, often working for charity efforts. He was also a promoter of air travel, and that interest was his undoing—in 1935 he died in a plane crash. The American people had lost a man who addressed the world and said what *they* would like to say—but said it funnier.

---

and Benjamin Gitlow of New York for vice-president. The Workers' Party is Communist. On the other hand, although it is not Communist, the Farmer-Labor Progressive Party has already nominated the same two men to head up their ticket. Having the Communists on their coattails will do nothing to aid the farmers.

4 NOVEMBER 1924

National Calvin Coolidge is elected president by an electoral vote of 382 to the Democrats' 136 and La Follette's 13. Coolidge receives 15,725,000 popular votes, Davis, 8,386,000, and La Follette receives a surprisingly large 4,823,000. Two women are elected governors: Nellie Ross in Wyoming, and Miriam Ferguson in Texas.

27 DECEMBER 1924

International The United States signs a treaty with The Dominican Republic which supersedes the one of 1907. In July, the U.S. had finally left the island.

5 JANUARY 1925

Regional Continuing its tradition of fairness in its

445

treatment of women, Wyoming inaugurates the country's first woman governor, Nellie Taylor Ross.

2 FEBRUARY 1925

Regional The country waits in suspense as men in relays of dog teams attempt to reach Alaska with an antidiphtheria serum. During the worst part of winter, the country's most northern territory has been swept by a deadly epidemic of diphtheria. Blinded by snow, Gunnar Kasson, in a superhuman final push, delivers the serum to Nome.

4 MARCH 1925

National Calvin Coolidge is inaugurated president. Although technically his second term, it is his first elected one, since he has previously served out the two years remaining upon Harding's death.

5 MAY 1925

National John T. Scopes, teacher in the public school system in Dayton, Tennessee, is arrested for teaching Darwin's theory of evolution. He will be brought to trial in July. Speaking for the prosecution will be the great fundamentalist thinker and orator William Jennings Bryan. The defense will be conducted by the able Clarence Darrow and Dudley Field Malone. The country is amused and excited by the clash between science and religion as to whether human beings are descended from monkeys or were made from clay and Adam's rib. On July 20 Bryan agrees to go on the witness stand where he is cross-examined on his strict interpretation of the Bible. Scopes loses the verdict and is fined $100. By the time Tennessee permits the teaching of Darwin's theory, the theory itself will have been modified by anthropological discoveries and interpretation.

17 DECEMBER 1925

National Colonel William "Billy" Mitchell is suspended from the Army for five years without pay. He has accused his superiors of "almost treasonable administration of national defense." Mitchell advocates a strong air arm, foreseeing that the next war will largely be fought in the air. Coolidge will not reverse the suspension but will reinstate Mitchell's pay; nonetheless, Mitchell, still impenitent, proceeds to resign from the Army.

OTHER EVENTS OF 1925

International Charles G. Dawes shares the Nobel Peace Prize with Sir Austen Chamberlain. Dawes receives his share for his plan for solving the German reparations problem.

Arts/Culture The Pulitzer Prize for fiction is presented to Edna Ferber for *So Big*; this seems a rather arbitrary choice because several important works are published this year, including Theodore Dreiser's *An American Tragedy*, John Dos Passos' *Manhattan Transfer* and Scott Fitzgerald's *Tender Is the Night*. This year also sees publication of Ezra Pound's *A Draft of XVI Cantos*, a monumental beginning to the main body of the poet's life's work.

CLARENCE DARROW, 1857-1938

When Americans think of the popular image of the trial lawyer—wise and canny, with utter devotion to his client and the ability to play a jury like a violin—they think of someone very much like Clarence Darrow. During the course of his long career in the public eye he achieved something of the status of a folk hero.

Darrow was born in Kinsman, Ohio, on April 18, 1857, the son of an agnostic ex-minister. He was admitted to the bar in 1878 and commenced a successful career as a corporation lawyer in Youngstown and Chicago. But his liberal sympathies pulled him into the courtroom in 1894 to defend Eugene Debs against contempt charges resulting from the Pullman strike. He went on to become a passionate and nationally-known defender of labor rights until a guilty plea he entered in a 1911 newspaper-bombing case turned organized labor against him; he returned to Chicago at the age of 56 with his career in ruins.

But in ten years Darrow built a new practice as a criminal lawyer. His shambling figure, his drawl and his acid wit in the courtroom reemerged into the headlines in 1924 with the Leopold-Loeb murder case, where his novel exploitation of psychiatric evidence averted a death sentence. In 1925 Darrow defended John Scopes, the Tennessee teacher who taught Darwin's theory, and although Darrow lost the case he succeeded in bringing the issue of evolution to national attention. Through a number of cases over the next few years, as well as a continuing flow of articles, books, films and lectures that continued through his retirement, Darrow debated before the public a number of vital questions—racism, socialism, atheism, Prohibition, capital punishment, child labor, and on and on. To those who agreed with him and those who did not, he was a major force in forming the conscience of his time.

---

27 JANUARY 1926

International Although the temper of the times is isolationist and xenophobic, the Senate adopts a resolution permitting the United States to join the World Court of International Justice, which is to be given jurisdiction over all international problems brought before it by its member nations. The resolution contains five reservations; four are accepted without question, but on the fifth, relating to advisory opinions from the Court relating to a dispute in which the United States is involved, the United States will not compromise. Further attempts during the next ten years to come to some agreement continue to fail. Although not a permanent member of either the World Court or the League of Nations, nonetheless The United States does take part in many international conferences and deliberations. Charles Evans Hughes will represent the U.S. at the Permanent Court of Arbitration at The Hague.

26 FEBRUARY 1926

National The Revenue Act is signed into law by Coolidge. Continuing the policy of "normalcy," which defines the general reduction of government at the Federal level, Coolidge reduces income taxes, surtaxes and other taxes, following Republican policies which tend to do little for the sickness already gnawing at the bowels of the nation in the way of unem-

OCTOBER 10, 1926

F. SCOTT FITZGERALD, 1896-1940

Francis Scott Key Fitzgerald yearned for wealth, fame, and the love of a beautiful woman; he got enough of all three to ruin and kill him. He wrote some bad books, a couple of not-so-bad books, and one very good book. This latter, *The Great Gatsby*, was so good that it may someday overshadow the pathetic story of his own life, which long after his death was his main claim to fame.

Descended from his namesake, the author of the *Star-Spangled Banner*, Fitzgerald was born in St. Paul, Minnesota, on September 24, 1896. His parents were somewhat-going-to-seed gentry, and that ambiguous background would mark Fitzgerald's consciousness. At Princeton he was a social whirlwind and not much of a student, finally leaving college for the army in 1917. While stationed in Alabama he met a vivacious Southern belle named Zelda Sayre; smitten fatally, he was obliged to finish *This Side of Paradise* to make himself rich and famous enough for her to consider marrying him. Published in 1920, this mediocre novel epitomized the Jazz Age, but otherwise did the trick: Zelda and Scott were married in 1920.

For a few years they lived a fancy and notorious existence all over the world. Meanwhile, Fitzgerald completed *The Beautiful and the Damned*, prophetically named and a better book at least than his first. His short fiction became a staple of popular magazines in America. But all along, Fitzgerald had the vision to see through the life he felt compelled to pursue; in 1925 this vision resulted in *The Great Gatsby*, the study of a rich man who finds himself in "a new world, material without being real, where poor ghosts, breathing dreams like air, drifted fortuitously about." A stunning literary achievement and critically acclaimed as such, the book was a flop with the public.

By 1931 they were broke, Zelda was in her first of several increasingly serious mental breakdowns and Scott was drinking heavily and writing as best he could. In 1934 appeared the flawed but deeply-felt *Tender Is the Night*, an evocation of his view of America and of his own broken life. The rest of the decade saw a steady decline. He died in 1940; hearing the news, Dorothy Parker pronounced his epitaph: "The poor son-of-a-bitch."

RICHARD BYRD, 1888-1957

Richard Byrd, aviator and pioneer explorer of Antarctica, was one of the authentic heroes of his time, and one of the last of such heroes to earn his fame from the charting of unknown areas of the earth. He was born in Winchester, Virginia, on October 25, 1888, a son of the most powerful family in Virginia politics. After graduating from the U.S. Naval Academy in 1912 he served on various ships until an ankle injury retired him to desk duty. However, he managed to be accepted for flight training and served as a patrol pilot in Canada during World War I.

After the war Byrd helped organize the first successful transatlantic flight, which was made by three Navy flying boats. In 1925 he was flying in the polar region on Greenland expeditions. In 1926, with private backing, he and Floyd Bennett made the first flight over the North Pole. After accompanying another successful three-man transatlantic flight in 1927, Byrd mounted a major expedition to the South Pole. The expedition in 1928 established the first "Little America" base camp on the Antarctic Ross Ice Shelf and wintered there; Byrd and Bernt Balchen flew over the South Pole in November 1929. On his return he was promoted to rear admiral and given the Navy Cross for extraordinary heroism.

Byrd's third Antarctic expedition began in 1933; during it he spent five months of the winter alone in an advance base and was rescued in 1934 near death from carbon monoxide poisoning. During this experience he wrote in his diary, "if I survive this ordeal I shall devote what is left of my life largely . . . to help further the friendship of my country with other nations of the world." He survived and kept his pledge. For the rest of his life he worked on issues of international peace, aided the war effort during World War II on secret missions in the Pacific and in Europe, and continued his pioneering work on the exploration and study of the Antarctic. He died in Boston in 1957.

ployment and the plight of the farmers. "Keep Cool With Coolidge" is his slogan, and helps keep the Republican Party intact throughout the scandalous revelations of corruption under Harding.

29 APRIL 1926
International The United States and France sign an agreement which will ultimately cancel 60 percent of the French debt. France agrees to repay $4 billion over 62 years at 1.6 percent interest.

9 MAY 1926
Aviation Rear Admiral Richard E. Byrd and Floyd Bennett make the first successful flight over the North Pole.

10 MAY 1926
International The United States Marines land in Nicaragua to quell a revolt. The U.S. military presence will remain there until 1933.

20 MAY 1926
Transportation Congress enacts the Air Commerce Act. Until now, the Federal Government has generally kept its hands off civil aviation except for subsidizing air mail; this act will give the Department of Commerce control over licensing of aircraft and pilots and this is a step toward federal regulation of many of society's activities.

2 JULY 1926
National Congress establishes the Army Air Corps.

18 SEPTEMBER 1926
Regional Florida has been exulting in one of the greatest land booms in history. The rush to get lots in the sunny state dwarfs all other land or gold rushes which the nation has witnessed. Suddenly into the feverish crush of prospective buyers sweeps a tornado, careening across Florida and the Gulf States. Over 6000 people are injured with another 372 killed. Some 18,000 families are left homeless, and the damage is ultimately estimated at $80,000,000.

10 OCTOBER 1926
Regional A naval ammunition depot at Lake Den-

447

EXPANDING RESOURCES 1901-1945

mark, New Jersey, explodes when hit by lightning. It is the worst such disaster in the history of the U.S. military. Thirty-one people lose their lives, and damage is estimated at $93,000,000. The explosions continue for several days.

25 OCTOBER 1926
National The Supreme Court rules that the president has the power to remove his own Cabinet members and other appointees. The ruling annuls an act of 1876, which Thaddeus Stevens and his Congressional colleagues had enacted to restrict the powers of President Andrew Johnson during the bitter days of Reconstruction.

OTHER EVENTS OF 1926
Life/Customs Gertrude Ederle, an American from New York, is the first woman to swim the English Channel; she makes her record swim in 14 hours, 31 minutes.

11 FEBRUARY 1927
Agriculture The McNary-Haugen bill is passed by the Senate after some three years of consideration. The plan is for the Federal Government to purchase agricultural surpluses to be sold at world market prices. If the world price is lower than the domestic price the producers would pay the government a token equalization fee. The plan is vetoed by Coolidge.

18 FEBRUARY 1927
International The United States and Canada establish diplomatic relations independent of Great Britain. The first Canadian Minister to present his credentials is Charles Vincent Massey. William Phillips will be the first minister to Canada from the United States. Later this year, on August 2, in ceremonies drawing the two countries ever closer, the Prince of Wales and Vice-President Dawes open the International Peace Bridge which links the U.S. with Canada at Buffalo, New York.

23 FEBRUARY 1927
National Continuing its policy of enlarging its right to regulate what some consider to be the private sector, Congress creates the Federal Radio Commission to oversee the newest field of national and international communications.

17 MARCH 1927
National The Teapot Dome and Elk Hills naval oil reserves, which had featured in the scandals of the Harding Administration, are returned to the jurisdiction of the Navy Department. The Supreme Court has ruled that the Mammoth Company has received them under fraudulent contracts which renders ownership invalid.

17 APRIL 1927
National Running in the early stages of the Presidential campaign, Alfred E. Smith, Governor of New York State, collides with the bigotry that underlies the political attitudes of the 20s. Asked by Charles C. Marshall where his loyalties would lie in a conflict involving the United States and the Vatican, Smith replies: "I recognize no power in the institution of my Church to interfere with the operations of the Constitution of the United States or the enforcement of the law of the land."

21 MAY 1927
Aviation Charles A. Lindbergh flies his monoplane

The Ku Klux Klan comes to Washington.

The *Spirit of St. Louis*.

the *Spirit of St. Louis*, from New York to Paris. It is the first such Atlantic crossing. Lindbergh covers the 3600 miles in 33 and a half hours. His solo flight is followed by millions, and when he lands at Orly airport, some 100,000 people are on hand to greet the new hero.

This same year on June 20, Clarence Chamberlain and Charles Levine fly their airplane *Colombia* 3905 miles in 43 hours to complete the journey between New York and Germany. A week later, on June 28, Lester J. Maitland and Albert F. Hegenberger, both lieutenants in the new Army Air Corps, make the flight from San Francisco to Honolulu. Next year on May 25, Amelia Earhart will be the first woman to fly the Atlantic. She takes two passengers with her.

2 AUGUST 1927
National Coolidge scotches any moves to induce him to run for what might be construed as a third term as president. In his laconic style he explains: "I do not choose to run."

29 SEPTEMBER 1927
Regional St. Louis is devastated by a tornado. In five minutes more than 1000 homes are a tangled mass of wreckage, 87 people are dead and more than 1500 injured. The cost of the fearful disaster will amount to some $50,000,000. This has not been the only natural disaster this year. In April the Mississippi has overflowed its banks to cause some $300,000,000 in property damage.

25 DECEMBER 1927
International The Mexican Congress reverses its Constitution of 1917 and grants unlimited concessions to foreigners for lands on which "positive" acts have been performed before May 1, 1917. The effect is to nullify the constitution's social and political reforms which had been enacted in an effort to curb foreign drain on Mexican natural resources. By a decree of 1918 the ownership of oil lands has been revoked and concessions are to be negotiated instead. The Ameri-

CHARLES A. LINDBERGH, 1902-1975

America in 1927 was still a place where a young and reticent loner could rise from utter obscurity to become in one day the most celebrated person on the planet. It is a lesson to be considered that Lindbergh wore the mantle of greatness as long and as gracefully as he did, given the reluctance with which he wore it and the sorrow it often brought him.

Lindbergh was born on February 4, 1902 in Detroit, Michigan. An indifferent student in his youth, he took up flying in the early 1920s. After a season of barnstorming, a year at an Army flying school and a brief stint as an airmail pilot, he determined to try for the Orteig Prize, which promised $25,000 to the first person to fly nonstop from New York to Paris. He helped design *The Spirit of St. Louis* for that purpose and tested the plane on a record-breaking flight from California to New York in 1927.

On May 20, 1927 the gasoline-stuffed little plane limped off the runway of Roosevelt Field in New York, barely clearing the telephone lines; inside, a sleepy Lindbergh had with him only a few sandwiches, a quart of water, and some letters of introduction that were unnecessary to say the least: his arrival in Paris 33½ hours later was met by a wave of shouting Frenchmen who greeted the astonished flier with a delirious enthusiasm that would mark his appearances everywhere for some time.

For years thereafter he lived in a public spotlight that he hated; his marriage to Anne Spencer Morrow, who became his flying partner and a noted writer, took place in a glare of publicity. Their notoriety made them the target of a kidnapping in 1932 that claimed the life of their first child. And there were more dark years; in the late 30s Lindbergh made a series of visits to Nazi Germany, where he was awarded a medal by Goering. Nonetheless, the love he still inspired spared him much censure, and he aided the war effort during the conflict. The rest of his life was spent as an airline consultant and conservationist. The spotlight that had brought him glory and sorrow slowly dimmed until his death in 1975.

U.S. Ambassador Herrick greets Lindbergh.

cans protest and when the new President Alvaro Obregon is recognized, it is on condition that he recognize American subsoil rights; otherwise, warns Secretary of State Frank B. Kellogg, the U.S. will not support the government in power. The Mexicans are in no mood to arbitrate under the circumstances. However, Coolidge sends Morgan & Company's Dwight W. Morrow as ambassador to Mexico to effect a settlement. On November 17 the Mexican Supreme Court finds Mexico's Petroleum Law unconstitutional and the oil lands effectively revert to American companies. Following the pattern of Mexican politics, Obregon will be assassinated July 17, 1928.

OTHER EVENTS OF 1927

Life/Customs The first "talkie," *The Jazz Singer*, starring Al Jolson, is released: movies—and America—will never be the same. Also this year, the Academy of Motion Picture Arts and Sciences is formed; it will not begin presentation of its awards, later to be known as "Oscars," until 1929.

16 JANUARY 1928

International The Sixth International Conference of American States opens in Havana. President Coolidge presides at the opening; however, this does not prevent the restless South American States from introducing a resolution aimed directly against the United States. The resolution proposes that "no state has the right to intervene in the internal affairs of another." This refers to the Roosevelt Corollary which has effectively made the United States policeman for the Western Hemisphere. For instance, at the time, U.S. troops are still in Nicaragua where they will remain until withdrawn by Hoover in 1933. Charles Evans Hughes, who has been named to represent the U.S. at the World Court but who is temporarily heading up the U.S. delegation to the Havana Convention, blocks passage of the resolution; however, he is merely buying time. On 17 December J. Reuben Clark of the State Department will redefine the Monroe Doctrine to apply to "a case of the U.S. v. Europe, and not the U.S. v. Latin America. . . The Doctrine does not concern itself with purely inter-American relations." The Roosevelt Corollary will have been repudiated in word if not in deed.

13 APRIL 1928

National The Socialist Party convenes in New York City to nominate Norman Thomas of New York for president and James H. Maurer of Pennsylvania for vice-president.

27 MAY 1928

National The Workers' Party, avowedly Communist, convenes in New York to nominate William Z. Foster of Illinois for president and Benjamin Gitlow of New York for vice-president.

15 JUNE 1928

National The Republican Party convenes in Kansas City, Missouri, to nominate Herbert Hoover of California for president and Charles Curtis of Kansas for vice-president. The Republican slogan is: "A chicken in every pot, a car in every garage." Hoover, who

---

NORMAN THOMAS, 1884-1968

In his long tenure as leader of the American Socialist movement, Norman Thomas managed to achieve a great deal of personal respect and fame in a cause that was highly suspect if not anathema to most of his countrymen. Perhaps this was because many of his basic positions—among them a commitment to pacifism, racial equality and disarmament—were inescapably right even if proclaimed before their time had come.

Thomas was born in Marion, Ohio, on November 20, 1884. He became in 1911 the third generation of his family to enter the Presbyterian ministry. As pastor of an East Harlem church in New York City, he worked with church social agencies, and at the outbreak of World War I became a pacifist and Socialist. In 1917 he helped found an organization that was to become the American Civil Liberties Union.

Resigning his ministry in 1918, Thomas observed that he was led to Socialism by the "grotesque inequalities, . . . exploitation, and unnecessary poverty all about me." In the 20s he became a tireless worker and writer for the cause, contributing to Socialist periodicals and issuing books as he would continue to do all his life. After several New York political bids Thomas in 1926 became leader of the Socialist party after the death of Eugene Debs; he first ran for president two years later. Of his six presidential campaigns the best he ever did was in 1932, when he polled fewer than 900,000 votes. Many of his campaign speeches were marked by public demonstrations and by the tossing of eggs and garbage.

In the 30s Thomas criticized the Soviet Union and allied himself with non-Marxists in the party. Though he opposed American entry into World War II, during the war he and the party supported the war effort while criticizing government actions, especially the internment of Japanese-Americans and the dropping of the atom bomb. Until his death in 1968 Thomas remained a prominent and much-admired leader of a movement that never made much headway but was nonetheless a platform for him to become a major voice of his country's conscience.

---

has done so much postwar relief work and cares about the welfare of people, seems to believe his own speech when, publicly accepting the nomination on August 11, he declares: "We in America today are nearer the final triumph over poverty than ever before in the history of the land."

29 JUNE 1928

National The Democratic Party convenes in Houston, Texas, to nominate Catholic Alfred E. Smith, now Governor of New York State, for president, and Joseph T. Robinson of Arkansas for vice-president. Religion will overshadow issues in the ensuing campaign.

25 AUGUST 1928

Exploration Richard E. Byrd, U.S. naval officer, begins the first leg of his flight to the South Pole. The Norwegian Roald Amundsen has already reached the pole in 1911, and Robert Scott has done so a month later, although he did not live through the journey home. Now Byrd attempts to conquer Antarctica, which is considered to be far more difficult than the

DECEMBER 21, 1928

AL SMITH, 1873-1944

As governor of New York and Presidential candidate, Al Smith was a much-loved Democratic progressive and social reformer, but his hopes for the White House were defeated partly by a bigotry and reactionism which left him disillusioned with his own ideals. Smith was born to a Catholic family in New York's Lower East Side on December 30, 1873, dropping out of school in the eighth grade to work at various small jobs. He entered politics by running errands for a saloon owner and Democratic precinct leader, working up in the Tammany Hall political machine to become a state assemblyman in 1903.

After the disastrous Triangle Waist Company fire of 1911, Smith helped lead a pathbreaking investigative commission, an experience that deepened his reformist sentiments and resulted in much vital social and labor legislation. His prominence on the committee led eventually to the New York governor's seat in 1918. He quickly appointed a number of women and minorities to his staff, including Frances Perkins and Belle Moskowitz. In spite of a successful term, a national Republican upsurge caused his defeat in 1920, but he returned to office in 1922 and was twice re-elected.

Smith by that time was the leading Democrat in New York politics; he thereby freed himself of machine loyalties and dominated the legislature to produce a wide-ranging progressive program including government reorganization, welfare, public housing, extended park facilities and pro-labor issues; somehow, at the same time he reduced taxes. His spectacular achievements made him a contender for the presidential nomination in the 1924 Democratic convention, where Franklin D. Roosevelt, nominating him, dubbed Smith "The Happy Warrior." After considerable wrangling marked by anti-Catholic undercurrents, Smith withdrew.

But by 1928 he was the unquestioned leader for the nomination, and received it on the first ballot at the convention. The Democratic campaign that ensued was marked by poor organization, Smith's unpopular anti-Prohibitionism and vitrolic anti-Catholic sentiment that left him personally shocked and bitter. Hoover won the election by a substantial margin. Smith never again found a political opening; he settled into business interests, becoming increasingly conservative as his political power slowly ebbed. He died in New York in 1944.

Arctic since the frozen continent is not populated. However, since it is also a land mass and not just frozen water, it is potentially far more important than the Arctic. By October, at latitude 78°30′, Byrd sets up base camp which he names Little America. There he methodically prepares for an air journey to the South Pole. On November 28, with a crew of three, he successfully reaches his goal and returns to his camp within 19 hours. Byrd will continue to explore the isolated continent bringing to public attention its wealth and strategic importance. His use of the airplane for exploration will be followed in the future.

27 AUGUST 1928
International The Pact of Paris, also known as the Kellogg-Briand Pact after its two formulators, is signed by the United States and 15 nations. The previous year in March, Aristide Briand, the French Foreign Minister, has had a conversation with Professor James T. Shotwell of Columbia University which leads Briand to publicly propose the "outlawry of war." In June of the same year, Secretary of State Frank B. Kellogg acknowledges the proposal and Briand proceeds to draft a bilateral treaty. As enthusiasm mounts for the idea, Kellogg submits a multinational agreement for discussion. On April 13 other nations are consulted on the idea. It is easy for nations to subscribe to the proposal because it commits neither men, money, nor machines. The idea is to outlaw war as a means to settle disputes and substitute the strength of world opinion and the skills of diplomats. The pact will ultimately be signed by 62 nations, just ten years prior to the outbreak of the most desolating war in history. (Kellogg will be awarded the Nobel Prize for Peace in 1929 for his part.)

6 NOVEMBER 1928
National Republican Herbert Hoover wins the election by 444 electoral votes to 87 for Al Smith, suggesting a decisive rejection of the Democrat on the grounds of religious prejudice. However, the popular vote tells a different story with a much closer 21,392,000 votes for Hoover to 15,016,000 for Smith. Foreshadowing events which will be of greater importance to the country, Democrat Franklin Delano Roosevelt is elected governor of New York State.

19 NOVEMBER 1928
International Herbert Hoover leaves for an extended goodwill tour of South America.

26 NOVEMBER 1928
International Although the mood of the country is essentially isolationist, so that the United States seems to be backing away from its international responsibilities, still at the diplomatic level it is extending its participation in international affairs. On this day, the United States is represented at the International Conference on Economic Statistics of the League of Nations; on December 10 the Pan-American Conference on Conciliation and Arbitration convenes in Washington at Coolidge's invitation; on December 12, the International Civil Aeronautics Conference opens in Washington with delegates from some 40 countries including the United States.

21 DECEMBER 1928
National The Federal Government takes its first big step and publicly enters the field of hydroelectric power, hitherto deemed the sector of private business. While paying lip-service to free enterprise, the government has proceeded to undertake ever larger projects for its citizens, ones larger than any one state can shoulder. On May 15, Congress has passed the Flood Control Act which provides $325,000,000 for control of flooding on the Mississippi. The project will take ten years to complete. On May 22 The Jones-White Merchant Marine Act is passed by Congress, providing subsidies to private shipping companies, thereby publicly blurring the edge between private enterprise

451

and government business. On May 25, Congress enacts the Muscle Shoals Bill, which provides for government ownership of the hydroelectric plant at Muscle Shoals, Tennessee. This last will be killed by a Coolidge pocket veto.

OTHER EVENTS OF 1928
Arts/Culture The Pulitzer Prize for fiction is awarded to Thornton Wilder for his *The Bridge of San Luis Rey*. The Ashcan School of painting dominates New York's Greenwich Village, now the art center of the country. The school, led by the painter John Sloan, proposes to treat the city as legitimate subject matter for the artist, who may bring the same lyricism to the bustling activity of city streets as others have brought to country life.

15 JANUARY 1929
International The U.S. Senate ratifies (85 to 1) the Kellogg-Briand Pact that was signed by 15 nations on August 27, 1928; the pact commits these nations to outlawing aggression and war.

2 FEBRUARY 1929
National The Federal Reserve Board forbids its member banks to make loans to anyone who wants to use the money to buy stocks on margin; this type of speculating is known to be contributing to the rise in stock prices but it is based on paper values.

11 FEBRUARY/7 JUNE 1929
International An international group of financial experts meets in Paris, elects Owen Young of the U.S.A. as its chairman and proceeds to revise the Dawes Plan under which Germany was supposed to pay reparations for World War I. Out of their deliberations will come a new schedule of reduced annual payments to be made through a Bank of International Settlements.

13 FEBRUARY 1929
National Congress passes the Cruiser Act, authorizing the construction of 19 new cruisers and 1 aircraft carrier. What it signifies is that the U.S., like all the world's powers, is signing peace treaties but nevertheless embarking on an armaments race.

14 FEBRUARY 1929
Regional In Chicago, six gangsters are lined up against a garage wall and shot to death by a rival gang; this will become known as "The St. Valentine's Day Massacre."

4 MARCH 1929
National Herbert Hoover is inaugurated as the 31st president with Charles Curtis as vice-president. In his address, Hoover assures the world that the U.S. has "no desire for territorial expansion, for economic or other domination of other people."

9 APRIL 1929
International A U.S. Coast Guard cutter sinks a

HERBERT HOOVER, 1874-1964

It is undoubtedly true that the accidents of history can make Presidents or break them. The disaster of the Depression broke Herbert Hoover; it is possible that without that he would have been a better–then–average President—he was clearly an extremely competent leader.

Hoover was born into an old Quaker family on August 10, 1874, in West Branch, Iowa. He graduated from Stanford with an engineering degree in 1895 and began a career as a mining engineer that took him to California, Australia, China and London; by 1910 he was a major international figure in the world of mining. His reputation led to appointments heading relief work during and after World War I; over a period of years he brilliantly directed efforts that fed and clothed millions of people devastated by the war. In 1920 he became Warren G. Harding's secretary of commerce; he worked at that post through the ensuing Coolidge administration.

His success was such that he was nominated on the first ballot of the 1928 Republican Convention. He ran on a platform that promised to widen existing prosperity, promote relief for farmers, strengthen protective tariffs and continue Prohibition. He swept the election, defeating liberal anti-Prohibition candidate Al Smith, and proceeded to guide his promised programs through Congress. Things were going relatively smoothly until October 29, 1929, when the stock market came tumbling down. Around America the breadlines began to form, the wandering jobless built ramshackle settlements which they dubbed "Hoovervilles." History has not blamed Hoover for the Depression as his own time did, but it is also true that his efforts to assuage the problem were ineffective and sometimes ill-advised, such as his aid to big business on the theory that the money would "trickle down" to the people—it never did. His foreign-policy initiatives, such as an important naval treaty in 1930, made little impact on the starving millions at home. In 1932 Franklin D. Roosevelt held out the promise of a New Deal, and America kicked Hoover out.

Bitter and disappointed, Hoover nonetheless stayed active for the rest of a long life, first as a critic of the New Deal and then as head of Truman's Commission on Organization of the Executive Branch. Over the years he produced a number of important books, including the 1958 *Ordeal of Woodrow Wilson*. He also lived to see his presidency to some extent vindicated by history.

AUGUST-SEPTEMBER 1929

ship, *I'm Alone*, about 200 miles offshore in the Gulf of Mexico on the suspicion that it is a rumrunner. As the ship turns out to be of Canadian registry, the Canadian government protests vigorously.

15 APRIL 1929
National A special session of Congress meets at President Hoover's request to deal with the mounting problems of the nation's economy; in particular, the farmers are becoming desperate for financial relief and the tariffs need revision.

20 MAY 1929
National The U.S.A. has become increasingly disturbed by the lawlessness and general defiance occasioned by the 18th Amendment—Prohibition. President Hoover has declared himself in favor of Prohibition, but he appoints a National Commission on Law Observance and Enforcement to study the effects of Prohibition on the nation; the commission is to be chaired by George Wickersham.

27 MAY 1929
National The Supreme Court, in *United States v. Schwimmer*, upholds a lower court's denial of citizenship to Rosika Schwimmer, a Hungarian immigrant who was an avowed pacifist. Justice Oliver Wendell Holmes Jr., in one of his famous dissents, argues that freedom to think unpopular notions is perhaps the most fundamental principle of the U.S. Constitution. On this day the Supreme Court also rules that the use of the "pocket veto" by a President is constitutional.

7 JUNE 1929
International The financial experts in Paris announce their agreement on the Young Plan—replacing the Dawes Plan—that sets up a new and reduced schedule of payments of German reparations. Germany and the other signatories will sign this agreement in January 1930.

15 JUNE 1929
National Congress passes the Agricultural Marketing Act, establishing a Federal Farm Board with a revolving fund to aid farmers' cooperatives and to help sell surplus agricultural produce at more stable prices. In 1930 several stabilization corporations will be set up by this Board to deal with different produce, but the nation's farmers will never fully cooperate.

1 JULY 1929
National The Immigration Act of 1924 (May 26) goes into effect (after being delayed from the original date called for, July 1, 1927); it institutes a quota system for immigrants in the U.S.A., based on the U.S. population in 1920; it is an overt attempt to keep the country's ethnic "composition" what it has been—that is, predominantly of Northern Europeans.

24 JULY 1929
International President Hoover formally proclaims that the Kellogg-Briand Pact is in effect.

PROHIBITION

Bootleg and hijack, speakeasies and flappers, stills and moonshine, gangsters and corrupt politicians—these are for many the images and associations of Prohibition in the United States. Yet the effort to halt drinking came largely from people who saw it as a threat to social stability. Attempts to control alcohol consumption had been made since colonial times in America, and as early as 1808 formal temperance organizations were active. The effort ebbed and flowed through the 19th century, with some states trying outright prohibition and others allowing local option laws. Clearly, restraints in one locale could be nullified by what was permitted in a neighboring area, so true prohibitionists were not satisfied. An actual Prohibition Party was organized in 1869, and although it attained little success at the polls, this party—along with the Womens Christian Temperance Union, the Anti-Saloon League and allies in other movements such as that for women's suffrage—made progress in popularizing the idea.

By the early 20th century, the ingredients necessary for passage of a national prohibition law were coming together. More than half the states, led by the South and West, were "dry." Congress outlawed the sale of liquor in the two areas it controlled—Indian reservations and the District of Columbia. The outbreak of World War I allowed for the cork to be pushed still farther: sales to soldiers and sailors were forbidden and other restrictions were placed on the making of alcohol (under the claim that it diverted resources from the war effort).

Finally, in December 1917, Congress passed the 18th Amendment, allowing Prohibition. It was soon adopted by large majorities in all but two states, and in January 1920, when the enforcement began under the Volstead Act, the United States found itself officially "dry." In fact, the law proved to be largely unenforcible. Bootleggers crossed the Mexican and Canadian borders with near impunity. Ocean-going ships waited outside the three-mile limit for high-speed "rum-runners" to carry the contraband liquors through the hopelessly inadequate blockade by U.S. government agencies. Domestic stills turned out an ever-increasing supply of local varieties of "white lightning," and most cities had speakeasies with virtually open hospitality for imbibers.

Ironically, if not predictably, the effect of Prohibition on society at large seemed to be the opposite of what had been intended. Drinking, alcohol abuse and lawlessness all increased during the 1920s. The great profits made available to illicit businessmen led to the organization of crime and its links with law enforcement agents, politicians and legal businesses that continue to plague American society. Even women, recently granted the right to elect by the 19th Amendment, cast their vote by violating the 18th. By the time the 21st Amendment repealed the 18th in December 1933, a social revolution had occurred, engendered by widespread violation of and disrespect for Prohibition; as a social experiment Prohibition had provided Americans with many provocative lessons.

AUGUST–SEPTEMBER 1929
National The nation's economy begins to crack along certain discontinuities. Steel and automobile production are declining and the whole economy shows signs of weakening. Yet stock market prices rise; in September, the common stock price index

EXPANDING RESOURCES 1901-1945

peaks at 216, the climax of a three-year bull market.

24 SEPTEMBER 1929
Aviation Lieutenant General James Doolittle successfully makes the first "blind" airplane flight at Mitchell Field, New York; he uses only instruments dependent on radio signals.

4-9 OCTOBER 1929
International Prime Minister Ramsay MacDonald of Great Britain comes to Washington, D.C., to discuss naval parity with President Hoover. In October Britain invites the U.S. and 3 other major naval powers (France, Italy, Japan) to a disarmament conference to open in London in January 1930; the U.S. will accept on October 10; meanwhile, on October 9, Hoover and MacDonald affirm their support of the Kellogg-Briand Pact.

22 OCTOBER 1929
National The President of New York's National City Bank states: "I know of nothing fundamentally wrong with the stock market or with the underlying business and credit structure." But not everyone agrees; just this month, there have been heavy withdrawals of capital from America as England raised its interest rate to 6.5 percent.

23 OCTOBER 1929
National There has been a steady decline in stock market prices since the peak in September and there are signs of panic in the New York Stock Exchange.

24 OCTOBER 1929
National There is a collapse of stock prices on the New York Stock Exchange: some 13,000,000 shares are sold, giving this day the label "Black Thursday." Wealthy investors such as J.P. Morgan and John D. Rockefeller have tried to prop up the market by buying, but they cannot check its fall.

29 OCTOBER 1929
National On what becomes known as "Black Tuesday," the New York Stock Exchange sees some 16,000,000 shares sold at declining prices. This is the most catastrophic day in the market's history and becomes the forerunner of the great Depression.

13 NOVEMBER 1929
National By this day, some $30,000,000,000 in value of listed stocks has been wiped out in the New York Stock Exchange; some of those who have seen their fortunes vanish will kill themselves, but most Americans will survive to work for a better future.

21 NOVEMBER 1929
National President Hoover, trying to reassure the nation, meets with representatives of big businesses and trade unions in two separate confidential sessions at the White House; two weeks later, several hundred representatives of both employers and workers will

---

THE AUTOMOBILE

Of all the inventions of the industrial age, none, perhaps, so changed American life as did the automobile. There was a simplicity to both the idea and to its application which appealed to just about everybody. Almost instantly thousands would begin to tinker with the little one–cylinder engines, and hundreds of factories would spring up to meet the extraordinary demand for what amounted to a new kind of freedom: mobility.

Paris had taken the "horseless carriage" to its heart some ten years before Americans did, and bad roads in the U.S. did much to dampen desire for the incredible machine for a time. However, when in 1908 Henry Ford brought out his Model T for some $825, and equally importantly when in 1916 Congress passed its matching appropriations bill for building roads, another one of those characteristically massive shifts in the American way of life was underway.

In 1893, the Duryea brothers of Springfield, Massachusetts, had been the first Americans to make a working gasoline engine. Modifications on the early one–cylinder, tiller-steered models soon followed: 1892, pneumatic tires; 1902, "H" slot gearshift; the same year, flexible front wheels attached to a stationary axle produced the steering wheel; 1904, automatic lubrication; 1906, front bumpers; 1907, V-8 engine; 1911, electric self-starter; 1912, steel frames; 1918, hydraulic brakes; 1923, ethyl gasoline.

Henry Ford sold over 15 million Model Ts by 1927 and had successfully invaded the European market. By 1929 revenues from exports on automobiles exceeded those on cotton. About half the families in Northern states owned cars. Ownership cut across class and racial barriers. Farmers were freed from their land. Not less importantly, the famous back seat on Lovers' Lane would do much to change the morals of America. There are respectable historians who still claim that more than any one other factor, cars ensured the stability and healthy growth of the American middle class.

---

ratify the general goals in an attempt to stop the collapse of the economy.

29 NOVEMBER 1929
Aviation Lieutenant Commander Richard E. Byrd and the Norwegian-American Bernt Balchen make the first airplane flight over the South Pole; they start from a base at Little America in Antarctica and will make one stop for fuel in their 19-hour flight.

2 DECEMBER 1929
International Secretary of State Henry Stimson writes to both the U.S.S.R. and China and appeals to them to resolve their dispute over Manchuria in the spirit of the Kellogg-Briand Pact that they have both signed.

3 DECEMBER 1929
National President Hoover delivers his annual message to Congress and declares that confidence in the nation's business has now been reestablished. The events of the coming decade will do nothing to justify this statement.

9 DECEMBER 1929
International The "Root formula" (so named after

its proposer, the American diplomat Elihu Root)—intended as the basis for U.S. adherence to decisions of the World Court of the League of Nations, is signed by an American representative in Switzerland. Secretary of State Stimson will accept this, but the U.S. Senate will refuse to ratify it.

OTHER EVENTS OF 1929

International The Nobel Prize for Peace is awarded to Frank Kellogg, the American Secretary of State who negotiated the Kellogg-Briand Pact for outlawing war.

Labor Ford Motor Company announces its minimum wage will increase from $6 to $7 a day.

Arts/Culture This year sees the publication of Thomas Wolfe's *Look Homeward, Angel*, William Faulkner's *Sartoris*, and Ernest Hemingway's *A Farewell to Arms*. The Academy of Motion Picture Arts and Sciences makes its first awards on May 16. (They will not be known as "Oscars" until 1931.) The award for the best picture of the 1927-28 season goes to *Wings*, to Janet Gaynor for best actress, and to Emil Jannings for best actor.

Life/Customs In New York City, Margaret Sanger's birth control clinic is raided by the police (after the Daughters of the American Revolution complain); two doctors and three nurses are arrested, and thousands of clients' records are confiscated. The case will later be dismissed on the grounds that it is an infringement on physicians' freedom to practice. In Radburn, New Jersey, the first American "garden community" is initiated; it is an attempt to design a community that is both aesthetic, natural and safe; roads, houses, public facilities, all elements have been designed.

2 JANUARY 1930

National With the economy sinking, agricultural and commodity prices falling, national income collapsing and unemployment approaching 4,000,000, President Hoover meets with Congressional leaders to discuss the advisability of developing a public works program.

21 JANUARY–22 APRIL 1930

International An international Naval Conference meets in London to continue the work begun at the Washington Conference of 1921-22. The U.S., Great Britain and Japan agree on ratios, sizes and schedules for enlarging their fleets but France and Italy reject the major provisions. The U.S. Senate will ratify this treaty on July 21, 1930.

3 FEBRUARY 1930

National Charles Evans Hughes is named by President Hoover to succeed William Howard Taft as Chief Justice of the Supreme Court. The appointment will be confirmed by the Senate on February 13.

13 MARCH 1930

National The trial of Edward Doheny begins in Washington, D.C.; he is charged with bribing former Secretary of the Interior Albert Fall to obtain a lease

WILLIAM FAULKNER, 1897-1962

Among the important and influential American writers of this century, few are as paradoxical as William Faulkner of Oxford, Mississippi. His books are full of violent and grotesque stories of Southern poor whites and blacks, yet in his Nobel Prize address he proclaimed that man will "prevail . . . because he has a spirit capable of compassion and sacrifice and endurance." His extravagant prose style was admired and condemned, often by the same critics. Beneath his self-created image of hard-drinking Southern farmer and story-teller, Faulkner was in fact an intensely idealistic and driven artist whose brilliant experiments with novelistic form influenced a whole generation of novelists.

Born in Mississippi on September 25, 1897, the young Faulkner increasingly neglected his schoolwork in favor of writing, finally dropping out of high school. After RAF flight training in Canada near the end of the war (he never saw action), Faulkner played the role of bohemian poet in Mississippi, New Orleans, and on rambles in Europe. In New Orleans Faulkner became friends with the novelist Sherwood Anderson and as a result tried his hand at a novel; published in 1926 as *Soldier's Pay*, this book had a modest success. After a weak second novel, Faulkner decided to follow Anderson's advice and write about his Mississippi background. The result, beginning with *Sartoris* in 1929, was an interconnected cycle of novels and stories set around the fictional town of Jefferson in Yoknapatawpha County. In effect, Faulkner's lifework was a single gigantic saga in which the same characters, families and events appear and reappear. Faulkner's fourth novel and first acknowledged masterpiece was *The Sound and the Fury* (1929). Despite the necessity of earning a living in Hollywood (where he wrote *The Big Sleep* among other films), there followed over the next 30 years a prolific and highly original output of novels and short stories including *As I Lay Dying*, *Light in August*, the sensationalistic *Sanctuary* and many others.

Faulkner did not achieve great fame and financial security until his 50s. During the lean years, however, his foreign reputation grew steadily and finally culminated in the Nobel Prize in 1949. The last years of Faulkner's life were marked by a flood of honors and the satisfaction of having achieved the status of a classic American writer.

for the Elk Hills naval oil reserve; Doheny will be acquitted on March 22.

31 MARCH 1930
National Acting upon its discussions with President Hoover to deal with the mounting unemployment problem, Congress adopts the Public Buildings Act (actually supplementing an act of 1926). It calls for $230,000,000, to be used for erecting public buildings.

4 APRIL 1930
National Congress votes to appropriate some $300 million for federal aid to states for road construction.

21 APRIL 1930
Regional In one of the worst fires in the nation's history, some 320 prisoners at the Ohio State Penitentiary are burned to death; there were some 4300 inmates in a prison designed to hold only 1500.

22 APRIL 1930
International The London Naval Treaty is signed by the U.S., Britain and Japan but France and Italy refuse to endorse its major provisions limiting the numbers and sizes of the ships each country can build. It is considered a step toward disarmament, but will soon enough prove meaningless.

4 MAY 1930
National The Hawley-Smoot Tariff Bill is moving toward Congressional acceptance; this bill will raise duties on many items imported into the U.S. and many people see this as a potential threat to international trade. This very day, a petition signed by some 1028 prominent economists is made public; they are protesting the passage of such a law and urging Hoover to veto it if it is passed. Congress, however, will pass the Hawley-Smoot Bill and Hoover will sign it on June 17.

24 MAY 1930
Life/Customs A poll taken by one of the nation's leading periodicals, the *Literary Digest*, shows that the majority of those polled favor the repeal of the 18th Amendment.

17 JUNE 1930
National President Hoover signs the Hawley-Smoot Tariff Act, raising duties on many items, in some cases so high that they are effectively prohibitive. As predicted by many economists, this soon leads other countries to raise their tariffs, setting off the economic warfare of the 1930s that intensifies the Depression and exacerbates nationalistic rivalries.

3 JULY 1930
National Congress passes the Veterans Administration Act, establishing the Veterans Administration so as to consolidate all federal programs for aiding ex-servicemen.

3 SEPTEMBER 1930
Transportation The first electric passenger train in the U.S. is run as an experiment by Thomas Edison; it goes between Hoboken and Montclair, New Jersey.

9 SEPTEMBER 1930
National The State Department issues an order prohibiting immigration of virtually all foreign laborers because of the mounting unemployment throughout the nation.

OCTOBER 1930
National Unemployment is now estimated to have reached at least 4,500,000, but President Hoover persists in his determination "to preserve the principles of individual and local responsibility." This month he appoints a Committee for Unemployment Relief, but it calls only for federal leadership of programs run by state and local agencies, not for much direct financial aid.

CHARLES EVANS HUGHES, 1862-1948

When Charles Evans Hughes resigned his first Supreme Court stint in 1916, fellow Justice Oliver Wendell Holmes, Jr. wrote, "I shall miss him consumedly, for he is not only a good fellow, experienced and wise, but funny, and with doubts that open vistas through the wall of a non-conformist conscience." In his long career as governor, cabinet officer, and Justice, Hughes maintained his progressive-Republican fervor for reform through a considerable variety of practical approaches.

Hughes was born on April 11, 1862 in Glens Falls, New York. After graduating from Brown, he attended law school at Columbia, where he graduated and entered the bar in 1884. His hard-working and meticulous style made him a successful commercial lawyer. In 1905 he came to prominence as head of committees that successfully rooted out corruption in the New York utilities and insurance industries.

These efforts led him to a gubernatorial bid; he defeated William Randolph Hearst to take the office in 1906, and as governor continued his progressive style. By his second term his regulatory and labor reforms slowed down due to his indifference to party politics. Named to the U.S. Supreme Court by Taft in 1910, he was a liberal influence on the bench. In 1916 he left the court in an unwise presidential bid against Wilson, but in 1920 the new President Harding took Hughes out of private practice to be secretary of state, where he worked with his usual alacrity for a naval treaty and for a relaxing of U.S. military occupation in Latin America. In 1925 he retired once more to private practice, but in 1930 was returned to the Supreme Court by Hoover, this time as Chief Justice. Even more than before he was an activist and a flexible jurist, believing the Constitution was not a static document but an idea in motion. Often at odds with the New Deal, he still made important decisions in Roosevelt's favor, such as approving the Wagner Labor Relations Act. Hughes retired in 1941, dying in Washington in 1948.

4 NOVEMBER 1930

National In midterm elections, the Democrats gain control of the House of Representatives; they add eight new seats in the Senate but the Republicans maintain their majority.

2 DECEMBER 1930

National President Hoover, seemingly recognizing the crisis of unemployment, asks Congress to appropriate up to $150,000,000 for constructing public works; Congress will appropriate $116,000,000 on December 20.

11 DECEMBER 1930

National The Bank of the U.S., a major private New York bank with some 60 branches and 400,000 depositors, closes. There have now been approximately 1300 U.S. bank closures since the late fall of 1929.

OTHER EVENTS OF 1930

Arts/Culture The Nobel Prize for Literature is awarded for the first time to an American, Sinclair Lewis.

Life/Customs A copy of James Joyce's new novel, *Ulysses*, sent from its Paris publisher to a New York publisher, is seized by the Bureau of Customs on the grounds that it is "obscene."

7 JANUARY 1931

National A report from the President's Emergency Committee for Unemployment Relief claims there are now between 4-5,000,000 unemployed; furthermore, the Depression is deepening daily.

19 JANUARY 1931

National The Wickersham Commission, which President Hoover had appointed in May 1929 to study the problems related to the 18th Amendment, submits its report; rather than recommending repeal, the commission simply suggests certain revisions in the laws enforcing the amendment. Hoover will submit this report to Congress on January 20 and indicate that he, too, is against outright repeal.

24 FEBRUARY 1931

National The U.S. Supreme Court rules that the procedures followed for adopting the 18th Amendment were constitutional and thus upholds the Prohibition amendment.

27 FEBRUARY 1931

National Congress, overriding President Hoover's veto of yesterday, passes the Bonus Loan Bill, allowing veterans to obtain cash loans up to 50 percent of the value of the veterans' bonus certificates they had been issued in 1924. Hoover sees this as favoring a special segment of the population while increasing the financial burdens of all Americans.

3 MARCH 1931

National President Hoover vetoes the Muscle Shoals Bill, calling for the Federal Government to take over operation of the hydroelectric facilities constructed during World War I at the Muscle Shoals section of the Tennessee River. Hoover is "opposed to government entering any business. . .in competition with our citizens." Later this very proposal will become the basis of President Roosevelt's Tennessee Valley Authority.

Life/Customs Congress passes, and Hoover signs, the act that designates "The Star Spangled Banner" as the national anthem; it was composed by Francis Scott Key during the bombardment of Fort McHenry on September 13-14, 1814.

20 MARCH 1931

Life/Customs The Federal Council of Churches of Christ of America gives qualified approval to some measures of birth control; as this is a relatively conservative denomination, it represents a major step in Americans' acceptance of this hitherto minority position.

25 MARCH 1931

Black Experience Nine young black boys are arrested in Scottsboro, Alabama, and are charged with raping a white woman; they will be found guilty in the course of three trials, but the Supreme Court will overturn the conviction on April 1, 1935. "The Scottsboro Boys" will become a *cause célèbre* for all determined to obtain justice for black Americans.

1 MAY 1931

Life/Customs The Empire State Building is formally dedicated; it will retain its claim as the world's tallest building until it loses it to Chicago's Sears Tower and New York City's World Trade Center in the 1970s.

20 JUNE 1931

International President Hoover proposes that all nations declare a one-year moratorium on all intergovernmental debts and reparations. Hoover is motivated in particular by the recent failure of a major Austrian bank that is beginning to have repercussions in international finance. Hoover's proposal will soon be accepted by all major nations and by July the moratorium is in effect. At first it has the desired effect of helping the world's stock markets and financial communities, but shortly the confidence wanes.

23 JUNE 1931

Aviation Wiley Post and Harold Gatty take off on what will be the first single–plane round-the-world flight; it will take 8 days, 15 hours, 51 minutes.

22 JULY 1931

Agriculture In Kansas, as farmers begin to produce a bumper crop of wheat, prices also begin to collapse; many counties grant a moratorium on taxes to tide these farmers over.

18 SEPTEMBER 1931

International Japan marches into Manchuria, a vast

EXPANDING RESOURCES 1901-1945

region of northeast China; this is in direct violation of the Kellogg-Briand Pact of 1928, which Japan signed, and effectively launches Japan on what will become World War II.

SEPTEMBER-OCTOBER 1931
International Despite Hoover's success in gaining the moratorium for debts and reparations, confidence in banks begins to slip again; this confidence further erodes when Great Britain goes off the gold standard on September 21. Many Americans fear that the U.S. will do the same and begin to withdraw their money from banks and hoard gold; in September and October, some 827 more U.S. banks will close.

18 SEPTEMBER 1931
International Meeting in their annual convention, the American Bar Association urges the U.S. Senate to ratify the "Root formula," introduced by Elihu Root in December 1929 to allow the U.S. to adhere to the decisions of the World Court. The lawyers see this as both a step toward world peace and as furthering economic recovery. The Senate will ignore them.

16 OCTOBER 1931
International The Council of the League of Nations in Geneva asks the U.S.A. to send a representative to the discussion of the crisis caused by the Japanese invasion of Manchuria. On October 18 Secretary of State Stimson will delegate the U.S. Consul General in Geneva to participate; on January 7, 1932 Secretary Stimson will announce that the U.S. will not recognize any situation that violates the Kellogg-Briand Pact; this places the U.S. on record as opposed to Japan's aggression but like the rest of the world's nations, the U.S. seems powerless to prevent it.

17 OCTOBER 1931
Regional The notorious gangster Al Capone, who has been able to evade prosecution for the many crimes he is alleged to have been involved in, is found guilty in the Federal Court in Chicago of income tax evasion. He will be sentenced to 11 years in prison and a $50,000 fine; he will be released from prison in 1939 due to his weakened health, and will die in 1947.

25 OCTOBER 1931
International French Premier Laval has been conferring in Washington D.C., and today he joins President Hoover in publicly declaring that both their countries will continue to hold to the gold standard.

7 DECEMBER 1931
National Hundreds of American "hunger marchers" have descended on Washington D.C., but they are turned away from the White House when they try to present their petition seeking employment at some minimum wage.

8 DECEMBER 1931
National President Hoover, in his annual message to Congress, asks Congress to establish an emergency reconstruction finance corporation; its prime goal would be to provide money to lend to banks, insurance companies and other bodies that would then lend the money to the nation's industries. Hoover also recognizes in his address that there is now some need for further public works to provide jobs.

OTHER EVENTS OF 1931
International The Nobel Prize for Peace is shared by two Americans, Jane Addams and Nicholas Murray Butler.

7 JANUARY 1932
International Prompted by Japan's occupation of Manchuria, Secretary of State Stimson sends notes to Japan and China saying that the U.S. will not recognize any territory taken contrary to the Kellogg-Briand Pact of 1928.

12 JANUARY 1932
Life/Customs Hattie W. Caraway is appointed Senator from Arkansas to fill the unexpired term of her late husband; later this year she will become the first woman elected to the U.S. Senate.

22 JANUARY 1932
National President Hoover signs the bill establishing a Reconstruction Finance Corporation (the bill having passed the Senate on January 11, the House on January 15); the agency will start operations on February 2 with $500,000,000 in funds and authorization to borrow up to $2,000,000,000 by tax exempt bonds. The plan is for the RFC to lend money to such institutions as banks, insurance companies, building and loan societies, agricultural credit corporations, farm mortgage associations and railroads so that these bodies can in turn stimulate the economy. This is President Hoover's belated recognition that the U.S. economy and work force need some government aid to get moving out of the Depression.

2 FEBRUARY 1932
International A World Disarmament Conference begins in Geneva, Switzerland, sponsored by the League of Nations. The U.S.A. does not formally belong to the League but it sends representatives to this conference; in the end, nothing comes of it.

27 FEBRUARY 1932
National The Glass-Steagall Banking Act is passed by Congress; it authorizes the Federal Reserve Bank to expand credit and to release some of the government's gold to business. There has been hoarding of both gold and currency as well as many withdrawals by foreign interest; this new act is an attempt to get more money circulating.

1 MARCH 1932
Regional Charles A. Lindbergh Jr., the 19-month-old child of Colonel Charles and Anne Morrow Lindbergh, is kidnapped from the family's home in

Hopewell, New Jersey. A note demanding a ransom of $50,000 is received and the sum is paid as directed but the infant is not returned; instead, he is found dead on May 12. Bruno Hauptmann is found with some of the ransom money in September; he will be convicted of murder and electrocuted on April 3, 1936 although he protests his innocence to the end. The Lindbergh case will lead· to Congress's adopting the death penalty in kidnapping cases that involve crossing state lines.

3 MARCH 1932

National The 20th Amendment is sent to the states for ratification; it calls for Congress to convene on January 3 and for the president to be inaugurated into a new term on January 20. Because it will eliminate the long period that has existed between elections and the taking of office, it is known as "the lame duck amendment."

23 MARCH 1932

Labor The Norris-LaGuardia Anti-Injunction Act is passed; it prohibits the use of injunctions in labor disputes except within certain restrictions; it is considered an important step in protecting the rights of labor to negotiate through their unions.

7 APRIL 1932

Regional Governor Franklin D. Roosevelt of New

H.L. MENCKEN, 1880-1956

Through his long and celebrated career as a journalist and "critic of ideas," Mencken spoke out for intelligence and common sense while flaying with gusto the follies of his countrymen. (Among his observations on the American scene, H.L. Mencken once wrote, "No one has ever gone broke underestimating the intelligence of the American public.")

Mencken was born into a comfortable German-American family in Baltimore, Maryland, on September 12, 1880. A studious youth, he graduated as valedictorian of his high school in 1896 and went into newspaper reporting. He rose rapidly and by 1906 was an editor-in-chief. When his paper failed he joined the *Baltimore Sun*, where he remained until 1948. In his articles there he began his tireless campaign against mindless Puritanism, blue laws and other features of American life. He claimed to speak for the "civilized minority" against the tyranny of the majority, whom he sometimes dubbed the "booboisie." In 1908 he found a national audience 'with *Smart Set*, a provocative and influential monthly, and was later editor of the *American Mercury*.

In his articles and books Mencken was a man fascinated with life, and he conveyed that fascination with vivid prose. The country came to know him as the iconoclast, the agnostic, the Darwinian, the ridiculer of Prohibition. At the same time he was a passionate and idealistic critic of music, books, and ethics, and a self-taught linguist who in *The American Language* examined for the first time the distinctions of American and British usage. He remained to his death in 1956 the man who said most to Americans of his time about the best and the worst of themselves.

York refers in a speech to "the forgotten man at the bottom of the economic pyramid." This sets the theme for what will become his campaign for the presidency.

20 MAY 1932

Aviation Amelia Earhart becomes the first woman to make a solo transatlantic flight; she flies from Newfoundland to Ireland, 2026 miles in 13½ hours.

22-24 MAY 1932

National The Socialist Party meets in Milwaukee and nominates Norman Thomas for the Presidency.

28 MAY 1932

National The Communist Party meets in Chicago and nominates William Z. Foster for the Presidency.

29 MAY 1932

National The first of what will eventually become a total of 17,000 veterans begin to arrive in Washington D.C., where they set up camp (some right in the center of the capital) to support their demand that they be allowed to cash in their bonus certificates from World War I in full value. By July 28-29, they will be driven out of Washington by U.S. Army troops, but in the meantime they become knows as "the Bonus Army."

14-16 JUNE 1932

National The Republican Party convenes in Chicago and nominates President Herbert Hoover and Vice–President Charles Curtis on the first ballot.

16 JUNE-9 JULY 1932

International Delegates from major European governments meet in Lausanne, Switzerland, and essentially agree to cancel all outstanding debts of Germany if the U.S.A. will cancel their own debts from World War I to the U.S. But the Hoover administration and the American people remain generally set against such an offer.

17 JUNE 1932

National The Senate rejects the Patman Bonus Bill that the House of Representatives passed on June 15; this is the bill that the Bonus Army demanded. Many of the veterans still camped now decide to leave, especially since the government offers some funds to pay for their return to their homes; but about 2000 will stay on until July 28-29.

27 JUNE-2 JULY 1932

National The Democratic Party meets in Chicago. There is a deadlock among three candidates—Alfred E. Smith, candidate in the previous election; John Nance Garner of Texas, Speaker of the House; and Governor Franklin D. Roosevelt of New York. Roosevelt wins on the fourth ballot when Garner throws his delegates to him in return for being named vice-presidential candidate. The party's platform endorses the repeal of the 18th amendment, but it also calls for

EXPANDING RESOURCES 1901-1945

AMELIA EARHART, 1897-1937

Pioneer aviator and feminist Amelia Earhart achieved the aims of the women's liberation movement long before it occured to most American women that they might need liberating. Hers was a personal, lighthearted and totally successful revolution, and in the course of it she became one of the most famous and well-loved figures of her time.

Born in Atchison, Kansas, on July 24, 1897, she followed her nomadic family through a succession of states and schools, graduating from high school in Chicago in 1915. Over the next ten years she wandered in search of a career, working at various jobs and briefly enrolling in various colleges. Meanwhile she took up flying, and in 1928 became the first woman to fly across the Atlantic, which she did with two men. From that point on, the buoyant, nonchalant Earhart was the preeminent woman flyer in the country, and the next few years saw her as an airline executive, aviation editor of *Cosmopolitan* and a record-breaking flyer. Her first records were "women's records," but in 1932 she set *the* record for transatlantic flight, which won her a medal from President Hoover and the adulation of the public (to which she characteristically observed, "I'll be glad when the zoo part is over").

Her achievements continued: further transatlantic records, the first flight from Hawaii to the U.S., first non-stop flight from Mexico City to Newark, and on and on. Though she said she flew "for the fun of it," she was seriously aware of her significance to the cause of feminism. On her marriage in 1931 to publisher G.P. Putnam, she made it clear that she was not going to tone down her career. But her legend was to end in tragedy and mystery: in July 1937 she and her navigator embarked on an around-the-world flight; after a few fragmentary radio messages over the Pacific there was silence. No trace was ever found. But her memory was to remain in her country's thoughts as a hero of her time and perhaps the most likable revolutionary of the century.

cutting back on government spending. In what is a first for American political life, Roosevelt flies to Chicago from Albany to give his acceptance speech in person; in this he declares, "I pledge you, I pledge myself, a new deal for the American people." Within 24 hours, this "new deal" will become the motto of Roosevelt's campaign and eventual administration.

21 JULY 1932
National President Hoover signs the Relief and Reconstruction Act, an emergency bill designed to enlarge the programs of the Reconstruction Finance Corporation, specifically by increasing the amount it can loan to $3,000,000,000 and by allowing the money to go to state and local agencies for supporting public works and relief.

22 JULY 1932
National Congress adopts the Federal Home Loan Bank Act, authorizing 8-12 regional banks to provide discounted, or cheaper, loans to existent lending institutions so that lower mortgages will be facilitated to homebuyers and more money available for home construction.

28-29 JULY 1932
National The Washington police force has tried to remove the remaining 2000 of the Bonus Army but in the confrontation two policemen and two veterans are killed. President Hoover now calls on U.S. Army Troops to evict the veterans from their encampment. The successful troops are led by the Chief of Staff, General Douglas MacArthur; his aide is a young major, Dwight D. Eisenhower.

26 AUGUST 1932
National The Controller of the Currency declares a moratorium on foreclosures of first mortgages; increasing numbers of unemployed Americans are unable to keep up payments.

2 OCTOBER 1932
International The League of Nations had earlier established the Lytton Commission to investigate Japan's invasion of Manchuria (and the U.S. had sent a representative); today the commission releases its report naming Japan the aggressor.

7 NOVEMBER 1932
National The Supreme Court rules, in *Powell v. Alabama*, that the "Scottsboro Boys" had not been properly represented by counsel and thus a retrial is granted.

8 NOVEMBER 1932
National Franklin Delano Roosevelt and the Democrats win the election by a landslide; Roosevelt gets 22,809,638 votes to Hoover's 15,758,901, and the Democrats take control of both houses of Congress. In the electoral college vote, Roosevelt's lead is even more impressive—472 to Hoover's 59. The election campaign had not presented the American people with an absolutely clear choice, especially as Roosevelt accused Hoover of "reckless and "extravagant" spending, even of trying "to center control of everything in Washington." But the American people were desperate for some alternative to Hoover's dilatory ways, and Roosevelt exuded confidence. As further evidence that Americans were simply wanting reasonably traditional solutions, they gave Norman Thomas, the Socialist, only some 882,000 votes, and William Foster, the Communist, only some 103,000 votes.

11 NOVEMBER 1932
National The Tomb of the Unknown Soldier is dedicated in Arlington National Cemetery.

OTHER EVENTS OF 1932
Economics The unemployed in the U.S.A. reach a peak of some 13,000,000 by the end of the year; total wages decline to some 60 percent less than in 1929; business losses are reported as up to $6,000,000,000; industry is operating at half the 1929 capacity; agricultural prices are dropping; banks are closing. The economy is close to rock bottom.

30 JANUARY 1933
International In Germany Adolph Hitler assumes

office as Chancellor on the invitation of President Von Hindenburg, who regards Hitler as the best alternative to the chaos now threatening Germany's government and society. But Hitler will move quickly to assert dictatorial power over all areas of German life, and then will mobilize Germans to launch a war of revenge and conquest that will change the history of modern times.

6 FEBRUARY 1933
National The 20th Amendment is formally adopted, eliminating from next year on the "lame-duck" Congress and Presidential administrations that result from the late turn-overs of government prescribed by the original Constitution.

15 FEBRUARY 1933
National President-elect Roosevelt is shot at by a would-be assassin, Giuseppe Zangara, while riding in an open vehicle in Miami, Florida; the bullets strike others—Mayor Anton Cermak of Chicago will die of wounds on March 6—but Roosevelt is untouched. Zangara is executed on March 20.

20 FEBRUARY 1933
National Congress votes to submit the 21st Amendment to the states; it will repeal the 18th Amendment and thus end Prohibition.

24 FEBRUARY 1933
International The Japanese delegation to the League of Nations in Geneva walks out of the assembly after voting to reject the Lytton Commission's report accusing Japan of being the aggressor in Manchuria.

25 FEBRUARY 1933
National The first U.S. aircraft carrier is launched at Newport News, Virginia; it is named the *Ranger*, after the ship commanded by the first American naval hero, John Paul Jones.

4 MARCH 1933
National Franklin Delano Roosevelt is inaugurated as 32nd president of the United States, with John Nance Garner as vice-president. In his address, he declares (in words borrowed from Thoreau): "Let me assert my firm belief that the only thing we have to fear is fear itself." In fact, Roosevelt inherits a country whose economy and social fabric are close to shreds. In particular, the nation's banks had been closing as depositors began to withdraw gold; stopping this will be his first order of business.

5 MARCH 1933
National President Roosevelt issues a proclamation declaring a four-day "bank holiday" throughout the nation, effective March 6; all banking transactions will stop and an embargo on the export of gold, silver and currency also goes into effect; this will have the desired result of stopping the panic "run" on the nation's banks. This same day Roosevelt also summons Congress to a special session on March 9.

FRANKLIN DELANO ROOSEVELT, 1882-1945

Simultaneously the most popular and the most reviled American President of the 20th century, Franklin Delano Roosevelt changed the thrust of his country's life and government, creating a partial welfare state and promoting government as an agent of social and economic reform.

FDR was born into an old, aristocratic family at Hyde Park, New York, on January 30, 1882. After an idyllic childhood he attended the upper-class Groton School in Massachusetts and then Harvard. During college he fell in love with Anna Eleanor Roosevelt, a fifth cousin, and they were married in 1905; their mutual relation, President Theodore Roosevelt, gave the bride away. After college, Roosevelt studied law at Columbia and entered the bar in 1907. His desire to find a more interesting field of endeavor than corporate law was realized in 1910, when he ran successfully as a Democrat for the New York state senate. His liberal efforts there brought him much attention and led to an appointment as an assistant navy secretary in 1913. In that post he gained valuable political contacts and experience, which resulted in his being on the 1920 national ticket as the vice-presidential nominee.

After the Republican victory by Warren G. Harding, FDR returned to law practice. In 1921 came a personal tragedy in the form of polio, which left him crippled for life. But the disease did not dampen his natural ebullience and optimism, and it had the effect of strengthening his partnership with Eleanor, who became his eyes and ears and whose own strengths began thereby to be revealed. In 1928 Roosevelt ran successfully for governor of New York. During two terms he pushed through programs for unemployment insurance, child labor laws and old age pensions, among others. As the Depression deepened, he set up a "Brain Trust" of advisors, who all came with him when he was elected President. That took place in 1932, when FDR defeated Herbert Hoover, whom the nation blamed for the Depression. In his first term he announced a New Deal, creating the "alphabet soup" of government agencies to fight the desperate situation. These programs provided much relief and several, such as the Social Security Act and the Tennessee Valley

Authority, remained through the century as vital social and economic measures.

But there was increasing resistance to his methods in his second term. The Depression had been assuaged but not ended. Tragically, it took a war to do that. As the conflict engulfed Europe, Roosevelt, by then in his third term, moved cautiously; but after the Japanese attack on Pearl Harbor in December 1941, he declared war on Japan, Germany and Italy. His sometimes disorganized but still charismatic leadership helped create miracles of production that turned the tide of the war; but the costs to his health mounted. As the election of 1944 approached, his advisers suspected he might not survive another term, and persuaded him to take on Harry Truman as a strong vice-president. The fears were justified: FDR won an unprecedented fourth term in 1944, but died at his retreat in Warm Springs, Georgia in April 1945, shortly before the armistice. He had been a leader of great strengths and great weaknesses, but his heritage to the nation was largely one of crucial and beneficial activism.

9 MARCH-16 JUNE 1933

National Congress meets in what will become known as Roosevelt's "Hundred Days," the session during which he will get a desperate and pliant Congress to enact many of the principal acts supporting his New Deal. This first day Congress passes the Emergency Banking Act, giving the President broad powers over all banking transactions and foreign exchange. It also allows banks to reopen as soon as they can prove they are solvent; starting on March 10, within three days, over 1000 banks will reopen; just as important, the nation's confidence will begin to pick up.

12 MARCH 1933

National President Roosevelt broadcasts over the radio in the first of his "fireside chats" to the nation; his informal approach and personal assurance will do much to allay Americans' "fear of fear itself."

20 MARCH 1933

National President Roosevelt signs the Economy Act, reducing the salaries of federal employees and of payments to veterans; it also calls for some reorganization of federal agencies in the interest of economy.

22 MARCH 1933

National Anticipating the repeal of the 18th Amendment, Congress amends the Volstead Act by passing the Beer and Wine Revenue Act: effective April 7 beer and wine with alcoholic content of 3.2 percent (by weight) will be legal. Roosevelt was also clever enough to put a solid tax on these beverages, thus satisfying two of his goals.

31 MARCH 1933

National Congress passes the Reforestation Relief Act, establishing the Civilian Conservation Corps (CCC); it will provide work immediately for some 250,000 young men (18-25) in reforestation projects, soil erosion and flood control, road construction and developing the national parks. Work camps soon

THE CIVILIAN CONSERVATION CORPS

In the "alphabet soup" of agencies created by Roosevelt and his New Deal, one of his personal favorites was the Civilian Conservation Corps—the CCC. Roosevelt came out of the class tradition that espoused conservation of land, forests and natural resources, and before he had been in office one month he had persuaded Congress to pass the act establishing the CCC. The basic idea was two-pronged: it would provide healthy work for unemployed young men and it would do necessary work in protecting, improving and increasing the nation's natural resources. By June 1933 camps were being built in forests and fields throughout the country and by August some 300,000 youths between the ages of 18 and 25 were living and working in these camps. Wages were low—$30 a month, of which up to $25 might have to be sent home to dependents; "assistant leaders" got $36, "leaders" got $45. But in addition they all received their food, clothing, shelter, transportation, medical care and even education or training: a little-publicized aspect of the CCC was its vocational training and remedial classes in elementary and secondary education. All were volunteers but the term was a minimum of six months and up to a maximum of two years. Thousands of American Indians and residents of American territories also participated. A typical camp had about 200, and up to 500,000 were employed at one time during the peak years.

By the time the CCC was phased out in 1941-42—when young men had a war to fight—over 2,500,000 youths had passed through some 1500 camps. They had planted some 200,000,000 trees to help reforest some 17,000,000 acres; they had worked on projects that helped check soil erosion and control floods; they had built miles of roads and trails in remote areas and had constructed cabins and campgrounds still enjoyed 50 years later; they had also fought many forest fires and worked to prevent others. One of the indirect results of the CCC was to bring the national parks and forests into the consciousness of millions of Americans, who would continue to appreciate and use them in ensuing decades.

Like so many New Deal programs, the CCC came in for its share of criticism. Although the U.S. Army was initially charged with setting up the camps and supervising the enrollees, the pervading neutralist sentiment of the country made sure that the volunteers were not taught drill or weaponry. And it did not escape the notice of some critics that the CCC's basic approach seemed vaguely similar to that of the Hitler Youth in Germany. But the spirit of the camps and participants was quite different: there was a minimum of pageantry, patriotism and propaganda. Ultimately most of the country felt that the CCC youth had improved both the nation's natural resources and themselves.

spring up, at first under the direction of Army officers. Those who participate are paid $30 per month (but part of this sum must go to any dependents). By the time the CCC ceases in 1941, some 2,000,000 young men will have been involved in its projects.

19 APRIL 1933

National By Presidential proclamation, Roosevelt takes the U.S. off the gold standard for its currency. The dollar inevitably declines sharply in exchanges abroad, while silver, commodities and stocks rise in the American market. But the net effect is to make money more available to Americans and so stimulate the economy.

21 APRIL 1933
International Prime Minister Ramsay MacDonald of Britain comes to Washington to discuss with President Roosevelt some of the problems that will be dealt with in the forthcoming World Monetary and Economic Conference in London (June 12).

12 MAY 1933
National Congress passes the Federal Emergency Relief Act, which authorizes immediate grants to states for relief projects—unlike Hoover's approach, which was to grant only loans. Unemployment has now reached some 14,000,000—over one-quarter of the nation's work force. President Roosevelt also signs the Agricultural Adjustment Act to provide immediate relief to farmers by establishing parity prices for certain agricultural products (with the government making up the difference) and by paying subsidies to farmers who curtailed production of crops that were in surplus. The program is to be administered through the Agricultural Adjustment Administration (AAA); some of its results—the literal plowing under of planted crops, the killing of surplus pigs—will bring the New Deal its harshest criticism; and in 1936 some of its provisions will be declared unconstitutional by the Supreme Court.

18 MAY 1933
National Congress establishes the Tennessee Valley Authority (TVA), an independent public corporation that will construct dams and power plants along the Tennessee Valley; the electricity will then go to the residents and enterprises within that valley, and fertilizer (and some explosives) will be sold. But there are broader goals than these—namely, to raise up the social and economic standards of a group of Americans in this remote region: critics will see the TVA as a Socialistic scheme, while its admirers will view it as one of the nation's most successful social projects.

27 MAY 1933
National Congress passes the Federal Securities Act, providing for the Federal Government to register and approve all issues of stocks and bonds and for the issuers (with some exceptions) to fully disclose all pertinent information about the firms to the public.

6 JUNE 1933
National Congress passes the National Employment System Act; it creates a U.S. Employment Service that is to cooperate with the states in providing employment services while providing matching funds to these state agencies.

12 JUNE-27 JULY 1933
International The London Economic Conference meets but in the end accomplishes little, largely due to the fact that the U.S.A. disagrees with most of the other major nations, who want to stress the need for

THE TENNESSEE VALLEY AUTHORITY

Often characterized as one of Franklin Delano Roosevelt's most significant and enduring legacies to America, the Tennessee Valley Authority is due at least as much to another individual, Senator George Norris of Nebraska. A veteran of Theodore Roosevelt's Progressive Party, a long-standing proponent of "The use of the earth for the good of man," Norris had tried and failed under two Presidents, Coolidge and Hoover, to develop a grand scheme for the development of the Tennessee River Valley. Including some 41,000 square miles in several states, the valley is spread out along the river that rises in North Carolina and southwestern Virginia and empties into the Ohio River. In 1917, at Muscle Shoals, in Alabama, where the Tennessee River drops some 137 feet in only 37 miles, the Federal Government had begun a dam and two plants that would employ the hydroelectric power to produce nitrates for munitions. The war ended, and there was some thought of leasing or selling these public works to private interests, but Norris persisted in his plan. Finally he succeeded with President Roosevelt, who on May 18, 1933, signed the act establishing the Tennessee Valley Authority.

This was to be an independent public body, directed by a board of three. All government-owned property already at Muscle Shoals was transferred to the Authority, which was charged with building and operating dams, generating and selling electricity, manufacturing and selling fertilizers produced, establishing flood control and developing navigation. The Authority proceeded on constructing dams; the Norris Dam was completed in 1936, and five more were built before World War II intervened; after the war, construction proceeded on many more on the Tennessee and its branches. Massive locks were built to allow far more and far larger boats to haul goods. Fertilizer was produced to be sold to farmers in the valley, which was also upgraded by reforestation and soil retention projects supported by the TVA. As for the primary goal—to provide cheap electricity to even the most remote parts of this area—this was achieved to a degree far beyond the original plan. TVA electricity would eventually be transmitted to an area at least twice as large as the valley, and it would be used not just to aid farms and homes but also to help develop mines, factories and many other enterprises. And by the 1980s the TVA region would be using over 100,000,000,000-kilowatt-hours of electricity annually—some 65 times as much as it used before the TVA started operations. Beyond these basic goals were many secondary and even unanticipated achievements, including the great reservoirs that provide water for leisure and sports activities. And it was at one TVA-powered facility at Oak Ridge, Tennessee, that the government built its center for atomic research and developed the atomic bomb that helped to end World War II.

To be sure, the TVA was controversial from the outset. To some Americans, a project of this type looked like a Socialist or Communist scheme. And the private companies that provided electricity both to the Tennessee Valley and other regions fought the project as unfair competition; the government's argument was that the disparate private interests were not capable of providing power to the more isolated people, let alone of developing all the supporting elements (such as reforestation or flood control). Eventually Washington prevailed, but a number of proposals for similar projects around the nation were defeated: ironically, the TVA would be imitated elsewhere in the world but remain unique domestically.

FRANCES PERKINS, 1880-1965

Given the hard-fighting and masculine climate of American labor relations, it is heartening to remember that one of the most significant government labor advocates of the 20th century was a gentle and methodical woman, Frances Perkins, FDR's secretary of labor. Although her relations with trade unions were often distant—she preferred labor legislation to unionism—she presided over an unprecedented growth in power of the American labor movement in the 30s and 40s.

Perkins was born in Boston, Massachusetts, on April 10, 1880, graduating from Mount Holyoke College in 1902. She quickly moved into social and philanthropic work with a series of organizations, meanwhile receiving a master's degree at Columbia (1910). As a lobbyist for the New York City Consumers League she was instrumental in working for a successful woman- and child-labor bill in 1912. During this work she became a friend and associate of New York politician Al Smith, for whom she worked during the teens on efforts to reform industrial conditions.

Over the next years Perkins was a noted expert and liberal activist in the field of labor relations, becoming a close advisor to New York governor Franklin D. Roosevelt in the late 20s. When FDR was elected President in 1932 he named Perkins as his secretary of labor. In the exciting early months of the New Deal she moved quickly to revive the Department of Labor and created the Division of Labor Standards. As one of the primary shapers of FDR's program against the Depression, she helped to form the Social Security Act of 1935 and the Fair Labor Standards Act of 1938.

Cognizant of her pioneering role in the world of politics, Perkins kept her image matronly; she observed that pretty dresses for women were attractive but "don't particularly invite confidence in their common sense." Her common sense made her an important trail-blazer for women in politics. Although her activism was subdued by the war, she remained a powerful cabinet figure into the beginning of the Truman administration. She resigned in 1945, and in 1946 published the popular reminiscence *The Roosevelt I Knew*. After many years of writing and teaching she died in 1965.

currency stabilization while the U.S.A. wants to solve the Depression by stimulating trade.

13 JUNE 1933

National Congress passes the Home Owners Refinancing Act; it sets up the Home Owners Loan Corporation (HOLC) to provide mortgage money and other aid to homeowners (as for taxes or even repairs). The HOLC will go out of business in June 1936, but by then it will have given loans for some 1,000,000 mortgages.

16 JUNE 1933

National On this, the final day of the 73rd Congress' "Hundred Days," a number of crucial bills are passed or signed. The New Deal's foundation has now been laid, and although few problems have been solved, the nation has clearly turned itself around. Among the most important bills signed today is the National Industrial Recovery Act (NIRA). It estab-

lishes the Public Works Administration (PWA) and the National Recovery Administration (NRA), two of the major elements in Roosevelt's recovery program. The PWA is authorized to supervise the construction of roads, public buildings, and other projects in order to increase employment and to "prime" the nation's economic pumps; Secretary of the Interior Harold Ickes is named to head the PWA, and in the ensuing years, he will direct the construction of many ambitious public works (including the Grand Coulee Dam, New York's Triborough Bridge and almost three-quarters of the country's new schools).

The NRA's goal is to stimulate competition so as to benefit both consumers and producers; it is to do this by superintending various codes—either drawn up by private industry or by the government—that would establish fair trade; compliance would be voluntary, but the NRA would encourage cooperation by supplying a sort of "seal of approval," with a "Blue Eagle" and the motto "We Do Our Part," so that consumers would support only those businesses and services displaying this seal. General Hugh Johnson will direct the NRA, but in May 1935 the NRA will be declared unconstitutional by the Supreme Court.

This last day, Congress will also pass the Farm Credit Act; its main goal is to help farmers get mortgages at low interest. And Congress will pass the Banking Act of 1933; it sets up the Federal Bank Deposit Insurance Corporation, empowered to insure bank deposits up to $5000.

1 AUGUST 1933

National The "Blue Eagle" of the NRA makes its first public appearance; very quickly, there are hundreds of codes being submitted, until they cover industries employing more than 22,000,000 workers and making every imaginable product (although Henry Ford, the nation's chief automobile maker, refuses to cooperate).

5 AUGUST 1933

National By executive order, President Roosevelt sets up the National Labor Board, with Senator Robert Wagner of New York as its chairman; this board is empowered to enforce the right of organized labor to bargain collectively.

10 OCTOBER 1933

International At Rio de Janeiro, the nations of the Western Hemisphere sign the Treaty of Non-Aggression and Conciliation; the U.S. Senate will ratify this on June 15, 1934.

14 OCTOBER 1933

International Germany withdraws from the Disarmament Conference in Geneva; it also announces that it will resign from the League of Nations in two years.

17 OCTOBER 1933

International Indicative of the rising tide of anti-

Semitism and anti-intellectualism in Hitler's Germany, Albert Einstein arrives in the U.S.A.; Einstein will make his home in Princeton, New Jersey, and is only one of many distinguished individuals who will take refuge in America in the coming years as the Nazi menace spreads.

25 OCTOBER 1933

National President Roosevelt authorizes the Reconstruction Finance Corporation to purchase newly mined gold at $31.36 an ounce; this is 27 cents above world market price and effectively devalues the U.S. dollar to 66 cents (in terms of gold).

7 NOVEMBER 1933

Regional Fiorello H. LaGuardia is elected as a fusion-reform mayor of New York City; this ends 16 years of domination of city government by the Tammany organization.

8 NOVEMBER 1933

National By executive order, President Roosevelt establishes the Civil Works Administration (CWA), with Harry Hopkins as administrator; the CWA's immediate goal is to provide jobs for some 4,000,000 unemployed over the imminent winter; the CWA will cease operations in March 1934.

16 NOVEMBER 1933

International After conferring at the White House with Soviet Commissar for Foreign Affairs Maxim Litvinov, President Roosevelt announces that the U.S. will resume diplomatic relations with the U.S.S.R., suspended since 1919.

5 DECEMBER 1933

National The 21st Amendment, repealing the 18th Amendment, goes into effect when Utah becomes the 36th state to ratify it. The "noble experiment" of Prohibition has been ended.

28 DECEMBER 1933

National President Roosevelt gives a speech in Washington, D.C., in which he states: "The definite policy of the United States from now on is one opposed to armed intervention."

OTHER EVENTS OF 1933

Arts/Culture In a major decision for free speech and the creative arts, Federal Judge John Woolsey in New York lifts the ban on the importation and sale of James Joyce's *Ulysses* (banned from the U.S. since its appearance in Paris in the 1920s); Judge Woolsey calls it "a sincere and honest book . . . I do not detect anywhere the leer of a sensualist."

Labor Although millions of Americans remain unemployed, labor makes certain gains: the National Labor Relations Board has supported its right to strike; there has been a move toward shortening the work week; and on October 13, labor showed another aspect when the AFL voted to boycott all German-made

---

HARRY HOPKINS, 1890-1946

Whether at the race track or at the head of New Deal agencies, Harry Hopkins played his hunches and spent a bundle, with exciting but variable results. Hopkins was born in Sioux City, Iowa, on August 17, 1890. After graduating from Iowa's Grinnell College in 1912 he became interested in social issues and worked in various social agencies in the 'teens and 20s. Having proven himself an able and honest administrator, he was appointed by then New York governor Franklin D. Roosevelt to head a state relief organization in 1931; in that post Hopkins supervised relief efforts for over a million New Yorkers crushed by the Depression.

When FDR became President he appointed Hopkins in 1933 to FERA and other New Deal agencies, Hopkins set a style of expensive, fast and dramatic action that put millions of people to work but received much criticism for inefficiency and waste. Though the various agencies did not end the Depression—the war did that—they had a major and lasting impact on the country, financing gigantic building programs, as well as efforts by artists, that became an American legend.

As his fragile health declined, Hopkins became increasingly important to FDR, whose own health was worsening. Named commerce secretary in 1938, Hopkins traveled all over the world to important conferences for the President. Though he resigned his cabinet post in 1940, he continued to work as FDR's alter ego; noting his forthright style, Churchill dubbed him "Lord Root of the Matter." After the death of FDR, Hopkins worked for Truman to help plan the United Nations. He returned to New York in ill health in 1945 and died there the following year.

---

products in protest against Nazi Germany's treatment of organized labor.

31 JANUARY 1934

National President Roosevelt signs the Farm Mortgage Refinancing Act. This calls for establishing the Federal Farm Mortgage Corporation, which is to assist farmers in refinancing their mortgages by providing easier credit terms backed by government bonds.

2 FEBRUARY 1934

National By executive order, President Roosevelt establishes the Export-Import Bank of Washington to encourage commerce between the U.S. and foreign nations. It is to do this by such means as short-term credits for exporting agricultural products, long-term credits for exporting industrial products, and loans to American exporters when the foreign buyers cannot obtain enough exchange to pay in dollars. The first bank will concentrate on encouraging trade with the U.S.S.R.; in March, a second bank will aid in trade with Cuba. By 1936 both of these operations will be consolidated and in the ensuing years the Export-Import Bank will concentrate on fostering trade between the U.S.A. and Latin American nations.

15 FEBRUARY 1934

National Congress passes the Civil Works Emergency Relief Act; this will provide funds for the Federal Emergency Relief Administration to run the

ELEANOR ROOSEVELT, 1884-1962

Born into the American aristocracy and condemned to the window-dressing role of the political wife, Eleanor Roosevelt gently but firmly burst those bonds to become one of the most active and beloved reformers of her time and the most controversial First Lady of any time. A niece of Theodore Roosevelt, she was born into an elite New York family on October 11, 1884. Her childhood was intensely unhappy; after the death of her parents she was raised strictly by her grandmother. But in finishing school in London she discovered qualities of leadership, and in 1905, while she was working with the poor in New York, she married her distant cousin Franklin D. Roosevelt.

For years she played the role of dutiful wife in the shadow of an autocratic mother-in-law and her husband's expanding political career. After bearing six children, she worked for the Red Cross during World War I and for the League of Women Voters and the Women's Trade Union League in the 20s. Her confidence increased steadily, and when FDR was crippled with polio in 1921 she was increasingly to become his political stand-in and closest partner.

By the time FDR became President in 1933, Eleanor was a fully-developed public figure; she called him the politician, herself the agitator, and they became one of the great teams in American political history. As First Lady she held press conferences, had her own radio program, and wrote a daily syndicated newspaper column and a number of books, including the 1937 *This Is My Story*. She was accused of betraying her social class, and indeed she had: now a passionate egalitarian, she worked tirelessly for the rights of labor, women, the disadvantaged and racial minorities. Crushed when her husband died in 1945, she nonetheless continued on to her most notable achievements, serving from 1945-1952 as a United Nations delegate, where she was a major force in drafting the U.N. Declaration of Human Rights and in supporting Israel. During the 50s she was an unofficial ambassador-at-large, and in favoring dialogue with Russia during the Cold War said, "all of us are going to die together or we are going to learn to live together, and if we are to live together we have to talk." In that timeless observation she perhaps epitomized women's wisdom in international relations. An activist to the end, she died in 1962.

new programs of civil works and direct relief.

4 JANUARY 1934
National In his message to Congress, President Roosevelt asks for $10,500,000,000 to advance his recovery programs during the next 18 months.

30 JANUARY 1934
National Congress passes the Gold Reserve Act, empowering the President to fix the value of the U.S. dollar between 50–60 cents in terms of gold. (On January 31 Roosevelt will issue a proclamation fixing the value of the dollar at 59.06 cents, with gold at $35 an ounce.) The Act also calls for the gold of the Federal Reserve Banks to be transferred to the U.S. Treasury and for the government to benefit from any increase in its value. All this is aimed at giving the Federal Government control over fluctuations in the value of the dollar.

23 FEBRUARY 1934
National Congress passes the Crop Loan Act; this continues the program of the Farm Credit Administration through 1934 by which farmers are given loans for their crop production and harvesting.

15 MARCH 1934
Labor Henry Ford, to show his confidence in the nation's economic recovery, restores the $5-per-day minimum wage to most of his workers.

24 MARCH 1934
International Congress passes the Tydings-McDuffie Act, which guarantees the Philippine Islands independence 10 years after the act's terms are approved by the Philippine legislature; this is achieved on May 1, 1934; independence formally comes on July 4, 1946.

7 APRIL 1934
National Congress adopts the Jones-Connally Farm Relief Act; this extends the number of agricultural commodities to be controlled by the Agricultural Adjustment Administration.

12 APRIL 1934
National The Senate establishes a committee to investigate the manufacture and sale of munitions in the U.S., specifically the extent to which this trade influenced and profited from the role taken by the U.S.A. in World War I. The committee will be headed by Senator Gerald Nye of North Dakota and its hearings will go on into 1936; its findings will tend to encourage the isolationist-neutralist elements in America, who will feel confirmed in their view that wars are fought for the goals and profits of a minority.

13 APRIL 1934
International Congress passes an act forbidding loans to any government in default on payments to the U.S.A.; within a few months it will emerge that all countries except for Finland have fallen behind in their debts from World War I.

21 APRIL 1934
National Congress passes the Cotton Control Act (Bankhead Act); this calls for mandatory controls on cotton crops, with a tax placed on every pound over the quotas allocated to the various cotton-growing states, counties and farmers. This represents a change from the voluntary compliance in quotas applied by the Agricultural Adjustment Administration.

9 MAY 1934
National Congress passes the Jones-Costigan Act, authorizing controls on both cane and beet sugar produced in the U.S. as well as on the amount of sugar imported. (A tax placed on the processing of sugar by this act will be declared unconstitutional in 1936.)

10–11 MAY 1934
Regional A severe dust storm blows an estimated

300,000,000 tons of topsoil from states such as Texas, Oklahoma, Arkansas, Kansas, and Colorado, much of it being blown all the way to the Atlantic Ocean. This is only one of many storms that have been stripping topsoil from what becomes known as "the Dust Bowl" due to improper plowing and farming practices; many of the inhabitants—some known as "Okies" and "Arkies"—will abandon their farms, pack their belongings and families into vehicles, and go off to California.

18 MAY 1934

National Congress passes a package of six bills aimed at controlling crime. Among them is the so-called Lindbergh Act: It calls for the death penalty in cases of kidnapping that involve crossing state lines.

29 MAY 1934

International The U.S. and Cuba sign a treaty releasing Cuba from the Platt Amendment (of May 22, 1903) that had effectively made Cuba a U.S. protectorate after the Spanish-American War.

6 JUNE 1934

National President Roosevelt signs the Securities Exchange Act; it establishes the Securities Exchange Commission that is empowered to regulate exchanges and transactions involving all securities. The first chairman of the SEC is Joseph Kennedy, a millionaire who owed much of his wealth to his own speculations in the stock market during the 1920s.

7 JUNE 1934

National Congress passes the Corporate Bankruptcy Act which will allow a corporation facing bankruptcy to reorganize itself if two-thirds of its creditors agree.

12 JUNE 1934

National Congress passes the Farm Mortgage Foreclosure Act to allow loans to farmers so that they can recover property they owned before foreclosure.
International Congress passes the Reciprocal Trade Agreement Act; this authorizes the President for the next three years to negotiate trade agreements with other nations without the consent of the Senate.

15 JUNE 1934

National Congress passes the National Guard Act; this makes the National Guard a part of the U.S. Army in time of war or a declared national emergency.

19 JUNE 1934

National Congress passes the Communications Act; this establishes the Federal Communications Commission (FCC) to supervise radio, telegraph, and telephone communications; the broad powers assigned to the FCC will only begin to take effect in later decades. Congress also passes the Silver Purchase Act that authorizes the President to increase the Treasury's silver holdings until they are one-third the value of the gold holdings; the President is also authorized to

---

HAROLD ICKES, 1874-1952

The feisty personality and fierce invective of long-time interior secretary Harold Ickes were at the service of an uncompromising struggle for honest and humane government; for many years he was a nagging voice of America's conscience. Ickes was born in Franklin Township, Pennsylvania, on March 15, 1874. After taking a BA and a law degree at the University of Chicago in the first decade of the century, he began a successful law practice and labored as a political committeeman, where he worked for Theodore Roosevelt's Progressive Party in 1912 and for progressive Republicans Charles Evans Hughes and Hiram Johnson in their Presidential bids in the 'teens and 20s.

In the election of 1932 Ickes headed a committee of liberal Republicans who turned away from Hoover and supported Roosevelt. As he had hoped to be, Ickes was rewarded for his labor by being named secretary of the interior. He quickly moved to improve government relations with Indians and to expand the National Park system. In the developing anti-Depression programs of the New Deal he headed the Public Works Administration, which engaged in an unprecedented building program. An ardent civil libertarian, Ickes belonged to the NAACP and arranged the historic Marian Anderson concert at the Lincoln Memorial; he also objected to government repression of Japanese-Americans during the war. His imaginative invective enlivened the newspapers of the day: he described Huey Long, for example, as having "halitosis of the intellect."

Ickes took an early and unpopular stand for military preparedness to face the growth of Fascism; his position was, needless to say, vindicated. In 1946, after 13 years as interior secretary, he resigned after a wrangle with Truman over an appointment. Thereafter he confined his crusading to print, most notably in his attacks on Senator Joseph R. McCarthy. In his last article he castigated corruption in both parties and concluded "The core of this people is yet sound and good." The truculent tone disguising an idealistic and hopeful heart was typical of Ickes. He died in 1952 in Washington.

---

nationalize the silver stocks and purchases of the U.S. (This is a victory for the Western-populist-free money element that has been fighting for many decades to get silver accepted.) Congress also passes a joint resolution that establishes the National Labor Relations Board (replacing the National Labor Board of 1933).

28 JUNE 1934

National Congress passes the National Housing Act, which establishes the Federal Housing Administration (FHA) to insure loans made by banks and other lending institutions for construction, renovation and repairs of private dwellings. Congress passes the Taylor Grazing Act; this sets aside some 8,000,000 of publicly owned land for grazing; eventually some 142,000,000 acres will be set aside for this purpose. Congress passes the Tobacco Control Act; this provides for mandatory quotas on tobacco crops with a tax on excess production. Congress passes the Federal Farm Bankruptcy Act (Frazier-Lemke Act); this places a moratorium on farm mortgage foreclosures.

EXPANDING RESOURCES 1901-1945

16 JULY 1934
Labor In San Francisco, where 12,000 members of the International Longshoremen's Association are out on strike, organized labor calls a "general strike," the first such in U.S. history. Throughout the U.S. this summer, there are numerous strikes.

22 JULY 1934
Regional John Dillinger, known as Public Enemy No. 1, is shot and killed by the FBI outside a Chicago Theater.

6 AUGUST 1934
International The last of the U.S. Marines leave Haiti, where they have been stationed since 1915.

9 AUGUST 1934
National By proclamation, President Roosevelt nationalizes silver and says the federal government will purchase it at 50.01 cents an ounce.

8 SEPTEMBER 1934
Regional A fire breaks out on the ship *Morro Castle* off New Jersey; some 130 people die.

6 NOVEMBER 1934
National In the midterm elections, the Democrats add nine seats in both the Senate and the House; among the new Senators is one from Missouri, Harry S. Truman.

3 DECEMBER 1934
National The Supreme Court, in *Hamilton v. Regents of the University of California*, upholds the right of land-grant colleges to require military training of their students.

29 DECEMBER 1934
International Japan denounces the Washington Naval Treaty of 1922 and the London Naval Treaty of 1930; Japan says it will withdraw completely from these treaties' terms as of December 1936.

OTHER EVENTS OF 1934
Life/Customs The Catholic Legion of Decency, recognizing the popularity and influence of movies, begins to censor them for Catholics.
Population In Ontario, Canada, five girls are born to the Dionne family; they become the first quintuplets known to survive and are immediately adopted by the world.

4 JANUARY 1935
National President Roosevelt delivers the annual State of the Union Message to Congress and effectively begins a second stage of his New Deal. He proposes legislation that has such long-term goals as providing for social security—for the aged, the unemployed, the ill—for better housing, for taxation reforms. At the same time, he demands that the government must "quit this business of relief" and provide jobs for the unemployed.

29 JANUARY 1935
National The Senate, by a vote of 52 to 36—a 2/3 majority being necessary for approving a treaty—ends up rejecting the proposal to ratify U.S. participation in the World Court. This kind of isolationism will not go unnoticed by countries such as Germany and Japan, which are waiting to move against international order.

8 APRIL 1935
National Congress adopts the Emergency Relief Appropriation Act, authorizing almost $5,000,000,000 for immediate relief and, more important, "to increase employment . . . by useful projects." It is this bill that will be used to set up various programs, the most important being the Works Progress Administration (WPA) that will commence on May 6.

27 APRIL 1935
National Congress establishes the Soil Conservation Service as a section within the Department of Agriculture. Its primary mission is to promote better use of the farmlands, particularly those in the West, where erosion and dust storms have been driving farmers off the land.

1 MAY 1935
National With an executive order, as empowered by the Emergency Relief Appropriation Act, President Roosevelt establishes the Resettlement Administration (RA). With Rexford Tugwell as its head, the RA will work to help farm families relocate in more productive areas and support them with loans and with projects such as reforestation and flood control. The RA will also aid some low-income city workers to relocate in specially constructed "greenbelt" towns. (The RA's work will essentially be taken over by the Farm Security Administration in 1937.)

6 MAY 1935
National The Works Progress Administration begins under the direction of Harry Hopkins. In many ways, the WPA becomes the best-known of the many New Deal programs, for it soon puts millions of Americans to work at reasonable wages while building thousands of miles of roads, constructing or repairing bridges, erecting thousands of public structures such as schools and post offices and building everything from parks to airfields. The WPA will also set up programs that provide employment for artists, musicians, actors, writers and scholars. In 1939 it will change its name to the Works Projects Administration but it will continue its efforts through June 1943, by which time it will have spent some $11,000,000,000 and employed at least 8,500,000 individual Americans. The WPA will inevitably be charged with waste and inefficiency and to critics of Roosevelt's New Deal it stands as the symbol of his misguided efforts. But for millions of Americans it provided work and income.

11 MAY 1935
National Again acting under the Emergency Relief

Appropriation Act, President Roosevelt uses an executive order to establish the Rural Electrification Administration. Its main function will be to provide loans at good terms for constructing plants and lines to bring electricity into those areas where the private utility companies had not found it profitable to provide service.

22 MAY 1935
National President Roosevelt vetoes the Patman Bill, which would allow veterans of World War I immediately to cash in bonus certificates (not due till 1945). Roosevelt becomes the first president to appear in person before Congress to give an explanation for his veto—he sees the results as inflationary—but the House of Representatives immediately overrides his veto. On May 23, however, the Senate will sustain the veto.

27 MAY 1935
National In what is immediately recognized as a major setback to Roosevelt's New Deal, the Supreme Court rules unanimously in *Schechter Poultry Corp. v. United States* that the National Industrial Recovery Act of 1933 was unconstitutional. The case itself seemed almost trivial, involving a small Brooklyn poultry firm charged with violations of National Recovery Administration code, but the Supreme Court ruled that Congress had given "virtually unfettered" powers to the NRA, and this was "utterly inconsistent" with the constitutional duties of Congress. This ruling is only one of many by the Supreme Court that will go against Roosevelt's plans and will lead to his "court-packing" proposal of 1937.

10 JUNE 1935
Life/Customs Alcoholics Anonymous is formally organized in New York City.

5 JULY 1935
National Roosevelt signs the National Labor Relations Act (also known by its sponsors' names, the Wagner-Connery Act). This is a major piece of labor legislation, setting up a National Labor Relations Board empowered to supervise elections by which workers vote for their own collective bargaining units. Other sections of the law support the right of employees to join labor organizations and set forth unfair labor practices by employers. The Supreme Court will uphold this law as constitutional in March 1937.

29 JULY 1935
Regional Thomas E. Dewey is appointed a special prosecutor in New York State to lead a drive against crime that will give him his national reputation and lead to his nomination for the presidency.

14 AUGUST 1935
National President Roosevelt signs the Social Security Act—by any standards, one of the most far-reaching pieces of legislation in American history. It sets up the system that will guarantee pensions to those retiring at 65 (starting in 1942), with contributions from both employees and employers. The act also assists the states in providing financial aid to dependent children, the blind and the aged who do not qualify for Social Security; beyond this, the act establishes a system of unemployment insurance. Although somewhat modified over the years, and occasionally attacked, this becomes the foundation of America's aged's security in the decades ahead.

23 AUGUST 1935
National Congress passes the Banking Act of 1935 that revises the operations of the Federal Reserve System, generally making banks both more responsible and responsive to the needs of the public.

26 AUGUST 1935
National Roosevelt signs the Public Utilities Act (or the Wheeler-Rayburn Act) requiring public utility holding companies to register with the Securities and Exchange Commission and giving other federal agencies new powers of regulating the gas and electric companies.

30 AUGUST 1935
National Congress passes the Revenue Act. It increases taxes on inheritances and gifts as well as on the higher incomes of individuals while adjusting taxes on corporations to favor smaller companies. When Roosevelt asked for such legislation, he explicitly stated, "Our revenue laws have operated . . . to the unfair advantage of the few, and they have done little to prevent an unjust concentration of wealth and economic power." The Revenue Act of 1935 clearly sets out to change that.

31 AUGUST 1935
National Roosevelt signs the Neutrality Act. It forbids the shipment of any arms and munitions to belligerents once the president has declared that a state of war exists. It also authorizes the President to prohibit American civilians from traveling on ships of belligerents.

8 SEPTEMBER 1935
Regional Huey Long, the Senator from Louisiana, is shot while visiting his state capitol in Baton Rouge; his assailant is Dr. Carl Weiss, Jr., angered at wrongs he feels Long has done to his family. Weiss is immediately killed by Long's bodyguards, but Long dies on September 10. Although Long failed to find a national constituency for his brand of populist-demagogic politics, he undeniably put pressure on Roosevelt to introduce certain reforms.

5 OCTOBER 1935
International Roosevelt proclaims that "a state of war unhappily exists" between Ethiopia and Italy as a result of Italy's invasion of Ethiopia on October 3 and declares the provisions of the Neutrality Act (passed only this August 31) to be in effect. On October 11 the League of Nations in Geneva will vote to declare Italy the aggressor, but the U.S. is not a member of

Among the bizarre and colorful characters in American history, Huey Long is a chapter unto himself. Populist and dictator, flagrantly corrupt but a keeper of election promises, a buffoon and a wily machine politician, his seven-year career in major office was a study in violent contrasts that inspired equally contrasting feelings about him.

Long was born near Winnfield, Louisiana, on August 30, 1892, son of a comfortable but populistic farming family who left him with an aversion to the privileged classes. For a time he was a travelling salesman, but by 1915 he had accumulated enough study to pass a special bar examination. After three years' law practice he was elected a state public service commissioner. In the early 20s an attack he mounted' on Standard Oil brought him public attention and a gubernatorial bid; defeated in 1924, he was successful four years later.

Long's first two years as governor of Louisiana were restrained by a hostile legislature, but he did enact programs for free schoolbooks and highway improvement. He also began immediately to excite controversy for assorted misconduct. In his second year of office he narrowly escaped impeachment, but soon silenced the legislature by running successfully for the Senate in 1930.

For the next two years he was both Senator and Governor. The nation came to know him by his nickname "Kingfish" and to be delighted and appalled by his antics. He supported Roosevelt in 1932, but after the President rejected his notions regarding redistribution of wealth, Long became a vituperative critic of the administration. This created a defection among leading Democrats back home. Threatened with the collapse of his power, Long went on the offensive with extraordinary effect: in 1934 and 1935 he pushed through the Louisiana legislature a series of measures giving him the most absolute power wielded by any politician in American history.

From that position he launched new attacks on Roosevelt, creating a "Share-Our-Wealth Society" with an impossible program which was nonetheless joined by millions of people who saw him as the messiah of the underdog. In August 1935 he announced he would challenge Roosevelt for the presidency. At that point fate intervened in the person of Dr. Carl A. Weiss, who assassinated Long in September 1935. Thus ended the career but by no means the legend of the closest thing to a dictator America ever had.

the League, which in any case is unable to take any concrete steps to stop Italy—another lesson that will not be lost on Adolph Hitler.

10 OCTOBER 1935
Arts/Culture *Porgy and Bess*, an opera by George Gershwin (based on a novel by DuBose and Dorothy Heyward) opens at the Alvin Theater in New York City (after a short tryout in Boston). It will run for 16 weeks in New York before a road tour of 3 months. With its story of black Americans and its music of indigenous rhythms and motifs, *Porgy and Bess* will gradually establish itself as arguably the greatest truly American opera.

26 OCTOBER 1935
Agriculture In 16 states that hold referendums,

corn-hog farmers vote 6 to 1 to continue the Agricultural Adjustment Administration at least through 1936. This is not only an important vote of endorsement for Roosevelt's policies but a crucial turning point in the way American farmers view their relations with the Federal Government.

9 NOVEMBER 1935
Labor John L. Lewis, president of the United Mine Workers, becomes chairman of the newly formed Committee for Industrial Organizations within the AFL. As the CIO soon challenges the more conservative AFL leadership and policies, it will be expelled in 1937 and then change its name to the Congress of Industrial Organizations, which will merge with the AFL in 1955.

15 NOVEMBER 1935
International The Commonwealth of Philippines inaugurates its first president, Manuel Quezon y Malina (who was elected on September 17).

9 DECEMBER 1935
International The Second London Naval Conference convenes in London, with the American delegation headed by Norman H. Davis. The goal is to control the expansion of the world's navies, but when Japan is denied its request to maintain a navy the equal of that of the U.S. and Britain, it will leave the conference.

OTHER EVENTS OF 1935
International The Saar is returned to Germany, a concession to Hitler's demands for restoring Germany's pre-World War I domain. Hitler also gets the Nazi party to pass the so-called Nuremberg Laws, depriving Jews of citizenship. In China, Mao Tse Tung and his Red Army complete their Long March to the north, where they will continue to resist both the Japanese and the Nationalist Chinese until the Communists assume control of China in 1949.

6 JANUARY 1936
National In *U.S. vs. Butler*, the Supreme Court rules 6-3 that the Agricultural Adjustment Act (of 1933) is unconstitutional on the grounds that the act did not levy a tax but an outright control over production and thus was exceeding the government's responsibilities. But the dissenting judges accuse the majority of substituting their own judgment for that of the legislators, and thus deepening the schism between the Supreme Court and the American people.

24 JANUARY 1936
National Congress passes the Adjusted Compensation Act by overriding President Roosevelt's veto earlier in the day. The bill allows for immediate cash redemption of the bonus certificates held by veterans of World War I. Roosevelt had vetoed a previous version of this bill on May 22,1935, but now, with the recession underway, Congress asserts itself.

GEORGE GERSHWIN, 1898-1937

George Gershwin was fated to die before he was very old, so the world was lucky that he started young. In a composing career that began in Tin Pan Alley and ended on the opera stage, he captured the ears of everyone from the unsophisticated listeners to the great musicians of his time.

Born in Brooklyn on September 26, 1898, Gershwin grew up a typical streetwise kid on New York's East Side. His occasional encounters with music stirred him deeply, and as a teenager he began picking out tunes on a neighbor's piano. Soon he was making up his own popular songs, but he was also studying the classics with various teachers. At the age of 15 he quit school to write songs for $15 a week; five years later came his first smash hit, "Swanee," for Al Jolson. The same year he wrote the first of his many musical comedies. During the 20s he rose to worldwide fame with his songs, most of them with lyrics by his brother Ira.

Gershwin was now rich and famous, but he was not satisfied. By 1922 he was experimenting with opera in jazz style. In 1924, under a commission by Paul Whiteman, Gershwin brought jazz into the concert hall and into the mainstream of music with *Rhapsody In Blue*; its influence was felt worldwide and it remains a monument of American music.

A prolific tunesmith and natural musician, Gershwin now began to study, to press classical composers such as Ravel and Stravinsky for lessons (comparing their incomes, Stravinsky suggested maybe Gershwin should give *him* lessons). His dual career continued: a series of Broadway musicals including *Lady Be Good* (1924) and *Of Thee I Sing*, which won the Pulitzer Prize in 1931; and a number of concert works including *An American in Paris* (1928).

But Gershwin had not finished growing. In 1935 came his greatest work, the immortal folk opera *Porgy and Bess*. Two years later he was dead of a brain tumor at the age of 38. One of the great songwriters of his time, he would be remembered not as a songwriter but as an artist, for whom popular success was never enough.

29 FEBRUARY 1936
National The Second Neutrality Act is passed, extending the act of 1935 to May 1, 1937 but adding a prohibition against granting any U.S. loans or credits to belligerents. Congress also passes the Soil Conservation and Domestic Allotment Act to take the place of the Agricultural Adjustment Act (declared unconstitutional on January 6, 1936). In this new version, farmers will be paid for withdrawing land planted with soil-depleting crops (such as cotton, tobacco, corn, wheat) and for efforts to control erosion and soil wastage (such as through planting soil-conserving crops).

2 MARCH 1936
International The U.S. signs a treaty with Panama that enlarges Panama's authority in the Canal Zone, but the U.S. Senate will not ratify it until July 25, 1939.

25 MARCH 1936
International Because Japan withdrew from the London Naval Conference (in December 1935), the U.S. joins Great Britain and France in a new agreement to set their own limits on naval forces.

9 MAY 1936
International With its capital, Addis Ababa, captured and the Emperor Hailie Selassie having fled, Ethiopia falls to the Italian Army. The fact that Mussolini is able to commit this aggression will encourage him—and Hitler—to proceed with plans to take other territory they want.
Aviation The German dirigible *Hindenburg* arrives at Lakehurst, New Jersey, completing the first scheduled transatlantic dirigible flight. (It will explode here on May 6, 1937.)

23 MAY 1936
National Meeting in Cleveland, the national convention of the Socialist Party nominates Norman Thomas as its presidential candidate.

9-12 JUNE 1936
National At its convention in Cleveland, the Republican Party nominates Alfred M. Landon, governor of Kansas, for president, with Frank Knox of Illinois for vice-president. Not unexpectedly, the Republicans adopt a platform that strongly opposes Roosevelt's New Deal and this will gain them some support from conservative Democrats.

19 JUNE 1936
National William Lemke, a Republican Representative from North Dakota, announces that he will run for president on the Union Party ticket. The Union Party is newly formed by those who oppose Roosevelt and his New Deal but are willing to incorporate various populist programs designed to win the support of the followers of such men as the Rev. Charles Coughlin, Francis Townsend and Gerald L. K. Smith. Father Coughlin's National Union for Social Justice will hold its own convention on August 14 and endorse Lemke, but his new populist movement will not attract many Americans.

20 JUNE 1936
National Congress adopts the Robinson-Patman Act, prohibiting stores and other firms from engaging in price-lowering and other practices intended to drive out competition and establish monopolies.

22 JUNE 1936
National Congress passes an act that grants the Virgin Islands, a U.S. territory, the right to elect its own legislature.

23-27 JUNE 1936
National At its national convention in Philadelphia, the Democratic Party nominates Franklin Delano Roosevelt for president by acclamation. John Nance Garner is selected again to be vice-president. The Democrats' platform generally supports the efforts and goals of the New Deal.

24-28 JUNE 1936
National In New York City, the Communist Party of the United States nominates Earl Browder for President.

26 JUNE 1936
National Congress passes the Merchant Marine Act, establishing the U.S. Maritime Commission to develop and regulate the nation's merchant marine with such means as subsidies (to compensate for cheaper foreign costs) and working standards for seamen.

17 JULY 1936
International Spanish Army units in Morocco proclaim a revolution against the government in Madrid, now headed by a leftist-oriented Popular Front that has been unable to stop the rising tide of violence among the various elements in Spain. General Francisco Franco soon emerges as the leader of the various conservative elements and a full-scale civil war is underway, one that prefigures World War II in its opposing ideologies and its use of new weapons and tactics. On August 7 the U.S. will announce that it will not interfere in this civil war—yet another signal to Hitler and Mussolini that the democracies are not prepared to stand up to the Fascist states.

SEPTEMBER-NOVEMBER 1936
National The Presidential campaign is now being hotly waged throughout the country, with Roosevelt and his New Deal being attacked from various sides. About 80 percent of American newspapers formally endorse the Republicans, some of whom become quite vitriolic in accusing Roosevelt of attempting to impose a centralized economy on America. Meanwhile, the minor parties of both the Left and Right try to appeal to those Americans still suffering from the Depression by offering even more drastic solutions. Roosevelt inspires so much strong feeling, in fact, that it becomes easy for some of his opponents to believe that he is about to be unseated; *The Literary Digest*, a prominent periodical, claims that its survey predicts a landslide for Landon.

3 NOVEMBER 1936
National In the election, Roosevelt defeats Landon by a landslide—27,751,612 popular votes to 16,681,913, and with an even more dramatic majority in the electoral college votes, 523 to 8 (only Maine and Vermont going to Landon). The Democrats also hold onto their majorities in the Senate (76-16) and House (331-89). Lemke gets 891,858 popular votes; Norman Thomas gets 187,342; and Browder, the Communist, gets 80,181. *The Literary Digest* folds.

11 DECEMBER 1936
International King Edward VIII of Great Britain abdicates his throne in favor of his love for the American divorcee, Wallis Warfield Simpson. As the Duke and Duchess of Windsor they will become the epitome of international celebritydom for a generation.

30 DECEMBER 1936
Labor The United Auto Workers begins a sit-down strike—literally sitting in the plant and defying management and authorities—at a General Motors plant in Michigan. Among other demands is one that the UAW be recognized as the sole bargaining agent for all employees. The strike will not end until February 11, 1937.

OTHER EVENTS OF 1936
Arts/Culture The Nobel Prize for Literature is awarded to the American Eugene O'Neill for his powerful dramas.
Sports At the summer Olympics in Berlin, staged by Hitler and his German supporters to enhance their image, the black American Jesse Owens wins four gold medals in field and track, somewhat discrediting Nazi theories of Aryan superiority.

6 JANUARY 1937
National Congress passes a resolution that prohibits the shipment of munitions to either of the sides now fighting a civil war in Spain. But this cannot stop individual Americans from taking sides; in particular, progressives, intellectuals and artists are sympathetic to the Loyalists and some will soon be going to Spain on their own to join in the fight against the forces led by General Franco.

20 JANUARY 1937
National Franklin Delano Roosevelt is inaugurated for his second term as president, with John Nance Garner as his vice-president. (This is the first time that the inauguration has occurred other than in March, a change due to the 20th Amendment adopted in February 1933.) In his Inaugural Address, Roosevelt continues to hammer away at the nation's economic problems and uses another phrase that will often be quoted: "I see one-third of a nation ill-housed, ill-clad, ill-nourished."

5 FEBRUARY 1937
National Roosevelt has been increasingly impatient, even outraged, at the Supreme Court, composed of nine men—all over 60 and generally conservative—whom he had come to regard as a small group thwarting the will of the nation. Emboldened by the extent of his victory at the polls, Roosevelt informs his Cabinet at a special meeting this morning that he will be sending a message to Congress that very noon proposing a reorganization of the federal judiciary system. Ostensibly it is designed to improve the efficiency of the entire system—by adding judges to all levels of the federal courts, by assigning judges to more congested courts, by adopting procedures to expedite the appeals process. But the heart of the proposal fools no one: it is that the Supreme Court should increase its membership by as many as six if any of the justices over 70 refused to retire. The proposal incites instant controversy, and Roosevelt is accused of wanting to "pack" the court and in so doing destroy the independence of the judiciary, to assert the supremacy of

EUGENE O'NEILL, 1888-1953

The life's work of playwright Eugene O'Neill was the desperate testament of a desperate man—the tragedy and despair of his plays was a direct reflection of his own life. O'Neill was born into a neurotic and tumultuous stage family in New York on October 16, 1888. After a failed term at Princeton, he wandered around the world for six aimless and drunken years, climaxed by a suicide attempt and a bout with tuberculosis, and including a failed marriage. At the tuberculosis sanitarium O'Neill tried his hand at a play; it became, he later said, his rebirth. From 1916 to 1920 he wrote, and produced, plays for the Provincetown Players. Then came his first Broadway production, *Beyond the Horizon*, which won the 1920 Pulitzer Prize and rocketed him to fame. Between 1918 and 1928 O'Neill wrote more than a dozen plays, winning two more Pulitzers and a reputation as the greatest tragic dramatist of his time. To those who criticized the gloom and squalor of his stories, O'Neill replied, "I love life. But I don't love life because it is pretty . . .There is beauty to me even in its ugliness."

He had gained wealth and fame, but by no means contentment. A second marriage broke up in 1928; he later disinherited the two children of that marriage. In 1929 he married Carlotta Monterey, his last wife, and began living a semi-reclusive existence in Georgia and California, where he wrote his only comedy and most-performed play, *Ah, Wilderness!* In 1936 he won the Nobel Prize for literature. But his personal tragedy was not over. After his 50th year he began to be afflicted with a degenerative nervous disorder that made it increasingly hard for him to work. Somehow, during the years 1935 to 1943, he produced, with enormous physical and emotional effort, his greatest and most deeply-felt plays, including the searing and autobiographical *Long Day's Journey Into Night*. Meanwhile, the world seemed nearly to forget him; his reputation fell and was not revived until after his death, following ten unproductive and painful years, in 1953. After his death, fellow playwright Arthur Miller said, "O'Neill was the great wrestler, fighting God to a standstill. The theater will forever need the towering rebuke of his life and his work and his agony."

the executive branch, and thus to subvert the Constitution. Even many of Roosevelt's longtime supporters will desert him on this issue as the debate moves into the Congress.

1 MARCH 1937

National Congress passes the Supreme Court Retirement Act, which simply permits the Justices to retire at 70 with full pay. This is clearly a compromise, a not very subtle attempt to buy off the elderly justices, and it will not lead to any immediate resignations. President Roosevelt signs the Reciprocal Trade Agreement Act, extending the Trade Agreement Act of 1934 to June 1940 and allowing the President to negotiate foreign trade agreements.

Labor In what comes as something of a surprise, John L. Lewis, head of the CIO, and the chairman of the board of U.S. Steel announce jointly that the U.S. Steel Corporation will accept a contract that includes recognition of the United Steel Workers. It will be several years before all the major steel companies follow suit, but this is a crucial breakthrough for organized labor in the U.S.

29 MARCH 1937

National The Supreme Court, in *West Coast Hotel v. Parrish*, reverses earlier decisions and upholds the principle of minimum wages for women.

12 APRIL 1937

National The Supreme Court, in a series of decisions by a narrow 5-4 majority, rules that the National Labor Relations Act (Wagner-Connery Act) of 1935 is constitutional. This will take some of the steam out of Roosevelt's move to revamp the court.

1 MAY 1937

National President Roosevelt signs the third Neutrality Act, extending the Neutrality Acts of 1935 and 1936, due to expire at midnight. It not only continues the prohibition on exporting arms to belligerents and prohibits these nations from selling their securities in the U.S., it also prohibits American ships from carrying arms into the belligerents' zones. It also requires that belligerent nations must pay with cash for certain non-military goods purchased in the U.S.A. and then carry them in their own ships—thus giving this the nickname of "the cash-and-carry law."

6 MAY 1937

Aviation The *Hindenberg*, the great German dirigible, while tying up at Lakehurst, New Jersey, explodes, killing 36 persons. This ends commercial airship traffic.

24 MAY 1937

National The Supreme Court, after considering three related cases, rules that the Social Security Act of 1935 is constitutional. This is a crucial victory for Roosevelt and takes still more steam out of his proposal to change the composition of the court.

22 JUNE 1937

Sports Joe Louis becomes World Heavyweight Boxing Champion by knocking out James J. Braddock in the 8th round in Chicago. Louis is the second black man to hold this title; he will retain the championship until his retirement in 1949.

2 JULY 1937

Aviation On her round-the-world flight, the noted American aviator Amelia Earhart vanishes over the Pacific Ocean after radio contact with her suddenly stops. Despite endless speculation and rumors, no trace of her plane or of her will ever be found.

12 AUGUST 1937

National President Roosevelt nominates Hugo L. Black of Alabama to the Supreme Court to replace retiring Justice Van Devanter. As a Senator he has been a liberal supporter of the New Deal, but he had belonged to the Klu Klux Klan in his youth and this will create considerable controversy.

18 AUGUST 1937
National Roosevelt signs the Miller-Tydings Enabling Act—actually he is forced to accept it as a "rider" to an appropriations bill for the District of Columbia—which amends federal antitrust laws by allowing for certain fixed-price items to be sold. But the act has considerable support on the grounds that price-cutting has become destructive of the very competition it is supposed to advance.

26 AUGUST 1937
National President Roosevelt signs the Judicial Procedure Reform Act, the compromise of his original judiciary reform proposal; basically it makes some changes in the lower courts. The Revenue Act of 1937 goes into effect this day; its main impact will be to close some loopholes in income tax laws that have allowed for tax evasion.

14 SEPTEMBER 1937
National By executive order, President Roosevelt bars U.S. ships from carrying arms to both China and Japan, engaged in war since Japan invaded China after a trumped-up incident in July.

11 DECEMBER 1937
International When the League of Nations, meeting in Geneva, votes against Italy because of its actions in Ethiopia, Italy simply withdraws from the League.

12 DECEMBER 1937
International The U.S. gunboat *Panay* is bombed by Japanese planes and sinks in the Yangtze River in China. There is an immediate outcry but on December 14 Japan apologizes, agrees to pay indemnity and promises that there will be no more such incidents.

OTHER EVENTS OF 1937
International In the U.S.S.R., hundreds of men and women are purged by being tried as "spies" by Stalin's Communist regime.
Economics A definite decline in economic output, coupled with a rise in labor unrest, makes clear that the worldwide Depression is still underway.

3 JANUARY 1938
National In his annual State of the Union message to Congress, President Roosevelt refers to the nation's need to be "adequately strong in self-defense," but most of his speech is concerned with the economic and social problems still crippling the nation.

10 JANUARY 1938
National Since 1935, Representative Louis Ludlow from Indiana has introduced into Congress on several occasions a resolution calling for a national referendum to decide whether Congress could declare war (except when the U.S. has been invaded). A poll has shown that a solid majority of Americans favored such a referendum, but President Roosevelt has long been opposed to it; as recently as January 6 he has

written to Senator Bankhead and said it would "cripple any President in his conduct of foreign relations." Today, the House of Representatives, by a majority of 209-188, returns Ludlow's resolution to a committee, and this will effectively end such a proposal.

28 JANUARY 1938
National President Roosevelt submits to Congress a recommendation calling for increased appropriations for building up the armed forces, particularly the Navy.

16 FEBRUARY 1938
National President Roosevelt signs the Agricultural Adjustment Act, an important effort by the federal government to stabilize agricultural prices and farmers' incomes. It provides for controls on acreage planted, on quotas of crops to be marketed, and on storage of surpluses; it also sets up the Federal Crop Insurance Corp, an agency of the Department of Agriculture, specifically to insure wheat crops by accepting wheat in payment of insurance taken out against losses from unavoidable natural causes. Behind this lies the concept of the "ever-normal granary," a favorite project of Secretary of Agriculture Henry Wallace, who feels the Federal Government should work directly to maintain agricultural supplies.

13 MARCH 1938
International After Austrian Chancellor Kurt von Schuschnigg is forced from office and German troops have been sent into Austria to "preserve order," Hitler declares Austria has been united with Germany, (the *Anschluss*), not conquered.

18 MARCH 1938
International Mexico nationalizes all oil properties of U.S. and other foreign-owned companies. (There will be no financial settlement until 1941.)

31 MARCH 1938
National Former President Herbert Hoover, in a speech to the Council on Foreign Relations, takes issue with President Roosevelt's Chicago speech (October 5, 1937) and advises the U.S. not to make any alliances with those European countries now lining up against the Fascist states such as Germany, Italy and Franco's Spain. Hoover warns that this will only lead to war.

11 MAY 1938
National Congress adopts the Revenue Act of 1938, which reduces corporate income taxes—purportedly to stimulate the economy; Roosevelt refuses to sign it, but it becomes law on May 27.

26 MAY 1938
National The House of Representatives sets up a committee to investigate un-American activities; it will be headed by Martin Dies from Texas. Supposedly the committee will investigate all un-American Groups—whether on the Right or Left, Nazis or Communists—

but eventually it will concentrate its attention on those of the radical Left.

21 JUNE 1938
National Roosevelt signs the Emergency Relief Appropriations Act, an extension of his previous efforts to deal with the economic recession that has taken over the country in the last 10 months.

22 JUNE 1938
National The Chandler Act is passed by Congress, amending the Federal Bankruptcy Act of 1898; it sets forth procedures under Chapter XI by which persons or businesses may settle their debts to avoid liquidation.

23 JUNE 1938
National Congress establishes the Civil Aeronautics Authority (CAA) to provide federal regulation of the nation's rapidly expanding air traffic—through licensing of pilots, rules of flight, assigning airways and standards for equipment.

24 JUNE 1938
National Congress passes the Food, Drug and Cosmetic Act to supersede the Pure Food Act of 1906. The new act calls for detailed disclosure of the ingredients of food, drugs and cosmetics on the labels, and sets stiff penalties for misbranding and for false advertising.

25 JUNE 1938
National President Roosevelt signs the Fair Labor Standards Act, a major piece of social legislation even though its requirements will sound tame within a few years: it sets the minimum wage at 40 cents an hour and the maximum work week at 44 hours (to be lowered to 40 in three years). Even these requirements are limited to businesses engaged in interstate commerce.

28 JUNE 1938
National Congress passes the Flood Control Act to support work on rivers and harbors.

1-3 JULY 1938
National On the 75th anniversary of the Battle of Gettysburg, President Roosevelt dedicates a memorial in the presence of many Civil War veterans.

14 JULY 1938
Aviation Howard Hughes sets a new record flying around the world in 3 days, 19 hours, 14.28 minutes.

17 JULY 1938
Aviation American aviator Douglas Corrigan lands in Dublin after his solo flight across the Atlantic. Since he had been unable to obtain an official flight exit-permit for Europe, he claims he made a mistake and thought he was heading for California. He is immediately dubbed Wrong-Way Corrigan and becomes a popular hero.

21 SEPTEMBER 1938
Environment A major tropical hurricane moves up the Atlantic coast, causing especially heavy damage in New England. Altogether, some 700 people lose their lives, millions of trees are downed and millions of dollars of damage is done.

27 SEPTEMBER 1938
International President Roosevelt sends a personal message to the governments of Great Britain, France, Germany and Czechoslovakia, asking that they negotiate a peaceful settlement to the Sudetenland crisis. The Sudetenland is an area of Czechoslovakia largely inhabited by German-speakers who, urged on by Hitler, are asking for autonomy.

30 SEPTEMBER 1938
International At a conference in Munich, British Prime Minister Neville Chamberlain and French Prime Minister Edouardo Daladier sign an agreement that allows Germany to take over the Sudetenland. Chamberlain returns to England and announces that this Munich Pact guarantees "peace in our time." Both Munich and that promise will instead go down in history as bitter reminders of the futility of appeasement. Yet a poll taken in the U.S. during October—even after Hitler triumphantly entered the Sudetenland on October 3—shows a minority of Americans disapproved of the Munich Pact.

30 OCTOBER 1938
Life/Customs Orson Welles broadcasts a radio play, "Invasion from Mars," that sounds so realistic (even though it was framed by announcements) that it leads many listeners to take to the highways in panic.

14 NOVEMBER 1938
International The U.S. ambassador to Germany is recalled for "report and consultation."

18 NOVEMBER 1938
International The German ambassador to the U.S.A. is recalled.
Labor John L. Lewis is elected the first president of the now formally organized independent Congress of Industrial Organizations.

6 DECEMBER 1938
International Anthony Eden, recently resigned as Britain's Foreign Minister to protest the action of Chamberlain at Munich, gives a radio speech in New York City and advises Americans that all democracies are being threatened by the now expanding fascist powers.

24 DECEMBER 1938
International Representatives of 21 nations of the Western Hemisphere meet at Lima, Peru, for the Eighth International American Conference and adopt the Declaration of Lima, reaffirming the principle of mutual consultation (as agreed at the Buenos Aires conference in 1936) but not stressing their mutual de-

EXPANDING RESOURCES 1901-1945

JOHN L. LEWIS, 1880-1969

The bulldog features, bristling eyebrows and extravagant oratory of John L. Lewis were familiar fixtures of the American scene during much of the 20th century; his ability to harangue, bully and often to threaten management into signing on the dotted line made him one of the most significant and controversial labor leaders of his time. Lewis was born into a mining family in Lucas, Iowa, on February 12, 1880. Dropping out of school after seventh grade to enter the mines, he soon began union work and rose to become president of the United Mine Workers of America in 1919. That year Lewis initiated a miners' strike which, though he canceled the strike after a government injuction, gave him a national reputation as a labor leader.

During the 20s the UMWA was torn by hard times and internal dissension, and membership dwindled. Things began to change during the 30s when the Roosevelt administration guaranteed more rights to unions. Angered by the American Federation of Labor's slowness in exploiting these opportunities, Lewis and seven other union leaders organized the Congress of Industrial Organizations in 1935. With Lewis as president, the CIO soon outnumbered the AFL. The next years saw intense wrangling between the two organizations, which was finally settled when they merged in 1955.

As CIO president, Lewis was one of the most powerful men in the country, though his truculent and sometimes self-serving style left many wondering whether he was working mainly for the membership or for himself. In 1937 a Lewis-led steel strike marked by violence on both sides inspired an angry Roosevelt to proclaim "a plague on both your houses." Partly as a result, Lewis changed from his previous support and strongly opposed Roosevelt in 1940; after Roosevelt was elected, Lewis resigned the CIO presidency in protest. Still president of the UMWA and still a formidable power, Lewis subsequently made several unsuccessful attempts to regain leadership of the CIO. During World War II he led several coal strikes that gained important concessions but alienated many union supporters. He remained an active and effective leader of the UMWA until his death in 1969.

fense against threats to the territorial integrity of any individual nation.

4 JANUARY 1939
National In his annual State of the Union address to Congress, President Roosevelt shifts his emphasis from domestic issues to the tense international scene, calling on all democracies to be prepared.

5 JANUARY 1939
National President Roosevelt formally submits his budget to Congress and requests $1,319,000,000 for defense out of a total of some $9,000,000,000.

30 JANUARY 1939
National The Supreme Court, in *Tennessee Electric Power Company v. Tennessee Valley Authority,* upholds the constitutionality of the TVA's competition with private utility companies.

13 FEBRUARY 1939
National Justice Louis Brandeis, one of the greatest of America's legal minds, retires from the Supreme Court at the age of 82. Appointed by President Wilson in 1916—and the first Jew to sit on the Supreme Court—Brandeis was generally one of the more liberal justices.

27 FEBRUARY 1939
National The Supreme Court, in *National Labor Relations Board v. Fansteel Metallurgical Corporation,* rules that sit-down strikes are unconstitutional.

14 MARCH 1939
International The German Army invades Czechoslovakia, having obtained the Sudetenland through the Munich appeasement pact.

1 APRIL 1939
International With the fighting in Spain effectively over, the U.S. recognizes the government headed by General Francisco Franco.

3 APRIL 1939
National President Roosevelt signs the Administrative Reorganization Act, which empowers the president to examine and then reorganize executive agencies with a view to eliminating overlapping functions and general waste. Roosevelt will submit five major plans—two in 1939, three in 1940—that will transfer, consolidate or abolish many executive units that had grown up over many decades. And since Congress does not vote against these plans, by the terms of this act they will all go into effect.

7 APRIL 1939
International The Italian Army invades tiny Albania, across the Adriatic Sea.

14 APRIL 1939
International Roosevelt writes to Hitler and Mussolini and requests that they offer a 10-year guarantee of peace for Europe and the Middle East in return for U.S. cooperation in talks on world trade and armaments. Neither Hitler nor Mussolini shows any interest in the proposal; indeed, Hitler revokes the German nonaggression pact with Poland and the Anglo-German Naval Agreement.

30 APRIL 1939
Life/Customs The New York World's Fair officially opens, with President Roosevelt in attendance. Billed as "The World of Tomorrow," the fair presents the prospect of many technological, social, cultural and other trends, soon to be shattered by a worldwide war.

10 MAY 1939
Ideas/Beliefs The Methodist Church—after major splits that had divided its members since 1830—forms a united body with some 8,000,000 members.

16 MAY 1939
National A food-stamp plan is begun in Rochester,

SEPTEMBER 3, 1939

New York, with the intention of distributing the nation's surplus food to the poor and needy. Within the next two years, a similar plan will be adopted in some 150 American cities. (During World War II the food-stamp plan will be discontinued, but on September 21, 1959, a similar plan to distribute surplus food will be reactivated.)

7-12 JUNE 1939
International King George VI and Queen Elizabeth visit the U.S. on what is called "a goodwill trip," but clearly it is designed to cement relations between the two countries against the growing Fascist menace.

28 JUNE 1939
Aviation With 22 people aboard, the Pan American Airways *Dixie Clipper* arrives in Lisbon, Portugal, after a flight from Long Island, New York, taking 23 hours, 52 minutes. This flight inaugurates transatlantic passenger air service.

14 JULY 1939
National President Roosevelt sends a special message to Congress to ask for the repeal of the arms embargo. It is hardly a secret that Roosevelt wants to be able to sell and send U.S. arms to countries such as England in order to help them resist the Fascist nations. On July 18 Roosevelt and his Secretary of State, Cordell Hull, will take the next step and ask Congress to revise the neutrality law. And on July 26 Hull will abrogate the trade treaty that the U.S. had signed with Japan back in 1911. All these actions will deepen the gap between the U.S. and the totalitarian-militaristic states and in turn make these latter regard the U.S.A. as a potential enemy.

2 AUGUST 1939
National Roosevelt signs the Hatch Act, which greatly restricts federal officeholders from participating in political campaigns. A major impetus for such a law has come from allegations that WPA workers in certain states had taken an active role in the 1938 elections.

10 AUGUST 1939
National President Roosevelt signs the Social Security Amendment, which moves up the date for starting monthly payments to January 1, 1940, and generally extends coverage in more generous terms. This is but the first of many amendments to be adopted over the years to expand the Social Security system.

23 AUGUST 1939
International Germany and the U.S.S.R. sign a non-aggression pact in Moscow. When word reaches the outside world the next day, it will create considerable disruption and dismay in both non-Communist and Communist circles.

1 SEPTEMBER 1939
World War II On the pretext that Polish personnel have attacked first, Germany launches a major invasion of Poland at 0445 hours. Before the day is over, Britain and France will have demanded that Germany withdraw from Poland, but the German forces will instead continue to overrun the unprepared Polish forces. It is now undeniable: the second great world war of the century, a war that has been increasingly provoked by aggressive actions, is now underway.

3 SEPTEMBER 1939
World War II Since Germany clearly has no intention of observing their ultimatum to cease the invasion of Poland, the British and the French formally declare war against Germany.
U.S. Approach to War The British liner *Athenia* is torpedoed by a German submarine off the Hebrides Islands, and 28 Americans die. This leads Secretary of State Hull the next day to limit Americans' travel to Europe to "imperative necessity." President Roosevelt, in one of his fireside chats this evening, declares that "this nation remains a neutral nation," and on September 5 the U.S. will make an official proclama-

EXPANDING RESOURCES 1901-1945

POPULAR CULTURE AND THE DEPRESSION

It would be understandable if later generations assumed that the Great Depression left the whole country no time or mind for anything other than concern over the state of the economy, both personal and national. In fact, American popular culture flourished during the 1930s and, to the extent that it responded to the times, it tended to do so in two contrary modes—escapism or criticism. Popular films, radio, music, fiction and other forms of expression led Americans either to forget their problems or to complain about what went wrong.

For the movies, it was the golden age of frivolity, glamour, spectacle and sentimentality. Hollywood was in its prime, and in general audiences preferred to revel in what they did not have in their lives. (Perhaps the best picture about the Depression itself, Preston Sturges' *Sullivan's Travels*, did not appear until 1941.) So the 1930s saw the suave glamour of Fred Astaire and his lovely dancing partners, the romantic images of stars like Clark Gable and Greta Garbo, the extravagant choreography of the Busby Berkeley musicals. Little Shirley Temple was the nation's sweetheart, appearing in a series of melodramas and musicals, and Walt Disney was amusing the public with his essentially childlike imagination. And if life seemed to offer little to laugh at, Hollywood regaled the world with comedies starring such as the Marx Brothers, Laurel and Hardy, W. C. Fields and Mae West. Perhaps the climax of the 1930s escapism came in 1939 with the delightful fantasy of *The Wizard of Oz* and its hit song, "Somewhere Over the Rainbow." America also got its great "palace" of movies, too, in the Radio City Music Hall, while in movie theaters throughout the land people flocked to "Bank Night," introduced in 1932 by a Charles Yeager in Colorado who got the notion of holding a lottery with prizes to attract people to the movies.

For movies also had to compete with another form of entertainment that was becoming an increasingly strong attraction—radio. Americans soon fell into the habit of listening to their favorite weekly radio shows such as "Fibber McGee and Molly" or "Gangbusters"; housewives diverted some of their hours at home with "soap operas," and children became attached to their various adventure "serials." In some respects, the archetypal 1930s radio show was "Amos 'n Andy," an affectionate comedy about blacks, but played by two white men in that more innocent era: the streets of many cities were said to be virtually deserted when "Amos 'n Andy" were on.

The 1930s saw the publication of the work of several of America's major writers—Faulkner, Hemingway, Steinbeck, Lewis, O'Hara. But if Steinbeck's *Grapes of Wrath* confronted the Depression head-on in this story of the "Okies," the most popular novel of the decade was the romantic epic *Gone With the Wind*, by Margaret Mitchell. In the theater, people went to see the sophisticated comedies of Philip Barry and Robert Sherwood or the antic comedies of Kaufmann and Hart. It was also a time of superb musical theater—by such as Cole Porter and Rodgers and Hart—and in George Gershwin America found a composer who united "popular" and "serious" in his opera *Porgy and Bess* (1935).

In popular music, the decade is characterized by the Big Bands and the Swing Era—evoked by such names as Benny Goodman, Jimmy and Tommy Dorsey, Glenn Miller, Duke Ellington, Louis Armstrong and Count Basie. People danced their cares away or tried to combine profit with pleasure by exhausting themselves for prizes in the bizarre "dance marathons." The hit songs of the day ranged from the wry "Brother, Can You Spare a Dime?" to the froth of "The Good Ship Lollipop." Even Roosevelt had his theme song—"Happy Days Are Here Again"—and in 1939 Irving Berlin wrote America's unofficial national anthem, "God Bless America."

But though escapism prevailed as usual in the popular arts, there was often beneath the surface—and sometimes well in view—an awareness of the suffering in this society. It was Louis Armstrong, supposedly the ebullient Uncle Tom, who also sang in the 1930s: "My only sin is the color of my skin. What did I do, to be so black and blue?"

tion of neutrality in the war now spreading across Europe.

8 SEPTEMBER 1939
U.S. Approach to War President Roosevelt proclaims a limited national emergency with the intention of giving himself certain powers to act more quickly.

28 SEPTEMBER 1939
International Germany and the U.S.S.R. sign a new treaty that divides up Poland between them—the Russians having invaded Poland from the east on September 17.

2 OCTOBER 1939
U.S. Approach to War Secretary of State Hull states that the U.S. does not recognize the partition of Poland by Germany and the U.S.S.R. but will maintain diplomatic relations with the Polish government now in exile in Paris.

2-3 OCTOBER 1939
International The Inter-American Conference, meeting in Panama City, issues its Declaration of Panama, establishing safety zones in the seas of the Western Hemisphere in which belligerent powers are told to refrain from any naval activities. In fact, the belligerents will ignore this warning.

11 OCTOBER 1939
Labor The AFL adopts a resolution that opposes the U.S.'s becoming involved in the war in Europe but at the same time proposes a boycott of goods from Germany, Russia and Japan.

18 OCTOBER 1939
U.S. Approach to War President Roosevelt issues a proclamation closing U.S. offshore waters and all U.S. ports to submarines of all belligerents.

4 NOVEMBER 1939
U.S. Approach to War Roosevelt signs the Neutrality Act of 1939, repealing the general embargo on arms of the previous neutrality acts and allowing for the sale of arms to belligerents as long as they pay cash and transport them in non-American ships. Again, although ostensibly a neutral plan, this is clearly designed by Roosevelt to allow the U.S. to aid Britain, France, and their allies.

478

30 NOVEMBER 1939
International The U.S.S.R. invades Finland and bombs its capital, Helsinki. The U.S. will extend both private and governmental aid to the Finnish people but by March 12, 1940 the Russians will have defeated and effectively annexed Finland.

23 DECEMBER 1939
World War II The first Canadian troops arrive in Great Britain—7500 men, the vanguard of what will eventually be millions of North Americans who will go to fight in Europe.

3 JANUARY 1940
National President Roosevelt submits a budget of $8,400,000,000, which includes some $1,800,000,000 for defense measures.

26 JANUARY 1940
International The trade treaty of 1911 between the U.S.A. and Japan expires and Secretary of State Hull informs Japan that the U.S. will not renew its special terms but will simply allow trade between their two nations to continue.

JANUARY-FEBRUARY 1940
World War II In the "Battle of the Atlantic," largely waged by German U-Boats, or submarines, against the ships of Britain and its allies, the losses are steadily mounting to near-disastrous proportions. In these two months alone, the Allies lose some 440,000 tons of shipping.

17 FEBRUARY 1940
U.S. Approach to War Undersecretary of State Sumner Welles leaves for Europe to survey conditions there among the belligerent nations. He will return and report to President Roosevelt on March 28.

13 MARCH 1940
International Finland signs an armistice and treaty with the U.S.S.R., putting a stop to the Russians' war against Finland but effectively neutralizing Finland. Meanwhile, the Allies as well as Hitler have taken note that tiny Finland seems to have inflicted terrific casualties on the Russian military; this will influence Hitler to invade Russia, and at first it will make the Allies and the U.S.A. slow to send aid to the Russians; the fear is that their military cannot stand up against the Germans.

18 MARCH 1940
World War II Mussolini meets Hitler at the Brenner Pass and agrees to join Germany and the other Axis powers in the war against Britain and France.

9 APRIL 1940
World War II The Germans invade Norway and Denmark. Copenhagen is taken within 12 hours. The Norwegians, with considerable help from British and French forces, put up an impressive resistance, but by June 9 the King of Norway and his prime minister order the loyal Norwegian forces to cease fighting.

29 APRIL 1940
U.S. Approach to War President Roosevelt makes yet another appeal to Mussolini to use his influence to bring about peace in Europe. Mussolini once again rejects this request.

10 MAY 1940
World War II Germany invades Luxembourg, the Netherlands and Belgium. President Roosevelt immediately orders that the assets of these three nations in the U.S. be frozen.
International Winston Churchill assumes the office of Prime Minister in Great Britain, replacing the now thoroughly discredited Neville Chamberlain. In fact, Churchill is far from widely admired by all his countrymen, but his decisiveness, resoluteness, powers of oratory and a soon-to-emerge charismatic appeal not only win over most of his British critics but also play a major role in bringing the United States into the war with a total commitment.
Life/Customs The New York World's Fair opens for a second year, and if few Americans can now accept that its rosy version of the future is just over the horizon, the fair continues to draw throughout the summer.

15 MAY 1940
U.S. Approach to War Prime Minister Churchill sends what turns out to be the first of many telegrams to President Roosevelt (all signed "Former Naval Person," less a military code than a personal appeal to Roosevelt's sympathies) in which Churchill requests America's aid and eventual participation in the war. The personal relationship between these two leaders will play a crucial part in the course of events.

16 MAY 1940
National President Roosevelt asks Congress to appropriate more money for defense, particularly to increase the production of aircraft.

25 MAY 1940
National President Roosevelt establishes the Office for Emergency Management. It is increasingly clear that he, at least, is going to be ready for a war that seems inevitable.

26 MAY-4 JUNE 1940
World War II Having been inexorably pushed westward by the German military might, thousands of British and French troops converge on Dunkirk, a coastal town in France. The British Royal Navy is immediately put in charge of Operation Dynamo, the evacuation of these troops, and all available naval and civilian ships are dispatched from Britain to assist in removing the troops who are exposed to German bombing and shelling. By the time the Germans move onto the beach to stop the operation, some 338,226 troops have been evacuated (but at the cost of some 80 merchant and naval vessels and many smaller craft and with 80 RAF pilots losing their lives). It is on

EXPANDING RESOURCES 1901-1945

June 4 that Churchill delivers his most famous radio speech—with its oft-quoted phrases: "We shall fight on the beaches, we shall fight on the landing grounds, we shall fight in the fields and in the streets . . . we shall never surrender"—and turns the retreat from Dunkirk into a symbol of the Allies' determination to win.

3 JUNE 1940
U.S. Approach to War The U.S. War Department agrees to sell Britain millions of dollars worth of surplus or outdated arms, munitions and aircraft in response to Churchill's request for aid.

5 JUNE 1940
World War II The Germans invade France; by June 14 Paris will fall to the Germans; by June 22 France will have capitulated to the Germans. But in London, on June 18, General Charles de Gaulle will pledge to carry on the fight against the Germans for a completely free France.

10 JUNE 1940
U.S. Approach to War President Roosevelt makes a speech at the University of Virginia in which he says that the U.S. policy is changing from "neutrality" to "non-belligerency." In practice, what he means is that the U.S. will now openly support the Allies without itself going to war against the Axis. The message is generally well received by Americans except for the last holdouts among the isolationists, who at least are correct in recognizing that this situation will inevitably lead to an outright war against the Axis powers.

11 JUNE 1940
National Congress passes the Naval Supply Act, authorizing almost $1,500,000,000 for naval defense.

13 JUNE 1940
National Congress passes the Military Supply Act, which includes some $1,800,000,000 for military defense projects.

20 JUNE 1940
National President Roosevelt appoints two prominent Republicans to his Cabinet—Henry L. Stimson as Secretary of War, and Frank Knox as Secretary of the Navy. This is patently an effort to form a "coalition government" to show the world that the U.S. is united; politically, too, it will enhance Roosevelt when he asks the American people to return him to an unprecedented third term.

24-28 JUNE 1940
National The Republican National Convention nominates Wendell L. Willkie as its presidential candidate, with Senator Charles McNary of Oregon for vice-president. Willkie, a corporation lawyer who has never held elective office, will prove a surprisingly appealing candidate, but since he supports Roosevelt's efforts to aid the Allies and even the basic principles

HENRY L. STIMSON, 1867-1950

The stern and moralistic personality of Henry L. Stimson guided him through a career that encompassed trustbusting for Theodore Roosevelt and authorizing the first atomic attacks. Born in New York City on September 21, 1867, Stimson attended Yale and Harvard Law, receiving his law degree in 1890, and thereafter developed into a noted trial lawyer. His abilities and connections brought him to Roosevelt's attention in 1906; as a U.S. attorney, Stimson and his staff successfully prosecuted for the President a number of major antitrust cases.

In 1911 Stimson was appointed Taft's secretary of war; resigning to enter active service as an artillery officer in 1917, he left a military that had been reorganized and strengthened during his tenure as secretary. After the war he pursued frustrating negotiations for the U.S. in Nicaragua and the Philippines. In 1929 another President called, and he became Hoover's secretary of state. This again was a period of frustration; the demands of the Depression left little time for foreign efforts, but Stimson did sign a major treaty (soon to be swept aside) at the 1930 London Naval Conference.

Viewing with alarm the rise of Fascism, Stimson during the 30s militated for preparedness, but the country resisted the thought of another war. When conditions were clearly on the brink in 1940, Stimson was appointed secretary of war by FDR. Working together with chief of staff George C. Marshall, Stimson brought his moral intensity and his organizational gifts to coordinate a miracle of mobilization and production that made the successful war effort possible. He also authorized the since-infamous evacuation of Japanese-Americans to concentration camps and, in 1945, oversaw the development of the atomic bomb; after a special committee report, he advised Truman to drop the bomb on Japan. Stimson resigned in 1945, soon after the war ended, and retired to Long Island, where he died in 1950.

of the New Deal, he has a hard time convincing the American people to "change horses in mid-stream."

28 JUNE 1940
National Congress passes the Alien Registration Act (Smith Act), not only requiring all aliens in the U.S. to register periodically but making it illegal for individuals or organizations to advocate the overthrow of the U.S. government by force.

2 JULY 1940
National Congress passes the Export Control Act, empowering the President to stop or restrict the export of any material considered vital to America's defense.

JULY-OCTOBER 1940
World War II This is the peak period of the German U-Boat successes against the Allied ships, with many of the 28 operational U-Boats now sinking ships virtually at will.

10 JULY 1940
National President Roosevelt submits another request to Congress calling for yet more money— $4,800,000,000—for defense.
World War II Today sees the first attack on Eng-

land by German warplanes, thus launching the Battle of Britain, the assault by the German Air Force and the heroic defense by the outnumbered defenders of Britain. When it ceases at the end of October, Hitler's plan of invading England essentially lies in ruins along with many aircraft and pilots. The Germans will continue to "blitz" England with their bombing raids, but they have failed to control the airspace of Britain.

15-19 JULY 1940

National The Democratic National Convention, meeting in Chicago, nominates Franklin Delano Roosevelt for president, an unprecedented bid for a third term. His vice-presidential running mate this time is Henry A. Wallace, formerly his Secretary of Agriculture.

20 JULY 1940

National Congress appropriates $4,000,000,000 to give the U.S. a two-ocean navy.

30 JULY 1940

International In Havana, Cuba, delegates of the Pan-American Union approve the Declaration of Havana, stating that the American states are prepared to take steps to make sure that any European colonies in the Western Hemisphere are not to be transferred to German control.

18 AUGUST 1940

U.S. Approach to War The U.S. joins Canada in setting up a Joint Board of Defense.

3 SEPTEMBER 1940

U.S. Approach to War The U.S. agrees to give 50 American destroyers to Britain in exchange for the rights to construct naval and air bases on various British possessions in the Western Hemisphere. This is the beginning of the so-called Lend-Lease agreement, and marks yet another stage in Roosevelt's efforts to accustom the American people to assuming an active role in the war.

16 SEPTEMBER 1940

U.S. Approach To War President Roosevelt signs the Selective Training and Service Act (or Burke-Wadsworth Act), requiring men between the ages of 21-35 to register for military training. Only the day before, Canada had begun to call up men between the ages 21-24, and the U.S.S.R. had announced its intention to conscript young men aged 19-20.

26 SEPTEMBER 1940

National President Roosevelt announces an embargo (effective October 16) on the export of scrap steel and iron outside the Western Hemisphere—except to Great Britain. It is obvious that the real intention is to cut Japan off from much-needed supplies and on October 8 Japan will officially protest. Although Japan was undoubtedly going to find some excuse anyway to make war, this will provide the rationalization for its later attack.

ERNEST HEMINGWAY, 1899-1961

When he was a child, someone asked Ernest Hemingway what he was afraid of. "Fraid o' nothin!" he shouted. Throughout his career as a self-proclaimed man's man and as a master writer, he would pursue and challenge the fears that fascinated but finally claimed him.

Hemingway was born in Oak Park, Illinois, on July 21, 1899, and spent a Tom-Sawyerish outdoor boyhood there and in the Michigan lake country. After high school he went to work for the Kansas City *Star*, later saying that newspaper writing helped forge his stark and precise prose style. At the outbreak of World War I he yearned to fight, but an eye injury kept him out of the Army. Becoming an ambulance driver in Italy, he was severely wounded in 1918. After the war he did more newspaper work and then went to Paris to be hungry and write; there he met Ezra Pound and Gertrude Stein, his first mentors. In 1925 he published *In Our Time*, a collection of stories, and in 1926 came a novel, *The Sun Also Rises*; its vivid depiction of the postwar "lost generation" made Hemingway world-famous. He was 27.

Hemingway's war experiences led to the disillusioned *A Farewell to Arms* in 1929. The 30s saw more writing—fiction and nonfiction—big-game hunting and deep-sea fishing expeditions and a growing obsession with bull-fighting, epitomized in his *Death in the Afternoon*. A reporter and Loyalist partisan in the Spanish Civil War, he turned his experiences there into the epic *For Whom the Bell Tolls* in 1940.

During the final decades of his life, Hemingway seemed to spend as much time cultivating his legend as he did on his serious writing. Yet in 1952 there appeared one of his finest works, *The Old Man and the Sea*, an acknowledgment of human courage and dignity in the face of defeat. Two years later Hemingway was awarded the Nobel Prize for Literature, with the commendation citing his "natural admiration for every individual who fights the good fight in a world . . . overshadowed by violence and death." But by now his health, both mental as well as physical, was slowly deteriorating and his writing was becoming more fitful. Hemingway had spent his life seeking out and standing in the face of death, and to be unable to write was for him a kind of death. Finally, exhausted, he gave up the fight, taking his own life in 1961.

EXPANDING RESOURCES 1901-1945

16 OCTOBER 1940
National This is the first day for registration under the selective service law (signed on September 16) and some 16,400,000 U.S. men will register for potentially a year of military training and service.

24 OCTOBER 1940
Labor The 40-hour work week (as provided by the Fair Labor Standards Act of 1938) goes into effect.

29 OCTOBER 1940
U.S. Approach to War The first number (158) is drawn by Secretary of War Stimson, thus initiating the draft.

5 NOVEMBER 1940
National In the election, Roosevelt receives 27,244,160 popular votes to Willkie's 22,305,198, and takes 449 electoral college votes to Willkie's 82. Despite the extent of the electoral college landslide, Willkie has proved to be a surprisingly effective opponent and he will continue to remain a public figure. The fact that the U.S. electorate was willing to go against the unwritten rule established by George Washington—and elect a man for a third term—simply registers the extent to which Roosevelt has carried the people with him in his efforts to confront the great domestic and international crises.

20 DECEMBER 1940
National President Roosevelt establishes the Office of Production Management to be headed by William S. Knudsen to coordinate and expedite defense production. It is clear that this is intended to support the Allies, and the next day Germany accuses the U.S. of "moral aggression" by providing aid to Britain.

29 DECEMBER 1940
National In an end-of-the-year fireside chat over the radio, President Roosevelt proclaims that the U.S. must be the "arsenal of democracy." But a nationwide poll taken in the U.S. this past month has revealed that 39 percent of Americans think that the U.S. made a mistake in taking part in World War I. However, this is down from the 64 percent who believed this in 1937, so there is clearly a growing shift away from isolationism.
Life/Customs Illiteracy in the U.S. has reached a new low of 4.2 percent (down from 15.8 percent in 1870). And an estimated 30,000,000 U.S. homes now have radios.

6 JANUARY 1941
National In his annual State-of-the-Union address, President Roosevelt asks Congress to support lend-lease for the Allies in their fight against the Axis powers. He also defines what he considers the "four essential freedoms" which Americans and all similarly inclined peoples are dedicated to preserving: freedom of speech and expression, freedom of worship, freedom from want, freedom from fear. These "four freedoms" will strike a responsive chord in Americans

THE ARSENAL OF DEMOCRACY

It was in December 1940 that President Roosevelt first announced publicly that he envisioned a role for America in the growing world conflict: it would be "the arsenal of democracy." In fact, F.D.R. and his closest advisers had already come to suspect that the U.S.A. was going to be more than an arsenal, but they had to go very slowly with the American public, many of whom still harbored deep isolationist and neutralist sentiments. Yet as early as September 1940, Roosevelt found a way to give Great Britain 50 aging destroyers and other armaments—the ostensible payment being the right of America to maintain bases on Bermuda, Newfoundland and the British West Indies. And that May he had also announced the then astonishing goal of producing 50,000 war planes a year—ostensibly, again, for defensive purposes only. But as the Germans quickly conquered most of Europe, it soon became apparent that only Great Britain and North America remained of the major industrial powers to provide materiél to fight the Axis. So in March 1941, Congress approved the crucial Lend-Lease program; at first it allocated only some $7,000,000,000 in aid for the Allies; by the end of the war, Lend-Lease aid had topped $50,000,000,000 (about one-half to Great Britain, and one–quarter to Russia).

With Pearl Harbor, all pretense that the U.S.A. would remain merely a supplier for others ended, and considering that the Axis had started with a considerable advantage in ships, planes, tanks and other armaments, the response of the Allies was all but miraculous. The Allies, for instance, would lose some 24,000,000 gross tons of shipping to the Axis—over half of this to German U-boats alone; in one month such as November 1942, the Allies would lose over 800,000 gross tons of shipping. The Japanese Navy far outnumbered and outweighed and outgunned the U.S. Navy—even before the losses at Pearl Harbor. And when the East Indies fell to the Japanese in early 1942, the Allies were cut off from such strategic materials as rubber, silk and quinine.

But those countries still free from and allied against the Axis lost little time in gearing up for war. Peacetime industries converted to war production with amazing speed, as sewing machine companies began to make bombs or vacuum cleaners were replaced by machine guns. Synthetic rubber was soon replacing natural rubber; synthetics such as nylon and rayon replaced silk and other natural fibers; atabrine, a synthetic drug, replaced quinine. Americans who only yesterday seemed mired in a Depression rose up and moved to where they were needed: some 1,200,000 are estimated to have relocated on the West Coast alone to work in the new war industries. Ships began to be produced at phenomenal rates: a *Liberty*-class merchant ship could be launched within 10 days of its start.

Before World War II would end, the U.S.A. alone produced some 297,000 airplanes, 86,000 tanks, 12,000 ships and vast quantities of other vehicles and armaments and munitions. A strong case would be made that in the long run the Allies won the war through the power of its factories, the superiority of its production. Whether this can be proven or not, the war did help America move up out of the Great Depression so that it was able to continue its role as the storehouse of the postwar recovery and reconstruction.

and, during the war that soon comes, will serve as a motto of sorts.

JUNE 25, 1941

8 JANUARY 1941
National Roosevelt submits a budget of $17,485,529,000, of which $10,811,000,000 is for defense.

20 JANUARY 1941
National Franklin Delano Roosevelt is inaugurated for his third term as president. His vice-president this term is Henry A. Wallace.

27 JANUARY-29 MARCH 1941
U.S. Approach to War Unknown to all except a few, high-level military staffs of the U.S. and Britain are holding secret talks in Washington, D.C., and they agree on strategy for war in the event the U.S.A. does join in the fight against Germany—and even against Japan. Known as the ABC-1 Plan, it calls for first concentrating on defeating Germany, then taking on Japan.

3 FEBRUARY 1941
National The Supreme Court, in *United States v. Darby Lumber Co.*, rules that the Fair Labor Standards Act (of June 25, 1938) is constitutional.

4 FEBRUARY 1941
U.S. Approach to War The United Service Organizations—soon to become widely known as the USO—is formed by six national organizations to serve the social, educational, welfare and religious needs of those in the armed forces and defense industries. Its best known activity will become the network of clubs throughout the world where service personnel can relax off-duty.

11 MARCH 1941
U.S. Approach to War Immediately after the House of Representatives passes it (the Senate having passed it on March 8), President Roosevelt signs the Lend-Lease Act, essentially the one he had requested in his message to Congress. It empowers the President to arrange to lend arms and other war material to any country determined to be vital to U.S. interests. Clearly it is designed to help Britain while pretending that the U.S. is not at war against the Axis. The initial appropriation (on March 27) will be some $7,000,000,000, but by the time the Lend-Lease program ends in September 1946, some $50,600,000,000 in aid will have been extended by the U.S. to the Allies.

11 APRIL 1941
National The Office of Price Administration (OPA) is established by executive order. Its stated task is to control prices, but its impact will eventually go far beyond this.
U.S. Approach to War As the German submarines, or U-Boats, have been taking an increasing toll on Allied and neutral merchant ships crossing the Atlantic, President Roosevelt announces that the U.S. will extend its patrols and security zone to west longitude 26° (which thus becomes known as "the sea frontier

of the U.S."). But Germany will simply ignore this, and on May 21 a U-Boat will sink the American merchant ship *Robin Moor* inside this line (just off the coast of Brazil).

21-27 APRIL 1941
U.S. Approach to War U.S. military officers meet with their British and Dutch counterparts in Singapore and draw up a plan for strategic operations against Japan in case it attacks the U.S.

15 MAY 1941
U.S. Approach to War President Roosevelt, while denouncing those French who are collaborating with the German occupation forces of their nation, has the U.S. government take into protective custody all French ships at present in U.S. ports. Among them is the great luxury liner, the *Normandie*.

27 MAY 1941
U.S. Approach to War President Roosevelt issues a proclamation declaring that a state of unlimited national emergency exists. He has come to this point after seeing Greece and Yugoslavia fall to the Axis, and he also realizes that the American people will be more receptive to this move since the sinking of the *Robin Moor*.

9 JUNE 1941
National President Roosevelt orders U.S. troops to take over the North American Aviation Company, in Ingleside, California, because striking workers are interfering with defense production.

12 JUNE 1941
National Associate Justice Harlan Fiske Stone is nominated Chief Justice of the Supreme Court.

14 JUNE 1941
U.S. Approach to War President Roosevelt, using the broad powers assigned to him in an emergency, freezes the assets of Germany and Italy in the U.S.

16 JUNE 1941
U.S. Approach to War Roosevelt now orders that all German consulates in the U.S. be closed by July 10. Germany and Italy inevitably retaliate by closing all U.S. consulates in locales under their control, and the U.S. orders closing Italian consulates on July 20.

24 JUNE 1941
U.S. Approach to War President Roosevelt promises that the U.S. will give aid to the U.S.S.R., which Hitler's armed forces invaded on June 22 (in outright violation of their countries' non-aggression pact of 1939).

25 JUNE 1941
National The Fair Employment Practices Committee is established by executive order to prevent discrimination due to race, creed or color in defense-related work.

483

GEORGE C. MARSHALL, 1880-1959

It was appropriate that the only career soldier ever to win the Nobel Peace Prize was George C. Marshall, who brilliantly led the U.S. Army through World War II but who was equally known for his peace efforts, most notably the European assistance plan that bore his name. Marshall was born in Uniontown, Pennsylvania, on December 31, 1880. After graduating from the Virginia Military Institute in 1901, he served in the Philippines and in the West in the early 1900s. He returned to the Philippines as a first lieutenant in 1914, where his leadership brought him to the attention of his superiors. By 1918 he was chief of operations for army commander Pershing.

After World War I Marshall continued for several years with Pershing, then served as an infantry officer in China, an instructor at Fort Benning, Georgia, and with the National Guard and the New Deal Civilian Conservation Corps. As Europe was on the brink of war, Marshall was called to Washington to become, the day Germany invaded Poland, army chief of staff. He remained in that post throughout the war, deeply involved in both the mammoth organizational problems of the army and air force and the large issues of Allied military strategy. In Churchill's admiring words, Marshall was "the true organizer of victory" in the war.

Directly after the war ended in 1945, Marshall tried to retire, but soon was sent to China by Truman in a hopeless effort to reconcile the Communists and Nationalists. Becoming Truman's secretary of state in 1947, Marshall helped develop what came to be known as the Marshall Plan, a program to aid postwar European recovery that was an historic success, the U.S. between 1948 and 1952 dispensing over 13 billion dollars to 16 European countries.

Marshall retired again in 1949, but the next year was back as secretary of defense, building up the army for the Korean conflict. In 1951 he was an advisor in Truman's unpopular decision to fire General MacArthur. The same year Marshall came under attack by Senator Joseph McCarthy, who, incredibly, accused him of being soft on Communism. Marshall's old subordinate Eisenhower, running for President, failed to defend him. Characteristically, the wise and soft-spoken Marshall soon forgave Eisenhower. He was awarded the Nobel Peace Prize in 1953, and died in Washington in 1959.

28 JUNE 1941
National Another executive order sets up the Office of Scientific Research and Development, with Vannevar Bush as its chairman. This OSRD will coordinate U.S. scientific-technological work related to defense and war–including radar, sonar and the first stage of developing the atomic bomb.

7 JULY 1941
U.S. Approach to War U.S. Marines land in Iceland, the first U.S. troops to move there after an agreement with Iceland's government that the U.S. will protect the island from any German attacks. The agreement calls for U.S. troops to leave immediately upon the end of the war in Europe.

25 JULY 1941
U.S. Approach to War President Roosevelt announces that all Japanese assets in the U.S. are frozen; this is in retaliation for the Japanese move into French Indochina (on July 24). This will effectively halt all trade between the U.S. and Japan, including the export of goods that Japan needs for its industries. This provides Japan with one more reason to advance its plans to attack the U.S.

26 JULY 1941
U.S. Approach to War President Roosevelt nationalizes the armed forces of the Philippines—still a U.S. dependency—and places them under the command of General Douglas MacArthur, who is named commander in chief of all U.S. forces in the Far East.

14 AUGUST 1941
International After secret meetings on August 9-12 on U.S. and British warships off the coast of Newfoundland, President Roosevelt and Prime Minister Winston Churchill of Britain issue the Atlantic Charter. It sets forth eight goals for the world, including the renunciation of all aggression, the right of peoples to choose their own governments, the support of access to raw materials, guarantees of freedom from want and from fear, freedom of the seas and the disarmament of aggressors. By September 24, 15 anti-Axis nations—including the U.S.S.R.—will endorse the Atlantic Charter and it will become in effect the blueprint for establishing the United Nations.

18 AUGUST 1941
National The Selective Service Extension Act extends active service in the army from one year to 18 months.

28 AUGUST 1941
U.S. Approach to War The Japanese ambassador to the U.S. presents a note to President Roosevelt in which Japan's Premier Konoye says his country wishes "to pursue courses of peace and harmony" with the U.S.

11 SEPTEMBER 1941
U.S. Approach to War As a result of increasing numbers of attacks on U.S. ships—naval and merchant—President Roosevelt orders U.S. Navy planes and ships to shoot on sight any Axis ships within the zone that the U.S. has declared it will defend (on April 11).

16 SEPTEMBER 1941
U.S. Approach to War The U.S. Navy announces it will become responsible for protecting all shipping as far east as Iceland.

20 SEPTEMBER 1941
National The Revenue Act of 1941 is passed, providing sharply increased taxes in order to raise the large sums now needed for the defense effort.

17 OCTOBER 1941
U.S. Approach to War The U.S. destroyer *Kearney* is torpedoed by a German U-Boat off Iceland;

DOUGLAS MacARTHUR, 1880-1964

As a man and as a general, Douglas MacArthur was a leader of great genius and great flaws. His career was one of the longest and most controversial in American military history; but as bold, flamboyant, and effective as he was as a fighting man, perhaps his greatest achievement was his peacetime administration of postwar Japan.

MacArthur was born in Little Rock, Arkansas, on January 26, 1880. His strong-willed mother inspired him with the achievements of his military family. He graduated from West Point in 1903 with one of the best records in Academy history. As a commander during World War I he gained a reputation as a fearless leader, was twice wounded and won many decorations. In 1919, becoming superintendent of West Point, he instituted a program of innovation and reform that revitalized the school. He was then on duty in the Philippines from 1922 until 1930, when Hoover appointed him army chief of staff. During this tenure he first became noted for his indiscreet conduct, especially in his violent criticism of pacifists.

As the threat of war with Japan increased in 1941, MacArthur was made commander of U.S. forces in the Far East, becoming a full general. His forces in the Philippines were driven out by the Japanese in 1942; MacArthur left in March saying, "I shall return." But late in 1942 he began to push the Japanese back in the Pacific Papuan Campaign and then in New Guinea during 1943-44. In 1945 he commanded the costly but successful invasion of Luzon. He had kept his promise to return. As the Allied Supreme Commander he presided over the Japanese surrender on September 2, 1945.

Named postwar leader of Japanese reconstruction, MacArthur pursued an enlightened policy of relief, democratization, demilitarization and reform. In 1950 he returned to military duties as chief of the United Nations Command in the Korean War. At Inchon he stopped and routed the North Korean advance. But then Communist China intervened, the war bogged down, and MacArthur's old troubles with superiors and his hostility to criticism ran afoul of Truman, who wished to avoid ex-

panding the conflict. In April 1951 the President abruptly cashiered MacArthur. The general returned to a hero's welcome in the U.S. and Truman's popularity plummeted; but history has tended to vindicate Truman. True to his statement to Congress that "old soldiers never die, they just fade away," MacArthur gradually retired from public life. He died in 1964.

although the destroyer does not sink, 11 Americans are killed. This attack comes only weeks after the U.S. Navy had announced its intention to protect all shipping as far east as Iceland.

27 OCTOBER 1941

Labor John L. Lewis, president of the United Mine Workers, announces a strike in what he calls the "captive" mines. Roosevelt will propose arbitration and this will be accepted by the UMW on November 27.

National In a broadcast to the nation on Navy Day, President Roosevelt flatly states: "America has been attacked, the shooting has started." But he realizes that many Americas are still reluctant to make the final step into open war, so he holds back from calling for such a declaration.

30 OCTOBER 1941

U.S. Approach to War The U.S. destroyer *Reuben James*, on convoy duty off Iceland, is sunk by a German U-Boat, with the loss of 100 Americans.

3 NOVEMBER 1941

U.S. Approach to War The U.S. ambassador to Japan, Joseph Grew, warns that the Japanese may be planning a sudden attack on U.S. positions. On November 7 Secretary of State Cordell Hull will repeat this warning to President Roosevelt and his cabinet.

17 NOVEMBER 1941

U.S. Approach to War The Japanese ambassador to the U.S., Kichisaburo Nomura, and a special envoy, Saburo Kurusu, begin negotiations with the U.S. State Department in Washington, D.C. On November 20 they will propose that the U.S. remove restrictions on trade with Japan and refrain from interfering with

President Roosevelt addresses the nation.

EXPANDING RESOURCES 1901-1945

Japan's activities in China and the Pacific. President Roosevelt, meanwhile, today signs a bill that amends the Neutrality Act of 1939 so as to permit U.S. merchant ships to be armed and also to call at ports of belligerents—clearly another move to provide U.S. aid to the Allies.

26 NOVEMBER 1941
U.S. Approach to War Secretary of State Hull rejects the Japanese proposals of November 20 and demands that first the Japanese withdraw their forces from China and Indochina and then the U.S. will remove trade restrictions.

1 DECEMBER 1941
U.S. Approach to War Japan rejects the proposals of the U.S. (of November 26) but will not formally announce this until December 7.

3 DECEMBER 1941
U.S. Approach to War Japanese consulates in the U.S. begin to burn their secret documents.

6 DECEMBER 1941
President Roosevelt appeals directly to Emperor Hirohito of Japan to exercise his influence to avoid war.

7 DECEMBER 1941
World War II On Sunday morning, 7:55 Honolulu time, Japanese bombers attack Pearl Harbor, the major U.S. naval base in Hawaii. Nineteen U.S. ships (including 6 battleships) are sunk or disabled; some 150 planes are destroyed; 2403 soldiers, sailors and civilians are killed, 1178 are wounded. Other Japanese planes and ships attack U.S. bases in the Philippines, Guam and Midway, as well as British bases in Hong Kong and the Malay Peninsula.

Meanwhile, the Japanese envoys in Washington, D.C., had been instructed to deliver the note rejecting the American proposal (of November 26) by 1:00 P.M. Washington time—just before the attack on Pearl Harbor. The envoys do not deliver the note until 2:05 P.M., by which time Washington has received reports of the attack on Pearl Harbor. And this evening, the Japanese will announce that they have officially declared war on the U.S.

From the moment the American people are informed of the attack on Pearl Harbor—many will learn when their favorite radio programs are interrupted on this Sunday afternoon—the country will be in a state of frustrated fury, and it is no wonder that the slogan "Remember Pearl Harbor!" will become from this day the rallying cry for the U.S. until the surrender of the Japanese.

8 DECEMBER 1941
National President Roosevelt appears before a special joint session of Congress and, declaring December 7 "a day that shall live in infamy," asks that the U.S. declare war against Japan. The Senate votes to approve 82-0, the House of Representatives 388-1 (the lone dissenter being the pacifist Jeanette Rankin, the first woman elected a Representative and who also voted against the U.S. entering the war in 1917). With this formal declaration of war, President Roosevelt begins to direct every branch of the U.S. military and government toward this one effort.

10 DECEMBER 1941
World War II Japanese forces invade the Philippines, landing first at Luzon.

11 DECEMBER 1941
World War II Germany and Italy declare war on the U.S. and Congress declares war on Germany and Italy.

15 DECEMBER 1941
National The Third Supplemental Defense Appropriation Act is passed, appropriating $10,000,000,000 more for what is now open warfare.

17 DECEMBER 1941
World War II Admiral Chester Nimitz is given command of the Pacific fleet, replacing Admiral Husband Kimmel, who had been in this command at Pearl Harbor and will eventually be found to have failed to take proper steps that might have at least lessened the extent of the disaster on December 7.

18 DECEMBER 1941
National President Roosevelt appoints a special commission to investigate the disaster at Pearl Harbor, with Associate Justice Owen Roberts as its chairman.

19 DECEMBER 1941
National An Office of Censorship is established by executive order to control all matters involving information vital to the war effort.

20 DECEMBER 1941
National President Roosevelt signs the Draft Act, which calls for all U.S. males between the ages of 18 and 65 to register, and for all men from ages 20 through 44 to be liable for active military duty.
World War II Admiral Ernest J. King is made commander in chief of the U.S. Navy.

22 DECEMBER 1941
World War II Prime Minister Winston Churchill joins President Roosevelt in Washington, D.C. for conferences about the joint war efforts.

23 DECEMBER 1941
World War II Wake Island, an American territory in the Pacific, falls to the Japanese.

25 DECEMBER 1941
World War II Hong Kong, the British colony, falls to the Japanese.

1 JANUARY 1942
International Representatives of 26 nations, includ-

ing the U.S., sign the Declaration of the United Nations, affirming their cooperation against the Axis. (These "United Nations" are more commonly designated the "Allies.")

2 JANUARY 1942
World War II Manila falls to the Japanese as U.S. and Philippine forces withdraw to the Bataan Peninsula. There General MacArthur will set up headquarters in the Corregidor ("The Rock"), a fortified island guarding the entrance to Manila Bay.

6 JANUARY 1942
National President Roosevelt, in his State-of-the-Union message, calls for production of vast numbers of planes, tanks, ships and guns in the effort to defeat the Axis. The next day he will submit a budget of $58,927,902,000, of which over $52,000,000,000 is for the war.

14 JANUARY 1942
National President Roosevelt, by proclamation, orders that all aliens in the U.S. register with the government. This takes on a new meaning now that the U.S.A. is at war against Germany, Italy and Japan, but all the suspicions and fears will tend to focus on the least assimilated group, the Japanese-Americans, or *nisei*, most of them residing on the West Coast. Plans are being made to move these Japanese-Americans to internment camps away from the coast on the claim that these people might provide aid to the enemy.

15-28 JANUARY 1942
International At the Rio de Janeiro Conference in Brazil, the foreign ministers of the 21 American nations, including the U.S., resolve to break relations with the Axis powers. (In fact, Chile will not do so until 1943, and Argentina will wait until 1944, when the fate of the Axis is clear.)

16 JANUARY 1942
National The War Production Board, established by executive order, replaces the Office of Production Management.

26 JANUARY 1942
National The commission that has been investigating the disaster at Pearl Harbor releases its findings. Both General Short, then commander of the Army's Hawaiian department, and Admiral Kimmel, then commander in chief of the U.S. fleet in the Pacific, are found to have been guilty of dereliction of duty. But both have already been dismissed from active duty, and the debate over the responsibility and blame for decisions taken or not taken will in fact never completely cease. Even 40 years later, historians and researchers will be writing to assign blame, some actually claiming that Roosevelt knew details of the imminent attack far enough in advance to warn the military but chose not to in order to force the U.S. into the war. But there is never any solid evidence of

such literal foreknowledge; what does seem apparent in the years that follow is that many men running the U.S. government and military were derelict in their duty.
World War II U.S. troops land in Northern Ireland, the first to arrive in the European theater since World War I.

28 JANUARY 1942
National The Office of Civil Defense is established to coordinate the various tasks that civilians will be asked to take on—from plane-spotting duty to keeping sand in the attic against bombing raids.

30 JANUARY 1942
National The Emergency Price Control Act goes into effect, authorizing the Office of Price Administration to place ceilings on prices and rents.

6 FEBRUARY 1942
World War II The U.S. War Department announces that the U.S.A. and Britain have established a combined chiefs of staff to coordinate their war efforts.

9 FEBRUARY 1942
National Clocks across the U.S.A. are turned ahead one hour for Daylight Saving Time; they will remain on this plan throughout the duration of the war.
Regional The French liner *Normandie*, having been seized by the U.S. and undergoing conversion to a troop ship, burns and capsizes at a dock in New York City. Although sabotage is suspected, it is never proven and it is eventually decided that carelessness by the workmen started the fire.

20 FEBRUARY 1942
National President Roosevelt formally authorizes a program to remove the Japanese-Americans from their homes and land in the Pacific Coast states (and Arizona) to internment camps in Colorado, Utah, Arkansas and other inland locales. There is only mild public reaction and few Americans see the full implications of such a scheme. Some 100,000 of the *nisei* will be "relocated," most of them in March 1942. Special army units of *nisei* will eventually be allowed, and they will perform exemplary duty, but even aside from this there is never any grounds for questioning the loyalty of the *nisei*.

23 FEBRUARY 1942
Regional An oil refinery near Santa Barbara, California, is shelled by a Japanese submarine—one of the few incidents during the war when the continental U.S. is attacked by the enemy.

27 FEBRUARY-1 MARCH
World War II During a major naval battle in the Java Sea, the Allied forces are virtually wiped out by the superior Japanese Navy.

11 MARCH 1942
World War II General MacArthur leaves the Philip-

Uprooted, a Japanese-American child leaves Los Angeles for a detention camp.

pines but makes his oft-quoted declaration, "I shall return!" He goes on to Australia in secret to assume command of the Allied Forces in the southwest Pacific. As ordered by Washington, he turns over the command in the Philippines to General Jonathan Wainright.

8 APRIL 1942
National The War Production Board stops all construction not essential to the war effort.

9 APRIL 1942
World War II After holding out for three months, some 75,000 Philippine and U.S. troops on Bataan Peninsula surrender to the Japanese. General Wainwright has meanwhile moved over onto Corregidor, the island fortress, with some troops. But the 75,000 taken prisoner on Bataan will now be forced by the Japanese to march some 100 miles to a prison camp; because of ill treatment and insufficient rations along the way, thousands of them will die on the so-called Death March.

18 APRIL 1942
World War II Sixteen U.S. bombers, led by Major General James Doolittle, take off from the carrier *Hornet* about 650 miles off Japan and raid Tokyo and three other Japanese cities. Those that are not shot down fly on to China to land. (To increase their range to the maximum, the bombers are practically unarmed.) It is not only a tremendous boost to the mo-

rale of the Allies; the raid diverts the Japanese defense efforts in several ways that will yet prove costly to their strategy.

28 APRIL 1942
National A "dim-out," or "black-out," to be observed nightly along a 15-mile strip of the Atlantic coast, goes into effect. Its immediate goal is to help stop German submarine activity.

4-8 MAY 1942
World War II In the Battle of the Coral Sea off southern New Guinea, the U.S. naval air force inflicts heavy losses on the Japanese fleet and prevents the Japanese from landing at Port Moresby. The U.S. loses its carrier *Lexington* and the carrier *Yorktown* is damaged, but the Japanese have lost many valuable planes and pilots. It is in fact the first naval battle in history in which surface ships did not engage one another—all the fighting having been done by planes from carriers.

7 MAY 1942
World War II General Jonathan Wainwright, having been captured by the Japanese, broadcasts the surrender of the forces on Corregidor and asks all U.S. forces in the Philippines to surrender.

15 MAY 1942
National President Roosevelt signs the Congressional act establishing the Women's Auxiliary Army

Corps (WAAC)—later to become simply the Women's Army Corps (WAC). And on July 30 Congress will establish a women's naval reserve, known as the WAVES. Gasoline rationing goes into effect in 17 states in the eastern U.S.

18 MAY 1942
National Price ceilings on retail products go into effect.

25 MAY 1942
World War II Both Japanese and U.S. ships from various ports throughout the Pacific begin the movements that will culminate in their convergence on Midway, a small island in the central Pacific. The Japanese intend not only to invade and capture Midway island but also to take the Aleutian islands off Alaska as part of this operation. Both sides will make decisions based on incomplete and misleading intelligence on each other but the two forces gradually sail to their confrontation.

3-6 JUNE 1942
World War II As aircraft, submarines, carriers and all kinds of other ships from both navies seek out and then engage each other, a tremendous battle develops off Midway. The Americans lose their carrier *Yorktown*, but not until after they have sunk four of the Japanese carriers and destroyed a significant portion of the better-trained pilot corps. The war is far from over, but the Japanese have now lost the initiative in terms of naval superiority.

3-21 JUNE 1942
World War II In conjunction with their naval action

off Midway, the Japanese invade two of the outermost Aleutian islands, Attu and Kiska and, meeting little resistance, soon conquer them.

13 JUNE 1942
National The Office of War Information is established by executive order, with a well-known news commentator, Elmer Davis, as director. The Office of Strategic Services (OSS), with William Donovan as director, is also established. (After the war, this will become the CIA.)

13-17 JUNE 1942
Regional Eight Germans land from submarines off the coasts of Long Island, New York, and Florida; they are supposed to engage in sabotage and spying, but they are all quickly apprehended. After a trial by a military tribunal, six are electrocuted (on August 8), and the other two imprisoned.

15-30 JUNE 1942
National All over the U.S., people join in a great scrap-rubber drive, scrounging through basements and dumps for every bit of this increasingly rare material essential to the war effort.

17 JUNE 1942
Life/Customs The first issue of *Yank*, an Army-sponsored newspaper, is published. It will soon become the favorite reading matter of millions of servicemen; it is staffed by many writers and artists who go on to make major careers after the war.

19 JUNE 1942
International Prime Minister Churchill joins Presi-

The carrier *Yorktown* under fire in the Battle of the Coral Sea.

dent Roosevelt in Washington, D.C., for conferences that, among other issues, plan the invasion of North Africa.

21 JUNE 1942
Regional The Oregon coast is shelled by a Japanese submarine.

25 JUNE 1942
World War II Major General Dwight D. Eisenhower is appointed commander of U.S. forces in the European theater.

30 JUNE 1942
National Congress appropriates $42,800,000,000 for the armed services. But with no more funds, the Civilian Conservation Corps (CCC)—one of the better known of Roosevelt's anti-Depression projects—comes to an end.

4 JULY 1942
World War II The first U.S. pilots participate with the Royal Air Force in a bombing raid on German targets on the Continent.

16 JULY 1942
National The War Labor Board gives a 15 percent wage increase to certain steel workers on the basis of the increase in cost of living; this becomes known as "the Little Steel Formula."

7 AUGUST 1942
World War II U.S. forces land on Guadalcanal and two other smaller islands in the Solomons in the Pacific. This is the first offensive operation in what will turn into the long, grueling, and murderous road to Tokyo.

12-15 AUGUST 1942
International In Moscow, Prime Minister Churchill and U.S. representative W. Averell Harriman confer with Premier Joseph Stalin on their joint war efforts.

17 AUGUST 1942
World War II The first all-U.S. bombing raid is made on German positions around Rouen, France. But it will be 1943 before the Eighth Air Force can build up to full strength and start bombing targets in Germany.

22 AUGUST 1942
World War II The Germans, having made major gains in Russia, now launch their massive assault on Stalingrad, intending to complete their conquest of Russia.

26 AUGUST 1942
International Wendell Willkie, defeated in his run against Roosevelt in November 1940, goes as the President's special envoy on a round-the-world trip to investigate conditions in general and to rally the Allied nations around the war effort. He will return to

the U.S. on October 14, and after making his report to the President, will proceed to write his best seller, *One World*.

10 SEPTEMBER 1942
National The Baruch-Compton-Conant Commission reports that the U.S. "will face both a military and civilian collapse" unless something is done immediately about the rubber supply. The next day, the U.S. signs an agreement to purchase the entire Mexican production of raw rubber for the next four years. But it is the almost overnight development of a synthetic rubber industry that comes to the rescue.

10-14 SEPTEMBER 1942
World War II German U-Boats have become among the most threatening and destructive of the Germans' many-sided attack on the Allies, and at times they seem to be almost invulnerable throughout the Atlantic. One of their more successful, but typical, operations occurs during these days as a group of 13 U-Boats stalks convoy ON-127, enroute from North America to Britain, and sinks 12 freighters and a destroyer escort, with the loss of only one U-Boat.

7 OCTOBER 1942
International President Roosevelt announces a plan to set up a United Nations Commission for the Investigation of War Crimes once the war is over. It is intended to let the Axis know that certain types of actions are not going to be excused as conventional acts of war.

21 OCTOBER 1942
National The Revenue Act of 1942 is passed, calling for taxes to be increased by some $9,000,000,000; this includes the so-called Victory Tax, a five percent tax on all income over $624, to be levied until the war ends.

25-26 OCTOBER 1942
World War II The Japanese Navy has mounted a major operation to support its forces on Guadalcanal Island, but the U.S. fleet meets it in the Battle of Santa Cruz; although the carrier *Hornet* is sunk and the carrier *Enterprise* damaged, the Japanese have to abandon their plans and they have suffered heavy losses in aircraft.

3 NOVEMBER 1942
National In the midterm elections in the U.S., Republicans gain significantly. Among the winners is Thomas Dewey, elected governor of New York, and immediately regarded as a presidential prospect.

7-8 NOVEMBER 1942
World War II Allied forces, some 400,000 strong, land at Morocco and Algeria, in North Africa, under the command of General Eisenhower.

12-15 NOVEMBER 1942
World War II In what is known as the Naval Battle of Guadalcanal, Admiral Halsey leads the U.S. fleet

in destroying the Japanese fleet; the Japanese lose some 28 warships and transports and thus are rebuffed in their efforts to stop the U.S. from taking Guadalcanal.

18 NOVEMBER 1942
National In a change in the Selective Service Act, U.S. males are now subject to active military duty at the age of 18; it is estimated that within the next year the U.S. Armed Forces will number some 10,000,000.

21 NOVEMBER 1942
International The 1523-mile Alcan International Highway, stretching from Alberta, Canada, to Alaska, officially opens. It will help in supplying the U.S. forces that will eventually recapture the Aleutians from the Japanese.

25 NOVEMBER 1942
World War II After some three months besieging Stalingrad, the German Army finds itself virtually surrounded by the Russians. Various German divisions begin to surrender, but it will be February 2, 1943 before the last German units surrender.

28 NOVEMBER 1942
National Coffee rationing is put into effect across the U.S.
Regional A fire in a Boston nightclub, the Coconut Grove, crowded with people celebrating a college football game, leaves 492 dead (a toll only exceeded in a single U.S.A. structure-fire by the Chicago Iroquois Theater fire of December 30, 1903).

1 DECEMBER 1942
National Gasoline rationing is now extended throughout the entire U.S.

4 DECEMBER 1942
National President Roosevelt, in what he calls "an honorable discharge" for a job well done, closes down the Works Projects Administration, one of the mainstays of his New Deal efforts to stem the Depression.

11 JANUARY 1943
National President Roosevelt submits a budget of $108,903,047,923, of which some $100,000,000,000 is for the war.

14-24 JANUARY 1943
International President Roosevelt attends a conference in Casablanca, Morocco, with Churchill and other representatives of the Allies. Several crucial decisions are announced, primarily with the authority of Roosevelt and Churchill. They will demand the unconditional surrender of the enemy (and not accept an armistice like that which ended World War I); their forces will first invade Sicily and Italy (while the U.S. preference for invading France from across the Channel, as opposed to an invasion of the Mediterranean coast, is left open); and General Dwight D.

Eisenhower is given command of the North African Theater.

27 JANUARY 1943
World War II The first all-American bombing raid on Germany takes place—a daylight attack on Wilhelmshaven.

2 FEBRUARY 1943
World War II The last German units surrounded at Stalingrad surrender to the Russians. In this campaign, some 330,000 Germans have been killed or captured, and Stalingrad clearly marks a turning point in the Germans' effort to take Russia: from now on, the Germans will essentially begin the long retreat from their Eastern Front until they end up surrounded in Berlin.

3 FEBRUARY 1943
Life/Customs The U.S. War Department bans hard liquor from all U.S. Army establishments.

7 FEBRUARY 1943
National Shoe rationing begins throughout the U.S., with each civilian limited to three pairs of leather shoes annually.

9 FEBRUARY 1943
World War II The U.S. Marines recapture Guadalcanal as the last of the Japanese troops evacuate it. This is considered an important step for the Allies, both strategically and psychologically.

14-25 FEBRUARY 1943
World War II U.S. Forces in North Africa are defeated by Rommel's Afrika Korps when they are pushed back at the Kasserine Pass in Tunisia, but by the 25th the U.S. troops have retaken their positions and stopped Rommel's drive.

1 MARCH 1943
National A point-rationing system is introduced for processed foods, with coupon books of varying points required to purchase such foods.

2-4 MARCH 1943
World War II In the Bismarck Sea off New Guinea, U.S. and Australian planes score a major victory over a Japanese convoy, sinking eight transports and four destroyers, shooting down at least 25 Japanese planes, and costing the Japanese some 3500 men. This Battle of the Bismarck Sea is a major setback to the Japanese plans for holding New Guinea.

8 MARCH 1943
International The U.S. Ambassador to the U.S.S.R., Admiral W. M. Standley, claims that the Russian leaders are not telling their people about all the aid the U.S. is sending. On March 11 the Russian Ambassador to the U.S., Maxim Litvinov, thanks the U.S. for its aid (although this does not quite deal with the U.S. ambassador's charge).

EXPANDING RESOURCES 1901-1945

Feverish wartime activity at Bethlehem-Fairfield Shipyards, Baltimore.

1 APRIL 1943
National Meats, fats and cheese are placed under rationing.

8 APRIL 1943
National President Roosevelt, by executive order, freezes prices, wages, and salaries in an effort to stem inflation.

13 APRIL 1943
National The Jefferson Memorial in Washington, D.C., is dedicated, with President Roosevelt delivering the main address.

1 MAY 1943
Labor John L. Lewis calls a strike among the United Mine Workers to protest the wage freeze, but Roosevelt immediately orders Secretary of Interior Ickes to take over the soft-coal mines; on May 2, Lewis calls off the strike.

7 MAY 1943
World War II American troops capture Bizerte, Tunisia, while British troops take that country's capital, Tunis. By May 10, the German and Italian troops will have ceased organized resistance in Tunisia and the commanders will begin the formal surrender. By

May 13, some 250,000 Axis troops will have surrendered.

11-27 MAY 1943
International Prime Minister Churchill comes to Washington, D.C. accompanied by some of his top military planners, and meets with Roosevelt and the American military planners in what is known as the Trident Conference. The main topics of discussion are the planned invasions of Europe and the commitment of forces to Europe and the Pacific; although there are numerous disagreements over details, both sides agree on the general strategy. On May 19 Churchill addresses a joint session of Congress and predicts the total defeat of Germany and Japan.

11 MAY 1943
World War II U.S. troops land on Attu, one of the Aleutian islands captured by the Japanese in June 1942. By May 31 all Japanese resistance on Attu will end.

13 MAY 1943
World War II With the surrender of the German and Italian commanders and hundreds of thousands of troops in North Africa (Rommel had left on March 9),

the Axis campaign in North Africa effectively ends. The Axis had spent some two years attempting to take North Africa and, most essentially, the Suez Canal, but they have only ended up losing some 500,000 men as casualties or prisoners.

16 MAY 1943
World War II After an uprising that began in April, the Jews in the ghetto of Warsaw—where they had been forced to gather by the German occupation forces—are captured by the Germans. The Jews will immediately be deported to concentration camps and the ghetto itself leveled.

27 MAY 1943
National President Roosevelt, by executive order, creates the Office of War Mobilization to coordinate the nation's total war efforts. Roosevelt also orders that all government contracts with war industries forbid racial discrimination.

9 JUNE 1943
National The Current Tax Payment Act, also known as the "Pay-As-You-Go-Act," goes into effect. It introduces the withholding of federal income taxes on wages and salaries before being paid; this will become a cornerstone of U.S. tax policy and the financing of government.

14 JUNE 1943
National The Supreme Court, in *West Virginia Board of Education v. Bernette*, rules it unconstitutional for a state to have a law requiring children to salute the flag and to be expelled if they don't.

20-22 JUNE 1943
Black Experience Whites protesting the employment of blacks in Detroit, Michigan, clash with blacks and before Federal troops can put down the ensuing riot and rampage, 34 people are dead.

25 JUNE 1943
National Congress adopts the War Labor Dispute Act (Smith-Connally Act) by overriding President Roosevelt's veto. The act requires a union to give 30-day notice before calling a strike in a war plant and outlaws any strike in government-operated plants.

5 JULY 1943
World War II German forces in Russia launch a massive attack on what is known as the Kursk salient in what will turn out, a week later, to be the final German initiative. Although the Soviet losses in men, tanks and planes are greater than those of the Germans, the Russians can now replenish their forces and the Germans cannot.

10 JULY 1943
World War II Sicily is invaded by U.S., British, Canadian and French troops; General Eisenhower is the supreme commander of the landing forces that include some 2500 ships and many airplanes. Several

cities in southern Sicily are captured before the day is over, and by August 17 Sicily will have fallen to the Allies. This will assure safer passage to Allied shipping in the Mediterranean and give the Allies a great advantage in their planned invasion of the Italian mainland.

16 JULY 1943
World War II President Roosevelt and Prime Minister Churchill issue a joint message—printed on millions of leaflets dropped from Allied planes over Italy—calling upon the Italian people to surrender.

19 JULY 1943
World War II Some 500 U.S. bombers carry out an air raid on selected targets in and around Rome. The Allies have deliberately not bombed Rome up to now because of the city's unique historical, religious and artistic significance, and special care is taken on this raid to avoid hitting any structures of such significance. (Only one church near a railroad yard is damaged.) Clearly the raid is designed to demonstrate to the Italian people that they should now give up resistance.

25 JULY 1943
World War II Mussolini is forced by King Victor Emmanuel to resign after 21 years as *Il Duce* of Italy. Marshal Badoglio is named Prime Minister, and although he will pretend to be loyal to the Axis he will immediately set about looking for a way to get the Italians out of the war.

1 AUGUST 1943
Black Experience A rumor of a murder in Harlem sparks a race riot that ends with five people killed, 410 injured, and some $5,000,000 in damage.

17-21 AUGUST 1943
World War II At Wewak, New Guinea, U.S. Air Force planes destroy or disable some 300 Japanese planes and kill 1500 Japanese pilots and ground crew. As Wewak is an important base for Japan's strategic plans in the Pacific, this is regarded as a major loss.

17 AUGUST 1943
World War II With the fall of Messina, Sicily is effectively conquered by the Allied forces. The Allies have lost some 25,000 men during the five weeks of the Sicilian campaign, but the Italians and Germans have lost 167,000.

3 SEPTEMBER 1943
World War II Allied forces now cross the Strait of Messina and invade the mainland of Italy. This same day, however, Marshal Badoglio signs a secret armistice with the Allies, agreeing to stop Italian military resistance on September 8. When Italy publicly surrenders on September 8, Germany will accuse Italy of betrayal and immediately begin to treat the country as an enemy.

EXPANDING RESOURCES 1901-1945

GEORGE S. PATTON, 1885-1945

Hard-fighting, hard-swearing, hard-living General George "Blood and Guts" Patton was a soldier in the old mold. Believing himself to be the reincarnation of ancient warriors, imposing of physique and packing two ivory-handled pistols, he was determined to live up to his concept of what a fighting man should be. The grandson of a Confederate general, Patton was born near Pasadena, California, on November 11, 1885. He spent his boyhood outdoors on the family ranch and was an avid reader of military adventure stories. After graduating from West Point in 1909, he became a cavalry lieutenant and, in 1912, an Olympic military pentathlon competitor.

Patton first saw action during Pershing's operations against Pancho Villa in 1916. A tank commander in World War I, his bravery and his innovations in tank warfare brought him many decorations before a wound in 1918 put him out of action. In the 20s and 30s he languished in various duties around the country while pursuing his combative instincts in sports and in extensive studies of military history. Then history gave Patton his war. At the outset of World War II he was given an armored division and by 1942 was commanding general of the I Armored Corps near Casablanca. In 1943 he worked successfully with the II Corps in Tunisia and along with British general Montgomery accomplished the invasion of Sicily in an astonishing 39 days. But his actions off the battlefield began to get him in trouble; after he slapped two shell-shocked American soldiers in August 1943, he nearly lost his command.

In the wake of D-Day in 1944, Patton's Third Army broke through German defenses in France in a bold operation; his advance outran its proposed goals as well as its supply lines. In the "Battle of the Bulge," Patton managed an historic turning of his army to shore up the southern shoulder of the Bulge. Crossing the Rhine in March 1945, the Third Army moved deep into the heart of Germany and then raced into Czechoslovakia and Austria, breaking the back of the Nazi army. As the war ended, Patton was promoted to four-star general. Exhilarated by his successes, Patton pressed his superiors to let him move against the Soviet Army in collaboration with German forces. This got him relieved from active duty. In December 1945, he died after an auto accident. Off the battlefield Patton was sometimes like a fish out of water, but on the battlefield he had been the supreme American field commander of the war.

---

9 SEPTEMBER 1943
World War II Allied troops—in some 700 ships—land at Salerno, south of Naples, where they encounter strong resistance from the Germans. But by September 14 the Germans will be forced to abandon Salerno. On September 19 Sardinia will fall to the Allies, and that same day the French on Corsica will rise up against the Italians and Germans who have been controlling this island.

21 SEPTEMBER 1943
International The House of Representatives adopts the Fulbright Concurrent Resolution calling for U.S. participation in a world organization to further peace.

1 OCTOBER 1943
World War II Naples, Italy, is captured by the U.S. 5th Army led by General Mark Clark. Before they evacuate the city, however, the Germans damage many of the major cultural institutions and burn many thousands of books—all to punish the Italians for their "betrayal."

13 OCTOBER 1943
World War II Italy, now led by Marshal Badoglio, declares war on Germany. But Italy will continue to remain under control of the Allied Military Government until the war officially ends.

19-30 OCTOBER 1943
International In Moscow, the foreign ministers of the U.S.S.R., Great Britain and the U.S., and the Chinese ambassador to Russia, gather to discuss various issues of mutual interst. They end by signing a declaration in which the four nations agree on how to treat the Axis powers once the war ends and also on the creation of an international organization to work for peace.

5 NOVEMBER 1943
International The Senate passes the Connally Resolution calling for the U.S. to support an international peace organization. This complements the Fulbright Resolution passed in the House of Representatives on September 21 and compensates for the "B₂H₂" resolution that was rejected on March 16.

22-26 NOVEMBER 1943
International President Roosevelt and Prime Minister Churchill converge on Cairo, Egypt, to meet with Generalissimo Chiang Kai-shek, the leader of the Nationalist Chinese. They agree to demand that Japan surrender unconditionally and accept these terms: Japan must restore all Chinese territory, it must give Korea its independence, and it must give up all islands in the Pacific that it has seized since 1914.

28 NOVEMBER-1 DECEMBER 1943
International Roosevelt and Churchill fly on to Teheran, Iran, and meet with Premier Joseph Stalin of the U.S.S.R. The leaders agree on the timing of the invasion of Europe. (This, by the way, is the first time these three leaders have met in person.)

4-6 DECEMBER 1943
International Roosevelt and Churchill return to Cairo and there hold discussions with President Ismet Inonu of Turkey over his country's intentions to join the Allied side.

17 DECEMBER 1943
National Congress repeals the Chinese Exclusion acts of earlier years, under which strict quotas had been set on immigrants from China.

24 DECEMBER 1943
National In his end-of-the-year message to the American people over the radio, President Roosevelt announces that General Dwight D. Eisenhower will be

THE WAR AND THE HOME FRONT

World War II became a war like no other before or since in America's history, one in which the entire resources and life of the country centered around the war effort. Even before the United States formally entered the war, the government began to make plans (some withheld from the mass of the people) for the conflict that seemed inevitable, and by 1942 many new government agencies were being formed to monitor every aspect of production and society. The Office of Price Administration controlled prices and rents, which were for the most part "frozen"; rationing was quickly introduced for a growing list of items—tires, gasoline, meat, sugar, coffee, butter, shoes—and many consumer products (such as metal appliances) essentially vanished from the stores. The National War Labor Board settled labor-management disputes (and by and large outlawed strikes in war-related industries). The Fair Employment Practice Committee attempted, if with limited success in a still segregated society, to eliminate racial discrimination in war industries and government jobs. Censorship was imposed as all mail overseas was opened and radio and newspaper reports of the war were controlled. Slogans like "Loose lips sink ships" appeared on posters along with caricatures of the brutal Nazis and bestial Japs (figures of whom became the targets of balls, darts, and pellets in amusement park games).

The Office of War Mobilization oversaw the allocation of home-front production and supply, but naturally most resources and labor went to war industries. Since so many men went into the services, some 2,000,000 American women were employed at the peak in 1943 in war-related industries, while many others pitched in on farms and other jobs to relieve men for the military: the figure of "Rosie the Riveter" entered the nation's popular imagination. Meanwhile, the Office of Civilian Defense, headed by New York City's Mayor LaGuardia, organized especially those living along the coasts, where enemy attacks from planes or ships seemed possible (and on a couple of occasions Japanese submarines did manage to land some shells on the West Coast, but with little effect). There were air-raid drills and school children crouched in basements and corridors with their geography texts (always the largest book) over their necks (to ward off falling debris) and erasers between their teeth (to soften the explosions). The coastal regions observed blackouts at night, and air raid wardens patrolled neighborhoods to enforce compliance; meantime, plane-spotters took turns nightly on rooftops to await the dreaded bombers, while families kept buckets of sand in attics to put out the incendiary fires. Plane-spotters' towers were erected in the hills of Vermont and other remote locales, but although every American boy grew adept at identifying his own planes from wing silhouettes, no one ever spotted an enemy plane. But this didn't stop Americans from conducting rubber drives, scrap metal drives (many a yard sacrificed its fine old iron fencing) and fat drives; from growing "victory gardens"; or from buying over $156,000,000,000 worth of war stamps and bonds—which in turn didn't stop the government from imposing new taxes on luxuries such as cosmetics and jewelry. And those who still had free time volunteered to serve by folding bandages or by entertaining service personnel at the many USO Clubs that sprang up.

Sports—both professional and collegiate—went on but there was pressure on athletes to enlist and the records and teams of the war years were generally regarded as less than high caliber. There was also pressure on many stars of the entertainment world to enlist or at least entertain the forces: Bob Hope's visits became a national institution, but he was only one of the many from the world of show business and the arts who did their part. The war inevitably became the primary theme of the popular arts. This was reflected in popular music, from "The White Cliffs of Dover" to "Praise the Lord and Pass the Ammunition." And every episode in the war was soon transferred to the movies, so that Americans seemed to have barely digested the news of the fall of Wake Island and Bataan and Corregidor when they were seeing Hollywood actors lose again in their local theaters; eventually, though, they watched the Allies recover and go on to win. The American home front's travails could in no way be compared to the sufferings of so many European civilians throughout these years, but Americans could claim to come through it by working, eating, hearing, wearing, looking at, singing and dancing World War II.

the Supreme Commander of the forces that will soon invade Europe. The planned area for the invasion is naturally left unstated.

27 DECEMBER 1943
Labor The Federal Government seizes the nation's railroads threatened with a shutdown by striking workers.

OTHER EVENTS OF 1943
Arts/Culture Wendell Willkie, having taken a trip around the world as Roosevelt's personal emissary, writes his *One World* and helps to convince many Americans of the need to abandon their old isolationist attitudes. The musical *Oklahoma*, by Richard Rodgers and Oscar Hammerstein, opens on Broadway and becomes an immediate and long-running popular and critical hit; it also stands as a milestone in American musical theater by leading musicals away from show business glitter and into more indigenous American subjects.

10 JANUARY 1944
National President Roosevelt submits a $70,000,000,000 budget, most of which is to go to the war effort.

16 JANUARY 1944
World War II General Dwight Eisenhower arrives in London to take up the post of Supreme Commander, Allied Expeditionary Force, and lead what will become known as "the crusade in Europe" to free the Continent from the German conquest.

19 JANUARY 1944
Labor With the final settlement of the wage dispute, the railroads that have been controlled by the Federal Government since December 27, 1943 are returned to their owners.

22 JANUARY 1944
World War II Allied forces land at Anzio and Nettuno, some 30 miles down the Italian coast from

Rome, to establish a beachhead intended to outflank the Germans aligned across central Italy.

National President Roosevelt, by executive order, sets up the War Refugee Board, a recognition of the problems that will increase as the war moves into its final phase.

31 JANUARY-22 FEBRUARY 1944
World War II U.S. forces invade the Marshall Islands in the Pacific and within these three weeks all of the Marshalls come under Allied control. This is the first territory captured from the Japanese that they had owned before they set out to take territory that belonged to other peoples.

3 FEBRUARY 1944
World War II U.S. warships shell the Kurile Islands of northern Japan, the first attack by ships on Japan's home territory.

6 FEBRUARY 1944
World War II Both at the Anzio beachhead and inland at Cassino, the Germans commit their full forces in an effort to stop the Allied advance on Rome.

12 FEBRUARY 1944
National Wendell Willkie, the Republican presidential candidate in 1940, announces he will run again for his party's nomination. Among those also being promoted as candidates is General Douglas MacArthur. President Roosevelt has not announced his intentions but his name has been entered in several primaries.

20-27 FEBRUARY 1944
World War II The U.S. Air Force conducts a series of massive air raids on the centers of the German aircraft industry; in what is known, as "Big Week," the U.S. suffers heavy losses but those of the Germans are much heavier and leave the German air capacity seriously weakened.

4 MARCH 1944
International Acting Secretary of State Edward Stettinius declares that the U.S. no longer recognizes the government of Argentina because Argentina has not cooperated with the rest of the Allies—and has not even declared war against Germany and Italy.

6 MARCH 1944
World War II With some 800 fighter planes supporting them, 660 U.S. bombers, make the first U.S. raid on Berlin. A second such raid will be made on March 8, and U.S. losses on both raids amount to some 10 percent. But these and the raids that follow almost daily on German cities will gradually weaken the Germans' will to resist.

15 MARCH 1944
World War II After a long stalemate at Cassino, the town and monastery in central Italy that serve as the keypoint to the Germans' Gustav Line across central Italy, the Allied forces launch a major offensive with a massive bombing raid and tank assault. Not only do the Germans put up stiff resistance but they have made their headquarters in the medieval monastery on the mountain, and the Allies are reluctant to bombard that. By March 26, the Allied offensive will have stalled, and it will be May before a new one can be launched.

21 MARCH 1944
International Secretary of State Cordell Hull reveals a 17-point program for a U.S. foreign policy that stresses international cooperation in the postwar world.

29 MARCH 1944
International The U.S. Congress approves a joint resolution authorizing up to $1,350,000,000 for the United Nations Relief and Rehabilitation Agency. This is the start of what will become the massive postwar effort to aid the millions of people whose lives were disrupted by the war.

3 APRIL 1944
National In *Smith v. Allwright*, the Supreme Court rules that a person cannot be denied the vote in the Democratic Party primary in Texas because of his color—namely, being black.

4 APRIL 1944
National Wendell Willkie has entered the Wisconsin primary in the hope of gaining the Republican nomination again for the presidency. But he has underestimated the depth of the isolationist spirit that still prevails, and he loses. On April 6 he will announce his withdrawal from the race.

17 APRIL 1944
International Congress extends the provisions of Lend-Lease aid to the Allies through June 30, 1945.

22 APRIL 1944
World War II The Allies launch a major invasion force and land in the Netherlands New Guinea. The Japanese are caught off–guard and the Allies are soon well established.

24 APRIL 1944
International In Cairo, Egypt, U.S. treasury representatives meet with financial experts from Great Britain and several Middle East nations in order to discuss financial problems anticipated in this region.

26 APRIL 1944
National Montgomery Ward & Company, the large retail mail order firm, has defied an order by the National Labor Relations Board to extend a contract with its union employees. U.S. Army troops move in today and physically carry Montgomery Ward's chairman, Sewell Avery, out of the plant.

30 APRIL 1944
National General MacArthur has been constantly

promoted as a possible Republican presidential candidate, but he now issues a statement that he neither wants nor intends to accept such a nomination.

3 MAY 1944
National Meat rationing, except for various choice cuts of beef, ends.

18 MAY 1944
World War II After two months of intensive attacks by the Allies, the Germans withdraw from the Monte Cassino monastery (which has been seriously damaged during the battle). The Germans' Gustav Line across central Italy is now pierced, although there is still considerable opposition at various points.

23 MAY 1944
World War II Having bogged down at Anzio since their landing there on January 22, the Allied forces now launch a major offensive in an effort to break out and move on to Rome. Day by day, the Allies advance, and by June 1 they are able to start a drive on Rome.

4 JUNE 1944
World War II Advance units of the U.S. Army enter Rome, but because it is Sunday the main Allied armies hold back. The German troops meanwhile have evacuated "the Eternal City" to spare it, treating it as an open city. On June 5 , the Allied armies sweep through Rome and pursue the Germans northward.

6 JUNE 1944
World War II D-Day Operation Overlord, the invasion of the Continent, begins just after midnight with the descent of two U.S. airborne divisions, and in the early hours of the morning with some 4000 invasion ships plus 600 warships, at least 10,000 planes (only one of which is shot down by the German Air Force) and about 176,000 Allied troops. It is the largest such invasion force in history, and the day itself is marked by both epic movements and statistics and by individual acts of heroism. The landings take place along a series of beaches in Normandy between Cherbourg and LeHavre, and although the Germans have had some warnings they have not concentrated on a unified strategy. Despite heavy casualties in some sectors—the U.S. lose at least 1000 men on Omaha Beach—by the end of this first day there are some 150,000 Allied troops dug in as well as thousands of vehicles and many tons of material. Americans will hear of the invasion over their radios during the morning and will go to bed knowing that it has evidently succeeded.

10 JUNE 1944
World War II The two U.S. beachhead armies—those from Omaha and Utah Beaches—link, and the Allies forces are now ready to present a solid line to move against the Germans. In effect, from this point on, and with many delays and a few setbacks, the

Allied forces will move inexorably eastward until Germany surrenders in May 1945.

13 JUNE 1944
World War II The first German V-I flying bombs, jet-propelled pilotless bombs launched from France and Belgium, cross the Channel; only one makes it to London.

15 JUNE 1944
World War II U.S. Superfortresses, B-29s based on China, bomb Yawatta, the first such air raid on a Japanese main island. In the Marianas, U.S. forces land on Saipan; by the time the island falls on July 9, the U.S. will have suffered some 3400 dead, but the Japanese will have 27,000 dead.

19-20 JUNE 1944
World War II In one of the more decisive air-naval battles of the War, the Battle of the Philippine Sea, the Japanese are soundly defeated, losing at least 400 planes and three carriers. U.S. losses are some 50 planes in battle and another 72 that crash while trying to land on their carriers in the darkness (but all except 49 pilots and crew are picked up).

22 JUNE 1944
National President Roosevelt signs the Servicemen's Readjustment Act, providing financial aid to veterans for education, housing, and other needs. This act will soon become widely known—and beloved—as the G.I. Bill of Rights.

27 JUNE 1944
World War II Cherbourg falls to U.S. forces, the first major French port to come under Allied control; although its facilities are virtually in ruins, it provides a vital foothold for the Allies.

28 JUNE 1944
National The Republican Party, meeting in Chicago, nominates Governor Thomas E. Dewey of New York for president and Governor John Bricker of Ohio for vice–president.

1-22 JULY 1944
International Delegates from 44 nations meet at a resort hotel at Bretton Woods, New Hampshire, for a monetary and financial conference. Before they leave, they will have agreed to set up an International Monetary Fund and an International Bank for Reconstruction and Development and many of their decisions will govern international finance for the next quarter-century.

6 JULY 1944
International General de Gaulle arrives in Washington, D.C., for several days of conferences seeking to gain U.S. support for his French forces fighting the Germans and for his plans to govern France once the Germans are driven out.
Regional In Hartford, Connecticut, a Ringling

Brothers & Barnum & Bailey circus tent catches fire; 168 people are killed and 250 seriously injured.

18 JULY 1944
World War II St. Lo, a crucial road junction linking Normandy and Brittany, effectively falls to U.S. forces; on July 25 the U.S. troops will launch a "break out," an armored thrust designed to isolate the German units in Brittany; by August 10, the U.S. Third Army under General George Patton will have achieved this: the Allies are then ready to move eastward toward Germany.

20 JULY 1944
World War II A bomb explodes near Hitler in his headquarters in East Prussia, but he escapes serious physical injury (although the whole incident makes him even more psychologically paranoid and erratic). It is immediately apparent that a group of officers and politicians have plotted to assassinate Hitler and seize power because they begin to take steps on the assumption that Hitler is dead. Instead he quickly reasserts command and before the day is over several of the leaders of the plot are executed; eventually thousands of the active or alleged conspirators will be executed.

21 JULY 1944
National Meeting in Chicago, the Democrats nominate Franklin Delano Roosevelt for an unprecedented fourth term as president. Some of his staff and insiders are generally aware of his failing health and urge that the vice–president be a man acceptable to a broad majority of Americans in case anything were to happen to Roosevelt. Senator Harry S. Truman from Missouri becomes the candidate for vice–president, but few Americans perceive him as a potential president.

25 JULY 1944
World War II The St. Lo "break out," officially known as Operation Cobra, begins as the Allies launch a coordinated offensive to cut off the German forces in Brittany.

10 AUGUST 1944
World War II The island of Guam is retaken by U.S. forces after some 20 days of fierce fighting; the Japanese have lost some 17,000 men (with only 500 surrendering) and the U.S. have lost 1214 killed and some 6000 wounded. Guam had fallen to the Japanese on December 13, 1941, so its recapture is of special significance to the Allied cause.

14 AUGUST 1944
National The production of various domestic appliances such as electric ranges, cooking utensils and vacuum cleaners is allowed to resume (but subject to the progress of the war).

15 AUGUST 1944
World War II The Allies launch a new front against the Germans by invading Southern France at beachheads between Cannes and Toulon. There is little German resistance and the Allies are immediately able to start their drive up the Rhone Valley.

21 AUGUST-7 OCTOBER 1944
International At Dumbarton Oaks, an estate in Washington, D.C., representatives from the U.S., Britain, the U.S.S.R. and China meet to discuss the formation of an international organization for promoting peaceful and legal solutions to international problems as soon as the war ends.

25 August 1944
World War II French General Leclerc leads his forces into Paris as the German commanding general, Chollitz, refuses Hitler's orders to resist. General de Gaulle appears in Paris on the 26th and marches in a ceremonial parade; General Eisenhower and other Allied leaders enter Paris on the 27th.

28 AUGUST 1944
World War II The Germans in Toulon and Marseilles surrender to the Allies, thus effectively ceding Southern France. The Allies have close to 190,000 men ashore by now and the American units are already pushing toward Lyons, the major French city on the Rhone.

8 SEPTEMBER 1944
World War II The first of the German V2 rockets land in England; these are much faster and more powerful than the V1 rockets and will take a considerable toll, both psychological and physical, on the British populace in the closing months of the war.

11-16 SEPTEMBER 1944
International At the second Quebec Conference (known as The Octagon Conference), Roosevelt and Churchill discuss the strategies for pursuing the Germans and Japanese as well as their status in the postwar world.

12 SEPTEMBER 1944
World War II The U.S. Army enters Germany for the first time, advancing only a few miles beyond the border between Trier and Aachen.

3 OCTOBER 1944
National Congress passes the Surplus War Property Act, indicating that the government is already thinking ahead to the end of the war. Congress also passes the War Mobilization and Reconversion Act to provide for the removal of various controls imposed during the war.

20 OCTOBER 1944
World War II U.S. forces invade Leyte Island in the Philippines; they are led by General MacArthur, who comes ashore within a few hours and broadcasts to the Philippine people, thus fulfilling his promise of March 1942, "I shall return."

23-26 OCTOBER 1944

World War II The Japanese have sent a major naval force into the Leyte Gulf with the intention of disrupting the American invasion. Instead, in the Battle of Leyte Gulf and the ensuing engagements, the Japanese suffer a major defeat, losing 24 large ships (including 4 carriers, 3 battleships and 10 cruisers). From this point on, the Japanese Navy is reduced to increasingly and literally suicidal engagements, as Kamikaze fighters—Japanese pilots who ritually dedicate themselves to piloting their planes onto the enemy's ships—begin to appear.

7 NOVEMBER 1944

National President Roosevelt wins an unprecedented fourth term with 25,602,504 popular votes against Thomas E. Dewey's 22,006,285; the electoral votes are 432 to 99.

19 NOVEMBER 1944

National President Roosevelt announces the 6th War Loan Drive, seeking to borrow some $14,000,000,000 immediately through the sale of war bonds.

15 DECEMBER 1944

National Congress passes an act establishing the new rank of General of the Army—which will soon become better known from the insignia as "5-star general"—and confers the rank on George Marshall, Dwight Eisenhower, Douglas MacArthur and Henry "Hap" Arnold.

16 DECEMBER 1944

World War II Led by General von Rundstedt, German forces launch a counteroffensive into the Ardennes Forest in Belgium. As the center of the Allied line falls back, it creates a "bulge," thus earning this episode the name of "Battle of the Bulge." It will be December 30 before the Allies can regroup and start their own counterattack, and it will be the end of January 1945 before this last German offensive is crushed.

22 DECEMBER 1944

World War II The U.S. 101st Airborne Division has been holding out in Bastogne in the Ardennes and the Germans have demanded they surrender. General Anthony McAuliffe is said to have replied today with one word, "Nuts!" The Americans in Bastogne will be relieved by the U.S. 3rd Army on December 26 and will begin a counterattack on December 30.

23 DECEMBER 1944

Sports The Director of War Mobilization & Reconversion announces that horse racing will be banned as of January 3, 1945, in an effort to save critical materials. But the ban will be removed on May 9, 1945 (the day after the war in Europe officially ends).

OTHER EVENTS OF 1944

Economics The cost of living has increased some 30 percent despite efforts to control wages and prices.

And a "black market" is estimated to have attracted at least $1,300,000,000 from Americans willing to pay extra for food, clothing, gasoline and other items rationed or in short supply.

20 JANUARY 1945

National Franklin Delano Roosevelt is inaugurated for his fourth term as president.

1 FEBRUARY 1945

World War II A force of some 1000 U.S. bombers raid Berlin.

4-11 FEBRUARY 1945

International At Yalta, in the Crimea, President Roosevelt joins Churchill and Stalin in discussing plans for the final phase of the Allies' assault on Germany. They also agree to call a meeting of the United Nations in San Francisco on April 25 to establish an international peace organization. (On April 9, a national poll reveals that 81 percent of Americans favor such an organization; this contrasts sharply with the 26 percent who supported such an organization in 1937.)

4-24 FEBRUARY 1945

World War II U.S. troops complete the capture of Manila, the capital of the Philippine Islands.

19 FEBRUARY-16 MARCH 1945

World War II In one of the hardest fought battles of the entire war, U.S. Marines capture the Pacific island of Iwo Jima; the raising of the flag on Mount Suribachi creates an image of triumph that will become a symbol of fighting in the Far East during World War II.

7 MARCH 1945

World War II Units of the U.S. Army cross the Rhine River at Remagen; by the 25th of March, all German forces will have been driven east of the Rhine.

1 APRIL-21 JUNE 1945

World War II Closing in on Japan, the U.S. Army wages a fierce battle to take the island of Okinawa, losing some 80,000 in casualties to Japanese losses of 120,000.

12 APRIL 1945

National While vacationing at Warm Springs, Georgia, President Roosevelt suffers a massive cerebral hemorrhage and dies. Vice President Harry S Truman is sworn in as President and must immediately assume the monumental tasks of replacing a major world leader in closing out the most costly war in history.

16 APRIL 1945

National The Lend-Lease Act is extended for an additional year. At a joint session of Congress, President Truman assures a quick termination of the war and promises that he will continue former President Roosevelt's policies, domestic and foreign.

EXPANDING RESOURCES 1901-1945

U.S. troops dig out survivors of a bombing.

25 APRIL 1945
International United States and Soviet troops make their first meeting in Germany. At San Francisco, representatives of 50 nations meet to draw up a document which will establish the United Nations Organization, a focal point for the hopes of a war-weary civilization.

7 MAY 1945
International The world rejoices as the Germans surrender to the Allies at Rheims, France. General Dwight D. Eisenhower accepts for the Allied forces.

8 MAY 1945
National A nationwide dimout invoked on January

15, 1945 is lifted as President Truman proclaims V-E Day. This follows the news of Germany's surrender on the previous day.

11 MAY 1945
World War II The United States aircraft carrier *Bunker Hill* is attacked by a Japanese kamikaze plane in waters off Okinawa. The death toll is reported at 373, a grim reminder that war continues.

5 JUNE 1945
International The Big Four (United States, Great Britain, France, U.S.S.R.) make arrangements to divide Berlin, together with the occupation of Germany.

21 JUNE 1945
World War II After 12,500 Americans die and 160,000 Japanese lose their lives, the Japanese surrender Okinawa to the U.S. Army.

5 JULY 1945
World War II The Philippine Islands are recaptured by General Douglas MacArthur's United States forces. This liberation occurs after ten months of fighting and the loss of over 12,000 American lives.

6 JULY 1945
National President Truman signs an Executive Order establishing the Medal of Freedom, to be awarded to civilians for meritorious service.

16 JULY 1945
National After months of secret research, atomic scientists see the results of their efforts on the Manhattan Project: the detonation of the first atomic bomb at Alamogordo, New Mexico. Among those contributing to the project are J. Robert Oppenheimer, in charge of the weapons laboratory at Los Alamos.

17 JULY 1945
International President Truman attends the first session of the Potsdam Conference, together with Britain's Prime Minister, Winston Churchill, and Russia's Joseph Stalin. Truman hopes to establish the ground rules for peacetime foreign policy by means of these summit conferences. In the middle of the conference, Clement Atlee replaces Churchill. The sessions establish a Council of Foreign Ministers to meet regularly, consisting of representatives from the United States, China, the Soviet Union, France and Britain.

26 JULY 1945
International The Potsdam Declaration of the U.S. and Britain, made in association with China, demands the unconditional surrender of Japan.

28 JULY 1945
International The United States Senate consents to the United Nations Charter by a vote of 89-2.

6 AUGUST 1945
World War II The United States Air Force drops an atomic bomb on the city of Hiroshima, Japan. This is the first application of atomic technology and the magnitude of destruction astounds even those working on the Manhattan Project.

Antitank gunners hold their position on Okinawa.

HARRY S TRUMAN, 1884-1972

To grasp the reins of power thrust suddenly into his hands during a time of national trial by the death of a legendary predecessor was, for a relatively unknown and untested vice-president from Independence, Missouri, a humbling assignment of fate. Undaunted, the diminutive, often feisty Harry S Truman vowed to himself and demonstrated to a nation that in his own way, a strong pragmatic hand would guide the nation through its continuing international and domestic crises.

Born to a family of Missouri farm pioneers, Harry Truman learned outspoken and assertive behavior from his parents. Forced, however, by an overly protective but loving mother to dress neatly, take piano lessons and babysit his younger sister, and excluded from rough boyhood games by poor eyesight, Truman was, by his own admission, "kind of a sissy" as a child. Unable to afford a college education, the quiet and bookish young man traveled down the road to Kansas City to earn his living as a clerk, bookkeeper and haberdasher, an undistinguished career interrupted by artillery duty in France during World War I.

Entering politics in the early 1920s, Truman maintained an almost puritanical integrity and honesty, both as a judge and a United States Senator while a cog in "Big Jim" Pendergast's corrupt Kansas City political machine. A loyal New Dealer with a noted penchant for barnyard epithets, the Missouri Senator remained an unassuming backbencher, a reputation only slightly elevated during World War II by his vigorous investigation of military contract abuses.

Privately questioning his own adequacy, Truman conducted himself self-confidently, even aggressively, as president. He stood fast against Soviet expansionism and spoke bluntly to its representatives, battled the conservative 80th Congress and Republican "gluttons of privilege" and fired administrators deemed more loyal to New Deal idealism than Fair Deal pragmatism. Though proving his political skill and personal mettle in the miraculous "give em hell" campaign of 1948, the Korean War, McCarthyism and the impending nomination of a military hero by the Republicans precluded another run for office in 1952.

Having grown and flourished in the presidency beyond all expectations, Harry Truman boarded a train with his beloved wife, Bess, after Eisenhower's inauguration, bound for his modest home in Independence, Missouri. There he resided as a common citizen, dispensing a kind of "cracker barrel" philosophy—lecturing to the press, the American people, current Chief Executives—until his death in 1972.

8 AUGUST 1945
World War II Russia enters the Eastern theater.

9 AUGUST 1945
World War II Nagasaki, Japan, is partly destroyed by a second atomic bomb. The United States awaits the response of the Japanese government to this show of force.

14 AUGUST 1945
National The War Manpower Commission lifts manpower controls.
World War II War ends in the Far East.

17 AUGUST 1945
International The Allies divide Korea at the 38th parallel, with United States troops moving into the southern portion. The North is occupied by Soviet troops.

29 AUGUST 1945
International General MacArthur is named Supreme Commander of Allied Powers in Japan.

31 AUGUST 1945
International President Truman asks Britain to allow another 100,000 Jewish refugees in Western Europe to enter Palestine, where the British are in control.

2 SEPTEMBER 1945
National Millions of Americans celebrate as the Japanese formally surrender aboard the USS *Missouri* in Tokyo Bay.

6 SEPTEMBER 1945
National President Truman recommends an economic recovery plan to Congress. The chief executive hopes that this plan will aid in employment and in the building of houses for a growing population.

28 SEPTEMBER 1945
Environmental The President issues executive orders proclaiming federal authority over all national resources beyond the continental shelf.

12 OCTOBER 1945
National Conscientious objector Private Desmond Doss receives a Medal of Honor from President Truman in recognition of heroism during World War II. Doss served in the Pacific Theater and was a medical corpsman acting with distinction and bravery.

19 OCTOBER 1945
National President Harry Truman is honored as the only United States President to become a 33rd Degree Mason. This degree is conferred on Truman at the House of the Temple, in Washington.

30 OCTOBER 1945
National Shoe rationing is ended nationwide.

19 NOVEMBER 1945
National President Truman requests that Congress establish a national compulsory health insurance program.
Military General Eisenhower is named Chief of Staff of the United States Army, replacing General George C. Marshall.

21 NOVEMBER 1945
National United Auto Workers go on strike at the General Motors plant in Detroit, Michigan, in the first postwar demonstration of labor unrest.

23 NOVEMBER 1945
National Meat and butter rationing ends.

OTHER EVENTS OF 1945

15 DECEMBER 1945
Military President Truman appoints General Marshall Special Ambassador to China to make peace between the Communist forces of Mao Tse-tung and National forces of Chiang Kai-shek.

20 DECEMBER 1945
National Nationwide rationing of tires ends.

31 DECEMBER 1945
National President Truman dismantles the War Labor Board. He establishes the Wage Stabilization Board to replace it, in an action aimed at putting the country on a peacetime footing.

OTHER EVENTS OF 1945
International The Nobel Peace Prize is awarded to former Secretary of State Cordell Hull.

The Japanese surrender aboard the battleship *Missouri*, September 2, 1945.

EMERGING AS A
WORLD POWER

1946–

ROBERT H. FERRELL
Professor of History, Indiana University

EMERGING AS A WORLD POWER 1946-

When Henry Adams attended the Chicago World's Fair of 1893 he was immediately convinced that the age in which he was living was the most fateful of all eras in the history of the world, and that the pace of events in the 1890s was increasing by a geometric progression; but he could not have conceived of the eventful years after World War II, when his observations were to make far better sense. Each generation, of course, considers its own time as being filled with a rush of history, one important event after another. But no period in world history can compare with the years since 1945.

The United States has dominated the affairs of the world since the close of World War II. America had become a world power before 1945, of course, but it was only in that year that it chose to exert this power, uncertainly in 1945-46, decisively with the Truman Doctrine, Marshall Plan, Berlin airlift, North Atlantic Treaty Organization and Korean and Vietnam Wars. During the presidency of Harry S Truman, who appropriately was from the Midwest, heretofore the most isolationist part of the country, the nation gave up the timeworn advice of Presidents George Washington and Thomas Jefferson about abstention and nonentanglement. These ideas were replaced by measures that were as revolutionary as was the Civil War and the other great domestic change of the preceding century, the Progressive movement that began with Theodore Roosevelt and (with a lapse of progress during the Republican 1920s) has continued, with the enlargement of government for social and economic purposes, to the present time. Truman's new foreign policy was followed by all his successors, even the Republicans, for although they sometimes liked to describe his measures as Democratic, perhaps even of his own invention, the new policy was essentially national and was avoidable only at dire peril to the Republic that his successors were sworn to preserve.

America as a world power had had a primary interest in Western Europe, in the rightful belief that the people and industrial capacity of that part of the world could not safely be allowed to pass under the control of the Soviet Union. To a lesser extent, the United States had seen the Middle East as an important but not crucial part of the world; American interest in the State of Israel led to talk of an alliance, but there has never been one, and none with any other nation of that region (in this respect, Turkey, a NATO nation, must be considered a part of Europe).

The Far East seemed an awkward area, a sort of politically faulted place with some countries, such as Japan, more secure than others. With the extraordinary growth

USS *Missouri* bombards shore targets near Chong Jin, Korea.

A naval helicopter crewman surveys a South Vietnamese village.

of the Japanese economy, the stability of Japan's postwar government and the wisdom of its policies, foreign and domestic, the United States has come to consider Japan essential to a power balance in the Far East. The opening of unofficial relations with the People's Republic of China in 1972 marked a dramatic reversal of a quarter century of confused policy.

Apart from this, dealings with the Far East have seemed fruitless and bitter. Led by columns of Soviet-built tanks, the North Korean army invaded South Korea on June 25, 1950. Korea had been divided at the end of World War II along the 38th parallel, with the Russians occupying the North and the U.S. controlling the South; two rival governments had been set up. The United Nations voted to send troops to help repel the invasion, but these troops were pushed back to the tiny Pusan perimeter where they held, while, on September 15, General Douglas MacArthur (commander of the NATO forces) staged a brilliant amphibious landing at Inchon, behind the enemy lines. Caught between the two forces, the North Koreans fled back across their border.

On October 8 the U.N. army crossed into North Korea and by the end of November, reached the Yalu River separating Korea from China. But then on November 26, the Chinese crossed the Yalu with some 200,000 men. They proceeded to clear North Korea of U.N. troops and on January 4, 1951, recaptured Seoul. MacArthur then complained that his efforts were being hampered by President Truman's refusal to allow bombing of supply depots in China. When the general refused Truman's order not to discuss the question publicly, he was fired by Truman. Meanwhile, the NATO forces had pushed the Communists back to the 38th parallel.

Peace talks began in July 1951, but were deadlocked. For the next two years the two sides fought a see-saw "Battle for the hills" of North Korea. Finally, in July 1953, the Chinese agreed to a cease-fire and the war came to an end. The conflict had come as a bitter shock to the American people, unaccustomed to a limited war instead of total victory. Instead, they turned against the Democrats and elected Dwight Eisenhower, a military hero, to replace the outgoing president.

Then came the Vietnam conflict, which had begun during the Truman years. Believing that a victory by Ho Chi Minh would lead to an expansion of world Communism, Truman backed France's attempt to reassert its colonial control over Vietnam. Despite U.S. aid, the French were defeated in 1954 and Vietnam was divided into two countries. The U.S. supported the non–Communist South Vietnam government. When the Communist Vietcong launched a campaign of political terrorism in the early 1960s, the Kennedy administration responded by increasing the number of military advisors stationed in the country and its financial aid to the government.

When North Vietnamese boats attacked two American ships in the Gulf of Tonkin in 1964, Congress reacted by passing the Gulf of Tonkin Resolution, that allowed the president to take whatever steps he deemed necessary to prevent further aggression against the U.S. President Johnson used this authorization to launch continuous aerial bombing of North Vietnam after a Vietcong attack killed seven Americans at Pleiku in February 1965. In March, he began a massive troop buildup with the result that in 1968, some 541,000 U.S. troops were in Vietnam.

This involvement came under strong criticism at

U.S. infantrymen deploy under fire to surround Bong Son, Vietnam.

home. Until early 1968 most people believed that the enemy was being defeated. Then in January, the Communists mounted a huge offensive. Johnson, realizing he was politically disabled, announced in March the cessation of the bombing and called upon Hanoi to begin peace talks. Richard Nixon, the incoming president, revealed his Vietnamization plan soon after taking office: U.S. troops would gradually be replaced by South Vietnamese soldiers. His action, in using U.S. air and ground forces to support South Vietnamese drives against Cambodia was, however, denounced. News about Napalm bombings, the My Lai massacre and the Pentagon Papers fueled anti-war sentiment, and on January 27, 1973 the administration signed an agreement providing for the complete withdrawal of U.S. troops.

In the early days of the Vietnam War Washington officials had considered the war essential in preventing the spread of Communism. The result, however, was a horrendous military, diplomatic, political, social, and moral defeat—57,000 American lives lost, and perhaps 150 billion dollars gone in useless expenditure—a tragic enterprise that was perhaps the greatest error in all of American history.

As for Latin America, terrible trouble arose with Cuba during the short-lived missile crisis of 1962. It was the worst international crisis since the end of the war and it was solved remarkably well by President John F. Kennedy. With other of the Caribbean and Central American countries where the United States had in the past often exercised heavy-handed influence—Haiti, the Dominican Republic, Mexico, Guatemala, Nicaragua, Costa Rica, El Salvador, Panama—relations became uneasy, and influence did not reach far. As Franklin D. Roosevelt had understood in the 1930s, the era of tutelage was over, whether Americans liked it or not.

By far the most intractable problem was the relationship with the Soviets, which, because of the implacable enmities of the Stalin era, seemed impossible of solution until Stalin's death in 1953, but even under his successors continued with the so-called Cold War. Perhaps the most interesting, and, in retrospect, attractive of the leaders of the U.S.S.R. was the ebullient and mercurial Nikita Khrushchev, who was premier from 1957 until 1964. In 1962, however, he appeared downright dangerous and relations seemed smoother under his phlegmatic successor, Leonid Brezhnev. One great problem with the Soviets was that of the two regimes in Germany—West and East—sponsored respectively by the U.S. and the U.S.S.R., with the divided city of Berlin a constant source of danger and possibly of a cataclysmic clash. In 1970-73 this was resolved with a series of bilateral and multilateral treaties and agreements that recognized regimes and borders and effectively removed Germany from international contention.

Underlying the tensions between Washington and Moscow was the arms race, especially in nuclear weapons and their carriers, a race in which for many years the genius of American science gave the advantage to the United States—each major advance in nuclear weapons and carriers was a triumph of American technology and came between four and six years or more before the Russians could respond: atomic bombs (U.S., 1945; U.S.S.R., 1949), hydrogen bombs (1952, 1956), operational ICBMs (early 1960s, late 1960s), MIRVs (1968, 1974), long-range cruise missiles (1975; by the early 1980s the Soviets were still without them). Efforts at arms limitation (never, to be sure, at disarmament) led to the SALT talks and, in 1972, a treaty and an executive agreement ending the emplacement of ABMs by both superpowers and roughly defining their respective missile strengths. But it proved impossible to make another SALT agreement and the race continued. With the superpowers unable to agree to further arms limitation, setting a poor example for ambitious non-nuclear nations, the danger that Secretary of State John Foster Dulles had described in the 1950s as "proliferation" appeared, the danger of so rapid a spread of nuclear arms and carriers that international equations would prove too complicated for human minds to calculate. A nuclear club of Britain, France, the People's Republic of China and India, in addition to the superpowers, was almost too much. What might happen with this addition of other industrial nations with sufficient technology to produce nuclear weapons—Argentina, Brazil, Pakistan, the Republic of China (Taiwan), South Korea, Japan, South Africa, Israel, Iran, Iraq? Or the addition of countries like Libya, led by the unpredictable Muammar el-Qaddafi, who publicly advertised his willingness to purchase nuclear weapons from any source, governmental or private?

Whether nuclear proliferation was about to take a great leap forward or backward was an open question at the beginning of the 1980s, but what was not arguable was that as the expense of being a superpower rose even higher—expense for both nuclear and non-nuclear arms—the security that supposedly came from paying for the very latest accoutrements of military power for purposes of national defense became even less certain. The nuclear overkill capacities of the U.S. and the U.S.S.R. became fantastically ridiculous, whatever the triumphs of American science.

Another unarguable international change was that the bipolarity with which the post-1945 era began—a world dominated by two superpowers—gave way in the 1950s to a structure outlined by what were loosely described as blocs, in such places as Latin America, Africa, the Middle East, or Asia. Another division of the time established what was known as the Third World, which varied in membership but excluded Europe and North America on the one hand and the Communist states on the other and seemed to comprise primarily non-industrial countries with non-white populations. Talk continued about blocs and the Third World, but the most notable sources of international influence, apart from the superpowers, gradually appeared to be such non-atomic industrial nations as Japan and West Germany. In the post-1945 world a superpower like the United States had to pay close attention to the needs and desires of smaller powers. Could it be possible, just barely possible, that the less powerful but nonetheless influential nations of the world might be able to find a way for the superpowers to end their senseless (so far as their own safety was concerned) competition?

As participation in international affairs produced a series of problems for the Government of the United States in the post-1945 years, so difficulties appeared in American domestic politics, but generally domestic matters were more placid. At the end of World War II it seemed obvious that the government had triumphed in every way, and that its organization in the progressive tradition of Theodore Roosevelt, carried to major achievement under his distant cousin Franklin, had proved itself. Big government seemed necessary to handle the multifarious economic and social purposes of a large population. Truman, the president from 1945 to 1953, announced a New Deal-like program in the autumn of his first presidential year, and set it out in detail after election in his own right in 1948, describing it as a Fair Deal. The Eisenhower Administration of 1953-61 essentially affirmed this New Deal-Fair Deal heritage, although for a while the general-president proposed to take government out of such activities as electrical-power generation, this when the Tennessee Valley Authority ran out of sites for generation of electricity by water power and proposed to build a steam-generating plant that would use coal. The Eisenhower Administration refused to permit this expansion of the TVA's activities beyond water power; the TVA's original design had been linked with conservation of the Tennessee Valley. It therefore gave construction of the proposed steam plant to a group of companies known as the Dixon-Yates syndicate. One problem led to another, a conflict of interest between a representative of Dixon-Yates and the government raised the possibility of scandal, the city of Memphis proposed to construct its own generating plant and the syndicate collapsed. With its end went most of the Republican talk of reducing socio-economic programs. Indeed, because of a combination of good weather and new fertilizers and the ingenuity of American farmers, the Eisenhower Administration spent many more billions on farm subsidies than had its profligate Democratic predecessor; despite the economizing talk of Secretary of Agriculture Ezra Taft Benson the administration bought up billions of excess bushels of wheat and corn, and storage silos rose everywhere in the Midwest, bursting at the seams with unsaleable produce.

In the 1960s the administrations of Kennedy and of Lyndon B. Johnson continued the New Deal heritage with the New Frontier and the Great Society, the new legislative measures combining with the rapidly rising standard of living to give evidence of the imminent abolition of poverty, until ever greater expenditures of Vietnam encouraged the Johnson Administration to undertake deficit financing, which produced sharp inflation by the end of the 1960s and when combined with rapid increases in energy costs, a rolling inflation

by the end of the 1970s—which was responsible, more than any other factor, for the election in 1980 of a conservative Republican, Ronald Reagan, as President of the United States. The Reagan Administration came into office with a mandate to reduce what the new president described as runaway New Deal measures. Actually, however, the president of the early 1980s did not interfere with the broad New Deal measures of his predecessors, although he weakened regulatory agencies through conservative appointments.

Big government—which was to say adequate government—thus became a part of American life after 1945, and the purpose was to bring a more equitable arrangement to American society. President Truman, one of the most attractive chief executives in the nation's history, was fond of describing his own party, the Democrats, as the party of the people, as compared to his Federalist-Whig-Republican opponents, men whom he often called economic royalists, seekers after their own good rather than the national welfare. Truman once said privately that he never could make a statement that was not partisan, that it "simply couldn't be done," and his description of the Democratic Party was always favorable. Leaving partisanship aside, however, the president was praising a development with which his countrymen agreed.

What was disquieting about American government on the national level in the post-World War II years was the sprawling nature of the bureaucracy, the tendency of offices, agencies, and departments to increase by Parkinson's Law. Truman, a master administrator, decided at the outset of his presidency that he could not control his administration through the appointive power—he could not appoint more than 3,000 officials in a civil service bureaucracy of 2.6 million (of which 1.3 million were civilian workers in the military and another 500,000 were in the post office)—figures, incidentally, that approximated the bureaucracy for 1980—2.7 million, with 960,116 in the military and 660,014 in the post office. Nor could he control the Federal Government through expanding his White House and executive office staffs. The system had simply become too unwieldy for successful management on the time-honored models. His only recourse was to pass authority to cabinet officials and demand that they not merely control their departments but behave responsibly toward the president. The system as he established it worked. His successor, Eisenhower, accustomed to military staff work, also controlled the government, although with a system that Truman was not fond of—the appointment of a chief of staff responsible to the president. Subsequent administrations tended to lose control, until in the 1970s and 1980s the presidency lost much of its effectiveness and became virtually an organ of public relations.

In the years immediately after World War II the American economy failed to go into the nose-dive that many Americans and the entire Soviet leadership expected—at least a recession (as G.O.P. partisans described depressions when they were in power), very probably a major depression. It was the first postwar era in American history without serious economic trouble, such as had followed, for example World War I in 1920-21. And beginning in 1950, with the onset of the Korean War, the American economy entered a period akin to what the economist Walt W. Rostow described as "take-off" (although his description properly applied to European and other nations that entered a consumer era similar to the one that the United States had experienced in the 1920s). In the years 1950-65 the economy produced as much as it had produced in the entire period since the founding of Jamestown in 1607. Here was a gigantic achievement, an enormous upswing in national wealth and power, evidenced on every hand—in the new interstate highway system begun in 1957, in the rapid increase in the number of automobiles, the spreading of suburbs around decaying city cores, and everywhere the new factories. Airports lengthened runways not merely for the new jets but to take increasing numbers of passengers. In the ensuing years, from 1965 to 1980, the national wealth again doubled. This second doubling was not noticed nearly so much as the first, because it was accompanied by inflation; the absolute increase in wealth and income seemed far less impressive because of much higher costs. Apart from what inflation meant for people on fixed incomes or who suffered from income tax inequities when inflation boosted them into higher brackets, life continued to be better.

It was in this generation of rapidly increasing affluence that American labor really came into its own. Admittedly, unions pushed wages up high in a few industries, notably steel and automobiles, that toward the end of the era were in trouble because of shrinking markets and foreign competition, and in those instances did their industries a large disservice by lessening competitive abilities. In the South, and in parts of the Midwest and trans-Mississippi West, where rural areas attracted industrial entrepreneurs because of cheap labor, unions showed the way to greater national wealth through organizing the new factories, raising the purchasing power of laboring men and women and thus producing more markets. Big labor had its ups and downs in confronting big government.

After World War II, President Truman initially was friendly to unions, for in his tight race in 1940 in Missouri for reelection to the Senate the railroad unions had helped produce his narrow primary victory, a plurality of 7,967 votes. In 1946 he discovered that in the rush to take advantage of postwar opportunities two of the most grasping unions were the leading railroad brotherhoods. He threatened to induct their members into the army and read a stern message to the House of Representatives, which passed the proposed "striker draft" with a whoop. Meanwhile, indeed in the middle of the president's speech, the two unions' leaders backed down and agreed to the government's proposals. Truman also "went to the mat," as he put it, with the aging leader of the United Mineworkers, John L. Lewis, who threw over an agreement with government negotiators because of a technicality and challenged the president to stop him ("no contract, no work"), knowing that in what then was a coal-dominated economy the president could get nowhere by putting the mines under military control, for the U.S. Army could not mine coal, a fairly technical operation. Truman cajoled and threatened and after the 1946 congressional elections, which Lewis had used as dramatic background (one might have said blackmail), he took the Mineworkers' leader to the mat and won.

In 1952, during the Korean War, the president seized the steel mills, but had to give them up after an adverse ruling by the Supreme Court. (The decision, *Youngstown Sheet and Tube Company v. Sawyer*, was to constitute, together with *United States v. Nixon* [1974], one of the two legal bulwarks against the imperial presidency of a later era.) Generally speaking, in the 1950s, 1960s, and 1970s the economy did so well that unions easily obtained most of their demands. They had no trouble with the Taft-Hartley Act passed by the Republican 80th Congress in 1947, over Truman's veto, which the president beheld as virulently antilabor. The act banned the closed shop, permitted employers to sue unions for broken contracts or damages inflicted during strikes, required a 60-day "cooling-off" period" before striking, forced unions to make public financial statements, forbade union contributions to political campaigns, ended the check-off system by which employers collected dues and required union leaders to take an oath that they were not members of the Communist Party. Union leaders later discovered that these requirements were less onerous than they sounded.

A further conservatively-inspired restriction on labor unions, the so-called "right to work" laws of the 1950s outlawing the union shop, got virtually nowhere when proposed to state legislatures; these laws were passed in Utah and Kansas in 1954, but were defeated in 31 states. The next year the United Auto Workers, the Ford Motor Company and General Motors pioneered in negotiating a guaranteed annual wage and provision for payments during layoff periods. The C.I.O. Steelworkers obtained similar contracts. That year the A.F. of L. and C.I.O. merged, bringing an end to contentions over craft versus industrial organization that had bitterly divided the ranks of labor in the 1930s, and actually reached back for decades to the turn of the century and before, when the perennial president of the A.F. of L., Samuel Gompers, had opted for craft unions.

In such ways, and with such accompaniments, the economy grew mightily, by every measure, absolute and per capita, in inflationary and real income. The population in 1945 was 139.9 million; in 1980 it was 226.5 million. Gross national product stood at $212.4 billion in 1945 ($560.4 billion in constant 1972 dollars); $286.5 billion in 1950 ($534.8 billion); $691.1 billion in 1965 ($929.3 billion); $2,626.1 billion in

EMERGING AS A WORLD POWER 1946-

1980 ($1,474.0 billion). The number of employed workers in the United States was 52.8 million in 1945, 58.9 million in 1950, 71 million in 1965, 97.2 million in 1980. Of workers in 1980, 41.2 million were women. Union membership increased from (1945) 14.7 million to (1950) 15 million to (1965) 18.5 million to (1978) 20.4 million. In the period 1945-80 the consumer price index rose from 53.9 (1967 = 100) to 246.8. Per capita disposable personal income in constant 1972 dollars was $2,416 in 1945, $2,392 in 1950, $3,171 in 1965, $4,473 in 1980.

Socially the single most important change in American life since the end of World War II lay in the rapid rise in the status of black Americans. The war of 1941-45 was fought by segregated units of the U.S. Armed Forces, and if segregation was not as marked as during World War II, it was apparent on all sides. In the war of 1917-18 the U.S. Army segregated blacks into two divisions in France, and the rest of the black Americans worked as stevedores and in other menial tasks in the Service of Supply. When the 42nd Rainbow Division was organized from units across the United States, a black unit sought to join, but its colonel was told that "black is not one of the colors of the rainbow." In World War II black units were largely supply organizations, but there were markedly more black fighting units, including one unit of pilots in the Air Force. After the war, President Truman decided for economic and political equality, which he believed would lead to progress in social matters. In 1947 he appointed a committee that drew up a document entitled "To Secure These Rights," and in a series of executive acts early in 1948 began desegregation of the armed forces and forbade discrimination in interstate transportation and in businesses engaged in interstate commerce. At the Democratic National Convention in 1948, the president boldly accepted a civil rights program, and lost support of parts of the Deep South, which formed the Dixiecrat Party under the governor of South Carolina, Strom Thurmond. After his victory, he ordered the complete desegregation of the military.

During the Eisenhower Administration, the Supreme Court, in *Brown v. Board of Education of Topeka* (1954), a landmark case in American constitutional history, forced a rapid integration of elementary schools, high schools, colleges and universities. Successive measures by the Kennedy and Johnson Administrations, ensuring the right of all black Americans to vote, completed the alienation of blacks from the Republican Party, a process begun during the Franklin Roosevelt Administration, and gave blacks such clear authority in the Democratic Party that their power in American politics was assured. Meanwhile, legislative measures ended open job discrimination and threatened employers with lawsuits if they did not hire a reasonable proportion of nonwhites.

In other ways American society changed greatly in the years beginning in 1945. The unwritten rule that Catholics were ineligible for the presidency, or their nomination too risky (seemingly evidenced in the defeat of the Democratic presidential candidate in 1928, Alfred E. Smith), was broken by the election of Kennedy in 1960. Bars to Jewish-Americans, which were largely unknown in the Midwest and Far West but highly noticeable in the East, vanished in the post-1945 period, in part because such discrimination became illegal, but largely because the anti-Semitism of the Hitler era in Germany so shocked Americans that it became no longer tolerable in any form. The rise to power of labor unions brought rapidly increasing income for blue-collar Americans, including opportunities for higher education for their children, and any stigmas that previously had attached to laboring men and women disappeared. Perhaps increasing numbers of automobiles, the similarity of suburban housing, and increased mobility of Americans also helped eradicate social distinctions.

As the 1980s dawned and the country began to approach the end of the century, pundits and preachers and students of American history looked to the past and future and some saw signs of social decay, notably in the increasing divorce rate and in the increasing acceptability of couples living together, even having children together, without benefit of clergy. It was difficult to draw wisdom of any sort from the statistics. For a while the number of divorces actually went down, from 3.8 per 1,000 population in 1945 to 2.6 in 1950 to 2.5 in 1965; admittedly they more than doubled by 1980, to 5.2. Marriages, apparently, were not lasting for very long. In 1980 there were 2,413,000 marriages and 1,182,000 divorces. Whether this meant anything other than a basically more honest arrangement for everyone concerned was hard to say.

Whatever conclusion one wanted to draw about the generation since the long-distant V-E and V-J Days of 1945, surely any lingering over the advance or retreat of the institution of marriage, or raising questions about the morality of divorce or cohabitation, was a waste of time. There were more important problems.

One of the most disturbing aspects of national life since 1945 was the way in which Americans allowed themselves to be distracted by crusades that resolved little or nothing. For a decade in the post-1945 period much attention had gone to anti-Communism, which from the benefit of a present-day perspective was mostly a waste of time. Communists admittedly were something of a threat in those bygone days, and the nation was indeed afflicted by several successful spy rings, which time and the ingenuity of the F.B.I. and C.I.A. revealed (the confession of the British physicist Klaus Fuchs told of penetration of the wartime atomic bomb project; the flight to the Soviet Union of three British intelligence officials, including the important operative Kim Philby, revealed penetration of the postwar bomb program and of the C.I.A.). But the witch hunts of the time, epitomized by the efforts of Senator Joseph R. McCarthy, uncovered few Communists. Then for a decade in the 1960s Vietnam mesmerized the country; the nation was transfixed by

512

Vietnam; scenes from the fighting were brought into American living rooms each night by television. This is not to say that the Vietnam War was not important, for the loss of so many soldiers' lives, not to mention the dollar expenditure, was no small sacrifice, but the entire involvement in Vietnam proved only a morass and a quagmire (to use the words of journalists of the time). The frightful result did not have much effect outside Southeast Asia—apart from a momentary, if marked, downturn in American prestige.

The continuing major trouble, and an intractable problem apparently, for the government and people of the United States from the year 1945 until the 1980s, was the arms race. Part of the difficulty was the cost of the military establishment, which was skewing the entire federal budget toward inflation. Much of the cost of the Department of Defense lay in salaries, pensions and housing of military personnel, almost one-third of the defense budget for the fiscal year 1981 (October 1980 through September 1981), which was an astronomical 159.1 billion dollars. But apart from the cost, and the danger of inflation, both of which were tolerable, was the threat to humanity itself of a nuclear war. The danger was great. The arms race had produced a latter-day Sword of Damocles, although the very image of a sword was an absurd anachronism.

With such thoughts Americans looked to the future.

MPs check Korean refugees for smuggled weapons.

CHRONOLOGY

9 JANUARY 1946
Labor Demanding an hourly wage increase of 5-7 cents, some 7700 Western Electric telephone mechanics go out on strike in 44 states.

10 JANUARY 1946
International The first General Assembly of the United Nations meets in London, England, with the United States delegation headed by Secretary of State James F. Byrnes and including Mrs. Eleanor Roosevelt.

15 JANUARY 1946
Labor Demanding an increase in daily pay of $2, United Electrical, Radio, and Machine Workers go out on strike in 16 states.

20 JANUARY 1946
National By executive order, President Truman establishes the Central Intelligence Group, the precursor of the Central Intelligence Agency (CIA).

21 JANUARY 1946
Labor The United Steelworkers Union closes down the country's steel mills over a wage disagreement. A pattern is clear: American labor, having held back demands because of the war, wants its share of the new prosperity.

24 JANUARY 1946
International In view of the effect of the atomic bombs dropped on Japan and the potential for destruction in atomic research, the United Nations establishes the international Atomic Energy Commission with the goal of restricting atomic energy to peaceful uses.

25 JANUARY 1946
National The Executive Council of the American Federation of Labor elects John L. Lewis as vice president as a sign that Lewis's United Mine Workers are returning to the A.F. of L. control.

20 FEBRUARY 1946
National The Employment Act of 1946 creates a Council of Economic Advisors and provides for an annual national economic report.

21 FEBRUARY 1946
National President Truman establishes the Office of Economic Stabilization to deal with conversion to a peacetime economy. Chester Bowles is named director.

5 MARCH 1946
International Former Prime Minister Churchill speaks at Fulton, Missouri, at Westminster College. In his address he cautions that "from Stettin in the Baltic, to Trieste .in the Adriatic, an iron curtain has descended across the Continent allowing 'police governments' to rule Eastern Europe."

13 MARCH 1946
National 175,000 United Auto Workers strikers end their successful 113-day walkout against General Motors Corporation.

1 APRIL 1946
National United Mine Workers, some 400,000 strong, go out on strike demanding wage increases and a health and welfare plan.

25 APRIL 1946
International Big Four foreign ministers begin to draw up peace treaties for Italy, Bulgaria, Romania, Hungary and Finland.

29 APRIL 1946
National In a report from the Department of Agriculture, Americans learn that farm prices are at record highs. Farmers are receiving more money for their goods than they have since July 1920.

23 MAY 1946
National The Railroad Trainmen and Locomotive Engineers Brotherhoods strike, causing national transportation to grind to a halt.

30 MAY 1946
National United Mine Workers end their strike after 59 days with a negotiated agreement providing wage increases and a welfare–retirement fund paid by the companies.

3 JUNE 1946
National The United States Supreme Court, in *Morgan* v. *Commonwealth*, rules that buses must allow seating without regard to race on vehicles in interstate commerce.

14 JUNE 1946
International Bernard Baruch submits a proposed United States plan at the United Nations for control of atomic energy.

21 JUNE 1946
National President Truman names Frederick Moore Vinson Chief Justice of the United States Supreme Court.

30 JUNE 1946
International The United States joins the United

Nations Educational, Scientific, and Cultural Organization (UNESCO).

1 JULY 1946
International The United States begins atomic tests at Bikini in the Marshall Islands.

4 JULY 1946
National Choosing Independence Day for its symbolism, President Truman proclaims the establishment of the Republic of the Phillipines.

7 JULY 1946
Ideas/Beliefs The first U.S. citizen to be canonized by the Roman Catholic Church is Mother Frances Xavier Cabrini, founder of the Missionary Sisters of the Sacred Heart of Jesus.

15 JULY 1946
National President Truman signs a bill extending wartime price controls for one more year.

1 AUGUST 1946
National The Atomic Energy Commission is established with the signing of the McMahon Act awarding civil control of nuclear material.
Education Creating a program for international education exchange, President Truman signs the Fulbright Act. The program will use foreign currency received from sales of American surplus commodities abroad.

2 AUGUST 1946
National Congress passes the Legislative Reorganization Act, a portion of which, Title III, requires registration of lobbyists and the reporting of expenses.

20 SEPTEMBER 1946
National Secretary of Commerce Henry Agard Wallace resigns. Wallace has recently spoken against the Truman administration's policies toward the Soviet Union.

1 OCTOBER 1946
International Under-Secretary of State Dean Acheson states unequivocally that the United States intends to remain in Korea until that country is united and free.

16 OCTOBER 1946
National The Truman administration lifts price controls on meat.

23 OCTOBER 1946
International In a second portion of its first General Assembly, the United Nations meets in New York City. There it agrees to accept $8,500,000 from financier John D. Rockefeller, Jr. to provide the United Nations with a site for its headquarters.

5 NOVEMBER 1946
National The Republicans make a sweep of both houses of Congress in the national elections.

9 NOVEMBER 1946
National Controls on most consumer goods are removed.

21 NOVEMBER 1946
National President Truman takes part in naval maneuvers off Key West, Florida, traveling in a captured German submarine.

7 DECEMBER 1946
Regional The worst hotel fire in the nation's history sweeps the Winecoff Hotel in Atlanta; 127 people die in this inferno; 100 are injured.

31 DECEMBER 1946
International President Truman issues a proclamation of formal cessation of World War II hostilities on this, the final day of 1946.

OTHER EVENTS OF 1946
Life/Customs Dr. Benjamin Spock, whose name is soon to become a household word, publishes *The Commonsense Book of Baby and Child Care*.
International John R. Mott, leader of the YMCA in America, and Emily Greene Balch, economist and president of the Women's International League for Peace and Freedom, are awarded the Nobel Peace Prize.

3 JANUARY 1947
National The first session of the 80th Congress convenes in the nation's capital. Representative Joseph W. Martin, Jr., of Massachusetts, is named Speaker of the House of Representatives.

8 JANUARY 1947
National President Truman names George C. Marshall Secretary of State. Marshall will assume his duties on January 21 and will soon become known to the American public, and to the world in general, as author of the Marshall Plan.

12 MARCH 1947
National Before a joint session of Congress, President Truman proposes a $400,000,000 aid program for Greece and Turkey to aid them in their recovery from the recent war and their resistance to any potential Russian-Communist efforts to exploit their weakened states. This program will become immediately known as "the Truman Doctrine."

21 MARCH 1947
National President Truman issues Executive Order 9835, establishing a Loyalty Program. This program institutes procedures requiring investigation of government employees and applicants for federal jobs. It reflects the rising fear of Communism.

24 MARCH 1947
National Congress proposes the 22nd Amendment to limit a United States President to two four-year terms.

7 APRIL 1947
National Striking telephone workers achieve wage hikes after a strike of only several weeks, an increase of $4.79 per week.

12 APRIL 1947
International The United Nations allows the United States trusteeship of Pacific Islands previously under mandate to Japan.

18 APRIL 1947
Regional The death toll reaches 500 as a result of a ship explosion at Texas City, Texas. Much of the city lies in ruins.

15 MAY 1947
National The Truman Doctrine aid program approved by Congress assures U.S. support for Greece and Turkey, and promises to prevent the spread of Communism.

22 MAY 1947
International President Truman signs a bill to aid Greece and Turkey.

31 MAY 1947
International President Truman allocates $350 million in relief for foreign countries devastated by recent war.

5 JUNE 1947
International At the Harvard commencement Secretary of State Marshall proposes a plan for European economic aid.

11 JUNE 1947
National In an action that elicits a sigh of relief from homemakers across the nation, sugar rationing ends after some five years.

17 JUNE 1947
International The first airline to offer a round-the-world service to its passengers, Pan American Airways, offers a flight fare of $1700.

23 JUNE 1947
National The Taft-Hartley Act is passed by the United States Congress despite a veto by President Truman three days earlier. This act bans the closed shop, permits employer lawsuits against unions for broken contracts or damages incurred during strikes, and establishes a Federal Mediation and Conciliation Service.

7 JULY 1947
National The Hoover Commission to study the organization of the executive branch of the Federal government is established with former President Herbert Hoover as chairman.

12 JULY-22 SEPTEMBER 1947
International A 16-nation conference is held in Paris to plan the United States-proposed Marshall Plan for economic aid to Europe. The Soviet Union and Communist-bloc nations decline to be involved.

18 JULY 1947
National The Presidential Succession Act passes Congress, revising the law of 1886 and making the Speaker of the House next in line of succession after the president and vice-president.

26 JULY 1947
National The National Security Act designates a National Military Establishment of all military services, administered by a secretary of defense, who receives Cabinet level status.

2 SEPTEMBER 1947
International President Truman flies to Petropolis, Brazil, and signs a hemispheric mutual defense pact at the Inter-American Defense Conference.

17 SEPTEMBER 1947
National James V. Forrestal, Secretary of the Navy, is sworn in as the first secretary of defense.
International The United States refers the issue of Korean independence to the United Nations, which passes a resolution to seek free elections in Korea.

19 SEPTEMBER 1947
International After a trip to China, General Albert C. Wedemeyer submits a report to President Truman concerning the possibility of a five–year United States military aid program.

5 OCTOBER 1947
Life/Customs Television is used for the first time by a president as a medium with which to communicate with the nation; Truman speaks on the world food crisis.

9 OCTOBER 1947
International President Truman supports a United Nations proposal for autonomous Jewish and Arab states in Palestine.

18 OCTOBER 1947
National The House Un–American Activities Committee opens an investigation into Communist influence in the American movie industry.

19 OCTOBER 1947
Aviation Supersonic speed is achieved for the first time by United States Air Force Captain Charles Yeager in an X-1 research plane built by Bell Aircraft.

24 OCTOBER 1947
National Senator Robert A. Taft announces he is a candidate for the GOP Presidential nomination in 1948.

25 OCTOBER 1947
Regional President Truman declares Maine a disas-

ter area in the aftermath of an extensive forest fire that destroys a large portion of Bar Harbor. Losses are estimated at $30,000,000.

29 OCTOBER 1947
National The findings of the President's Commission on Civil Rights are made public.

25 NOVEMBER 1947
International The Council of Foreign Ministers meets in London to discuss the economy and government of Germany.

3 DECEMBER 1947
Arts/Culture New Orleans sees the opening of a new play by Tennessee Williams—*A Streetcar Named Desire*.

19 DECEMBER 1947
International President Truman asks Congress for the first installment of a proposed $17,000,000,000 for a four-year European Economic Recovery Program.
International The Nobel Peace Prize is shared by the Friends Service Council and the American Friends Service Committee.
Sports Jackie Robinson becomes the first black athlete to play for a major league baseball team when he is signed by the Brooklyn Dodgers.

27 DECEMBER 1947
Regional In New York City, the greatest snowfall on record causes work in the metropolitan area to grind to a halt; 80 deaths result from this record 25.8-inch snowfall.

29 DECEMBER 1947
National Running on a third party ticket, one-time Vice-President Henry Wallace makes known his candidacy for the presidency.

OTHER EVENTS OF 1947
Science/Technology An American husband-wife team, Carl and Gerty Cori, share the Nobel Prize for physiology and medicine with the Argentinian Bernardo Houssay.

12 JANUARY 1948
National A United States Supreme Court decision dictates, in *Sipeul* v. *Board of Regents of the University of Oklahoma*, that no state can discriminate against a law school applicant on the basis of race.

23 JANUARY 1948
International The United Nations Temporary Commission on Korea receives notification from the Soviet Union that it cannot enter North Korea. The Commission is responsible for elections in Korea.

2 FEBRUARY 1948
National President Truman introduces a civil rights package to Congress in which he calls for an end to

segregated schools and employment discrimination. Wallace's Progressive Party candidacy will not receive American Federation of Labor support, according to a decision by that body's Executive Council.

7 FEBRUARY 1948
National General Eisenhower retires from active duty in the United States Army, and will become president of Columbia University.

21 FEBRUARY 1948
National President Truman begins a five-day trip to Puerto Rico, the Virgin Islands and Cuba, where he inspects the Naval base at Guantanamo Bay.

8 MARCH 1948
National The Supreme Court rules that religious training conducted in public schools is unconstitutional.

15 MARCH 1948
National Coal miners strike in hope of gaining a more liberal pension plan, taking more than 200,000 workers out of the mines.

22 MARCH 1948
International The United States announces a land reform program for Korea.

2 APRIL 1948
National The Economic Assistance Cooperation Administration, established by Congress, provides over $5,000,000 in aid to Western Europe under the Marshall Plan.

12 APRIL 1948
National Striking soft-coal miners reach a compromise in their pension plan negotiations and return to work at the request of United Mine Workers President John L. Lewis.

20 APRIL 1948
National A Federal judge levies a $20,000 fine against Lewis, head of the United Mine Workers. The union must pay $1,250,000 for contempt of court following the March 1947 coal strike.

30 APRIL 1948
International The Organization of American States, a 21-member group, begins meetings in Bogota, Colombia. The United States is among OAS members.

10 MAY 1948
National President Truman, dealing with a nationwide rail strike, orders the Army to operate the nation's railroads.
International In United States-occupied South Korea, elections occur under the jurisdiction of the United Nations Temporary Commission. North Korea authorities refuse cooperation.

14 MAY 1948
International Israel declares itself an independent

EMERGING AS A WORLD POWER 1946-

nation and the United States becomes the first nation to recognize it.

19 MAY 1948
National The United States House of Representatives passes the Mundt-Nixon Bill requiring Communists in the United States to register. The Senate does not act on this bill.

25 MAY 1948
National The United Auto Workers benefit from a General Motors escalator clause in contracts for auto industry workers. This clause provides for a cost-of-living increase, and is the first sliding-scale contract negotiated with General Motors.

3 JUNE 1948
Science At ceremonies on Mount Palomar in California the astronomers dedicate the world's largest reflector telescope.

7 JUNE 1948
National General Dwight D. Eisenhower becomes president of Columbia University.

HENRY A. WALLACE, 1888-1965

He was a proud, incorruptible visionary to his followers, a naive political dreamer to his detractors. Whether secretary of agriculture, vice-president, secretary of commerce, or presidential candidate, Henry Wallace remained steadfast in his evangelical devotion to internationalism abroad and social justice at home, even as the political winds shifted and swirled about him.

Raised on the broad, fertile plains of Iowa, son of a noted agriculturalist, Wallace acquired early in life the traits of hard work, dedication to agricultural research, love of the land and its people and strong Christian faith. A nationally respected plant geneticist and farm journalist, he arrived in Depression era Washington, D.C., intent upon saving the American farmer from ruin. With his blunt Midwestern manner, Wallace quickly established himself as a favorite New Dealer of Franklin Roosevelt and was chosen as FDR's vice-president in 1941. An aloof demeanor and unconcealed disdain for the compromises of practical politics, however, left him a political outcast in the corridors of power occupied by urban bosses and conservative Southern Democrats. Such an incautious attitude cost this tall, rumpled man dearly when he was ultimately replaced (by his less idealistic opponents) by Harry Truman in 1945.

His ego bruised, Wallace found only temporary solace in the Commerce secretariat. Politically isolated and personally bitter, he regained vigor in 1948 when he embarked in his righteous crusade to capture the White House as the Progressive Party candidate and true descendant of F.D.R. Promising his followers a "century of the common man," Wallace vowed to raise a "Gideon's Army" in the cause of international peace and domestic equality. An unabashed New Dealer in an era of caution, Wallace grew frustrated yet resigned to defeat. His public career at an end, Henry Wallace lived the remainder of his days in quiet solitude, returning to his first love, the study of the plants and soil of agrarian America.

WHITTAKER CHAMBERS, 1901-1961

Few lives better typify the shifting sands of radical American political ideology than that of Whittaker Chambers. Raised on Long Island, New York, Whittaker Chambers flirted briefly with academia, attending Columbia University before immersing himself in the activities of the American Communist Party. With the zeal of the newly converted, Chambers served the party both as a secret agent and by writing for various Communist journals and publications. His personal instability caused him to become disillusioned with Communism and he left the party in 1938, at once becoming a fervent anti-Communist. As if to further atone for his former Communist party affiliation, Chambers joined the staff of *Time* magazine in 1939.

Chambers, anxious to prove himself a loyal citizen, attained national prominence in the summer of 1948 as a "namer of names" in the Federal Government's search for past Communist connections of government employees. Chambers implicated State Department official Alger Hiss before the House Un-American Activities Committee (HUAC), and repeated those charges of Hiss's past Communist espionage on the National Broadcasting Company's *Meet the Press* television show. Sued for slander by Hiss in December 1948, Chambers produced (from their hiding place in a pumpkin) microfilms of secret documents alledgedly typed by Hiss, and thus became the chief witness against Hiss in two perjury trials in 1948.

Leaving *Time* in 1948, Chambers wrote *Witness,* his autobiography, and completed his journey from political Left to Right by writing for the conservative *National Review.* Attempting to free himself from the notoriety and controversy with which his past activities had surrounded him, Chambers enrolled as an undergraduate at Western Maryland College. But the man who had spent the bulk of his adult life in pursuit of a cause was destined to be forever identified with the bitterly divisive issues rife during the government witch-hunts of the post-war years. Two years after his matriculation at Western Maryland College, Chambers died of a heart attack in Westminister, Maryland.

---

11 JUNE 1948
National The Vandenberg Resolution passes the Senate allowing the United States to enter collective security pacts with non-Western Hemisphere nations.

24 JUNE 1948
National President Truman signs a Selective Service Act to register all males between the ages of 18 and 25 for service in the armed forces. At the GOP National Convention, Republicans nominate New York Governor Thomas E. Dewey to be their presidential candidate, with California Governor Earl Warren as vice–presidential nominee.

26 JUNE 1948
International American European Command aircraft are ordered to respond to Berlin's need for food and fuel denied them by the two-day Soviet blockade of the city's Western Sectors.

15 JULY 1948
National At the Democratic National Convention,

President Truman receives the nomination, with Alben Barkley of Kentucky as his running mate. The addition of a civil rights plank to the party platform provokes some Southern delegates to walk out.

17 JULY 1948
National Southern Democrats who walked out of the party convention two days earlier, over a dispute concerning civil rights, form the States' Rights Party (Dixiecrats) which nominates Strom Thurmond of South Carolina for president. The Dixiecrats propose a platform of racial segregation.

22 JULY 1948
National In Philadelphia dissident Democrats form a third party. Adopting the name "Progressive" they nominate Henry Wallace, a former vice–president.

26 JULY 1948
National An executive order bars segregation in the United States armed forces and calls for an end to racial discrimination in Federal employment. In a special session of Congress called by President Truman, there is an unsuccessful attempt to pass measures to control inflation, enact civil rights legislation and repeal the Taft-Hartley Act.

31 JULY 1948
Regional President Truman dedicates New York City's Idlewild International Airport, later known as John F. Kennedy International Airport.

3 AUGUST 1948
National Fear increases of Communism in government and elsewhere in the United States. Former Communist Whittaker Chambers names Alger Hiss as a former Party member. Hiss subsequently sues Chambers for slander, an action that leads to his conviction for perjury.

14 AUGUST 1948
Sports After having been cancelled in 1940 and 1944 because of the world war, the Olympic Games have been held in London, England. As they come to a close on this day, the United States is the unofficial team champion with 547.5 points.

15 AUGUST 1948
International Seoul, South Korea, is the site of a proclamation establishing the Republic of South Korea. Syngman Rhee is the president of the new republic.

9 SEPTEMBER 1948
International In North Korea, as a response to developments in the South, a People's Republic is established. This government claims jurisdiction over the entire country in conflict with Rhee's United States-backed administration in Seoul.

24 OCTOBER 1948
National Bernard Baruch, speaking before a Senate committee, points out that "we are in the midst of a cold war which is getting warmer."

2 NOVEMBER 1948
National The Presidential elections result in a surprise victory for incumbent Harry S. Truman, who defeats New York Governor Thomas E. Dewey by 2.2 million popular votes and 114 electoral votes. This victory is due, in part, to the 10,000 miles of campaigning logged on his "Whistle Stop" tour of the United States. The Dixiecrat candidate, Strom Thurmond, receives 39 electoral votes and a little over one million popular votes. Henry Wallace, Progressive Party candidate, receives no electoral college votes but garners some one million popular votes.

6 DECEMBER 1948
National In connection with the Alger Hiss case, Richard M. Nixon of the House Un–American Activities Committee charges that the Truman administration has invested in the concealment of "embarrassing facts" rather than "finding out who stole the documents."

OTHER EVENTS OF 1948
Arts/Culture The Nobel Prize for Literature goes to the Anglo-American writer T.S. Eliot. The Pulitzer Prize for Fiction goes to James Michener for *Tales of the South Pacific* (the basis for the later Broadway musical).
Life/Customs The long-playing (LP) phonograph record is introduced by Columbia Records.

3 JANUARY 1949
National The United States Supreme Court rules that states have the right to ban the closed shop. This order is based on the controversial Taft-Hartley Act which President Truman had attempted unsuccessfully to veto in the spring of 1947. As the 81st Congress begins its second term, the United States House of Representatives elects Sam Rayburn of Texas as House Speaker.

7 JANUARY 1949
National Secretary of State Marshall resigns effective January 20, the day Truman is to be inaugurated.

12 JANUARY 1949
Korean War Under-Secretary of State–designate Dean Acheson reaffirms the United Nations' responsibility to provide military security to Pacific area nations. He does not consider Korea as within the U.S. defense perimeter.

14 JANUARY 1949
National The Department of Justice files an anti-trust suit against American Telephone and Telegraph, intended to divide AT&T from the manufacturing component of the company, Western Electric.

19 JANUARY 1949
National Congress raises the salary for Presidents to

An exuberant Harry Truman confounds the prognosticators.

$100,000 per year. The chief executive will also receive a tax-free expense allowance of $50,000.

20 JANUARY 1949
National In his inaugural address, Harry S. Truman discusses foreign policy and its role in world peace. Emphasizing the part played by American aid to foreign technological and economic development, he proposes several points designed to help developing nations. The "Point Four" section of this proposal, for the sharing of industrial and scientific expertise, goes to Congress four days later.

21 JANUARY 1949
National Dean Acheson is sworn in as Secretary of State.

7 FEBRUARY 1949
National The *Hoover Commission on Organization of the Executive Branch of the Government* submits an initial report recommending changes changes in the Postal Department to remove it from political patronage.

13 FEBRUARY 1949
National In opposition to President Truman's proposed compulsory health insurance plan, the American Medical Association favors a voluntary plan.

25 FEBRUARY 1949
National General Motors drops automobile prices,

THE FAIR DEAL

For Truman, the war had only postponed the Administration's commitment to domestic reform; it had not ended it. Although the new President was prepared to agree with some critics that FDR's New Deal had been ad hoc and eclectic in its approach, he believed that had been because of the urgent need to recover from a crippling depression. Now that the war was over and the nation was no longer distracted by the threat of imminent economic collapse, however, the Federal Government could settle down to a cohesive program of longer-range reform.

Although Truman did not give a name to his domestic program until January 1949, he had laid down most of its points by the end of 1945. In September of that year, he sent a lengthy message to Congress which included 21 specific suggestions for legislative action. He called for a substantial raise in the minimum wage, a dramatic extension of the Social Security System, national health insurance, federal aid to education and a government-sponsored housing project for the poor.

The president also pushed hard for civil rights legislation to protect blacks from discrimination. He asked Congress to extend the wartime Fair Employment Practices Commission, to pass a strong anti-lynching law and to take action to abolish poll taxes. To further demonstrate his commitment to ending discrimination, he issued an executive order in 1948 which provided for the desegregation of the Armed Forces.

Aside from this important accomplishment, however, the president's plans for domestic reform brought few tangible results. Lacking the tact necessary to win converts, and faced by a Congress dominated by Republicans and conservative Southern Democrats, Truman succeeded in getting only two of his proposals: one established the Atomic Energy Commission and the other, the Employment Act, pledged the Federal Government to use all "practical" means to guarantee full employment. After his upset victory in the 1948 election, Truman again put pressure on Congress to act on the Fair Deal. This time the federal legislators responded by raising the minimum wage and by greatly expanding the Social Security system. They also passed the National Housing Act, which established a slum clearance program and provided for the construction of some 800,000 housing units for the poor.

After 1950, with the beginning of the Korean War and economic prosperity at home, the government quickly shifted its attention away from domestic legislation. Although the bulk of Truman's Fair Deal failed to secure passage, it remained the basic blueprint for liberal Democrats for more than a generation afterward and in the 1960s inspired many of Lyndon Johnson's Great Society bills. Truman's vigorous commitment to civil rights, in particular, helped establish the Democratic Party as the champion of the nation's oppressed black population.

the first cut in car prices since World War II.
Science The United States launches the *WAC-Corporal* at White Sands, New Mexico, achieving a record missile altitude of 250 miles.

2 MARCH 1949
National United Mine Workers president John L.

Lewis orders a two-week walkout of soft-coal workers to protest naming Dr. James Boyd director of the Federal Bureau of Mines.
Science The United States Air Force completes its first nonstop, around-the-world flight. Refueling four times while aloft, the B-50 bomber proves that the United States has unlimited air strike capabilities.

4 APRIL 1949
International Twelve nations sign the North Atlantic Treaty, a mutual defense pact. Among those signing are the United States, Great Britain, France and Canada. This defense agreement lays a foundation for the North Atlantic Treaty Organization (NATO).

8 APRIL 1949
International The United States occupation zone in Germany is to merge with the occupied zones of France and Britain, contingent on the establishment of a federal government.

20 APRIL 1949
Science After many years of research, scientists announce the discovery of a process to produce the hormone cortisone in quantities adequate for use by many patients. Cortisone's greatest benefits will be enjoyed by those suffering from rheumatoid arthritis, asthma and other allergic reactions and certain skin diseases.

12 MAY 1949
International The Soviet Union lifts its blockade of Berlin.

20 MAY 1949
National The Executive Council of the American Federation of Labor rejects a bid for reaffiliation proposed by the United Mine Workers.

21 MAY 1949
International The Federal Republic of Germany is established.

20 JUNE 1949
National The Reorganization Act, signed by President Truman, allows reorganization of the executive branch of the Government. Changes made by a chief executive become effective in 60 days if not vetoed during that time by Congress.

27 JUNE 1949
National The United States Supreme Court hears the case *Wolf* v. *Colorado*. The Court rules that prosecutors may continue using evidence gained through illegal search and seizure.

29 JUNE 1949
International The United States removes the last of its troops from Korea, leaving a group of approximately 500 advisers.

15 JULY 1949
National President Truman signs the Housing Act.

EMERGING AS A WORLD POWER 1946-

This provides for extended Federal aid for public housing throughout the United States, which many hope will alleviate the shortage experienced across the nation.

21 JULY 1949
International The North Atlantic Treaty passes the United States Senate. The vote is 82 to 13.

5 AUGUST 1949
International A White Paper issued by the State Department announces that the United States blames the Chiang regime as corrupt and indicates that its ineptitude lost mainland China to the Communists.

10 AUGUST 1949
National President Truman signs the National Security Act, creating a Department of Defense and giving subcabinet status to the secretaries of the Army, Navy and Air Force.

11 AUGUST 1949
National General Omar Bradley becomes chairman of the Joint Chiefs of Staff.

24 AUGUST 1949
National President Truman appoints Thomas Clark of Texas as Associate Justice of the United States Supreme Court.

21 SEPTEMBER 1949
International In order to provide military aid to United States allies in NATO, President Truman signs the Mutual Defense Assistance Act.

23 SEPTEMBER 1949
International President Truman announces to the American people that the Soviet Union now has nuclear capabilities, having just tested an atomic device.

1 OCTOBER 1949
National A steel strike brings out 500,000 workers who demand, and later receive, increased retirement benefits.
International The United States refuses to recognize the Communist Chinese Government under Mao Tsetung. America does not follow the lead of its allies, Britain and France, both of whom give immediate recognition.

6 OCTOBER 1949
National Foreign aid appropriations are given a boost as President Truman signs a bill of $5,810,000.

12 OCTOBER 1949
National Sherman Minton of Indiana receives an appointment as Associate Justice of the Supreme Court.

14 OCTOBER 1949
National Eleven Communists, on trial for conspiracy to advocate violent overthrow of the Federal Government, are found guilty under the Smith Act. The

---

THE KOREAN WAR

Led by columns of Soviet-built tanks, the North Korean army, in the early morning hours of June 25, 1950, launched a full-scale invasion of South Korea. Korea had been temporarily divided at the end of World War II along the 38th parallel, with the Russians occupying the North and the U.S. controlling the South. When the two sides had not been able to agree on a plan for reunification, two rival governments had been set up. Now, the North Korean Communists, strongly supported by the Soviet Union, were determined to bring unity to the country' on their terms.

Unobstructed by the Russians, who were boycotting the meetings at the time, the United Nations voted to send troops to help repel the invasion. The allies were pushed back to the tiny Pusan Perimeter where they held while, on September 15, General Douglas MacArthur (commander of the allied forces) staged a brilliant amphibious landing at Inchon, behind the enemy's lines. Caught between two large enemy forces, the North Koreans fled back across their border.

On October 8 the UN army crossed into North Korea and by the end of November had reached the Yalu River, separating Korea from China. MacArthur thought the fighting might be over by Christmas. But then on November 26 the Chinese crossed the Yalu River and hurled some 200,000 men at the allies. With massive reinforcements from China, the Communists cleared North Korea of UN troops and on January 4, 1951, recaptured Seoul.

As the allies went back on the defensive, a controversy erupted in Washington. General MacArthur complained that his efforts were being hampered by Truman's rufusal to allow bombing of Communist supply depots in China. Republicans rallied to the support of MacArthur, but Truman, supported by his Joint Chiefs of Staff, refused to budge. When the general disregarded the President's order not to discuss the question publicly, Truman fired him. Many in the U.S. bitterly condemned the action and even more so the president's refusal to wage war against China.

Meanwhile, the allies had again pushed the Communists back to the 38th parallel, inflicting heavy casualties on the enemy. Peace talks began in July 1951 but were soon deadlocked and for the next two years, the two sides fought a see-saw "Battle for the Hills" of Korea. Finally in July 1953 the Chinese agreed to a cease-fire and the war came to an end.

The Korean War came as a bitter shock to Americans. Accustomed to total victories, it was not easy for them to accept Truman's policy of limited war. Instead they turned against the party that espoused it and chose a military hero to replace the outgoing President (although part of Eisenhower's appeal was that he promised to go to Korea and end the war). Still, most were beginning to realize the necessity of mutual coexistence with Communism, and that realization would continue to govern the policy of the succeeding administrations.

---

presiding judge, Harold Medina, has been subject to extensive personal attacks by critics of the Truman administration's stance on Communism.

24 OCTOBER 1949
International New York City sees the dedication of

United Nations headquarters at the East River location.

26 OCTOBER 1949
National The Fair Labor Standards Act is amended to increase the minimum wage to 75¢ an hour from 40¢, to go into effect in January 1950.

31 OCTOBER 1949
National United Auto Workers president Walter Reuther starts purging the Congress of Industrial Organizations (CIO) of allegedly Communist-dominated unions.

9 DECEMBER 1949
National House Un-American Activities Committee chairman J. Parnell Thomas is found guilty of payroll padding, fined and given an 8- to 24-month prison sentence.

OTHER EVENTS OF 1949
Science/Technology The Nobel Prize in Chemistry goes to William F. Giauque.
Arts/Culture The Nobel Prize for Literature goes to William Faulkner.

2 JANUARY 1950
National The Department of Commerce reports that since July 1945, foreign nations received nearly $25,000,000,000 in the form of grants and credits from the U.S.

3 JANUARY 1950
National The second session of the 81st Congress of the United States opens.

19 JANUARY 1950
National Oscar Chapman becomes Secretary of the Interior.

21 JANUARY 1950
National President Truman chooses Paul Larsen to head the Civilian Mobilization Office, an agency to upgrade civil defense.

31 JANUARY 1950
National President Truman notifies the public that government scientists are at work on a hydrogen bomb under the Atomic Energy Commission.

7 FEBRUARY 1950
National In Wheeling, West Virginia, Senator

Marines attack a Communist emplacement in Korea.

EMERGING AS A WORLD POWER 1946-

Joseph R. McCarthy of Wisconsin speaks to a Woman's Club gathering and charges the State Department with harboring Communists.

20 FEBRUARY 1950
National McCarthy reveals another list of persons under suspicion of Communist connections. The accusations provoke a Senate subcommittee investigation. The Supreme Court rules that police have the right to seize property without a search warrant, in *United States* v. *Rabinowitz.*

7 MARCH 1950
International Charges brought against Valentin Gubitchev lead to the Soviet consular official's being found guilty of conspiracy and attempted espionage against the United States. He is later expelled from the United States.

13 MARCH 1950
National General Motors Corporation announces earnings of $656,434,232, the largest profit ever reported by any United States corporation.

17 MARCH 1950
Science Researchers at the University of California at Berkeley announce the discovery of Californium, the heaviest known element.

8 MAY 1950
National A further reflection of the preoccupation with Communism in government and private business appears when the United States Supreme Court rules, in *American Communications Association v. Douds,* that the non-Communist statement required by the Taft-Hartley Act does not violate the Constitution.

11 MAY 1950
National President Truman travels to Washington State to dedicate the Grand Coulee Dam.

25 MAY 1950
Regional The Brooklyn-Battery tunnel opens in New York City, the longest tunnel in the United States.

5 JUNE 1950
National Foreshadowing future civil rights suits, the Supreme Court makes two rulings upholding black Americans' rights to attend a state law school and receive full educational benefits from such schools.
International President Truman puts his signature on the International Development Act—his Point Four Program.

25 JUNE 1950
International North Korean troops cross the 38th parallel, invading South Korea, equipped with Soviet-made weapons. This invasion sets the stage for United Nations military involvement.

26 JUNE 1950
Korean War President Truman authorizes the

McCARTHYISM

Waving a sheet of paper in his hand, Joseph McCarthy told his Wheeling, West Virginia, audience that he was holding a list of 205 people who, though known Communists, were still "working and shaping the policy of the State Department." Refusing either to prove or retract his charge, the junior Senator from Wisconsin within weeks had established himself as the unofficial leader of the national crusade against Communism.

The post-war campaign against internal subversion was actually well under way by the time McCarthy joined its ranks with his Wheeling speech in February 1950. Closely tied to the international situation, the hysteria over domestic subversion escalated as the fear of worldwide Communist expansion increased. In March 1947, only nine days after enunciating his Truman Doctrine, the President issued an executive order requiring security checks of all government employees. The same year, the House Un-American Activities Committee launched a series of sensational hearings aimed at uncovering Communists in the entertainment industry which resulted in the blacklisting of a number of Hollywood personalities. In 1948, Alger Hiss, a former official in the State Department, was accused of passing on secrets to the Russians. As the public followed the subsequent trials, China fell to the Communists. Republicans, like McCarthy, openly charged that the Truman Administration, influenced by unpatriotic advice, had "lost" China.

Then the beginning of the Korean War in June triggered a full-scale assault on domestic "Reds." Congress passed the McCarran Internal Security Act requiring the registration of all members of the Communist party. McCarthy also stepped up his attacks on "subversives." After 1952, as chairman of a Senate subcommittee, he conducted over 150 investigations into Communist activity in the U.S. Waves of character assassinations and blacklistings engulfed universities, businesses and professional organizations as McCarthy subjected each to his scrutiny. Then in 1954 the Senator charged the army with harboring Communists; in a series of nationally televised hearings which followed, McCarthy was completely discredited, revealing himself to his audience as both a bully and a liar. His complete lack of decorum also led to his censure by the Senate. But his influence did not entirely end with his political career.

By that time, the anti-Communist crusade had largely spent itself. The end of the Korean War and a thaw in the Cold War had helped ease domestic fears; then McCarthy's excesses exposed the dark side of the crusade in a way that few could overlook. But McCarthy had never been completely to blame; the thousands who had suffered as a result of the hysteria did so because the public was willing to disregard constitutional and legal safeguards. America's legal system had not really been corrupted by McCarthyism—just ignored.

United States Navy and Air Force to aid South Korean troops operating south of the 38th parallel.

27 JUNE 1950
Korean War Acting in the absence of the Soviet representative, the United Nations Security Council adopts a resolution calling for armed intervention in Korea on the eve of Seoul's collapse to the North Koreans.

30 JUNE 1950

Korean War United States ground troops are sent to South Korea by President Truman. He signs a bill extending the draft for another year, and orders the United States Navy to blockade the Korean coast.

8 JULY 1950

Korean War General Douglas MacArthur is named to command United Nations troops in South Korea.

20 JULY 1950

National President Truman asks Congress to pass a $10,000,000,000 rearmament program, and pressures for a partial mobilization of United States resources. These actions are taken by the President in light of the Korean conflict. The Senate Foreign Relations Committee publishes a report that finds Senator Joseph R. McCarthy's statements of February 7 without basis in fact.

4 AUGUST 1950

National The United States Army calls 62,000 reservists.

18 AUGUST 1950

National The Special Committee to Investigate Crime in Interstate Commerce issues a report that organized crime is taking over legitimate businesses.

25 AUGUST 1950

National Threat of a railroad strike prompts President Truman to order the United States Army to operate the rail lines.

28 AUGUST 1950

National Amendments in the Social Security Act provide expanded benefits. There is an increase in the number of workers in the system; some 9 million additional persons are eligible for Social Security benefits.

8 SEPTEMBER 1850

National The Defense Production Act passes Congress, authorizing wage and price controls.

15 SEPTEMBER 1950

Korean War United Nations troops in South Korea land at Inchon and press toward Seoul.

21 SEPTEMBER 1950

National Former Secretary of State George Marshall becomes Secretary of Defense.

23 SEPTEMBER 1950

National Congress passes the Internal Security Act over the President's veto. The Act requires Communists to register with the government and to be detained in event of a national emergency and establishes a Subversive Activities Control Board.

26 SEPTEMBER 1950

Korean War United Nations troops recapture Seoul, South Korea.

29 SEPTEMBER 1950

Korean War United States-supported South Korean troops reach the 38th parallel.

7 OCTOBER 1950

Korean War United Nations forces invade North Korea.

11 OCTOBER 1950

Korean War The United States crossing of the 38th

NATIVE AMERICANS

In 1950, the Bureau of Indian Affairs (BIA) got a new commissioner; he was Dillon S. Myer—wartime director of the "relocation" of Japanese-Americans into internment camps.

There could hardly have been a more graphic omen of what the future held for the country's Native Americans. If any did miss the significance of the appointment, Myer's Termination Policy—designed to withdraw all special federal assistance to Indian tribes—soon demonstrated the government's new attitude.

During the 1930s, the Roosevelt Administration had tried to arrest the steady disintegration of Indian culture that had taken place since the 19th century by giving legal recognition to the tribal system and allocating funds to buy back Indian lands. After the war, however, this concern for Indian culture quickly evaporated. Instead, the Federal Government launched a vigorous effort to integrate Native Americans into American society. As part of this program, the BIA worked diligently to sell off reservation land and to find jobs for Indians in urban centers. Although most tribes strenuously objected to this policy, it remained in effect throughout the 1950s and by the end of the decade some 40 percent of all American Indians were city dwellers.

The return of Democrats to power in 1960, however, again saw a renewed effort by the government to preserve Indian culture and tribal integrity. To achieve this, Washington strongly encouraged businesses to locate on Indian lands to help bring employment and prosperity to the people. In 1968, Congress created the National Council of Indian Opportunity to channel money into health and educational programs for Indians. Grants were also provided to tribes to help them develop their own resources.

Despite such programs, by 1970 almost three-fourths of the country's Native Americans lived in cities. Although still maintaining a strong ethnic pride, these "modern" Indians had far different concerns than those living on reservations. They were also more aggressive in pushing the government to address those problems. In 1969, a group of militant Indians seized the abandoned Alcatraz Penitentiary and demanded that the unused island be turned over to them. Three years later, 600 members of the American Indian Movement (AIM) occupied and ransacked the BIA office in Washington to dramatize their demand for programs for urban Indians. The most dramatic confrontation took place at Wounded Knee, South Dakota, the site of the notorious Indian massacre in 1890. Members of AIM took over the town and held it for over two months in 1973. This time a massacre was narrowly averted, but when it was over it still remained to be seen whether it would be possible for Indians to maintain their cultural identity in a White America.

parallel in Korea provokes a denouncement by Red Chinese, who state that China will not "stand idly by."

Science The Columbia Broadcasting System receives its authorization to begin television broadcasts in color, beginning on November 2, 1950.

15 OCTOBER 1950
Korean War President Truman and General Douglas MacArthur meet on Wake Island to plan the Korean conflict. The two men agree on strategy.

20 OCTOBER 1950
Korean War A two-day fight for the capital of North Korea, Pyongyang, brings about the capture of the city by United Nations troops, allowing them to advance farther north.

1 NOVEMBER 1950
National In an assassination attempt at Blair House, where he lives while the White House is renovated, President Truman is shaken but not hurt. Two Puerto Rican Nationalists, Griselio Torresola and Oscar Collazo, attempt to take the president's life. Torresola is killed, and Collazo wounded. He ultimately receives a life sentence. A White House guard, Leslie Coffelt, is killed, and two other guards are wounded.

6 NOVEMBER 1950
Korean War Chinese Communist troops attack in North Korea and then pull back in what later appears to have been a warning.

7 NOVEMBER 1950
National In Congressional elections across the country, the Republicans are encouraged by a gain of 5 House and 31 Senate seats. Democrats maintain control over both the Senate and the House of Representatives. Richard M. Nixon is elected to the Senate from California.

20 NOVEMBER 1950
Korean War United Nations troops reach the Yalu River, on the border of Manchuria.

26 NOVEMBER 1950
Korean War The Chinese Communists stage a massive counteroffensive in North Korea. United Nations troops begin a retreat.

5 DECEMBER 1950
Korean War Pyongyang, North Korea's capital, is abandoned by the United Nations troops.

8 DECEMBER 1950
International President Truman announces a ban on United States shipment of goods to Communist China.

16 DECEMBER 1950
National President Truman declares a national emergency. Anticipating his immediate appointment to the NATO command, Dwight D. Eisenhower receives an indefinite leave of absence from his post as president of Columbia University.

19 DECEMBER 1950
International The North Atlantic Council names Eisenhower supreme commander of Western European defense forces.

29 DECEMBER 1950
National The Clayton Anti-Trust Act is amended by the Celler-Kefauver Act, which seeks to prevent corporations from acquiring property that might lead to a decrease in competition.
International General Douglas MacArthur states that United States troops ought to attack Communist China.
Arts/Culture The Nobel Prize for Peace goes to Ralph Bunche.

1 JANUARY 1951
National The United States Congress allows President Truman to place a freeze on prices.

3 JANUARY 1951
National The 82nd Congress of the United States convenes in its first session.

15 JANUARY 1951
National The United States Supreme Court rules, in *Feiner* v. *United States*, that a speaker who displays "a clear and present danger" of incitement to riot can be arrested.

1 FEBRUARY 1951
International The United Nations charges that Communist China is responsible for aggression against Korea.

8 FEBRUARY 1951
National Nationwide rail service resumes after a 12-day strike. Railroad workers win a pay raise as a result of this walk-off.

26 FEBRUARY 1951
National The 22nd Amendment to the United States Constitution becomes law as Nevada is the 36th state to ratify. "No person shall be elected to the office of the President more than twice." The Supreme Court invalidates state laws proscribing union activities. This ruling, in *Bus Employees* v. *Wisconsin Employment Relations Board*, affects union issues protected by the National Labor Relations Act.

14 MARCH 1982
Korean War Seoul, South Korea, is recaptured by United Nations forces.

21 MARCH 1951
National Defense Secretary George Marshall announces that the United States armed forces stand at 2,900,000, twice what they were prior to the Korean conflict.

4 APRIL 1951
International General Dwight D. Eisenhower sets up Supreme Headquarters, Allied Powers in Europe (SHAPE), in Paris.

5 APRIL 1951
National After a controversial trial in which they have been found guilty of giving top-secret information on nuclear weapons to the Soviet Union, Julius Rosenberg and his wife, Ethel, are sentenced to death.

Korean War General Douglas MacArthur states, in a letter to Joseph Martin, House Minority Leader, that as far as Korea is concerned "there is no substitute for victory." MacArthur is responding to Truman's plans to negotiate a truce.

11 APRIL 1951
Korean War In an action both criticized and ap-

General Eisenhower visits the 5th Field Artillery.

plauded by the public, President Truman removes MacArthur from his command in the Far East and appoints General Matthew Ridgway in his place.

19 APRIL 1951
National Speaking to a joint session of Congress, General Douglas MacArthur explains the urgency of the country's military situation in Korea. MacArthur urges that the United States expand the war against Communist China.

28 APRIL 1951
National The Office of Price Stabilization fixes prices on beef.

3 MAY 1951
National The Senate Armed Services and Foreign Relations Committees meet to consider General MacArthur's address to Congress.

15 MAY 1951
National American Telephone and Telegraph announces that it has over 1,000,000 stockholders, a first for any United States corporation.

4 JUNE 1951
National The United States Supreme Court rules, in *Dennis* v. *United States*, that the Smith Act (passed in 1949 and dealing with Communists in government) is constitutional. In another ruling, *Garner* v. *Los Angeles*, the justices uphold a state's right to require job applicants to sign non–Communist affadavits.

19 JUNE 1951
National The military draft is extended to July 1, 1955. Congress lengthens military service to 2 full years and lowers the draft age to 18½.

10 JULY 1951
International The United States takes part in truce talks at Kaesang between the United Nations and the Chinese Communists.

11 JULY 1951
Regional A flood covers more than 1,000,000 acres in Kansas, Oklahoma, Missouri and Illinois when the Mississippi River overflows. Flood waters rise over a period of nearly 2 weeks, causing over $1,000,000,000 damage.

1 AUGUST 1951
National President Truman cancels tariff concessions to Soviet-bloc nations.

30 AUGUST 1951
International The United States and the Philippines sign a trade agreement between the two nations until 1954.

1 SEPTEMBER 1951
International The Tripartite Agreement by the United States, Australia and New Zealand provides for mutual defense, in anticipation of signing of the Japanese peace treaty.

8 SEPTEMBER 1951
International In San Francisco, California, 49 nations sign the Japanese Peace Treaty recognizing Japan's "full sovereignty." The United States and Japan agree that the United States can maintain mili-

---

THE ROSENBERG CASE

The Soviet explosion of an atomic bomb in August 1949 sent a collective shudder through the fabric of U.S. society. As the Cold War had intensified in the years following World War II, Americans had come to view "the bomb" as their primary defense against an aggressive Russian army. Now the solace that mighty weapon had once given them was dramatically compromised.

But how could a country as industrially backward as the Soviet Union so quickly have erased the technological gap between herself and the U.S.? In January 1950, Klaus Fuchs, a former physicist on the Manhattan Project, provided an answer. While working on the top secret project to develop the atomic bomb, Fuchs told Scotland Yard inspectors in Britain that he and a group of co-conspirators had been assiduously passing on information to the Communists.

In the aftermath of Fuchs's revelations, the FBI picked up David Greenglass, another former employee on the Manhattan Project, his wife, and a chemist named Harry Gold. Charged with espionage, the three all agreed to testify for the prosecution in exchange for the promise that their own lives would be spared. They then told the federal investigators that Greenglass's sister Ethel and her husband Julius Rosenberg had been at the center of the spy ring.

The fact that Julius had been dismissed from the Signal Corps in 1945 for being a member of the Communist Party (which he denied), gave some credence to the Greenglass's story, and in the wake of the accusation the Rosenbergs were arrested and charged with passing on top secret information to the Soviets, including details concerning the atomic bomb. Although both steadfastly maintained their innocence throughout the trial, they were convicted and sentenced to death in 1951. Promised lenience if they admitted their guilt, the couple continued to deny any involvement in an espionage ring. On June 19, 1953, after President Eisenhower had twice denied pleas for clemency, the Rosenbergs were electrocuted— the first Americans ever to be executed for espionage during peacetime.

Set in an atmosphere of intense anti-Communist hysteria at home and with the Korean war raging abroad, many felt that the Rosenbergs had little chance for a fair trial. Their execution brought a storm of protests from all over the world. Critics claimed that the FBI had doctored evidence to bolster their case and had allowed Gold and Greenglass to collaborate in order to clear up inconsistencies in their stories. The fact that the prosecution's case had rested so heavily on the testimony of these self-confessed spies, as well as the Rosenbergs' unwavering insistence on their innocence, also led many to doubt that justice had been served by their execution. Years later, the couple's sons won an appeal to the courts for a release of the FBI's files in the case, but the Rosenberg trial still remains shrouded in mystery and recrimination.

---

tary forces in Japanese territory.

10 OCTOBER 1951
National President Truman signs the Mutual Security Act, $7,000,000,000 in aid to foreign countries. At Englewood, New Jersey, the first transcontinental dial telephone service goes into effect.

20 DECEMBER 1951
Science In Idaho, at the United States Reactor Testing Station, researchers generate electricity from nuclear fuel.

24 DECEMBER 1951
Arts/Culture Gian-Carlo Menotti's opera *Amahl and the Night Visitors* is broadcast by National Broadcasting Corporation, having been commissioned by the network.

OTHER EVENTS OF 1951
Science For their discovery of plutonium, Edwin McMillan and Glenn Seaborg win the Nobel Prize for Chemistry.

5 JANUARY 1952
International Prime Minister Winston Churchill of Great Britain, back in office since 1951, and United States President Harry S. Truman begin several days of meetings in the nation's capital. Churchill hopes to "re-establish the close and intimate relationship that he had with President Roosevelt in wartime and to seek a common policy and approach on the grave problems facing the Western Alliance."

7 JANUARY 1952
National General Dwight D. Eisenhower makes known his willingness to accept a draft for the Republican Presidential nomination.

8 JANUARY 1952
International President Truman and Britain's Churchill wind up their conference in Washington. They issue a statement concerning the United States airbases in Britain. The United States agrees not to launch an atomic attack on Communist Europe without the consent of Britain.

24 JANUARY 1952
International United Nations negotiators in Tokyo announce that Korean truce talks have stalled.

18 FEBRUARY 1952
Regional Storms off the coast of Cape Cod, Massachusetts, wreck two tankers, the *Fort Mercer* and the *Pendleton*, resulting in the deaths of 14 men.

20 FEBRUARY 1952
International In a statement at the opening of the North Atlantic Council meeting in Lisbon, United States Secretary of State Dean Acheson points out the focus and function of the organization. He reminds NATO members of the defensive, rather than offensive, nature of the alliance, and rejects the idea of preventive warfare.

2 MARCH 1952
National The United States Supreme Court rules that persons termed subversives may be barred from teaching in public schools.

18 MARCH 1952
National Senator William Benton of Connecticut at-

LILLIAN HELLMAN, 1905-

By the time her third play, *The Little Foxes*, appeared in 1939, Lillian Hellman had been hailed as one of America's foremost playwrights and by far its leading female dramatist. A writer of biting social commentary, Hellman expressed her emotions, which were often explosive, and her political views with burning conviction.

Raised in New Orleans, Louisiana, Hellman experienced the flavor of both wealth and poverty. Traveling north to school, she attended New York University and Columbia University. Hellman worked for publishers in New York City between 1924 and 1934 when her first play, *The Children's Hour*, was produced. It was during this time that she became associated with Dashiell Hammett, the author with whom she had a close personal relationship for over 30 years.

Lillian Hellman, outspoken and often obstinate, aligned herself early with left-wing politics. In the 1930s she went to Spain during the Civil War, relishing her experiences as a radical while candidly admitting her deficiencies as a revolutionary. Nevertheless, Hellman's contacts with leftist politics and her association with those more strongly committed to the Left were to bring her a great deal of hardship in later years. In 1944 she travelled to the Soviet Union to produce her plays, writing later of her gut-level fear and her exhilaration in viewing the war from the Russian front.

Lillian Hellman's fame as a dramatist receded in the early 1950s to be replaced by notoriety when she testified before the House Un-American Activities Committee concerning her possible connection to Communism in Hollywood screenwriting circles. Her adamant refusal to comply with the Committee's requests nearly cost her her personal freedom. Unlike many others, Hellman was not convicted nor was she imprisoned; her close friend and mentor, Dashiell Hammett, spent several years in jail for his refusal to answer questions put before him by HUAC. During this most painful period, Hellman's strength of character gained her the respect of many; it also reduced her fortune, causing her to sell the farm in upstate New York that she and Hammett had shared together, a sale to which she later referred with a poignant yet resigned wistfulness.

Writing during a time when many women encountered gender discrimination, Lillian Hellman attained acceptance for her work by the public and critics alike. That she seized the opportunity to defend free speech during a time of grotesque political inquiry—and that many respected and accepted her after she did so—further enabled Lillian Hellman to prove that she was resilient yet unbending, sensitive but tough. This was perhaps the secret of her success, and this was confirmed by the wide public she reached with her autobiographical writings in her later years.

tempts to discredit Senator Joseph McCarthy's anti-Communist campaign tactics. Benton charges that McCarthy is using a Hitler-like approach.

20 MARCH 1952
International On a vote of 66 to 10, the Japanese Peace Treaty passes the United States Senate.

26 MARCH 1952
National Senator Joseph McCarthy brings suit against Senator William Benton for libel, slander, and conspiracy against him (Benton has attempted to have McCarthy expelled from the Senate).

30 MARCH 1952
National President Truman announces that he will "not be a candidate for re-election." This presents the Democratic Party with a wide-open race for the presidential nomination for the first time since 1932.

2 APRIL 1952
International George F. Kennan becomes United States ambassador to the Soviet Union.

8 APRIL 1952
National To avoid a steel strike, President Truman orders a federal takeover of steel mills in Youngstown, Ohio. The Supreme Court rules this seizure unconstitutional June 2 in *Youngstown Sheet and Tube* v. *Sawyer*, the most important decision limiting the power of the president save for *U.S.* v. *Nixon* (1974).

9 APRIL 1952
National The federal courts deny three major steel companies the temporary restraining orders they request after President Truman's takeover of steel mills.

26 APRIL 1952
Regional After colliding with the aircraft carrier *Wasp*, the United States destroyer *Hobson* sinks in mid-Atlantic.

28 APRIL 1952
International President Truman formally announces the end of a state of war between the U.S. and Japan. General Ridgway is named supreme commander of Allied troops in Europe, replacing General Eisenhower.

8 MAY 1952
Science Secretary of the Army Frank Pace announces the development of an atomic cannon.

12 MAY 1952
International General Mark Clark receives appointment to head United Nations troops in the Far East. The first woman ambassador to the United States is received in the nation's capital—her Excellency Shrimati Vijaya Lakshmi Pandit, of India.

23 MAY 1952
National Railroad owners regain control of lines

that have been under United States Army jurisdiction since August 27, 1950.

26 MAY 1952
International The United States, Britain, France and West Germany sign a peace treaty at Bonn.

1 JUNE 1952
National President Truman meets with General Eisenhower after the latter returns from Europe as commander of Allied Forces.

2 JUNE 1952
National In a 6-3 decision, the United States Supreme Court rules against President Truman's takeover of the steel industry. As the latter reverts to private ownership once more, over 600,000 workers go out on strike.

14 JUNE 1952
Science At ceremonies in Groton, Connecticut, President Truman lays the keel of the first United States atomic-powered submarine, *Nautilus*.

25 JUNE 1952
National President Truman vetoes the McCarran-Walter Bill, legislation to limit immigration.

27 JUNE 1952
National The McCarran-Walter Act becomes law as the United States Senate passes it, 57-26. The act retains a quota system for determining immigration levels, a system derived from a count of nationalities in the country made in 1920.

28 JUNE 1952
National Congress votes to extend existing wage and rent controls.

7 JULY 1952
National The Republican National Convention meets at Chicago. Eisenhower successfully wins the presidential nomination on the first ballot, against Senator Robert A. Taft. Richard M. Nixon of California is chosen as Eisenhower's running mate. The Republican platform includes a balanced budget, reduced national debt and retention of the Taft-Hartley Act.

14 JULY 1952
National Price controls on virtually all fresh and processed vegetables and meats are removed.

16 JULY 1952
National To provide for veterans of the Korean conflict, Congress passes the Korean GI Bill of Rights to ensure educational benefits, loan guarantees and similar provisions.

21 JULY 1952
National The Democratic National Convention opens in Chicago. Running for six days, it yields Adlai Stevenson as the third-ballot winner of the nom-

ADLAI E. STEVENSON, 1900-1965

Among the Presidential also-rans in American history, few have commanded the enduring respect of Adlai Stevenson. Although he was elected to only one major political office in his lifetime, he is still regarded as one of the century's great statesmen. Stevenson was born on February 5, 1900 in Los Angeles, where his father was a newspaper manager. The family had long been prominent in Illinois; Stevenson's grandfather was Grover Cleveland's vice-president and his great-grandfather a close friend of Lincoln. Stevenson returned to Illinois for part of his schooling, later studying at Princeton and at Harvard Law. Receiving his law degree from Northwestern in 1926, he began practice in 1927.

Over the next 15 years Stevenson alternated private law practice with political appointments in Washington and Illinois. By 1945 he was an assistant to the Secretary of State and centrally involved in organizing the new United Nations, where he was a delegate in 1946 and 1947. Stevenson emerged from comparative obscurity in 1948 to run successfully for governor of Illinois. He was a remarkably effective and popular governor, and in the four years of his term his national reputation became such that by 1952 he was considered the leading Democratic Presidential candidate. Having promised to run for a second term in Illinois, Stevenson did not seek the Democratic nomination. Nonetheless, the 1952 Democratic Convention drafted him as the party candidate to run against Dwight D. Eisenhower.

Stevenson's calm and intelligent manner—he was often called an "egghead"—could not quite capture the imagination of the nation as did the popular General Eisenhower; in 1952 and again in 1956 he lost the election. But Stevenson continued to be regarded as leader of his party throughout the 50s until the rise of John F. Kennedy. In 1960 the *Washington Post* observed, "holding no public office for nearly eight years, he has nevertheless remained a symbol of what American leadership can mean in intellect, idealism, and courage." In 1961 President Kennedy appointed Stevenson as Ambassador to the United Nations; although he often seemed out of step with the Kennedy and Johnson administrations, he served with distinction in that post until his death on July 14, 1965.

ination for president. Stevenson's running mate is Senator John Sparkman of Alabama.

24 JULY 1952
National The steel strike, has immobilized the industry for weeks and ends as labor and management reach a agreement on wage and price increases.

25 JULY 1952
International Puerto Rico becomes a Commonwealth under United States jurisdiction.

31 JULY 1952
National Former commander of United Nations forces in Korea General Douglas MacArthur becomes chairman of the board of Remington Rand.

4 AUGUST 1952
International In Honolulu, United States Secretary

of State Acheson addresses the first session of the Pacific Council. He calls the Japanese peace treaty "one building block in the structure of peace."

23 SEPTEMBER 1952
National Richard Nixon, under pressure to step aside as Eisenhower's vice–presidential candidate because of charges that he has had a "secret slush fund," makes a television appearance in which he says he has never profited personally from the contributions. This "Checkers Speech"—in reference to the Nixon family's dog, a gift that Nixon says he will never give back—is blatantly emotional, but the Republicans and Eisenhower reaffirm their support of Nixon.

13 OCTOBER 1952
National Julius and Ethel Rosenberg have their appeal of espionage conviction rejected by the United States Supreme Court.

23 OCTOBER 1952
Regional In New York City, eight teachers are dismissed by the Board of Education for alleged Communist activities.

4 NOVEMBER 1952
National Dwight D. Eisenhower wins the 1952 race for President, garnering 33,927,549 votes out of 61,547,861 votes cast. He received the electoral votes of all but nine states—442 to 89.
Regional In the Senate race in Connecticut, William Benton loses his seat to William Purtell. In part, Benton suffers defeat because of his encounter with Senator Joseph McCarthy and the resulting lawsuit brought by McCarthy against Benton.

10 NOVEMBER 1952
National The United States Supreme Court rules in favor of a lower court decision barring segregation in interstate railway travel.

16 NOVEMBER 1952
Science The United States Atomic Energy Commission announces that it has completed hydrogen bomb testing at Eniwetok Atoll in the Marshall Islands.

18 NOVEMBER 1952
National President Truman meets with President-elect Eisenhower to discuss the transition of administrations.

20 NOVEMBER 1952
National President-elect Eisenhower names John Foster Dulles as Secretary of State.

21 NOVEMBER 1952
National American Federation of Labor president William Green dies in Coshocton, Ohio. Green was 82.

25 NOVEMBER 1952
National To fill the vacancy created by William

EMERGING AS A WORLD POWER 1946-

Green's death, George Meany is appointed AFL president.

4 DECEMBER 1952
National United Auto Workers president Walter Reuther is chosen to head the CIO.

5 DECEMBER 1952
International President-elect Eisenhower visits Korea in the hope of breaking a stalemate in truce talks. He also visits front lines.

17 DECEMBER 1952
National John Foster Dulles meets in New York City with President-elect Eisenhower and General Douglas MacArthur. They discuss the threat of Communism and the current situation in the Korean truce negotiations.

OTHER EVENTS OF 1952
Science Drs. Felix Bloch and Edward Mills Purcell receive the Nobel Prize in Physics. The Nobel Prize in Medicine and Physiology goes to Dr. Selman Waksman, whose research led to the discovery of streptomycin.
Arts/Culture Herman Wouk's novel *The Caine Mu-*

tiny receives the Pulitzer Prize.

7 JANUARY 1953
National President Truman gives his State of the Union message, warning in particular of the dangers of atomic war.
Senator John W. Bricker of Ohio proposes a Constitutional Amendment to limit United States participation in treaties.

9 JANUARY · 1953
National Federal budget estimates are projected at $78,587,000,000; total expected Federal revenues for the year are $68,665,000,000.

16 JANUARY 1953
National Prior to his departure from office, President Truman sets aside offshore oil reserves as Federal property.

20 JANUARY 1953
National Dwight D. Eisenhower is inaugurated President of the United States.

21 JANUARY 1953
National A federal jury in New York convicts 13

President-elect Eisenhower reviews the Korean conflict, December 1952.

JOHN FOSTER DULLES, 1888-1959

John Foster Dulles was one of the primary architects of America's midcentury crusade against the Communist Menace, a crusade which was born within the apparent moral certainties of two world wars and which died for a time within the moral uncertainties of the Vietnam War. Dulles was born in Washington, D.C. on February 25, 1888; his ancestry included several ministers and two secretaries of state. He was admitted to the bar in 1911 and for much of his life was a prominent international lawyer and financial advisor. In 1919 he gained his first major diplomatic experience as a member of the Reparations Commission of the Versailles Conference.

In the 20s and 30s Dulles was involved in a number of international conferences dealing with finance and peace. A deeply religious man, he came to feel that "the nations of the West must recover their lost sense of spiritual purpose." In the late 40s he was a U.S. delegate to the new United Nations, and in 1951 was chief negotiator of the peace treaty with Japan. His growing reputation led to his appointment as Secretary of State by Eisenhower in 1953.

This period was the heart of the Cold War with Russia and of the McCarthy period in America. It was appropriate that it should be Dulles leading the American assault against Communism. He said that when necessary the country must go to the brink of war to achieve its goal of disrupting Communism wherever it appeared, anywhere in the world, and it was Dulles who gave the thrust to the foreign policy of the Eisenhower administration. The full support of the Nationalist Chinese against the Communist Chinese, of the South Vietnamese against the North Vietnamese, of almost any government so long as it opposed Communism—these were largely the result of Dulles's commitment. To his death in 1959, he remained the vigilant Cold Warrior, convinced of the righteousness of his cause and of its ultimate triumph.

Communists on charges of conspiracy to overthrow the United States government.

1 FEBRUARY 1953
National President Eisenhower is received into membership in the National Presbyterian Church in Washington, D.C.

2 FEBRUARY 1953
National In his State of the Union message, President Eisenhower says that the Seventh Fleet can "no longer be employed to shield Communist China." This is to allow the forces of Chiang Kai-Shek on Taiwan to take the offensive against the mainland.

5 FEBRUARY 1953
National The American Iron and Steel Institute reports the United States steel production is at 117,500,000 short tons yearly.

6 FEBRUARY 1953
National The Office of Price Stabilization lifts controls on wages and salaries.

12 FEBRUARY 1953
National Price controls on eggs, poultry, tires and gasoline are lifted.

13 FEBRUARY 1953
National Senator Joseph McCarthy states that Eisenhower's foreign policy is being "sabotaged" by the Voice of America radio network.

20 FEBRUARY 1953
National Secretary of State John Foster Dulles proposes a resolution to Congress that decries "the forcible absorption of free peoples."

5 MARCH 1953
International Joseph Stalin, dictator Premier of the U.S.S.R., dies in Moscow.

17 MARCH 1953
National The Office of Price Stabilization ends its controls on all prices.

18 MARCH 1953
National The Eisenhower administration protests the Soviet Union's firing upon a United States bomber in international waters.

25 MARCH 1953
National Senator Joseph McCarthy attempts to block confirmation of Charles Bohlen, nominated as Ambassador to the Soviet Union. McCarthy charges that Bohlen has a past of close ties to FDR's and Truman's foreign policies, enough to disqualify him.

26 MARCH 1953
International In talks with French Premier René Mayer, President Eisenhower makes a commitment of aid to France in the latter's war in Indo–China.

27 MARCH 1953
National Charles Bohlen is confirmed as Ambassador to the Soviet Union by a vote of 74-13.

1 APRIL 1953
National An Act of Congress establishes the Department of Health, Education and Welfare (HEW).

6 APRIL 1953
National Secretary of State John Foster Dulles speaks out against the proposed Bricker Amendment, saying that it would be "dangerous to our peace and security."

11 APRIL 1953
National President Eisenhower names Oveta Culp Hobby of Texas as HEW Secretary.

24 APRIL 1953
National In a report issued by the Internal Revenue Service, taxes collected by the IRS in the previous year reach a record high of $68,500,000,000.

25 APRIL 1953
National As a response to President Truman's action

of January 16 concerning the Federal authority over off-shore oil, Senator Wayne Morse of Oregon heads the opposition to a bill which would reverse Truman's decision and return those off-shore rights to individual states.

5 MAY 1953

National The United States Senate votes on off-shore rights, preserving the states' control over the petroleum reserves. The vote is 56-35 despite Senator Morse's filibuster of 22½ consecutive hours.

11 MAY 1953

Regional A series of tornadoes sweeps through Waco and San Antonio, Texas, leaving 124 dead.

22 MAY 1953

National President Eisenhower signs the Submerged

DWIGHT D. EISENHOWER, 1890-1969

Preceded by his reputation as supreme commander of Allied forces in Europe during World War II, Dwight D. Eisenhower was swept into his first elected office as the nation's 34th President. And although "Ike" seemed exactly right for both positions, few would have predicted this when he was growing up in his poor, hardworking and pious family in the frontier town of Abilene, Kansas. Eisenhower went on to graduate from West Point in 1915 and then spent the early years of his Army career in training posts. As General Douglas MacArthur's Chief of Staff, Eisenhower spent some years in the mid-30s in the Philippines. By the time the United States entered World War II, Eisenhower had already been picked as a leader by his superiors, but his meteoric rise to the position of commanding general of American forces in Europe was due to his thoroughness as well as a keen sense of strategy. He then met the many challenges presented by the post of Supreme Commander of Allied Forces in Europe, directing an incredibly complex consortium of staff, personnel and materiel that eventually produced the surrender of the Germans in May 1945. No one individual could take full credit, but Eisenhower deserves as much credit as any single person.

Given a hero's welcome, Eisenhower's return to civilian life saw him installed as president of Columbia University, a tenure which was interrupted by his appointment as NATO commander. Eisenhower, well-liked and with a strong public following, received the Republican nomination for president in 1952. Winning the November election by a landslide, Eisenhower scored 33.9 million popular votes to Adlai Stevenson's 27.3 million. In office, Eisenhower concerned himself primarily with challenges to national security, an area with which he was most familiar. While his foreign policy emphasized the containment of Communism, he was careful to place limits on defense spending even as he was successful in bringing the Korean conflict to a halt. These combined factors contributed to his continued popularity. In the area of domestic security, Eisenhower signed the Communist Control Act, but acted with a sense of caution, attempting to keep a distance from the Army--McCarthy hearings, the execution of the Rosenbergs, and the denial of security clearance for J. Robert Oppenheimer, former AEC head.

Eisenhower suffered a mild heart attack on September 24, 1955, but was healthy enough to once more defeat Adlai Stevenson in the 1956 race for President. During his second term of office, United States efforts to monitor Soviet military developments caused embarrassment in May 1960 when an American U-2 spy plane was shot down within Soviet air space. Eisenhower left office in 1961 warning the nation of the political dangers inherent in a growing military-industrial complex. Having seen the nation through the initial phases of a period of rapid economic growth, Eisenhower was regarded by most Americans as a genial and competent chief executive whose administration was remarkably free from controversy. After he left the White House he returned to his Gettysburg, Pennsylvania, farm where he devoted his time to improving his golf game and to writing his recollections of his military and political career. He died of a heart attack on March 28, 1969.

Lands Act. This legislation allows jurisdiction to coastal states over submerged and reclaimed land.

25 MAY 1953

Science At United States military testing grounds in Nevada, the first atomic artillery shell is fired.

8 JUNE 1953

Regional Ohio and Michigan experience tornadoes that leave 139 dead.

9 JUNE 1953

Regional In yet another tornado, 86 people are killed as a twister rips through central Massachusetts.

12 JUNE 1953

National The CIO signs a contract with United States Steel Corporation providing for an 8½¢ hourly wage increase for steelworkers.

14 JUNE 1953

National President Eisenhower, in an address at Dartmouth College in New Hampshire, warns against "book burners" and thought control.

18 JUNE 1953

International In a message to South Korean President Syngman Rhee, President Eisenhower states that Rhee has violated United Nations command authority. Rhee has released North Korean prisoners of war. In another area of Asia a United States Air Force plane crashes near Tokyo. In this, the worst air mishap in history up to now, 129 lives are lost.

19 JUNE 1953

National At a Federal prison in Ossining, New York, convicted spies Julius and Ethel Rosenberg are executed in the electric chair. They are the first Americans executed for treason during peacetime.

23 JUNE 1953

International United Nations member countries sign a protocol limiting opium production to world scientific and medical needs.

27 JULY 1953
International At Panmunjon, Korea, an armistice is signed by United Nations and North Korean officials, halting the Korean conflict.

29 JULY 1953
International A United States B-50 bomber is shot down by Soviets off the coast of Vladivostok, Siberia.

31 JULY 1953
Population Ohio Senator Robert A. Taft dies in New York City at the age of 63. Known as "Mr. Republican," he was one of the co-authors of the Taft-Hartley Act of 1947.

5 AUGUST 1953
International John Foster Dulles, United States Secretary of State, and Korean President Syngman Rhee meet to discuss policy in Seoul.

7 AUGUST 1953
National Congress signs the Refugee Relief Act, admitting 214,000 more foreign nationals to the U. S.

15 AUGUST 1953
National General Matthew Ridgway becomes United States Army Chief of Staff.

2 SEPTEMBER 1953
Population General Jonathan Wainwright dies at age 70. He commanded United States forces on Corregidor in the Philippines during World War II.

4 SEPTEMBER 1953
International Former commander of the United States 24th Division in Korea, Major General William Dean, captured in 1950, is released at Panmunjon.

8 SEPTEMBER 1953
Population Frederick Vinson, United States Supreme Court Chief Justice, dies at age 63.

10 SEPTEMBER 1953
National Martin Durkin resigns his Cabinet post as

President Dwight D. Eisenhower.

Secretary of Labor over disputes with the Eisenhower administration's enforcement of the Taft-Hartley Act.

16 SEPTEMBER 1953
Science/Technology 20th Century-Fox releases *The Robe*, the first film made in CinemaScope, a process that enhances the depth of the film image.

18 SEPTEMBER 1953
International Big Three foreign ministers, representing the United States, Great Britain and France, call on the Soviet Union to meet at Lugano, Switzerland, to discuss issues of world peace.

26 SEPTEMBER 1953
International The United States pledges military and economic aid to Spain in exchange for air and naval bases in that country.

1 OCTOBER 1953
National President Eisenhower employs the Taft-Hartley Law to prevent a dockworkers' strike.

JONAS SALK, 1914-

For many generations of children and adults before 1954, summers had been a time of pleasure but also of fear. For all those years people never went through a summer without warnings of polio, without seeing people, often friends and family members, in wheelchairs, braces, crutches, iron lungs. In 1952 a polio epidemic in America struck 57,626 people, killing 3300 and crippling many of the rest. It has been given to few human beings in history to eradicate that much fear and suffering, but that is what Dr. Jonas Salk and his associates did.

Salk was born in New York City on October 28, 1914. An exceptional student in his youth, he attended City College in New York and received his MD from NYU Medical School in 1939. During the 40s he worked for the Army on a vaccine for influenza, which was eventually to result in a successful vaccine in the early 50s. The experience gained in this research stood him in good stead when he and his team, working at the University of Pittsburgh's Virus Research Laboratory, turned their attention to polio in the late 40s.

Over a period of years, with funding from the March of Dimes, research went on. In 1953, Salk cautiously announced that the vaccine had been experimentally successful, and massive field trials were begun. To questions of the vaccine's safety, Salk replied that he had vaccinated himself and his family and would take personal responsibility for the results of the tests.

Although there were some deaths from poorly-prepared vaccine samples, the tests were successful and starting in 1955 millions of people around the world began to take the Salk vaccine. In 1961, another polio vaccine, developed by Dr. Albert B. Sabin, also came into widespread use and together these vaccines came to virtually eradicate this great scourge of history. Salk received numerous honors but refused to make any personal profit from his work. In 1963 the Salk Institute for Biological Studies was founded in La Jolla, California, and Salk became its director, leading an international group in their researches.

---

5 OCTOBER 1953
National Earl Warren takes the oath as Chief Justice of the United States Supreme Court.

16 OCTOBER 1953
Regional The Boston Naval Shipyard is the scene of an explosion and fire on the aircraft carrier *Leyte*, with 37 men killed and 40 injured.

3 NOVEMBER 1953
International The Soviet Union refuses to honor Big Three requests for a meeting of foreign ministers unless it includes a representative of Communist China.

23 NOVEMBER 1953
National In reference to the tactics used by Senator Joseph McCarthy, President Eisenhower says that all Americans have the right to confront their accusers "face to face."

24 NOVEMBER 1953
National In a radio and television broadcast, Senator Joseph McCarthy attacks the administration of former President Truman, saying it was "crawling" with Communists.

4 DECEMBER 1953
International President Eisenhower begins a four-day conference in Bermuda, the subject of which is the exchange of atomic information. The United States joins Britain and France.

8 DECEMBER 1953
International President Eisenhower speaks to the United Nations General Assembly in New York City. The President addresses many issues, among them the use of nuclear research in the world community. Eisenhower suggests an "Atoms for Peace" program.

9 DECEMBER 1953
National Following precedents set by other businesses and by the actions of the Federal Government, General Electric Corporation reports that it will dismiss all Communist employees.

16 DECEMBER 1953
National A White House press conference attended by 161 reporters is the first to allow direct quotations in later news reports. The text of the conference is broadcast, and copies are printed in several newspapers.

26 DECEMBER 1953
International The United States announces it will pull two military divisions out of Korea.

OTHER EVENTS OF 1953
Science/Technology The Nobel Prize for Medicine and Physiology goes to American Fritz Lipmann and his English colleague, Hans A. Krebs. Their work is in living cell mechanisms.

Arts/Culture Ernest Hemingway is the recipient of the Pulitzer Prize for his novel *The Old Man and the Sea*.

International George Marshall, former United States Secretary of State, is the winner of the Nobel Peace Prize. He is given this award in recognition for his work on the so-called Marshall Plan of economic aid to Europe.

7 JANUARY 1954
National President Eisenhower delivers his State-of-the-Union message, proposing cuts in military spending.

11 JANUARY 1954
National In hope of better providing for the current and future needs of the American farmer, President Eisenhower proposes replacing rigid farm price supports with those based on "modernized parity." The Department of Agriculture would, under this revamped program, have the power to barter with foreign countries—surplus crops in exchange for strategic goods. Eisenhower, in an address to Congress, asks for changes in the Taft-Hartley Labor law.

12 JANUARY 1954
International Secretary of State John Foster Dulles announces the United States' commitment to a policy of "massive retaliation." The new doctrine meets with severe criticism, foreign and domestic.

19 JANUARY 1954
National General Motors Company announces a $1,000,000,000 program to expand production.

21 JANUARY 1954
Science The first United States nuclear submarine, the *Nautilus*, is launched at Groton, Connecticut.

23 JANUARY 1954
International The Berlin Conference of Big Four foreign ministers opens in Germany.

26 JANUARY 1954
International The Senate consents to a defense treaty between the United States and South Korea.

2 FEBRUARY 1954
Science President Eisenhower makes a report on the first United States hydrogen bomb test in 1952 at Eniwetok Atoll in the Pacific.

18 FEBRUARY 1954
International Meeting in Berlin, the United States, Britain, France and Russia discuss the issues arising from a deteriorating French military position in Indochina. In another, separate, issue, the Big Four ministers find they are unable to reach agreement on reunification of Germany.

23 FEBRUARY 1954
Science Polio vaccine is administered to school children in Pittsburgh, Pennsylvania, after Dr. Jonas E. Salk develops a serum.

1 MARCH 1954
National Puerto Rican nationalists attack five Congressmen in a shooting affray in the House of Representatives; the five are wounded, not critically.

International The United States meets in Caracas, Venezuela, with members of the Organization of American States (OAS) to explore the threat of Communism in member countries.

Science The Marshall Islands in the Pacific are subject to a hydrogen bomb test that exceeds expected proportions.

8 MARCH 1954
International The United States signs a mutual defense treaty with Japan.

10 MARCH 1954
National The United States House of Representatives votes to reduce by 50 percent most excise taxes and federal luxury taxes.

16 MARCH 1954
International France calculates that the greater portion of its expenses in Indochina has been borne by United States military support. The United States has been active in opposing a negotiated settlement as it feels that Southeast Asia would then be doomed to Communist domination.

24 MARCH 1954
Science President Eisenhower reports on the hydrogen bomb test of March 1.

1 APRIL 1954
National President Eisenhower establishes a United States Air Force Academy, similar to West Point and Annapolis. The new military college will be near Colorado Springs, Colorado.

2 APRIL 1954
Regional The International Longshoremen's Association ends a New York City strike, in effect since March 3, 1954.

3 APRIL 1954
International Congress is reluctant to commit the United States to further involvement in Indochina unless Great Britain makes a similar commitment. This decision comes after Secretary of State John Foster Dulles repeatedly urges United States air support to prevent the fall of Dien Bien Phu, the base in northern Vietnam where the French have chosen to make a major stand against the Communist forces.

7 APRIL 1954
International In a statement to the press, President Eisenhower gives his support to continued use of foreign aid for France in Indochina. He reasons that to lose influence in Indochina would encourage South-

east Asia to succumb to Communism like a "falling row of dominoes."

22 APRIL 1954
National The Senate begins hearings over a dispute between Senator Joseph McCarthy and the United States Army, specifically over McCarthy's investigations at Fort Monmouth, New Jersey.

7 MAY 1954
International Dien Bien Phu falls to the Communist Vietnamese and the United States begins to prepare for limited military intervention in Indochina, despite Britain's continued opposition.

13 MAY 1954
National The United States Congress passes the Wiley-Dondero Act providing for a United States-Canadian project of construction of a channel between Montreal and Lake Erie. This act establishes the St. Lawrence Seaway Development Corporation.

17 MAY 1954
National In a landmark ruling having ramifications

Senator Joseph McCarthy at 1954 Army hearings.

for civil rights, the United States Supreme Court finds, in *Brown* v. *Board of Education of Topeka*, that the "separate but equal" doctrine does not offer equal protection under the laws providing public education. The Brown case deals with elementary education, and results in a unanimous decision that desegregation in public schools be accomplished with "all deliberate speed." There is widespread reaction to this ruling and it causes hostility in many areas of the South.
International The United States State Department terms the support of arms from Czechoslovakia to Arbenz–Guzman's Guatemalan government "a development of gravity." The United States had previously taken part in an OAS agreement to discuss ways of curbing Communist infiltration of the Western Hemisphere.

19 MAY 1954
Population Composer Charles Ives dies in New York City. Winner of the 1947 Pulitzer Prize in music, he was 79 years old.

21 MAY 1954
National The United States Senate votes down a proposed Constitutional amendment that would allow 18-year-olds to vote.

26 MAY 1954
Regional In a fire on the U.S.S. *Bennington* in waters off Quonset, Rhode Island, 103 men are killed.

1 JUNE 1954
National A three-man board reviews J. Robert Oppenheimer's request for reinstatement as a consultant for the Atomic Energy Commission. The board denies Oppenheimer's request on a 2-1 vote. Oppenheimer headed the Los Alamos laboratory for atomic research during World War II.

2 JUNE 1954
National Senator Joseph McCarthy charges that the Central Intelligence Agency (CIA) has been infiltrated by Communists.

9 JUNE 1954
International President Eisenhower names Defense Secretary Charles Wilson to head the St. Lawrence Seaway Development Corporation.

15 JUNE 1954
International In response to a French slowdown in military operations in Indochina, the United States refuses further military aid to the French efforts in Southeast Asia.

18 JUNE 1954
International A CIA-supported military force, led by Colonel Carlos Castillo Armas, invades Guatemala from neighboring Honduras.

20 JUNE 1954
International The United Nations Security Council,

meeting at its New York headquarters, calls for cessation of hostilities in Guatemala. The Security Council asks that other nations withhold aid to the attackers of the Arbenz–Guzman regime.

25 JUNE 1954
International President Eisenhower meets with Great Britain's Prime Minister Winston Churchill. At this conference in Washington, the two heads of state

---

CHARLES IVES, 1864-1954

After a New Haven church service before the turn of the century, a lady of the congregation rushed up to the young organist who had just premiered his new Thanksgiving prelude; perhaps he expected some decorous congratulations, but what he heard instead was, "Mr. Ives, it was awful!" For his whole creative life Charles Ives heard little else but condemnation of his astonishingly innovative and deeply personal style. It took the musical world many years to stretch its ears and catch up with the eccentric Yankee, and to finally recognize him as America's first great composer, "our Washington, Lincoln and Jefferson of music."

Ives was born in Danbury, Connecticut, on October 20, 1874, the son of a bandmaster with a taste for experimentation. His father, George Ives, tinkered incessantly with new instruments, new harmonies, and the like, with sometimes uproarious results, as when he had two bands march past one another playing different tunes. It was his son who later brought these scattered experiments to fruition. In 1894 Ives entered Yale, where he soon learned to keep his already radical notions to himself and to write the kind of "nice" music expected of him.

Upon leaving college, Ives faced the fact that the world was not ready to listen to the music he wanted to write. Thus in 1898 he entered the insurance business in New York; within 15 years he and a partner had developed the largest agency in the country. Incredibly, during this same period he was a prolific composer, using his evenings and weekends to turn out a series of works, written at white-hot intensity, that anticipated every later musical innovation of the century. Into his music he poured his musical experience: the popular hymns and marches of his youth, along with the experiments of his father and the wrong notes and scattered rhythms that the common people added to their music, which to Ives were not mistakes but rather signs of human feeling. Allied with these concepts was the transcendental philosophy of Emerson and Thoreau, which began with the ordinary to discover the sublime.

By 1918, after completing his greatest and most far-reaching work, the *Fourth Symphony,* Ives was exhausted, worn down by his double life and by the continual rejection of his music. Often his wife, Harmony Ives, was his only supporter. That year he suffered a serious heart attack and was never healthy again. By 1921 he had virtually ceased composing. But slowly the world began to notice; the 1939 premier of the *Concord Sonata* was greeted as "the greatest music composed by an American," and in 1947 he won the Pulitzer Prize for the *Third Symphony,* finished back in 1911. Ives's music was to remain controversial, as he surely would have wished, but by his death in 1954 he was acclaimed both as a prophet and as a unique and peculiarly American genius.

---

discuss matters pertaining to world peace.

29 JUNE 1954
National The Atomic Energy Commission concurs with the decision made on June 1 to deny security clearance to J. Robert Oppenheimer. The AEC vote is 4-1. The CIO and U.S. Steel Corporation sign a two-year labor agreement that provides wage increases and expanded welfare benefits.

International Due, in part, to aid provided by the CIA, the Arbenz–Guzman government in Guatemala is overthrown by anti-Communist insurgents. The latter install a junta. President Eisenhower and Prime Minister Winston Churchill wind up their discussions in Washington, D.C.

12 JULY 1954
National President Eisenhower proposes a highway modernization program by state and Federal governments.

13 JULY 1954
National The Department of Commerce announces the 1953 gross national product to be $365,000,000,000.

21 JULY 1954
International The Geneva agreement is signed by Big Four countries, signaling an end to the Indochina war after French troop withdrawal.

26 JULY 1954
National Henry Cabot Lodge, Jr. is renamed to the head of the United States delegation to the United Nations.

2 AUGUST 1954
National President Eisenhower signs the Housing Act of 1954, which will help alleviate housing shortages. The new bill will provide 35,000 housing units. A Senate committee to investigate charges of misconduct against Senator Joseph McCarthy is organized by senators concerned over possible damage to their legislative body.

11 AUGUST 1954
International After Eisenhower's February 2, 1953 statement, which lifted the United States blockade of Taiwan, Communist Chinese Foreign Minister Chou En-lai indicates Red Chinese intentions to attack Taiwan.

17 AUGUST 1954
International In response to Chou En-lai's declaration of an intended attack on Taiwan, President Eisenhower states that "any invasion of Formosa would have to run over the 7th Fleet."

24 AUGUST 1954
National President Eisenhower signs the Communist Control Act that strips the Communist Party in America of privileges and immunities, and subjects the Party to penalties under the Internal Security Act (Mc-

EMERGING AS A WORLD POWER 1946-

Carran Act).

30 AUGUST 1954
National President Eisenhower signs the Atomic Energy Bill, which will allow for private ownership of atomic reactors to produce electrical power. The act provides for the sharing of information on atomic weaponry with the European allies.

1 SEPTEMBER 1954
National Social Security Act amendments add another seven million workers to those already covered by Social Security. It primarily affects self-employed farmers.
Regional New England and much of Long Island, New York, is struck by a hurricane with 68 reported dead, and property losses near $500,000,000.

HENRY CABOT LODGE, JR., 1902-

A man of distinguished lineage with a seemingly unerring instinct for the appropriate, Henry Cabot Lodge, Jr. became a key figure in both the early years of United States involvement in Vietnam and the Vietnam Peace talks of the 1960s.

The tradition of commitment to a cause—handed down from his Massachusetts colonial ancestors and maintained by his father (outspoken Massachusetts Senator Henry Cabot Lodge, Sr.)—endowed Lodge with the drive necessary for the public life he began as a United States Senator. His successful 1936 bid for a Massachusetts seat was repeated in 1942, but with the United States in World War II, Lodge resigned and joined the military, thus becoming the first United States Senator since the Civil War to do so. Lodge attained the rank of major general in the Army, but his tour of duty was shortened by the Secretary of State who deemed Lodge more valuable to America's war efforts as a Senator than as a military officer. Lodge subsequently headed up Eisenhower's Presidential campaign, despite the drain on his own political career. Lodge was edged out in the 1952 Senate race by John F. Kennedy, but Eisenhower named him Ambassador to the United Nations, a position he held from 1953 to 1960. It was here that Lodge made his mark as an able diplomat, deftly debating the controversy surrounding Suez and Lebanon, and the dramatic upheaval in Hungary during the mid-1950s.

Henry Cabot Lodge vied again, unsuccessfully, for elected office in 1960 as vice-president on the Nixon ticket. Ever the implacable New Englander, Lodge was recruited as Ambassador to South Vietnam by President Kennedy, who wished to provide bi-partisan support for his Vietnam policy-making. Lodge was groomed by heredity and decades of public service for this diplomatic berth. He left South Vietnam when the war began to escalate and became United States Ambassador-at-Large, the United States Ambassador to Germany. Called on to utilize his diplomatic skills and his knowledge of Vietnam, Lodge was named chief negotiator at the Paris Peace Talks in 1969, where he served for 12 months. Then after nearly 40 years in public life, Henry Cabot Lodge withdrew from his formerly significant role in Republican national politics, dedicating himself to his personal affairs and family business interests.

---

3 SEPTEMBER 1954
National Congress approves a measure to impose the death penalty for espionage during peacetime.

6 SEPTEMBER 1954
Regional President Eisenhower attends groundbreaking for the first atomic power plant in Pittsburgh.

8 SEPTEMBER 1954
International The United States joins seven other countries in the signing of a collective defense treaty for the Pacific. The Southeast Asian Treaty Organization (SEATO) is to be comprised of Australia, Great Britain, New Zealand, Pakistan, the Philippines, Thailand and the United States. Secretary of State Dulles makes provision for United States involvement in this SEATO pact conditional: The United States will respond "only to Communist aggression."

10 SEPTEMBER 1954
Regional A hurricane rips through Cape Hatteras, North Carolina, and leaves 22 dead and $50,000,000 worth of damage.

12 SEPTEMBER 1954
National President Eisenhower meets with the National Security Council, concerned about the possibility of atomic war, and decides against military action in the Red China-Taiwan conflict.

27 SEPTEMBER 1954
National Senator Arthur Watkins heads the Special Senate Committee that calls, unanimously, for Senator Joseph McCarthy's censure.
International As a means of improving the radar stations protecting the United States and Canada from surprise attack, the two nations agree on a Distant Early Warning (DEW) line, the third string of radar stations north of the United States-Canadian border, to reach from Arctic Canada to Greenland.

11 OCTOBER 1954
National As a result of passage of the Communist Control Act on August 24, the Civil Service Commission has dismissed over 2600 persons from federal employment.

13 OCTOBER 1954
Science The United States Air Force approves production of the first supersonic bomber, the B-58.

25 OCTOBER 1954
National A Cabinet meeting is televised for the first time.

30 OCTOBER 1954
International The United States Government promises nearly $6,500,000 in support of recently-elected Guatemalan president Carlos Castillo Armas.

2 NOVEMBER 1954
National In mid-term elections, the House and the

Senate are once more under Democratic control. Democrats in the Senate have a 1-seat margin, while in the House they enjoy a 29-seat margin over Republicans.

16 NOVEMBER 1954
Science Enrico Fermi wins the special award of the Atomic Energy Commission, the sum of $25,000, for his many contributions to nuclear physics.

27 NOVEMBER 1954
National Alger Hiss, convicted of perjury, leaves prison after serving 44 months. He received national attention in 1948 when questioned, first by the House Un-American Activities Committee and then by a Federal Grand Jury, about Communist activities while a government employee. Hiss was found guilty in November 1950 and despite appeals was sent to prison.

2 DECEMBER 1954
National Senator Joseph McCarthy is condemned by his Senate colleagues because of his conduct during the recent Army-McCarthy hearings. This marks an end to his four-year campaign against domestic Communism.
International The United States and Taiwan sign a mutual defense treaty.

11 DECEMBER 1954
National The U.S.S. *Forrestal* is launched at Newport News, Virginia, a 59,650-ton aircraft carrier, the largest ever constructed.

16 DECEMBER 1954
National President Eisenhower names Nelson A. Rockefeller as special assistant to the administration in foreign policy.

31 DECEMBER 1954
National In its highest volume of trading since 1933, the New York Stock Exchange reports 573,374,622 shares traded during the past year.

OTHER EVENTS OF 1954
Science The Nobel Prize for Medicine and Physiology goes to Doctors John Enders, Thomas Weller, and Frederick Robbins. The three receive the award for their research in polio virus culture. Dr. Linus Pauling receives the Nobel Prize in Chemistry.
Arts/Culture The Nobel Prize for Literature goes to Ernest Hemingway.

1 JANUARY 1955
International The United States Foreign Operations Administration begins sending aid to Southeast Asia. Cambodia, Laos and South Vietnam will receive $216,000,000 from the United States this year.

5 JANUARY 1955
National Sam Rayburn of Texas is elected Speaker of the House of Representatives as the 84th Congress opens its first session.

6 JANUARY 1955
National In his State of the Union message, President Eisenhower calls for cooperation by Democrats and Republicans in making the United States a leader in world peace.

8 JANUARY 1955
Science Medical researchers announce the discovery of two new drugs, reserpine and thorazine, both having been used with some success in treating patients with mental disorders.

9 JANUARY 1955
National The Atomic Energy Commission announces that private industry will soon be able to operate atomic power plants.

14 JANUARY 1955
National Reaffirming the government's commitment

JOSEPH McCARTHY, 1908-1957

Joseph McCarthy's star rose in 1950 from near obscurity into the national political sky, burned furiously for four years, and ended in decline. Few politicians ever monopolized the attention of the nation and threw into such turmoil its most prestigious legislative assembly as did this aggressive, flamboyant Red-hunter' from rural Wisconsin.

An ungainly, withdrawn child, McCarthy as an adolescent, and later as an adult, concealed his insecurities behind a facade of overwhelming amiability and irreverent bellicosity. After an undistinguished Pacific tour of duty as a Marine during World War II, an unsophisticated yet cocky Joe McCarthy turned from law practice to Republican politics as a way of employing his restless energies. First as a circuit court judge and then as a first-term United States Senator, McCarthy's audacious flaunting of the rules of judicial and legislative decorum gained quick notoriety but little respect from his colleagues.

Seizing upon the anti-Communist issue to regain his Senate seat, McCarthy dominated the headlines month after month following his attack on the State Department on February 9, 1950 at Wheeling, West Virginia. McCarthy's statement, "I have here in my hand a list of 205 that were known . . . as being members of the Communist Party," increased his political attention and further stimulated the calculated demagogue in the man. No individual, however exalted his office or illustrious his career, was safe from McCarthy's verbal assaults or tempestuous behavior. His search for Communists in the government led ultimately to televised Senate hearings beginning in April, and lasting until June 17, 1954.

Growing ever more wild in his accusations and arrogant in his treatment of the President, the United States Army and the Senate itself, Joe McCarthy's conduct became too destructive for all but his closest associates to tolerate. Ultimately censured by the Senate in a 67 to 22 vote of condemnation, McCarthy declined into alcoholic obscurity. He died at Bethesda, Maryland, on May 2, 1957, remembered chiefly for his violation of democratic procedure, his name having become synonymous with an era of suspicion, fear and investigative excess.

to rid the nation of Communism, the United States Senate votes 84-0 to continue its investigation of Communist activities by government employees.

17 JANUARY 1955

National The Federal Government announces its projected 1955 fiscal year budget: expenditures total $62,408,000,000 while revenues are projected at $60,000,000,000.

19 JANUARY 1955

National President Eisenhower takes part in the first televised press conference.

25 JANUARY 1955

International The Republic of Panama and the United States sign a treaty in which both agree to cooperate over issues pertaining to the Panama Canal.

29 JANUARY 1955

National Congress passes a resolution permitting President Eisenhower to call for troop mobilization in the event Taiwan is attacked by Communist China.

1 FEBRUARY 1955

International The Southeast Asian Collective Defense Treaty passes Congressional ratification. The SEATO Council prepares to meet.

15 FEBRUARY 1955

National According to an Atomic Energy Commission report, a hydrogen bomb explosion has the capacity to devastate a 700-square-mile area.

23 FEBRUARY 1955

International SEATO Council members convene for a three-day meeting in Bangkok, Thailand.

1 MARCH 1955

National The salaries of Congressmen and Federal Judges are increased by nearly 50 percent in a bill passed by the House.

10 MARCH 1955

National President Eisenhower indicates that, in event of war, the United States would use nuclear weapons.

28 MARCH 1955

National President Eisenhower names John Marshall Harlan an Associate Justice of the United States Supreme Court.

1 APRIL 1955

International After the Senate consents to negotiations concerning the future of West Germany, the Federal Republic of Germany receives sovereignty.

12 APRIL 1955

Science In a report from the Polio Vaccine Evaluation Center at the University of Michigan, the Salk vaccine is termed successful after numerous tests made nationwide during 1954.

10 MAY 1955

National After some consideration of statehood for Alaska and Hawaii, the House of Representatives refers legislation back to committee.

International Continuing in his quest for a summit conference to promote world peace, President Eisenhower states he will meet "anyone, anywhere."

15 MAY 1955

International The Big Four ministers gather in Vienna to sign the Austrian State Treaty, restoring the country's boundaries to their pre-1938 positions and prohibiting economic union with Germany. The treaty provides for the withdrawal of occupation forces.

19 MAY 1955

National The Federal Trade Commission indicates that business mergers have tripled during the past five years.

23 MAY 1955

Ideas/Beliefs The General Assembly of the Presbyterian Church announces that it will permit ordination of women ministers.

27 MAY 1955

Regional Tornadoes devastate areas of Kansas, Arkansas, Oklahoma, Missouri and Texas, leaving 121 persons dead.

31 MAY 1955

National With reference to the *Brown* v. *Board of Education* ruling made in 1954, the United States Supreme Court decrees that school desegregation will be under Federal District Court jurisdiction. Desegregation of public schools is not to be carried out by any specified time.

6 JUNE 1955

National Ford Motor Company and the UAW reach agreement on contract negotiations that include a supplemental unemployment proviso.

10 JUNE 1955

National Employees of the United States Postal Service receive an eight percent salary hike.

16 JUNE 1955

National The United States House of Representatives votes to extend Selective Service until June 30, 1959.

17 JUNE 1955

International The United States Senate agrees to the Austrian State Treaty in a vote of 63-3.

20 JUNE 1955

International At San Francisco, member countries gather for a tenth anniversary meeting of the United Nations.

22 JUNE 1955
International Soviet fighter planes shoot down a United States Navy patrol plane over the Bering Strait off the coast of Alaska, injuring seven United States airmen.

1 JULY 1955
National 600,000 striking steelworkers go back to work after a 12–hour walkout.

7 JULY 1955
International The Soviet Union offers compensation for the Navy patrol plane shot down over the Bering Strait on June 22.

11 JULY 1955
Regional At its temporary site at Denver, the United States Air Force Academy accepts its first class of 306 cadets. The Academy will later relocate to a permanent site near Colorado Springs.

13 JULY 1955
National The House of Representatives approves a bill to give $1,365,613,520 to the Atomic Energy Commission, the Tennessee Valley Authority and the Public Works Program. In a Cabinet-level change, Oveta Culp Hobby, named to head the HEW office by President Eisenhower, resigns effective August 1.

18 JULY 1955
International President Eisenhower attends a summit conference in Geneva, Switzerland, the first since 1945. Also attending are Great Britain's Prime Minister Anthony Eden; Edgar Faure, French Premier; Soviet Premier N.A. Bulganin. The Soviet Union is also represented by First Secretary of the Communist Party, Nikita Khrushchev. One of the most important results of this conference is the atmosphere of accommodation and cooperation that is achieved by the participants—termed by some the "spirit of Geneva."

21 JULY 1955
Regional The second of the United States' nuclear submarines, the *Sea Wolf*, is launched at Groton, Connecticut.

29 JULY 1955
National The United States government makes known its plans for launching earth–orbiting satellites. The projected date for these launchings is 1957.

1 AUGUST 1955
National President Eisenhower names Marion Bayard Folsom of Georgia Secretary of HEW following Oveta Culp Hobby's resignation earlier in the year.

2 AUGUST 1955
National Congress votes 187-168 to build 45,000 public housing units by July 31, 1956.

8 AUGUST 1955
International At Geneva, the United States meets with members of the International Conference on the Peaceful Uses of Atomic Energy.

12 AUGUST 1955
National In signing a bill that amends the Fair Labor Standards Act, President Eisenhower increases the minimum wage to $1.00 an hour, effective March 1, 1956.

19 AUGUST 1955
Regional After two days of rain and high winds in six Northeastern states, a hurricane leaves 179 dead and property damage of $458,000,000.

24 SEPTEMBER 1955
National President Eisenhower is hospitalized in Denver following a heart attack. The President remains in the hospital for nearly three weeks.

26 SEPTEMBER 1955
National The New York Stock Exchange announces its heaviest single–day dollar loss in history, $44,000,000,000.

6 OCTOBER 1955
National In the worst commercial airline disaster to date, a United Airlines DC-4 crashes in Laramie, Wyoming, killing 66.

7 OCTOBER 1955
National At New York's Naval Shipyard in Brooklyn, the U.S.S. *Saratoga* is launched, displacing 59,600 tons.

18 OCTOBER 1955
Science Nuclear physicists working at the University of California discover a new nuclear particle—the antiproton.

2 NOVEMBER 1955
National President Eisenhower names Rear Admiral Richard E. Byrd to head Antarctic affairs.

22 NOVEMBER 1955
International United States representatives attend the opening session of members of the Baghdad Pact—a mutual defense treaty including Turkey, Pakistan, Iran, Iraq and Great Britain. Although the United States representatives do not sign this treaty, they maintain a position as observers and sit on several committees including the defense committee.

25 NOVEMBER 1955
National The Interstate Commerce Commission bans segregation on trains and buses crossing state lines.

5 DECEMBER 1955
National In a merger of United States labor unions, the American Federation of Labor and Congress of Industrial Organizations combine to form the AFL-CIO. This new group is to be led by former AFL

head George Meany.

12 DECEMBER 1955
National The Ford Foundation announces that it has given a record $500,000,000 to colleges, universities and medical institutions.

17 DECEMBER 1955
International The United States offers Egypt a loan of $56,000,000 for its proposed Aswan High Dam. This project will provide electric power and allow irrigation. Secretary of State John Foster Dulles will later revoke U.S. aid due to Egyptian-Soviet ties.

26 DECEMBER 1955
Regional After five days of floods in California, Nevada and Oregon, the death toll is at 74.
National The reported number of traffic fatalities for the Christmas holiday is a record 609 lives.

OTHER EVENTS OF 1955
Science The Nobel Prize in Chemistry goes to Cornell Medical College researchers Vincent du Vigneaud for hormone studies. For their research in atomic measurements, Polykarp Kusch and Willis Lamb, Jr. receive the Nobel Prize in Physics.

9 JANUARY 1956
Regional In a vote that appears to support segregation, the Virginia legislature passes an amendment allowing state support for private education. This amendment follows the United States Supreme Court ruling ordering desegregation of public schools. The ruling has resulted in the temporary closing of Virginia's schools.

6 FEBRUARY 1956
Civil Rights The University of Alabama enrolls its first black student, Autherine Lucy, who is suspended after three days of violent unrest and near rioting.

15 FEBRUARY 1956
Regional A Federal court in New Orleans rules against all state laws supporting segregation, banned by the Supreme Court in 1954.

17 FEBRUARY 1956
National After disclosures that Senator Francis Case of South Dakota was offered campaign funding by oil interests, President Eisenhower vetoes a bill that would have removed Federal price controls from independent natural gas production.

29 FEBRUARY 1956
National President Eisenhower announces he is willing to serve a second term.

1 MARCH 1956
Civil Rights The National Association for the Advancement of Colored People (NAACP) has brought suit against the University of Alabama on behalf of Autherine Lucy, suspended on February 6. Ms. Lucy is expelled from the university.

7 MARCH 1956
International President Eisenhower turns down a request by Israel to purchase military arms from the United States. It comes after the Soviet Union has provided military equipment to Egypt.

20 MARCH 1956
National A 156-day strike at Westinghouse Electric Corporation ends as union and company spokesmen agree on a contract.

27 MARCH 1956
National The *Daily Worker* is seized by the Internal Revenue Service. The IRS claims nonpayment of taxes, and in New York, Chicago and Detroit, members of the newspaper staff post funds sufficient for reopening.

3 APRIL 1956
Regional Michigan, Wisconsin, Oklahoma, Kansas,

WALTER REUTHER, 1907-1970

Walter Reuther, long-time president of the United Auto Workers, was one of the preeminent labor leaders of his time. He was born in Wheeling, West Virginia on September 1, 1907 and would become the third generation of labor activists in his family. Dropping out of high school to apprentice as a tool and die maker, his union-organizing activities got him fired from his first job. Unable to find work after a second firing—by Ford in 1933—Reuther toured Europe on a bicycle, finally working for 16 months at the Gorky auto plant in Russia. He returned to Detroit in 1935 and within a year was president of Local 174 of the UAW, which soon affiliated with the Congress of Industrial Organizations during a period of intensive organizing and strikes. At this time he renounced his earlier Socialist beliefs, thereafter promoting the idea of a "mixed" economy involving both private and public ownership.

Reuther came to national attention in 1940 when he proposed an elaborate plan, later partially adopted, for utilizing facilities of the auto industry for the mass production of military airplanes. During the war he was appointed to the labor-management committee of the War Manpower Commission. As soon as the war ended, Reuther helped organize a major strike against General Motors; during this successful and precedent-setting 113-day strike he was elected president of the UAW, which post he held until his death. Over the next few years his union made massive gains in collective-bargaining rights, cost-of-living increases and unemployment benefits. Reuther was also at this time a member of the NAACP executive board and an active opponent of racial discrimination in jobs.

In 1952 Reuther became president of the CIO, which merged with the American Federation of Labor in 1955. However, impatient with that organization's progress in various reforms, Reuther took the UAW out of the CIO in 1969, affiliating with the Teamsters to form the Alliance for Labor Action. In the midst of his continuing activities he was killed in a plane crash in 1970.

Mississippi, Arkansas and Tennessee are hit by tornadoes, leaving over 45 people dead or missing, thousands homeless and extensive property losses.

5 APRIL 1956
National Labor columnist Victor Riesel, an oppo-

CIVIL RIGHTS MOVEMENT

It hardly seemed like a very remarkable incident, but when Mrs. Rosa Parks was arrested on December 1, 1955, for refusing to yield her seat to a white man on a Montgomery bus, it triggered a ten-year campaign by blacks against the South's segregation laws. Encouraged by a Supreme Court decision the previous year (*Brown* v. *Board of Education at Topeka*) outlawing segregated public schools, the NAACP took Mrs. Parks's case to test Alabama's "Jim Crow" busing law. Local black leaders, including a young pastor named Martin Luther King Jr., also organized a city-wide bus boycott to protest the arrest. For the next year, the city's blacks walked, carpooled or taxied to work while bus company revenues plummeted to 35 percent of their former level. Then in November 1956 the Supreme Court struck down Alabama's laws requiring segregated buses.

The boycott had been so successful that in 1957 black leaders formed the Southern Christian Leadership Conference to continue a "direct action" assault on segregation. Strictly adhering to a philosophy of nonviolence, the organization sponsored a wide range of protests against "Jim Crow" public facilities. Then in February 1960, a "sit-in" by four black college students at a "whites only" lunch counter in Greensboro, North Carolina, brought a wave of similar demonstrations throughout the South. The following year, the newly formed Student Nonviolent Coordinating Committee helped sponsor a series of "freedom rides" to implement a federal directive ordering desegregation on all interstate buses.

The freedom rides, like most of the other black demonstrations, brought violent reprisals from Southern whites; the terrorism, however, generated a huge groundswell of support for the civil rights movement in the North and put pressure on Congress to act on behalf of the blacks. A brutal assault by Birmingham police on nonviolent marchers in the spring of 1963 particularly outraged public sentiment and led Kennedy to push for the passage of a strong Civil Rights Bill. That summer, some 250,000 demonstrators staged a march on Washington to rally support for the law, and in July 1964 Congress responded by passing the comprehensive Civil Rights Act outlawing discrimination in all public facilities. The murder of three civil rights workers in the summer of 1964 during a massive black voter registration drive again underscored the need for federal intervention. In 1965, Congress enacted a tough Voting Rights Act, making possible for the first time since Reconstruction the full participation of blacks in state and federal elections.

After the passage of the Voting Rights Act, discrimination still remained, but it was now more economic and informal than legal. Although King wished to continue the struggle, his leadership and nonviolent tactics came under increasing criticism after 1965 from more militant black crusaders. The splintering of the black movement, rising black militancy and the ghetto riots of the late 1960s all combined to undermine support for further reforms, but there could never again be any legal denial of the fundamental civil rights of American minorities.

---

nent of racketeering, loses sight in both eyes as the result of acid thrown in his face by an attacker.

8 APRIL 1956
Regional Six Marine recruits drown at Parris Island, South Carolina, while on a disciplinary march. Platoon sergeant Matthew McKeon is charged with negligent homicide.

11 APRIL 1956
Regional President Eisenhower gives approval to a power project for the upper Colorado River. It will provide irrigation for the region.

19 APRIL 1956
International One of the most publicized marriages of the century occurs between Hollywood actress Grace Kelly and Prince Rainier III of Monaco. Kelly won an Academy Award in 1954 for Best Actress.

2 MAY 1956
Ideas/Beliefs At its annual conference at Minneapolis, the Methodist Church calls for an end to all segregation in the church. This reflects a growing concern for civil rights among spiritual as well as secular leaders.

4 MAY 1956
Science Two private nuclear power plants are approved by the Atomic Energy Commission. One will be built by Consolidated Edison at Indian Point, New York, and will cost $55,000,000.

28 MAY 1956
National President Eisenhower signs an Agricultural Act to establish a soil bank. This will aid in the reduction of farm surpluses, which will help United States farmers maintain price stability.

9 JUNE 1956
National The President is hospitalized after an attack of ileitis and undergoes surgery.

11 JUNE 1956
Science The American Medical Association convenes at Chicago. Doctors Jonas Salk and Leonard Schule announce that they expect the Salk vaccine to eliminate polio within three years.

30 JUNE 1956
Aviation A record disaster over the Grand Canyon kills 128 people when two airliners, a TWA Super-Constellation and a United Airlines DC-7, crash in flight.

17 JULY 1956
International Egypt accepts an offer of financial aid from the United States for the Aswan High Dam. The United States has offered $56,000,000; the World Bank will add $100,000,000.

19 JULY 1956
International Because of Egypt's connection with

the Soviet Union and the latter's sale of arms to the Middle Eastern country, United States Secretary of State John Foster Dulles withdraws financial aid for the Aswan Dam. This provokes the World Bank to withdraw its offer.

22 JULY 1956

International President Eisenhower signs the Panama Declaration along with 18 other heads of state, confirming the principles set by the Organization of American States guaranteeing the use of the Panama Canal.

26 JULY 1956

International In retaliation for United States action the previous week in withdrawing funding of the Aswan Dam project, President Gamal Abdel Nasser of Egypt nationalizes the Suez Canal. Nasser's announcement cautions that Israel will not receive protection for its shipping.

1 AUGUST 1956

National President Eisenhower signs legislation to increase Social Security coverage.
Science The Salk polio vaccine, developed by Dr. Jonas Salk, is now available to the public.

7 AUGUST 1956

National President Eisenhower authorizes federal support of another 70,000 housing units and relaxes mortgage requirements.

11 AUGUST 1956

Population Jackson Pollock, among the more avant garde contemporary painters, dies at the age of 44 in an auto accident at East Hampton, New York. He is best known for his "drip" painting.

13 AUGUST 1956

National Chicago is the site of the Democratic National Convention, which nominates Adlai Stevenson as the presidential candidate. His running mate is Estes Kefauver.

20 AUGUST 1956

National President Eisenhower and Vice–President Richard M. Nixon are nominated for re-election by the GOP at the party's national convention at San Francisco.

7 SEPTEMBER 1956

National Labor racketeer Johnny Dio and five other men are indicted by a Federal Grand Jury for the attack on Victor Riesel, the outspoken columnist and crusader against gambling, blinded by acid thrown in his face.

24 SEPTEMBER 1956

International The first transatlantic telephone cable stretches 2250 miles, from Oban, Scotland, to Claren-

Civil rights demonstration in Birmingham.

ville, Newfoundland and will increase by three times the circuits between the United States and Europe.

26 OCTOBER 1956
International Seventy nations send representatives to New York City for the signing of the Statute of the International Atomic Energy Agency.

31 OCTOBER 1956
International President Eisenhower opposes force in settling the crisis surrounding Israeli occupation of the Sinai Peninsula and a British-French-Israeli attack on Egypt.

5 NOVEMBER 1956
International After days of fighting by Britain, France and Israel against Egypt, the United States achieves a ceasefire in the Sinai Peninsula. A United Nations force is sent to prevent further clashes between Egypt and Israel.

6 NOVEMBER 1956
National The presidential elections result in Eisenhower's victory. He defeats Adlai Stevenson with 457 electoral votes to 73. The Republican Party is not as successful in the Congressional elections—Democrats retain control of the Senate and the House of Representatives.

8 NOVEMBER 1956
International Following recent violent anti-government demonstrations in Hungary, and the subsequent flood of refugees seeking admission to the United States, the Eisenhower administration offers to admit individuals wishing to leave Hungary.

13 NOVEMBER 1956
National The United States Supreme Court invalidates a Montgomery, Alabama law that provides for segregation in interstate bus travel.

OTHER EVENTS OF 1956
Science Two Americans, Andre Cournand and Dickinson Richards Jr., share the Nobel Prize for Medicine and Physiology with a German colleague, Werner Forssmann. The three have completed research in catheterization of the heart.
Arts/Culture The Pulitzer Prize in fiction goes to MacKinlay Kantor for *Andersonville*.

5 JANUARY 1957
International President Eisenhower speaks to a joint session of Congress, presenting a proposal for United States aid to Middle Eastern nations threatened by Communism. Known as the Eisenhower Doctrine, it promises arms for any country requesting aid.

10 JANUARY 1957
National President Eisenhower makes his State-of-the-Union speech and calls on Congress to pass his Middle East proposal. He warns of the dangers of inflation to the nation's economy.

14 JANUARY 1957
National In a speech to the Senate, Secretary of State John Foster Dulles says that the threat of Communism in the Middle East is at its most critical point in years.

18 JANUARY 1957
Aviation Averaging speeds of over 500 miles per hour, three United States Air Force jets complete a nonstop around-the-world flight.

20 JANUARY 1957
National Dwight D. Eisenhower is inaugurated for his second term of office as President of the United States. This inauguration is a private one, due to its falling on a Sunday.

21 JANUARY 1957
National President Eisenhower follows up yesterday's private inauguration with a public swearing–in at the east portico of the White House. Over 750,000 watch the inaugural parade.

28 JANUARY 1957
National Speaking to the House Armed Services Committee, Secretary of Defense Charles E. Wilson states that the National Guard harbored draft-dodgers during the Korean conflict.

8 FEBRUARY 1957
International The United States agrees to continue military support of Saudi Arabia in return for a lease of the Dhahran airfield. Negotiations for this arrangement are concluded by President Eisenhower and King Ibn Saud.

12 FEBRUARY 1957
National The United States Communist Party convenes in New York City and votes to remain a political party independent of Soviet control.

26 FEBRUARY 1957
National A Senate committee opens hearings concerning the International Brotherhood of Teamsters and allegations that the union harbors corruption.

7 MARCH 1957
International The United States Congress approves the Eisenhower Doctrine.

18 MARCH 1957
International In London the United Nations Disarmament Subcommittee Talks open. Harold E. Stassen is the United States' delegate.

21 MARCH 1957
International After a three–week tour of African nations, Vice–President Richard M. Nixon returns to the United States.

24 MARCH 1957
Regional The Midwest and the Southwest are hit by

a blizzard that kills at least 40 people.
International President Eisenhower meets with Great Britain's Prime Minister Harold Macmillan in Bermuda to discuss Anglo-American ties.

1 APRIL 1957
International The United States lifts a ban on travel to Egypt, Israel, Jordan and Syria.

16 APRIL 1957
National President Eisenhower appropriates an additional $41,000,000 for the United States Postal Service.

29 APRIL 1957
National The nation's first nuclear power reactor, at Fort Belvoir, Virginia, is dedicated by Army Secretary Wilbur N. Brucker.

30 APRIL 1957
National In an action taken by a Special Senate Committee, five Senators from the past become members of the Senate Hall of Fame. They are: Henry Clay, Daniel Webster, John Calhoun, Robert La Follette and Robert Taft.

2 MAY 1957
International John Foster Dulles informs the North Atlantic Council meeting in Bonn that the United States intends to maintain its military forces in Europe at current levels.
Population Senator Joseph McCarthy dies in the naval hospital at Bethesda, Maryland.

6 MAY 1957
Arts/Culture Massachusetts Senator John F. Kennedy wins the Pulitzer Prize for his biographical sketches *Profiles in Courage*.

11 MAY 1957
International President Eisenhower and South Vietnamese President Ngo Dinh Diem meet in Washington and affirm their commitment to prevent the spread of world Communism.

16 MAY 1957
Regional The nation's third atomic-powered submarine, the *Skate*, is launched at Groton, Connecticut.

20 MAY 1957
National The AFL-CIO expels David Beck from its Executive Committee. Beck is charged with "gross misuse of union funds."

24 MAY 1957
International In Taipei, Taiwan, rioters mob the United States Embassy after the release of an American soldier held on a charge of killing a Chinese national.

26 MAY 1957
International President Eisenhower receives "pro-

found regrets" from Chiang Kai-Shek over the recent rioting in Taipei, Taiwan.

28 MAY 1957
International President Eisenhower and West German Chancellor Konrad Adenauer end three days of meetings on disarmament and German unification.

2 JUNE 1957
International Nikita Khrushchev of the U.S.S.R. advises that the first phase of a world disarmament program should begin with an agreement between the Soviets and the United States.

7 JUNE 1957
International Poland and the United States make arrangements for loans for the development of mining and agriculture in Poland.

13 JUNE 1957
Life/Customs After duplicating the Pilgrim's original voyage across the Atlantic Ocean in 1620, the *Mayflower II* arrives in Plymouth, Massachusetts. The voyage began in Plymouth, England, and took 54 days.

15 JUNE 1957
Regional 17 people die as flash floods hit St. Louis.

28 JUNE 1957
Regional Along the coast of Texas and Louisiana, 531 are dead or missing in the wake of a hurricane.
International Secretary of State John Foster Dulles emphasizes the fact that the United States will not recognize Red China. He also claims that the Communist government there is of a temporary nature.

12 JULY 1957
National The Housing Act of 1957 is signed by President Eisenhower. Passage of this bill will help liberalize mortgage benefits and extend public housing benefits to the elderly.

16 JULY 1957
National Secretary of Defense Charles E. Wilson cuts the United States Armed Forces by 100,000 men, a reduction to be completed by the end of 1957.

29 JULY 1957
International President Eisenhower signs a bill agreeing to U.S. membership in the International Atomic Energy Agency.

13 AUGUST 1957
International Three United States Embassy officials are asked to leave Syria on charges of having plotted against the government of President Shukri al-Kuwatly.

21 AUGUST 1957
National President Eisenhower proposes that the United States will impose a two-year nuclear test ban.

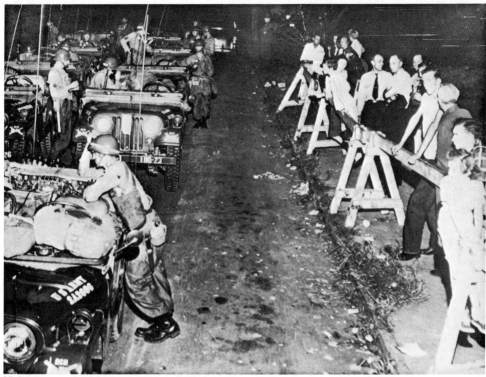

Violence over school integration brings Federal troops to Little Rock, Arkansas.

Regional Congress passes the Niagara Power Act enabling the New York State Power Authority to build a hydroelectric facility at Niagara Falls, New York, a plant second in size only to the Grand Coulee Dam in Colorado.

27 AUGUST 1957
National Democrat William Proxmire wins a special election to fill the vacant Senate seat from Wisconsin.

28 AUGUST 1957
National After being removed from the AFL-CIO Executive Council on May 20, David Beck is charged with tax evasion by a Federal grand jury in Tacoma, Washington.

29 AUGUST 1957
Civil Rights The Civil Rights Commission is established as President Eisenhower signs the Civil Rights Act of 1957. It provides penalties for violation of the voting rights of any United States citizen. The act faces stiff opposition, and in an effort to block passage South Carolina Senator Strom Thurmond sets a filibuster record, speaking for 24 hours, 27 minutes.

30 AUGUST 1957
National The United States Supreme Court makes a ruling, in *Jencks v. United States*, that a defendant in a Federal trial may only have access to FBI file material relating to testimony given in direct examination.

4 SEPTEMBER 1957
Civil Rights In Little Rock, Arkansas, the state militia blocks black students seeking entrance to Central High School. Governor Orval Faubus calls out the Arkansas National Guard to prevent desegregation in direct violation of the 1954 Supreme Court decision in *Brown v. Board of Education*, which ordered states to desegregate the public schools "with all deliberate speed."

14 SEPTEMBER 1957
Civil Rights To prevent further violence and to bring about the desegregation of Arkansas schools, President Eisenhower confers with Arkansas Governor Orval Faubus.

19 SEPTEMBER 1957
National Nevada nuclear testing grounds are used for the nation's first underground atomic testing.

20 SEPTEMBER 1957
Civil Rights In response to a Federal injunction, Governor Orval Faubus orders Arkansas State troops out of Central High School in Little Rock.

23 SEPTEMBER 1957
Civil Rights As a result of rioting, black students at

EMERGING AS A WORLD POWER 1946-

Central High School in Little Rock, Arkansas, withdraw from school.

25 SEPTEMBER 1957
Civil Rights President Eisenhower orders United States Army troops to Little Rock, Arkansas, where they escort nine black students to the classes.

4 OCTOBER 1957
Science/Technology The U.S.S.R. launches the first

THE SPACE PROGRAM

The launching of Sputnik by the Soviet Union, in October 1957, left most Americans dumbfounded. Overnight, their smug self-confidence in the superiority of United States technical know-how had been all but destroyed. A flurry of activity followed as Washington scrambled to regain its lost pre-eminence. Plans were immediately implemented for a quick launch of an American scientific satellite (which took place three months after Sputnik) and on November 7, Eisenhower created a panel of experts to study the scope and direction of America's space program. As a result of its recommendation, Congress founded the National Aeronautics and Space Administration (NASA), in July 1958, to oversee space exploration. By the end of October, the new agency had already launched its first satellite.

The biggest boost to the United States space program came after John Kennedy took office. Capitalizing on the excitement created by Alan Shepard's successful flight into space in May 1961, the President announced his goal of putting a man on the moon before the end of the decade. Such an ambitious project, he hoped, would help restore America's prestige as the world's foremost technological power. Kennedy's objective of a manned lunar landing by 1970 quickly assumed dominance over other space projects. Although scientists at NASA complained that manned flights were several times more expensive and much slower in realizing scientific rewards, they did provide a spectacular way for Americans to measure their achievements. An appeal to the people's chauvinism also made it easier for the government to justify the high costs involved ($25,000,000,000) to put a man on the moon. Congress was so generous in financing the space program in the 1960s that NASA was also able to carry out a variety of unmanned projects. While public attention was focused on the spectacular missions of Mercury, Gemini and Apollo that led up to the lunar landing in 1969, unmanned satellites gathered vital scientific knowledge and also vastly improved world-wide communication. Mariner, an interplanetary space project begun in the 1960s, also provided a wealth of information about earth's nearest neighbors.

The dichotomy in the United States space program—to provide a symbol of American technological supremacy and to do meaningful scientific exploration—continued throughout the 1970s. Even after Neil Armstrong's successful landing on the moon in July 1969, NASA's manned projects (first Skylab and later, the Space Shuttle) consumed most of its budget while the unmanned program (notably Mariner, Viking and Voyager) accumulated scientific laurels. But whatever the inconsistencies or the interruptions, it was certain that the United States would seek to remain in the forefront of the exploration of space.

---

satellite, known as *Sputnik*, into space, and provokes the U.S. to speed up its space program. It will also lead to a commitment to science and mathematics education in American schools.

6 OCTOBER 1957
International After ratification of United States membership in the International Atomic Energy Agency, Sterling W. Cole is named director general.

16 OCTOBER 1957
Regional Great Britain's Queen Elizabeth II and her husband, Prince Philip, visit Jamestown, Virginia, celebrating the 350th anniversary of the first English settlement.

7 NOVEMBER 1957
National President Eisenhower names James R. Killian, Jr. as a special presidential aide for space technology.

25 NOVEMBER 1957
National President Eisenhower suffers a minimal stroke.

6 DECEMBER 1957
National Alleged corruption in its ranks forces the expulsion of the Teamsters' Union from the AFL-CIO.
Science At Cape Canaveral, Florida, a United States Vanguard rocket explodes on the launching pad.

15 DECEMBER 1957
National The United States Air Force tests its first Atlas Intercontinental Ballistic Missile (ICBM).

16 DECEMBER 1957
International President Eisenhower and Secretary of State Dulles leave for Paris to attend a 4-day NATO summit meeting.

OTHER EVENTS OF 1957
Science/Technology The Nobel Prize for physics goes to American scientists C. N. Yang and T. D. Lee, for disproving the law of conservation of parity.
Life/Customs Wham-O, a company in San Gabriel, California, produces a plastic disc to be used for spinning through the air; it is called a Frisbee, after an old American pie-plate of this name.

3 JANUARY 1958
National The Air Force forms two squadrons of the Strategic Air Command (SAC) armed with medium-range ballistic missiles.

7 JANUARY 1958
National The 85th Congress convenes with a Democratic majority in both Senate and House. President Eisenhower asks Congress to appropriate $1,370,000,-000 for air defense and missile research.

9 JANUARY 1958
National The President gives his State-of-the-Union

message and advocates continuation of foreign aid and missile programs.

13 JANUARY 1958
Ideas/Beliefs *The Daily Worker* reduces publication to a weekly basis, a decision based on declining income.

15 JANUARY 1958
Life/Customs A Gallup poll survey reports that Eleanor Roosevelt, widow of President Franklin D. Roosevelt, heads the list of most admired women in the United States.

16 JANUARY 1958
International Expressing concern for increased use of outer space by major world powers, Secretary of State Dulles calls for an international agreement to guarantee its peaceful use.

20 JANUARY 1958
National President Eisenhower warns Congress of the economic perils in wage and price increases.

23 JANUARY 1958
National President Eisenhower urges more legisla-

tion to prevent illegal labor union practices. Eisenhower wants to cut down on racketeering and other abuses.

27 JANUARY 1958
International The United States signs a pact with the Soviet Union that will encourage exchanges in education, sports, culture and technology.

31 JANUARY 1958
Science/Technology America's first satellite, *Explorer 1*, is launched at Cape Canaveral, Florida, by the United States Army.

7 FEBRUARY 1958
Science/Technology The Advance Research Projects Agency is set up by the Defense Department in order to promote space exploration.

28 FEBRUARY 1958
National United States Postal Service rates increase; first class mail goes from three to six cents per ounce.

5 MARCH 1958
Science/Technology The atomic submarine *Skate*

Great Britain's Queen Elizabeth II visits Washington.

EMERGING AS A WORLD POWER 1946-

docks at Portsmouth, England. It has crossed the Atlantic in an undersea voyage that took less than eight days, 11 hours.

17 MARCH 1958
Science/Technology The three-and-one-quarter-pound *Vanguard I* satellite is launched by the United States Navy. It goes into a wider orbit than any previous satellite.

1 APRIL 1958
National The Emergency Housing Act is signed by President Eisenhower to stimulate housing, an action deemed necessary to bolster the nation's flagging economy.

28 APRIL 1958
Science/Technology The United States begins atomic tests at Eniwetok Atoll in the Marshall Islands.

12 MAY 1958
International The United States establishes an arrangement with Canada for the North American Air Defense Command (NORAD).

13 MAY 1958
International In Caracas, Venezuela, Vice–President Richard Nixon encounters hostile mobs. His trip to eight South American countries is part of a goodwill tour. He leaves Venezuela for San Juan, Puerto Rico, the following day.

14 MAY 1958
International The U.S. Navy's 6th Fleet doubles its strength in the Mediterranean. Arms are sent in to Lebanon via an airlift to safeguard Lebanese independence and United States citizens.

30 MAY 1958
National At Arlington National Cemetery, ceremonies honor the burial of Unknown Soldiers of World War II and the Korean War.

8 JUNE 1958
International A United States Army helicopter makes an emergency landing in East Germany.

17 JUNE 1958
National Presidential aide Sherman Adams goes before a Special House Subcommittee on Legislative Oversight, testifying that he did not influence Federal regulatory agencies to aid a friend, Bernard Goldfine.

18 JUNE 1958
National Speaking on behalf of Sherman Adams, President Eisenhower makes clear his faith in Adams' integrity, saying of his aide, "I need him."

20 JUNE 1958
International The United States demands the release of a nine-member helicopter crew forced down over East Germany on June 7.

27 JUNE 1958
Aviation A New York-to-London speed record is set by United States Air Force pilot Colonel Harry Burrell. He makes the trip in five hours, 27 minutes, and averages 630.2 miles per hour.

29 JUNE 1958
Civil Rights In Birmingham, Alabama, a bomb explodes outside of the Bethel Baptist Church where the minister, Fred Shuttlesworth, is an active civil rights leader.

30 JUNE 1958
National On a vote of 64-20, the United States Senate approves the admission of Alaska to the Union.

1 JULY 1958
International United States delegates attend an international conference in Geneva, Switzerland, dealing with nuclear weapons tests and disarmament.

7 JULY 1958
National President Eisenhower signs the bill making Alaska the 49th State in the Union.

15 JULY 1958
International Due to the crisis in the Middle East, the Marines of the 6th Fleet begin landing in Lebanon at the request of that country's government.

19 JULY 1958
International The International Red Cross arranges for the release of nine helicopter crew members detained in East Germany after a forced landing.

29 JULY 1958
National The National Aeronautics and Space Administration (NASA) is created as President Eisenhower signs a bill providing millions of dollars for a United States space program.

5 AUGUST 1958
Science The *Nautilus,* an atomic–powered submarine, makes the world's first undersea crossing of the North Pole. The trip takes 96 hours and carries the sub under a 50-foot-thick ice cap.

6 AUGUST 1958
National The Defense Reorganization Act is signed by the president to give the Secretary of Defense more control over three "separately organized departments,": the Army, Navy and Air Force.

13 AUGUST 1958
National Bernard Goldfine is cited for contempt of Congress for refusal to answer questions concerning his connection to President Eisenhower's aide, Sherman Adams. Goldfine eventually receives a prison sentence for his role in corrupt Federal regulatory agency practices.
International The United States withdraws 1700 Marines from Lebanon where they have been sent as

part of a force aiding the preservation of Lebanese independence.

18 AUGUST 1958
Arts/Culture Vladimir Nabokov's *Lolita* is published in the United States and quickly receives much attention due to its controversial subject: the love of an older man for a 12-year-old girl.

25 AUGUST 1958
National A law awarding pensions to former presidents goes into effect.

26 AUGUST 1958
National Alaskan voters turn out for an election in which they approve statehood by a 5-1 margin.

28 AUGUST 1958
National The Labor Pension Reporting Act makes mandatory the reporting of employee welfare and pension plans covering more than 25 individuals.

2 SEPTEMBER 1958
National President Eisenhower signs the National Defense Education Act for government-backed student loans and the support of education in the sciences.

4 SEPTEMBER 1958
Civil Rights The Civil Rights Act of 1957 allows the United States Supreme Court to act on alleged violations of black voters' rights in Columbus, Georgia.

12 SEPTEMBER 1958
Civil Rights The United States Supreme Court denies a Little Rock, Arkansas, school board request to postpone integration at Central High School.

15 SEPTEMBER 1958
Regional In a train accident near Bayonne, New Jersey, 48 people are killed.

22 SEPTEMBER 1958
National Sherman Adams resigns as President Eisenhower's assistant. In a nationally televised resignation he relates that he has "done no wrong" in dealing with Boston industrialist Bernard Goldfine.

29 SEPTEMBER 1958
Civil Rights Chief Supreme Court Justice Earl Warren presides over a unanimous ruling which bars "evasive schemes" on the question of public school integration.

30 SEPTEMBER 1958
Civil Rights Arkansas governor Orval Faubus closes four high schools in Little Rock, in defiance of a Supreme Court ruling against segregated public education.

6 OCTOBER 1958
Science/Technology The atomic submarine *Seawolf* surfaces after a 60-day underwater voyage. It sets a world record for undersea endurance.

12 OCTOBER 1958
Science/Technology The United States fails in an attempt to circle the moon with a Pioneer rocket. The launching attains a record–setting altitude of 79,193 miles.
Ideas/Beliefs A synagogue in Atlanta, Georgia, is bombed. No one is hurt.

25 OCTOBER 1958
International The United States withdraws the last of its troops from Lebanon.

31 OCTOBER 1958
International An international meeting on the suspension of nuclear testing at Geneva, Switzerland, is attended by the United States, Great Britain and the Soviet Union.

4 NOVEMBER 1958
National Democrats capture 15 Senate seats and 48 seats in the House of Representatives. Among those winning in nation–wide mid-term elections is John F. Kennedy, who receives a second term as Senator from Massachusetts; Kennedy wins by 860,000 votes. Elsewhere, in New York, Republican Nelson Rockefeller is elected governor in a surprising victory.

15 NOVEMBER 1958
International The Eisenhower administration rejects a Soviet proposal for a permanent atomic test ban.

18 NOVEMBER 1958
Regional In Lake Michigan, a cargo vessel founders in stormy waters and sinks; 33 men lose their lives.

1 DECEMBER 1958
Regional A devastating school fire in Chicago claims the lives of 95 children and three nuns at the Our Lady of the Angels Parochial School. It ranks as the third most serious school fire in United States history.

10 DECEMBER 1958
Aviation National Airlines inaugurates jet passenger service, employing two Boeing 707s.

19 DECEMBER 1958
International The United States, Great Britain and the Soviet Union end their conference on the prohibition of nuclear testing. It has been in session since October 31, but has produced small gains in the advance of a world free of atomic weapons and atomic testing.

OTHER EVENTS OF 1958
Science University of Wisconsin researcher Joshua Lederberg shares the Nobel Prize in Physiology and Medicine with George Beadle of California Institute of Technology and Edward Tatum of the Rockefeller Institute.
Arts/Culture James Agee's novel *A Death in the*

EMERGING AS A WORLD POWER 1946-

Family wins the Pulitzer Prize.

3 JANUARY 1959
National Alaska becomes the 49th state of the Union as a result of legislation passed during the latter part of 1958.

6 JANUARY 1959
National In a 74-70 vote, Representative Charles Halleck, Republican from Indiana, is elected House Republican leader, ending Joseph W. Martin's 20-year tenure in that position.

7 JANUARY 1959
National The first session of the 86th Congress convenes in Washington. There are 64 Democrats and 34 Republicans in the Senate, 283 Democrats and 153 Republicans in the House of Representatives.
International The United States recognizes a new government in Cuba. The island nation's new leader is Fidel Castro.

2 FEBRUARY 1959
Civil Rights Public schools in Arlington and Norfolk, Virginia, are desegregated with no significant disruption.

10 FEBRUARY 1959
Regional A tornado rips through St. Louis, leaving thousands homeless; 22 people are killed and over 300 injured. President Eisenhower declares St. Louis a disaster area after learning of damages estimated at $12,000,000.

16 FEBRUARY 1959
International The United States rejects a Soviet proposal for a 28-nation conference on Germany, calling for a Big Four foreign ministers meeting.

18 FEBRUARY 1959
International The President begins several days of discussion with Mexican President Lopez Mateos at Acapulco. It results in the agreement between the United States and Mexico to begin a dam project on the Rio Grande.

5 MARCH 1959
International The United States signs bilateral defense pacts with Iran, Pakistan and Turkey to ensure military aid for those countries.

18 MARCH 1959
National President Eisenhower signs a bill to admit Hawaii as a state.

31 MARCH 1959
National President Eisenhower enacts a three month extension of a Federal employment compensation program providing further benefits to those covered.

5 APRIL 1959
Science According to a report by the United States Naval Research Laboratory there has been a three-fold increase in radioactivity over the eastern part of the nation, a result of atmospheric tests by the Soviet Union during a two–month period in 1958.

7 APRIL 1959
National Prospects for an improved national economic scene appear on the horizon as the Commerce and Labor Departments announce a drop in unemployment. Figures indicate that unemployment went from 4,749,000 in February to 4,362,000 in March.
Regional In Oklahoma, 51 years of prohibition draw to a close as a voter margin of 80,000 repeals the ruling that has kept the state liquor-free since 1908.

15 APRIL 1959
National Secretary of State John Foster Dulles resigns, suffering from cancer.

18 APRIL 1959
National President Eisenhower names Christian A. Herter to fill the vacancy resulting from John Foster Dulles' resignation. The Senate confirms Herter's nomination, 93-0.

25 APRIL 1959
International The St. Lawrence Seaway opens, stretching through the eastern portion of the United States-Canadian border.

3 MAY 1959
Ideas/Beliefs The American Unitarian Association and the Universalist Church of America merge.

20 MAY 1959
National In recognition of his contributions and dedicated service to the nation, John Foster Dulles receives the Medal of Freedom. The award is presented by President Eisenhower and is the highest civilian award given.
Life/Customs American citizenship is restored to nearly 5000 Japanese Americans who renounced it during World War II.

22 MAY 1959
International In signing an agreement with Canada, the United States agrees to cooperate in research and development of nuclear energy.
Black Experience Brigadier General Benjamin O. Davis Jr., of the Air Force, is appointed to Major General, the first black American appointed to the rank.

24 MAY 1959
Population Former Secretary of State John Foster Dulles dies at age 71. President Eisenhower comments that he was "one of the truly great men of our time."

8 JUNE 1959
National In a continued emphasis on routing Communists from government service, the United States

Supreme Court upholds a previous ruling concerning the right of Congress to investigate Communist activity. The Court also supports individual states in similar inquiries.

9 JUNE 1959
Science/Technology At Groton, Connecticut, the *George Washington* is launched. This atomic submarine is capable of firing a Polaris missile.

11 JUNE 1959
National United States Postmaster General Arthur Summerfield bans from the mails D. H. Lawrence's novel, *Lady Chatterley's Lover.*

15 JUNE 1959
National A United States Stock Exchange report indicates that nearly 13,000,000 people own stock in publicly held corporations in the United States.

18 JUNE 1959
Civil Rights The Arkansas law permitting Governor Orval Faubus to close Little Rock schools is declared unconstitutional by a Federal court.

21 JUNE 1959
National United States Secretary of State Christian Herter returns to Washington after the Geneva Conference. Herter states that the Soviet Union appears intent on dominating West Berlin and absorbing all Germany into the Communist bloc.

22 JUNE 1959
National The United States Supreme Court upholds a 1957 Congressional statute dealing with pretrial statements. The statute restricts a defendant's access to such statements made by witnesses.

27 JUNE 1959
National The Senate refuses to confirm Lewis Strauss as Secretary of Commerce, the first Cabinet nominee since 1925 to be rejected by the Senate. Opposition has to do with his role as chairman of the Atomic Energy Commission and denial of J. Robert Oppenheimer's security clearance by the AEC.

30 JUNE 1959
National President Eisenhower signs a bill extending the temporary Federal debt ceiling to $295 billion.

9 JULY 1959
International At Bienhoa, South Vietnam, two American soldiers are killed by Communist guerillas.

14 JULY 1959
National A rise in unemployment during a 30-day period, from mid-May, shows an increase of nearly 1,400,000 persons.

15 JULY 1959
National Despite attempts to negotiate a settlement,

United Steelworkers go out on strike. This walkout affects 28 companies which produce nearly 95 percent of the country's steel.

21 JULY 1959
Science/Technology The first nuclear merchant ship is launched at Camden, New Jersey. President Eisenhower's wife, Mamie, christens the vessel the *Savannah.*

7 AUGUST 1959
Science/Technology A 142–pound satellite, *Explorer IV*, is launched from Cape Canaveral. This satellite is the first to be built and placed in orbit by the National Aeronautics and Space Administration.

12 AUGUST 1959
Civil Rights Nearly 250 demonstrators assemble near Central High School in Little Rock, protesting the opening of integrated schools there.

24 AUGUST 1959
National Hawaii sends two Senators and one Representative to Congress. This puts House membership at 437 and the Senate at 100.

26 AUGUST 1959
International President Eisenhower sets out on a visit to Europe during which he will meet with heads of state in West Germany, Britain and France.

27 AUGUST 1959
National The State Department announces an increase in military supplies to the Laotian Army.

29 AUGUST 1959
National The Veteran's Pension Act causes revisions in benefits, increasing payments for non-service–related disabilities.

4 SEPTEMBER 1959
National Congress passes the Labor Reform Act of 1959 which restricts unions' power.

5 SEPTEMBER 1959
National The Senate approves a bill to increase the current federal gasoline tax by one cent per gallon for highway construction.

7 SEPTEMBER 1959
Ideas/Beliefs According to a United Council of Churches report, 64 percent of Americans are church members.

11 SEPTEMBER 1959
National A legislative bill empowers the Secretary of Agriculture to distribute surplus food, through food stamps, to designated "depressed areas" of the country.

14 SEPTEMBER 1959
National Congress passes the Landrum-Griffin Act

to help curb racketeering and blackmail in labor organizations.

15 SEPTEMBER 1959
International Soviet Premier Nikita Khrushchev arrives in the United States on a six-day visit.
Civil Rights Congress approves an extension of the Civil Rights Commission for two years.

9 OCTOBER 1959
National To break the nationwide steel strike, President Eisenhower invokes the Taft-Hartley Act, causing an injunction to be served against striking steelworkers.

13 OCTOBER 1959
Regional At ceremonies in Abilene, Kansas, President Eisenhower breaks ground for the Dwight David Eisenhower Library.

2 NOVEMBER 1959
National In a statement to the House Special Committee on Legislative Oversight, Charles Van Doren says that his 1956 role on the quiz show "$64,000 Question" was "fixed."

10 NOVEMBER 1959
Science/Technology The *Triton* nuclear submarine is commissioned at Groton, Connecticut, the largest atomic sub ever built.

21 NOVEMBER 1959
International The United States signs an agreement to a two year exchange program with the Soviet Union in science, sports and culture.

22 DECEMBER 1959
National President Eisenhower returns after an eleven-nation tour of Europe, Asia and Africa.

3 JANUARY 1960
National Senator John F. Kennedy announces that he is a candidate for the Democratic presidential nomination.

7 JANUARY 1960
National President Eisenhower delivers his State-of-the-Union message, showing a $200,000,000 surplus in the budget for 1960 and predicts this year will "be the most prosperous year in our history."
Science/Technology A small submarine, the *Trieste,* sets a new record when it descends 24,000 feet into Pacific waters off Guam.

9 JANUARY 1960
National Vice–President Richard M. Nixon declares he is a candidate for the 1960 Republican presidential nomination.

19 JANUARY 1960
International The United States signs a mutual defense treaty with Japan. Demonstrations in Tokyo

cause President Eisenhower to cancel a proposed trip to Japan.

1 FEBRUARY 1960
Civil Rights In Greensboro, North Carolina, four black students stage a sit-in at a lunch counter to protest a "whites only" serving policy.

2 FEBRUARY 1960
National The Senate approves 70-18 the 23rd Amendment to the Constitution, which would ban a poll tax requirement for voting in Federal elections.

16 FEBRUARY 1960
National In a message to Congress, President Eisenhower asks for a $4,000,000,000 foreign aid and military assistance program for 1961.

15 MARCH 1960
Civil Rights A Civil Rights Commission statement makes public the fact that, since 1957, 436 Americans in 23 states have filed complaints concerning denial of voting rights; 140 of these complaints come from Alabama, 105 from Louisiana, 66 from Mississippi and 47 from California.
International Ten nations, including the United States, the Soviet Union, Britain and France, meet at Geneva for a disarmament conference.

17 MARCH 1960
National President Eisenhower asks Congress to increase the annual immigration quota from 260,000 to 500,000 per year.

18 APRIL 1960
National In a reply to a question concerning his Roman Catholic faith, Senator John F. Kennedy, on the campaign trail in West Virginia, says "I don't think that my religion is anyone's business."

26 APRIL 1960
National John F. Kennedy, Democratic candidate for president, wins the write-in Democratic primary in both Pennsylvania and Massachusetts.

5 MAY 1960
International A U-2 Air Force plane, employed for photographic reconnaissance, is shot down inside Soviet territory, according to an announcement by Premier Nikita Khrushchev.

6 MAY 1960
Civil Rights The Civil Rights Act of 1960 is signed by the President, promoting voter registration for referees.

7 MAY 1960
International Two days after the Soviet Union has shot down a United States Air Force U-2 reconnaissance plane, the United States admits to its intelligence mission. The plane had been described as on a weather observation mission.

OTHER EVENTS OF 1960

11 MAY 1960
International President Eisenhower publicly states that the United States has been conducting reconnaissance missions over Soviet territory for the past four years.

16 MAY 1960
International A summit conference in Paris, France, disbands after Soviet Premier Khruschev states that Russia cannot take part until the United States apologizes for the U-2 incident.

12 JUNE 1960
International President Eisenhower leaves on an eight–day tour of the Philippines, Taiwan, South Korea and Alaska.

13 JUNE 1960
Arts/Culture Theaters on Broadway re-open after a contract is signed between Actor's Equity and the New York Theater League. The ten–day strike was the longest since a 30–day shutdown in 1919.

16 JUNE 1960
National The 23rd Amendment to the Constitution is sent to the states for ratification. This amendment will change Federal voting rights, and allow citizens of the District of Columbia full voting privileges.

22 JUNE 1960
International The Senate consents to the United States-Japenese mutual defense treaty.

27 JUNE 1960
International The ten–nation disarmament conference begun in mid-March disperses after failure to reach agreement on nuclear arms.

6 JULY 1960
International Due to an increasingly hostile attitude on the part of Cuban Premier Fidel Castro, the United States cuts its imports of sugar from the island nation by 95 percent.

11 JULY 1960
National At the Democratic National Convention in Los Angeles, Senator John F. Kennedy is nominated on the first ballot. His running mate is Texas Senator Lyndon Johnson.

27 JULY 1960
National The Republicans hold their National Convention at Chicago and nominate Vice–President Richard M. Nixon with Henry Cabot Lodge of Massachusetts as his running mate.

10 AUGUST 1960
International The Senate consents to a treaty designating Antarctica as a "peaceful scientific preserve." The United States joins five other nations—Belgium, Japan, Norway, South Africa and Great Britain—in this treaty.

23 AUGUST 1960
International President Eisenhower asks Congress to cut the import of sugar from the Dominican Republic, in response to an Organization of American States (OAS) decision to break diplomatic relations with the Dominican Republic.

26 SEPTEMBER 1960
The first of four, hour-long televised debates between the two presidential candidates is held in studios in Chicago. These debates are made possible, in part, by a suspension of the "equal time" section of the 1934 Communications Act. Newsmen ask Nixon and Kennedy questions on foreign and domestic issues. Kennedy appears to have a slight edge in popularity.

7 OCTOBER 1960
National The second Presidential Debate is televised from Washington, D.C.

13 OCTOBER 1960
National Nixon and Kennedy debate for the third time, Nixon from a studio in Hollywood, and Kennedy from studios in New York City.

19 OCTOBER 1960
International President Eisenhower announces that the United States and Canada have signed a ten-year pact for a Columbia River water and power project.

21 OCTOBER 1960
National The fourth and final televised debate between Kennedy and Nixon occurs, this one from New York City.

26 OCTOBER 1960
Civil Rights Senator Robert F. Kennedy calls Mrs. Coretta Scott King, wife of Dr. Martin Luther King Jr. who has been jailed on a traffic violation.

8 NOVEMBER 1960
National Voters send Massachusetts Senator John Fitzgerald Kennedy to the White House, 303 electoral votes to Nixon's 219. Kennedy is elected by a slim margin of little more than 100,000 popular votes.

12 DECEMBER 1960
National John F. Kennedy announces that Dean Rusk, president of the Rockefeller Foundation, is to be the new Secretary of State.

19 DECEMBER 1960
National The Supreme Court upholds a ruling under the 1956 Narcotics Control Act that requires testimony from witnesses promised immunity from prosecution.

OTHER EVENTS OF 1960
Science/Technology The Nobel Prize for Physics goes to Donald Glaser. The Nobel Prize for Chemistry goes to Willard F. Libby. The first laser is demonstrated by the American Theodore Maiman, although several scientists in the U.S.A. and the U.S.S.R.

have been working on the idea. The laser, a means of intensifying light to provide great energy, will have countless applications.

Arts/Culture The Pulitzer Prize for Fiction goes to Allen Drury for *Advise and Consent*.

3 JANUARY 1961

National The first session of the 87th Congress meets.

International President Eisenhower directs that the United States will break diplomatic relations with Cuba.

17 JANUARY 1961

National President Eisenhower, in a farewell speech to the country, warns of the increasing power of a "military-industrial complex."

20 JANUARY 1961

National John F. Kennedy is inaugurated as the nation's 35th President, and urges the nation to stand as a world power. The United States should "never negotiate out of fear . . . but let us . . . never fear to negotiate." He calls for domestic harmony, telling Americans to "ask what you can do for your country."

MARTIN LUTHER KING, JR., 1929-1968

A relentless crusader against the brutality of racism, Martin Luther King, Jr. dedicated his adult life to the quest for securing equal rights for black Americans. The son and grandson of well-liked and respected Baptist ministers in Atlanta, Georgia, King carried his Christian inheritance out of the pulpit and into the world of unjust laws. In the early 1950s at Crozier Theological Seminary in Chester, Pennsylvania, and at Boston University where he received his doctorate, King combined the tenets of Christianity with a passionate desire for racial harmony. This intense yet gentle leader soon captured the imagination and hearts of urban and rural blacks throughout the nation.

Emphatic in his message, Martin Luther King adhered to the Gandhian principles he had absorbed at Crozier, organizing and encouraging boycotts and sit-ins as part of non-violent resistance to segregation. In 1955, King led Montgomery, Alabama's boycott of city buses, protesting the arrest of Rosa Parks for violating segregation laws. During the following weeks King and his family and friends were subjected to every type of harassment. Dr. King was jailed on conspiracy charges and his home was bombed. His response to the latter event was to counsel his followers, "We must love our white brothers no matter what they do to us." In January 1957 he helped form the Southern Christian Leadership Committee, one of the most powerful forces in the early civil rights movement, and was named president of this organization. As a Baptist minister, and as a national symbol, King reached hundreds of thousands of black Americans with his words of encouragement and staunch determination.

That desegregation would provoke violence, despite Dr. King's pleas to avoid direct confrontation, was inevitable. The extremism resulting from this often placed King in the role of mediator. His unquestioning resolve helped those around him—both those dedicated to non-violence and the more militant members of the movement (who later broke off angrily to promote their brand of Black Power)—to push further in their demands. By the early 1960s, King had earned the respect of thousands, both black and white, and prompted the Kennedy administration to view him as a formidable leader of a powerful group. In the summer of 1961, Freedom Rides (conceived to mobilize the sit-in) were initially encouraged by Dr. King as a way of publicizing black demands in a non-violent way.

Martin Luther King gave the civil rights movement power and credence by virtue of his own integrity, and in August 1963 at Washington, D.C., he delivered his "I have a dream" speech to the hundreds of thousands assembled there. Viewed by his supporters and foes as a tireless and idealistic leader, King was honored by the world community with the Nobel Peace Prize in December 1964. The full irony of his position was made clear when, despite this coveted award, the FBI harassed King and his family by wiretapping and other surveillance methods throughout the 1960s. J. Edgar Hoover, director of the FBI, was anxious to discredit King by connecting his SCLC with alleged Communist-infiltrators, evidence of which was never found.

Despite his personal dedication to non-violence, Martin Luther King seemed destined to a violent death. On April 4, 1968, he was in Memphis, Tennessee, on behalf of a sanitation workers' strike, and was shot in the head by assassin James Earl Ray. The black community's grief was characterized by riots in 63 cities nationwide; 150,-000 mourners gathered at his funeral in Atlanta, Georgia on April 9. The tragedy of Dr. King's death helped promote even further the cause of civil rights, and his assassination consecrated the mission to which he had dedicated his life—that of equality for all black Americans.

---

21 JANUARY 1961

National President Kennedy names his younger brother, Robert Francis Kennedy, as Attorney General, the first chief executive to appoint a brother to a Cabinet post.

25 JANUARY 1961

National President Kennedy takes part in the first live televised press conference.

13 MARCH 1961

International President Kennedy sends a request to Latin American countries to join with the United States in a development project, the Alliance for Progress, which will hold its first meeting on August 17 of this year.

23 MARCH 1961

International The United States takes a stand against the increased involvement of Communist troops in Laos.

1 MARCH 1961

International President Kennedy creates the Peace Corps by Executive Order.

26 MARCH 1961
International To discuss the ways of averting further escalation of the problems in Laos, President Kennedy meets with Britain's Prime Minister Harold Macmillan at Key West.

29 MARCH 1961
National The 23rd Amendment is adopted. Citizens of the District of Columbia will now have the right to vote in presidential elections.

17 APRIL 1961
International CIA-trained Cuban refugees invade Cuba at the Bay of Pigs. Within 48 hours, the force is defeated.

5 MAY 1961
National The Fair Labor Standards Act, signed by President Kennedy, raises the minimum wage to $1.15 in September of 1961 and to $1.25 by September of 1963.
Science/Technology After several years of preparation, NASA puts a man in space, Commander Alan Shepard Jr., who makes a suborbital flight of 300 miles in a Mercury capsule.

6 MAY 1961
Sports The Kentucky Derby is won by the colt, Carry Back, ridden by John Sellers; Carry Back will go on to win over $1.2 million in his career.

16 MAY 1961
International President Kennedy leaves on a three-day trip to Ottawa.

25 MAY 1961
Science/Technology Speaking to Congress, Presi-

Dr. Martin Luther King, Jr. and associates at Memphis Hotel balcony where he was shot.

dent Kennedy commits the United States to "landing a man on the moon and returning him safely to earth" by the end of the decade.

31 MAY 1961
International President Kennedy travels to Paris to confer with President Charles de Gaulle.

4 JUNE 1961
International In Vienna, President Kennedy has a two-day meeting with Premier Nikita Khrushchev.

19 JUNE 1961
National The Supreme Court rules against the use of illegal evidence in prosecuting state court cases.

30 JUNE 1961
National President Kennedy signs the Housing Act of 1961.

25 JULY 1961
International President Kennedy, in a show of force against the Soviet Union, calls for $3-1/2 billion and an additional contingent of reserve troops.

17 AUGUST 1961
International At the first meeting of the Alliance for Progress in Punta del Este, Uruguay, the United States and other member nations draw up a charter of economic aid and developmental support.

5 SEPTEMBER 1961
National Legislation makes airplane hijacking a Federal offense.
International The Agency for International Development is established by the Foreign Assistance Act of 1961.

15 SEPTEMBER 1961
National The United States begins underground nuclear testing per the atmospheric testing ban recently agreed to by the United States and Britain.
International At Washington, Big Four ministers meet to discuss the situation in Berlin.

22 SEPTEMBER 1961
International President Kennedy puts his signature on an Act of Congress formally establishing the Peace Corps. Kennedy had created the Corps in March by executive order.

9 OCTOBER 1961
Sports The New York Yankees defeat the Cincinnati Reds, four games to one, to become World Series champions.

15 DECEMBER 1961
International President Kennedy leaves for a visit to Colombia, Puerto Rico and Venezuela.

21 DECEMBER 1961
International At Hamilton, Bermuda, President

JOHN F. KENNEDY, 1917-1963

It is understandable that the popular appeal enjoyed by John F. Kennedy arose, in part, from his vigorous personal style. At age 43, Kennedy was the youngest elected President in American history, and he and his wife Jacqueline projected a vitality that would soon characterize his entire administration. Son of the former United States Ambassador to Great Britain, Joseph P. Kennedy, this energetic, engaging man with the flashing grin was a member of an indomitable Irish-Catholic clan from which he emerged as a leader after the death of his older brother, Joe, Jr., during World War II.

The Massachusetts-born Kennedy distinguished himself during World War II as a Navy torpedo boat commander, and it was here that he gained his reputation as a war hero. Elected to the United States Congress in 1947, he defeated Henry Cabot Lodge in the 1952 Senate race in his home state, a political coup that forecast his future success. Running against then Vice-President Richard M. Nixon in 1960, Kennedy won the race for President with 303 electoral votes to his opponent's 219; the 118,550 popular vote margin made this contest an extremely close one, however. At his inauguration Kennedy advised: "Ask not what your country can do for you; ask what you can do for your country," thus setting the tone for his entire administration—one of service and optimism.

In April 1961, Kennedy's judgment was criticized when a CIA-sponsored invasion of Cuba failed. Kennedy, realizing that a cover-up would precipitate far more trouble than it might prevent, shouldered full blame for the Bay of Pigs fiasco; he regained the confidence and respect of many of his detractors by doing so. In October of 1962, his firm-handed response to the Soviet Union's missile installation in Cuba was to order a naval blockade, and his deft manipulation of this potentially disastrous incident served to enhance his growing popularity. During this relatively brief time in office, Kennedy managed to project a broad-based appeal, largely because of his charisma and confident ability. His economic programs were supportive of the disadvantaged—he raised the minimum wage, proposed increased social security benefits, signed an act funding further re-development programs and asked Congress to approve a medical program for the nation's elderly.

At what seemed the zenith of his career, he was obliterated from the political scene by assassin Lee Harvey Oswald. His death, on November 22, 1963, was for most Americans an incomprehensible tragedy. In the day immediately following his death, a stunned nation watched on television as Kennedy's young son saluted his dead father's passing. While the thousand days of Kennedy's administration were too brief to establish his precise imprint on history, John F. Kennedy symbolized the hopes of many that a better America could be built. The President, who was so fond of the musical *Camelot,* and seemed the embodiment of "that one brief shining moment," had almost effortlessly captured the dream and confidence of the entire nation.

Kennedy meets with Prime Minister Macmillan.

OTHER EVENTS OF 1961
Science/Technology The Nobel Prize for Physics goes to Robert Hofstadter and the award for Chemistry to Melvin Calvin. George von Bekesy receives the

Nobel Prize for Medicine and Physiology.

Arts/Culture The Pulitzer Prize for Fiction goes to author Harper Lee for *To Kill a Mockingbird*.

1 JANUARY 1962

National Over 6000 members of the UAW at Studebaker-Packard in South Bend, Indiana, stage a walkout over stalled contract negotiations.

2 JANUARY 1962

Civil Rights NAACP executive secretary Roy Wilkins speaks out in praise of President Kennedy's "personal role" in advancement of civil rights.

9 JANUARY 1962

National President Kennedy meets with the nation's Democratic leaders. The President points out that the national debt limit must be raised.

10 JANUARY 1962

National The 87th Congress reconvenes.

11 JANUARY 1962

National President Kennedy delivers his State-of-the-Union message to a joint session of Congress and speaks confidently about the United States' role in the world, but emphasizes that "both the successes and the setbacks of the past year remain on our agenda of unfinished business."

10 FEBRUARY 1962

International The Russians release Air Force pilot Francis Gary Powers, shot down over the Soviet Union in May 1960.

20 FEBRUARY 1962

Science/Technology Astronaut John Glenn is the first American to orbit the earth; he circles the earth three times in a Mercury space capsule.

22 FEBRUARY 1962

International Meeting with West Berlin Mayor Willy Brandt, Robert Kennedy denounces the Communist wall dividing the city.

1 MARCH 1962

National President Kennedy speaks to Congress concerning "renewed interest and momentum" in developing the country's natural resources. Kennedy urges the establishment of a Land Conservation Fund which would enable the acquisition of new recreational land nationwide.

Aviation The crash of an American Airlines Boeing 707 at New York's Idlewild Airport kills 95 people, including all eight crew members, the nation's worst single-plane aviation disaster.

2 MARCH 1962

Science/Technology To press the Soviets into banning the testing of nuclear weapons, President Kennedy announces the United States intention of more atmospheric nuclear tests.

GEORGE MEANY, 1894-1980

While he was not as vivid as John L. Lewis or as innovative as Walter Reuther, George Meany shared the spotlight with his two rivals as one of the most influential labor leaders of his time. Born in New York City on August 16, 1894, Meany quit school at 16 to become a plumber like his father. He soon became active in union work and by 1934 had risen through the ranks to become president of the 1,000,000-member New York Federation of Labor. In that position he distinguished himself as a labor advocate in Albany, pushing for a number of successful bills including an unemployment insurance act.

In 1939 Meany became secretary-treasurer of the American Federation of Labor, and during the Second World War was a prominent member of the National Defense Mediation Board. When in 1941 John L. Lewis and others broke their industry-oriented Congress of Industrial Organizations away from the craft-oriented AFL, Meany made it a major goal to bring the two organizations back together. The two finally joined in 1955, again unifying the American labor movement; by that time Meany had been president of the AFL for three years. A passionate anti-Communist in a time when the labor movement itself was often accused of Communist tendencies, Meany was a powerful lobbyist for labor issues, saying he wanted "economic dignity" for workers within the capitalist system. He also challenged corruption within the labor movement, presiding over the expulsion of the Teamsters from the AFL-CIO in 1957. Meany retired as president of the AFL-CIO in 1979; he died in 1980.

---

13 MARCH 1962

National President Kennedy asks Congress to allocate $4,878,500,000 for foreign aid in fiscal 1963.

26 MARCH 1962

National The United States Supreme Court rules in *Baker v. Carr* that the Federal court has the power to order reapportionment of seats in a state legislature.

10 APRIL 1962

National The President vociferously denounces a hike in steel prices as "wholly unjustified and irresponsible." Within several days steel industry leaders cancel increases.

International President Kennedy and Great Britain's Harold Macmillan appeal to the Soviet Union to agree to an international test ban.

12 MAY 1962

International Renewed fighting in Laos, Southeast Asia, prompts the United States to send naval and ground forces to support anti-Communist Laotian troops.

17 MAY 1962

International President Kennedy defends American troops in Laos as a "diplomatic solution."

24 MAY 1962

Science/Technology Malcolm Scott Carpenter orbits the earth three times in a Mercury space capsule.

25 JUNE 1962
National The Supreme Court rules in *Engel v. Vitale* that the reading of prayers in the New York public schools is unconstitutional.

29 JUNE 1962
International President and Mrs. Kennedy pay a state visit to Mexico.

10 JULY 1962
Science/Technology A communications satellite, *Telstar,* is placed in orbit.

17 AUGUST 1962
Science/Technology The Senate passes the Kennedy administration's communications satellite bill by 66-11. Researcher and FDA official Frances Kelsey is cited by the medical profession for her stance against the tranquilizer thalidomide; the drug has been found responsible for numerous birth defects and Dr. Kelsey's opposition to its use soon prompts the FDA to enact stiffer drug control regulations.

29 AUGUST 1962
National President Kennedy names Labor Secretary Arthur Goldberg to fill the post left vacant by Felix Frankfurter's retirement.

17 SEPTEMBER 1962
Science/Technology According to reports from Kennedy administration officials, there are no dangerous levels of fallout in the United States from nuclear testing.

30 SEPTEMBER 1962
Civil Rights Black student James Meredith is admitted to the University of Mississippi against severe opposition.

3 OCTOBER 1962
Science/Technology Astronaut Walter Schirra orbits the earth nearly six times in a Mercury capsule.

10 OCTOBER 1962
Science/Technology President Kennedy signs a drug bill designed to safeguard the public against harmful drugs. This comes in the wake of the tragedies in West Germany and other European countries where thalidomide induced birth defects.

11 OCTOBER 1962
International President Kennedy signs the Trade Expansion Act, a bill intended to encourage foreign commerce by allowing certain tariff reductions.

16 OCTOBER 1962
Sports The New York Yankees take the World Series after defeating the San Francisco Giants four games to three.

22 OCTOBER 1962
International President Kennedy announces that the

THE CUBAN MISSILE CRISIS

On October 14, 1962 a U-2 flying a routine reconnaissance mission over Cuba uncovered the existence of fully equipped missile bases capable of attacking the United States with nuclear warheads. Shown the photographs two days later, President Kennedy quickly assembled his top security advisers and, while news of the bases was carefully kept from the public, the group debated what action should be taken.

The Joint Chiefs of Staff leaned strongly toward an air strike and even suggested an invasion to topple the Castro regime. Robert Kennedy, the Attorney General, argued vigorously against such action. The United States had already backed the ill-fated Bay of Pigs invasion a year earlier and the Administration was still recovering from the political fallout; a full scale assault on Cuba, the President's brother insisted, would completely destroy America's moral position in the world. Finally, the President decided on a naval quarantine of the island to block the further introduction of offensive weapons. While demonstrating that the United States would not tolerate the presence of the missiles so close to its shores, a quarantine would also give the Soviets a way out if they wanted one.

On the evening of October 22, Kennedy revealed to the world the existence of the missile bases. Emphasizing Russia's repeated assurances that it would not introduce offensive weapons in Cuba, Kennedy then announced his decision to quarantine the island. The Soviets immediately denounced the United States action and Premier Nikita Khrushchev warned that Russia would not accept the quarantine. With Soviet ships steaming toward the blockade, people around the world nervously awaited a confrontation.

Then a break came. On October 26, a top Soviet diplomat unofficially approached John Scali, a United States newsman, with a proposal: The Russians would dismantle their bases in exchange for a public promise by the United States not to invade Cuba. That evening a telegram arrived from Khrushchev suggesting the same thing. A follow up letter from the Premier the next day, though, demanded the withdrawal of NATO missiles from Turkey in exchange. The President would not agree to this, but cleverly chose to ignore the second letter altogether and respond to the first offer. This formula worked and, on October 28, the Soviets agreed to the terms.

The confrontation had been averted but the missile crisis had graphically demonstrated the ease with which the two super-powers might slip into nuclear war. The realization, however, awakened both sides to a determination to prevent a similar incident in the future. The Cuban missile bases were soon dismantled and withdrawn; a telephone hotline was installed between Moscow and Washington guaranteeing instant communication between the two governments; and in July 1963 the two nations signed a nuclear Test Ban Treaty.

U.S. has photographic evidence that Russia is building missile bases in Cuba, capable of launching a nuclear attack on American cities. Kennedy demands that Russia remove all missiles and dismantle the bases; he asks the UN Security Council and the Organization of American States to take a stand and announces that the U.S. is placing a naval quarantine, or blockade, around Cuba to prevent Russian ships from bringing missiles or materials for the bases. Russian ships are in fact heading for Cuba, and there follow several days of nervous fear on the part of the world, with intense negotiations by the leaders of the U.S., Russia and the UN.

28 OCTOBER 1962

International As Russian ships draw near to the U.S. naval blockade off Cuba, Premier Khrushchev announces that Russia will remove the missiles and bases, for the U.S. has agreed not to attack Cuba (the ostensible reason for putting the missiles there).

6 NOVEMBER 1962

National In midterm elections Democrats retain majorities in both houses of Congress. Former Vice–President Richard Nixon loses his bid for election as governor of California. In Massachusetts, Edward M. Kennedy is elected to the Senate.

20 NOVEMBER 1962

International President Kennedy announces that the U.S. is ending its naval quarantine of Cuba now that all Russian missiles have been removed and the bases dismantled, and that Khrushchev has promised to remove all Soviet jet bombers in the next 30 days.
Civil Rights By executive order, President Kennedy orders all federal agencies to eliminate discrimination based on race or religion in any federally funded housing.

1 DECEMBER 1962

Sports Navy defeats Army, 34-14, in their annual football game in Philadelphia.

14 DECEMBER 1962

Science/Technology After traveling for some 3½ months, the U.S. unmanned spacecraft *Mariner II* passes within 21,600 miles (34,760 kilometers) of the planet Venus, the first successful interplanetary mission.

21 DECEMBER 1962

International Meeting in Nassau, President Kennedy and Prime Minister Macmillan announce a nuclear force within NATO.

23 DECEMBER 1962

International Cuba announces that it will release the 1113 prisoners from the 1961 Bay of Pigs invasion; in return, the U.S. agrees to give Cuba $62,000,000 worth of medical supplies, food and farming equipment.

OTHER EVENTS OF 1962

Science/Technology The Nobel Prize for Medicine and Physiology is shared by the American James Watson and two Britons, Frances Crick and Maurice Wilkins, for discovering the "double helix" structure of DNA.
International The Nobel Prize for Peace is awarded to Linus Pauling, who in 1954 had received the prize

in chemistry.
Arts/Culture The Nobel Prize in Literature goes to John Steinbeck.

7 JANUARY 1963

National The United States postal service announces higher rates: five cents for first-class postage on letters.

29 JANUARY 1963

Population Pulitzer Prize-winning poet Robert Frost dies at age 88.

14 FEBRUARY 1963

National The President proposes a comprehensive program to provide job opportunities for American youth. This program includes the establishment of a Youth Conservation Corps and a domestic Peace Corps.

17 MARCH 1963

Ideas/Beliefs Mother Elizabeth Ann Bayley Seton, founder of the religious order of Sisters of Charity of St. Joseph, is beatified by Pope John XXIII in Rome, the second American to be thus honored.

JOHN GLENN, 1921-

Pilot, astronaut and politician, John Glenn is one of the rare people who managed to make a successful transition from old-fashioned hero to effective political leader. He was born in Ohio on July 18, 1921, and spent his school years in Cambridge, a town he later described as "a real-life version of *The Music Man.* Everyone . . . took patriotism very seriously."

After graduating from a local college, Glenn took flight training and joined the Marine Air Corps early in the Second World War. He became a crack fighter pilot, earning two Distinguished Flying Crosses in the Pacific. Also during the war he married his high school sweetheart. Glenn won two more DFC medals as a fighter ace in the Korean conflict, flying 90 missions and shooting down three MiGs. After Korea he became a military test pilot and was credited with the first transcontinental supersonic flight. In 1959 he was named one of the team of seven first-generation American astronauts, making his country's first earth-orbital flight in the *Friendship 7* in 1962. His engaging, modest, clean-cut image made him the most popular of the early astronauts.

Strongly affected by Kennedy's assasination in 1963, Glenn resigned from the space program to pursue a political career. His first two efforts for an Ohio Senate seat in 1964 and 1970 were unsuccessful. In 1974 he mounted a bitter attack on wealthy incumbent Howard Metzenbaum's income tax record, billing himself as "someone your children can look up to." He took the Democratic primary and then won the Senatorial election by one of the largest margins in Ohio history. As a moderate-to-liberal Senator, Glenn pursued issues of campaign financing, tax reform, national health insurance, and energy policy among others. In 1976 he was a keynote speaker at the Democratic National Convention, and after that time became mentioned with increasing frequency as a potential Presidential candidate for his party.

EMERGING AS A WORLD POWER 1946-

18 MARCH 1963
National The United States Supreme Court rules in *Gideon v. Wainwright,* that indigent defendants are entitled to court-appointed legal counsel in criminal cases.

19 MARCH 1963
International A seven-nation agreement, signed at San Jose, Costa Rica, pledges the United States, Costa Rica, Guatemala, Honduras, Nicaragua, Panama and El Salvador to joint efforts against Soviet aggression in the Western Hemisphere.

2 APRIL 1963
National The President speaks to Congress and submits a foreign aid program for fiscal 1964, $4,525,000,000

5 APRIL 1963
Science/Technology For his contributions to research and development in the field of nuclear energy, J. Robert Oppenheimer receives the Fermi Prize of the United States Atomic Energy Commission, $50,000.

9 APRIL 1963
International Winston Churchill is granted honorary United States citizenship.

10 APRIL 1963
National The atomic submarine *Thresher* sinks in Northern Atlantic waters; 129 crew members die. Admiral Hyman Rickover says there is "no danger of radioactive contamination."

12 APRIL 1963
Civil Rights The Reverend Martin Luther King Jr. is arrested in Birmingham after his participation in a civil rights march.

2 MAY 1963
Civil Rights Thousands of blacks, many of them school children, are arrested while taking part in a nonviolent demonstration in Birmingham.

7 MAY 1963
Science/Technology Another communications satellite, *Telstar II,* is launched from Cape Canaveral, Florida.

10 MAY 1963
Civil Rights After days of civil rights-related violence and the arrest of hundreds of demonstrators in Birmingham, United States Attorney General Robert F. Kennedy calls a halt to police action in that city.

16 MAY 1963
Science/Technology NASA launches astronaut Gordon Cooper in a space flight of 22 earth orbits.

11 JUNE 1963
Civil Rights Alabama Governor George Wallace, faced with the specter of federal intervention by National Guard troops and the possibility of continued racial violence, allows two black students to enroll at the University of Alabama.

12 JUNE 1963
Civil Rights Civil rights leader Medgar Evers is shot in Mississippi.
Arts-Culture President Kennedy signs an Executive Order creating the President's Advisory Council on the Arts.

17 JUNE 1963
Ideas/Beliefs The United States Supreme Court rules that Bible reading in public schools is unconstitutional.

20 JUNE 1963
International The United States and the Soviet Union agree to the establishment of a "hot line" link between the two nations.

26 JUNE 1963
International President Kennedy receives a welcome by 2,000,000 citizens of West Berlin, at the outset of a European tour.

3 JULY 1963
International President Kennedy returns home after his visit to Germany, Great Britain and Italy.

5 AUGUST 1963
International A nuclear test ban treaty, agreed upon by the United States, Great Britain and the Soviet Union, is signed by the three countries. It now remains for the United States Senate to consent to the treaty, which bans atmospheric, underwater and outer-space testing.

28 AUGUST 1963
Civil Rights The March on Washington, organized by civil rights leaders who wish to work peacefully for desegregation and equal opportunity for all Americans, takes place. Over 200,000 people participate. Dr. Martin Luther King Jr. delivers a moving speech: "I have a dream that one day the nation will rise up and live out the true meaning of its creed . . . all men are created equal."

30 AUGUST 1963
International A "hot line" between the United States and the Soviet Union goes into operation to prevent accidental triggering of military responses.

24 SEPTEMBER 1963
National The President leaves on a tour of eleven western states.
International The United States Senate consents to the nuclear test ban treaty signed by the United States, Great Britain and Russia.

10 OCTOBER 1963
International The nuclear test ban treaty, ratified by

THE KENNEDY ASSASSINATION

The trip had gone very well—much better than expected. The President had traveled to Texas to help bolster his sagging popularity in the state and now, as the motorcade wound its way through the downtown streets, even the people of Dallas seemed enthusiastic. But then it happened; as the President's limousine passed the Texas School Book Depository, a shot was fired from the sixth floor. Kennedy stiffened and lurched forward. Seconds later, a second bullet struck and the President collapsed into his wife's lap with a fatal wound to his head. The motorcade sped off to Parkland Memorial Hospital where, a half-hour later, at 1 P.M., November 22, 1963, Kennedy was pronounced dead.

The assassination stunned the nation. Most schools closed and the children were sent home. For the next few days, millions of Americans sat in front of their televisions watching the solemn events which culminated with a stirring funeral procession through the streets of the capital. Around the world, non-Americans mourned Kennedy's death. In New Delhi, India, people cried in the streets when they heard the news of his death.

The weekend also brought more dramatic news from Dallas. As Lee Harvey Oswald, the accused assassin, was being transferred to another jail, he was shot and killed by a local nightclub owner named Jack Ruby. Immediately there were charges of conspiracy. Oswald, an ex-marine, had lived in the Soviet Union and even married a Russian and, since returning to the U.S., had been active in the pro-Castro Fair Play for Cuba Committee. These facts, coupled with his murder, suggested to some that he had been part of the Communist conspiracy.

A week after taking office, President Johnson appointed a commission, headed by Chief Justice Earl Warren, to investigate the Kennedy assassination. Ten months later, the commission reported its findings: Oswald and Ruby had both acted alone; there had been no conspiracy. Despite the mass of detail, there were gaps in the report and it soon became clear that it had not satisfied everyone. Instead, speculation on the assassination became almost a national pastime. In 1967, Jim Morrison, the New Orleans district attorney, created a sensation by announcing that he had proof that a conspiracy had existed. Although that case fizzled out in court, doubts would continue to haunt many for years to come.

Equally fascinating was the way Kennedy's death transformed him, almost instantly, into a universal idol. As President, he had always had panache, but he had been only modestly successful in getting his legislation enacted. The world, however, preferred not to judge him on what he had accomplished, but rather on what they thought he represented. As Prime Minister Harold Macmillan suggested: "He seemed, in his own person, to embody all the hopes and aspirations of this new world that is struggling to emerge—to rise Phoenix-like out of the ashes of the old." It would appear that the assassination of Kennedy, like that of Lincoln a century earlier, would guarantee the survival of a mythical man beyond the historical personage.

the Senate on September 24, takes effect.

2 NOVEMBER 1963
International South Vietnamese generals overthrow the government and kill President Ngo Dinh Diem and his brother, Ngo Dinh Nhu.

22 NOVEMBER 1963
National President and Mrs. Kennedy go to Texas to mend some "political fences" and are riding from the airport into Dallas when, at 12:30 P.M., shots ring out; Kennedy slumps, mortally wounded; Texas Governor John Connally is wounded; the car rushes to the hospital as Mrs. Kennedy holds her husband. Kennedy is pronounced dead at 1 P.M. Dallas police capture Lee Harvey Oswald in a movie theater where he has fled after shooting a policeman who had noticed his suspicious behavior; Oswald was a former expatriate to Russia who has returned to the U.S.A., and will be charged with having shot Kennedy and Connally from the sixth-floor window of the Dallas Book Depository. At 2:30 P.M., Lyndon B. Johnson is sworn in as President.

24 NOVEMBER 1963
National The alleged assassin Lee Harvey Oswald, protesting innocence, is removed from the Dallas Police Headquarters to a safer jail; as he is being led through a basement passage, Jack Ruby, a Dallas nightclub owner, shoots him fatally.

25 NOVEMBER 1963
National President Kennedy's funeral takes place at St. Matthew's Cathedral in Washington; 102 nations are represented. The President is buried in Arlington National Cemetery with military honors.

27 NOVEMBER 1963
National President Lyndon Johnson addresses a joint session of Congress; he assures the American people and the world that he will continue the policies of Kennedy.

29 NOVEMBER 1964
National President Johnson appoints a commission to investigate every aspect of the assassination of President Kennedy. Chief Justice Earl Warren will head it.

17 DECEMBER 1963
International The U.S. Senate consents to the Chamizal Treaty which cedes a small section of El Paso to Mexico, in dispute for 90 years. And President Johnson addresses the United Nations and calls for a "peaceful revolution" to stamp out hunger, disease and poverty that afflict "one-third of mankind."

OTHER EVENTS OF 1963
Science/Technology The Nobel Prize for Physics is shared by two Americans, Eugene Wigner and Maria Goeppert-Mayer, and a German, J. Hans Jensen.
Arts/Culture The Pulitzer Prize for Fiction goes to William Faulkner for *The Reivers*.

8 JANUARY 1964
National President Johnson delivers his State-of-the-Union message to Congress on budget reductions and

a national "war against poverty."

11 JANUARY 1964
Science/Technology The Surgeon General announces proof that cigarette smoking causes lung disease.

13 JANUARY 1964
Science/Technology The Federal Trade Commission announces that it will require statements concerning the hazards of smoking on all packages of cigarettes.

23 JANUARY 1964
National The 24th amendment, eliminating the poll tax for eligibility in Federal elections, is ratified.

28 JANUARY 1964
International Soviet planes down a United States Air Force jet training plane over Erfurt, East Germany, killing three crew members.

13 FEBRUARY 1964
Arts/Culture President Johnson asks Congress to appropriate partial funding for the John F. Kennedy Center for the Performing Arts in Washington. The cost of the new center is estimated at $34 million, of

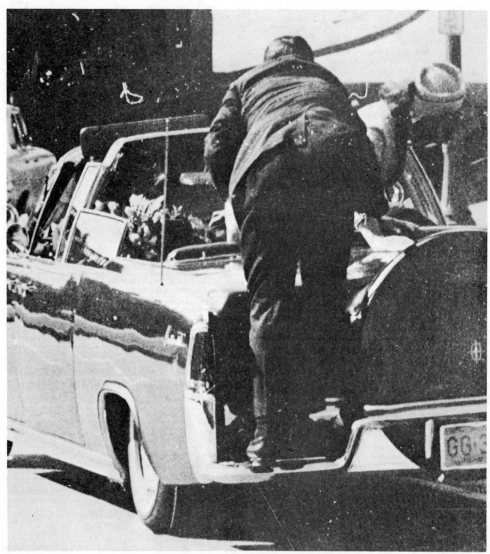

Secret Service man leaps onto car bearing stricken President Kennedy and his wife.

which half will be provided by the government.

25 FEBRUARY 1964
Sports The World Heavyweight Championship boxing title is won by Cassius Marcellus Clay, who defeats Charles (Sonny) Liston, the current titleholder.

29 FEBRUARY 1964
Science/Technology At a press conference, President Johnson reports that Lockheed Aircraft has succeeded in developing a jet capable of 2000 miles per hour.

9 MARCH 1964
National The Supreme Court, in *New York Times Co. v. Sullivan,* rules that public officials may not recover payment in libel suits unless they can prove actual malice was involved in publishing defamatory falsehoods about their public actions.

LYNDON BAINES JOHNSON, 1908-1973

As the tears of a mourning nation greeted him, Lyndon Baines Johnson assumed the Presidency with a confidence based on the knowledge of his past success in public office. This tireless Southern Democrat's approach as a legislator had been a direct one; he would use the same open, aggressive tactics in dealing with the pain and frustration experienced by a country. It worked until the country became embroiled in the bitter controversy over a war, and then these tactics proved inadequate.

Raised in rural Texas and the son of a schoolteacher, Johnson's marriage to Claudia "Lady Bird" Taylor helped to smooth out some of the rougher edges of this man's hearty personal style. First elected as a United States Representative from Texas in 1938, Johnson served five full terms before his election to the Senate. Respected by his colleagues for his persistence, he used his influence and shrewd political maneuvering to gain passage for various legislative packages. His reputation helped him gain the post of Senate Majority Leader and made him the popular choice for John Kennedy's running mate in the 1960 election. Upon his assumption of the presidency after Kennedy's assassination Johnson steadfastly followed his predecessor's lead in providing opportunities for the disadvantaged, declaring a Federal "war on poverty."

With Hubert Humphrey as his running mate in the 1964 race for President, "LBJ" as he was familiarly known, proved his overwhelming popularity (even as the Vietnam War began to surface on the political horizon); he garnered 486 electoral votes to Barry Goldwater's 52. In the month following his inauguration, Congress passed a raft of legislation. Among these measures were acts protecting voting and housing rights for black Americans, establishing an anti-poverty program, and funding medical care for the aged. But despite this forward-thinking domestic legislation, there lurked the unavoidable issue of Johnson's stepped-up war in Vietnam. Taking a consistently hawkish position on the war, Johnson used the Gulf of Tonkin Resolution to initiate the bombing of North Vietnam, and despite increasing protest across the country from doves and liberals, the president systematically increased the number of Americans troops serving in South Vietnam. He did so in the belief that this was the one way to prevent the spread of Communism in Southeast Asia. But after three years of dissent and civil disruption, Johnson faced the results of his investment in an unpopular war. In March 1968 he called for a cease fire and, at the same time, surprised the nation with the announcement that he would not be up for re-election. The heavy toll on Johnson during his years in office was clearly apparent during this televised speech; his lined, tired face bespoke days and nights of conflict and anxiety endured on behalf of the nation.

Considered a politically tragic figure at the end of his term, Lyndon Johnson was nevertheless proud of his record. His social welfare programs had upgraded the lives of many Americans, and many considered that his unswerving energies in this area at least partially exonerated him from the more severe criticism surrounding his Vietnam War policies. In the four years remaining to him after he left the White House, LBJ wrote his memoirs and spent time on his Texas ranch. He suffered a heart attack in April 1972 and died on January 22, 1973, at San Antonio, Texas.

16 MARCH 1964
National President Johnson sends a special message to Congress for a $962,000,000 "war on poverty."

23 MARCH 1964
International The United States joins 115 nations at Geneva for a United Nations conference on Trade and Development.

27 MARCH 1964
Regional A severe earthquake in Alaska kills 66 people, with damage of nearly $500 million.

5 APRIL 1964
Population General Douglas MacArthur dies at Walter Reed Hospital. He is 84.

8 MAY 1964
Regional The President winds up a two-day tour of Appalachia. At a speech in Rocky Mount, North Carolina, Johnson asserts "the time has come for us to see that every American gets a decent break."

19 JUNE 1964
Civil Rights The Senate passes 73-27 the Civil Rights Bill of 1964. President Johnson terms this passage "a challenge to all Americans to transform the commands of our laws into the customs of our land."

22 JUNE 1964
Civil Rights Three young civil rights workers, in Mississippi for the summer voter registration drive, are reported missing after being released from a jail. Their bodies will be found on August 4 in a newly built earth dam near Philadelphia, Mississippi. And on December 4, 21 white men—most of them members of the Ku Klux Klan, and including a local sheriff and his deputy—will be arrested for conspiring to abduct and kill the three youths.

2 JULY 1964
Civil Rights President Johnson signs the Civil

Rights Act of 1964 into law. He states that "its purpose is not to divide, but to end divisions."

15-16 JULY 1964
National Senator Barry Goldwater wins the GOP nomination on the first ballot at the Republican National Convention at San Francisco, California. Representative William Miller of New York is named as Goldwater's running mate.

23 JULY 1964
National The Senate passes President Johnson's anti-poverty bill which calls for $947,000,000 of aid for various measures to combat illiteracy, unemployment and other conditions associated with poverty.

24 JULY 1964
National President Johnson meets with Barry Goldwater to discuss civil rights and the presidential campaign.

2-5 AUGUST 1964
Vietnam: War Two U.S. destroyers patrolling in

SAM RAYBURN, 1882-1961

To many Americans of the 1980s "Mr. Sam" Rayburn is the first Speaker of the House of Representatives who comes to mind. He was a member of the House continuously for 49 years, longer than any other member in history, and was its Speaker for more than twice as long as anyone else. It is a testament to his personal and political abilities that he retained the affection and power he commanded long after the ideas he believed in had passed from fashion. Rayburn was born in Tennessee on January 6, 1882, but his family soon moved to Texas. He was the son of a Confederate veteran and Hard-Shell Baptist; the religiously fundamentalist and populist leanings of his agrarian upbringing would never leave him. He decided early to enter politics and after earning his law degree was elected to the Texas House in 1906. From there he moved to the U.S. House of Representatives in 1912.

To Rayburn the House was the closest governmental connection to the common people, and he was to become the consummate House politician and party man. His motto was, "If you want to get along, go along." He kept his personal sympathies largely to himself, never failing to support a Democratic Presidential candidate. During the 30s he was an effective partner for Roosevelt in the New Deal and piloted through the House in that decade a number of major bills including the Securities Exchange Act of 1934 and the Rural Electrification Act of 1936. He became Speaker of the House in 1940 and held the post until his death. Chief among his Texas protegés during his career was Lyndon Johnson, whose power in the House and presidential ambitions were supported by Rayburn. When Kennedy won the nomination over Johnson in 1960, Rayburn typically campaigned hard for the nominee, but in taking the vice-presidency, after Kennedy's assasination Johnson was to achieve his goal.

Rayburn's gregariousness transcended party lines, and his commitment to slow progress, moderation and accommodation kept him above ideological battles throughout his career. Thus he remained an undramatic but nonetheless popular and effective leader to the end of his life.

THE GREAT SOCIETY

The theory behind Johnson's domestic program was really quite simple: that in an integrated and inter-related society, what hurts one group affects the whole community and that poverty and ignorance anywhere vitiates the strength of the nation as a whole. Although the President did not give a label to his program until May 1964, at a University of Michigan campaign speech, the foundation for the "Great Society" had been laid in his first six months in office.

In January 1964, less than two months after taking office, the President declared his War on Poverty and backed his words by creating the Office of Economic Opportunity to oversee a wide range of projects aimed at aiding the poor. The emphasis of the program was on preparing people through job training programs and educational aid to become useful and productive members of the community. Johnson also made civil rights a major objective in his domestic program. Openly playing on Kennedy's death, the President secured the passage in 1964 of his predecessor's Civil Rights Bill. The bill, which outlawed discrimination in all public accomodations, was the most far-reaching of its kind to be passed since Reconstruction. The next year, it was followed up by the Voting Rights Act, making possible for the first time the widespread participation of Southern blacks in state and federal elections.

Although many of his bills were anticipated by Kennedy, it was Johnson's political skills, honed by years of parliamentary maneuvering in Congress, that made their passage possible. Also important was the overwhelming victory Johnson and the Democratic party won in the 1964 election. Conscious that his strength would never be greater, Johnson inundated his new Congress with a flood of domestic legislation. He secured the passage of Medicare, which provided government financed medical care to the elderly. He also dramatically increased spending on education and adopted programs designed to help students finance their way through college. Conservation also received attention as Congress passed the Water Quality Act, establishing federal pollution standards for the nation's waterways.

By the end of 1965, the bulk of Johnson's domestic program had been enacted. With the country's growing involvement in Vietnam, the administration's attention was increasingly diverted away from domestic legislation. After 1965 also, the spiraling financial demands of the war and a white backlash to the rising black militancy made it difficult for the President to secure sufficient funds for those projects already implemented. In any realistic sense, the "Great Society" would always remain a goal but there was no denying that Johnson himself had helped derail the nation from its journey towards that end.

---

the Gulf of Tonkin off North Vietnam are attacked by North Vietnamese P.T. boats; the U.S. forces sink two of the P.T. boats and then bomb their nearby bases on August 5.

7 AUGUST 1964
Vietnam: War Congress passes the Gulf of Tonkin Resolution, giving President Johnson power "to take all necessary measures to repel any armed attack

against the forces of the United States and to prevent further aggression."

8 AUGUST 1964

National The House passes the Johnson Anti-poverty bill 226-184. The legislation now goes to the President for his signature.

26 AUGUST 1964

National President Johnson is nominated at the Democratic National Convention and Hubert Humphrey of Minnesota is named as his running mate.

MALCOLM X, 1925-1965

Demands and grievances of American blacks were numerous during the 1950s and 1960s, and one of the most forceful voices in the chorus of protest was that of Malcolm X, a name that at one period actually struck fear in the hearts of many Americans.

The man who was known as the crusader for the freedom of urban blacks had been born Malcolm Little in Omaha, Nebraska, the heart of America's farm country. He moved as a teenager to the crisis-ridden milieu of Harlem, where he soon fell afoul of the law. And it was while serving time that he fell under the influence of the Black Muslims, and upon his release in 1952 became a minister and then a close aide of the sect's leader, Elijah Muhammad. Lacking formal education, Malcolm X—the name he adopted upon rejecting the past he so resented—compensated for this with the power he brought to his public appearances where he spoke angrily against the institutions and traditions that he felt had been responsible for the economic and social poverty that had enslaved his fellow blacks. But in 1963, after his bitter remarks on the assassination of President Kennedy, Malcom X was suspended by Elijah Muhammad; the next year, after a visit to Mecca, Malcolm X returned to America and completed the split with the Black Muslims by announcing that his vision of Islam allowed for cooperation among whites and blacks. But his newly formed Organization for Afro-American Unity now served to polarize the rivalries among the blacks who endorsed the conventional Black Muslims and Malcolm X's new message, and there were a series of violent confrontations between the various adherents. They came to a climax in New York City on February 21, 1965, when Malcolm X was speaking to a rally of his supporters and was shot to death, a murder for which blacks identified as Black Muslims were eventually convicted (but which has been seriously disputed in the years since).

Those who agreed with Malcolm X's personal philosophy were dismayed at his death, but many Americans were undeniably relieved that so fiery a figure would no longer be able to encourage blacks to take arms against threats and attacks, both literally and figuratively. Yet his message and person found a still broader audience through the autobiography that he had written (with much help from Alex Haley, later to become famous for his own story, *Roots*), and as the years passed Malcolm X came to appear far less threatening and far more prescient. He was undoubtedly controversial, even potentially dangerous; but his death was a reminder of how costly were the problems that called him forth.

EARL WARREN, 1891-1974

In mid-20th-century America the unprecedented expansion of civil rights and liberal law was presided over and sanctioned by a "progressive conservative" Republican and former prosecuter named Earl Warren, and the Supreme Court he led as Chief Justice has gone down as one of the boldest, most humane and most controversial in our history. Born in Bakersfield, California on March 19, 1891, Warren earned degrees in law at Berkeley in 1912 and 1914. Starting in the 20s he rose through district attorney posts to the position of Attorney General of California in 1939. From 1941 he went on to become the first man to be elected governor of the state three times in succession. As governor he worked successfully and with bipartisan support to reduce taxes and improve state services.

In 1953 Warren was appointed Chief Justice of the Supreme Court by President Eisenhower, who commended his "integrity, honesty, (and) middle-of-the-road philosophy." Warren certainly reflected all those qualities, but he was also a man preoccupied with "fairness," his sense of justice transcending fine points of legal scholarship. Diligent prosecutor that he had been, he once confessed, "I never heard a jury bring in a verdict of guilty but that I felt sick at the pit of my stomach." In 1954, speaking for the unanimous Court decision in the epochal civil-rights case *Brown v. Board of Education,* Warren said, "the doctrine of "separate but equal" has no place. Separate educational facilities are inherently unequal." This decision was the death knell of legally sanctioned segregation in America. The Warren Court went on to make many other important decisions on civil rights, freedom of the press and rights of the accused; one of its most far-reaching came in 1964 with the ruling that states must apportion their legislatures on the basis of equal population. In 1964 Warren also headed the committee that investigated the assassination of President Kennedy; the so-called Warren Report that named Oswald as the lone assassin only increased the controversy that followed Warren. But from his retirement in 1969 to his death in 1974, Earl Warren maintained a low profile, leaving it to history to judge his contributions to American society.

---

24 SEPTEMBER 1964

National The conclusion of the Warren Commission is that Lee Harvey Oswald "acted alone" in the assassination of John F. Kennedy. The 296,000-word report denies "any conspiracy, domestic or foreign."

14 OCTOBER 1964

Civil Rights The Reverend Martin Luther King, Jr. is honored as an advocate of black civil rights and of world peace by the award of the Nobel Peace Prize. King says "every penny" will go to the civil rights movement.

3 NOVEMBER 1964

National In a landslide win, a 15½ million vote plurality, the Johnson-Humphrey ticket defeats Goldwater-Miller.

OTHER EVENTS OF 1964

Science/Technology The Nobel Prize for Physics is

| ELECTION FINAL | DAILY ☀ NEWS | 7¢ |

NEW YORK'S PICTURE NEWSPAPER ®

Vol. 46. No. 113 Copr. 1964 News Syndicate Co Inc.   New York, N.Y. 10017, Wednesday, November 4, 1964*   WEATHER: Sunny and pleasant.

LBJ WINS BIG

President Lyndon B. Johnson after his landslide victory in 1964.

shared by the American Charles Townes and two Russians, Nikolai Basov and Alexander Prokhorov. The Nobel Prize for Medicine and Physiology is shared by the American Konrad Bloch and the German Feodor Lynen. The first basic patent for miniaturized electronic circuits is granted.

4 JANUARY 1965
National In his State of the Union address, President Johnson describes his goals for the "Great Society," by the improvement of the quality of life in America. He calls for federal efforts in education, health care and the arts as well as projects to improve cities, to break down regional pockets of poverty and reduce pollution of rivers and lakes. He appeals to Congress to eliminate obstacles to the right to vote. Before the end of the month the President will call on Congress to provide health care to the elderly and dis-

MARCH 23, 1965

HUBERT HUMPHREY, 1911-1978

Hubert Horatio Humphrey was an honorable man, and an ebullient and much-loved public figure. He came to national attention as a fighting liberal Senator, without whom some of the most important progressive legislation of the century might never have been enacted. But his honor led him to stand behind his friend and President, Lyndon Johnson, another good liberal, and together they were defeated by what their country came to suspect was a dishonorable war.

Humphrey was born in Wallace, South Dakota, on May 27, 1911. He attended the University of Minnesota, graduating in 1939 with high honors in political science; he continued on to graduate degrees and taught political science at several colleges. His first try for office was in 1943, when he ran for mayor of Minneapolis. Defeated then, he was successful in 1945, and in his two terms became a highly effective and popular liberal mayor. Among his achievements was the nation's first municipal fair employment practices ordinance. This prefigured his impassioned and successful demand for a strong civil rights plank in the 1948 Democratic platform.

In the same year Humphrey was elected to the Senate. During his long career there he was associated with the most progressive ideas—health care for the aged, a nuclear test ban treaty, the Civil Rights Act of 1964 and a flood of other bills. In 1961 he became the assistant Democratic leader (called the Whip) in the Senate. Throughout, Humphrey's career was encouraged by the more moderate Senator Lyndon Johnson. It was only natural that Johnson would pick Humphrey as his running mate in the 1964 election. As Vice-President, Humphrey worked hard for his boss in the trail-blazing civil rights and poverty programs. But then came the Vietnam War; loyal as ever, Humphrey turned his ebullient advocacy to that cause, too.

When Johnson, sensing the national mood turning against the war, declined to run in 1968, Humphrey was chosen as the Democratic nominee in the stormy Chicago Convention. In the campaign he turned on his old-fashioned if sincere liberal rhetoric, but his support of the war was an albatross, and Nixon won. Re-elected to the Senate in 1970, Humphrey was passed over for the 1972 nomination. Already suffering from cancer, he was returned to the Senate in 1976; the nation saw on their screens a ravaged and shrunken but somehow still smiling Humphrey. He died in 1978 and was given a state funeral in the Capitol rotunda; his ideals, like many of his country's, had been swept away by war, but the nation still remembered him as an honorable man.

abled (Medicare), grants for public schools and appropriations for a new submarine missile (the Poseidon).

20 JANUARY 1965
National Lyndon B. Johnson is sworn in by Chief Justice Earl Warren. Johnson says in his inaugural address that "Our destiny in the midst of change will rest on the unchanged character of our people—and on their faith." Hubert H. Humphrey is sworn in today by Speaker of the House John McCormack.

6 FEBRUARY 1965
War: Vietnam Vietcong guerrillas attack a U.S.

military base at Pleiku, killing eight Americans and wounding 126. The next day, in response to the attack, President Johnson orders the bombing of North Vietnamese positions, including the Dong Hoi base. The bombings mark a significant enlargement of the U.S. role in Vietnam.

18 FEBRUARY 1965
National Defense Secretary Robert S. McNamara, testifying before the House Armed Services Committee, calls for a nationwide network of bomb shelters, which he believes could save the lives of up to 27,000,000 Americans in the event of a Russian attack. McNamara also says more lives could be saved if the U.S. developed an antiballistic missile system and improved defenses against manned bombers.

21 FEBRUARY 1965
Black Experience Malcolm X, former leader of the Black Muslims, is shot and killed as he is preparing to address an audience in New York City. Three men, all Black Muslims, are arrested. Malcom X, born Malcolm Little, had been relieved of his position in the Black Muslims by Elijah Muhammad in 1964. Returning from a trip to the Mideast to study the Islamic faith, Malcolm founded the Organization for Afro-American Unity. All three arrested will be convicted.

7 MARCH 1965
Civil Rights Close to 200 state troopers attack 525 civil rights demonstrators in Selma as they are preparing to begin a march to Montgomery to protest voting rights discrimination. After a second march is also blocked, federal court judge Frank Johnson rules on March 17 that the demonstration may proceed. After President Johnson federalizes the state national guard and sends another 2200 troops to protect demonstrators, the walk begins on March 21, with 3200 participating.

8 MARCH 1965
War: Vietnam U.S. Marines land in Vietnam. The two batallions are the first combat forces in that country. Some 23,000 U.S. personnel already are in Vietnam as military advisers. The role of the Marines is to protect the Air Force base at Danang.

11 MARCH 1965
Civil Rights The Reverend James J. Reeb of Boston dies in Selma, Alabama, following a beating. Two other white Unitarian ministers were injured in the attack. On April 13 three men will be indicted on charges of killing Reeb.

23 MARCH 1965
Science-Technology *Gemini 3*, the first manned mission of the Gemini project, is launched from Cape Kennedy. After three orbits around the earth, which include some course-changing manuevers, the spacecraft splashes down in the Atlantic Ocean. On June 3 *Gemini 4* will be launched on a much longer journey, which will include the first American spacewalk (the

THE VIETNAM WAR

America's involvement in Vietnam actually began in the Truman years. Believing that a victory by the nationalist (and pro-Communist) forces of Ho Chi Minh would lead to an expansion of world Communism, Truman backed France's attempt to reassert its colonial control over Vietnam. Despite U.S. aid, however, the French were defeated in 1954 and Vietnam divided into two countries. The U.S. then transfered its support to the non-Communist government in the South; when the Communist Vietcong in that country launched a full-scale campaign of political terrorism in the early 1960s to topple the government, the Kennedy Administration responded by dramatically increasing both the number of military advisers stationed in the country and its financial aid to the government.

Then in 1964, North Vietnamese boats attacked two American ships in the Gulf of Tonkin. Congress reacted by passing the Gulf of Tonkin Resolution allowing the President to take whatever steps he deemed necessary to prevent further aggression against the U.S. When a Vietcong attack at Pleiku the following February resulted in the deaths of seven Americans, Johnson used the Congressional authorization to launch a continuous aerial bombing of North Vietnam. The next month, the President also began a massive troop buildup which would peak in 1968, when some 541,000 U.S. soldiers were stationed in Vietnam.

From the first landing of troops, U.S. involvement had come under strong criticism at home. Although Johnson was able to maintain the support of most Americans by repeatedly assuring them that the enemy was being steadily defeated, a huge offensive by the Communists in January 1968 forced a major re-evaluation of the U.S. war effort. The President, now politically disabled, announced in March the immediate cessation of bombing and called on Hanoi to begin peace talks.

In 1969, Nixon came to the White House already pledged to ending the war. Soon after taking office, he announced his plan of Vietnamization: to gradually replace U.S. troops with South Vietnamese soldiers. Despite American troop reductions, however, protest at home continued; when the President used U.S. air and ground forces to support South Vietnamese drives against enemy bases in Cambodia and Laos the action was loudly denounced as an enlargement of the war. The revelation, late in 1969, that U.S. troops had massacred over a hundred civilians at My Lai, and then the publication of the Pentagon Papers in 1971, proving blatant deception on the part of U.S. administrations, further fueled anti-war sentiment. Under mounting pressure, the Nixon Administration finally signed an agreement on January 27, 1973, providing for the complete withdrawal of U.S. troops.

The Vietnam War had severely challenged Americans' image of themselves as moral guardians of the world. Forced to admit that the U.S. was probably guilty of killing thousands of civilians in its routine bombings of the North as well as in untold massacres in the South, it became increasingly difficult for them to justify their involvement in a conflict that had taken the lives of some 57,000 young Americans and seriously injured many more thousands. The rights and wrongs of the Vietnam War would long be debated, but all sides tended to agree that it failed to gain the necessary support of the American people.

first walk will be by a Soviet during the spring). Meanwhile, two lunar space probes, *Ranger 8* (in February) and *Ranger 9* (in March) will be sent into space to radio pictures of the moon's surface, in preparation for manned landing.

2 APRIL 1964
War: Vietnam At a military meeting with his security advisers, President Johnson agrees to step up military and economic aid to South Vietnam, which will include troops to protect bases and train the South Vietnamese military. On April 7 the President will announce that the U.S. is willing to participate in "unconditional" talks with Hanoi to bring an end to the war.

6 APRIL 1965
Communications NASA launches *Early Bird*, the first commercial satellite to be put up in space. The spacecraft transmits telephone and television signals.

28 APRIL 1964
International President Johnson sends the first contingent of Marines to the Dominican Republic to protect Americans during a civil war between the U.S.-supported government forces of Donald Reid Cabral and rebel troops backing ex-President Juan Bosch. On May 2, President Johnson charges that the leftist guerrilla movement has been taken over by Communists who wish to exploit the civil war to gain power. To avert a rebel victory, the U.S. will send 20,000 troops. On May 26 the Organization of American States agrees to provide a peace-keeping force to enforce a truce; as OAS troops arrive, American forces withdraw.

29 APRIL 1965
Civil Rights Francis Keppel, the U.S. Commissioner of Education, announces that all public school districts are to desegregate their schools by the fall of 1967. The announcement is based on the 1964 Civil Rights Act barring federal aid to schools practicing racial discrimination.

9 MAY 1965
War: Vietnam The government announces the total U.S. fighting force is 42,200 men. Deployment of another 21,000 U.S. soldiers will be announced on June 26. On June 28 American troops will take part in an attack 20 miles northeast of Saigon.

30 JUNE 1964
National In its final report, the Senate Ethics Committee recommends that Robert (Bobby) Baker, former secretary for the Democratic majority, be indicted for violations of the Senate's conflict of interest laws. Baker is believed to have accepted a $5000 payment from a lobbyist in exchange for his efforts to secure passage of a bill licensing a freight company. Next year Baker will be indicted by a federal court on charges of income tax evasion arising out of alleged illegal gifts.

14 JULY 1965

Population U.N. Ambassador Adlai Stevenson dies of a heart attack in London at the age of 65. He has served in the U.N. as ambassador since his appointment by President Kennedy in January 1961. He will be succeeded at that post by Supreme Court Associate Justice Arthur Goldberg.

26 JULY 1965

War: Vietnam President Johnson announces his decision to increase U.S. strength in Vietnam from 75,000 to 125,000 men. To support the buildup, draft quotas double from 17,000 to 35,000. Johnson will tell the nation that the non-Communist countries of Asia are incapable of resisting "the growing ambition of Asian Communism." On August 4 the president will ask Congress for an additional $1,700,000,000 to support the war.

30 JULY 1965

National In Independence, Missouri, with ex-President Harry Truman looking on, President Johnson signs the Medicare bill. It provides limited health care insurance for the elderly and disabled through an increase in the social security tax, and allows for an additional optional medical insurance plan for enroll-

ing members.

6 AUGUST 1965

National The President signs the Voting Rights Act empowering the Federal Government to suspend all literacy, knowledge or character tests for voting in areas where less than 50 percent of the voting age population is registered. The bill allows the National Government to send registrars to supervise enrollment of voters where tests have been suspended.

11 AUGUST 1965

Black Experience A major race riot breaks out in the Watts district of southwest Los Angeles, triggered by a minor incident—a white highway patrolman pulling over a black motorist on suspicion of drunken driving. Behind the event, according to blacks, is police brutality. Rioters loot and burn stores and other buildings, causing $40,000,000 in damages. Before the violence is quelled on August 16, 34 people will be killed and thousands arrested. Some 15,000 law enforcement officials, including over 12,000 national guardsmen, will be called to deal with the mobs; most of the deaths (overwhelmingly blacks) will be attributed to the guardsmen's lack of experience. Governor Pat Brown will appoint a commission to investigate

U.S. paratroopers seek out Viet Cong guerrillas.

THE GHETTO RIOTS

The great achievements of the civil rights movement in the decade after 1955 left the urban blacks of the North virtually untouched. After World War II, hundreds of thousands of blacks had migrated north, settling primarily in large urban centers. By moving, they had escaped neither poverty nor discrimination, but the exact sources of that discrimination were much harder to locate. They still lived in inferior housing and attended all-black schools and they were still largely untrained and poorly educated but the cause of these problems no longer seemed legal or even particularly personal. As they watched the heroic progress of the civil rights movement in the South, their own frustration mounted.

There were some signs of discontent among urban blacks in 1963, when over 200,000 marched in Detroit to protest discrimination and almost half of the children in Chicago boycotted their schools to help bring an end to *de facto* segragation in public education. The next year, rioting broke out in Harlem. Then in 1965, a devastating six-day riot in Watts, the black neighborhood of Los Angeles, left 34 dead and caused $40,000,000 worth of property damage. There were more disturbances in 1966, but the worst summer of violence occurred in 1967, when racial unrest hit over 100 cities across the country. The largest riots took place in Newark and Detroit, with the violence in Detroit lasting a full week and resulting in 43 deaths and over 7000 arrests. Following the assassination of Martin Luther King Jr. in April 1968, another round of black-ghetto upheavals swept the U.S. and left 50 people dead.

Except for the disorders following King's death in 1968, the violence was almost always precipitated by local incidents, often involving police arrests. Despite what many whites thought, there was little evidence in most cases to link the riots to outside agitators. Those killed in the disturbances, too, were overwhelmingly blacks (all of those in Watts, three-fourths in Detroit and nine-tenths in the 1966 riots), and the evidence suggests that police and national guardsmen did most of the shooting.

The ghetto riots produced a strong backlash among whites. Inspired by the heroic nonviolence of the Southern civil rights movement, many whites had supported President Johnson's ambitious anti-poverty program. When they saw blacks pour out their hatred in the urban riots, however, they quickly turned their backs on such schemes. Ironically, the Kenner Commission, appointed by Johnson in 1967 to study the riots, reached exactly the opposite conclusion. Only by a vigorous commitment by the government to provide jobs, better housing and more educational opportunities, it decided, could such violence be prevented in the future.

the riot to be headed by John McCone, but the commission's report will provide few answers, suggesting only that the violence was caused by delinquency and high unemployment. Unemployment rate among black males in Watts is 30 percent.

9 SEPTEMBER 1965
National President Johnson signs a law creating the Department of Housing and Urban Development. The new Cabinet-level department will be headed by Robert C. Weaver, the first black Cabinet member.

16 SEPTEMBER 1965
Communication Most of New York City's major newspapers go out on strike. The walkout will last three weeks and will cost between $10,000,000 and $15,000,000.

1 OCTOBER 1965
National Congress passes an anti-pollution bill which empowers the Secretary of Health, Education and Welfare to set emission standards on toxic pollutants in new diesel and gasoline powered automobiles. The bill prohibits the sale of vehicles that do not meet government standards.

3 OCTOBER 1965
National President Johnson signs a major immigration act abolishing the quota system for immigrants established on the basis of national origin.

15 NOVEMBER 1965
National In a decision that seriously weakens the McCarran Internal Security Act, the Supreme Court rules that individuals may refuse to register as members of the Communist Party as part of their Constitutional right against self-incrimination. The McCarran Act not only required registration of Communist Party members but authorized emergency detention of potential subversives in the event of an attack or internal insurrection.

27 NOVEMBER 1965
Sports Army and Navy play to a 7-7 tie in their annual football rivalry.

4 DECEMBER 1965
Science/Technology *Gemini 7* is launched into space on a 14-day mission, the longest manned flight to date. On 15 December, *Gemini 6* will also go into orbit where it will maneuver to within 100 feet of *Gemini 7* and remain for six hours. Another Gemini flight (*Gemini 5*) in August lasted for eight days. Both *Gemini 7* and *Gemini 5* were designed to prove that men could function in space long enough to make a roundtrip to the moon.

OTHER EVENTS OF 1965
Science/Technology The Nobel Prize for Physics is shared by two Americans, Richard Feynman and Julian Schwinger, and a Japanese, Sin-itiro Tomonaga. The Nobel prize in Chemistry goes to Robert Woodward.
Life/Customs The mini-skirt is introduced, with its hemline several inches above the knee.

1 JANUARY 1966
Transportation Members of the AFL-CIO's Transport Workers Union in New York City go out on strike, crippling that city's bus and subway transit system. Although Union leader Michael Quill will be jailed on January 3 for refusing to call off the strike, the shutdown remains in effect until January 13. The agreement which ultimately will settle the strike

against the city's Transit Authority includes a 15 percent wage hike. The strike begins hours before John V. Lindsay is sworn in as mayor of New York, the first Republican in 20 years.

12 JANUARY 1966

National In his third State of the Union message, President Johnson pledges to continue with his "Great Society" program while maintaining the commitment to South Vietnam. Johnson proposes a Constitutional amendment increasing Congressional terms to four years, legislation outlawing discrimination in sale or rental of housing, strengthening federal jurisdiction over assaults against civil rights workers, and a Cabinet-level department of transportation. On January 24, Johnson will present his proposed budget to Congress, calling for federal expenditures of $112,000,000,000 (including a $1,800,000,000 deficit). Although the budget incorporates allocations for his "Great Society," the President will admit that the rate of advance is less than it would have been if it were not for the Vietnam War.

31 JANUARY 1966

War: Vietnam Johnson announces resumption of U.S. bombing raids over North Vietnam, after a 37-day pause. The cessation of the raids was part of an administration "peace offensive" to open peace talks. The peace effort has brought "only denunciation and rejection" from the Communists. In pursuit of the peace initiative, according to Secretary of State Dean Rusk, the administration conferred with heads of 115 governments, as well as the Vatican, the U.N., OAS and NATO. Despite the renewal of the aerial attacks, Johnson calls on the U.N. to continue its efforts to procure a peaceful settlement.

8 FEBRUARY 1966

War: Vietnam President Johnson finishes three days of talks in Honolulu with South Vietnam Premier Nguyen Cao Ky on the progress of the war as well as the need for social reforms. Ky announces that he is not willing to participate in negotiations with the Vietcong.

23 FEBRUARY 1966

National President Johnson presents a special message to Congress dealing with conservation and environmental protection. The President calls for projects to clean America's waterways, federal grants to preserve historical landmarks and funds to finance pollution-control research. On November 3, Johnson will sign the Clean Waters Restoration Act, for purifying the nation's lakes and rivers.

1 MARCH 1966

National In a special message on health and education, the president calls for a commitment to provide "full education for every citizen to the limits of his capacity to absorb it and good health for every citizen to the limits of our ability to provide it." Included among his proposals are grants to fund health educa-

tion and research, an expansion of "operation headstart" (educational opportunities to disadvantaged children) and more money for primary, secondary and higher education.

3 MARCH 1966

National President Johnson signs the Cold War GI Bill of Rights, allowing special education, housing and health and job benefits to veterans who have spent at least 180 days in service since January 31, 1955. The bill will benefit hundreds of thousands of veterans of the Vietnam War.

16 MARCH 1966

Science/Technology *Gemini 8* becomes the first spacecraft to dock in space when it maneuvers into the forward opening of an Agena, launched just prior to the Gemini capsule. After 26 minutes of docked flight, however, a thruster rocket in the manned Gemini craft malfunctions, causing the spacecraft to spin wildly. The astronauts on board pull the craft out of orbit, making an emergency re-entry and splashdown in the Pacific, after completing only seven of its scheduled 44 orbits. Another manned Gemini flight (*Gemini 9*) will be completed on June 6, after featuring the world's longest spacewalk (two hours and nine minutes). On May 30, the unmanned *Surveyor I* will make the U.S.'s first soft landing on the moon, three months after the Soviets accomplished their first soft landing.

26 MARCH 1966

National In the second day of nationwide protests against the war, demonstrations are staged in San Francisco, Chicago, Boston, Philadelphia and Washington.

27 APRIL 1966

Industry The Interstate Commerce Commission allows the merger of the Pennsylvania and New York Central Railroads, the largest merger in U.S. corporate history. It will make the new rail company (Pennsylvania and New York Central Transportation Company) one of the 10 largest nonfinancial corporations in the country, with assets of $4,000,000,000.

13 JUNE 1966

National In an important decision affecting the rights of suspects in criminal cases, *Miranda v Arizona*, the Supreme Court rules (5-4) that an accused must be apprised of his or her rights before interrogation. Arguing from the Fifth Amendment guarantee against self-incrimination, the majority decrees that a suspect must be told that his remarks may be used against him and that he has a right to a lawyer during the interrogation. The ruling will place the burden of proof on the prosecution to demonstrate that the suspect voluntarily waived his rights in cases where a statement is elicited.

29 JUNE 1966

War: Vietnam Pointing to the increase in North Vietnamese infiltration to the South to aid the Vietcong, the U.S. announces the commencement of bombing raids against Haiphong and Hanoi. On June 11, Secretary of Defense Robert McNamara had announced that the U.S. troop total in Vietnam had reached 285,000 men.

12 JULY 1966
Black Experience Rioting erupts in Chicago's West Side after a fire hydrant being used by the district's black children to keep cool in the 98 degree temperatures is shut off. The violence will last until July 15, when Mayor Richard Daley calls in the National Guard. More riots will occur in six other U.S. cities—Baltimore, San Francisco, Cleveland, Omaha, Nebraska, Brooklyn and Jacksonville. Not all the violence, though, will be carried out by blacks. In Baltimore, on July 28 and 29, white teenagers will overrun a black district after a National States' Rights Party convention is held in the city; in Chicago's Gage Park district, whites will attack civil rights marchers demonstrating against unfair real estate practices.

6 SEPTEMBER 1966
Black Experience Two days of rioting break out in Atlanta after a white detective wounds a black youth suspected of car theft. A police officer will later testify that a Student Nonviolent Coordinating Committee sound truck traveled the district following the shooting announcing that the youth had been murdered by the police, and Stokely Carmichael (chairman of S.N.C.C.) will be arrested and charged with inciting a riot. Another round of violence will erupt on September 10 after the killing of another black teenager; it will last for three days. Altogether 35 people will be wounded in five days of violence and 135 arrested.

12 SEPTEMBER 1966
Civil Rights A mob of whites in Grenada, Mississippi, armed with axe handles, metal pipes and chains, attacks black students attempting to integrate two neighborhood schools. The violence, which continues tomorrow, leads to accusations that local police officials allowed the beatings by refusing to intervene to protect the blacks. Tomorrow, news and cameramen in town to cover the unrest will also be attacked by local whites as they film the assaults. Grenada officials will be charged with willful neglect of their duty and 13 men will be arrested for conspiring against the civil rights of the blacks. On September 20, 300 local white citizens will publish a statement condemning mob violence.

15 OCTOBER 1966
National President Johnson signs a bill creating the Department of Transportation. The law establishing the 12th Cabinet-level department will become effective on April 1, 1967, and Johnson will appoint Alan Boyd as first Secretary of DOT.

20 OCTOBER 1966
National Congress passes a major piece of "Great Society" legislation, providing federal funds to finance the planning and rebuilding of large urban areas. Between 60 and 70 "demonstration" cities will receive up to 80 percent of the local expense of undertaking the renovation programs. The bill calls for the expenditure of $25,000,000 for fiscal 1967 for planning the projects and $900,000,000 the following year for the renewal projects.

25 OCTOBER 1966
War: Vietnam President Johnson concludes a conference in Manila with heads of six other nations involved in Vietnam. A four-point declaration of peace is issued declaring the goals of the allied nations (Australia, the Philippines, Thailand, New Zealand, South Korea and South Vietnam) as being to foster political self-determination as well as economic, social and cultural cooperation and breaking of the "bonds of poverty, illiteracy and disease." The six allies also pledge to withdraw troops within six months after North Vietnam has ceased its aggression.

3 NOVEMBER 1966
National President Johnson signs a Truth-in-Packaging bill requiring labeling of supermarket items to provide information on contents and manufacturer. The law bans label phraseology such as "jumbo ounces" and "giant half-quart," but does not set weight and measure standards. It urges manufacturers to develop standards "voluntarily."

8 NOVEMBER 1966
National In the national mid-term elections, the G.O.P. picks up three seats in the Senate and 47 in the House. Edward Brooke of Massachusetts becomes the first black elected to the Senate since Reconstruction. In state elections the Republicans pick up eight governors. Although the Democratic party still holds a margin of 65 in the House of Representatives and 30 in the Senate, the strong showing gives comfort to Republicans who feared that the landslide victory of the Democrats in 1964 might signal the permanent decline of their party.

OTHER EVENTS OF 1966
Science/Technology The Nobel Prize in Chemistry goes to Robert Milliken. The Nobel prize for Physiology and Medicine goes to Charles Huggins and Francis Rous.

5 JANUARY 1967
War: Vietnam The State Department announces 5008 Americans killed and 30,093 wounded in Vietnam in 1966. Losses raise total American casualties since January 1, 1961 to 6664 killed and 37,738 wounded. Current troop strength in the Southeast Asian country (January 1) is 380,000 U.S. soldiers. On January 8, American troops will launch their largest offensive to date with 16,000 U.S. and 14,000 South Vietnamese soldiers participating in "Operation Cedar Falls," a drive against enemy positions in an area known as the Iron Triangle, 25 miles northwest of Saigon. The offensive will last

until January 19.

6 JANUARY 1967
National In his fourth State of the Union message, President Johnson asks Congress for a 6 percent surcharge on individual and corporate income taxes to help fund his "Great Society" programs. He calls for more federal spending on Head Start, model cities and job training programs begun during his administration; he asks for a 20 percent increase in Social Security, a law barring the use of wiretapping and electronic eavesdropping and extension of anti-pollution programs. In foreign affairs, the President reminds Americans of the need for a slowdown of the arms race.

27 JANUARY 1967
Science/Technology A fire breaks out in the *Apollo I* spacecraft during ground testing at Cape Kennedy. The three astronauts (Virgil Grissom, Edward White and Roger Chafee) are killed as the fire spreads to the pure oxygen atmosphere of the capsule. The deaths are the first tied directly to the space program testing. (Three others have been killed in airplane crashes.) A report released on April 9, will blame the fire on a defective electrical wire and criticize deficiencies in Apollo project design and construction.

1 MARCH 1967
National The House of Representatives, by a tally of 307 to 116, votes to exclude Representative-elect Adam Clayton Powell, Jr. from the 90th Congress. A black representing New York's Harlem district, Powell is accused of using government money for private and personal use.

18 MAY 1967
Ideas/Beliefs Tennessee's Governor Buford Ellington signs a bill repealing the state's famous "Monkey Law" (which prohibited the teaching of "any theory that denies the story of divine creation of man as taught in the Bible"), made famous in 1925 by the trial in which John T. Scopes was charged with teaching evolution. The trial pitted William Jennings Bryan against the celebrated defense lawyer Clarence Darrow and brought a conviction, overturned by the state supreme court on technical grounds. The law had remained on the books.

12 JUNE 1967
National In a Supreme Court decision enhancing the protection of the press against libel suits, the court rules in *Curtis Publishing Co. v. Butts* that the Constitution not only safeguards the news media against such suits by public officials but also other people prominent in the public eye. To prove libel in such cases, it must be shown that misstatements were either deliberate or made with reckless disregard for the truth.

In another decision rendered today (*Loving v. Virginia*), the court unanimously strikes down a Virginia law banning interracial marriages. The High Court also declares similar laws in 15 other states as violating the Constitution.

23 JUNE 1967
National Senator Thomas Dodd of Connecticut is censured by the Senate for using public funds from political testimonials and campaign contributions for personal expenses.

25 JUNE 1967
International President Johnson and Alexsei Kosygin meet for the second time in three days at the house of the president of Glassboro College in New Jersey.

30 JUNE 1967
International Meeting at the so-called Kennedy Round in Geneva, 53 nations of the world agree to dramatic cuts in tariff duties to stimulate world trade. The agreement calls for 35 percent reduction on industrial products, 50 percent on chemical goods and cuts on agricultural products. The accord also pledges a world-wide food program, 4,500,000 tons of grain a year to developing countries.

16 JULY 1967
Transportation In the most extensive rail strike in history, members of the A.F.L.-C.I.O.'s International Association of Machinists go out on strike, idling some 600,000 railroad employees and affecting 95 percent of the nation's railroad tracks. To end the strike, Congress will pass a bill demanding that workers return to work and authorizing the President to establish a board to settle the dispute if the two sides are unable to agree within 90 days.

23 JULY 1967
Black Experience Rioting erupts in Detroit following a police raid on an after-hours drinking club on the city's west side. The violence is provoked by charges of police brutality during the raid and will last until July 30, leaving 41 people dead and 2000 injured. On July 24 President Johnson will call in federal troops. The property damage during the week will be estimated between $250,000,000 and $400,000,000 and will leave 5000 people without homes. The Detroit riot will be the bloodiest and most destructive riot in the worst year of racial violence yet. Earlier another major riot took place in Newark that killed 26 people (24 blacks) and caused $15,000,000 to $30,000,000 in damage.

26 JULY 1967
Black Experience H. Rap Brown, chairman of the Student Nonviolent Coordinating Committee, is arrested by police on charges of inciting a riot following an outbreak of racial violence in Cambridge, Maryland. Before the rioting Brown had told an audience to "burn this city down."

29 JULY 1967
War: Vietnam 134 crewmen are killed aboard the

USS *Forrestal* in the Gulf of Tonkin as fire sweeps across the ship's deck, after a punctured Skyhawk fuel tank ignites. This is the worst naval accident in a war zone since World War II and takes place seven minutes before the ship's aircraft were scheduled to take off on a bombing mission over North Vietnam.

30 AUGUST 1967
National Thurgood Marshall is confirmed by the Senate as the first black justice of the Supreme Court. Marshall was the Solicitor General before appointment to the bench by Johnson on June 13. He is the great-grandson of a slave.

18 SEPTEMBER 1967
National In a speech in San Francisco, Secretary of Defense Robert McNamara announces that the U.S. will develop a "thin" antiballistic missile system composed of Nike X and Spartan missiles, designed to shield the U.S. from a possible nuclear attack from Communist China. The missile system, expected to cost $5,000,000,000 over the next five years, is preferred by the administration over a "heavy" system (costing $40,000,000,000), according to McNamara, because a "heavy" system would encourage the Soviet Union to step up its missile production.

19 OCTOBER 1967
Science/Technology NASA's *Mariner 5* interplanetary space probe passes within 2500 miles of Venus and transmits data back on the planet's atmosphere. According to *Mariner*'s findings, Venus's atmosphere contains no appreciable quantity of oxygen, a discovery that contradicts information provided by the Soviet *Venera 4* which landed on Venus yesterday.

On September 10, NASA's *Surveyor 5* landed on the moon's surface and began testing lunar soil. Results showed that the moon's surface is made up of basaltic and volcanic rock.

21 OCTOBER 1967
National Two days of antiwar demonstrations begin in Washington which will involve some 35,000 protestors and lead to the arrest of at least 647 people. On October 31 President Johnson will reiterate his determination to maintain the U.S. commitment to South Vietnam.

7 NOVEMBER 1967
National State and municipal elections are held throughout the country today. Despite the fact that black rioting and busing were high on the list of issues discussed in a number of the mayoral elections, voters do not show a strong tendency toward racial backlash. Carl Stokes and Richard Hatcher, both blacks, are elected respectively as mayors of Cleveland and Gary, Indiana, while in Boston the moderate Kevin White defeats the anti-busing candidate Louise Day Hicks. In Mississippi, Louisiana and Virginia the effects of increased black voting are evident as Robert Clark (Mississippi), Stephen K. Morial (Louisiana) and Dr. William Ferguson (Virginia) become the first blacks in this century to serve in their states' legislatures.

14 NOVEMBER 1967
National Congress passes the Air Quality Act, setting aside $428,300,000 over the next three years to fight air pollution. The bill empowers the HEW Secretary to initiate court action to secure an injunction shutting down sources of air contamination during an emergency. In signing the bill on November 14, President Johnson will tell his audience, "either we stop poisoning our air or we become a nation of gas masks, groping our way through the dying cities and a wilderness of ghost towns."

20 NOVEMBER 1967
National President Johnson signs a bill creating the National Commission on Product Safety. The agency's task will be to keep the public informed concerning potentially hazardous products on the market and also to investigate and report on the current state and federal laws protecting consumers against harmful products.

8 DECEMBER 1967
National Four days of antiwar demonstrations end in New York after some 585 protestors are arrested, including Dr. Benjamin Spock and the poet Alan Ginsberg. Those arrested were trying to disrupt the activities of an army induction center by blocking the entrance to the building. The action was part of a nationwide "Stop-the-Draft" movement organized by 40 antiwar groups. Protestors have also been arrested during the week in Madison, Wisconsin; Manchester, New Hampshire; New Haven, Connecticut and Cincinnati.

OTHER EVENTS OF 1967
Science/Technology The Nobel Prize in Physics goes to Hans Bethe. The Nobel Prize in Physiology and Medicine is shared by two Americans, George Wald and H. Keffer Hartline, and the Swede Ragnar Granit.

17 JANUARY 1968
National President Lyndon Johnson calls for a ten percent income tax surcharge in his State of the Union message. He speaks out on the need for aiding the unemployed, on condition of America's urban areas, and on the $25,000,000,000 annual cost of the Vietnam war.
Sports In Superbowl II at Miami, Florida, the Green Bay Packers defeat the Oakland Raiders, 33-14.

21 JANUARY 1968
War: Vietnam American troops at Khesanh in Vietnam are attacked by Communist guerrillas.

22 JANUARY 1968
National A Strategic Air Command (SAC) B-52 crashes and explodes in North Star Bay off the coast of Greenland. The plane was carrying four unarmed

MAY 10, 1968

hydrogen bombs, and although radioactive material was distributed over a large area there was no nuclear explosion. One crewman dies but six survive the crash.

23 JANUARY 1968
International A United States Navy intelligence vessel, *Pueblo*, is seized along with an 83-man crew, by North Korean patrol boats in the Sea of Japan. The American ship has allegedly violated the territorial limit, claimed by the North Koreans to be 12 miles.

25 JANUARY 1968
International The United States aircraft carrier *Enterprise* is sent to the Sea of Japan in a show of force. President Johnson hopes that this buildup off the coast of North Korea will forestall direct military action over the *Pueblo* incident.

30 JANUARY 1968
National The United States Senate confirms Clark Clifford as Secretary of Defense to succeed Robert S. McNamara.
War: Vietnam The Communists in Vietnam launch a major offensive on the eve of Tet, the lunar New Year, as a brief holiday truce is about to take effect.

1 FEBRUARY 1968
National Richard M. Nixon, former vice-president under Dwight D. Eisenhower, declares his intention to run for the Republican presidential nomination.

12 MARCH 1968
National Senator Eugene McCarthy, an ardent opponent of the war in Vietnam, wins 42 percent of the votes in the Democratic primary in New Hampshire.

16 MARCH 1968
National New York Senator Robert Kennedy announces his intention of running for the Democratic presidential nomination.

22 MARCH 1968
War: Vietnam General William Westmoreland is named by the President as Army Chief of Staff.

31 MARCH 1968
National President Johnson announces the cessation of bombing north of the 21st parallel in Vietnam, and his decision not to run for re-election.

4 APRIL 1968
Civil Rights At Memphis, Tennessee, Civil Rights leader and former Nobel Peace Prize winner Martin Luther King, Jr., is assassinated.

8 APRIL 1968
National A Bureau of Narcotics and Dangerous Drugs will oversee narcotics and other drugs.

23 APRIL 1968
Social Change At Columbia University in New

ROBERT F. KENNEDY, 1925-1968

Combining bravado with shyness, toughness with vulnerability, Robert Kennedy fashioned a career which traversed the post-war political landscape from McCarthyism to the "New Frontier," coming to rest amid the tumult and turbulence of 1968. Although possessed of wealth and privilege from birth, by the mid-1960s few politicians on the national scene had allied themselves more closely with the plight of the poor and the disadvantaged than "Bobby" Kennedy.

Born to a large Irish-Catholic family ruled by a stern diplomat-businessman father who pressured his sons to compete and to excel both mentally and physically, Kennedy attended both Harvard College and the University of Virginia Law School. With neither doubt nor hesitation he launched a career in public service. In the 1950s, after a brief stint with the Justice Department, Kennedy joined the staff of the Senate Permanent Investigations Subcommittee of Red-hunter Joseph McCarthy. After McCarthy's condemnation by the Senate, Kennedy quietly slipped out of this association and briefly gained national prominence as the youthfully agressive chief counsel to the Senate investigation of corruption in the Teamsters' Union.

After skillfully directing his older brother John's hard-fought 1960 campaign for the presidency, Kennedy entered the Cabinet as Attorney General, although he served more as John's closest confidant than as the nation's highest legal officer. Constantly at the President's side, he played crucial roles in defusing the Cuban Missile Crisis and in mollifying civil rights activists in the South. Traumatized by his brother's assassination and upset with Lyndon Johnson, a restless Bobby Kennedy came out from under the constraining shadows of both men in 1964, when he captured a Senate seat from New York.

Deeply moved by the national problems made manifest by the civil rights and student protest movements, the tousle-haired Kennedy spoke out in the accent of his native Massachusetts against racial discrimination, economic injustice and the Vietnam War. His quest for the 1968 Democratic presidential nomination neared triumph following his victory in the crucial California primary but ended in tragedy. Kennedy fell, mortaly wounded, when assassin Sirhan Sirhan shot him as he was leaving the Hotel Ambassador in Los Angeles, California. In a national outpouring of emotion usually reserved for fallen presidents, thousands lined the tracks and millions watched on television as a train carried Robert Kennedy's body from New York City to Washington, D.C., transporting with it the shattered dreams of a generation.

York City, student protestors seize five buildings. Most of these students are members of the Students for a Democratic Society, and are protesting Columbia's involvement in research connected with the Vietnam war.

24 APRIL 1968
Social Change At Boston University, some 300 black students take over the administration building, demanding a stronger emphasis on black history in the curriculum and increased financial aid for blacks.

10 MAY 1968
War: Vietnam Peace talks begin in Paris, France,

579

with Averell Harriman representing the United States and Xuan Thuy representing North Vietnam.

15 MAY 1968
National The United States Postal Service commemorates the 50th anniversary of air mail service.

1' JUNE 1968
Population Helen Keller dies at age 87 in Westport, Connecticut; deaf and blind since infancy, she overcame her handicap and was respected throughout the world for her humanitarian contributions and the powerful example she set for others similarly cut off from the hearing and sighted world.

6 JUNE 1968
National Robert Kennedy dies of wounds received

STUDENT UNREST

The 1960s might be characterized as a decade when various subgroups within American society demanded recognition, and among these it was college students who staged some of the most vehement protests on behalf of their interests and aims. Student protest in the 1960s was an international phenomenon—it virtually brought the French government to a halt—and had various roots and results, but in the United States it probably took its inspiration from the civil rights protests; indeed, student unrest often overlapped or intertwined with the civil rights movement. But the distinctive "unrest" that ran through student life is usually considered to have started with the protests that erupted in 1964 at the University of California at Berkeley over the issue of free speech and right of assembly. Meanwhile, such phenomena as the explosion of rock music and the adoption of drugs such as marijuana and LSD were giving rise to a new youth counterculture that was reshaping at least the more evident aspects of student life—leading to new fads in everything from writers (such as Hermann Hesse) to food (such as the macrobiotic diet). Adults, too, were being encouraged to "let it all hang out," and new fashions, therapies and lifestyles were sweeping the land.

But none of this would necessarily have produced the actual protests that spilled out onto the campuses and streets were it not for the Vietnam War. Some student protests seemed to be about such issues as demands for changes in the curriculum or more recognition of minorities, but it was the Selective Service Act, alias the draft, that became the spark that ignited most students. Hundreds of thousands of young American males chose to defy the draft (few were ever tried, and even fewer jailed), and by 1968 the draft protesters and general antiwar movement were disrupting campus life across America. The violence that occurred at the Democratic convention in Chicago that summer involved many other than students, but young people were clearly the "troops" of the movement.

As antidraft protests, student takeovers of university buildings, black ghetto riots and assassinations of prominent leaders seemed to be leading the nation to the edge of anarchy, a strange event occurred. In August 1969, at Bethel, New York, some 400,000 young people gathered for a rock concert that was known as Woodstock. Although violence and worse were predicted, the gathering was actually quite peaceful, and it seemed to put American youth into a new less confrontational mode. Not that the students ceased protesting. After Nixon ordered the invasion of Cambodia in April 1970, students at Kent State in Ohio were marching across campus in protest on May 4 when the National Guard fired on them, killing four and wounding nine. Ten days later, at Jackson State in Mississippi, two black students were killed and 12 wounded in what was clearly a gratuitous racial assault. Some 488 campuses across America either shut down or went on strike as a result of this violence, and it appeared that student unrest' would continue. But on June 29 came the announcement that U.S. ground troops would be removed from Cambodia, and as American troops were also being withdrawn from the front lines in Vietnam, the nation's campuses began to quiet down that fall.

The students had learned some lessons not found in conventional classrooms, but the changes demanded by many were not especially appreciated by all Americans. Yet the demands that college curricula reflect the times helped institute Afro-American and women's studies at many schools, and many schools were forced to re-examine their priorities. Student unrest was disruptive and flawed, but it effected undeniable changes in American society.

---

in Los Angeles several hours earlier while campaigning. A Jordanian immigrant, Sirhan Sirhan, is charged with the murder.

8 JUNE 1968
National James Earl Ray, accused of shooting Martin Luther King, Jr., is arrested in London.

14 JUNE 1968
National Doctor Benjamin Spock is convicted of conspiracy to abet draft evasion along with three others.

26 JUNE 1968
National President Johnson indicates Chief Justice Earl Warren's intention to submit his resignation "solely because of age." Johnson nominates Justice Abe Fortas.

16 JULY 1968
National Justice Abe Fortas begins three days of testimony before the Senate Judiciary Committee, the first time a nominee has been obliged to testify to fitness before confirmation.

21 JULY 1968
Arts/Culture One of the early figures in modern dance, Ruth St. Denis, dies in Hollywood, California, at age 91.

8 AUGUST 1968
National Richard M. Nixon receives his party's nomination for president. Maryland Governor Spiro T. Agnew is chosen as Nixon's running mate.

26 AUGUST 1968
National The Democratic National Convention opens in Chicago.
Education A report issued by the National Student

EVERETT DIRKSEN, 1896-1969

The mellifluous and florid oratory of Illinois Senator Everett Dirksen was one of the most familiar sounds in media political coverage of the 50s and 60s. Serving in Congress for 34 years, he was a classic but highly individual old-style Washington politician.

Dirksen was born in Pekin, Illinois, on January 4, 1896. After military service overseas in World War I he worked at various business and town offices until his election to the U.S. House of Representatives in 1932. There he became a leading Republican critic of Roosevelt's New Deal, though he supported the President's foreign policy. He remained in the House until 1948, helping to frame the Congressional Reorganization Act of 1946. After two years practicing law back in Illinois he was elected to the Senate in 1952.

In 1954, Dirksen was a major supporter of Joseph R. McCarthy during the Army-McCarthy hearings; he later dissociated himself from McCarthy's attacks on Eisenhower. Considered a firm member of the Republican old guard, he became the Senate Republican leader in 1959. Though he was generally a conservative, he occasionally allied himself with Senate liberals on such issues as civil rights and the nuclear test ban treaty. He once astutely described himself thusly: "I'm just an old-fashioned garden variety of Republican who believes in the Constitution, the Declaration of Independence, in Abraham Lincoln, who accepts the challenges as they arise from time to time, and who is not unappreciative of the fact that this is a dynamic economy . . . and sometimes you have to change your position." He died still in office in 1969.

Association indicates that during the first six months of the year there have been 221 major demonstrations at 101 colleges and universities.

28 AUGUST 1968

National The Democrats adopt a Vietnam plank for the party platform that represents the "hawkish" elements at the convention. The plank calls for a halt to the Vietnam bombing only when "this action would not endanger" American troops there. Hubert Humphrey receives the presidential nomination in the midst of police action against antiwar demonstrations outside the convention hall.

29 AUGUST 1968

National Maine Senator Edmund Muskie receives the Democratic nomination for vice-president.

2 OCTOBER 1968

National President Johnson withdraws his nomination of Abe Fortas to be Chief Supreme Court Justice.

31 OCTOBER 1968

War: Vietnam President Johnson announces an end to all United States bombing of North Vietnam. This is a move intended to break a stalemate in the Paris Peace talks.

6 NOVEMBER 1968

National The election returns indicate that Richard M. Nixon will be the next chief executive. The final tally in this, one of the closest elections ever held—Nixon: 31,710,470; Humphrey: 30,898,055; Wallace; 9,446,167—shows 302 electoral votes for Nixon, 191 for Hubert Humphrey.

11 DECEMBER 1968

National A Labor Department report shows that the unemployment rate for the nation is at its lowest in 15 years—a rate of 3.3 percent.

27 DECEMBER 1968

Science/Technology After a six-day orbital flight around the moon and back, astronauts Borman, Lovell and Anders land safely on earth.

OTHER EVENTS OF 1968

Science/Technology The Nobel Prize for Physics goes to Luis Alvarez. The Nobel Prize for Chemistry goes to Lars Onsager. The Nobel Prize for Physiology and Medicine is shared by Robert Holley, H. Gobind Khorana and Marshall Nirenberg. It was in this year that the U.S. oceanographic vessel *Glomar Challenger* began its long series of drillings deep into the ocean floor and came up with evidence in support of the revolutionary theory of the earth's geological formation known as plate tectonics.

14 JANUARY 1969

National President Johnson delivers his last State of the Union address. The outgoing President emphasizes his "Great Society" programs at home and peace abroad.

20 JANUARY 1969

National Richard Nixon is sworn in as the 37th president of the U.S, and Spiro T. Agnew takes the oath of office as vice-president. In his inaugural address, Nixon tells the nation: "We have found ourselves rich in goods, but ragged in spirit; reaching with magnificent precision for the moon, but falling into raucous discord on earth. We are caught in war, wanting peace. We are torn by divisions, wanting unity."

5 FEBRUARY 1969

Regional A huge oil slick off the coast of Santa Barbara closes the harbor of that city.

2 MARCH 1969

International President Nixon returns to Washington after an eight-day trip to Europe, to visit leaders in five western countries: Belgium, Britain, Italy, France and West Germany.

10 MARCH 1969

Civil Rights James Earl Ray pleads guilty to the murder of Dr. Martin Luther King, Jr. and is sentenced to 99 years in prison.

14 MARCH 1969

National President Nixon announces his plans to

EMERGING AS A WORLD POWER 1946-

build a modified ABM system designed primarily to protect U.S. offensive missile bases against either Soviet or Chinese attack. The new "Safeguard" system replaces the "Sentinel" plan offered by the Johnson administration designed to protect U.S. cities against an attack by unsophisticated Chinese missiles. "Safeguard" calls for immediate construction of two ABM sites, but foresees as many as 12. The open-ended nature of the plan, as well as fears that it will provoke an escalation of the arms race, precipitates debate in Congress, but the system will be approved ultimately by both houses.

RICHARD MILHOUS NIXON, 1913-

While nothing in his early political life predicted the humiliating disgrace that Richard Nixon was to experience later, he was a man who seemed uncomfortable in public life even after attaining the Presidency of the United States. Born in Yorba Linda, California, Nixon graduated from Whittier College, subsequently attending Duke University Law School from which he graduated in 1937. Serving in the United States Navy during World War II, Nixon was elected to the Congress in 1946 upon his return to civilian life. It was as a Representative from California that Nixon served as a member of the House UnAmerican Activities Committee during the Alger Hiss case. His political integrity was called into question by allegations of improper use of campaign funds for his Senate campaign in 1950, and Nixon was forced to defend himself as a proper running mate for Eisenhower in 1952. The speech Nixon gave on nationwide television, a speech in which Nixon utilized considerable emotional manipulation—even to the point of invoking a family pet, Checkers, the dog for whom the speech was later named—only further emphasized the man's inability to command respect and confidence.

After serving for eight years in Eisenhower's shadow, then Vice-President Nixon narrowly lost the 1960 Presidential election to Senator John F. Kennedy. Another defeat followed two years later, as Nixon lost to Edmund "Pat" Brown in his bid for the California governorship. For the next six years Nixon lived the quiet life of a corporate lawyer in New York City, but all the while he maintained contact with the Republican Party. He resurfaced politically in 1968; Nixon and running mate Maryland Governor Spiro Agnew led the Republicans to victory in their Presidential campaign over a divided Democratic party led by Vice-President Humphrey. To fulfill campaign promises as quickly as possible, Nixon removed American ground forces from the conflict in Vietnam by employing vastly increased bombing of both the North and the South. Simultaneously, he established detente with the Soviet Union, and opened diplomatic contact with the People's Republic of China.

His apparent personal insecurity, admitted intolerance of anti-war demonstrators and willingness to employ questionable political practices led Nixon to authorize a series of illegal wiretaps and other acts of harassment against his political opponents, culminating in the June 1972 Watergate burglary. While defeating Senator George McGovern in the 1972 Presidential election with 521 electoral votes to McGovern's 17, Nixon spent much of the next two years attempting to ward off investigations into his conduct by the Senate Watergate Committee and Special Prosecutors Archibald Cox and Leon Jaworski. Following a Supreme Court Order to release crucial White House tape-recordings and a House Judiciary Committee Impeachment Resolution, Nixon announced on August 8, 1974 his resignation from the Presidency of the United States effective the following day. Withdrawing to his San Clemente, California, estate, Nixon devoted himself, through television interviews and writing his memoirs, to giving a personal, if defensive, account of his years in office. But little that this former chief executive could say would erase the stain that many Americans felt he had so carelessly left on the highest elected office in the country. Nixon would be remembered for many things—his "Checkers" speech, his trip to Red China, his vehement opposition to anti-war agitators— but he would be recalled first and foremost for the Watergate scandal.

---

28 MARCH 1969
Population Dwight David Eisenhower, 78, the 34th President of the U.S., dies of heart failure at Walter Reed Hospital in Washington.

7 APRIL 1969
National In a unanimous decision, the Supreme Court rules unconstitutional laws that try to prohibit the reading or viewing of obscene material in the privacy of one's home. "Our whole constitutional heritage," Justice Thurgood Marshall insists, "rebels at the thought of giving the government the power to control men's minds."

9 APRIL 1969
Education Close to 300 students, mainly members

Richard Milhous Nixon.

Vice-President Nixon nominated for re-election with President Eisenhower in 1956.

of the militant Students for a Democratic Society (SDS), take over Harvard University's administration building, evicting eight deans as well as staff members, and locking themselves in the building. At least 45 will be injured and 184 arrested. In this harrowing season of student unrest, disorders also take place at New York City College, San Francisco State College, Brandeis, Berkeley and hundreds of other colleges around the country.

6 MAY 1969

National Overruling a naval court of inquiry, Navy Secretary John Chafee announces that none of the members of the *Pueblo* crew will be disciplined. The *Pueblo*, a U.S. intelligence-gathering vessel, was seized by the North Koreans in January 1968 and released 11 months later. The court of inquiry had recommended court-martial of Commander Lloyd M. Bucher on several charges, including failure to defend the ship, and Lieutenant Stephen Harris, the intelligence officer, for failing to destroy secret material.

14 MAY 1969

National Supreme Court Justice Abe Fortas resigns amidst strong criticism of alleged financial misdealings. The associate justice had agreed to a $20,000 a year stipend from a charitable foundation created by Louis Wolfson, who is currently serving a prison sentence for stock market manipulation.

26 MAY 1969

Science-Technology After 18 days in space, including 31 orbits around the moon, *Apollo 10* splashes down in the Pacific. The mission, which was designed as a complete rehearsal for a manned lunar landing, included a descent by a landing module (dubbed Snoopy) to within nine miles of the moon's surface to get a close-up look at the projected landing site for *Apollo 11*.

8 JUNE 1969

War: Vietnam President Nixon meets with South Vietnam President Nguyen Van Thieu on the island of

Midway to discuss the war in Vietnam. After the conference, Nixon announces that 25,000 American troops will be withdrawn from that country, the first troop reduction since President Johnson introduced combat troops in March 1965. The action is part of the administration's plan to deescalate American military involvement in the war by turning over combat to the South Vietnamese.

23 JUNE 1969

National   Warren Burger takes the oath of office as the Supreme Court's 15th Chief Justice. Burger had been confirmed by the Senate, by a vote of 74-3, on June 9.

18 JULY 1969

National   A car driven by Senator Edward M. Kennedy, of Massachusetts, goes off a narrow bridge on Chappaquiddick Island (part of Martha's Vineyard) plunging into a salt water pond below. The Senator manages to escape, but 28-year-old Mary Jo Kopechne drowns.

20 JULY 1969

National   At 10:56 PM (EDT), Neil Armstrong steps onto the lunar surface, the first man to walk on the moon. *Apollo 11*, which carried Armstrong, Colonel Buzz Aldrin and Lieutenant Colonel Michael Collins on this historic journey, was launched on July 16 from Cape Kennedy and went into lunar orbit three days later. Early today a lunar landing module, manned by both Armstrong and Aldrin, made the final descent to the moon. The two astronauts deposit a lunar capsule and an American flag on the moon while Americans view the ceremony from television screens. A plaque, to be left on the moon, is read to the audience as the astronauts hold it before the cameras: "Here men from the planet Earth first set foot upon the moon July, 1969, AD. We came in peace for all mankind." At 12:56 tomorrow morning the landing craft (the "Eagle") will return to the command module and on July 24, *Apollo 11* will return to earth.

3 AUGUST 1969

International   President Nixon returns to Washington, ending a 12-day trip around the world, in which he signaled an important new direction in American foreign policy. The President not only outlined his self-help policy for Asian countries as he made stops in Thailand, India, Pakistan, Indonesia and South Vietnam, but pledged willingness to negotiate with Communist countries in an atmosphere of "mutual respect." In the first visit to a Communist country by a president since World War II, Nixon told the Romanian people yesterday that "nations can have widely different internal orders and live in peace."

Science-Technology   NASA's *Mariner 7* passes within 2200 miles of Mars and transmits back to earth a series of breathtaking pictures of that planet.

18 AUGUST 1969

Arts/Culture   A three-day music concert attended by

NEIL ARMSTRONG, 1930-

Of all those connected with the NASA space program, no one had the opportunity to capture the attention of the American public more than Neil Armstrong. This boyish astronaut with the engaging grin stirred the imagination of millions world-wide as he became the first human being to walk on the moon. Living what seemed the realization of a childhood fantasy—Armstrong was capitivated by airplanes from thè age of nine on—he was part of the three-man Apollo 11 crew. Symbolizing the aspirations of Americans for United States space technology, Neil Armstrong also served as a reminder of the human effort involved in such projects.

Growing up in Ohio, Armstrong led an uneventful childhood that was shadowed by the Depression. Attending Purdue University, where he met his wife Jan, Armstrong pursued a lifelong interest in piloting planes, and it was not until 1962 that he joined the NASA program. When he did so, he had been a test pilot for several years, flying as a civilian at Edwards Air Force Base. He entered the space program with a sense of commitment to his personal ambitions and also to the ideals of his nation. (Nowhere were these two factors more clearly highlighted than when, as a freshman at Purdue, he worked belatedly on the completion of his Eagle Scout requirements.)

With his fierce sense of privacy Armstrong's role in the Apollo project afforded him satisfaction of a personal nature that was sometimes obscured by his role as a team player. While not evident at the time of the moon flight, several colleagues later commented on Armstrong's intense desire to be in the forefront. Neil Armstrong seized world-wide attention as he emerged on July 20, 1969, from the lunar module *Eagle*; satellite pictures of the moon landing reached anyone with a television set. Climbing down a ladder onto lunar rock, Armstrong was heard to say, "One small step for man, a giant leap for mankind." By so doing, he became the object of wonder and admiration that must surely have fed the ego of this man who, as a small boy, did little else but build model airplanes and dream of the day when he could fly.

Americans everywhere reacted with pride and excitement over such an amazing feat. This smiling, though reticent, astronaut had cast himself forever into the realm of heroes. While he later would teach engineering at the University of Cincinnati and live on a quiet farm, away from the glamour of a hero's life, he would never be able to escape from the fact that he was the first man to walk on the moon.

---

close to 300,000 youths, ends in Bethel, New York. The festival, known simply as Woodstock (where it was intended to be held), was plagued by problems, but the principal ones were the lack of adequate food and sanitation facilities as well as rains that drenched the audience throughout the weekend. Despite the crowds, the ubiquity of drugs and adverse conditions, the festival was free from violence and became a symbol of the counter-culture movement.

16 SEPTEMBER 1969

War: Vietnam   President Nixon announces the withdrawal of another 35,000 Americans from Vietnam. The reductions are part of Nixon's policy of Vietnamization, which he will unveil to the American public on November 4. By the end of the year, the president will have reduced American fighting strength in the Southeast Asian country by 110,000 men.

29 OCTOBER 1969

National In its first major decision rendered under Chief Justice Warren Burger, the Supreme Court rules that it is the "obligation of every school district . . . to terminate dual systems at once." The decision, which supersedes the court's previous call for integrating with "all deliberate speed," comes as a setback to the Nixon administration, which had sought to delay desegregation in 33 Mississippi school districts for several months.

15 NOVEMBER 1969

National The largest antiwar rally in the history of the U.S. takes place in Washington, as 250,000 people gather to protest involvement in the Vietnam War.

17 NOVEMBER 1969

International The U.S. and the Soviet Union begin strategic arms limitation talks (SALT) in Helsinki. The Helsinki negotiations are a preliminary to talks in Vienna beginning April 16, 1970. On November 24, a breakthrough will limit nuclear weapons when the two superpowers sign the U.N.-sponsored Nuclear Non-proliferation Treaty, which pledges not to spread nuclear weapons know-how or material.

19 NOVEMBER 1969

National The Lunar landing module (Intrepid) of *Apollo 12* lands on the moon, the second manned landing on the lunar surface. After some 31½ hours on the moon, astronauts Charles Conrad, Jr. and Alan Bean will return to the command module (Yankee Clipper) and on November 21 begin their journey back to earth. Splashdown will take place on November 24 in the Pacific.

20 NOVEMBER 1969

Indian Affairs Some 78 militant Indians seize Alcatraz Island in San Francisco Bay and demand that it be given to the Indian community.

21 NOVEMBER 1969

National By a vote of 55-45, the Senate rejects the nomination of Clement Haynesworth as Supreme Court justice. Opposition to the South Carolinian appellate judge stems primarily from questionable financial investments, but many are displeased by his record on civil rights and labor-related issues.

24 NOVEMBER 1969

War: Vietnam The Army announces that Lieutenant William L. Calley has been charged with premeditated murder in the massacre of Vietnam civilians in the hamlet of My Lai, on March 16, 1968. Sergeant David Mitchell has already been tried and acquitted of killing 30 people in the massacre, but Calley will be

President Nixon tours South Vietnam, 1969.

convicted and sentenced to life in prison. The revelation that American soldiers were responsible for murder of civilians in Vietnam will discredit the war and add to the antiwar movement in the U.S.

25 NOVEMBER 1969
National President Nixon orders all U.S. germ warfare stockpiles destroyed and asks the Senate to consent to the 1925 Geneva protocol prohibiting biological and chemical warfare. The president reserves the right to use lethal chemical weapons in retaliation if they are used on American troops. Encased in concrete coffins, two trainloads of nerve gas will be sunk in the Atlantic Ocean next August.

1 DECEMBER 1969
War: Vietnam With New York Representative Alexander Pirnie performing the task of withdrawing capsules, the first draft lottery since World War II is held in New York City. The lottery, proposed by Nixon in May, is an attempt to quell mounting criticism of inequities in selective service. The lottery establishes eligibility of 19-year-olds according to birthdays, with each day in the year represented by a capsule. The order in which birthdate capsules are withdrawn from the glass bin determines the order in which men will enter service.

30 DECEMBER 1969
National The most far-reaching tax reform bill in the country's history is signed into law by President Nixon. It is estimated that the law will reduce individual tax rates by 5 percent and remove some 9,000,000 low income Americans from the tax roles.

OTHER EVENTS OF 1969
Science/Technology Three Americans, Max Delbrook, Alfred Hershey and Salvador Luria, receive this year's Nobel Prize in Medicine or Physiology, while Murray Gell-Mann is awarded the Prize for Physics.

22 JANUARY 1970
National In his State of the Union message, President Nixon calls for a "new American experience" of equality of opportunity and government responsiveness to citizens' needs. The President calls for the nation to "begin to make reparations for the damage we have done to our air, to our land and to our waters," and asks Congress to enact a Family Assistance plan in place of the present welfare system, which would guarantee a minimum income to every family. Nixon, however, asserts that the nation's first priority must be to "bring an end to the war in Vietnam."

18 FEBRUARY 1970
Regional The jury in the trial of the "Chicago Seven" finds the defendants not guilty of charges of conspiring to incite a riot, in connection with the violence that took place in Chicago during the Democratic National Convention in 1968. Five of the men (Tom Hayden, Abbie Hoffman, Rennie Davis, Jerry Rubin and David Dellinger) are found guilty on a lesser charge of crossing state lines with the intent of inciting a riot.

18 MARCH 1970
Labor Postal workers in New York City go out on strike, in a demand for higher wages. The strike spreads to several cities (including Akron, Philadelphia, Chicago, Boston and Denver as well as the state of California), and will eventually involve 200,000 (out of 750,000) post office employees.

8 APRIL 1970
National By a vote of 51-45, the Senate rejects the nomination of Harold Carswell of Florida as Supreme Court associate justice, the second nominee named by Nixon to fill the seat vacated by Abe Fortas. Opposition stems principally from the judge's earlier statements endorsing segregation as well as his lackluster record as an appellate judge.

17 APRIL 1970
National Apollo 13 lands safely in the Pacific after a near catastrophic journey to the moon. The mission, which was scheduled to include the third manned lunar landing, was suddenly interrupted on April 13, about two and one-half days after takeoff, by an explosion in the service module that deprived the command module of power. The astronauts (James Lovell, John L. Swigert and Fred Haise) had to use the engines of the lunar landing craft (nicknamed Aquarius) to provide propulsion for the return flight to earth. For the next three and one-half days Apollo 13 rounded the moon and then completed its journey back to earth. As preparations got underway to recover the crippled spacecraft, messages from the Soviet Union as well as several other countries arrived in Washington volunteering assistance. The splashdown turns out to be amazingly accurate, occurring 4.6 miles from the USS *Iwo Jima*.

20 APRIL 1970
War: Vietnam President Nixon, continuing the Vietnamization program, promises to withdraw another 150,000 men from Indochina before the end of the year. American manpower in Vietnam by the end of December will be 340,000 men, down by 210,000 from its peak in 1968. The dramatic decrease in troop strength, combined with a more defensive posture by those U.S. units still in Vietnam, will have a strong effect on casualty rates. During 1968 an average of 280 Americans were killed each week, but by the end of this year, U.S. deaths will average 25 a week.

30 APRIL 1970
War: Vietnam President Nixon announces that U.S. troops have been sent into Cambodia to attack enemy bases. The decision to send troops follows the deposing of Prince Sihanouk in favor of a regime under Lon Nol. Both Hanoi and Peking support Sihanouk's effort to regain power and the U.S. is aiding Lon Nol in driving out Communist troops in the northern sec-

tion of his country. U.S. involvement in Cambodia (close to 31,000 men), which will last until June 29, generates criticism.

4 MAY 1970
Education Four students are killed and nine others wounded at Kent State University when national guardsman, called in to disperse a student antiwar demonstration, fire on the crowd. Protests have taken place at Ohio State University, Stanford, Penn State and the University of Kansas.

12 MAY 1970
National Harry Blackmun of Minnesota, a lifelong friend of Chief Justice Warren Burger, is unanimously approved by the Senate as associate justice of the Supreme Court.

14 MAY 1970
Black Experience In the second day of violent demonstrations at Jackson State College—a predominantly black school in Mississippi—state law enforcement officials fire into a crowd of bottle-and-rock-throwing youths, killing two and injuring 12.

18 JUNE 1970
National President Nixon signs into law a bill giving 18-year-olds the right to vote in federal elections.

1 JULY 1970
Regional The country's most liberal abortion law goes into effect in New York State. During the first 24 weeks of pregnancy, the law leaves the decision concerning abortion to the woman; after that time the law provides that abortions can only be performed in instances where the woman's life is in danger. In the past few years, feminist groups have lobbied extensively for the liberalization of abortion laws as a necessary step toward sexual equality.

12 AUGUST 1970
National President Nixon signs into law a bill making the U.S. Post Office an independent government corporation. The Post Office has been a Cabinet-level department since 1829 and is being made an independent agency to increase its efficiency. Reorganization is also designed to bring self-sufficiency.

15 SEPTEMBER 1970
Labor Over 340,000 members of the United Auto Workers begin a strike against General Motors in both the United States and Canada. The strike, which is the industry's largest in 20 years, will last until November 11.

20 OCTOBER 1970
Agriculture Norman Borlaug, an Iowa-born American, receives the Nobel Peace Prize for his efforts in perfecting and introducing around the world new strains of high-yield, disease-resistant wheat and rice crops. Borlaug heads the International Maize and Wheat Improvement Center of Mexico, which in-

cludes scientists from 17 different countries, and is supported by the Rockefeller Foundation.

3 NOVEMBER 1970
National In the national midterm elections, neither Democrats nor Republicans win a clear victory; in the Senate the GOP picks up two more seats, but in the House the Democrats increase their majority by nine. In state elections the Democratic Party gains nine governorships.

23 NOVEMBER 1970
War: Vietnam Secretary of Defense Melvin Laird announces a daring raid by American troops to rescue U.S. prisoners 23 miles west of Hanoi. American soldiers overran the camp where the prisoners were reportedly held, but found none. To provide cover U.S. planes conducted a seven-hour bombing raid. The bombing apparently was intended as a warning to North Vietnam, that despite troop reductions the U.S. still maintains a military presence.

10 DECEMBER 1970
Transportation Four unions, representing close to 500,000 employees, begin a walkout against the nation's railroads, the third national rail strike in the last 50 years. Two hours after the strike begins at 12:01 A.M., Nixon signs a bill, passed by Congress to deal with the crisis, increasing wages by 13.5 percent (effective immediately) and postponing the strike for 80 days.

OTHER EVENTS OF 1970
Science/Technology Julius Axelrod of the U.S. shares the Nobel Prize in Medicine or Physiology with Ulf von Euler of Sweden and Bernard Katz of Britain. On 16 October, the second presentation of the Nobel Prize in Economics is made, with Paul A. Samuelson of MIT named as this year's winner.

Population The 19th census shows a population of 203,184,722. One of the most noteworthy facts gleaned from the latest census is the strikingly diminished birth rate during the 1960s, one of the lowest in the nation's history. The slowing population growth is mainly the result of later marriages, more divorces and smaller families.

1971
22 JANUARY 1971
National President Nixon delivers his State of the Union address, proposing revenue sharing with the state and local governments for urban and rural development, education, job training, law enforcement and transportation.

8 FEBRUARY 1971
War: Vietnam The South Vietnamese army, aided by heavy U.S. air support, launches an attack in Laos.

9 FEBRUARY 1971
National Apollo 14 splashes down in the Pacific after nine days in space, including 33 hours on the

moon's surface. Apollo 15, another lunar landing mission, will be launched on July 26.

Regional An earthquake strikes the San Fernando Valley of California, killing 64 people and injuring 1000 others.

21 FEBRUARY 1971

Regional Tornadoes sweep through sections of Louisiana, Mississippi and west Tennessee, killing 93 people and causing an estimated $10,000,000 in damages.

23 MARCH 1971

National The Senate cuts off funds for a supersonic plane (SST) designed to carry 300 passengers and travel at speeds up to 1800 m.p.h.

29 MARCH 1971

Regional Charles Manson and three female members of his "family" are sentenced to death after being found guilty of murder in connection with the gruesome Tate-LaBianca slayings in Los Angeles on August 9 and 10, 1969.

20 APRIL 1971

National In a unanimous decision, the Supreme Court upholds busing as the primary way of achieving school integration.

24 APRIL 1971

National A massive antiwar demonstration in Washington draws close to 200,000 people to protest involvement in Vietnam.

1 MAY 1971

Transportation The National Railroad Passenger Corporation (Amtrak), a semi-public corporation, begins operation of intercity rail service. Designed to improve service and reduce losses, the corporation continues to rely on Congress for subsidies.

2 JUNE 1971

Regional Juan V. Corona pleads not guilty to the charge of killing 25 people—mostly migrant workers—in Northern California, the largest mass murder in recent history.

10 JUNE 1971

International The administration announces the lifting of a 21-year embargo of trade to Mainland China. On July 15, Nixon will announce that he has accepted "with pleasure" an invitation by Premier Chou En-lai to visit that country. On October 2 the U.S. will call for seating of Mainland China in the United Nations.

28 JUNE 1971

National The Supreme Court rules, eight to one, that the Constitution forbids states from reimbursing private schools for nonreligious education.

30 JUNE 1971

National The Supreme Court rules that the *New*

BUSING

Busing to achieve school integration extends back to 1954, when the Supreme Court ruled (in *Brown* v. *the Board of Education at Topeka, Kansas*) that segregated public schools violated the Constitution. Although the decision was seen originally as an attack on the South's codified dual school systems, by the late 1960s, federal courts were turning increasingly to busing to overcome residential segregation. ·In 1971 the Supreme Court validated such a strategy as a primary way of achieving racial balance.

As the number of court-ordered busing plans multiplied, however, so did the opposition to them. In March 1972 President Nixon called on Congress to put a halt on future orders for busing until July 1973, or until legislation could be devised to control them. An education bill, passed in June, included an amendment barring the implementation of court-ordered busing plans until all appeals were exhausted or the deadline for them expired. In 1974 President Ford signed a bill which prohibited the busing of students farther than the second closest school unless the courts decided it was necessary to protect an individual's Constitutional rights.

Congressional action reflected widespread public disaffection with busing. To many, such plans seemed at least wasteful; they also clashed with the ideal of the "neighborhood school." In 1972 George Wallace ran an impressive race for the Democratic nomination, in part, because of the stress he placed on the busing issue. Although an assassination attempt left Wallace paralyzed and effectively ended his presidential bid, the message was not lost on the other candidates.

The public also expressed its dissatisfaction with busing in other ways. Boston, Massachusetts (1974), and Louisville, Kentucky (1975), were the scenes of bloody confrontations when busing plans were implemented in those cities. Rather than submit to court plans, many parents kept their children at home. But boycotts were only a short term protest; enrollment figures in places where busing had been implemented showed that "white flight" was another response to forced integration. By 1976 17,216 white students had left the Boston public schools either for the suburbs or for private schools.

In this atmosphere, even the Supreme Court seemed to waver. In 1974 the court threw out a plan which called for busing children between overwhelmingly white suburban districts and the predominantly black inner-city district in Detroit. In the years following, however, the court approved busing plans for Denver, Columbus, Ohio, and Louisville, Kentucky. The court's ambivalence, perhaps, was a gauge of the public's misgivings: for many, busing remains an unsatisfactory answer to a problem that deserves a better solution

---

York Times and *Washington Post* may resume publication of the top secret Pentagon Papers on Vietnam.

15 AUGUST 1971

National To help deal with a sluggish economy and rising prices, President Nixon announces a wide variety of measures including a 90-day freeze on prices, wages and rents.

8 SEPTEMBER 1971

Arts/Culture The $70,000,000 Kennedy Center

opens in Washington. The premiere performance at the new culture center is Leonard Bernstein's *Mass*.

13 SEPTEMBER 1971
Regional Some 1000 state troopers storm Attica state prison in New York, ending a four-day prison revolt. Altogether 43 people are killed, including 31 prisoners and nine hostages.

17 SEPTEMBER 1971
National Supreme Court Justice Hugo Black, appointed by Franklin Roosevelt in 1937, resigns because of illness.

12 OCTOBER 1971
International President Nixon announces he will travel to Moscow next year to meet Soviet leaders. The trip will mark the first time a U.S. President has visited that country since World War II. Soviet-U.S. tensions eased last month (September 3) when the USSR guaranteed in writing Western access to West Berlin. In exchange, the U.S. promised that West Germany would not try to incorporate the western section of that city. Berlin has been a source of friction between the two superpowers since the Blockade of 1948-1949.

As another sign of reduced tension, the administration will announce (November 5) the sale to the Soviets of $136,000,000 in feed grains.

12 NOVEMBER 1971
War: Vietnam President Nixon announces withdrawal of another 45,000 men from Vietnam, which will leave a force of 139,000. Since Nixon's policy of Vietnamization, casualties have dropped dramatically, with 1302 U.S. deaths compared with 14,592 in 1968.

14 NOVEMBER 1971
National Phase II of Nixon's economic program goes into effect, flexible guidelines for wage and price rises in the hope of slowing annual inflation to 2.5 percent.

18 DECEMBER 1971
Finance The U.S. devalues the dollar by 8.57 percent, making dollars "cheaper" in comparison to foreign currencies, designed to increase U.S. exports and change a $5,000,000,000 negative balance in trade (imports exceeding exports) into an $8,000,000,000 surplus.

OTHER EVENTS OF 1971
Science/Technology Earl Sutherland receives the Nobel Prize in Medicine and Physiology. Another American, Simon Kuznets, is awarded the Nobel Prize in Economics.

5 JANUARY 1972
National President Nixon gives approval to the space shuttle, a NASA project to develop a reusable spacecraft fired into space on a rocket but landing like an airplane. The bill calls for $5,500,000,000 over the next six years to build and test such a craft.

13 JANUARY 1972
War: Vietnam Although there is no peace agreement in sight and the enemy continues to attack South Vietnamese positions, President Nixon announces that an additional 70,000 American troops will be withdrawn from Vietnam by January 13. With these departures, U.S. strength will be 69,000.

24 JANUARY 1972
National President Nixon announces his proposed budget for fiscal 1973, deficit of $25,500,000,000, the largest deficit in peacetime American history.

25 JANUARY 1972
War: Vietnam The Nixon Administration makes public an eight-point peace proposal to the North Vietnamese and Vietcong at the next session of the Paris Peace talks scheduled for February 3. The proposal calls for a ceasefire and release of all American prisoners in exchange for U.S. withdrawal. Following the departure of the American troops, South Vietnam is to hold new elections in which the U.S. would remain neutral. The President reveals that secret negotiations between Henry Kissinger and the Communists have been going on since June.

15 FEBRUARY 1972
National Attorney General John Mitchell resigns from the Nixon Cabinet to become chairman of the Committee to Reelect the President. He will be succeeded by the deputy assistant in the Justice Department, Richard Kleindienst of Arizona. It is while Mitchell is chairman of CRP that the Watergate break-in takes place. Soon afterward he will resign, ostensibly to spend time with his family.

21 FEBRUARY 1972
International President Nixon begins an epochal visit to China, which he describes as a "journey for peace." Since 1949, when the Communists seized control of the mainland and forced the Nationalists to flee to the island of Formosa, the U.S. has had no diplomatic relations with mainland China. At the end of Nixon's visit the U.S. and the Communist Chinese government will issue a joint statement pledging "normalization" of relations.

28 FEBRUARY 1972
Black Experience The murder trial of black militant Angela Davis begins in San Jose, California.

17 MARCH 1972
National President Nixon proposes to Congress a moratorium on busing to achieve racial balance. Accusing federal judges of over-reaching themselves and helping generate "turmoil" in local communities, the President proposes improving neighborhood schools.

22 MARCH 1972
National The Senate consents to the Equal Rights

Amendment by a vote of 84 to 8. The amendment will now go to the states.

30 MARCH 1972

War: Vietnam North Vietnamese troops cross the Demilitarized Zone to launch a massive attack against South Vietnam. After five weeks of fighting the Communists will have penetrated 22 miles into the south. The U.S. will renew bombing raids of the North, suspended for over three years. On May 9 Nixon will order the mining of major ports in North Vietnam.

THE WOMEN'S RIGHTS MOVEMENT

At the end of World War II, most working women quickly abandoned their jobs and war-inflated paychecks and settled comfortably into a life of domesticity. The baby boom of the next ten years, which raised the country's birthrate by 50 percent, suggested that most women were willing to accept motherhood as their highest ambition.

By the early 1960s, there were a few signs that things might change. In 1961 President John Kennedy established a Commission on the Status of Women, and two years later, as a result of its work, Congress passed an Equal Pay act. Although many important categories were excluded, the bill at least recognized the glaring inequality in income between the sexes. Then in 1964 the establishment of the Equal Employment Opportunity Commission, set up primarily to handle cases of racial discrimination, brought a flood of complaints (40 percent of the total) from women.

Only a year earlier, Betty Friedan had published *The Feminine Mystique,* an eloquent appeal for a wider role for women in American society. Although originally regarded by some as the solitary outcry of a disgruntled housewife, it soon became evident that the book articulated the discontent of many other women. Within three years, Friedan had set up the National Organization for Women (NOW) to push for greater political and economic equality for women.

Like the suffrage movement of the 19th century, feminism in the 1960s was partly a spin-off of other political movements. Involvement in civil rights and anti-war activity awakened many women to the sexual discrimination practiced by society. Their experiences also helped radicalize them in their thinking and behavior. Charging that NOW was too conservative, many young feminists formed their own groups committed to the complete overthrow of what they considered a sexist society. They attempted in various ways to protest their image as sexual objects. The media were only too happy to highlight some of their more outrageous and flippant activities—the bra-burners and beauty pageant protesters were in a distinct minority, although they received ample television coverage. Some women advocated lesbianism as the only way to escape male domination and this split in sexual preference and sexual politics was eventually to produce a schism in the women's movement itself.

Easy access to contraceptives and abortion on request remained important objectives in the feminists' goals of achieving complete control over their bodies and their lives. The Supreme Court greatly aided this cause in 1973 when it ruled that states could not, among other things, outlaw voluntary abortions before the sixth month of pregnancy.

The Women's Movement, however, continued to meet strong resistance. Many women enjoyed their separate spheres, and resisted efforts to interfere with practices which they believed benefited them. Thus, when the Equal Rights Amendment, passed by Congress in 1970, was sent to the states for ratification, conservative women's groups helped carry the amendment down to defeat. Nevertheless, a great number of women of all ages continue to support the ideas that first helped the post-war Women's Movement gain momentum—that equal pay for equal work is the right of every American citizen, and that opportunities in all areas of society should be available to all men and women.

13 APRIL 1972

International President Nixon and Canadian Prime Minister Pierre Trudeau agree to a joint effort to free the Great Lakes of pollution.

16 APRIL 1972

National NASA launches Apollo 16. The lunar mission, the fifth manned expedition to land on the moon, is to collect rock samples from the mountainous Descartes region. After 11 days in space, including three on the moon, American astronauts return to earth. In a less publicized project, the U.S. launched Pioneer 10 on March 2. This unmanned interplanetary spacecraft will make a 620,000,000-mile voyage past Jupiter to gather information about the solar system's largest planet.

2 MAY 1972

Population J. Edgar Hoover, director of the FBI since its establishment 48 years ago, dies.

15 MAY 1972

National Governor George C. Wallace is shot by Arthur H. Bremer, 21, while campaigning for the Presidency at a shopping center in Laurel, Maryland.

22 MAY 1972

International In the first peacetime visit to the Soviet Union by an American president, Nixon begins a week of talks with Communist leaders in Moscow. Nixon will sign, on May 26, a pact pledging the two countries to freeze nuclear arsenals at current levels. He will also work out a trade agreement and agree to a joint Soviet-U.S. space mission in 1975.

8 JUNE 1972

National Congress passes a bill for federal aid to college and university students. The bill includes a provision delaying court-ordered busing for up to 18 months and allocates $2,000,000,000 to help elementary and high schools desegregate.

14 JUNE 1972

Agriculture The Environmental Protection Agency announces a ban on the chemical pesticide DDT to take effect on December 31.

17 JUNE 1972

National Police arrest five men at the Democratic National Headquarters in the Watergate complex in

J. EDGAR HOOVER, 1895-1972

A name synonymous for decades with the vigilance of the FBI, J. Edgar Hoover, from his obscure beginnings in a minor government post, quickly rose to become the right-hand man of Attorney General A. Mitchell Palmer in 1919. Born in the nation's capital, Hoover was educated there, earning his law degree at George Washington University in 1917. His one and only interest was the upgrading of federal law enforcement practices—and toward that end he focused his life. In 1924, Hoover assumed the post of FBI director and soon gave full play to his passion for detail by establishing a crime lab, a fingerprint file and a training school for FBI detectives and other law enforcement personnel. The tenacious behavior which propelled Hoover's career led him, in the 1930s and 1940s, to launch a series of investigations into suspected espionage and sabotage against the government.

Hoover's intense desire to rid the United States of undesirable elements was fueled by a limited personal vision of what was politically appropriate. Viewed by the public with an awe and fascination which combined to make him an almost legendary figure in his own time, Hoover thrived on the mystique which he built for himself and his agency. This image was further perpetrated by Hollywood films of the era which dwelt upon the FBI's dedication to apprehending lawbreakers. J. Edgar Hoover was admired by most Americans as a man who would stop at nothing to deter the criminal element in society. But Hoover, a solitary individual with virtually no personal involvements outside of his career, was caricatured by other Americans, along with his agency, as a silent, almost sinister figure.

Hoover acted as an informant to administrations, a role he thoroughly enjoyed. In this capacity, he increased surveillance on such persons as Eleanor Roosevelt, William O. Douglas, and later, Martin Luther King Jr., individuals of a more liberal persuasion than the arch-conservative Hoover, a man suspicious of any views not coinciding with his own.

Hoover's efforts to build an agency which worked to preserve justice were successful in terms of size and effectiveness: the agency employed 16,000 by 1960. This seeming success was marred, however, by the alleged illegal practices conducted by the FBI in the mid- and late-1960s. The director was at that time asked by the Attorney General's office to cease tampering with mail, illegal break-ins and wire-taps. While there were numerous calls for Hoover's dismissal during this period, due to his arbitrary, imperious attitude concerning legal violations, both Presidents Johnson and Nixon supported him. His advancing age did little to budge him from the position of influence and power that he had carved out for himself, and he was allowed to remain at his post long past mandatory retirement age. He died in the nation's capital, alone and virtually reclusive to the end, a secretive man whose life's energy had been spent in service to his country.

Washington. All five men are employed by the Committee to Reelect the President and the attempted burglary is an effort to obtain political material. Two other men on the CRP staff will be arrested in connection with the break-in. The fact that these two, G. Gordon Liddy and E. Howard Hunt, had worked as aides in the White House will begin an investigation

that ultimately leads to Nixon's resignation. The seven men will be indicted on September 15.

19 JUNE 1972
Regional A hurricane begins 10 days of devastation along the Eastern Coast of the U.S., which will affect major damage in Florida, Virginia, Maryland, Pennsylvania and New York. The hurricane will kill some people and cause extensive damage.

29 JUNE 1972
National In a landmark decision, the Supreme Court rules, in *Furman v. Georgia,* that the death penalty can constitute cruel and unusual punishment and violates the 8th Amendment to the Constitution. The ruling affects the fate of many currently on death row and will lead to a flurry of activity by state legislatures to revise laws on capital punishment to meet the

GEORGE WALLACE, 1919-

The stocky figure of George Wallace, governor of Alabama, first appeared on the nation's television screens in June 1963, as he stood at the door of the University of Alabama in a dramatic but unsuccessful attempt to bar the registration of the school's first black students. At that point he became one of the leaders of the last stand of American segregationists. Although he later retreated from his earlier proclamations of "segregation forever," he remained into the 70s a highly visible leader of the conservative cause.

Wallace was born on the family farm in Clio, Alabama, on August 25, 1919. In high school he was a champion Golden Gloves boxer. Later he paid his way through Alabama Law School partly by boxing professionally. After receiving his law degree in 1942 he served three years in the Air Force. Returning after the war to Alabama, he was elected to the state legislature in 1947; there he became a noted speaker and an effective promoter of various bills relating to trade, health and education. Also in the legislature he began his series of struggles to stem the rising tide of integration, fighting against civil rights planks in the 1949 Democratic Convention and in the next two conventions. As a district court judge in the mid-50s he refused to turn over voting registration records to the federal courts. The attention these efforts brought him led to an unsuccessful gubernatorial bid in 1958 and a successful one in 1962; he had, in his own words, learned to "out-seg" his opponents, a traditional Southern method of gaining office.

After failing to prevent blacks from registering at the university in 1962, Wallace made several other stands against integration, all frustrated by President Kennedy, who repeatedly used the National Guard to restore order, keep schools open and proceed with integration. Still, Wallace became a national hero to segregationists, conservatives and states-righters, and this led to a 1968 Presidential bid on an independent ticket; he polled 13 percent of the popular vote in the election. While campaigning again for the Presidency in 1972, Wallace was shot by Arthur Bremer and was partially paralyzed. Failing to win a presidential nomination in 1972 and 1976, Wallace ran again for governor of Alabama in 1982 and won, thus reestablishing himself as one of the political phenomena of the century.

court's objections.

8 JULY 1972
International The Nixon administration announces a deal with the Soviet Union for the U.S. to sell $750,000,000 of corn, wheat and other grain. The President hopes that trade between the two countries can reduce tensions.

10 JULY 1972
National The Democratic Convention begins in Miami Beach. Candidates for the presidential nomination are Hubert Humphrey and George McGovern. McGovern has won the largest number of delegates in state primaries and will win the nomination and name Senator Thomas F. Eagleton as his running mate. He has long been an opponent of the Vietnam War and campaigned throughout the year for the "immediate and complete withdrawal" of U.S. troops.

1 AUGUST 1972
National Democratic vice-presidential nominee Thomas Eagleton announces withdrawal from the race. On July 25 the Missouri Senator confirmed that he had undergone psychiatric therapy, including electric shock. Although McGovern continued to support

him, unfavorable public reaction convinced Eagleton to abandon the contest. On October 8 R. Sargent Shriver, brother-in-law of the late John and Robert Kennedy and best known for heading the Peace Corps, will fill the number two slot on the Democratic ticket.

3 AUGUST 1972
National By a vote of 88 to 2, the Senate agrees to a strategic arms treaty with the Soviet Union. The pact, signed by Nixon while he was in Moscow, sets limits on antiballistic missile systems of the two countries. A second agreement, placing ceilings on offensive weapons arsenals of the superpowers, will be approved by the Senate on September 14.

12 AUGUST 1972
War: Vietnam The last units of U.S. ground forces withdraw from Vietnam.

21 AUGUST 1972
National The Republican Convention opens in Miami Beach. President Nixon and Vice-President Spiro Agnew both will be renominated by almost unanimous votes. On the 23rd, some 1129 anti-war protestors picketing outside the convention hall will

U.S. soldiers pinned down by snipers near Long Dinh, Vietnam.

JANUARY 11, 1973

A third-rate burglary is how one Nixon aide described the break-in at the National Democratic Headquarters at the Watergate on June 17, 1972. For some nine months afterward, it seemed that the event would remain just that; although it had been quickly established that all seven men arrested worked for the Committee to Reelect the President (CRP), which maintained close ties with the White House, there was no direct evidence to prove involvement by Nixon's staff. And none of the seven was talking.

Then the conspiracy of silence was suddenly broken. In March 1973 James McCord, one of the convicted burglars, identified CRP chairman (and former Attorney General) John Mitchell as having directed the break-in. Then the next month, FBI director Patrick Gray admitted destroying Watergate evidence on the advice of Nixon aides. The twin revelations brought a string of resignations which included the President's closest aides, John Erlichman and Robert Haldeman as well as Presidential Counsel John Dean. Then Nixon himself came under attack. In June 1973 John Dean charged before a Senate committee that Nixon had personally authorized the payment of hush money to the "Watergate Seven." Then, three weeks later, the committee was told that all conversations in the President's office were taped. There now was a way to verify Dean's story.

For the next year, all three branches of the government were embroiled in a battle for the Presidential tapes. Nixon tried, in October, to end the legal action by firing special prosecutor Archibald Cox but the move badly misfired; Congress was so outraged that it immediately took up consideration of impeachment charges. Also, though Nixon turned over some tapes after firing Cox (one with a mysterious 18-minute gap), the new special prosecutor, Leon Jaworski, continued to press for the release of additional tapes, refusing to accept an edited transcript which the President provided in April 1974.

Then in July the President was dealt two severe blows: The Supreme Court ordered him to turn over the subpoenaed evidence; and the House Judiciary Committee approved three articles of impeachment. Pressed from all aides, Nixon released the tapes on August 5. Four days later, on the advice of key Republicans in Congress, he resigned.

The tapes proved conclusively that Nixon had obstructed justice by ordering the FBI to halt its Watergate investigation only six days after the break-in. But even more shocking was the discovery that the Watergate incident was not an isolated event, but part of a vast network of activity which included break-ins, wiretaps and political sabotage. With the great powers at his disposal, Nixon had orchestrated an insidious program of domestic espionage which mocked the democratic process itself. He had also made "Watergate" a synonym for scandal in high places.

be arrested for trying to prevent delegates from entering.

11 SEPTEMBER 1972
Sports At the Summer Olympics in Munich, 11 Israeli atheletes are killed by Arab terrorists.

26 OCTOBER 1972
War: Vietnam Returning from South Vietnam, Secretary of State Henry Kissinger says that peace is "within reach in a matter of weeks or less." The announcement is two weeks before the national elections.

30 OCTOBER 1972
National President Nixon signs an amendment to the Social Security Act providing an additional $5,300,000,000 in benefits for the elderly. The bill makes important changes, including an increase in the annual amount a beneficiary can earn and extension of Medicare benefits to disabled under 65. On July 1 Nixon signed a bill increasing Social Security benefits by 20 percent.

7 NOVEMBER 1972
National Nixon wins an overwhelming victory over Senator George McGovern. The President captures 60.8 percent of the popular vote and 520 out of 537 electoral ballots (only Massachusetts going to McGovern). The Republicans gain 13 seats in the House of Representatives but remain the minority party in that chamber. In the Senate, Democrats gain one seat, increasing their majority to 14.

28 NOVEMBER 1972
National Nixon begins a major Cabinet reorganization. George Romney, Secretary of Housing and Urban Development, and Melvin Laird, the Defense Secretary, are both dropped, while Elliot Richardson and James T. Lynn shift to fill these positions. The President makes changes in his White House staff.

18 DECEMBER 1972
War: Vietnam President Nixon orders the resumption of bombings over North Vietnam. Intense fighting by South Vietnamese soldiers, supported by bombing by the U.S., had helped stall the last major assault on the South.

OTHER EVENTS OF 1972
Science/Technology The Nobel Prize in Physics goes to three Americans, John Bardeen, Leon Cooper and John R. Schrieffer, for their work on superconductivity. The Nobel Prize for Chemistry goes to three other Americans, Christian B. Anfinsen, Stanford Moore and William H. Stein, for their contributions to the study of enzymes. Gerald M. Edelman, an American, shares the Nobel Prize for Physiology or Medicine with Rodney R. Porter of England for their work on the chemical structure of antibodies.
Economics The Nobel Award for Economics is shared by the American Kenneth J. Arrow and the Briton Sir John Hicks.

11 JANUARY 1973
National President Nixon ends mandatory wage and price controls. The controls have been in effect since the passage of the Economic Stabilization Act 17 months ago and were designed to slow the country's inflation rate. Except for food, health and housing, the administration will rely on voluntary compliance with its anti-inflationary guidelines. The new plan,

EMERGING AS A WORLD POWER 1946-

HENRY KISSINGER, 1923-

Regarded by many people both in the United States and abroad as one of the most effective statesmen in this century, Henry Kissinger was also one of the most controversial public figures. From the moment he appeared in Washington as Nixon's special assistant for national security affairs and then moved on to become the Secretary of State, Kissinger—with his German-accented speech and his detached humor—provided the media with a constant stream of news and images. Much of this tended to create an aura around the man that his admirers felt reflected his achievements but which his critics felt obscured his failings.

Kissinger was born in Germany and fled the Nazis with his Jewish family to arrive in New York City in 1938. After serving with the United States Army in World War II, Kissinger attended Harvard College, graduating summa cum laude in 1950. While pursuing his graduate studies there, he became executive director of Harvard's International Seminar and came to know young people from all over the world with whom he would later deal as their nations' leaders. Accepting a post on Harvard's government faculty, Kissinger began to publish his views on contemporary affairs and was soon serving as an unofficial adviser to Nelson Rockefeller. But when Rockefeller lost his race for the presidency, Kissinger found himself invited by newly elected President Nixon to serve as an adviser on foreign affairs. Kissinger's dynamic approach soon brought him into conflict with the more reserved approach of the Secretary of State, but it would be 1973 before Nixon would promote Kissinger to that post.

Meanwhile Kissinger had taken a direct role in the secret negotiations with the North Vietnamese that eventually led to the cease-fire agreement of January 1973, thus ending that grim war—and winning Kissinger the Nobel Peace Prize (along with the chief North Vietnamese negotiator). Kissinger's admirers inevitably focused on these attainments as proof of his greatness; critics noted that Kissinger himself had helped to promote and prolong that very war. Few could deny, however, that he helped to pave the way for Nixon's historic trip to China in 1972. More controversial again was Kissinger's role in negotiating with the principals in the Israeli-Arab conflict: as with so much of Kissinger's diplomacy, there was more than a little suggestion that there was more form than substance, more personality than policy, behind his apparent attainments.

But Kissinger seemed to thrive on such contradictions. Given to secrecy in his diplomatic negotiations, he seemed to court the limelight as soon as he emerged from the inner chambers of power. Described as arrogant and cold by many who worked alongside him, he could be urbane and witty in his dealings with the most casual reporter. Sometimes appearing like a committed idealogue whose whole life was centered around stemming the spread of totalitarian regimes, Kissinger in other respects seemed like a person more interested in advancing his own career. History might well label him "the Great Manipulator."

Kissinger did serve to give the waning and disastrous days of the Nixon administration whatever stability they had and then continued to serve as Ford's Secretary of State. With Carter's election, Kissinger stepped down, and his subsequent activities included some teaching, a great deal of lecturing, consulting and writing his version of the events he had participated in. By this time he

could name—and get—his own price for almost anything he chose to do, but in fairness to the man it had to be admitted that he kept a surprisingly low profile. Ironically, he was regarded by some of Reagan's more conservative supporters as even more heinous than by many Democrats and liberals, so it seemed that his active role in American foreign affairs was over.

known as "Phase III" of the President's economic program, will remain, with modifications, until summer.

20 JANUARY 1973
National Nixon delivers his Sate of the Union message. Signaling his aim of reducing the role of the Federal Government in the lives of its citizens, the President tells the nation: "In our own lives, let each of us ask not just what will the government do for me, but what can I do for myself?"

22 JANUARY 1973
National In a landmark decision of *Roe v. Wade*, the Supreme Court rules unconstitutional all state laws that prohibit voluntary abortions before the third month (and sets limits on prohibitions during the second three months). The decision, which is greeted by feminists as an important breakthrough for their cause, will help fuel a strong "right to life" movement to obtain a constitutional amendment banning abortions.

27 JANUARY 1973
War: Vietnam Henry Kissinger signs a four-party pact in Paris (the signers are North Vietnam, the Vietcong, South Vietnam and the U.S.) providing for withdrawal of U.S. troops within 60 days. An immediate ceasefire will begin and all American prisoners are to be freed. Although cease-fire violations will occur on virtually a daily basis, and although the U.S. will continue bombing Cambodia until August 14, the public sees the Paris peace agreement as ending American military involvement in Southeast Asia, and in the aftermath of the signing the President's approval rating will jump to 68 percent.

Secretary of Defense Melvin Laird announces the end of the draft. The U.S. will rely on voluntary enlistment.

5 FEBRUARY 1973
National Roy Ash, Nixon's director of the Office of Management and Budget, reveals that the administration has impounded $8,700,000,000 appropriated by Congress for federal programs. The announcement will spark a bitter argument over the authority of the executive to withhold appropriated funds.

7 FEBRUARY 1973
National The Senate establishes a Select Committee on Presidential Campaign Activities, chaired by Sam Ervin, to investigate the Watergate conspiracy. The committee, which will begin public hearings on May 17, will eventually hear testimony implicating the

Henry Kissinger.

man, domestic affairs assistant John Erlichman and Presidential Counsel John Dean III resign. Attorney General Richard Kleindienst submits his resignation. President Nixon makes a public broadcast announcing the resignations but denying knowledge of the Watergate cover-up.

11 MAY 1973
National Charges against Daniel Ellsberg and Anthony J. Russo for theft and circulation of the Pentagon Papers are dismissed by Judge William Byrne. The allegations stem from their alleged role in "leaking" the classified papers to the press. The judge's action does not settle the constitutional questions concerning freedom of the press, but comes after the Attorney General's office had revealed to Byrne that two government agents, E. Howard Hunt and G. Gordon Liddy, had broken into the office of Ellsberg's psychiatrist in an attempt to steal the defendant's medical records.

13 JUNE 1973
National President Nixon announces a price freeze on all retail goods. The freeze does not include rents, interest rates or raw agricultural products. After dramatic increases in consumer and wholesale prices, Nixon is moving back toward controls. On July 18 he will unveil "Phase IV" of his economic program.

16 JUNE 1973
International Soviet leader Leonid Brezhnev begins a series of talks with President Nixon. Before Brezhnev leaves Washington the two will agree to avoid confrontations that might precipitate a nuclear war. They will sign an accord setting down rules for negotiation of a strategic arms limitation treaty to replace the temporary agreement instituted in 1972. On June 24 Brezhnev will address this nation in a television broadcast, the first Soviet leader to do so.

21 JUNE 1973
National In five separate Supreme Court cases, all decided by a 5-to-4 vote, the court sets rules for suppression of pornography. Reversing a 15-year trend narrowing the legal definition of pornography, it decides that local community standards are a yardstick of what is pornographic.

25 JUNE 1973
National Testifying before the Senate Watergate Committee, John Dean III, former Presidential Counsel, accuses Nixon of involvement in the Watergate cover-up and charges the President with authorizing payment of hush money to the seven men accused of breaking into Democratic National Headquarters. On July 24, though, John Erlichman will tell the committee that Dean's charges are undermining Nixon's attempts to present the public with a factual account of the Watergate conspiracy.

16 JULY 1973
National The Senate Armed Forces Committee be-

President in the Watergate cover-up.

12 FEBRUARY 1973
Finance George P. Shultz, Secretary of the Treasury, announces a 10 percent devaluation of the American dollar against the world's major currencies. The second of its kind in 14 months, it is an attempt to improve the foreign trade balance.

27 FEBRUARY 1973
Indian Affairs Close to 300 members of the militant American Indian Movement (AIM) take over Wounded Knee, South Dakota—the site of a massacre of Indians by federal soldiers in 1890.

23 MARCH 1973
National In a breakthrough in the Watergate case, James W. McCord, one of the convicted men in the attempted burglary, admits, in a letter to Judge John Sirica, that he and the other six defendants have been under pressure to remain silent about the case. McCord tells the judge that others who have escaped punishment were involved in the break-in. McCord will name former CRP chairman John Mitchell as "overall boss."

20 APRIL 1973
National Patrick E. Gray, director of the FBI, resigns after admitting he destroyed Watergate evidence on the advice of Nixon aides.

30 APRIL 1973
National Presidential Chief of Staff H. R. Halde-

gins hearings into charges that the U.S. made secret bombing raids into Cambodia during 1969 and 1970, while that nation was recognized as a neutral country. Tomorrow Secretary of Defense James Schlesinger will tell the committee that the raids (some 3500 in number) were "fully authorized" and necessary to protect U.S. troops from attack. On the 20th, Pentagon officials admit that they gave the Senate false reports about the bombings.

Alexander P. Butterfield, former deputy assistant to the President, tells the Senate Watergate Committee that all conversations in the Oval Office were routinely recorded. The startling news provides the committee with a way of substantiating testimony implicating President Nixon on the cover-up of the Watergate conspiracy. The Senate panel will subpoena the President's tapes but on July 23 Nixon will reject the subpoena, arguing that the tapes are "privileged" executive information and to turn them over would infringe the independence of that branch of government.

14 AUGUST 1973
Regional In the largest multi-murder in American history, David Brooks and Elmer Henley are indicted for killing 27 men over a period of three years. The police uncovered the murders seven days ago when Henley confessed to killing Dean Corll, a sexual pervert for whom he and Brooks had secured the other victims.
International The U.S. officially halts its bombing raids into Cambodian territory. For several months, the U.S. had been publicly bombing the Southeast Asian country to help defeat rebel forces. Although the White House, on June 27, vetoed a Congressional bill that would have immediately cut off funds for such bombings, Nixon later agreed to a compromise date of August 15 for cessation of the raids.

6 SEPTEMBER 1973
Labor W. A. "Tony" Boyle, the 71-year-old former president of the United Mine Workers, is charged with the murder of Joseph A. Yablonski and his wife and daughter. Yablonski was a leading opponent of Boyle in the UMW.

6 OCTOBER 1973
International Just as the Hebrew holy days of Yom Kippur are to begin, Egyptian troops invade the Israeli-occupied territory in the Sinai Peninsula and Syrian troops cross over into the Israeli-occupied Golan Heights. The Israelis are caught by surprise but quickly rally.

10 OCTOBER 1973
National Vice-President Spiro Agnew resigns after pleading "no contest" to a charge of tax evasion stemming from illegal payments by contractors who sought favors while he was governor of Maryland. Agnew is only the second vice-president to resign (the first having been John C. Calhoun, who left Andrew Jackson's administration for political reasons). In two days Nixon will nominate House minority leader Gerald R. Ford to succeed Agnew—invoking for the first time the provisions of the 25th Amendment (ratified in 1967) allowing the President to fill a vacancy in the office of vice-president.

15 OCTOBER 1973
International The U.S. announces that it is resupplying Israel with military equipment to counter support given by the U.S.S.R. to Arab forces.

16 OCTOBER 1973
International In a controversial decision, Dr. Henry Kissinger and Le Duc Tho of North Vietnam receive the Nobel Peace Prize for negotiating the Paris peace accord, ending fighting in Vietnam. Although Kissinger will travel to Stockholm for the ceremonies, Le Duc Tho declines the award until peace is established in his country.

20 OCTOBER 1973
National President Nixon orders his Attorney General, Elliot Richardson, to dismiss special prosecutor Archibald Cox, who has refused to accept the President's compromise offer to release a synopsis of Presidential tapes subpoenaed by the prosecutor instead of the tapes themselves. Rather than comply with the order, Richardson and his assistant, William D. Ruckelshaus, resign. Cox is then fired by Solicitor General Robert Bork, third in line in the Justice Department. Dubbed the Saturday Night Massacre, the resignations of Richardson and Ruckelshaus and the firing of Cox will bring a storm of protest and lead Congress to consider impeachment of the President.
International The Arab oil-producing nations declare an embargo on oil exports to the U.S. and a 10 percent cut in production, part of an attempt to put pressure on the U.S. and its West European allies to force Israel to withdraw from occupied Arab lands. After their initial successes since invading Israeli-occupied lands on October 6, the tide of the war has turned against them. They hope that the U.S., Israel's greatest source of military equipment, will withdraw its support.

THE ENERGY CRISIS

There were some signs early in 1973 of an impending energy shortage. In the winter, for example, the lack of sufficient heating oil in some midwestern states forced the shutdown of a number of factories and schools. In June, President Nixon created the Energy Policy Office to help the administration better manage the country's energy resources. An oil embargo, however, imposed by the Arab oil producing nations in October, brought matters to a head. Early in November, the President went on national television to propose a series of energy saving measures to deal with the crisis, including year-round daylight savings time, a relaxation of environmental standards and a cutback on fuel allocations. Later in the month, he called for a 50 mph speed limit and Sunday closings of gas stations to further ease the shortage. During the winter,

William Simon (who became the administration's energy "czar" in December) managed the country's fuel resources by restricting the production and distribution of gasoline in order to concentrate on the refining of industrial fuel and home heating oil. Although the winter saw long lines at most of America's gas stations and many grumbled that the shortage had been deliberately manufactured to drive up prices, the nation's critical oil needs were met.

The shortage, too, stimulated a move for energy independence. In November, Nixon signed a bill providing for the construction of a 789-mile oil pipeline from Alaska to the lower 48 states, a move which he insisted would help the U.S. become self-sufficient by 1980. Measures were also taken to increase the exploitation of the nation's oil and coal reserves and to speed up the construction of nuclear energy reactors. Although environmentalists were often critical of these steps, they were more supportive of the steps taken to develop the nation's alternative energy sources such as wind power or solar energy.

The end of the Arabs' embargo in March 1974 helped ease the shortage considerably but, in December 1978, the nation was again caught short when Iran—following a revolution in that country—stopped all oil exports. To make matters worse, a major nuclear power accident at Three Mile Island, near Harrisburg, Pennsylvania, early the next spring, not only closed that reactor but also served to slow the construction of many other plants. In April President Carter called on Congress to phase out price controls on oil and gasoline in order to stimulate conservation. He also asked for an emergency gas-rationing plan and a concerted effort by the government to develop alternative energy sources.

Although prices almost doubled before they leveled off, the shortages and the measures taken to alleviate them did produce some positive results. Not only did the U.S. increase its energy producing capabilities but it became much less wasteful of the resources it had. Americans, for example, not only began to drive less, but they turned increasingly to fuel-efficient automobiles to provide their transportation; oil shortage had turned into a surplus. Although the transition away from wasteful energy practices would not be easy, this was an unmistakable sign that it could be done.

22 OCTOBER 1973

International The U.S. and Soviet Union jointly sponsor a UN resolution calling for a cease-fire in the two-week-old war in the Middle East. Both sides accept the ceasefire and the fighting will come to an end on the 24th.

23 OCTOBER 1973

National Congressional leaders agree that the House Judiciary Committee should begin investigation into impeachment charges against the President. Outrage over the firing of Cox leads Nixon to reverse his position on release of the tapes. His lawyer announces that subpoenaed evidence will be turned over. On October 30 the White House will reveal that two of the tapes do not exist. On November 21, a mysterious 18½ minute gap on another reel will be reported. Although Nixon's personal secretary will testify that she might have accidentally erased the tape, a panel of experts will report on January 15, 1974 that the gap could not have been caused by accidental erasure.

7 NOVEMBER 1973

National Congress passes the War Powers Act over the President's veto. The bill is an attempt by the legislative branch to restrain the executive's power to commit U.S. troops into foreign countries for indefinite periods without Congressional approval.

Today also, Nixon addresses the nation on the energy crisis in a television broadcast. The President proposes stringent measures to ease the country's energy demands, including the instigation of year-round daylight savings time and the relaxation of environmental standards.

International The U.S. and Egypt announce resumption of diplomatic relations after a break that extends back to the 1967 war.

9 NOVEMBER 1973

National Six of the Watergate defendants are sentenced by Judge John Sirica for their role in the break-in at the Democratic National Headquarters in June 1972. E. Howard Hunt receives a sentence ranging from 2½ to 8 years and a fine of $10,000. The others are given lesser sentences. G. Gordon Liddy has been sentenced to 20 years for his involvement. The penalty resulted from Liddy's refusal to cooperate with the prosecution.

13 NOVEMBER 1973

National Representatives of Gulf and Ashland Oil Companies plead guilty to illegal contributions to President Nixon's reelection fund. Tomorrow Commerce Secretary Maurice Stans will admit that such contributions were expected from major corporations. On November 15, Braniff International, American Airlines and Goodyear will testify to similar donations.

16 NOVEMBER 1973

National President Nixon signs the controversial Alaska Pipeline Bill ,to build a 789-mile pipeline across Alaska to carry oil to the rest of the U.S. Opposed by environmental groups, the law is praised by the President as the first major step toward making the U.S. self-sufficient in energy by 1980.

30 NOVEMBER 1973

National Egil Krogh Jr., former leader of the White House "plumbers," pleads guilty to charges stemming from his break-in of the office of Daniel Ellsberg's psychiatrist.

6 DECEMBER 1973

National Gerald Ford is sworn in as the nation's 40th vice-president. Because of the ongoing investigation into Nixon's possible role in the Watergate cover-up, many Congressmen have insisted that Ford be evaluated as the Chief Executive. After rigorous investigation into his background, Congress ratifies Nixon's selection.

OTHER EVENTS OF 1973

Science/Technology   The Nobel Prize for Physics is shared by an American, Ivar Giaever, a Japanese, Leo Esaki, and a Briton, Brian Josephson. Procedures are developed for laboratory production of recombinant DNA molecules.

Economics   The Nobel Prize for Economics is awarded to Wassily Leontief, a professor at Harvard University.

Transportation   Americans from coast to coast find themselves in long lines at gas stations and frequently traveling distances to find stations open "after hours" or on weekends—an unprecedented situation in a land with a seemingly bottomless gas tank. Although triggered by the oil embargo imposed by the Arab nations in October, the shortage, in fact, traced back several years—for the world's oil surplus of many years was diminishing. The Arab oil-producing countries sensed this development, and used the occasion of the Arab-Israeli War to raise their prices. American consumers often failed to see these long-term causes of the oil crisis, and many people considered it a creation of the oil companies to drive up prices and force smaller independent producers out of business. Many areas impose gas allocation programs such as the "odd-even" system—cars with even-numbered plates buy gas on even-numbered days, odd-numbered plates on odd-numbered days. The crisis will ease by March 1974, when the Arab countries lift their embargo against the U.S., but by that time it is clear that the energy crisis is going to be around much longer.

4 JANUARY 1974

National   President Nixon refuses to surrender 500 tapes and documents subpoenaed by the Senate Watergate Committee. Nixon tells Committee chairman Sam Ervin that to accede would "unquestionably destroy any vestige of confidentiality of presidential communications, thereby irreparably impairing the constitutional functions of the office of the presidency." The committee is still awaiting court action on previously subpoenaed tapes.

30 JANUARY 1974

National   In his State of the Union address, Nixon outlines his goals for the remaining years of his administration, a ten-point program to reduce the energy crisis, slow inflation, promote world peace and initiate domestic reform in transportation, health care and education. The President again pledges he will not resign but will cooperate with the House Judiciary Committee in its investigation in any way that does not weaken the Presidency.

4 FEBRUARY 1974

Regional   Patricia Hearst, granddaughter of the newspaper tycoon William Randolph Hearst, is kidnapped from her Berkeley apartment by a group calling itself the Symbionese Liberation Army. On February 12, the SLA will demand that her father,

Randolph Hearst, begin a massive program of food distribution to the poor.

8 FEBRUARY 1974

Science/Technology   After a record space journey of 84 days, the three-man crew of Skylab 3 returns to earth, the last of three NASA projects to test humans' ability to live and work in space.

1 MARCH 1974

National   Seven former White House staff members, including H. R. Haldeman, John Erlichman and John Mitchell, are indicted for conspiring to obstruct investigation into the Watergate break-in. The trials of five of the seven will begin on October 1, and on January 1, 1975, Erlichman, Haldeman, Mitchell and Robert Mardian will be found guilty of the charges. A fifth man, Kenneth Parkinson, will be acquitted; the Watergate charges against Charles Colson will be dropped after he pleads guilty to crimes in connection with the break-in of the office of Daniel Ellsberg's psychiatrist. Gorden Strachen, the seventh defendent, will be tried separately.

18 MARCH 1974

International   In a meeting in Vienna, Arab oil-producing nations agree to end the embargo against the U.S. imposed last October. The embargo has caused widespread shortages and stimulated the government to a program of energy self-sufficiency.

3 APRIL 1974

National   President Nixon announces he will pay $432,787.13 in back taxes, after months of investigation by a joint Congressional Committee charged with looking into Nixon's tax payments. Controversy stems from revelations last year that Nixon, despite a yearly income of $200,000, paid taxes for the last three years equivalent to those levied on a yearly income of $15,000. In December the President released his files to the committee, admitting that two deductions he had used to reduce his liability might be controversial. In releasing the files he had promised to abide by decision of the committee. A few days earlier the Congressional panel placed the President's tax delinquency for 1969-1972 at $476,431.

29 APRIL 1974

National   To avoid handing over tapes subpoenaed by the House Judiciary Committee and special prosecutor Leon Jaworski, Nixon issues a 1200-page edited transcript. On May 1 the committee will decline to accept the transcript. Jaworski had been appointed by the Justice Department on October 23, after the firing of Cox, and will refuse to accept the transcript. Both he and the House committee will continue legal action to secure the tapes.

16 MAY 1974

National   Former Attorney General Richard Kleindienst pleads guilty to a misdemeanor charge of failing to testify fully and accurately before a Senate committee. The charges stem from Senate investigation into alleged wrongdoing in an antitrust case against IT&T. Watergate prosecutor Leon Jaworski has agreed to drop any possible charges of perjury in connection with the Watergate cover-up. Kleindienst is the first attorney general convicted of a crime.

12 JUNE 1974
International President Nixon begins a week-long tour of the Middle East in hope of promoting peace. Since the Yom Kippur War (October 1973), the U.S. has taken a prominent role in trying to secure peace in the region. Last month Secretary of State Henry Kissinger mediated a troop disengagement agreement between Syria and Israel (whose troops had remained in the field since the ceasefire eight months earlier).

27 JUNE 1974
International President Nixon visits the Soviet Union for five days of summit talks. Although the two countries will sign agreements concerning nuclear weapons on July 3, the talks fail to produce breakthroughs. *Pravda*, however, will praise the negotiations as "an essential movement forward on the path of strengthening peace and mutual trust."

24 JULY 1974
National The Supreme Court issues a unanimous decision demanding that President Nixon turn over the tapes subpoenaed by special prosecutor Leon Jaworski in April. The case is the first time the Supreme Court has deliberated over a legal action in which a president is accused of criminal misconduct. Eight hours after the decision, the White House announces that the President will comply.

27 JULY 1974
National The House Judiciary Committee approves two Articles of Impeachment against the President, one charging him with obstructing justice and the other accusing him of repeatedly violating his oath of office. In three days, the committee will recommend a third charge, of unconstitutional defiance of committee subpoenas.

5 AUGUST 1974
National In preparation for release of all the subpoenaed tapes, President Nixon gives out three transcripts of a conversation with former chief of staff H. R. Haldeman on June 23, 1972. The transcripts show that six days after the Watergate break-in, Nixon had ordered a halt to an FBI investigation into the affair. The President concedes that in his earlier statements he had failed to include this information and thus had been guilty of "a serious act of ommission." As a result of this revelation, what remains of the President's support in Congress evaporates.

8 AUGUST 1974
National In a nationally televised speech, Nixon announces his resignation effective at noon tomorrow. The decision to step down comes as a result of advice

by key Republicans in Congress following his revelation three days ago. Meeting with the President after that revelation, such conservative Republicans as Barry Goldwater told Nixon he would be impeached and convicted if he remained and that a long drawn-out trial would hurt the country.

9 AUGUST 1974
National The resignation of President Nixon as the nation's Chief Executive becomes effective at noon today. Before leaving Washington for California, Nixon bids his staff farewell: "Always remember, others may hate you, but those who hate you do not win unless you hate them—and then you destroy yourself." Soon afterwards, he is driven to the airport where he hands Henry Kissinger his letter of resignation as he boards the plane. At 12:03, with Nixon in flight to California, Gerald R. Ford is sworn in as president by Chief Justice Warren Burger. In his inaugural address the new President asks Americans to pray that the man "who brought peace to millions" shall "find it for himself."

21 AUGUST 1974
National President Ford nominates Nelson Rockefeller as vice-president of the U.S. Governor of New York for 15 years, Rockefeller has failed three times to secure his party's nomination for President. Because of his long experience in government the public reaction is overwhelmingly positive.

Ford signs a bill providing some $25,000,000,000 to support primary and secondary schools over the next four years. Included in the bill is a restriction on busing to achieve desegregation. It decrees that no one should be transported farther than the school next closest to his neighborhood school unless a court decides it necessary to preserve the individual's constitutional right against segregation.

8 SEPTEMBER 1974
National Ford grants former President Nixon "a full, free and absolute pardon . . . for all offenses against the United States which he . . . has committed or may have committed or taken part in while President." Ford's action brings a storm of criticism accusing him of interfering with legal process and sometimes alleging that he made a "deal" with Nixon to secure the latter's resignation. Ford contends that a continued fixation on Watergate is bad for the nation and refers to Nixon's health as a motive in his decision.

12 SEPTEMBER 1974
Black Experience Violent protests erupt at South Boston High School as court ordered busing goes into effect. Five youths are arrested for disorderly conduct and the vast majority of white students fail to attend classes. Disturbances will continue for the rest of the year, with racial violence reaching a peak in October.

16 SEPTEMBER 1974
National President Ford announces a Presidential

amnesty for Vietnam War draft evaders and military deserters. The program is conditional, requiring an oath of allegiance from returning fugitives and a commitment to work for up to two years in a public service position. The plan is fairly popular but draws fire from veterans groups. Americans in Canada who fled the draft will complain that the program is punitive and implies admission of guilt.

17 SEPTEMBER 1974
National The Senate Foreign Relations Committee orders investigation into allegations that the Central Intelligence Agency spent $8,000,000 to overthrow former Chilean President Salvador Allende Gossens. On September 19 Kissinger will tell the committee that money spent in Chile by the CIA was to keep political parties alive and not to overthrow the government. Allende died in a military coup in 1973 and was the first freely elected Marxist leader in Chilean history.

15 OCTOBER 1974
National President Ford signs a campaign reform law which sets new regulations for federal election campaigns. It provides public funds for major presidential candidates and sets limits on spending in both presidential and congressional elections. The bill has been the subject of long debates in Congress and stems in part from public outrage over reports of gross abuses in the 1972 election. Revelations that U.S. corporations made large illegal contributions to Nixon's reelection committee convinced many citizens that reform was necessary.

5 NOVEMBER 1974
National In the midterm elections held today, Democrats increase their majorities in both houses of Congress, winning 291 seats out of 435 in the House and 61 out of 99 in the Senate (one seat remains vacant from New Hampshire due to disputed election returns). Altogether, 42 Congressional incumbents go down to defeat—38 Republicans and 4 Democrats. The blow to the Republicans, anticipated by four congressional races held earlier in the year, is widely attributed to the Watergate scandal. Dissatisfaction over the state of the economy probably contributes to the GOP's losses. In August the government reported that, for the second consecutive quarter, the gross national product had fallen. Increasing unemployment and run-away inflation convinces many voters that all is not well.

24 NOVEMBER 1974
International President Ford ends an eight-day world trip with stops in Japan, South Korea and Vladivostok, where he and Soviet leader Leonid Brezhnev sign a tentative agreement limiting offensive weapons until 1985. Further negotiations are scheduled to take place in Geneva.

26 NOVEMBER 1974
National President Ford signs into law a bill pledg-

NELSON ROCKEFELLER, 1908-1979

Part of the third generation of one of the wealthiest and most prominent families in America, Nelson Rockefeller during his long career worked diligently to uphold his family tradition of public service. He was born in Bar Harbor, Maine, on July 8, 1908, grandson of John D. Rockefeller Sr., founder of Standard Oil and the originator of a family fortune estimated somewhere between one and two billion dollars. Reared comparatively simply and strictly, Nelson became an excellent student at Dartmouth and was the editor of a school arts magazine, having absorbed his family's love of the arts.

During the 40s Rockefeller was appointed by President Roosevelt as coordinator of the office of Inter-American Affairs. In 1944 and 1950 he again dealt with underdeveloped countries in Washington appointments. Later he worked for President Eisenhower on a committee dealing with government organization; from this committee came plans for the Department of Health, Education and Welfare, the U.S. Information Agency, and other reorganization proposals. In all these posts he established himself as a dynamic and effective leader.

These experiences led him to the next logical step, that of elective office; in 1958 he won the first of four consecutive terms as governor of New York State. During his tenure he initiated a series of bold and largely successful programs in state services while maintaining a blanced budget. He came to be considered a leading liberal Republican and a national political figure. The next logical step, clearly, was the presidency.

But this final goal was to elude him; he failed to win the nomination in 1960 and in the next two presidential campaigns. Meanwhile, he became increasingly conservative, perhaps to build his appeal to mainstream Republicans. He ordered the bloody suppression of the Attica prison riot in 1971, for which he was severely criticized by liberals. He resigned the governorship in 1973; the following year he was named to the last political post of his career when President Ford appointed him vice-president. He brought to the office his customary industriousness, but the enmity of conservatives led him to decline the vice-presidential nomination when Ford ran in 1976. Returning to his private interests in business and the arts, he died in New York in 1979.

---

ing $11,800,000,000 in federal money over the next six years to improve mass transit.

19 DECEMBER 1974
National Nelson Rockefeller takes the oath of office as vice-president. Rockefeller's nomination had been originally greeted with widespread public support; but revelations that the multi-millionaire had made large gifts and loans to prominent political figures and that he helped finance a derogatory biography of one-time Supreme Court Justice Arthur Goldberg greatly weakened support for his nomination.

OTHER EVENTS OF 1974
Science/Technology The Nobel Prize for Chemistry goes to the American Paul J. Flory. The Nobel Prize for Physiology and Medicine is shared by the Americans Albert Claude and George Palade with the

Belgian Christian de Duve.

1 JANUARY 1975
National H. R. Haldeman, John Mitchell, John Erlichman and Robert C. Mardian, all former members of the Nixon administration, are convicted of obstructing the Watergate investigation. Erlichman was already convicted last July on charges connected with the break-in into the office of Daniel Ellsberg's psychiatrist.

8 JANUARY 1975
National The President appoints an eight-man commission to investigate charges that the CIA had been involved in a wide range of illegal domestic activity. On December 21 the *New York Times* had charged that the government intelligence agency had orchestrated a vast operation of domestic espionage in violation of its charter. The next day, Ford announced that he would not tolerate such activities during his administration. The commission, which is headed by Nelson Rockefeller, will report its findings in June.

15 JANUARY 1975
National President Ford delivers his first State of the Union message, proposing a $16,000,000,000 cut in income tax. He calls for a three-pronged attack against energy dependence, inflation and recession. Ford's concern comes in the wake of increasing unemployment. On January 4 the Bureau of Labor Statistics reported that unemployment reached 7.1 percent, a 13-year high. By June, the rate will climb to a 33-year high of 9.2 percent.

14 FEBRUARY 1975
International The U.S. and officials of the Northern Marianas Islands sign a pact making those islands a U.S. commonwealth. The agreement will be ratified by the people of the islands on June 17 by a margin of four to one. The treaty marks the first territorial acquisition by the U.S. since the purchase of the Danish West Indies in 1917.

12 MARCH 1975
National Former Commerce Secretary Maurice Stans pleads guilty to charges that he violated federal campaign laws. Stans has already admitted collecting millions of dollars in illegal contributions from major American corporations, and says that his actions "were not willful and at the time they occurred were not believed to be violations."

22 MARCH 1975
International After two weeks of shuttle diplomacy, Secretary of State Henry Kissinger announces that "irreconcilable differences" between Israel and Egypt have led him to suspend efforts for an agreement between the two Middle East countries.

31 MARCH 1975
National President Ford's clemency program, to repatriate draft evaders and deserters in exchange for

GERALD R. FORD, 1913-

As Gerald Ford assumed the Presidency of the United States in 1974, he faced the seemingly Herculean task of re-establishing trust in the Executive branch of the government. Ford, chosen as vice-president by Richard Nixon in part for the qualities of perserverance, tact, discretion and integrity, soon made it clear that he would live up to these, if no more lofty, expectations.

Gerry Ford was a genial, well-liked Representative serving from the Fifth Michigan District in the 81st through the 93rd Congresses when Nixon appointed him to the vice-presidency. His popularity with both Democrats and fellow Republicans notwithstanding, Ford's effectiveness as a president was diminished by several factors—among the more critical was his assumption of leadership while the country's economy suffered under the burden of inflation. Also, the painful political and social divisions engendered by the Vietnam War and the Watergate scandal remained. Ford's "full, free and absolute pardon" of Richard Nixon failed to heal these too recent wounds, and was damaging to Ford's political future. When he launched an economic program designed to encourage confidence and optimism in America's potential, his detractors termed it too little, too late, and despite his intentions, *Whip Inflation Now* (WIN) was considered a failure.

As Ford's ability to direct sound fiscal policy was seriously questioned, his foreign policy was tested in May 1975 when the American merchant ship *Mayaguez* was seized by Cambodia. Ford responded by ordering United States Naval forces to attack Cambodia. This prompted the release of the *Mayaguez* and its crew, temporarily bolstering confidence in his leadership, but did little to help his image in any significant way.

Gerald Ford had been chosen for his stability and personal integrity, and in that sense he served the nation well. Though neither a brilliant economic strategist nor an innovator in foreign policy, Ford did give America a needed respite from political corruption. After what could be termed an adequate but undistinguished tenure as president, Gerald Ford lost his bid for a full term of office in the November 1976 elections, garnering 240 electoral votes compared to the 297 cast for Jimmy Carter.

Ford returned to his home state after Carter's inauguration, to write and to lecture, having earned the unique distinction of being the 'only man to serve both as vice-president and as president but having been elected to neither office.

civil service work, ends today. Some 22,500 men out of a possible 124,400 have applied for the program while it has been in operation.

17 APRIL 1975
National Former Secretary of Treasury John Connally is acquitted of charges of bribery stemming from allegations that Connally had accepted $10,000 from the American Milk Producers Company in exchange for a recommendation to Nixon to raise government price supports on milk.

30 APRIL 1975
International The U.S. completes its evacuation program in South Vietnam as the Saigon government

President Gerald R. Ford.

surrenders to the Communists. The final phase of the Vietnam War began in January, as Communists made their first military gains since the Paris peace agreement two years ago. Thousands of "boat people" will flee South Vietnam as the Communists consolidate their hold; many of the fugitives will be eventually picked up by U.S. ships patrolling off Vietnam.

14 MAY 1975

International Ford orders a ground, air and sea operation to recover the U.S. cargo vessel *Mayaguez*, seized by the Khmer Rouge government of Cambodia two days ago. Both the *Mayaguez* and its crew are rescued but some 15 American Marines are killed. Ford's forceful handling of the *Mayaguez* incident will be widely applauded by both Congress and the American public who view the seizure as piracy. The Cam-

bodian government charges that the U.S. vessel was part of a spying operation by the U.S. against their country.

29 MAY 1975

National President Ford vetoes a $5,300,000,000 jobs bill passed by Congress to create 1,000,000 jobs.

10 JUNE 1975

National The Rockefeller Commission investigating charges of domestic spying by the CIA documents a wide range of covert operations violating the agency's charter and it recommends a joint Congressional committee to oversee intelligence.

30 JUNE 1975

National President Ford signs into law a bill extending unemployment benefits to a maximum of 65 weeks. The action comes after unemployment reached 9.2 percent of the work force in May.

8 JULY 1975
National Ford formally announces his candidacy for the 1976 presidential election. He tells the press that he has decided to run "in order to finish the job I have begun." Tomorrow, his campaign chairman, Howard Calloway, will announce that Ford's campaign organization will make no effort to win support for vice-president Nelson Rockefeller as Ford's running mate.

15 JULY 1975
International As a sign of U.S.-Soviet detente, the two countries begin the Apollo/Soyuz space mission. On July 17 the American spacecraft Apollo will link up in space with the Soviet Soyuz and the two spaceships remain in orbit together for two days. Both sets of astronauts will ultimately return to earth safely, though the Americans will experience side effects from breathing noxious fumes during re-entry.

28 JULY 1975
Civil Rights Congress approves a bill extending the Voting Rights Act of 1965 for seven years, including provisions safeguarding voting rights of Spanish-speaking and other "language minority" groups.

31 JULY 1975
Labor Former President of the Teamsters Union, James Hoffa, is reported missing in Detroit. A subsequent investigation by the FBI will fail to locate Hoffa.

18 AUGUST 1975
Labor Six member unions in the AFL-CIO announce a boycott on loading of grain bound for the U.S.S.R. The boycott will end on September 9, after Ford and union president George Meany reach an agreement concerning future grain deals with the Soviets.

27 AUGUST 1975
Regional Ohio Governor James Rhodes and 27 Ohio national guardsmen are exonerated of blame in the shootings of 13 Kent State students in May 1970.

10 SEPTEMBER 1975
National Congress overrides a presidential veto on a $7,900,000,000 education appropriation bill. Congress, controlled by Democrats, strongly objects to Ford's attempts to slash spending in order to reduce inflation.

18 SEPTEMBER 1975
Regional After a 19-month search, police capture Patricia (Patty) Hearst, who had been kidnapped by members of the Symbionese Liberation Army (SLA) in February 1974. After announcing in April 1974 that she had joined her captors to help fight for "the free-

dom of the oppressed people," she was identified as having taken part in two robberies. In May, the FBI reclassified her as an armed fugitive and, although six SLA members were killed in a shootout that month, Hearst had remained at large until today. Police also apprehend William and Emily Harris, with whom Hearst has been living. All three will be charged with armed robbery. The Harrises will also be convicted of kidnapping.

22 SEPTEMBER 1975
National Sarah Jane Moore, a 45-year-old political activist, shoots at President Ford as he walks out of the St. Francis Hotel in San Francisco. A bystander sees the gun before it is fired, and deflects Ms. Moore's hand as she is taking aim. The President, unharmed, is hurried off by car to the airport.

20 OCTOBER 1975
International The U.S. announces an agreement with the Soviet Union to sell between 6,000,000 and 8,000,000 tons of grain yearly.

12 NOVEMBER 1975
National William O. Douglas, Supreme Court Justice, resigns after 36 years on the Court.

26 NOVEMBER 1975
National President Ford announces his decision to help New York City meet its financial obligations and avoid defaulting on loans. Although only a month earlier Ford had threatened to veto any federal bailout, he now says that "by what they have done in conjunction with New York State (and others) they have bailed themselves out." Only yesterday, the New York State Legislature passed a $200,000,000 tax bill as part of a larger program aimed at financing the New York City debt.

4 DECEMBER 1975
National The Senate Select Committee on Intelligence issues its findings on the role of the CIA in the overthrow of Chile's President Salvador Allende Gossens in 1973. The report concludes that while there is no evidence to directly tie the agency to the coup itself, the CIA had "created the atmosphere" favorable for the ousting of Allende. The Senate had begun the investigation in September 1974, following charges that the CIA had spent some $8,000,000 to finance the overthrow of the Marxist leader.

5 DECEMBER 1975
International President Ford concludes a five-day tour of the Far East which included stops in China, Indonesia and the Philippines. In Peking, Ford talked with Mao Tse-tung and was warned by leaders of the potential dangers of war by trying to "appease" the Soviet Union. China has become alarmed by U.S. detente with Moscow.

OTHER EVENTS OF 1975
Science/Technology The Nobel Prize for Physics is

shared by the American L. James Rainwater and two Danes, Aage Bohr and Ben Mottelson. The Nobel Prize for Physiology or Medicine goes to three Americans, David Baltimore, Renato Dulbecco and Howard Temin.

Economics The Nobel Award for Economics is shared by the American Tjalling Koopmans and the Russian Leonid Kantorovich.

Social Change The year 1975 is observed around the world as International Woman's Year. The U.S. military academies open their doors to females. At West Point, 118 women are admitted as entering cadets, while the Navy and Air Force Academies include 81 and 157 women respectively.

19 JANUARY 1976
National In his second State of the Union Address, President Ford exhorts Congress to practice fiscal restraint in order to curb inflation.

27 JANUARY 1976
National Defying President Ford's call for fiscal restraint, Congress overrides his veto on a bill providing $45,000,000,000 for health, welfare and manpower programs.

30 JANUARY 1976
National In an important Supreme Court case, the Justices rule unconstitutional parts of the 1974 Federal Campaign Act. The court decides that in almost all cases (except where public money is involved) federally imposed limits on campaign spending violate the First Amendment guaranteeing free speech.

17 FEBRUARY 1976
National President Ford announces a sweeping reform of U.S. intelligence gathering agencies, including the FBI and CIA. Included among the changes is the establishment of an independent "oversight board."

20 MARCH 1976
Regional Patricia Hearst, who was kidnapped by the SLA in 1974 and subsequently joined her abductors in a series of burglaries, is found guilty of armed robbery. The defense had maintained that Hearst had been subjected to extreme psychological pressure by her captors, including prolonged confinement and forced intercourse, to force her to cooperate with them.

29 MARCH 1976
National The Supreme Court upholds, by a vote of six to three, a lower court ruling allowing states to outlaw homosexual acts, even if committed in private by consenting adults. The decision, which will bring strong criticism from civil liberties groups as well as gay activists, is a marked departure from a 10-year trend by the courts to expand safeguards of privacy.

5 APRIL 1976
Population Multi-millionaire Howard Hughes, who

has long shunned all public exposure, dies.

26 APRIL 1976
National The Senate Select Committee on Intelligence Activities ends a 15-month investigation into the various intelligence agencies of the Federal Government. Its report details a wide assortment of questionable activities by the FBI, CIA, IRS and the Army, which seriously infringed on the civil rights of American citizens. The Committee recommends Congressional legislation to restrict such abuses in the future. On 19 May, in response to suggestions made by this panel, Congress will establish a permanent 15-person board to oversee government intelligence activities.

25 MAY 1976
National In one of the busiest days of presidential primaries, President Ford defeats his conservative opponent, former governor Ronald Reagan, in Kentucky, Tennessee and Oregon.

Meanwhile former Governor Jimmy Carter of Georgia, almost unknown a year ago, passes the halfway point in delegate support as he wins in Arkansas, Tennessee and Kentucky.

28 MAY 1976
International The U.S. and Soviet Union sign a five-year agreement limiting underground nuclear explosions and providing on-site inspection.

2 JULY 1976
National The U.S. Supreme Court rules the death penalty not inherently in violation of the Constitution. The 7-2 court decision opens the way for the execution of convicts currently on death row.

4 JULY 1976
National The U.S. officially observes its 200th birthday with parades, fireworks and festivals. During the day President Ford travels to Philadelphia and then New York City.

15 JULY 1976
National The Democratic National Convention in New York City nominates Jimmy Carter for the presidency. Although Carter had been assured of nomination by his victory in the Ohio primary, Governor Jerry Brown of California had given the Democratic front-runner a scare by winning in Maryland, Nevada and his home state. Carter, who chooses Senator Walter Mondale as his running mate, will receive endorsement from labor unions and black leaders.

22 JULY 1976
National Congress passes a $3,950,000,000 jobs bill over the veto of President Ford, to offset unemployment (still high, standing at 7.5 percent in June).

1 AUGUST 1976
Regional A flash flood in the Colorado River Canyon kills 139 people and causes extensive damage.

NOVEMBER 2, 1976

JAMES EARL CARTER, JR., 1924-

The first American President from the Deep South since 1848, "Jimmy" Carter was considered an unlikely candidate for the Executive Office. A relative newcomer to politics, Carter carried with him a personal commitment strengthened by deep moral convictions. His image was that of an educated but basically homespun individual whose first intention was to serve his country.

A native of Georgia and a graduate of Annapolis, Carter's personal and professional backgrounds were intertwined. After serving in the United States Navy, Jimmy returned to Plains, Georgia, and took charge of the lucrative family peanut business. He used this base of operation to launch a successful bid for the Georgia State Senate, holding a Democratic seat from 1963 to 1967. After this he served one term as Georgia's Governor, stepping some years later into the national limelight as a candidate for the Democratic presidential nomination. A virtual unknown outside of the South, Carter's sincerity and simplicity impressed many Americans who were impatient with the Republican administration's seemingly endless failings. Carter's inexperience only served to enhance his image; for many he was the antithesis of the jaded politician. The Carter-Mondale campaign took advantage of this popular view, and made certain that personal appearances and town-meeting type discussions were sprinkled liberally along the campaign trail in order to further establish Jimmy's home-grown image.

Once in office, Carter issued pardons to nearly 10,000 who had evaded the military draft during the Vietnam conflict, a move calculated to have broad public appeal. Similarly, Carter launched an energy program which was to decrease the United States' dependence on foreign oil imports. Although he created a Cabinet-level energy post, Jimmy Carter was unable to push his energy package through Congress.

Among Carter's successful policy-making strategies was the arrangement of a meeting at Camp David between Israel's Prime Minister Menachem Begin and Egypt's Anwar Sadat in the fall of 1978. His success in this area of foreign policy was overshadowed by the tragedy of the Iranian hostage crisis. Despite Carter's tireless efforts, he was unable to make sufficient headway in negotiations. This lack of resolution for such a serious problem hurt Carter badly in the polls. Carter's sincerity was plainly there, but what had been considered a virtue was now seen as a defect: Carter's relaxed, informal style seemed to suggest incompetence or, at best, inability. He was defeated in the 1980 presidential race by Republican Ronald Reagan who seemed to represent the politics of influence and money as much as Carter had attempted to embody the values of independence and plain hard work.

President Carter speaks on the hostage crisis.

special tax shelters and also increase the tax burden on the wealthy by raising the minimum required tax payment. For the first time in 30 years, significant changes are also made in the estate tax laws. The Tax Reform Act will become law before the end of the year.

30 SEPTEMBER 1976
National Congress overrides a presidential veto on a $56,000,000,000 appropriations bill for social services including manpower, education and health projects.

7 OCTOBER 1976
National In the second in a series of three nationally-televised presidential debates, Ford makes what most believe to be a serious political gaffe when he insists that there is "no Soviet domination of Eastern Europe and there never will be under a Ford administration."

21 OCTOBER 1976
National With the announcement of Saul Bellow as this year's recipient of the Nobel Prize for Literature, the U.S. makes a clean sweep of awards in all categories for the first time.

2 NOVEMBER 1976
National James Earl Carter defeats Gerald Ford to become the nation's 39th president. Of 80,000,000 votes Carter polls 2,000,000 more than Ford, winning 297 electoral votes to the incumbent's 241. Despite the narrow victory, the Democrats maintain a 61-to-38 edge in the Senate (where there is one independent) while gaining slightly in the House, to improve their

19 AUGUST 1976
National President Ford is nominated at the Republican National Convention for this year's presidential race. The convention opened three days ago with both Ford and challenger Ronald Reagan claiming victory.

16 SEPTEMBER 1976
National Congress completes work on a bill incorporating revisions in the tax code. The reform bill will reduce the number of individuals who can claim

two-to-one majority over the Republicans. In the state governors' contests, the Democrats pick up seats, controlling three times as many governorships as the GOP.

3 DECEMBER 1976
National President-elect "Jimmy" Carter announces Cyrus Vance as Secretary of State.

6 DECEMBER 1976
National Thomas P. O'Neill, Jr. of Massachusetts becomes Speaker of the House for the 95th Congress, replacing Carl Albert of Oklahoma.

20 DECEMBER 1976
Population Mayor Richard Daley of Chicago, leader of one of the most effective political machines in America, dies of a heart attack at the age of 74.

OTHER EVENTS OF 1976
Science/Technology The Nobel Prize for Physics is awarded to two Americans, Burton Richter and Samuel Chao Ching Ting. The Nobel Prize for Chemistry goes to the American William Lipscomb. The Nobel Prize for Physiology or Medicine goes to Baruch Blumberg and D. Carleton Gajdusek.
Economics The Nobel Award for Economics goes to Milton Friedman.
Arts/Culture The Nobel Prize for literature is awarded to the American novelist Saul Bellow. Bellow also wins the Pulitzer Prize in fiction for *Humboldt's Gift*.
Ideas/Beliefs Jacqueline Means, 40, becomes the first woman to be ordained a priest by the Episcopal Church.

12 JANUARY 1977
National Gerald Ford delivers his last State of the Union message, emphasizing the progress of the country in handling the energy crisis and economic recession.

17 JANUARY 1977
Life/Customs Gary Mark Gilmore becomes the first prisoner to be executed in 10 years.

20 JANUARY 1977
National Jimmy Carter is sworn in as the 39th president. Carter sends a message to the nations of the world pledging "a world order that is more responsive to human aspirations."

21 JANUARY 1977
National Carter grants unconditional pardon to almost all draft evaders during the Vietnam War.

26 JANUARY 1977
National With the Eastern and Central States suffering one of the coldest winters in history, President Carter asks Congress to authorize the emergency reallocation of the nation's natural gas supplies to help states experiencing severe energy shortages. Many

areas have been forced to close schools and factories.

27 JANUARY 1977
National The Carter administration sends Congress a $31,000,000,000 proposal to stimulate the economy.

24 FEBRUARY 1977
International The Carter administration announces that foreign aid will be reduced to countries guilty of human rights violations.

2 MARCH 1977
National The House of Representatives adopts a stringent new ethics code governing finances of members. Income and gifts over $100 must be reported and a representative's outside income cannot exceed 15 percent of his salary.

5 MARCH 1977
National Carter conducts a radio-broadcasted question-and-answer program from the White House.

11 MARCH 1977
Labor Cesar Chavez's United Farm Workers sign an agreement with the Teamsters Union.

1 MAY 1977
Regional Some 1400 members of the Clamshell Alliance (a group opposed to the construction of nuclear power plants) are arrested in Seabrook, New Hampshire, the proposed site of a nuclear reactor.

3 MAY 1977
International The U.S. and Vietnam begin talks in Paris to normalize relations. Although both sides will express satisfaction over the two-day discussions, the U.S. still refuses to provide financial assistance.

9 MAY 1977
National President Carter calls for an increase in Social Security taxes to help "restore" the program's "financial integrity." Specifically, Carter proposes an increase in the tax rate from 7 to 7.5 percent as well as higher limits on those wages subject to tax. The most controversial point of the package, however, is the provisional transfer of money from other federal revenues if unemployment levels render the Social Security fund inadequate. Congress will pass a modified version of Carter's plan in December.

3 JUNE 1977
International The U.S. and Cuba agree to exchange diplomatic missions in each other's countries

13 JULY 1977
Regional A blackout occurs throughout New York City and in parts of Westchester County after an electrical storm north of the city.

20 JULY 1977
National Leon Jaworski, formerly special prosecutor in the Watergate conspiracy, is again called upon by

the Federal Government to investigate charges of political corruption. Jaworski's appointment by the House Ethics Committee is part of a Congressional effort to investigate charges that a South Korean lobbyist had tried to gain political favors from Senators and Representatives through gifts and campaign contributions. Five days ago, the committee's former counsel Philip Lacovara had resigned, complaining that panel members, particularly chairman John Flynt Jr. of Georgia, were dragging their feet in the investigation. The House hopes that Jaworski's appointment will help restore public confidence in their diligence in probing the Congressional scandal. By mid-October, the Justice Department, which is also looking into the "Koreagate" scandal, will have returned indictments against both the lobbyist Park and an assistant as well as former House Representative Richard T. Hanna of California. The investigations, which will continue into 1978, will be seriously impeded by the South Korean government's unwillingness to return Kim Dong Jo, the former ambassador to the U.S., for questioning in connection with the scandal.

4 AUGUST 1977
National Agreeing to a request by President Carter, Congress creates the Department of Energy, the 12th Cabinet-level executive department in the Federal Government and the first to be created since 1966; Congress also confirms James Schlesinger as its first Secretary.

12 AUGUST 1977
Science/Technology The Space Shuttle *Enterprise* completes its first test flight. For today's test the *Enterprise* is carried up by a Boeing 747 and released to make a landing.

7 SEPTEMBER 1977
International President Carter and General Omar Torrijos Herrera of Panama sign treaties for gradual return of the Panama Canal Zone and ultimately the canal itself to Panamanian control and for perpetual neutrality of the waterway. The treaties both will be ratified (March 16 and April 18, 1978) by one vote more than the needed two-thirds majority.

8 SEPTEMBER 1977
International The U.S. and Canada sign a pact for a $10,000,000,000 pipeline to carry natural gas from Alaska to the United States Midwest.

22 SEPTEMBER 1977
Immigration A repatriation program, signed by the U.S. and Cuba on August 29, gets under way as 29 Americans and 26 Cuban relatives arrive in Florida from the Caribbean island.

31 OCTOBER 1977
National Former director of the CIA Richard Helms pleads "no contest" to charges that he failed to testify "fully, completely and accurately" before a Senate committee. The charges stem from remarks Helms made to a Senate committee investigating CIA involvement in the overthrow of Chilean President Salvador Allende.

7 APRIL 1978
National President Carter announces a decision to postpone production of the neutron bomb—a weapon that relies on enhanced radiation to kill people while doing relatively little property damage.

6 JUNE 1978
Regional By a vote of almost two to one, California voters approve Proposition 13, an amendment to the state constitution imposing strict limits on property tax rates.

28 JUNE 1978
National In a much-publicized case, the Supreme Court rules that, while flexible affirmative action plans by colleges do not violate the Constitution, strict racial quotas are flatly illegal. The case before the Court involves the rejection of Allan Bakke's application to the medical school at the University of California at Davis. According to Bakke, he had been denied admission while less qualified minority students were admitted.

8 AUGUST 1978
National Carter signs a bill providing for a federal guarantee on $1,600,000,000 in loans to the city of New York. The action is part of an attempt to help that city fight off bankruptcy. Similar aid had been approved during the Ford administration.

22 AUGUST 1978
National Congress passes an amendment to the Constitution giving the District of Columbia full voting rights in Congress. The proposed amendment will now go to the states where it must be ratified by three-fourths of the states' legislatures.

17 SEPTEMBER 1978
International Private talks, mediated by President Carter, between Egyptian President Anwar Sadat and Israeli Prime Minister Menachem Begin, end today at Camp David, Maryland, with two sides signing the "Camp David Accords." The agreement establishes a timetable for peace negotiations.

6 OCTOBER 1978
National The Senate votes to extend the deadline for the ratification of the Equal Rights Amendment. The extension gives states until June 1982 to ratify.

20 OCTOBER 1978
Financial Wall Street ends the worst week in its history, the Dow-Jones closing at an average of 838.01 per share, down 59.08 points from a week ago. The frantic selling spree is largely the result of continually escalating interest rates which investors fear will bring on a recession. On October 31 the Federal Reserve Board, in an attempt to stifle inflation, will raise the

discount rate (the rate at which money is lent to member banks) to 9.5 percent.

18 NOVEMBER 1978
International Representative Leo Ryan of California and others traveling with him are murdered near Jonestown, Guyana, by members of an American religious sect. These deaths precede the suicide of 911 cult members. The dead are part of a "Temple" based in California.

27 NOVEMBER 1978
Immigration The U.S. will permit another 15,000 Indochinese refugees to enter the country. The ceiling, raised in May, now allows 47,000 "boat people" to settle in the U.S. Government action comes after Southeast Asian countries closed their doors to hundreds of thousands of people fleeing Laos, Cambodia and Vietnam to escape persecution.

16 DECEMBER 1978
Regional Cleveland, Ohio, becomes the first American city to default since the depression. The city's financial problems, exacerbated by feuding between the city council and mayor, include a $14,000,000 debt to six area banks.

1 JANUARY 1979
International The U.S. opens diplomatic relations with mainland China and severs ties with Taiwan. Since the Communist takeover in 1949, the U.S. has recognized the nationalist government on Taiwan as the legitimate government of China. The process toward recognition of the Communist regime was begun during the Nixon administration when the President visited China and sought normal relations. On February 26 the Senate will confirm Leonard Woodcock as ambassador to Peking.

1 FEBRUARY 1979
Regional Patricia Hearst is released from jail after President Carter commutes her sentence. Hearst, who had been kidnapped by the terrorist Symbionese Liberation Army five years ago, later joined her kidnappers in a series of burglaries. She has served 22 months of a seven-year term for armed robbery.

5 FEBRUARY 1979
Agriculture To dramatize demand for higher price supports, 3000 farmers drive campers, tractors and trucks into Washington, causing a massive traffic jam.

26 FEBRUARY 1979
National President Carter asks Congress to pass legislation enabling him to impose gas rationing and other emergency conservation measures to cut U.S. oil consumption. His action comes in response to Iran's stoppage of oil exports in December as well as the decision of Kuwait and Venezuela to raise prices.

5 MARCH 1979
Science/Technology *Voyager I* passes within 172,-000 miles of Jupiter. The American interplanetary spacecraft radios back vivid pictures of the planet and its moons, providing evidence of geological eruptions on that planet. On September 1 another U.S. spacecraft, *Pioneer II*, will fly past Saturn, discovering an 11th moon as well as additional rings around the planet.

26 MARCH 1979
International In a formal ceremony in Washington, Israeli Prime Minister Menachem Begin and Egyptian President Anwar Sadat sign a peace treaty between their countries, bringing to an end the state of war existing since 1948.

28 MARCH 1979
Regional A major nuclear power accident occurs at the Three Mile Island reactor, near Harrisburg, Pennsylvania. The failure of a cooling valve to open triggers the incident, allowing the radio-active core to overheat. A pressure relief valve then sticks, causing the water level to plummet and creating the risk of a nuclear melt-down—the worst possible nuclear disaster. As workers battle to reduce a large gas bubble that develops inside the reactor and restricts the water circulation, clouds of radio-active steam pour out of the plant into the atmosphere.

5 APRIL 1979
National President Carter orders the gradual elimination of all controls on domestic oil prices.

25 MAY 1979
Transportation In the worst aviation accident in American history, 273 people are killed as a DC-10 crashes after takeoff from Chicago's O'Hare Airport. Investigators decide that the crack in the engine mount was the result of a labor-saving assembly technique.

7 JUNE 1979
National President Carter gives his approval to a new guided missile system—called the MX—which is expected to cost $30,000,000,000.

18 JUNE 1979
International President Carter and Soviet President Leonid Brezhnev sign the SALT II agreement in Vienna. The treaty, if ratified, would limit long-range nuclear missiles and bombers of the two countries to 2250 apiece. One of the major points of dispute since the two superpowers began negotiations in 1974 was whether a Soviet supersonic bomber should come under the agreement; in exchange for the exclusion of these planes, Brezhnev gave Carter oral and written assurance that production of the bomber would not exceed 30 per year.

28 JUNE 1979
International OPEC countries announce another hike in oil prices which, with previous increases during the last 12 months, will bring the price of the

commodity to a rate 50 percent higher than a year ago. The action will bring further inflationary pressure to an economy plagued by a spiraling cost of living. Tomorrow, leaders of the major oil-consuming nations, including the U.S., will agree to set ceilings on oil imports through 1985.

27 SEPTEMBER 1979
National Congress approves Carter's proposal for the creation of a Department of Education. The new Cabinet-level department was strongly favored by the National Education Association. Shirley Hufstedler will be appointed as the department's first head on October 30.

1 OCTOBER 1979
International The U.S. formally gives up the Panama Canal Zone. The canal is to revert to Panamanian control on the last day of this century. The Senate consented to the treaties providing for transfer as well as neutrality of the canal on March 16 and April 18, 1978.
Ideas/Beliefs Pope John Paul II begins a week-long trip to the U.S., which will include stops in Boston, New York City, Philadelphia, Chicago and Washington D.C. The pontiff will also make a visit to Des Moines, Iowa. The Roman Catholic Church, over which the Pope rules, has 50,000,000 members in the U.S., over 20 percent of the country's population.

4 NOVEMBER 1979
International Muslim students in Iran storm the U.S. embassy in Teheran, taking 66 Americans hostage. The action comes in response to the admission of the former Shah of Iran, Muhammed Reza Pahlavi, into the U.S. to undergo a gall bladder operation. The students demand that the Shah—who fled Iran in a violent revolution—return to face trial. In retaliation for this government-supported takeover, Carter will issue an order calling for deportation of all Iranian students who were in the country illegally. In the next few days the President will take further action: barring oil imports from Iran on November 12, and freezing Iranian assets in American banks.

19 DECEMBER 1979
National The Senate approves a $1,500,000,000 loan to the Chrysler Corporation. In July, the chairman of that company, John J. Ricardo, announced that Chrysler had lost $200,000,000 in the second quarter of 1979.

18 JANUARY 1980
Finance The price of gold soars to $802 on the New York market, a $159 increase in a week's time.

24 JANUARY 1980
International In a major shift by the U.S., President Carter announces that the administration is willing to sell weapons to China. The decision is part of the administration's response to the Soviets' armed intervention in Afghanistan.

THE HOSTAGE CRISIS

On November 4, 1979, some 500 Iranian students stormed the American embassy in Teheran, capturing 90 diplomatic personnel, including 66 Americans. The students then demanded that the U.S. turn over the former Shah of Iran, Muhammed Reza Pahlavi, who had been overthrown in a revolution late in 1978 and was now temporarily in the U.S. undergoing surgery for the removal of a gall stone. Although the Iranian government had not explicitly called for the takeover, it soon became clear that it was backing the students. On November 18 the leader of the Iranian government, Ayatollah Ruhollah Khomeini, announced that some of the embassy personnel might be tried as spies.

In response to the takeover, President Carter froze all Iranian assets in American banks, cut off oil imports from that country and called for the deportation of Iranian students in the U.S. illegally. The U.S. also pressured the international community to take steps against the Mideast country. On December 4, the UN unanimously approved a resolution calling for the release of the hostages, and in February it sent a fact-finding mission to the country to listen to Iranian grievances. Then on May 24, 1980 the International Court of Justice demanded the immediate surrender of the hostages and ruled that Iran would be liable for reparations claims arising from the takeover. Six days earlier, the European Economic Community (EEC) voted to cancel all contracts with Iran negotiated since the embassy seizure. Canada, which had earlier smuggled six American embassy personnel out of Iran, and Japan, had also adopted sanctions against that country in April.

Meanwhile, on April 1 the Iranian government announced that it would assume control over the remaining 53 American hostages (all the others, including 13 American women and blacks, had been released by the students late in November). At home President Carter, who was in the middle of a campaign for the Democratic nomination, was coming under increasing criticism for his handling of the situation. During April he stepped up the pressure on Iran. On April 7, he severed diplomatic relations and 10 days later barred all travel to that country and prohibited imports from Iran. Then on April 24, frustrated by the diplomatic stalemate, the President ordered a rescue attempt to recover the hostages. The mission, however, was aborted when one helicopter developed a fuel leak and two others failed to arrive at the rendezvous point.

With the Shah's death of cancer in July (in Egypt), one important issue obstructing the negotiations was removed. In November Iran presented a series of new demands which ultimately served as the basis for the final agreement. With Algeria acting as an intermediary during the last two months of negotiations, the U.S. finally agreed, on January 19, 1981, to unfreeze Iranian assets, locate and freeze the late Shah's wealth, lift all trade restrictions between the two countries and refrain from interfering in Iran's internal affairs. The next day, the hostages were released after 444 days in captivity.

---

25 JANUARY 1980
National Labor statistics reveal that the 1979 inflation rate was the highest in 33 years.

3 FEBRUARY 1980
National The press reveals the existence of the most

far-reaching investigation into political corruption ever undertaken by the FBI. Federal agents, posing as Arab businessmen, reportedly gave bribes to some 31 public officials, including a Senator and seven U.S. Congressmen. By the end of June five Congressmen will have been indicted in connection with the Abscam investigation.

27 MARCH 1980
Financial   The price of silver drops by $5, to $10.80 an ounce, in a single day of trading. The drastic decline threatens to destroy the multi-billion dollar fortune of Nelson and W. Herbert Hunt of Dallas. To escape contracts pledging them to buy 19,000,000 ounces of the metal at $35 an ounce, the Hunt brothers will turn over vast silver holdings as well as Canadian oil properties worth $500,000,000.

31 MARCH 1980
National   President Carter signs a bill deregulating the banking industry. The law raises the interest rates that banks may offer small depositors and permits interest on checking accounts. It also raises the limit on federally insured accounts to $100,000 (the former limit was $40,000).

2 APRIL 1980
National   President Carter signs the Crude Oil Windfall Profits Tax Act. The bill, which Carter suggested to Congress last year, is probably the largest tax ever imposed on a single industry. Since Carter lifted controls on oil prices last year, oil industry profits have skyrocketed. Revenues from the tax are estimated at $227,000,000,000 by 1990.

24 APRIL 1980
International   After several months of diplomatic maneuvers to gain the release of the American hostages in Iran, President Carter orders a military rescue mission. He calls off the mission after two helicopters fail to arrive at the rendezvous and another develops a leak which prevents it from taking off. Eight Americans are killed as another helicopter collides with a transport plane. The ill-fated rescue attempt leads Secretary of State Cyrus Vance (who has opposed the scheme) to resign.

17 MAY 1980
Black Experience   Three days of rioting begin in Miami, Florida, shortly after an all-white jury acquits four white policemen of killing Arthur McDuffie, a black insurance executive in Miami. Before it is over 18 people will be killed, 400 injured and nearly 1000 arrested.

18 MAY 1980
Regional   Mount St. Helens, a volcano in southwestern Washington, erupts, killing at least 26 people and showering ash over the countryside for 120 miles. The eruption, which will be estimated by scientists as having a force some 500 times as great as the atomic bomb dropped over Hiroshima, will be followed by a

RONALD REAGAN, 1911-

Known first to the American public as a film star, Ronald Reagan defied his celluloid beginnings to become President of the United States. But the man whose identity was so closely connected with the screen characters he played, who cannily exploited his popularity when campaigning, found that some resisted accepting the film star as chief executive.

Working first as a radio sports announcer after his 1932 graduation from Eureka College in Illinois, Reagan enjoyed film popularity throughout the 1930s and 1940s, insisting all the while that he was "a plain guy with a set of homespun features." His 1940 marriage to actress Jane Wyman further enhanced his Hollywood image. After serving in the United States Air Force from 1942 to 1945, Reagan became involved in liberal Democratic politics. He moved from a liberal to a more conservative outlook during the McCarthy era, a shift which foreshadowed his later jump to the GOP. Beginning in 1966, Reagan's tenure as California's governor proved that he had an austere, almost driven attitude concerning funding of state welfare and educational programs. Accordingly, Reagan was viewed as a hardline conservative. While he was disliked by liberals for the limitations his fiscal policies imposed, he was applauded by others for the $4,000,000 reduction in California state taxes between 1971 and 1975. On the strength of his conservative reputation, Ronald Reagan campaigned vigorously for the GOP Presidential nomination in 1968, promising support for school prayer and opposition to Federally funded abortions. Due to a late start, Reagan was unable to garner sufficient GOP support. Undaunted, he felt continued confidence in his abilities and in the image he conveyed to the American people—that of "a plain guy."

He optimistically launched a well-organized effort to unseat President Ford in 1976, but this, too, failed. However, the determination that helped Reagan implement his budget packages in California served him well as he fought for the Republican nomination in 1980. Winning both the nomination and the election, Reagan swept confidently into the White House. He and his second wife, Nancy (Reagan divorced Wyman in 1948), brought with them both the glitter of Hollywood and the entrenched conservatism that had been the hallmark of their political and social lifestyle. True to his reputation and campaign pledges, Ronald Reagan cut federal spending, attacking various government programs indiscriminately. These actions sparked public outcry, particularly from liberals who had fought hard during the 1960s and 1970s to establish these programs. The invective hurled at the President had, by the mid-point of his first term, made considerable impact on his public image. Reagan accordingly sought to build support for his actions by employing his talents in front of the camera, making a series of television broadcasts further underscoring his determination to balance the federal budget.

His opponents watching with dismay, Ronald Reagan rode roughshod over welfare programs that had been years in the making, but the President continued to follow his fiscal plans.

series of lesser eruptions in the next months. By June 10, it will be estimated that the volcano has caused damages of $2,700,000,000.

20 JUNE 1980
National Congress deregulates the trucking industry, allowing freedom in establishing rates and relaxing regulations widely believed to restrict service.

27 JUNE 1980
National President Carter signs a bill allowing for the draft registration of all the nation's 19- and 20-year-old men. The peacetime registration is one of the many steps taken by Carter in response to the Soviet invasion of Afghanistan.

16 JULY 1980
National The Republican National Convention, meeting in Detroit, selects Ronald Reagan as the party's nominee for president. Reagan aides will launch a strong but unsuccessful effort to entice former President Gerald Ford to run as Reagan's vice-presidential candidate.

14 AUGUST 1980
National The Democratic National Convention meeting in New York City renominates James Earl Carter and Walter Mondale to head the party's ticket in 1980.

28 OCTOBER 1980
National President Carter and Ronald Reagan debate in Cleveland in a nationally televised broadcast. Pollsters claim that viewers rate Reagan the winner.

4 NOVEMBER 1980
National In a landslide victory, Ronald Reagan defeats Jimmy Carter for president, winning almost 52 percent of the popular vote to 41.6 percent for Carter (the remainder goes to independent John Anderson). Reagan captures 489 electoral votes to 49 for Carter. The Republican victory extends to the legislature as the GOP gains a 53 to 47 majority in the Senate while decreasing the Democratic majority in the House to five seats. Most analysts see the Democratic defeat as a result of voter dissatisfaction with the Democrats' handling of domestic and international affairs. Although the economy rebounded in October from a recession, inflation plagues the country. The Soviet invasion of Afghanistan and the frustration over the stalemated Iranian hostage situation troubles Americans.

20 JANUARY 1981
National Ronald Reagan is sworn in as the country's 40th President. In his address, the new President tells the nation that "we are not, as some would have us believe, doomed to an inevitable decline."
International After 444 days of captivity the 52 Americans held hostage by Iran are released. The negotiations leading to release revolved around Iran's demand for return of the late Shah's wealth and release of Iranian assets frozen late in 1979. In exchange for the hostages, the U.S. agrees to release most of Iran's assets (some will be held until legal claims can be settled), and to locate and freeze the

President Ronald Reagan.

estate of the former Shah (who died of cancer in Egypt last July). It also promises not to interfere in the internal affairs of Iran and removes trade restrictions between the two nations. Former President Carter, acting as an emissary for Reagan, will greet the returning hostages in West Germany.

17 FEBRUARY 1981
Industry Chrysler Corporation announces that its losses for 1980 amounted to $1,710,000,000, the largest in American business history. Both Ford and General Motors also report heavy losses for the year as Americans increasingly purchased fuel-efficient foreign cars.

2 MARCH 1981
International With civil war in El Salvador between leftist guerrillas and government troops supporting President José Napoleon Durate, the Reagan administration announces its intention to send 20 more advisers and $25,000,000 in military equipment to help support the Duarte junta.

10 MARCH 1981
National President Reagan submits his proposed budget for fiscal 1982, which calls for federal expenditures of $695,000,000,000. The budget projects a deficit of $45,000,000,000 and includes some $48½ billion in spending cuts. The programs hardest hit by the cuts are mass transit and synthetic fuels projects as well as federally sponsored programs encouraging the arts.

23 MARCH 1981
National The Supreme Court decides, 6 to 3, that a state can pass legislation prohibiting physicians from performing abortions on teenagers unless the parents are notified.

30 MARCH 1981
National President Reagan is shot. The President had just finished giving a speech at the Washington Hilton Ballroom and was walking toward his limousine just outside the hotel exit when John W. Hinckley Jr. steps through a crowd of reporters and begins firing his 22-caliber handgun. Three others are

EMERGING AS A WORLD POWER 1946-

also hit by the shower of bullets, including Reagan's press secretary, James Brady. As police wrestle the gun from Hinckley, the President is rushed to George Washington University Hospital where he is treated for a possible lung collapse and goes into surgery. Miraculously, none of the four men is killed. Brady is shot in the forehead and suffers extensive damage to brain tissue, but ultimately recovers. The would-be assassin will be acquitted when a jury decides that he is mentally incompetent.

12 APRIL 1981
Science/Technology The Space Shuttle *Columbia* is launched on its first voyage from Cape Canaveral, Florida. Shortly after takeoff, astronauts John Young and Captain Robert Crippen discover that a number of heat resistant panels have been torn from the craft, probably during takeoff. The missing panels pose no threat to the flight and *Columbia* will safely land at Edwards Air Force Base, in California, on April 14. A second test flight will take place in November.

24 APRIL 1981
International Fulfilling a campaign promise, President Reagan lifts the grain embargo on the Soviet Union.

30 APRIL 1981
National Senator Harrison Williams of New Jersey is convicted of bribery in connection with the Abscam investigation uncovered in February 1980. With his conviction, all seven of the Congressional members accused of involvement in the scandal have been found guilty. Yesterday, Raymond Lederer, one of the convicted, resigned his seat in the House of Representatives in order to avoid expulsion.

12 JUNE 1981
Sports Major League baseball players go on the longest strike in sports history. Games will begin on August 9.

21 JUNE 1981
Regional Wayne Williams, a 28-year-old black man, is arrested and charged with the murder of two blacks in Atlanta, Georgia. Although he is formally accused of only two killings, Williams is believed responsible for the deaths of 28 young blacks over the last two years.

9 JULY 1981
Regional Battling a potentially disastrous infestation of the Mediterranean fruit fly, California Governor Jerry Brown announces the beginning of aerial spraying.

18 JULY 1981
Regional Two aerial walkways collapse at the Hyatt Regency Hotel in Kansas City, while the ballroom below is packed with some 1500 guests. The worst hotel accident in U.S. history leaves 113 people dead and injures 190.

SANDRA DAY O'CONNOR, 1930-

It is an interesting historical curiosity that it was conservative president, Ronald Reagan, who took what many perceived to be the radical step of appointing the first woman Supreme Court justice, Sandra Day O'Connor. Born in El Paso, Texas, on March 26, 1930, O'Connor took her law degree from Stanford in 1952 and soon after married a law school classmate. After living in Germany during her husband's army service, the couple returned to Phoenix, Arizona, in 1957, where they both settled down to practice law and to raise their family of three children.

By the mid-60s O'Connor had actively entered politics as a Republican, serving first as an assistant attorney general and than as a state senator, becoming Arizona's senate majority leader in 1973. The following year she left the senate on being elected a superior court judge, where she gained a reputation as a tough and methodical jurist. When in 1982 President Reagan was looking to fulfill his campaign promise to put a woman on the bench, O'Connor came to his attention as being both of the right gender and, perhaps, of the right conservative persuasion. In her Senate confirmation hearings she skillfully deflected grilling on touchy issues such as abortion and the Equal Rights Amendment, stating that she was opposed to judicial "activism"—meaning the kind of liberal pathbreaking represented by the Warren Court of the 50s, but perhaps also including such pathbreaking from the conservative side. She was confirmed as associate justice by the Senate in September 1981.

---

22 JULY 1981
Industry Chrysler announces $11,600,000 in profit for the previous quarter. The net gain by the company follows two years of record-breaking losses.

3 AUGUST 1981
Transportation After rejecting a contract offer by the government, 13,000 members of the U.S. Professional Air Traffic Controllers Organization (PATCO) go out on strike. The Reagan administration retaliates, announcing that all those who remain off the job after August 5 will be fired. Gradually, air traffic returns to normal and the FAA begins an extensive training program to replace the fired controllers.

21 SEPTEMBER 1981
National Sandra Day O'Connor becomes the first woman member of the Supreme Court.

2 OCTOBER 1981
National President Reagan presents a five-point program for strengthening America's military defense system. The plan calls for the building of 100 B-1 bombers (which the Carter administration had earlier opposed) and 100 MX missiles. Carter had also endorsed the MX missile system but had favored an intricate underground rail system to shuttle the missiles between silos so their location could never be pinpointed by the enemy. Instead of this scheme, Reagan proposes that the missiles be placed in fixed sites in superhardened silos capable of withstanding a direct nuclear strike. In August the Reagan administration

had also announced that the U.S. would begin production of the neutron bomb. Carter had deferred production of the enhanced-radiation weapon during his term.

28 OCTOBER 1981
International The Senate approves the Reagan administration plans to sell Saudi Arabia several billion dollars worth of military equipment—including five sophisticated Airborne Warning and Control Systems (AWAC) surveillance planes.

28 DECEMBER 1981
International Following announcement by the Polish government of a crackdown on its independent labor union Solidarity, Reagan imposes sanctions against the Soviet Union, whom he holds responsible for the hard-line policy of the Polish regime. Reagan calls for a ban on high technology equipment to the U.S.S.R., as well as other, primarily symbolic, measures. The President does not cut off grain shipments, a move for which he had criticized Carter after the invasion of Afghanistan.

OTHER EVENTS OF 1981
Science/Technology The Nobel Prize for Physics is shared by two Americans, Nicolaas Bloembergen and Arthur Schlawlow, and the Swede Kai Siegbahn. The Nobel Prize for Chemistry is shared by the American Ronald Hoffman and the Japanese Kenichi Fukui. The Nobel Prize for Physiology or Medicine is awarded to three Americans, David Hubel, Torsten Wiesel, and Roger Sperry.
Economics The Nobel Prize for Economics is awarded to the American James Tobin.

JANUARY 1982
Regional In one of the worst winters on record, many parts of the U.S. are battered by freezing temperatures, winds, blizzards and tornadoes.

5 JANUARY 1982
National A ruling by a Federal judge in Arkansas overturns a state law requiring that public schools teach both creationism and evolutionary theory.

8 JANUARY 1982
National In the settlement of an antitrust suit, American Telephone and Telegraph agrees to relinquish provision of local telephone service provided by 22 Bell System companies. This is one of the largest, most significant such actions in years. It allows AT&T to begin data processing sales and to develop its provision of computer communications to customers. The Labor Department reports that the unemployment rate rose to 8.9 percent during the last month of 1981.

13 JANUARY 1982
Regional After an unsuccessful takeoff in a snowstorm, an Air Florida Boeing 737 crashes in the icy Potomac River in Washington, D.C. Of 79 people on board, five survive the crash. Four people are killed on the 14th Street bridge as the plane plunges into the river.

26 JANUARY 1982
National In his State of the Union Message, President Reagan states his intention to transfer many Federal programs to state and local control. Included in this change are the food stamp program and many other social welfare programs currently administered by the Federal Government.

27 FEBRUARY 1982
Regional Wayne Williams is found guilty of killing two of the 28 young blacks found murdered in and around Atlanta, Georgia, in the last three years. (He is suspected of killing most if not all of the others, but the evidence is not strong enough.) Williams is given two consecutive life terms.

28 FEBRUARY 1982
Labor The United Auto Workers negotiate a new contract for Ford Motor Company employees; workers agree to give up certain wage and benefit increases in return for job security clauses. On March 21 General Motors will announce a similar agreement with the UAW.

1 MAY 1982
Regional The World's Fair opens in Knoxville, with President Reagan attending the ceremonies.

21 MAY 1982
International The first British troops land on the Falklands; by June 14, all Argentine forces there will have surrendered. The U.S. will come in for intense criticism by Argentines and many others for lending support to Britain.

6 JUNE 1982
International The Israeli army invades southern Lebanon, claiming it must drive out the Palestinians who have shelled Israelis from this area.

12 JUNE 1982
National An estimated 500,000 people wind for three miles through the streets of New York City into Central Park for a demonstration on behalf of nuclear arms control.

15 JUNE 1982
National The Supreme Court rules that all children are entitled to public education, whatever their citizenship, in response to a Texas law that did not guarantee such a right to young aliens.

30 JUNE 1982
National The Equal Rights Amendment is defeated as it falls three states short of the 38 states required for ratification.

9 JULY 1982
Regional A Pan American jetliner crashes after take-

off from New Orleans International Airport in Louisiana; 154 people are killed in this disaster—146 passengers and crew and another eight people on the ground—as the plane ripped through numerous houses before it exploded.

19 JULY 1982
National According to Census Bureau statistics, the United States has a poverty rate of 14 percent, highest since 1967. The study indicates a 7.4 percent increase over 1980.

28 JULY 1982
Regional San Francisco becomes the first city in the United States to ban the sale and possession of handguns.

5 AUGUST 1982
International The House of Representatives votes to reject a resolution that would freeze United States and Russian arsenals at their present levels.

11 AUGUST 1982
National Federal Judge Harold Greene rules that AT&T cannot provide service in the field of electronic information until it is clear that the giant corporation cannot dominate the market. This ruling comes as a result of the January 8, 1982, Federal Court decision concerning AT&T's relationship with the Bell System.

19 AUGUST 1982
National Both houses of Congress approve of the bill submitted by President Reagan calling for over $98 billion in taxes. Critics of Reagan see a concession that tax decreases and general economic policies are failing, but he emphasizes that only a small part of the total represents new taxes.

26 AUGUST 1982
National As a result of more than 10,000 claims against their company by those attributing their medical problems to exposure to asbestos, the Manville Corporation—the nation's largest producer of asbestos—files for bankruptcy.

8 SEPTEMBER 1982
National President Reagan announces that he will not block a bill proposed by North Carolina Senator Jesse Helms to allow prayer in public schools.

13 SEPTEMBER 1982
National In a merger that will consolidate over 22,000 miles of track, the ICC approves the combination of Union Pacific, Missouri Pacific, and Western Pacific railroads.

26 OCTOBER 1982
National President Reagan's administration shows a record budget deficit of more than $110,000,000,000 for fiscal 1982.

2 NOVEMBER 1982
National Mid-term elections show gains for Democrats who win 75 percent of the governors' races and 60 percent of the Congressional seats.

16 NOVEMBER 1982
Sports After a 57-day strike, NFL members reach a tentative contract settlement.

23 NOVEMBER 1982
National A Labor Department report indicates a 6 percent rise in the cost of living over a twelve-month period, based on a .5 percent increase in October.

16 DECEMBER 1982
National According to Federal Reserve Board figures, the nation's factories are operating at 67.8 percent capacity, the lowest since 1948 when the Bureau first began to compile records on factory output.

21-23 DECEMBER 1982
National Congress approves the Reagan administration's gasoline tax bill; with a new federal tax of 5 cents per gallon, it is expected to bring in nearly $5,500,000,000 a year for highway and bridge repairs.

OTHER EVENTS OF 1982
Science/Technology The Nobel Prize in Physics goes to Kenneth Wilson. Scientists at the Jet Propulsion Laboratory in California announce they have found four, possibly six, more small moons around Saturn. A team of scientists from The Ohio State University announce they have found the first fossil remains of a land mammal on the continent of Antarctica.

The Truman Library: 520.
USDA—National Park Service: 263.
U.S. Army Photo: 500, 501, 503, 504-505, 508, 513, 532, 535, 551, 573, 592.
U.S. Marine Corps Photo: 253.
U.S. Navy Photo: 118, 120, 127 (top), 282, 407, 489.
U.S. Steel Corporation: 339.
University of Wyoming, American Heritage Center: 298-299.
White House Photo: 585, 611 (Jack Kightlinger).
Wide World Photos: 559, 566, 605.

ACKNOWLEDGEMENTS

The publisher would like to thank the following people who have helped in the preparation of this book: Lynn Cadwallader, Jane Eliot, Judith Hawkins, Michael Kirkby, Jan Swafford, Eva Weber, who contributed to the chronology; Thomas G. Aylesworth, who edited it; Chris Simon, who designed it; John K. Crowley, who did the picture research; Cynthia Klein, who prepared the index.

INDEX

621